July 23-27, 2018
Egham, United Kingdom

Association for
Computing Machinery

Advancing Computing as a Science & Profession

PODC '18

Proceedings of the 2018 ACM Symposium on
Principles of Distributed Computing

Sponsored by:

ACM SIGACT & ACM SIGOPS

Supported by:

Amazon Web Services, IBM Research, Oracle Labs, and VMware

Association for Computing Machinery

Advancing Computing as a Science & Profession

The Association for Computing Machinery
2 Penn Plaza, Suite 701
New York, New York 10121-0701

ISBN: 978-1-4503-5795-1 (Digital)

ISBN: 978-1-4503-5955-9 (Print)

Additional copies may be ordered prepaid from:

ACM Order Department
PO Box 30777
New York, NY 10087-0777, USA

Phone: 1-800-342-6626 (USA and Canada)
+1-212-626-0500 (Global)
Fax: +1-212-944-1318
E-mail: acmhelp@acm.org
Hours of Operation: 8:30 am – 4:30 pm ET

PODC 2018 Chairs' Preface

Welcome to the 37th ACM SIGACT-SIGOPS Symposium on Principles of Distributed Computing (PODC 2018), held July 23-27, 2018, at Royal Holloway, University of London, Egham, United Kingdom. This year's symposium continues its tradition of being the premier forum for presentation of research on all aspects of distributed computing, including the theory, design, implementation, and applications of distributed algorithms, systems, and networks.

This volume contains 41 regular papers and 18 brief announcements selected by the Program Committee for presentation at PODC 2018, as well as the abstracts of three keynote lectures – by Robert Peglar, Graham Cormode, and Keren Censor-Hillel – and four tutorials. The volume also includes the citations for two awards jointly sponsored by PODC and the EATCS Symposium on Distributed Computing (DISC): the Edsger W. Dijkstra Prize in Distributed Computing, and the Principles of Distributed Computing Doctoral Dissertation Award.

The 2018 Edsger W. Dijkstra Prize in Distributed Computing, was presented at PODC 2018 to Bowen Alpern and Fred B. Schneider for their paper *Defining Liveness*, and the 2018 Principles of Distributed Computing Doctoral Dissertation Award will be presented at DISC 2018 in New Orleans, LA, USA, to Rati Gelashvili, for his dissertation titled "On the Complexity of Synchronization," written under the supervision of Prof. Nir Shavit at the Massachusetts Institute of Technology.

This year, 163 regular papers and 13 brief announcements were submitted to the symposium, where some regular submissions asked to be considered also as brief announcements. The Program Committee accepted 41 papers and 18 brief announcements that cover a wide variety of topics. Every submitted paper was read and evaluated by at least three reviewers. The final decisions regarding acceptance were made in a meeting held on April 23-24 2018 at Yahoo Research, Oath, in Haifa, in which most Program Committee members participated via videoconferencing. Revised and expanded versions of a few selected papers will be considered for publication in a special issue of the journal Distributed Computing and in the Journal of the ACM.

The Best Paper Award was presented to Leonid Barenboim, Michael Elkin, and Uri Goldenberg for their paper *Locally-Iterative Distributed (Δ+1)-Coloring below Szegedy-Vishwanathan Barrier, and Applications to Self-Stabilization and to Restricted-Bandwidth Models*. The Best Student Paper Award was shared between two papers; it was jointly awarded to Guy Goren for his paper *Silence* co-authored with Yoram Moses; and Thibault Rieutord and Yuan He for their paper *An Asynchronous Computability Theorem for Fair Adversaries* co-authored with Petr Kuznetsov.

Six workshops were co-located with PODC: BDA – Biological Distributed Algorithms, BTT – Workshop on Blockchain Technology and Theory, SISOSN – Workshop on Social Issues in Online Social Networks, ApPlied – Advanced tools, programming languages, and PLatforms for Implementing and Evaluating algorithms for Distributed systems, LADIS – Workshop on Large-Scale Distributed Systems and Middleware, and TOPIC – Theory and Practice for Integrated Cloud, Fog and Edge Computing Paradigms. In addition, the 60th birthday of Jennifer Welch was celebrated via five talks highlighting her contributions to the theory of distributed computation and the impact of her work.

Many thanks to the authors for submitting their high-quality work to PODC; to the Program Committee members and external reviewers for reviewing the papers and providing valuable feedback to the authors; to the Conference Committee who ensured everything will go smoothly, including local arrangements, finances, proceedings production, publicity, and workshops; and to the Steering Committee for ensuring the continuity and long-term excellence of the conference. Finally, we thank our sponsors for their support. We hope that you find PODC 2018 enjoyable and intellectually stimulating.

Idit Keidar
PODC'18 Program Committee Chair
Technion, Israel

Calvin Newport
PODC'18 General Chair
Georgetown University, USA

Table of Contents

Session 1D: Graph Algorithms

Keynote 2

Session 2A: Approximation and Learning

Session 2B: Routing and Leader Election

Session 3A: Congest

Session Chair: Idit Keidar *(Technion)*

Session 3B: Concurrency

Session 3C: Coloring

Session Chair: Magnús Halldórsson *(Reykjavik University)*

Session 3D: Graphs and Population

Session Chair: Michael Elkin *(Ben-Gurion University of the Negev)*

Tutorials

PODC 2018 Symposium Organization

General Chair: Calvin Newport *(Georgetown University, USA)*

Program Committee Chair: Idit Keidar *(Technion, Israel)*

Organizing Chair: Gregory Chockler *(Royal Holloway, University of London, UK)*

Treasurer: Peter Robinson *(Royal Holloway, University of London, UK)*

Publicity Chair: Mark Tuttle *(Amazon, USA)*

Communication Chair: Jukka Suomela *(Aalto University, Finland)*

Workshop Chair: Amitabh Trehan *(Loughborough University, UK)*

Proceedings Chair: Lewis Tseng *(Boston College, USA)*

Student Travel Grant Coordinator: Hsin-Hao Su *(Boston College, USA)*

Steering Committee Chair: Nitin H. Vaidya *(University of Illinois, USA)*

Steering Committee:
Lorenzo Alvisi *(Cornell University, USA)*
Idit Keidar *(Technion, Israel)*
Calvin Newport *(Georgetown University, USA)*
Andrzej Pelc *(Université du Québec en Outaouais, Canada)*
Peter Robinson *(Royal Holloway, University of London, United Kingdom)*
Alexander A. Schwarzmann *(University of Connecticut, USA)*

Program Committee:
Dan Alistarh *(IST, Austria)*
Leonid Barenboim *(Open University, Israel)*
Joffroy Beauquier *(Université Paris-Sud, France)*
Anastasia Braginsky *(Yahoo Research, Israel)*
Janna Burman *(Université Paris-Sud, France)*
Gregory Chockler *(Royal Holloway University of London, UK)*
Swan Dubois *(UPMC Sorbonne Universités, France)*
Michael Elkin *(Ben Gurion University of the Negev, Israel)*
Yuval Emek *(Technion, Israel)*
Ittay Eyal *(Technion, Israel)*
Vijay Garg *(UT Austin, USA)*
Rati Gelashvili *(University of Toronto, Canada)*
Chryssis Georgiou *(University of Cyprus, Cyprus)*
Mohsen Ghaffari *(ETH Zurich, Switzerland)*
Wojciech Golab *(University of Waterloo, Canada)*
Alexey Gotsman *(IMDEA, Spain)*
Bernhard Haeupler *(Carnegie Mellon University, USA)*

Program Committee: (continued)

Magnus Halldorsson *(Reykjavik University, Iceland)*
Prasad Jayanti *(Dartmouth College, USA)*
Idit Keidar *(Technion, Israel)*
Eddie Kohler *(Harvard, USA)*
Igor Konnov *(TU Wien, Austria)*
Eric Koskinen *(Stevens Institute, USA)*
Dariusz Kowalski *(University of Liverpool, UK)*
Alexander Matveev *(MIT, USA)*
Adam Morrison *(Tel Aviv University, Israel)*
Achour Mostéfaoui *(Université de Nantes, France)*
Rotem Oshman *(Tel Aviv University, Israel)*
Roberto Palmieri *(Lehigh University, USA)*
Merav Parter *(Weizmann Institute, Israel)*
Boaz Patt-Shamir *(Tel Aviv University, Israel)*
Maria Potop-Butucaru *(UPMC Sorbonne Universités, France)*
Sergio Rajsbaum *(UNAM, Mexico)*
Binoy Ravindran *(Virginia Tech, USA)*
Peter Robinson *(Royal Holloway University of London, UK)*
Nicola Santoro *(Carleton University, Canada)*
Stefan Schmid *(Aalborg University, Denmark)*
Ulrich Schmid *(TU Wien, Austria)*
Michael Spear *(Lehigh University, USA)*
Marko Vukolić *(IBM Zurich, Switzerland)*
Haifeng Yu *(National University of Singapore, Singapore)*

External Reviewers:

Amr Abdelnabi
Andres Abeliuk
Chrysovalandis Agathangelou
Dan Alistarh
Luciana Arantes
Maya Arbel
Sergio Arevalo
James Aspnes
Chen Avin
Mathias Bæk Tejs Knudsen
Leonid Barenboim
Joffroy Beauquier
Luca Becchetti
Oren Becker
Allan Borodin
Sébastien Bouchard
Marjorie Bournat
Zohir Bouzid
Quentin Bramas
Janna Burman
Costas Busch
Eleni C. Akrida
Roberto Calvo-Palomino
Armando Castañeda
Arnaud Casteigts
Himanshu Chauhan.
Vicent Cholvi
Koen Claessen
Andrea Clementi
Natacha Crooks
Andrzej Czygrinow
Bernardo M. David
Shantanu Das
Ajoy Datta
Gianluca De Marco
Antonella Del Pozzo
Argyrios Deligkas
Roman Dementiev

External Reviewers: (continued)

Stéphane Devismes
Giuseppe Di Luna
Yoann Dieudonne
Anaïs Durand
Adem Efe Gencer
Michael Elkin
Yuval Emek
Ittay Eyal
Luis F. Chiroque
Sergey Frenkel
Leszek Gasieniec
Cyril Gavoille
Rati Gelashvili
Ran Gelles
Golnaz Ghasemiesfeh
Theodoros Gkountouvas
Alexey Gotsman
Vincent Gramoli
Theophanis Hadjistasi
Nicolas Hanusse
Maurice Herlihy
Lisa Higham
Heidi Howard
Justin Hsu
Nicole Immorlica
Taisuke Izumi
Colette Johnen
Nikolaos Kallimanis
Xiaohan Kang
Liran Katzir
Idit Keidar
Alex Kogan
Christian Konrad
Amos Korman
Petr Kuznetsov
Arnaud Labourel
Ioannis Lamprou
Christoph Lenzen
Nikos Leonardos
Quanquan Liu
Zhiyu Liu
Adrian Loch
Federico Lombardi
Zvi Lotker
Víctor M. López Millán
Mahyar Malekpour
Frederik Mallmann-Trenn
Ioannis Marcoullis
Darryl Mcadams
Themistoklis Melissourgos
Hammurabi Mendes
George Mertzios
Othon Michail
Matthew Milano
Adam Morrison
Achour Mostéfaoui
Cameron Musco
Danupon Nanongkai
Prakash Narayana Moorthy
Ofer Neiman
Nicolas Nicolaou
Rotem Oshman
Roberto Palmieri
Giorgos Panagiotakos
Gopal Pandurangan
David Peleg
Richard Peng
Thomas Petig
Seth Pettie
Tsvetomira Radeva
Sergio Rajsbaum
Christoforos Raptopoulos
Netanel Raviv
Peter Robinson
Paolo Romano
Thomas Ropars
Stephane Rovedakis
Alexander Russell
Joel Rybicki
Jared Saia
Nicola Santoro
Vikram Saraph
Nicholas Schiefer
Johannes Schneider
Gregory Schwartzman
Michele Scquizzato
Kevin Sekniqi
Andres Sevilla

External Reviewers: (continued)

Isaac Sheff
Umair Siddique
Shikha Singh
Yannis Stamatiou
Aikaterini-Panagiota Stouka
Hsin-Hao Su
Jukka Suomela
Nathalie Sznajder
Sebastien Tixeuil
Corentin Travers
Lewis Tseng
José Verschae
Laurent Viennot
Giovanni Viglietta
Vincent Villain
Wojciech Wawrzyniak
Qin Xin
Thomas Zacharias
Akka Zemmari
Hong-Sheng Zhou
Leqi Zhu
Dionysis Zindros

Sponsors:

SIGACT
acm SIGOPS

Supporters:

amazon webservices™
IBM Research
Oracle Labs
vmware®

2018 Edsger W. Dijkstra Prize in Distributed Computing

The Dijkstra Prize Committee has decided to grant the 2018 Edsger W. Dijkstra Prize in Distributed Computing to Bowen Alpern and Fred B. Schneider for their paper:

B. Alpern, F.B. Schneider: Defining liveness, published in Information Processing Letters 21(4), October 1985, pages 181-185.

The Prize is awarded for outstanding papers on the principles of distributed computing, whose significance and impact on the theory and/or practice of distributed computing have been evident for at least a decade.

Concurrent and distributed algorithms today are characterized in terms of safety ("bad things" don't happen) and liveness ("good things" do happen). This seminal paper is what gave semantic legitimacy to that decomposition. Safety and liveness for concurrent programs had been suggested earlier by Lamport, but liveness was only formally defined for the first time in the winning paper, where it was accompanied by a compelling justification – that every (what we today call a) "trace property" is the conjunction of a safety and a liveness property. The liveness definition and accompanying decomposition theorem thus establish that safety and liveness are not only intuitively appealing but are also formally orthogonal. As a consequence, they constitute the basic building blocks of all (trace) properties and thus underly a substantial number of papers that appeared at PODC and DISC so far.

Moreover, subsequent work has shown that invariants suffice for verifying safety properties and that variant functions on well-founded domains are suitable for verifying liveness properties. So, of the possible ways to decompose properties, the decomposition into safety and liveness provides the added value of also suggesting approaches for verifying each property. Further evidence of the importance of this work is that its topological characterizations and decomposition proof have since been scaled-up to safety and liveness hyperproperties, which express confidentiality and other important correctness concerns that trace properties cannot.

The E.W. Dijkstra Prize is sponsored jointly by the ACM Symposium on Principles of Distributed Computing (PODC) and the EATCS Symposium on Distributed Computing (DISC). The prize is presented annually, with the presentation taking place alternately at PODC and DISC. This year it will be presented at PODC to be held at Royal Holloway, University of London, Egham, United Kingdom, July 23-27, 2018.

The 2018 Dijkstra Prize Committee:

Yehuda Afek
Tel-Aviv University

Idit Keidar
Technion

Boaz Patt-Shamir
Tel-Aviv University

Sergio Rajsbaum
UNAM

Ulrich Schmid, Chair
TU Wien

Gadi Taubenfeld
IDC Herzliya

2018 Doctoral Dissertation Award

The winner of the 2018 Principles of Distributed Computing Doctoral Dissertation Award is Dr. **Rati Gelashvili**, for his dissertation titled "On the Complexity of Synchronization," written under the supervision of Prof. Nir Shavit at the Massachusetts Institute of Technology.

The field of distributed algorithms revolves around efficiently solving *synchronization tasks*, such as leader election and consensus in different models. Gelashvili's thesis provides an extraordinary study of the complexity of solving synchronization tasks, which is both deep and broad. It makes significant contributions towards understanding the complexity of solving synchronization tasks in various models. In particular, it pushes the boundary of our understanding of consensus, the algorithmic process by which asynchronous computation threads coordinate with each other, which has been the subject of extensive research for over 30 years.

In one part of his thesis, Gelashvili challenges the underpinnings of Herlihy's consensus-based computability hierarchy, which has been the theoretical basis for classifying the computational power of concurrent data structures and synchronization primitives in multiprocessors and multicore machines for two and a half decades. He observes that Herlihy's classical hierarchy treats synchronization instructions as distinct objects, an approach that is far from the real-world, where multiprocessors do let processes apply supported atomic instructions to arbitrary memory locations. Gelashvili shows that, contrary to common belief, solving consensus does not require multicore architectures to support "strong" synchronization instructions such as compare-and-swap. Rather, combinations of "weaker" instructions such as decrement and multiply suffice. He goes on to propose an alternative complexity-based hierarchy for concurrent objects. The dissertation further opens a new line of research by proving a linear-space bound for the anonymous case of randomized consensus, the first major progress on this problem in 15 years, which won the Best Paper Award at DISC 2015, and for which Gelashvili developed novel lower bound techniques. Apart from their great importance, these results are also technically complex and mathematically beautiful.

The award. The award is sponsored jointly by the ACM Symposium on Principles of Distributed Computing (PODC) and the EATCS Symposium on Distributed Computing (DISC). This award is presented annually, with the presentation taking place alternately at PODC and DISC. The 2018 award will be presented at DISC 2018, to be held in New Orleans, LA, USA.

The 2018 Principles of Distributed Computing Doctoral Dissertation Award Committee:

Lorenzo Alvisi
Cornell University

Idit Keidar, Chair
Technion

Andrea Richa
Arizona State University

Alex Schwarzmann
University of Connecticut

Overview of Persistent Memory in Distributed Systems Architecture – Past, Present, Future

Robert Peglar
Advanced Computation and Storage LLC
rob@advanced-c-s.com

ABSTRACT

During the past half-century, persistent memory has had an interesting history and relationship to the design of computing and storage systems. In this talk, the history of systems design using persistent memory (as well as non-persistent, aka volatile memory) will be briefly discussed, as well as approaches to data storage. The majority of the talk will focus on two areas. First, the current state of the persistent memory art, as well as a taxonomy of persistent memory. Second, current methods and issues surrounding the use of persistent memory in systems, in particular distributed systems. The relationship between processing (e.g. CPUs) and persistent memory will be discussed in detail, illustrating certain challenges and opportunities with regard to several forms of distributed computation, in particular concerning large-scale multi-processor designs using shared persistent memory technology.

Categories and Subject Descriptors
E.0 [General]

Keyword
Persistent Memory

BIO
Robert Peglar is currently the President of Advanced Computation and Storage LLC, after a distinguished 40-year career serving the compute and storage technology industries, spanning six companies. His most recent post was Senior Vice President and CTO of Formulus Black, leading development efforts in next-generation software for persistent in-memory computing. Before that, he was Vice President of Advanced Storage at Micron Technology, where he led efforts in advanced storage systems strategy, led the CTO function and executive-level planning with key customers and partners worldwide for

Micron's Storage Business Unit, and defined future storage portfolio offerings.

Prior to joining Micron in February 2015, Mr. Peglar was Chief Technology Officer, Americas at EMC Isilon for four years. Prior to EMC, he was a Senior Fellow and Vice President of Technology at Xiotech for 11 years. Prior to Xiotech, he held key technology specialist and engineering leadership positions over a 10-year period at StorageTek and its subsidiary, Network Systems Corporation. Prior to StorageTek, he held engineering development and product management positions for a decade at Control Data and its supercomputer division, ETA Systems.

Mr. Peglar serves on the Board of Directors of the SNIA, is the former co-chair the SNIA Tutorials, and is the former director of the SNIA Solid State Storage Initiative. He also serves as an advisor to the Flash Memory Summit. Mr. Peglar has extensive experience in persistent memory architecture, data management and analysis, high-performance computing, nonvolatile systems, distributed cluster architectures, file systems, I/O performance optimization, cloud storage, replication and archiving strategy, networking protocols, and storage virtualization. He is a sought-after keynote speaker and panelist at leading storage and computing-related seminars and conferences worldwide.

Mr. Peglar holds a B.S. degree in computer science from Washington University, St. Louis, Missouri, and performed graduate work at Washington University's Sever Institute of Engineering.

PODC'18, July 23-27, 2018, Egham, United Kingdom

ACM ISBN 978-1-4503-5795-1/18/07.
https://doi.org/10.1145/3212734.3212796

Nesting-Safe Recoverable Linearizability: Modular Constructions for Non-Volatile Memory*

Hagit Attiya
Department of Computer Science,
Technion
hagit@cs.technion.ac.il

Ohad Ben-Baruch
Department of Computer Science,
Ben-Gurion University
ohadben@cs.bgu.ac.il

Danny Hendler
Department of Computer Science,
Ben-Gurion University
hendlerd@cs.bgu.ac.il

ABSTRACT

We presents a novel abstract individual-process crash-recovery model for non-volatile memory, which enables *modularity*, so that complex recoverable objects can be constructed in a modular manner from simpler recoverable base objects. Within the framework of this model, we define *nesting-safe recoverable linearizability* (NRL) – a novel correctness condition that captures the requirements for nesting recoverable objects. Informally, NRL allows the recovery code to extend the interval of the failed operation until the recovery code succeeds to complete (possibly after multiple failures and recovery attempts). Unlike previous correctness definitions, the NRL condition implies that, following recovery, an implemented (higher-level) recoverable operation is able to complete its invocation of a base-object operation and obtain its response.

We present algorithms for *nesting-safe recoverable primitives*, namely, recoverable versions of widely-used primitive shared-memory operations such as read, write, test-and-set and compare-and-swap, which can be used to implement higher-level recoverable objects. We then exemplify how these recoverable base objects can be used for constructing a recoverable counter object.

Finally, we prove an impossibility result on wait-free implementations of recoverable test-and-set (TAS) objects from read, write and TAS operations, thus demonstrating that our model also facilitates rigorous analysis of the limitations of recoverable concurrent objects.

CCS CONCEPTS

• **Theory of computation → Shared memory algorithms**;

KEYWORDS

Concurrency; shared memory; multi-core algorithms; wait-freedom; lock-freedom; nonblocking.

ACM Reference Format:
Hagit Attiya, Ohad Ben-Baruch, and Danny Hendler. 2018. Nesting-Safe Recoverable Linearizability: Modular Constructions for Non-Volatile Memory. In *PODC '18: ACM Symposium on Principles of Distributed Computing, July 23–27, 2018, Egham, United Kingdom.* ACM, New York, NY, USA, 10 pages. https://doi.org/10.1145/3212734.3212753

*This research was partially supported by the Israel Science Foundation (grant 1749/14) and by the Lynne and William Frankel Center for Computing Science at Ben-Gurion University.

ACM ISBN 978-1-4503-5795-1/18/07...$15.00
https://doi.org/10.1145/3212734.3212753

1 INTRODUCTION

Shared-memory multiprocessors are asynchronous in nature. Asynchrony is related to reliability, since algorithms that provide non-blocking progress properties (e.g., lock-freedom or wait-freedom [15]) in an asynchronous environment with reliable processes continue to provide the same progress properties in the presence of *crash failures*. This happens because a process that crashes permanently during the execution of the algorithm is indistinguishable to the other processes from one that is merely very slow. Owing to its simplicity and intimate relationship with asynchrony, the crash-failure model is almost ubiquitous in the treatment of concurrent algorithms.

The attention to the crash-failure model has so far mostly neglected the *crash-recovery* model, in which a failed process may be resurrected after it crashes. Recent developments foreshadow the emergence of new systems, in which byte-addressable *non-volatile main memory* (*NVRAM*), combining the performance benefits of conventional main memory with the durability of secondary storage, co-exists with (or eventually even replaces) traditional volatile memory. Traditional log-based recovery techniques can be applied correctly in such systems but fail to take full advantage of the parallelism and efficiency that may be gained by allowing processing cores to access recovery data directly using memory operations rather than by performing slow block transfers from secondary storage. Consequently, there is increased interest in *recoverable concurrent objects* (also called *persistent* or *durable*): objects that are made robust to crash-failures by allowing their operations to recover from such failures.

In this paper, we present a novel abstract individual-process crash-recovery model for non-volatile memory, inspired by a model introduced by Golab and Ramaraju for studying the *recoverable mutual exclusion* (RME) problem [13]. Our model enables nesting of recoverable objects, so that complex recoverable objects can be constructed in a modular manner from simpler recoverable base objects. We assume that processes communicate via persistent shared-memory variables. Each process also has local variables stored in volatile processor registers. At any point, a process may incur a crash-failure, causing all its local variables to be reset to arbitrary values. A key challenge with which recovery code must cope in our model is that operation response values are returned via volatile processor registers. Hence, they may become inaccessible to the calling process if it fails just before persisting the response value.

Each recoverable operation *Op* is associated with a *recovery function* that is responsible for completing *Op* upon recovery from a crash-failure.

Several correctness conditions for the crash-recovery model were defined in recent years (see, e.g., [2, 3, 14, 17], further discussed in Section 4). The goal of these conditions is to maintain the state of concurrent objects consistent in the face of crash failures. However, guaranteeing object consistency is insufficient for operation nesting. To illustrate this point, consider a base object $\mathcal{B}$ that supports atomic *compare&swap* (CAS) and *read* operations. Suppose that an operation *Op* by some recoverable object *O* invokes $\mathcal{B}$*.compare&swap(old,new)* in its algorithm which, upon completion, should return a success or failure response. Suppose also that some process *p* crashes inside *Op*, immediately after it invokes $\mathcal{B}$*.compare&swap(old,new)*. Since the CAS operation is atomic, the consistency of $\mathcal{B}$ is ensured in spite of *p*'s failure: either the CAS took effect before the failure, or it did not. However, the consistency of $\mathcal{B}$ is insufficient, since once *p* recovers from the crash, it has no way of knowing whether the CAS succeeded or not, as its response was written to a volatile local variable that was lost because of the crash. Reading $\mathcal{B}$ will not help, since even if *new* was written before the crash, it may have been overwritten by other processes since then. *Op* may therefore not be able to proceed correctly.

To address this issue, we define within the framework of our model the notion of *nesting-safe recoverable linearizability* (NRL), a novel correctness condition that captures the requirements for nesting recoverable objects. Informally, NRL allows the recovery code to extend the interval of the failed operation until the recovery code succeeds to complete (possibly after multiple failures and recovery attempts). NRL implies that, following recovery, an implemented (higher-level) recoverable operation is able to complete its invocation of a base-object operation and obtain its response.

We present several algorithms for *nesting-safe recoverable primitive objects*, recoverable versions of widely-used primitive shared-memory operations such as read, write, test-and-set and compare-and-swap, that can be used by higher-level recoverable objects. We also provide an example of how these recoverable base objects can be used for constructing a recoverable counter object.

In addition, we prove an impossibility result on wait-free implementations of recoverable test-and-set (TAS) objects from read, write and TAS operations, thus demonstrating that our model also facilitates rigorous analysis of the limitations of recoverable concurrent objects.

2 MODEL AND DEFINITIONS

We consider a system where *N* asynchronous *processes* $p_1, \ldots, p_N$ communicate by applying operations to *concurrent objects*. The system provides *base objects* that support atomic read, write, and read-modify-write operations. Base objects can be used for implementing more complex concurrent objects (e.g. counters, queues and stacks), by defining access procedures that simulate each operation on the implemented object using operations on base objects. These may be used in turn similarly for implementing even more complex objects, and so on.

The state of each process consists of non-volatile *shared-memory variables*, which serve as base objects, supporting read, write and read-modify-write operations, as well as *local variables stored in volatile processor registers* which support read and write only. Each process can incur at any point during the execution a *crash-failure* (or simply a *crash*) that resets all its local variables to arbitrary values, but preserves the values of all its non-volatile variables. A process *p invokes an operation Op* on an object by performing an *invocation step*. Upon *Op*'s completion, a *response step* is executed, in which *Op's response is stored to a local variable of p*. It follows that the response value is lost if *p* incurs a crash before persisting it.

Operation *Op* is *pending* if it was invoked but was not yet completed. For simplicity, we assume that, at all times, each process has at most a single pending operation on any one object.[1] A *recoverable operation Op* is associated with a *recovery function*, denoted *Op*.Recover, that is responsible for completing *Op* upon recovery from a crash. The execution of operations (and recoverable operations in particular) may be nested, that is, an operation Op_1 can invoke another operation Op_2. Following a crash of process *p* that occurs when *p* has one or more pending recoverable operations, the system may eventually resurrect process *p* by invoking the recovery function of the inner-most recoverable operation that was pending when *p* failed. This is represented by a *recover step for p*.

More formally, a *history H* is a sequence of *steps*. There are four types of steps:

(1) an *invocation step*, denoted (INV, p, O, Op), represents the invocation by process *p* of operation *Op* on object *O*;
(2) an operation *Op* can be completed either normally or when, following one or more crashes, the execution of *Op*.Recover is completed. In either case, a *response step s*, denoted (RES, p, O, Op, ret), represents the completion by process *p* of operation *Op* invoked on object *O* by some step s' of *p*, with response *ret* being written to a local variable of *p*. We say that *s is the response step that matches s'*;
(3) a *crash step s*, denoted $(CRASH, p)$, represents the crash of process *p*. We call the inner-most recoverable operation *Op* of *p* that was pending when the crash occurred the *crashed operation of s*. $(CRASH, p)$ may also occur while *p* is executing some recovery function *Op*.Recover and we say that *Op* is the crashed operation of *s* also in this case;
(4) a *recovery step s for process p*, denoted (REC, p), is the only step by *p* that is allowed to follow a $(CRASH, p)$ step s'. It represents the resurrection of *p* by the system, in which it invokes *Op*.Recover,[2] where *Op* is the crashed operation of s'. We say that *s is the recovery step that matches* s'.

When a recovery function *Op*.Recover is invoked by the system to recover from a crash represented by step *s*, we assume it receives the same arguments as those with which *Op* was invoked when that crash occurred. We also assume that *Op*.Recover has access to a designated per-process non-volatile variable LI_p, identifying the instruction of *Op* that *p* was about to execute in the crash represented by *s*. An object is a *recoverable object* if all its operations

[1] This assumption can be removed, but this would require substantial changes to the notions of sequential executions and linearizability, which we chose to avoid in this work.

[2] A history does not contain invocation/response steps for recovery functions.

are recoverable. In the following definitions, we consider only histories that arise from operations on recoverable objects or atomic primitive operations.

Consider a scenario in which p incurs a crash (represented by a crash step s) immediately after a recoverable operation Op completes (either directly or through the completion of Op.Recover) – an event represented by a response step r. In this case, the response value is lost and, moreover, Op.Recover will not be invoked by the system, since the crashed operation of s is no longer Op but, rather, the operation Op' that invoked Op. In general (although there are exceptions to this rule as we will see in Section 3), Op' may therefore not be able to proceed correctly. Hence, it is sometimes required to guarantee that a recoverable operation returns only once its response value gets persisted. This is defined formally as follows.

Definition 1. *A recoverable operation Op is a* strict recoverable operation *if whenever it is completed, either directly or by the completion of Op.*Recover *(an event represented by a (RES,p,O,Op,ret) step), ret is stored in a designated persistent variable accessed only by process p.*

For a history H, we let $H|p$ denote the subhistory of H consisting of all the steps by process p in H. We let $H|O$ denote the subhistory of H consisting of all the invoke and response steps on object O in H, as well as any crash step in H, by any process p, whose crashed operation is an operation on O and the corresponding recover step by p (if it appears in H). H is *crash-free* if it contains no crash steps (hence also no recover steps). We let $H|<p,O>$ denote the subhistory consisting of all the steps on O by p. A crash-free subhistory $H|O$ is well-formed, if for all processes p, $H|<p,O>$ is a sequence of alternating, matching invocation and response steps, starting with an invocation step.

Given two operations op_1 and op_2 in a history H, we say that op_1 *happens before* op_2, denoted by $op_1 <_H op_2$, if op_1's response step precedes the invocation step of op_2 in H. If neither $op_1 <_H op_2$ nor $op_2 <_H op_1$ holds then we say that op_1 and op_2 are *concurrent* in H. $H|O$ is a *sequential object history*, if it is an alternating series of invocations and the matching responses starting with an invocation (that may end by a pending invocation). The *sequential specification* of an object O is the set of all possible (legal) sequential histories over O. H is a *sequential history* if $H|O$ is a sequential object history for all objects O.

A crash-free history H is *well-formed* if: 1) $H|O$ is well-formed for all objects O, and 2) For all p, if i_1, r_1 and i_2, r_2 are two matching invocation/response steps in $H|p$ and $i_1 <_H i_2 <_H r_1$ holds, then $r_2 <_H r_1$ holds as well. The second requirement guarantees that if operation Op_1 invokes operation Op_2, Op_2's response must precede Op_1's response. Two histories H and H' are *equivalent*, if $H|<p,O> = H'|<p,O>$ for all processes p and objects O. A history H is *sequential*, if $H|O$ is sequential for all objects O that appear in H. Given a history H, a *completion* of H is a history H' constructed from H by selecting separately, for each object O that appears in H, a subset of the operations pending on O in H and appending matching responses to all these operations, and then removing all remaining pending operations on O (if any).

Definition 2 (Linearizability [16], rephrased). *A finite crash-free history H is* linearizable *if it has a completion H' and a legal sequential history S such that:*

L1. H' is equivalent to S; and

L2. $<_H \subseteq <_S$ (i.e., if $op_1 <_H op_2$ and both ops appear in S then $op_1 <_S op_2$).

Thus, a finite history is linearizable, if we can linearize the subhistory of each object that appears in it. Next, we define a more general notion of well-formedness that applies also to histories that contain crash/recovery steps. For a history H, we let $N(H)$ denote the history obtained from H by removing all crash and recovery steps.

Definition 3 (Recoverable Well-Formedness). *A history H is* recoverable well-formed *if the following holds.*

(1) Every crash step in $H|p$ is either p's last step in H or is followed in $H|p$ by a matching recover step of p.

(2) $N(H)$ is well-formed.

We can now define the notion of nesting-safe recoverable linearizability.

Definition 4 (Nesting-safe Recoverable Linearizability (NRL)). *A finite history H satisfies* nesting-safe recoverable linearizability *(NRL) if it is recoverable well-formed and $N(H)$ is a linearizable history. An object implementation satisfies NRL if all of its finite histories satisfy NRL.*

3 NESTING-SAFE RECOVERABLE BASE OBJECTS

In this section, we present algorithms for recoverable base objects that support primitive operations such as read, write, compare-and-swap (CAS) and test-and-set. As described in Section 2, this consists in implementing a recovery function Op.Recover for each such operation, which may be invoked by the system upon a crash-failure when Op is the crashed operation. In the pseudo-code, we use names that start with a capital letter for shared-memory variables and lower-case names for local variables. We also use capital-letter names for implemented operations and lower-case names for primitive operation names.

We remind the reader that, as defined in our model, we only consider recoverable objects or base objects provided by the system that support atomic read, write or read-modify-write (RMW) operations. Before presenting our algorithms we prove that, under these assumptions, our model guarantees that all histories are recoverable well-formed.

Lemma 1. *Let H be a history in which all operations are applied to either recoverable objects or atomic base objects. Then H is recoverable well-formed.*

Proof. Consider an execution α of any algorithm and the corresponding history $H(\alpha)$. If an atomic read, write or RMW is executed in α, then its invocation and response steps appear in H consecutively hence cannot violate well-formedness, so it suffices to consider invocation/response steps on recoverable objects and crash/recovery steps.

When a process p invokes an operation Op on a recoverable object O, a corresponding invocation step i is appended to $H(\alpha)$. If p crash-fails inside Op, a $(CRASH,p)$ step c is appended to $H(\alpha)$ and its crashed operation is Op. If and when the system eventually resurrects p and invokes Op.RECOVER, a recovery step r that matches c is appended to $H(\alpha)$. If p undergoes additional failures before Op completes, then additional pairs of a crash step and its matching recovery step are appended to $H(\alpha)$. Otherwise, if and when Op completes, a response step r that matches i is appended to $H(\alpha)$. It follows from Definition 3 that $H(\alpha)$ is a recoverable well-formed history. □

3.1 Read-Write Object

Our recoverable read-write object algorithm assumes that all values written to the object are distinct. This assumption can be easily satisfied by augmenting each written value with a tuple consisting of the writing process' ID and a per-process sequence number. In some cases, such as the example of a recoverable counter that we present later, this assumption is satisfied due to object semantics and does not require special treatment.

Algorithm 1 presents pseudo-code for process p of a recoverable read-write object R. It supports non-strict (see Definition 1) recoverable READ and WRITE operations. Both READ and READ.RECOVER simply return R's current value (lines 7-9, 18-20).

Our implementation of WRITE "wraps" the write primitive with code that allows the recovery function WRITE.RECOVER to conclude whether p's write in line 4, or a write by a different process, took place since p's invocation of WRITE. This is done using a single-reader-single-writer shared-memory variable S_p that stores a pair of values – R's previous value (read in line 2) and a flag that allows the recovery function to infer the location in WRITE where the failure occurred. Specifically, $flag = 0$ holds whenever p is either not performing a WRITE operation on R (since it is initialized to 0 and set to 0 in line 5 before WRITE returns) or p has performed line 5 but WRITE was not yet completed.

The intuition for correctness is the following. A crash before line 3 is executed implies that both $S_p = \langle 0, curr \rangle$ and $curr \neq val$ hold, since we assume each value written to R is distinct. In this case, WRITE.RECOVER simply re-executes WRITE (lines 12-13). If a crash occurs after p writes to S_p in line 3 but before it writes to it in line 5 and no process writes to R since p reads it in line 2, then the condition of line 14 holds and so p re-executes WRITE also in this case (in line 15).

Otherwise neither of the conditions of lines 12, 14 holds. Hence, either p already executed line 4, or another process wrote to R between when R was read by p in line 2 and in line 14. In either of these cases, we may linearize WRITE, so the recovery function updates S_p and returns *ack* (lines 16-17). A formal correctness proof follows.

Lemma 2. *Algorithm 1 satisfies NRL.*

Proof. First observe that R is a recoverable object since each of its two operations has a corresponding RECOVER function. Consider an execution α of the algorithm and the corresponding history $H(\alpha)$. From Lemma 1, $H(\alpha)$ is recoverable well-formed. Hence, $H'(\alpha) = N(H(\alpha))$ is a well-formed (non-recoverable) history. Following definition 4, it remains to prove that $H'(\alpha)|R$ is linearizable.

Since neither of R's recovery functions write to variables read by other processes, they have no effect on their execution. We can therefore ignore crashes that occur during the execution of the recovery functions, as long as S_p is not written (which only occurs in line 16 of WRITE.RECOVER).

Assume p applies a WRITE(val) operation to R in α. If p does not fail during its execution, then clearly p writes to R exactly once in line 4 and this is the operation's linearization point. Otherwise, assume that p fails when executing the WRITE operation. A crash before line 3 implies that p did not yet write to neither S_p nor R, hence WRITE was not linearized yet. Upon recovery, p reads $S_p = \langle 0, curr \rangle$, where $curr \neq val$ holds, since we assume all written values are distinct. Hence, WRITE.RECOVER re-executes WRITE.

A crash between the two writes to S_p (in lines 3 and 5) implies that $S_p = \langle 1, curr \rangle$ and $curr \neq val$ holds. Upon recovery, if the condition of line 14 is satisfied, then $curr = R$ ensures that no process wrote to R between the two reads of R (in lines 2 and 14). In particular, p did not write to R (so WRITE was not linearized) and the operation is re-executed.

Otherwise $curr \neq R$, i.e., there was a write to R between the two reads of R by p. If p wrote to R in line 4, then the operation was already linearized at this point. Otherwise, there was a write by a different process q that occurred between the two reads by p, hence within the execution interval of p's WRITE. Thus, p's WRITE can be linearized immediately before q's, causing q to immediately overwrite val (if it was indeed written by p in line 4), resulting in an execution that is indistinguishable to all processes from one in which p does not write to R at all. It follows that, in both these cases, p's WRITE operation can be linearized correctly and WRITE.RECOVER returns *ack*.

The last case to consider is when WRITE.RECOVER reads $\langle 0, val \rangle$ in line 11 and then performs lines 16-17 and returns. This can occur either if p crashed after executing line 5, or if it crashed before line 5 but a subsequent WRITE.RECOVER failed after updating S_p (in line 16). The latter case can happen only if a previous invocation of WRITE.RECOVER by p read $S_p = \langle 1, curr \rangle$, for $curr \neq R$, executed line 16 and then failed. Our previous analysis established that WRITE can be linearized also in this case. This concludes our discussion of linearization points of WRITE operations. As for READ, if and when it returns (in lines 9 or 20), it is linearized when it last read R (in line 8 or line 19, resp.). □

3.2 Compare-and-Swap Object

A Compare-and-Swap (CAS) object supports the CAS(old, new) operation, which atomically swaps the object's value to new only if the value it stores is old. The operation returns true and we say it is *successful* if the swap is performed, otherwise it returns false and we say it *fails*. A CAS object also supports a READ operation which returns the object's value. Algorithm 2 presents pseudo-code for process p of a recoverable CAS object C. C stores two fields, both initially *null*. The first is the ID of the last process that performed a successful CAS and the second is the value it wrote.

Both READ and READ.RECOVER simply return $C.val$. To perform the CAS operation, process p first reads C. If it reads a value v other

Algorithm 1 Nesting-safe recoverable read/write object R, program for process p

Shared variables: S_p - pair of values, initially $< 0, null >$

```
procedure WRITE(val)
    temp ← R
    S_p ←< 1, temp >
    R ← val
    S_p ←< 0, val >
    return ack
procedure READ()
    temp ← R
    return temp
procedure WRITE.RECOVER(val)
    < flag, curr >← S_p
    if flag = 0 ∧ curr ≠ val then
        proceed from line 2
    else if flag = 1 ∧ curr = R then
        proceed from line 2
    S_p ←< 0, val >
    return ack
procedure READ.RECOVER()
    temp ← R
    return temp
```

Algorithm 2 Nesting-safe recoverable CAS object C, program for process p

Shared variables: R[N][N] - all elements initially *null*

```
1:  procedure CAS(old,new)
2:      <id,val> ← C.read()
3:      if val ≠ old then
4:          return false
5:      if id ≠ null then
6:          R[id][p] ← val
7:      ret ← C.cas(<id,val >,<p,new>)
8:      return ret
9:  procedure READ()
10:     <id,val> ← C
11:     return val
12: procedure CAS.RECOVER(old, new)
13:     if C = <p,new> ∨
          new ∈ {R[p][1],...,R[p][N]} then
14:         return true
15:     else
16:         proceed from line 2
17: procedure READ.RECOVER()
18:     <id,val> ← C
19:     return val
```

than *old*, p returns *false* and is linearized at the read (lines 2-4). Otherwise, if $v \neq null$, p helps the process (say, q) that wrote v by informing it that its CAS took effect. This is done by writing v to $R[q][p]$ (lines 5-6), which is a SRSW shared variable used by p to inform q. This allows processes to inform each other which CAS operations were successful. We assume that CAS is never invoked with $old = new$ and that values written to C by the same process are distinct. (This assumption can be easily satisfied by augmenting each written value with a per-process sequence number.) The helping mechanism described above guarantees that, upon recovery, process p is able to determine that its CAS operation took effect if the value it wrote is still stored in C or is written in $R[p][j]$, for some j.

If p crash-fails inside CAS without modifying C, either because it crashes before line 7 or because it crashed after its *cas* in line 7 failed, then $<p, new>$ is never written to C or to any of $R[p][*]$. In this case, CAS.RECOVER simply re-executes CAS. A key point in the correctness argument is that a CAS operation that crashed after a failed (primitive) *cas* can be re-executed, since it did not affect other processes, hence we may assume it was not linearized yet and re-execute it without violating the sequential specification of CAS.

Lemma 3. *Algorithm 2 satisfies NRL.*

Proof. First observe that C is a recoverable object since each of its two operations has a corresponding RECOVER function. Consider an execution α of the algorithm and the corresponding history $H(\alpha)$. From Lemma 1, $H(\alpha)$ is recoverable well-formed. Hence, $H'(\alpha) = N(H(\alpha))$ is a well-formed (non-recoverable) history. Following definition 4, it remains to prove that $H'(\alpha)|C$ is linearizable. Since none of the recovery functions writes to a variable read by other processes, they have no effect on their executions. We can therefore ignore crashes that occur during the execution of the recovery function.

For presentation simplicity, when we refer to *the value of* C we refer to the value of its second field, which represents the state of the object, and when we refer to *the content of* C, we refer to both fields as a pair. Since no process writes the same value twice, it follows that the content of C is unique, while the value of C is not necessarily unique, since different processes may write the same value.

Assume p applies a CAS(old, new) operation to C in α. First assume that p does not crash during the CAS operation. In line 2, p reads C and then compares the value of C to *old*. If the values differ, then the operation is linearized at the read in line 2 and indeed at this point the value of C is different from *old*, so p returns *false* in line 4. Otherwise, p informs the last process q to have performed a successful CAS that its operation took effect. It does so by writing to $R[q][p]$ the value it read from C. Then, p tries to change the value of C by performing *cas* in line 7.

The following two possibilities exist. Assume first that a successful CAS to C was linearized between p's execution of line 2 and line 7. In this case, the first such operation must change C's value to a value other than *old*, and we can linearize p's operation right after it. Since the content of C is unique, p's *cas* operation in line 7 fails, and it returns *false* in line 8. Otherwise, there was no successful CAS to C between the read in line 2 and the *CAS* in line 7, and thus the *cas* in line 7 is successful, and this is also the linearization point and p returns *true* in line 8.

Assume now that p crashed during a CAS operation. Assume first that either p crashed before executing line 7, or it crashed after line 7 but its *cas* operation in line 7 failed. In both cases, <p,*new*> was never written to C, since p writes distinct values to C. As processes write to R only values they read from C, no process wrote *new* to $R[p][*]$. Consequently, CAS.RECOVER re-executes CAS. A failed *cas* operation does not affect other processes, that is, removing the operation is indistinguishable to other processes. Therefore, in both cases, considering the operation as not having a linearization point so far and re-executing it does not violate the sequential specification of CAS.

If p did perform a successful CAS in line 7 before the crash, then this is also the operation's linearization point. We argue that the next process q to perform a successful CAS on C, if any, must write *new* to $R[p][q]$ before its CAS takes effect. Assume there exists such a process q. Then, consider the time when the successful CAS of q in line 7 occurs. It must be that q executes lines 2-7 without crashing, since any crash before writing to C will cause the re-execution of the CAS operation, as we have already shown. In addition, q reads <p,*new*> from C in line 2, since by our assumption it succeeds in replacing p's value, that is, it performed a successful *CAS* when C's content was <p,*new*>. As the content of C is unique, reading any other content implies the *CAS* in line 7 fails, a contradiction. Hence, before q's successful CAS in line 7, it writes *new* to $R[p][q]$ in line 6. We assume that the left term in the condition of line 13 of CAS.RECOVER is evaluated before the right term. Consequently, in line 13, p either reads C = <p,*new*> or, otherwise, some process q already replaced C's content but wrote *new* to $R[p][q]$ before that, thus p observes *new* in $R[p][q]$. In both cases, p considers the CAS operation as successful and returns true in line 14.

As for READ, if and when it returns (in lines 11 or 19), it is linearized when it last read C (in line 10 or line 18, respectively). □

3.3 Test-and-Set Object

A non-resettable Test-and-Set (TAS) object is initialized to 0 and supports the T&S operation, which atomically writes 1 and returns the previous value. In the following, we present a recoverable non-resettable test-and-set algorithm that uses a (non-recoverable) non-resettable (and non-readable) TAS object and read/write shared variables. Before that, however, we present an impossibility result on such implementations of recoverable TAS algorithms.

We say that an operation (or a recovery function) is *wait-free* [15], if a process that does not incur failures during its execution completes it in a finite number of its own steps. Our implementation of TAS has a wait-free T&S operation but its recovery code is blocking. The following theorem proves that this is inevitable: any recoverable TAS object from these primitives cannot have both a wait-free T&S operation and a wait-free T&S.RECOVER function.

THEOREM 4. *There exists no recoverable non-resettable TAS algorithm satisfying NRL, from read/write and (non-recoverable) non-resettable TAS base objects only, such that both the* T&S *operation and the* T&S.RECOVER *function are wait-free.*

PROOF. We prove the theorem using valency arguments [10]. Let $\mathcal{A}$ be an NRL recoverable non-resettable TAS implementation using the base objects assumed by the theorem, and assume towards a contradiction that both T&S and T&S.RECOVER are wait-free. We say that a configuration C is p-valent (resp. q-valent) if there exists a crash-free execution starting from C in which p (resp. q) returns 0 or has already returned 0. C is bivalent if it is both p-valent and q-valent, and univalent otherwise. Observe that any configuration C is either p-valent or q-valent (or both), because in a solo execution of p followed by a solo execution of q from C where both complete their operations (if they haven't done so already), exactly one must return (or already returned) 0.

The initial configuration C_0, in which both p and q invoke the *TAS* operation, is bivalent – a solo execution of each process returns 0. Using valency arguments and as we assume that T&S is wait-free, there is an execution starting from C_0 that leads to a bivalent configuration C_1, in which both p and q are about to perform a critical step. This step must be an application of the *t&s* primitive to the same base object. Moreover, a step by any of the processes leads to a different univalent configuration. Assume wlog that configuration $C_1 \circ p$ is p-valent whereas $C_1 \circ q$ is q-valent.

Let p and then q perform their next *t&s* steps, followed by a crash step of p. Since p's response from the *t&s* primitive is lost due to the crash, upon recovery p does not know whether the *t&s* primitive was performed, and if it was, what the response value was. Specifically, configurations $C_1 \circ p \circ q \circ CRASH_p$ and $C_1 \circ q \circ p \circ CRASH_p$ are indistinguishable to p. Consequently, a solo execution of T&S.RECOVER by p after both configurations (which will complete since we assume that T&S.RECOVER is wait-free) returns the same value *ret*. This implies that both configurations are u-valent for some u.

Wlog assume $u = p$ (the other case is symmetric), then we consider configuration $C_1' = C_1 \circ q \circ p \circ CRASH_p$. Note that C_1' is indistinguishable from configuration $C_1 \circ q \circ p$ for q, since q is not aware of p's crash. Therefore, C_1' is both q-valent and p-valent, that is, it is bivalent. Since we assume that both processes are only allowed to use read, write and t&s primitives, we can repeat the same argument again and show that there is an extension of C_1' leading to a bivalent configuration C_2, where both p and q are about to perform a critical step. Moreover, this step must be the application of a t&s primitive to the same base object. This must be a TAS base object other than those previously used in the execution, since those would always return 1, contradicting criticality.

Continuing in this manner, we construct a crash-free execution of q in which it executes an infinite number of steps while performing a single T&S operation. This is a contradiction. □

Algorithm 3 presents pseudo-code for process p of a recoverable TAS object T that uses a base atomic *non-readable and non-resetable t&s* operation. T supports a strict recoverable T&S operation. We assume a process invokes the T&S operation at most once, as any additional operations are bound to return 1.

T uses a shared-memory array R, where $R[i]$ (initialized to 0) stores the state of process i, as well as shared variables *Winner* and *Doorway* whose usage we describe soon. Process p first sets its state to 1 (in line 2) to indicate it is trying to enter the algorithm's doorway. If the doorway is closed (line 3), implying that another process closed it (in line 7) before p performed line 3, then p "loses" the T&S operation, so it sets its return value to 1 (in line 4) and proceeds to persist its response value, indicate it completed its operation and return (lines 11-13).

If the doorway is still open, p updates its state (line 6), closes the doorway (line 7), and attempts to win the (non-recoverable) atomic *t&s* operation (line 8). It p wins, then it declares that it is the winner by writing its identifier to the *Winner* variable in line 10. Regardless of whether p wins or loses, it proceeds to persist its state and return its response in lines 11-13.

As we prove, the doorway mechanism guarantees that any T&S operation invoked after *Doorway* is set (in line 7) will return 1.[3] This implies that an operation that returns 0 can be linearized before all other operations. Once a process writes to *Winner*, any process can recover by simply reading *Winner*. Hence, the main difficulty is to ensure that at most a single process writes to *Winner*.

We now proceed to describe the recovery function, which uses $R[p]$ for determining at which point in the execution p crashed. If the condition of line 15 is satisfied, then p crashed before executing line 6, implying that its operation did not yet affect any other process, so T&S.RECOVER simply re-executes T&S (line 16). If the condition of line 17 is satisfied, then p crashed after writing 3 to $R[p]$, in either line 12 or line 33, implying that p already computed its response and wrote it to Res_p. In this case, T&S.RECOVER simply returns the value stored in Res_p (in lines 18-19). If the condition of line 20 is satisfied, then a winner already declared itself, thus p recovers by determining its response accordingly, persisting it, and returning (lines 21, 31-34).

If none of the above cases holds, then p still needs to compete to win the TAS. In order to do so, it closes the doorway in line 22, in case it is still open, announces it is recovering and competing for the TAS by writing 4 to $R[p]$ in line 23, and attempts to win the *t&s* operation in line 24.

The difficulty in determining the winner of the T&S operation is that a process may win the atomic *t&s* operation (in line 8 or in line 24) and then fail before writing its identifier to *Winner*. In order for a unique winner to be determined in this case, p now has to pass two busy-waiting loops, in lines 25-26 and 27-28. In the first loop, p waits for all lower-indexed processes that started an operation to complete it. In the second loop, p waits for all higher-indexed processes that started an operation to either complete it or to announce that they are recovering. As we prove, these busy-waiting loops guarantee that if there is a process writing to *Winner* in line 10, then p must wait for it to do so. Also, only the process with the smallest identifier out of those that reach these loops is able to compete and possibly win and write to *Winner* in lines 29-30, while the rest of the recovering processes must wait for it to complete. As we prove, this implies that at most a single process writes to *Winner*.

[3] We note that the doorway mechanism could have been replaced by simply reading T if a *readable* atomic TAS object would have been used by the algorithm.

Claim 1. *Algorithm 3 satisfies NRL.*

Proof. First observe that T is a recoverable object since each of its two operations has a corresponding RECOVER function. Consider an execution α of the algorithm and the corresponding history $H(\alpha)$. From Lemma 1, $H(\alpha)$ is recoverable well-formed. Hence, $H'(\alpha) = N(H(\alpha))$ is a well-formed (non-recoverable) history. Following definition 4, it reamins to prove that $H'(\alpha)|T$ is linearizable.

The proof relies on the following simple observations:

(1) If there is a process that completes its operation, there must be a write to *Doorway*.
(2) Once a process writes to *Doorway*, any operation that did not yet execute line 2 can no longer return 0. Moreover, such an operation can only set $R[p]$ to either 1 or 3.
(3) Once a process writes 3 to $R[p]$ (in line 12 or line 33), its response is persistent in Res_p. In addition, the value $R[p]$ is fixed for the rest of the execution, and if p runs sufficiently long without crashing it returns the value stored in Res_p.
(4) A process that returns 0 must have previously written to *Winner*.
(5) Assume that process p is the only process that wrote to *Winner*. Then, if p runs long enough without crashing, it eventually returns 0.

If no T&S operation completes in α, then H' is obviously linearizable. Therefore, assume that there is a T&S operation that completes in α, either normally or by completing a T&S.RECOVER execution. By Observation (1), there is a write to *Doorway* in α. Let β be the prefix of α up to, and including, the first such write. No operation completes in β, otherwise there is an earlier write to *Doorway* in α, contradicting our definition of β. Also, by Observation (2), any operation that did not yet execute line 2 in β can only return 1, and would set $R[p]$ to either 1 or 3.

The proof is based on the following two claims: 1) at most a single operation returns 0, and 2) if all operations are allowed to execute sufficiently long without crashing, then some operation returns 0. It follows from these two claims that either there is a single operation pending at β which returns 0 in α, or there is no such operation, but there is an operation, pending at β, that is also pending at α. In both cases we can linearize one operation right after β as returning 0, while the rest can be linearize after it, and they all return 1. This would prove that H' is linearizable.

Following Observation (4), proving there can be no two processes writing to *Winner* would establish that only a single operation may return 0. Assume there is a process p that writes to *Winner* in line 10. Then no other process can write to *Winner* in line 10, since $T.t\&s$ may return 0 at most once. Assume towards a contradiction that some process q writes to *Winner* in line 30. Then, by the definition of β, q did not yet execute line 23 in β. In order to write to *Winner*, q must pass the busy-waiting loops in the T&S.RECOVER function,

Algorithm 3 Nesting-safe recoverable TAS object T, program for process p

Shared variables: R[N]: an array, initially [0,...,0]; Winner, Doorway: read/write registers, initially *null*, *true* resp.

```
1:  procedure T&S()
2:      R[p] ← 1
3:      if Doorway = false then
4:          ret ← 1
5:          proceed from line 11
6:      R[p] ← 2
7:      Doorway ← false
8:      ret ← T.t&s()
9:      if ret = 0 then
10:         Winner ← p
11:     Res_p ← ret
12:     R[p] ← 3
13:     return ret

14: procedure T&S.RECOVER()
15:     if R[p] < 2 then
16:         proceed from line 2
17:     if R[p] = 3 then
18:         ret ← Res_p
19:         return ret
20:     if Winner ≠ null then
21:         proceed from line 31
22:     Doorway ← false
23:     R[p] ← 4
24:     T.t&s()
25:     for i from 0 to p − 1 do
26:         await(R[p] = 0 or R[p] = 3)
27:     for i from p + 1 to N do
28:         await(R[p] = 0 or R[p] > 2)
29:     if Winner = null then
30:         Winner ← p
31:     ret ← (Winner ≠ p)
32:     Res_p ← ret
33:     R[p] ← 3
34:     return ret
```

and thus has to wait for p to set $R[p] > 2$. By Observation (2), p executed line 2 in β. Also, p cannot set $R[p]$ to 4 in line 23, as this would imply that p crashed after executing line 6 and before writing to *Winner* (since it reads *null* in line 20). In particular, p does not re-execute any part of T&S upon recovery, contradicting the fact it writes to *Winner* in line 10, since the condition in line 16 can no longer hold for it. Therefore, it must be that p sets $R[p] \leftarrow 3$ (in line 12 or in line 33), and this happens only after p writes to *Winner*. As a result, q gets to line 29 only after p writes to *Winner*, and therefore does not write to *Winner* in line 30, a contradiction.

Assume now there is a process p that writes to *Winner* in line 30. As proved above, no process can write to *Winner* in line 10 in this case. Assume towards a contradiction there exists another process q which writes to *Winner* in line 30. WLOG, assume $p < q$. After β, both p and q are after executing line 2 and before executing line 25. Hence, in order to get to line 30, q has to wait for p to set $R[p] \leftarrow 3$, that is, to complete its operation. This happens only after p writes to *Winner*, thus q reads in line 20 a value different from *null* and does not write to *Winner*, which is a contradiction. This concludes the proof of the first claim

To prove the second claim, we show that if every active process is eventually allowed to execute sufficiently long without crashing, then eventually some process writes to *Winner*. Assume towards a contradiction that no process writes to *Winner*. If no operation crashes after setting $R[p] \leftarrow 2$ in line 6, then the first operation to execute line 8 also writes to *Winner*, which is a contradiction. Thus, there must be such an operation, and it eventually executes T&S.RECOVER and sets $R[p] \leftarrow 4$ in line 23. Let q be the process with the smallest identifier to do so. Any operation that does not execute line 23, when executing for a sufficiently long time without crashing eventually sets $R[p]$ to 3 and returns. Hence, eventually the following holds: for all $i < q$ $R[i] \in \{0,3\}$ holds (since q is the smallest to execute line 23), and for all $i > q$ $R[i] \in \{0,3,4\}$ holds. Consequently, eventually q complete the busy-waiting loops in T&S.RECOVER and writes to *Winner* in line 30, which is a contradiction. □

3.4 Using Nesting-Safe Recoverable Base Objects: an Example

A *Counter* object supports an INC operation that atomically increments its value and a READ operation. We start by describing a simple linearizable implementation of a *Counter* object and then discuss the changes required for making it a recoverable *Counter* satisfying NRL. Each process p has its own entry $R[p]$ in an array R of integers, initialized to 0. To perform INC, p simply increments $R[p]$. In the READ operation, p reads all array entries, sums up the values and returns the sum.

Claim 2. *The Counter algorithm described above is linearizable.*

Proof. The correctness argument is as follows. Assume process p completes a READ operation. Let v be the value it read from $R[q]$. Since $R[q]$ is monotonically increasing, it must be that $R[q] \leq v$ immediately after the READ's invocation and $R[q] \geq v$ immediately before the READ's response. Therefore, at most v INC operations by q have been linearized before the READ's invocation, and at least v INC operations were linearized before the READ's response. As this is true for any q, it implies that, as p computes value val, then there are at most val INC operations that were linearized before its

READ invocation, and at least *val* INC operations that were linearized before its READ response. In particular, there is a point during READ's execution when exactly *val* INC operations were linearized, so the READ operation can be correctly linearized at that point. □

Making this implementation recoverable necessitates equipping both INC and READ operations with a RECOVER function. The pseudo-code of the recoverable implementation is shown by Algorithm 4. As we described in Section 2, our system model assumes that a recovery function *Op*.RECOVER has access to LI_p - a designated per-process non-volatile variable identifying the instruction of *Op* that *p* was about to execute when it incurred the crash that triggered *Op*.RECOVER. Our implementation of the INC operation, which we now describe, exemplifies how LI_p is used.

The INC operation's write to $R[p]$ in line 4 is its linearization point. In order to ensure that $R[p]$ is incremented exactly once in each INC operation, we use an array *R* of recoverable read/write objects, such as the one we described previously, instead of an array of (non-recoverable) read/write variables. Recall that our implementation of recoverable WRITE requires that distinct values will be written, but this imposes no overhead here, since it is ensured by the counter's algorithm.

Consider a crash that occurs between INC's invocation and response. If *p* crashes inside WRITE (invoked by INC in line 4), then WRITE is the inner-most recoverable operation that was pending. Consequently, if and when *p* is resurrected by the system, it does so by invoking WRITE.RECOVER and, once its recovery is completed, INC returns in line 5 (unless it crashes again). Otherwise, the system invokes INC.RECOVER, which uses LI_p in line 7 to determine whether the last crash inside INC occurred before line 4 - in which case INC is re-executed, or after it - in which case INC.RECOVER simply returns.

We chose to implement the counter's READ operation as strictly recoverable. This was accomplished in our implementation by having READ write its response value, immediately before it returns, to a shared-memory variable Res_p, used by *p* only. This ensures that a recoverable operation that invokes the counter's READ operation is able to access its response even if the process fails immediately after *N*.READ returns.

Algorithm 4 demonstrates how recoverable base objects that satisfy the NRL condition can be used in our model for constructing more complex recoverable objects (satisfying the same condition) relatively easily. Modular constructions, such as that of Algorithm 4, leverage the following key property guaranteed by NRL: base recoverable operations are guaranteed to be linearized correctly before they return, even in the presence of multiple crashes, allowing the implemented recoverable operation to proceed correctly.

4 RELATED WORK

Golab and Ramaraju [13] define an abstract individual-process crash-recovery model to study the *recoverable mutual exclusion* (RME) problem. RME is a generalization of the standard mutual exclusion problem, whereby a process that crashes while accessing a lock is resurrected eventually and allowed to execute recovery actions. The RME problem was further studied in [12, 18]). Additional work investigated lock recoverability in different models [1, 5–7, 23].

A *consistency* condition specifies how to derive the semantics of a concurrent implementation of a data structure from its *sequential specification*. This requires to disambiguate the expected results of concurrent operations on the data structure, as done for example in *linearizability* [16]. Linearizability guarantees a locality property required for nesting, but it cannot be directly used for specifying recoverable objects, since it has no notion of an aborted or failed operation, and hence, no notion of recovery.

Several consistency conditions for the crash-recovery model were suggested, aiming to maintain the consistent state of concurrent objects. However, none of them ensures that a process is able to infer whether the failed operation completed and, if so, to obtain its response value, hence they cannot be directly used as a correctness condition for modular constructions of recoverable objects.

Aguilera and Frølund [2] proposed *strict linearizability* as a correctness condition for recoverable objects. It treats the crash of a process as a response, either successful or unsuccessful, to the interrupted operation. Strict linearizability preserves both *locality* [15] and program order. Guerraoui and Levy [14] define *persistent atomicity*. It is similar to strict linearizability, but allows an operation interrupted by a failure to take effect before the subsequent invocation of the same process, possibly after the failure. They also proposed *transient atomicity*, which relaxes this criterion even further and allows an interrupted operation to take effect before the subsequent write response of the same process. Both conditions ensure that the state of an object will be consistent in the wake of a crash, but they do not provide locality.

Berryhill et al. [3] present an alternative condition, called *recoverable linearizability*, which achieves locality but may compromise program order following a crash. Whereas [2, 3, 14] consider an *individual process failures* model in which any subset of the processes may crash-fail at any time, Izraelevitz et al. [17] consider a *simultaneous failures* model, in which processes always crash-fail together. Under this model, persistent atomicity and recoverable linearizability are indistinguishable.

Several previous works investigated transactional access of persistent shared objects and NVRAM-based system recovery [4, 19–22, 24, 25]. Coburn et al. [8] presented *NV-heaps*, a software user-level library that allows using NVRAM directly for storing object state and recovery data. Cohen et al. [9] recently presented an efficient logging protocol for NVRAM. Friedman et al. [11] presented three concurrent lock-free queue algorithms exhibiting different tradeoffs between consistency and efficiency.

5 DISCUSSION

We presented a novel abstract model and correctness criterion for non-volatile memory, supporting modular construction of complex recoverable objects from simpler recoverable base objects. We gave algorithms for recoverable versions of widely-used primitive shared-memory operations such as read, write, test-and-set and compare-and-swap, and showed they can be used to construct a recoverable counter object.

An intriguing research direction is to devise and prove the correctness of more complex data structures (such as lists, stacks, queues and search trees), whose (non-recoverable) lock-free implementations from reads, writes, and CAS operations are known.

Algorithm 4 Nesting-safe recoverable Counter object N, program for process p

Shared variables: R[N]: an array of recoverable read/write objects, initially [0, . . . , 0]

```
1: procedure INC()
2:     temp ← R[p].READ
3:     temp ← temp + 1
4:     R[p].WRITE(temp)
5:     return ack
6: procedure INC.RECOVER()
7:     if LI_p < 4 then
8:         proceed from line 2
9:     else
10:        return ack
11: procedure READ()
12:     val ← 0
13:     for i from 1 to N do
14:         val ← val + R[i].READ
15:     Res_p ← val
16:     return val
17: procedure READ.RECOVER()
18:     proceed from line 12
```

The model we presented in this paper assumes that the system provides recovery functions with access to a per-process non-volatile variable identifying the instruction that the process was about to execute when it crashed. In future work, we plan to investigate how best to relax this requirement while allowing the algorithm to explicitly label critical "check-points" (typically corresponding to write operations) for facilitating correct recovery.

6 ACKNOWLEDGEMENTS

We thank the anonymous reviewers for their helpful comments.

REFERENCES

[1] U. Abraham, S. Dolev, T. Herman, and I. Koll. Self-stabilizing l-exclusion. *Theor. Comput. Sci.*, 266(1-2):653–692, 2001.

[2] M. K. Aguilera and S. Frølund. Strict linearizability and the power of aborting. In *Tech. Rep. HPL-2003-241*, 2003.

[3] R. Berryhill, W. M. Golab, and M. Tripunitara. Robust shared objects for non-volatile main memory. In *19th International Conference on Principles of Distributed Systems, OPODIS*, pages 20:1–20:17, 2015.

[4] H.-J. Boehm and D. R. Chakrabarti. Persistence programming models for non-volatile memory. In *Proceedings of the 2016 ACM SIGPLAN International Symposium on Memory Management*, ISMM, pages 55–67, 2016.

[5] P. Bohannon, D. F. Lieuwen, and A. Silberschatz. Recovering scalable spin locks. In *Proceedings of the Eighth IEEE Symposium on Parallel and Distributed Processing, SPDP 1996, New Orleans, Louisiana, USA, October 23-26, 1996.*, pages 314–322, 1996.

[6] P. Bohannon, D. F. Lieuwen, A. Silberschatz, S. Sudarshan, and J. Gava. Recoverable user-level mutual exclusion. In *Proceedings of the Seventh IEEE Symposium on Parallel and Distributed Processing, SPDP 1995, San Antonio, Texas , USA, October 25-28, 1995*, pages 293–301, 1995.

[7] D. R. Chakrabarti, H. Boehm, and K. Bhandari. Atlas: leveraging locks for non-volatile memory consistency. In *Proceedings of the 2014 ACM International Conference on Object Oriented Programming Systems Languages & Applications, OOPSLA 2014, part of SPLASH 2014, Portland, OR, USA, October 20-24, 2014*, pages 433–452, 2014.

[8] J. Coburn, A. M. Caulfield, A. Akel, L. M. Grupp, R. K. Gupta, R. Jhala, and S. Swanson. NV-Heaps: Making persistent objects fast and safe with next-generation, non-volatile memories. In *Proceedings of the Sixteenth International Conference on Architectural Support for Programming Languages and Operating Systems*, ASPLOS, pages 105–118, 2011.

[9] N. Cohen, M. Friedman, and J. R. Larus. Efficient logging in non-volatile memory by exploiting coherency protocols. *PACMPL*, 1(OOPSLA):67:1–67:24, 2017.

[10] M. J. Fischer, N. A. Lynch, and M. Paterson. Impossibility of distributed consensus with one faulty process. *J. ACM*, 32(2):374–382, 1985.

[11] M. Friedman, M. Herlihy, V. Marathe, and E. Petrank. Brief announcement: A persistent lock-free queue for non-volatile memory. In *Distributed Computing - 31st International Symposium (DISC)*, 2017.

[12] W. M. Golab and D. Hendler. Recoverable mutual exclusion in sub-logarithmic time. In *Proceedings of the ACM Symposium on Principles of Distributed Computing PODC*, pages 211–220, 2017.

[13] W. M. Golab and A. Ramaraju. Recoverable mutual exclusion: [extended abstract]. In *Proceedings of the 2016 ACM Symposium on Principles of Distributed Computing, PODC*, pages 65–74, 2016.

[14] R. Guerraoui and R. R. Levy. Robust emulations of shared memory in a crash-recovery model. In *24th International Conference on Distributed Computing Systems (ICDCS)*, pages 400–407, 2004.

[15] M. Herlihy. Wait-free synchronization. *ACM Trans. Program. Lang. Syst.*, 13(1):124–149, 1991.

[16] M. Herlihy and J. M. Wing. Linearizability: A correctness condition for concurrent objects. *ACM Trans. Program. Lang. Syst.*, 12(3):463–492, 1990.

[17] J. Izraelevitz, H. Mendes, and M. L. Scott. Linearizability of persistent memory objects under a full-system-crash failure model. In *Distributed Computing - 30th International Symposium, DISC*, pages 313–327, 2016.

[18] P. Jayanti and A. Joshi. Recoverable FCFS mutual exclusion with wait-free recovery. In *31st International Symposium on Distributed Computing, DISC 2017, October 16-20, 2017, Vienna, Austria*, pages 30:1–30:15, 2017.

[19] A. Kolli, S. Pelley, A. Saidi, P. M. Chen, and T. F. Wenisch. High-performance transactions for persistent memories. In *Proceedings of the Twenty-First International Conference on Architectural Support for Programming Languages and Operating Systems*, ASPLOS, pages 399–411, 2016.

[20] V. J. Marathe, M. Seltzer, S. Byan, and T. Harris. Persistent memcached: Bringing legacy code to byte-addressable persistent memory. In *9th USENIX Workshop on Hot Topics in Storage and File Systems (HotStorage)*, 2017.

[21] D. Narayanan and O. Hodson. Whole-system persistence. In *Proceedings of the 17th International Conference on Architectural Support for Programming Languages and Operating Systems, ASPLOS 2012, London, UK, March 3-7, 2012*, pages 401–410, 2012.

[22] D. Schwalb, M. Dreseler, M. Uflacker, and H. Plattner. Nvc-hashmap: A persistent and concurrent hashmap for non-volatile memories. In *Proceedings of the 3rd VLDB Workshop on In-Memory Data Mangement and Analytics, IMDM@VLDB 2015, Kohala Coast, HI, USA, August 31, 2015*, pages 4:1–4:8, 2015.

[23] G. Taubenfeld. *Synchronization Algorithms and Concurrent Programming.* Prentice-Hall, Inc., Upper Saddle River, NJ, USA, 2006.

[24] S. Venkataraman, N. Tolia, P. Ranganathan, and R. H. Campbell. Consistent and durable data structures for non-volatile byte-addressable memory. In *FAST*, volume 11, pages 61–75, 2011.

[25] H. Volos, A. J. Tack, and M. M. Swift. Mnemosyne: Lightweight persistent memory. In *Proceedings of the Sixteenth International Conference on Architectural Support for Programming Languages and Operating Systems*, ASPLOS, pages 91–104, 2011.

Recoverable Mutual Exclusion Under System-Wide Failures

Wojciech Golab*
Department of Electrical and Computer Engineering
University of Waterloo
wgolab@uwaterloo.ca

Danny Hendler†
Department of Computer Science
Ben-Gurion University
hendlerd@cs.bgu.ac.il

ABSTRACT

Recoverable mutual exclusion (RME) is a variation on the classic mutual exclusion (ME) problem that allows processes to crash and recover. The time complexity of RME algorithms is quantified in the same way as for ME, namely by counting remote memory references – expensive memory operations that traverse the processor-to-memory interconnect. Prior work has established that the RMR complexity of the RME problem for n processes is $\Theta(\log n)$ for the class of algorithms that use read/write registers and single-word comparison primitives such as Compare-And-Swap (Golab and Ramaraju 2016), $O(\log n/\log\log n)$ for the class of algorithms that use read/write registers and additional single-word read-modify-primitives such as Fetch-And-Store (Golab and Hendler 2017), and $\Theta(1)$ for the class of algorithms that use read/write registers and specialized double-word read-modify-write primitives (Golab and Hendler 2017). These complexity bounds hold in a model of computation where processes may fail independently, and where a process that fails while accessing the mutex is required to recover eventually. This body of work leaves open two important questions: (i) what is the tight bound on the RMR complexity of RME for the class of algorithms that use read/write registers and commonly supported single-word read-modify-primitives; and (ii) how is the RMR complexity of RME affected by variations in the failure model? This paper answers both questions partially by showing that RME can be solved using $O(1)$ RMRs per passage in the worst case in a model where failures are system-wide (i.e., all processes crash simultaneously), and processes receive additional information from the environment regarding the occurrence of the failure. The upper bound algorithm we present relies crucially on a novel RMR-efficient barrier that processes use to synchronize recovery actions after each failure. The barrier uses read/write registers and single-word Compare-And-Swap only. Additionally, we present a transformation that can add properties such as critical section re-entry and a strong notion of starvation freedom to any RME algorithm while preserving its asymptotic RMR complexity.

*Wojciech Golab is supported in part by the Natural Sciences and Engineering Research Council (NSERC) of Canada, Discovery Grants Program, and by a Google Faculty Research Award.
†Danny Hendler is supported in part by the Israel Science Foundation (grant 1749/14).

PODC '18, July 23–27, 2018, Egham, United Kingdom

ACM ISBN 978-1-4503-5795-1/18/07...$15.00
https://doi.org/10.1145/3212734.3212755

CCS CONCEPTS

• **Theory of computation → Shared memory algorithms**; • **Software and its engineering →** *Mutual exclusion*; • **Computer systems organization →** Reliability;

KEYWORDS

Mutual exclusion; recovery; fault tolerance; concurrency; shared memory; multi-core algorithms; non-volatile main memory; persistent data structures.

ACM Reference Format:
Wojciech Golab and Danny Hendler. 2018. Recoverable Mutual Exclusion Under System-Wide Failures. In *PODC '18: ACM Symposium on Principles of Distributed Computing, July 23–27, 2018, Egham, United Kingdom.* ACM, New York, NY, USA, 10 pages. https://doi.org/10.1145/3212734.3212755

1 INTRODUCTION

Non-volatile main memory (NVRAM) will soon become available commercially. This novel storage medium will challenge the traditional coupling of volatile main memory with non-volatile secondary storage in computer architectures, which has long led to a separation of program state into operational data stored using disposable in-memory data structures, and recovery data stored using durable but sequential on-disk structures such as transaction logs. The eventual convergence of primary and secondary storage into a single layer in the memory hierarchy will allow computer systems to simultaneously harness the performance benefits of main memory and the durability of secondary storage, provided that software design adapts accordingly. In particular, system designers must rethink traditional log-based recovery techniques, which restrict parallelism during recovery, and embrace techniques that allow multiple processing cores to recover concurrently using state saved in NVRAM.

One of the fundamental research problems related to constructing fault-tolerant data structures for NVRAM pertains to hardening mutual exclusion locks against crash-recovery failures. Research on this topic was revived recently by Golab and Ramaraju, who formulated and solved the Recoverable Mutual Exclusion (RME) problem [18]. RME is a modern take on the classic mutual exclusion (ME) problem formulated by Dijkstra [11] that allows a process to crash while accessing (i.e., acquiring, releasing, or holding) a lock provided that it recovers eventually and resumes execution, beginning with recovery actions that restore the internal state of the lock. In contrast, the ME problem assumes that a process never fails while accessing a lock, as otherwise a conventional lock becomes vulnerable to starvation.

Recent work on the RME problem [16, 18, 22] precipitated a flurry of upper bounds on time complexity, which in this context is quantified by counting *remote memory references* (RMRs) – expensive memory operations that cause traffic on the interconnect joining processors with memory. In the model with independent process failures, Golab and Ramaraju proved that RME can be solved for N processes using only atomic reads and writes in $O(\log N)$ RMRs, which matches the tight bound known for conventional ME [5, 32]. However, the tight bound on RMR complexity is not known for the class of algorithms that use commonly supported single-word Read-Modify-Write primitives, some of which are known to be sufficiently powerful to solve ME using only $O(1)$ RMRs. In particular, only two solutions to the RME problem have been published that beat that logarithmic bound: Golab and Hendler presented an $O(\log N/\log\log N)$ RMRs algorithm that uses single-word Fetch-And-Store and Compare-And-Swap, and an $O(1)$ RMRs algorithm that uses specialized double-word Read-Modify-Write operations [16].

This paper advances the state of the art by providing partial answers to two fundamental questions: (i) what is the tight bound on the RMR complexity of RME for the class of algorithms that use read/write registers and commonly supported single-word read-modify-primitives; and (ii) how is the RMR complexity of RME affected by variations in the failure model? Specifically, we show that RME can be solved using only $O(1)$ RMRs in the worst case in a model where failures are system-wide and processes receive additional information from the environment regarding the occurrence of the failure. The algorithms we present rely crucially on a novel RMR-efficient barrier that processes use to synchronize recovery actions after each failure. The barrier uses read/write registers and single-word Compare-And-Swap only. Additionally, we present a transformation that can add properties such as critical section re-entry and a strong notion of starvation freedom to any RME algorithm while preserving its asymptotic RMR complexity.

2 MODEL

We consider N asynchronous unreliable processes, $p_1, p_2, \ldots, p_N$, that communicate by accessing variables in shared memory. These processes compete for an exclusive lock (recoverable mutex [18]), which protects a shared resource, by executing an infinite loop whose body comprises the following sections: the *non-critical section* (NCS), where processes do not access the lock or the shared resource; the *recovery protocol* (**Recover**), where a process repairs up the internal structure of the lock following a crash failure; the *entry protocol* (**Enter**), where a process waits for access to the shared resource; the *critical section* (CS), where a process accesses the shared resource; and finally the *exit protocol* (**Exit**), where a process makes the shared resource available to others.

Correctness properties for recoverable mutex algorithms are expressed in reference to *histories* that record the actions of processes. Formally, a history H is a sequence of *steps* that come in two varieties. An *ordinary step* is a shared memory operation combined with bounded local computation (e.g., arithmetic, accessing private variables, advancing the program counter). A *crash step* is a system-wide failure that resets the private variables of all processes to their initial values, and transitions the program counters to the NCS. The next step a process takes after a crash step is either another crash step, or the first step of **Recover**. A *passage* is a sequence of steps taken by a process from when it begins **Recover** to when it completes **Exit**, or crashes, whichever occurs first. A passage is called *failure-free* if it does not end with a crash step. A *super-passage* is a maximal non-empty collection of consecutive passages executed by the same process where (only) the last passage in the collection is failure-free. A history H is *fair* if it is finite, or if it is infinite and every process that participates either executes infinitely many steps or stops taking steps after completing a failure-free passage.

The fairness property implies that a process always recovers eventually following a crash in the middle of a passage. This aspect of the model makes it possible to maintain liveness properties in the presence of process failures without relying on accurate failure detection, and is inherited from Golab and Ramaraju [18]. It can be viewed as a generalization of the traditional assumption that a process participating in mutual exclusion never halts permanently outside of the NCS.

The fundamental correctness properties of RME algorithms include the following [18]:

Mutual Exclusion (ME): For any finite history H, at most one process is in the CS at the end of H.

Starvation Freedom (SF): For any infinite fair history H, if a process p_i leaves the NCS in some step of H then eventually p_i itself enters the CS, or else there are infinitely many crash steps in H.

Critical Section Re-entry (CSR): For any history H and for any process p_i, if p_i crashes inside the CS then no other process may enter the CS before p_i re-enters the CS after the crash failure.

Bounded Recovery (BR): There exists an integer $b > 0$ such that for any history H and for any process p_i, any execution of the recovery protocol by p_i incurs at most b steps.

Bounded Exit (BE): There exists an integer $b > 0$ such that for any history H and for any process p_i, any execution of the exit protocol by p_i incurs at most b steps.

The time complexity of RME algorithms is defined as the number of *remote memory references* (RMRs) executed by a process per passage. An RMR is any memory operation that traverses the processor-to-memory interconnect, and is defined in an architecture-specific manner. In this paper we consider both the cache-coherent (CC) and distributed shared memory (DSM) models [3]. In the CC model, we (conservatively) count each shared memory operation as an RMR with the exception of an *in-cache* read, which occurs when a process p_i reads a variable v that it has already read in an earlier step, following which step no process has accessed v except by a read operation. In the DSM model, each shared variable is local to exactly one process, which is determined statically at initialization.

The algorithms presented in this paper assume that processes have knowledge of an *epoch number* parameter, which is a positive integer that increases after each system-wide failure. For example, the epoch number can be the value of a counter that is incremented by the operating system after every failure, or the time of the last system boot.[1] This parameter augments the model introduced in [18], and is given as input to the pseudo-code procedures **Recover**, **Enter**, and **Exit**. All passages executed between successive failures

[1]The counter-based method of computing epoch numbers does not guarantee monotonicity in cases where failures occur in rapid succession as there may be insufficient time between such failures to save the updated value of the counter to NVRAM. This limitation does not break the algorithms presented in this paper.

use the same epoch number, whereas passages made after a particular failure use a higher epoch number than passages made before this failure. Thus, epoch numbers increase monotonically, but need not reflect the exact number of failures that have occurred since the beginning of the execution. A practical algorithm that records epoch numbers in registers of finite size can only tolerate a finite (but very large) number of failures.

3 BARRIER

This section presents the implementation of an RMR-efficient synchronization barrier, which is used heavily in the transformations presented later on in this paper. A barrier is accessed by executing a *barrier procedure* whose specification is captured in Definition 3.1 below. Two variations of this barrier are presented, and one is used as a building block of the other. Both variations are based on the premise that some distinguished process called the *barrier leader* (*leader* for short) must open the barrier before other processes, called non-leaders, are able to progress beyond the barrier. The barrier leader is fixed for the duration of a given epoch. The barrier can be reused in different epochs with different leaders.

Definition 3.1. A barrier procedure satisfies the following properties for any given epoch e:

(i) no call to the barrier procedure in epoch e terminates before the leader has begun its call;
(ii) in a fair history, the leader's call in epoch e eventually terminates (or a failure occurs); and
(iii) in a fair history, if the leader's call in epoch e terminates then every other call in epoch e eventually terminates (or a failure occurs).

3.1 Barrier Variation 1: Known Leader

In the first variation, the barrier procedure is called **BarrierSub**, and is invoked with two arguments: the epoch number *epoch*, and the process ID of the leader, which is decided using some external mechanism. The leader opens the barrier at line 3 by writing a global shared variable, and then uses a distributed signaling mechanism to wake up non-leader processes that may be waiting on the barrier. The signaling mechanism borrows ideas from [17], except that it uses Compare-And-Swap for handshaking among two processes as opposed to implementing leader election from reads and writes. This barrier variation is designed for and needed in the DSM model only, where it achieves $O(1)$ RMR complexity.

After writing R, the leader executes the helper procedure **BSub-Leader** in which it synchronizes with non-leader processes that may be accessing the barrier. This helper procedure begins with a handshaking mechanism at lines 8–13, which uses the array $C[lid][1..N]$ of CAS objects to settle a potential race condition between the leader and non-leaders executing line 10 and line 18. If the leader is the first to swap *epoch* into $C[lid][j]$ (i.e., wins the handshake) then p_j will progress through the barrier without blocking, otherwise p_j will wait for a signal. The for loop at lines 8–13 generates a list of non-leaders who win the handshake (i.e., with whom the leader loses the handshake) and stores their IDs in consecutive elements of $L[lid][1..N]$ at line 11. The position of a process p_j in this array is recorded in $I[lid][j]$ at line 12. Finally, the leader signals the first process in this list at line 16, and sets off a chain reaction by which the kth process in the list signals process number $k+1$.

A non-leader process p_i calls **BSub-NonLeader** if $R < epoch$ at line 1, and executes the handshake at line 18. If p_i swaps *epoch* into $C[lid][i]$ before the leader (i.e., p_i wins the handshake) then p_i waits for a signal at line 17, and then signals the next process in the list created by the leader at lines 21–24. Otherwise, if the leader already swapped *epoch* into $C[lid][i]$ then p_i returns immediately since the barrier is open and p_i is not required to participate in the distributed signaling mechanism.

Theorem 3.2 asserts the correctness properties of the barrier. The proof is omitted due to lack of space.

THEOREM 3.2. **BarrierSub** *satisfies its specification (Definition 3.1).*

3.2 Barrier variation 2: Unknown Leader

The second variation of the barrier is designed for both the CC and DSM models, where it also achieves $O(1)$ RMR complexity. The barrier procedure is called **Barrier**, and is invoked with two arguments: the epoch number *epoch*, and a Boolean *isLeader* indicating whether the caller is the barrier leader. Thus, each process knows whether it is the leader, but non-leader processes do not know the ID of the leader. The barrier is opened by the leader by writing the current epoch number to a shared variable R. The variable R persists across failures but does not need to be reset since the epoch number grows monotonically. Synchronization with non-leader processes is straightforward in the CC model, and is contained in procedure **BarrierCC**. The algorithm for the DSM model is contained in procedure **BarrierDSM**, and is much more involved. This procedure uses **BarrierSub** as a subroutine, which we refer to as the *secondary barrier.*

The implementations of **Barrier**, **BarrierCC**, and **BarrierDSM** are presented in Figure 2. In the CC model, synchronization is achieved easily using a global spin variable R. The leader increases the value of R to the current epoch number at line 30, and the other processes wait for this state change at line 32. The execution path in the DSM model is more involved since a global spin variable cannot be used in an RMR-efficient manner. Synchronization is instead achieved using a combination of two mechanisms. First, the leader increases the value of the shared variable R to the current epoch number at line 48, which opens the barrier for any other process that reads R at line 41 after R is updated. A secondary mechanism is needed to handle the situation where the other process arrives at the barrier before the leader, and does not know who the leader is. This is dealt with by electing a secondary leader using the CAS object C at line 49 and line 54. Once the barrier is opened by the barrier leader, the secondary leader is unblocked at line 52, and all processes meet at the secondary barrier **BarrierSub** at line 58.

The DSM execution path begins with resetting the CAS object C at lines 42–45. The algorithm cannot rely on the leader from the previous epoch to reset C at the end of **BarrierDSM** because a crash failure can prevent the leader from progressing that far.[2] Resetting C is difficult because one has to distinguish between the case when C holds the ID of the leader from a prior epoch

[2]The algorithm can be simplified under the assumption that a crashed process eventually recovers and reaches the barrier again, but in this section we present a more general solution that does not rely on this assumption.

Shared variables:

- R: read/write register, **init** 0
- $C[1..N][1..N]$: **array** of readable **CAS** objects, **init** 0, elements $C[i][1..N]$ local to process p_i
- $I[1..N][1..N]$: **array** of read/write registers, **init** 0, elements $I[i][1..N]$ local to process p_i
- $L[1..N][1..N]$: **array** of read/write registers, **init** 0, elements $L[i][1..N]$ local to process p_i
- $S[1..N]$: **array** of read/write registers, **init** 0, element i local to process p_i

Private variables:

- j, k, tmp: integer, uninitialized

Procedure BarrierSub (*epoch, lid*) for process p_i

```
// try fast path
if R = epoch then return
// take slow path
if lid = i then
    R := epoch
    BSub-Leader (epoch)
else
    BSub-NonLeader (epoch, lid)
```

Procedure BSub-Leader (*epoch*) for process p_i

```
k := 1
for j in 1..N do
    tmp := C[i][j]
    if CAS(&C[i][j], tmp, epoch) = epoch then
        L[i][k] := j
        I[i][j] := k
        k := k + 1
if k > 1 then
    tmp := L[i][1]
    S[tmp] := epoch
```

Procedure BSub-NonLeader (*epoch, lid*) for process p_i

```
tmp := C[lid][j]
if CAS(&C[lid][j], tmp, epoch) < epoch then
    await S[i] = epoch
    k := I[lid][i]
    if k < N then
        tmp := L[lid][k + 1]
        if tmp ≠ 0 then
            S[tmp] := epoch
```

Figure 1: RMR-efficient barrier with known leader.

(which must be reset), versus the case when C holds the ID of the current leader (which must not be reset). The algorithm makes the distinction by appending a binary tag to the process ID, which is why C holds an ordered pair of the from $\langle ID, tag \rangle$. The tag is toggled when process p_i reaches line 46, and is recorded implicitly by storing a pair of epoch numbers in the array $E[i][0..1]$. The two array elements hold distinct values (except in the initial state), and the index of the higher value indicates the state of the tag after p_i's last call to **SetTag**. The value of the tag a process p_i will hold in the current epoch after calling **SetTag** is determined by calling **GetTag** at line 44. This procedure reads $E[i][0..1]$ at lines 33–34, and searches for an array element that holds the current epoch number. If such an element exists, its index is the value of the tag for p_i in the current epoch (line 36 and line 38). If not, then the value of p_i's tag in the current epoch is different than in the last epoch where p_i toggled its tag, and is computed at line 40.

To reset C, process p_i first checks whether C holds the ID of some process p_j and its tag (as opposed to $\perp$ and a tag) at lines 42–43. If so, and the tag stored in C does not match the tag computed for p_j for the current epoch (line 44), then p_i attempts to reset C using CAS at line 45. The tag prevents the ABA problem in case some other process resets C and p_j then wins the secondary leader election at line 49 or line 54 in the current epoch after p_i reads C at line 42 and before p_i executes the CAS at line 45.

Theorem 3.3 asserts the correctness properties of the barrier. The proof is omitted due to lack of space.

THEOREM 3.3. **Barrier** *satisfies its specification (Definition 3.1) and has worst-case $O(1)$ RMR complexity in the CC and DSM models.*

4 TRANSFORMATIONS

This section presents several RMR-efficient transformations for mutual exclusion (ME) and recoverable mutual exclusion (RME) algorithms. Applying these to the MCS lock [27], we obtain an $O(1)$ RMRs RME algorithm that uses read/write registers as well as single-word Fetch-And-Store and Compare-And-Swap.

4.1 Transformation 1: Conventional ME to RME

The first transformation, presented in Figure 3, converts a conventional mutex (base mutex) to a recoverable mutex (target mutex) by resetting the base mutex after each failure. The main algorithmic idea is similar to [18], except that the overhead of resetting the base mutex is reduced greatly by taking advantage of the stronger failure model. Internally, the transformation uses a conventional base mutex B, a CAS object C, and the RMR-efficient barrier described

Shared variables:

- R: read/write register, **init** 0
- C: readable/writable **CAS** object, **init** $\langle \perp, 0 \rangle$
- $E[1..N][0..1]$: **array** of read/write register, **init** 0, element $E[i][0..1]$ local to process p_i
- $S[1..N]$: **array** of **Boolean** spin variables, element $S[i]$ local to process p_i, **init** 0

Private variables:

- $secldr, tag, ltag, e0, e1$: integer, uninitialized

Procedure Barrier (*epoch, isLeader*) for process p_i

```
if CC model then
    BarrierCC (epoch, isLeader)
else if DSM model then
    BarrierDSM (epoch, isLeader)
```

Procedure BarrierCC (*epoch, isLeader*) for process p_i

```
if isLeader then
    R := epoch
else
    await R = epoch
```

Procedure GetTag (*epoch, i*) for process p_i

```
e0 := E[i][0]
e1 := E[i][1]
if e0 = epoch then
    return 0
else if e1 = epoch then
    return 1
else
    if e0 > e1 then return 1 else return 0
```

Procedure BarrierDSM (*epoch, isLeader*) for process p_i

```
// try fast path
if R := epoch then return
// slow path, reset CAS object first
⟨secldr, ltag⟩ := C
if secldr ≠ ⊥ then
    if ltag ≠ GetTag(epoch, secldr) then
        CAS(&C, ⟨secldr, ltag⟩, ⟨⊥, 0⟩)
// elect secondary leader
tag := SetTag(epoch)
if isLeader then
    // open the barrier
    R := epoch
    ⟨secldr, ltag⟩ := CAS(&C, ⟨⊥, 0⟩, ⟨i, tag⟩)
    if secldr = ⊥ then
        secldr := i
    // signal secondary leader
    S[secldr] := epoch
else
    ⟨secldr, ltag⟩ := CAS(&C, ⟨⊥, 0⟩, ⟨i, tag⟩)
    if secldr = ⊥ then
        secldr := i
        await S[i] = epoch
// wait for secondary leader
BarrierSub(epoch, secldr)
```

Procedure SetTag (*epoch*) for process p_i

```
tag := GetTag(epoch, i)
E[i][tag] := epoch
return tag
```

Figure 2: RMR-efficient barrier with unknown leader.

earlier in Section 3. The target entry and exit protocols simply invoke their counterparts on the base mutex B. The recovery protocol uses the shared variable C to determine who will be responsible for resetting B, and the barrier to ensure that no process accesses B unsafely while it is being reset.

In steady-state failure-free operation, C holds the current epoch number, and so the body of the recovery protocol is bypassed due to the conditional statements at line 63 and line 71. Following the first failure, C holds a value ≥ 0 and less than the current epoch number. Under this condition, processes proceed to line 64 to elect a leader, and the latter process updates the value of C to a negative value ($-epoch$), indicating that recovery is in progress. The leader then resets B at line 66, and updates C to a positive value (*epoch*) at line 67, indicating that recovery is complete. The leader then enters the barrier at line 68. A process that lost the leader election at line 64 enters the barrier as a non-leader at line 70.

Some processes may begin executing the recovery protocol after the leader has already been chosen in the current epoch, and before the leader reaches line 67. Such processes read a negative value ($-epoch$) from C at line 62, and then enter the barrier as a non-leader at line 72. If the recovery protocol in the previous epoch was interrupted by a failure, then a process may also read a negative value $> -epoch$ and < 0 from C at line 62, in which case it proceeds to line 64, similarly to the case when C holds a value ≥ 0 and $< epoch$. The leader election is then repeated for the current epoch.

Theorem 4.1 asserts the correctness properties of the transformation presented in Figure 3.

THEOREM 4.1. *The target mutex implemented using the transformation presented in Figure 3 satisfies mutual exclusion, ensures starvation freedom if B ensures starvation freedom in failure-free histories, ensures bounded exit if B ensures bounded exit, and has*

Procedure Recover (*epoch*) for process p_i

```
62 cur := C
63 if −epoch < cur < epoch then
64 |   ret := CAS(&C, cur, −epoch)
65 |   if ret = cur then
66 |   |   reset B to its initial state
67 |   |   C := epoch
68 |   |   Barrier (epoch, true)
69 |   else
70 |   |   Barrier (epoch, false)
71 else if cur = −epoch then
72 |   Barrier (epoch, false)
```

Shared variables:

- B: conventional mutex (base mutex)
- C: readable/writable **CAS** object, **init** 0

Private variables:

- cur, ret: integers, uninitialized

Procedure Enter (*epoch*) for process p_i

```
73 B.Enter( )
```

Procedure Exit (*epoch*) for process p_i

```
74 B.Exit( )
```

Figure 3: Transformation of conventional mutex to recoverable mutex.

RMR complexity $O(f(B))$ where $f(B)$ denotes the sum of the RMR complexity of B and the RMR cost of resetting B at line 66.

The statement of Theorem 4.1 intentionally omits the bounded recovery property because the recovery protocol presented in Figure 3 may perform busy-waiting inside the barrier operations. In particular, a process that enters the barrier as a non-leader may busy-wait at lines 70 or 72. However, the recovery protocol is bounded in passages that begin in a state where C holds the value of the current epoch. This includes all passages occurring in failure-free histories, provided that the initial epoch number matches the initial value of the shared variable C. It also includes passages that begin after some process has completed lines 66–67 after the most recent failure.

The remainder of this section is dedicated to the proof of Theorem 4.1. The analysis begins with a proof that the base mutex B is accessed correctly.

Lemma 4.2. *No process executes B.***Enter**() *or B.***Exit**() *while another process is resetting B at line 66. Furthermore, B is reset at most once in each epoch, and no process executes B.***Enter**() *or B.***Exit**() *in a given epoch e before B is reset in epoch e at line 66.*

Proof. Consider an arbitrary epoch e. Suppose that processes continue to take steps, not necessarily in a fair order, in epoch e. Since C can only be assigned a value of $-e$ (line 64) or $+e$ (line 67) in epoch e, and since C is initialized to a value less than any epoch number, it follows that $-e < C < e$ holds at the beginning of epoch e. Assuming that processes continue to take steps and there is no failure, the next two transitions in the value of C are $C = -e$ at line 64 and $C = e$ at line 67. Furthermore, at most one process p_i succeeds in swapping $-e$ into C at line 64, and only this process reaches lines 66–67 in epoch e. Due to the conditional statements at lines 63 and 71, no process can complete the recovery protocol until p_i reaches line 67, and after p_i has done so, both conditions are false. As a result, at most one process p_i resets B at line 66 in epoch e, no process completes the recovery protocol until after p_i reaches line 67 after resetting B, and no process executes lines 66–67 again after p_i has done so. These statements imply the lemma since B is only reset at line 66. □

Lemma 4.3. *The target mutex algorithm ensures mutual exclusion.*

Proof. The base mutex B maintains its correctness properties because it is accessed correctly by Lemma 4.2 and the structure of the transformation (lines 73 and 74). Therefore, the critical section of the target algorithm is protected by B. □

Lemma 4.4. *If B ensures starvation freedom in failure-free histories, then the target mutex algorithm satisfies starvation freedom.*

Proof. Consider any fair execution history H of the target mutex. Suppose for contradiction that some process p_i leaves the NCS in H and never enters the CS despite a finite number of failures in H. Let e be the epoch number corresponding to the suffix of H after the last failure. Since p_i has an incomplete super-passage after this last failure, and since H is fair, it follows that p_i takes infinitely many steps in epoch e but does not enter the CS. This implies that p_i is stuck forever in epoch e. Then p_i must be stuck in a barrier or in some access to the base mutex B since the rest of the algorithm is wait-free.

Case 1: p_i is stuck in a barrier at line 68, line 70, or line 72. The barrier leader never gets stuck by the correctness properties of the barrier (Theorem 3.3), and so p_i must be stuck at line 70 or line 72 where it accesses the barrier as a non-leader. If p_i is stuck at line 70 then it read $-e < C < e$ at line 62, and then failed to swap $-e$ into C at line 64, which implies that some other process p_j won the CAS operation. Then p_j is the barrier leader who eventually completes line 68 and opens the barrier. In that case the fact that p_i is stuck forever contradicts the correctness of the barrier (Theorem 3.3). On the other hand, if p_i is stuck at line 72 then it read a value $\leq -e$ or $> e$ from C at line 62. Values $< -e$ and $> e$ are not possible in epoch e, and so p_i must have read $C = -e$. Once again, this implies that some process p_j won the CAS at line 64, and eventually opens the barrier at line 68, so the assumption that p_i is stuck contradicts the correctness of the barrier.

Case 2: p_i is stuck in some access to B at line 66, line 73, or line 74. Since line 66 is wait-free sequential code, p_i must be stuck at line 73 or line 74. It follows from Lemma 4.2 that B is first reset exactly once at line 66 before p_i can reach line 73 or line 74, and so the steps executed by all processes at line 73 and line 74 in epoch e constitute some failure-free execution history H of the base mutex B. Furthermore, H is fair and failure-free as well. This follows from several observations: the execution over the target mutex is fair, processes access B in the correct order (i.e., entry first, then exit, in an alternating sequence), and Case 1 rules out the possibility of a process getting stuck outside of line 73 or line 74. As a result, the fact that p_i is stuck forever in H executing the entry or exit protocol of B contradicts the starvation freedom of B. □

Lemma 4.5. *Letting $f(B)$ denote the sum of the RMR complexity of the base mutex and the RMR cost of resetting B at line 66, the target mutex has worst-case RMR complexity $O(f(B))$.*

Proof. The RMR complexity of the target mutex in one passage is the sum of several components. First, each process accesses the barrier at most once per passage, and this incurs $O(1)$ RMRs by Theorem 3.3. Second, each process accesses B at most three times per passage – to reset it at line 66, to acquire it at line 73, and to release it at line 74 – and each such access costs $O(f(B))$ RMRs. (Recall that B is accessed correctly by Lemma 4.2 and the structure of the transformation, namely the order of lines 73 and 74.) Finally, each process incurs $O(1)$ additional RMRs per passage executing other lines of code. □

Proof of Theorem 4.1. The mutual exclusion property follows from Lemma 4.3. Preservation of starvation freedom follows from Lemma 4.4. Preservation of bounded exit follows from the simple structure of the exit protocol (line 74). The RMR complexity property follows from Lemma 4.5. □

In addition to the properties stated in Theorem 4.1, the transformation has a feature not provided by prior RME algorithms: it guarantees a weak form of starvation freedom even when processes are not required to recover following a failure. This new liveness property is stated formally in Definitions 4.6–4.7.

*Definition 4.6 (**Weak Fairness**).* A history H is *weakly fair* if it is finite, or if it is infinite and every process that participates either executes infinitely many steps, or stops taking steps after completing a failure-free passage, or stops taking steps after a crash step.

*Definition 4.7 (**Weak Starvation Freedom**).* For any infinite weakly fair history H, if a process p_i leaves the NCS in some step of H then eventually p_i itself enters the CS, or p_i stops taking steps after a crash step, or else there are infinitely many crash steps in H.

Theorem 4.8. *The target mutex implemented using the transformation presented in Figure 3 ensures weak starvation freedom if B ensures starvation freedom in failure-free histories.*

Proof. The theorem follows by the same proof as for Lemma 4.4. □

4.2 Transformation 2: RME to CSR RME

The second transformation adds the CSR property to an existing RME algorithm (base mutex). Its pseudo-code is presented in Figure 4 in black-colored font. The figure contains also pseudo-code in gray-colored font for Transformation 3 (described later) which should be disregarded for now. Critical section ownership is tracked using a pair of shared variables: *inCSpid* stores the ID of the process currently in the CS, or the negation of this ID if that process is re-entering the CS following a failure; *inCSepoch* stores the epoch number of the process who last entered the CS.

A process p_i accessing the target mutex first executes the recovery protocol of the base mutex at line 75. Next, it determines whether another process is currently in (or dangerously near) the CS. If p_i reads its own ID, or its negation, from *inCSpid* at line 76, then this indicates that p_i must re-enter the CS before any other process enters the CS. In that case, p_i proceeds to execute the base entry protocol at line 88. Then, p_i ensures that the current epoch number is recorded in *inCSepoch* at line 89. This additional information helps other processes distinguish between the case when a process failed in the CS in a prior epoch and must be allowed to re-enter the CS, versus the case when this process entered the CS in the current epoch and does not require any special treatment. Next, p_i writes the negation of its ID to *inCSpid* at line 91, indicating that it is about to re-enter the CS. In the exit protocol, p_i first checks at line 100 whether it had re-entered the CS after an earlier failure, which is the case when $inCSpid = -i$ (see line 91). If so, then p_i opens the $BR1$ barrier at line 102. This barrier is used to barricade other processes inside the recovery protocol (see line 80) in order to allow p_i to re-enter the CS unimpeded. Finally, p_i resets *inCSpid* to $\perp$ at line 102 and completes the base exit protocol at line 105.

A process p_i that does not read its own ID or its negation from *inCSpid* at line 76 of the recovery protocol must check whether another process p_j may be recovering from a failure in the CS, in which case p_i must wait for p_j instead of competing for the base mutex. This case is identified at lines 78–79, which check whether $inCSpid \neq \perp$ and $inCSepoch \neq epoch$. The latter condition implies that p_j must re-enter the CS, and must be given priority over p_i. In that case p_i waits for p_j at a barrier at line 80. Even if $inCSepoch = epoch$, it is possible that p_j is also re-entering the CS and has progressed beyond line 89, however in that case p_j has already cleared the base entry protocol at line 88 and so it is safe for p_i to race against p_j without waiting on the barrier. If p_i does wait, then p_j eventually opens the barrier at line 102 of the exit protocol, at which point p_i is free to compete for the base mutex with other processes. In the entry protocol, p_i then executes the base entry protocol at line 88, ensures that the *inCSepoch* variable stores the current epoch number at line 89, and then writes its ID to *inCSpid* at line 93. In the exit protocol, p_i resets *inCSpid* at line 104 and then completes the base exit protocol at line 105.

Theorem 4.9 asserts the correctness properties of the transformation. The proof is omitted due to lack of space.

Theorem 4.9. *The target mutex implemented using the transformation presented in Figure 4 satisfies mutual exclusion, ensures CSR, ensures SF if B ensures SF, and has the same RMR complexity asymptotically as B.*

Shared variables:

- B: base mutex, recoverable
- $BR1$,$BR2$: Barrier object
- $inCSpid$: read/write register, **init** $\bot$
- $inCSepoch$: read/write register, **init** 0
- $h[1..N]$: array of Boolean, **init false**
- $hInd$: read/write register, **init** 1
- $hEpoch$: read/write register, **init** 0

Procedure Recover (*epoch*) for process p_i

```
75 B.Recover(epoch)
76 if inCSpid = i ∨ inCSpid = −i then
       // CS re-entry after failure
77     proceed to entry protocol
78 else if inCSpid ≠ ⊥ then
79     if inCSepoch ≠ epoch then
80         BR1.Barrier (epoch, false)
81 if hEpoch ≠ epoch ∧ h[|hInd|] = true ∧ inCSpid ∉
   {hInd, −hInd} then
82     if |hInd| = i then
           // Privileged process recovery
83         hInd := −i
84         proceed to entry protocol
85     else
86         BR2.Barrier (epoch, false)
```

Procedure Enter (*epoch*) for process p_i

```
87 h[i] := true
88 B.Enter(epoch)
89 inCSepoch := epoch
90 if inCSpid = i ∨ inCSpid = −i then
       // CS re-entry after failure
91     inCSpid := −i
92 else
93     inCSpid := i
94 h[i] := false
95 if hEpoch ≠ epoch ∧ ¬(inCSpid < 0 ∧ |inCSpid| ≠
   |hInd| ∧ h[|hInd|] = true) then
96     hEpoch := epoch
97     if hInd < 0 then
98         BR2.Barrier (epoch, true)
99     hInd = (|hInd| mod N) + 1
```

Procedure Exit (*epoch*) for process p_i

```
100 if inCSpid = −i then
        // CS re-entry after failure
101     inCSpid := ⊥
102     BR1.Barrier (epoch, true)
103 else
104     inCSpid := ⊥
105 B.Exit(epoch)
```

Figure 4: Transformation of recoverable mutex to CSR and FRF recoverable mutex.

The statement of Theorem 4.9 intentionally omits the bounded exit property because the transformation presented in Figure 4 does not preserve BE. This is due to the barrier operation at line 102 of the exit protocol, which may internally perform busy-waiting. However, if the barrier is implemented using the algorithm described in Section 3 then the transformation does ensure BE in two special cases: (1) in the CC model, where the barrier algorithm for the leader is wait-free; and (2) in the DSM model, in a passage where a process does not re-enter the CS following a failure, which includes all failure-free executions.

Similarly to BE, the transformation does not preserve bounded recovery due to the barrier operation at line 80. BR is guaranteed only in passages where the recovery of B at line 75 completes in a bounded number of steps, and where the value of *inCSepoch* matches the current epoch number, which enables barrier bypass at line 79.

4.3 Transformation 3: CSR RME to CSR and Failures-Robust Fair RME

Transformations 1 and 2 do not guarantee fairness in executions containing infinitely many failures in the sense that some processes may enter the CS infinitely often while other processes starve. This is because Transformation 1 resets the base mutex to its initial state after each failure, and Transformation 2 only preserves the starvation freedom (SF) property defined in Section 2, which does not guarantee progress to every process when failures occur infinitely often. Transformation 3, which we present next, prevents this problem by ensuring that a waiting process can be overtaken only a finite number of times even in these executions. We call this new property *Failures-Robust Fairness* (FRF):

*Definition 4.10 (**Failures-Robust Fairness (FRF)**).* For any fair history H containing infinitely many super-passages, if a process p_i leaves the NCS in some step of H then p_i eventually itself enters the CS.

The idea underlying the transformation is a recovery-time helping mechanism. This helping mechanism ensures that once a process p_i starts the base entry section, after at most n epochs in which there are new entries to the CS, p_i is guaranteed to be the next process to enter the CS. The pseudo-code of Transformation 3 is presented in Figure 4 in gray-colored font.[3] The transformation

[3] We note that a transformation adding the FRF property can be applied directly to a recoverable mutex obtained using Transformation 1, resulting in a recovable mutex that satisfies FRF but not CSR.

ensures that if the base mutex is starvation-free, then the target mutex satisfies both the CSR and the FRF properties.

The transformation uses the following shared variables. The h array stores a flag per every process, indicating whether or not the process requires recovery-time helping. The $hInd$ variable is an index to the h array, storing the entry number of the *privileged process*, that is, the next process that should be helped (if its flag is set). A process sets its flag in the h array immediately before invoking the base entry code (line **87**). The flag is reset at line **94**, before entering the CS but after variable $inCSpid$ is set (at line **91** or line **93**), thus guaranteeing that p would be the next to enter the CS even in case of a failure immediately after it is reset. The $hInd$ index is initialized to 1 and is incremented (modulo N) at line **99** upon a new epoch (line **95**). The $BR2$ barrier (see Section 3) is used for guaranteeing the uninterrupted CS entry of the privileged process upon recovery, if its flag is set.

When a process p_i performs a steady-state failure-free passage, lines **81–86** in the recovery protocol are skipped (because $hEpoch = epoch$) and p_i proceeds to the entry code. In the entry code, p_i sets its h flag at line **87** before invoking the base entry code and resets it at line **94** when it is logically in the CS. Lines **95–99** are also skipped in steady-state failure-free passages. No additional logic is required in the exit section to support the recovery-time helping mechanism.

Upon recovery from a new failure, we consider first the simpler case in which $inCSpid = \perp$ holds. In this case, p_i skips lines **77–80**, and proceeds to evaluate the condition at line **81**. If this is a new epoch and the privileged process requires help, then the condition is true since $inCSpid = \perp$, so the condition of line **82** is evaluated. If $|hInd| = i$, then p_i is the privileged process and it requires help. In this case, p_i sets $hInd = -i$ in order to remember that it needs to execute special actions in the entry section and proceeds into it (lines **83–84**). The other possibility is that p_i is not the privileged process. In this case, p_i waits for the privileged process at line **86**, permitting the latter's unobstructed entry to the CS.

If p_i reaches the entry section from line **84**, then it executes the base entry protocol. After completing the base entry section, p_i sets $inCSpid = i$ and then resets its h flag (lines **93–94**); it no longer requires help, since it is already logically in the CS and the re-entry mechanism ensures it would return to it if the system fails before it exits. Since this is a new epoch and $inCSpid = hInd$ now holds, the condition at line **95** is satisfied and so p_i updates the epoch number, increments $hInd$ modulo N and opens the $BR2$ barrier (lines **96–99**), allowing those processes that may wait at line **86** to proceed to the entry section.

The other possible case is that $|inCSpid| = j$ holds upon recovery, for some process ID j. If there is no privileged process, then the CSR code ensures that p_j re-enters the CS. Otherwise there are two subcases to consider. If there is a privileged process $p_i \neq p_j$ then, as we prove, Transformation 3 ensures that the next two entries to the CS are by p_j followed by p_i. If $i = j$, then the algorithm ensures that p_i enters the CS via the CSR code and the helping code is not executed. In all cases, lines **95–99** guarantee that once the privileged process enters the CS (or does not require help in the first place), $hInd$ is incremented modulo N, thus ensuring the FRF property.

Theorem 4.11 asserts the correctness properties of Transformation 3. The proof is omitted due to lack of space.

THEOREM 4.11. *The target mutex generated by Transformation 3 maintains the CSR property. If the base mutex satisfies SF, then the target mutex obtained from it by Transformation 3 satisfies the FRF property. The target mutex has the same RMR complexity asymptotically as the base mutex.*

The transformation presented in Figure 4 preserves the bounded exit property in the same special cases as the recoverable-to-CSR version, which omits the additional lines of pseudo-code typeset in gray-colored font. These cases are discussed at the end of Section 4.2. Similarly, the full transformation does not preserve bounded recovery due to the barrier operations at lines **80** and **86**. This is true even in some passages where $inCSepoch$ matches the current epoch number because of the additional synchronization performed at line **86** for the FRF property.

5 RELATED WORK

Mutual exclusion (ME) is one of the oldest topics in distributed computing [3, 11, 30, 31]. Recent research in this space has focused on *local spin* algorithms, which guarantee bounded RMR complexity per passage by busy-waiting only on locally accessible shared variables. Local spinning bounds the communication overhead associated with synchronization and supports multi-core scalability [4, 10]. For the class of N-process algorithms that use reads, writes and comparison primitives (defined in [3]), the tight bound on worst-case RMRs is $\Theta(\log N)$. Yang and Anderson [32] proved the upper bound in the CC and DSM models using an arbitration tree modeled after Kessels [23]. Attiya, Hendler, and Woelfel [5] later proved the matching lower bound, building on a series of earlier results [2, 9, 12, 15]. Sub-logarithmic RMR complexity is attainable on expectation using randomization [6, 13, 14, 20], and $O(1)$ RMR complexity is attainable deterministically if additional atomic primitives are available, such as Fetch-And-Store or Fetch-And-Add [4, 19, 26, 27].

Solutions to the ME problem generally assume reliable processes since synchronization is achieved by busy-waiting, although variations of the problem are solvable in some failure models. Lamport and Taubenfeld define several such models for algorithms based on single-writer registers, assuming that failures affect the values of such shared variables in specific ways [25, 31]. Lamport's Bakery [24] tolerates crash failures provided that any registers owned by the failed process are reset to zero [24]. Bohannon et al. instead consider a failure model in which process crashes are permanent and do not affect the values of shared variables, which complicates recovery [7, 8]. Their solutions rely on operating system support for failure detection and assume for simplicity that recovery is performed in a dedicated process that is itself reliable. Michael and Kim's fault-tolerant mutex similarly relies on failure detection but does not require a dedicated recovery process [28]. Instead, a process that is waiting for a lock may "usurp" the lock if it determines that the previous lock holder has crashed permanently.

Recoverable mutual exclusion (RME) was formalized by Golab and Ramaraju [18]. Two of Golab and Ramaraju's RME solutions are local-spin in both the CC and DSM models, and both incur $\Omega(\log N)$ RMRs per passage in the worst case. Ramaraju's earlier RME algorithm incurs $\Theta(N)$ RMRs in the worst case and relies on a specialized Fetch-And-Store-And-Store (FASAS) instruction, which is equivalent to the atomic composition of a Fetch-And-Store followed by a write that saves the fetched value in NVRAM [29]. The best upper bound proved by Golab and Ramaraju is $O(\log N)$ RMRs in the CC and DSM models, and requires atomic reads and writes only. Golab and Hendler broke the logarithmic barrier by presenting an RME algorithm that uses single-word Fetch-And-Store and Compare-And-Swap and incurs $O(\log N/\log\log N)$ RMRs per passage in the CC model, as well as an algorithm that uses specialized double-word Read-Modify-Write operations (FASAS and CAS) and incurs $O(1)$ RMRs per passage in the CC and DSM models [16].

Jayanti and Joshi recently proposed an RME algorithm that uses reads, writes, and single-word Compare-And-Swap operations, and incurs $O(\log N)$ RMRs per passage in the CC and DSM models. The new breakthrough in this work is the use of wait-free recovery code, achieved using an f-array – a shared object type that generalizes multi-writer snapshots by supporting the computation of a user-specified function f (e.g., min or max) over the array elements [21]. Operations on the f-array are naturally idempotent, which allows the algorithm to avoid busy-waiting in the recovery protocol.

Published solutions to the RME problem [16, 18, 22] assume independent failures, and work correctly if failures are system-wide, but do not benefit from the stricter failure model in terms of RMR complexity. It is not known whether RME is inherently less costly in the model with system-wide failures because the tight RMR complexity bound for RME has not yet been established for the model with independent failures.

The epoch numbers used in our algorithms are inspired by prior work on fault-tolerant computation. The failure detector $\diamond S_e$ proposed by Aguilera, Chen and Toueg associates an epoch number with each process deemed to be currently up [1]. The completeness property of this failure detector requires that the epoch number of an unstable process eventually increases monotonically as long as the process is included in the failure detector's output. Epoch numbers in this paper are used somewhat similarly for detecting system-wide failures, but our model does not use a formal failure detector abstraction in which every process has access to its own failure detector module. We assume instead that processes have common knowledge of the current epoch number, which is obtained by querying the operating system during process initialization.

6 CONCLUSION

We considered an RME model where failures are system-wide and processes receive additional information from the environment regarding the occurrence of the failure. We proved that, in this model, an $O(1)$ RMRs conventional mutex can be transformed to an $O(1)$ RMRs recoverable mutex using only commonly supported single-word synchronization primitives. In future work, we intend to investigate the gap in RMR complexity between our upper bounds for the model with system-wide failures and prior results in the model with individual failures [16, 18, 22].

REFERENCES

[1] M. K. Aguilera, W. Chen, and S. Toueg. Failure detection and consensus in the crash-recovery model. *Distributed Computing*, 13(2):99–125, 2000.

[2] J. Anderson and Y.-J. Kim. An improved lower bound for the time complexity of mutual exclusion. *Distributed Computing*, 15(4):221–253, 2002.

[3] J. Anderson, Y.-J. Kim, and T. Herman. Shared-memory mutual exclusion: Major research trends since 1986. *Distributed Computing*, 16(2-3):75–110, 2003.

[4] T. Anderson. The performance of spin lock alternatives for shared-memory multiprocessors. *IEEE Transactions on Parallel and Distributed Systems*, 1(1):6–16, 1990.

[5] H. Attiya, D. Hendler, and P. Woelfel. Tight RMR lower bounds for mutual exclusion and other problems. In *Proc. of the 40th ACM Symposium on Theory of Computing (STOC)*, pages 217–226, 2008.

[6] M. A. Bender and S. Gilbert. Mutual Exclusion with $O(\log^2 \log n)$ Amortized Work. In *Proc. of the 52nd Symposium on Foundations of Computer Science (FOCS)*, pages 728–737, 2011.

[7] P. Bohannon, D. F. Lieuwen, and A. Silberschatz. Recovering scalable spin locks. In *Proc. of the 8th IEEE Symposium on Parallel and Distributed Processing (SPDP)*, pages 314–322, 1996.

[8] P. Bohannon, D. F. Lieuwen, A. Silberschatz, S. Sudarshan, and J. Gava. Recoverable user-level mutual exclusion. In *Proc. of the 7th IEEE Symposium on Parallel and Distributed Processing (SPDP)*, pages 293–301, 1995.

[9] R. Cypher. The communication requirements of mutual exclusion. In *Proc. of the 7th ACM Symposium on Parallel Algorithms and Architectures (SPAA)*, pages 147–156, 1995.

[10] T. David, R. Guerraoui, and V. Trigonakis. Everything you always wanted to know about synchronization but were afraid to ask. In *Proc. of the 24th ACM SIGOPS Symposium on Operating Systems Principles (SOSP)*, pages 33–48, 2013.

[11] E. W. Dijkstra. Solution of a problem in concurrent programming control. *Communications of the ACM*, 8(9):569, 1965.

[12] R. Fan and N. Lynch. An $\Omega(n \log n)$ lower bound on the cost of mutual exclusion. In *Proc. of the 25th ACM Symposium on Principles of Distributed Computing (PODC)*, pages 275–284, 2006.

[13] G. Giakkoupis and P. Woelfel. A tight RMR lower bound for randomized mutual exclusion. In *Proc. of the 44th Symposium on Theory of Computing (STOC)*, pages 983–1002, 2012.

[14] G. Giakkoupis and P. Woelfel. Randomized mutual exclusion with constant amortized RMR complexity on the DSM. In *Proc. of the 55th Symposium on Foundations of Computer Science (FOCS)*, pages 504–513, 2014.

[15] W. Golab, V. Hadzilacos, D. Hendler, and P. Woelfel. RMR-efficient implementations of comparison primitives using read and write operations. *Distributed Computing*, 25(2):109–162, 2012.

[16] W. Golab, and D. Hendler. Recoverable mutual exclusion in sub-logarithmic time. In *Proc. of the 36th Annual ACM Symposium on Principles of Distributed Computing (PODC)*, pages 211–220, 2017.

[17] W. Golab, D. Hendler, and P. Woelfel. An O(1) RMRs leader election algorithm. *SIAM J. Comput.*, 39(7): 2726–2760, 2010.

[18] W. Golab, and A. Ramaraju. Recoverable mutual exclusion. In *Proc. of the 35th Annual ACM Symposium on Principles of Distributed Computing (PODC)*, pages 65–74, 2016.

[19] G. Graunke and S. Thakkar. Synchronization algorithms for shared-memory multiprocessors. *IEEE Computer*, 23(6):60–69, 1990.

[20] D. Hendler and P. Woelfel. Randomized mutual exclusion with sub-logarithmic RMR-complexity. *Distributed Computing*, 24(1):3–19, 2011.

[21] P. Jayanti. F-arrays: Implementation and Applications. In *Proc. of the 21st Annual ACM Symposium on Principles of Distributed Computing (PODC)*, pages 270–279.

[22] P. Jayanti and A. Joshi. Recoverable FCFS mutual exclusion with wait-free recovery. In *Proc. of the 31st International Symposium on Distributed Computing (DISC)*, pages 30:1–30:15, 2017.

[23] J. Kessels. Arbitration without common modifiable variables. *Acta Informatica*, 17:135–141, 1982.

[24] L. Lamport. A new solution of Dijkstra's concurrent programming problem. *Communications of the ACM*, 17(8):453–455, 1974.

[25] L. Lamport. The mutual exclusion problem: part II – statement and solutions. *Journal of the ACM*, 33(2):327–348, 1986.

[26] P. Magnusson, A. Landin, and E. Hagersten. Queue locks on cache coherent multiprocessors. In *Proc. of the 8th International Parallel Processing Symposium (IPPS)*, pages 165–171, 1994.

[27] J. Mellor-Crummey and M. Scott. Algorithms for scalable synchronization on shared-memory multiprocessors. *ACM Transactions on Computer Systems*, 9(1):21–65, 1991.

[28] M. Michael and Y. Kim. Fault tolerant mutual exclusion locks for shared memory systems. US Patent 7,493,618, 2009.

[29] A. Ramaraju. RGLock: Recoverable mutual exclusion for non-volatile main memory systems. Master's thesis, University of Waterloo, 2015. https://uwspace.uwaterloo.ca/handle/10012/9473.

[30] M. Raynal. *Algorithms for Mutual Exclusion*. MIT Press, 1986.

[31] G. Taubenfeld. *Synchronization Algorithms and Concurrent Programming*. Prentice Hall, 2006.

[32] J.-H. Yang and J. Anderson. A fast, scalable mutual exclusion algorithm. *Distributed Computing*, 9(1):51–60, 1995.

Deterministic Abortable Mutual Exclusion with Sublogarithmic Adaptive RMR Complexity

Adam Alon
Blavatnik School of Computer Science
Tel Aviv University

Adam Morrison
Blavatnik School of Computer Science
Tel Aviv University

ABSTRACT

We present a deterministic abortable mutual exclusion algorithm for a cache-coherent (CC) model with read, write, Fetch-And-Add (F&A), and CAS primitives, whose RMR complexity is $O(\log_W N)$, where W is the size of the F&A registers. Under the standard assumption of $W = \Theta(\log N)$, our algorithm's RMR complexity is $O(\frac{\log N}{\log \log N})$; if $W = \Theta(N^\epsilon)$, for $0 < \epsilon < 1$ (as is the case in real multiprocessor machines), the RMR complexity is $O(1)$. Our algorithm is adaptive to the number of processes that abort. In particular, if no process aborts during a passage, its RMR cost is $O(1)$.

ACM Reference Format:
Adam Alon and Adam Morrison. 2018. Deterministic Abortable Mutual Exclusion with Sublogarithmic Adaptive RMR Complexity. In *PODC '18: ACM Symposium on Principles of Distributed Computing, July 23–27, 2018, Egham, United Kingdom.* ACM, New York, NY, USA, 10 pages. https://doi.org/10.1145/3212734.3212759

1 INTRODUCTION

Mutual exclusion [9] is a fundamental problem in distributed computing. A mutual exclusion object (henceforth, *lock*) prevents simultaneous entry to a *critical section* of code, in which some shared resource is accessed. To execute the critical section, a process must first *acquire* the lock by executing an *entry section.* The lock algorithm guarantees that at any time, at most one process holds the lock. After acquiring the lock and executing the critical section, a process *releases* the lock by executing an *exit section.*

Classic locks do not allow a process waiting in the entry section to abort its lock acquisition attempt and quit the lock protocol. Several use cases, however, require this feature: (1) a process blocked on a lock may wish to abandon its work chunk and switch to working on a different work chunk not subjected to serialization [8]; (2) database systems use aborts to recover from deadlocks and to deal with preemption of a lock holding process [25]; and (3) low-priority processes can abort to expedite lock handoff to a high-priority process [8, 24]. To meet these demands, an *abortable lock* [24, 25] additionally allows a process to abort its lock acquisition attempt in a finite number of its own steps.

We investigate the *remote memory references* (RMR) complexity of abortable locks. The RMR complexity measure captures the fact that the cost of a memory reference on shared-memory multiprocessor machines is not uniform. Some references can be satisfied quickly from memory local to the processor, whereas the rest must be satisfied from remote memory. For example, in a *cache-coherent* (CC) system, each processor stores local copies of the shared variables it accesses in its cache; a cache coherence protocol maintains the consistency of the copies in the different caches. A memory access to a cached variable is local; otherwise, it is remote. In a *distributed shared-memory* (DSM) system, each shared variable is permanently locally accessible to a single processor and remote to all other processors. References to remote memory are orders of magnitude slower than local memory accesses, as they must traverse the system's interconnect, and so the performance of lock algorithms critically depends on the number of remote memory references they generate [5, 21]. The RMR complexity measure (or *RMR cost*) therefore charges an algorithm only for RMRs; local memory accesses are considered free. RMR cost has been used almost exclusively as the complexity measure in shared-memory mutual exclusion research over the last 20 years [4, 6, 7, 10–12, 14, 15, 17, 23].

There is a gap between the known RMR cost of locks and of abortable locks. For an N-process system with read, write, comparison primitives [4] such as Compare-And-Swap (CAS), or LL/SC, Yang and Anderson's lock [26] and Jayanti's abortable lock [17] both have $O(\log N)$ RMR cost, which is optimal [6]. For mutual exclusion, the $\Omega(\log N)$ lower bound can be defeated by leveraging additional synchronization primitives. The MCS lock [21], for example, uses Fetch-And-Store (SWAP) in addition to the aforementioned primitives, and has RMR cost of $O(1)$. For abortable mutual exclusion, however, no algorithm with worst-case sublogarithmic RMR cost is known. Lee's abortable lock [19] leverages SWAP and Fetch-And-Add (F&A) primitives to obtain an RMR cost of $O(A^2)$, where A is the number of processes that abort. Lee's algorithm therefore incurs $O(1)$ RMRs if no process aborts, but its worst-case RMR cost is $O(N^2)$. Sublogarithmic RMR cost can also be achieved using randomization, both for locks [7, 11, 14, 15] and for abortable locks [12, 23], but this paper considers deterministic algorithms.

Our Contribution. We show that, as with mutual exclusion, abortable locks can leverage additional primitives to obtain sublogarithmic worst-case RMR cost. We present an abortable lock algorithm for a CC model with F&A in addition to read, write, and CAS primitives, whose worst-case RMR cost is $O(\log_W N)$, where W is the size of the F&A registers. Under the standard assumption of $W = \Theta(\log N)$, this time/space tradeoff implies that our algorithm's RMR cost is $O(\frac{\log N}{\log \log N})$. The RMR cost becomes $O(1)$ if $W = \Theta(N^\epsilon)$ for some $0 < \epsilon < 1$, as is the case in realistic multiprocessor systems.[1] Our algorithm is *adaptive to the number of*

PODC '18, July 23–27, 2018, Egham, United Kingdom

ACM ISBN 978-1-4503-5795-1/18/07...$15.00
https://doi.org/10.1145/3212734.3212759

[1] E.g., for a system with a billion processes and 64-bit memory words, $W \approx N^{1/5}$.

<table>
<tr><th rowspan="2" colspan="2">Algorithm</th><th rowspan="2">Model</th><th rowspan="2">Primitives</th><th rowspan="2">Space (#words)</th><th rowspan="2">Fairness Guarantee</th><th colspan="3">RMR cost of a passage through CS</th></tr>
<tr><th>Worst-case</th><th>No aborts</th><th>Adaptive bound</th></tr>
<tr><td colspan="2">Scott [24]</td><td>CC/DSM</td><td>SWAP, CAS</td><td>unbounded</td><td>FCFS</td><td>unbounded</td><td>$O(1)$</td><td>$O(\#A)$, where $\#A$ is the number of aborts during the execution</td></tr>
<tr><td colspan="2">Jayanti [17]</td><td>CC/DSM</td><td>LL/SC or CAS</td><td>$O(N)$</td><td>FCFS</td><td>$O(\log N)$</td><td>$O(\min(k, \log N))$</td><td>$O(\min(k, \log N))$, where k is the maximum number of processes active concurrently during the passage (i.e., point contention)</td></tr>
<tr><td colspan="2">Lee [19]</td><td>CC</td><td>F&A, SWAP</td><td>$O(N^2)$</td><td>FCFS</td><td>$O(N^2)$</td><td>$O(1)$</td><td>$O(A_i \cdot A_t)$</td></tr>
<tr><td rowspan="2">This Work</td><td>One-Shot</td><td>CC/DSM</td><td>F&A</td><td>$\mathbf{O(N)}$</td><td>FCFS</td><td rowspan="2">$\mathbf{O(\log_W N)}$</td><td rowspan="2">$\mathbf{O(1)}$</td><td rowspan="2">$\mathbf{O(\log_W A_i)}$ for complete passage
$\mathbf{O(\log_W A_t)}$ for aborted passage</td></tr>
<tr><td>Long-Lived</td><td>CC</td><td>F&A, CAS</td><td>$\mathbf{O(N^2)}$</td><td>Starvation Freedom</td></tr>
</table>

Table 1: ***Comparison of abortable locks, showing their system model, required primitives, complexity, and fairness.***

processes that abort. The RMR cost of a complete *passage* (entry and corresponding exit of the critical section) is $O(\log_W A_i)$, where A_i is the number of processes that abort during the passage. If no process aborts during a passage, its RMR cost is $O(1)$. The RMR cost of an aborted passage is $O(\log_W A_t)$, where A_t is the number of processes that abort during the entire execution. (Note that our notion of adaptivity differs from that of Jayanti's algorithm [17], in which the RMR cost of a passage depends on the maximum number of processes that are concurrently active during the passage, not only on those that abort.)

We obtain our algorithm by composing two constructions. We first design a *one-shot* abortable lock, which each process can attempt to acquire at most once. This lock has the aforementioned RMR cost and linear space complexity. We next present a generic transformation that converts a one-shot abortable lock algorithm with space complexity $s(N)$, where $s(N)/2^W = O(1)$, into a long-lived algorithm with the same asymptotic RMR cost and space complexity $O(N \cdot s(N) + N^2)$. Our final algorithm thus uses $O(N^2)$ memory words. The transformation does not maintain fairness guarantees. While our one-shot algorithm is first-come-first-served (FCFS) [18], the final algorithm is starvation-free. Table 1 compares the final algorithm to prior work.

2 MODEL AND PROBLEM STATEMENT

Model. We consider an asynchronous shared-memory model, in which a set of N deterministic processes communicate by executing atomic operations on shared W-bit words that support read, write, CAS, and F&A operations. *CAS*(w, o, n) atomically changes w's value to n if w contains o, and returns *true*; otherwise, it returns *false* without modifying w. *F&A*(w, x) atomically updates the value stored in w from v to $v + x$, and returns v. A *configuration* consists of the state of all processes and memory words. An *execution* is a (possibly infinite) sequence of *steps*. Each *step* consists of a process invoking an operation on a shared variable and receiving its return value, thereby moving the system to a new configuration.

RMR complexity. In a cache-coherent (CC) model, each processor maintains local copies of shared variables it accesses in its cache, and a coherence protocol ensures the consistency of cached variables by invalidating cached copies when a variable is written. A memory access to an uncached variable is called a *remote memory reference* (RMR): Each write, CAS, or F&A incurs an RMR. A read by process p of a shared variable w incurs an RMR if (1) it is p's first read of w, or (2) after p's last read of w, another process performed a write, CAS, or F&A to w. In a distributed shared-memory (DSM) model, each register is (forever) local to some processor and remote to all others. An access to a remote register is an RMR.

Abortable mutual exclusion. An *abortable lock* supports the methods *Enter* and *Exit*. A process *attempts* to acquire the lock by executing *Enter*. If *Enter* returns *true*, the process *acquires* the lock and *enters* the critical section (CS). While inside *Enter*, a process can receive an external signal to *abort* its attempt, in which case *Enter* may return *false.*[2] Once a process completes the CS, it *exits* the CS by invoking *Exit* and thereby *releases* the lock. A *passage* is the sequence of steps in which a process executes *Enter*, the CS, and *Exit*. A process not executing *Enter*, *Exit*, or the CS is said to be in the *remainder section.*

Problem statement. The goal is to design an abortable lock algorithm satisfying the following requirements: (1) *mutual exclusion:* at any time, at most one process is in the CS; (2) *starvation-freedom:* if no process crashes outside the remainder section and every process that enters the CS eventually leaves it, then if a process p invokes *Enter* and does not abort its attempt, p eventually enters the CS in that attempt; (3) *bounded exit:* a process completes an *Exit* call in a finite number of its own steps; and (4) *bounded abort:* if a process p busy waiting in *Enter* receives a signal to abort its attempt, then p's execution of *Enter* returns (either *true* or *false*) within a finite number of p's steps.

3 ONE-SHOT ALGORITHM

Here, we describe our one-shot abortable lock, which is the main building block of our algorithm. Unless noted otherwise, we assume the CC complexity model.

The one-shot lock implements an array-based queue lock [5, 13], augmented with a data structure that tracks which processes have aborted and thus given up their place in the queue. Our high-level design is similar to Jayanti's algorithm [17], with the main difference being in the augmenting data structure. Whereas Jayanti uses a linearizable priority queue [16], we use a tree-based ordered set that is *not* linearizable. The semantics of our *Tree* data structure cannot be cleanly captured by a sequential specification, as they depend on the concurrency between operations.

Figure 1 shows the pseudo-code of the lock algorithm. Its underlying data structures are an array-based queue, *go*, and a *Tree* whose implementation we describe in Section 4. We assume that each process attempts to perform at most one pass through the critical section. To acquire the lock, a process first increments *Tail* using F&A to obtain an index to a slot in the *go* array. We will identify each process with its index $0 \leq i \leq N - 1$. Process i spins

[2]Returning *false* is not mandatory because a process can receive the signal after being handed the lock, but before noticing the handoff. Formulations in which an abort signal moves the process to some *Abort* method [17] similarly require this method to detect and handle such a scenario.

Shared Variables:
$Head = 0; Tail = 0; LastExited = -1; go = [1, 0, \ldots, 0]; Tree$ (see Section 4)

Algorithm 3.1 *Enter*()

```
i ← F&A(Tail, 1)
while ¬go[i] do
    if AbortSignal then
        Abort(i)
        return false
Head ← i
return true
```

Algorithm 3.2 *Exit*()

```
head ← Head
LastExited ← head
SignalNext(head)
```

Algorithm 3.3 *Abort*(*i*)

```
Tree.Remove(i)
head ← Head
if head ≠ LastExited then
    return
SignalNext(head)
```

Algorithm 3.4 *SignalNext*(*head*)

```
j ← Tree.FindNext(head)
if j ∈ {⊤, ⊥} then
    return
go[j] ← true
```

Figure 1: *One-shot abortable lock algorithm*

on its slot until being signaled that it owns the lock, and then sets the queue's *Head* to *i* and enters the CS. (Initially, *go*[0] is set, so process 0 immediately enter the CS.)

When process *i* exits the CS, it hands the lock off to the *next slot* in the queue, which is the minimal $j > i$ such that slot *j* has not been abandoned by its process due to an abort. The *Tree* data structure facilitates this handoff. It maintains the (ordered) set of queue slots that have not been abandoned by aborting processes. (Initially, $Tree = \{0, \ldots, N-1\}$.) The handoff of process *i*'s lock ownership to the next slot is performed by *SignalNext*(*i*). This procedure calls *Tree.FindNext*(*i*) to find the next slot, *j*, in order to set *go*[*j*] to *true*. *FindNext*(*i*) might return $\bot$, indicating that all possible successor slots have been abandoned and thus the lock is now unusable. Finally, *FindNext*(*i*) may also return $\top$, indicating that its successor search "crossed paths" with an aborting process *k* removing itself from *Tree*. In such a case, as described next, some aborting process will *assume responsibility* for performing the handoff on behalf of process *i*.

Aborts are performed by the *Abort*() procedure, which a process busy waiting in *Enter* calls when it detects the external *AbortSignal*. An aborting process *i* abandons its queue slot by removing itself from *Tree*. It then reads *Head* to obtain the id of the process in the CS, *h*, and compares *h* to the *LastExited* variable, which contains the id of the last process to release the lock. If $h = LastExited$, then process *h* may be in the middle of exiting the CS, and its *FindNext*() might have crossed paths with process *i*'s *Remove* and thus returned $\top$. Therefore, process *i* *assumes responsibility* for *h*'s lock handoff and executes *SignalNext*(*h*). Of course, it can then cross paths with some aborting process *j* and so fail to complete the handoff, but then process *j* would assume responsibility for the handoff. The crux of our correctness proofs is to show that eventually, some aborting process that assumes responsibility for the handoff manages to complete it.

DSM variant. In the DSM model, we cannot guarantee that the *go* slot of a process is local, since the slot is determined at run time. As a result, a process might incur an unbounded number of RMRs while busy waiting. We use indirection to address this problem, by having the process spin on a local spin bit that it publishes in an *announce* array. To synchronize with a concurrent lock handoff, process *i* publishes its spin bit *s* by writing $announce[i] = s$, and then, if $go[i] \neq 1$, spinning locally on *s* . A *SignalNext*() hands the lock to process *i* by writing $go[i] = 1$, reading $s = announce[i]$, and if $s \neq \bot$, writing $s = 1$.

4 TREE DATA STRUCTURE

The *Tree* data structure maintains a *W*-ary tree with *N* leafs, whose height is $H = \lceil \log_W N \rceil$. A tree node *u* contains a *W*-bit word, initially 0, in which the *j*-th most significant bit is associated with *u*'s *j*-th child, counting from the left (so the leftmost bit in *u* is associated with *u*'s leftmost child). We number the leafs from left to right starting with 0, and identify leaf *p* with process *p* (equivalently, queue slot *p*). *Tree* has the property that if some queue slot in the subtree rooted at *u* has not been abandoned by an aborting process, then the bit associated with *u* in *u*'s parent is clear. To maintain this property, an aborting process *p* ascends the tree starting from its leaf, performing a F&A to set the bit associated with its subtree in each visited node *u*. If all bits in *u* are then set, the process keeps ascending to *u*'s parent; otherwise, it stops.

FindNext(*p*) needs to find the first leaf to the right of *p* that has not been abandoned. To find this leaf, it simply walks up the tree until finding a clear bit to the right of *p*, and then walks down towards the relevant leaf. If *FindNext*(*p*) does not find a zero bit during its ascent, it returns $\bot$. If it encounters a node in which all bits are set after starting to descend, then it has "crossed paths" with a *Remove*() ascending the subtree and so returns $\top$. Figure 2 depicts these scenarios.

Figure 3 presents the pseudo-code of the algorithm. Because the tree structure is static, we do not need pointers in the nodes; parent or child nodes are computed by the processes. Leaf nodes act as static sentinels. Only the values stored in non-leaf nodes need to be stored in shared memory. The size of the tree is thus $O(\frac{N}{W})$ words. For $0 \leq j \leq W - 1$, we denote the *j*-th child (from left to right) of node *u* by *Child*(*u*, *j*); if *u* is a leaf, $Child(u, j) = \bot$. We denote the parent of node *u* by *Parent*(*u*); if *u* is the root, $Parent(u) = \bot$. The *i*-th leaf is denoted *Leaf*(*i*). The *W* bits maintained in a node are stored in a field named *value*. For leafs, *value* contains the id of the associated process (i.e., $Leaf(p).value = p$ for $0 \leq p \leq N - 1$).

We use the following notation to associate bits with processes (equivalently, queue slots). The *level* of node *u*, denoted *Lvl*(*u*), is 0 if *u* is a leaf; otherwise, $Lvl(u) = Lvl(Child(u, 0)) + 1$. Let $1 \leq l \leq H$. The *node of process p in level l*, denoted *Node*(*p*, *l*), is *Leaf*(*p*) if $l = 0$; otherwise, $Node(p, l) = Parent(Node(p, l - 1))$. The *offset of process p in level l*, denoted *Offset*(*p*, *l*) is the number *o* such that $Child(Node(p, l), o) = Node(p, l - 1)$. The *bit of process p in level l*, denoted *Bit*(*p*, *l*), is the *o*-th MSB of *Node*(*p*, *lvl*).*value*, where $o = Offset(p, l)$.

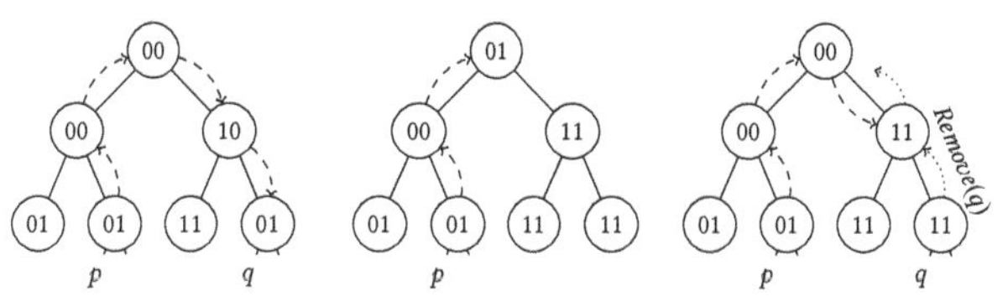

(a) Found successor (return *q*)

(b) No successor (return $\bot$)

(c) Cross paths with ascending *Remove* (return $\top$)

Figure 2: *Possible FindNext(p) scenarios*

Algorithm 4.1 *Tree.FindNext(p)*

```
20: for lvl ← 1 to H do
21:     node ← Node(p, lvl)
22:     offset ← Offset(p, lvl)
23:     snap ← node.value
24:     if HasZeroToTheRight(snap, offset) then
25:         break
26: if HasZeroToTheRight(snap, offset) = false then
27:     return ⊥        // reached root and found no candidate
28: index ← GetFirstZeroToTheRight(snap, offset)
29: node ← Child(node, index)
30: for dummy ← lvl − 1 to 1 do
31:     snap ← node.value
32:     if snap = EMPTY then
33:         return ⊤
34:     index ← GetFirstZero(snap)
35:     node ← Child(node, index)
36: return node.value
```

Algorithm 4.2 *Tree.Remove(p)*

```
37: for lvl ← 1 to H do
38:     j ← word with only Offset(p, lvl)-th MSB set
39:     snap ← F&A(Node(p, lvl).value, j)
40:     if snap + j ≠ EMPTY then
41:         break
```

Algorithm 4.3 *Tree.AdaptiveFindNext(p)*

```
42: node ← Node(p, 1)
43: offset ← Offset(p, 1)
44: for lvl ← 1 to H do
45:     if offset = W − 1 then
46:         node ← RightCousin(node)
47:         offset ← −1
48:     snap ← node.value
49:     if HasZeroToTheRight(snap, offset) then
50:         break
51:     if offset = −1 then
52:         offset ← offsetAtParent(node) − 1
53:     else
54:         offset ← offsetAtParent(node)
55:     node ← Parent(node)
56: Continue as in FindNext() (from Line 26 of Algorithm 4.1)
```

- *HasZeroToTheRight(snap, offset)* returns **true** if and only if there is a zero bit in *snap* to the right of *offset*.
- *GetFirstZeroToTheRight(snap, offset)* returns the offset of the first zero bit in *snap* to the right of *offset*.
- *GetFirstZero(snap)* returns the offset of the first zero bit in *snap*.
- *EMPTY* is the all-ones word, $2^W - 1$.
- *RightCousin(node)* is the node to the right of *node* at the same level.
- *offsetAtParent(node)* is the offset of the bit associated with *node* at its parent, i.e., o such that *Child(Parent(node), o) = node*.

Figure 3: ***Tree data structure***

4.1 Adaptive *FindNext()*

It is easy to see that the RMR cost of *Remove()* is $O(\log_W A_t)$, where A_t is the number of processes that abort during the execution. However, *FindNext()* is not adaptive to the number of aborts. When invoked on a leaf v that is the rightmost node in its subtree, *FindNext()* ascends to the root of the subtree—which can be of height $\log_W N$—even if the leaf of the next non-aborted process is immediately to the right of v (just in another subtree).

We introduce a novel (though small) change to the way *FindNext(p)* walks up the tree that improves its RMR cost to $O(\log_W A_i(p))$, where $A_i(p)$ is the number of processes that abort during process p's passage. Algorithm 4.3 presents the pseudo-code of the adaptive algorithm. Instead of ascending along a path from the leaf to the root, whenever we reach a node u that is the rightmost child of its parent, we "sidestep" to v, the node right to u's parent at the same level, as depicted in Figure 4. The idea is that because we cannot hope to find a zero bit to the right of u's bit in *Parent(u)*, we instead optimistically check whether v has a zero bit. If this is the case, then *FindNext(p)*'s ascent would have stopped at w, the lowest common ancestor of u and v, and would have then started descending until eventually reaching v. If, however, v does not contain a zero bit, then all leafs between p and the rightmost leaf in v's subtree have been abandoned. Therefore, it is safe to resume the ascent from v.

A subtle point in Algorithm 4.3 is that if we "sidestep" to v, fail to find a zero bit there, and ascend to v's parent, we still need the search for a zero bit in v's parent to include v's subtree. (Hence the use of $offsetAtParent(v) - 1$ in line 52, after "sidestepping.") The reason is that the *Remove()* which has set the last bit in v might not have set v's bit in the parent yet. In such a case, *FindNext()* would have returned ⊤, as it would descend towards v (which it would find *EMPTY*) after going through *Parent(v)* (where v's bit is zero). Therefore, *AdaptiveFindNext()* mimics this property.

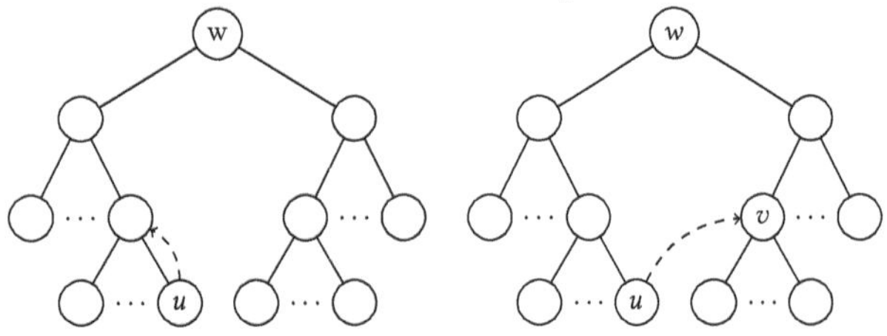

(a) *FindNext* ascent (b) *AdaptiveFindNext* ascent

Figure 4: ***Comparison of*** *FindNext()* ***ascent algorithms***

We can thus show that *AdaptiveFindNext()* is equivalent to *FindNext()* in the following sense: (The proof appears in the full version [3].)

Lemma 1. *Let E be an execution of the one-shot algorithm using AdaptiveFindNext(). Then there exists an execution E′ of the one-shot algorithm using FindNext(), such that (1) process p invokes FindNext(q) in E′ if and only if it invokes AdaptiveFindNext(q) in E; (2) process p's FindNext(q) in E' returns* $x \in [N] \cup \{\bot, \top\}$ *if and only if its AdaptiveFindNext(q) in E returns x; and (3) the order of FindNext() invocation/responses in E′ is the same as the order of AdaptiveFindNext() invocation/responses in E.*

5 CORRECTNESS AND COMPLEXITY OF THE ONE-SHOT ALGORITHM

Here, we prove that our one-shot algorithm satisfies mutual exclusion, starvation freedom, and the first-come-first-served (FCFS) fairness condition (formally defined later). Then we show that the algorithm has sublogarithmic adaptive RMR cost. We assume that $W \geq \lceil \log N \rceil$. The following theorem summarizes these properties.

Theorem 2. *The one-shot lock of Figure 1 and Figure 3 satisfies mutual exclusion, starvation freedom, bounded exit, bounded abort, and FCFS. Each passage of the algorithm incurs* $O(\log_W A_i)$ *RMRs, where* A_i *is the number of processes that abort during the passage. An aborted attempt incurs* $O(\log_W A_t)$ *RMRs, where* A_t *is the number of processes that abort during the entire execution.*

Lemma 1 implies that any correctness result obtained for the one-shot algorithm using *FindNext()* (Algorithm 4.1) also holds for *AdaptiveFindNext*() (Algorithm 4.3). Therefore, for simplicity, the following proofs consider the one-shot lock with *FindNext*().

Notation. Let E be an execution. We denote by E_t the prefix of E consisting of the first t steps in E. The *value of variable* v *at time* t is the value of v in the configuration following E_t. Step s *occurs at time* t if it is the t-th step in E. We identify a process with the index it obtains from the F&A on *Head* (Algorithm 3.1, line 1).

5.1 Tree Properties

We begin the proof of Theorem 2 by proving some properties of the *Tree* data structure. We assume a *well-formed* execution, in which (1) each process invokes *FindNext*() at most once; (2) *Remove(p)* is invoked only by process p, and at most once; and (3) if process p invokes both *Remove(p)* and *FindNext(u)*, then it invokes them in this order. An execution of the one-shot algorithm is well-formed.

5.1.1 Preliminaries. Abusing notation, we say that $p \in u$ if $Node(p, Lvl(u)) = u$, i.e., if $Leaf(p)$ is in the subtree rooted at u.

Definition 1. *The* lowest common level *of leafs* p *and* q*, denoted* $LCL(p,q)$*, is the lowest level in which* p *and* q *have a common ancestor, i.e.,* $LCL(p,q) = \min\{lvl \parallel Node(p,lvl) = Node(q,lvl)\}$*. The* lowest common level *of leaf* p *and internal node* u *is* $LCL(p,u) = LCL(p,q)$ *for some leaf* $q \in u$*.*

The structure of the tree immediately implies that for any leafs $p < q$ with $L = LCL(p,q)$, the following hold: (1) $Offset(p,L) < Offset(q,L)$; (2) $\forall lvl > L.\, Offset(p,lvl) = Offset(q,lvl)$; (3) $\forall lvl \geq L.\, Node(p,lvl) = Node(q,lvl)$; and (4) $\forall p < r < q.\, LCL(p,r) \leq L,\, LCL(r,q) \leq L$.

Claim 3. *In any execution* E*,* $Bit(p,lvl) = 1$ *if and only if some process performs* $F\&A(Node(p,lvl).value, j)$ *in Remove() (Algorithm 4.2, line 39), where* j *is a word whose only set bit is the* $Offset(p,lvl)$*-th MSB.*

Proof. Appears in the full version of the paper [3]. □

Lemma 4. *For every execution* E*, process* p*, and* $1 \leq lvl \leq H$*, if* $Bit(p,lvl) = 1$ *at time* t*, then for all* $l < lvl$ *and* $m \in Node(p, lvl-1)$*,* $Bit(m,l) = 1$ *at time* t*.*

Proof. We prove by induction over lvl. The base case of $lvl = 1$ is vacuously true. For the induction step, assume the claim holds for levels $1, \ldots, lvl-1$. Suppose that $Bit(p,lvl) = 1$ at time t. Claim 3 implies that $Bit(p,lvl) = 1$ because of a F&A performed on $Node(p,lvl).value$ by some process q. Then $Node(q,lvl) = Node(p,lvl)$ and $Offset(q,lvl) = Offset(p,lvl)$. Therefore, $q \in Node(p, lvl-1)$. For process q to have accessed $Node(p,lvl)$ to set $Bit(p,lvl)$, it must have reached iteration lvl in *Remove(q)*. Consider iteration $lvl-1$ of *Remove(q)*. Process q wrote $Node(q, lvl-1).value = EMPTY$ at time $t_1 < t$. Because $Node(q, lvl-1) = Node(p, lvl-1)$, this means that for every $m \in Node(p, lvl-1)$, $Bit(m, lvl-1) = 1$ at time $t_1 < t$. Let $m \in Node(p, lvl-1)$. We know $Bit(m, lvl-1) = 1$ at time t_1. Since $m \in Node(m, lvl-2)$, by the induction assumption, for every $l < lvl-1$, $Bit(m,l) = 1$ at time t_1. The claim follows, as $t_1 < t$. □

Corollary 5 (Remove Invariant). *For every execution* E*, process* p*, and* $1 \leq lvl \leq H$*, if* $Bit(p,lvl) = 1$ *at time* t*, then (1) for every* $q \in Node(p, lvl-1)$*, process* q *invokes Remove(q) at some time* $t' \leq t$*; and (2) if Remove(p) is not invoked in* E_t*, then for all* $1 \leq lvl \leq H$*,* $Bit(p,lvl) = 0$ *in* E_t*.*

5.1.2 FindNext() Properties. Let E be an execution of the algorithm. We now prove several properties provided by *Tree* during E. We identify the *invocation* (respectively, *completion*) of a *Tree* method with the first (respectively, last) memory operation performed by the method's code. If process p invokes method M, we denote by M_p the subsequence of E that starts at M's invocation and ends at its completion (or, if M does not complete, at the end of E). We say that M_p *happens before* M'_q, denoted $M_p \to M'_q$, if the completion of M_p occurs before the invocation of M'_q (i.e., p performs the last memory operation in M_p's code before q performs the first memory operation of M'_q). We say that a method M_p *starts before method* M'_q *completes*, denoted $M_p \rightsquigarrow M'_q$, if the invocation of M_p occurs before the completion of M'_q in E. Note that $M_p \rightsquigarrow M'_q \iff \neg(M'_q \to M_p)$. We use the fact implied by this equivalence, that if $A \rightsquigarrow B$ and $B \to C$, then $A \rightsquigarrow C$.

The first three properties say that $FindNext(p)_a$ returns the first process $q > p$ that did not yet invoke *Remove(v)*.

Property 6. *If* $FindNext(p)_a$ *returns* $q \notin \{\bot, \top\}$*, then* $p < q$*.*

Property 7. *If* $FindNext(p)_a$ *returns* $q \notin \{\bot, \top\}$ *and Remove(q) is invoked in* E*, then* $FindNext(p)_a \to Remove(q)$*.*

Proof. Let t_1 be the time a executes the last step of $FindNext(p)$. Code inspection shows that this step reads $Bit(q,1) = 0$. The first step of *Remove(q)* is a F&A that sets $Bit(q,1)$ to 1. It follows that *Remove(q)* cannot perform its first step before t_1, i.e., $FindNext(p)_a \to Remove(q)$. □

Corollary 8. *If* $Remove(q) \rightsquigarrow FindNext(p)$ *then* $FindNext(p)$ *does not return* q*.*

Property 9. *If* $FindNext(p)_a$ *returns* $q \notin \{\bot, \top\}$*, then for all* $p < w < q$*,* $Remove(w) \rightsquigarrow FindNext(p)_a$*.*

Proof. Let t be the time a executes the last step of $FindNext(p)$. Assume towards a contradiction, that for some $p < w < q$, *Remove(w)* does not perform its first memory operation in E_t. It follows from the remove invariant that for all $1 \leq lvl \leq H$, $Bit(w,lvl) = 0$ at time t. Let $l_{p,q} = LCL(p,q)$, $l_{p,w} = LCL(p,w)$, and $l_{w,q} = LCL(w,q)$. Code inspection shows that a ascends until level $l_{p,q}$, observing only 1 bits to the right of $Offset(p,l)$ at all levels $l < l_{p,q}$. At level $l_{p,q}$, a observes 0 at bit $Offset(q, l_{p,q})$ and 1 at every bit between $Offset(p, l_{p,q})$ and $Offset(q, l_{p,q})$. Then a starts descending. In each level l, a observes 0 at bit $Offset(q,l)$ and 1 at every bit to the left of that offset. Finally, a reaches $Leaf(q)$ and returns q.

If $l_{p,w} < l_{p,q}$, then $Offset(w, l_{p,w}) > Offset(p, l_{p,w})$. Yet a ascends through level $l_{p,w}$, implying that it observes $Bit(w, l_{p,w}) = 1$ during E_t, a contradiction. If $l_{p,w} = l_{p,q} = l_{w,q}$, then $Offset(p, l_{p,w}) < Offset(w, l_{p,q}) < Offset(q, l_{p,w})$. Thus, a reads $Bit(w,l) = 1$ during E_t, a contradiction. Otherwise, $l_{p,q} > l_{w,q} > 0$, and therefore $Offset(w, l_{w,q}) < Offset(q, l_{w,q})$. Yet

a descends level $l_{w,q}$, implying that it observes $Bit(w, l_{w,q}) = 1$ during E_t, a contradiction. □

The next property says that if $FindNext(p)$ returns $\perp$, then every process $q > p$ has invoked $Remove(q)$ (and thus no next process should be signaled).

Property 10. *If $FindNext(p)_a$ returns $\perp$, then for all $p < q < N$, $Remove(q) \rightsquigarrow FindNext(p)_a$.*

Proof. Assume towards a contradiction, that for some $p < w < n$, $Remove(w)$ does not perform its first step in E_t. It follows from the remove invariant that for all $1 \leq lvl \leq H$, $Bit(w, lvl) = 0$ at time t. Let $l_{p,w} = LCL(p, w) \leq H$. At level $l_{p,w}$, a observes 1 at all offsets greater than $Offset(p, l_{p,w})$ at some time $t_1 \leq t$. We know $Offset(p, l_{p,w}) < Offset(w, l_{p,w})$, implying a observed $Bit(w, l_{p,w}) = 1$ at time $t_1 \leq t$, which is a contradiction. □

The next property says that the process ids returned by non-overlapping $FindNext(p)$ executions are monotonically increasing.

Property 11. *If $FindNext(p)_a \rightarrow FindNext(p)_b$ and $FindNext(p)_a, FindNext(p)_b$ respectively return $q_a, q_b \notin \{\top, \perp\}$, then $q_a \leq q_b$.*

Proof. Assume towards a contradiction that $q_a > q_b$. From code inspection, a ascends until level $l_{p,q_a} = LCL(p, q_a)$ and then descends until level 0, and b ascends until level $l_{p,q_b} = LCL(p, q_b)$ and then descends until level 0. From Property 6, we have $p < q_b < q_a$, and therefore $l_{p,q_b} \leq l_{p,q_a}$. If $l_{p,q_b} < l_{p,q_a}$, then (1) a reads $Bit(q_b, l_{p,q_b}) = 1$, as a ascends past level l_{p,q_b}; and (2) b reads $Bit(q_b, l_{p,q_b}) = 0$, as it stops its ascent at level l_{p,q_b}. However, $FindNext(p)_a \rightarrow FindNext(p)_b$, and therefore any bit observed by a as 1 cannot be observed by b as 0, so this is a contradiction.

If $l_{p,q_b} = l_{p,q_a}$, then both a and b stop their ascent at this level, but descend into different subtrees. Let $l = LCL(q_a, q_b)$. If $l = l_{p,q_b} = l_{p,q_a}$, then clearly $Offset(p, l) < Offset(q_b, l) < Offset(q_a, l)$, and therefore a reads $Bit(q_b, l) = 1$ but b reads $Bit(q_b, l) = 0$, which is a contradiction, since $FindNext(p)_a \rightarrow FindNext(p)_b$. Therefore, $l < l_{p,q_b} = l_{p,q_a}$ and $Offset(q_b, l) < Offset(q_a, l)$. Thus, a reads $Bit(q_b, l) = 1$, as it descends towards a, but b reads $Bit(q_b, l) = 0$. Since $FindNext(p)_a \rightarrow FindNext(p)_b$, this is a contradiction. □

The last property refers to scenarios in which process a's $FindNext(p)$ is about to return some value $q > p$, but a $Remove(q)$ crosses paths with a's $FindNext(p)$ execution and causes it to return $\top$. The property says that in such a case, there exists a process b that assumes responsibility for p's lock handoff. We reason about the responsibility for the handoff with the following *responsibility relation*.

Definition 2 (Responsibility relation). *Given processes a, b, we say that process a* has less p-responsibility than b, *denoted $a <_p^R b$, if the following 4 conditions hold in E:*

1. *$Remove(b)$ is invoked by b in E.*
2. *$FindNext(p)_a$ is invoked by a in E.*
3. *$FindNext(p)_a \rightsquigarrow Remove(b)$.*
4. *For every $p < d < max\{a, b\}$, $Remove(d) \rightsquigarrow Remove(b)$.*

Lemma 12. *The relation $<_p^R$ is a strict partial order.*

Proof. A strict partial order is irreflexive and transitive.

Irreflexive: Assume $Remove(a)$ and $FindNext(p)_a$ are both invoked in E by some process a. The execution is well-formed, and so we have $Remove(a) \rightarrow FindNext(p)_a$. Therefore, $\neg(FindNext(p)_a \rightsquigarrow Remove(a))$. Therefore, Conditions 1–3 in Definition 2 cannot all hold together for a, and thus $a <_p^R a$ cannot hold.

Transitive: Assume $a <_p^R b$ and $b <_p^R c$ for some processes a, b, and c. From Conditions 1 and 2 in Definition 2, $Remove(c)$ and $FindNext(p)_a$ are invoked in E. Therefore, Conditions 1 and 2 also hold for a and c. From Condition 1, $Remove(b)$ is invoked by b in E. From Condition 2, $FindNext(p)_b$ is invoked by b in E. The execution is well-formed, so we have $Remove(b) \rightarrow FindNext(p)_b$. From Condition 3, $FindNext(p)_a \rightsquigarrow Remove(b)$. From Condition 3, $FindNext(p)_b \rightsquigarrow Remove(c)$. Therefore, we conclude that $FindNext(p)_a \rightsquigarrow Remove(b) \rightarrow FindNext(p)_b \rightsquigarrow Remove(c)$, and thus $FindNext(p)_a \rightsquigarrow Remove(c)$ holds. Therefore Condition 3 holds for a, c. Let d such that $p < d < max\{a, c\}$. If $p < d < max\{b, c\}$, then from Condition 4 we get $Remove(d) \rightsquigarrow Remove(c)$ as needed. Otherwise, $p < d < max\{a, b\}$, and from Condition 4, we know $Remove(d) \rightsquigarrow Remove(b)$. We can thus conclude that $Remove(d) \rightsquigarrow Remove(b) \rightarrow FindNext(p)_b \rightsquigarrow Remove(c)$, which implies $Remove(d) \rightsquigarrow Remove(c)$ as needed. Therefore, Condition 4 holds for a, c, implying $a <_p^R c$.

□

Corollary 13. *If $a <_p^R b$, then there exists a maximal u for a, i.e., u such that $a <_p^R u$ and for all c, $\neg(u <_p^R c)$.*

Property 14. *Fix processes p and $a \geq p$. If for every $p < d < a$, $Remove(d) \rightsquigarrow Remove(a)$, and $FindNext(p)_a$ returns $\top$, then for some process $b \neq a$, $a <_p^R b$*

Proof. Since $FindNext(p)_a$ returns $\top$, a reads $EMPTY$ from $node.value$ for some node $node$ at time t (Algorithm 4.1, line 31). Let b be the process whose F&A in $Remove(b)$ writes $EMPTY$ to $node.value$. Clearly, $b \in node$ and $b \neq a$. We claim that $a <_p^R b$.
Condition 1: Let l^- be the level of $node$, i.e., the level in which p stops its descent. Then at time t_1, a reads $Bit(l^- + 1, b) = 0$, and at time $t_2 > t_1$, a reads $Bit(b, l^-) = 1$. The latter fact implies, from the remove invariant, that $Remove(b)$ is invoked by b in E.
Condition 2: Immediate from the premise.
Condition 3: Consider $Remove(b)$'s execution. Since b sets $node.value$ to $EMPTY$, it ascends to level $l^- + 1$, with the intent to set $Bit(l^- + 1, b)$ to 1. However, at time t_1, a reads $Bit(l^- + 1, b) = 0$, implying that $Remove(b)$ did not perform a F&A at level $l^- + 1$ by then. Therefore, $Remove(b)$ does not complete before $FindNext(p)_a$ is invoked, i.e., $FindNext(p)_a \rightsquigarrow Remove(b)$.
Condition 4: Let $p < d < max\{a, b\}$. Suppose $p < d < a$. We have $Remove(d) \rightsquigarrow Remove(a)$, $Remove(a) \rightarrow FindNext(p)_a$ and $FindNext(p)_a \rightsquigarrow Remove(b)$. Therefore, $Remove(d) \rightsquigarrow Remove(b)$, as needed. Otherwise, $p \leq a \leq d < b$. Let l^+ be the level at which a stops its ascent and starts descending towards b. Let $l_{d,b} = LCL(d, b)$, and $l_{p,d} = LCL(p, d)$.

Suppose that $l_{d,b} > l^-$. If $l_{d,b} < l^+$, a descends through $Node(b, l_{d,b}) = Node(d, l_{d,b})$ and observes $Bit(d, l_{d,b}) = 1$ since it descends towards b. If $l_{d,b} = l^+$ and $l_{p,d} < l^+$, a ascends through

$Node(p, l_{p,d}) = Node(d, l_{p,d})$ and observes $Bit(d, l_{p,d}) = 1$, as it keep ascending. If $l_{d,b} = l^+$ and $l_{p,d} = l^+$, a stops ascending at $Node(b, l_{d,b}) = Node(d, l_{p,d})$ and observes $Bit(d, l_{p,d}) = 1$, as a then descends towards b. In any case, we have that at some time $t_3 \leq t_1$, a reads $Bit(d, l_{d,b}) = 1$ or $Bit(d, l_{p,d}) = 1$. The remove invariant implies that d performs the first step of *Remove*(d) at some time $t_4 \leq t_3$. Above we have established that *Remove*(b) does not complete before $t_1 \geq t_3 \geq t_4$, implying that *Remove*(d) $\rightsquigarrow$ *Remove*(b).

Suppose, then, that $l_{d,b} \leq l^-$. Then *Remove*(b) ascends through level $l_{d,b}$ before setting *node.value* to *EMPTY* at time $t_5 < t_1$. Thus, at time t_5, $Bit(d, l^-) = 1$, and so the remove invariant implies that d performs the first step of *Remove*(d) at some time $t_6 < t_5$. Above we have established that *Remove*(b) does not complete before $t_1 > t_5 > t_6$, and so *Remove*(d) $\rightsquigarrow$ *Remove*(b).

Thus all four conditions of Definition 2 hold, and indeed $a <_p^R b$. □

5.2 Mutual Exclusion

Lemma 15. *For every execution E and process i, if go[i] =* ***true*** *at time t_0 then for all $j < i$, j performs the first step of either Abort() or Exit() at time $t < t_0$.*

Proof. We prove by contradiction. Let E be an execution in which the claim is false, and let t_0 be the first time in which the above condition is violated. Then at time t_0, some process k writes $go[i]$ = **true**, but there exists some process $j < i$ that has not yet performed the first step of either *Abort*() or *Exit*().

We claim that *LastExited* $< j$ at all times $t < t_0$. Otherwise, at some time $t < t_0$, some process $k' \geq j$ writes *LastExited* $= k'$, implying that k' exits the CS. By definition of j, $k' \neq j$. Process k' reads $go[k']$ = **true** at time $t' < t < t_0$, even though $j < k'$ and j has not performed the first step of either *Abort*() or *Exit*() at t'. This contradicts t_0 being the first time in which such a violation occurs.

Now, since k writes $go[i]$ = **true** at time t_0, it completes a *FindNext*(h) invocation, for some h, at time $t_1 < t_0$ and receives i as the response. Clearly, $k \neq j$, because by time t_0, process k has invoked *FindNext*() but j has not. Process k invokes *SignalNext*(h) either from *Abort*() or from *Exit*(). In either case, for *SignalNext*(h) to be invoked, it must hold that at some time $t_2 < t_1$, process k reads *LastExited* and observes its value to be h (either because of line 13 in Algorithm 3.3 or line 9 of Algorithm 3.2). Thus, $h < j$. Now, *FindNext*(h)$_k$ returns i at time $t_1 < t_0$. Since $h < j < i$, it follows from Property 9 that *Remove*(j) $\rightsquigarrow$ *FindNext*(h)$_k$, i.e., that process j performs the first step of *Remove*(j) at some time $t' < t_1 < t_0$, which is a contradiction. □

Corollary 16. *The one-shot algorithm satisfies mutual exclusion.*

5.3 FCFS and Starvation Freedom

For a one-shot abortable lock, the *first-come-first served* (FCFS) fairness condition [17] requires that (1) *Enter* starts with a *doorway*, which is a wait-free section of code (i.e., that can be completed in a finite number of the executing process' steps); and (2) if process p completes the doorway before q starts executing the doorway, and if p does not abort, then p enters the CS before q does.

Lemma 17. *The one-shot algorithm satisfies FCFS.*

Proof. We define the doorway to be the F&A operation (Algorithm 3.1, line 1). Process j receives index j from this F&A and proceeds to the "waiting" section, in which it waits for $go[j]$ to become **true**. Let i be a process that executes the doorway after process j, receiving index $i > j$. Suppose that at time t, process i observes $go[i]$ = **true** and enters the CS. Lemma 15 implies that by time t, process j has invoked either *Exit*() or *Abort*(), which establishes FCFS. □

Lemma 18. *The one-shot algorithm satisfies starvation freedom.*

Proof. By contradiction. Let E be an execution in which no process crashes outside the remainder section and every process that enters the CS eventually leaves it, but there exists a minimal i such that process i invokes but does not complete the execution of *Enter*(). This means that i does not invoke *Abort*(), *Exit*(), or *SignalNext*(). It is easy to verify that *LastExited* and *Head* are both strictly increasing. Let m be the largest value of *Head* in E. Then $m < i$. Otherwise, some process $m > i$ writes to *Head*, and the assumption on E implies that m eventually enters the CS, which violates FCFS. It is easy to verify that at any time *LastExited* $\leq$ *Head* and so *LastExited* $\leq m$ in E. The assumption on E implies that process m eventually, at some time t_0, reaches line 9 and sets *LastExited* $= m$. Therefore, from time t_0 onwards, *LastExited* $=$ *Head* $= m$. Let k be the maximal value such that $go[k]$ = **true** in E. Then $m \leq k < i$.

Claim 19. *There exists q such that $k <_m^R q$.*

Proof. Suppose that $k = m$. Then process k executes *Exit*(), invoking *FindNext*(k)$_k$, which returns b. If $b \notin \{\top, \bot\}$, then from Property 6, $b > k$ and k eventually writes $go[b]$ = **true**, contradicting k's maximality. If $b = \bot$, then Property 10 implies that i invokes *Remove*(i), which can only be invoked from *Abort*(i), which is a contradiction. Therefore, $b = \top$. The preconditions for Property 14 hold vacuously, as there is no d such that $m = k < d < k$. It follows that for some process q, $k <_m^R q$.

Alternatively, suppose that $k > m$. We will show that the preconditions of Property 14 hold, and thus for some process q, $k <_m^R q$. Process k does not enter the CS, as that would contradict m's maximality. Therefore, process k invokes *Abort*(k) and, in turn, *Remove*(k). Consider the process p that wrote $go[k]$ = **true**. p executes *FindNext*(v)$_p$ and receives k. From the definition of m, $v \leq m$. If $v < m < k$, then Property 9 implies that m invoked *Abort*, which is a contradiction. Therefore, $v = m$ and p executes *FindNext*(m)$_p$, receiving k in response. From Property 7, *FindNext*(m)$_p$ $\rightarrow$ *Remove*(k). Process k executes *Remove*(k) and then *FindNext*(m)$_k$, receiving b. Therefore *FindNext*(m)$_p$ $\rightarrow$ *FindNext*(m)$_k$. If $b \notin \{\top, \bot\}$, then from Property 11, $k \leq b$. From Corollary 8, $b \neq k$. Thus, $b > k$ and k writes $go[b]$ = **true**, contradicting k's maximality. If $b = \bot$, Property 10 implies that i invokes *Remove*(i), which is a contradiction. Therefore $b = \top$. Consider any d such that $m < d < k$. By Property 9, *Remove*(d) $\rightsquigarrow$ *FindNext*(m)$_p$. We also have *FindNext*(m)$_p$ $\rightarrow$ *Remove*(k). Therefore, *Remove*(d) $\rightsquigarrow$ *Remove*(k). The preconditions of Property 14 thus hold. □

Claim 19 shows that $k <^R_m q$ for some q. By Corollary 13, there exists a maximal r such that $k <^R_m r$. The definition of $<^R_m$ implies that $Remove(r)$ is invoked in E and that $FindNext(m)_k \rightsquigarrow Remove(r)$. Therefore, at time t_0 (when m sets $LastExited = m$), $Remove(r)$ has not yet completed. Once $Remove(r)$ returns, r thus reads $Head = LastExited = m$ at line 13 of Algorithm 3.3 and invokes $FindNext(m)_r$, receiving some value c.

If $c = \bot$, this again implies i invokes $Remove(i)$, which is a contradiction. If $c = \top$, let d such that $m < d < r$. We have $u < d < max\{k, r\}$ and $k <^R_m r$, and so by the definition of $<^R_m$, $Remove(d) \rightsquigarrow Remove(r)$. The preconditions for Property 14 thus hold for m and $r > m$. This implies that for some process $\hat{r} \neq r$, $r <^R_m \hat{r}$, contradicting r's maximality.

Finally, suppose that $c \notin \{\top, \bot\}$. If $c > k$ then process r writes $go[c]$ = **true**, contradicting k's maximality. Therefore $c \leq k$. From condition 3 in the definition of $<^R_m$, we have $FindNext(m)_k \rightsquigarrow Remove(r)$. So $Remove(k) \rightarrow FindNext(m)_k \rightsquigarrow Remove(r) \rightarrow FindNext(m)_r$, and therefore $Remove(k) \rightsquigarrow FindNext(m)_r$. From Corollary 8, we have that $FindNext(m)_r$ does not return k, and therefore $c < k$. From Property 6, we have $c > m$. So $m < c < max\{k, r\}$. Condition 4 in the definition of $<^R_m$ implies that $Remove(c) \rightsquigarrow Remove(r)$. Therefore, $Remove(c) \rightsquigarrow FindNext(m)_r$. From Corollary 8, $FindNext(m)_r$ does not return c, which is a contradiction. □

5.4 Complexity Analysis

The one-shot algorithm performs $O(1)$ RMRs in addition to the RMRs performed by $Tree$ operations. Each $Tree$ operation is wait-free and takes $O(\log_W N)$ steps, and thus at most $O(\log_W N)$ RMRs. Given an execution E, let R denote the number of processes that invoke $Remove()$ in E. In the following, some proofs are relegated to the full version [3] due to space limitations.

Claim 20. *The RMR cost of Remove() is* $O(\log_W R)$.

Denote by $R_p(t)$ the number of processes $r \geq p$ that invoke $Remove(r)$ in E_t.

Claim 21. *The RMR cost of* $AdaptiveFindNext(p)_q$ *is* $O(\log_W R_p(t))$, *where t is the time in which* $AdaptiveFindNext(p)_q$ *completes.*

Proof. Consider an execution of $AdaptiveFindNext(p)$ by process q that performs $l > 2$ iterations of the loop at line 44 of Algorithm 4.3. Consider the execution of $HasZeroToTheRight$ at line 49 in iteration $l-1$, and let $node$ be the node q accesses at this iteration. The check at line 45 guarantees that the value of the $offset$ argument is less than $W-1$, and that $p \notin Child(node, W-1)$ (i.e., p is not the rightmost child). Since process q does not break at this iteration, we have that it receives **false** from this $HasZeroToTheRight$. This implies that the least significant (rightmost) bit of $node.value$ is 1. It follows from the remove invariant that for all $r \in Child(node, W-1)$, process r invokes $Remove(r)$ before $AdaptiveFindNext(p)_q$ completes at time t, i.e., in E_t. Because $p \notin Child(node, W-1)$, for every $r \in Child(node, W-1)$, $r > p$. There are W^{l-2} leafs in the subtree rooted at $Child(node, W-1)$. The number of processes $r \geq p$ that invoke $Remove(r)$ in E_t is $R_p(t)$. Therefore, $W^{l-2} \leq R_p(t)$, and so $l \leq 2 + \log_W R_p(t)$. Each iteration of the loop performs a constant number of RMRs, and the claim follows. □

Corollary 22. *Each successful passage of the one-shot algorithm incurs* $O(\log_W A_i)$ *RMRs, where* A_i *is the number of processes that abort during the passage. An aborted attempt incurs* $O(\log_W A_t)$ *RMRs, where* A_t *is the number of processes that abort during the entire execution.*

6 FROM ONE-SHOT TO LONG-LIVED LOCK

We present a generic transformation that converts a one-shot abortable lock algorithm L, with space complexity $s(N)$ (where $s(N)/2^W = O(1)$) into a long-lived algorithm with the same asymptotic RMR cost as L, and space complexity $O(N \cdot s(N) + N^2)$. Our transformation preserves starvation-freedom, but not FCFS.

Figure 5 presents the pseudo-code of the transformation. For simplicity, we assume a system with unbounded word and memory size, in which allocating a new (and initialized) instance of the one-shot lock L is free of charge. Section 6.2 removes these assumptions.

The long-lived lock uses an instance of L to solve mutual exclusion, and dynamically switches to new instances to keep processes from accessing the same one-shot lock instance twice. We represent the long-lived lock as a tuple $(Lock, Spn, Refcnt)$, where $Lock$ is a pointer to the instance of L; Spn is a pointer to a *spin node* associated with this instance, which contains a single boolean field go; and $Refcnt$ is a $\lceil \log N \rceil$-bit *reference count*, indicating the number of processes currently accessing the one-shot lock instance. The tuple is stored in a single memory word $LockDesc$, which enables its fields to be manipulated atomically, as follows.

We store $Refcnt$ in the lower bits of $LockDesc$, allowing processes to use F&A to increment/decrement it while simultaneously obtaining a snapshot of the tuple. To acquire the lock, a process p uses F&A on $LockDesc$ to increment $Refcnt$, obtaining the instance l pointed to by $Lock$ in response (line 62), which p then attempts to acquire. Once p finishes its attempt (either due to aborting or after releasing l), it uses a F&A on $LockDesc$ to decrement $Refcnt$ (line 70). If p decrements $Refcnt$ to 0, it uses a CAS to atomically switch $Lock$ and Spn to point to new one-shot lock and spin node instances, conditioned on $Refcnt = 0$ (line 76).

However, p will fail to switch the lock from l if another process increments $Refcnt$ between lines 70 and 76. This scenario can lead to p's next acquisition attempt occurring while $Lock$ still points to l, but p cannot access the one-shot lock l again. We use the spin node spn associated with l to efficiently prevent processes from accessing l again: p saves spn in a local variable when its attempt to acquire l finishes (line 70), and in the next acquisition attempt, p busy waits on $spn.go$ if $LockDesc.Spn = spn$ (lines 57–59). Once the lock is switched from (l, spn) to new instances, $spn.go$ is set (line 77), signalling the processes busy waiting on $spn.go$ that $LockDesc.Lock \neq l$, and so they may attempt to acquire the one-shot lock. Using the spin nodes thus establishes that $LockDesc.Lock$ changed in $O(1)$ RMRs. Without them, it would require accessing $LockDesc$, which could incur $N-1$ RMRs, as $Refcnt$ can change N times before $LockDesc.Lock$ changes.

6.1 Correctness of the Transformation

Here, we prove:

Theorem 23. *Let L be a one-shot starvation-free abortable lock. Our transformation yields a long-lived starvation-free abortable lock.*

Shared variables:
LockDesc : (*Lock* : ptr to *L* instance, *Spn* : ptr to *SpinNode*, *Refcnt* : int)
initially, *LockDesc* = (fresh *L* instance, fresh *SpinNode*, 0)
Local variables: *oldSpn* : ptr to *SpinNode*, initially *oldSpn* = ⊥

Algorithm 6.1 *Enter*()

```
57: (l, spn, v) ← LockDesc
58: if spn = oldSpn then
59:     while ¬spn.go do
60:         if AbortSignal then
61:             return false
62: (l, spn, refcnt) ← F&A(LockDesc, 1)        // read Lock, Spn & inc Refcnt
63: completed ← l.Enter()
64: if completed = false then
65:     Cleanup()
66: return completed
```

Algorithm 6.2 *Exit*()

```
67: (l, spn, r) ← LockDesc
68: l.Exit()
69: Cleanup()
```

Algorithm 6.3 *Cleanup*()

```
70: (oldLock, oldSpn, refcnt) ← F&A(LockDesc, −1)
71: if refcnt = 1 then
72:     newLock ← AllocateOneShotLockInstance()
73:     newSpn ← AllocateSpinNode()
74:     old ← (oldLock, oldSpn, 0)
75:     new ← (newLock, newSpn, 0)
76:     if CAS(LockDesc, old, new) then
77:         oldSpn.go ← true
```

Figure 5: Transformation of a one-shot abortable lock algorithm *L* into a long-lived abortable lock

Claim 24. *Suppose process p invokes l.Enter() (line 63). Let (l, s, r) be the LockDesc value p obtains at line 62 prior to this l.Enter() call. Then LockDesc remains (l, s, _) until p executes the F&A at line 70.*

Proof. Every process increments and decrements *LockDesc.Refcnt* once per acquisition attempt (lines 62 and 70, respectively). Therefore, $LockDesc.Refcnt \geq 1$ from *p*'s F&A execution at line 62 prior to invoking *l.Enter*() and until it executes the F&A at line 70 afterwards (after either aborting or releasing *l*). Now, *LockDesc.Spn* and *LockDesc.Lock* change only if a CAS at line 76 succeeds. However, a *CAS* at line 76 can succeed only if $LockDesc.Refcnt = 0$. The claim follows. □

Claim 25. *Let E be an execution of the long-lived algorithm. Then no process executes Enter() twice on the same one-shot lock object.*

Lemma 26. *The long-lived algorithm satisfies mutual exclusion.*

Proof. Assume towards a contradiction that processes *p*, *q* are both in the CS at time *t*. Prior to entering the CS of the one-shot lock, both processes execute the *F&A* at line 62 and obtain *LockDesc* values $(l_p, s_p, \_)$ and $(l_q, s_q, \_)$. WLOG, assume that *p* performs its *F&A* first, at time t_0. Since *p* is in the CS at time *t*, Claim 24 implies that $LockDesc.Lock = l_p$ at time *t*. Therefore, $l_q = l_p$, as *q* performs its *F&A* at time t_1, $t_0 < t_1 < t$. Both processes are thus in *l*'s CS at time *t*, contradicting mutual exclusion of the one-shot lock *l*. □

Lemma 27. *The long-lived algorithm satisfies starvation freedom.*

Proof. Let *E* be an execution in which no process crashes outside the remainder section and every process that enters the CS eventually leaves it. Suppose that some process *p* is spinning at line 59 at time *t*. Let *l* be the one-shot lock instance pointed to by *p*'s *oldSpn* variable at time *t*. Then at some time $t' < t$, *p* executed a F&A at line 70 that returned $(l, \_, \_)$. Claim 24 implies that if a process executes a F&A at line 70 that returns $(l, \_, \_)$, then the previous execution of line 63 by the process invoked *l.Enter*(). Therefore, Claim 25 implies that each process executes a F&A at line 70 that returns $(l, \_, \_)$ at most once. Let *q* be the last process to execute such a F&A. Since *q* is last, this F&A returns $(l, \_, 1)$, and so eventually *q* executes the *CAS* at line 76. This CAS cannot fail because some process increments *LockDesc.Refcnt* (while $LockDesc.L = l$) as such a process will later call *Cleanup*() and execute line 70, in contradiction. Therefore, either *q*'s CAS succeeds or it fails because another process executes a CAS at line 76 that succeeds. In either case, eventually some process sets *oldSpn.go* to **true**, and so eventually *p* breaks out of its spin loop and invokes *Enter*() on some instance *l'* of the one-shot lock. Starvation-freedom of *l'* implies that if *p* does not abort, it will enter the CS. □

6.2 Bounding Space and RMR Complexity

We augment the long-lived lock with memory management schemes that safely recycle one-shot lock and spin node instances, so that the overall number of objects used by the algorithm is $O(N)$ one-shot locks and $O(N^2)$ spin nodes. These bounds enable maintaining *LockDesc* in a *W*-bit memory word, assuming that $W = \Omega(\log N)$. We only provide an overview of the schemes, due to space constraints. Details appear in the full version [3].

Recycling one-shot locks. A process that successfully installs a new one-shot lock instance holds on to the instance *l* that it replaced, and uses *l* to satisfy its next allocation. (This is safe because other processes attempt to acquire *l* only if *LockDesc.Lock* points to it, which is not the case after switching to a new one-shot lock instance.) The main problem is how to reset the *variables* of *l* so that when *l* gets reused they contain their initial values, but without having a single reset operation that incurs $s(N)$ RMRs. To this end, we use a *lazy* reset scheme, in which the processes reset the variables of *l* as they are accessed inside the one-shot algorithm.

Our scheme borrows ideas from the scheme of Aghazadeh et al. [1, § 4], but does not "steal" bits from the words being reset. The idea of their scheme is to add a version number for *l*, which is incremented each time *l* is reused, and to encode a version number in each of *l*'s memory words, enabling processes to detect "stale" values. A process reading value *x* from a word uses *x* only if the version encoded in it equals *l*'s current version; otherwise, the process proceeds as if it read the word's initial value. A process that writes to a word augments the write with *l*'s current version. In our scheme, for each word *w* of *l* we maintain a word V_w that contains a pair (v_w, b_w), where v_w is *w*'s version and b_w is an *incarnation* bit. We also maintain two words, w_0 and w_1, and guarantee that *w*'s *next incarnation*, w_{1-b_w}, always contains *w*'s initial value. When a process *p* first needs to access *w*, it reads (v_w, b) from V_w. If $v_w = v$, where *v* is *l*'s current version, *p* will access w_b whenever it needs to access *w* from then on. Otherwise, if $v_w \neq v$, *p* updates V_w to $(v, 1-b)$ and resets w_b to *w*'s initial value. It will subsequently access w_{1-b} whenever it needs to access *w*.

To prevent wraparound of l's version from making a stale word appear valid, we (like Aghazadeh et al. [1, § 4]) additionally reset $s(N)/2^W$ of l's words each time l gets reused, which guarantees that after l's version wraps around, each word has been reset. In summary, our scheme (1) increases the one-shot lock's space complexity from $s(N)$ to $O(s(N))$; (2) adds $O(1)$ RMRs to the first access a process makes in the one-shot algorithm; and (3) adds $O(s(N)/2^W)$ RMRs to the cost of allocating a one-shot lock instance.

Recycling spin nodes. Since a spin node might be accessed by a busy waiting process even after *LockDesc* no longer points to it, recycling spin nodes requires a *safe memory reclamation* scheme that recycles a spin node only if no process busy waits on it. We use the memory reclamation scheme of Aghazadeh et al. [2], which is similar to hazard pointers [22] but has constant worst-case RMR cost. Each process allocates spin nodes from a local pool. The reclamation scheme replenishes the pool as follows: A process p that switches *LockDesc.Spn* to point from spin node *spn* to another node *retires* the node *spn*. Once the scheme ascertains that no process is busy waiting on *spn*, it places *spn* into p's pool. The reclamation scheme guarantees that a process can have at most N spin nodes that it retired but have not yet been placed into its pool. We therefore guarantee that pools never become empty by using pools of size $N + 1$. Overall, we manage $O(N^2)$ spin nodes, and the reclamation scheme requires $O(N)$ words for its shared variables.

The following result follows from the above discussion.

Claim 28. *If L has RMR cost $t(A_i, A_t)$ and space complexity $s(N)$, and if $s(N)/2^W = O(1)$, then the long-lived lock has RMR cost $O(t(A_i, A_t))$ and space complexity $O(N \cdot s(N) + N^2)$.*

7 RELATED WORK

Randomized abortable locks can obtain $O(\frac{\log N}{\log \log N})$ expected RMR cost [23] or $O(1)$ expected amortized RMR cost [12]. Both algorithms are for the CC model; use reads, writes, and CAS; and work against an adversary that is slightly weaker than the *strong adaptive adversary*, which can make scheduling decisions based on all past events, including the latest coin-flips.

Lee [20] obtains an $O(\log N)$-RMR (non-adaptive) abortable lock by modifying Yang and Anderson's lock [26], making each two-process lock in their binary tree abortable. It is thus not clear that his construction can be generalized to make the tree W-ary. Jayanti's adaptive $O(\log N)$-RMR abortable lock [17] hinges on a binary tree-based f-array [16]. While the f-array can be made W-ary, the RMR complexity of such a W-ary tree of height $H = \log_W N$ is $O(W \cdot H)$, which is not sublogarithmic. In contrast, with F&A we can aggregate certain information about a node's children with one RMR, while the LL/SC-based f-array requires $O(\#\text{ children})$ RMRs. Further, unlike prior work, we simplify the problem to a one-shot variant, which we then (generically) transform to a long-lived lock.

8 CONCLUSION

Applying the transformation of Section 6 to the one-shot abortable lock of Section 3 yields a starvation-free (but not FCFS) abortable lock with space complexity $O(N^2)$, in which the RMR cost of a successful passage is $O(\log_W A_i)$ and the RMR cost of an aborted attempt is $O(\log_W A_t)$. Assuming $W = \Theta(\log N)$, the worst-case RMR cost of the composed lock is $O(\frac{\log N}{\log \log N})$. This paper thus shows that, as with mutual exclusion, abortable locks can leverage additional primitives (beyond read, write and CAS) to obtain sublogarithmic worst-case RMR cost.

Several interesting questions remain. Our algorithm is for the CC model; the problem in the DSM model remains open. Our algorithm achieves $O(1)$ RMR cost only if $W = \omega(\log N)$, whereas lock algorithms such as the MCS lock [21] obtain $O(1)$ RMR cost with $W = \Theta(\log N)$. Is this an inherent difference between abortable locks and regular locks? Finally, Jayanti's $O(\log N)$-RMR abortable lock [17] satisfies FCFS and is adaptive to point contention; our algorithm does not have these properties. Can this gap be bridged?

ACKNOWLEDGMENTS

This research was funded in part by the Israel Science Foundation (grant 2005/17). Adam Morrison is supported by Len Blavatnik and the Blavatnik Family Foundation.

REFERENCES

[1] Zahra Aghazadeh, Wojciech Golab, and Philipp Woelfel. Making Objects Writable. In *PODC*, 2014.
[2] Zahra Aghazadeh, Wojciech M. Golab, and Philipp Woelfel. Brief announcement: resettable objects and efficient memory reclamation for concurrent algorithms. In *PODC*, 2013.
[3] Adam Alon. Deterministic Abortable Mutual Exclusion with Sublogarithmic Adaptive RMR Complexity. Master's thesis, Tel Aviv University, June 2018.
[4] James H. Anderson and Yong-Jik Kim. An Improved Lower Bound for the Time Complexity of Mutual Exclusion. *Distributed Computing*, 15(4), December 2002.
[5] T. E. Anderson. The Performance of Spin Lock Alternatives for Shared-Memory Multiprocessors. *IEEE TPDS*, 1(1), January 1990.
[6] Hagit Attiya, Danny Hendler, and Philipp Woelfel. Tight RMR Lower Bounds for Mutual Exclusion and Other Problems. In *STOC*, 2008.
[7] Michael A. Bender and Seth Gilbert. Mutual Exclusion with $O(Log^2 LogN)$ Amortized Work. In *FOCS*, 2011.
[8] Milind Chabbi, Abdelhalim Amer, Shasha Wen, and Xu Liu. An Efficient Abortable-locking Protocol for Multi-level NUMA Systems. In *PPoPP*, 2017.
[9] E. W. Dijkstra. Solution of a Problem in Concurrent Programming Control. *CACM*, 8(9), September 1965.
[10] George Giakkoupis and Philipp Woelfel. A Tight RMR Lower Bound for Randomized Mutual Exclusion. In *STOC*, 2012.
[11] George Giakkoupis and Philipp Woelfel. Randomized Mutual Exclusion with Constant Amortized RMR Complexity on the DSM. In *FOCS*, 2014.
[12] George Giakkoupis and Philipp Woelfel. Randomized Abortable Mutual Exclusion with Constant Amortized RMR Complexity on the CC Model. In *PODC*, 2017.
[13] G. Graunke and S. Thakkar. Synchronization algorithms for shared-memory multiprocessors. *IEEE Computer*, 23(6), June 1990.
[14] Danny Hendler and Philipp Woelfel. Adaptive Randomized Mutual Exclusion in Sub-logarithmic Expected Time. In *PODC*, 2010.
[15] Danny Hendler and Philipp Woelfel. Randomized mutual exclusion with sub-logarithmic RMR-complexity. *Distributed Computing*, 24(1), Sep 2011.
[16] Prasad Jayanti. F-arrays: Implementation and Applications. In *PODC*, 2002.
[17] Prasad Jayanti. Adaptive and Efficient Abortable Mutual Exclusion. In *PODC*, 2003.
[18] Leslie Lamport. The Mutual Exclusion Problem: PartII&Mdash;Statement and Solutions. *JACM*, 33(2), April 1986.
[19] Hyonho Lee. Fast Local-spin Abortable Mutual Exclusion with Bounded Space. In *OPODIS*, 2010.
[20] Hyonho Lee. *Local-spin Abortable Mutual Exclusion*. PhD thesis, University of Toronto, January 2012.
[21] John M. Mellor-Crummey and Michael L. Scott. Algorithms for scalable synchronization on shared-memory multiprocessors. *ACM TOCS*, 9(1), February 1991.
[22] Maged M. Michael. Hazard Pointers: Safe Memory Reclamation for Lock-Free Objects. *IEEE TPDS*, 15(6), June 2004.
[23] Abhijeet Pareek and Philipp Woelfel. RMR-Efficient Randomized Abortable Mutual Exclusion. In *DISC*, 2012.
[24] Michael L. Scott. Non-blocking Timeout in Scalable Queue-based Spin Locks. In *PODC*, 2002.
[25] Michael L. Scott and William N. Scherer. Scalable Queue-based Spin Locks with Timeout. In *PPoPP*, 2001.
[26] Jae-Heon Yang and James H. Anderson. A fast, scalable mutual exclusion algorithm. *Distributed Computing*, 9(1), Mar 1995.

Brief Announcement: Persistent Multi-Word Compare-and-Swap

Matej Pavlovic*
EPFL
matej.pavlovic@epfl.ch

Alex Kogan
Oracle Labs
alex.kogan@oracle.com

Virendra J. Marathe
Oracle Labs
virendra.marathe@oracle.com

Tim Harris*
tim.harris@gmail.com

ABSTRACT

This brief announcement presents a fundamental concurrent primitive for persistent memory – a persistent atomic multi-word compare-and-swap (PMCAS). We present a novel algorithm carefully crafted to ensure that atomic updates to a multitude of words modified by the PMCAS are persisted correctly. Our algorithm leverages hardware transactional memory (HTM) for concurrency control, and has a total of 3 persist barriers in its critical path. We also overview variants based on just the compare-and-swap (CAS) instruction and a hybrid of CAS and HTM.

ACM Reference Format:
Matej Pavlovic, Alex Kogan, Virendra J. Marathe, and Tim Harris*. 2018. Brief Announcement: Persistent Multi-Word Compare-and-Swap. In *PODC '18: ACM Symposium on Principles of Distributed Computing, July 23–27, 2018, Egham, United Kingdom.* ACM, New York, NY, USA, 3 pages. https://doi.org/10.1145/3212734.3212783

1 INTRODUCTION

Emerging persistent memory (PM) technologies such as Intel and Micron's 3D XPoint [1] will offer the persistence of traditional storage technologies (NAND flash and disks), DRAM-like byte-addressability, and performance approaching that of DRAM (100-1000x faster than state-of-the-art NAND flash). The combination of these features of PM could profoundly affect the way we manage persistent data in modern applications. Traditionally, DRAM-resident data structures can be hosted in persistent memory. However, this task is complicated by the fact that the processor cache hierarchy will remain *nonpersistent* in the foreseeable future. Processor vendors, such as Intel [10], have proposed new hardware instructions to order persistence of stores to PM.

With the new instructions (flush/writeback cache lines, persist barriers), programmers are expected to rebuild applications to leverage PM. This is, however, a non-trivial endeavor. The principal challenge in building such algorithms centers around the fact that the caching layers in processor memory hierarchy are not persistent, and cache lines can be evicted (thus, persisted) in an arbitrary order. Algorithms must carefully order persistence of stores, using the aforementioned instructions, for correct recovery after failures.

Recognizing these programming challenges, several researchers and practitioners have proposed the use of various forms of transactions to access and manipulate data in persistent memory [4, 5, 16]. While transactions are a powerful abstraction to program PM, they incur significant performance overheads, which is why the field continues to be a subject of active research [12, 13]. In addition, more efficient concurrent data structure implementations can be built without transactions [6] or with a simple multi-word compare-and-swap (MCAS) primitive [7, 8, 14].

Wang et al. [17] recently proposed a lock-free persistent multi-word compare-and-swap (PMCAS) based on Harris et al's. MCAS algorithm [8]. Although an important advance, the algorithm is complex and suffers from significant performance overheads – for every PMCAS, it uses 5 CASes and 2 persist barriers per modified word in the critical path. In this brief announcement, we present new *durably linearizable* [2, 11] variants of a persistent multi-word compare-and-swap (PMCAS) primitive, where multiple words in PM can be updated atomically and in a crash-tolerant manner. Our algorithm, though blocking, requires just 1 CAS per modified word and 3 persist barriers in total in the critical path.

2 PERSISTENT MCAS ALGORITHM

We assume a conventional shared memory multicore system with deterministic threads that read and write shared memory using load, store, and CAS instructions as well as HTM transactions. We assume a fail-stop failure model, where a failure crashes all threads accessing the shared memory. The system can contain both persistent and nonpersistent (DRAM) memory. Processor buffers and caches are nonpersistent.

For simplicity, we focus on PMCAS-htm, a PMCAS variant that leverages the hardware transactional memory (HTM) feature available in some of the contemporary processors [9, 15]. In this variant, reads from memory locations being updated by a concurrent PMCAS block and wait for the PMCAS to complete. Toward the end, we briefly mention nonblocking reads, and two variants of PMCAS, one that uses the compare-and-swap (CAS) instruction instead of HTM, and another that uses both HTM and CAS.

For each PMCAS, the application creates a persistent *update structure* that holds old and new values of the target addresses. We assume that the application persistently tracks all these structures in use by potentially multiple threads (e.g. by having a persistent pool of update structures reachable from a designated "root" of a persistent region). These structures must be reachable from the recovery subsystem.

*Author was employeed at Oracle Labs during this work.

PODC '18, July 23–27, 2018, Egham, United Kingdom

ACM ISBN 978-1-4503-5795-1/18/07.
https://doi.org/10.1145/3212734.3212783

In a nutshell, PMCAS-htm uses a HTM transaction to acquire "ownership" of each target address. It then applies (and persists) the updates on the owned addresses, thereby releasing the ownership. This trivial approach turns out to be surprisingly tricky when we consider (fail-stop) failures at arbitrary points in the algorithm: How can recovery determine if an operation was already applied or failed? How can recovery determine the state of a partially persisted PMCAS-htm and then complete or rollback that state?

PMCAS-htm's pseudocode appears in Figure 1. Our main algorithm begins at line 50. It uses the least significant bit of each target word to represent a "transitory" state of the address being modified; we assume that this bit is not used by the application. In addition to the target addresses, their expected old values, and the new values, PMCAS-htm takes an *update structure* as its argument. Internally, the update structure itself contains a status field and a set of M *update records* (M can vary between different PMCAS-htms), each of which contains a target address, expected old value, and the new value to be applied in the PMCAS (lines 1 – 15). First, the update structure is updated with addresses, old and new values. These updates are persisted before proceeding with the PMCAS (lines 55 – 61). We note that depending on the actual programming interface, this initialization of the update structure (including the persist barrier in line 61) might be done by the application code invoking PMCAS.

PMCAS-htm goes through two states during its execution. It always begins with the ACTIVE state, and eventually switches over to either the SUCCESS or the FAILURE state, denoting success or failure, respectively, of the PMCAS-htm operation. The state transitions must also be correctly persisted for recovery to determine the action to perform on in-flight PMCAS-htm operations – roll forward or roll back.

After initializing and persisting the update structure, PMCAS-htm uses a HTM transaction[1] (the atomic block at lines 70 – 80) to first check if all targets have the expected values. In the same transaction, if the check succeeds, we acquire exclusive ownership of the target addresses by installing a "marked" pointer pointing to the PMCAS-htm's update structure in the target addresses. Ownership acquisition success is indicated by a local committed flag. On success, the ownership acquisitions are all persisted (lines 83 – 86), the status of PMCAS-htm is updated to SUCCESS and persisted. Finally, new values are written back to the targets and persisted (line 92 and 28 – 37). If the PMCAS-htm operation fails, the status is updated to FAILURE and persisted (lines 94 – 96). No roll back is needed since ownership acquisition of the target addresses did not happen on the failure path (line 73).

Recovery proceeds as follows: For all the updates supplied by the application to the PMCAS-htm recovery subsystem, it rolls forward the PMCAS-htm operations whose status is SUCCESS, and rolls back the rest. Rolling forward simply requires calling write_new_values() for the PMCAS-htm operation. Rolling backward applies to only the ACTIVE PMCAS-htm operations since their partial updates may have persisted (between lines 80 and 89). Rolling back such a PMCAS-htm operation may sound like a conservative approach, however it is correct and keeps recovery simple, logically serializing the crash before the rolled back PMCAS-htm operations.

[1] We assume that all hardware transactions will eventually succeed. This can be enforced with a hybrid TM runtime system with progress guarantees; e.g., one that uses a global lock after several failed transactions.

PMCAS variants: PMCAS-htm blocks any readers from reading an address that is owned by a concurrent updater (lines 18 – 26). However, we can avoid blocking by accessing the old value through the marked pointer written by the updater. This optimization however requires a lazy reclamation or garbage collection based scheme for persistent memory management [3]. The HTM transaction can be avoided using a loop that uses CAS instructions to acquire ownership of target addresses. We must ensure that the target addresses are ordered in a global total order to avoid conflicts between concurrent updaters resulting in *spurious* failures of PMCAS-htms. A HTM-CAS hybrid algorithm would attempt to acquire ownerships with a transaction and fall back to the CAS version if the hardware transaction fails to commit. In all these variants, the recovery algorithm remains unchanged.

This work is ongoing, and we plan to evaluate these algorithms going forward. Our future work will also focus on developing *lock-free* variants of this algorithm.

3 CONCLUSION

We presented a simple PMCAS algorithm that guarantees failure-atomic updates to multiple words resident in persistent memory. Our algorithm is simpler than the state-of-the-art lock-free algorithm by Wang et al. [17], and far more efficient in terms of the number of CASes and persist barriers needed per PMCAS. Our algorithm, however, is blocking, and in future work we will explore its lock-free variants.

REFERENCES

[1] 3dxpoint 2015. 3D XPoint Technology Revolutionizes Storage Memory. http://www.intel.com/content/www/us/en/architecture-and-technology/3d-xpoint-technology-animation.html.

[2] Ryan Berryhill, Wojciech M. Golab, and Mahesh Tripunitara. 2015. Robust Shared Objects for Non-Volatile Main Memory. In *19th International Conference on Principles of Distributed Systems.* 20:1–20:17.

[3] Kumud Bhandari, Dhruva R. Chakrabarti, and Hans-Juergen Boehm. 2016. Makalu: fast recoverable allocation of non-volatile memory. In *Proceedings of the 2016 ACM SIGPLAN International Conference on Object-Oriented Programming, Systems, Languages, and Applications.* 677–694.

[4] Dhruva R. Chakrabarti, Hans-Juergen Boehm, and Kumud Bhandari. 2014. Atlas: leveraging locks for non-volatile memory consistency. In *Proceedings of the 2014 ACM International Conference on Object Oriented Programming Systems Languages & Applications, OOPSLA 2014, part of SPLASH 2014, Portland, OR, USA, October 20-24, 2014.* 433–452. https://doi.org/10.1145/2660193.2660224

[5] Joel Coburn, Adrian M. Caulfield, Ameen Akel, Laura M. Grupp, Rajesh K. Gupta, Ranjit Jhala, and Steven Swanson. 2011. NV-Heaps: Making Persistent Objects Fast and Safe with Next-generation, Non-volatile Memories. In *Proceedings of the Sixteenth International Conference on Architectural Support for Programming Languages and Operating Systems.* 105–118.

[6] Michal Friedman, Maurice Herlihy, Virendra Marathe, and Erez Petrank. 2018. A Persistent Lock-free Queue for Non-volatile Memory. In *Proceedings of the 23rd ACM SIGPLAN Symposium on Principles and Practice of Parallel Programming.* 28–40.

[7] Michael Greenwald. 2002. Two-handed emulation: how to build non-blocking implementation of complex data-structures using DCAS. In *Proceedings of the Twenty-First Annual ACM Symposium on Principles of Distributed Computing.* 260–269.

[8] Timothy L. Harris, Keir Fraser, and Ian A. Pratt. 2002. A Practical Multi-word Compare-and-Swap Operation. In *Distributed Computing, 16th International Conference.* 265–279.

[9] IBM. [n. d.]. AIX transactional memory programming. *https://www.ibm.com/support/knowledgecenter/en/ssw_aix_71/com.ibm.aix.genprogc/transactional_memory.htm.*

[10] intel-isa 2015. Intel Architecture Instruction Set Extensions Programming Reference. *https://software.intel.com/sites/default/files/managed/0d/53/319433-022.pdf.*

```
struct UpdateRecord {
  uint64_t *ad;
  uint64_t old_val;
  uint64_t new_val;
};

enum {
  ACTIVE = 0,
  SUCCESS,
  FAILURE
} State;

__thread struct Upd {
  State status;
  UpdateRecord ur[M];
} my_upd;

uint64_t read(
  uint64_t *ad){

  uint64_t val = *ad;
  while(is_marked(val)) {
      val = *ad;
  }
  return val;
}

void write_new_values(Upd *u) {
  for(int i = 0; i < M; i++) {
    if(unmark(*u->ur[i].ad) == u){
      *u->ur[i].ad
        = u->ur[i].new_val;
      flush(u->ur[i].ad);
    }
  }
  persist_barrier();
}

void restore_old_values(Upd *u) {
  for(int i = 0; i < M; i++) {
    if(unmark(*u->ur[i].ad) == u){
      *u->ur[i].ad
        = u->ur[i].old_val;
      flush(u->ur[i].ad);
    }
  }
  persist_barrier();
}

State PMCAS-htm(Upd &my_upd,
                uint64_t* ad[],
                uint64_t old[],
                uint64_t new[]) {
  // Assume my_upd.status == ACTIVE
  for(int i = 0; i < M; i++) {
    my_upd.ur[i].ad = ad[i];
    my_upd.ur[i].old_val = old[i];
    my_upd.ur[i].new_val = new[i];
  }
  flush(&my_upd);
  persist_barrier();

  return PMCAS-htm-run(my_upd);
}

State PMCAS-htm-run(
  Upd &my_upd) {

  bool committed = false;
  atomic {
    for(int i = 0; i < M; i++) {
      if(read(ad[i]) != old[i]) {
        commit_tx();
      }
    }
    for(int i = 0; i < M; i++) {
      *ad[i] = mark(&my_upd);
    }
    committed = true;
  }

  if(committed) {
    for(int i = 0; i < M; i++) {
      flush(ad[i]);
    }
    persist_barrier();

    my_upd.status = SUCCESS;
    flush(&my_upd.status);
    persist_barrier();

    write_new_values(&my_upd);
  } else {
    my_upd.status = FAILURE;
    flush(&my_upd.status);
    persist_barrier();
  }

  return my_upd.status;
}

void recover() {
  for(Upd *upd : all_updates) {
    if (upd->status == SUCCESS) {
      write_new_values(upd);
    } else
    if (upd->status == ACTIVE) {
      restore_old_values(upd);
    }
  }
}
```

Figure 1: PMCAS-htm: Persistent MCAS using HTM

[11] Joseph Izraelevitz, Hammurabi Mendes, and Michael L. Scott. 2016. Linearizability of Persistent Memory Objects Under a Full-System-Crash Failure Model. In *Distributed Computing - 30th International Symposium.* 313–327.

[12] Mengxing Liu, Mingxing Zhang, Kang Chen, Xuehai Qian, Yongwei Wu, Weimin Zheng, and Jinglei Ren. 2017. DudeTM: Building Durable Transactions with Decoupling for Persistent Memory. In *Proceedings of the Twenty-Second International Conference on Architectural Support for Programming Languages and Operating Systems.* 329–343.

[13] Amirsaman Memaripour, Anirudh Badam, Amar Phanishayee, Yanqi Zhou, Ramnatthan Alagappan, Karin Strauss, and Steven Swanson. 2017. Atomic In-place Updates for Non-volatile Main Memories with Kamino-Tx. In *Proceedings of the Twelfth European Conference on Computer Systems.* 499–512.

[14] Faisal Nawab, Dhruva R. Chakrabarti, Terence Kelly, and Charles B. Morrey III. 2015. Procrastination Beats Prevention: Timely Sufficient Persistence for Efficient Crash Resilience. In *Proceedings of the 18th International Conference on Extending Database Technology, EDBT 2015.* 689–694.

[15] James Reinders. 2012. Transactional Synchronization in Haswell. *https://software.intel.com/en-us/blogs/2012/02/07/transactional-synchronization-in-haswell.*

[16] Haris Volos, Andres Jaan Tack, and Michael M. Swift. 2011. Mnemosyne: lightweight persistent memory. In *Proceedings of the 16th International Conference on Architectural Support for Programming Languages and Operating Systems.* 91–104.

[17] Tianzheng Wang, Justin Levandoski, and Per-Ake Larson. 2018. Easy Lock-Free Indexing in Non-Volatile Memory. In *34th IEEE International Conference on Data Engineering.*

Separating Lock-Freedom from Wait-Freedom

Hagit Attiya*
Department of Computer Science, Technion
hagit@cs.technion.ac.il

Armando Castañeda†
Instituto de Matemáticas, UNAM
armando.castaneda@im.unam.mx

Danny Hendler‡
Department of Computer Science, Ben-Gurion University
hendlerd@cs.bgu.ac.il

Matthieu Perrin§
LS2N, Université de Nantes
matthieu.perrin@univ-nantes.fr

ABSTRACT

A long-standing open question has been whether lock-freedom and wait-freedom are fundamentally different progress conditions, namely, can the former be provided in situations where the latter cannot? This paper answers the question in the affirmative, by proving that there are objects with lock-free implementations, but without wait-free implementations—using objects of any finite power.

We precisely define an object called *n-process long-lived approximate agreement* (*n-LLAA*), in which two sets of processes associated with two *sides*, 0 or 1, need to decide on a sequence of increasingly closer outputs. We prove that 2-LLAA has a lock-free implementation using reads and writes only, while n-LLAA has a lock-free implementation using reads, writes and $(n-1)$-process consensus objects. In contrast, we prove that there is no wait-free implementation of the n-LLAA object using reads, writes and specific $(n-1)$-process consensus objects, called $(n-1)$-window registers.

CCS CONCEPTS

• **Theory of computation → Shared memory algorithms; Concurrent algorithms;**

KEYWORDS

concurrency; shared memory; multi-core algorithms; wait-freedom; lock-freedom; nonblocking.

ACM Reference Format:
Hagit Attiya, Armando Castañeda, Danny Hendler, and Matthieu Perrin. 2018. Separating Lock-Freedom from Wait-Freedom. In *PODC '18: ACM Symposium on Principles of Distributed Computing, July 23–27, 2018, Egham, United Kingdom.* ACM, New York, NY, USA, 10 pages. https://doi.org/10.1145/3212734.3212739

1 INTRODUCTION

Asynchronous shared-memory algorithms capture the behavior of concurrent systems, where failure-prone processes, each running at its own speed, communicate by applying primitives to shared base objects. Such algorithms are often used to *implement* higher-level objects, supporting ongoing invocations. These implementations withstand adverse system behavior, due to scheduling anomalies and failures.

Two main progress conditions have been studied for asynchronous shared-memory implementations [11]. The first, *wait-freedom*, ensures individual progress to each process, i.e., its operations complete as long as it takes an infinite number of steps. The second, *lock-freedom*, requires only global progress, namely, if a process takes an infinite number of steps then some (possibly other) processes complete their operations.[1] Clearly, every wait-free implementation is also lock-free.

Many wait-free implementations, starting with the universal construction [11] and recently [13], are derived by first presenting a fairly simple lock-free implementation, which is then made wait-free through sophisticated techniques. It is therefore natural to ask whether every object with a lock-free implementation also has a wait-free implementation. For *one-shot* (or *bounded*) objects, which each process accesses at most once (or a bounded number of times), the answer is trivially positive: Every lock-free algorithm is also wait-free, since once a process completes its operation (or a bounded number thereof), it takes no more steps, and the global progress condition implies that other processes are guaranteed to complete their operations.

The question, however, is challenging for long-lived objects, as there are objects with a lock-free implementation but without a known wait-free implementation *using the same primitives* (e.g., queues from test&set primitives [2]). The fundamental nature of wait-freedom and lock-freedom, and their use in numerous papers, makes this an important question.

The question was seemingly answered by Herlihy [10], who argued that there is an object for which there is a lock-free implementation for two processes using only reads and writes, and there is no wait-free algorithm in the same setting. Besides several inaccuracies in the proofs (see below), the answer provided by [10] is

*Partially supported by the Israel Science Foundation (grant 1749/14).
†Partially supported by project PAPIIT UNAM IA102417.
‡Partially supported by the Israel Science Foundation (grant 1749/14).
§Part of this work was done while this author was at the Department of Computer Science, Technion, supported by the Israel Science Foundation (grant 1749/14).

ACM ISBN 978-1-4503-5795-1/18/07...$15.00
https://doi.org/10.1145/3212734.3212739

[1] Implementations of this kind were initially called *nonblocking* [11], but we use the more contemporary terminology.

limited: it does not show a separation for more than two processes and it does not show a separation when primitives stronger than reads and writes can be used.

This paper paints a more complete picture of the separation between lock-freedom and wait-freedom. We precisely define an object called *n-process long-lived approximate agreement* (in short, *n-LLAA*), supporting a single operation called output(), which has no argument and returns a real number. Each of the n processes is assigned a *side*, either 0 or 1. Let S be a sequential execution with invocations of output(). The *current position* of side i in S is the output value of the last operation of a process in side i, or i if there are no operations of processes in side i. The sequential specification of n-LLAA includes every sequential execution in which the distance between the current positions of the two sides is at most $\frac{1}{2^r}$, where r is the total number of operations in the execution.

We present a lock-free linearizable implementation of 2-LLAA, a restriction of n-LLAA for two processes, using reads and writes only (Section 3). This implementation is extended to a lock-free linearizable implementation of n-LLAA, using reads, writes and $(n-1)$-process consensus objects (Section 4).[2]

A specific consensus object that can be used is a *window register*. These registers support read and write primitives: the write primitive is standard, but the read primitive, parameterized with an integer $k > 1$, returns a k-tuple composed of the last k values written, in the order in which they were written. A k-window register supports read primitives with parameter $\leq k$; note that a 1-window register is a standard register supporting read and write primitives. This object was initially defined in [14] to illustrate causal consistency. A similar object was defined concurrently in the context of space lower bounds for concurrent objects [8]. It is proved in [1] that a k-window register can solve consensus among exactly k processes, i.e., its *consensus number* is k.

Our main impossibility result shows that there is no wait-free implementation of the n-LLAA object, that uses only k-window registers, for $k < n$ (Section 5). Note that this includes read/write registers.

Related Work: The 2-LLAA object is a stronger version of the *iterated approximate agreement* object studied in [10], and its implementation is the same, except for a few small details. However, as explained in Section 3.2, 2-LLAA requires a more elaborate correctness proof, which determines the linearization points dynamically. Differently from 2-LLAA, the convergence requirement of the iterated approximate agreement object is that the r-th output operation of p_i is at distance at most $1/2^r$ from the the current position of the other process. Furthermore, the impossibility result for wait-free implementations in [10] relies on an unstated assumption (in the second paragraph of the proof of Lemma 14) that an infinite number of steps by one process must eventually fix the decision of the other process. Although this behavior, often referred to as *helping*, is a common way to turn lock-free implementations into wait-free ones, it is not a priori known to be a necessary condition for wait-freedom. The notion of helping was recently formalized [5, 6] and was shown to be a nontrivial property, allowing to prove nontrivial results not known to hold otherwise. Additionally, the final step of the impossibility proof in [10] (in the proof of Theorem 15) needs a stronger convergence requirement than the one required by the iterated approximate agreement object. Our impossibility proof addresses these challenges and extends to the general case of systems with $(n-1)$-consensus objects.

Aspnes and Herlihy [4] defined a class of objects for which there are wait-free implementations from read/write objects, as well as lock-free ones. Another class of objects, called *Common2*, includes the set of objects that have a wait-free implementation from objects with consensus number 2, e.g., test&set [2, 3].

Strong linearizability [9] was introduced as a way to circumvent some anomalies when used with randomized implementations. It was shown that there are deterministic lock-free and strongly linearizable implementations of snapshot, max-register or counter from multi-writer multi-reader registers, while there are no such wait-free implementations [7].

2 MODEL OF COMPUTATION

We consider a standard shared memory system with n asynchronous processes, $p_0, \ldots, p_{n-1}$, which may crash at any time during an execution. Processes communicate with each other by applying atomic *primitives* to *base objects*. The base objects we consider are *window registers* of size $k \in \{1, \ldots, n-1\}$ (in short, k-window registers) to which *read* and *write* primitives are applied. The *write* primitive has a single parameter, the value to be written. The *read* primitive returns a k-tuple composed of the last k values written, in the order in which they were written. Missing values are replaced by a default value $\perp$. Each window register can be read and written to by all processes, i.e., they are *multi-reader multi-writer.* Note that a 1-window register is the standard register, supporting ordinary read and write operations.

A *(high-level) concurrent object*, or *data type*, is defined by a state machine consisting of a set of states, a set of operations, and a set of transitions between states. Such a specification is known as *sequential.* An *implementation* of a data type T is a distributed algorithm $\mathcal{A}$ consisting of a local state machine $\mathcal{A}_p$, for each process p. For any process p, $\mathcal{A}_p$ specifies which primitives p applies in order to return a response when it invokes an operation of T. Each of these primitive invocations is a step. For the rest of this section, fix an implementation $\mathcal{A}$ of some data type T.

A *configuration* C of the system contains the states of all registers and processes. In an *initial* configuration, registers and processes are in their initial states. Given a configuration C and process p, $p(C)$ is the configuration after p takes its next step in C. Moreover, $p^0(C) = C$ and for every $n \in \mathbb{N}$, $p^{n+1}(C) = p(p^n(C))$.

An *execution* of $\mathcal{A}$ is a possibly infinite sequence of steps (namely, invocations of primitives) and invocations and responses of high-level operations in $\mathcal{A}$, with the following properties: (1) Each process first invokes a high-level operation, and only when it has a corresponding response, it can invoke another high-level operation, i.e., executions are *well-formed.* (2) A process takes steps only between an invocation and a response. (3) For any invocation of

[2] The separation question is trivial if n-process consensus objects are available since they support a wait-free implementation for n-processes of every object with a sequential specification [11].

process p, the steps of p between that invocation and the following response of p, if there is one, correspond to steps of p that are specified by $\mathcal{A}$.

An operation in an execution is *complete* if both its invocation and response appear in the execution. An operation is *pending* if only its invocation appears in the execution. An implementation is *wait-free* if every process completes each of its operations in a finite number of its steps. Formally, if a process executes infinitely many steps in an execution, all its operations are complete. An implementation is *lock-free* if whenever processes execute steps, at least one of the operations terminates. Formally, in every infinite execution, infinitely many operations are complete. Thus, a wait-free implementation is lock-free but not necessarily vice versa.

An operation OP *precedes* another operation OP' if OP completes before OP' starts. OP and OP' are *concurrent* (or *overlapping*) if neither OP precedes OP' nor OP' precedes OP. OP *does not precede* OP' if either OP is concurrent with OP' or OP' precedes OP.

Linearizability [12] is the standard notion used to identify a correct implementation. Roughly speaking, an implementation is linearizable if each operation appears to take effect atomically at some time between its invocation and response, hence operations' real-time order is maintained. Formally, let $\mathcal{A}$ be an implementation of a data type T. An execution α of $\mathcal{A}$ is *linearizable* if there is a sequential execution S of T (i.e., a sequence of matching invocation-response pairs, starting with an invocation) such that: (1) S contains every complete operation of α and some pending operations. Hence, the output value in the matching responses of an invocation in S and α are the same. (2) For every pair of operations op and op' in α, if the response of op precedes the invocation of op' in α, then op appears before op' in S; namely, S respects the real-time order in α. $\mathcal{A}$ is *linearizable* if each of its executions is linearizable.

3 READ/WRITE LOCK-FREE 2-LLAA

This section presents a read/write lock-free 2-LLAA implementation, as well as a sketch of its correctness proofs. Some proofs are deferred to the appendix.

Definition 1. *Let S be a sequential execution with invocations of two processes p_0 and p_1 to an operation* output(), *each returning a real number. The* current position *of p_i in S is the output value of the last operation of p_i, or i if there are no operations of p_i. We say that S satisfies the* convergence requirement *if the distance between the current positions of the processes is at most $1/2^r$, where r is the total number of operations in the execution. The sequential specification of the* 2-LLAA object *contains every sequential execution of* output() *operations by p_0 and p_1 such that each of its prefixes satisfies the convergence requirement.*

The algorithm in Figure 1 is a lock-free implementation of 2-LLAA using read/write primitives. Each process p_i locally stores its current position and round (number of complete and pending operations of p_i, so far) in its local variable *me*, and stores the position and round of the other process, denoted p_j, in *you*. The initial position and round of p_i are i and 0. Processes communicate through the shared array M by writing and reading positions and rounds. Additionally, p_i uses two (closed) intervals *prev* and *range*: *prev* stores the interval committed in p_i's previous operation, which indicates where any future position of p_i might be, and *range* stores

```
Shared variables:
    M[0, 1] ← [⟨pos = 0, round = 0⟩, ⟨pos = 1, round = 0⟩]

Local variables:
    myID ← i
    yourID ← 1 − i
    me.⟨pos, round⟩ ← ⟨myID, 0⟩ %% My position and round
    you.⟨pos, round⟩ ← ⟨yourID, 0⟩ %% Other's position and round
    prev, range ← [myID ± 1]

Function output():
(01) me.round ← me.round + 1
(02) M[myID].round ← me.round
(03) while true do
(04)     M[myID].pos ← me.pos
(05)     you ← M[yourID]
(06)     rounds ← me.round + you.round
(07)     range ← [me.pos ± 1/2^rounds]
(08)     if you.pos ∈ range ∨ you.pos ∉ prev then
(09)         prev ← range
(10)         return me.pos
(11)     elseif me.pos < you.pos then
(12)         me.pos ← me.pos + 1/2^rounds
(13)     else
(14)         me.pos ← me.pos − 1/2^rounds
(15)     endif
(16) endwhile
endFunction
```

Figure 1: A lock-free 2-LLAA algorithm for processes p_0 and p_1. Code of process p_i.

the current interval the position of p_j should belong to in order for p_i to decide.

When executing output(), p_i first increments its round counter and writes the new value in M (lines 01 and 02) and then iterates the while loop (lines 03 to 15). Each iteration tries to get closer to the position of p_j in M, until the condition in line 08 is satisfied. There are two (disjoint) cases that can make p_i's current operation decided. In the first case, called *closeness rule*, the position of p_j read by p_i is in the interval *range* computed in line 07, hence the distance between the positions is at most $1/2^r$, where r is the total number of operations p_i is aware of. This ensures that the distance between the positions of the processes obeys the convergence requirement of 2-LLAA. In the second case, called *invalid position rule*, the position of p_j is out of the previously-committed range *prev* of p_i. Observe that this can happen because of asynchrony: p_i might have completed several operations getting closer to a position of p_j in M that is different from the position p_j is about to write. The rationale behind the invalid position rule is that as p_j was slow and its position is not in *prev* of p_i, it would have to "catch up" and decide by the closeness rule in its current operation. As shown below (Lemma 1), whenever p_i decides by the invalid position rule, the current operation of p_j is pending and p_j decides by the closeness rule in every extension in which its operation is complete.

3.1 Correctness Proof

In the analysis of the algorithm, for simplicity and without loss of generality, the invocation of an operation is identified with its first shared-memory write operation outside the **while** loop of the output function (line 02), that is, it is executed atomically together with the local operations of line 01. The response of a decided operation is identified with its last shared-memory read step inside the loop (line 05). We also assume that the local computation inside the **while** loop (lines 05-15) is executed atomically together with the shared-memory read step in line 05.

For an execution α, we use the following notation and terminology. The k-th operation of a process p_i in α is denoted $P_i^k(\alpha)$, if there is such an operation. $P_i^0(\alpha)$ denotes a fictitious operation whose output is the initial position of p_i. An operation $P_i^k(\alpha)$ of p_i is *decided* if it takes its response (read) step in α. In this case, $v_i^k(\alpha)$ denotes the value of variable v at the end of $P_i^k(\alpha)$. We let $rad(prev_i^k(\alpha))$ denote the radius of the interval $prev_i^k(\alpha)$ with center $me_i^k.pos(\alpha)$. A decided operation $P_i^k(\alpha)$ decides *by the closeness rule on* $P_j^m(\alpha)$ (with $j = 1 - i$) if $you_i^k.pos(\alpha) \in range_i^k(\alpha)$ and $you_i^k.round(\alpha) = m$. $P_i^k(\alpha)$ decides *by the invalid position rule on* $P_j^m(\alpha)$ if $you_i^k.pos(\alpha) \notin prev_i^k(\alpha)$ and $you_i^k.round(\alpha) = m$. We omit α from the above definitions when it can be understood from the context.

To see that Algorithm 1 is lock-free, we note that two operations P_i^k and P_j^m cannot both take an infinite number of steps without completing, since eventually they agree on $rounds = k + m$ and their positions get sufficiently close to each other. The formal proof is omitted for lack of space

Algorithm Linearize (Figure 2) specifies how we linearize a quiescent execution (i.e. an execution without pending operations) α. Lemma 1 stated below (whose proof is in the appendix) forms the basis for showing that Algorithm Linearize produces correct linearizations. Linearize considers the operations of α in the order they decide. Let P_i^k and P_j^m be the operations considered at the beginning of the ℓ-th iteration of the while loop of Linearize. If P_j^m is decided, then P_j^m is already in seq_ℓ, and, as we shall see, P_i^k decides by the closeness rule. This implies that P_i^k and P_j^m satisfy the convergence requirement. If P_j^m is not decided (hence pending), then P_j^m can be safely placed before or after P_i^k because Lemma 1 implies that P_j^m will decide by the closeness rule. Finally, as the proof of Lemma 3 argues, if none of P_i^k and P_j^m are in seq_ℓ, then P_i^k and P_j^m start from a quiescent state of the algorithm (operations P^2 and Q^1 in Figure 3 are an example of this situation) and their order is decided considering the outputs of the previous operations.

Lemma 1. *Let α be a finite execution whose last step is a read (in line 05) of an operation P_i^k of p_i that makes that operation decided (by either the closeness or the invalid position rules) on some undecided operation P_j^m of p_j, with $j = 1 - i$. Let $\alpha\beta$ be any extension of α in which P_j^m is decided. Then, P_j^m decides by the closeness rule in $\alpha\beta$ and $dist(me_i^k.pos, me_j^m.pos) \leq 1/2^{m+k}$.*

It follows directly from Algorithm Linearize that the latest point in which an operation is linearized is when it decides (by reading in line 05 of Figure 1). Moreover, once an operation is linearized, the operation (by the other process) it decides on is also linearized (if it was not linearized before).

Function Linearize(α):
(01) $seq_0 \leftarrow \epsilon$, $\ell \leftarrow 0$
(02) **while** α has more than ℓ operations **do**
(03) $\beta_{\ell+1} \leftarrow$ shortest prefix of α with $\ell + 1$ decided operations
(04) $P_i^k \leftarrow$ operation that decides in the last (read) step of $\beta_{\ell+1}$
(05) $P_j^m \leftarrow$ operation that P_i^k decides on in α (i.e. $you_i^k.round = m$)
(06) **if** P_i^k is in seq_ℓ **then**
(07) **if** P_j^m is in seq_ℓ **then**
(08) $seq_{\ell+1} \leftarrow seq_\ell$
(09) **else**
(10) $seq_{\ell+1} \leftarrow seq_\ell \cdot P_j^m$
(11) **else**
(12) **if** P_j^m is in seq_ℓ **then**
(13) $seq_{\ell+1} \leftarrow seq_\ell \cdot P_i^k$
(14) **else if** $dist(me_i^k.pos, me_j^{m-1}.pos)$ $\leq dist(me_j^m.pos, me_i^{k-1}.pos)$ **then**
(15) $seq_{\ell+1} \leftarrow seq_\ell \cdot P_i^k \cdot P_j^m$
(16) **else**
(17) $seq_{\ell+1} \leftarrow seq_\ell \cdot P_j^m \cdot P_i^k$
(18) **endif**
(19) **endif**
(20) $\ell \leftarrow \ell + 1$
(21) **endwhile**
(22) Remove the (fictitious) operations P_0^0 and P_1^0 from seq_ℓ
(23) **return** seq_ℓ
endFunction

Figure 2: A sequential algorithm to linearize an execution α without pending operations.

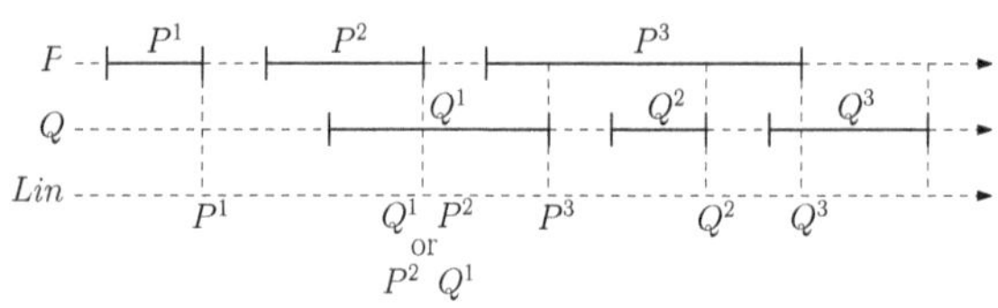

Figure 3: An example of the linearization produced by Algorithm Linearize.

Lemma 2. *Let α be a finite execution without pending operations. The sequential execution produced by* Linearize(α) *respects the real-time order in α.*

Proof. Consider two operations P_i^k and P_j^m in α, $k, m > 0$. Suppose that P_i^k precedes P_j^m in α. The latest point at which Algorithm Linearize linearizes P_i^k is when β_{l+1} in line 03 of Algorithm Linearize ends in the read step which makes P_i^k decide in α. None of the steps of P_j^m appear in β_{l+1}, hence P_i^k does not decide on P_j^m and consequently P_j^m is not linearized in lines 10, 15 or 17 of Algorithm Linearize (which are the only places operations are linearized). Furthermore, no prior operation by p_i could have decided on P_j^m in β_{l+1}, hence it was not linearized before. □

Lemma 3, is the key technical lemma in the algorithm's correctness proof, establishing that Algorithm Linearize outputs correct linearizations.

LEMMA 3. *Let α be any finite execution without pending operations. Then,* $\mathsf{Lin}(\alpha)$ *is a sequential execution of the 2-LLAA object.*

PROOF SKETCH. We consider a linearization $\mathsf{Lin}(\alpha)$ of an execution α which, as we assume towards a contradiction, is not a sequential execution of 2-LLAA, and consider the first operation P_i^k that violates convergence. Let P_j^{m-1} be the latest preceding operation of p_j in $\mathsf{Lin}(\alpha)$. Then, $dist(me_i^k.pos, me_j^{m-1}.pos) > 1/2^{m+k-1}$. Since $\mathsf{Lin}(\alpha)$ respects the real-time order in α (Lemma 2), P_i^k does not precede P_j^{m-1} in α.

If P_j^{m-1} and P_i^k are concurrent in α, let β be the shortest prefix of α in which the first of them, say P_i^k, is decided. Hence P_j^{m-1} is pending and P_i^k decides on P_j^{m-1}. By Lemma 1,

$$dist(me_i^k.pos, me_j^{m-1}.pos) \leq 1/2^{m+k-1},$$

and the convergence requirement holds.

We therefore know that P_j^{m-1} precedes P_i^k in α. It can be shown that at the end of the previous (possibly fictitious) operation P_i^{k-1} of p_i, $rad(prev_i^{k-1}) \geq 1/2^{m+k-2}$. Moreover, when P_i^k starts, $prev_i = prev_i^{k-1}$, $me_i.pos = me_i^{k-1}.pos$ and $M[j].pos = me_j^{m-1}.pos$. Now, if no operation of p_j overlaps P_i^k, then if P_i^k decides by the invalid position rule, it does so in the very first iteration of the while loop, without any change to its position $me_i.pos$, and thus $me_i^k.pos = me_i^{k-1}.pos$. Hence, $me_j^{m-1}.pos \notin prev_i^{k-1}$ and $dist(me_i^{k-1}.pos, me_j^{m-1}.pos) > 1/2^{m+k-2}$, implying that either P_i^{k-1} or P_j^{m-1} (both preceding P_i^k in $\mathsf{Lin}(\alpha)$) do not satisfy the convergence requirement, which is a contradiction. And if P_i^k decides by the closeness rule, the code implies that

$$dist(me_i^k.pos, me_j^{m-1}.pos) \leq 1/2^{m+k-1},$$

and the convergence requirement holds.

We are left with the case that operation P_j^m exists and overlaps with P_i^k (and P_j^{m-1} precedes P_i^k). We first prove that

$$dist(me_i^k.pos, me_j^{m-1}.pos) \leq dist(me_j^m.pos, me_i^{k-1}.pos) \quad (1)$$

$$dist(me_i^k.pos, me_j^m.pos) \leq 1/2^{m+k} \quad (2)$$

To prove (1), note that P_j^m cannot precede P_i^{k-1} because it is concurrent with P_i^k. Also, it is easy to show that P_i^{k-1} precedes P_j^m in α. Thus, P_j^{m-1} precedes P_i^k and P_i^{k-1} precedes P_j^m, and hence *both* P_i^{k-1} *and* P_j^{m-1} *are complete when the first among* P_i^k *and* P_j^m *starts in* α. Without loss of generality, suppose that P_i^k decides before P_j^m, then, since they overlap, P_i^k decides on P_j^m. Since P_j^{m-1} precedes P_i^k and P_i^{k-1} precedes P_j^m, in the while iteration of Algorithm Linearize that linearizes P_i^k, the conditions of lines 06 and 12 are false, namely, P_i^k and P_j^m were not linearized yet, and they are linearized in lines 14-18. It can be shown that P_j^m is not linearized before P_i^k, and the condition of line 14 holds, implying (1).

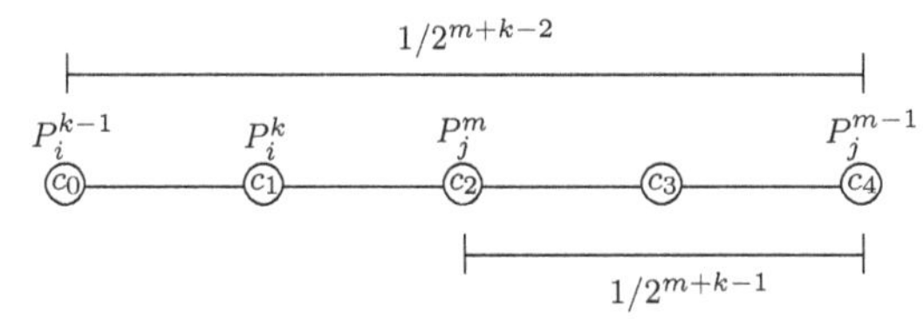

Figure 4: An example of the last case in the proof of Lemma 3: P_i^k decides before P_j^m and outputs c_1, whose distance to the output of P_j^{m-1} is strictly larger than $1/2^{m+k-1}$. By (2), the output of P_j^m is in the interval $[c_0, c_2]$. This is a contradiction since the distance between any point in $[c_0, c_2]$ and the output of P_i^{k-1} is at most $1/2^{m+k-1}$, and thus $dist(me_i^k.pos, me_j^{m-1}.pos) > dist(me_j^m.pos, me_i^{k-1}.pos)$.

Lemma 1 implies (2), since P_i^k are P_j^m are concurrent, similarly to the case when P_i^k and P_j^{m-1} are concurrent, handled before.

Finally, consider the outputs $me_i^{k-1}.pos$ and $me_j^{m-1}.pos$ of P_i^{k-1} and P_j^{m-1}. Suppose that $me_i^{k-1}.pos \leq me_j^{m-1}.pos$ (the other case is similar). Let $\mathcal{I} = [me_i^{k-1}.pos, me_j^{m-1}.pos]$. It can be shown that $me_i^k.pos, me_i^m.pos \in \mathcal{I}$. By assumption, P_i^{k-1} and P_j^{m-1} do satisfy the convergence requirement, namely,

$$dist(me_i^{k-1}.pos, me_j^{m-1}.pos) \leq 1/2^{m+k-2},$$

and hence $|\mathcal{I}| \leq 1/2^{m+k-2}$. The interesting case is when $|\mathcal{I}| = 1/2^{m+k-2}$. Lemma 12 (in the appendix) implies that the first to decide among P_i^k and P_j^m must decide a position (in $\mathcal{I}$) that is an integer multiple of $1/2^{m+k}$. There are only five integer multiples of $1/2^{m+k}$ in $\mathcal{I}$.[3] A case by case analysis shows that if $dist(me_i^k.pos, me_j^{m-1}.pos) > 1/2^{m+k-1}$, then inequality (2) implies that $dist(me_i^k.pos, me_j^{m-1}.pos) > dist(me_j^m.pos, me_i^{k-1}.pos)$, which is a contradiction, given inequality (1) (see an example in Figure 4). □

Consider any finite execution α of the algorithm from Figure 1. Let $\alpha\beta$ be an extension of α in which all operations in α are complete (and no new operation is started). This extension exists since the algorithm is lock-free. By Lemma 2, the sequential execution $seq(\alpha\,\beta)$ produced by $\mathsf{Lin}(\alpha\beta)$ respects the real-time order of $\alpha\,\beta$; by Lemma 3, it is a sequential execution of the 2-LLAA object. Thus, $seq(\alpha\,\beta)$ is a linearization of $\alpha\,\beta$, and of α as well, implying the main theorem of this section:

THEOREM 4. *Algorithm 1 is a lock-free linearizable implementation of the 2-LLAA object, using reads and writes.*

3.2 A Simpler Linearization Proof?

This section discussed whether a simpler linearization argument exits. The linearization proof in the previous subsection is nontrivial, partly because Algorithm Linearize may place operations that are pending in α before operations that are complete. Furthermore, as we described previously, to linearize a non-quiescent execution α,

[3] It is useful to consider the initial configuration, where $m = k = 1$ and $me_i^{k-1}.pos = 0$, $me_j^{m-1}.pos = 1$.

we first complete all pending operations in α and then apply Algorithm Linearize to the resulting quiescent execution. Consequently, it is possible that the linearization S' we obtain for an extension α' of α is not an extension of the linearization S we obtain for α, implying that our implementation is not necessarily strongly linearizable [9].[4]

In contrast, the linearizability order used in the correctness proof of the lock-free algorithm [10, Figure 5, Section 4] is simple and shows that the algorithm is strongly linearizable. Below we argue that this simple approach does not work for our stronger 2-LLAA object.

The linearization order used in [10] (right above Lemma 11) is the following. For every operation OP in an execution, let $rounds(OP)$ be the first value the operation sets to the local variable $rounds$ (that variable is called i in [10]). Then, if $rounds(OP) < rounds(OP')$, OP is linearized before OP', and if $rounds(OP) = rounds(OP')$, OP and OP' can be linearized in any order.

Consider the following execution of the algorithm in Figure 1: (1) p_0 starts an invocation to output(), completes one iteration of the loop (note that it does not decide as $1/2^{rounds} = 1/2^1$) and stops before writing its new preference at the first step of the second iteration of the loop. Note that p_0 is about to write 1/2 and the position of p_0 in M is still 0. (2) p_1 executes, until completion, two consecutive invocations to output() (p_0 takes no steps while p_1 completes the two invocations). Observe that p_1 obtains 1/4 and 1/8 from the two invocations, respectively. (3) p_0 runs solo until it completes its pending output() invocation. Note that p_0 obtains 1/4 from the invocation.

It is easy to see that, for the execution α defined above, $rounds(P_0^1) = 1$, $rounds(P_1^1) = 2$ and $rounds(P_1^2) = 3$, and thus, using the linearization order defined in [10], α would be linearized as follows: $\langle P_0^1 : 1/4\rangle\langle P_1^1 : 1/4\rangle\langle P_1^2 : 1/8\rangle$. However, this linearization is incorrect because $\mathsf{lin}(\alpha)$ is not a sequential execution of 2-LLAA: the prefix $\langle P_0^1 : 1/4\rangle$ of the sequential execution is invalid, because the distance between the current position of p_0 and the current (initial) position of p_1, which are respectively 1/4 and 1, is larger than $1/2^1$. Consequently, $\mathsf{lin}(\alpha)$ is not a valid sequential execution of 2-LLAA either.

Finally, it can be verified that Algorithm Linearize produces the linearization $\langle P_1^1 : 1/4\rangle\langle P_0^1 : 1/4\rangle\langle P_1^2 : 1/8\rangle$ from α, which is a sequential execution of 2-LLAA.

4 LOCK-FREE n-LLAA, USING $(n-1)$-CONSENSUS OBJECTS

We formally define the n-LLAA object and explain how it can be implemented in a lock-free manner using $(n-1)$-process consensus objects; full correctness proofs are omitted for lack of space.

Definition 2. *Each of the n processes belongs to a* side, *either 0 or 1. The n-LLAA object supports a single operation called* output(). *Let S be a sequential execution with invocations of* output(), *each returning a real number. The* current position *of side i in S is the output value of the last operation of a process in side i, or i if there are no operations of processes in side i. We say that S satisfies the* convergence requirement *if the distance between the current positions of the two sides is at most $\frac{1}{2^r}$, where r is the total number of operations in the execution. The sequential specification of the n-LLAA object contains every sequential execution of* output() *operations by the n processes such that each of its prefixes satisfies the convergence requirement.*

[4] An algorithm is *strongly linearizable* if there is a function f from executions of the algorithm to sequential executions such that (1) for every execution α, $f(\alpha)$ is a linearization of α and (2) for every execution $\alpha\beta$, $f(\alpha)$ is a prefix of $f(\alpha\beta)$.

The lock-free implementation of n-LLAA is based on the lock-free 2-LLAA algorithm. Consider first the case in which there is at least one process in each side. Then, using $(n-1)$-process consensus objects, the $\leq n-1$ processes in side i simulate operations of process p_i in Algorithm 1; each time an operation terminates, the processes decide who takes this output value, also using consensus objects. When there are n processes in the same side, the processes can safely decide on the initial value of the other side.

Figure 5 shows how processes in the same side i simulate process p_i of Algorithm 1. Lines 05–31 simulate a single operation output() of p_i; each time this loop starts, a new operation of p_i is simulated. Lines 08 and 11 correspond to the write operations of Algorithm 1 and Lines 12–16 simulate the read operation of Algorithm 1, with the help of the consensus objects in *READS*. Each process first reads the pair $(pos, round)$ of the processes in the other side and considers the most current one (from its point of view), with the help of the timestamps in the local variables me. This is its proposal to the consensus which decides the next read value of the simulated process p_i. Once the output value of the current simulated operation of p_i has been computed (the condition in Line 19 is true), the processes in the same side i compete for that output value in Line 22, with the help of the consensus objects in *OPS*. The winning process outputs that value for its current operation, while the others start a new simulated operation of p_i. The goal of Lines 01–04 is to handle the case in which all processes belong to the same side: when a process discovers that all processes are in its side, it knows that the other side is not moving (it has not moved since the beginning of the execution) hence it can safely decide the initial position of the other side.

The way processes advertise their side in Line 01, and then check the others' side in Line 03, ensures that in every execution, at most $n-1$ processes invoke the same consensus object (in Lines 16 and 22). The following property directly follows from the agreement property of consensus.

Lemma 5. *Consider an execution of Algorithm 5. Then, for every pair of processes p_ℓ and p_j in the same side, if both p_ℓ and p_j assign the kth value to a local variable v, which is either $me, you, prev$ or $range$, then $v_j^k = v_\ell^k$.*

Using this lemma, we can now precisely define the notion of a *simulated operation.* Let α be a (finite or infinite) execution of Algorithm 5. For every side i and integer $k \geq 1$, the *k-th simulated operation of side i*, denoted sOP_i^k, is the subsequence of α containing all steps corresponding to steps in Lines 08, 11, 12, 16 or 22 of any process such that when it executes the step, its $me.round$ local variable is equal to k. The following lemma relates the executions of Algorithms 1 and 5, where the two processes in Algorithm 1 are denoted q_0 and q_1.

Lemma 6. *For every finite or infinite execution α of Algorithm 5, there is an execution α^* of Algorithm 1 such that:*

```
Shared variables:
    M[0, 1][0, ..., n − 1] ← each entry of M[j], j ∈ {0, 1},
initialized to ⟨pos = j, round = 0, tmst = 0⟩
    SIDE[0, ..., n − 1] ← each entry initialized to ⊥
    READS[0, 1][∞] ← bi-dimensional array
with infinitely many (n − 1)-process consensus objects
    OPS[0, 1][∞] ← bi-dimensional array
with infinitely many (n − 1)-process consensus objects

Local variables:
    mySide ← initialized to 0 or 1
    otherSide ← 1 − mySide
    me.⟨pos, round, tmst⟩ ← ⟨mySide, 0, 0⟩
%% My side's position, round and timestamp
    you.⟨pos, round, tmst⟩ ← ⟨otherSide, 0, 0⟩
%% Other's position, round and timestmp
    prev, range ← [mySide ± 1]
    count_reads, count_ops ← 0

Function output():
(01) SIDE[ID] ← mySide
(02) s ← snapshot(SIDE)
(03) if |{ID : s[ID] = mySide}| = n then
(04)   return otherSide
(05) while true do
(06)   me.round ← me.round + 1
(07)   me.tmst ← me.tmst + 1
(08)   M[mySide][ID] ← me
(09)   decided ← false
(10)   while ¬decided do
(11)     M[mySide][ID] ← me
(12)     t ← snapshot(M[otherSide])
(13)     max ← max({tmst′ : t[ID].tmst = tmst′})
(14)     prop ← any t[ID] such that t[ID].tmst = max
(15)     count_reads ← count_reads + 1
(16)     you ← READS[mySide][count_reads].decide(prop)
(17)     rounds ← me.round + you.round
(18)     range ← [me.pos ± 1/2^rounds]
(19)     if you.pos ∈ range ∨ you.pos ∉ prev then
(20)       prev ← range
(21)       count_ops ← count_ops + 1
(22)       owner ← OPS[mySide][count_ops].decide(ID)
(23)       if owner = ID then
(24)         return me.pos
(25)       decided ← true
(26)     elseif me.pos < you.pos then
(27)       me.pos ← me.pos + 1/2^rounds
(28)       me.tmst ← me.tmst + 1
(29)     else
(30)       me.pos ← me.pos − 1/2^rounds
(31)       me.tmst ← me.tmst + 1
(32)     endif
(33)   endwhile
(34) endwhile
endFunction
```

Figure 5: A lock-free n-process LLAA object algorithm.

(1) There is a function f from the set of operations of α onto the set of operations in α^*; moreover, for each operation OP in side i, $f(OP)$ is an operation of q_i.

(2) An operation OP is pending if and only if $f(OP)$ is pending; moreover, OP has infinitely many steps if and only if $f(OP)$ has infinitely many steps too.

(3) The outputs of a completed operation OP and its associated completed operation $f(OP)$ are the same.

(4) If OP precedes OP' in α then $f(OP)$ precedes $f(OP')$ in α^*.

Proof Sketch. By Lemma 5, every pair of processes performing the steps of the same simulated operation *sOP*, write the same sequence of values (possibly at distinct times, due to asynchrony). Thus, for each simulated operation *sOP* in α, we can map an operation $g(sOP)$ in an execution of α^* of Algorithm 1 by removing redundant steps from α (essentially, we keep the first ℓth simulated step of *sOP*, for every ℓ). For any operation *OP* of process p_i in α, let $h(OP)$ be the simulated operation in α, the last step of *OP* by p_i belongs to. Then, if *OP* is completed, $h(OP)$ is the simulated operation p_i is simulating when it wins in the consensus at Line 22. Finally, we let $f(OP) = g(h(OP))$ □

Theorem 7. *Algorithm 5 is a lock-free linearizable implementation of the n-LLAA object, using reads, writes and $(n-1)$-process consensus objects.*

Proof. Lemma 6 implies that if there is an infinite execution α of Algorithm 5 in which only finitely many operations are completed, then there is an infinite execution α^* of Algorithm 1 in which only finitely many operations are completed, in contradiction to the lock-freedom of Algorithm 1. This implies that Algorithm 5 is lock-free as well.

Next, consider any finite execution α and let $\alpha\beta$ be an extension in which all operations in α are completed. Let λ be an execution of Algorithm 1 associated with $\alpha\beta$, as in Lemma 6. The output of a completed operation *OP* is equal to the output of its associated completed operation $f(OP)$, and if *OP* precedes OP' in $\alpha\beta$ then, by Lemma 6, $f(OP)$ precedes $f(OP')$ in λ. Thus, by replacing each *OP* with $f(OP)$, we can obtain a linearization $\mathrm{lin}(\alpha\beta)$ of $\alpha\beta$ from any linearization $\mathrm{lin}(\lambda)$ of λ, since the convergence requirement in both 2-LLAA and n-LLAA is a function of the number of all previous operations. Thus, Algorithm 5 is linearizable. □

5 IMPOSSIBILITY OF WAIT-FREE n-LLAA USING $(n-1)$-WINDOW REGISTERS

An execution β is an *extension* of a finite execution α if α is a prefix of β. A configuration C is *reachable* if there is a finite execution that ends with all processes and variables in the same states as in C. A configuration C' is *reachable* from a configuration C if there is a finite execution α that ends with C' and a prefix of the execution α ends with C. Two configurations C and C' are *indistinguishable* to process p, denoted $C \overset{p}{\sim} C'$, if the state of every shared variable and the state of p are the same in C and C'.

Fix an implementation $\mathcal{A}$ of the n-LLAA object. Below, we consider only executions of $\mathcal{A}$ in which process p_0 is on side 0, performing a single output() operation, and all other processes are on side 1.

Let α be a finite execution of $\mathcal{A}$; α is *v-potent* if there is an extension α' of α in which the operation of p_0 is complete and returns v; α is *v-univalent* (or just *univalent* when v is irrelevant) if α is v-potent and for all $w \neq v$, α is not w-potent; α is *bivalent* if it is both v-potent and w-potent, for two values $v \neq w$.

Definition 3. *An execution α is* ambivalent for process $q \neq p_0$ *(or simply* ambivalent *when q is immaterial), if α is v-univalent and for some $w \neq v$, there is a w-univalent execution α' that is indistinguishable from α to process q. If α ends with a configuration C, we say that C* is ambivalent for process q.

Definition 4. *An execution α, ending with configuration C, has a* critical q-extension *(or simply* critical extension *when q is immaterial) for a process $q \neq p_0$, if there is a process $q' \notin \{p_0, q\}$ such that, for all $\ell \geq 0$, $p_0(q^\ell(C))$ is v-univalent and $p_0(q'(q^\ell(C)))$ is w-univalent with $v \neq w$.*

Definition 5. *An execution α, ending with configuration C, is* (v, q, v')-critical *(or simply* critical *if v, q and v' are immaterial), if $p_0(C)$ is v-univalent, there is a process $q \neq p_0$ such that $p_0(q(C))$ is v'-univalent, for $v' \neq v$, and for all finite extensions $\alpha\beta$ of α ending in configuration C', $p_0(C')$ is univalent.*

Lemma 8. *If α is a (v, p_1, v')-critical execution of $\mathcal{A}$ ending in configuration C, then either some extension of α is ambivalent or some extension of α has a critical extension.*

Proof. The proof considers the next steps that p_0 and p_1 are about to take in C. If both p_0 and p_1 access different window registers, or p_1's step is a read, then $p_1(p_0(C))$ and $p_0(p_1(C))$ are indistinguishable to p_0. Hence, a solo execution of p_0 after both configurations returns the same value, contradicting the fact that α is (v, p_1, v')-critical, that is, $p_1(p_0(C))$ is v-univalent and $p_0(p_1(C))$ is v'-univalent.

If p_0's next step is a read of a window register, then $p_1(p_0(C))$ and $p_0(p_1(C))$ are indistinguishable to all processes other than p_0, $p_1(p_0(C))$ is v-valent and $p_0(p_1(C))$ is v'-valent, so $p_1(p_0(C))$ and $p_0(p_1(C))$ are both ambivalent for all processes other than p_0.

The remaining case is when both steps are writes to the same window register R. If $n = 2$, then R is an ordinary register, so $p_0(p_1(C))$ and $p_0(C)$ are indistinguishable to p_0. Since α, ending with C, is (v, p_1, v')-critical, $p_0(C)$ is v-valent and $p_0(p_1(C))$ is v'-valent, which is a contradiction.

For $n > 2$, we can prove the following claim:

Claim 9. *Let $\alpha\beta$ be a finite extension of α ending in configuration C', such that p_0 and p_1 do not take steps in β and no process writes to R in β. Then $p_0(C')$ is v-univalent and $p_0(p_1(C'))$ is v'-univalent.*

Proof. The proof is by induction on the length of β, with a trivial base case when β is empty. Suppose the lemma holds for when the length of β is ℓ, and let us consider an extension $\alpha\beta\gamma$ of α, where γ is a single step of some process $q \notin \{p_0, p_1\}$. Let C' be the configuration at the end of $\alpha\beta$, and C'' be the configuration at the end of $\alpha\beta\gamma$. By the induction hypothesis, $p_0(C')$ is v-univalent and $p_0(q(C'))$ is v'-univalent. Note that no process writes to R in $\beta\gamma$.

If q applies a primitive to a window register different than R, then $p_0(C'') = p_0(q(C')) = q(p_0(C'))$ is v-univalent and $p_0(p_1(C'')) = p_0(p_1(q(C'))) = q(p_0(p_1(C')))$ is v'-univalent.

Otherwise, since no process writes to R in $\beta\gamma$, q reads R. Then $p_0(C'') = p_0(q(C'))$ and $p_0(C')$ are indistinguishable to p_0. As $p_0(C')$ is v-univalent, $p_0(C'')$ is v-potent, since the solo executions by p_0 starting from C'' and from C' are the same, hence both must return v. Moreover, since α is critical, $p_0(C'')$ is univalent. Therefore, $p_0(C'')$ is v-univalent. Similarly, $p_0(p_1(C'')) = p_0(p_1(q(C')))$ and $p_0(p_1(C'))$ are indistinguishable to p_0 and $p_0(p_1(C'))$ is v'-univalent by the induction hypothesis. Hence, $p_0(p_1(C''))$ is v'-univalent. □

Assume first that we can let each process $p_2, \ldots, p_{n-1}$, in turn, take steps until it is about to write to R, reaching a configuration D in which the next step of every process is a write to R. By Claim 9, $p_0(D)$ is v-valent and $p_0(p_1(D))$ is v'-valent. However, since R is an $(n-1)$-window register, $p_{n-1}(\ldots(p_2(p_0(D)))\ldots)$ and $p_{n-1}(\ldots(p_2(p_0(p_1(D))))\ldots)$ are indistinguishable to all processes except p_1, contradicting the fact that $p_{n-1}(\ldots(p_2(p_0(D)))\ldots)$ is v-valent, whereas $p_{n-1}(\ldots(p_2(p_0(p_1(D))))\ldots)$ is v'-valent.

Otherwise, for some process $q \neq p_1$, there is an infinite extension $\alpha\beta\gamma$ of α such that q runs solo in γ and no process writes to R in $\beta\gamma$. Let C' be the configuration at the end of $\alpha\beta$. By Claim 9, for all $\ell \geq 0$, $p_0(q^\ell(C'))$ is v-univalent and $p_0(p_1(q^\ell(C')))$ is v'-univalent, i.e., γ is a critical q-extension of $\alpha\beta$. □

We next use a standard valency argument to prove that if $\mathcal{A}$ is wait-free, then it has a critical execution.

Lemma 10. *If $\mathcal{A}$ is a wait-free linearizable implementation of the n-LLAA object, then it has a critical execution.*

Proof. Since $\mathcal{A}$ is linearizable, in a solo execution by p_0 starting from C_0 and completing one output operation, the current position of side 0 must be at least $\frac{1}{2}$. On the other hand, in the execution from C_0 in which p_1 first executes solo two complete output operations and then p_0 runs solo and executes its output operation to completion, the current position of side 0 can be at most $\frac{3}{8}$. It follows that the empty execution (from C_0) is bivalent.

Starting with the empty execution as α, we repeatedly extend α to a bivalent execution $\alpha\alpha''$, such that p_0 executes a step in α'' (α'' may include steps by other processes). Since $\mathcal{A}$ is wait-free, eventually we reach a bivalent execution $\alpha\alpha'$ ending with configuration C' such that for any extension $\alpha\alpha'\beta$ of $\alpha\alpha'$ ending with configuration C'', $p_0(C'')$ is univalent. In particular, this holds for the empty β.

It follows that $p_0(C')$ is univalent, so it is v-valent for some v. Since $\alpha\alpha'$ is bivalent, it has an extension $\alpha\alpha'\beta_1$, ending with a configuration C_1, such that $p_0(C_1)$ is v'-valent, for some $v' \neq v$. Let β_2 be the longest prefix of β_1 such that $\alpha\alpha'\beta_2$ ends with a configuration C_2 for which $p_0(C_2)$ is v-valent. Let q be the process that takes the next step in $\alpha\alpha'\beta_1$ after the execution of $\alpha\alpha'\beta_2$. From our construction, $p_0(C_2)$ is v-valent, $p_0(q(C_2))$ is v'-valent for $v' \neq v$, and for any finite extension $\alpha\alpha'\beta_3$ of $\alpha\alpha'\beta_2$, ending with a configuration C_3, $p_0(C_3)$ is univalent. It follows from Definition 5 that $\alpha\alpha'\beta_2$ is (v, q, v')-critical. □

Theorem 11. *There is no wait-free linearizable implementation of the n-LLAA object, which uses only $(n-1)$-window registers. (Note that this includes read and write registers.)*

Proof. Assume, by way of contradiction, that $\mathcal{A}$ is a wait-free linearizable implementation of the n-LLAA object. By Lemma 10, $\mathcal{A}$ has a critical execution α. By Lemma 8, we have two cases:

Case 1: Some extension α' of α, ending with a configuration C', is ambivalent for a process $q \neq p_0$. By Definition 3, α' is v-valent for some v, and there is a $w \neq v$ and an execution α_w, ending with a configuration C_w, such that α_w is w-univalent and configurations C' and C_w are indistinguishable to q.

Pick an integer k such that $\frac{1}{2^k} < |v-w|$. Let $\alpha'\beta_v^q$ be an extension of α' such that, in β_v^q, q runs solo and executes to completion $k+3$ output operations. Let x be the value returned by the last operation of q. Let $\alpha'\beta_v^q\beta_v^{p_0}$ be an extension of $\alpha'\beta_v^q$ such that, in $\beta_v^{p_0}$, p_0 runs solo until it completes its output operation. Since α' is v-univalent, p_0's operation returns v.

Consider a linearization of $\alpha'\beta_v^q\beta_v^{p_0}$. It contains at least $k+3$ operations of processes in side 1, including all the ones by q, and one operation by p_0. Suppose first that the last operation of q is linearized after the operation of p_0. By Definition 2, $|x-v| \leq \frac{1}{2^{k+4}} < \frac{1}{2^{k+1}}$.

Suppose now that the last operation of q is linearized before the operation of p_0. Let k' denote the number of operations in side 1 linearized between the last operation of q and the operation of p_0 and let y be the value returned by the operation linearized right before the operation of p_0. By Definition 2,

$$\begin{aligned} |x-v| &\leq |x-0| + |0-y| + |y-v| \\ &\leq 2^{-(k+3)} + 2^{-(k+3+k')} + 2^{-(k+3+k'+1)} \\ &< 2^{-(k+1)}. \end{aligned}$$

Let $\alpha_w\beta_w^q$ be an extension of α_w such that, in β_w^q, q runs solo after α_w and executes to completion $k+3$ output operations. Since α' and α_w are indistinguishable to q, $\beta_w^q = \beta_v^q$ and so q's $(k+3)$'th output operation in β_w^q also returns x. Now consider the extension $\alpha_w\beta_w^q\beta_w^{p_0}$ such that, in $\beta_w^{p_0}$, p_0 runs solo until it completes its output operation. Since α_w is w-univalent, p_0's output operation returns w. Consider a linearization of $\alpha_w\beta_w^q\beta_w^{p_0}$. Using a similar reasoning as above, we can show that $|w-x| < 2^{-(k+1)}$. Therefore,

$$|w-v| \leq |w-x| + |x-v| < \frac{2}{2^{k+1}} = \frac{1}{2^k},$$

which is a contradiction.

Case 2: Some extension α' of α, ending with configuration C', has a critical q-extension. That is, there are two processes $q \neq q'$, different from p_0, and two values $v \neq w$, such that for all $\ell \geq 0$, $p_0(q^\ell(C'))$ is v-univalent and $p_0(q'(q^\ell(C')))$ is w-univalent.

The rest of the reasoning is similar to the previous case. Pick an integer k such that $\frac{1}{2^k} < |v-w|$. Let $\alpha'\beta$ be an extension of α' ending in a configuration C'', such that in β, q runs solo and executes $k+3$ output operations to completion. Let x be the value returned by q's last operation.

Let $\alpha'\beta\gamma_v$ and $\alpha'\beta\gamma_w$ be two extensions of $\alpha'\beta$ such that, in γ_v, p_0 runs solo until it completes its output operation, returning v, since $p_0(C'')$ is v-univalent; and in γ_w, q' executes a single step and then p_0 runs solo until it completes its output operation, returning w, since $p_0(q'((C'')))$ is w-univalent. Considering a linearization of $\alpha'\beta\gamma_v$ and a linearization of $\alpha'\beta\gamma_w$, it can be shown that

$$|v-w| \leq |v-x| + |w-x| < \frac{2}{2^{k+1}} = \frac{1}{2^k},$$

which is a contradiction. □

6 SUMMARY AND FUTURE WORK

This paper shows a computational separation between lock-freedom and wait-freedom, two dominant progress conditions of concurrent algorithms: while there is no wait-free implementation of the n-LLAA object from k-window registers, with $k < n$ (whose consensus number is exactly k), there is a lock-free implementation of the n-LLAA object using read/write primitives and $(n-1)$-process consensus objects. To the best of our knowledge, this is the first time such a separation is shown.

An interesting open question is whether there exists an n-LLAA implementation from x-process consensus objects for $x < n-1$, e.g., reads and writes, which would strengthen the separation. Noting that the n-LLAA object is non-deterministic, a second avenue for future research is to investigate whether or not the separation that we have shown holds also for *deterministic* long-lived objects. Finally, the n-LLAA specification assumes that the object "knows" the ID of the process invoking an operation on it. It would be interesting to see if the separation holds also for objects that do not assume this.

REFERENCES

[1] M. R. Achour Mostéfaoui, Matthieu Perrin. A simple object that spans the whole consensus hierarchy. *Parallel Processing Letters*, 2018 (in press).
[2] Y. Afek, E. Gafni, and A. Morrison. Common2 extended to stacks and unbounded concurrency. *Distributed Computing*, 20(4):239–252, 2007.
[3] Y. Afek, E. Weisberger, and H. Weisman. A completeness theorem for a class of synchronization objects. In *PODC*, pages 159–170, 1993.
[4] J. Aspnes and M. Herlihy. Wait-free data structures in the asynchronous pram model. In *SPAA*, pages 340–349, 1990.
[5] H. Attiya, A. Castañeda, and D. Hendler. Nontrivial and universal helping for wait-free queues and stacks. In *OPODIS*, 2015.
[6] K. Censor-Hillel, E. Petrank, and S. Timnat. Help! In *PODC*, pages 241–250, 2015.
[7] O. Denysyuk and P. Woelfel. Wait-freedom is harder than lock-freedom under strong linearizability. In *DISC*, pages 60–74, 2015.
[8] F. Ellen, R. Gelashvili, N. Shavit, and L. Zhu. A complexity-based hierarchy for multiprocessor synchronization. In *Proceedings of the 2016 ACM Symposium on Principles of Distributed Computing*, pages 289–298, 2016.
[9] W. Golab, L. Higham, and P. Woelfel. Linearizable implementations do not suffice for randomized distributed computation. In *STOC*, pages 373–382, 2011.
[10] M. Herlihy. Impossibility results for asynchronous pram. In *SPAA*, pages 327–336, 1991.
[11] M. Herlihy. Wait-free synchronization. *ACM Trans. Prog. Lang. Syst.*, 13(1):124–149, Jan. 1991.
[12] M. P. Herlihy and J. M. Wing. Linearizability: A correctness condition for concurrent objects. *ACM Trans. Prog. Lang. Syst.*, 12(3):463–492, July 1990.
[13] A. Kogan and E. Petrank. A methodology for creating fast wait-free data structures. In *PPoPP*, pages 141–150, 2012.
[14] M. Perrin, A. Mostefaoui, and J. Claude. Causal consistency: beyond memory. In *Proceedings of the 21st ACM SIGPLAN Symposium on Principles and Practice of Parallel Programming*, 2016.

A ADDITIONAL PROOFS FOR SECTION 3

We present additional details for the correctness analysis of Algorithm 1; some technical proofs are omitted for lack of space.

For an execution α, we use the following notation and terminology. If α is finite, v_i^α denotes the value of local variable v of a process p_i at the end of α, while M^α denotes the value of the shared array M at the end of α. I_i^α denotes the interval

$[M^\alpha[i].pos \pm 1/2^{me_i^\alpha.round+you_i^\alpha.round}]$. If α is finite and ends with a read step of p_i that makes its current operation decided, then $rad(prev_i^\alpha)$ is the radius of the interval $prev_i^\alpha$ with center $me_i^\alpha.pos$.

The following lemma can be easily proved by induction on the length of the execution α.

Lemma 12. *In every finite execution α, for $i \in \{0,1\}$, $M^\alpha[i].pos = y/2^{me_i^\alpha.round+you_i^\alpha.round}$, for some integer $y \geq 0$.*

Lemma 13. *Let $\lambda = \alpha e_1 e_2 \cdots e_\ell$ be a finite execution. Then, $I_i^\lambda \subseteq prev_i^\alpha$.*

Proof. The proof of the lemma is based on the following two claims.

Claim 14. *For every finite execution α, $I_i^\alpha \subseteq prev_i^\alpha$.*

Proof Sketch. By induction on the length of the prefixes of α, one can prove that $me_i^\alpha.pos \in prev_i^\alpha$ and the distance between $me_i^\alpha.pos$ and any extreme of $prev_i^\alpha$ is at least $1/2^{me_i^\alpha.round+you_i^\alpha.round}$. This invariant proves the lemma when $M^\alpha[i].pos = me_i^\alpha.pos$, because then $I_i^\alpha \subseteq prev_i^\alpha$ by definition. Otherwise, it must be that the last step of p_i in α is a read step in line 05 that modifies its position $me_i.pos$ after executing lines 11-15, in which case we consider the execution α' obtained from α by removing the last step of p_i and proceed as in the first case. □

Claim 15. *For every finite execution αe, $prev_i^{\alpha e} \subseteq prev_i^\alpha$.*

Proof. We prove the claim by induction on the length of the prefixes of αe. Note that the first step f in αe must be a write in line 02, which does not change the value of any local variable, and hence $prev_i^f = prev_i^\epsilon$, where ϵ is the empty execution. This is the base of the induction.

Suppose that $prev_i^{\beta f} \subseteq prev_i^\beta$, for a prefix βf of α. We show that $prev_i^{\beta f g} \subseteq prev_i^{\beta f}$, where g is the next step in αe. If g is not a step of p_i or is a write step of p_i (in line 02 or line 04), then such a step does not change the local variables of p_i, and $prev_i^{\beta f g} = prev_i^{\beta f}$.

Otherwise, g is a read step of p_i (Line 05) and the local variables of p_i might change when p_i executes lines 07–15. The claim clearly holds if p_i does not decide, since it executes line 07 and then lines 11–15; therefore, $prev_i$ is not modified, namely, $prev_i^{\beta f g} = prev_i^{\beta f}$.

If p_i decides, that is, the condition of line 08 is satisfied, then note that p_i does not modify its position after the read step, hence $me_i^{\beta f g}.pos = me_i^{\beta f}.pos = M^{\beta f}[i].pos$. By Claim 14, $I_i^{\beta f} \subseteq prev_i^{\beta f}$ holds. Also, following the execution of line 07, $range^{\beta f g} = I_i^{\beta f g} \subseteq I_i^{\beta f}$ holds (note that the containment may be proper, because $you_i^{\beta f g}.round \geq you_i^{\beta f}.round$) and $prev^{\beta f g} = range_i^{\beta f g}$ (line 09), and thus $prev^{\beta f g} \subseteq prev^{\beta f}$. □

By Claim 14, $I_i^\lambda \subseteq prev_i^\lambda$. By repeatedly applying Claim 15, $prev^{\alpha e_1 e_2 \cdots e_\ell i} \subseteq prev^{\alpha e_1 e_2 \cdots e_{\ell-1} i} \subseteq \ldots \subseteq prev^\alpha$. Therefore, $I_i^{\alpha e_1 e_2 \cdots e_\ell} \subseteq prev_i^\alpha$ and the lemma follows. □ □

Lemma 16. *Let α be a finite execution. Then, for each $i \in \{0,1\}$ and $j = 1 - i$, either $M^\alpha[i].pos \in prev_j^\alpha$ or $M^\alpha[j].pos \in prev_i^\alpha$.*

Proof Sketch. By strong induction on the length of the executions, we can show that either $me_i^\alpha.pos \in prev_j^\alpha$ or $me_j^\alpha.pos \in prev_i^\alpha$. This proves the lemma because if neither $M^\alpha[i].pos \in prev_j^\alpha$ nor $M^\alpha[j].pos \in prev_i^\alpha$, then we consider the execution α' obtained from α by removing, if necessary, the last read step of each process so that $M^{\alpha'}[i].pos = me_i^{\alpha'}.pos$ and $M^{\alpha'}[j].pos = me_j^{\alpha'}.pos$, hence reaching a contradiction. □

Proof of Lemma 1. First, we show that if $M^\alpha[i].pos \in prev_j^\alpha$, then P_j^m must decide by the closeness rule in $\alpha\beta$. Note that $me_i^\alpha.pos = M^\alpha[i].pos$. Assume otherwise towards a contradiction, then P_j^m decides by the invalid position rule, hence at some point in the execution p_j evaluates $you_j.pos \notin prev_j$ as true in line 08. Thus, there must exist a prefix λ of $\alpha\beta$ such that p_i's last read in λ (in line 05) results in it executing lines 11–15 and writing to $me_i^\lambda.pos$ a value such that $me_i^\lambda.pos \notin prev_j^\lambda$ (with α a prefix of λ and $prev_j^\alpha = prev_j^\lambda$). Observe that p_i changes $me_i^\lambda.pos$ in order to get closer to p_j's position, hence $you_i^\lambda.pos = M^\lambda[j].pos \notin prev_j^\lambda$, implying that $I_j^\lambda \not\subseteq prev_j^\lambda$, contradicting Lemma 13. Thus, P_j^m cannot decide by the invalid position rule.

We prove that $M^\alpha[i].pos \in prev_j^\alpha$, by considering two possibilities. (1) P_i^k decides by the closeness rule Note that $me_i^\alpha.pos = M^\alpha[i].pos$ and $you_i^\alpha.pos = M^\alpha[j].pos$. The fact that P_i^k decides by the closeness rule implies that at the end of α, when p_i executes line 08, it sees that $M^\alpha[j].pos = you_i^\alpha.pos \in range_i^\alpha$. Since the round counter of each process increases monotonically, we have that $rad(range_i^\alpha) \leq rad(I_j^\alpha)$, hence $M^\alpha[i].pos = me_i^\alpha.pos \in I_j^\alpha$. By Lemma 13, $I_j^\alpha \subseteq prev_j^\alpha$, from which follows that $M^\alpha[i].pos \in prev_j^\alpha$. (2) P_i^k decides by the invalid position rule. Hence, at the end of α, when p_i executes Line 08, it sees that $you_i^\alpha.pos = M^\alpha[j].pos \notin prev_i^\alpha$. Lemma 16 directly implies that $M^\alpha[i].pos \in prev_j^\alpha$. In both cases, $M^\alpha[i].pos \in prev_j^\alpha$ and hence P_j^m decides by the closeness rule.

Now, since the last step in α is a read by p_i in line 05 that makes P_i^k decided, p_i executes lines 07–10 at the end of α, and so we have that $me_i^\alpha.pos$ is the center of $prev_i^\alpha$, $rad(prev_i^\alpha) = 1/2^{m+k}$, $me_i^k.pos = me_i^\alpha.pos$ and $prev_i^k = prev_i^\alpha$. We prove that $me_j^m.pos \in prev_i^\alpha$, which implies that $dist(me_i^k.pos, me_j^m.pos) \leq 1/2^{m+k}$.

Let λ be the shortest prefix of $\alpha\beta$ in which P_j^m is decided (hence α is a prefix of λ). The last step of λ is a read step by p_j in line 05 that makes P_j^m decided. Let $x = you_j^\lambda.round$. Thus, P_j^m decides (by the closeness rule) on the operation P_i^x, for $x \geq k$. At the end of λ, after p_j executes lines 07–10, we have that $me_j^m.pos = me_j^\lambda.pos$.

By Lemma 13, $I_i^\lambda \subseteq prev_i^\alpha$. Since P_j^m decides by the closeness rule, at the end of λ the condition of line 08 is satisfied when p_j checks it, and thus $dist(me_j^\lambda.pos, you_j^\lambda.pos) \leq 1/2^{m+x}$. Notice that $you_j^\lambda.pos = M^\lambda[i].pos$, and hence $me_j^m.pos \in I_i^\lambda \subseteq prev_i^\alpha$, which concludes the proof. □

Passing Messages while Sharing Memory

Marcos K. Aguilera
VMware Research

Naama Ben-David*
CMU

Irina Calciu
VMware Research

Rachid Guerraoui
EPFL

Erez Petrank
Technion

Sam Toueg
University of Toronto

ABSTRACT

We introduce a new distributed computing model called m&m that allows processes to both pass messages and share memory. Motivated by recent hardware trends, we find that this model improves the power of the pure message-passing and shared-memory models. As we demonstrate by example with two fundamental problems—consensus and eventual leader election—the added power leads to new algorithms that are more robust against failures and asynchrony. Our consensus algorithm combines the superior scalability of message passing with the higher fault tolerance of shared memory, while our leader election algorithms reduce the system synchrony needed for correctness. These results point to a wide new space for future exploration of other problems, techniques, and benefits.

ACM Reference Format:
Marcos K. Aguilera, Naama Ben-David, Irina Calciu, Rachid Guerraoui, Erez Petrank, and Sam Toueg. 2018. Passing Messages while Sharing Memory. In *PODC '18: ACM Symposium on Principles of Distributed Computing, July 23–27, 2018, Egham, United Kingdom.* ACM, New York, NY, USA, 10 pages. https://doi.org/10.1145/3212734.3212741

1 INTRODUCTION

The distributed computing community has a dichotomy between shared-memory and message-passing models. Books, courses, and papers explicitly separate these models to present results and algorithms. These models differ based on how processes communicate. In the shared-memory model, processes can write and read data in a common area of memory. In the message-passing model, processes can send and receive messages to and from each other.

In this paper, we investigate the benefits of a hybrid model, called *message-and-memory model* or simply *m&m model*, where processes can both pass messages and share memory. We are motivated by recent technologies that permit exactly that, such as Remote Direct Memory Access (RDMA) [39, 41, 65], disaggregated memory [55], and Gen-Z [33]. By using both methods of communication, one can devise a new genre of algorithms that could potentially combine the advantages of shared-memory and message-passing algorithms.

*Work done in part while the author was at VMware Research.

PODC '18, July 23–27, 2018, Egham, United Kingdom

ACM ISBN 978-1-4503-5795-1/18/07...$15.00
https://doi.org/10.1145/3212734.3212741

It has been proven that the message-passing and shared-memory models are equivalent [11], by demonstrating that one model can simulate the other. If that is so, what could be the benefit of combining two models that are equivalent? Closer inspection of the equivalence result reveals that it holds only in a certain sense and under some assumptions. In particular, the equivalence is computational: it shows how algorithms for a problem in one model can be translated to the other using an emulation. However, the emulation does not preserve efficiency or synchrony (e.g., a timely process in one model can become untimely as it waits for other processes). Moreover, the emulation requires the assumption that the message-passing model has a majority of correct processes, and that processes know each other's identities as well as the number of processes in the system. In many cases these assumptions do not hold.

In fact, we find that each model has its own advantages and they benefit algorithms in different ways. Our contribution is to propose the new m&m model that merges the capabilities of the pure models, to identify some of the advantages of each pure model, and to show that they can be combined in the m&m model.

To illustrate the advantages of combining the models, consider the fundamental problem of mutual exclusion [26]. In this problem, there is a doorway and a critical section. The goal is to ensure that at most one process in the doorway enters the critical section at a time. The traditional algorithms for this problem, such as the bakery algorithm or Dijkstra's algorithm, have been designed in the shared-memory read-write model [51]. In that abstract model, these algorithms have a common drawback: while some process is in the critical section, other processes in the doorway must spin on one or more shared-memory locations to know when the critical section becomes empty again. Much work was devoted to mitigate this problem, by making the spin local to each process (e.g., [23, 46–48]).

By allowing an algorithm to share memory and pass messages in the m&m model, one finds very simple solutions that do not have to spin: upon leaving the critical section, a process could send a message to the processes in the doorway; those processes, rather than spinning, go to sleep and resume execution when a message arrives. This ability to react to data without spinning is a characteristic of message passing. In practice, by avoiding the spin, the CPU can be better utilized to run other processes. Such benefits escape the abstract equivalence of the message-passing and shared-memory models in [11].

Besides benefits, each model has limitations that the m&m model can overcome. Shared-memory systems have worse scalability than message-passing systems due to hardware limitations. For example, a typical shared-memory system today has tens to thousands of processes, while message-passing systems can be much larger (e.g., map-reduce systems with tens of thousands of hosts [25], peer-to-peer systems with hundreds of thousands of hosts, the SMTP email system and DNS with hundreds of millions of hosts, etc).

On the other hand, message-passing systems have limitations on fault tolerance and synchrony. On fault tolerance, some fundamental problems in distributed computing—such as consensus and atomic storage—require a majority of correct processes to be solvable in the message-passing model, even under strong partial synchrony assumptions, whereas the same problems can be solved in shared memory with an arbitrary number of correct processes using wait-free algorithms under partial synchrony, randomization, or stronger hardware primitives. With respect to synchrony, due to engineering reasons, message-passing systems have larger variances in their timing than shared memory: the slowest and fastest message delays can be eight orders of magnitude apart (microseconds to tens of seconds), while the variance in the execution speeds of processes in shared memory is much smaller. As a result, partial synchrony bounds tend to be much worse in message-passing systems.

In this paper, we make these advantages and drawbacks more precise. We show that the m&m model can enhance the *robustness* of algorithms. We consider two aspects of robustness: the number of process crashes that algorithms can tolerate and the synchrony assumptions required by them. We illustrate how we improve the first aspect through the consensus problem and the second through the eventual leader election problem. In short, we show that message passing and shared memory complement each other when combined, allowing algorithms that have inherent advantages over the pure message-passing and shared-memory models.

For consensus, we give an algorithm called Hybrid Ben-Or or simply HBO that tolerates more than a majority of failures (like shared-memory algorithms can), while scaling to a large system size (like message-passing systems can). To scale to a large system, the algorithm limits the number of processes that share a given shared-memory location to a small constant number. We define an undirected *shared-memory graph*, whose nodes are processes and there is an edge between processes p and q if they share a memory location. Due to hardware limitations, to scale the system we must limit the maximum degree d of this graph [28, 43]. Our algorithm employs expander graphs to tolerate a majority of crash failures—up to $f < (1-\frac{1}{2(1+h)})n$ of them—in a system with n processes, where h is the expansion of the graph as measured by the *vertex expansion ratio*. Roughly, this ratio indicates by how much a set of vertices expands each time we add their neighbors to the set. The higher the expansion, the more failures the algorithm can tolerate. Our algorithm is a simulation of a pure message-passing consensus algorithm that requires a majority of correct processes, without having that majority in reality. To do that, we use a wait-free shared-memory consensus algorithm among each local neighborhood in the shared-memory graph to emulate a virtual process in the larger message-passing algorithm. This virtual process fails only if all processes in its neighborhood fail. By taking a shared-memory graph with high expansion, we ensure that even with a small d, many processes can fail without affecting a majority of virtual processes. Here, the topology of the shared-memory graph determines the fault tolerance of consensus: graphs with higher expansion allow for higher fault tolerance, because correct processes are adjacent to (and thus can simulate) more processes. We show that this relation is inherent by giving an impossibility result relating graph expansion and fault tolerance.

We next turn our attention to the (eventual) leader election problem. This problem is traditionally considered in message-passing systems, and much effort has been devoted to find the weakest synchrony needed to solve it [5, 6, 38]. Prior algorithms required some timeliness on processes *and* communication links. We show that in the m&m model, we can do better by using both shared memory and message passing to obtain different benefits. We use shared memory to reduce the timeliness requirement to processes only: our leader election algorithms require only that a *single* process, the leader, increments its local heartbeat in a timely fashion; other processes can be asynchronous—in particular, they can be arbitrarily slow to read the heartbeat. We use message passing to provide a trade-off between message reliability and amount of work in steady state: we give two algorithms for different types of links. (1) With *reliable* links[1], the only steady-state work is that the leader periodically increments a local heartbeat counter in shared memory, while other processes read the counter; (2) With *fair lossy* links[2], in addition to the above, the leader also periodically *reads* a shared register. In either algorithm, no messages are exchanged in the steady state, and all the communication links can be *asynchronous*. We further prove that the two leader election algorithms are optimal in the following sense. For systems with a timely process and asynchronous links, any algorithm requires the leader to write a shared register periodically (as in both our algorithms). This result holds whether links are reliable or fair lossy. Moreover, with fair lossy links, there are more requirements: either the leader writes and reads shared registers periodically (as our second algorithm), or some process keeps sending messages forever.

To summarize, the contributions of this paper are the following:

- We motivate and introduce the m&m model of distributed computing, which allows processes to both share memory and pass messages.
- We study the consensus problem under the m&m model. We give a new algorithm that improves on the fault tolerance of message-passing algorithms, while limiting memory sharing to allow for scalability. We show that the algorithm's fault tolerance is improved by a shared-memory graph with high expansion, and prove an impossibility result showing that this relationship to expansion is inherent.
- The new consensus algorithm introduces a simulation technique that combines shared memory and message passing. We believe this technique is interesting in its own right, as it could be used to improve other algorithms, to show impossibility results, etc.
- We study the leader election problem under the m&m model and give algorithms that reduce the synchrony required, while maintaining a low communication complexity. We show that these algorithms are tight in their communication.

[1] I.e., links that do not drop messages.

[2] I.e., links that can drop messages, but if a message is repeatedly sent then it is eventually received.

While we focus on two problems and some benefits of the m&m model, we believe the paper opens a large space for future research on other problems and benefits.

Due to space limitations, we omit proofs and some details. They will be included in the full version of this paper.

2 RELATED WORK

The m&m model is motivated by emerging technologies, such as Remote Direct Memory Access (RDMA) [39, 41, 65], disaggregated memory [31, 55], Gen-Z [33], and OmniPath [40]. These technologies provide remote memory [4] and can be unified under higher-level abstractions [3]. RDMA permits a process to access the memory of a remote host without interrupting the remote processor. It has been widely used in high-performance computing [72] and is now being adopted in modern data centers [34]. Work on RDMA shows how it can improve the performance of important applications, such as key-value storage systems [28, 43, 60], database systems [13, 73], distributed file systems [58], and more [29, 36, 67, 68]. Recent work uses RDMA to improve performance of consensus [64, 70] assuming a majority of processes are correct. Disaggregated memory separates compute and memory, and connects them using a fast network; prior work proposes new architectures for disaggregated memory [9, 22, 62] and studies the network [35] and system [4, 56] requirements for a practical implementation. Gen-Z and OmniPath are commercial technologies under development that offer memory semantics and low-latency access to remote data.

The shared-memory and the message-passing models are well studied in academic research, and have been compared under both theoretical and practical considerations [17, 18, 49, 54]. The two models have been shown to be computationally equivalent [11], though for efficiency, simplicity, or hardware availability, one might prefer one model over the other. For instance, Barrelfish [14] uses message passing to improve performance on a shared-memory multicore machine [24]. Conversely, distributed shared-memory systems [8, 16, 66] offer the abstraction of shared memory on top of a message-passing system. Recent work improves the performance of such systems using RDMA [45, 61]. Integrating message passing and shared memory in hardware has been explored in the MIT Alewife machine [50]. Our work differs in that (1) we propose a new abstract distributed computing model, which encapsulates low-latency remote access technologies, such as RDMA and disaggregated memory, and (2) we show that this model can improve the robustness of algorithms, rather than the performance or simplicity of applications.

Consensus is a fundamental problem in distributed computing. Following the well-known FLP result [32] showing that it cannot be solved in an asynchronous crash-prone message-passing system, much work has focused on getting around the impossibility by using randomization [10, 12, 15], partial synchrony [27, 30], or unreliable failure detectors [19, 20]. In fact, the eventual leader election problem, Ω, is the weakest failure detector that can solve consensus, and is used in several algorithms [53, 63]. This is the problem that we study in the second part of the paper. The eventual leader election problem is known to require some synchrony to implement. We show that the m&m model permits solutions with less synchrony than before, while minimizing the work done.

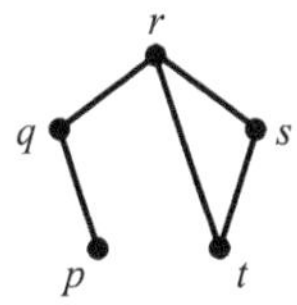

$S_p = \{p, q\}$ $\quad S_s = \{r, s, t\}$
$S_q = \{p, q, r\}$ $\quad S_t = \{r, s, t\}$
$S_r = \{q, r, s, t\}$

$$\mathcal{S} = \{S_p, S_q, S_r, S_s, S_t\} = \{\{p, q\}, \{p, q, r\}, \{q, r, s, t\}, \{r, s, t\}\}$$

Figure 1: Example of a shared-memory graph G_{SM} and the resulting shared-memory domain $\mathcal{S}$, where p, q, r, s, t are processes. This shared-memory graph permits registers that can be shared among any of the S_x sets in $\mathcal{S}$. The graph is intended to model the underlying physical connections that implement the shared memory. For example, a register shared among S_r is physically kept in the host containing process r, and processes q, s, t access this register over the connections to r in the graph, while process p cannot access this register.

Expander graphs are graphs that are sparse, yet well-connected. They are well-studied and have applications in many areas of computer science, including distributed computing [21, 71]. In this paper, we show that the fault tolerance of the m&m model is tightly coupled with the expansion of its shared-memory connections, highlighting another problem in which expander graphs apply.

3 MODEL

We consider a distributed system with n processes $\Pi = \{0, \ldots, n-1\}$ that can communicate with each other using message passing and shared memory. Processes may fail by crashing, in which case they stop taking steps. If a process does not fail, it is said to be *correct* and it keeps taking steps forever. Some algorithms require a bound on the maximum number of processes that can crash; we denote this bound by f. A process has a local state that is private to itself, and it may communicate with others through message passing and shared memory.

Message passing. Processes can send messages over directed links. The link from p to q, denoted $p \longrightarrow q$, is an *output link* of p and an *input link* of q. Each link $p \longrightarrow q$ satisfies the following property in every run:

- *[Integrity]:* If q receives m from p k times then p previously sent m to q at least k times.

Some links may satisfy additional properties which are described next. We consider two types of links: reliable and fair lossy. Roughly, a reliable link does not drop messages, while a fair lossy link may drop messages but ensures that if a process sends a message repeatedly then it is eventually received.

More precisely, we say that a link $p \longrightarrow q$ is *reliable* if it satisfies Integrity and the following property:

- *[No loss]:* If p sends a message m to q and q is correct then eventually q receives m from p.

We say that a link $p \longrightarrow q$ is *fair lossy* if it satisfies Integrity and the following property:

- *[Fair loss]:* If p sends a message m infinitely often to q and q is correct, then q receives m infinitely often from p.

In this paper, we consider a fully connected network, that is, for any two processes $p \neq q$, there is a link from p to q.

Shared memory. Processes can also communicate via a set of *shared registers*. Here, we consider only atomic read-write registers.

In practice, a shared register is provided by the hardware, but not all processes may be able to access all registers, as there may be limits on the number of processes that can share the same memory [28, 43, 44, 69]. We define the *shared-memory domain* $\mathcal{S}$ as a set of process subsets; intuitively, $\mathcal{S}$ determines what subsets of processes can share memory. More precisely, for each set $S \in \mathcal{S}$, the model permits having any number of registers shared among processes in S. In general, $\mathcal{S}$ can be arbitrary. However, in practice memory sharing is simpler, as the hardware technology naturally imposes a structure on $\mathcal{S}$: for example, a process might be able to share memory only with processes that connect to it over the underlying hardware. We say that $\mathcal{S}$ is *uniform* if it can be represented by an undirected graph G_{SM} of processes, such that registers can be shared by a process and its neighbors in G_{SM}; intuitively, G_{SM} is the graph of connections of the underlying hardware that implements the shared memory. Formally, G_{SM} is a graph $G_{SM} = (\Pi, E_{SM})$ and the sets in $\mathcal{S}$ are exactly the sets consisting of a process p and its neighbors in G_{SM}. That is, if we let $S_p = \{p\} \cup \{q : (p, q) \in E_{SM}\}$ then $\mathcal{S} = \{S_p : p \in \Pi\}$. For a uniform $\mathcal{S}$, we say that G_{SM} is its *shared-memory graph*. Figure 1 gives an example. In this paper, we are interested in the uniform model, and all our results work with the graph G_{SM}. The broader model based on $\mathcal{S}$ is provided to allow for future theoretical work and potential new hardware platforms. Note that, while the model does not constrain the number or size of registers that can be shared, algorithms may choose to reduce their shared-memory usage for efficiency.

In systems with few processes (e.g., in the tens), G_{SM} could be a fully connected graph, but systems with lots of processes may have to limit the maximum degree of G_{SM} (e.g., limit the connections over the hardware).

We assume that the shared memory does not fail, as in the pure shared-memory model. This assumption can be supported by the hardware: with RDMA, the shared memory can be registered with the kernel so that it remains accessible after processes crash; disaggregated memory can similarly preserve memory accesses after process crashes.

Synchrony. For some results, we make some partial synchrony assumptions about the relative execution speed of processes. We first define what it means for a process p to be timely with respect to another process q:

- *[Pairwise timeliness]:* We say that p is q-*timely* (in a run) if p is correct and there is an integer $i \geq 1$ such that every time interval containing i steps of q has at least one step of p.

The timeliness bound i above is not known to processes: it may depend on each run and each pair of processes p and q. We now define what it means for a process p to be timely:

- *[Timeliness]:* We say that p is *timely* (in a run) if p is q-timely for every process $q \in \Pi$ (in this run).

Intuitively, timeliness means that eventually the process executes within a bounded rate relative to other processes. This is a weak requirement in many ways. First, it is relative to the speed of other processes, so a process can be timely even if it slows down arbitrarily in real time. Second, the bound on execution rate need not be known. Third, the bound is arbitrary and not fixed a priori, so timeliness can be satisfied even if a process is initially arbitrarily slow relative to others.

We consider two types of systems: (1) asynchronous systems, which might not have any timely processes, and (2) systems with little synchrony, that is, systems where at least one process is timely; this process can vary from run to run and is not known to the processes. We make no assumptions about the timeliness of messages.

Consensus problem. In the consensus problem, each process begins with an input value $v \in \{0, 1\}$ which it *proposes*, and it *decides* on an output value in the end. The output values must satisfy three properties:

- *[Uniform Agreement]:* No two processes decide on a different value.
- *[Validity]:* If a process decides on a value v then v was proposed by some process.
- *[Termination]:* Every correct process eventually decides.

We allow randomized solutions, where the above Termination property must hold with probability 1 under a *strong adversary*—one that can schedule processes based on their current state and past history.

A *consensus object* is a shared-memory object with one operation, *propose*(v), which takes a value v and returns the first value that was proposed to the object.

The eventual leader election problem. This problem is formally defined in [20] as the Ω failure detector. Informally, each process p outputs a single process denoted $leader_p$, such that the following property holds:[3]

- There is a correct process ℓ and a time after which, for every correct process p, $leader_p = \ell$.

Note that, at any given time, processes do not know if there is a commonly agreed leader; they only know that eventually there will be a common leader.

4 CONSENSUS

We show that the m&m model can be used improve the fault tolerance of algorithms compared to a pure message-passing system. It is known that consensus cannot be solved deterministically in an asynchronous system subject to failures, even if processes can only fail by crashing and at most one process may fail; this is true in both message-passing and shared-memory models [32, 57]. We thus consider asynchronous systems where processes can toss coins. Then, in a shared-memory system, consensus can be solved (with probability 1) with up to $n-1$ crash failures [1] (n is the number of processes in the system), whereas in a message-passing system, a consensus algorithm can tolerate at most $\lfloor (n-1)/2 \rfloor$ crash failures [15]. We show that the m&m model can strike a balance between shared memory and message passing.

First note that if the shared-memory graph G_{SM} is fully connected then any fault-tolerant shared-memory algorithm also works in the m&m model—the algorithm simply never sends messages. Thus, there are algorithms in the m&m model that can tolerate up to $n-1$ crash failures. However, in a large system, it is impractical to connect all processes over shared memory (§3). When fewer

[3]Henceforth, when we say that there is a time after which some property C holds, we mean that there is a time t such that, for every time $t' \geq t$, property C holds at time t'.

processes can share memory, we show that the m&m model provides a range of choices, where the fault tolerance increases as we improve the shared-memory graph. Specifically, we present an algorithm for the m&m model that tolerates anywhere between $\lfloor (n-1)/2 \rfloor$ and $n-1$ crash failures, depending on the topology of the shared-memory graph (§4.1). We discuss how to best choose this topology (§4.2), building on expander graphs [37]. We then give an impossibility result about the fault tolerance of consensus in the m&m model (§4.3).

4.1 Algorithm

The algorithm for the m&m model is based on Ben-Or's randomized algorithm [15], which can tolerate up to $f < n/2$ process crashes in the message-passing model. This is one of the simplest consensus algorithms, but not the most efficient one. Our goal here is to show feasibility; designing more efficient algorithms for the m&m model is future work.

Ben-Or's algorithm. In Ben-Or's algorithm, each process has an estimate of the decision value, which starts with the process's initial value. The algorithm proceeds in rounds, each with two phases. In the first phase (phase R), each process p sends its current estimate to all processes, waits to receive at least $n-f$ messages, and checks if more than $n/2$ messages have the same value v. If so, p sends this value to all processes in the second phase (phase P). Otherwise, p sends a special value '?' to all processes in the second phase. Process p then waits to receive at least $n-f$ messages. If at least $f+1$ of them have the same non-'?' value, p decides on this value. If at least one of them is a non-'?' value, p changes its estimate to that value. Otherwise, p changes its estimate to a random bit.

Ben-Or's algorithm satisfies the validity and uniform agreement properties of consensus (§3), and it satisfies the termination property with probability 1 if a majority of the processes are correct [7].

Simulating Ben-Or's algorithm in the m&m model. We modify Ben-Or's algorithm, so that correct processes simulate the actions of their neighbors in the shared-memory graph G_{SM}. The idea of the simulation is simple: when sending a message in any phase, process p sends not only its own value, but also the value that its neighbors are supposed to send. That is, p ensures that its neighbors progress at least as much as it does. To do so, for each neighbor q, p reaches agreement with q and q's neighbors on what q's message should be. Then, p sends a message of the form (*phase*, *round*, $[\langle q, val\rangle : q \in neighbors(p)]$), where *phase* is a phase (either R or P), *round* is a round number, and the last entry is an array with a tuple for each neighbor q indicating the agreed value of q's message. We say that the message *represents* each of the processes whose ids appear in the tuple. For a set of such messages, we say that the messages represent the union of the processes that are represented by each message separately.

To reach agreement on the message of a neighbor q, there are two arrays of consensus objects, one array for each phase, indexed by q and the round. All of q's neighbors use the same consensus object to determine what q's message might be for a given phase and round. Process q and its neighbors propose their own value to that consensus object. The consensus objects themselves are implemented using known wait-free randomized shared-memory

---

SHARED OBJECTS:

RVals$[p, i]$: consensus object accessible by $\{p\} \cup neighbors(p)$,
  $\forall p \in \Pi, \forall i \in \{1, 2, \ldots\}$
PVals$[p, i]$: consensus object accessible by $\{p\} \cup neighbors(p)$,
  $\forall p \in \Pi, \forall i \in \{1, 2, \ldots\}$

CODE FOR PROCESS p:

```
procedure Consensus(v_p)
  message ← []
  k ← 1
  for q ∈ {p} ∪ neighbors(p) do
    message[q] ← ⟨q, RVals[q, k].propose(v_p)⟩
  while true
    send (R, k, message) to all
    wait for messages of the form (R, k, *) representing more than
        n/2 processes
    if received more than n/2 tuples with different ids and
        and the same value v
    then for q ∈ {p} ∪ neighbors(p) do
        message[q] ← ⟨q, PVals[q, k].propose(v)⟩
    else for q ∈ {p} ∪ neighbors(p) do
        message[q] ← ⟨q, PVals[q, k].propose(?)⟩

    send (P, k, message) to all
    wait for messages of the form (P, k, *) representing more than
        n/2 processes
    if received more than n/2 tuples with different ids and
        the same value v ≠ ?
    then decide(v)
    k ← k + 1
    if at least one tuple has value v ≠ ?
    then for q ∈ {p} ∪ neighbors(p) do
        message[q] ← ⟨q, RVals[q, k].propose(v)⟩
    else for q ∈ {p} ∪ neighbors(p) do
        v ← 0 or 1 randomly
        message[q] ← ⟨q, RVals[q, k].propose(v)⟩
```

Figure 2: Hybrid Ben-Or (HBO) consensus algorithm.

algorithms [10, 12], which work in the m&m model because neighbors in G_{SM} share memory.

We call this algorithm the *Hybrid Ben-Or* or *HBO* algorithm. Figure 2 shows the pseudocode. There, processes do not terminate after deciding, but it is easy to modify the algorithm so that they do. This algorithm always satisfies the safety properties of consensus, irrespective of the number of crash failures:

THEOREM 4.1. *The HBO algorithm in Figure 2 satisfies the Validity and Uniform Agreement properties of consensus in the m&m model with reliable links.*

The proof of this theorem is given in the full paper. There, we also show that the HBO algorithm terminates as long as a majority of the processes are *represented.*

THEOREM 4.2. *The HBO algorithm in Figure 2 satisfies the Termination property of consensus with probability 1 in the m&m model with reliable links where a majority of the processes are represented.*

In the next section, we consider how many failures may occur while still ensuring that a majority of processes are represented.

4.2 Shared-memory expanders

In this section, we consider the fault tolerance of the HBO algorithm: how many crash failures can it tolerate while ensuring that processes decide. In the algorithm, correct processes represent their neighbors in G_{SM}, so the fault tolerance depends on G_{SM} and how many neighbors correct processes have. We show that, by choosing G_{SM} to be a graph with *high expansion*, we obtain the best trade-off between maintaining low degree and achieving high fault tolerance. Having a low degree is important because the degree indicates the number of connections that a process must have to establish a shared memory, and that number is limited by the hardware (§3).

Roughly, expander graphs are graphs with the property that every sufficiently small set of vertices has many neighbors. To define these graphs more precisely, we follow the survey by Hoory, Linial and Wigderson [37]; we refer the reader to this survey for a detailed treatment.

Definition 1. *Let $G = (V, E)$ be an undirected graph.*

1. *The* vertex boundary *of a set $S \subseteq V$ is*
$$\delta S = \{ u \in V : \{u, v\} \in E, v \in S \} \setminus S.$$
2. *The* vertex expansion ratio *of G, denoted $h(G)$, is defined as*
$$h(G) = \min_{S \subseteq V : |S| \leq |V|/2} \frac{|\delta S|}{|S|}$$

Intuitively, the higher the vertex expansion ratio, the larger the vertex boundary and the better connected the graph.

To apply this definition to the fault tolerance of HBO, consider a system with shared-memory graph G_{SM} and vertex expansion ratio $h(G_{SM})$, where up to f processes may crash. The set of vertices of interest to us is the set C of correct processes. If C has many neighbors, then it can simulate many extra processes in HBO. The adversary may pick *any* set of at least $n - f$ processes to be correct; regardless of the set it picks, that set has a vertex boundary of at least $(n-f) \cdot h(G_{SM})$.

The fault tolerance of HBO improves with the vertex expansion ratio of the graph. This is made precise by the following:

Theorem 4.3. *Consider the m&m model with shared-memory graph G_{SM} where links are reliable and f processes may crash. The HBO algorithm in Figure 2 satisfies the Termination property of consensus with probability 1 if $f < (1 - \frac{1}{2(1+h(G_{SM}))}) \cdot n$.*

Proof. Recall that Ben-Or's algorithm requires that $f < n/2$ for termination. The HBO algorithm simulates the correct processes and the processes in their vertex boundary. Given G_{SM} has vertex expansion ratio $h(G_{SM})$, the number of processes simulated by the algorithm is at least $(n-f) \cdot (1+h(G_{SM}))$. Rearranging the terms leads to the theorem. □

In the full paper, we give an example of graphs we can use, by discussing a construction of a family of expander graphs and showing their expansion ratio $h(G)$.

4.3 Impossibility result

We now show an impossibility result about the fault tolerance of consensus in the m&m model. The impossibility depends on the topology of the shared-memory graph G_{SM}. Intuitively, the impossibility indicates that the expander construction is the correct approach: we show that the fault tolerance of the system is related to the minimum cut that separates a large subgraph from the rest of the G_{SM} graph. In graphs with high expansion, the size of such a cut it guaranteed to be large, and thus many failures can be tolerated.

To establish the impossibility, we extend the well-known *partitioning argument* [59] to the m&m model. Basically, if two processes cannot communicate during the execution of an algorithm, then they cannot decide the same value. Thus, if the adversary can partition the system into two disjoint subgraphs A and B, each of size $\geq n - f$, where processes in A do not communicate with processes in B, then agreement cannot hold. This argument works in message-passing models, where the adversary can arbitrarily delay messages on the network, but it breaks in a shared-memory model, in which communication between processes cannot be delayed without blocking the processes themselves. Thus, in the m&m model, to create such a partition the adversary must get rid of all shared-memory edges of G_{SM} on the cut between A and B.

We now formalize the intuition to arrive at the impossibility. Given a graph $G = (V, E)$, we say that $C = (B, S, T)$ is an *SM-cut* in G if B, S, and T are disjoint subsets of V such that $B \cup S \cup T = V$, and there is a way to partition B into two disjoint subsets B_1 and B_2 such that $(B_1 \cup S, B_2 \cup T)$ is a cut of the graph G, and for every $b_1 \in B_1$, $b_2 \in B_2$, $s \in S$ and $t \in T$, $\{s, t\} \notin E$, $\{b_1, t\} \notin E$, and $\{b_2, s\} \notin E$. Intuitively, B is the set of vertices on the boundary of the cut, and S and T are the remaining vertices on each side.

Theorem 4.4. *Consider the m&m model with shared-memory graph G_{SM}, where links are reliable and f processes may crash. Consensus cannot be solved if G_{SM} has an SM-cut (B, S, T) with $|S| \geq n-f$ and $|T| \geq n-f$.*

We prove this theorem in the full paper. Note that, in a graph with high expansion, there are no *SM-cuts* (B, S, T) with $|S| \geq n-f$ and $|T| \geq n-f$. Intuitively, this is because if we want to build an *SM-cut* and we start with some set S with $|S| \geq n - f$, we must include δS in B_1, and then include $\delta(S \cup B_1)$ in B_2. As these sets expand quickly, we are then left with fewer than $n - f$ vertices to put in T. In the full paper, we formalize the above intuition to relate the impossibility to the expansion properties of G_{SM}.

5 LEADER ELECTION

We now show that the m&m model allows us to not only improve the fault tolerance of message-passing systems, but also to reduce the synchrony needed to solve certain problems. To demonstrate that, we turn our attention to the (eventual) leader election problem. In this problem, each process has a leader, and the goal is for all correct processes to eventually have the *same* correct leader (this is also known as the Ω failure detector [19]). Leader election is used in several well-known consensus algorithms, such as Paxos [52], Raft [63], and CT [20]. To be solvable, leader election requires the system to have some partial synchrony (because it can be used to solve consensus, and consensus is impossible in asynchronous systems [32]). Finding the weakest models of synchrony for solving this problem was the goal of several papers, but all known leader election algorithms for message-passing systems require some synchrony on at least some of the network communication links. In practice, it can be hard to guarantee small bounds on network delays, thus leading to high recovery time when a leader crashes.

We show that the m&m model permits solutions with almost no synchrony: the only requirement is that some process be timely. We give two algorithms: one assumes reliable links (§5.1), and the other relaxes that requirement and assumes only fair lossy links (§5.2). In both algorithms, the leader regularly increments a heartbeat counter in shared memory, and other processes verify that the leader is alive by monitoring and timing out on this counter. With fair lossy links, the leader in addition periodically reads a register. We can make it easier for the leader to be timely, by placing the shared registers so that eventually the leader accesses only local registers (§5.3). We show that our algorithms are tight in efficiency (§5.4). In this section, we assume that G_{SM} is the complete graph.

5.1 Algorithm for reliable links

The basic idea of the first algorithm is that each process p has a "badness" counter that it shares with other processes. Intuitively, this badness counter represents the number of times that other processes suspected p of having crashed. To pick its leader, p keeps a set of processes, called *contenders*, that are contending for leadership; this set always includes p and initially contains no other processes. If there are no other contenders, p picks itself as the leader; otherwise, it picks the process with the smallest badness counter. Note that at this point, different processes could pick different leaders. We show that our algorithm always eventually realizes and corrects such situations.

When p becomes its own leader, it announces its leadership to other processes using a notification mechanism; here, this mechanism simply sends a message to the other processes (in our next algorithm, the mechanism is more complex because messages can be lost). If p thinks it is the leader, it sets an *active* bit in shared memory to indicate that it believes itself to be the leader. Then, it periodically increments a heartbeat counter in shared memory to tell others that it is alive. Process p also periodically checks whether it got any notifications from another process q; if it did, this means that q also wants to be the leader. So, p adds q to the contenders set, and p starts a timer on q; in effect, p now monitors q to see if it remains timely. Lastly, upon adding q to its contenders set, p also notifies q that p is also a contender, in case q does not know.

Whether p is a leader or not, p monitors the processes in its contender set other than itself. Intuitively, p expects each contender $q \neq p$ to periodically increment q's heartbeat counters in shared memory. If q fails to do so within a timeout,[4] p removes q from its contenders set; p then checks whether q has the active bit set in shared memory; if it does, that means q thinks it is the leader, so p sends an accusation to q and increments the timeout value. While p is its own leader, it also checks whether it received any accusation messages. If p receives an accusation, it increments its badness counter. If p stops thinking it is the leader, it clears the active bit in shared memory. The active bit is critical for correctness; it prevents processes from sending an accusation to p after it relinquishes leadership and stops incrementing its heartbeat.

Processes who believe themselves to be the leader fight among themselves for leadership: as described above, they notify each other about their desire to be the leader, adding each other to their contender set, and they pick the contending process with the smallest badness counter as the winning leader. We now explain how all correct processes eventually choose the same leader forever.

First note that every timely process eventually stops being accused (because it increases its heartbeat in a timely fashion when it thinks it is the leader, and it clears its active bit when it thinks it is not the leader). By assumption, the system has at least one timely process, thus there is at least one correct process that stops receiving accusations, and so its badness counter stops growing. Let ℓ be such a correct process whose badness counter is smallest. Therefore, for every process $q \neq \ell$: either q has a badness counter that eventually grows larger than ℓ's badness counter, or q crashes (and so every correct process eventually times out on q and removes q from its contender set). Since the contender set of ℓ contains ℓ forever, it is clear that ℓ eventually selects itself as the leader forever. When ℓ becomes leader, it notifies all the correct processes. Eventually other processes stop thinking they are leader: if a process $q \neq \ell$ thought it were leader infinitely often, it would check notifications infinitely often and eventually get a notification from ℓ, add ℓ to its contender set, see that ℓ has a smaller badness counter, and then pick ℓ rather than itself as its leader. This implies that every correct process eventually selects ℓ as a leader forever.

This algorithm performs little work in steady state, as eventually the following happens: (1) processes stop sending notifications because they do so only when they become a leader or when they are leader and receive a notification; (2) processes stop sending accusations, because eventually ℓ is their only contender (other than themselves), and no process times out on ℓ; (3) ℓ is the only process who writes to a shared register, because only a process who thinks it is the leader does so; (4) ℓ does not read any shared register, because processes stop sending notifications; (5) processes $p \neq \ell$ read only the shared register written by ℓ, because ℓ is their only contender. Also note that each shared register in this algorithm is written only by a single process (single-writer multi-reader shared register).

Figures 3 and 4 show the detailed algorithm. In the text below, when necessary for clarity, we use subscripts on a local variable to denote its process, and possibly superscripts to denote a time (e.g., $state_p$ is *state* variable of p, while $state_p^t$ is the value of this variable at time t).

Figure 4 shows the notification mechanism, which is very simple in this case (where links are reliable): the NOTIFY(q) procedure just sends a notification message to q, while the GET_NOTIFICATIONS() procedure returns the processes from which p got a notification message since the last invocation. Figure 3 has the main pseudocode. Each process p has a $STATE[p]$ shared register, which is a triple with p's heartbeat counter, badness counter, and active bit. Process p has a local variable $state_p[q]$ containing p's local view of $STATE[q]$. Process p executes forever in a loop. In this loop, p first picks its leader (line 9). Then p checks if it has just become the leader and, if so, notifies others (lines 10–11). Next p checks if it has just lost leadership and, if so, clears its active bit (lines 12–14). Next, if p is the leader (line 15), it increments its heartbeat counter and sets the active bit in shared memory (lines 16–18), and checks from whom it received notifications (line 19). For each such process q, it adds q to

[4]In the code, p checks the timer of *all* processes for expiration, but it is easy to see that only processes in p's contender set have an ongoing timer at p.

```
SHARED OBJECTS:
1  STATE[p] ← (0, 0, FALSE): register accessible by all, ∀p ∈ Π
                                          { fields (hb, counter, active) }
VARIABLES OF PROCESS p:
2  state[q] ← (0, 0, FALSE), ∀q ∈ Π { local var with fields (hb, counter, active) }
3  hbtimeout[q] ← η + 1, ∀q ∈ Π \ {p};   hbtimer[q] ← off, ∀q ∈ Π \ {p}
4  notifiers ← ∅; competitors ← ∅
5  contenders ← {p}
6  leader ← ⊥
CODE FOR EACH PROCESS p:
7  repeat forever
8    previous_leader ← leader
9    leader ← ℓ s.t.
       (state[ℓ].counter, ℓ) = min{(state[q].counter, q) : q ∈ contenders}
10   if previous_leader ≠ p and leader = p then        { if p becomes leader }
11     for each q ∈ Π \ {p} do NOTIFY(q)                  { p tells all others }
12   if previous_leader = p and leader ≠ p then  { if p loses its leadership }
13     state[p].active ← FALSE                    { p indicates it is not active }
14     STATE[p] ← state[p]                 { p updates its STATE shared variable }
15   if leader = p then                                      { if p is leader }
16     state[p].hb ← state[p].hb + 1             { p increments its heartbeat }
17     state[p].active ← TRUE                         { p indicates it is active }
18     STATE[p] ← state[p]                 { p updates its STATE shared variable }
19     competitors ← GET_NOTIFICATIONS() { p checks if others are leaders }
20     for each q ∈ competitors do   { for each q competing for leadership }
21       contenders ← contenders ∪ {q}             { p adds q to contenders }
22       hbtimer(q) ← hbtimeout[q]                  { p starts a timeout on q }
23       state[q] ← STATE[q]             { p reads q's STATE shared variable }
24       NOTIFY(q)          { p tells q that p is also competing for leadership }
25     if received ACCUSATION do                                 { if p accused }
26       state[p].counter ← state[p].counter + 1      { inc accusation count }
27       STATE[p] ← state[p]               { p updates its STATE shared variable }
28   for each q ∈ Π \ {p} do
29     if hbtimer(q) expired
30       previous_hb[q] ← state[q].hb    { p records q's previous heartbeat }
31       state[q] ← STATE[q]             { p reads q's STATE shared variable }
32       current_hb[q] ← state[q].hb      { p records q's current heartbeat }
33       if current_hb[q] > previous_hb[q] then      { if q's heartbeat grew }
34         hbtimer(q) ← hbtimeout[q]               { p restarts a timeout on q }
35       else
36         contenders ← contenders − {q}   { p removes q from contenders }
37         if state[q].active then                               { if q active }
38           send ACCUSATION to q                                  { p accuses q }
39           hbtimeout[q] ← hbtimeout[q] + 1 { p increments q's timeout }
```

Figure 3: Leader election algorithm.

```
procedure NOTIFY(q) { send NOTIFY to q }
procedure GET_NOTIFICATIONS() {
  notifiers ← {q ∈ Π \ {p} : received new NOTIFY message from q }
  return notifiers }
```

Figure 4: Notification mechanism (reliable links).

```
SHARED OBJECTS:
NOTIFICATIONS[p] ← FALSE          { register written by all, read by p }
for each q ∈ Π do NOTIFIES[p][q] ← FALSE
                                     { register written by all, read by p }
CODE FOR EACH PROCESS p:
procedure NOTIFY(q)
  NOTIFIES[q][p] ← TRUE                  { tell q that it was notified by p }
  NOTIFICATIONS[q] ← TRUE                     { tell q that it was notified }
  return
procedure GET_NOTIFICATIONS()
  notifiers ← ∅
  if NOTIFICATIONS[p] = TRUE then do    { if someone notified p then }
    NOTIFICATIONS[p] ← FALSE            { p resets its notifications flag }
    for each q ∈ Π \ {p} do                    { p checks who notified it }
      if NOTIFIES[p][q] = TRUE then do   { if p was notified by q then }
        NOTIFIES[p][q] ← FALSE { p resets the notification flag set by q }
        notifiers ← notifiers ∪ {q}           { add q to its notifiers set }
  return notifiers
```

Figure 5: Notification mechanism (fair lossy links).

contenders, starts a timer on q,[5] reads *STATE*[q], and notifies q that it is also a leader contender (lines 20–24). Then p checks whether it received accusations and, if so, increments its badness counter (lines 25–27).

Next, whether p is leader or not, it checks whether the timer on each process $q \neq p$ has expired (lines 28–29). If it has, p checks whether q's heartbeat increased since p started the timer (lines 30–33). If so, p restarts the timer (line 34). Otherwise, p removes q from its contender set; if q is active, p sends an accusation to q and increments its timeout value (lines 35–39).

THEOREM 5.1. *The algorithm in Figures 3 and 4 solves the eventual leader election problem in the m&m model where links are reliable and at least one process is timely. Eventually, no messages are sent, and the only accesses to shared memory is that the leader periodically writes a shared register and other processes periodically read this register.*

The proof is in the full paper.

5.2 Algorithm for fair lossy links

We now present an algorithm that works with fair lossy links. This algorithm has an added cost: the leader not only keeps writing a shared register, but also keeps reading a shared register. This cost is necessary, as we see later (§5.4).

The algorithm is similar to the previous one, except that it uses a different notification mechanism. Instead of sending a message, a process p notifies q by setting a bit in a *NOTIFIES*[q][p] matrix in shared memory; p also sets a bit in a *NOTIFICATIONS*[q] vector; this is an optimization so that q can monitor just one bit instead of a row of the matrix. More precisely, to know whether p has any notifications, p first examines the *NOTIFICATIONS*[p] bit; if it is

[5] The timer is a local variable with a counter that is decremented at each step of p (this is not shown in the code for clarity), until it reaches 0 (it "expires").

clear, it need not check anything else; otherwise, it examines the row *NOTIFIES*[p][$-$] of the matrix to find out which process sent the notification. Figure 5 has the detailed code. By combining it with in Figure 3, we obtain the leader election algorithm.

THEOREM 5.2. *The algorithm in Figures 3 and 5 solves the eventual leader election problem in the m&m model where links are fair lossy and at least one process is timely. Eventually, no messages are sent, and the only accesses to shared memory is that the leader periodically writes a shared register and periodically reads a shared register, and other processes periodically read a shared register.*

5.3 Locality

Our leader election algorithms are also efficient in terms of the *locality*, where each register is local to some process. This model corresponds well to the reality of an RDMA network, in which each process and each register are on some machine. In this case, if a process p is on the same machine as some register r, we say that r is *local* to p, and that p *owns* r. We say that the owner can read and write the register *locally*, while others read and write *remotely*.

Both leader election algorithms ensure that eventually the leader ℓ accesses registers only locally, by writing *STATE*[ℓ] (first algorithm), or by writing *STATE*[ℓ] and reading *NOTIFICATIONS*[ℓ] (second algorithm). This property further decreases the synchrony needed in practice: recall that we require only one process to be timely (the leader). By making the leader accesses local, the algorithms make it easier for the leader to be timely, since its steps involve only local accesses. On the other hand, the other processes access shared registers remotely, which is slower, but they are not required to be timely.

5.4 Impossibility result

In the full paper, we show that our algorithms are tight in the following sense. For systems with a timely process and asynchronous links, the leader must write shared registers forever. This result holds even if links are reliable and, a fortiori, if links are fair lossy. If, however, links are fair lossy, there is an additional requirement: either the leader writes and reads shared registers forever, or some process keeps sending messages forever.

THEOREM 5.3. *Let A be any eventual leader election algorithm for the m&m model with $n \geq 2$ processes, where links are reliable and at least one process is timely. There is a run of A whose leader writes shared registers infinitely often.*

THEOREM 5.4. *Let A be any eventual leader election algorithm for the m&m model with $n \geq 3$ processes, where links are fair lossy and at least one process is timely. Either (1) there is a run of A whose leader writes and reads shared registers infinitely often, or (2) there is a run of A in which some process sends messages infinitely often.*

6 CONCLUSION

The m&m model provides some inherent advantages over the pure message-passing and shared-memory models. In this paper, we demonstrated advantages in two aspects, fault tolerance and synchrony, and we focused on two problems, consensus and leader election. There are many exciting directions for future work in this space: discovering other benefits of the m&m model, developing better algorithms, studying other problems beyond consensus and leader election, evaluating algorithms in practice, and considering more failure models. On the last point, we addressed only process crashes, but it would be interesting to consider Byzantine failures, where the ability to pass messages and share registers selectively could overcome the difficulties of dealing with Byzantine processes in shared memory. Also interesting is to consider failures of the shared memory, especially if only parts of the memory fails [2, 42].

REFERENCES

[1] K. Abrahamson. On achieving consensus using a shared memory. In *ACM Symposium on Principles of Distributed Computing*, pages 291–302, Aug. 1988.

[2] Y. Afek, D. S. Greenberg, M. Merritt, and G. Taubenfeld. Computing with faulty shared objects. *Journal of the ACM*, 42(6):1231–1274, Nov. 1995.

[3] M. K. Aguilera, N. Amit, I. Calciu, X. Deguillard, J. Gandhi, S. Novakovic, A. Ramanathan, P. Subrahmanyam, L. Suresh, K. Tati, R. Venkatasubramanian, and M. Wei. Remote regions: a simple abstraction for remote memory. In *USENIX Annual Technical Conference*, July 2018.

[4] M. K. Aguilera, N. Amit, I. Calciu, X. Deguillard, J. Gandhi, P. Subrahmanyam, L. Suresh, K. Tati, R. Venkatasubramanian, and M. Wei. Remote memory in the age of fast networks. In *ACM Symposium on Cloud Computing*, pages 121–127, Sept. 2017.

[5] M. K. Aguilera, C. Delporte-Gallet, H. Fauconnier, and S. Toueg. Communication-efficient leader election and consensus with limited link synchrony. In *ACM Symposium on Principles of Distributed Computing*, pages 328–337, July 2004.

[6] M. K. Aguilera, C. Delporte-Gallet, H. Fauconnier, and S. Toueg. On implementing Omega in systems with weak reliability and synchrony assumptions. *Distributed Computing*, 21(4):239–314, Oct. 2008.

[7] M. K. Aguilera and S. Toueg. The correctness proof of Ben-Or's randomized consensus algorithm. *Distributed Computing*, 25(5):371–381, Oct. 2012.

[8] C. Amza, A. L. Cox, S. Dwarkadas, P. Keleher, H. Lu, R. Rajamony, W. Yu, and W. Zwaenepoel. TreadMarks: Shared memory computing on networks of workstations. *IEEE Computer*, 29(2):18–28, Feb. 1996.

[9] K. Asanovic and D. Patterson. FireBox: A hardware building block for 2020 warehouse-scale computers. In *Keynote of USENIX Conference on File and Storage Technologies*, Feb. 2014.

[10] J. Aspnes and M. Herlihy. Fast randomized consensus using shared memory. *Journal of algorithms*, 11(3):441–461, Sept. 1990.

[11] H. Attiya, A. Bar-Noy, and D. Dolev. Sharing memory robustly in message-passing systems. *Journal of the ACM*, 42(1):124–142, Jan. 1995.

[12] H. Attiya and K. Censor. Tight bounds for asynchronous randomized consensus. *Journal of the ACM*, 55(5):20, Oct. 2008.

[13] C. Barthels, S. Loesing, G. Alonso, and D. Kossmann. Rack-scale in-memory join processing using RDMA. In *International Conference on Management of Data*, pages 1463–1475, May 2015.

[14] A. Baumann, P. Barham, P.-E. Dagand, T. Harris, R. Isaacs, S. Peter, T. Roscoe, A. Schüpbach, and A. Singhania. The multikernel: A new OS architecture for scalable multicore systems. In *ACM Symposium on Operating Systems Principles*, pages 29–44, Oct. 2009.

[15] M. Ben-Or. Another advantage of free choice (extended abstract): Completely asynchronous agreement protocols. In *ACM Symposium on Principles of Distributed Computing*, pages 27–30, Aug. 1983.

[16] J. K. Bennett, J. B. Carter, and W. Zwaenepoel. Munin: Distributed shared memory based on type-specific memory coherence. In *ACM Symposium on Principles and Practice of Parallel Programming*, pages 168–176, Mar. 1990.

[17] I. Calciu, D. Dice, T. Harris, M. Herlihy, A. Kogan, V. Marathe, and M. Moir. Message passing or shared memory: Evaluating the delegation abstraction for multicores. In *International Conference on Principles of Distributed Systems*, pages 83–97, Dec. 2013.

[18] S. Chandra, J. R. Larus, and A. Rogers. Where is time spent in message-passing and shared-memory programs? In *International Conference on Architectural Support for Programming Languages and Operating Systems*, pages 61–73, Oct. 1994.

[19] T. D. Chandra, V. Hadzilacos, and S. Toueg. The weakest failure detector for solving consensus. *Journal of the ACM*, 43(4):685–722, July 1996.

[20] T. D. Chandra and S. Toueg. Unreliable failure detectors for reliable distributed systems. *Journal of the ACM*, 43(2):225–267, Mar. 1996.

[21] C. Cooper, T. Radzik, N. Rivera, and T. Shiraga. Fast plurality consensus in regular expanders. In *International Symposium on Distributed Computing*, pages

13:1–13:16, Oct. 2017.

[22] A. Daglis, D. Ustiugov, S. Novakovic, E. Bugnion, B. Falsafi, and B. Grot. SABRes: Atomic object reads for in-memory rack-scale computing. In *International Symposium on Microarchitecture*, pages 1–13, Oct. 2016.

[23] R. Danek and V. Hadzilacos. Local-spin group mutual exclusion algorithms. In *International Symposium on Distributed Computing*, pages 71–85, Oct. 2004.

[24] T. David, R. Guerraoui, and M. Yabandeh. Consensus inside. In *International Middleware Conference*, pages 145–156, Dec. 2014.

[25] J. Dean and S. Ghemawat. MapReduce: Simplified data processing on large clusters. In *Symposium on Operating Systems Design and Implementation*, pages 137–150, Dec. 2004.

[26] E. W. Dijkstra. Solution of a problem in concurrent programming control. *Communications of the ACM*, 8(9):569, Sept. 1965.

[27] D. Dolev, C. Dwork, and L. Stockmeyer. On the minimal synchronism needed for distributed consensus. *Journal of the ACM*, 34(1):77–97, Jan. 1987.

[28] A. Dragojević, D. Narayanan, M. Castro, and O. Hodson. FaRM: Fast remote memory. In *Symposium on Networked Systems Design and Implementation*, pages 401–414, Apr. 2014.

[29] A. Dragojević, D. Narayanan, E. Nightingale, M. Renzelmann, A. Shamis, A. Badam, and M. Castro. No compromises: distributed transactions with consistency, availability, and performance. In *ACM Symposium on Operating Systems Principles*, pages 54–70, Oct. 2015.

[30] C. Dwork, N. A. Lynch, and L. Stockmeyer. Consensus in the presence of partial synchrony. *Journal of the ACM*, 35(2):288–323, Apr. 1988.

[31] P. Faraboschi, K. Keeton, T. Marsland, and D. Milojicic. Beyond processor-centric operating systems. In *Workshop on Hot Topics in Operating Systems*, pages 17–17, May 2015.

[32] M. J. Fischer, N. A. Lynch, and M. S. Paterson. Impossibility of distributed consensus with one faulty process. *Journal of the ACM*, 32(2):374–382, Apr. 1985.

[33] Gen-Z draft core specification—december 2016. http://genzconsortium.org/draft-core-specification-december-2016.

[34] C. Guo, H. Wu, Z. Deng, G. Soni, J. Ye, J. Padhye, and M. Lipshteyn. RDMA over commodity ethernet at scale. In *ACM SIGCOMM Conference on Applications, Technologies, Architectures, and Protocols for Computer Communications*, pages 202–215, Aug. 2016.

[35] S. Han, N. Egi, A. Panda, S. Ratnasamy, G. Shi, and S. Shenker. Network support for resource disaggregation in next-generation datacenters. In *Workshop on Hot Topics in Networks*, pages 10:1–10:7, Nov. 2013.

[36] B. Holt, J. Nelson, B. Myers, P. Briggs, L. Ceze, S. Kahan, and M. Oskin. Flat combining synchronized global data structures. In *International Conference on PGAS Programming Models*, pages 76–92, Oct. 2013.

[37] S. Hoory, N. Linial, and A. Wigderson. Expander graphs and their applications. *Bulletin of the American Mathematical Society*, 43(4):439–561, Aug. 2006.

[38] M. Hutle, D. Malkhi, U. Schmid, and L. Zhou. Chasing the weakest system model for implementing Ω and consensus. *IEEE Transactions on Dependable and Secure Computing*, 6(4):269–281, Oct. 2009.

[39] InfiniBand. http://www.infinibandta.org/content/pages.php?pg=about_us_infiniband.

[40] Intel Omni-Path. http://www.intel.com/content/www/us/en/high-performance-computing-fabrics/omni-path-architecture-fabric-overview.html.

[41] iWARP. https://en.wikipedia.org/wiki/IWARP.

[42] P. Jayanti, T. D. Chandra, and S. Toueg. Fault-tolerant wait-free shared objects. *Journal of the ACM*, 45(3):451–500, May 1998.

[43] A. Kalia, M. Kaminsky, and D. G. Andersen. Using RDMA efficiently for key-value services. In *ACM SIGCOMM Conference on Applications, Technologies, Architectures, and Protocols for Computer Communications*, pages 295–306, Aug. 2014.

[44] A. Kalia, M. Kaminsky, and D. G. Andersen. FaSST: Fast, scalable and simple distributed transactions with two-sided (RDMA) datagram RPCs. In *Symposium on Operating Systems Design and Implementation*, pages 185–201, Nov. 2016.

[45] S. Kaxiras, D. Klaftenegger, M. Norgren, A. Ros, and K. Sagonas. Turning centralized coherence and distributed critical-section execution on their head: A new approach for scalable distributed shared memory. In *IEEE International Symposium on High Performance Distributed Computing*, pages 3–14, June 2015.

[46] P. Keane and M. Moir. A simple local-spin group mutual exclusion algorithm. *IEEE Transactions on Parallel and Distributed Systems*, 12(7):673–685, July 2001.

[47] Y.-J. Kim and J. H. Anderson. Adaptive mutual exclusion with local spinning. In *International Symposium on Distributed Computing*, pages 29–43, Oct. 2000.

[48] Y.-J. Kim and J. H. Anderson. Timing-based mutual exclusion with local spinning. In *International Symposium on Distributed Computing*, pages 30–44, Oct. 2003.

[49] A. C. Klaiber and H. M. Levy. A comparison of message passing and shared memory architectures for data parallel programs. In *International Symposium on Computer Architecture*, pages 94–105, Apr. 1994.

[50] D. Kranz, K. Johnson, A. Agarwal, J. Kubiatowicz, and B.-H. Lim. Integrating message-passing and shared-memory: Early experience. In *ACM Symposium on Principles and Practice of Parallel Programming*, pages 54–63, 1993.

[51] L. Lamport. On interprocess communication part I–II. *Distributed Computing*, 1(2):77–101, May 1986.

[52] L. Lamport. The part-time parliament. *ACM Transactions on Computer Systems*, 16(2):133–169, May 1998.

[53] L. Lamport. Paxos made simple. *ACM SIGACT News (Distributed Computing Column)*, 32(4):51–58, Dec. 2001.

[54] T. LeBlanc and E. Markatos. Shared memory vs. message passing in shared-memory multiprocessors. In *IEEE Symposium on Parallel and Distributed Processing*, pages 254 – 263, Dec. 1992.

[55] K. Lim, J. Chang, T. Mudge, P. Ranganathan, S. K. Reinhardt, and T. F. Wenisch. Disaggregated memory for expansion and sharing in blade servers. In *International Symposium on Computer Architecture*, pages 267–278, June 2009.

[56] K. Lim, Y. Turner, J. R. Santos, A. AuYoung, J. Chang, P. Ranganathan, and T. F. Wenisch. System-level implications of disaggregated memory. In *IEEE Symposium on High Performance Computer Architecture*, pages 189–200, Feb. 2012.

[57] M. C. Loui and H. H. Abu-Amara. Memory requirements for agreement among unreliable asynchronous processes. *Advances in Computing Research*, 4:163–183, 1987.

[58] Y. Lu, J. Shu, Y. Chen, and T. Li. Octopus: an RDMA-enabled distributed persistent memory file system. In *USENIX Annual Technical Conference*, pages 773–785, July 2017.

[59] N. A. Lynch. *Distributed Algorithms*. Morgan Kaufmann, 1996.

[60] C. Mitchell, Y. Geng, and J. Li. Using one-sided RDMA reads to build a fast, CPU-efficient key-value store. In *USENIX Annual Technical Conference*, pages 103–114, June 2013.

[61] J. Nelson, B. Holt, B. Myers, P. Briggs, L. Ceze, S. Kahan, and M. Oskin. Latency-tolerant software distributed shared memory. In *USENIX Annual Technical Conference*, pages 291–305, July 2015.

[62] S. Novakovic, A. Daglis, E. Bugnion, B. Falsafi, and B. Grot. Scale-out NUMA. In *International Conference on Architectural Support for Programming Languages and Operating Systems*, pages 3–18, Mar. 2014.

[63] D. Ongaro and J. Ousterhout. In search of an understandable consensus algorithm. In *USENIX Annual Technical Conference*, pages 305–320, June 2014.

[64] M. Poke and T. Hoefler. DARE: High-performance state machine replication on RDMA networks. In *IEEE International Symposium on High Performance Distributed Computing*, pages 107–118, June 2015.

[65] RDMA over converged ethernet. https://en.wikipedia.org/wiki/RDMA_over_Converged_Ethernet.

[66] D. J. Scales, K. Gharachorloo, and C. A. Thekkath. Shasta: A low overhead, software-only approach for supporting fine-grain shared memory. In *International Conference on Architectural Support for Programming Languages and Operating Systems*, pages 174–185, Oct. 1996.

[67] J. Shi, Y. Yao, R. Chen, H. Chen, and F. Li. Fast and concurrent RDF queries with rdma-based distributed graph exploration. In *Symposium on Operating Systems Design and Implementation*, pages 317–332, Nov. 2016.

[68] P. Stuedi, A. Trivedi, B. Metzler, and J. Pfefferle. DaRPC: Data center RPC. In *ACM Symposium on Cloud Computing*, pages 1–13, Nov. 2014.

[69] S.-Y. Tsai and Y. Zhang. LITE kernel RDMA support for datacenter applications. In *ACM Symposium on Operating Systems Principles*, pages 306–324, Oct. 2017.

[70] C. Wang, J. Jiang, X. Chen, N. Yi, and H. Cui. APUS: Fast and scalable PAXOS on RDMA. In *ACM Symposium on Cloud Computing*, pages 94–107, Sept. 2017.

[71] U. Wijetunge, S. Perreau, and A. Pollok. Distributed stochastic routing optimization using expander graph theory. In *Australian Communications Theory Workshop*, pages 124–129, Jan. 2011.

[72] T. S. Woodall, G. M. Shipman, G. Bosilca, R. L. Graham, and A. B. Maccabe. High performance RDMA protocols in HPC. In *Recent Advances in Parallel Virtual Machine and Message Passing Interface, 13th European PVM/MPI User's Group Meeting*, pages 76–85, Sept. 2006.

[73] E. Zamanian, C. Binnig, T. Kraska, and T. Harris. The end of a myth: Distributed transactions can scale. *Proceedings of the VLDB Endowment*, 10(6):685–696, Feb. 2017.

Revisionist Simulations: A New Approach to Proving Space Lower Bounds

(Extended Abstract)

Faith Ellen
University of Toronto
faith@cs.toronto.edu

Rati Gelashvili
University of Toronto
gelash@cs.toronto.edu

Leqi Zhu
University of Toronto
lezhu@cs.toronto.edu

ABSTRACT

Determining the number of registers required for solving x-obstruction-free (or randomized wait-free) k-set agreement for $x \leq k$ is an open problem that highlights important gaps in our understanding of the space complexity of synchronization. In x-obstruction-free protocols, processes are required to return in executions where at most x processes take steps. The best known upper bound on the number of registers needed to solve this problem among $n > k$ processes is $n - k + x$ registers. No general lower bound better than 2 was known.

We prove that any x-obstruction-free protocol solving k-set agreement among $n > k$ processes must use $\lfloor \frac{n-x}{k+1-x} \rfloor + 1$ or more registers. Our main tool is a simulation that serves as a reduction from the impossibility of deterministic wait-free k-set agreement. In particular, we show that, if a protocol uses fewer registers, then it is possible for $k + 1$ processes to simulate the protocol and deterministically solve k-set agreement in a wait-free manner, which is impossible. An important aspect of the simulation is the ability of simulating processes to revise the past of simulated processes. We introduce an *augmented snapshot object*, which facilitates this.

We also prove that any lower bound on the number of registers used by obstruction-free protocols applies to protocols that satisfy nondeterministic solo termination. Hence, our lower bound of $\lfloor \frac{n-1}{k} \rfloor + 1$ for the obstruction-free case (i.e., $x = 1$) also holds for randomized wait-free protocols. In particular, we get a tight lower bound of exactly n registers for solving obstruction-free and randomized wait-free consensus.

KEYWORDS

set agreement; space complexity; lower bounds; obstruction-freedom

ACM Reference Format:
Faith Ellen, Rati Gelashvili, and Leqi Zhu. 2018. Revisionist Simulations: A New Approach to Proving Space Lower Bounds : (Extended Abstract). In *PODC '18: ACM Symposium on Principles of Distributed Computing, July 23–27, 2018, Egham, United Kingdom.* ACM, New York, NY, USA, 10 pages. https://doi.org/10.1145/3212734.3212749

ACM ISBN 978-1-4503-5795-1/18/07...$15.00
https://doi.org/10.1145/3212734.3212749

He who controls the past controls the future. He who controls the present controls the past.

George Orwell, 1984

1 INTRODUCTION

The k-set agreement problem is a classical synchronization task, introduced by Chaudhuri [19], in which n processes, each with an input value, are required to return at most k different input values. This is a generalization of the consensus problem, which is the case $k = 1$.

Two celebrated results in distributed computing are the impossibility of solving consensus deterministically when at most one process may crash [25, 37] and, more generally, the impossibility of solving k-set agreement deterministically when at most k processes may crash [14, 34, 40], using only registers. One way to bypass these impossibility results is to design protocols that are obstruction-free [33]. *Obstruction-freedom* is a termination condition that requires a process to terminate given sufficiently many consecutive steps, i.e., from any configuration, if only one process takes steps, then it will eventually terminate. x-*obstruction-freedom* [43] generalizes this condition: from any configuration, if only x processes take steps, then they will all eventually terminate. It is known that k-set agreement can be solved using only registers in an x-obstruction-free way for $1 \leq x \leq k$ [44]. Another way to overcome the impossibility of solving consensus is to use randomized wait-free protocols, where non-faulty processes are required to terminate with probability 1 [13].

It is possible to solve consensus for n processes using n registers in a randomized wait-free way [1, 3, 5, 39] or in an obstruction-free way [16, 17, 30, 45]. A lower bound of $\Omega(\sqrt{n})$ was proved by Ellen, Herlihy, and Shavit in [23]. Recently, Gelashvili proved an $\Omega(n)$ lower bound for *anonymous* processes [28]. Anonymous processes [7, 23] have no identifiers and run the same code: all processes with the same input start in the same initial state and behave identically until they read different values. Then Zhu proved that any obstruction-free protocol solving consensus for n processes requires at least $n-1$ registers [46]. All these lower bounds are actually for protocols that satisfy *nondeterministic solo termination* [23], which includes both obstruction-free and randomized wait-free protocols.

In contrast, there are big gaps between the best known upper and lower bounds on the number of registers needed for k-set agreement. The best obstruction-free protocols require $n - k + 1$ registers [16, 45]. Bouzid, Raynal, and Sutra [16] also give an x-obstruction-free protocol that uses $n-k+x$ registers, improving on the $min(n + 2x - k, n)$ space complexity of Delporte-Gallet, Fauconnier, Gafni, and Rajsbaum's obstruction-free protocol [20]. All of these algorithms work for anonymous processes. Delporte-Gallet, Fauconnier, Kuznetsov, and Ruppert [21] proved that it is impossible to solve k-set agreement using 1 register. For anonymous processes, they also proved a lower bound of $\sqrt{x(\frac{n}{k}-2)}$ for x-obstruction-free protocols, which still leaves a polynomial gap between the lower and upper bounds.

There are good reasons why proving lower bounds on the number of registers needed for k-set agreement may be difficult. At a high level, the impossibility results for k-set agreement consider some representation (for example, a simplicial complex) of all possible process states in all possible executions. Then, a combinatorial property (Sperner's Lemma [42]) is used to prove that, roughly speaking, for any given number of steps, there exists an execution leading to a configuration in which $k+1$ outputs are still possible. Although there is ongoing work to develop a more general theory [26, 27, 41], we do not know enough about the topological representation of protocols that are x-obstruction-free or use fewer than n multi-writer registers [32] to adapt topological arguments to prove space lower bounds for k-set agreement. There are similar problems adapting known proofs that do not explicitly use topology [4, 10].

Our contribution. In this paper, we prove a lower bound of $\lfloor \frac{n-x}{k+1-x} \rfloor + 1$ on the number of registers necessary for solving n-process x-obstruction-free k-set agreement. As corollaries, we get a tight lower bound of n registers for obstruction-free consensus and a tight lower bound of 2 for obstruction-free $(n-1)$-set consensus. In the full version of the paper, we also prove a lower bound of $\lfloor \frac{n}{2} \rfloor + 1$ registers for obstruction-free ϵ-approximate agreement [22], for sufficiently small $\epsilon > 0$. This is another important task for which no good space lower bound was known.

In addition, in Section 5, we prove that any lower bound on the number registers needed for obstruction-free protocols to solve a task also applies to nondeterministic solo terminating protocols and, in particular, to randomized wait-free protocols solving that task. Hence, our space lower bounds for obstruction-free protocols also apply to such protocols.

Technical Overview. Using a novel simulation, we convert any obstruction-free protocol for k-set agreement that uses too few registers to a protocol that solves wait-free k-set agreement using only registers. Since solving wait-free k-set agreement is impossible using only registers, this reduction gives a lower bound on the number of registers needed to solve obstruction-free k-set agreement. This simulation technique, described in detail in Section 4, is the main technical contribution of the paper. It is the first technique that proves lower bounds on space complexity by applying results obtained by topological arguments. In the full version of the paper, we also use this new technique to prove a lower bound on the number of registers needed for ϵ-approximate agreement by a reduction from a step complexity lower bound for ϵ-approximate agreement.

The executions of the simulated processes in our simulation are reminiscent of the executions constructed by adversaries in covering arguments [6, 18]. In those proofs, the adversary modifies an execution it has constructed by revising the past of some process, so that the old and new executions are indistinguishable to the other processes. It does so by inserting consecutive steps of the process starting from some carefully chosen configuration. In our simulation, a real process may revise the past of a simulated process, in a way that is indistinguishable to other simulated processes. This is possible because each simulated process is simulated by a single real process. In contrast, in the BG simulation [15], different steps of simulated processes can be performed by different real processes, so this would be much more difficult to do.

A crucial component of our simulation is the use of an *augmented snapshot object*, which we implement in a non-blocking manner from registers. Like a standard snapshot object, this object consists of a fixed number of components and supports a `Scan` operation, which returns the contents of all components. However, it generalizes the `update` operation to a `Block-Update` operation, which can update multiple components of the object. In addition, a `Block-Update` returns some information, which is used by our simulation. The specifications of `Block-Update` and our implementation of an augmented snapshot object appears in Section 3.

2 PRELIMINARIES

An asynchronous shared memory system consists of a set of processes and instances of base objects, which processes use to communicate. An *object* has a set of possible values and a set of operations, each of which takes some fixed number of inputs and returns a response. The processes take steps at arbitrary speeds and may fail, at any time, by crashing. Every step consists of an operation on some base object by some process plus local computation by that process to determine its next state from the response returned by the operation.

Configurations and Executions. A *configuration* of a system consists of the state of each process and the value of each object. An *initial* configuration is determined by the input value of each process. Each object has the same value in all initial configurations. A configuration C is *indistinguishable* from a configuration C' to a set of processes $\mathcal{P}$ in the system, if every process in $\mathcal{P}$ is in the same state in C as it is in C' and each object in the system has the same value in C as in C'.

A step e by a process p is *applicable* at a configuration C if e can be the next step of process p given its state in C. If e is applicable at C, then we use Ce to denote the configuration resulting from p taking step e at C. A sequence of steps $\alpha = e_1, e_2, \dots$ is *applicable* at a configuration C if e_1 is applicable at C and, for each $i \geq 1$, e_{i+1} is applicable at $Ce_1 \cdots e_i$. In this case, α is called an *execution from* C. An execution $\alpha\beta$ denotes the execution α followed by the execution β. A configuration C is *reachable* if there exists a finite execution from an initial configuration that results in C.

For a finite execution α from a configuration C, we use $C\alpha$ to denote the configuration reached after applying α to C. If α is empty, then $C\alpha = C$. We say an execution α is $\mathcal{P}$*-only*, for a set of processes $\mathcal{P}$, if all steps in α are by processes in $\mathcal{P}$. A $\{p\}$-only execution, for some process p, is also called a *solo execution by* p. Note, if configurations C and C' are indistinguishable to a set of processes $\mathcal{P}$, then any $\mathcal{P}$-only execution from C is applicable at C'.

Implementations and Linearizability. An *implementation* of an object specifies, for each process and each operation of the object, a deterministic procedure describing how the process carries out the operation. The *execution interval* of an invocation of an operation in an execution is the subsequence of the execution that begins with its first step and ends with its last step. If an operation does not complete, for example, if the process that invoked it crashed before receiving a response, then its execution interval is infinite. An implementation of an object is *linearizable* if, for every execution, there is a point in each operation's execution interval, called the *linearization point* of the operation, such that the operation can be said to have taken place atomically at that point [35]. This is equivalent to saying that the operations can be ordered (and all incomplete operations can be given responses) so that any operation which ends before another one begins is ordered earlier and the responses of the operations are consistent with the sequential specifications of the object [35].

Progress Conditions. An implementation of an object is *wait-free* if every process is able to complete its current operation on the object after taking sufficiently many steps, regardless of what other processes are doing. An implementation is *non-blocking* if infinitely many operations are completed in every infinite execution.

A protocol is *x-obstruction-free* if, from any configuration C and for any subset P of at most x processes, every process in P that takes sufficiently many steps after C outputs a value, as long as only processes in P take steps after C. A protocol is *obstruction-free* if it is 1-obstruction-free and *wait-free* if it is n-obstruction-free.

Registers and Snapshot objects. A *register* is an object that supports two operations, `write` and `read`. A `write(v)` operation writes value v to the register, and a `read` operation returns the last value that was written to the before the read. A *multi-writer register* allows all processes to write to it, while a *single-writer register* can only be written to by one fixed process. A process is said to be *covering* a register if its next step is a write to this register. A *block write* is a consecutive sequence of `write` operations to different registers performed by different processes.

An *m-component multi-writer snapshot* object [2] stores a sequence of m values and supports two operations, `update` and `scan`. An `update`(j, v) operation sets component j of the object to v. A `scan` operation returns the current *view*, consisting of the values of all components. A *single-writer* snapshot object shared by a set of processes has one component for each process and each process may only `update` its own component. A process is said to be covering component j of a snapshot object if its next step is an update to the component j. A *block update* is a consecutive sequence of `update` operations to different components of a snapshot object performed by different processes.

It is easy to implement m registers from an m-component multi-writer snapshot object, by replacing each `write` to the j'th register by an `update` to the j'th component and replacing a `read` to the j'th register by a `scan` and then discarding all but the value of the j'th component. An m-component snapshot object can also be implemented from m registers [2].

Tasks and Protocols. A *task* specifies a set of allowable combinations of inputs to the processes and, for each such combination, what combinations of outputs can be returned by the processes. A *protocol* for a task provides a procedure for each process to compute its output, so that the task's specifications are satisfied. In particular, in *k-set agreement*, each process begins with an arbitrary value as its input and, if it does not crash, must output a value such that at most k values are output (*k-agreement*) and each output value is the input of some process (*validity*).

The *space complexity* of a protocol is the maximum number of registers used in any execution of the protocol. Each m-component snapshot object it uses counts as m registers. The *space complexity* of a task is the minimum space complexity of any protocol for the task.

2.1 Our Setting

We consider two asynchronous shared memory systems, the simulated system and the real system.

Simulated system. The *simulated system* consists of n simulated processes, $p_1, \ldots, p_n$, that communicate through an m-component multi-writer snapshot object. Thus, any task that can be solved in the simulated system has space complexity at most m.

Without loss of generality, we assume that each process p_i alternately performs `scan` and `update` operations on the snapshot object: Between two consecutive `update` operations, p_i can perform a `scan` and ignore its result. If p_i is supposed to perform multiple consecutive `scan`s, it can, instead, perform one `scan` and use its result as the result of the others. This is because it is possible for all these `scan`s to occur consecutively in an execution, in which case, they *would* all get the same result.

Real system. The real system consists of $k + 1$ real processes, $q_0, \ldots, q_k$, that communicate through a single-writer snapshot object. For clarity of presentation, real processes use single-writer registers in addition to the single-writer snapshot object. The single-writer registers to which a particular process writes can be treated as additional separate fields of the component of the snapshot object belonging to that process. In Section 3, we define and implement an *m-component augmented snapshot object* shared by the real processes.

In our simulation, the processes in the simulated system are partitioned into $k + 1$ sets, $P_0, \ldots, P_k$, and real process q_i is solely responsible for simulating the actions of all processes in P_i in the simulated system. This is illustrated in Figure 1.

The following impossibility result applies to our real system.

Theorem 1 ([14, 34, 40]). *In a system of $k + 1$ processes sharing a single-writer snapshot object, there is no deterministic wait-free protocol that allows these processes to solve k-set agreement.*

3 AUGMENTED SNAPSHOT OBJECT

In this section, we define an augmented snapshot object and show how it can be deterministically implemented in the real system. This object plays a central role in our simulation. It is used by real processes to simulate steps performed by simulated processes. In particular, a real process q_i uses this object to simulate an `update` or a `scan` by any simulated process in P_i, or a block update by any subset of processes in P_i. Our simulation, which is explained in Section 4, is non-standard. Unfortunately, to satisfy its technical requirements, the augmented snapshot has to satisfy some non-standard properties.

An m-component augmented snapshot object is a generalization of an m-component multi-writer snapshot object. A `Scan` operation returns the current *view*, consisting of the values of all components. The components can be updated using a `Block-Update` operation. The key difference between a multi-writer snapshot and

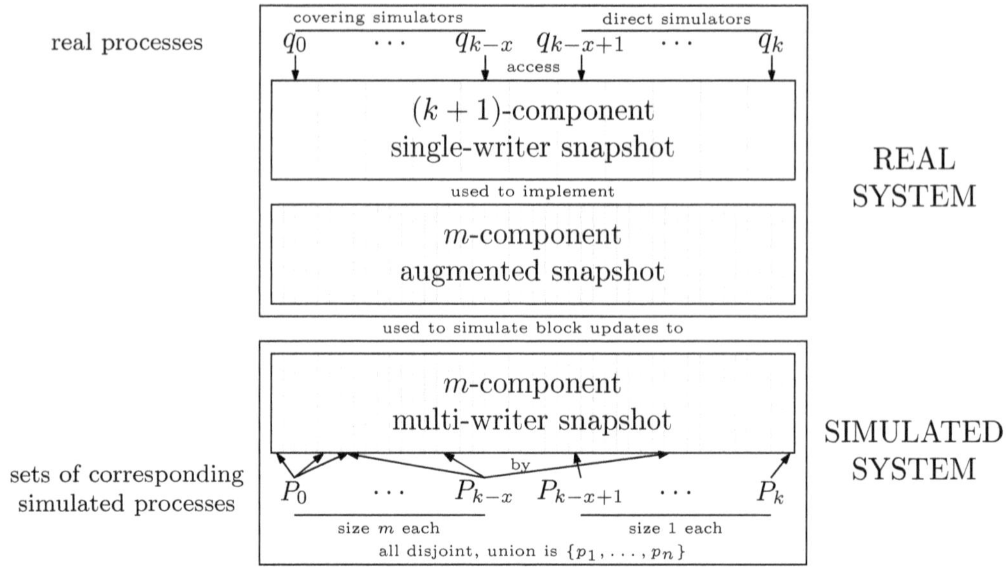

Figure 1: High-level overview of real and simulated systems.

an augmented snapshot is that a Block-Update may update *multiple* components, although not necessarily atomically. In addition, a Block-Update may return a view from some earlier point in the execution. Otherwise, it returns a special *yield* symbol, $\triangledown$.

A linearizable, non-blocking implementation of an augmented snapshot object in the real system is impossible. This is because a Block-Update operation that updates 2 components would then be the same as a 2-assignment operation. However, 2-assignment, together with read or Scan, can be used to deterministically solve wait-free consensus among 2 processes [31], which is impossible in the real system [2, 37].

Instead, a Block-Update operation can be considered to be a sequence of atomic Update operations, which each update one component of the augmented snapshot object. (Analogously, a *collect* operation [9, 12] is not atomic, but the individual reads that comprise it are atomic.)

3.1 Specification

An *m-component augmented snapshot object*, $\mathcal{M}[1..m]$, shared by $k+1$ processes, $q_0, q_1, \ldots, q_k$, consists of m components and supports two operations, Scan and Block-Update, which can be performed by all processes. A *view* of the augmented snapshot consists of the value of each of the m components at some point in an execution. A Scan operation returns the current view. A Block-Update operation to a sequence of $r \geq 1$ different components $[j_1, \ldots, j_r]$ of $\mathcal{M}$ with a sequence of r values $[v_1, \ldots, v_r]$ is comprised of a sequence of Update operations $U_1, \ldots, U_r$. Each Update U_c atomically sets $\mathcal{M}[j_c]$ to v_c. These Update operations may occur in any order. A Block-Update operation also returns either $\triangledown$ or a view of $\mathcal{M}$.

A Block-Update that does not return $\triangledown$ is called *atomic*. We require that every execution has a linearization in which the Update operations comprising each atomic Block-Update are linearized consecutively.

Consider any atomic Block-Update, B. Let Z be the first Update in B. Let Z' be the last Update prior to Z that is part of an atomic Block-Update or the beginning of the execution, if there is no such Update. Then B must return a view of $\mathcal{M}$ at some point T between Z' and Z such that no Scan occurs between T and Z.

We prove that, in our implementation, a Block-Update only returns $\triangledown$ under certain circumstances, as described in Theorem 3. For example, a Block-Update by process q_0 will always be atomic and, if a Block-Update experiences no step contention [8], it will be atomic. The simulation in Section 4 relies on this property of our implementation.

3.2 Implementation

Figure 2 contains the pseudocode for our non-blocking implementation of an m-component augmented snapshot object, $\mathcal{M}$, shared by $k+1$ processes, $q_0, q_1, \ldots, q_k$. Every Block-Update is wait-free. A Scan can only be blocked by an infinite sequence of concurrent Block-Update operations.

The implementation uses a single-writer snapshot object H[0..k]. All $k+1$ components of H are initially $\perp$. The i'th component of H is used by q_i to record a list of every Update it performs, each represented by a *triple*. A triple contains a component of $\mathcal{M}$, a value, and a *timestamp* we associate with a Block-Update. For a Block-Update to r components of $\mathcal{M}$, q_i appends r triples to H[i], all with the same timestamp. For clarity of presentation, we also use $n(n-1)$ unbounded arrays of single-writer registers, $\mathsf{L}_{i,j}$, for all $i \neq j$, each indexed by non-negative integers. Each register is initially $\perp$. Only process q_i can write to $\mathsf{L}_{i,j}[b]$ and only process q_j reads from it. The registers $\mathsf{L}_{i,j}[b]$ are used by q_i to help q_j determine the return value of its b'th Block-Update. As discussed in Section 2, these single-writer registers are actually implemented as part of the single-writer snapshot object provided by the real system.

```
procedure New-timestamp(h) by q_i
    for j ∈ {0, ..., k} do
        t_j ← #h_j
    t_i ← t_i + 1
    return (t_0, ..., t_k)
procedure Get-view(h) by q_i
    for j ∈ {1, ..., m} do
        if there is an update triple in h with first
          component j then
            t ← max{t' : (j, v', t') is a triple in h}
            let (j, v, t) be the unique triple in h with
              component j and timestamp t
            v_j ← v
        else v_j ← ⊥
    return (v_1, ..., v_m)
procedure Scan() by q_i
    repeat
        h ← H.scan()
        for j ∈ {0, ..., k} − {i} do
            L_{i,j}[#h_j].write(h)
        f ← H.scan()
    until h = f
    return Get-view(h)
procedure Block-Update([j_1, ..., j_c], [v_1, ..., v_c]) by q_i
    h ← H.scan()
    t ← New-timestamp(h)
    H.update(i, h_i · [(j_1, v_1, t), ..., (j_c, v_c, t)])
    f ← H.scan()
    for j ∈ {0, ..., i − 1} do
        L_{i,j}[#f_j].write(f)
    // Check for a conflicting Block-Update by a
       process with lower identifier
    g ← H.scan()
    if there exists 0 ≤ j < i such that #g_j > #h_j then
        return ▽
    last ← h
    for j ∈ {0, ..., k} − {i} do
        r[j] ← L_{j,i}[#h_i].read()
        if r[j] ≠ ⊥ and last is a proper prefix of r[j] then
            last ← r[j]
    return Get-view(last)
```

Figure 2: Pseudocode for Augmented Snapshot Object Implementation.

Notation. We use upper case letters to denote instances of scan and update on H, instances of read and write on single-writer registers, and instances of Scan, Block-Update and Update on $\mathcal{M}$. The corresponding lower case letter denotes the result of a scan, read, or Block-Update operation. For example, h denotes the result of a scan H. We use h_i to denote the value of the i'th component of h and $\#h_i$ to denote the number of Block-Update operations q_i has performed on $\mathcal{M}$, which is exactly the number of different timestamps associated with the triples recorded in h_i.

Auxiliary Procedures. A *timestamp* is a label from a partially ordered set, which can be associated with an operation, such that, if one operation completes before another operation begins, the first operation has a smaller timestamp [36]. We use a variant of vector timestamps [11, 24, 38]: Each *timestamp* is a $(k+1)$-component vector of non-negative integers, with one component per process. Timestamps are ordered lexicographically. We use $t' > t$ to denote that timestamp t' is lexicographically larger than timestamp t and $t' \geq t$ to denote that t' is lexicographically at least is large as t.

Let h be the result of a scan. Process q_i *generates a new timestamp* $t = (t_0, t_1, \ldots, t_k)$ from h using the locally computed function New-timestamp(h). It sets t_j to $\#h_j$ for all $j \neq i$ and sets t_i to $\#h_i + 1$.

For each $j \in \{1, \ldots, m\}$, let v_j be the value with the lexicographically largest associated timestamp among all update triples (j, v, t) in all components of h, or $\perp$ if no such triple exists. The *view* of h, denoted view(h), is the vector $(v_1, \ldots, v_m)$. It is obtained using the locally computed function Get-view(h).

Main Procedures. To perform a Scan() of $\mathcal{M}$, process q_i repeatedly performs scans of H until two consecutive results are the same. Then q_i returns the view of its last scan. Notice that Scan is not necessarily wait-free. However, it can only be blocked by an infinite sequence of Block-Update operations that modify H between every two scan operations performed by the Scan. To help other processes determine what to return from a Block-Update, q_i records the result, h, of each scan in register $L_{i,j}[\#h_j]$, for all $j \neq i$.

To perform a Block-Update($[j_1, \ldots, j_c], [v_1, \ldots, v_c]$) of $\mathcal{M}$, q_i first performs a scan H of H. Then it generates a timestamp, t, from the result, h, of H and appends the triples $(j_1, v_1, t), \ldots, (j_c, v_c, t)$ to H[i] via an update. This associates the same timestamp, t, with the Block-Update and each of the Update operations comprising it. Next, process q_i helps processes with lower identifiers by performing another scan F of H and recording its result, f, in $L_{i,j}[\#f_j]$ for all $j < i$. Then q_i performs a third scan to check whether any process with a lower identifier has performed an update after H. If so, q_i returns $\triangledown$. This is the only way in which a Block-Update can return $\triangledown$. Consequently, all Block-Update operations performed by q_0 are atomic.

If q_i does not return $\triangledown$, it reads $L_{j,i}[b]$ for all $j \neq i$, where b is the number of Block-Update operations that q_i had previously performed. It determines which among these and h is the result of the latest scan and returns its view. The mechanism for determining the latest scan is described next.

If h and h' are the results of two scans of H and, if h_j is a prefix of h'_j for all $j \in \{0, 1, \ldots, k\}$, we say that h is a *prefix* of h'. In addition, if $h_j \neq h'_j$ for some $j \in \{0, 1, \ldots, k\}$, we say that h is a *proper* prefix of h'. Since each update to the single-writer snapshot H appends one or more update triples to a component, the following is true.

Observation 2. *Let H and H' be* scans *of* H *with results h and h', respectively. If H occurred before H', then h is a prefix of h'. Conversely, if h is a proper prefix of h', then H occurred before H'.*

Thus, by Observation 2, for any set of scans, the result of the earliest of these scans is a prefix of the result of every other scan in the set.

Linearization Points. A complete Scan operation is linearized at its last scan of H, performed on Line 19. Now consider a Block-Update, with associated timestamp t, that updates components $j_1, \ldots, j_c$. For $1 \leq i \leq c$, the Update to component j_i is linearized at the first point in the execution at which H contains a triple beginning with j_i and ending with a timestamp $t' \geq t$. If multiple Update operations are linearized at the same point, then they are ordered by their associated timestamps (from earliest to latest) and then in increasing order of the components they update.

Each Update of a Block-Update, B, performed without step contention is linearized at B's update to H on Line 25. However, it is not possible to do this for all Block-Update operations; otherwise, we would be implementing a linearizable, non-blocking augmented snapshot, which, as discussed earlier, is impossible. In our linearization, if an Update, U, that is part of B updates a component which is also updated by an Update, U', that is part of a concurrent Block-Update by a process with a lower identifier, then U may be linearized before U'.

In the full version of the paper, we prove the following theorem.

Theorem 3. *Figure 2 gives a non-blocking implementation of an m-component augmented snapshot object. A* Block-Update *by q_i returns $\triangledown$ only if its execution interval contains an* update *by a process q_j with $j < i$ to* H *on Line 25 (performed as a part of a* Block-Update *by q_j).*

As part of the proof, we show each Update, U, that is part of a Block-Update, B, is linearized between the scan of H in B on Line 23 and the update, u, to H in B on Line 25. To see why, suppose that U updates component j to value v and has associated timestamp t. Since u appends the triple (j, v, t) to a component of H, U is linearized no later than u. However, U could be linearized at an update, u', prior to u. This happens if u' appends a triple (j, v', t') to a component of H, where $t' \geq t$. Note that the scan of H in B on Line 23 occurs before u'; otherwise, the view, h, this scan returns includes (j, v', t'). Since $t =$ New-Timestamp(h), we can show that $t > t'$, which is a contradiction.

Let q_i be the process that performs B. Then $t_i = \#h_i + 1$. Since u' occurs before u, it follows that $t'_i \leq \#h_i$. But $t \geq t$ and timestamps are ordered lexicographically, so there exists $0 \leq \ell < i$ such that $t'_\ell > t_\ell$. Let g be the result of the scan of H in B on Line 29, which occurs after u and, hence, after u'. Then $\#g_\ell \geq t'_\ell > t_\ell = \#h_\ell$. This is detected by the test in B on Line 30, so B returns $\triangledown$. Thus, all Update operations that comprise an atomic Block-Update are linearized at Line 25 of the Block-Update.

In addition, we show that different timestamps are associated with different Block-Update operations. This implies the Update operations comprising an atomic Block-Update are linearized consecutively.

4 THE SIMULATION

In this section, we prove the following theorem:

Theorem 4. *For $1 \leq x \leq k$, any x-obstruction-free protocol for solving k-set agreement among $n > k$ processes must use at least $\lfloor \frac{n-x}{k-x+1} \rfloor + 1$ registers.*

The standard approach for proving space complexity lower bounds is to use a *covering argument* [18]. Such an argument involves showing that it is possible to schedule the processes so that they perform block writes and cover successively more registers. The main difficulty with this approach is proving that processes do not terminate prematurely. In particular, when inserting *hidden* steps by a process before a block write, one must show that it does, in fact, write to a register that is not covered. Moreover, after a block write, one must show that the processes have not yet gained enough information to output a value and terminate.

In contrast, in our proof, we show that, if an x-obstruction-free protocol Π for k-set agreement among $n > k$ processes uses $m \leq \frac{n-x}{k-x+1}$ registers, then $k + 1$ real processes can simulate an execution of Π in the simulated system. The real processes will also be solving k-set agreement in the real system. Each process q_i will initialize all the simulated processes that it is responsible for (the processes in P_i) with its own input, and will simulate their steps according to Π. It will simulate them in an order so that the resulting execution in the simulated system satisfies certain properties. Intuitively, it will be very much like performing a covering argument inside a simulation. This approach avoids the problem of processes terminating prematurely because, when a simulated process outputs a value and terminates, the real process simulating it will be able to output the same value and terminate. We will use x-obstruction-freedom of the simulated protocol, combined with properties satisfied by the simulated execution, to ensure that each real process can return a correct output in a wait-free manner.

This gives a protocol for $k + 1$ real processes to solve k-set agreement in a wait-free manner, which contradicts Theorem 1. Hence, our lower bound may be viewed as a "black-box" reduction from Theorem 1.

4.1 Simulation algorithm

Fix any x-obstruction-free protocol Π for k-set agreement among $n > k$ processes that uses $m \leq \frac{n-x}{k+1-x}$ registers. As discussed in Section 2, we may assume that the protocol uses one single m-component multi-writer snapshot object, M, on which each process alternately performs scan and update, until it performs a scan on M whose result allows it to output a value and terminate.

We now describe how the real processes simulate Π. The real processes are partitioned into $k + 1 - x$ *covering* simulators, each responsible for m distinct simulated processes, and x *direct* simulators, each responsible for one simulated process. Notice that the total number of simulated processes is $x + m(k + 1 - x) \leq n$, since $m \leq \frac{n-x}{k+1-x}$.

Both types of simulators use a non-blocking implementation of an m-component augmented snapshot object, $\mathcal{M}$, for simulating the steps of processes they are responsible for. A direct simulator directly simulates its single process in a step-by-step manner. A covering simulator attempts to simulate its set of processes so that they all cover different components of M. We note that the algorithm of a covering simulator, which we will shortly describe in detail, is similar to a covering argument, i.e. a covering simulator tries to simulate its processes so that they perform block updates and cover successively more components. This involves *locally* simulating certain steps by simulated processes, i.e. without performing any operations on $\mathcal{M}$.

We will guarantee that for each *real execution* of the simulators (i.e. an execution by the real processes in the real system) there exists a corresponding *simulated execution* of the protocol Π. However, because of the locally simulated steps, the exact correspondence between these executions is too complex to be described here without proper formalism.

Direct simulator's algorithm. A direct simulator q *directly* simulates its process p as follows. Initially, q sets the input of p to its input. To simulate a `scan` on M by p, q performs a `Scan` on $\mathcal{M}$. To simulate an `update`(j, v) on M by p, q performs a one component `Block-Update`$([j], [v])$ on $\mathcal{M}$, ignoring the value returned. At any point, if p outputs a value and terminates, then q outputs the same value and terminates.

A covering simulator q uses a `Block-Update` operation, $\mathcal{B}$, to attempt to simulate a block update by a subset of its processes. If $\mathcal{B}$ returns a view $\mathcal{V} \neq \triangledown$, then q knows that $\mathcal{B}$ was *atomic*, i.e. the individual `Update`s in $\mathcal{B}$ can be linearized consecutively. Moreover, q knows that $\mathcal{V}$ is a view of $\mathcal{M}$ at some earlier point in the real execution such that, between this point and the first `Update` in $\mathcal{B}$, there are no `Scan` operations and no `Update` operations that are part of atomic `Block-Update` operations. At this point, q may choose to simulate *hidden steps* by one of its processes, p, effectively *revising* the past in the corresponding simulated execution. The resulting simulated execution will be indistinguishable to all other simulated processes, so p *could have* taken those steps. We emphasize that the real execution does not change. If $\mathcal{B}$ returns $\triangledown$, then q knows that the the `Update` operations comprising $\mathcal{B}$ have occurred, but not necessarily consecutively. In this case, q does not use $\mathcal{B}$ to hide steps. Note that any two sequences of hidden steps are separated by at least one atomic `Block-Update` and, hence, do not interfere with each other.

Covering simulator's algorithm. Let $P = \{p'_1, \ldots, p'_m\}$ be the set of simulated processes that a particular covering simulator q is responsible for. Initially, q sets the input of each process in P to its input. The goal of q is to simulate P such that, eventually, P covers all components of M. This corresponds to q *constructing* a `Block-Update` to all components of $\mathcal{M}$. In general, *constructing* a `Block-Update` to r components of $\mathcal{M}$ involves q simulating $p'_1, p'_2, \ldots, p'_r$ until they are covering r different components of M. We describe a recursive procedure for doing so. Note that, at any point in q's construction procedure, if a process in P outputs a value and terminates, then q outputs the same value and terminates.

As a base case, to construct a `Block-Update` to a single component of $\mathcal{M}$, q directly simulates p'_1 until it is about to perform an `update`(j_1, v_1) to M (or it terminates). If p'_1 does not terminate, then q has constructed `Block-Update`$([j_1], [v_1])$.

To construct a `Block-Update` to $r + 1$ components of $\mathcal{M}$, q constructs and performs a sequence of `Block-Update` operations $\mathcal{B}_1, \mathcal{B}_2, \ldots$ to r components of $\mathcal{M}$. It continues until (one of its simulated processes terminates or) it constructs a `Block-Update` $\mathcal{B}_t$ to r components of $\mathcal{M}$ that updates the same set of components as some atomic `Block-Update` earlier in the sequence, i.e. for some $t' < t$, $\mathcal{B}_{t'}$ updates the same set of components as $\mathcal{B}_t$ and $\mathcal{B}_{t'}$ returns a view $\mathcal{V} \neq \triangledown$. Let $j_1, \ldots, j_r$ be the components that $\mathcal{B}_t$ updates and let $v_1, \ldots, v_r$ be the corresponding values. After constructing $\mathcal{B}_t$, q continues its simulation of p'_{r+1} by *locally* simulating a solo execution of p'_{r+1}, assuming that the contents of M are $\mathcal{V}$ at the beginning of this execution. It does so until p'_{r+1} (terminates or is about to perform an `update`(j_{r+1}, v_{r+1}) to M, where $j_{r+1} \notin \{j_1, \ldots, j_r\}$). This has the effect of inserting hidden steps by p'_{r+1} at the point in the simulated execution corresponding to $\mathcal{V}$ in the real execution. If none of q's simulated processes terminate, then q has constructed `Block-Update`$([j_1, \ldots, j_r, j_{r+1}], [v_1, \ldots, v_r, v_{r+1}])$.

If q constructs a `Block-Update` to all m components of $\mathcal{M}$, then q locally simulates this block update by P followed by the terminating solo execution of p'_1. This execution is applicable at any point in the future, since the block update completely overwrites M. Then process q terminates and returns the value that p'_1 returns in its simulated solo execution. This termination condition is crucial for showing that the k-set agreement algorithm for the real processes is wait-free.

4.2 Sketch of correctness proof

The formal correctness proof of the simulation is fairly technical, so we only give a sketch here. A complete proof appears in the full version of the paper.

At a high level, we would like to prove that every real execution $\boldsymbol{\sigma}$ corresponds to a valid execution σ of Π by the simulated processes. We would like the states of the simulated processes at the end of σ to be stored by their respective simulators at the end of $\boldsymbol{\sigma}$. However, this property is not strong enough as an inductive hypothesis. In particular, when we inductively add one more step to $\boldsymbol{\sigma}$, the corresponding execution σ may have to change significantly to accommodate hidden, locally simulated steps. This is a significant technical hurdle.

The implementation of $\mathcal{M}$, described in Section 3, is non-blocking and, while `Block-Update` operations are not necessarily atomic, the `Update` operations that comprise them are. This lets us guarantee that the contents of $\mathcal{M}$ throughout a real execution match the contents of M at certain configurations in the corresponding simulated execution. However, because of the revisionist nature of the simulation (i.e. the locally simulated steps by the covering simulators), there are configurations in the simulated execution in which the contents of M do not match the contents of $\mathcal{M}$ in any configuration of the real execution. This is a reason why there is no short and easy way to capture the correspondence between the real and simulated executions. It requires a complex invariant with proper formalism and a rigorous proof, which is done in the full version of the paper. In particular, we capture properties of σ that hold at points where the locally simulated steps may be inserted.

Once we have shown that σ corresponds to a valid execution σ of the protocol, we prove that the simulation is wait-free and satisfies k-agreement and validity. To see that the simulation satisfies k-agreement, notice that any value that is output by a simulator is output by a process in σ. Since the protocol satisfies k-agreement, the set of values output by the simulated processes has size at most k. Moreover, because each simulator initially sets the inputs of its simulated processes to its own input and the protocol satisfies validity, the output of a simulator must be the input of some simulator. Hence the simulation satisfies validity.

Wait-freedom. Consider any Q-only execution and any Block-Update that begins during this execution. If this Block- Update is performed by the simulator $q \in Q$ with the lowest identifier, then, by Theorem 3, it will not return $\bigtriangledown$. Since covering simulators have lower identifiers than direct simulators, if covering simulators continue to perform Block-Update operations, then some covering simulator, q, will continue to perform atomic Block-Update operations. The number of different sets of components that may be covered by r processes is $\binom{m}{r}$. So, to construct a Block-Update to $r+1$ components, q needs to construct and perform at most $\binom{m}{r}$ atomic Block-Update operations to r components. Thus, q performs finitely many Block-Update operations. After q stops performing Block-Update operations, if covering simulators continue to perform Block-Update operations, then some other covering simulator will continue to perform atomic Block-Update operations. Thus, inductively, every covering simulator performs only finitely many Block-Update operations.

After covering simulators stop performing Block-Update operations, they will no longer apply update operations and, hence, cannot be observed by the x processes simulated by the x direct simulators. Since the simulated protocol is x-obstruction-free, these x processes and, hence, their direct simulators will return within a finite number of subsequent steps. Using these ideas and our invariant, we prove that no real process q_i, whether it is a covering simulator or a direct simulator, can apply infinitely many operations on $\mathcal{M}$.

If there is an infinite execution of the simulation, then some processes apply infinitely many accesses to the underlying single-writer snapshot object used to implement $\mathcal{M}$. Since our implementation of $\mathcal{M}$ is non-blocking, this means that infinitely many operations on $\mathcal{M}$ will complete. But this is impossible, since every real process applies only finitely many operations on $\mathcal{M}$. Thus the simulation is wait-free.

5 FROM NONDETERMINISTIC SOLO TERMINATION TO OBSTRUCTION-FREEDOM

A protocol is *nondeterministic solo terminating* if, for any process p and any configuration C, there exists a solo execution by p from C in which p outputs a value (and terminates) [23]. In this section, we prove the following theorem.

THEOREM 5. *If there is a nondeterministic solo terminating protocol for a task that only uses a multi-writer snapshot with m components, then there is an obstruction-free protocol for the task that only uses a multi-writer snapshot with m components.*

First, we need to formalize the notion of a nondeterministic solo terminating protocol. A nondeterministic protocol specifies a nondeterministic state machine M_p for each process p. Each state machine M_p is a 5-tuple $(S_p, \nu_p, \delta_p, I_p, F_p)$, where

- S_p is a set of states,
- $I_p \subset S_p$ is a set of initial states, one for each possible input to p,
- $F_p \subseteq S_p$ is a set of final states, one for each possible output of p,
- ν_p specifies the next step that p will perform in each non-final state $s \in S_p - F_p$, and
- δ_p is a transition function mapping each non-final state $s \in S_p - F_p$ and possible response from step $\nu_p(s)$ to a nonempty subset of S_p.

A state machine is *deterministic* if δ_p maps each non-final state and possible response to a state, rather than a subset of states.

In every configuration, each process p is in some state $s \in S_p$. Initially, each process is in one of its initial states and each component of the snapshot contains $\perp$. When allocated a step by the scheduler, p does nothing if it is in a final state. If p is in state $s \in S_p - F_p$, it performs step $\nu_p(s)$ and, if a is the response it receives from this step, p nondeterministically chooses its next state s' from $\delta_p(s, a)$. If s' is in F_p, we consider p to have output the value corresponding to s'.

Without loss of generality, we assume that each state $s \in S_p$ contains a possible view, $E_p(s)$, of the snapshot. It is $(\perp, \ldots, \perp)$ for each initial state in I_p and is updated as follows. Suppose that, when p performs $\nu_p(s)$, it gets response a and enters state $s' \in \delta(s, a)$. If $\nu_p(s)$ = update(j, v), then $E_p(s')$ is the same as $E_p(s)$ except component j is set to v. Otherwise, $\nu_p(s)$ is a scan and $E_p(s') = a$. Intuitively, $E_p(s)$ is what p expects to see in its next scan, if no other process has taken steps since its last step.

A *p-solo path* from a state s of length t is an alternating sequence of states in S_p and responses, $s_0, a_0, s_1, \ldots, a_{t-1}, s_t$, such that $s_0 = s$, $s_t \in F_p$, and, for each $0 \leq i < t$,

$s_{i+1} \in \delta_p(s_i, a_i)$,
if $\nu_p(s_i)$ is an update, then a_i = ACK, and
if $\nu_p(s_i)$ is a scan, then $a_i = E_p(s_i)$.

A p-solo path represents a solo terminating execution by p from a configuration C where p is in state s and $E_p(s)$ is the view of the snapshot at C.

If p is in state s in a reachable configuration C, then there exists a p-solo path from s. To see why, consider the execution σ from the initial configuration C_0 that is used to reach C. Let σ'' be the longest suffix of σ containing no scans by p and write $\sigma = \sigma'\sigma''$. Then σ' is either empty or ends with the last scan by p in σ. Let β be the subsequence of p's steps in σ'' and let $C' = C_0\sigma'\beta$. Note that C' is a reachable configuration of Π in which the state of p is s and the view of the snapshot is $E_p(s)$. Since Π is nondeterministic solo terminating, p has a solo terminating execution from C' and, hence, there is a p-solo path from s.

Given a nondeterministic solo terminating protocol, Π, we build a deterministic state machine $M'_p = (S_p, \nu_p, \delta'_p, I_p, F_p)$ from $M_p = (S_p, \nu_p, \delta_p, I_p, F_p)$, for each process p. The result is a deterministic protocol, Π', which uses the same snapshot. For each state $s \in S_p - F_p$ and response a, we define $\delta'_p(s, a)$ as follows. If there is a

p-solo path from s such that the response of step $v_p(s)$ is a, then we define $\delta'_p(s,a) = s_1$, where $\sigma(s,a) = s_0, a_0, s_1, \ldots, a_{t-1}, s_t$ is a shortest p-solo path with $s_0 = s$ and $a_0 = a$. Otherwise, we define $\delta'_p(s,a)$ to be any fixed state $s' \in \delta_p(s,a)$.

Correctness of Π': Observe that every execution of Π' is an execution of Π. This is because, for each process p, each state $s \in S_p - F_p$, and each response a to $v_p(s)$, $\delta'_p(s,a) \in \delta_p(s,a)$, so $\delta'_p(s,a)$ is a state that p could be in after performing $v_p(s)$ in Π. It follows that if Π is a protocol for a task, Π' is also a protocol for the task.

Obstruction-freedom of Π': Assume, for a contradiction, that there is an infinite solo execution α by some process p from a reachable configuration C_0. In this execution, p never enters a final state and, so, does not output a value. Let $C_0, e_0, C_1, e_1, \ldots$ be the alternating sequence of configurations and steps corresponding to α and, for $i \geq 0$, let $f_i \in S_p - F_p$ be the state of p in C_i and let a_i be the response of e_i. Since C_i is a reachable configuration in which p has state f_i, there is a p-solo path from f_i.

First, suppose that α contains only update steps, i.e. $e_i = v_p(f_i)$ is an update step, for all $i \geq 0$. Hence, there is a p-solo path from f_i where the response of $v_p(f_i)$ is a_i = ACK. By definition, $\sigma(f_i, a_i) = f_i, a_i, \sigma'(f_i, a_i)$, where $\sigma'(f_i, a_i)$ is a p-solo path from f_{i+1}. Since $v(f_{i+1})$ is an update step, the first response in $\sigma'(f_i, a_i)$ is a_{i+1} = ACK. Thus, for $i \geq 0$, the length of $\sigma(f_{i+1}, a_{i+1})$ is at most the length of $\sigma'(f_i, a_i)$, which is less than the length of $\sigma(f_i, a_i)$.

Now suppose that α contains a scan step. Let e_j be the first scan step in α. Then a_j is view of the snapshot at C_j and C_{j+1} and, by definition, $E_p(f_{j+1}) = a_j$. Since α is a solo execution by process p, $E_p(f_i)$ is the view in configuration C_i for all $i \geq j+1$. It follows that, for each $i \geq j+1$, f_i has a solo path where the response of step $v_p(f_i)$ is a_i. By definition, $\sigma(f_i, a_i) = f_i, a_i, \sigma'(f_i, a_i)$, where $\sigma'(f_i, a_i)$ is a p-solo path from f_{i+1}. Since $E_p(f_i)$ is the view of the snapshot at C_i, $\sigma(f_i, a_i)$ represents a solo execution from C_i, so each response following a state s in $\sigma(f_i, a_i)$ matches the response from the corresponding step $v_p(s)$ in the solo execution. In particular, the first response in $\sigma'(f_i, a_i)$ is a_{i+1}. Thus, for $i \geq j+1$, the length of $\sigma(f_{i+1}, a_{i+1})$ is at most the length of $\sigma'(f_i, a_i)$, which is less than the length of $\sigma(f_i, a_i)$.

In both cases, there is a $k \geq 0$ such that, for all $i \geq k$, the length of $\sigma(f_i, a_i)$ is decreasing. Let t be the length of $\sigma(f_k, a_k)$. Then there exists $k' \leq k+t$ such that the length of $\sigma(f_{k'}, a_{k'})$ is 0. Hence, $f_{k'} \in F_p$. This is a contradiction.

6 CONCLUSIONS AND FUTURE WORK

We conjecture that the space complexity of x-obstruction-free k-set agreement is $n - k + x$, matching the upper bound of [16]. Our paper makes significant progress by proving the first non-constant lower bound for non-anonymous processes. This lower bound is asymptotically tight when k and x are constant and tight when $x = 1$ and either $k = 1$ (obstruction-free consensus) and $k = n - 1$ (obstruction-free $(n-1)$-set agreement). Equally importantly, our simulation technique uses a new approach. It is conceivable that this approach can be extended to obtain a tight lower bound when $k > 1$ and $1 \leq x \leq k$.

Extending the techniques introduced in this paper and applying them to other problems may be fruitful. We demonstrate this in the full version of the paper by applying the simulation with minor modifications to get a space lower bound for approximate agreement that is within a factor of 2 of optimal. It is possible to generalize our approach to obtain space lower bounds for a class of *simulatable* tasks, which are either not deterministically solvable in a wait-free manner or have large lower bounds on their step complexity. It would be great to generalize our approach to a larger class of tasks.

We proved that a space lower bound for obstruction-free protocols implies a space lower bound for protocols that satisfy nondeterministic solo termination (including randomized wait-free protocols). by converting any nondeterministic solo terminating protocol to an obstruction-free protocol that uses the same number of registers. This allows researchers to focus on deriving space lower bounds for obstruction-free protocols.

It is known how to convert any deterministic obstruction-free protocol for n processes that has solo step complexity b into a randomized wait-free protocol against an oblivious adversary, which has expected step complexity polynomial in n and b [29]. However, our construction provides no bound on the solo step complexity of the resulting obstruction-free protocol. It would be interesting to improve the construction to bound the solo step complexity of the resulting protocols.

ACKNOWLEDGEMENTS

Part of this work was performed when Rati Gelashvili was a Ph.D. student at MIT. This work was supported by an NSERC Discovery Grant, an NSERC Postgraduate Scholarship, a University of Toronto Faculty of Arts & Science Postdoctoral Fellowship, NSF grants IIS-1607189, IIS-1447786, and CCF1563880, a donation from SUN Microsystems, and a grant from Intel Corporation.

REFERENCES

[1] Karl Abrahamson. 1988. On achieving consensus using a shared memory. In *Proceedings of the 7th ACM Symposium on Principles of Distributed Computing (PODC '88)*. 291–302.
[2] Yehuda Afek, Hagit Attiya, Danny Dolev, Eli Gafni, Michael Merritt, and Nir Shavit. 1993. Atomic snapshots of shared memory. *J. ACM* 40, 4 (1993), 873–890.
[3] James Aspnes and Maurice Herlihy. 1990. Fast randomized consensus using shared memory. *Journal of Algorithms* 11, 3 (1990), 441–461.
[4] Hagit Attiya and Armando Castañeda. 2013. A non-topological proof for the impossibility of k-set agreement. *Theoretical Computer Science* 512 (2013), 41 – 48.
[5] Hagit Attiya and Keren Censor. 2008. Tight bounds for asynchronous randomized consensus. *J. ACM* 55, 5 (2008), 20.
[6] Hagit Attiya and Faith Ellen. 2014. Impossibility Results for Distributed Computing. *Synthesis Lectures on Distributed Computing Theory* 5, 1 (2014), 1–162.
[7] Hagit Attiya, Alla Gorbach, and Shlomo Moran. 2002. Computing in totally anonymous asynchronous shared memory systems. *Information and Computation* 173, 2 (2002), 162–183.
[8] Hagit Attiya, Rachid Guerraoui, and Petr Kouznetsov. 2005. Computing with Reads and Writes in the Absence of Step Contention. In *Proceedings of the 30th International Symposium on Distributed Computing (DISC '05)*. 122–136.
[9] Hagit Attiya, Nancy Lynch, and Nir Shavit. 1994. Are wait-free algorithms fast? *J. ACM* 41, 4 (1994), 725–763.
[10] Hagit Attiya and Ami Paz. 2016. Counting-based Impossibility Proofs for Set Agreement and Renaming. *J. Parallel and Distrib. Comput.* 87, C (2016), 1–12.
[11] Hagit Attiya and Jennifer Welch. 2004. *Distributed Computing: Fundamentals, Simulations, and Advanced Topics.* John Wiley & Sons, USA.
[12] Paul Beame. 1986. Limits on the power of concurrent-write parallel machines. In *Proceedings of the 18th ACM Symposium on Theory of Computing (STOC '86)*. 169–176.
[13] Michael Ben-Or. 1983. Another Advantage of Free Choice (Extended Abstract): Completely Asynchronous Agreement Protocols. In *Proceedings of the 2nd ACM Symposium on Principles of Distributed Computing (PODC '83)*. 27–30.

[14] Elizabeth Borowsky and Eli Gafni. 1993. Generalized FLP impossibility result for t-resilient asynchronous computations. In *Proceedings of the 25th Annual ACM Symposium on Theory of Computing (STOC '93)*. 91–100.
[15] Elizabeth Borowsky, Eli Gafni, Nancy Lynch, and Sergio Rajsbaum. 2001. The BG distributed simulation algorithm. *Distributed Computing* 14, 3 (2001), 127–146.
[16] Zohir Bouzid, Michel Raynal, and Pierre Sutra. 2015. Anonymous obstruction-free (n, k)-set agreement with $n - k + 1$ atomic read/write registers. *Distributed Computing* 31, 2 (2015), 1–19.
[17] Jack R. Bowman. 2011. *Obstruction-free Snapshot, Obstruction-free Consensus, and Fetch-and-add Modulo k.* Technical Report TR2011-681. Dartmouth College.
[18] James E Burns and Nancy A Lynch. 1993. Bounds on shared memory for mutual exclusion. *Information and Computation* 107, 2 (1993), 171–184.
[19] Soma Chaudhuri. 1993. More choices allow more faults: Set consensus problems in totally asynchronous systems. *Information and Computation* 105, 1 (1993), 132–158.
[20] Carole Delporte-Gallet, Hugues Fauconnier, Eli Gafni, and Sergio Rajsbaum. 2013. Black Art: Obstruction-free k-set agreement with |MWMR registers| < |processes|. In *Proceedings of the 1st International Conference on Networked Systems (NETYS '13)*. 28–41.
[21] Carole Delporte-Gallet, Hugues Fauconnier, Petr Kuznetsov, and Eric Ruppert. 2015. On the Space Complexity of Set Agreement. In *Proceedings of the 34th ACM Symposium on Principles of Distributed Computing (PODC '15)*. 271–280.
[22] Danny Dolev, Nancy Lynch, Shlomit Pinter, Eugene Stark, and William Weihl. 1986. Reaching approximate agreement in the presence of faults. *J. ACM* 33, 3 (1986), 499–516.
[23] Faith Fich, Maurice Herlihy, and Nir Shavit. 1998. On the space complexity of randomized synchronization. *J. ACM* 45, 5 (1998), 843–862.
[24] Colin Fidge. 1991. Logical time in distributed computing systems. *Computer* 24, 8 (1991), 28–33.
[25] Michael J. Fischer, Nancy A. Lynch, and Michael S. Paterson. 1985. Impossibility of distributed consensus with one faulty process. *J. ACM* 32, 2 (1985), 374–382.
[26] Eli Gafni, Yuan He, Petr Kuznetsov, and Thibault Rieutord. 2016. Read-Write Memory and k-Set Consensus as an Affine Task. In *Proceedings of the 20th International Conference on Principles of Distributed Systems (OPODIS '16)*. 6:1–6:17.
[27] Eli Gafni, Petr Kuznetsov, and Ciprian Manolescu. 2014. A Generalized Asynchronous Computability Theorem. In *Proceedings of the 33rd ACM Symposium on Principles of Distributed Computing (PODC '14)*. 222–231.
[28] Rati Gelashvili. 2015. On the optimal space complexity of consensus for anonymous processes. In *Proceedings of the 29th International Symposium on Distributed Computing (DISC '15)*. 452–466.
[29] George Giakkoupis, Maryam Helmi, Lisa Higham, and Philipp Woelfel. 2013. An $O(\sqrt{n})$ Space Bound for Obstruction-Free Leader Election. In *Proceedings of the 27th International Symposium on Distributed Computing (DISC '13)*. 46–60.
[30] Rachid Guerraoui and Eric Ruppert. 2005. What can be implemented anonymously?. In *Proceedings of the 19th International Conference on Distributed Computing (DISC '05)*. 244–259.
[31] Maurice Herlihy. 1991. Wait-free synchronization. *ACM Transactions on Programming Languages and Systems* 13, 1 (1991), 124–149.
[32] Maurice Herlihy, Dmitry Kozlov, and Sergio Rajsbaum. 2013. *Distributed Computing Through Combinatorial Topology.* Morgan Kaufmann Publishers Inc.
[33] Maurice Herlihy, Victor Luchangco, and Mark Moir. 2003. Obstruction-Free Synchronization: Double-Ended Queues as an Example. In *Proceedings of the 23rd International Conference on Distributed Computing Systems (ICDCS '03)*. 522–.
[34] Maurice Herlihy and Nir Shavit. 1999. The topological structure of asynchronous computability. *J. ACM* 46, 6 (1999), 858–923.
[35] Maurice Herlihy and Jeannette Wing. 1990. Linearizability: A correctness condition for concurrent objects. *ACM Transactions on Programming Languages and Systems* 12, 3 (1990), 463–492.
[36] Leslie Lamport. 1978. Time, clocks, and the ordering of events in a distributed system. *Commun. ACM* 21, 7 (1978), 558–565.
[37] M. Loui and H. Abu-Amara. 1987. Memory Requirements for Agreement among Unreliable Asynchronous Processes. In *Advances in Computing Research.* Vol. 4. JAI Press, Inc., 163–183.
[38] Friedemann Mattern. 1989. Virtual time and global states of distributed systems. *Parallel and Distributed Algorithms* 1, 23 (1989), 215–226.
[39] Michael Saks, Nir Shavit, and Heather Woll. 1991. Optimal Time Randomized Consensus - Making Resilient Algorithms Fast in Practice. In *Proceedings of the Second Annual ACM-SIAM Symposium on Discrete Algorithms (SODA '91)*. 351–362.
[40] Michael Saks and Fotios Zaharoglou. 2000. Wait-free k-set agreement is impossible: The topology of public knowledge. *SIAM J. Comput.* 29, 5 (2000), 1449–1483.
[41] Vikram Saraph, Maurice Herlihy, and Eli Gafni. 2016. Asynchronous Computability Theorems for t-Resilient Systems. In *Proceedings of the 30th International Symposium on Distributed Computing (DISC '16)*. 428–441.
[42] Lefschetz Solomon. 1949. *Introduction to Topology.* Princeton University Press, New Jersey, United States.
[43] Gadi Taubenfeld. 2017. Contention-sensitive data structures and algorithms. *Theoretical Computer Science* 677 (2017), 41–55.
[44] Jiong Yang, Gil Neiger, and Eli Gafni. 1998. Structured derivations of consensus algorithms for failure detectors. In *Proceedings of the 17th ACM Symposium on Principles of Distributed Computing (PODC '98)*. 297–306.
[45] Leqi Zhu. 2015. Brief Announcement: Tight space bounds for memoryless anonymous consensus. In *Proceedings of the 29th International Symposium on Distributed Computing (DISC '15)*. 665.
[46] Leqi Zhu. 2016. A tight space bound for consensus. In *Proceedings of the 48th ACM Symposium on Theory of Computing (STOC '16)*. 345–350.

On the Classification of Deterministic Objects via Set Agreement Power

David Yu Cheng Chan
University of Toronto
Department of Computer Science
Toronto, Ontario, Canada
davidchan@cs.toronto.edu

Vassos Hadzilacos
University of Toronto
Department of Computer Science
Toronto, Ontario, Canada
vassos@cs.toronto.edu

Sam Toueg
University of Toronto
Department of Computer Science
Toronto, Ontario, Canada
sam@cs.toronto.edu

ABSTRACT

Since the early days of the shared memory model for distributed computing, researchers have sought a simple and precise characterization of an object's ability to implement other objects in a wait-free manner.

The first candidate for such a characterization was the object's *consensus number* [14]. But a characterization based on consensus numbers is *not* precise: there are pairs of objects with the *same* consensus number that are *not* equivalent (i.e., one cannot be implemented by instances of the other and registers). This was first shown for non-deterministic objects [24] and much later for deterministic objects as well [2].

A more recent candidate for such a characterization is the object's *set agreement power* [10]. In PODC 2017, it was shown that this characterization is also *not* precise: there are two objects with the *same* set agreement power that are *not* equivalent [6]. One of these two objects, however, is non-deterministic. So this left open one remaining final question: when restricted to *deterministic* objects, does the set agreement power of an object fully characterize its ability to implement other objects? More precisely: are any two *deterministic* objects with the same set agreement power equivalent? In this paper, we show the answer is again no. In fact, we prove the following stronger result: every level $n \geq 2$ of *Herlihy's consensus hierarchy* [14] contains two deterministic objects with the same set agreement power that are *not* equivalent (i.e., one of these two objects cannot be implemented using instances of the other and registers).

We also leverage the above result and a result in [12] to show that in any system with $n > 2$ processes, there is a deterministic wait-free object that is *not* equivalent to any wait-free task.

CCS CONCEPTS

• **Theory of computation → Concurrency**; *Parallel computing models*; *Distributed computing models*;

KEYWORDS

asynchronous system; shared memory; set agreement; consensus hierarchy

ACM Reference Format:
David Yu Cheng Chan, Vassos Hadzilacos, and Sam Toueg. 2018. On the Classification of Deterministic Objects via Set Agreement Power. In *PODC '18: ACM Symposium on Principles of Distributed Computing, July 23–27, 2018, Egham, United Kingdom.* ACM, New York, NY, USA, 10 pages. https://doi.org/10.1145/3212734.3212775

1 INTRODUCTION

Background, Motivation, and Result. Since the early days of the shared memory model for distributed computing, researchers have sought a simple and precise characterization of an object's ability to implement other objects in a wait-free manner.[1] The first candidate for such a characterization was the object's *consensus number* [14]: the maximum number of processes for which instances of the object and registers can solve the *consensus* problem. The consensus number of an object, however, is not a *precise* characterization of the object's ability to implement other objects: some objects have the *same* consensus number but are *not* equivalent (we say two objects are *equivalent* if each can be implemented by instances of the other and registers in a wait-free manner). This was first shown for non-deterministic objects [24] and later for deterministic objects as well [2].

Since the consensus number of an object does not fully characterize its ability to implement other objects, one may ask whether some natural extension of the consensus number, namely the *set agreement power* of an object [6, 10], does so (a conjecture along these lines was given in [10]). Intuitively, the set agreement power of an object is the infinite sequence $(n_1, n_2, \ldots, n_k, \ldots)$ where n_k is the maximum number of processes for which instances of the object and registers can solve the *k-set agreement* problem.[2] Note that the first component of the set agreement power of an object is simply its consensus number.

Is the set agreement power of an object indeed a precise characterization of its ability to implement other objects? In [6], we proved that the answer is no: we exhibited two objects that have the same set agreement power but are not equivalent. One of these two objects, however, is non-deterministic. So this left open one remaining final question: when restricted to *deterministic* objects,

[1] Unless otherwise specified, we consider objects, algorithms, and implementations that are *wait-free* [14, 21]. Moreover, we assume that all algorithms and implementations can use registers.

[2] In the k-set agreement problem [8], each process has an input value and must decide on one of the input values such that there are at most k distinct decision values.

PODC '18, July 23–27, 2018, Egham, United Kingdom

ACM ISBN 978-1-4503-5795-1/18/07...$15.00
https://doi.org/10.1145/3212734.3212775

does the set agreement power of an object fully characterize its ability to implement other objects? More precisely:

> Are any two *deterministic* objects with the same set agreement power equivalent?

In this paper, we show the answer is again no. In fact, we prove the following stronger result: every level $n \geq 2$ of *Herlihy's consensus hierarchy* [14] has two deterministic objects with the same set agreement power that are *not* equivalent (i.e., one of these two objects cannot be implemented using instances of the other and registers).

We also leverage the above result and a result in [12] to shed some light on the relation between wait-free objects and tasks: we show that in any system with $n > 2$ processes, there is a deterministic wait-free object that is not equivalent to any wait-free task.

Our Deterministic Objects. The objects at the core of our result are both fairly simple. The first is just the n-consensus object, the standard object that allows up to n processes to solve the consensus problem directly. The second, which we call *n-P&G* (for "Propose&Get"), is an n-consensus object that we weaken as follows: (1) *proposing* a value and *getting* the agreed upon value are two separate operations, (2) roughly speaking, the object forces two of the n processes to compete to obtain the agreed upon value and returns ? to losers, and (3) the other $n-2$ processes can get the agreed upon value unhindered. We give a precise definition of the n-P&G object in Section 3.

Proof Outline. We show that for all $n > 2$: (a) the n-P&G and $(n-1)$-consensus objects have the same set agreement power, but (b) the n-P&G object cannot be implemented using only $(n-1)$-consensus objects and registers.

To prove (a), we show that the set agreement power of both the n-P&G object and the $(n-1)$-consensus object is $(n_1, n_2, \ldots, n_k, \ldots)$ where $n_k = k(n-1)$. For the $(n-1)$-consensus object, this follows directly from results of Chaudhuri and Reiners [9]. For the n-P&G object, we first show that it solves the $(n-1)$-consensus problem, and so it has set agreement power $(n_1, n_2, \ldots, n_k, \ldots)$ where $n_k \geq k(n-1)$. We then prove that it has set agreement power $(n_1, n_2, \ldots, n_k, \ldots)$ where $n_k \leq k(n-1)$, and so $n_k = k(n-1)$. We do so by deriving a novel extension of the Borowsky-Gafni (BG) simulation algorithm [4, 5] that allows the simulated algorithm to use n-P&G objects (in addition to registers); we then apply this simulation algorithm to transform the known impossibility result that $k+1$ processes cannot solve the k-set agreement problem using only registers [4, 5, 15, 25], into a new impossibility result that $k(n-1)+1$ processes cannot solve the k-set agreement problem using only n-P&G objects and registers, and so $n_k \leq k(n-1)$.

To prove (b), we introduce a problem called the *n-SLC problem* and show that (i) the n-SLC problem can be solved using the n-P&G object, and (ii) the n-SLC problem can*not* be solved using only $(n-1)$-consensus objects and registers. To show (ii), we leverage a result of Hadzilacos and Toueg [13] that $(n-1)$-consensus objects and registers cannot solve the *n-DAC problem*, a problem that is no harder than the n-SLC problem.

By (a) and (b), the deterministic n-P&G and $(n-1)$-consensus objects have the same set agreement power but are not equivalent.

Roadmap. The rest of this paper is organized as follows. We sketch the model in Section 2 and describe our n-P&G object in Section 3. In Section 4 we prove that the n-P&G object and the $(n-1)$-consensus object have the same set agreement power. In Section 5 we prove that the n-P&G object cannot be implemented using only $(n-1)$-consensus objects and registers. In Section 6, we show that the deterministic n-P&G object is not equivalent to any task. We discuss some related BG simulation work in Section 7, and we conclude the paper with some brief remarks in Section 8.

2 MODEL SKETCH

We consider systems with asynchronous processes that apply operations on objects and may fail by crashing [14]. In our model, objects have ports [23]: each operation *op* is invoked on a specific port of an object, and the response it receives may depend on the port chosen. Processes can choose to invoke an operation on any port of any object, but no two operations may be applied on the same port of an object concurrently. Thus the number of ports of an object effectively limits the number of processes that may access it concurrently. Henceforth, we consider only algorithms that are *well-formed*, i.e., algorithms that never apply concurrent operations on the same port of an object.

The *sequential specification* of an object describes its behavior when operations are applied sequentially. We consider objects that are *linearizable* (with respect to their sequential specification): they behave as if *all* operations, including concurrent ones, are applied sequentially, so that each operation appears to take effect instantaneously at some distinct point between its invocation and response [17].

For example, the *n-consensus object* has n ports. Each process can apply a PROPOSE(v) operation on any port $i \in [1..n]$ of this object for any $v \in \mathbb{Z}^+$. Since no two processes may apply operations on the same port concurrently, up to n processes can access an n-consensus object concurrently. The sequential specification of the n-consensus object states that all operations return the proposal value of the first operation that was applied on the object. It is clear that an n-consensus object can be used solve the *n-consensus problem.*

3 n-P&G OBJECTS

In this section, we define deterministic and linearizable *n-P&G* objects for $n > 2$. Intuitively, the n-P&G object is a modified n-ported consensus object, where: (1) *proposing* a value and *getting* the agreed upon value are two separate operations, and (2) two of the n processes have to compete to get the agreed upon value, while the other processes can get the agreed value without competition. Roughly speaking, the competition works as follows. A process that tries to obtain the consensus value from port $i \in \{1, 2\}$ of the object, must apply *two* consecutive get operations on that port: the first acquires a token that gives it the right to obtain the consensus value, and the second obtains the consensus value *if the token was not taken away by another process.* A process that applies a get operation on any port $i > 2$ of the object, obtains the consensus value immediately (without competing for the token). We now define the n-P&G object more precisely.

The n-P&G object has $n > 2$ ports. It supports operations PROPOSE(v) for $v \in \mathbb{Z}^+$, and GET(), each of which can be applied to any port $i \in [1..n]$. A PROPOSE(v) operation applied to port i is denoted

Figure 1 Sequential specification of the n-P&G object

```
1: procedure PROPOSE(v, i) { v ∈ ℤ⁺; i ∈ [1..n] }
     {* PROPOSE(v) operation applied to port i *}
2:   if val = ⊥ then
3:     val ← v
4:   return DONE

5: procedure GET(i) { i ∈ [1..n] }
     {* GET() operation applied to port i *}
6:   if i ≤ 2 and pri + i is odd then
7:     pri ← pri + 1
8:     return ?
9:   else
10:    return val
```

PROPOSE(v, i); similarly, a GET() operation applied to port i is denoted GET(i). The *sequential specification* of the n-P&G object describes how the object behaves when it is accessed sequentially. It can be defined as a deterministic automaton (which has a set of states, a set of operations, a set of responses, and a deterministic state transition function) whose behavior is described in Figure 1.

The state of the n-P&G object is a tuple (val, pri), such that:

- val $\in \mathbb{Z}^+ \cup \{\perp\}$ is initially $\perp$.
- pri $\in \mathbb{Z}^+$ is initially 1.

The val field is used to store the agreed upon value, and it is set by the first PROPOSE$(-,-)$ operation. The pri field is an integer counter that specifies which one of GET(1) and GET(2) has the token: if pri is odd then GET(1) has the token, if it is even then GET(2) has the token. From lines 6 to 10 of Figure 1, if a GET(i) operation has the token, or $i > 2$, then it returns the consensus value stored in val; otherwise, it changes the parity of the pri counter (to get the token for the next GET(i) operation) and returns ?.

Intuitively, a GET(i) operation is prioritized if it has the token or $i > 2$ (so it has the right to obtain the consensus value). More precisely, a GET(i) operation is *prioritized* if and only if, immediately before it is applied, either pri $+\, i$ is even or $i > 2$.

From Figure 1, it is easy to see that:

OBSERVATION 1. *The sequential specification of an n-P&G object satisfies the following properties:*

(1) *If a* GET$(-)$ *operation is preceded by a* PROPOSE$(-,-)$ *operation, then it does not return* $\perp$.
(2) *All* GET$(-)$ *operations that do not return* $\perp$ *or ? return the proposal value of the first* PROPOSE$(-,-)$ *operation.*
(3) *If, for some* $i \in \{1,2\}$, *there is a time after which there are no* GET(i) *operations, then only finitely many* GET$(-)$ *operations return ?.*
(4) *For all* $i \in [3..n]$, *no* GET(i) *operation returns ?.*

We consider n-P&G objects that are *linearizable* (with respect to their sequential specification): they behave as if *all* operations, including concurrent operations on different ports, are applied sequentially, so that each operation appears to take effect instantaneously at some distinct point between its invocation and response [17].

Algorithm 2 Solving the $(n-1)$-consensus problem using an n-P&G object $\mathcal{D}$.

```
   Code executed by each process q ∈ [1..n − 1] with input v_q ∈ ℤ⁺:
1: D.PROPOSE(v_q, q + 1)
2: repeat
3:   val ← D.GET(q + 1)
4: until val ≠ ?
5: decide val
```

4 THE SET AGREEMENT POWER OF THE n-P&G OBJECT

We now show that the n-P&G object has the same set agreement power as the $(n-1)$-consensus object. It is known that:

THEOREM 2 (CHAUDHURI AND REINERS [9]). *For all* $n > 2$, *the* $(n-1)$*-consensus object has set agreement power* $(n_1, n_2, \ldots, n_k, \ldots)$ *such that, for all* $k \geq 1$, $n_k = k(n-1)$.

4.1 Lower Bound

THEOREM 3. *For all* $n > 2$, *the* $(n-1)$*-consensus problem can be solved using an n-P&G object.*

PROOF. Without loss of generality, let the $n-1$ processes be numbered 1 to $n-1$, and let v_q denote the input value of each process q. To solve the $(n-1)$-consensus problem with an n-P&G object $\mathcal{D}$, each process q executes Algorithm 2. Note that each process $q \in [1..n-1]$ performs operations only on port $q+1$ of the n-P&G object $\mathcal{D}$. Thus, this algorithm satisfies the requirement that no two operations are applied on the same port of $\mathcal{D}$ concurrently. Furthermore, no process performs an operation on port 1 of $\mathcal{D}$.

In Algorithm 2, each process performs a PROPOSE$(-,-)$ operation on $\mathcal{D}$ with its own input value (line 1), and repeatedly performs GET$(-)$ operations until it receives a non-? value (lines 2 to 4), which it then decides in line 5. We now show that the Validity, Agreement, and Termination properties of the consensus problem hold.

Since each process performs a PROPOSE$(-,-)$ before performing any GET$(-)$ operation, by Observation 1(1) no GET$(-)$ operation on $\mathcal{D}$ returns $\perp$. Thus, if a process decides a value v (in line 5), then v was returned by a GET$(-)$ operation in line 3, and $v \notin \{\perp, ?\}$. So, by Observation 1(2), v was proposed by the first PROPOSE$(-,-)$ operation on $\mathcal{D}$, and therefore Validity and Agreement hold. Finally, since there are no GET(1) operations on $\mathcal{D}$, by Observation 1(3), every correct process will eventually exit the loop of lines 2-4, and decide; so Termination holds. □ Theorem 3

It is clear that any solution for the $(n-1)$-consensus problem can be used to implement the $(n-1)$-consensus object. So the n-P&G object has *at least* the set agreement power of the $(n-1)$-consensus object. Thus, by Theorems 2 and 3:

COROLLARY 4. *For all* $n > 2$, *the n-P&G object has set agreement power* $(n_1, n_2, \ldots, n_k, \ldots)$ *such that, for all* $k \geq 1$, $n_k \geq k(n-1)$.

4.2 Upper Bound

It now suffices to show that for all $n > 2$, the n-P&G object has *at most* the set agreement power of the $(n-1)$-consensus object, i.e., that it has set agreement power $(n_1, n_2, \ldots, n_k, \ldots)$ such that, for all $k \geq 1$, $n_k \leq k(n-1)$.

THEOREM 5. *For all $n > 2$ and $k \geq 1$, the $(k(n-1)+1, k)$-SA problem cannot be solved using n-P&G objects and registers.*

The proof of this theorem is the technically hardest result in this paper, and it is given in detail in the full paper. In the following, we outline this proof.

Suppose, for contradiction, that there exists a wait-free well-formed algorithm A_P that solves the $(k(n-1)+1, k)$-SA problem in a system P that has $|P| = k(n-1)+1$ processes, and n-P&G objects and registers. Without loss of generality, we assume that in system P, every process $p \in [1..|P|]$ owns a single-writer multi-reader register, and there are no other registers.[3]

Using the algorithm A_P, we construct a wait-free algorithm A_Q that solves the $(k+1, k)$-SA problem in a system Q that has $|Q| = k+1$ processes and *only* registers — which is known to be impossible [4, 5, 15, 25]. Intuitively, in the algorithm A_Q, the $k+1$ *real* processes of the system Q simulate an execution of A_P by the $k(n-1)+1$ *virtual* processes of the system P. This algorithm A_Q is a novel extension of the Borowsky-Gafni (BG) simulation algorithm introduced in [4, 5]: the original BG simulation algorithm showed how to simulate the algorithm A_P if A_P only uses registers; since A_P also uses n-P&G objects, the extension adds code to also simulate n-P&G objects. In contrast to the original BG simulation algorithm, where each real process that crashes "blocks" the simulation of at most one virtual process, in our simulation each real process crash can block at most $n-1$ virtual processes.

The simulation algorithm A_Q. Intuitively, each real process $q \in [1..|Q|]$ simulates an execution of the algorithm A_P by the virtual processes in P. More precisely, for each virtual process $p \in [1..|P|]$, each real process q has a thread q_p that simulates the steps of virtual process p in A_P.

To ensure that all real processes simulate the *same* execution of A_P, they use *safe agreement objects* [4, 5], which are consensus-like objects that can be implemented using registers but are *not* wait-free. Each safe agreement object supports PROPOSE(v) and DECIDE() operations that satisfy the following properties:

- **Agreement:** If two invocations of DECIDE() return v_1 and v_2 then $v_1 = v_2$.
- **Validity:** If some invocation of DECIDE() returns v then some process previously invoked PROPOSE(v).
- **Termination (a):** Every PROPOSE($-$) operation invoked by a correct process eventually completes.
- **Termination (b):** If no process crashes during a PROPOSE($-$) operation, then every DECIDE() operation invoked by a correct process eventually completes.

The threads of the real processes that simulate (the execution of the algorithm A_P by) a virtual process p use safe agreement objects to agree on the steps of p. Reaching this agreement, however, comes at a cost: by Termination (b), if a real process q crashes while one of its threads q_p is executing a PROPOSE($-$) operation on a safe agreement object, the thread q'_p of every other real process q' that simulates p could be stuck executing a non-terminating DECIDE() operation on that object, thereby preventing progress in the simulation of virtual process p by *all* real processes.

[3] It is known that arbitrarily many multi-writer multi-reader registers can be implemented from a single array of single-writer multi-reader registers, one for each process [20, 26].

Algorithm 3 Implementation of a safe agreement object O_{safe} by the real processes of system Q.

Shared Memory:
$V[1..|Q|]$: A snapshot object; all fields initially $(\bot, 0)$.

A real process $q \in [1..|Q|]$ performs PROPOSE(v) and DECIDE() operations on the safe agreement object O_{safe} as follows:

```
procedure PROPOSE(v)
    V[q].WRITE((v, 1))
    snap ← V.SNAPSHOT()
    if snap does not contain (−, 2) then
        V[q].WRITE((v, 2))
    else
        V[q].WRITE((v, 0))
    return DONE

procedure DECIDE()
    repeat
        snap ← V.SNAPSHOT()
    until snap does not contain (−, 1)
    Let ṽ be the smallest value s.t. (ṽ, 2) ∈ snap.
    return ṽ
```

To prevent the crash of a real process q from blocking the progress of too many virtual processes, the threads of q use a local lock LOCK_q to ensure that at most one of them is within a PROPOSE($-$) operation on a safe agreement object at any time.

Algorithm 3 shows an implementation of a safe agreement object O_{safe} that uses a $\{0, 1, 2\}$-level mechanism [4, 5]. This implementation uses a *snapshot* object, which is a linearizable object that can be implemented using registers [1]. Roughly speaking, a snapshot object is composed of an array of registers referred to as the fields of the snapshot object. Each field supports standard WRITE(v) operations that replace the field's current value with the parameter v, and the object as a whole supports SNAPSHOT() operations that return the current value of every field in the array.

In addition to safe agreement objects, the simulation algorithm A_Q also requires base objects for simulating the n-P&G objects and registers used by the simulated algorithm A_P. To simulate the registers of A_P, we use an array of snapshot objects such that for each virtual process $p \in [1..|P|]$, $MEM[1..|Q|][p]$ is a snapshot object that simulates the register owned by p. To simulate an n-P&G object O, we use the following base objects:

- A *snapshot object* $VAL_O[1..|Q|][1..|P|]$:
  Intuitively, VAL_O simulates the `val` field of the n-P&G object O. In our simulation algorithm, all fields of VAL_O are initially $(\bot, 0)$.[4] For each $q \in [1..|Q|]$, the real process q owns (is the only writer of) the field $VAL_O[q][p]$ for every $p \in [1..|P|]$.
- A *max register* PRI_O:
  Intuitively, PRI_O simulates the `pri` field of the n-P&G object O. Note that linearizable max registers can be implemented using registers [3]. Roughly speaking, max registers are modified registers that support READMAX() and WRITEMAX(v) operations instead of standard READ() and WRITE(v) operations of registers. READMAX() is identical to READ(), but WRITEMAX(v) differs from WRITE(v) in that the value of the

[4] We consider $\bot < v$, for all $v \in \mathbb{Z}^+ \cup \{0\}$.

register is replaced with v if and only if v is larger than the current value; otherwise the value of the register remains the same. Thus the value of a max register is simply the maximum of all values that have been written into it, including its initial value. In our simulation algorithm, PRI_O has initial value 1.

Since the snapshot and max register base objects are linearizable, we assume that they are atomic (i.e., operations on them are instantaneous).

Algorithms 4 and 5 present the code for this extended simulation algorithm A_Q, with accesses of the local lock LOCK_q highlighted in red. Algorithm 4 also displays in black the code of the BG simulation algorithm (as given in [22]), with our additional code for simulating n-P&G objects shown in blue.

For each real process $q \in [1..|Q|]$ and each virtual process $p \in [1..|P|]$, thread q_p executes algorithm A_Q as follows. First, thread q_p acquires LOCK_q to propose v_q, the input value of the real process q, to a safe agreement object (lines 4 to 8); this is to agree with every other thread q'_p on the input value v_p of virtual process p. Then thread q_p enters an unbounded loop where in each loop iteration $x \geq 1$, thread q_p simulates the x-th step of virtual process p according to algorithm A_P. This step is simulated as follows.

- If the step of p is to write a value u to the register owned by p, thread q_p writes the pair (u, x) into the field $MEM[q][p]$ of the snapshot object $MEM[1..|Q|][p]$ (line 12).
- If the step of p is to read a value from the register owned by a virtual process p', thread q_p first finds the value u paired with the largest step number in the snapshot object $MEM[1..|Q|][p']$ (lines 15 to 17). Thread q_p then acquires LOCK_q to propose u to a safe agreement object to ensure that all simulations of this read step of p read the same value (lines 18 to 21).
- If the step of p is to decide a value u, and the real process q that created thread q_p has not yet decided, thread q_p makes the real process q also decide u (lines 26 to 27).
- If the step of p is to perform a $\text{PROPOSE}(v, i)$ operation op on an n-P&G object O (Algorithm 5, lines 30 to 41), then intuitively, thread q_p competes with other threads to set the `val` field of O, which is simulated by the snapshot object VAL_O (lines 31 to 39). The mechanism used to win this competition is essentially the {0,1,2}-level mechanism used by safe agreement objects (as shown in Algorithm 3). More precisely:

(1) Thread q_p checks whether VAL_O already contains level 1 or 2 proposals (lines 31 to 32); if so, thread q_p simply returns DONE (line 41) without changing VAL_O.
(2) Otherwise, thread q_p acquires LOCK_q (line 33).
(3) Thread q_p elevates its proposal v from level 0 to level 1 by writing $(v, 1)$ into $VAL_O[q][p]$ (line 34).
(4) Thread q_p checks whether VAL_O already contains level 2 proposals (lines 35 to 36). If not, thread q_p elevates its proposal v from level 1 to level 2 by writing $(v, 2)$ into $VAL_O[q][p]$ (line 37); otherwise, thread q_p reduces its proposal v from level 1 to level 0 by writing $(v, 0)$ into $VAL_O[q][p]$ (line 39).
(5) Thread q_p releases LOCK_q (line 40), and then returns DONE (line 41).

Algorithm 4 The Algorithm A_Q executed by the real processes of system Q to simulate the execution of the Algorithm A_P by the virtual processes of system P.

```
Shared Memory:
MEM[1..|Q|][1..|P|]: For each p ∈ [1..|P|], MEM[1..|Q|][p] is a snapshot
object, all fields initially (u_p, 0) where u_p is the initial value of the register owned
by p in A_P.
SAFE[1..|P|][0..∞][1..∞]: An array of safe agreement objects, all initially in
the fresh state.
Max registers and snapshot objects for simulating each n-P&G object O, as listed
in Algorithm 5.

Local Variables for each real process q ∈ [1..|Q|]:
For each virtual process p ∈ [1..|Q|], state_p: state of p according to q.
LOCK_q: a lock that is held by at most one of the |P| threads of q at any time.

Code executed by each real process q ∈ [1..|Q|] with input v_q ∈ ℤ⁺:
1:  Create local lock LOCK_q.
2:  For every virtual process p ∈ [1..|P|], create a thread q_p.
3:  parallel for each thread q_p, p ∈ [1..|P|], do
      {* Each thread q_p simulates the execution of virtual process p *}
4:    LOCK_q.ACQUIRE()
5:    SAFE[p][0][1].PROPOSE(v_q)
6:    LOCK_q.RELEASE()
7:    v_p ← SAFE[p][0][1].DECIDE()
8:    state_p ← initial state of p in A_P with input value v_p.
9:    for x ← 1 to ∞ do
        {* Simulate the x-th step of virtual process p in algorithm A_P *}
10:     Let op be the next operation of p in state_p according to algorithm A_P.
11:     case op is a WRITE(u) operation on the register of p.
12:       MEM[q][p].WRITE((u, x))
13:       ret ← DONE
14:     case op is a READ() operation on the register of some p' ∈ [1..|P|].
15:       snap ← MEM[1..|Q|][p'].SNAPSHOT()
16:       y ← x', where x' is largest (−, x') ∈ snap.
17:       u ← ṽ, such that (ṽ, y) ∈ snap.
18:       LOCK_q.ACQUIRE()
19:       SAFE[p][x][1].PROPOSE(u)
20:       LOCK_q.RELEASE()
21:       ret ← SAFE[p][x][1].DECIDE()
22:     case op is a PROPOSE(v, i) or GET(i) operation on some n-P&G object O.
23:       Simulate the execution of op on O as described by Algorithm 5.
24:       ret ← response of O to op by this simulation.
25:     case op is a DECIDE(u)
26:       if q has not decided then
27:         decide u
28:       ret ← DONE
29:     state_p ← the new state of p in A_P after receiving ret from its x-th step
```

- If the step of p is to perform a $\text{GET}(i)$ operation on an n-P&G object O, thread q_p repeatedly attempts to obtain the state (`val`, `pri`) of O so that it can return the correct value. To obtain the value of the `pri` field of O from the max register PRI_O, thread q_p performs a $\text{READMAX}()$ operation on PRI_O (line 51).

The mechanism used to obtain the value of the `val` field of O from VAL_O is a modification of the {0,1,2}-level mechanism used by safe agreement objects, as we now explain. With a safe agreement object, a process attempting to obtain the value of the object by performing a $\text{DECIDE}()$ operation on that object must loop until there are no level 1 proposals. Thus if a proposal remains at level 1 forever, then every process performing a $\text{DECIDE}()$ operation may loop forever, so all $\text{DECIDE}()$ operations may never return. In our case, we take advantage of the fact that a $\text{GET}(i)$ operation that is not prioritized, i.e., one such that $i \leq 2$ and `pri` + i is odd, does *not* need to find out the value of the `val`, because

Algorithm 5 Code executed to simulate a n-P&G object O.

```
    Shared Memory:
    VAL_O[1..|Q|][1..|P|]: A snapshot object; all fields initially (⊥, 0).
    PRI_O: A max register; initially 1.
    Code executed by the thread q_p of real process q to simulate the x-th step of
    virtual process p when this step is a PROPOSE(v, i) or GET(i) operation on O:
30: procedure PROPOSE(v, i) { v ∈ Z+; i ∈ [1..n] }
      {* PROPOSE(v) operation applied to port i of O *}
31:   snap ← VAL_O.SNAPSHOT()
32:   if all fields of snap are (−, 0) then
33:       LOCK_q.ACQUIRE()
34:       VAL_O[q][p].WRITE((v, 1))
35:       snap ← VAL_O.SNAPSHOT()
36:       if snap does not contain (−, 2) then
37:           VAL_O[q][p].WRITE((v, 2))
38:       else
39:           VAL_O[q][p].WRITE((v, 0))
40:       LOCK_q.RELEASE()
41:   return DONE

42: procedure GET(i) { i ∈ [1..n] }
      {* GET() operation applied to port i of O *}
43:   for j ← 1 to ∞ do
44:       val ← ?
45:       snap ← VAL_O.SNAPSHOT()
46:       if all fields of snap are (−, 0) then
47:           val ← ⊥
48:       else if snap contains (−, 2) but not (−, 1) then
49:           Let ṽ be the smallest value s.t. (ṽ, 2) ∈ snap
50:           val ← ṽ
51:       pri ← PRI_O.READMAX()
52:       LOCK_q.ACQUIRE()
53:       SAFE[p][x][j].PROPOSE((val, pri))
54:       LOCK_q.RELEASE()
55:       (val, pri) ← SAFE[p][x][j].DECIDE()
56:       if i ≤ 2 and pri + i is odd then
57:           PRI_O.WRITEMAX(pri + 1)
58:           return ?
59:       if val ≠ ? then
60:           return val
```

by the sequential specification of the n-P&G object, such a GET(i) operation simply returns ?. Thus in our modified {0,1,2}-level mechanism, the thread q_p that simulates a GET(i) operation by virtual process p only loops until either (a) there are no level 1 proposals, as in the original safe agreement mechanism, *or* (b) it finds that the GET(i) operation is not prioritized (in which case it returns ?). So even if a proposal remains at level 1 forever, the GET(i) operation may still be able to return.

More precisely, to simulate a GET(i) operation that is the x-th step of a virtual process p, thread q_p enters a loop where in each loop iteration $j \geq 1$ (Algorithm 5, lines 42 to 60):

(1) Thread q_p attempts to determine the value of the `val` field of O from VAL_O as follows (lines 44 to 50): if there are only level 0 proposals, it sets *val* to $\perp$ (line 47), indicating that the `val` field of O still has its initial value $\perp$; if there are level 2 proposals but no level 1 proposals, it sets *val* to the smallest value u such that u is a level 2 proposal (line 50); otherwise, *val* remains ? (as initially set in line 44), indicating that so far thread q_p has failed to find the value of the `val` field of O.

(2) Thread q_p determines the value of the `pri` field of O by performing a READMAX() operation on PRI_O and assigning the response to *pri* (line 51).

(3) Thread q_p acquires LOCK$_q$ to propose (*val*, *pri*) to a safe agreement object to ensure that all of the threads that execute the j-th loop iteration while simulating this GET(i) operation agree on the (`val`, `pri`) state of O to use for this j-th loop iteration (lines 52 to 55).

(4) Thread q_p uses the agreed (`val`, `pri`) state of O for this j-th loop iteration to determine if this GET(i) operation is prioritized (line 56).
   - If it is not prioritized, thread q_p performs a WRITEMAX(`pri`+ 1) operation on PRI_O to increment the `pri` field of O (line 57), and then returns ? (line 58).
   - If it is prioritized and `val` ≠ ? (line 59), thread q_p returns `val` (line 60).

(5) If thread q_p does not return in the j-th loop iteration (line 58 or 60), it goes to the $j+1$-th loop iteration.

The simulated history of algorithm A_P. We assume that in the system Q, there is at least one real process that is *correct*, i.e. it does not crash. Let H_Q be an arbitrary infinite history of A_Q (Algorithm 4) by the $k+1$ real processes in the system Q. Note that in this history, because of the use of safe agreement objects, the simulations of each virtual process p by different real processes cannot diverge: if two real processes simulate the x-th step of p, then that step is the application of the same operation on the same object and with the same return value. So from H_Q we can construct a well-defined simulated history H_P of the $k(n-1)+1$ virtual processes in the system P such that for each operation *op* of virtual process p:

- The execution interval of *op begins* at the earliest time that thread q_p of any real process q begins simulating *op*.
- The execution interval of *op ends* at the earliest time that thread q_p of any real process q completes simulating *op*. (If no real process ever completes simulating *op*, then *op* is *incomplete* in H_P.)
- If *op* is complete, then *op* returns the value returned by every complete simulation of *op*.

Liveness of the simulation algorithm. We now outline the proof that every correct real process in the history H_Q of the simulation algorithm A_Q simulates infinitely many steps of some virtual process in the history H_P of the simulated algorithm A_P. Henceforth, the lines of the simulation code that are protected by a local lock, namely, lines 5, 19, 53, and lines 34 to 39 are called the *critical parts* of the simulation.

Let q be an arbitrary correct real process, and recall that it has $|P| = k(n-1)+1$ threads, each simulating a distinct virtual process. First, suppose no real process crashes within a critical part of the simulation. Then it is easy to show that for each virtual process p, thread q_p simulates infinitely many steps of p. Roughly speaking, this is because in the simulation algorithm A_Q, thread q_p can only become stuck in two ways, both of which require some real process q' to crash within a critical part of the simulation:

- For some integers $x \geq 0$ and $j \geq 1$, thread q_p could invoke a DECIDE() operation that never completes on the safe agreement object *SAFE*[p][x][j]. This however, requires a real process to crash while performing a PROPOSE(−) operation on *SAFE*[p][x][j] (in line 5, 19, or 53).

- Within the simulation of some GET(−) operation invoked by p on some n-P&G object O, thread q_p could execute infinitely many loop iterations of the for loop on lines 43 to 60. This however, requires a real process to crash while it has a level 1 proposal in VAL_O (within lines 34 to 39). Otherwise, thread q_p will eventually find the value of the `val` field of O, and return it on line 60.

Our goal is to show that even if all $|Q| - 1 = k$ real processes other than q crash, at least one of the $|P| = k(n-1)+1$ threads of q is *not blocked*, i.e., at least one of the threads of q simulates infinitely many steps of some virtual process. So intuitively, it suffices to show that each real process crash blocks at most $n - 1$ threads of q.

In the simulation algorithm A_Q, every real process q' uses its local lock $\text{LOCK}_{q'}$ to ensure that *at most one* of its threads is within a critical part of the simulation at any time. Thus, if a real process q' crashes, it does so within at most one critical part of the simulation. There are two cases: either (1) this critical part involves a safe agreement object (line 5, 19, or 53), or (2) this critical part is within the simulation of a PROPOSE(−, −) operation on an n-P&G object O (lines 34 to 39).

First consider case (1); i.e., suppose that a real process q' crashes within a critical part involving a safe agreement object $SAFE[p][x][j]$ for some virtual process p and some integers $x \geq 0$ and $j \geq 1$ (line 5, 19, or 53). This crash may leave an incomplete PROPOSE(−) operation that could cause a DECIDE() operation invoked by thread q_p on $SAFE[p][x][j]$ to never complete; so this crash would block thread q_p. However, it would not affect the other threads of q, since they do not access $SAFE[p][x][j]$. So if a real process crashes within a critical part involving a safe agreement object, at most one thread of q is blocked.

Next, consider case (2); i.e., suppose that a real process q' crashes within the critical part of the simulation of a PROPOSE(−, −) operation on an n-P&G object O (lines 34 to 39). This crash may leave a level 1 proposal in VAL_O forever. We claim that this may block at most $n - 1$ threads of q. Suppose, for contradiction, that n threads of q are blocked. Intuitively, each of these n threads of q is stuck in a simulation of a distinct GET(−) operation on O: it is executing infinitely many loop iterations of the for loop on lines 43 to 60 because, in every iteration, the level 1 proposal left in VAL_O prevents it from finding the value of the `val` field of O. Since A_P is well-formed, in the full paper we show that these n GET(−) operations are on distinct ports of O. Let op_i be the GET(−) operation on port $i \in [1..n]$.

We claim that no simulation of op_i completes. This is because if a simulation of op_i completes in some loop iteration j, the use of the safe agreement object on lines 53 to 55 ensures that the thread of q simulating op_i will also complete in loop iteration j (contradicting our assumption that this thread of q is blocked). Thus op_i is incomplete in H_P.

Since A_P is well-formed and every port $i \in [1..n]$ of O has an incomplete operation op_i, in the full paper we show that there is a time after which no other operation is invoked on O. So there is a time after which the `pri` field of O stops changing; let r be the final value of `pri`. Without loss of generality, suppose r is even (a symmetric argument holds for the case where r is odd). Since $r + i$ is odd for $i = 1$, there is a time after which the thread of q simulating op_1 (which loops forever in lines 43 to 60) will find that the `pri` field of O contains r, evaluate the conditional on line 56 as true, and return ? on line 58 — contradicting our earlier claim that no simulation of op_1 completes. So if a real process crashes within the critical part of the simulation of a PROPOSE(−, −) operation on an n-P&G object O, at most $n - 1$ threads of q are blocked.

Since the crash of a real process blocks at most $n-1$ threads of q, even if k out of the $|Q| = k + 1$ real processes of Q crash, at least one of the $|P| = k(n - 1) + 1$ threads of q is not blocked, i.e., this thread simulates infinitely many steps of a virtual process in P.

Safety of the simulation algorithm. We need to prove that the real processes that execute our extended BG simulation algorithm A_Q in system Q (which has only registers) correctly simulate an execution of the algorithm A_P by the virtual processes of system P (which has registers and n-P&G objects). If the algorithm A_P is such that no process in P ever accesses n-P&G objects, then the correctness of A_Q follows directly from the correctness of the original BG simulation algorithm [4, 5, 22]. This is because, in this case, no real process would ever execute the code of A_Q that we added to the original BG simulation to simulate accesses to n-P&G objects by the virtual processes of P (lines 22 to 24 and lines 30 to 60). So to prove the correctness of our extended BG simulation algorithm A_Q, it suffices to show that this additional code correctly simulates accesses to n-P&G objects by the virtual processes of P. More precisely, we must show that for each n-P&G object O, the history H_P^O of the operations on O in the simulated history H_P is linearizable with respect to the sequential specification of the n-P&G object. The detailed proof is given in the full paper, and we only convey the main ideas here.

Below we explain how to linearize H_P^O assuming that it contains at least one GET(−) operation on O that returns a value other than ? or $\perp$.[5] Note that all such GET(−) operations return the same value, denoted v_O^{win}; this is because they obtain the value of the `val` field of O from VAL_O via a modification of the {0,1,2}-level mechanism used by safe agreement objects.

Recall that: (i) the state of the n-P&G object O consists of two fields `val` and `pri` (as defined in Figure 1), and (ii) the `val` field of O is simulated by the snapshot object VAL_O, while the `pri` field of O is simulated by the max register PRI_O. Intuitively, at any time t:

- If all fields of the snapshot object VAL_O still contain $(-, 0)$, i.e., there are no level 1 or 2 proposals, then the `val` field of O contains $\perp$; otherwise it contains v_O^{win}.
- The value of the max register PRI_O is the value of the `pri` field of O.

We first construct a completion $H_P'^O$ of the history H_P^O of the operations on O: For each incomplete operation op, if op changes the state of O, we complete op immediately after it does so; otherwise we remove op.

We then linearize the operations of $H_P'^O$ as follows: We first linearize the PROPOSE(−, −) operations on O, and then we linearize the GET(−) operations on O. In both cases, we begin by linearizing the operations that *change* the state of O, and then we linearize the operations that *only read* the state of O, as described below.

[5] If this assumption does not hold, the linearization of H_P^O is simpler; intuitively, this is because in this case the values proposed to O are not "visible".

Let op_O^{win} be the PROPOSE(v_O^{win}, −) operation with the earliest invocation time among all PROPOSE(v_O^{win}, −) operations on O in H_P^O. Intuitively, op_O^{win} is the first PROPOSE(−, −) operation to take effect, by changing the `val` field of O from $\bot$ to v_O^{win}. Thus, we linearize op_O^{win} at the earliest time t when VAL_O is changed, i.e., when a (−, 1) is first written into VAL_O (line 34). Note that this time t is within the execution interval of op_O^{win}:

- Time t cannot be after op_O^{win} is completed, because every simulation of op_O^{win} either finds that VAL_O has been changed from its initial value (lines 31 to 32), or it changes VAL_O (line 34).
- If time t is before op_O^{win} is invoked, then every simulation of op_O^{win} would evaluate the conditional on line 32 as false and return without changing VAL_O. The same would hold for all subsequent PROPOSE(v_O^{win}, −) operations, so v_O^{win} would never be written into VAL_O — contradicting our definition of v_O^{win} as the agreed upon value determined by the $\{0, 1, 2\}$-level mechanism on VAL_O.

Let op be any PROPOSE(−, −) operation that is not op_O^{win}. Intuitively, op should be linearized after op_O^{win} (and it should return DONE without changing the state of O). So we linearize op at its completion time. Note that the completion time of op is after the earliest time VAL_O is changed (the linearization time of op_O^{win}), because every simulation of op either finds that VAL_O has been changed from its initial value (lines 31 to 32), or it changes VAL_O (line 34). Thus op is linearized *after* op_O^{win} is linearized, as wanted.

Next, let op be any GET(−) operation that performs a WRITEMAX(−) operation on PRI_O (line 57). Intuitively, op is an unprioritized GET(−) operation, which changes the `pri` field of O. Roughly speaking, since safe agreement objects are used to agree on the values read from PRI_O (lines 51 to 55), all simulations of op that perform WRITEMAX(−) operations on PRI_O (line 57) write the same value. Since PRI_O is a max register that contains the largest value ever written to it, only the earliest of these WRITEMAX(−) operations changes the state of PRI_O. Thus we linearize op at the earliest time t when a simulation of op performs a WRITEMAX(−) operation on PRI_O (line 57). Clearly, this time t is within the execution interval of op.

Finally, let op be any GET(−) operation that does *not* perform a WRITEMAX(−) operation on PRI_O (line 57). Intuitively, op is a prioritized GET(−) operation, which returns the current value $u \neq ?$ of the `val` field of O without changing the state of O. Thus we linearize op at the earliest time within its execution interval when (a) the `val` field of O contains u, and (b) the `pri` field of O contains an integer r such that op is prioritized. We now explain why such a time exists.

First observe that before op returns $u \neq ?$, some simulation of op reads u from the `val` field of O (lines 45 to 50), and then reads an integer indicating that op is prioritized from the `pri` field of O (line 51). Let t be the time when this simulation of op takes a snapshot of VAL_O (line 45), and t' be the time when this simulation of op performs a READMAX() operation on PRI_O (line 51). Note that the interval $[t, t']$ is within the execution interval of op: op returns u after time t', and op is invoked before time t, because some simulation of op executes line 45 at time t. Clearly, (a) is true at time t, while (b) is true at time t'. We claim that (b) is also true at time t, as wanted.

Suppose, for contradiction, that (b) is not true at time t. This implies that op is on a port $i \leq 2$; otherwise, (b) would be true at *all* times. Without loss of generality, assume that op is on port 1 (a symmetric argument applies in the case where op is on port 2). Since op is a GET(1) operation, the integer r that indicates that op is prioritized is odd. From lines 56-57, it clear that only GET(1) operations can write odd integers to PRI_O. Since (b) is not true at time t, PRI_O does not contain r at time t. Thus (a thread simulating) some GET(1) operation op' writes r into PRI_O at some time between t and t', i.e., within the execution interval of op. Since PRI_O is a max register, and PRI_O does not contain r at time t, it is clear that no thread of op' writes r into PRI_O before time t. Thus op' completes after time t. Furthermore, since a thread simulating op' writes r into PRI_O before time t', op' is invoked before time t'. So op and op' are *concurrent* operations, and they are both on port 1 of O. In the full paper, we show that this contradicts the fact that the simulated algorithm A_P is well-formed. Thus, (b) is true at time t; and so our linearization of op is well-defined.

The proof that the above linearization of the operations on O respects the sequential specification of the n-P&G object is given in the full paper. This implies that the $k + 1$ real processes that execute A_Q in system Q (which has only registers) correctly simulate an execution of A_P by the virtual processes of system P (which has registers and n-P&G objects). Recall that A_P is a *wait-free* algorithm that solves the k-set agreement problem. Earlier, we explained why every correct real process $q \in Q$ simulates infinitely many steps of some virtual process $p \in P$ which executes A_P. So each correct real process $q \in Q$ eventually simulates a virtual process $p \in P$ deciding some value u (line 25), and decides u itself (line 27). Thus A_Q is a *wait-free* algorithm that also solves the k-set agreement problem among $k + 1$ real processes even though it only has registers, which is known to be impossible [4, 5, 15, 25]. Therefore there is no wait-free algorithm A_P that solves the k-set agreement problem among $k(n - 1) + 1$ processes using only n-P&G objects and registers.

This completes our outline of the proof of Theorem 5. By Corollary 4, Theorem 5, and Theorem 2:

COROLLARY 6. *For all $n > 2$, the n-P&G object has the same set agreement power as the $(n - 1)$-consensus object.*

5 $(n - 1)$-CONSENSUS CANNOT IMPLEMENT THE n-P&G OBJECT

In this section, we show that the n-P&G and $(n - 1)$-consensus objects are not equivalent. To do so, we first introduce for all $n > 2$, a variation of the n-consensus problem that we call *n-SLC* (for "Semi-Live Consensus"). The n-SLC problem is identical to the wait-free n-consensus problem, except that two distinguished processes are only required to be obstruction-free, instead of wait-free. We define this problem more precisely below.

Without loss of generality, let the processes be numbered 1 to n. Then an algorithm solves the n-SLC problem if every execution of the algorithm satisfies the following properties:

- **Agreement:** No two processes decide different values.
- **Validity:** If a process decides v, then v is the input of some process.

Algorithm 6 Solving the n-SLC problem using an n-P&G object $\mathcal{D}$

Code executed by each process $q \in [1..n]$ with input v_q:

$\mathcal{D}$.PROPOSE(v_q, q)
repeat
  $val \leftarrow \mathcal{D}$.GET$(q)$
until $val \neq$?
decide val

- **Termination:**
  (a) If any process $q \in \{1, 2\}$ takes infinitely many steps solo (i.e., not interleaved with steps of other processes), then q eventually decides.
  (b) If any process $q \in [3..n]$ takes infinitely many steps, then q eventually decides.

It is straightforward to see that n processes can solve the n-SLC problem by running Algorithm 6 which uses a single n-P&G object (the proof is in the full paper). Thus we have the following:

THEOREM 7. *For all $n > 2$, the n-SLC problem can be solved using an n-P&G object.*

THEOREM 8. *For all $n > 2$, the n-SLC problem cannot be solved using only $(n-1)$-consensus objects and registers.*

PROOF. Consider the *n-DAC* problem introduced by Hadzilacos and Toueg [13]. This problem is identical to the obstruction-free consensus problem, except that there is a distinguished process p that is wait-free, but *may abort instead of deciding* if any other process takes a step. It is easy to see that the n-SLC problem is a stronger version of the n-DAC problem where: (i) no process can abort, and (ii) there are $n-2$ distinguished processes that are wait-free. The theorem follows from the fact that the n-DAC problem cannot be solved using only $(n-1)$-consensus objects and registers [13].[6] □ Theorem 8

Theorems 7 and 8 imply:

COROLLARY 9. *For all $n > 2$, the n-P&G object cannot be implemented using only $(n-1)$-consensus objects and registers.*

Corollary 6 and Corollary 9 imply:

COROLLARY 10. *For all $n > 2$, level $n-1$ of Herlihy's consensus hierarchy contains two deterministic objects, namely the n-P&G object and the $(n-1)$-consensus object, that have the same set agreement power but are not equivalent.*

Thus the set agreement power classification of deterministic objects is not precise.

6 A RELATED RESULT: OBJECTS VS. TASKS

Wait-free *objects* and *tasks* [16] are fundamental concepts of distributed computing, and a natural question is whether objects and tasks are equivalent. By combining our result with a result of Gafni and Kuztnetsov [12], we now show that, in general, the answer is no: more precisely, we prove that in systems with $m > 2$ processes, there is a *deterministic* object that is not equivalent to *any* task.

[6] A proof of a slightly stronger result is also given in [6] (Theorem 4.2).

THEOREM 11. *For systems with $m > 2$ processes, the deterministic wait-free object m-P&G is not equivalent to any wait-free task.*

PROOF. Suppose, for contradiction, that in a system with $m > 2$ processes, there is a task T that is equivalent to the m-P&G object, i.e., (a) T can be solved in a wait-free manner using m-P&G objects and registers, and (b) the m-P&G object can be implemented in a wait-free manner using any wait-free solution for T and registers. By Corollary 6, there is no algorithm that solves the consensus problem for m processes using only m-P&G objects and registers.

Gafni and Kuztnetsov proved the following result [12]: "Let A be a deterministic object such that no protocol solves consensus among $n+1$ processes using copies of A and read-write registers. If a task T is wait-free solvable by $n+1$ processes using read-write shared-memory and copies of A, then T is also wait-free solvable when copies of A are replaced with n-consensus objects."

Let $n+1 = m$ and A be our deterministic object m-P&G. By the above result and (a), T can be solved in a wait-free manner using $(m-1)$-consensus objects and registers. So by (b), the m-P&G object can be implemented in a wait-free manner using $(m-1)$-consensus objects and registers — contradicting Corollary 9. □ Theorem 11

7 BG SIMULATION AND EXTENSIONS

The original BG simulation algorithm introduced by Borowsky and Gafni [4] was designed to simulate algorithms that use registers to solve *colorless* tasks (intuitively, in a colorless task, each process can adopt the input and/or output value of any process).[7] In that simulation, each real process that crashes can block at most one virtual process. Chaudhuri and Reiners [9] extended the BG simulation algorithm to simulate algorithms that use (n, k)-set agreement objects in addition to registers, and Imbs and Raynal [19] presented a simpler extension for the special case where $k = 1$, i.e., for simulating n-consensus objects. In both [9, 19], however, the simulation of n-consensus objects comes at a cost: each real process crash may now block up to n virtual processes. In this paper, we extended the BG simulation algorithm to simulate the access to n-P&G objects, which are slightly weaker than n-consensus objects. Our simulation was carefully crafted to take advantage of this weakness to reduce the number of processes that may be blocked: in our simulation, each real process crash can block at most $n-1$ virtual processes. Roughly speaking, this reduction in the number of blocked processes was achieved as follows.

When a virtual process accesses an n-consensus object C, it can never return without getting the agreed upon proposal value. So if the crash of a real process prevents this agreed upon proposal value from being determined, *every* virtual process that accesses C may be forever prevented from returning, i.e., may be blocked. In fact, if C is simulated by a safe-agreement object O_{safe} (as in [9, 19]), and a real process crashes while proposing a value to O_{safe}, all operations on C may loop forever, unable to return because they cannot determine the agreed upon proposal value.

In contrast to an n-consensus object, a virtual process that performs a GET(-) operation on an n-P&G object returns ? without getting the agreed upon proposal value, if this GET(-) operation is not prioritized. So we simulated each n-P&G object by adding an

[7] The BG simulation algorithm was later generalized to algorithms that use registers to solve colored tasks in [11, 18].

escape clause to the loop of the safe agreement algorithm: in each loop iteration, a real process also checks the `pri` field of the n-P&G object to determine whether the GET(−) operation it is simulating is prioritized. If it is not, the operation returns ?, and thus the process escapes the unbounded loop. Note that whenever n virtual processes perform concurrent GET(-) operations on (distinct ports of) an n-P&G object, either the operation on port 1 or the operation on port 2 is not prioritized: it can thus return ? without getting the agreed upon proposal value. So the crash of a real process that prevents this agreed upon proposal value from being determined, can block at most $n-1$ virtual processes.

It is worth noting, however, that the `pri` field of the n-P&G object which is critical to the escape clause, makes the linearization of the operations of an n-P&G object significantly more complex than the linearization of the operations of an n-consensus object.

8 CONCLUSION

Since the early days of the shared memory model for distributed computing, researchers have sought a simple way to classify objects in a precise manner, i.e., such that a pair of objects is in the same class if and only if each can be implemented by instances of the other (and registers) in a wait-free manner. It is known that the classification of objects given by Herlihy's wait-free consensus hierarchy [14] is not precise [24], even when it is restricted to deterministic objects [2].

In [7], we showed that the precise classification of linearizable objects divides them into *uncountably* many classes, and in [6] we proved that the classification of linearizable objects (into uncountably many classes) based on their set agreement power is not precise. In this paper, we focused on the subset of linearizable objects that are *deterministic*, and we proved that their classification by set agreement power is also not precise. It remains an open question whether the precise classification of such objects has uncountably many classes, and whether they can be classified by a simple scheme.

ACKNOWLEDGMENTS

We thank the anonymous referees for their comments and suggestions. This work was partially supported by the Natural Sciences and Engineering Research Council of Canada.

REFERENCES

[1] Yehuda Afek, Hagit Attiya, Danny Dolev, Eli Gafni, Michael Merritt, and Nir Shavit. 1993. Atomic Snapshots of Shared Memory. *J. ACM* 40, 4 (Sep. 1993), 873–890.

[2] Yehuda Afek, Faith Ellen, and Eli Gafni. 2016. Deterministic Objects: Life Beyond Consensus. In *Proceedings of the 2016 ACM Symposium on Principles of Distributed Computing (PODC '16)*. ACM, New York, NY, USA, 97–106.

[3] James Aspnes, Hagit Attiya, and Keren Censor. 2009. Max Registers, Counters, and Monotone Circuits. In *Proceedings of the 28th ACM Symposium on Principles of Distributed Computing (PODC '09)*. ACM, New York, NY, USA, 36–45.

[4] Elizabeth Borowsky and Eli Gafni. 1993. Generalized FLP Impossibility Result for t-resilient Asynchronous Computations. In *Proceedings of the 25th Annual ACM Symposium on Theory of Computing (STOC '93)*. ACM, New York, NY, USA, 91–100.

[5] Elizabeth Borowsky, Eli Gafni, Nancy Lynch, and Sergio Rajsbaum. 2001. The BG Distributed Simulation Algorithm. *Distributed Computing* 14, 3 (Oct. 2001), 127–146.

[6] David Yu Cheng Chan, Vassos Hadzilacos, and Sam Toueg. 2017. Life Beyond Set Agreement. In *Proceedings of the 2017 ACM Symposium on Principles of Distributed Computing (PODC '17)*. ACM, New York, NY, USA, 345–354.

[7] David Yu Cheng Chan, Vassos Hadzilacos, and Sam Toueg. 2017. On the Number of Objects with Distinct Power and the Linearizability of Set Agreement Objects. In *Proceedings of the 31st International Symposium on Distributed Computing (DISC '17)*. Schloss Dagstuhl–Leibniz-Zentrum fuer Informatik, Dagstuhl, Germany, Article 12, 14 pages.

[8] Soma Chaudhuri. 1993. More Choices Allow More Faults: Set Consensus Problems in Totally Asynchronous Systems. *Information and Computation* 105, 1 (Jul. 1993), 132–158.

[9] Soma Chaudhuri and Paul Reiners. 1996. Understanding the Set Consensus Partial Order Using the Borowsky-Gafni Simulation (Extended Abstract). In *Proceedings of the 10th International Workshop on Distributed Algorithms (WDAG '96)*. Springer-Verlag, London, UK, 362–379.

[10] Carole Delporte-Gallet, Hugues Fauconnier, Eli Gafni, and Petr Kuznetsov. 2017. Set-Consensus Collections are Decidable. In *Proceedings of the 20th International Conference on Principles of Distributed Systems (OPODIS '16)*. Schloss Dagstuhl–Leibniz-Zentrum fuer Informatik, Dagstuhl, Germany, Article 7, 15 pages.

[11] Eli Gafni. 2009. The Extended BG-simulation and the Characterization of t-resiliency. In *Proceedings of the Forty-first Annual ACM Symposium on Theory of Computing (STOC '09)*. ACM, New York, NY, USA, 85–92.

[12] Eli Gafni and Petr Kuznetsov. 2007. N-consensus is the Second Strongest Object for $N+1$ Processes. In *Proceedings of the 11th International Conference on Principles of Distributed Systems (OPODIS'07)*. Springer-Verlag, Berlin, Heidelberg, 260–273.

[13] Vassos Hadzilacos and Sam Toueg. 2013. On Deterministic Abortable Objects. In *Proceedings of the 2013 ACM Symposium on Principles of Distributed Computing (PODC '13)*. ACM, New York, NY, USA, 4–12.

[14] Maurice Herlihy. 1991. Wait-free Synchronization. *ACM Trans. Program. Lang. Syst.* 11, 1 (Jan. 1991), 124–149.

[15] Maurice Herlihy and Nir Shavit. 1993. The Asynchronous Computability Theorem for t-resilient Tasks. In *Proceedings of the 25th Annual ACM Symposium on Theory of Computing (STOC '93)*. ACM, New York, NY, USA, 111–120.

[16] Maurice Herlihy and Nir Shavit. 1999. The Topological Structure of Asynchronous Computability. *J. ACM* 46, 6 (Nov. 1999), 858–923.

[17] Maurice Herlihy and Jeannette Wing. 1990. Linearizability: A Correctness Condition for Concurrent Objects. *ACM Trans. Program. Lang. Syst.* 12, 3 (Jul. 1990), 463–492.

[18] Damien Imbs and Michel Raynal. 2009. Visiting Gafni's Reduction Land: From the BG Simulation to the Extended BG Simulation. In *Proceedings of the 11th International Symposium on Stabilization, Safety, and Security of Distributed Systems (SSS '09)*. Springer-Verlag, Berlin, Heidelberg, 369–383.

[19] Damien Imbs and Michel Raynal. 2010. The Multiplicative Power of Consensus Numbers. In *Proceedings of the 29th ACM SIGACT-SIGOPS Symposium on Principles of Distributed Computing (PODC '10)*. ACM, New York, NY, USA, 26–35.

[20] Amos Israeli and Amnon Shaham. 1992. Optimal Multi-writer Multi-reader Atomic Register. In *Proceedings of the 11th Annual ACM Symposium on Principles of Distributed Computing (PODC '92)*. ACM, New York, NY, USA, 71–82.

[21] Leslie Lamport. 1977. Concurrent Reading and Writing. *Commun. ACM* 20, 11 (Nov. 1977), 806–811.

[22] Daniel Lister. 2013. *A Pedagogical Presentation of the BG-Simulation*. Master's thesis. University of Toronto.

[23] Nancy Lynch. 1996. *Distributed Algorithms*. Morgan Kaufmann Publishers Inc., San Francisco, CA, USA.

[24] Ophir Rachman. 1994. Anomalies in the Wait-Free Hierarchy. In *Proceedings of the 8th International Workshop on Distributed Algorithms (WDAG '94)*. Springer-Verlag, London, UK, 156–163.

[25] Michael Saks and Fotios Zaharoglou. 2000. Wait-Free k-Set Agreement is Impossible: The Topology of Public Knowledge. *SIAM J. Comput.* 29, 5 (Mar. 2000), 1449–1483.

[26] Paul M. B. Vitanyi and Baruch Awerbuch. 1986. Atomic Shared Register Access by Asynchronous Hardware. In *Proceedings of the 27th Annual Symposium on Foundations of Computer Science (SFCS '86)*. IEEE Computer Society, Washington, DC, USA, 233–243.

Brief Announcement: Specification and Implementation of Replicated List: The Jupiter Protocol Revisited*

Hengfeng Wei
State Key Laboratory for Novel Software Technology, Nanjing University
Nanjing, China
hfwei@nju.edu.cn

Yu Huang
State Key Laboratory for Novel Software Technology, Nanjing University
Nanjing, China
yuhuang@nju.edu.cn

Jian Lu
State Key Laboratory for Novel Software Technology, Nanjing University
Nanjing, China
lj@nju.edu.cn

ABSTRACT

The replicated list object is frequently used to model the core functionality of replicated collaborative text editing systems. Recently, Attiya et al. proposed the strong/weak list specification and conjectured that the well-known Jupiter protocol satisfies the weak list specification. The major obstacle to proving this conjecture is the mismatch between the global property on all replica states prescribed by the specification and the local view each replica maintains in Jupiter using data structures like 1D buffer or 2D state space. To address this issue, we propose CJupiter (Compact Jupiter) based on a novel data structure called n-ary ordered state space for a replicated client/server system with n clients. At a high level, CJupiter maintains only a single n-ary ordered state space which encompasses exactly all states of each replica. We prove that CJupiter and Jupiter are equivalent and that CJupiter satisfies the weak list specification, thus solving the conjecture above.

KEYWORDS

Collaborative text editing systems; Replicated list; Strong/weak list specification; Operational transformation; Jupiter protocol.

ACM Reference Format:

Hengfeng Wei, Yu Huang, and Jian Lu. 2018. Brief Announcement: Specification and Implementation of Replicated List: The Jupiter Protocol Revisited. In *PODC '18: ACM Symposium on Principles of Distributed Computing, July 23–27, 2018, Egham, United Kingdom.* ACM, New York, NY, USA, 3 pages. https://doi.org/10.1145/3212734.3212778

1 INTRODUCTION

Collaborative text editing systems, like Google Docs [5] and Apache Wave [1], allow multiple users to concurrently edit the same document. For availability, such systems often replicate the document at several *replicas*. For low latency, replicas are required to respond to user operations immediately without any communication with others and updates are propagated asynchronously.

The *replicated list object* has been frequently used to model the core functionality (e.g., insertion and deletion) of collaborative text editing systems [2, 7, 8]. Recently, Attiya et al. [2] proposed the strong/weak list specification, which specifies global properties on intermediate states going through by replicas. It is ***conjectured*** [2] that the Jupiter protocol [7, 8], which is behind Google Docs [5] and Apache Wave [4], satisfies the weak list specification.

Jupiter adopts a *centralized server* replica for propagating updates. [1] Client replicas are connected to the server replica via FIFO channels (Figure 1). Jupiter relies on the technique of operational transformations (OT) to achieve convergence [7]. The basic idea of OT is for each replica to execute any local operation immediately and to transform a remote operation so that it takes into account the concurrent operations previously executed at the replica.

The major obstacle to proving that Jupiter satisfies the weak list specification is the *mismatch* between the *global property* on all states prescribed by such a specification and the *local view* each replica maintains in the protocol. On the one hand, the weak list specification requires that states across the system are pairwise compatible. That is, for any pair of (list) states, there cannot be two elements a and b such that a precedes b in one state but b precedes a in the other. On the other hand, Jupiter uses data structures like 1D buffer or 2D state space [8] which are not "compact" enough to capture all replica states in one. The replica states are dispersed in multiple data structures maintained locally at individual replicas.

To resolve the mismatch, we propose CJupiter (Compact Jupiter), which uses a novel data structure called *n-ary ordered state space* for a system with n clients. CJupiter is compact in the sense that at a high level, it maintains only a single n-ary ordered state space which encompasses exactly all states of each replica. Each replica behavior corresponds to a path going through this state space. This makes it feasible for us to reason about global properties and finally prove that Jupiter satisfies the weak list specification, thus solving the conjecture of Attiya et al. The roadmap is as follows:

- (Section 3) We propose CJupiter based on the n-ary ordered state space data structure.
- (Section 4) We prove that CJupiter is equivalent to Jupiter in the sense that the behaviors of their corresponding replicas are the same under the same schedule of operations.
- (Section 5) We prove that CJupiter satisfies the weak list specification. Due to the "compactness" of CJupiter, we are able to focus on a single n-ary ordered state space which provides a global view of all possible replica states.

*The full version is available at https://arxiv.org/abs/1708.04754 (v3, 12 May 2018).

PODC '18, July 23–27, 2018, Egham, United Kingdom

ACM ISBN 978-1-4503-5795-1/18/07.
https://doi.org/10.1145/3212734.3212778

[1] Since replicas are required to respond to user operations immediately, the client/server architecture does not imply that clients process operations in the same order.

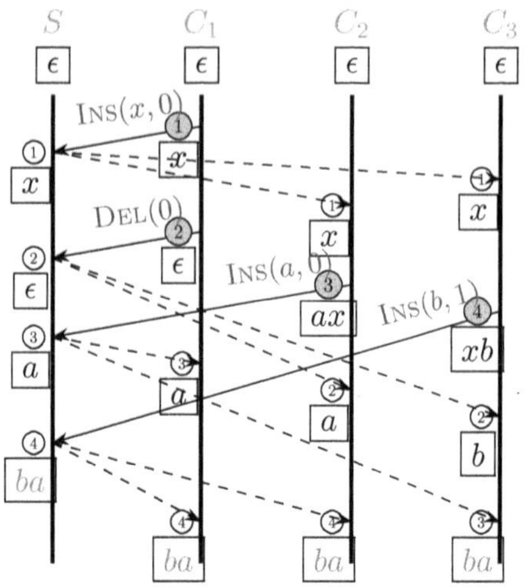

Figure 1: A schedule of four operations adapted from [2], involving a server replica and three client replicas. The lists produced by CJupiter (Section 3) are shown in boxes.

2 PRELIMINARIES

We follow the framework proposed by Burckhardt et al. [3] for specifying replicated data types. A ***replica*** is a state machine R, driven by three kinds of *events*: *1)* $\text{do}(o, v)$: accepts an operation o from a user and immediately returns a value v; *2)* $\text{send}(m)$: sends a message m to some replicas; *3)* $\text{receive}(m)$: receives a message m. A ***protocol*** is a collection $\mathcal{R}$ of replicas. An ***execution*** α of a protocol $\mathcal{R}$ is a sequence of all events occurring at the replicas in $\mathcal{R}$. We denote by $R(e)$ the replica at which an event e occurs, and by $e \prec_\alpha e'$ that e precedes e' in α. The causally happens-before relation $\xrightarrow{\text{hb}_\alpha}$ on the events in α is defined as usual [6]. The ***behavior*** of a replica R in α is a sequence of the form: $\sigma_0, e_1, \sigma_1, e_2, \ldots$, where $\langle e_1, e_2, \ldots \rangle \triangleq \alpha|_R$ is the subsequence of events at R and for all i, σ_i is the state obtained by applying e_i on σ_{i-1}. A ***state*** σ of R in α is represented by the events in a prefix of $\alpha|_R$ it has processed.

An ***abstract execution*** records the operations performed by users and visibility relationships between them [2]. Formally, it is a pair $A = (H, \text{vis})$, where H is a sequence of do events and $\text{vis} \subseteq H \times H$ is an acyclic visibility relation such that *1)* if $e_1 \prec_H e_2$ and $R(e_1) = R(e_2)$, then $e_1 \xrightarrow{\text{vis}} e_2$; *2)* if $e_1 \xrightarrow{\text{vis}} e_2$, then $e_1 \prec_H e_2$; *3)* vis is transitive. A ***specification*** $\mathcal{S}$ is a prefix-closed set of abstract executions. A protocol $\mathcal{R}$ ***satisfies*** a specification $\mathcal{S}$, denoted $\mathcal{R} \models \mathcal{S}$, if any execution α of $\mathcal{R}$ *complies with* some abstract execution $A = (H, \text{vis})$ in $\mathcal{S}$, namely $\forall R \in \mathcal{R} : H|_R = \alpha|_R^{\text{do}}$, where $\alpha|_R^{\text{do}}$ is the subsequence of do events of replica R in α.

A replicated list object supports three types of user operations [2]:

- $\text{Ins}(a, p)$: inserts a unique element a at position p and returns the updated list.
- $\text{Del}(a, p)$: deletes an element at position p and returns the updated list. The parameter a is to record the deleted element.
- Read: returns the contents of the list.

We denote by $\text{elems}(A) = \{a \mid \text{do}(\text{Ins}(a, \_), \_) \in H\}$ the set of all elements inserted into the list in an abstract execution $A = (H, \text{vis})$.

The weak list specification requires the ordering between elements that are not deleted to be consistent across the system [2].

Definition 1. An abstract execution $A = (H, \text{vis})$ belongs to the ***weak list specification*** $\mathcal{A}_{\text{weak}}$ iff there is a relation $\text{lo} \subseteq \text{elems}(A) \times \text{elems}(A)$, called the *list order*, such that:

(1) Each event $e = \text{do}(o, w) \in H$ returns a sequence of elements $w = a_0 \ldots a_{n-1}$, where $a_i \in \text{elems}(A)$, such that:
  (a) w contains exactly the elements visible to e that have been inserted, but not deleted.
  (b) lo is consistent with the order of the elements in w.
  (c) Elements are inserted at the specified position: $o = \text{Ins}(a, k) \implies a = a_{\min\{k, n-1\}}$.
(2) lo is irreflexive and for all events $e = \text{do}(op, w) \in H$, it is transitive and total on $\{a \mid a \in w\}$.

Example 2. In the execution of Figure 1, there exist three states with lists $w_1 = ba$, $w_2 = ax$, and $w_3 = xb$, respectively. This is allowed by the weak list specification with the list order lo: $b \xrightarrow{\text{lo}} a$ on w_1, $a \xrightarrow{\text{lo}} x$ on w_2, and $x \xrightarrow{\text{lo}} b$ on w_3.

3 THE CJUPITER AND JUPITER PROTOCOLS

CJupiter adopts a client/server architecture, where the server serializes operations and propagates them from one client to others. For a client/server system with n clients, CJupiter maintains $(n+1)$ ***n-ary ordered state spaces***, one per replica (CSS_s for the server and CSS_{c_i} for client c_i). Each CSS is a directed graph whose vertices represent states and edges are labeled with operations of type *Op*. Each *operation* of type *Op* consists of a globally unique operation identifier *oid* and an operation context *ctx* which is a set of *oids*, denoting the operations it "knows". The state in a vertex is represented by the set *oids* of operations that have been executed. The edges from a vertex are ***totally ordered*** by the operations associated with them, which are in turn totally ordered by the server.

Each replica keeps the most recent vertex *cur* of its n-ary ordered state space S. We briefly describe CJupiter in three parts.

Local Processing. When a client receives a list operation o from a user, it applies o locally, generates $op \in Op$ with the operation context $S.cur.oids$, creates a vertex v with $v.oids = S.cur.oids \cup \{op.oid\}$, links v to $S.cur$ via an edge labeled with op, and finally sends op to the server.

Server Processing. When the server receives an operation $op \in Op$ from a client, it transforms op with an operation sequence in S to obtain op' by calling $S.\text{xForm}(op)$ (see below), applies op' locally, and then sends op (not op') to other clients.

Remote Processing. When a client receives an operation $op \in Op$ from the server, it transforms op with an operation sequence in S to obtain op' by calling $S.\text{xForm}(op)$, and applies op' locally.

OTs in CJupiter. The procedure $S.\text{xForm}(op : Op)$ first locates the vertex u whose *oids* matches the *ctx* of *op*, and then iteratively transforms *op* with an operation sequence consisting of operations along the ***first*** edges from u to the final vertex *cur* of S. The choice of the "first" edges in OTs is necessary for establishing the equivalence of CJupiter and Jupiter at the server side.

Although $(n+1)$ n-ary ordered state spaces are maintained by CJupiter for a system with n clients, they are all the same (Figure 2).

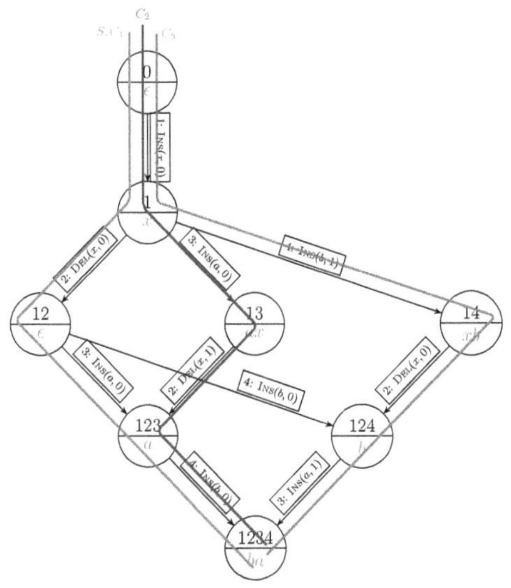

Figure 2: The same final n-ary ordered state space constructed by CJupiter for each replica under the schedule of Figure 1. Each replica behavior corresponds to a path going through this state space.

Proposition 3. *In* CJupiter, *the replicas that have processed the same set of operations have the same n-ary ordered state space.*

Jupiter is similar to CJupiter with three major differences: *1)* For a client/server system with n clients, Jupiter [8] maintains $2n$ ***2D state spaces***, each consisting of a *local* dimension and a *global* dimension. In particular, the server maintains n 2D state spaces, one for each client; *2)* In xForm(op : $Op, d \in \{\textit{LOCAL}, \textit{GLOBAL}\}$) of Jupiter, the operation sequence with which op transforms is determined by the parameter d; *3)* In Jupiter, the server propagates the *transformed* operations to other clients.

4 CJUPITER IS EQUIVALENT TO JUPITER

We prove that CJupiter is equivalent to Jupiter from perspectives of both the server and clients. ***At the server***, the n-ary ordered state space CSS_s of CJupiter equals the *union* (in terms of graphs as sets of vertices and edges) of all 2D state spaces maintained at the server for each client in Jupiter. The equivalence of ***clients*** follows since the final transformed operations executed at each client in Jupiter and CJupiter are the same (although the original operations are propagated in CJupiter). Thus, we have that

Theorem 4. *Under the same schedule, the behaviors of corresponding replicas in* CJupiter *and* Jupiter *are the same.*

5 CJUPITER SATISFIES THE WEAK LIST SPECIFICATION

The following theorem, together with Theorem 4, solves the conjecture of Attiya et al. [2].

Theorem 5. CJupiter *satisfies the weak list specification* $\mathcal{A}_{\text{weak}}$.

Proof. For each execution α of CJupiter, we first construct an abstract execution $A = (H, \text{vis})$ with $\text{vis} = \xrightarrow{\text{hb}_\alpha}$. It is easy to prove the conditions 1(a) and 1(c) of $\mathcal{A}_{\text{weak}}$. Then, we define the ***list order relation*** lo: For $a, b \in \text{elems}(A)$, $a \xrightarrow{\text{lo}} b$ iff there exists an event $e \in \alpha$ with returned list w such that a precedes b in w. By definition, lo satisfies conditions 1(b).

It remains to show the *irreflexivity* of lo, which is equivalent to the ***pairwise state compatibility property***: lo is irreflexive iff any two list states w_1 and w_2 in A are compatible, namely, for any two common elements a and b of w_1 and w_2, their relative orderings are the same in w_1 and w_2. By Proposition 3, it suffices to show that the state space CSS_s at the server satisfies the pairwise state compatibility property. Given a pair of states/vertices in CSS_s, we consider the paths to them from their LCA. [2]

Lemma 6. *Every pair of vertices in CSS_s has a unique LCA.*

Lemma 7. *Let v_0 be the unique LCA of a pair of vertices v_1 and v_2 in CSS_s. Then, the path $P_{v_0 \rightsquigarrow v_1}$ from v_0 to v_1, as well as $P_{v_0 \rightsquigarrow v_2}$ from v_0 to v_2, is* ***simple****, namely, there are no duplicate operations along it. Furthermore, the set of operations $O_{v_0 \rightsquigarrow v_1}$ along $P_{v_0 \rightsquigarrow v_1}$ is* ***disjoint*** *from the set of operations $O_{v_0 \rightsquigarrow v_2}$ along $P_{v_0 \rightsquigarrow v_2}$.*

The desired pairwise state compatibility property follows, when we take the common vertex v_0 in the next Lemma as the LCA of the two vertices v_1 and v_2 under consideration.

Lemma 8. *Let $P_{v_0 \rightsquigarrow v_1}$ and $P_{v_0 \rightsquigarrow v_2}$ be two paths from vertex v_0 to vertices v_1 and v_2, respectively in CSS_s. If they are* ***disjoint simple paths****, then the list states of v_1 and v_2 are* ***compatible****.*

□

6 ACKNOWLEDGMENTS

This work is supported by the National 973 Program of China (2015CB352202), the National Natural Science Foundation of China (61702253), and the Fundamental Research Funds for the Central Universities (020214380031).

REFERENCES

[1] [n. d.]. Apache Wave. https://incubator.apache.org/wave/.
[2] Hagit Attiya, Sebastian Burckhardt, Alexey Gotsman, Adam Morrison, Hongseok Yang, and Marek Zawirski. 2016. Specification and complexity of collaborative text editing. In *Proceedings of the 2016 ACM Symposium on Principles of Distributed Computing (PODC '16)*. ACM, 259–268.
[3] Sebastian Burckhardt, Alexey Gotsman, Hongseok Yang, and Marek Zawirski. 2014. Replicated Data Types: Specification, Verification, Optimality. In *Proceedings of the 41st ACM SIGPLAN-SIGACT Symposium on Principles of Programming Languages (POPL '14)*. ACM, 271–284.
[4] The Apache Wave Foundation. 2015. *Apache Wave (incubating) Protocol Documentation (Release 0.4)*.
[5] Google. 2010. What's different about the new Google Docs: Making collaboration fast. https://drive.googleblog.com/2010/09/whats-different-about-new-google-docs.html.
[6] Leslie Lamport. 1978. Time, Clocks, and the Ordering of Events in a Distributed System. *Commun. ACM* 21, 7 (July 1978), 558–565.
[7] David A. Nichols, Pavel Curtis, Michael Dixon, and John Lamping. 1995. High-latency, Low-bandwidth Windowing in the Jupiter Collaboration System. In *Proceedings of the 8th Annual ACM Symposium on User Interface and Software Technology (UIST '95)*. ACM, 111–120.
[8] Yi Xu, Chengzheng Sun, and Mo Li. 2014. Achieving Convergence in Operational Transformation: Conditions, Mechanisms and Systems. In *Proceedings of the 17th ACM Conference on Computer Supported Cooperative Work and Social Computing (CSCW '14)*. ACM, 505–518.

[2]The LCA (Lowest Common Ancestor) of two vertices v_1 and v_2 in CSS_s, which is a DAG, is the lowest (i.e., deepest) vertex that has both v_1 and v_2 as descendants.

Leveraging Indirect Signaling for Topology Inference and Fast Broadcast

Magnús M. Halldórsson
ICE-TCS, School of Computer Science,
Reykjavik University
Reykjavik, Iceland
mmh@ru.is

Tigran Tonoyan
ICE-TCS, School of Computer Science,
Reykjavik University
Reykjavik, Iceland
ttonoyan@gmail.com

ABSTRACT

The physical (or SINR) model of wireless communication is more intricate than radio networks and still not well understood. If two neighbors of a node are transmitting, the node may be able to decode one of the transmissions, depending on the *relative nearness* of the transmitters. Thus, even the lack of proper reception carries *indirect information*. We explore here the power of such indirect signaling to infer the approximate topology of the network. In particular, we obtain a polylogarithmic time algorithm to compute a *backbone*: a set of nodes of constant density that dominates every ϵ-neighborhood. A backbone has wide utility for information dissemination, functioning as a sparse spanner. It also leads to fast broadcast, running in O(Diameter) time after a polylogarithmic precomputation, which previously was only known when additional features such as carrier sense, collision detection, geometric coordinates, or power control were available.

CCS CONCEPTS

• **Networks** → **Ad hoc networks**; **Network control algorithms**; • **Theory of computation** → **Distributed algorithms**;

KEYWORDS

Wireless Network, Backbone, SINR, Broadcast

ACM Reference Format:
Magnús M. Halldórsson and Tigran Tonoyan. 2018. Leveraging Indirect Signaling for Topology Inference and Fast Broadcast. In *PODC '18: ACM Symposium on Principles of Distributed Computing, July 23–27, 2018, Egham, United Kingdom.* ACM, New York, NY, USA, Article 4, 9 pages. https://doi.org/10.1145/3212734.3212766

1 INTRODUCTION

Cumulative interference models of wireless networks, such as the *physical (SINR)* model [8], pose significant *challenges* for distributed computing. Here are two examples. In graph-based models (e.g., [2]), in order to push its message through, a node must compete with its immediate neighborhood only, while in the physical model, no local communication can be achieved if there is too much cumulative interference from outside the given neighborhood. Another example is unreliable links: the longer a link, the less likely it is to operate under even moderate external interference, and the challenge is to detect such links. Hence, most research effort has focused on addressing those issues, by careful adaptation of known techniques to the model, and introduction of new methods. In many instances, this has been achieved by augmenting the basic model with additional features, such as carrier sensing, power control, knowledge of coordinates in a common system, or restricting the structure of the input network.

On the other hand, some research has successfully utilized the intrinsic *advantages* of the physical model, stemming from the underlying geometry and the fact that signals decay with the distance from the transmitter. The works [4, 6, 10, 18] are based on the fundamental observation that when all nodes transmit with constant probability, the shortest links in the network succeed with constant rate. Hence, if one filters out the successful links, the process can be re-iterated, eventually handling all links. A related observation is used in [14]: Suppose that in the neighborhood of node v, the contention (the total mass of transmission probabilities) is just right for node v to receive messages with constant rate. Now, if all transmission probabilities are increased by an appropriate factor, then the only way v can receive messages with good rate is from its *close* neighborhood. This allows us, in particular, to estimate the density of the close neighborhood.

This work builds on yet another trick: inferring local topology via *indirect signalling*. Consider three nodes u, v, w, and assume there is no external interference. The basic observation is that if nodes u, w transmit simultaneously, and node v is able to receive, say, the transmission of u, then we can deduce that node v is "considerably" closer to u than to w. Thus, if v knows that the other two nodes are transmitting, it can deduce a useful information about the relative placement of those nodes. Performing such measurements in a controlled way, nodes can deduce an approximate picture of their neighborhood topology, namely a (crude) skeleton of the relative locations of the nodes in space, which we call *topology sketches*. The basic observation above, albeit without the "considerable" part (which is crucial to our work), was previously used in [15, 17]. Although the purpose and use was different, their successes with deterministic algorithm provided the initial spark for our investigations.

As a proof of concept, we show how topology sketches can be used systematically to build an ϵ-*backbone*: a set of nodes of constant density that dominates every ϵ-neighborhood. This can be done for any fixed precision $\epsilon \in (0, 1)$ in $\tilde{O}(\log^2 n)$ rounds[1]

[1] $\tilde{O}$ hides doubly-logarithmic factors.

PODC '18, July 23–27, 2018, Egham, United Kingdom

ACM ISBN 978-1-4503-5795-1/18/07...$15.00
https://doi.org/10.1145/3212734.3212766

(n is the number of nodes), without using carrier sensing, power control or node coordinates. A backbone is a sparse spanner of the network, and can be used for faster communication. For instance, our results give a spontaneous single-message broadcast algorithm with runtime $O(D) + \tilde{O}(\log^2 n)$ (the algorithm consists of simply flooding the message over the backbone), where D Δ is the diameter of the network. This improves the previous best $O(D \log n + \log^2 n)$ runtime for broadcast [14] (under model assumptions similar to ours) for graphs of diameter $D = \omega(\log^{1+\tau} n)$, for any constant $\tau > 0$.

Related Work. There have been several attempts to achieve sparsification of the network, in particular for the purpose of efficient broadcast, but most of them used additional facilities. Scheideler et al. [22] give a backbone construction in time $O(\log n)$, assuming the nodes can do carrier sensing. An efficient sparsification algorithm can be extracted from the papers of Jurdzinski et al. [13, 16], under the assumption that the nodes know their coordinates in a common coordinate system. Yu et al. [23] assume that the nodes can perform power control, in particular that the power can be set to such a small value that only nodes at ϵ fraction of the maximum communication range can communicate. Chlebus and Vaya [3] construct in time $O(\Delta \log^7 n)$ a structure that can be viewed as a fixed precision backbone, but assume a restricted variant of the SINR model (called *weak sensitivity*). The only work we are aware of that achieves some degree of sparsification efficiently and without the use of additional features is [14], (a slight modification of) which transforms the input network of n nodes into a subset which is "everywhere dense" but has maximum degree $O(\log^2 n)$. We reduce the latter to a constant.

The "capture effect" of the SINR model – the ability to receive in the presence of other nearby transmissions has been shown to yield several surprises. Theoretically, leader election can be achieved in only two rounds [9], and experimentally, information from multiple transmitters can be received simultaneously at the sub-packet level [19]. These require, however, more advanced features than we depend on: (lots of) power control, or advanced decoding, respectively.

Roadmap. We start with basic definitions in Sec. 2, followed by the introduction of topology sketches and their properties in Sec. 3. Sec. 4 provides a description of the ingredients used to construct a backbone, as well as a simple algorithm with runtime $\tilde{O}(\log^3 n)$. The details of implementation of the backbone algorithm, including basic communication primitives, construction of sketches etc. is presented in Sec. 5. Sec. 6 presents a refined construction of a backbone with runtime $\tilde{O}(\log^2 n)$. Some applications, including an improved broadcast algorithm, are discussed in Sec. 7. We conclude with a short discussion of future work.

2 DEFINITIONS AND ASSUMPTIONS

Let V denote the input set of n wireless nodes, represented as distinct points in the Euclidean plane. The transmission power of all nodes is set to a static value P.

An *r-disk* is a closed disk of radius r centered at a node in V; we shall denote it by indicating the center as a subscript, e.g. B_v. The *maximum degree* (or simply, degree) Δ_S of a set S of nodes is the maximum number of nodes of S in a single 1-disk. We work with partial neighborhoods that nodes discover through an "imperfect" neighborhood discovery algorithm. An *η-neighborhood $N_v \subseteq S$ of a node v in a set S* of nodes, for $\eta \leq 1$, is an arbitrary subset of nodes in the 1-disk B_v that contains all the nodes of S in the η-disk E_v.

A *δ-core* of network V, for $\delta \in (0, 1)$, is a subset $U \subseteq V$ of nodes such that: a) U is a *δ-dominating set*: every δ-disk contains at least one node of U, b) U is *sparse*, of degree $\delta^{-O(1)}$, and c) Every node $v \in V$ knows its *dominator*, i.e., a node $u \in U$ in the δ-disk of v.

A *reliable δ-communication graph* over a set U of nodes, for $\delta \in (0, 1)$, is a simple graph $G = (U, E)$, such that a) every pair of nodes at distance at most $1 - \delta$ is adjacent, b) there is a constant $c > 0$, such that for any assignment of transmission probabilities $\{p_v\}$ to nodes $v \in U$ with the property that the total probability mass in every 1-disk B_u is at most $\sum_{v \in B_u \cap U} p_v \leq c\delta$, it holds that if every node $v \in U$ transmits independently w.p.[2] p_v, then the transmission of each node w is successfully received by all its neighbors in G w.p. $\Omega(p_w)$.

An *ϵ-backbone* of network V, for a constant $\epsilon > 0$, is an ϵ-core, together with a reliable ϵ-communication graph over it. The idea behind this definition is to provide a structure that dominates the network with a given resolution and has a constant-degree reliable communication graph over it, which can transfer data with constant throughput (see also the applications in Sec. 7).

SINR model. According to the *physical* or *SINR* model of communication, if the nodes of a subset U are transmitting simultaneously, then the transmission of a node $u \in U$ is successfully received by a *listening* node v, iff $\frac{P}{d(u,v)^\alpha} > \beta \cdot (N + I_v)$, where d denotes the (Euclidean) distance, $\alpha > 2$ is the *path-loss* constant, $\beta > 1$ is the *reception threshold*, $N > 0$ is the *ambient noise*, and $I_v = \sum_{w \in U \setminus \{u\}} \frac{P}{d(w,v)^\alpha}$ is the *interference* on node v by nodes in $U \setminus \{u\}$. We denote by $d_{max} = \left(\frac{P}{\beta N}\right)^{1/\alpha}$ the maximum distance at which a communication between two nodes is possible, in the absence of interference. We assume, for simplicity, that $d_{max} = 1$, by scaling the power to $P = \beta N$.

Assumptions. We assume *spontaneous* mode of operation, where the nodes simultaneously start executing a protocol at a prespecified time. The computations are performed in synchronous rounds, where in each round, a node can transmit (or try to receive, but not both) a packet of $O(\log n)$ bits. Nodes have unique IDs, and know the SINR parameters α, β, N. They also know the precision parameter ϵ and a polynomial bound on n. We assume the "plain" SINR model, without power control, carrier sensing, coordinates knowledge, or channel coding techniques. The last one is necessary to ensure that β is strictly greater than 1 during the execution of the ConstructCore algorithm (see Sec. 5.4).

3 TOPOLOGY SKETCHES

Indirect signalling. We first observe that if two nodes u, w in the 1-disk of node v are known to be simultaneously transmitting, and the interference from all other nodes on v is small, then v can learn the relative distance to u *vis-à-vis* w.

[2]We use w.p. and w.h.p. for "with probability" and "with high probability" (namely, w.p. $1 - n^{-c}$, for a constant $c \geq 1$), respectively.

Lemma 3.1. *Let $\check{\tau} = \beta^{1/\alpha}$ and $\hat{\tau} = (\beta+2)^{1/\alpha}$. Consider a time slot where nodes u, w in the 1-disk B_v transmit, node v listens, and the interference at v from nodes $V \setminus \{u, v, w\}$ is smaller than P/β. Then:*

$$\frac{d(w,v)}{d(u,v)} > \hat{\tau} \Rightarrow (v \text{ receives the transmission of } w) \Rightarrow \frac{d(w,v)}{d(u,v)} > \check{\tau}\,.$$

Proof. In order for v to decode the message of u, it is necessary and sufficient that:

$$\frac{P}{d(u,v)^\alpha} > \beta\left(N + I + \frac{P}{d(w,v)^\alpha}\right),$$

where $I \leq P/\beta$ is the interference from nodes in $V \setminus \{u, v, w\}$. Recalling that $P = \beta N$, the inequality simplifies to: $d(u,v)^{-\alpha} > 2 + \beta d(w,v)^{-\alpha}$, leading to the condition:

$$d(w,v)^\alpha > \beta d(u,v)^\alpha + 2(d(w,v)d(u,v))^\alpha.$$

Now, clearly, this condition implies $d(w,v) > \beta^{1/\alpha} d(u,v)$, and is implied by $d(w,v)^\alpha > (\beta+2)d(u,v)^\alpha$ because $d(w,v) < 1$. □

Detection. By performing all pairwise transmissions, the nodes can learn the approximate topology of their vicinity, in the form of approximate distance relationships. For technical reasons (see the analysis of ConstructCore), we only aim for learning the topology of the 1/3-disk of a node. Let N_v be a 1/3-neighborhood of v in V. The topology information is encoded as a pair $(N_v, \prec_v)$ called *topology sketch*, where $\prec_v$ is a partial order over the set N_v, such that for given constants $\check{\tau} < \hat{\tau}$,

$$\frac{d(w,v)}{d(u,v)} \geq \hat{\tau} \quad \Rightarrow \quad u \prec_v w \quad \Rightarrow \quad \frac{d(w,v)}{d(u,v)} \geq \check{\tau}\,.$$

Roughly, $u \prec_v w$ means that v is "considerably" closer to u than to w. The topology sketches are then used to conservatively decide *ϵ-adjacency*, i.e., if two nodes are within distance at most ϵ. A chain in $\prec_v$ is *long* if its length is at least $\log_{\check{\tau}} \frac{1}{\epsilon}$. We say node v *detects* node $u \in N_v \setminus \{v\}$ if there is a long chain in $\prec_v$ starting at u, with all nodes contained in the 1/3-disk of v. By convention, node v detects itself.

Lemma 3.2. *If v detects u then they are ϵ-adjacent.*

Proof. Since v detects u, there is a long chain $u = w_0 \prec_v w_1 \prec_v w_2 \prec_v \cdots \prec_v w_s$ starting at u. This implies that $d(w_i, v) \geq \check{\tau} \cdot d(w_{i-1}, v)$, for all $i = 1, 2, \ldots, s$. Hence, $d(u,v) \leq d(w_s, v)/\check{\tau}^s \leq \check{\tau}^{-s} \leq \epsilon$, as required. □

Detection graph. We can now form, for any subset $U \subseteq V$ of nodes, the undirected *detection graph* $G = (U, E)$ with edges between nodes u, v if and only if either u detects v or v detects u.

The following result exhibits the connection between sketches and ϵ-backbones, and is closely related to the classic results of Hochbaum and Shmoys on facility location problems [12]. A *2-MIS* (Maximal Independent Set) of a graph G is a maximal subset of vertices of mutual hop-distance at least 3.

Lemma 3.3. *Every 2-MIS M of the detection graph $G = (U, E)$ is a 2ϵ-dominating set for U of size at most that of a minimum (graph) dominating set of G.*

Proof. M is a 2ϵ-dominating set, since only ϵ-adjacent nodes detect each other. Each node dominates at most a single node of a 2-MIS, hence the size bound. □

Detecting Everyone with a Few Nodes. We crucially show that few nodes suffice to detect all nodes, i.e., that the detection graph has a small dominating set. Lemma 3.3 then leads the way toward finding such a set.

Theorem 3.4. *The detection graph of every 1-disk contains a dominating set of size at most $12 \cdot (8\hat{\tau}+1)^{4\lceil \log_{\check{\tau}}(\hat{\tau}/\epsilon)\rceil} = \epsilon^{-O(1)}$.*

The proof is based on the concept of exponential trees, defined as follows. Given a set X of nodes and a number $t > 1$, a *t-exponential tree* $T = (X, E_T)$ with vertex set X is a rooted tree with the following property: If $v \in X$ is a node with parent p and child c, and w is a proper descendant of c, then the distance from c to p is at least t times the distance from w to c: $d(p,c) > t \cdot d(c,w)$.

First, we prove that every set U of nodes can be partitioned into a constant number of bounded degree t-exponential trees. We use the following two simple facts. A set X of nodes is *r-spread* if the distance between every two nodes in X is more than r.

Fact 1. *For every $r < R$, an r-spread set within an R-disk contains at most $(2R/r+1)^2$ nodes.*

The claim follows by comparing the total area of the (disjoint) $r/2$-disks centered at nodes of X with the area of the expanded $(R + r/2)$-disk containing all those $r/2$-disks.

Fact 2. *Let X be a maximal r-spread subset of a disk F_v. The distance from each node $w \in F_v$ to its nearest node in X is at most r, while the distance to any other node in X is more than $r/2$.*

Proof. The first claim follows by maximality. For the second, consider a node $w \in F_v$, let $u \in X$ be its closest node in X, and $u' \in X$ be another node. If $d(u,w) \leq r/2$, then by the triangle inequality, $d(u',w) \geq d(u',u) - d(u,w) > r - r/2 = r/2$. Otherwise, $d(u',w) \geq d(u,w) > r/2$. □

Lemma 3.5. *Let U be a set of nodes and $t > 1$ be a number. There is a spanning forest over U with at most $(8t+1)^2$ different t-exponential trees of degree at most $(8t+1)^2$.*

Proof. If U contains a single node or none, then we are done, so assume there are at least two nodes. Let F be an r-disk containing U, for some $r > 0$. Let $t' = 4t$, $r_0 = r$ and $r_1 = \frac{r_0}{t'}$. Let L_1 be a maximal r_1-spread set of nodes in F. By Fact 1, L_1 contains at most $(2t'+1)^2$ nodes, and by maximality, every other node u in $F \setminus L_1$ is within distance r_1 of a node in L_1. If $|L_1| = 1$, then all nodes are located in a single disk of radius r_1, so we let $r_0 \leftarrow r_1$, $r_1 \leftarrow \frac{r_1}{t'}$, and repeat, until $|L_1| \geq 2$. The latter will eventually happen, since the nodes occupy distinct positions in space, and their number is at least 2.

We set the nodes of L_1 as the roots of the forest and denote them by $L_1 = \{u_0, u_1, \ldots, u_{|L_1|-1}\}$. Partition the remaining nodes $F \setminus L_1$ into $|L_1|$ subsets $S_0, S_1, \ldots, S_{|L_1|-1}$, where for every i, the set S_i contains the nodes whose closest point in L_1 is u_i, ties broken arbitrarily. By Fact 2, $d(w, u_i) \leq r_1$, for each $w \in S_i$. In particular, each S_i is contained in a disk of radius r_1. For each subset S_i, recursively compute a forest of at most $(2t'+1)^2$ trees spanning S_i. Let L_2^i be the roots of the forest of S_i. We assign the node $u_{i+1 \bmod |L_1|}$ as the parent of nodes in L_2^i. Namely, when assigning parents, we shift the indices by one. Since $|L_1| \geq 2$, the parent $u_{i+1 \bmod |L_1|}$ of nodes in

L_2^i is different from u_i, which implies, by Fact 2, that the distance from $u_{i+1 \mod |L_1|}$ to its children is at least $r_1/2$.

Thus, as observed above, for every node $u \in L_2^i$, the distance from u to its parent $p \in L_1$ is between $r_1/2$ and $2r_0 = 2t'r_1$ (since all nodes of L_1 and L_2^i are in the same r_0-disk). Let c be a child of u, and w be any descendant of c. Then by the same reasoning as above, $d(c,w) \leq 2r_2$, where $r_2 = \frac{r_1}{t'}$, and $d(p,c) \geq r_1/2$ (by Fact 2). Hence, $d(p,c) \geq r_1/2 = t'r_2/2 = 2tr_2 \geq td(c,w)$. By induction, the latter extends to every node-parent-child-descendant configuration, as required. Also, by construction, the number of roots, as well as the number of children of every node is at most $(2t'+1)^2 = (8t+1)^2$. □

Proof of Thm. 3.4. Since the nodes in a 1-disk can be covered with at most 12 of 1/3-disks, it is enough to show that in every 1/3-disk E_v, there is a set U of at most $(8\hat{\tau}+1)^{4\lceil \log_{\hat{\tau}}(\hat{\tau}/\epsilon)\rceil}$ nodes, such that every node in E_v is detected by some node in U. Let $T_1, T_2, \ldots, T_k$ be a spanning $\hat{\tau}$-exponential forest over the nodes in E_v, as provided by Lemma 3.5, where $k = (8\hat{\tau}+1)^2$. We focus on tree T_1, the case of others being similar. Let p_0 be a node in T_1 at tree-distance $d = 2 \cdot \lceil \log_{\hat{\tau}} \frac{1}{\epsilon} \rceil$ from the root, w be a descendant of p_0, and $p_0, p_1, p_2, \ldots, p_d$ be the path to the root. We claim that p_0 detects all of its descendants. Indeed, by the definition of exponential trees, we have: $d(p_2,p_0) \geq \hat{\tau}d(w,p_0)$, $d(p_4,p_0) \geq \hat{\tau}d(p_2,p_0)$, and generally, $d(p_{2i},p_0) > \hat{\tau}d(p_{2i-2},p_0)$, for $i = 2,\ldots,d$. Thus, by definition, the sequence $w, p_2, p_4, \ldots, p_d$ is a long $<_{p_0}$-chain starting with w and contained in the 1/3-disk E_v, so p_0 indeed detects w.

The argument above shows that the set of nodes at tree-distance at most d from the root indeed detects the whole tree T_1. The maximum degree of T_1 is at most k, by Lemma 3.5, so the number of nodes at tree-distance at most d from the root is less than k^{d+1}. Considering all trees together, we obtain a subset of at most $k^{d+2} = (8\hat{\tau}+1)^{4\lceil \log_{\hat{\tau}}(\hat{\tau}/\epsilon)\rceil}$ nodes that detect all nodes in E_v. □

4 THE MAIN ALGORITHM

A backbone is constructed in several stages, each formulated as a separate subroutine below. Roughly, the algorithm is as follows. First, we sparsify the network using an extension of the algorithm of [14], reducing the degree of the network to roughly logarithmic. Next, nodes collect their neighborhood information and organize and schedule paired transmissions, thus building neighborhood sketches (via Lemma 3.1). Finally, the detection graph is formed and the backbone is obtained by computing a 2-MIS of the detection graph.

Concrete steps are described below, where we describe a simple formulation of the algorithm that has runtime $\tilde{O}(\log^3 n)$. In Sec. 6 we show how using the same building blocks in a divide-and-conquer approach can further reduce this to $\tilde{O}(\log^2 n)$, leading to the main result, stated below.

Theorem 4.1. *There is a randomized distributed algorithm that for any constant $\epsilon \in (0, 1/3)$ constructs an ϵ-backbone in $\tilde{O}(\log^2 n)$ rounds, w.h.p.*

Algorithm 1 Backbone(ϵ)

1: $S \leftarrow$ Sparsify($\epsilon/(2\hat{\tau})$)
2: $S' \leftarrow$ ConstructCore(S, V, $\epsilon/(2\hat{\tau})$, $\epsilon/(4\hat{\tau})$)
3: ConstructGraph(S', ϵ)

Sparsify(δ) is an extension of the probabilistic sparsification algorithm of Jurdzinski et al. [14], augmented with a "sample-and-repeat" step in order to reduce the degree of the network. The output is a δ-dominating set of V of degree $O(\delta^{-\alpha} \log n \log\log n)$. The runtime of Sparsify(δ) is $O(\delta^{-\alpha} \cdot \log^2 n)$. In the simple implementation of Backbone, we take $\delta = \epsilon/(2\hat{\tau})$.

ConstructCore is the central piece of our algorithm. The input to ConstructCore(S, U, δ', δ) is two parameters $\delta, \delta' > 0$ such that $2\delta+\delta' \leq 1/(3\hat{\tau})$, a subset $U \subseteq V$, and a δ'-dominating set $S \subseteq U$ of U, such that the nodes in S know a constant-factor approximate upper bound on Δ_S. The output is a subset $S' \subseteq S$ that is a $\hat{\tau}\cdot(2\delta+\delta')$-core of U. The runtime is $O(\Delta_S^2 \log n)$.

ConstructGraph(S', δ) constructs a reliable δ-communication graph over the set S'. The runtime is $O(\Delta_{S'}^2 \log n)$, assuming δ is constant.

It follows directly from the properties of the algorithms above that Backbone(ϵ) w.h.p. computes an ϵ-backbone in $O(\log^3 n \cdot (\log\log n)^2)$ rounds.

5 IMPLEMENTATION

Here we present the implementation of the subroutines used in Backbone. In addition, we adapt previous work on *coloring* and *local broadcast* to our setting, which are used as basic scheduling and message dissemination primitives in our algorithms.

5.1 Sparsify

Algorithm Sparsify(δ) constructs a δ-dominating set of V of degree $O(\delta^{-\alpha} \log n \log\log n)$. The algorithm is based on a "probabilistic sparsification" procedure StabilizeProbability due to Jurdzinski et al. [14, Lemmas 1, 2], that establishes a probability assignment $\{p_v\}$ of the nodes in the network, as follows. StabilizeProbability(U, δ, $\tilde{\Delta}$) takes as input a set U, and parameters $0 < \delta < 1$ and $\tilde{\Delta}$, and terminates in $O(\delta^{-\alpha} \log\tilde{\Delta} \log n)$ rounds, where $\tilde{\Delta}$ is an upper bound on Δ_U that the nodes have:[3] At the initial application below, $\tilde{\Delta}$ is simply the polynomial upper bound on n that the nodes have. The output is a probability assignment $\{p_v\}$ to the nodes in U, such that for constants $c_U, c_L > 0$ it holds that: a) The probability mass in every 1-disk B_v is at most $c_U \log\tilde{\Delta}$, and b) For every δ-disk E_v, the probability mass in E_v is at least $c_L\delta^{\alpha}$. We assume that $1/\delta = polylog(n)$, and use the notation $\gamma = 2(\delta/2)^{-\alpha}/c_L$ in the algorithm and analysis.

[3]The dependence on $\tilde{\Delta}$ is obtained by slightly modifying the algorithm, by changing the initial probabilities from $O(1/n)$ to $O(1/\tilde{\Delta})$. The dependence on δ is also implicit in [14], but can be recovered by inspecting the proofs.

Algorithm 2 SPARSIFY(δ)

1: $\{p_v\} \leftarrow$STABILIZEPROBABILITY(V, $\delta/2$, n)
2: Construct set S', where each node $v \in V$ joins S' w.p. $1-(1-p_v)^{\gamma \log n}$
3: $\{p'_v\} \leftarrow$STABILIZEPROBABILITY(S', $\delta/2$, $O(\delta^{-\alpha}\log^2 n)$)
4: Return set R, where each node $v \in S'$ joins R w.p. $1-(1-p'_v)^{\gamma \log n}$

Clearly, the runtime of SPARSIFY(δ) is $O(\delta^{-\alpha}\cdot\log^2 n)$.

LEMMA 5.1. *S' is a $\frac{\delta}{2}$-dominating set of degree $O(\delta^{-\alpha}\log^2 n)$ of V, w.h.p.*

PROOF. First note that the act of a node joining S' is equivalent to the following procedure (not actually performed): for $\gamma \log n$ rounds, every node v in every round (re-)joins S' w.p. p_v, independently from others. Let B_v be a 1-disk, and E_v be a $\delta/2$-disk. Since the probability mass in B_v is upper-bounded by $c_U \log n$, the expected number X_i of "joins" by nodes in B_v during this process is $\mathbb{E}[X] \le \gamma \log n \cdot c_U \log n = (2c_U(\delta/2)^{-\alpha}/c_L)\log^2 n$. By a similar reasoning, the expected number Y of "joins" by nodes in E_v is $\mathbb{E}[Y] \ge c_L\delta^\alpha\gamma\log n = 2\log n$. This implies, using standard Chernoff bounds for Binomial r.v.s, that w.h.p., every $\delta/2$-disk E_v, $v \in V$, contains at least one node from S', and every 1-disk B_v, $v \in V$, contains at most $O(\delta^{-\alpha}\log^2 n)$ nodes from S', as required. □

Now, it should be clear that the second application of STABILIZEPROBABILITY is correct, since the degree of S' is $O(\delta^{-\alpha}\log^2 n)$, w.h.p. Hence, by the same argument as in the lemma above, R is a $\delta/2$-dominating set of S', and by the simple observation below (Obs. 5.2), R is a δ-dominating set of V, as required. Moreover, the degree of R is $O(\delta^{-\alpha}\log n \log\log n)$.

OBSERVATION 5.2. *If a set X is an a-dominating set of Y, and Y is a b-dominating set of Z, then X is an $(a+b)$-dominating set for Z.*

5.2 LocalBroadcast

Most of our algorithms can be seen as sequences of local computations, calls to external algorithms, and operations of the form "every node sends t messages to all nodes within its $1-\delta$-disk". The latter is achieved through a local broadcast algorithm LOCALBROADCAST(U, δ), which guarantees, w.h.p., that each node in a set U successfully transmits a single message to all nodes in its $1-\delta$-disk (note that nodes outside the $1-\delta$-disk may, but are not required to, receive the message as well). The algorithm simply consists of each node in U transmitting independently w.p. $p = c\delta/\Delta_U$ in each of $c'\delta^{-1}\Delta_U \log n$ rounds, where c, c' are appropriate constants (in our case, nodes will know a constant-factor upper bound on Δ_U). This algorithm has been analyzed in, e.g., [7], where it is shown that after its execution, each node has delivered its message to its $1-\delta$-disk w.h.p. The following lemma can be extracted from [7] (where the dependence on δ is implicit), and in combination with a standard Chernoff bound easily implies the proof.

LEMMA 5.3. *Assume the nodes transmit independently, using a probability assignment $\{p_v\}$, such that the probability mass in every 1-disk is bounded by $a\delta$, for a small enough constant a. The probability that a node u successfully delivers its message to all nodes in its $1-\delta$-disk is $\Theta(p_u)$.*

We let $T_{LB}(\Delta_U, \delta) = O(\delta^{-1}\Delta_U \log n)$ denote the runtime of LOCALBROADCAST(U, δ) in a set U with at most n nodes.

5.3 DeltaColor

We use an $O(\Delta)$-coloring algorithm, DELTACOLOR(U, δ), which assigns the nodes in the input set U colors in the range $1, 2, \ldots, t = O(\Delta_U)$ so that pairs of nodes within distance $1-\delta$ receive different colors. For this purpose, we use the coloring algorithm of [21], adopted to the SINR model in [5]. The runtime of the algorithm is $O(\Delta_U \log n)$, for any constant $\delta \in (0,1)$. The implementation of [5] works under certain assumptions. One assumption is that the nodes know a constant factor approximate upper bound on the degree Δ_U, which holds in our application. A more subtle issue is the assumption that a node cannot receive a message from another node at distance greater than $1-\delta$, even without interference. This is a restriction of the SINR model. The reason for this assumption is that message reception between nodes at distances arbitrarily close to 1 may be inconsistent due to the sensitivity to external interference, so such pairs of nodes may prevent each other from committing to their colors for a long time, delaying the runtime of the algorithm and increasing the number of colors.

In order to overcome this limitation, we make the following observations about the coloring algorithm in [5, 21]: 1. Each round of the algorithm consists of each node v independently transmitting a message according to a probability assignment $\{p_v\}$, 2. In every round, the probability mass in each 1-disk is bounded by a constant, which can be made arbitrarily small by only changing constant factors in the runtime, and 3. The analysis is based on the assumption that in each round, a node transmitting w.p. p_v successfully delivers its message to all nodes in its $1-\delta$-disk, w.p. $\Omega(p_v)$.

These observations readily suggest the following solution: we add a preprocessing step, where we call CONSTRUCTGRAPH(U, δ) to compute a reliable δ-communication graph over the set U (see Sec. 5.5), then apply the coloring algorithm, where a node accepts messages only from its neighbors in the graph (and ignores the rest). The observations above and the properties of reliable communication graphs imply that the modified algorithm will correctly compute an $O(\Delta_U)$-coloring.

The only caveat is that CONSTRUCTGRAPH takes $O(\Delta_U^2 \log n)$ time. This does not increase the runtime of BACKBONE significantly, but it would be an obstacle for the optimized variant presented in Sec. 6. Note that CONSTRUCTGRAPH first computes a *directed* communication graph in $O(\Delta_U \log n)$ rounds, then removes the directed edges in $O(\Delta_U^2 \log n)$ rounds. The directed edges are still reliable, and they are only between nodes that are at distance larger than $1-\delta$. It can be checked, by inspecting the proofs in [21], that the modified coloring algorithm works correctly even with such a directed communication graph, giving us a coloring algorithm with runtime $O(\Delta_U \log n)$.

5.4 ConstructCore

The input to CONSTRUCTCORE(S, U, δ', δ) consists of parameters $\delta, \delta' > 0$, such that $2\delta + \delta' \le 1/(3\hat{\tau})$, a subset $U \subseteq V$, and a δ'-dominating set S of U, such that the nodes in S that know a constant-factor approximate upper bound on Δ_S. The output is a subset $S' \subseteq S$ that is a $\hat{\tau} \cdot (2\delta + \delta')$-core of U.

The algorithm consists of two parts. The goal of the first part is for all nodes in U to learn their topology sketches with respect to S and parameter δ. We are only interested in the topology sketch of the 1/3-disk of each node. The main idea is, as described in Lemma 3.1, for each pair of nodes u, w to transmit together alone so that nodes in their vicinity can deduce their topology sketches. In the second part, the nodes compute the detection graph $G = (S, E)$, based on the sketches, and compute a 2-MIS of G, which, by Lemma 3.3 and Thm. 3.4, is a sparse dominating set of S.

We use sub-routines OnYourMarks(i, j) and Go(i, j). In the former, the color-i, j nodes establish paired transmission schedules, while the latter includes the execution of those schedules and the construction of sketches by the listening nodes. All nodes mentioned in the algorithm are assumed to be in S, except when explicitly stated otherwise. Nodes in $U \setminus S$ never transmit in this algorithm.

Algorithm 3 ConstructCore(S, U, δ', δ)

DeltaColor(S, 1/3): Assign every node a color in $[k] = \{1, 2, \ldots, k = O(\Delta_S)\}$
LocalBroadcast(S, 1/3): Each node v learns a 2/3-neighborhood N'_v in S, and their colors
For each pair of colors $\{i, j\}$, in some well-defined order, run phase $\{i, j\}$: OnYourMarks(i, j), then Go(i, j)
Each node learns, via calls to LocalBroadcast(S, 1/3), its 2-hop neighborhood in the detection graph G
Compute a 2-MIS M of G and run LocalBroadcast(M, 1/3)
Every node in S sets its 2-hop neighbor in M as its dominator. Every node $v \in U$ identifies a 2-MIS node u that is minimal in v's partial order w.r.t. S, and sets u as its dominator

OnYourMarks(i, j) consists of $cT_{LB}(32, 1/3)$ rounds, for a constant c. It uses constants $c, c', p = \Omega(1)$, specified in the analysis. Go(i, j) consists of $c' \log n$ rounds. In both subroutines, all transmissions are performed via LocalBroadcast(X, 1/3) by the corresponding sets X of nodes.

Algorithm 4 OnYourMarks(i, j)

Every color-i (symmetrically, color-j) node v sends a random string $s_v(w)$ of $c' \log n$ bits, each bit set w.p. p, independently from all other strings and bits, to each color j node in N'_v (by Fact 1, there are at most 16 of them)
Every color i (color j) node sends a confirmation message, containing the set of IDs from which it received a random string assigned to itself
Every node v, upon receiving a confirmation message from a node $w \in N'_v$ computes a shared random string (*schedule*) s_{wv} that is the bitwise OR of $s_v(w)$ and $s_w(v)$

Algorithm 5 Go(i, j)

for rounds $r = 1, 2, \ldots, c' \log n$ **do**
  Every color-i (color-j) node v forms the subset A^r_v of color-j (color-i) nodes $w \in N'_v$ that share a random string s_{vw} with it, such that $s_{vw}[r] = 1$
  if $A^r_v \neq \emptyset$ **then**
    v transmits A^r_v
  end if
  Every node $v \in U$, upon receiving $A^r_u = \{w_1, w_2, \ldots\}$ from node u, adds, for each $t \geq 1$, the relation $u <_v w_t$ to its partial order, if v has overheard confirmation messages from both u and w_t in OnYourMarks(i, j).
end for

In order to compute a 2-MIS of the detection graph G, we use a variant of the MIS algorithm of [20], adapted to the SINR model in [24], with the modification that nodes ignore all messages coming from nodes that are not within their 2-hop neighborhood in G. It should be noted that [24] assumes a restricted SINR model, where nodes at distance greater than 2/3 (in our case) can not communicate. However, as said above, the nodes ignore messages from outside of their 2-hop neighborhoods (which includes all nodes at distance greater than $2\delta \leq 2/3$), so there is no need for model restriction.

Correctness. We begin by showing that the algorithm correctly computes the sketches of 1/3-disks, w.h.p. First, Lemma 3.1 implies that if a node v hears a scheduled transmission of two nodes u, w in its vicinity and the external interference is low, then it can learn their order in its sketch. Thus, it remains to argue that this will happen for all pairs u, w that are not far from v.

We say a pair of nodes u, v of colors i, j respectively, *is set up* for round r of phase $\{i, j\}$, if they share a string s_{uv}, with $s_{uv}[r] = 1$. Note that if u, v are set up for round r, they will transmit simultaneously in round r. Nodes in the same area could also transmit simultaneously, even if they are not set up for the given round, but this will be a "random accident", since the strings s_{uv} are mutually independent.

Observation 5.4. *Every pair $\{u, v\}$ of nodes of colors $\{i, j\}$ that share a random string s_{uv} are set up in each round r of phase $\{i, j\}$ w.p. $2p$, independently from all other pairs $\{u', v'\} \neq \{u, v\}$ of nodes.*

With this observation, the transmissions in Go(i, j) by pairs of nodes that are set up together, are almost identical to a LocalBroadcast in a bounded degree network, with the only difference that instead of single nodes in separate neighborhoods, coordinated pairs of nodes execute transmissions, independently from other pairs (note that by Fact 1, there can be at most 16 nodes of the same color in a 1-disk). Hence, by choosing the constants c and p appropriately, we can ensure that every pair of nodes in the 1/3-disk B_v of a node v (which contains its δ-disk) is measured by v, as per Lemma 3.1, since every pair of nodes in B_v are at reliable local broadcast distance, and hence discover each other via sets N'_v, and share and execute a common schedule, w.h.p. The formal analysis is nearly identical to that of LocalBroadcast, and is omitted.

One possible concern with the argument above is that the nodes outside the 1/3-disk of a node v might introduce false relations into $<_v$, namely relations $u <_v w$ for which the condition $d(w, v) >$

$\check{\tau}d(u, v)$ does not hold. This could only happen if v receives a message from u, that contains the ID of w, while w does not transmit in this stage. This in turn means that one of them did not confirm the schedule of the other. However, by design, node v does not draw conclusions from unconfirmed communications (or ones that it didn't hear to be confirmed both ways).

Finally, let us show that the output M of the algorithm is a $\hat{\tau} \cdot (2\delta + \delta')$-core of U, w.h.p. First, M is a 2δ-core of S, by Lemma 3.3 and Thm. 3.4. On the other hand, S is a δ'-dominating set for U, which means that M is a $(\delta' + 2\delta)$-dominating set for U (Obs. 5.2). It is possible that a node $u \in U \setminus S$ does not detect any of the 2-MIS nodes, but by selecting a 2-MIS node that is minimal in its partial order w.r.t. S guarantees that the selected node is at most $\hat{\tau}$ times further than the nearest 2-MIS node (which is within $\delta' + 2\delta \leq 1/(3\hat{\tau})$), as otherwise the selected node would not be minimal. Hence, M is a $\hat{\tau} \cdot (\delta' + 2\delta)$-core of U.

Runtime. The coloring step takes $O(\Delta_S \log n)$ rounds. Computation of neighborhood sets N'_v takes $T_{LB}(\Delta_S, 1/3) = O(\Delta_S \log n)$ rounds. As observed above, every 1-disk contains at most 32 active nodes in each phase, hence in OnYourMarks, the random string and confirmation message transmissions take $O(T_{LB}(32, 1/3)) = O(\log n)$ time. On the other hand, Go has runtime $c' \log n$, by definition. Since the number of phases is $O(\Delta_S^2)$, the total runtime of OnYourMarks and Go is $O(\Delta_S^2 \log n)$. The 2-hop neighborhood discovery in G takes $O(\Delta_S^2 \log n)$ rounds ($O(\Delta_S)$ local broadcasts). The 2-MIS computation takes $O(\log \Delta_S \log n)$ rounds [20, 24]. [4] Hence, the total runtime is $O(\Delta_S^2 \log n)$.

5.5 ConstructGraph

The input to ConstructGraph(U, δ) is a parameter $\delta \in (0, 1)$ and a subset U of V, such that the nodes in U know a constant-factor upper bound on Δ_U. The output is a reliable δ-communication graph over the set U, w.h.p. The basic strategy is to first find a *balanced* probability assignment $\{p_v\}$, such that the probability mass in every 1-disk is $\Theta(\delta)$, then simulate transmissions according to the assignment $\{p_v\}$, and select the edges that "work" consistently, i.e., edges that deliver messages with sufficient rate (the latter part is related to what is done in [4] for creating their *SINR-Induced Graphs*). The main purpose of the assignment $\{p_v\}$ is to make sufficient "noise" so that only reliable links are selected.

In order to achieve a balanced probability assignment, we use a contention balancing procedure ContentionBalance(U, δ), which is related but different from the ones used in [11, 14, 20]. The runtime of the procedure is $O(\log \Delta_U \log n)$. The algorithms below use tunable constants c_i, $1 \leq i \leq 5$.

Each node v starts with initial probability $p_v = c_1\delta/\Delta_U$. Time is divided into $\log \Delta_U$ phases of $c_2\delta^{-1} \log n$ rounds each. During each round of each phase, every node v independently transmits w.p. p_v. If v receives at least $c_3 \log n$ messages during a phase, then it *freezes* the probability p_v for the remaining phases. If p_v has not been frozen (in this or previous phases), then it is doubled at the end of the phase.

We claim that after the procedure completes, every 1-disk has probability mass $\Theta(\delta)$. The claim follows from the following two observations. The following lemma, whose variation appears in nearly every work on distributed SINR algorithms, provides a key ingredient for the proof.

Lemma 5.5. *Assume the nodes transmit independently, using a probability assignment $\{p_v\}$, such that the probability mass in every 1-disk is bounded by $a\delta$, for a small enough constant a. If the probability mass in the $1 - \delta$-disk of a node w is $p_w + q_1$, and the probability mass in the 1-disk of w is $p_w + q_2$, then w successfully receives a message w.p. in $\Omega(q_1) \cap O(q_2)$.*

Observation 5.6. *On termination, the probability mass in every 1-disk is $\Omega(\delta)$, w.h.p.*

Proof sketch. Let v be a node. If v never froze its probability, then p_v reached $c_1\delta$, which implies the claim. So, we may assume there was a phase i in which v received at least $c_3 \log n$ messages. Let q denote the probability mass in the 1-disk B_v in phase i. We show that if q was too small, then the reception of at least $c_3 \log n$ messages would be a low probability event. By Lemma 5.5, in each round of phase i, the probability that v receives a message is at most $c'q$, for a constant c'. Hence, the expected number of messages that v receives is at most $c'qc_2\delta^{-1} \log n$. By choosing the constants c_2 and c_3 appropriately and using a standard Chernoff bound, we see that if it was $q \leq c''\delta$ for a small enough constant, then the probability of receiving at least $c_3 \log n$ messages could be made inversely polynomial in n. □

Observation 5.7. *The probability mass in every 1/3-disk stays at most $2c_1\delta$ after every phase, w.h.p.*

Proof sketch. The proof is by induction on the number of phases. We have that before the first phase, the probability mass in every 1-disk is at most $c_1\delta$. This implies the base case, if we consider the initial phase to be the trivially empty one. Now consider a phase i and a 1/3-disk B_v. If the probability mass in B_v was less than $c_1\delta/2$ after phase $i - 1$, it will be at most $c_1\delta$ after phase i. So, suppose it reaches $c_1\delta/2$ for the first time at the start of phase i. Let S be the set of nodes in B_v that have not frozen their probabilities. If $|S| = 1$, then we are done, since the maximum probability of a node is $c_1\delta$. So assume $|S| \geq 2$. Note that all nodes in S use the same probability in phase i, which is at most half of the probability mass in B_v, since $|S| \geq 2$. Hence, for each node $u \in S$, the probability mass in B_v is at least $p_u + c_1\delta/4$. By the inductive hypothesis, the probability mass in each 1/3-disk at the beginning of phase i is at most $2c_1\delta$, so by an appropriate choice of c_1, we can apply Lemma 5.5, to see that in each round, node u receives a message w.p. at least $c'c_1\delta$, for a constant c'. The expected number of messages received by u in the phase i is then at least $c'c_1\delta \cdot c_2\delta^{-1} \log n$. By choosing the constants c_2, c_3 appropriately, we can apply a standard Chernoff bound to show that u receives at least $c_3 \log n$ messages, w.h.p., and hence it freezes its probability at the end of phase i. Applying the union bound over all nodes and all phases, we find that the probability mass within each 1/3-disk never exceeds $2c_1\delta$, w.h.p. □

Having the probability assignment $\{p_v\}$ from ContentionBalance, we are ready to perform the procedure Simulate$(U, \delta, \{p_v\})$, which constructs the graph. The procedure consists of

[4]The dependence on the degree is implicit in [20, 24], but can be obtained by a simple modification of the algorithm, assuming the nodes have an estimate of the degree.

$c_4\delta^{-1}\Delta_U \log n$ rounds, where in each round, every node v transmits probe message w.p. $q_v = c_1\delta/(2\Delta_U)$, transmits noise message w.p. $p_v/2$, and stays silent w.p. $1-p_v/2-q_v$, for an appropriate constant c_4. If node v receives at least $c_5 \log n$ probe messages from a node u, it adds the directed edge (u, v) to its graph neighborhood.

It is easy to see that during the whole run of the algorithm, the probability mass in each 1-disk is $\Theta(\delta)$. Hence, by choosing the constants c_4, c_5 appropriately, we can use an analysis similar to the one for ContentionBalance to prove, with the help of Lemmas 5.3 and 5.5, the following properties.

Observation 5.8. *If $d(u, v) \le 1 - \delta$, then both edges (u, v) and (v, u) are added, w.h.p.*

Observation 5.9. *If an edge (u, v) is added, then w.h.p., the probability that u delivers its* probe *message to v in a single round is $\Omega(q_v)$.*

The two properties above show that the graph G output by Simulate is indeed a reliable δ-communication graph, with the caveat that it may contain directed edges between some pairs of nodes at distance larger than $1 - \delta$. This is fixed by the procedure FixDirectedEdges(G, δ), where the nodes locally broadcast lists of their neighbors, and remove directed edges or add the missing directions. [5] This part of the algorithm is the most expensive, taking $O(\Delta_U^2 \log n)$ rounds.

Algorithm 6 ConstructGraph(U, δ)

$\{p_v\} \leftarrow$ ContentionBalance(U, δ)
$G \leftarrow$Simulate(U, δ, $\{p_v\}$)
$G' \leftarrow$FixDirectedEdges(G, δ)
return G'

Proposition 5.10. *Algorithm ConstructGraph constructs a reliable δ-communication graph in $O(\Delta_U^2 \log n)$ rounds, w.h.p.*

6 FASTER COMPUTATION OF BACKBONE

As mentioned in Sec. 4, a divide and conquer approach can be used to improve the runtime of Backbone to $\tilde{O}(\log^2 n)$. The idea is to split the instance into low-degree sub-instances, call ConstructCore on each one separately, merge the obtained solutions, and repeat. Since the runtime of ConstructCore is quadratic in the degree, this gives us the improvement. Note however, that after each iteration, the domination radius of the dominating set increases (cf. Obs. 5.2), so we need to start with a small value of δ.

Recall that the algorithm ConstructCore(S, U, δ', δ) outputs a $\hat{\tau}(2\delta + \delta')$-core of U, which is a $\hat{\tau}(2\delta + \delta')$-dominating set of degree δ^{-c}, for a constant $c > 0$. We also note that by calling ConstructCore(S, S, 0, δ), we obtain a 2δ-dominating set of S, since each node in S has a 2-hop neighbor in the constructed 2-MIS (see the analysis in Sec. 5.4). The algorithm FastBackbone below uses notation $\delta = \frac{\epsilon}{2\hat{\tau}\log\log n}$, and $t = \delta^{-c} \cdot \log\log n$.

[5] It can be shown with the tools used here that if an edge is reliable in one direction, it is also reliable in the opposite direction, with a difference only in constant factors.

Algorithm 7 FastBackbone(ϵ)

$S_0 \leftarrow$ Sparsify(δ)
$i \leftarrow 0$
while $\Delta_{S_i} > t$ **do**
  DeltaColor(S_i, 1/3): Each node $v \in S_i$ is assigned a color $col(v) \in [1, O(\Delta_{S_i})]$
  for $j = 1, 2, \dots, O(\Delta_{S_i}/t)$ **do**
    $R_j \leftarrow \{v \in S_i : col(v) \in [(j-1)\cdot t + 1, j \cdot t]\}$
    $C_j \leftarrow$ConstructCore(R_j, R_j, 0, $\delta/2$)
  end for
  $S_{i+1} \leftarrow \cup_j C_j$
  $i \leftarrow i + 1$
end while
$S' \leftarrow$ConstructCore(S_i, V, $\epsilon/(2\hat{\tau})$, $\epsilon/(4\hat{\tau})$)
ConstructGraph(S', ϵ)

Correctness. The following lemma shows how the domination radius and degree evolve during a run of the algorithm.

Lemma 6.1. *S_i is an $i\delta$-dominating set of S_0 of degree $\Delta_{S_i} \le \Delta_{S_0} \cdot (c'/\log\log n)^i$, for a constant c'.*

Proof. Consider the first iteration. The set S_0 is partitioned into $c'\Delta_{S_0}/t$ subsets R_j for a constant c', each of degree t. By running ConstructCore on R_j, we obtain a δ-dominating set of R_j. Note that the nodes in $V \setminus R_j$ stay idle during this call, so there is no factor of $\hat{\tau}$ involved in the domination radius. Hence, at the end of the first iteration, S_1 is a δ-dominating set of S_0, of degree $c'\delta^{-c}\Delta_{S_0}/t = \Delta_{S_0} \cdot c'/\log\log n$. The claim follows by induction, using Obs. 5.2. □

The lemma above implies, in particular, that the loop iterates at most $O(\log \Delta_{S_0}/\log\log\log n) \le \log\log n$ times (assuming n is large enough), since $\Delta_{S_0} = O(\delta^{-\alpha}\log n \cdot \log\log n) = O(\log n \cdot (\log\log n)^{\alpha+1})$. Hence, after the loop breaks, S_i is a $\delta \log\log n = \frac{\epsilon}{2\hat{\tau}}$-dominating set of S_0, which implies that S' is an ϵ-core of V.

Runtime. Sparsify(δ) takes $O(\delta^{-\alpha}\log^2 n) = O(\log^2 n(\log\log n)^\alpha)$ time. Each application of ConstructCore($R_j, \dots$) takes $O(t^2 \log n)$ rounds, so the total runtime of the ith iteration is $\frac{\Delta_{S_i}}{t} \cdot O(t^2 \log n) = O(t\Delta_{S_i} \log n)$ (this subsumes the runtime of DeltaColor). Using the lemma above, we see that the total runtime of the loop is $O(t\Delta_{S_0}\log n) = O(\log^2 n(\log\log n)^{\alpha+c+1})$. The last application of ConstructCore takes $O(\log n \cdot t^2) = O(\log^2 n)$ time, since the degree of S_i is at most t at this point. The final step takes $O(\log n)$ time. Overall, the algorithm takes $O(\log^2 n \cdot (\log\log n)^{c+\alpha+1}) = \tilde{O}(\log^2 n)$ rounds.

7 APPLICATIONS

7.1 Broadcast

In the (single-source) *broadcast problem*, a source node s intends to transmit a message to all nodes in the network V. Given a parameter $\epsilon \in (0, 1)$, we define the *ϵ-diameter D_ϵ* of the network as the diameter of the graph $G_\epsilon = (V, E_\epsilon)$ over V, where two nodes are adjacent iff their distance is at most $1-\epsilon$. Consider an $\epsilon/4$-backbone of V. It is easy to see that whenever two nodes in V are adjacent in G_ϵ, their corresponding dominators in in the $\epsilon/4$-core U are at distance at most $1 - \epsilon/2$, and hence are adjacent in the backbone.

Thus, the backbone is a 1-*spanner* of G_ϵ. Simple flooding achieves broadcast from any source to all nodes in V within $O(D_\epsilon + \log n)$ rounds: a) The source broadcasts the message once, and b) Every node in U, upon receiving the message, re-transmits it for $c \log n$ rounds, with i.i.d. probability $p = \Omega(1)$ in each round, where the probability p obeys the conditions in the definition of the communication graph. The proof of the runtime is essentially same as [1, Lemma 6].

7.2 Graph simulation

An ϵ-backbone provides a *probabilistic broadcast* CONGEST (PB-CONGEST) layer over the corresponding ϵ-core: in each round of this model, a node v can transmit the same message to all its neighbors in the communication graph G; with a constant probability $q > 0$ (irrespective of other nodes, but not independent), the transmission will succeed and v learns of its success. This can be implemented as follows. Recall that there is a constant probability p, such that if every node in the ϵ-backbone transmits w.p. p, then all neighbors of a given node v receive the message of v with $\Omega(p)$ probability. Now, each round of PB-CONGEST consists of a single transmission round of the physical model, followed by $O(1)$ ack rounds. In the transmission round, every node transmits a message w.p. p, as per normal operation of the protocol. In every ack round, every node transmits an acknowledgment for the last message it has received, again w.p. p. It is easy to see that if the number of ack rounds is a sufficiently large constant, then a node that successfully transmitted in a transmit round, will receive acknowledgments from all its neighbors in the following ack rounds, w.p. in $\Omega(1)$.

This also means that we can simulate a round of a CONGEST algorithm that involves bandwidth $\Omega(\log^2 n)$ with only constant factor overhead. More generally, a CONGEST round with bandwidth $b(n)$ bits can be simulated in time $\Theta(b(n)/\log n + \log n)$.

8 FUTURE WORK

It remains to see if the time complexity of backbone construction can be improved; $O(\log^2 n)$ time seems plausible. We also leave further applications of the backbone, such as local broadcast, faster multi-message broadcast and aggregation, to the future work.

ACKNOWLEDGMENTS

This work was supported by grants nos. 152679-05 and 174484-05 from the Icelandic Research Fund. The first author is also supported by the Research Institute for Mathematical Sciences, a Joint Usage/Research Center located in Kyoto University. We are grateful to the anonymous referees for their constructive comments.

REFERENCES

[1] Marijke H. L. Bodlaender, Magnús M. Halldórsson, and Pradipta Mitra. 2013. Connectivity and aggregation in multihop wireless networks. In *PODC*. ACM, 355–364.

[2] Imrich Chlamtac and Shay Kutten. 1985. On Broadcasting in Radio Networks-Problem Analysis and Protocol Design. *IEEE Trans. Communications* 33, 12 (1985), 1240–1246.

[3] Bogdan S. Chlebus and Shailesh Vaya. 2016. Distributed communication in bare-bones wireless networks. In *ICDCN*. ACM, 1:1–1:10.

[4] Sebastian Daum, Seth Gilbert, Fabian Kuhn, and Calvin C. Newport. 2013. Broadcast in the Ad Hoc SINR Model. In *DISC*. Springer, 358–372.

[5] Bilel Derbel and El-Ghazali Talbi. 2010. Radio Network Distributed Algorithms in the Unknown Neighborhood Model. In *ICDCN*. Springer, 155–166.

[6] Jeremy T. Fineman, Seth Gilbert, Fabian Kuhn, and Calvin C. Newport. 2016. Contention Resolution on a Fading Channel. In *PODC*. ACM, 155–164.

[7] Olga Goussevskaia, Thomas Moscibroda, and Roger Wattenhofer. 2008. Local broadcasting in the physical interference model. In *DIALM-POMC*. ACM, 35–44.

[8] Piyush Gupta and P. R. Kumar. 2000. The capacity of wireless networks. *IEEE Trans. Information Theory* 46, 2 (2000), 388–404.

[9] Magnús M. Halldórsson, Stephan Holzer, and Evangelia Anna Markatou. 2017. Leader Election in SINR Model with Arbitrary Power Control. In *SIROCCO*. Springer, 3–14.

[10] Magnús M. Halldórsson and Pradipta Mitra. 2012. Distributed connectivity of wireless networks. In *PODC*. ACM, 205–214.

[11] Magnús M. Halldórsson and Pradipta Mitra. 2012. Towards tight bounds for local broadcasting. In *FOMC*. ACM, 2.

[12] Dorit S Hochbaum and David B Shmoys. 1986. A unified approach to approximation algorithms for bottleneck problems. *Journal of the ACM (JACM)* 33, 3 (1986), 533–550.

[13] Tomasz Jurdzinski, Dariusz R. Kowalski, Michal Rozanski, and Grzegorz Stachowiak. 2013. Distributed Randomized Broadcasting in Wireless Networks under the SINR Model. In *DISC*. Springer, 373–387.

[14] Tomasz Jurdzinski, Dariusz R. Kowalski, Michal Rozanski, and Grzegorz Stachowiak. 2014. On the impact of geometry on ad hoc communication in wireless networks. In *PODC*. ACM, 357–366.

[15] Tomasz Jurdzinski, Dariusz R. Kowalski, Michal Rozanski, and Grzegorz Stachowiak. 2017. Deterministic Digital Clustering of Wireless Ad Hoc Networks. *CoRR* abs/1708.08647 (2017).

[16] Tomasz Jurdzinski, Dariusz R. Kowalski, and Grzegorz Stachowiak. 2013. Distributed Deterministic Broadcasting in Uniform-Power Ad Hoc Wireless Networks. In *FCT*. Springer, 195–209.

[17] Tomasz Jurdzinski, Michal Rozanski, and Grzegorz Stachowiak. 2017. Token Traversal in Ad Hoc Wireless Networks via Implicit Carrier Sensing. In *SIROCCO*. Springer, 15–33.

[18] Tomasz Jurdzinski and Grzegorz Stachowiak. 2015. The Cost of Synchronizing Multiple-Access Channels. In *PODC*. ACM, 421–430.

[19] Michael König and Roger Wattenhofer. 2016. Effectively Capturing Attention Using the Capture Effect. In *SenSys*. ACM, 70–82.

[20] Thomas Moscibroda and Roger Wattenhofer. 2005. Maximal independent sets in radio networks. In *PODC*. ACM, 148–157.

[21] Thomas Moscibroda and Roger Wattenhofer. 2008. Coloring unstructured radio networks. *Distributed Computing* 21, 4 (2008), 271–284.

[22] Christian Scheideler, Andréa W. Richa, and Paolo Santi. 2008. An O(log n) dominating set protocol for wireless ad-hoc networks under the physical interference model. In *MobiHoc*. ACM, 91–100.

[23] Dongxiao Yu, Qiang-Sheng Hua, Yuexuan Wang, Haisheng Tan, and Francis C. M. Lau. 2012. Distributed Multiple-Message Broadcast in Wireless Ad-Hoc Networks under the SINR Model. In *SIROCCO*. Springer, 111–122.

[24] Dongxiao Yu, Yuexuan Wang, Qiang-Sheng Hua, and Francis C. M. Lau. 2014. Distributed (Δ+1)-coloring in the physical model. *Theor. Comput. Sci.* 553 (2014), 37–56.

The Energy Complexity of Broadcast*

Yi-Jun Chang
University of Michigan
Ann Arbor, MI

Varsha Dani
University of New Mexico
Albuquerque, NM

Thomas P. Hayes†
University of New Mexico
Albuquerque, NM

Qizheng He
IIIS, Tsinghua University
Beijing, China

Wenzheng Li
IIIS, Tsinghua University
Beijing, China

Seth Pettie‡
University of Michigan
Ann Arbor, MI

ABSTRACT

Energy is often the most constrained resource in networks of battery-powered devices, and as devices become smaller, they spend a larger fraction of their energy on *communication* (transceiver usage) not computation. As an imperfect proxy for true energy usage, we define *energy complexity* to be the number of time slots a device transmits/listens; idle time and computation are free.

In this paper we investigate the energy complexity of fundamental communication primitives such as Broadcast in *multi-hop* radio networks. We consider models with collision detection (CD) and without (No-CD), as well as both randomized and deterministic algorithms. Some take-away messages from this work are as follows.

Time lower bounds imply energy lower bounds.
The *energy* complexity of Broadcast in a multi-hop network is connected to the *time* complexity of LeaderElection in a single-hop (clique) network. Many existing lower bounds on time complexity immediately transfer to energy complexity. For example, in the CD and No-CD models, Broadcast requires $\Omega(\log n)$ and $\Omega(\log^2 n)$ energy, respectively, w.h.p.

Energy- and time-efficient broadcasting.
It requires $\Omega(D)$ time to solve Broadcast even allowing unlimited energy budget, where D is the diameter of the network. The complexity measures of energy and time are in conflict, and it is an open problem whether both can be minimized simultaneously. We show that it is possible to achieve near optimality in time complexity with only poly log n energy cost. For any constant $\epsilon > 0$, Broadcast can be solved in $O(D^{1+\epsilon} \log^{O(1/\epsilon)} n)$ time with $O(\log^{O(1/\epsilon)} n)$ energy.

CCS CONCEPTS

• **Theory of computation → Distributed algorithms**;

*The full version of this paper is available at [9].
†Supported by NSF CAREER award CCF-1150281
‡Supported by NSF grants CCF-1514383 and CCF-1637546

PODC '18, July 23–27, 2018, Egham, United Kingdom

ACM ISBN 978-1-4503-5795-1/18/07.
https://doi.org/10.1145/3212734.3212774

KEYWORDS

Broadcast; energy-aware computing; wireless network; distributed algorithm

ACM Reference Format:
Yi-Jun Chang, Varsha Dani, Thomas P. Hayes, Qizheng He, Wenzheng Li, and Seth Pettie. 2018. The Energy Complexity of Broadcast. In *PODC '18: ACM Symposium on Principles of Distributed Computing, July 23–27, 2018, Egham, United Kingdom,* Idit Keidar (Ed.). ACM, New York, NY, USA, 10 pages. https://doi.org/10.1145/3212734.3212774

1 INTRODUCTION

In many networks of small wireless devices the scarcest resource is energy, and the majority of energy is often spent on *radio transceiver usage*—sending and receiving packets— not on computation. See, e.g., [35, Fig. 2], [6, Tab. 1], and [37, §3]. Rather than account for the energy profile of every mode of operation, we assume for simplicity that devices spend one unit of energy to send/listen and nothing for computation. It is not uncommon to use transceiver usage as a proxy for total energy [10, 19, 22].

1.1 The Model

The network is a connected undirected graph $G = (V, E)$ with devices associated with vertices. Each vertex knows nothing about the topology of G, except for some general parameters such as the number of vertices $n = |V|$, the maximum degree $\Delta = \max_v \deg(v)$, and the diameter $D = \max_{u,v} \mathrm{dist}(u, v)$. Each of Δ and D can be upper bounded by n if it is unknown.

Time is partitioned into discrete slots, and all vertices agree on time slot zero, i.e., they simultaneously start at the same time. In each time slot, each device can choose to either (i) send a message, (ii) listen, or (iii) remain idle, where (i) and (ii) cost one unit of energy and (iii) is free. We allow unbounded message size and local computation power. A device is not allowed to simultaneously send and listen; and a sender does not know whether its message has been successfully delivered to its neighbors.

If a device chooses to send a message or remain idle, it gets no feedback from the environment. If a device chooses to listen and *exactly one* neighbor sends a message m, it receives m. The other cases depend on how the model handles collisions.

No-CD: If zero or at least two neighbors transmit, a listener hears a signal λ_S, indicating *silence.*

CD: If zero neighbors transmit, a listener hears λ_S; if at least two neighbors transmit, a listener hears λ_N, indicating *noise.*

LOCAL: Every listener hears *every* message transmitted by any neighbor. There are no collisions.[1]

All the models come in randomized and deterministic variants. In the deterministic setting, vertices are assigned distinct IDs in $\{1, \ldots, N\}$ and can use them to break symmetry. Unless otherwise stated, by default the maximum allowed failure probability for a randomized algorithm is $f = 1/\text{poly}(n)$. Randomized algorithms can generate private random bits to break symmetry, e.g., they can assign themselves $O(\log n)$-bit IDs, which are distinct w.h.p.

Energy Metrics. The energy cost E_v of a vertex v is defined as the number of time slots v transmits/listens; the energy complexity of an algorithm is $\max_{v \in V} E_v$. Thus, we aim to optimize the worst case energy cost per device, and not the total energy expenditure of all devices.

In this paper we assume that (i) transmitting and listening incur the same energy cost, and (ii) whether or not a message is received, the cost of listening is the same. While some works [3, 8, 17, 24] assume that only transmitting costs energy, a number of other papers consider the model where both transmitting and listening cost the same amount of energy [7, 10, 21, 25, 28].

The validity of these assumptions depends on the underlying wireless network technology. To cite a specific example, for a sender node called *Mica2*, the current consumption of transmitting ranges from 3.7mA (transmission power at -20dBm) to 21.5mA (at +10dBm); the current consumption for listening is always 7mA, regardless of whether a message is received (see [36]). That is, the costs of transmitting and listening are roughly of the same order. In fact, in networking and system research, "idle listening" (i.e., the device is in listening mode, but no message is received) has been identified as a major cause of energy loss [1, Section 9.1]. There are a number of papers on reducing idle listening [38, 40].

1.2 Our Contribution

In this paper we consider fundamental problems in arbitrary *multi-hop* network topologies, primarily Broadcast. At time zero there is a distinguished *source* device $s \in V$ holding a message m. By the end of the computation all vertices should know m. We establish lower and upper bounds on Broadcast in all collision-detection models, both randomized and deterministic. Some of the more interesting findings are as follows.

Time lower bounds on LeaderElection in single-hop networks extend to *energy* lower bounds on Broadcast in multihop networks. As a consequence, we get energy lower bounds on Broadcast of $\Omega(\log n)$ and $\Omega(\log \Delta \log n)$ in CD and No-CD, respectively. These lower bounds reflect the difficulty of local *contention resolution*, not on broadcasting *per se*. We give a more robust energy lower bound of $\Omega(\log D) = \Omega(\log n)$ that reflects the difficulty of getting a message across a long path. It applies to any collision-detection model, even LOCAL.

Even with an infinite energy budget we need $\Omega(D)$ time. We show that it is possible to achieve near optimality in both energy and time simultaneously. For any $\epsilon > 0$, there is a Broadcast algorithm taking $O(D^{1+\epsilon} \log^{O(1/\epsilon)} n)$ time and $O(\log^{O(1/\epsilon)} n)$ energy.

Given sufficient (slightly super-linear) time, regardless of the diameter D, the energy lower bounds can almost be achieved. For example, we give an algorithm for No-CD using time $O(n \log \Delta \log^2 n)$ and energy $O(\log \Delta \log^2 n)$.

[1]Lower bounds in the LOCAL model are robust since they capture the difficulty of synchronization, not on the subtleties of any particular collision-detection model. This model bears the same name as Linial's LOCAL model [29, 34] and is very similar to it. In the traditional LOCAL model vertices do not have to choose between transmitting and listening, and there is no cost associated with communication.

1.3 Related Work

Single-hop Networks. In theory research, previous work on energy complexity has focused on fundamental problems in single-hop (clique) networks like LeaderElection (i.e., choose exactly one device as the leader) and ApproximateCounting (approximating the number of devices n to within a constant factor) [7, 10, 19–23, 31]. In the study of single-hop networks, it is typical to assume that n is unknown.

Nakano and Olariu [31] showed that in No-CD, n initially identical devices can assign themselves distinct IDs in $\{1, \ldots, n\}$ with $O(\log \log n)$ energy per device. Bender, Kopelowitz, Pettie, and Young [7] gave a randomized method for circuit-simulation in the CD model, which led to algorithms for LeaderElection and ApproximateCounting using $O(\log(\log^* n))$ energy and $n^{o(1)}$ time, w.h.p. An earlier algorithm of Kardas et al. [23] solves the problem in $O(\log^{\epsilon} n)$ time using $O(\log \log \log n)$ energy, *but only in expectation.* Chang et al. [10] proved that for these problems, $\Theta(\log(\log^* n))$ and $\Theta(\log^* n)$ energy are optimal in CD and No-CD, respectively, for poly(n)-time algorithms. They also give tradeoffs between time and energy, e.g., in No-CD, with $O\left(\log^{2+\epsilon} n\right)$ time we can use just $O\left(\epsilon^{-1} \log \log \log n\right)$ energy, w.h.p. For deterministic LeaderElection protocols, $\Theta(\log N)$ is optimal in CD and No-CD [10, 21], but if senders can also detect collisions, the energy complexity drops to $\Theta(\log \log N)$ [10].

Multi-hop Networks. Energy efficiency of multi-hop networks have also been studied in theory research. Berenbrink et al. [8] studied broadcasting and gossiping algorithms, and they measured energy cost by the total number of messages transmitted. They presented a Broadcast algorithm that takes $O\left(D \log(n/D) + \log^2 n\right)$ time with expected $O\left(\log^2 n / \log(n/D)\right)$ transmissions per vertex. Gasieniec et al. [17] considered the following problem in a *known* graph topology. Given a graph with a distinguished source vertex, design a transmission schedule to minimize broadcasting time, subject to the requirement that each device only transmits at most k times. For $k = 1$, they showed that $D + \Omega(\sqrt{n - D})$ time is necessary and that $D + O(\sqrt{n} \log n)$ is sufficient. The lower bound extends to $D + \Omega((n - D)^{1/(2k)})$, and the upper bound to $O\left(n^{1/(k-2)} \log^2 n\right)$.

Some papers in the literature consider optimization problems related to energy efficiency. Kirousis et al. [24] studied the following problem. Given stations in d-dimensions, $d \in \{1, 2, 3\}$, pick transmission radii to satisfy some network properties (e.g., the network should be connected and have small diameter). The objective is to minimize the sum of the broadcasting energies. A related problem is the minimum energy broadcast routing problem (MEBR) [4]. Given coordinates of stations and a distinguished source, come up with transmission power and transmission schedule to broadcast a message. The goal is to minimize total power of all transmitters. A

6-approximation algorithm via MST heuristic has been shown by Ambühl [3].

Broadcasting Protocols. Broadcast is a well-studied problem in multi-hop networks. The seminal *decay* algorithm of Bar-Yehuda et al. [5] solves Broadcast in No-CD in $O\left(D\log n + \log^2 n\right)$ time. This bound was later improved to $O\left(D\log\frac{n}{D} + \log^2 n\right)$ [12, 26]. The $\log^2 n$ term is known to be necessary [2], and the $D\log\frac{n}{D}$ term is known to be optimal [27] for a restricted class of algorithms that forbid "spontaneous transmission" (i.e., vertices that have yet to learn the message are forbidden from transmitting).

Haeupler and Wajc [18] recently gave a broadcast algorithm in the No-CD model that runs in $O\left(D\frac{\log n\log\log n}{\log D} + \log^{O(1)} n\right)$ time, demonstrating that spontaneous transmissions *are* useful. Czumaj and Davies [11] improved this to $O\left(D\frac{\log n}{\log D} + \log^{O(1)} n\right)$ and gave a LeaderElection algorithm of the same complexity, improving [15]. See [16] for an $O(D + \log^6 n)$-time Broadcast algorithm in the CD model.

1.4 Organization and Technical Overview

In Section 2 we show two simple lower bounds. We prove that even for a simple network topology—a path—and the strongest model—randomized LOCAL—the Broadcast problem still requires $\Omega(\log n)$ energy. We then present a generic reduction showing that the *energy* complexity of Broadcast in a multi-hop network is at least the *time* complexity of LeaderElection in a single-hop network, with the other aspects of the model being the same (CD or No-CD, deterministic or randomized). The take-away message from these lower bounds is that the cost of Broadcast arises from two causes: (i) the cost of synchronization, for propagating messages along long paths (when D is large), and (ii) the cost of contention-resolution in a vertex's 2-hop neighborhood (when Δ is large).

In Section 3 we introduce the basic tool SR-comm used by all our algorithms. In Section 4 we show a simple randomized algorithm in No-CD based on iterative clustering. For graphs of unbounded degree, our algorithm takes $O(n\log^3 n)$ time and $O(\log^3 n)$ energy in No-CD, which is actually the product of our two lower bounds. In Section 5, we present an algorithm in nearly diameter time.

2 LOWER BOUNDS

We prove two lower bounds on the energy-complexity of Broadcast.

THEOREM 1. *Consider a path graph $P = (v_1, \ldots, v_n)$, where each vertex v_i does not know its position i. Suppose that v_1 attempts to broadcast a message m. For any randomized* LOCAL *Broadcast algorithm $\mathcal{A}$, with probability $1/2$, at least one vertex spends $\log_{13} n - 1$ energy before receiving the message m.*

PROOF. We may assume, without loss of generality, that the algorithm $\mathcal{A}$ works as follows. Every vertex begins in exactly the same state, except for v_1, which knows the message m. Each vertex v locally generates a string r_v of random bits, and afterward, behaves deterministically.[2] At any moment in time, each vertex v_l maintains an interval $[\alpha, \beta]$ such that v_l knows r_{v_j} if and only if $j \in [\alpha, \beta]$. Whenever v_l transmits a message, it transmits every useful piece of information it knows, namely the concatenation of $r_{v_\alpha}, \ldots, r_{v_\beta}$. After each wakeup, a vertex decides the time of its next wakeup and mode (transmit or listen) based on all the information it has learned so far. It is easy to see that any algorithm in this model can be simulated with the same round- and energy-complexity if vertices only communicate the r_{v_j}-strings they know.

Let I be an interval of the path $(v_1, \ldots, v_n)$ not including v_1. Intuitively, the event $\mathcal{E}_i[I]$ holds if there is some device in I that, after its ith wakeup, knows of no information outside I. This definition has two undesirable properties. First, it necessarily depends on the behavior of (i.e., random bits generated by) vertices outside I. Second, even if we could make it independent of the random bits outside I, the event may still depend subtly on *where* the path I is embedded within $(v_2, \ldots, v_n)$. The actual event $\mathcal{E}_i[I]$ assumes "worst case" embedding of I and "best case" behavior of vertices outside I. Therefore, $\mathcal{E}_i[I]$ depends *only* on the strings of random bits generated by I-vertices. In particular:

$$\begin{aligned}\mathcal{E}_i[I]\ :\ & \exists(v^\star \in I)\ \forall(\text{embedding of } I \text{ in } (v_2, \ldots, v_n))\\ & \forall(r_{v_j} \mid v_j \notin I)\ \forall(v_k \notin I):\\ & \text{After its } i\text{th wakeup, } v^\star \text{ does not know } r_{v_k}.\end{aligned}$$

Observe that because of the quantification over all random strings outside I and the embedding of I in $(v_2, \ldots, v_n)$, we are considering a large class of *potential* executions of $\mathcal{A}$, which necessarily includes the actual execution. If $\mathcal{E}_i[I]$ occurs, we write $v^\star[I]$ to denote the leftmost vertex $v^\star \in I$, satisfying the statement of $\mathcal{E}_i[I]$.

The lower bound is by induction, with an induction hypothesis that is probabilistic. In particular, we assume, for each interval I of length $(13)^i$, that

$$\Pr(\mathcal{E}_i[I]) \geq 1/2.$$

The assumption is valid in the base case $i = 0$, since $\Pr(\mathcal{E}_0[I]) = 1$ when I contains a single node that has yet to wakeup. Let I be an interval of length $(13)^{i+1}$ partitioned into 13 subintervals $I_1, \ldots, I_{13}$ of length $(13)^i$. We apply the inductive hypothesis to each subinterval and conclude that $\Pr(\mathcal{E}_i[I_j]) \geq 1/2$. Moreover, since these events are independent (they depend on disjoint sets of random strings),

$$\Pr\left(\sum_{j=1}^{13} \mathbf{1}_{\{\mathcal{E}_i[I_j]\}} \geq 5\right) \geq \Pr(\text{Binom}(13, \tfrac{1}{2}) \geq 5) > 5/6.$$

Suppose that the number of subintervals I_j satisfying $\mathcal{E}_i[I_j]$ is, in fact, at least 5, and let $J_1, \ldots, J_5$ be the first 5 such subintervals. At this point in the proof $J_1, \ldots, J_5$ have no distinguishing characteristics. Because of this, the *times* of the ith wakeups for the vertices $v^\star[J_1], \ldots, v^\star[J_5]$ are independent and identically distributed random variables. Among these 5 vertices, suppose the one whose ith wakeup is earliest is some $v^\star \in \{v^\star[J_2], v^\star[J_3], v^\star[J_4]\}$. After this wakeup, $v^\star$ could not have learned any random string outside I. Every such string must have been communicated through either $v^\star[J_1]$ or $v^\star[J_5]$, and each of these vertices has only been awake at most $i - 1$ times. Thus, assuming $J_1, \ldots, J_5$ exist, with probability $3/5$ there is a vertex $v^\star$ that wakes up i times and knows of no information outside I. Since $J_1, \ldots, J_5$ exist with probability $5/6$,

[2] For example, if the algorithm $\mathcal{A}$ assumes that vertices have distinct $O(\log n)$-bit IDs, these can be generated without communication, with probability $1 - 1/\text{poly}(n)$.

the probability that such a $v^\star$ exists is at least $(5/6)(3/5) = 1/2$, which concludes the induction. □

Next, we prove Broadcast lower bounds for the No-CD and CD models, which hold even in constant diameter graphs. There are some very subtle issues about the randomized No-CD lower bound, see the end of the section for discussion.

Theorem 2. Broadcast *is subject to the following energy lower bounds, where the failure probability is fixed at* $f = 1/\text{poly}(n)$ *for randomized algorithms. (i) deterministic* No-CD: $\Omega(\Delta)$; *(ii) randomized* No-CD: $\Omega(\log\Delta\log n)$; *(iii) randomized* CD: $\Omega(\log n)$.

Proof. Consider the LeaderElection problem in a single-hop network, where the number of vertices is unknown, but is guaranteed to be upper bounded by n'. The goal of LeaderElection is to have a time slot τ where exactly one vertex transmits, and all remaining vertices listen. In the single-hop network model, we allow all vertices to send and listen simultaneously, i.e., we are in the *full duplex* model. We also make a distinction between randomized and deterministic models.

- **Randomized Model.** Each vertex is anonymous, i.e., they do not have IDs. We allow all vertices to have *shared randomness*, but each vertex still has its own private randomness. The maximum allowed failure probability is f'. Let $T_r(n', f')$ be the time complexity for LeaderElection this model. It is known that $T_r(n', f') = \Omega(\log\log n' + \log\frac{1}{f'})$ for CD [33, 39],[3] and also $T_r(n', f') = \Omega(\log n' \log\frac{1}{f'})$ for No-CD [14].
- **Deterministic Model.** Each vertex has a distinct ID in $[n']$. The algorithm is not allowed to fail for any possible assignment of distinct IDs. Let $T_d(n')$ be the deterministic time complexity. It is known that $T_d(n') = \Omega(n')$ [19, Theorem 1.6].

There is a very subtle issue regarding the $\Omega(\log\log n' + \log\frac{1}{f'})$ lower bound; see the end of this section for discussion.

Let G_k be the bipartite graph $K_{2,k}$ with two parts $\{s, t\}$ and $\{v_1, \ldots, v_k\}$, where the vertex s is attempting to broadcast a message. Let $\mathcal{A}$ be any Broadcast algorithm that applies to the graphs G_k, for all $1 \le k \le \Delta$. If $\mathcal{A}$ is randomized and has failure probability at most f, then we claim that $\mathcal{A}$ uses at least $T_r(\Delta, f)/2$ energy. If $\mathcal{A}$ is deterministic, then we claim that it $\mathcal{A}$ uses at least $T_d(\Delta)/2$ energy. These two claims imply the statement of the lemma (with $f = 1/\text{poly}(n)$).

A Generic Reduction. These claims are proved by the following generic reduction. Let $\mathcal{A}$ be any Broadcast algorithm on G_k, for all $1 \le k \le \Delta$, that takes E energy. We transform it into a LeaderElection algorithm $\mathcal{A}'$ in the aforementioned single-hop network model with $n' = \Delta$ that takes $2E$ time.

For the algorithm $\mathcal{A}$ to solve Broadcast, the vertex t has to receive a message from s, and so there must be one time slot $\tau^\star$ where exactly one vertex in $\{v_1, \ldots, v_k\}$ transmits and t listens.

We call the vertices in the corresponding single-hop network $\{v'_1, \ldots, v'_k\}$. Intuitively, each vertex v'_i in the single-hop network simulates v_i in the multi-hop network, and we treat $\{s, t\}$ as the communication channel. Each v'_i uses its private random bits to simulate the private random bits of v_i.

[3]The randomized CD $\Omega(\log\frac{1}{f'})$ lower bound, which applies even for $k = 2$, is folklore.

Assumptions about $\mathcal{A}$. Without loss of generality, we make the following assumptions about $\mathcal{A}$. If we are in the randomized model, we let the two vertices s and t announce all their local random bits in the first two rounds of $\mathcal{A}$.

If we are in the deterministic model, we assume that the IDs of the vertices in $\{v_1, \ldots, v_k\}$ are chosen from the range $\{1, \ldots, \Delta\}$, and we let the two vertices s and t announce their IDs in the first two rounds of $\mathcal{A}$.

Simulation of Time Slot τ *of* $\mathcal{A}$. We show how to simulate a time slot τ of $\mathcal{A}$ in the single-hop network model. The simulation of the first two special rounds are straightforward, as follows. In the randomized model, we use the shared randomness in the single-hop network to simulate the random bits of s and t. In the deterministic model, we simply set $\text{ID}(s) = n'+1 = \Delta+1$ and $\text{ID}(t) = n'+2 = \Delta+2$.

In what follows, we assume $\tau > 2$. If at least one of s and t listens at time slot τ in $\mathcal{A}$, the simulation costs 1 round; otherwise, the simulation skips this round. Thus, the total amount of time for the simulation is at most $2E$.

During the simulation, we maintain an inductive hypothesis that each vertex v'_i (in the single-hop network, right before they simulate the time slot τ of $\mathcal{A}$) already knows the entire history and information of the three vertices v_i, s, and t during all time slots $\{1, \ldots, \tau - 1\}$ in $\mathcal{A}$ in the multi-hop network.

The inductive hypothesis, together with the above assumption, implies that v'_i is able to perfectly predict the actions of the three vertices v_i, s, and t at time τ in $\mathcal{A}$ in the multi-hop network.

If both s and t do not listen at time τ in $\mathcal{A}$, then nothing needs to be done in the simulation. The reason is that at time τ in $\mathcal{A}$, the channel feedback must be silence for everyone.

If at least one of s and t listens at time τ in $\mathcal{A}$, we use one round in the single-hop network to simulate the time slot τ in $\mathcal{A}$. Specifically, for each vertex v'_i, all we need to do is to let v'_i calculate the channel feedback of v_i, s, and t at time τ in $\mathcal{A}$.

Note that v'_i already knows the channel feedback of v_i (at time τ in $\mathcal{A}$) since it knows the actions of s and t. To let v'_i learn the channel feedback of s and t (at time τ in $\mathcal{A}$), we simply let each $v'_i \in \{v'_1, \ldots, v'_k\}$ do what v_i does at time τ in $\mathcal{A}$, and then the channel feedback in the single-hop network that each v'_i receives is the same as the channel feedback received by s and t in the multi-hop network model. □

Theorem 2 complements Theorem 1 by showing another $\Omega(\log n)$ energy lower bound (by setting $f = 1/\text{poly}(n)$) in CD, even when $D = O(1)$. On graphs with unbounded degree, Theorem 2 implies $\Omega(\log^2 n)$ energy lower bounds in No-CD, and $\Omega(n)$ lower bounds in *deterministic* No-CD.

Remark. Our $\Omega(\log\Delta\log n)$ lower bound relies on the existence of an $\Omega(\log n' \log 1/f')$ lower bound for the LeaderElection problem in single-hop networks, where we set $n' = \Delta$ and $f' = 1/\text{poly}(n)$. The known lower bound [14] for this result only applies to uniform algorithms. There is another lower bound [33] that works for all algorithms but requires $f' = 1/n' = 1/\Delta$. If we use [14], then the $\Omega(\log\Delta\log n)$ lower bound only applies to uniform algorithms. If we use [33], then we get an $\Omega(\log^2\Delta)$ lower bound that applies to all algorithms.

Next, we discuss an issue about applying the lower bound of [14] in the proof of Theorem 2. First of all, we are only interested in the regime of $f' = 1/\text{poly}(n)$, and so we assume $f' < 1/n^2 < 1/\Delta^2$. Recall that we consider a single-hop network with at most $n' = \Delta$ vertices.

The randomized No-CD $\Omega(\log n' \log \frac{1}{f'})$ lower bound of [14] only applies to *uniform* algorithms in the sense that for each round τ, there is a sending probability p_τ such that each vertex sends with probability p_τ using fresh randomness independently at round τ. Notice that in the No-CD model the channel feedback for all vertices must be silence all the time before the first successful transmission.

We show that this lower bound can still be applied in our setting. The only issue that we need to deal with is that we allow shared randomness. Let $\mathcal{A}$ be any algorithm (with shared randomness) that solves LeaderElection with failure probability f', and let $\mathcal{A}[r]$ be the algorithm with respect to a string r that serves as the shared randomness. Then $\mathcal{A}[r]$ must be uniform.

In what follows, we show that there exists a string $r^\star$ such that the failure probability of $\mathcal{A}[r^\star]$ is at most $n'f' < \sqrt{f'}$, and so the $\Omega(\log n' \log \frac{1}{f'})$ lower bound of [14] also applies to $\mathcal{A}$. We say that a string r is *good* for a number $k \in [n']$ if the failure probability of $\mathcal{A}[r]$ is at most $n'f'$ when we run $\mathcal{A}[r]$ on a single-hop network with k vertices. It suffices to show that there is a string $r^\star$ that is good for all $k \in [n']$. Suppose that such $r^\star$ does not exist. Then there exists a number $k^\star \in [n']$ such that with probability at least $1/n'$ a uniformly random string r is not good for $k^\star$. This implies that for an execution of $\mathcal{A}$ on a single-hop network of $k^\star$ vertices, the failure probability is higher than $(1/n')(n'f') = f'$, which is a contradiction.

3 BASIC BUILDING BLOCKS

Given two disjoint vertex sets S and R, the task SR-comm is defined as follows. Each vertex $u \in S$ attempts to transmit a message m_u, and each vertex in R attempts to receive one message. An SR-comm algorithm guarantees that for every $v \in R$ with $N(v) \cap S \neq \emptyset$, with probability $1 - f$, v receives a message m_u from at least one vertex $u \in N(v) \cap S$.

Lemma 3. *In the randomized* No-CD *model,* SR-comm *can be solved with high probability, i.e., $f = 1/\text{poly}(n)$, in time $O(\log \Delta \log n)$ and energy $O(\log \Delta \log n)$.*

Proof. Use the $O(\log \Delta \log 1/f)$-time algorithm of [5], which is also known as *decay.* □

For the randomized CD model, we present a generic transformation which turns an algorithm $\mathcal{A}$ for LeaderElection in single-hop networks (satisfying some additional requirements) to an algorithm $\mathcal{A}'$ that solves SR-comm.

Requirements for $\mathcal{A}$. We require that in an execution of $\mathcal{A}$, within time $T(n', f)$ there is a successful communication with probability $1 - f$. The algorithm $\mathcal{A}$ is executed on a single-hop network, where the number of vertices is unknown, but is guaranteed to be at most n'. The vertices in the single-hop network are allowed to simultaneously send and listen. Since we do not measure the energy of $\mathcal{A}$, we simply assume that all vertices (including senders) always listen to the channel.

We assume that algorithm $\mathcal{A}$ is *uniform* in the following sense. For each time slot t, there is an integer $k_t \in \{0, 1, \ldots, \lceil \log n' \rceil\}$ such that each vertex transmits with the same probability $p = 2^{-k_t}$ independently at the time slot t. The number k_t depends solely on the history (i.e., channel feedback) of the algorithm execution before time t. Since all vertices always listen to the channel, they have the same history.

The Generic Transformation. We show how to obtain a randomized algorithm $\mathcal{A}'$ that solves SR-comm in time $T(\Delta, f) \cdot \lceil \log \Delta \rceil$ with energy cost $2 \cdot T(\Delta, f)$, but in a multi-hop network, where vertices cannot simultaneously send and listen.

The algorithm $\mathcal{A}'$ consists of $T(\Delta, f)$ epochs, each of which consists of $\lceil \log \Delta \rceil$ time slots.

The protocol for vertices in S is as follows. In each epoch, each vertex $v \in S$ transmits at the ith time slot of this epoch with probability 2^{-i} in such a way that the total number of transmissions of v during an epoch is at most 2. This can be achieved since $1 + \frac{1}{2} + \frac{1}{4} + \frac{1}{8} + \ldots = 2$.

Each vertex $u \in R$, in parallel, simulates the algorithm $\mathcal{A}$ executed on a single-hop network of size $|N(u) \cap S|$, as follows. We simulate the ith time slot of $\mathcal{A}$ during the ith epoch. In the simulation, u serves as the communication channel. By inductive hypothesis, we assume that before the ith epoch, u already knows the history of the execution up to time $i - 1$, and so u has enough information to calculate the number k_i. During the ith epoch, u only listens at the k_ith slot. Notice that the channel feedback that u receives simulates the ith time slot of the execution of $\mathcal{A}$ on a single-hop network of size $|N(u) \cap S|$, as each vertex in $N(u) \cap S$ transmits with probability 2^{-k_i} at the k_ith slot of an epoch.

Recall that in an execution of $\mathcal{A}$, with probability $1 - f$, there is some successful communication by time $T(|N(u) \cap S|, f) \leq T(\Delta, f)$. Thus, for each $u \in R$, with probability $1 - f$, there must be one epoch where exactly one vertex in $N(u) \cap S$ is transmitting, and so the vertex $u \in R$ receives a message. Based on this generic transformation, we obtain Lemma 4.

Lemma 4. *In the randomized* CD *model,* SR-comm *can be solved with energy $O(\log \log \Delta + \log 1/f)$ and runtime $O(\log \Delta(\log \log \Delta + \log 1/f))$. For the special case where each $v \in S$ is adjacent to at most one vertex in R, the energy cost is $O(\log \log \Delta) + X$, where X is a random variable drawn from an exponential distribution* Exponential(λ), *for some $\lambda = O(1)$.*

Proof. Apply the generic transformation to the uniform leader election protocol of [32]. The runtime of the algorithm of [32] is actually $O(\log \log n' + \log 1/f)$, *for every f*. That is, the runtime is can be written as $O(\log \log n') + X$, where X is a random variable drawn from an exponential distribution Exponential(λ), for some $\lambda = O(1)$. This already implies the energy cost of each $u \in R$ is $O(\log \log n') + X$, since each $u \in R$ can simply terminates after its simulation is done. However, in general, we cannot obtain this improvement for vertices in S, since a vertex $v \in S$ can be adjacent to many R-vertices.

For the special case where each $v \in S$ is adjacent to at most one vertex $u \in R$, the vertex v is only involved in the simulation associated with u. In this case, we are able to show that the energy cost of $O(\log \log n') + X$ can be achieved for all vertices. Consider the following modifications to the above generic transformation. In the first round, all vertices in R speak, and all vertices in S listen. This allows each vertex in S to check whether it is adjacent to a vertex in R. Those vertices in S that are not adjacent to a vertex in R terminate after the first round. For each epoch i, we allocate an additional time slot at the end of the ith epoch to let each vertex $u \in R$ inform all its neighbors in S whether or not the simulation associated with u has finished (i.e., u has already received a message from a vertex in $u \in N(v) \cap S$). If it is done, then all vertices in $S \cap N^+(v)$ terminate. □

Remark 5. *In Lemma 4, if a vertex v satisfies either (i) $v \in S$ and $N(v) \cap R = \emptyset$, or (ii) $v \in R$ and $N(v) \cap S = \emptyset$, then the energy cost of v can be lowered to $O(1)$ in the* CD *model. Due to the ability of a vertex to distinguish between noise and silence, in $O(1)$ time, each $v \in S$ can check whether $N(v) \cap R = \emptyset$, and similarly each $v \in R$ can check whether $N(v) \cap S = \emptyset$ in $O(1)$ time. We will make use of this observation to reduce the energy cost of algorithms in the* CD *model.*

4 BASIC ENERGY-EFFICIENT RANDOMIZED ALGORITHMS

In this section we show that Broadcast can be solved using $O(\log^3 n)$ energy in randomized No-CD.

Layers of Vertices. A labeling $\mathcal{L} : V(G) \mapsto \{0, \ldots, n-1\}$ is said to be *good* if it has the following property. Each vertex v with $\mathcal{L}(v) > 0$ must have a neighbor u such that $\mathcal{L}(u) = \mathcal{L}(v) - 1$. A vertex v is called a *layer-i* vertex if $\mathcal{L}(v) = i$. The intuition underlying the definition of a good labeling is that it represents a clustering of vertices. If we let each layer-i vertex select a layer-$(i-1)$ neighbor as its parent, then we obtain a partition of $V(G)$ into $|\mathcal{L}^{-1}(0)|$ clusters. Each cluster C is a rooted tree T, where the root r is the unique layer-0 vertex in the cluster C. However, it is possible that a vertex has multiple choices of its parent, so the clustering resulting from a good labeling is, in general, not unique.

We say that two layer-0 vertices u and v are *$\mathcal{L}$-adjacent* if there exists a path $P = (u, u_1, \ldots, u_a, v_b, \ldots, v_1, v)$ such that $\mathcal{L}(u_i) = i$ for all $i \in [a]$ and $\mathcal{L}(v_j) = j$ for all $j \in [b]$. The graph $G_{\mathcal{L}}$ is on vertex set $\mathcal{L}^{-1}(0)$ and edge set $\{\{u, v\} \mid u \text{ and } v \text{ are } \mathcal{L}\text{-adjacent}\}$.

In the following lemma we show that Broadcast can be solved energy-efficiently if we already have a good labeling $\mathcal{L}^\star$ with small number of layer-0 vertices.

Lemma 6. *Let $\mathcal{L}^\star$ be a good labeling of G. Each vertex knows its $\mathcal{L}^\star$-label and two integers $d, L \geq 1$ such that (i) d is an upper bound on the diameter of $G_{\mathcal{L}^\star}$, and (ii) L is an upper bound on the number of layers. Then* Broadcast *can be solved by a randomized algorithm with high probability in time $T = T_{n,d,L}$ using energy $E = E_{n,d,L}$.*

LOCAL :	$T = O(Ld)$	$E = O(d)$
CD :	$T = O(Ld \log n \log \Delta)$	$E = O(d + \log n)$
No-CD :	$T = O(Ld \log n \log \Delta)$	$E = O(d \log n \log \Delta)$

Proof. Let v be the vertex that attempts to broadcast some message m. The goal of the Broadcast problem is to relay the message m to all vertices in the graph. This can be solved by first (1) do Up-cast to relay the message from v to some layer-0 vertex; (2) repeat (Down-cast, All-cast, Up-cast) for d times to let all layer-0 vertices receive the message m; and then (3) do Down-cast to ensure that all vertices in the graph have the message m.

- Down-cast. For $i = 0, \ldots, L-2$, do SR-comm with S being the set of layer-i vertices that hold the message m, and R being the set of all layer-$(i+1)$ vertices that have not received the message m. Each vertex in S attempts to broadcast the message m.
- All-cast. Do SR-comm with S being the set of all vertices that hold the message m, and R being the set of all vertices that have not received the message m. Each vertex in S attempts to broadcast the message m.
- Up-cast. For $i = L-1, \ldots, 1$, do SR-comm with S being the set of layer-i vertices that hold the message m, and R being the set of all layer-$(i-1)$ vertices that have not received the message m. Each vertex in S attempts to broadcast the message m.

We use SR-comm with $f = 1/\text{poly}(n)$. Thus, the Broadcast problem can be solved in $O(Ld) \cdot T'(n, \Delta)$ time and $O(d) \cdot E'(n, \Delta)$ energy, where $T'(n, \Delta)$ and $E'(n, \Delta)$ are the runtime and the energy cost of SR-comm; see Lemmas 3 and 4. By the observations made in Remark 5, the energy cost can be further reduced to $O(d + E'(n, \Delta)) = O(d + \log n)$. In the above algorithm, each vertex v is involved in $O(d)$ invocations of SR-comm, and all but $O(1)$ of them satisfy either (i) $v \in S$ and $N(v) \cap R = \emptyset$, or (ii) $v \in R$ and $N(v) \cap S = \emptyset$. □

In what follows, we show that a good labeling $\mathcal{L}^\star$ with small number of layer-0 vertices can be computed efficiently. Our strategy is to begin with the trivial all-0 good labeling, and then in each iteration use the current good labeling $\mathcal{L}$ to obtain a new good labeling $\mathcal{L}'$ such that (i) each layer-0 vertex remains layer-0 with some probability (to be determined), and (ii) no new layer-0 vertex is created.

Computing a New Labeling $\mathcal{L}'$ from $\mathcal{L}$. Let $p \in (0, 1)$ and $s \geq 1$ be two parameters to be chosen later. The algorithm for computing $\mathcal{L}'$ is as follows: (1) initially, set $\mathcal{L}'(v) = \perp$ for all vertices, but each layer-0 vertex v sets $\mathcal{L}'(v) = 0$ independently with probability p; (2) repeat (Down-cast, All-cast, Up-cast) s times, and then do Down-cast; (3) any vertex v that has yet to obtain a new $\mathcal{L}'$ label (i.e., $\mathcal{L}'(v) = \perp$) retains its old label, setting $\mathcal{L}'(v) = \mathcal{L}(v)$.

- Down-cast. For $i = 0, \ldots, n-2$, do SR-comm with S being the set of layer-i vertices of $\mathcal{L}$ such that its $\mathcal{L}'$ label is not $\perp$, and R being the set of all layer-$(i+1)$ vertices of $\mathcal{L}$ such that its $\mathcal{L}'$ label is $\perp$. Each vertex in S attempts to broadcast its $\mathcal{L}'$ label. Each vertex in R that receives the message m sets its $\mathcal{L}'$ label to be $m+1$.
- All-cast. Do SR-comm with S being the set of all vertices such that its $\mathcal{L}'$ label is not $\perp$, and R being the set of all vertices such that its $\mathcal{L}'$ label is $\perp$. Each vertex in S attempts to broadcast its $\mathcal{L}'$ label. Each vertex in R that receives the message m sets its $\mathcal{L}'$ label to be $m+1$.
- Up-cast. For $i = n-1, \ldots, 1$, do SR-comm with S being the set of layer-i vertices of $\mathcal{L}$ such that its $\mathcal{L}'$ label is not $\perp$, and R being the set of all layer-$(i-1)$ vertices of $\mathcal{L}$ such that its $\mathcal{L}'$ label is $\perp$. Each vertex in S attempts to broadcast its

$\mathcal{L}'$ label. Each vertex in R that receives the message m sets its $\mathcal{L}'$ label to be $m + 1$.

We use SR-comm with $f = 1/\text{poly}(n)$. It is straightforward to verify that the algorithm indeed computes a good labeling $\mathcal{L}'$, w.h.p. The algorithm takes $O(ns) \cdot T'(n, \Delta)$ time and $O(s) \cdot E'(n, \Delta)$ energy, where $T'(n, \Delta)$ and $E'(n, \Delta)$ are the runtime and the energy cost of SR-comm; see Lemmas 3 and 4. In the CD model, the energy cost is $O(s + \log n)$; see Remark 5.

We show that each layer-0 vertex in $\mathcal{L}$ remains layer-0 in $\mathcal{L}'$ with probability at most $p + (1 - p)^{\min\{s+1, w\}} + 1/\text{poly}(n)$, where $w = |\mathcal{L}^{-1}(0)|$. Assuming all invocations of SR-comm succeed, which happens with probability $1 - 1/\text{poly}(n)$, there are two ways for a layer-0 vertex v in $\mathcal{L}$ to remain layer-0 in $\mathcal{L}'$.

- The vertex v sets $\mathcal{L}'(v) = 0$ at Step (1), and this occurs with probability p.
- All vertices u within distance s to v (in $G_{\mathcal{L}}$) have $\mathcal{L}'(u) = \perp$ at Step (1), and this occurs with probability at most $(1 - p)^{\min\{s+1, w\}}$.

We are in a position to prove the main theorems of this section.

Theorem 7. *The* Broadcast *problem can be solved by a randomized algorithm with high probability in the following runtime $T = T(n, \Delta)$ and energy cost $E = E(n, \Delta)$.*

LOCAL :	$T = O(n \log n)$	$E = O(\log n)$
CD :	$T = O(n \log \Delta \log^2 n)$	$E = O(\log^2 n)$
No-CD :	$T = O(n \log \Delta \log^2 n)$	$E = O(\log \Delta \log^2 n)$

Proof. Set $p = 1/2$ and $s = 1$. As long as the number of layer-0 vertices in $\mathcal{L}$ is greater than 1, each layer-0 vertex in $\mathcal{L}$ remains layer-0 in $\mathcal{L}'$ with probability at most $p + (1 - p)^{\min\{s+1, w\}} + 1/\text{poly}(n) \leq 1/2 + 1/4 + 1/\text{poly}(n) = 3/4 + 1/\text{poly}(n)$. Thus, after $O(\log n)$ iterations of computing a new labeling from an old labeling, we obtain a good labeling $\mathcal{L}^\star$ such that the number of layer-0 vertices is exactly 1, with high probability. Applying Lemma 6 (with $L = n$ and $d = 0$) gives the theorem. □

Recall that the energy cost for computing $\mathcal{L}'$ from $\mathcal{L}$ is $O(s + \log n)$ (instead of $O(s \log n)$) in the CD model. Using this fact, the energy cost can be improved in the CD model without affecting the time too much. This result is omitted from this extended abstract. Refer to the full version of the paper [9].

5 ENERGY-EFFICIENT BROADCAST WITH NEARLY OPTIMAL TIME

In this section, we show that it is possible to achieve near diameter time $O(D^{1+\epsilon}\text{poly}(\log n))$ while keeping relatively low energy complexity $O(\text{poly}(\log n))$. Throughout this section we are working in the No-CD model for simplicity. A couple log factors can be saved by adapting our algorithm to the CD model.

Our algorithm is based on a subroutine Partition(β), described by Miller, Peng, and Xu [30] and further analyzed by Haeupler and Wajc [18]. The goal of Partition(β) is to produce the following random clustering. Each vertex v picks $\delta_v \sim \text{Exponential}(\beta)$, $\beta \in (0, 1)$, and assigns v to the cluster of u that minimizes $\text{dist}(u, v) - \delta_u$. This algorithm is as follows [18].

Partition(β). Every vertex v picks a value $\delta_v \sim \text{Exponential}(\beta)$. Let v's start time be $\text{start}_v \leftarrow \max\{1, \frac{2\log n}{\beta} - \lceil \delta_v \rceil\}$. There are $\frac{2\log n}{\beta}$ epochs numbered 1 through $\frac{2\log n}{\beta}$. At the beginning of epoch t, if v is not yet in any cluster and $\text{start}_v = t$, v becomes the cluster center of its own cluster. During the epoch, we execute SR-comm with failure probability $f = 1/\text{poly}(n)$, where S is the set of all clustered vertices and R the set of all as-yet unclustered vertices. Any vertex $v \in R$ receiving a message (we call this "merging request") from $u \in S$ joins the cluster of u.

The algorithm Partition(β) can be implemented in No-CD, and it takes $O(\frac{\log^3 n}{\beta})$ time and $O(\frac{\log^3 n}{\beta})$ energy.

The cluster graph is defined as the graph resulting from contracting each cluster to a vertex. Our strategy for solving Broadcast is to iteratively apply the clustering algorithm Partition(β) to the cluster graph until it has diameter poly($\log n$).

Lemma 8 presents some useful properties of Partition(β). In Lemma 9 we prove that the diameter of the cluster graph shrinks by a factor of $O(\beta)$ with high probability.

Lemma 8 ([18, 30]). *The algorithm* Partition(β) *partitions the vertices into clusters with the following properties.*

1. *The probability of any edge $\{u, v\}$ having its endpoints in different clusters is at most 2β.*
2. *Let u be any vertex. The probability that vertices in $N^d(u) \cup \{u\}$ are in at least t distinct clusters is at most $\left(1 - e^{-(2d+1)\beta}\right)^{t-1}$. As a special case, for $d = 1$ (i.e., if we only care about u and its neighbors) this probability is at most $\left(1 - e^{-3\beta}\right)^{t-1}$.*

Proof. The two properties are due to [18, Corollary 3.7] and [18, Corollary 3.8], respectively. □

Lemma 9 (Concentration bound on diameter). *Suppose that the diameter of the graph G is $D = \frac{\alpha \log^2 n}{\beta^4}$, for some number α. Then the diameter of the cluster graph resulting from* Partition(β) *is at most $3\beta D$, with probability $1 - n^{-\Omega(\alpha)}$.*

Proof. Let $k = 2 \cdot \frac{2\log n}{\beta}$ be twice the number of epochs, and so the maximum diameter of any cluster is at most k. Consider any two vertices u and v such that $\text{dist}(u, v) > 3\beta D = 3\beta \cdot \frac{\alpha \log^2 n}{\beta^4} = \frac{3\alpha \log^2 n}{\beta^3}$. Let $P = (w_1, w_2, \ldots, w_\ell, w_{\ell+1})$ be a shortest path from $u = w_1$ to $v = w_{\ell+1}$ of length ℓ. Define X_i to be the indicator random variable that w_i and w_{i+1} are contained in different clusters. Then $X = \sum_{i=1}^{\ell} X_i$ is an upper bound on the distance between the cluster of u and the cluster of v in the cluster graph.

If $|i - j| > k = \frac{4\log n}{\beta}$, then X_i and X_j are independent. Thus, we can color $\{X_i\}_{i=1,\ldots,\ell}$ by $\chi = \frac{4\log n}{\beta}$ colors in such a way that variables of the same color are independent. By [13, Theorem 3.2], we have the following inequality: $\Pr[X \geq \mathrm{E}[X] + t] \leq \exp(-2t^2/(\chi \cdot \ell))$. By linearity of expectation and Lemma 8(1), $\mathrm{E}[X] \leq 2\beta\ell$. Thus, by setting $t = \beta\ell$, we have

$$\Pr[X \geq 3\beta\ell] \leq \exp(-\Omega(\beta^3 \ell / \log n)) = n^{-\Omega(\alpha)}.$$

The lemma follows by a union bound over all $O(n^2)$ possible pairs $\{u, v\}$. Notice that if $\text{dist}(u, v) \leq 3\beta D$, then the distance between the cluster of u and the cluster of v in the cluster graph is already at most $3\beta D$. □

5.1 Outline of the Algorithm

We fix the parameter $\beta = \frac{1}{\log^{1/\epsilon} n}$. Our randomized No-CD algorithm for Broadcast consists of two phases. The first phase is to iteratively run Partition(β) on the current cluster graph $\log_{1/(3\beta)} D$ times. The second phase is to apply Lemma 6 to the last clustering to solve Broadcast.

Throughout the procedure, the cluster graph is implemented as a good labeling, and each layer-0 vertex is responsible for simulating a cluster. The communication between clusters can be done using Down-cast, All-cast, Up-cast in a way similar to that in Section 4.

Details of the First Phase. After performing Partition(β) to get a new clustering, we will later see that the maximum number of layers in any cluster is multiplied by at most $\frac{4\log n}{\beta} + 1 < \frac{5\log n}{\beta} = 5\log^{1+\frac{1}{\epsilon}} n$. Recall that there are in total $\frac{2\log n}{\beta}$ epochs. In each epoch, when we merge a cluster C into another cluster C', the number of layers in C is increased by at most two times the number of layers in C'. See Section 5.4 for implementation details of merging clusters.

Using the above number, throughout the first phase, the maximum number of layers of the underlying good labeling is at most

$$\mathcal{D} = \left(\frac{5\log n}{\beta}\right)^{\log_{1/(3\beta)} D} = D^{\left(\frac{\log \frac{5\log n}{\beta}}{\log \frac{1}{3\beta}}\right)} = D^{1+\epsilon(1+O(1/\log\log n))}.$$

By Property 2 of Lemma 8, with high probability, for each vertex u, the number of distinct clusters that vertices in $N^+(u) = N(u) \cup \{u\}$ belong to is at most

$$C = O\left(\log_{1/3\beta} n\right) = O\left(\log_{\log^{1/\epsilon} n} n\right) = O\left(\frac{\epsilon \log n}{\log\log n}\right).$$

We will later see that, based on the implementation of the cluster structure in Section 5.2, we can simulate one round of Partition(β) on the cluster graph using $O(\mathcal{D}C\log^3 n)$ rounds and $O(C\log^3 n)$ energy in the underlying graph G. The simulation of Partition(β) on the cluster graph is given in Section 5.3. The maintenance of good labeling underlying the clustering is described in Section 5.4. To summarize, the performance for the first phase is:

Time:	$\log_{1/(3\beta)} D \cdot O(\log^{3+1/\epsilon} n) \cdot O(\mathcal{D}C\log^3 n)$,
Energy:	$\log_{1/(3\beta)} D \cdot O(\log^{3+1/\epsilon} n) \cdot O(C\log^3 n)$.

Details of the Second Phase. Consider the cluster graph resulting from the first phase, and let $\mathcal{L}^\star$ be the underlying good labeling. Recall that $\mathcal{D}$ is the maximum number of layers of $\mathcal{L}^\star$. In view of Lemma 9, after the first phase, the diameter of the cluster graph is less than $O(\frac{\log^2 n}{\beta^4}) = O(\log^{2+4/\epsilon} n)$. Notice that the diameter of the cluster graph must be greater than or equal to the diameter of $G_{\mathcal{L}^\star}$. We apply Lemma 6 with $d = O(\log^{2+4/\epsilon} n)$ and $L = \mathcal{D} = D^{1+\epsilon(1+O(1/\log\log n))}$, to solve Broadcast with the following cost:

Time:	$O(D^{1+\epsilon(1+O(1/\log\log n))}\log^{4+4/\epsilon} n)$,
Energy:	$O(\log^{4+4/\epsilon} n)$.

By doing a variable change $\epsilon' = \epsilon(1 + O(1/\log\log n))$, we have the following theorem.

Theorem 10. *For any $\epsilon \in (0,1)$, there is a randomized* No-CD *algorithm that, w.h.p., solves* Broadcast *in time $O(D^{1+\epsilon}\log^{O(\frac{1}{\epsilon})} n)$ using energy $O(\log^{O(\frac{1}{\epsilon})} n)$.*

5.2 Cluster Structure

We assume that each vertex v has a unique number ID(v), and has a good labeling $\mathcal{L}(v)$. Recall that a good labeling, in general, does not give rise to a unique clustering. To fix a specific clustering, consider the following modifications. We define the cluster id of a cluster C by ID(r), where r is the unique layer-0 vertex in C. We assume that each vertex $v \in C$ knows the cluster id CID(v) = ID(r). We assume the cluster center r has generated a sufficiently long random string $R(r)$, and each vertex $v \in C$ knows $R(v) \overset{\text{def}}{=} R(r)$. We call this the *shared random string* of the cluster C.

Suppose that all vertices agree on the two parameters C and $\mathcal{D}$ meeting the following conditions. For each vertex u, the vertices in $N^+(u)$ belong to at most C distinct clusters. The number $\mathcal{D}$ is an upper bound on the number of layers of the good labeling. We claim that the following two tasks can be done with $O(C\log^3 n)$ time and $O(C\log^3 n)$ energy.

- Downward transmission. Let $i \geq 0$ and V' be a subset of layer-i vertices that have some messages to send. The goal is to have each layer-$(i+1)$ vertex with at least one V'-neighbor *in the same cluster* receive a message from any such neighbor, with high probability.
- Upward transmission. Let $i > 0$ and V' be a subset of layer-i vertices that have some messages to send. The goal is to have each layer-$(i-1)$ vertex with at least one V'-neighbor *in the same cluster* receive a message from any such neighbor, with high probability.

Lemma 11. *In the* No-CD *model, both* Downward transmission *and* Upward transmission *can be solved by a randomized algorithm that takes $O(C\log^3 n)$ time and $O(C\log^3 n)$ energy.*

Proof. We only present the proof for Downward transmission, since Upward transmission can be solved analogously. The algorithm is as follows. Repeat the following procedure for $O(C\log n)$ iterations. Each layer-i vertex $v \in V'$ joins the set S with probability $\frac{1}{C}$, using the shared random string $R(v)$. Thus, for any two layer-i vertices $u, v \in V'$ in a cluster C, we must have either $u, v \in S$ or $u, v \notin S$. Run SR-comm with S being the above set, and R being the set of all layer-$(i+1)$ vertices. This algorithm takes $O(C\log^3 n)$ time and $O(C\log^3 n)$ energy.

Now we prove the correctness of this algorithm. Consider any layer-$(i+1)$ vertex v in cluster C, let $u_1, \ldots, u_x$ be all layer-i neighbors of v in C that are transmitting, and let $u_{x+1}, \ldots, u_k$ be all layer-i neighbors of v not in C that are transmitting. The vertices $u_1, \ldots, u_k$ are contained in at most C distinct clusters. Within $O(C\log n)$ iterations, with high probability, there is an iteration where (i) $u_1, \ldots, u_x \in S$, and (ii) $u_{x+1}, \ldots, u_k \notin S$. Thus, v is able to receive a message from a neighbor in C in this iteration. We assume any message contains the cluster id, so that v can check whether a message it receives comes from a neighbor in C. □

5.3 Simulating Algorithms on the Cluster Graph

In view of the definition of SR-comm, we define the $CD^\star$ model as follows. This model is basically the same as CD, but for the case where at least two neighbors are transmitting, the listener receives any one of these messages instead of receiving noise. The choice of the message that the listener receives can be arbitrary. Observe that Partition(β) works in $CD^\star$.

Consider one round of $CD^\star$ on the *cluster graph* (the graph resulting from contracting each cluster into a vertex). Let $\mathcal{S}$ be the set of all clusters that are transmitting, and let $\mathcal{R}$ be the set of all clusters that are listening. This round can be simulated in the underlying graph G by the following three operations: (i) Down-cast allows the layer-0 vertex representing each cluster $C \in \mathcal{S}$ to broadcast a message to the entire cluster; (ii) All-cast allows messages to be transmitted between the clusters; (iii) Up-cast allows the layer-0 center of each cluster $C \in \mathcal{R}$ to obtain one message sent to the cluster, if any. Recall that the number of layers is at most $\mathcal{D}$.

- Down-cast. For each $C \in \mathcal{S}$, the center r of C generates some message m, and the goal is to let all vertices in C know m. This can be done by transmitting the message layer by layer. The algorithm is as follows. For $i = 0, \ldots, \mathcal{D} - 2$, suppose all layer-$i$ vertices have received the message, and then execute Downward transmission to let all layer-$(i + 1)$ vertices to receive the message. This operation takes $O(\mathcal{D}C \log^3 n)$ time and $O(C \log^3 n)$ energy.
- All-cast. Let S be the set of all vertices that belong to a cluster in $\mathcal{S}$, and let R be the set of all vertices that belong to a cluster in $\mathcal{R}$. Each $v \in S$ has a message to transmit, and the goal is to let each $u \in R$ such that $N(u) \cap S \neq \emptyset$ to receive some message. This can be solved in a way similar to Lemma 11, and takes $O(C \log^3 n)$ time and $O(C \log^3 n)$ energy.
- Up-cast. For each $C \in \mathcal{R}$, some vertices in a cluster C hold a message, and the goal is to let the center know any one of them, if at least one exists. The algorithm is similar to Down-cast. For $i = \mathcal{D} - 1, \ldots, 1$, run Upward transmission to let layer-$(i - 1)$ vertices receive messages from layer-i vertices. This takes $O(\mathcal{D}C \log^3 n)$ time and $O(C \log^3 n)$ energy.

LEMMA 12. *In the* No-CD *model, we can simulate any* $CD^\star$ *algorithm on the cluster graph, where each round of the* $CD^\star$ *algorithm is simulated in* $O(\mathcal{D}C \log^3 n)$ *time using* $O(C \log^3 n)$ *energy.*

5.4 Maintaining a Good Labeling

In this section, we show the details of maintaining the good labeling $\mathcal{L}$ as well as other information, such as the cluster id CID(v) and shared random string $R(v)$, while some clusters are being merged.

Let W denote the set of all vertices that successfully received "merging requests" at some time during an execution of Partition(β) (more precisely, at an All-cast operation in Section 5.3). We assume that the merging request sent from a vertex v in a cluster C' contains the following information: ID(v), CID(v), $R(v)$, and $\mathcal{L}(v)$. For each $u \in W$, let $\phi(u)$ be the vertex in a neighboring cluster that successfully sent the merging request to u.

If a cluster C satisfies $C \cap W \neq \emptyset$, then it needs to accept one merging request, and merges itself to a neighboring cluster. More specifically, this is done as follows. First, within the cluster C, we select one leader vertex $v^\star \in C \cap W$, and then we re-root the cluster C at $v^\star$, and assign a new good labeling $\mathcal{L}'$ to all C-nodes.

For example, suppose that the accepted merging request is sent from the vertex $\phi(v^\star) = u^\star \in C'$. Then we need to merge C into C'. If the vertex label of $u^\star$ is 18, then we need to set the new label of $v^\star$ as 19. The rest of the vertices in C will receive labels $20, 21, \ldots$. This can be done via Up-cast and Down-cast in Section 5.3 on the old labeling $\mathcal{L}$. That is, this task can be accomplished in $O(\mathcal{D}C \log^3 n)$ time using $O(C \log^3 n)$ energy. The algorithm is as follows.

Step 1: Electing $v^\star$. Perform an Up-cast to let the cluster center of C elect a vertex $v^\star \in C \cap W$, and then perform a Down-cast to let all vertices in C know the decision.

Step 2: Update Labeling $\mathcal{L}'$. Initially, all vertices $v \in C$ have $\mathcal{L}'(v) = \perp$, except that $\mathcal{L}'(v^\star)$ is initialized as the layer number of $\phi(v^\star)$ plus 1. The $\mathcal{L}'$-label of all remaining vertices in C can be assigned using Up-cast and Down-cast as follows.

- Perform an Up-cast. The message of $v^\star$ is its $\mathcal{L}'$-label. Each vertex v that receives a message m sets $\mathcal{L}'(v) = m+1$, and it will transmit the message $m + 1$ during the next Upward transmission.
- Perform a Down-cast. For each vertex v that has obtained a $\mathcal{L}'$-label, its message is its $\mathcal{L}'$-label (and it will not reset its $\mathcal{L}'$-label). Each vertex v that has not obtained a $\mathcal{L}'$-label sets $\mathcal{L}'(v) = m + 1$, where m is the message it receives.

After the Down-cast in Step 2, everyone in C is guaranteed to receive a vertex label. Information about cluster id and shared random string can also be transmitted through this procedure.

Suppose that in this epoch of Partition(β), the clusters $C_1, \ldots, C_k$ are merged into a cluster C'. Before merging, we let L be maximum number of layers in a cluster $C_1, \ldots, C_k$, and let L' be the number of layers of C'. Then, the number of layers in the new cluster resulting from merging $C_1, \ldots, C_k$ into C' is at most $L' + (2L - 1)$.

Since Partition(β) has $(2 \log n)/\beta$ epochs, the maximum number of layers in any cluster is multiplied by at most $1 + (4 \log n)/\beta$ after Partition(β).

6 CONCLUSION AND OMITTED RESULTS

Energy complexity is a natural and attractive concept in wireless radio networks. In this work we presented (to our best knowledge) the first algorithm that solved Broadcast in poly $\log n$ energy. Several results were omitted from this extended abstract. We briefly summarize these below. Refer to the full version [9] for details.

Simulation of LOCAL *Algorithms.* With a preprocessing step, one can simulate any LOCAL algorithm in No-CD by scheduling all transmissions to avoid collisions. Specifically, we show that any algorithm $\mathcal{A}$ for the LOCAL model taking time T and energy E can be simulated in randomized No-CD using $O(\Delta^2 T + \Delta \log \Delta \log n)$ time and $O(\Delta(E + \log \Delta \log n))$ energy. In particular, when $\Delta = O(1)$, the Broadcast problem can be solved by a randomized No-CD algorithm in $O(n \log n)$ time with energy cost $O(\log n)$, which shows that the LOCAL lower bound on path graphs of Theorem 1 is matched by a No-CD algorithm on bounded-degree graphs.

Improved Randomized Algorithms for the CD *Model.* The energy complexity for the randomized CD model in Section 4 can be further improved to nearly match the lower bound, up to a small $O(\log\log\Delta/\log\log\log\Delta)$ factor. Specifically, we demonstrate a CD algorithm that takes $O\left(\frac{\log n(\log\log\Delta+(1/\xi))}{\log\log\log\Delta}\right)$ energy and $O\left(\Delta n^{1+\xi}\right)$ time, for any $\xi=\omega(\log\log n/\log n)$.

Time and Energy Optimal Algorithm for Path Graphs. We design a Broadcast algorithm for path graphs that has $O(n)$ worst case runtime with $O(\log n)$ expected energy cost. This shows that optimality in time and energy can be simultaneously achieved.

Deterministic Algorithms. We have a deterministic algorithm for the CD model, also based on iterative clustering. Its energy complexity is $O(\log^3 N\log n)$ but the runtime is $O(nN^2\log n\log N)$.

Open Problems. Assuming energy usage is paramount, can one design Broadcast algorithms meeting our lower bounds: $\Omega(\log n)$ in CD and $\Omega(\log\Delta\log n)$ in No-CD? Can we get the best of both worlds: near optimality in time and energy? Specifically, is there a small constant c for which $O(D\log^c n)$ time and $O(\log^c n)$ energy suffice to solve Broadcast? Can we simultaneously achieve $O(n)$ time and $O(\log n)$ per-vertex energy on *arbitrary* graphs?

REFERENCES

[1] I. F. Akyildiz, T. Melodia, and K. R. Chowdhury. 2007. A survey on wireless multimedia sensor networks. *Computer Networks* 51, 4 (2007), 921–960.

[2] N. Alon, A. Bar-Noy, N. Linial, and D. Peleg. 1991. A lower bound for radio broadcast. *J. Comput. System Sci.* 43, 2 (1991), 290–298.

[3] C. Ambühl. 2005. An Optimal Bound for the MST Algorithm to Compute Energy Efficient Broadcast Trees in Wireless Networks. In *Automata, Languages and Programming*, L. Caires, G. F. Italiano, L. Monteiro, C. Palamidessi, and M. Yung (Eds.). Springer Berlin Heidelberg, Berlin, Heidelberg, 1139–1150.

[4] C Ambühl. 2008. *Minimum Energy Broadcasting in Wireless Geometric Networks.* Springer US, Boston, MA, 1–99.

[5] R. Bar-Yehuda, O. Goldreich, and A. Itai. 1992. On the time-complexity of broadcast in multi-hop radio networks: An exponential gap between determinism and randomization. *J. Comput. System Sci.* 45, 1 (1992), 104–126.

[6] M. Barnes, C. Conway, J. Mathews, and D. K. Arvind. 2010. ENS: An Energy Harvesting Wireless Sensor Network Platform. In *Proceedings of the 5th International Conference on Systems and Networks Communications (ICSNC).* 83–87.

[7] M. A. Bender, T. Kopelowitz, S. Pettie, and M. Young. 2016. Contention Resolution with Log-logstar Channel Accesses. In *Proceedings of the 48th Annual ACM Symposium on Theory of Computing (STOC).* 499–508.

[8] P. Berenbrink, C. Cooper, and Z. Hu. 2009. Energy efficient randomised communication in unknown AdHoc networks. *Theoretical Computer Science* 410, 27 (2009), 2549 – 2561.

[9] Yi-Jun Chang, Varsha Dani, Thomas P. Hayes, Qizheng He, Wenzheng Li, and Seth Pettie. 2017. The Energy Complexity of Broadcast. *CoRR* abs/1710.01800 (2017). arXiv:1710.01800 http://arxiv.org/abs/1710.01800

[10] Y.-J. Chang, T. Kopelowitz, S. Pettie, R. Wang, and W. Zhan. 2017. Exponential separations in the energy complexity of leader election. In *Proceedings of the 49th Annual ACM SIGACT Symposium on Theory of Computing (STOC).* 771–783.

[11] A. Czumaj and P. Davies. 2017. Exploiting Spontaneous Transmissions for Broadcasting and Leader Election in Radio Networks. In *Proceedings of the 2017 ACM Symposium on Principles of Distributed Computing (PODC).*

[12] A. Czumaj and W. Rytter. 2003. Broadcasting algorithms in radio networks with unknown topology. In *Proceedings of 44th Annual IEEE Symposium on Foundations of Computer Science (FOCS).* 492–501.

[13] D. P. Dubhashi and A. Panconesi. 2009. *Concentration of Measure for the Analysis of Randomized Algorithms.* Cambridge University Press.

[14] M. Farach-Colton, R. J. Fernandes, and M. A. Mosteiro. 2006. Lower Bounds for Clear Transmissions in Radio Networks. In *Proceedings of the 7th Latin American Symposium on Theoretical Informatics (LATIN).* 447–454.

[15] M. Ghaffari and B. Haeupler. 2013. Near Optimal Leader Election in Multi-Hop Radio Networks. In *Proceedings of the 24th Annual ACM-SIAM Symposium on Discrete Algorithms (SODA).* 748–766.

[16] M. Ghaffari, B. Haeupler, and M. Khabbazian. 2015. Randomized broadcast in radio networks with collision detection. *Distributed Computing* 28, 6 (2015), 407–422.

[17] L. Gsieniec, E. Kantor, D. R. Kowalski, D. Peleg, and C. Su. 2007. Energy and Time Efficient Broadcasting in Known Topology Radio Networks. In *Distributed Computing*, A. Pelc (Ed.). Springer Berlin Heidelberg, Berlin, Heidelberg, 253–267.

[18] B. Haeupler and D. Wajc. 2016. A faster distributed radio broadcast primitive. In *Proceedings of the 2016 ACM Symposium on Principles of Distributed Computing (PODC).* ACM, 361–370.

[19] T. Jurdzinski, M. Kutylowski, and J. Zatopianski. 2002. Efficient algorithms for leader election in radio networks. In *Proceedings of the 21st Annual ACM Symposium on Principles of Distributed Computing (PODC).* 51–57.

[20] T. Jurdzinski, M. Kutylowski, and J. Zatopianski. 2002. Energy-Efficient Size Approximation of Radio Networks with No Collision Detection. In *Proceedings of the 8th Annual International Conference on Computing and Combinatorics (COCOON).* 279–289.

[21] T. Jurdzinski, M. Kutylowski, and J. Zatopianski. 2002. Weak Communication in Radio Networks. In *Proceedings of the 8th International European Conference on Parallel Computing (Euro-Par).* 965–972.

[22] T. Jurdzinski, M. Kutylowski, and J. Zatopianski. 2003. Weak communication in single-hop radio networks: adjusting algorithms to industrial standards. *Concurrency and Computation: Practice and Experience* 15, 11–12 (2003), 1117–1131.

[23] M. Kardas, M. Klonowski, and D. Pajak. 2013. Energy-efficient leader election protocols for single-hop radio networks. In *Proceedings of the 42nd International Conference on Parallel Processing (ICPP).* 399–408.

[24] L. M. Kirousis, E. Kranakis, D. Krizanc, and A. Pelc. 2000. Power consumption in packet radio networks. *Theoretical Computer Science* 243, 1 (2000), 289 – 305.

[25] M. Klonowski, M. Kutylowski, and J. Zatopianski. 2012. Energy efficient alert in single-hop networks of extremely weak devices. *Theoretical Computer Science* 453 (2012), 65 – 74. http://www.sciencedirect.com/science/article/pii/S0304397512001016 Algorithmic Aspects of Wireless Sensor Networks.

[26] D. R. Kowalski and A. Pelc. 2005. Broadcasting in undirected ad hoc radio networks. *Distributed Computing* 18, 1 (2005), 43–57.

[27] E. Kushilevitz and Y. Mansour. 1998. An $\Omega(D\log(N/D))$ Lower Bound for Broadcast in Radio Networks. *SIAM J. Comput.* 27, 3 (1998), 702–712.

[28] M. Kutyłowski and W. Rutkowski. 2003. Adversary Immune Leader Election in ad hoc Radio Networks. In *Algorithms - ESA 2003*, Giuseppe Di Battista and Uri Zwick (Eds.). Springer Berlin Heidelberg, Berlin, Heidelberg, 397–408.

[29] N. Linial. 1992. Locality in Distributed Graph Algorithms. *SIAM J. Comput.* 21, 1 (1992), 193–201.

[30] G. L. Miller, R. Peng, and S. C. Xu. 2013. Parallel graph decompositions using random shifts. In *Proceedings of the twenty-fifth annual ACM symposium on Parallelism in algorithms and architectures (SPAA).* ACM, 196–203.

[31] K. Nakano and S. Olariu. 2000. Energy-Efficient Initialization Protocols for Single-Hop Radio Networks with No Collision Detection. *IEEE Trans. Parallel Distrib. Syst.* 11, 8 (2000), 851–863.

[32] K. Nakano and S. Olariu. 2002. Uniform leader election protocols for radio networks. *IEEE Transactions on Parallel and Distributed Systems* 13, 5 (2002), 516–526.

[33] C. Newport. 2014. Radio Network Lower Bounds Made Easy. In *Proceedings of the 28th International Symposium on Distributed Computing (DISC).* 258–272.

[34] D. Peleg. 2000. *Distributed Computing: A Locality-Sensitive Approach.* SIAM.

[35] J. Polastre, R. Szewczyk, and D. Culler. 2005. Telos: enabling ultra-low power wireless research. In *Proceedings of the 4th International Symposium on Information Processing in Sensor Networks (IPSN).* 364–369.

[36] V. Shnayder, M. Hempstead, B.-r. Chen, G. W. Allen, and M. Welsh. 2004. Simulating the Power Consumption of Large-scale Sensor Network Applications. In *Proceedings of the 2nd International Conference on Embedded Networked Sensor Systems (SenSys).* ACM, New York, NY, USA, 188–200.

[37] K. M. Sivalingam, M. B. Srivastava, and P. Agrawal. 1997. Low power link and access protocols for wireless multimedia networks. In *Proceedings of the IEEE 47th Vehicular Technology Conference (VTC)*, Vol. 3. 1331–1335.

[38] Y. Wang, F. Nunez, and F. J Doyle. 2012. Energy-efficient pulse-coupled synchronization strategy design for wireless sensor networks through reduced idle listening. *IEEE transactions on signal processing* 60, 10 (2012), 5293–5306.

[39] D. E Willard. 1986. Log-logarithmic selection resolution protocols in a multiple access channel. *SIAM J. Comput.* 15, 2 (1986), 468–477.

[40] W. Ye, J. Heidemann, and D. Estrin. 2002. An energy-efficient MAC protocol for wireless sensor networks. In *Proceedings.Twenty-First Annual Joint Conference of the IEEE Computer and Communications Societies*, Vol. 3. 1567–1576 vol.3.

Deterministic Digital Clustering of Wireless Ad Hoc Networks

Tomasz Jurdziński
Institute of Computer Science
University of Wrocław, Poland

Dariusz R. Kowalski
Department of Computer Science
University of Liverpool, United Kingdom

Michał Różański
Institute of Computer Science
University of Wrocław, Poland

Grzegorz Stachowiak
Institute of Computer Science
University of Wrocław, Poland

ABSTRACT

We consider deterministic distributed communication in wireless ad hoc networks of identical devices in the SINR model without predefined infrastructure. Most algorithmic results in this model rely on additional features or capabilities, e.g., randomization, access to geographic coordinates, power control, carrier sensing with various precision of measurements, and interference cancellation. We study a *pure* scenario, when no such features are available.

Several distributed algorithms have been presented in recent years for the local and global broadcast problems considered in this paper. However, all these solutions were either randomized or relied on the assumption that nodes of a network know their own coordinates in a given metric space or devices has signal sensitivity limited to some area (typically smaller than transmission range). In contrast, the aim of this paper is to check how efficient could be solutions without randomization, availability of locations, limited sensitivity, power control, carrier sensing, interference cancellation or other features. Our research objective is motivated twofolds. Firstly, examination of necessity and impacf of randomization is a natural research topic in algorithm design. Moreover, as wireless ad hoc networks are usually built from computationally limited devices run on batteries, it is desirable to use simple and energy efficient algorithms which do not need access to several sensing capabilities or true randomness.

As a general tool, we develop a deterministic distributed *clustering* algorithm, which splits nodes of a multi-hop ad hoc network into clusters of constant diameter. Our solution relies on a new type of combinatorial structures (called witnessed strong selectors), which might be of independent interest.

Using the clustering, we develop a deterministic distributed *local broadcast* algorithm accomplishing this task in $O(\Delta \log^* N \log N)$ rounds, where Δ is the density of a network. This is the first solution in pure scenario which is only polylog(n) away from the universal lower bound $\Omega(\Delta)$, valid also for scenarios with randomization and other features. Therefore, we conclude that none of these features substantially helps for the local broadcast task. Using clustering, we also build a deterministic *global broadcast* algorithm that terminates within $O(D(\Delta + \log^* N) \log N)$ rounds, where D is the diameter of the network. This result is complemented by a lower bound $\Omega(D\Delta^{1-1/\alpha})$, where $\alpha > 2$ is the path-loss parameter of the environment. This lower bound, in view of previous work, shows that randomization or knowledge of own location help substantially (by a factor polynomial in Δ) in *the global broadcast*. Similar cluster-based techniques can be used to build efficient (comparing to the lower bound) solutions to the wake-up problem and the global leader election problem. Summarizing, our results prove that additional model/environment features may help substantially in design of time-efficient solutions for global communication problems, but not much in case of local problems.

KEYWORDS

ad hoc networks, wireless networks, broadcast, clustering, selectors, deterministic algorithms

ACM Reference Format:
Tomasz Jurdziński, Dariusz R. Kowalski, Michał Różański, and Grzegorz Stachowiak. 2018. Deterministic Digital Clustering of Wireless Ad Hoc Networks. In *PODC '18: ACM Symposium on Principles of Distributed Computing, July 23–27, 2018, Egham, United Kingdom.* ACM, New York, NY, USA, 10 pages. https://doi.org/10.1145/3212734.3212752

1 INTRODUCTION

We study distributed algorithms in ad hoc wireless networks in the SINR (*Signal-to-Interference-and-Noise Ratio*) model with uniform transmission power. We consider the *ad hoc* setting where both capability and knowledge of nodes are limited – nodes know only the basic parameters of the SINR model (i.e., $\alpha, \beta, \varepsilon, \mathcal{N}$) and upper bounds Δ, n on the degree and the size of the network, such that the actual maximal degree is $O(\Delta)$ and the size is $n^{O(1)}$. Such a setting appears in networks without infrastructure of base stations, access points, etc., reflecting scenarios where large sets of sensors are distributed in an area of rescue operation, environment monitoring, or in prospective internet of things applications. Among others, we study basic communication problems – global and local broadcast, as well as primitives designed to coordinate computation and communication in networks (e.g., leader election and wake-up).

1.1 The Network Model.

We consider a wireless network consisting of nodes located on the 2-dimensional Euclidean space. We model transmissions in the network with the SINR constraints. The model is determined by fixed parameters: path loss $\alpha > 2$, threshold $\beta > 1$, ambient noise $\mathcal{N} > 0$ and transmission power $\mathcal{P}$. The value of $SINR(v, u, \mathcal{T})$ for

ACM ISBN 978-1-4503-5795-1/18/07...$15.00
https://doi.org/10.1145/3212734.3212752

given nodes u, v and a set of concurrently transmitting nodes $\mathcal{T}$ is defined as

$$SINR(v, u, \mathcal{T}) = \frac{\mathcal{P}/d(v,u)^\alpha}{\mathcal{N} + \sum_{w \in \mathcal{T} \setminus \{v\}} \mathcal{P}/d(w,u)^\alpha}, \quad (1)$$

where $d(u, v)$ denotes the distance between u and v. A node u successfully receives a message from v iff $v \in \mathcal{T}$ and $SINR(v, u, \mathcal{T}) \geq \beta$, where $\mathcal{T}$ is the set of nodes transmitting at the same time. *Transmission range* is the maximal distance at which a node can be heard provided there are no other transmitters in the network. Without loss of generality we assume that the transmission range is all equal to 1. This assumption implies that the relationship $\mathcal{P} = \mathcal{N}\beta$ holds. However, it does not affect generality and asymptotic complexity of presented results.

Communication graph. In order to describe the topology of a network as a graph, we set a connectivity parameter $\varepsilon \in (0, 1)$. The *communication graph* $G = (V, E)$ of a given network consists of all nodes and edges $\{v, u\}$ connecting nodes that are in distance at most $1 - \varepsilon$, i.e., $d(u, v) \leq 1 - \varepsilon$. Observe that a node can receive a message from a node that is not its neighbor in the graph, provided interference from other nodes is small enough. The communication graph, defined as above, is a standard notion in the analysis of the SINR model, cf., [8, 12, 15, 18, 29].

Synchronization and content of messages. We assume that algorithms work synchronously in rounds. In a single round, a node can transmit or receive a message and perform local computation. The size of a single message is limited to $O(\log N)$.

Knowledge of nodes. Each node has a unique identifier from the set $[N] = \{1, \ldots, N\}$, where $N = n^{O(1)}$ is the upper bound on the size n of the network. Moreover, nodes know N, the SINR parameters – $\alpha, \beta, \mathcal{N}, \mathcal{P}, \varepsilon$, the linear upper bounds on the diameter D and the degree Δ of the communication graph.

Communication problems. The *global broadcast* problem is to deliver a message from the designated source node s to all the nodes in the network, perhaps through relay nodes. At the beginning of an execution of a global broadcast algorithm, only the source node s is active. A node $v \neq s$ starts participating in an execution of the algorithm only after receiving the first message from another node. (This is so-called non-spontaneous wake-up model, popular in the literature.) In the *local broadcast problem*, the goal is to make each node to successfully transmit its own message to its neighbors in the communication graph. Here, all nodes start participating in the execution of an algorithm at the same round.

1.2 Related Work

In the last years the SINR model was extensively studied, both from the perspective of its structural properties [2, 16, 23] and algorithm design [4, 8, 12, 14, 24, 29]. The first work on local broadcast [12] presented an $O(\Delta \log n)$ and $O(\Delta \log^3 n)$ randomized algorithms with respectively known and unknown degree Δ. After that, the problem was studied in various settings. In [15], an $O(\Delta + \log^2 n)$ round algorithm in a model with feedback was given, further improved to $O(\Delta + \log n \log\log n)$ in [4]. For the scenario when the degree Δ is not known, Yu et al. [29] improved the $O(\Delta \log^3 n)$ bound from [12] to $O(\Delta \log n + \log^2 n)$. Deterministic efficient algorithms using information about own locations of nodes were given e.g. in [11]. However, no deterministic algorithm for local broadcast was known in the scenario that nodes do not know their coordinates.

For the global broadcast problem, a few deterministic solutions are known and all of them use the information about location of nodes. Broadcast can be accomplished deterministically in time $O(D \log^2 n)$ in such setting [20]. If messages cannot be delivered to nodes which are close to the range boundary, complexity of global broadcast is much higher [21, 26]. In the harsh scenario, where connectivity of a network might rely on so-called weak links, deterministic global broadcast requires $\Theta(n \log N)$ rounds [22]. Randomized results on global broadcast in ad hoc settings were given in [8, 18]. Solutions with complexity, respectively $O((D \log n) \log^{\alpha+1} g)$ and $O(D \log^2 n)$ are presented, where g is a parameter depending on the geometry of the network. More efficient solutions for local broadcast and related problems has been obtained in stronger models, by sensing the idle/busy channel and estimating the total interference using signal measurements [13, 14, 27]. The global broadcast and related problems were studied in the related radio networks model [3, 5, 7, 9, 25, 25] and even weaker beeping networks [6]. For the closest to our model geometric unit-disk-graph radio networks, the complexity of broadcast is $\Theta(D\Delta)$ [10].

1.3 Our Contribution

As a general tool, we develop a clustering algorithm which splits nodes of a multi-hop network into clusters such that: (i) each cluster is included in a ball of constant diameter; (ii) each ball of diameter 1 contains nodes from $O(1)$ clusters. Using the clustering algorithm, we develop a *local broadcast* algorithm for ad hoc wireless networks, which accomplishes the task in $O((\Delta + \log^* N) \log N)$ rounds, where Δ is the density of the network. This is the first solution in the considered scenario which is only polylog(N) away from the universal lower bound $\Omega(\Delta)$.

Using clustering, we also build a deterministic global broadcasting algorithm that terminates within $O(D(\Delta + \log^* N) \log N)$ rounds, where D is the diameter of the network graph. This result is complemented by a lower bound $\Omega(D\Delta^{1-1/\alpha})$. This lower bound, in view of previous work, shows that randomization or knowledge of own location substantially help in *the global broadcast*. Previous results on global broadcast were independent of the networks density Δ. However, they relied on either randomization, or access to coordinates of nodes or carrier sensing. Without these capabilities, as we show, the polynomial dependence of Δ is unavoidable.

We also provide efficient solutions to the wake-up problem and the global leader election problem.

1.4 High Level Description of Our Technique

The key challenge in designing efficient algorithm in the ad hoc wireless scenario is the interference from dense areas of a network. If randomization was available, nodes could adjust their transmission probabilities and/or signal strength such that the expected interference from each ball of radius 1 is bounded by a constant. Another problem in the considered model stems from the fact that it is impossible to distinguish received messages which are sent by close neighbors from those sent by nodes on boundaries of the transmission range. This issue could be managed if nodes had access to their geographic coordinates or were equipped with carrier sensing capabilities. In the pure ad hoc model considered in this paper, all those tools are not available.

Our algorithmic solutions rely on the notion of *r-clustering*, i.e., a partition of nodes into clusters such that: (i) each cluster is included in a ball of radius r; (ii) each ball of radius 1 contains nodes from $O(1)$ clusters.

Two communication primitives are essential for efficient implementation of our approach: *Sparse Network Schedule* (SNS) and *Close Neighbors Schedule* (CNS). **Sparse Network Schedule (SNS)** is a communication protocol of length $O(\log N)$ which guarantees that, given an arbitrary set of nodes X with constant density, each $v \in X$ performs local broadcast (i.e., the message transmitted by v is received in distance $1 - \varepsilon$). **Close Neighbors Schedule (CNS)** is a communication protocol of length $O(\log N)$ which guarantees that, given an arbitrary set of nodes X of density Γ with r-clustering of X for $r = O(1)$, each close enough pair of elements of X from each sufficiently dense cluster can hear each other. For efficient implementation of these primitives, we build new selectors, called *witnessed (cluster aware) strong selectors*. These selectors implement algorithmically an implicit collision detection mechanism in SINR model, which filters out most connections on large distance in an execution of CNS. Therefore, properties of the new selectors might be applicable in other contexts.

Given the above described primitives, we develop tools for (partially) clustered networks — in order to build r-clustering of the whole network gradually. In particular, we design the ***sparsification*** algorithm, which, given a set of clustered nodes W, gradually decreases the largest number of nodes in a cluster and eventually ends with a set $W' \subset W$ such that $O(1)$ (and at least one!) nodes from each cluster of W belong to W'. Using sparsification algorithm, we develop a tool for ***imperfect labeling*** of clusters, which results in assigning temporary IDs (tempID) in range $O(\Delta)$ to nodes such that $O(1)$ nodes in each cluster have the same tempID. Moreover, an efficient ***radius reduction*** algorithm is presented, which transforms r-clustering for $r > 1$ into a 1-clustering.

Given the tools for a clustered set of nodes, we build a *global broadcasting* algorithm, which works in phases. In the ith phase all nodes awaken* in the phase $(i-1)$ perform local broadcast. In this way, the set of nodes awaken in the first i phases contains all nodes in communication graph of distance i from the source. Moreover, we assure that all nodes awaken in a phase are 1-clustered. (We start with the cluster formed by nodes in distance ≤ 1 from the source s, awaken in a round in which s is the unique transmitter.) A phase consists of three stages. In Stage 1, an imperfect labeling of each cluster is done. In Stage 2, Sparse Network Schedule is executed $O(\Delta)$ times. A node with label j participates in the jth execution of SNS only. In this way, all nodes transmit successfully on distance $1 - \varepsilon$. All nodes awaken in Stage 2 inherit cluster ID from nodes which awaken them. In this way, we have 2-clustering of all nodes awaken in Stage 2. In Stage 3, a 1-clustering of awaken nodes is formed by using an efficient algorithm that reduces the radius of clustering.

Our algorithm for *local broadcast* builds a 1-clustering of the whole network, assigns tempIDs to nodes in clusters with use of the imperfect labeling algorithm, and eventually performs local broadcast by applying SNS for each prospective tempID separately. (Recall that, in the local broadcast problem, all nodes are awaken simultaneously, just at the beginning of a protocol.) Thus, the key challenge here is to build a 1-clustering starting from an unclustered network. First, we use our sparsification technique to build a sparse set of *leaders* and a schedule S such that each node of the network is in distance of $O(\log N)$ hops from some leader with respect to the schedule S. Then, starting from clusters containing neighbors of leaders, we gradually build clustering of the whole network.

Missing proofs and details are available in the arXiv report [19].

*A node is awaken in the phase j if it receives the broadcast message for the first time in that phase.

2 PRELIMINARIES

Geometric definitions. Let $B(x, r)$ denote the ball of radius r around the point x on the plane. That is, $B(x, r) = \{y \mid d(x, y) \leq r\}$. We identify $B(x, r)$ with the set of nodes of the network that are located inside $B(x, r)$. A *unit ball* is a ball with radius 1. Let $\chi(r_1, r_2)$ denote the maximal size of a set of points S located in a ball of radius r_1 such that $d(u, v) \geq r_2$ for each $u, v \in S$ such that $u \neq v$.

Clustered and unclustered sets of nodes. Assume that each node from a given set is associated with a pair of numbers (v, ϕ), where $v \in [N]$ is its unique ID and $\phi \in [N]$ is the ID of the *cluster* of v, $\phi = \text{cluster}(v)$. A set X of pairs (v, ϕ) associated with nodes is called a *clustered set* of nodes. The *cluster* ϕ denotes the set $\{(v, \phi') \in X \mid \phi' = \phi\}$.

An *unclustered* set X of nodes is just a subset of $[N]$, which might be also considered as a clustered set, where each node's cluster ID is equal to 1, i.e., cluster$(v) = 1$ for each $v \in X$.

Geometric clusters. Consider a clustered set of nodes X such that each node is located in the Euclidean plane (i.e, it has assigned coordinates determining its location). The clustering of X is an r-clustering, for $r \geq 1$, if the following conditions are satisfied:

- For each cluster ϕ, all of nodes from the cluster ϕ are located in the ball $B(x, r)$, where x is an element of ϕ called the *center* of ϕ.
- For each clusters ϕ_1, ϕ_2, the centers x_1, x_2 of ϕ_1, ϕ_2 are located in distance at least $1 - \varepsilon$, i.e., $d(x_1, x_2) \geq 1 - \varepsilon$.

The *density* Γ of an unclustered network/set denotes the largest number of nodes in a unit ball. For a clustered network/set G, the *density* is equal to the largest number of elements of a cluster. One can observe that the density of a network and the degree of its communication graph are linearly dependent. Therefore, we use Δ/Γ to denote both the density and the degree of the communication graph.† For a clustered set of density Γ, a cluster is *dense* when it contains at least $\Gamma/2$ elements. For an unclustered set of density Γ, a unit ball $\mathcal{B}$ is *dense* when it contains at least $\Gamma/2$ elements.

Now, we define the notion of a *close pair*, essential for our network *sparsification* technique. Let $d_{\Gamma,r}$ be the smallest number satisfying the inequality $\chi(r, d_{\Gamma,r}) \geq \Gamma/2$. Thus, according to the definition of the function χ and the definition of a dense cluster/ball, the smallest distance between nodes of a dense cluster (unit ball, resp.) in an r-clustered (unclustered, resp.) network is at most $d_{\Gamma,r}$ ($d_{\Gamma,1}$, resp.).

†This abuse of notations has no impact on asymptotic upper bounds on complexity of algorithms designed in this paper.

Definition 1. *Nodes u, w form a* close pair *in an r-clustered network of density Γ for $r \geq 1$ if the following conditions hold for some $\zeta \in (0, 1]$ and cluster ϕ:*

a) cluster(u) = cluster(w) = ϕ,
b) $d(u, w) = \zeta d_{\Gamma,r} \leq 1 - \varepsilon$,
c) $d(u, x) \geq d(u, w)$ and $d(w, x) \geq d(u, w)$ for each $x \notin \{u, w\}$ from the cluster ϕ = cluster(u) = cluster(w);
d) $d(u', w') \geq d(u, w)/2$ for any $u', w' \in B(u, \zeta) \cup B(w, \zeta)$, such that $u' \neq w'$ and cluster(u') = cluster(w') = ϕ.

The nodes u, w form a close pair *in an unclustered network of density Γ iff the above conditions (a)–(d) hold provided cluster(x) = 1 for each node x of a network and $r = 1$. A node v is a* close neighbor *of u iff (u, v) is a close pair.*

An intuition behind the requirements of the definition of a close pair is as follows. In the clustered case, only the pairs inside the same cluster are considered to be a close pair, by (a)). The requirement (b)) states that $d(u, w)$ is at most the upper bound on the smallest distance between closest nodes of a dense cluster/ball. The item (c)) assures that u is the closest node to w and w is the closest node to u. Finally, (d)) states that the distances between nodes in the close neighborhood of u and w are not much smaller than $d(u, w)$. Polynomial attenuation of strength of signals with the power $\alpha > 2$ in the SINR model will assure that, for a close pair u, w, a successful reception of a message from u to w will depend on behaviour of some constant number of the nodes which are closest to u and w. We formalize this intuition in further part of this work (Lemmas 4 and 5). In the following lemma we observe presence of close pairs in dense areas of a network.

Lemma 1. *Assume that the density of a set of nodes X is Γ. Then,*

(1) If X is unclustered, then there is a close pair in each ball $B(x, 5)$ such that $B(x, 1)$ is dense.
(2) If X is clustered, then there is a close pair in each dense cluster.

Imperfect labeling. Assume that a clustering of a set X of nodes with density Γ is given. Then, *c-imperfect labeling* of X is a labeling of all elements of X such that label(x) $\leq \Gamma$ for each $x \in X$ and, for each cluster $\phi \in [N]$ and each label $l \in [N]$, the number of nodes from the cluster ϕ with label l is at most c, where c is a fixed co nstant.

3 COMBINATORIAL TOOLS FOR SINR COMMUNICATION

In this section, we introduce combinatorial structures and communication primitives using them.

3.1 Combinatorial tools

In this section we will use families of sets with specific combinatorial properties as communication protocols in such a way that the nodes from the ith set of the family are transmitters in the ith round. Below, we give necessary definitions to apply this approach, recall some results and build new combinatorial structures.

A *transmission schedule* for unclustered (clustered, resp.) sets is defined by a sequence $S = (S_1, ..., S_t)$ of subsets of $[N]$ ($[N] \times [N]$, resp.), where the ith set determines nodes transmitting in the ith round of the schedule; i.e., a node with ID $v \in [N]$ (and cluster(v) = ϕ, resp.) transmits in round i if and only if $v \in S_i$ ((v, cluster(v)) $\in S_i$, resp.).

A set $S \subseteq [N]$ *selects* $x \in X$ from $X \subseteq [N]$ if $S \cap X = \{x\}$. The family $\mathcal{S}$ of sets over $[N]$ is called (N, k)-strongly selective family (or (N, k)-ssf) if for each subset $X \subseteq [N]$ such that $|X| \leq k$ and each $x \in X$ there is a set $S \in \mathcal{S}$ that selects x from X. It is well known that there exist (N, k)-ssf of size $O(k^2 \log(N/k))$ for each $k \leq N$ [5].

We introduce a combinatorial structure generalizing ssf in two ways. Firstly, it will take the clustering into account, allowing that some clusters might be "in conflict". Secondly, selections of elements from a given set X will be "witnessed" by all nodes outside of X. As we show later, this structure helps to build a sparse graph in a SINR network, such that each close pair is connected by an edge. We start from a basic variant called *witnessed strong selector (wss)*, which does not take clustering into account. (A restricted variant of wss has been recently presented in [22].) Then, we generalize the structure to clustered sets. We call this variant *witnessed cluster aware strong selector (wcss).*

Witnessed strong selector. A sequence $\mathcal{S} = (S_1, \ldots, S_m)$ of sets over $[N]$ satisfies *witnessed strong selection property for a set $X \subseteq [N]$*, if for each $x \in X$ and $y \notin X$ there is a set $S_i \in \mathcal{S}$ such that $X \cap S_i = \{x\}$ and $y \in S_i$. One may think that y is a "witness" of a selection of x in such a case. A sequence $\mathcal{S} = (S_1, \ldots, S_m)$ is a *(N, k)-witnessed strong selector* (or (N, k)-wss) of size m if, for every subset $X \subseteq [N]$ of size k, the family $\mathcal{S}$ satisfies the witnessed strong selection property for X.

Note that any (N, k)-wss is also, by definition, an (N, k)-ssf. Additionally, (N, k)-wss guarantees that each element outside of a given set X of size k has to be a "witness" of selection of every element from X.

Now, we generalize the notion of (N, k)-wss to the situation that witnessed strong selection property is analyzed for each cluster separately, assuming that each cluster might be in *conflict* with l other clusters.

The conflict between the clusters ϕ_1 and ϕ_2 means that a selection of an element from ϕ_1 by a set S is possible only in the case that the considered set S does not contain any element from ϕ_2.

(N, k, l)-witnessed cluster aware strong selector. We say that a set $S \subseteq [N]^2$ is *free* of cluster ϕ if for all $(x, \phi') \in S$ we have $\phi' \neq \phi$. A set S is free of the set of clusters C if it is free of each cluster $\phi \in C$. Let $X \subseteq [N] \times \{\phi\}$ be a set of nodes from the cluster ϕ and $C \subseteq [N] \setminus \{\phi\}$ be a set of clusters in conflict with the cluster ϕ. Then, a sequence $\mathcal{S} = (S_1, ..., S_m)$ of subsets of $[N]^2$ satisfies *witnessed cluster aware selection property (wcss property)* for X with respect to C if for each $x \in X$ and each $y \notin X$ from cluster ϕ (i.e., $y \in [N] \times \{\phi\}$) there is a set S_i such that $S_i \cap X = \{x\}$, $y \in S_i$ and $S_i \cap ([N] \times C) = \emptyset$. In other words, wcss property requires that for each $x \in X$ and each $y \notin X$ from ϕ = cluster(x), x is selected by some S_i, y is a witness of a selection of X by S_i (i.e., $y \in S_i$), and S_i is free of the clusters from C. A sequence $\mathcal{S} = (S_1, ..., S_m)$ of subsets of $[N]^2$ is a (N, k, l)-witnessed cluster aware strong selector (or (N, k, l)-wcss) if for any set of clusters $C \subseteq [N]$ of size l, any cluster $\phi \notin C$ and any set $X \subseteq [N] \times \{\phi\}$ of size k, $\mathcal{S}$ satisfies wcss property for X with respect to C.

Lemma 2. *For each natural N, and $k, l \leq N$ such that $k \geq 1$ and $l \geq 0$, there exists a (N, k, l)-wcss of size $O((k+l)(l+1)k^2 \log N)$.*

Proof. We use the probabilistic method [1]. Let $\mathcal{S} = (S_1, ..., S_m)$, when the length m of the sequence will be specified later, be a sequence of sets built in the following way. The sets S_i are chosen independently at random as follows. First, the set C_i of "allowed" clusters is determined by adding each cluster ID from $[N]$ to C_i with probability $\frac{1}{l+1}$. Then, the set S_i is determined by adding independently (x, ϕ) to S_i for each $x \in [N]$ and $\phi \in C_i$ to the set S_i, with probability $1/k$. Let $\mathcal{T}$ be the set of tuples (X, C, ϕ, x, y) such that $X, C \subset [N]$, $|X| = k$, $|C| = l$, $\phi, x, y \in [N]$, $\phi \notin C$, $x \in X$, $y \notin X$. The size of $\mathcal{T}$ is $|\mathcal{T}| = \binom{N}{k}\binom{N}{l}(N-l)k(N-k) < N^{k+l+3}$. For a fixed tuple $(X, C, \phi, x, y) \in \mathcal{T}$, let $\mathbb{E}_i$ be the conjunction of the following three events:

- $\mathbb{E}_{i,0}$: $\phi \in C_i$ and $C \cap C_i = \emptyset$,
  [thus, $\text{Prob}(\mathbb{E}_{i,0}) = \frac{1}{l+1}\left(1 - \frac{1}{l+1}\right)^l \geq \frac{1}{4} \cdot \frac{1}{l+1}$;
  for $l = 0$, recall that $0^0 = 1$],
- $\mathbb{E}_{i,1}$: $(X \times \{\phi\}) \cap S_i = \{(x, \phi)\}$,
  [thus, $\text{Prob}(\mathbb{E}_{i,1} \mid \mathbb{E}_{i,0}) = \frac{1}{k}\left(1 - \frac{1}{k}\right)^{k-1} \geq \frac{1}{4} \cdot \frac{1}{k}$],
- $\mathbb{E}_{i,2}$: $(y, \phi) \in S_i$
  [thus, $\text{Prob}(\mathbb{E}_{i,1} \mid \mathbb{E}_{i,0} \cap \mathbb{E}_{i,1}) = 1/k$].

Then, $\mathbb{E}_i$ occurs with probability

$$\begin{aligned} p = \text{Prob}(\mathbb{E}_i) &= \text{Prob}(\mathbb{E}_{i,0} \cap \mathbb{E}_{i,1} \cap \mathbb{E}_{i,2}) \\ &= \text{Prob}(\mathbb{E}_{i,0}) \cdot \text{Prob}(\mathbb{E}_{i,1} \mid \mathbb{E}_{i,0}) \cdot \text{Prob}(\mathbb{E}_{i,2} \mid \mathbb{E}_{i,0} \cap \mathbb{E}_{i,1}) \\ &= \frac{1}{l+1}\left(1 - \frac{1}{l+1}\right)^l \cdot \frac{1}{k}\left(1 - \frac{1}{k}\right)^{k-1} \cdot \frac{1}{k} \\ &= \Omega\left(\frac{1}{(l+1)k^2}\right). \end{aligned}$$

The sequence $S_1, S_2, \ldots, S_m$ is a (N, k)-wcss when the event $\mathbb{E}_i$ occurs for each element of $\mathcal{T}$ for some index $i \in [m]$. The probability that, for all indices $i \in [m]$, $\mathbb{E}_i$ does not occur for the tuple (ϕ, X, C, x, y) is equal to

$$(1 - \text{Prob}(E_i))^m = (1-p)^m \leq e^{-mp}.$$

Thus, by the union bound, the probability that there exists a tuple (X, C, ϕ, x, y) for which E_i does not occur for all i is smaller or equal to $|\mathcal{T}|(1-p)^m \leq N^{k+l+3}e^{-mp} = e^{O((k+l)\log N) - mp}$. By choosing $m = \Theta((k+l)(l+1)k^2 \log N)$ large enough, the above expression gets strictly smaller than 1 and therefore the probability of obtaining (N, k, l)-wcss is positive. Hence, by using the probabilistic method, such an object exists. □

Observe that, by applying Lemma 2 for $l = 0$, we see that there exists a (N, k)-wss of size $O(k^3 \log n)$.

3.2 Basic communication under SINR interference model

Using introduced selectors, we provide some basic communication primitives on which we build our sparsification and clustering algorithms.

Lemma 3. *(Sparse Network Lemma) Let $\gamma \in \mathbb{N}$ be a fixed constant and $\varepsilon \in (0, 1)$ be the parameter defining the communication graph. There exists a schedule $\mathbf{L}_\gamma$ of length $O(\log N)$ such that each node u transmits a message which can be received (at each point) in distance $\leq 1 - \varepsilon$ from u in an execution of $\mathbf{L}_\gamma$ on a set with density γ.*

The schedule $\mathbf{L}_\gamma$ defined in Lemma 3 will be informally called Sparse Network Schedule or shortly SNS. The following lemmas imply that, for a successful transmission of a message on a link connecting a close pair, it is sufficient that some set of constant size of close neighbors is not transmitting at the same time (provided a round is free of some set of conflicting clusters of constant size). This fact will allow to apply wss (and wcss) for efficient communication in the SINR model.

Lemma 4. *There exists a constant κ (which depends merely on the SINR parameters and ε) which satisfies the following property. Let u, v be a close pair of nodes in an unclustered set A. Then, there exists a set $A' \subseteq A$ such that $u, v \in A'$, $|A'| \leq \kappa$ and v receives a message transmitted from u provided u is sending a message and no other element from A' is sending a message.*

Lemma 5. *Let A be an r-clustered set for a fixed $r = O(1)$. Then, there exists constants κ, ρ (depending only on r, ε and SINR parameters) satisfying the following condition. For each cluster ϕ and each close pair of nodes u, v from ϕ, there exists $A' \subseteq A$ of size $\leq \kappa$ and a set of clusters C of size $\leq \rho$ such that u receives a message transmitted by v in a round satisfying the conditions:*

- *no node from A' (except of v) transmits a message in the round,*
- *the round is free of clusters from C (that is, for each cluster $\phi' \in C$, no node from ϕ' transmits in the round).*

3.3 Proximity graphs

The idea behind sparsification algorithm extensively applied in our solutions is to repeat several times the following procedure: identify a graph including as edges all close pairs and "sparsify this" graph (switch off some nodes) appropriately. To this aim, we introduce the notion of *proximity graph*. For a given (clustered) set of nodes X, a *proximity graph* $H(X)$ of X is any graph on this set such that:

(i) vertices of each close pair u, v are connected by an edge,
(ii) the degree of each node of the graph is bounded by a fixed constant,
(iii) $\text{cluster}(u) = \text{cluster}(v)$ for each edge (u, v) of $H(X)$.

Using well-known strongly selective families (ssf) and Lemma 4, one can build a schedule S of length $O(\log N)$ such that each close pair of an unclustered network *exchange* messages during an execution of S. However, this property is not sufficient for fast construction of a proximity graph, since nodes may also receive messages from distant neighbors during an execution of S which migh result in large degrees. Moreover, each node v knows only received messages after an execution of S, but it is not aware of the fact which of its messages were received by other nodes. Finally, a direct application of ssf for clustered network/set requires additional increase of time complexity. In order to build proximity graphs efficiently, we use the algorithm ProximityGraphConstruction (Alg. 1). This algorithm relies on properties of witnessed (cluster aware) strong selectors.

Our construction (Alg. 1) builds on the following observations. Firstly, if u can hear v in a round in which w is transmitting as well, then (u, w) is for sure not a close pair (otherwise, w generates interference which prevents reception of the message from v

by u). Secondly, given a close pair (u, v), u can hear v in a round in which v transmits, provided none of the other κ closest to u nodes (from cluster(u)) transmits and no node from ρ conflicting clusters transmits, where κ, ρ are the constants from Lemmas 4, 5.

Given an

- (N, κ)-wss S in an unclustered network (for constant κ from Lemma 4), or
- (N, κ, ρ)-wcss S in a clustered network (for constants κ, ρ from Lemma 5),

one can build a proximity graph in $O(\log N)$ rounds using Alg. 1, assuming that cluster(v) $=\perp$ for each node v in the unclustered case. The algorithm consists of three phases: Exchange Phase, Filtering Phase, and Confirmation Phase (see Fig. 1 and Alg. 1). In Exchange Phase, all nodes execute S. In Filtering Phase, each node v determines the set C_v of all nodes u such that v has received a message from u during S and v has not received any other message in rounds in which u is transmitting (messages from other clusters are ignored). At the end of Filtering Phase, v removes all elements from C_v if $|C_v| > \kappa$. In Confirmation Phase, v sends information about the content of C_v to other nodes in consecutive $|C_v|$ repetitions of S. The set of neighbors of v in the final proximity graph is $E_v = \{w \in C_v \mid v \in C_w\}$. (Note that v can exchange messages with its neighbours in the constructed graph during an execution of S.)

Algorithm 1 ProximityGraphConstruction(v, cluster(v))

Pseudo-code for the node v:
$E_v \leftarrow \emptyset$,
if cluster(v) $=\perp$ **then**
  S $\leftarrow (N, \kappa)$-wss ▷ κ – constants from Lemma 4
else
  S $\leftarrow (N, \kappa, \rho)$-wcss ▷ κ, ρ – constants from Lemma 5
▷ Remark: all nodes use the same schedule S
Exchange Phase:
Execute S with message containing ID of v and cluster(v).
$U_v \leftarrow$ the set nodes which successfully delivered a message to v during Exchange Phase.
Filtering Phase:
$C_v \leftarrow U_v$
for each $u, w \in U_v$ **do**
  if in some round u and w transmitted **and** v heard u **then**
    $C_v \leftarrow C_v \setminus \{w\}$ ▷ lookup in the schedule S
if $|C_v| > \kappa$: $C_v \leftarrow \emptyset$
Confirmation Phase:
for each $u \in C_v$ **do**: execute S with $\langle v, u \rangle$ as the message.
for each message $\langle w, v \rangle$ received in confirmation phase **do**
  if $w \in C_v$ **then** $E_v \leftarrow E_v \cup \{w\}$

Using Lemmas 4, 5 and properties of witnessed selectors, one can prove the following lemma.

Lemma 6. *(Close Neighbors Lemma) ProximityGraphConstruction executed on a (clustered) set X builds a proximity graph $H(X)$ of constant degree in $O(\log N)$ rounds. Moreover, ProximityGraphConstruction builds a schedule* S *of size $O(\log N)$ such that u and v exchange messages during* S *for each edge (u, v) of $H(X)$.*

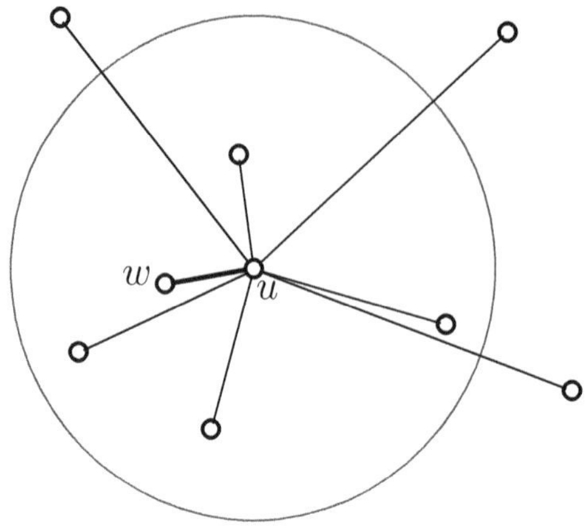

(a) Exchange Phase: edges connect u with elements of U_u.

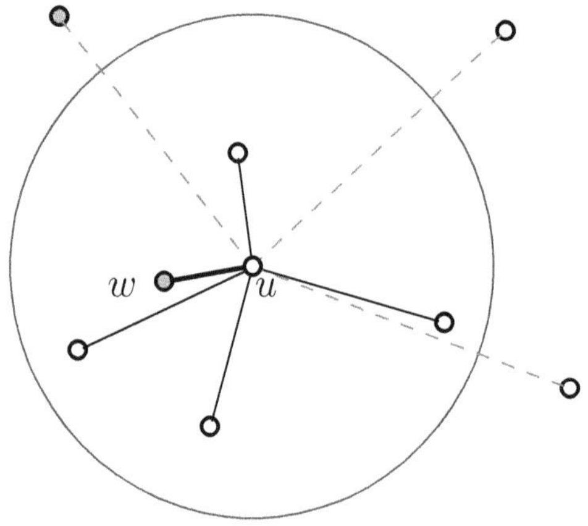

(b) Filtering Phase: If u hears w, it can remove all other nodes (dashed edges) that transmitted at the same time.

Figure 1: Proximity graph construction (Alg. 1). The blue circle contains κ closest nodes to u.

4 NETWORK SPARSIFICATION AND ITS APPLICATIONS

In this section we describe a sparsification algorithm which decreases density of a network by removing some nodes from dense areas and assigning them to their "parents" which are not removed. Simultaneously, the algorithm builds a schedule in which removed nodes exchange messages with their parents. Using sparsification as a tool, we develop other tools for (non)sparsified networks. Finally, a clustering algorithm is given which partitions a network (of awaken nodes) into clusters in time independent of the diameter of a network.

4.1 Sparsification

A c-sparsification algorithm for a constant $c \leq 1$ is a distributed ad-hoc algorithm S which, executed on a set X of density Δ determines a set $Y \subseteq X$ such that:

a) density of Y is at most $c\Delta$,

b) each $v \in X$ knows whether $v \in Y$ and each $v \in X \setminus Y$ has assigned parent$(v) \in Y$ such that v and parent(v) exchange messages during an execution of S on X.

Moreover, if X is a clustered set, cluster(v)=cluster(parent(v)) for each $v \in X \setminus Y$.

Alg. 2 contains a pseudocode of our sparsification algorithm. The algorithm builds a proximity graph of a network several times. Each time a proximity graph H is determined, an independent set Y of H is computed such that:

(A) for each dense cluster ϕ, at least one element of ϕ is in Y (clustered case) or

(B) for each dense unit-ball $\mathcal{B}$, there is an element in Y located close to (the center of) $\mathcal{B}$ (unclustered case).

Then, some elements of Y are linked with their neighbours in Y by parent/child relation and removed from the set of nodes attending consecutive executions of ProximityGraphConstruction. In this way, the density of the set of nodes attending the algorithm gradually decreases. Details of implementation of the algorithm (including differences between clustered and unclustered variant) and analysis of its efficiency are presented below.

Algorithm 2 Sparsification(Γ, X) ▷ Γ - density

```
1: For each v ∈ X: parent(v) = ⊥, children(v) = ∅
2: Active ← X, Prnts ← ∅, GlobChl ← ∅
3: for i = 1, 2, . . . , Γ do
4:     For each v ∈ Active: ProximityGraphConstruction(v, cluster(v))
5:     H ← the proximity graph built in line 4
6:     Y ← IndependentSet(H)
7:     NewChl ← {v ∈ Active | v ∉ Y and N_v^H ∩ Y ≠ ∅}
                       ▷ N_v^H denotes the set of neighbors of v in H
8:     for each v ∈ NewChl do
9:         parent(v) ← min(N_v^H ∩ Y)
10:        children(parent(v)) ← children(parent(v)) ∪ {v}
11:    Prnts ← Prnts ∪ {v ∈ Active | children(v) ≠ ∅}
12:    GlobChl ← GlobChl ∪ NewChl
13:    Active ← Active \ (Prnts ∪ GlobChl)
14: return Active ∪ Prnts
```

For a clustered network, IndependentSet(G) is chosen as the set of local minima in a proximity graph, that is, $Y \leftarrow \{v \mid \text{ID}(v) < \min(\{\text{ID}(u) \mid u \in N_v^H\})\}$. Using properties (A) and (B) one can show that, in each iteration of the main for-loop, at least one new child-parent relationship is build in each dense cluster. Based on this observation and properties of ProximityGraphConstruction, one can prove the following lemma.

Lemma 7. *Alg. 2 is a $\frac{3}{4}$-sparsificaton algorithm for clustered networks, it works in time $O(\Gamma \log N)$.*

For unclustered networks IndependentSet(G) is determined by a simulation of the distributed Maximal Independent Set (MIS) algorithm for the LOCAL model [28] which, for graphs of constant degree, works in time $O(\log^* n)$. As ProximityGraphConstruction builds an $O(\log N)$ time schedule in which each pair of neighbors u, v (of a built proximity graph) exchange messages, we can simulate each step of the algorithm from [28] in $O(\log N)$ rounds. In contrast to the clustered networks, we are unable to guarantee that a **single** execution of Sparsification reduces the density in an unclustered network. This is due to the fact that a node from dense unit ball might become a parent of a node outside of this ball; as a result the number of elements in the considered unit ball is not reduced during an execution of Sparsification. Therefore, we have to deal with unclustered case more carefully. Let $l \leftarrow \chi(5, 1-\varepsilon)$ and let SparsificationU(Γ, X) be an algorithm which executes Sparsification(Γ, X_i) for $i = 0, \ldots, l-1$, where $X_0 = X$, X_i is the set returned by Sparsification(Γ, X_{i-1}) and X_l is the set returned as the final result (see Alg. 3).

Algorithm 3 SparsificationU(Γ, X)

```
X_0 ← X
l ← χ(5, 1 − ε)
for i = 0, . . . , l − 1 do
    X_{i+1} ← Sparsification(Γ, X_i)
    S_i: the schedule of Sparsification(Γ, X_i)
return (X_1, . . . , X_l), (S_0, . . . , S_{l−1})
```

Lemma 8. *An execution of SparsificationU(Γ, U) on an unclustered set U of density Γ returns a sequence of set $X_0 \supseteq X_1 \supseteq \cdots \supseteq X_l$ and schedules $S_0, \ldots, S_{l-1}$ such that the density of X_l is at most $\frac{3}{4}\Gamma$, each node $x \in X_i \setminus X_{i+1}$ exchange messages with parent$(x) \in X_{i+1}$ during S_i. Moreover, SparsificationU(Γ, U) works in time $O(\Gamma \log N \log^* N)$.*

Proof. The analysis of the sparsification algorithm for clustered networks relies on the fact that there is a close pair in each dense cluster ϕ and therefore the number of active elements in ϕ is reduced after each iteration of the for-loop in Alg. 2. In the unclustered network, it might be the case that there is no close pair in a dense unit-ball. That is why the reasoning from Lemma 7 does not apply here.

We define an auxiliary notion of *saturation*. For a unit ball $\mathcal{B} = B(x, 1)$, the saturation of $\mathcal{B}$ with respect to the set of nodes X is the number of elements of X in $B(x, 5)$. As long as $\mathcal{B}$ contains at least $\Gamma/2$ nodes in an execution of ProximityGraphConstruction, there is a close pair u, v in $B(x, 5)$ (Lemma 1) and therefore u, v are connected by an edge in H. Thus, u or v is not in the computed MIS (line 6); wlog assume that u is not in MIS. Thus, u is dominated by a node from MIS and therefore it becomes a member of GlobChl and it is switched off. This in turn decreases saturation of $B(x, 5)$. Thus, an execution of Sparsification results either in decreasing the number of nodes in $\mathcal{B}$ to $\leq \Gamma/2$ or in reducing saturation of $\mathcal{B}$ by at least Γ. As $B(x, 5)$ might be covered by $l = \chi(5, 1)$ unit balls, there are at most $l\Gamma$ nodes in $B(x, 5)$ and saturation can be reduced at most $l\Gamma$ times. Hence, l repetitions of Sparsification eventually leads to the reduction of the number of active elements located in $\mathcal{B}$ to $\leq \Gamma/2$. □

4.2 Full Sparsification

A full sparsification algorithm is a distributed ad hoc schedule $S = S_1 S_2 \ldots S_k$ which, executed on an r-clustered set of nodes A of density Γ determines sets $A_0, A_1, \ldots, A_k$ such that $k = \log_{4/3} \Gamma$, $A_{i+1} \subseteq A_i$ (each node $v \in A$ knows whether $v \in A_i$), $A_0 = A$ and, for each $i \in [k]$:

a) the density of A_i is at most $\max\{\Gamma(3/4)^i, \chi(r, 1-\varepsilon)\}$,

b) each $v \in A_i \setminus A_{i+1}$ has assigned parent(v) $\in A_{i+1}$ such that v and parent(v) exchange messages during S_i and cluster(v) = cluster(parent(v)).

Alg. 4 contains a pseudocode of our full sparsification algorithm. In Lemma 9, the properties of this algorithm (following directly from Lemma 7) are summarized.

Algorithm 4 FullSparsification(Γ, A)

$A_0 \leftarrow A, X \leftarrow A, \Lambda \leftarrow \Gamma, k \leftarrow \log_{\frac{4}{3}} \Gamma$
for $i = 1, 2, \ldots, k$ **do**
  $Y \leftarrow$ Sparsification(Λ, X)
  $S_i \leftarrow$ the schedule of Sparsification(Λ, X)
  $A_i \leftarrow X \setminus Y, \Lambda \leftarrow \frac{3}{4}\Lambda$
  $X \leftarrow Y$
return $(A_0, \ldots, A_k), (S_1, \ldots, S_k)$

Lemma 9. *Algorithm 4 is a full sparsificaton algorithm for clustered networks which works in time $O(\Gamma \log N)$.*

4.3 Imperfect labelings of clusters

Using r-clustering of a set X with density Γ, it is possible to build an imperfect c-labeling of X for $c = O(1)$.

Lemma 10. *Assume that an r-clustering of a set X of density Γ is given. Then, it is possible to build c-imperfect labeling of X in $O(\Gamma \log N)$ rounds, where c depends merely on r and SINR parameters.*

Proof. Let $S = S_1, \ldots, S_k$ and $A_1, \ldots, A_k$ be the schedules and the sets obtained as the result of an execution of the procedure FullSparsification(Γ, X). It splits each cluster in $O(1)$ trees, defined by the child-parent relation build during an execution of FullSparsification. (Indeed, the elements of A_k are the roots of the trees.) The schedule S (and its reverse S^R) of length $O(\Gamma \log N)$ allows for bottom-up (top-down, resp.) communication inside these trees. Using S and S^R one can implement tree-labeling algorithm as follows. First, each node learns the size of its subtree (and subtrees of its children) in a bottom-up communication. Then, the root starts top-down phase, where each node assigns the smallest label in a given range to itself and assigns appropriate subranges to its children. The root starts from the range $[1, m]$, where m is the size of the tree. Given $[a, b]$, each node assigns a as its own ID and splits $[a + 1, b]$ into its subtrees. □

4.4 Reduction of radius of clusters

In this section we show how to reduce the radius of a clustering. Given an r-clustering of a set X of density Γ, our goal is to build an 1-clustering of X. The idea is to repeat the following steps several times. First, X is fully sparsified, i.e., $O(1)$ nodes remain from each cluster. Then, a minimum independent set (MIS) of this sparse set is determined on the graph with edges (u, v) connecting u, v which exchange messages during an execution of Sparse Network Schedule (see Lemma 3). The elements of MIS become the centers of new clusters in the new 1-clustering and they execute Sparse Network Schedule. A node v (not in MIS) which receives a message from w during this execution of SNS, becomes an element of cluster(w) and it is removed from further consideration. As we show below, a 1-clustering of X can be obtained in this way efficiently by Alg. 5.

Algorithm 5 RadiusReduction(Γ, X, r)

1: For each $v \in X$: newcluster(v) $\leftarrow \perp$ ▷ $\perp$ - "undetermined"
2: **for** $i = 1, 2, \ldots, \chi(r + 1, 1 - \varepsilon)$ **do**
3:   $(X_0, \ldots, X_k), (S_0, \ldots, S_k) \leftarrow$ FullSparsification(Γ, X)
4:   Execute Sparse Network Schedule L_Y from Lemma 3 on X_k
5:   $E \leftarrow \{(u, v) \mid u, v$ exchange messages during $L_Y\}$
6:   Let $G(Y, E)$, where $Y = \{v \mid \exists_u (u, v) \in E\}$
7:   $D \leftarrow$ MIS(G) ▷ simulation of MIS alg. from [28]
8:   Execute SNS L_Y from Lemma 3 on D
   ▷ Local Broadcast from D, using Lemma 3
9:   **for** each $v \in X \setminus D$ **do**
10:     **if** a message from $u \in D$ received **then**
11:       newcluster(v) $\leftarrow u$
12:   $X \leftarrow X \setminus (D \cup \{v \mid \text{newcluster}(v) \neq \perp\})$

Lemma 11. *Assume that a r-clustering of a set X of density Γ is given for a fixed constant $r \geq 1$. Then, Algorithm 5 builds 1-clustering of X in $O((\Gamma + \log^* N) \log N)$ rounds.*

Proof. By Lemma 7, the set X_k has density $c' = O(1)$ and it contains at least one element from each nonempty cluster of X. Each pair of nodes from X_k in distance $\leq 1 - \varepsilon$ exchange messages during step 4, therefore the graph G contains the communication graph of X_k. As D computed in step 7 is a MIS of X_k in the graph G and X_k contains at least one element from each nonempty cluster, there is an element of D in close neighborhood of each cluster. More precisely, for a dense cluster ϕ with nodes located inside $B(x, r)$, there is an element of the computed maximal independent set (MIS) in $B(x, r + 1)$. Indeed, by Lemma 9, there is y from ϕ in Y. Thus, $y \in B(x, r)$, where x is the center of the cluster ϕ. Either y is in the computed MIS or y is in distance ≤ 1 from an element z from the MIS. In the latter case, $z \in B(x, r + 1)$. Then, steps 8–11 assign all nodes in distance $\leq 1 - \varepsilon$ (and some in distance ≤ 1) from elements of D (including the above defined y or z) to new clusters included in unit balls (with centers at the elements of D). Thus, the nodes from each "old" cluster are assigned to new clusters after $\chi(r + 1, 1 - \varepsilon)$ repetitions of the main for-loop. □

4.5 Clustering algorithm

In this section we provide an algorithm which, given an unclustered set A, builds a 1-clustering of A. The algorithm consists of two main parts. In the former part, the sequence of sets $A_0 \supseteq \cdots \supseteq A_{kl}$ is built using SparsificationU, for $k = \log_{4/3} \Gamma$ and $l = \chi(5, 1 - \varepsilon)$. By Lemma 8, the density of A_{il} is at most $\Gamma(\frac{3}{4})^i$. Moreover, a sequence of schedules $S_0, \ldots, S_{kl}$ is built such that each $v \in A_i \setminus A_{i+1}$ exchange messages with parent(v) $\in A_{i+1}$. In the latter part, we start from 1-clustering of A_{kl}, which is obtained by assigning each node $v \in A_{kl}$ to a separate cluster. Then, given an 1-clustering of A_i for $i > 0$, we get 2-clustering of A_{i-1} by executing S_{i-1} with messages equal to cluster IDs of transmitting nodes. The elements of A_{i-1} choose clusters of their parents. Using RadiusReduction (Lemma 11), the obtained 2-clustering is transformed into an 1-clustering. A pseudocode is presented in Alg. 6.

Properties of SparsificationU and RadiusReduction (Lemmas 8 and 11) give the following theorem.

Algorithm 6 Clustering(Γ, A)

$k \leftarrow \log_{4/3}\Gamma$, $X \leftarrow A$, $A_0 \leftarrow A$
$\Lambda \leftarrow \Gamma$, $l \leftarrow \chi(5, 1-\varepsilon)$
for $i = 1, 2, \ldots, k$ **do**
  $j \leftarrow (i-1)l + 1$
  $(A_j, \ldots, A_{il}), (S_j, \ldots, S_{il}) \leftarrow$ SparsificationU(Λ, X)
  $X \leftarrow A_{il}$, $\Lambda \leftarrow \frac{3}{4}\Lambda$
For each $v \in A_{kl}$: cluster(v) $\leftarrow$ ID(v)
$X \leftarrow A_{kl}$, $\Lambda \leftarrow 1$
for $i = 0, 1, 2, \ldots, kl$ **do**
  Execute S_{kl-i}, on A_{kl-i} where each v sends cluster(v)
  For each $v \in A_{kl-i-1}$: cluster(v) $\leftarrow$ cluster(parent(v))
  $X \leftarrow X \cup A_{kl-i-1}$
  RadiusReduction($\Lambda, X, 2$)
  if $i \bmod l = 0$ **then** $\Lambda \leftarrow \frac{4}{3} \cdot \Lambda$

THEOREM 1. *The algorithm Clustering builds 1-clustering of an unclustered set A of density Γ in time $O(\Gamma \log N \log^\star N)$.*

5 COMMUNICATION PROBLEMS

In this section, we use sparsification and clustering in algorithms for the local and global broadcast.

We solve the local broadcast problem by the following Local-Broadcast algorithm (see pseudocode Alg. 7).

Algorithm 7 LocalBroadcast(V, Δ)

Clustering(Δ, V) ▷ Theorem 1
Imperfect labeling of V ▷ Lemma 10
for $l = 1, \ldots, \Delta$ **do**
  Run SNS on nodes with label equal to l ▷ Lemma 3

First, the clustering algorithm is applied, which builds a 1-clustering of V in time $O(\Delta \log N \log^\star N)$ (Th. 1). Then, an imperfect labeling of clusters can be formed in time $O(\Delta \log N)$ (Lemma 10). Finally, an algorithm which executes Δ times Sparse Network Schedule (see Lemma 3), the lth execution of SNS is performed by the nodes with label l (they use own IDs during SNS). As each label appears $O(1)$ times in each cluster, the density of the set of nodes with label l is $O(1)$ for each $l \in [N]$. Thus, consecutive executions of SNS accomplish the local broadcast task.

THEOREM 2. *The algorithm LocalBroadcast performs local broadcast in time $O(\Delta \log N \log^\star N)$.*

The algorithm for global broadcast works in phases. Let V_i denote the set of nodes in the graph-distance i from the source s, i.e., $v \in V_i$ if a shortest path from s to v has length i. In Phase 1, the source s transmits a message. After receiving the message from s, a node $v \in V \cap B(s, 1)$ assigns itself to the cluster s. Hence, the set of awaken nodes L_1 contains V_1 and we have 1-clustering of L_1.

In Phase $i > 1$, local broadcast is executed on L_i, the set of nodes awaken in Phase $i-1$. In this way, the set of nodes awaken in the first i phases contains all nodes in graph distance i from s, i.e., $\bigcup_{j\in[i]} V_j \subseteq \bigcup_{j\in[i]} L_j$. Moreover, we assure that all nodes awaken in a phase are 1-clustered at the end of the phase.

A phase consists of three stages. In Stage 1 of phase i, an *imperfect labeling* of each cluster of L_i is built. This means that each node v is assigned a label l_v such that, for each cluster, the number of nodes with the same label in the cluster is $O(1)$ (Lemma 10). In Stage 2, Sparse Network Schedule (Lemma 3) is executed Δ times. A node with label l participates in the lth execution of SNS only. In this way, all nodes from L_i transmit on distance $1-\varepsilon$. All nodes awaken in Stage 2 inherit cluster numbers from nodes which awaken them. In this way, we obtain a 2-clustering of L_{i+1}, the set of nodes awaken in Stage 2. The goal of Stage 3 is (given the obtained 2-clustering) to build an 1-clustering of awaken nodes.

Algorithm 8 GlobalBroadcast(V, s)

s transmits the broadcast message
$L_1 \leftarrow$ nodes awaken by s, with cluster IDs equal to s
for $i = 1, 2, \ldots, D$ **do**
  Stage 1: imperfect labeling of L_i ▷ Lemma 10
  Stage 2: local broadcast from L_i, using labels ▷ Lemma 3
  Stage 3: RadiusReduction($\Delta, L_{i+1}, 2$) ▷ Lemma 11.

Using Lemmas 10, 3 and 11, we obtain the following result.

THEOREM 3. *Algorithm GlobalBroadcast solves the global broadcast problem in $O(D(\Delta + \log^* N)\log N)$ rounds.*

Using similar techniques as for the global and local broadcast, we can efficiently solve the related wake-up and leader election problems in the model with global clock (see [19] for details).

In the wake-up problem [17], some nodes are *activated* at various rounds by an adversary and the goal is to activate the whole network. Nodes which are not activated by the adversary should be activated by a message successfully delivered to them.

THEOREM 4. *The wake-up problem in networks with global clock can be solved in $O(D(\Delta + \log^* N)\log N)$ rounds.*

The *leader election* problem is to choose (exactly) one node in the whole network as the leader, assuming that nodes can be awaken in various rounds by an adversary.

THEOREM 5. *The leader election problem in networks with global clock can be solved in $O(D(\Delta + \log^* N)\log^2 N)$ rounds.*

6 LOWER BOUND

We also show that, in the model considered in this paper, complexity of global broadcast depends polynomially on the density Δ. The sketch of the proof of this result is given in Appendix.

THEOREM 6. *Each deterministic algorithm for the global broadcast in the SINR network with non-spontaneous wake-up works in time $\Omega(D\Delta^{1-1/\alpha} + \Delta)$, provided $N = \Omega(D\Delta)$ and the connectivity parameter $\varepsilon > 0$ is small enough.*

In order to prove the above theorem, we build a family of networks called *gadgets*. Each network from the family consists of nodes $s, v_0, \ldots, v_{\Delta+1}, t$ located on the line (see Fig. 2, 3) Thus, in particular, s is connected in the communication graph with $v_0, \ldots, v_{\Delta+1}$, t is connected merely with $v_{\Delta+1}$ and only messages from $v_{\Delta+1}$ can be received by t. One can show that, for each deterministic algorithm, one can assign IDs to the nodes $s, v_0, \ldots, v_{\Delta+1}$ such that the broadcast message originating at s will be delivered to t after $\Omega(\Delta)$ rounds. For the purpose of the lower bound, the main property of the locations of nodes in the gadget are:

(a) v_i does not receive any message, provided at least two nodes from the set $\{v_j \mid j < i\}$ transmit at the same time;
(b) t can receive a message from $v_{\Delta+1}$ ($v_{\Delta+1}$ is the only node from the gadget in distance ≤ 1 from t) only in the case that no other node from the gadget transmits at the same time.

Using (a), we assign IDs to consecutive nodes $v_1, v_2, \ldots$ such that, after i rounds, the nodes v_k for $k > 2i$ do not have any information about their location inside the set $\{v_l \mid l > 2i\}$. Thus, the only available information differentiating them are their IDs. Using this property, we prevent a transmission of $v_{\Delta+1}$ in a round in which other nodes from the gadget do not transmit for $\Omega(\Delta)$ rounds.

A natural idea to generalize such a result to $\Omega(D\Delta)$ is to connect sequentially consecutive gadgets such that the target (t) of the ith gadget is identified with the source s of the $(i+1)$st gadget. However, under the SINR constraints, the interference from distant nodes might potentially help, since it differentiates history of communication for nodes in various locations (even the close ones). Therefore, the applicability of this idea under the SINR constraints is limited. Instead of identifying the target t of the ith gadget with the source of the $(i+1)$st gadget s, we separate each two consecutive gadgets by a long "sparse" path of nodes such that consecutive nodes are in distance $1 - \varepsilon$ (Fig. 4). In this way, we limit the impact of nodes located outside of a gadget on communication inside the gadget. Finally, our result is $\Omega(D\Delta^{1-1/\alpha})$ (see [19]).

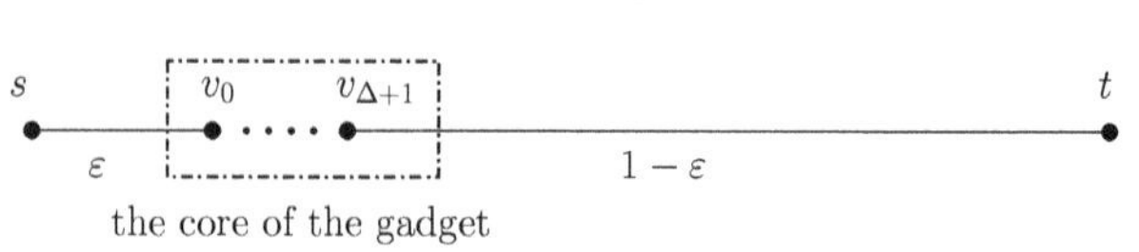

Figure 2: The gadget, satisfies $d(v_i, t) > 1$ for $i < \Delta + 1$.

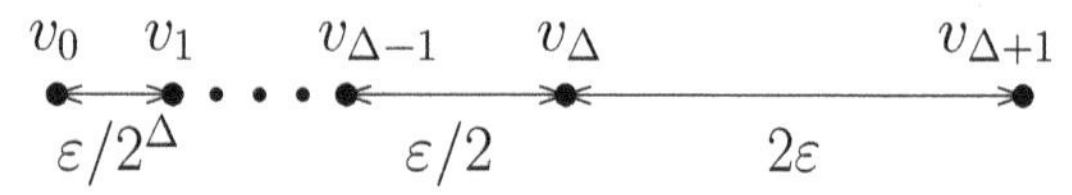

Figure 3: The core of the gadget, $d(v_i, v_{i+1}) = \varepsilon/2^{\Delta-i}$ for $i < \Delta$. Observe that $2\varepsilon < d(v_0, v_{\Delta+1}) < 3\varepsilon$.

Figure 4: Network of diameter $\Theta(D)$ formed by D/κ gadgets, where $\kappa = \frac{\Delta^{1/\alpha}}{1-\varepsilon}$.

7 CONCLUSIONS

We build an efficient clustering algorithm without use of randomization, in a very harsh model of wireless SINR networks. Using the clustering algorithm, we developed an efficient local broadcast algorithm. On the other hand, we exhibited importance of randomization for the global broadcast. Exact complexity of global broadcast remains open as well as the impact of availability of other model features.

ACKNOWLEDGMENTS

The authors would like to thank anonymous reviewers for helpful comments. This work was supported by the National Science Centre, Poland grants DEC-2012/07/B/ST6/01534 and 2014/13/N/ST6/01850.

REFERENCES

[1] N. Alon and J. H. Spencer. *The Probabilistic Method.* Wiley Publishing, 4th edition, 2016.
[2] B. Aronov, M. J. Katz. Batched point location in SINR diagrams via algebraic tools. ICALP 2015, Part I, p. 65–77, Springer, 2015.
[3] R. Bar-Yehuda, O. Goldreich, and A. Itai. On the time-complexity of broadcast in multi-hop radio networks: An exponential gap between determinism and randomization. *JCSS*, 45(1):104–126, 1992.
[4] L. Barenboim, D. Peleg. Nearly optimal local broadcasting in the SINR model with feedback. SIROCCO 2015, p. 164–178, Springer, 2015.
[5] A. E. F. Clementi, A. Monti, and R. Silvestri. Selective families, superimposed codes, and broadcasting on unknown radio networks. *SODA*, p. 709–718. ACM/SIAM, 2001.
[6] A. Cornejo, F. Kuhn. Deploying Wireless Networks with Beeps. DISC 2010, p. 148–162, Springer.
[7] A. Czumaj and W. Rytter. Broadcasting algorithms in radio networks with unknown topology. In *FOCS*, p. 492–501. IEEE, 2003.
[8] S. Daum, S. Gilbert, F. Kuhn, and C. C. Newport. Broadcast in the ad hoc SINR model. DISC 2013, LNCS 8205, p. 358–372. Springer, 2013.
[9] G. DeMarco. Distributed broadcast in unknown radio networks. *SIAM J. Comput.*, 39(6):2162–2175, 2010.
[10] Y. Emek, L. Gasieniec, E. Kantor, A. Pelc, D. Peleg, C. Su. Broadcasting in udg radio networks with unknown topology. *Distr. Comp.*, 21(5):331–351, 2009.
[11] F. Fuchs, D. Wagner. On Local Broadcasting Schedules and CONGEST Algorithms in the SINR Model. ALGOSENSORS 2013, p. 170-184.
[12] O. Goussevskaia, T. Moscibroda, R. Wattenhofer. Local broadcasting in the physical interference model. *DIALM-POMC*, p. 35–44, ACM, 2008.
[13] H. Gudmundsdottir, E.I. Asgeirsson, M.H.L. Bodlaender, J.T. Foley, M.M. Halldórsson, Y. Vigfusson. Extending wireless algorithm design to arbitrary environments via metricity. *MSWiM'14*, p. 21-26, ACM, 2014.
[14] M. M. Halldórsson, S. Holzer, N. A. Lynch. A local broadcast layer for the SINR network model. PODC 2015, ACM, p. 129–138, 2015.
[15] M. M. Halldórsson and P. Mitra. Towards tight bounds for local broadcasting. In *FOMC*, p. 2. ACM, 2012.
[16] M. M. Halldórsson and T. Tonoyan. How well can graphs represent wireless interference? In STOC 2015, p. 635–644, ACM, 2015.
[17] T. Jurdzinski and D. R. Kowalski. Wake-up problem in multi-hop radio networks. In *Encyclopedia of Algorithms*, pages 2352–2354. Springer, 2016.
[18] T. Jurdzinski, D. R. Kowalski, M. Rozanski, G. Stachowiak. On the impact of geometry on ad hoc communication in wireless networks. PODC 2014, p. 357–366, ACM, 2014.
[19] T. Jurdzinski, D. R. Kowalski, M. Rozanski, G. Stachowiak. Deterministic digital clustering of wireless ad hoc networks. *CoRR*, abs/1708.08647, 2017.
[20] T. Jurdzinski, D. R. Kowalski, and G. Stachowiak. Distributed deterministic broadcasting in uniform-power ad hoc wireless networks. *FCT*, LNCS 8070, p. 195–209, Springer, 2013.
[21] T. Jurdzinski, D. R. Kowalski, and G. Stachowiak. Distributed Deterministic Broadcasting in Wireless Networks of Weak Devices. *ICALP*, LNCS 7966, p. 632–644, Springer, 2013.
[22] T. Jurdzinski, M. Rozanski, G. Stachowiak. Token traversal in ad hoc wireless networks via implicit carrier sensing. SIROCCO 2017, LNCS 10641, p. 15–33, Springer, 2017.
[23] E. Kantor, Z. Lotker, M. Parter, and D. Peleg. The minimum principle of SINR: A useful discretization tool for wireless communication. FOCS 2015, p. 330–349, IEEE, 2015.
[24] T. Kesselheim. A constant-factor approximation for wireless capacity maximization with power control in the sinr model. In *SODA 2011*, p. 1549–1559. , SIAM, 2011.
[25] D. R. Kowalski and A. Pelc. Broadcasting in undirected ad hoc radio networks. In PODC 2003, p. 73–82, ACM, 2003.
[26] S. P. Reddy, S. Vaya. Brief Announcement: Multi-Broadcasting under the SINR Model. PODC 2016: 479-481.
[27] A.W. Richa, C. Scheideler. Jamming-Resistant MAC Protocols for Wireless Networks. Encyclopedia of Algorithms, 999–1002, 2016, Springer.
[28] J. Schneider, R. Wattenhofer. A log-star distributed maximal independent set algorithm for growth-bounded graphs. PODC, p. 35–44, ACM, 2008.
[29] D. Yu, Q. Hua, Y. Wang, and F. C. M. Lau. An o(log n) distributed approximation algorithm for local broadcasting in unstructured wireless networks. DCOSS 2012, p. 132–139, IEEE, 2012.

Brief Announcement: Broadcast in Radio Networks Time vs. Energy Tradeoffs.

Extended Abstract*

Marek Klonowski†
Wroclaw University of Science and Technology
Wroclaw, Poland
marek.klonowski@pwr.edu.pl

Dominik Pajak‡
Massachusetts Institute of Technology
Cambridge, MA, USA
pajak@csail.mit.edu

ABSTRACT

In wireless networks, consisting of battery-powered devices, energy is a costly resource and most of it is spent on transmitting messages. Broadcast is a problem where a message needs to be transmitted from one node to all other nodes of the network. We study algorithms that can work under limited energy measured as the maximum number of transmissions among all the stations. The goal of the paper is to study tradeoffs between time and energy complexity of broadcast problem in unknown multi-hop radio networks with no collision detection.

We propose and analyse two new randomized energy-efficient algorithms. Our first algorithm works in time $O((D + \varphi) \cdot n^{1/\varphi} \cdot \varphi)$ with high probability and uses $O(\varphi)$ energy per station for any $\varphi \leq \log n/(2 \log\log n)$ for any graph with n nodes and diameter D. Our second algorithm works in time $O((D + \log n) \log n)$ with high probability and uses $O(\log n/\log\log n)$ energy.

We prove that our algorithms are almost time-optimal for given energy limits for graphs with constant diameters by constructing lower bound on time of $\Omega(n^{1/\varphi} \cdot \varphi)$. The lower bound shows also that any algorithm working in polylogaritmic time in n for all graphs needs energy $\Omega(\log n/\log\log n)$.

CCS CONCEPTS

• **Theory of computation → Distributed computing models**;
• **Networks → Ad hoc networks**;

KEYWORDS

broadcast; radio networks; energy efficiency; algorithm

ACM Reference Format:

Marek Klonowski and Dominik Pajak. 2018. Brief Announcement: Broadcast in Radio Networks Time vs. Energy Tradeoffs.: Extended Abstract. In *PODC '18: ACM Symposium on Principles of Distributed Computing, July 23–27, 2018, Egham, United Kingdom.* ACM, New York, NY, USA, 3 pages. https://doi.org/10.1145/3212734.3212786

*The full version of the paper is available at https://arxiv.org/abs/1711.04149.

†Supported by Polish National Science Center grant 2013/09/B/ST6/02258.
‡Supported by Polish National Science Center grant 2015/17/B/ST6/01897.

PODC '18, July 23–27, 2018, Egham, United Kingdom

ACM ISBN 978-1-4503-5795-1/18/07.
https://doi.org/10.1145/3212734.3212786

1 INTRODUCTION

The problem of broadcast consists in delivering a single message from a source to all the nodes of a communication network. In multi-hop networks, neighboring stations can send messages to each other but when two neighbors of one station are sending at the same time, then these transmissions interfere and the messages are not delivered. A station can locally distinguish only the case where exactly one neighbor transmits from all the other situations (no collision detection).

Two most important parameters of an algorithm in radio networks is the time complexity, measured as the number of steps necessary to complete the execution, and energy complexity, which is the maximum number of rounds in which a station is transmitting. We want to also show a tradeoff between time and energy for broadcasting protocols. This will allow greater flexibility when designing algorithms by decreasing the maximum energy expenditure of a station at a cost of the runtime of the algorithm. Clearly, minimizing the energy cost can sometimes be a critical aspect of real-life systems as they are often composed of small, cheap, battery-powered devices whose batteries cannot be easily recharged or replaced. For such systems it may be reasonable to sacrifice time and save some energy of the stations.

1.1 Model and Problem Statement

In this paper we consider a radio network represented as an undirected, connected graph $G = (V, E)$, where the nodes symbolize stations and the edges are bidirectional communication links between them. By n we denote the number of nodes of the graph and by D its diameter. We assume that the nodes are given value of n and the energy limit. The stations do not know the topology of the network, are identical and do not have any labels. Symmetry between the stations can be in our model broken as the stations have access to independent sources of random bits.

Time is divided into discrete *rounds* and all the stations know the number of the current round. The model is synchronous and in each round each node either transmits a message or listens. Each station receives a packet from its neighbors only if it listens in a given round and **exactly one** of its neighbors is transmitting. We say that Single occurs in such a round. If zero or more than one neighbor of v transmits, then v receives no message.

The single-message broadcast problem is defined as follows. Initially some node, called *originator* has a message and the goal is to deliver this message to all the nodes in the network. We assume that the nodes that have not received the message are not allowed to make any transmissions.

Energy metrics. We define e_v, an *energetic effort* of a station $v \in V$, as the number of rounds when v transmitted. Note that both successful as well as unsuccessful (due to collisions) transmissions count. We will say that algorithm uses energy at most E if $\max_{v \in V} e_v \leq E$. In other words we aim at limiting the energetic expenditure of **all** stations that are present in the network since we need all stations working. Broadcast problem with the goal of minimizing the time and with a bounded number of transmissions per station is sometimes called k-shot broadcasting problem.

1.2 Related work

Energy aspects of broadcast in known and unknown networks has been investigated by Kantor and Peleg in [3] using the same energy-efficiency metric as in our paper. For the model with unknown topology they presented a protocol that uses k energy and is completed in $O\Big((D + \min\{D \cdot k, \log n\}) \cdot n^{1/(k-1)} \log n\Big)$ rounds for $k > 1$ and $O(D \cdot n^2 \log n)$ for $k = 1$ w.h.p. Moreover they demonstrated $\Theta(\log n)$-shot broadcasting protocol that terminates in $O\Big(D \log n + \log^2 n\Big)$ rounds. Berenbrink *et al.* [2] presented a broadcast algorithm with optimal time $O\Big(D \log(n/D) + \log^2 n\Big)$ with expected $O\Big(\log^2 n / \log(n/D)\Big)$ transmissions per node.

Since authors of [2, 3] use the same model, the results can be compared with ours. First, let us note that their protocols are based on a different constructions. For time $O\Big(D \log n + \log^2 n\Big)$ our algorithm Green-Decay uses $\log \log n$ times less energy than [3]. We also show our energy bound is tight and energy $\Theta(\log n / \log \log n)$ is the always required for any algorithm has time polylogarithmic in n. We can also compare our results that use any energy. Algorithm of Kantor and Peleg [3] works with probability $1 - n^{-1/(k-1)}$. If we use the same probability of success then our algorithm BB-Broadcast will have time complexity $O\Big((D + k)n^{1/(k-1)}k\Big)$ which is by a factor of $\log n / k$ faster. Algorithm by Berenbrink *et al.* [2] works in a different regime of energies – our algorithms work with energy $o(\log n)$ and time $\Omega(D \log n + \log^2 n)$.

2 ENERGY-EFFICIENT ALGORITHMS

In this section we present two new algorithms. BB-Broadcast ("Balls-into-Bins Broadcast") can work with arbitrarily small (also constant) available energy. Of course smaller energy leads to higher running time. The second algorithm GD-Broadcast ("Green Decay Broadcast") is built based on classical Broadcast by Bar-Yehuda et al. [1] that has energy complexity $O(\log n \log \log n)$. Our GD-Broadcast algorithm works in the same asymptotic time as the original one, but has reduced energy complexity $O(\log n / \log \log n)$.

2.1 Balls into Bins

Here we introduce a subprocedure Balls-into-Bins(k) that will be used in both our algorithms. In this subprocedure each participating station transmitts in one, randomly chosen out of k time slots. Balls into Bins is a classical concept in probability theory with applications in load balancing where the studied value is usually the maximum number of balls in any bin. In our setting, balls correspond to transmissions by the stations and bins are the time slots, hence we are interested whether some bin contains exactly one ball as this corresponds to a successful transmission.

```
Let t be the first time slot of the subprocedure
Choose a random number i ∈ [0, 1, .., k − 1]
Transmit in slot t + i
```

Algorithm 1: Balls-into-Bins(k)

In the following lemma we bound the probability that in a procedure Balls-into-Bins(k) there is a slot that is chosen by exactly one station.

Lemma 2.1. *If m neighbors of any fixed node v are performing procedure* Balls-into-Bins(k) *with $k = 24\lceil n^{1/\varphi} \rceil + 1$ if $1 \leq \varphi < \frac{\log n}{\log \log n}$ and if $1 \leq m \leq 12/\varphi \cdot n^{1/\varphi} \ln n$ then v receives the message with probability at least $1 - \frac{1}{2n^{1/\varphi}}$ for sufficiently large n.*

2.2 Balls into Bins Broadcast

The goal of this section is to design an algorithm that uses at most $O(\varphi)$ transmissions and has time complexity roughly $O\Big(D \cdot n^{1/\varphi} \cdot \varphi\Big)$ for any $\varphi > 0$. The idea of the algorithm is as follows. We consider the algorithm from the perspective of a fixed node u at the first step when at least one of its neighbors v has the message. The goal is to deliver the message to u with high probability in time $O\Big(n^{1/\varphi}\Big)$. Each participating station (neighbor of u that has the message) chooses a phase being a number chosen according to geometric distribution with parameter $\varphi / n^{1/\varphi}$. We will show that regardless of how many participants are there, some value will be chosen by at most $O\Big(n^{1/\varphi}/\varphi \cdot \ln n\Big)$ stations. Each phase is a Balls-into-Bins($n^{1/\varphi}$) procedure. We already know that if the number of participants is $O\Big(n^{1/\varphi}/\varphi \cdot \ln n\Big)$, then the failure probability of such procedure (i.e. no Single transmission occurs) is at most $n^{-1/\varphi}$. Then, repeating it $\left\lceil \varphi \cdot \left(1 + \frac{\log \frac{2}{\epsilon}}{\log n}\right) \right\rceil$ times will give us the desired probability. This intuition is further specified in the following pseudocode and formalized in the theorem.

```
a ← ⌈ φ log n / (log n − φ log φ) ⌉
k ← 24⌈n^{1/φ}⌉ + 1
t_ph ← ak
Wait until receiving the message;
repeat
    Wait until (Time mod t_ph) = 0
    Choose a number x ~ Geo(φ/n^{1/φ})
    Skip (min{x, a} − 1) · k rounds
    Balls-into-Bins(k)
until ⌈ φ · (1 + log(2/ε) / log n) ⌉ times;
```

Algorithm 2: BB-Broadcast(φ, ϵ)

THEOREM 2.2. *For any* $1 \le \varphi < \frac{\log n}{\log\log n}$ *and* $\epsilon > 2n^{-3}$, *if* $n \ge 4$, *then Algorithm* BB-Broadcast(φ, ϵ) *completes broadcast in time* $O\left((D+\varphi)\cdot n^{1/\varphi}\cdot\frac{\varphi\log n}{\log n - \varphi\log\varphi}\right)$ *using at most* $\left\lceil \varphi\left(1+\frac{\log(2/\epsilon)}{\log n}\right)\right\rceil$ *energy per station, with probability at least* $1-\epsilon$.

2.3 Green-Decay Broadcast

Algorithm BB-Broadcast can operate under a wide range of energy limits, however for the optimal energy $\log n/(\log\log n + 1)$ it has time $O\left(\left(D + \frac{\log n}{\log\log n}\right)\cdot\frac{\log^2 n}{\log\log\log n}\right)$, which is slower than the algorithms from the literature. In this section we want to develop an algorithm that is less universal (i.e. does not offer parametrized energy vs. time trade-off) but achieves an almost-optimal time $O((D + \log n)\log n)$ using optimal energy $O(\log n/\log\log n)$.

We will first present Green-Decay which is a simple modification of classical procedure Decay introduced in [1]. It will serve as a subprocedure to our energy-efficient algorithm GD-Broadcast. In original Decay, each station transmits for a number of rounds being a geometric random variable. We note that instead of broadcasting in each round of the procedure it is sufficient to broadcast only in the last one. With this we save energy whilst the probability of success remains the same.

```
Transmit;
repeat
    x ← 0 or 1 with equal probability;
    if x = 1 then
        Transmit;
until x = 1 but at most k times;
```

Algorithm 3: Green-Decay(k)

The high-level idea of GD-Broadcast is as follows. In Broadcast algorithm from [1] each station participates in $\Theta(\log n)$ Decay procedures and the expected maximum energy is $\Theta(\log n \log\log n)$. By simply replacing it with Green-Decay (that takes always at most a constant energy per participant) we can reduce the energy complexity from $\log n \log\log n$ to $\log n$. In order to reduce the energy complexity further we observe that a station does not necessarily need to participate in all the $\log n$ procedures Decay. If some number x of neighbors of v have the message and want to transmit it to v it is sufficient that in at least a constant fractionof the $\Theta(\log n)$ procedures Decay at least one among the x stations participate. In our algorithm each station participates in $\Theta(\log n/\log\log n)$ procedures Decay chosen at random. If x is sufficiently large, at least a constant fraction of procedures Decay will have at least one participant and the algorithm will work correctly with high probability. On the other hand if x is small we can use procedure Balls-into-Bins which gives a probability of success of order $1 - 1/\log n$, for $\varphi = \log n/\log\log n$. Hence for small x, $O(\log n/\log\log n)$ procedures Balls-into-Bins is sufficient to obtain the high probability of successful transmission. Our algorithm combines Green-Decay and Balls-into-Bins to cover both cases of small and large number of neighbors trying to deliver the message. One more difficulty we need to overcome is that the number of participating (i.e., holding the message) neighbors of v might increase over time.

```
ll ← ⌈log log n⌉
k ← 24⌈log n⌉ + 1
state ← new
Wait until receiving the message;
repeat
    Wait until (Time mod 3·k) = 0
    phase ← Time/(3·k) mod ll
    if phase = 0 and state = new then
        state ← normal
    endif
    if state = new then
        Balls-into-Bins(k)
        Skip k rounds
    else if phase = 0 then
        Skip k rounds
        Balls-into-Bins(k)
    endif
    if phase = 0 or state = new then
        if state = new then state ← normal ;
        myPhase ← Random([0, 1, ..., ll − 1])
    endif
    if phase = myPhase then
        Green-Decay(k)
    endif
until 2⌈log n⌉ + 2 times;
```

Algorithm 4: GD-Broadcast

THEOREM 2.3. *If* $n \ge 32$ *then algorithm* GD-Broadcast *completes broadcast in time* $O((D + \log n)\log n)$ *using* $O(\log n/\log\log n)$ *energy per station with probability at least* $1 - 2/n$.

3 LOWER BOUND

Our algorithm BB-Broadcast has a surprisingly large multiplicative factor $n^{1/\varphi}$. In this section we want to prove that such a factor is sometimes necessary by showing that time $\Omega(n^{1/\varphi}\cdot\varphi)$ is needed for any algorithm using energy φ. Our lower bound also shows that energy $\Omega(\log n/\log\log n)$ is required for any algorithm that works in time polylogarithmic in n which shows energy-optimality of GD-Broadcast in this class of algorithms.

THEOREM 3.1. *For any randomized broadcast algorithm* $\mathcal{A}$ *successful with probability at least* $(1 - e^{-1})/2$ *in all multi-hop radio networks there exists a graph* G *with constant diameter and* n *nodes, such that if* T *is the runtime and* E *is the energy used by the algorithm then the expected value of* $E\cdot\log(T/E)$ *is* $\Omega(\log n)$.

REFERENCES

[1] Reuven Bar-Yehuda, Oded Goldreich, and Alon Itai. 1992. On the Time-Complexity of Broadcast in Multi-hop Radio Networks: An Exponential Gap Between Determinism and Randomization. *J. Comput. Syst. Sci.* 45, 1 (1992), 104–126. DOI: http://dx.doi.org/10.1016/0022-0000(92)90042-H

[2] Petra Berenbrink, Colin Cooper, and Zengjian Hu. 2009. Energy efficient randomised communication in unknown AdHoc networks. *Theor. Comput. Sci.* 410, 27-29 (2009), 2549–2561. DOI: http://dx.doi.org/10.1016/j.tcs.2009.02.002

[3] Erez Kantor and David Peleg. 2016. Efficient k-shot broadcasting in radio networks. *Discrete Applied Mathematics* 202 (2016), 79–94. DOI: http://dx.doi.org/10.1016/j.dam.2015.08.021

Round- and Message-Optimal Distributed Graph Algorithms*†

Bernhard Haeupler
Carnegie Mellon University
Pittsburgh, Pennsylvania, USA
haeupler@cs.cmu.edu

D. Ellis Hershkowitz
Carnegie Mellon University
Pittsburgh, Pennsylvania, USA
dhershko@cs.cmu.edu

David Wajc
Carnegie Mellon University
Pittsburgh, Pennsylvania, USA
dwajc@cs.cmu.edu

ABSTRACT

Distributed graph algorithms that separately optimize for either the number of rounds used or the total number of messages sent have been studied extensively. However, algorithms simultaneously efficient with respect to both measures have been elusive. For example, only very recently was it shown that for Minimum Spanning Tree (MST), an optimal message and round complexity is achievable (up to polylog terms) by a single algorithm in the CONGEST model of communication.

In this paper we provide algorithms that are simultaneously round- and message-optimal for a number of well-studied distributed optimization problems. Our main result is such a distributed algorithm for the fundamental primitive of computing simple functions over each part of a graph partition. From this algorithm we derive round- and message-optimal algorithms for multiple problems, including MST, Approximate Min-Cut and Approximate Single Source Shortest Paths, among others. On general graphs all of our algorithms achieve worst-case optimal $\tilde{O}(D + \sqrt{n})$ round complexity and $\tilde{O}(m)$ message complexity. Furthermore, our algorithms require an optimal $\tilde{O}(D)$ rounds and $\tilde{O}(n)$ messages on planar, genus-bounded, treewidth-bounded and pathwidth-bounded graphs.[1]

CCS CONCEPTS

• **Theory of computation** → **Distributed algorithms**; • **Mathematics of computing** → *Graph algorithms*; Approximation algorithms;

KEYWORDS

Distributed graph algorithms; Low-congestion shortcuts; CONGEST; Part-wise Aggregation

ACM Reference Format:
Bernhard Haeupler, D. Ellis Hershkowitz, and David Wajc. 2018. Round- and Message-Optimal Distributed Graph Algorithms. In *PODC '18: ACM Symposium on Principles of Distributed Computing, July 23–27, 2018, Egham, United Kingdom.* ACM, New York, NY, USA, 10 pages. https://doi.org/10.1145/3212734.3212737

1 INTRODUCTION

Over the years, a great deal of research has focused on characterizing the optimal runtime for distributed graph algorithms in the CONGEST model of communication. Fundamental problems that have been studied include Shortest Paths [10, 23, 24, 28, 29, 31], MST [13, 25, 27, 36], Min-Cut [17, 32], and Max Flow [16]. Runtime is measured by the number of synchronous rounds of communication, and for these problems $\tilde{\Theta}(D + \sqrt{n})$ rounds are known to be necessary and sufficient [5, 7, 17, 36].

Another common performance metric optimized for in the CONGEST model is the total number of messages sent. For MST, an $\tilde{\Omega}(m)$ lower bound is known [2].[2] However, for several decades the only MST algorithms known to match this message lower bound had sub-optimal round complexity [1–3, 9, 11, 12]. The question of whether algorithms attaining both optimal round and message complexity has been a long-standing problem. For instance, Peleg and Rubinovich [36] asked whether it might be achievable for MST. In a recent breakthrough work Pandurangan et al. [34] answered this question in the affirmative, providing a randomized MST algorithm with simulataneously optimal round and message complexities (up to polylog terms). Shortly thereafter Elkin [8] provided the same result without randomization. However, simultaneously round- and message-optimal algorithms for other fundamental problems have remained elusive.

1.1 Our Main Result

In this paper we advance the study of simultaneously round- and message-optimal distributed algorithms. In particular, we provide such algorithms for multiple distributed graph problems. Underlying these contributions is our main result – a round- and message-optimal algorithm for a fundamental distributed problem, which we refer to as Part-Wise Aggregation (or PA for short). We elaborate on some applications of this algorithm in Section 1.2. Informally, Part-Wise Aggregation is the problem of computing the result of a function applied to each part of a graph partition. Formally, the problem is as follows.

Definition 1.1 (Part-Wise Aggregation). *The input to* Part-Wise Aggregation (PA) *is:*

(1) *a graph $G = (V, E)$;*

*All authors supported in part by NSF grants CCF-1527110, CCF-1618280 and NSF CAREER award CCF-1750808.
†Full version available at [18].
[1]Throughout this paper, n, m and D denote respectively the number of nodes, number of edges and the graph diameter respectively. In addition, we use tilde notation, $\tilde{O}$, $\tilde{\Omega}$ and $\tilde{\Theta}$, to suppress polylogarithmic terms in n.

ACM ISBN 978-1-4503-5795-1/18/07...$15.00
https://doi.org/10.1145/3212734.3212737

[2]Strictly speaking, the $\tilde{\Omega}(m)$ message lower bound for MST only holds if the algorithm is (1) deterministic (2) in the KT0 model, or (3) "comparison-based". (Our deterministic algorithm satisfies (1),(2) and (3).) If these conditions are not met it is possible to solve MST using $\tilde{O}(n)$ messages – beating the $\tilde{\Omega}(m)$ bound for sufficiently dense graphs. For more see Mashreghi and King [30].

(2) *a partition* $(P_i)_{i=1}^N$ *of* V, *where each* P_i *induces a connected subgraph on* G. *Each node* $v \in P_i$ *knows an* $O(\log n)$*-bit value associated with it, val(v), and which of its neighbors are in* P_i;

(3) *a function* f *that takes as input two* $O(\log n)$*-bit inputs, outputs an* $O(\log n)$*-bit output and is commutative and associative.*

The problem is solved if for every P_i *every* $v \in P_i$ *knows its part's aggregate value* $f(P_i) := f(val(v_1), f(val(v_2), \ldots))$, *where* $P_i = \{v_1, v_2, \ldots\}$.

The performance of our algorithm is determined by the quality of the *shortcuts* that the input graph admits. Shortcuts, as well as the parameters which determine their quality – termed the *block parameter*, b, and *congestion*, c – are formally defined in Section 2. For now, we note only that every graph admits a shortcut with $b = 1$ and $c = \sqrt{n}$. Our main result is as follows.

Theorem 1.2. *There exists a Part-Wise Aggregation on a graph* G *admitting a tree-restricted shortcut with congestion* c *and block parameter* b *w.h.p.*[3] *in* $\tilde{O}(bD + c)$ *rounds and* $\tilde{O}(m)$ *messages, and deterministically in* $\tilde{O}(b(D + c))$ *rounds and* $\tilde{O}(m)$ *messages.*

1.2 Applications of Our Main Result

The power of Part-Wise Aggregation – and by extension Theorem 1.2 – is that numerous distributed primitives can be cast as instances of this problem. For example, it is not hard to see that electing a leader, computing the number of nodes in each tree in a forest or having every part of a graph partition agree on a minimum value are all instances of this problem. Consequently, many previous algorithms rely on subroutines which are implementable using Part-Wise Aggregation [5, 6, 12–17, 21, 27, 32]. Perhaps unsurprisingly then, using our new PA algorithm as a subroutine in some of these previous works' algorithms, we obtain round- and message-optimal solutions to numerous problems.

In the following three corollaries we highlight three such applications of our algorithm: round- and message-optimal algorithms for MST, Approximate Min-Cut and Approximate SSSP. We defer the proofs of these corollaries (and other corollaries of our main result and algorithmic approach) to the paper's full version. For a flavor of these corollaries' proofs, we note that Borůvka's MST algorithm [33] can be implemented easily using $O(\log n)$ applications of Part-Wise Aggregation, implying Corollary 1.3. Corollaries 1.4 and 1.5 are obtained by using our PA algorithm in the algorithms of [15] and [21], respectively.

The input to all three problems is an undirected weighted graph with edge weights in $[1, \text{poly}(n)]$. Initially, every node knows the weight associated with each of its incident edges. Recall that since every graph has a shortcut with $b = 1$ and $c = \sqrt{n}$, our algorithms simultaneously achieve a message complexity of $\tilde{O}(m)$ and a runtime of essentially worst-case optimal $\tilde{O}(D + \sqrt{n})$.

MST. MST is solved when every node knows which of its incident edges are in the MST.

Corollary 1.3. *Given a graph* G *admitting a tree-restricted shortcut with congestion* c *and block parameter* b, *one can solve MST w.h.p in* $\tilde{O}(bD + c)$ *rounds and* $\tilde{O}(m)$ *messages and deterministically in* $\tilde{O}(b(D + c))$ *rounds with* $\tilde{O}(m)$ *messages.*

Approximate Min-Cut. Min-cut is $(1 + \epsilon)$-approximated when every node knows whether or not it belongs to a set $S \subset V$ such that the size of the cut given by $(S, V \setminus S)$ is at most $(1 + \epsilon)\lambda$, where λ is the size of the minimum cut of G with the prescribed weights.

Corollary 1.4. *For any* $\epsilon > 0$ *and graph* G *admitting a tree-restricted shortcut with congestion* c *and block parameter* b, *one can* $(1 + \epsilon)$*-approximate min-cut w.h.p. in* $\tilde{O}(bD + c) \cdot \text{poly}(1/\epsilon)$ *rounds and* $\tilde{O}(m) \cdot \text{poly}(1/\epsilon)$ *messages.*

Approximate SSSP. An instance of α-approximate single source shortest paths (SSSP) consists of an undirected weighted graph G as above and a source node s, which knows that it is the source node. For $v \in V$ we denote by $d(s, v)$ the shortest path length between s and v in G and $L = \max_{u,v} d(u, v)$. The problem is solved once every node v knows d_v such that $d(s, v) \leq d_v \leq \alpha \cdot d(s, v)$.

Corollary 1.5. *For any* $\beta = O(1/\text{poly} \log n)$, *given a graph* G *admitting a tree-restricted shortcut with congestion* c *and block parameter* b, *one can* $L^{O(\log \log n)/\log(1/\beta)}$*-approximate SSSP w.h.p in* $\tilde{O}\left(\frac{1}{\beta}(bD + c)\right)$ *rounds and* $\tilde{O}\left(\frac{m}{\beta}\right)$ *messages.*

The value of β determines a tradeoff between the quality of the SSSP approximation and the round and message complexity of our algorithm. Taking $\beta = \log^{-\Theta(1/\epsilon)} n$, Corollary 1.5 yields an $O(L^{\epsilon})$-approximation algorithm using $\tilde{O}(bD + c)$ rounds and $\tilde{O}(m)$ messages.

1.3 Discussion of Our Results

There are a few salient points worth noting regarding our results, on which we elaborate below.

Round- and Message-Optimality of our Algorithms. As all graphs admit a tree-restricted shortcut with block parameter $b = 1$ and congestion $c = \sqrt{n}$, our algorithms all terminate within $\tilde{O}(D + \sqrt{n})$ rounds, which is optimal for all our applications of our PA algorithm, by [5]. As for message complexity, our $\tilde{O}(m)$ bound is tight for MST in the KT_0 model by [2]. For the other problems an $\Omega(n)$ message lower bound is trivial; for sparse graphs, then, our message complexity bound is tight for these problems. Finally, we note that our proof of Corollary 1.3 relies on solving Part-Wise Aggregation $O(\log n)$ times to solve MST, which implies that our algorithms for PA are both round- and message-optimal (again, up to polylog terms).

Beyond Worst-Case Optimality. As stated above, every graph admits tree-restricted shortcuts with block parameter $b = 1$ and congestion $c = \sqrt{n}$, which implies an $\tilde{O}(D + \sqrt{n})$ bound for our algorithms' round complexity on general graphs. However, as observed in prior work, a number of graph families of interest – planar, genus-bounded, bounded-treewidth and bounded-pathwidth graphs – admit shortcuts with better parameters [15, 19, 20]. As a result, our algorithms have a round complexity of only $\tilde{O}(D)$ times the relevant parameter of interest (e.g., genus, treewidth or pathwidth). Provided these parameters are constant or even polylogarithmic, our algorithms run in $\tilde{O}(D)$ rounds. Another recent

[3]Throughout the paper, by w.h.p. we mean with probability $1 - \frac{1}{\text{poly}(n)}$.

result [22] implies that our algorithms run in $\tilde{O}(D^2)$ time on minor-free graphs. We also note that our algorithms need not know the optimal values of block parameter and congestion, as a simple doubling trick can be used to approximate the best values (see [19]). In particular, our algorithms perform as well as the parameters of the best shortcut that the input graph admits.

Future Applications of This Work. Non-trivial shortcuts likely exist for graph families beyond those mentioned above. As such, demonstrating even better runtimes for our algorithms on many networks may be achieved in the future by simply proving the *existence* of efficient shortcuts on said networks. Moreover, given the pervasiveness of PA in distributed graph algorithms, the applications of our PA algorithm we present are likely non-exhaustive. We are hopeful that our PA algorithm will find applications in deriving round- and message-optimal bounds for even more problems.

Due to space constraints, we give several proof sketches rather than full proofs. Full proofs anywhere a proof sketch is given and further discussion of applications of our main result are available in the paper full version of our paper [18].

2 PRELIMINARIES

Before moving onto our formal results, we explicitly state the model of communication we consider and then review relevant concepts from previous work in low-congestion shortcuts.

2.1 CONGEST Model of Communication

Throughout this paper we work in the classic CONGEST model of communication [35]. In this model, the network is modeled as a graph $G = (V, E)$ of diameter D with $n = |V|$ nodes and $m = |E|$ edges. Communication is conducted over discrete, synchronous rounds. During each round each node can send an $O(\log n)$-bit message along each of its incident edges. Every node has an arbitrary and unique ID of $O(\log n)$ bits, first only known to itself (this is the KT_0 model of Awerbuch et al. [2]).

2.2 (Tree-Restricted) Shortcuts

Low-congestion shortcuts were originally introduced by Ghaffari and Haeupler [15] to solve PA. These shortcuts allow high-diameter parts to communicate efficiently, by using edges outside of parts; this effectively decreases the diameter of the parts. Ghaffari and Haeupler [15] showed how, given a simple low-congestion shortcut, PA can be solved in an optimal number of rounds – i.e. $\tilde{O}(D + \sqrt{n})$ – w.h.p. Formally, a low congestion shortcut is defined as follows.

Definition 2.1 (Low-Congestion Shortcuts [15]). *Let $G = (V, E)$ be a graph and $(P_i)_{i=1}^N$ be a partition of G's vertex set. $\mathcal{H} = H_1, \ldots, H_N$ where $H_i \subseteq E$ is a* c-congestion shortcut with dilation d *with respect to $(P_i)_{i=1}^N$ if it satisfies*

1. *Each $e \in E$ belongs to at most c of the H_i.*
2. *The diameter of $(P_i \cup V(H_i), E[P_i] \cup H_i)$ for any i is at most d.*[4]

[4] Here $V(H_i)$ denotes all endpoints of edges in H_i and $E[P_i]$ denote the edges of G with both endpoints in P_i.

Ghaffari and Haeupler [15] also showed how to compute near-optimal $\tilde{O}(D)$-congestion and $\tilde{O}(D)$-dilation shortcuts for planar graphs, given an embedding of such a graph. This allowed them to obtain $\tilde{O}(D)$-round MST algorithms for this problem, among other results. However, it was not until the work of Haeupler, Izumi, and Zuzic [19] that it was demonstrated that shortcuts could be efficiently computed in general. This work showed that high quality instances of a certain type of shortcut – *tree-restricted shortcuts* – can be efficiently approximated. These types of shortcuts are defined as follows.

Definition 2.2 (Tree-Restricted Shortcuts [19]). *Let $G = (V, E)$ be a graph and $(P_i)_{i=1}^N$ be a partition of G's vertex set. A shortcut $\mathcal{H} = (H_i)_{i=1}^N$ is a* T-restricted shortcut *with respect to $(P_i)_{i=1}^N$ if there exists a rooted spanning tree T of G with $H_i \subseteq E[T]$ for all $i \in [N]$.*

Since a rooted BFS tree has minimal depth, and the $\tilde{O}(D)$-round $\tilde{O}(m)$-message deterministic leader election algorithm of Kutten et al. [26] allows us to compute a BFS tree in the same bounds, throughout this paper T will be a rooted BFS tree. The same work that introduced tree-restricted shortcuts also introduced a convenient alternative to dilation, block parameter.

Definition 2.3 (Block Parameter [19]). *Let $\mathcal{H} = (H_i)_{i=1}^n$ be a T-restricted shortcut on the graph $G = (V, E)$ with respect to parts $(P_i)_{i=1}^n$. For any part P_i, we call the connected components of $(P_i \cup V(H_i), H_i)$ the* blocks *of P_i, and the number of blocks of P_i its* block parameter. *The* block parameter *of $\mathcal{H}$, b, is the maximum block parameter of any part P_i.*

As shown in [19], if T is a depth-D tree, the dilation of a T-restricted shortcut with block parameter b is at most $O(bD)$. As such, block parameter is a convenient alternative to dilation. See Figure 1 for an example of a T-restricted shortcut.

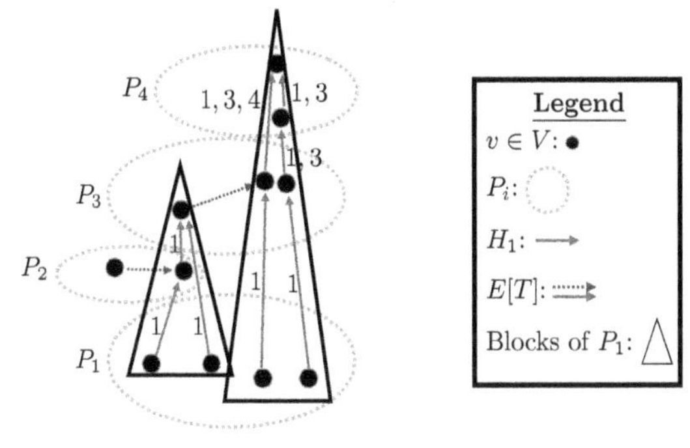

Figure 1: An example of a T-restricted shortcut on 4 parts. $e \in E[T]$ labeled with $\{i : e \in H_i\}$. Edges directed towards T's root. Here $c = 3$ and $b = 2$.

3 TECHNIQUES

In this section we outline our general algorithmic approach. We begin by demonstrating the message sub-optimality of previous shortcut algorithms for Part-Wise Aggregation on a particular example. We then give a workaround for this example and sketch how we develop this workaround into a full-fledged algorithm.

3.1 Bad Example for Previous Shortcut-Based Algorithms

Several prior round-optimal randomized algorithms for PA used tree-restricted shortcuts [19, 20]. To solve PA, these algorithms repeatedly aggregate within blocks. To aggregate within a block, every node in the block transmits its value up the block (along the tree's edges); when values from the same part arrive at a node in the block, they are aggregated by applying f and then forwarded up the block as a single value. By the end of this process, the root of the block has computed f of the block and can broadcast the result back down. This approach can be implemented using an optimal $\tilde{O}(D + \sqrt{n})$ rounds.

Unfortunately, there exist PA instances for which the above approach requires $\omega(m)$ messages. For example, consider the $D \times (n-1)/D$ grid graph with an additional node, r, neighboring all of the top row's nodes. Suppose each row is its own part, and all the column edges are shortcut edges, forming a single block rooted at r. See Figure 2. Aggregating within this block requires $\Omega(nD)$ messages: a message cannot be combined with other messages in its part until it has at least reached r and so each node is responsible for sending a unique message to r along a path of length $D/2$ on average. Thus, aggregating in blocks in this way to solve PA requires $\Omega(nD)$ messages, which is sub-optimal for any $D = \omega(1)$, since $m = O(n)$ for this network.

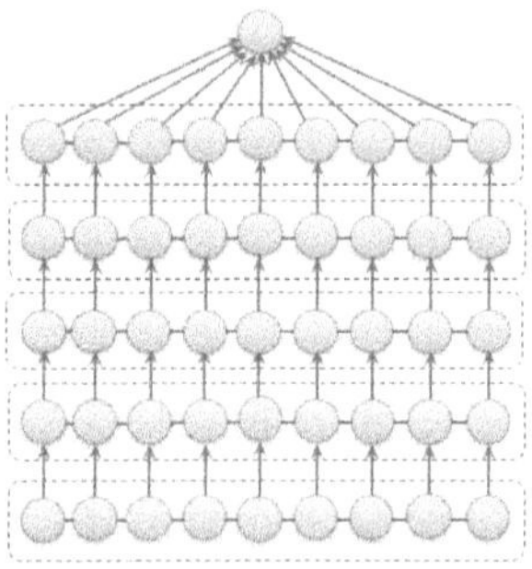

Figure 2: $\Omega(nD)$ message example. Parts are indicated by dashed rectangles. Tree edges are directed towards the root.

A Workaround. We can improve the poor message complexity of aggregating within blocks on this particular network as follows. Partition each of the D parts into *sub-parts*, each with $O(D)$ connected nodes; we have $O(n/D)$ sub-parts in total. See Figure 3. First, sub-parts aggregate: the right-most node in the sub-part broadcasts its value left and every other node broadcasts left the aggregation of its own value and what it receives from its neighbor to the right. The leftmost node of a sub-part then uses the block's edges to transmit the sub-part's aggregate value to r, which then computes the aggregate value for each part. Symmetrically to the above, r then broadcasts to every node the aggregate value for its part.

Aggregating within each sub-part requires $O(n)$ messages, as it requires each node to broadcast at most once. Moreover, there are $O(n/D)$ sub-parts, each responsible for broadcasting up and down the block once and so using the shortcut requires $O(n/D) \cdot O(D) =$

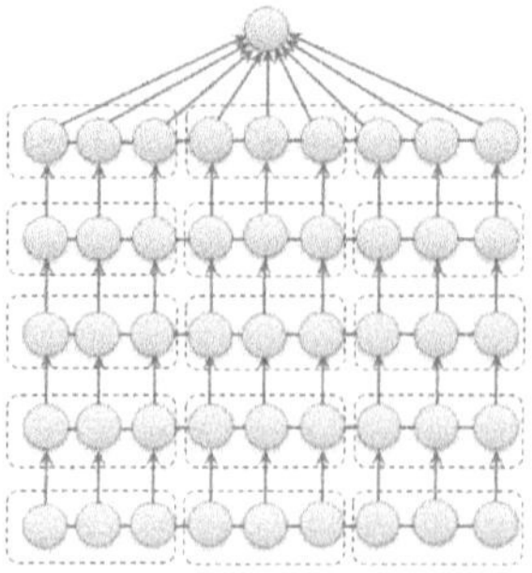

Figure 3: A workaround. Sub-parts are indicated by (smaller) dotted rectangles.

$O(n)$ messages. Therefore, for this network, our workaround requires an optimal $O(m) = O(n)$ messages.

3.2 Overview of Our Approach

The workaround of the previous subsection is heavily tailored to the particular example of Figure 2. Moreover, it requires that nodes know significantly more about the network topology than we allow. However, the above example and workaround motivate and highlight some of the notable strategies of our algorithm for Part-Wise Aggregation.

Sub-Part Divisions. As illustrated in the example, having all nodes use a shortcut in order to send their private information to their part leader rapidly exhausts our $\tilde{O}(m)$ message budget. To solve this issue, we refine the partition of our network into what we call a *sub-part division.* In a sub-part division each part P_i containing more than D nodes is partitioned into $\tilde{O}(|P_i|/D)$ sub-parts each with a spanning tree rooted at a designated node termed the *representative* of the sub-part. In the preceding example the representatives are the left-most nodes of each sub-part. Each sub-part uses its spanning tree to aggregate towards its representative, who then alone is allowed to use shortcut edges to forward the result toward the part leader. This decreases the number of nodes that use the shortcut from $O(n)$ to $\tilde{O}(n/D)$, thereby reducing the message complexity of aggregating within a block from $O(nD)$ to $\tilde{O}(n)$. Applying this observation and some straightforward random sampling ideas to previous work on low-congestion shortcuts to solve PA almost immediately implies our message-efficient randomized solutions to PA.

Message-Efficient (and Deterministic) Shortcut Construction. If our algorithms are to use shortcuts as we did in the preceding example, they must construct them message efficiently; i.e., with $\tilde{O}(m)$ messages. No previous shortcut construction algorithm achieves low message complexity. We show that not only do sub-part divisions allow us to use shortcuts message efficiently, but they also allow us to construct shortcuts message efficiently. In particular, we give both randomized and deterministic message-efficient shortcut construction algorithms. The latter is the first round-optimal deterministic shortcut construction algorithm and is based on a divide-and-conquer strategy that uses heavy path decompositions [37]. Though the general structure of our deterministic shortcut construction algorithm is similar to that used in previous low-congestion shortcut work—nodes try to greedily claim the shortcut edges they get to use—the techniques used to deterministically implement this structure are entirely novel with respect to past work in low-congestion shortcuts.

Star Joinings. To use sub-part divisions as above, we must demonstrate how to compute them within our bounds. To do so, we begin with every node in its own sub-part and repeatedly merge sub-parts until the resulting sub-parts are sufficiently large. However, it is not clear how many sub-parts can be efficiently merged together at once, as obtained sub-parts can have arbitrarily large diameter, rendering communication within a sub-part infeasible. We overcome this issue by always forcing sub-parts to merge in a star-like fashion; this limits the diameter of the new sub-part, enabling the new sub-part to adopt the representative of the center of the star. We call this behavior *star joinings.* As we show, enforcing this behavior is easily accomplished with random coin flips. We also accomplish the same behavior deterministically but with significantly more technical overhead, drawing on the coloring algorithm of Cole and Vishkin [4].

4 SOLVING PA

In this section we show how to solve PA, given shortcuts and a sub-part division. The subroutines necessary to compute shortcuts and sub-part divisions randomly and deterministically within our time and message bounds are given in Section 5 and Section 6, respectively. Those subroutines together with our algorithm for PA given a sub-part division and shortcuts imply our main result, Theorem 1.2.

For our purposes it is convenient to assume that in our PA instance each part P_i also has a *leader* $l_i \in P_i$ where every $v \in P_i$ knows the ID of l_i. As we show in the full version of our paper, we can dispense with this assumption at the cost of logarithmic overhead in round and message complexity. As we ignore multiplicative polylogarithmic terms, for the remainder of the paper we assume that a leader for each part is always known in our PA instances.

One of the crucial ingredients we will rely on to solve PA instances as above is sub-part divisions.

Definition 4.1 (Sub-part division). *Given partition $(P_i)_{i=1}^N$ of V, a* sub-part division *is a partition of every part P_i into $\tilde{O}\left(\frac{|P_i|}{D}\right)$ sub-parts $S_1, \ldots, S_{k_i}$. Each sub-part S_j also has a spanning tree of diameter $O(D)$ rooted at a node $r \in S_j$, termed the sub-part's* representative.

We note that sub-parts are not necessarily related to blocks in any way; e.g. a single sub-part might span multiple blocks and blocks need not contain sub-part representatives.

4.1 Aggregating on Families of Sub-trees

The second ingredient we rely on is tree-restricted shortcuts, along which we will route (some of) our messages. To do so, we must first restate an algorithm of Haeupler, Izumi, and Zuzic [19] which we refer to as BlockRoute, that convergecasts/broadcasts within shortcut blocks. As convergecast and broadcast are symmetric, we only discuss convergecast.

Lemma 4.2. *([19, Lemma 2]) Let T be a tree of depth D. Given a family of subtrees such that any edge of T is contained in at most c subtrees, there is a deterministic algorithm that can perform a convergecast/broadcast on all of the subtrees in $O(D + c)$ CONGEST rounds.*

Specifically, for convergecasts, if multiple messages are scheduled over the same edge, the algorithm forwards the packet with the smallest depth of the subtree root, breaking ties with the smallest ID of the subtree.

One observation we make about this algorithm, and which will prove crucial since we only allow representatives to use shortcuts, is the following.

Observation 4.3. *Let S be the set of nodes with a value to be convergecasted in the algorithm described in Lemma 4.2. Then the number of messages used by the algorithm is $O(|S|D)$.*

4.2 Solving PA and Verifying Block Parameter

We now show how given a sub-part division and a T-restricted shortcut, we can round- and message-efficiently solve PA with and without randomization. Our method is given by Algorithm 1 (which contains both our deterministic and randomized algorithm), and works as follows. First, each leader l_i of part P_i broadcasts an arbitrary message m_i to all nodes in P_i. Then, symmetrically to how m_i was broadcast, each l_i computes $f(P_i)$ and then broadcasts $f(P_i)$ to all nodes of P_i. The most technically involved aspect of our algorithm is how l_i broadcasts m_i to all nodes in P_i. If $|P_i|$ is smaller than D, broadcast can be trivially performed along the spanning tree of the single sub-part of P_i in $O(D)$ rounds with $O(|P_i|)$ messages. However, if $|P_i|$ is larger than D, we use shortcuts, as follows.

For our deterministic algorithm, we repeat the following b times: every representative in a block which received the message m_i spreads m_i to other representatives in its block using BlockRoute along the shortcut. Next, representatives with m_i spread m_i to nodes in their sub-part. Lastly, nodes with m_i spread m_i to neighboring nodes in adjacent sub-parts. Crucially, only our representatives use shortcuts, thereby limiting our message complexity, by Observation 4.3. We illustrate the broadcast of m_i in Figure 4.

Our randomized algorithm works similarly, with the following modification: each part leader independently delays itself – and subsequently, its entire part – before sending its first message at the beginning of the algorithm, by a delay chosen uniformly in the range $[c]$ (here c is the shortcut's congestion). This limits the number of parts which would use any given edge during any round to $O(\log n)$ w.h.p. As only one message can be sent along an edge, we execute BlockRoute as before, but rather than break ties as in Lemma 4.2, we simply spend $O(\log n)$ rounds between each "meta-round", to allow each node to forward all of its $O(\log n)$ messages. This broadcast within blocks requires $O(D \log n)$ CONGEST rounds. The following lemma states the performance of our algorithms.

Lemma 4.4. *Given a sub-part division and a T-restricted shortcut with congestion c and block parameter b, Algorithm 1 uses $\tilde{O}(m)$ messages to solve PA either w.h.p in $\tilde{O}(bD + c)$ rounds or deterministically in $\tilde{O}(b(D + c))$ rounds.*

Proof. We first prove our round complexities. We start by proving the stated round complexity for broadcasting m_i. Any part that

Algorithm 1 PA given shortcut and sub-part division.

Input: PA instance;
sub-part division;
T-restricted shortcut
Output: solves PA
Notation: $S(v) \subseteq V := v \in V$'s sub-part;
$r(v) \in V := v \in V$'s representative;
$S(U) := \bigcup_{u \in U} S(u)$ for $U \subseteq V$;
$R(U) := \{r(U) \mid u \in U\}$ for $U \subseteq V$;
$R_i := r(P_i)$;
$B_i(v) \subseteq V :=$ the block of part P_i containing $v \in V$

1: **for** Part P_i **do**
2:   **if** $|P_i| < D$ **then**
3:     Broadcast m_i from l_i to all of P_i on P_i's spanning tree.
4:   **else**
5:     **if** Randomized algorithm **then**
6:       Delay part P_i by (independent) $\sim U(c)$;
7:       Blow up calls to BlockRoute by $O(\log n)$.
8:     Route m_i from l_i to $r(l_i)$ using BlockRoute.
9:     $\mathcal{A} \leftarrow \{r(l_i)\}, \mathcal{I} \leftarrow \{\}$. ▷ "active"/"inactive" reps.
10:     **for** b iterations **do**
11:       BlockRoute ($\mathcal{A}$) to send m_i to $\bigcup_{r \in \mathcal{A}} B_i(r) \cap R_i$.
12:       $\mathcal{A} \leftarrow \mathcal{A} \bigcup_{r \in \mathcal{A}} B_i(r) \cap R_i$.
13:       **for all** $r \in \mathcal{A}$ **do**
14:         Broadcast m_i from r to $S(r)$ along $S(r)$'s tree.
15:       Broadcast m_i over edges in E that exit $S(\mathcal{A})$.
16:       **for all** Vertex $v \notin S(\mathcal{A}) \cup S(\mathcal{I})$ **do**
17:         **if** v received a message in line 15 **then**
18:           v routes m_i to $r(v)$.
19:       $\mathcal{I} \leftarrow \mathcal{I} \cup \mathcal{A}$.
20:       $\mathcal{A} \leftarrow$ reps. that received a message in line 18.
21: Symmetrically to lines 1-20, compute $f(P_i)$ at l_i.
22: Symmetrically to lines 1-20, b'cast result of $f(P_i)$ from l_i to P_i.

is of fewer than D nodes clearly only requires $O(D)$ rounds. For any part of more than D nodes, we argue that each of the b iterations requires only $\tilde{O}(D+c)$ rounds or $O(D \log n)$ if a random delay of $U(c)$ is added. Routing m_i from l_i to $r(l_i)$ requires $O(D)$ rounds. Running BlockRoute only requires $O(D+c)$ rounds by Lemma 4.2. Moreover, if a random delay is added, a Chernoff and union bound show that w.h.p an edge never has more than $O(\log n)$ distinct parts' aggregate messages that should be transmitted along it. By allowing each node to send up to $O(\log n)$ parts' aggregate message in each meta-round, BlockRoute requires $O(D \log n)$ rounds, and therefore this approach requires $\tilde{O}(bD + c)$ rounds overall. Next, broadcasting m_i within any sub-part requires $\tilde{O}(D)$ rounds as sub-parts are of diameter $\tilde{O}(D)$. Broadcasting m_i to adjacent subparts requires only a single round. Lastly, computing $f(P_i)$ and broadcasting $f(P_i)$ symmetrically require $\tilde{O}(b(D+C))$ rounds.

We now prove a message complexity of $\tilde{O}(m)$. We start by proving this message complexity for broadcasting m_i. Message complexity is trivial if the part is of fewer than D nodes. Next consider parts of more than D nodes. Notice that nodes in a given sub-part only send messages in those rounds where the sub-part is active.

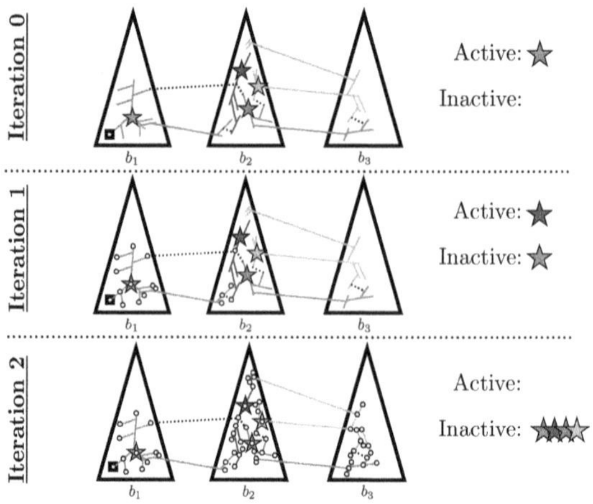

Figure 4: Nodes with m_j (yellow circles) and (in)active representatives at the end of each broadcast iteration for a part with 3 blocks b_1, b_2 and b_3. The leader l_i is indicated by a black square, l_i, while sub-part representatives are indicated by stars; solid lines and dotted black lines correspond to intra- and inter-sub-part edges.

Moreover, once a sub-part becomes inactive, it never again becomes active. Routing m_i from l_i to $r(l_i)$ requires $O(D)$ messages. Moreover, each of the $\tilde{O}\left(\frac{|P_i|}{D}\right)$ sub-parts in part P_i use BlockRoute at most once, using $O(D)$ messages per sub-part by Observation 4.3; as a result this step uses $\tilde{O}(|P_i|)$ messages for part P_i and so $\tilde{O}(n)$ messages total. Broadcasting within all sub-parts requires $O(n)$ messages since each sub-part only does so once and has a spanning tree with which to do so. Broadcasting across sub-parts uses each edge at most twice and so uses $O(m)$ messages. Lastly, computing $f(P_i)$ and broadcasting $f(P_i)$ symmetrically require $O(m)$ messages.

Correctness of broadcasting m_i is trivial if $|P_i| < D$. Moreover, if $|P_i| \geq D$, a simple argument by induction over blocks shows that b iterations suffices for parts of more than D nodes. Correctness of computing $f(P_i)$ and broadcasting $f(P_i)$ symmetrically follow. □

Because our PA algorithm is essentially the same algorithm we use to verify that our shortcuts have good block parameter, we now describe this second algorithm, Algorithm 2. We verify the block parameter of a fixed part P_i as follows. Run Algorithm 1 to broadcast an arbitrary message m_i. If our block parameter is sufficiently small then every node will receive m_i and assume it as such. Moreover, if our block parameter is too large but Algorithm 1 succeeds we can still use Algorithm 1 to inform all nodes in P_i of P_i's block parameter symmetrically to how m_i was broadcast. However, if Algorithm 1 fails –i.e. some node does not receive m_i – then we must somehow inform all nodes that the block parameter is too large. We do so by having each node that does not receive m_i inform its neighbors in P_i that it did not receive m_i. There must be some such neighbor in P_i that did receive m_i. By one additional call to Algorithm 1 this neighbor can inform all nodes that did receive m_i that the block parameter is, in fact, too large. This algorithm gives the following lemma.

Algorithm 2 Block parameter verification.

Input: partition of V, $(P_i)_{i=1}^N$, where $v \in P_i$ knows leader l_i;
sub-part division;
T-restricted shortcut, $\mathcal{H}$;
desired block parameter b
Output: for all i, $v \in P_i$ learns if P_i has block param. b in $\mathcal{H}$
for part P_i **do**
  Run Alg. 1 to broadcast arbitrary m_i from l_i.
  for $v \in P_i$ that did not receive m_i **do**
    v broadcasts $\bar{m}_i$ to neighbors in P_i.
  Run Alg. 1 to broadcast if $\exists v \in P_i$ with m_i and $\bar{m}_i$.
  for every i and $v \in P_i$ **do**
    if v did not receive m_i or received $\bar{m}_i$ **then**
      v decides block parameter of P_i exceeds b.
    else Run Alg. 1 to compute the block number of P_i.

Lemma 4.5. *Given parts $(P_i)_{i=1}^N$, a sub-part division, a c-congestion T-restricted shortcut, $\mathcal{H}$, and desired block parameter b, one can deterministically (resp., w.h.p.) inform every node whether its part's block parameter in $\mathcal{H}$ exceeds b in $\tilde{O}(b(D+c))$ (resp. $\tilde{O}(bD+c)$) rounds with $\tilde{O}(m)$ messages.*

Proof. Round and message complexities follow trivially from Lemma 4.4 and Lemma 4.2. We now argue correctness. If a node does not receive m_i when Algorithm 1 is first run then the block parameter of P_i is certainly larger than b. When this occurs, all nodes will either be told by l_i that the block parameter is larger than b or they will not receive m_i, implicitly informing them that the block parameter of P_i is larger than b. If all nodes receive m_i, then l_i clearly distributes to all nodes in P_i the number of blocks incident to P_i and so the block number of P_i is correctly determined to be above or below b as desired. □

5 RANDOMIZED SUBROUTINES

In this section we outline how we construct sub-part divisions and shortcuts round- and message-optimally using randomization.

5.1 Computing Sub-Part Divisions

We first show how a sub-part division can be computed with randomization, by randomly sampling sub-part representatives in Algorithm 3. In particular, for large parts ($|P_i| \geq D$), every node decides to be a representative with probability $\min\{1, \frac{\log n}{D}\}$ and then representatives claim balls of radius D around them as their sub-part. Algorithm 3's properties are given below.

Lemma 5.1. *Algorithm 3 computes a sub-part division of a part with a known leader w.h.p in $O(D)$ rounds with $O(m)$ messages.*

Proof. Runtime and message complexity are trivial. Correctness is trivial for parts of fewer than D nodes, so consider parts of more than D nodes. By construction, each claimed sub-part has diameter $O(D)$. It remains to show that every node has a representative and there are $\tilde{O}\left(\frac{|P_i|}{D}\right)$ sub-parts in P_i. Fix node v and consider the ball of radius D around v. Since P_i has at least D nodes, this ball is of size at least D and so a Chernoff bound shows that w.h.p $\Theta(\log n)$ nodes in this ball will elect themselves a representative, meaning v will have a representative. A union bound over all v shows this to hold for every node. Moreover, the expected number of representatives in part P_i is $\frac{|P_i| \log n}{D}$ and so a Chernoff bound shows that w.h.p there are $\tilde{O}\left(\frac{|P_i|}{D}\right)$ sub-parts in P_i. A union bound shows this holds for all parts w.h.p. □

Algorithm 3 Randomized sub-part division.

Input: partition of V, $(P_i)_{i=1}^N$, where $v \in P_i$ knows leader l_i
Output: sub-part division
for part P_i **do**
  if $|P_i| \leq D$ **then**
    Let P_i have one sub-part with representative l_i.
    Compute sub-part spanning tree by a BFS in P_i from l_i.
  else
    for $v \in P_i$ **do**
      if Coin flip with bias $\min\{1, \frac{\log n}{D}\}$ is heads: **then**
        v is a representative.
        v sends its ID to P_i neighbors.
      for $O(D)$ rounds **do**
        v transmits first ID it hears to P_i neighbors.
        v's sub-part parent ← first neighbor v hears.
        v computes for which neighbors it is a parent.

5.2 Computing Shortcuts

We now show in Algorithm 4 how we message-efficiently construct a T-restricted shortcut with randomization. We rely on the CoreFast shortcut construction algorithm of Haeupler et al. [19]. In CoreFast, a sub-sampled set of vertices broadcast up T, attempting to "claim" edges; edges with too many vertices trying to claim them are discarded. To control the message complexity, we only have the $\tilde{O}(n/D)$ sub-part representatives attempt to claim edges. The correctness and runtime of Algorithm 4 is given by Lemma 5.2.

Algorithm 4 Randomized shortcut construction.

Input: partition of V, $(P_i)_{i=1}^N$ where $v \in P_i$ knows leader l_i;
BFS tree T;
sub-part division
Output: T-restricted shortcut with congestion $\tilde{O}(c)$ and block parameter $< 3b$
1: Set all P_i *active*.
2: **for** $O(\log n)$ iterations **do**
3:   Run CoreFast [19] on representatives in active parts.
4:   Run Alg. 2 on line 3 result to check if block params. $< 3b$.
5:   **for** each P_i **do**
6:     **if** block parameter of P_i is $< 3b$ in line 4 **then**
7:       Set P_i *inactive*.
8:   **for** each newly inactive P_i **do**
9:     P_i uses the edges line 3 gives it as shortcut edges.

Lemma 5.2. *Given partition partition of V, $(P_i)_{i=1}^N$ where $v \in P_i$ knows leader l_i, a sub-part division, spanning tree T and the existence of a T-restricted shortcut with congestion c and block parameter b, Algorithm 4 computes a T-restricted shortcut with congestion at most*

$\tilde{O}(c)$ and block parameter at most $3b$ in $\tilde{O}(bD + c)$ rounds with $O(n)$ messages w.h.p.

Proof (Sketch). Since only the $\tilde{O}(n/D)$ sub-part representatives broadcast up a tree of depth $O(D)$, each uses $O(D)$ messages and so we use $O(n)$ messages. Round complexity is trivial. Congestion of the shortcut follows by construction. The block parameter can be shown by arguing that we can only discard so many extra edges relative to the optimal shortcut and each extra discarded edge induces a new block. □

6 DETERMINISTIC SUBROUTINES

In this section we show how to construct sub-part divisions and shortcuts deterministically.

6.1 Computing Star Joinings

Our algorithm for constructing sub-part divisions repeatedly merges together sub-parts until they are of sufficient size. However, if sub-parts are allowed to merge arbitrarily, the resulting sub-parts may have prohibitively large diameter. The diameter of resulting sub-parts can be limited by forcing sub-parts to always join in a star-like fashion. As such, we begin by providing a deterministic algorithm to enable such behavior. We term this behavior a *star joining*.

Definition 6.1 (Star joining). *Let $(P_i)_{i=1}^N$ partition V. We say a* star joining *is computed over parts $(P_i)_{i=1}^N$ if the following holds: a constant fraction of the parts P_i are designated as* receivers, *and the other parts P_i are designated as* joiners. *For every joiner part P_i, all $v \in P_i$ knows some (common) edge with one endpoint in P_i and another end-point in some receiver part P_j.*

We now show how a star joining can be computed deterministically, given a deterministic PA solution. We use as a sub-routine the 3-coloring algorithm of Cole and Vishkin [4]. Roughly, the Cole and Vishkin [4] algorithm works as follows. Every node begins with its ID as its color, meaning there are initially n colors. Next, every node updates its color based on its neighbors' colors, logarithmically reducing the number of possible colors. This is then repeated $\log^* n$ times. For more, see Cole and Vishkin [4]. The properties of this algorithm are as follows.

Lemma 6.2. *([4, Corollary 2.1]) An oriented n-vertex graph with maximum out-degree of one can be 3-colored in $O(\log^* n)$ rounds with $O(m \log^* n)$ messages.*

We give our algorithm for deterministically computing star joinings in Algorithm 5 which works as follows. Take the super-graph whose nodes are parts and whose edges are the chosen (directed) edges. First, designate parts with at least two incoming edges receivers and all parts with an outgoing edge into one such part a joiner. These parts constitute all trees in our super-graph and so we next remove them from the super-graph, leaving only (directed) paths and (directed) cycles. On the remaining paths and cycles, simulate the Cole-Vishkin algorithm to compute a 3-coloring of the remaining nodes in the super-graph. For colors $k = 1, 2, 3$ make all k-colored parts receivers, their neighbors joiners and remove these parts from this process. The properties of our deterministic star joining algorithm are given by the following lemma.

Algorithm 5 Deterministic star joining.

Input: $(P_i)_{i=1}^N$ s.t. $v \in P_i$ knows $e_i \in E$ exiting P_i and leader l_i; PA algorithm $\mathcal{A}$
Output: a star joining on $(P_i)_{i=1}^N$

- $\mathcal{J}, \mathcal{R} \leftarrow \emptyset$ ▷ Initialize joiners and receiver
- $G' \leftarrow \left(((P_i)_{i=1}^N), \{e_i\}_{i=1}^N\right)$
- $\mathcal{R} \leftarrow \mathcal{R} \cup \{P_i : \delta^-_{G'}(P_i) \geq 2\}$ by $\mathcal{A}$.
- $\mathcal{J} \leftarrow \mathcal{J} \cup \{P_i : P_i \notin \mathcal{R} \wedge e_i = (P_{i'}, P_i)$ s.t. $P_{i'} \in \mathcal{R}\}$ by $\mathcal{A}$.
- $G' \leftarrow G' \setminus (\mathcal{R} \cup \mathcal{J})$.
- Run the 3-coloring algorithm of [4] on G'.
- **for** color $k = 1, 2, 3$ **do**
    - $\mathcal{R} \leftarrow \mathcal{R} \cup \{P_i : P_i$ colored $k\}$ by $\mathcal{A}$.
    - $\mathcal{J} \leftarrow \mathcal{J} \cup \{P_i : P_i \notin \mathcal{R} \wedge e_i = (P_{i'}, P_i)$ s.t. $P_{i'} \in \mathcal{R}\}$ by $\mathcal{A}$.

Lemma 6.3. *Let $(P_i)_{i=1}^N$ partition V and suppose every $v \in P_i$ knows some edge $e_i \in E$ exiting P_i. If algorithm $\mathcal{A}$ solves PA over $(P_i)_{i=1}^N$, then Algorithm 5 computes a star joining over $(P_i)_{i=1}^N$ with $O(\log^* n)$ calls to $\mathcal{A}$.*

Proof (Sketch). Standard graph-theoretic arguments show that a constant fraction of nodes are receivers. Moreover, it is not too hard to see that the Cole-Vishkin algorithm can be efficiently simulated within our bounds. □

6.2 Computing Sub-Part Divisions

We now use star joinings to deterministically compute sub-part divisions in Algorithm 6 as follows: start with each node in its own sub-part; compute star joinings and merge stars of joiners centered around receivers $O(\log n)$ times, fixing sub-parts once they have at least D nodes. Correctness and runtime of Algorithm 6 are given by the following lemma.

Algorithm 6 Deterministic sub-part division.

Input: partition of V, $(P_i)_{i=1}^N$
Output: a sub-part division

- **for** part P_i **do**
    - $\mathcal{I}_i \leftarrow \{\{v\} : v \in P_i\}$ ▷ Initialize incomplete sub-parts
    - $C_i \leftarrow \{\}$ ▷ Initialize complete sub-parts
    - **for** $O(\log n)$ iterations **do**
        - **for** $F_j \in \mathcal{I}_i$ **do**
            - **if** $\exists$ edge $(u, v) \in F_j \times (\bigcup_{F_{j'} \in \mathcal{I}_i} F_{j'} \setminus F_j)$ **then**
                - $e_j \leftarrow e$ for such edge $e = (u, v)$ by PA.
            - **else**
                - $e_j \leftarrow$ any $e = (u, v) \in F_j \times (\bigcup_{F_{j'} \in C_i} F_{j'})$ by PA.
        - Run Alg. 5 on $\mathcal{I}_i$ sub-parts with edges $\{e_j\}$.
        - **for** Joiner F_j with edge $e_j = (u, v)$ with $v \in F_{j'}$ **do**
            - F_j merges with $F_{j'}$ by PA.
            - u remembers v as its parent.
            - F_j orients its tree edges to v by PA.
        - $C'_i \leftarrow \{F_j \in \mathcal{I}_i : |F_j| \geq D\}$ by PA.
        - $C_i \leftarrow C_i \cup C'_i$.
- **return** Division given by $\{C_i\}_{i=1}^N$.

Lemma 6.4. *Given partition $(P_i)_{i=1}^N$ of V, Algorithm 6 computes a sub-part division of $(P_i)_{i=1}^N$ in $\tilde{O}(D)$ rounds with $\tilde{O}(n)$ messages.*

6.3 Computing Shortcuts

Having shown how sub-part divisions can be computed in a deterministic fashion, we now turn to our deterministic shortcut construction. We rely on heavy path decompositions [37].

Definition 6.5 (Heavy Path Decomposition [37]). *Given a directed tree T, an edge (u, v) of T is* heavy *if the number of v's descendants is more than half the number of u's descendants; otherwise, the edge is* light. *A* heavy path decomposition *of T consists of all the heavy edges in T.*

It is immediate from the definition that each leaf-to-root path on an n-node tree T intersects at most $\lfloor \log_2 n \rfloor$ different paths of T's heavy path decomposition. Given a rooted tree T of depth D, a heavy path decomposition of T can be easily computed in $O(D)$ rounds using $O(n)$ messages.

Our deterministic shortcut construction algorithm, Algorithm 8, first computes a heavy path decomposition and then computes shortcuts on the obtained paths in a bottom-up order. Thus, we first provide a sub-routine, Algorithm 7, that computes shortcuts of congestion $O(c \log D)$ on a path P. Algorithm 7 assumes every node v begins with a set $S(v)$ of part IDs that would like to use v's parent edge in the path. For simplicity, we assume vertices of $\mathcal{P}$ are numbered by their height, $v = 1, 2, \ldots$ (i.e., the source of the path is number 1, its parent is numbered 2, etc'). Algorithm 7 iteratively extends paths used for shortcuts, repeatedly doubling them in length, unless too much congestion results. See Figure 5. This algorithm's properties are as follows.

Algorithm 7 Deterministic shortcut construction for paths.

Input: Path $P \subseteq V$;
Mapping $S : V \to 2^{(P_j)_{j=1}^N}$;
Desired congestion c
Output: Mapping $S_f : V \to 2^{(P_j)_{j=1}^N}$

for $v \in V$ **do**
  Set $S_0(v) \leftarrow S(v)$.
for $i = 0, 1, 2, \ldots, \log_2 D - 1$ **do**
  for every node $v \equiv 2^i \mod 2^{i+1}$ **do**
    if $|S_i(v)| \geq 2c$ **then**
      Break $(v, v+1)$ and set $S_i(v) \leftarrow \emptyset$.
    else
      $u \leftarrow v + 2^i$
      if no broken edges between v and u **then**
        Transmit $S_i(v)$ from v to u along P.
        Set $S_{i+1}(u) \leftarrow S_i(u) \cup S_i(v)$.
return $S_f = S_{\log_2 D}$.

Lemma 6.6. *Given directed path P of length D, desired congestion c and $S : V \to 2^{(P_i)_{i=1}^N}$ which denotes for each vertex v which parts want to use v's parent edge in P, Algorithm 7 returns $S_f : V \to 2^{(P_i)_{i=1}^N}$ s.t. for every $v \in P$ it holds that $|S_f(v)| = O(c \log D)$ in $O(c \log D + D)$ rounds.*

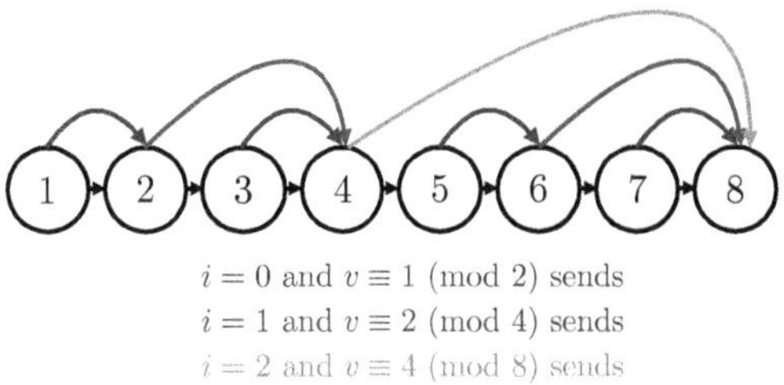

Figure 5: Illustration of Algorithm 7. Source of colored edge is vertex v that transmits $S_i(v)$ and sink is vertex u that updates $S_{i+1}(u)$ (assuming no edges broken). Black edges are path edges.

Proof. To bound the running time, observe that iteration i of the algorithm can be implemented in $c + 2^i$ rounds. Summing over all iterations $i = 0, 1, \ldots, \log_2 D - 1$, the bound on the number of rounds follows. To bound the congestion of the output shortcuts, we prove by induction that before the i-th iteration the congestion on any edge is at most $2ci$. This clearly holds for $i = 0$. Assume as an inductive hypothesis that before iteration i all edges are used by at most $2ci$ parts. In iteration i the only edges whose congestion are potentially increased are those edges exiting u (i.e. edge $(u, u+1)$) such that $u \equiv 0 \mod 2^{i+1}$. The congestion on this edge increases by $|S_i(v)|$ where $v \equiv 2^i \mod 2^{i+1}$. Applying our inductive hypothesis we get that the total congestion on such an edge is at most $|S_i(v)| + |S_i(u)| = 2ci$, implying the claimed bound on the congestion. □

We now turn to describing the overall shortcut construction algorithm, Algorithm 8, and analyze the resulting block parameter there. We limit message complexity by only allowing sub-part representatives to send a message requesting that an edge be used in their part's shortcut. As we show, each bottom-up computation yields good shortcuts for a constant fraction of parts. Thus, after each bottom-up computation, we can use our block parameter verification algorithm – Lemma 4.5 – to identify the parts for which our shortcut construction succeeded and freeze the shortcut edges of said parts. The correctness and runtime of Algorithm 8 is given by Lemma 6.7.

Lemma 6.7. *Given: partition $(P_i)_{i=1}^N$ where $v \in P_i$ knows leader $l_i \in P_i$; a tree T of depth D which admits a T-restricted shortcut of congestion c and block parameter b; and a sub-part division, Algorithm 8 deterministically computes in $\tilde{O}(b(c + D))$ rounds and $\tilde{O}(m)$ messages, a shortcut with congestion $O(c \log n)$ and block parameter $O(b)$.*

Proof (Sketch). The stated round complexity comes from summing sub-routines. The message complexity follows similarly and requires noting that only the $\tilde{O}(n/D)$ sub-part representatives forward their part ID up at most D nodes when running Algorithm 7. Lastly, there can only be a constant number of parts with bad block parameter in each iteration. Each extra block we introduce corresponds to a broken edge that is not broken by the original shortcut. However, each such edge also corresponds to some number of parts that tried to use it and since a part can only try to use so many edges in our shortcut we have that not that many extra edges can be broken. □

Algorithm 8 Deterministic shortcut construction.

```
Input: partition of V, (P_i)_{i=1}^N with leader l_i known by v ∈ P_i;
       sub-part division
       BFS-tree T
Output: T-restricted shortcut with congestion Õ(c) and block
        parameter < 3b
1:  Initially all P_i are active.
2:  Compute heavy path decomposition of T.
3:  for j = 1, 2, ..., O(log n) do
4:      for all v ∈ V do
5:          if v is representative in active part P_i then
6:              S_j(v) ← {l_i}.
7:          else
8:              S_j(v) ← ∅.
9:      Set each heavy path with no incoming light edges active.
10:     for ⌊log n⌋ repetitions do
11:         S_f ← output of Alg. 7 run on all active heavy paths.
12:         for active path sink node v and light edge (v, u) do
13:             S_j(u) ← S_{j−1}(u) ∪ ⋃_v S_f(v).
14:         Set active paths inactive.
15:         Set heavy paths with source u as in line 13 active.
16:     Run Alg. 2 on active parts to check if block params. < 3b.
17:     Set parts with block parameter < 3b inactive.
18: return ∪_j S_j(v) as v's shortcut edges
```

REFERENCES

[1] Baruch Awerbuch. 1987. Optimal distributed algorithms for minimum weight spanning tree, counting, leader election, and related problems. In *Proceedings of the 19th Annual ACM Symposium on Theory of Computing (STOC)*. 230–240.

[2] Baruch Awerbuch, Oded Goldreich, Ronen Vainish, and David Peleg. 1990. A Trade-off Between Information and Communication in Broadcast Protocols. *Journal of the ACM (JACM)* 37, 2 (1990), 238–256.

[3] F Chin and HF Ting. 1985. An almost linear time and $O(n \log n + e)$ messages distributed algorithm for minimum-weight spanning trees. In *Proceedings of the 26th Symposium on Foundations of Computer Science (FOCS)*. 257–266.

[4] Richard Cole and Uzi Vishkin. 1986. Deterministic coin tossing with applications to optimal parallel list ranking. *Information and Control* 70, 1 (1986), 32–53.

[5] Atish Das Sarma, Stephan Holzer, Liah Kor, Amos Korman, Danupon Nanongkai, Gopal Pandurangan, David Peleg, and Roger Wattenhofer. 2012. Distributed verification and hardness of distributed approximation. *SIAM Journal on Computing (SICOMP)* 41, 5 (2012), 1235–1265.

[6] Michael Elkin. 2006. A faster distributed protocol for constructing a minimum spanning tree. *J. Comput. System Sci.* 72, 8 (2006), 1282–1308.

[7] Michael Elkin. 2006. An unconditional lower bound on the time-approximation trade-off for the distributed minimum spanning tree problem. *SIAM Journal on Computing (SICOMP)* 36, 2 (2006), 433–456.

[8] Michael Elkin. 2017. A Simple Deterministic Distributed MST Algorithm, with Near-Optimal Time and Message Complexities. *Proceedings of the 36th ACM Symposium on Principles of Distributed Computing (PODC)* (2017).

[9] Michalis Faloutsos and Mart Molle. 2004. A linear-time optimal-message distributed algorithm for minimum spanning trees. *Distributed Computing* 17, 2 (2004), 151–170.

[10] Silvio Frischknecht, Stephan Holzer, and Roger Wattenhofer. 2012. Networks cannot compute their diameter in sublinear time. In *Proceedings of the 23rd Annual ACM-SIAM Symposium on Discrete Algorithms (SODA)*. 1150–1162.

[11] Eli Gafni. 1985. Improvements in the time complexity of two message-optimal election algorithms. In *Proceedings of the 4th ACM Symposium on Principles of Distributed Computing (PODC)*. 175–185.

[12] Robert G. Gallager, Pierre A. Humblet, and Philip M. Spira. 1983. A distributed algorithm for minimum-weight spanning trees. *ACM Transactions on Programming Languages and systems (TOPLAS)* 5, 1 (1983), 66–77.

[13] Juan A Garay, Shay Kutten, and David Peleg. 1998. A sublinear time distributed algorithm for minimum-weight spanning trees. *SIAM Journal on Computing (SICOMP)* 27, 1 (1998), 302–316.

[14] Mohsen Ghaffari. 2014. Near-optimal distributed approximation of minimum-weight connected dominating set. In *Proceedings of the 41nd International Colloquium on Automata, Languages and Programming (ICALP)*. 483–494.

[15] Mohsen Ghaffari and Bernhard Haeupler. 2016. Distributed Algorithms for Planar Networks II: Low-congestion Shortcuts, MST, and Min-Cut. In *Proceedings of the 27th Annual ACM-SIAM Symposium on Discrete Algorithms (SODA)*. 202–219.

[16] Mohsen Ghaffari, Andreas Karrenbauer, Fabian Kuhn, Christoph Lenzen, and Boaz Patt-Shamir. 2015. Near-optimal distributed maximum flow. In *Proceedings of the 34th ACM Symposium on Principles of Distributed Computing (PODC)*. 81–90.

[17] Mohsen Ghaffari and Fabian Kuhn. 2013. Distributed minimum cut approximation. In *Proceedings of the 27th International Symposium on Distributed Computing (DISC)*. 1–15.

[18] Bernhard Haeupler, D Ellis Hershkowitz, and David Wajc. 2018. Round- and Message-Optimal Distributed Graph Algorithms. *arXiv preprint arXiv:1801.05127* (2018).

[19] Bernhard Haeupler, Taisuke Izumi, and Goran Zuzic. 2016. Low-congestion shortcuts without embedding. In *Proceedings of the 35th ACM Symposium on Principles of Distributed Computing (PODC)*. 451–460.

[20] Bernhard Haeupler, Taisuke Izumi, and Goran Zuzic. 2016. Near-Optimal Low-Congestion Shortcuts on Bounded Parameter Graphs. In *Proceedings of the 30th International Symposium on Distributed Computing (DISC)*. 158–172.

[21] Bernhard Haeupler and Jason Li. 2018. Beating $O(\sqrt{n} + D)$ for Distributed Shortest Path Approximations via Shortcuts. *arXiv preprint arXiv:1802.03671* (2018).

[22] Bernhard Haeupler, Jason Li, and Goran Zuzic. 2018. Minor Excluded Network Families Admit Fast Distributed Algorithms. *arXiv preprint arXiv:1801.06237* (2018).

[23] Stephan Holzer and Roger Wattenhofer. 2012. Optimal distributed all pairs shortest paths and applications. In *Proceedings of the 31st ACM Symposium on Principles of Distributed Computing (PODC)*. 355–364.

[24] Taisuke Izumi and Roger Wattenhofer. 2014. Time Lower Bounds for Distributed Distance Oracles. In *International Conference on Principles of Distributed Systems (OPODIS)*. 60–75.

[25] Maleq Khan and Gopal Pandurangan. 2006. A fast distributed approximation algorithm for minimum spanning trees. In *Proceedings of the 20th International Symposium on Distributed Computing (DISC)*. 355–369.

[26] Shay Kutten, Gopal Pandurangan, David Peleg, Peter Robinson, and Amitabh Trehan. 2015. On the complexity of universal leader election. *Journal of the ACM (JACM)* 62, 1 (2015), 7.

[27] Shay Kutten and David Peleg. 1995. Fast distributed construction of k-dominating sets and applications. In *Proceedings of the 14th ACM Symposium on Principles of Distributed Computing (PODC)*. 238–251.

[28] Christoph Lenzen and Boaz Patt-Shamir. 2015. Fast partial distance estimation and applications. In *Proceedings of the 34th ACM Symposium on Principles of Distributed Computing (PODC)*. 153–162.

[29] Christoph Lenzen and David Peleg. 2013. Efficient distributed source detection with limited bandwidth. In *Proceedings of the 32nd ACM Symposium on Principles of Distributed Computing (PODC)*. 375–382.

[30] Ali Mashreghi and Valerie King. 2017. Time-communication Trade-offs for Minimum Spanning Tree Construction. In *Proceedings of the 18th International Conference on Distributed Computing and Networking (ICDCN)*.

[31] Danupon Nanongkai. 2014. Distributed approximation algorithms for weighted shortest paths. In *Proceedings of the 46th Annual ACM Symposium on Theory of Computing (STOC)*. 565–573.

[32] Danupon Nanongkai and Hsin-Hao Su. 2014. Almost-tight distributed minimum cut algorithms. In *Proceedings of the 28th International Symposium on Distributed Computing (DISC)*. 439–453.

[33] Jaroslav NeÅąetÅŹil, Eva MilkovÃą, and Helena NeÅąetÅŹilovÃą. 2001. Otakar BorÅŕvka on Minimum Spanning Tree Problem Translation of Both the 1926 Papers, Comments, History. *Discrete Mathematics* 233, 1 (2001), 3–36.

[34] Gopal Pandurangan, Peter Robinson, and Michele Scquizzato. 2017. A time- and message-optimal distributed algorithm for minimum spanning trees. In *Proceedings of the 49th Annual ACM Symposium on Theory of Computing (STOC)*. 743–756.

[35] David Peleg. 2000. *Distributed computing: a locality-sensitive approach.* SIAM.

[36] David Peleg and Vitaly Rubinovich. 2000. A Near-Tight Lower Bound on the Time Complexity of Distributed Minimum-Weight Spanning Tree Construction. *SIAM Journal on Computing (SICOMP)* 30, 5 (2000), 1427–1442.

[37] Daniel D Sleator and Robert Endre Tarjan. 1983. A data structure for dynamic trees. *J. Comput. System Sci.* 26, 3 (1983), 362–391.

Improved Massively Parallel Computation Algorithms for MIS, Matching, and Vertex Cover

Mohsen Ghaffari
ETH Zurich
ghaffari@inf.ethz.ch

Themis Gouleakis
MIT
tgoule@mit.edu

Christian Konrad
University of Bristol
christian.konrad@bristol.ac.uk

Slobodan Mitrović
EPFL
slobodan.mitrovic@epfl.ch

Ronitt Rubinfeld
MIT and Tel Aviv University
ronitt@csail.mit.edu

ABSTRACT

We present $O(\log\log n)$-round algorithms in the Massively Parallel Computation (MPC) model, with $\tilde{O}(n)$ memory per machine, that compute a maximal independent set, a $1+\varepsilon$ approximation of maximum matching, and a $2+\varepsilon$ approximation of minimum vertex cover, for any n-vertex graph and any constant $\varepsilon > 0$. These improve the state of the art as follows:

- Our MIS algorithm leads to a simple $O(\log\log\Delta)$-round MIS algorithm in the CONGESTED-CLIQUE model of distributed computing, which improves on the $\tilde{O}(\sqrt{\log\Delta})$-round algorithm of Ghaffari [PODC'17].
- Our $O(\log\log n)$-round $(1+\varepsilon)$-approximate maximum matching algorithm simplifies or improves on the following prior work: $O(\log^2\log n)$-round $(1+\varepsilon)$-approximation algorithm of Czumaj et al. [STOC'18] and $O(\log\log n)$-round $(1+\varepsilon)$-approximation algorithm of Assadi et al. [arXiv'17].
- Our $O(\log\log n)$-round $(2+\varepsilon)$-approximate minimum vertex cover algorithm improves on an $O(\log\log n)$-round $O(1)$-approximation of Assadi et al. [arXiv'17].

CCS CONCEPTS

• **Theory of computation** → **Massively parallel algorithms**; **Distributed algorithms**;

KEYWORDS

Maximal Independent Set; Maximum Matching; Vertex Cover; Massively Parallel Computation; Congested Clique

ACM Reference Format:
Mohsen Ghaffari, Themis Gouleakis, Christian Konrad, Slobodan Mitrović, and Ronitt Rubinfeld. 2018. Improved Massively Parallel Computation Algorithms for MIS, Matching, and Vertex Cover. In *PODC '18: ACM Symposium on Principles of Distributed Computing, July 23–27, 2018, Egham, United Kingdom.* ACM, New York, NY, USA, 10 pages. https://doi.org/10.1145/3212734.3212743

ACM ISBN 978-1-4503-5795-1/18/07...$15.00
https://doi.org/10.1145/3212734.3212743

1 INTRODUCTION

A growing need to process massive data led to development of a number of frameworks for large-scale computation, such as MapReduce [16], Hadoop [43], Spark [44], or Dryad [28]. Thanks to their natural approach to processing massive data, these frameworks have gained great popularity. In this work, we consider the *Massively Parallel Computation* (MPC) model [32] that is abstracted out of the capabilities of these frameworks.

In our work, we study some of the most fundamental problems in algorithmic graph theory: maximal independent set (MIS), maximum matching and minimum vertex cover. The study of these problems in the models of parallel computation dates back to PRAM algorithm. A seminal work of Luby [39] gives a simple randomized algorithm for constructing MIS in $O(\log n)$ PRAM rounds. When this algorithm is applied to the line graph of input graph G, it outputs a maximal matching of G, and hence a 2-approximate maximum matching of G. The output maximal matching also provides a 2-approximate minimum vertex cover. Similar results, also in the context of PRAM algorithms, were obtained in [3, 29, 30]. Since then, the aforementioned problems were studied quite extensively in various models of computation. In the context of MPC, we design simple randomized algorithms that construct (approximate) instances for all the three problems.

1.1 The Models

We consider two closely related models: *Massively Parallel Computation* (MPC), and the CONGESTED-CLIQUE model of distributed computing. Indeed, we consider it as a conceptual contribution of this paper to (further) exhibit the proximity of these two models. We next review these models.

1.1.1 The MPC model. The MPC model was first introduced in [32] and later refined in [4, 9, 23]. The computation in this model proceeds in synchronous *rounds* carried out by m machines. At the beginning of every round, the data (e.g. vertices and edges) is distributed across the machines. During a round, each machine performs computation locally without communicating to other machines. At the end of the round, the machines exchange messages which are used to guide the computation in the next round. In every round, each machine receives and outputs messages that fit into its local memory.

Space: In this model, each machine has S words of space. If N is the total size of the data and each machine has S words of space, the typical settings that are of interest are when S is sublinear in N

and $S \cdot m = \Theta(N)$. That is, the total memory across all the machines suffices to fit all the data, but is not much larger than that. If we are given a graph on n vertices, in our work we consider the regimes in which $S \in \Theta(n/\text{polylog}\, n)$ or $S \in \Theta(n)$.

Communication vs. computational complexity: Our main focus is the number of rounds required to finish the computation, which is essentially the complexity of the communication needed to solve the problem. Although we do not explicitly state the computational complexity in our results, it will be apparent from the description of our algorithms that the total computation time across all the machines is nearly-linear in the input size.

1.1.2 CONGESTED-CLIQUE. A second model that we consider is the CONGESTED-CLIQUE model of distributed computing, which was introduced by Lotker, Pavlov, Patt-Shamir, and Peleg[38] and has been studied extensively since then, see e.g.,[10, 11, 13, 14, 17, 18, 20–22, 24–27, 31, 33, 35, 41, 42]. In this model, we have n players which can communicate in synchronous rounds. In each round, every player can send $O(\log n)$ bits to every other player. Besides this communication restriction, the model does not limit the players, e.g., they can use large space and arbitrary computations; though, in our algorithms, both of these will be small. Furthermore, in studying graph problems in this model, the standard setting is that we have an n-vertex graph $G = (V, E)$, and each player is associated with one vertex of this graph. Initially, each player knows only the edges incident on its own vertex. At the end, each player should know the part of the output related to its own vertex, e.g., whether its vertex is in the computed maximal independent set or not, or whether some of its edges is in the matching or not.

We emphasize that CONGESTED-CLIQUE provides an all-to-all communication model. It is worth contrasting this with the more classical models of distributed computing. For instance, the LOCAL model, first introduced by Linial [36], allows the players to communicate only along the edges of the graph problem G (with unbounded size messages).

1.2 Related Work

Maximum Matching and Minimum Vertex Cover: If the space per machine is $O(n^{1+\delta})$, for any $\delta > 0$, Lattanzi et al. [34] show how to construct a maximal matching, and hence a 2-approximate minimum vertex cover, in $O(1/\delta)$ MPC rounds. Furthermore, in case the machine-space is $\Theta(n)$, their algorithm requires $O(\log n)$ many rounds to output a maximal matching. In their work, they apply *filtering* techniques to gradually sparsify the graph. Ahn and Guha [2] provide a method for constructing a $(1+\varepsilon)$-approximation of weighted maximum matching in $O(1/(\delta\varepsilon))$ rounds while, similarly to [34], requiring that the space per machine is $O(n^{1+\delta})$.

If the space per machine is $\tilde{O}(n\sqrt{n})$, Assadi and Khanna [7] show how construct an $O(1)$-approximate maximum matching and an $O(\log n)$-approximate minimum vertex cover in two rounds. Their approach is based on designing randomized composable coresets.

Recently, Czumaj et al. [15] designed an algorithm for constructing a $(1 + \varepsilon)$-approximate maximum matching in $O((\log \log n)^2)$ MPC rounds of computation and $O(n/\text{polylog}\, n)$ memory per machine. To obtain this result, they start from a variant of a PRAM algorithm that requires $O(\log n)$ parallel iterations, and showed how to compress many of those iterations (on average, $O(\log n/(\log \log n)^2)$ many of them) into $O(1)$ MPC rounds. Their result does not transfer to an algorithm for computing $O(1)$-approximate minimum vertex cover.

Building on [15] and [7], Assadi [5] shows how to produce an $O(\log n)$-approximate minimum vertex cover in $O(\log \log n)$ MPC rounds when the space per machine is $O(n/\text{polylog}\, n)$. The work by Assadi et al. [6] also addresses these two problems, and provides a way to construct a $(1 + \varepsilon)$-approximate maximum matching and an $O(1)$-approximate minimum vertex cover in $O(\log \log n)$ rounds when the space per machine is $\tilde{O}(n)$. Their result builds on techniques originally developed in the context of dynamic matching algorithms and composable coresets.

Maximal Independent Set: Maximal independent set has been central in the study of graph algorithms in both the parallel and the distributed models. The seminal work of Luby [39] and Alon, Babai, and Itai [3] provide $O(\log n)$-round parallel and distributed algorithms for constructing MIS. The distributed complexity in the LOCAL model was first improved by Barenboim et al.[8] and consequently by Ghaffari [20], which led to the current best round complexity of $O(\log \Delta) + 2^{O(\sqrt{\log \log n})}$. In the CONGESTED-CLIQUE model of distributed computing, Ghaffari [21] gave another algorithm which computes an MIS in $\tilde{O}(\sqrt{\log \Delta})$ rounds. A deterministic $O(\log n \log \Delta)$-round CONGESTED-CLIQUE algorithm was given by Censor-Hillel et al. [14].

It is also worth referring to the literature on one particular MIS algorithm, known as the *randomized greedy MIS*, which is relevant to what we do for MIS. In this algorithm, we permute the vertices uniformly at random and then add them to the MIS greedily. Blelloch et al. [12] showed that one can implement this algorithm in $O(\log^2 n)$ parallel/distributed rounds, and recently Fischer and Noever [19] improved that to a tight bound of $\Theta(\log n)$. We will show a $O(\log \log \Delta)$-round simulation of the randomized greedy MIS algorithm in the MPC and the CONGESTED-CLIQUE model.

1.3 Our Contributions

As our first result, in Section 3 we present an algorithm for constructing MIS.

Theorem 1.1. *There is an algorithm that with high probability computes an MIS in $O(\log \log \Delta)$ rounds of the MPC model, with $\tilde{O}(n)$-bits of memory per machine. Moreover, the same algorithm can be adapted to compute an MIS in $O(\log \log \Delta)$ rounds of the CONGESTED-CLIQUE model.*

As our second result, in Section 4, we first design an algorithm that returns a $(2+\varepsilon)$-approximate fractional maximum matching and a $(2+\varepsilon)$-approximate integral minimum vertex cover in $O(\log \log n)$ MPC rounds. In the full version of this paper we show how to round this fractional matching to a $(2 + \varepsilon)$-approximate integral maximum matching. In comparison to previous work: our result has somewhat better round-complexity than [15], provides a stronger approximation guarantee than [6], and appears to be simpler than both. After applying vertex-based random partitioning (that was proposed in this context in [15]), the algorithm repeats only a couple of simple steps to perform all its decisions.

Theorem 1.2. *There is an algorithm that with high probability computes a $(2+\varepsilon)$-approximate integral maximum matching and a $(2+\varepsilon)$-approximate integral minimum vertex cover in $O(\log\log n)$ rounds of the MPC model, with $\tilde{O}(n)$-bits of memory per machine.*

Following similar observations as Assadi et al. [6], it is possible to apply the techniques of [40] on Theorem 1.2 to obtain the following result.

Corollary 1.3. *There exists an algorithm that with high probability constructs a $(1+\varepsilon)$-approximate integral maximum matching in $O(\log\log n)\cdot(1/\varepsilon)^{O(1/\varepsilon)}$ MPC rounds, with $\tilde{O}(n)$-bits of memory per machine.*

As noted by Czumaj et al. [15], the result of Lotker et al. [37] can be used to obtain the following result.

Corollary 1.4. *There exists an algorithm that outputs a $(2+\varepsilon)$-approximation to maximum weighted matching in $O(\log\log n\cdot(1/\varepsilon))$ MPC rounds and $\tilde{O}(n)$-bits of memory per machine.*

For the sake of clarity, we present our algorithms for the case in which each machine has $\tilde{O}(n)$-bits of memory (or $O(n)$ words of memory). However, similarly to [15], our algorithm for matching and vertex cover can be adjusted to still run in $O(\log\log n)$ MPC rounds even when the memory per machine is $O(n/\text{polylog}\, n)$.

1.4 Our Techniques

Maximal independent set: Our MPC algorithm for MIS is based on the randomized greedy MIS algorithm. We show how to efficiently implement this algorithm in only $O(\log\log n)$ MPC and CONGESTED-CLIQUE rounds.

Maximum matching and vertex cover: In Section 4.1, we start from a sequential algorithm that outputs a $(2+\varepsilon)$-approximate fractional maximum matching and a $(2+\varepsilon)$-approximate integral minimum vertex cover. The algorithm maintains edge-weights. Initially, every edge-weight is set to $1/n$. Then, gradually, at each iteration the edge-weights are simultaneously increased by a multiplicative factor of $1/(1-\varepsilon)$. Each vertex whose sum of the incident edges becomes $1-2\varepsilon$ or larger is frozen, and its incident edges do not change their weights afterward. The vertices that are frozen in this process constitute the desired vertex cover. It is not hard to see that after $O(\log n/\varepsilon)$ iterations every edge will be incident to at least one frozen vertex, and at this point the algorithm terminates.

In Section 4.3, we show how to simulate this sequential algorithm in the MPC model, by on average simulating $\Theta(\log n/\log\log n)$ iterations in $O(1)$ MPC rounds. As the first step, motivated by [15], we apply vertex-based sampling. Namely, the vertex-set is randomly partitioned across the machines into disjoint sets, and each machine considers only the induced graph on its local copy of vertices. Then, during each MPC round, every machine simulates several iterations of the sequential algorithm on its local subgraph. During this simulation, each machine estimates weights of the vertices that it maintains locally in order to decide which vertices should be frozen. However, even if the estimates are sharp, only a slight error could potentially cause many vertices to largely deviate from their true behavior. To alleviate this issue, instead of having a fixed threshold $1-2\varepsilon$, for each vertex and in every iteration we choose a random threshold from the interval $[1-4\varepsilon, 1-2\varepsilon]$. For most vertices, this prevents slight errors in estimates from having large effects. Then, vertices are frozen only if their estimated weight is above their randomly chosen threshold. Intuitively, this significantly reduces the chance of these decisions (on whether to freeze a vertex or not) deviating from the true ones

As our final component, in the full version of the paper, we provide a rounding procedure that for a given fractional matching produces an integral one of size only a constant-factor smaller than the size of the fractional matching. Furthermore, every vertex in that rounding method chooses edges based only on its neighborhood, i.e., makes local decision. Thus it is straightforward to parallelize the rounding procedure.

2 PRELIMINARIES

For a graph $G=(V,E)$ and a set $V'\subseteq V$, $G[V']$ denotes the subgraph of G *induced* on the set V', i.e. $G[V']=(V', E\cap(V'\times V'))$. We use $N(v)$ to refer to the neighborhood of v in G. Throughout the paper, we use $n:=|V|$ to denote the number of vertices in the input graph.

Independent Sets: An *independent set* $I\subseteq V$ is a subset of non-adjacent vertices. An independent set I is *maximal* if for every $v\in V\setminus I$, $I\cup\{v\}$ is not an independent set. Given an independent set I, we call the graph $G'=G[V\setminus\Gamma_G[I]]$ the residual graph with respect to I. If clear from the context, we may simple call G' the residual graph. We say that a vertex $u\in V$ is *uncovered* with respect to I, if u is not adjacent to a vertex in I, i.e., $u\in V\setminus\Gamma_G[I]$. Again, if clear from the context, we simply say u is uncovered without specifying I explicitly.

Ghaffari gave the following result that we will reuse in this paper:

Theorem 2.1 (Ghaffari [21]). *Let G be an n-vertex graph with $\Delta(G)=\text{poly}\log(n)$. Then, there exists a distributed algorithm that runs in the* CONGESTED-CLIQUE *model and computes an MIS on G in $O(\log\log\Delta)$ rounds.*

Routing: As a subroutine, our algorithm needs to solve the following simple routing task: Let $u\in V$ be an arbitrary vertex. Suppose that every other vertex $v\in V\setminus\{u\}$ holds $0\le n_v\le n$ messages each of size $O(\log n)$ that it wants to deliver to u. We are guaranteed that $\sum_{v\in V} n_v\le n$. Lenzen proved that in the CONGESTED-CLIQUE model there is a deterministic routing scheme that achieves this task in $O(1)$ rounds [35]. In the following, we will refer to this scheme as Lenzen's routing scheme.

3 MAXIMAL INDEPENDENT SET

The Greedy algorithm for maximal independent set processes the vertices of the input graph in arbitrary order. It adds the current vertex under consideration to an initially empty independent set I if none of its neighbors are already in I.

This algorithm progressively thins out the input graph, and the rate at which the graph loses edges depends heavily on the order in which the vertices are considered. Consider a sequential random greedy algorithm that ranks/permutes vertices 1 to n randomly and then greedily adds vertices to the MIS, while walking through this permutation. As it was observed in [1] in the context of correlation clustering in the streaming model, the number of edges in the residual graph decreases relatively quickly with high probability. In this section, we simulate this algorithm in $O(\log\log\Delta)$ rounds of the CONGESTED-CLIQUE model, thus proving the following result:

THEOREM 1.1. *There is an algorithm that with high probability computes an MIS in $O(\log\log\Delta)$ rounds of the MPC model, with $\tilde{O}(n)$-bits of memory per machine. Moreover, the same algorithm can be adapted to compute an MIS in $O(\log\log\Delta)$ rounds of the CONGESTED-CLIQUE model.*

3.1 Randomized Greedy Algorithm for MIS

Let us first consider a randomized variant of the sequential greedy MIS algorithm described below, that we show how to implement in the CONGESTED-CLIQUE and the MPC model. We remark that this algorithm has been studied before in the literature of parallel algorithms[12, 19].

Greedy Randomized Maximal Independent Set:

- Initially, choose a permutation $\pi : [n] \rightarrow [n]$ uniformly at random.
- Repeat until the next rank is at least $n/\log^{10} n$ and the maximum degree is at most $\log^{10} n$:

(A) Mark the vertex v which has the smallest rank among the remaining vertices according to π, and add v to the MIS.

(B) Remove all the neighbors of v.

- Run $O(\log\log\Delta)$ rounds of the Sparsified MIS Algorithm of [21] in the remaining graph. Remove from the graph the constructed MIS and its neighborhood.
- Deliver the remaining graph on a single machine and find its MIS.
- At the end, output the constructed MIS sets.

3.2 Simulation in $O(\log\log\Delta)$ rounds of MPC and CONGESTED-CLIQUE

Simulation in the MPC model: We now explain how to simulate the above algorithm in the MPC model with $O(n\log n)$-bits of memory per machine, and also in the CONGESTED-CLIQUE model. In each iteration, we take an induced subgraph of G that is guaranteed to have $\tilde{O}(n)$ edges and simulate the above algorithm on that graph. We show that the total number of edges drops fast enough, so that $O(\log\log\Delta)$ rounds will suffice. More concretely, we first consider the subgraph induced by vertices with ranks 1 to n/Δ^{α}, for $\alpha = 3/4$. This subgraph has $O(n)$ edges, with high probability. So we can deliver it to one machine, and have it simulate the algorithm up to this rank. Now, this machine sends the resulting MIS to all other machines. Then, each machine removes its vertices that are in MIS or neighboring MIS. In the second phase, we take the subgraph induced by remaining vertices with ranks n/Δ^{α} to n/Δ^{α^2}. Again, we can see that this subgraph has $O(n)$ edges (a proof is given below), so we can simulate it in $O(1)$ rounds. More generally, in the i-th iteration, we will go up to rank n/Δ^{α^i}. Once the next rank becomes $n/\log^{10} n$, which as we show happens after $O(\log\log\Delta)$ rounds, the maximum degree of the graph is some value $\Delta' \leq O(\log^{11} n)$ (see Lemma 3.1). Note that clearly also $\Delta' \leq \Delta$. At that point, we apply the MIS Algorithm of [21] for sparse graphs to the remaining graph. This algorithm is applicable whenever the maximum degree is at most $2^{O(\sqrt{\log n})}$ (see Theorem 1.1 of [21]). After $O(\log\log\Delta')$ rounds, w.h.p., that algorithm finds an MIS which after removed along with its neighborhood results in the graph having $O(n)$ edges. Now we deliver the whole remaining graph to one machine where it is processed in a single MPC round.

We note that the Algorithm of [21] performs only simple local decisions with low communication, and hence every iteration of the algorithm can be implemented in $O(1)$ MPC rounds, with $\tilde{O}(n)$ memory per machine, by using standard techniques.

Simulation in CONGESTED-CLIQUE: We now argue that each iteration can be implemented in $O(1)$ rounds of CONGESTED-CLIQUE. To simulate the first step of the algorithm, all vertices agree on a uniform random order as follows: the vertex with the smallest ID choses a uniform random order locally and informs all other vertices about their positions within the order. Then, all vertices broadcast their positions to all other vertices. As a result, all vertices know the entire order. Also, in each iteration, we make all vertices with permutation rank in the selected range send their edges to the leader vertex. Here, the leader is an arbitrarily chosen vertex, e.g., the one with the minimum identifier. As we show below, the number of these edges per iteration is $O(n)$ with high probability, and thus we can deliver all the messages to the leader in $O(1)$ rounds using Lenzen's routing method[35]. Then, the leader can compute the MIS among the vertices with ranks in the selected range. It then reports the result to all the vertices in a single round, by telling each vertex whether it is in the computed independent set or not. A single round of computation, in which the vertices in the independent set report to all their neighbors, is then used to remove all the vertices that have a neighbor in the independent set (or are in the set). After these steps, the algorithm proceeds to the next iteration.

Regarding the round-complexity of the algorithm once the rank becomes $n/\log^{10} n$: The work [21] already provides a way to solve MIS in $O(\log\log\Delta')$ CONGESTED-CLIQUE rounds for any $\Delta' = 2^{O(\sqrt{\log n})}$. Here, Δ' is the maximum degree of the graph remained after processing the vertices up to rank $n/\log^{10} n$, and, as we show by Lemma 3.1, that $\Delta' \leq \text{polylog}\, n \ll 2^{O(\sqrt{\log n})}$. Hence, the overall round complexity is again $O(\log\log\Delta)$ rounds.

3.3 Analysis

Since by the i-th iteration the algorithm has processed the ranks up to n/Δ^{α^i}, the rank $n/\log^{10} n$ is processed within $O(\log\log\Delta)$ iterations. In the proof of Theorem 1.1 presented below, we prove that with high probability the number of edges sent to one machine per phase is $O(n)$. Before that, we present a lemma that will aid in bounding the degrees and the number of edges in our analysis. A variant of this lemma was proved in [1].

Lemma 3.1. *Suppose that we have simulated the algorithm up to rank r. Let G_r be the remaining graph. Then, the maximum degree in G_r is $O(n\log n/r)$ with high probability.*

Proof. We first upper-bound the probability that G_r contains a vertex of degree at least d. Then, we conclude that the degree of every vertex in G_r is $O(n \log n/r)$ with high probability.

Consider a vertex whose degree is still d. When the sequential algorithm considers one more vertex, which is like choosing a random one among the remaining vertices, one of this vertex or its neighbors gets hit with probability at least d/n. If that happens, this vertex would be removed. The probability that this does not happen throughout ranks 1 to r is at most $(1 - d/n)^r \leq \exp(-rd/n)$. Now, the probability that a vertex in G_r has degree more than $20n \log n/r$ is at most $1/n^5$, which implies that, the maximum degree of G_r is at most $20n \log n/r$ with probability at least $1 - n^{-4}$. □

We are now ready to prove the main theorem of this section.

Proof of Theorem 1.1. We first argue about the MPC round-complexity of the algorithm, and then show that it requires $\tilde{O}(n)$ memory.

Round complexity: Recall that the algorithm considers ranks of the form $r_i := n/\Delta^{\alpha^i}$, until the rank becomes $n/\log^{10} n$ or greater. When that occurs, it applies other algorithms for $O(\log\log\Delta)$ iterations, as described in Section 3.2. Hence, the algorithm runs for at most $i^\star + \log\log\Delta$ iterations, where $i^\star$ is the smallest integer such that rank $r_{i^\star} := n/\Delta^{\alpha^{i^\star}} \geq n/\log^{10} n$. A simple calculation gives $i^\star \leq \log_{4/3}\log\Delta$, for $\alpha = 3/4$. Furthermore, every iteration can be implemented in $O(1)$ rounds as discussed above.

Memory requirement: We first discuss the memory required to implement the process until the rank becomes $O(n/\log^{10} n)$. By Lemma 3.1 we have that after the graph up to rank r_i is simulated, the maximum degree in the remaining graph is $O(n \log n/r_i)$ w.h.p. Observe that it also trivially holds in the first iteration, i.e. the initial graph has maximum degree $O(n)$. Let G_i be the graph induced by the ranks between r_i and r_{i+1}. Then, a neighbor u of vertex v appears in G_i with probability $(r_{i+1} - r_i)/(n - r_i) \leq r_{i+1}/n$. Hence, the expected degree of every vertex in this graph is at most

$$\mu := \Theta(n \log n/r_i \cdot r_{i+1}/n) = \Theta\left(\Delta^{(1-\alpha)\alpha^i} \log n\right).$$

Since $\mu \geq \log n$, by Chernoff bound we have that every vertex in G_i has degree $O(\mu)$ w.h.p. Now, since there are $O(r_{i+1})$ vertices in G_i, we have that G_i contains

$$O\left(r_{i+1}\Delta^{(1-\alpha)\alpha^i} \log n\right) = O\left(n\Delta^{-\alpha^i/2} \log n\right) \quad (1)$$

many edges w.h.p., where we used that $\alpha = 3/4$. Recall that the algorithm iterates over the ranks until the maximum degree becomes less than $\log^{10} n$. Also, $\Theta(n \log n/r_i)$ upper-bounds the maximum degree (see Lemma 3.1). Hence, we have

$$\Theta(n \log n/r_i) \geq \log^{10} n \implies \Delta^{\alpha^i} \geq \Omega\left(\log^9 n\right).$$

Combining the last implication with Eq. (1) provides that G_i contains $O(n)$ edges w.h.p.

After the rank becomes $n/\log^{10} n$ or greater, we run the CONGESTED-CLIQUE algorithm of [21] for $O(\log\log\Delta)$ iterations. Since that algorithm performs only simple local decisions with low communication, every iteration of the algorithm can be implemented in $O(1)$ MPC rounds, with $\tilde{O}(n)$ memory per machine, by using standard techniques. Finally, using Theorem 2.1, we conclude that the MIS will be computed after $O(\log\log\Delta)$ rounds in the MPC or the CONGESTED-CLIQUE model.

□

4 MATCHING AND VERTEX COVER, SIMPLE APPROXIMATIONS

In this section, we describe a simple algorithm that leads to a fractional matching of weight within a $(2+\varepsilon)$-factor of (integral) maximum matching and, the same algorithm, leads to a $2+\varepsilon$ approximation of minimum vertex cover, for any small constant $\varepsilon > 0$. In Section 4.4 we prove our main technical lemma, while the complete proof of correctness of the algorithm is deferred to the full version of this paper. Also in the full version, we design an algorithm that efficiently constructs an integral $(2+\varepsilon)$-approximate maximum matching from a fractional one. That result along with standard techniques underlined in Section 1.3 provides $1+\varepsilon$ approximation of maximum matching.

In Section 4.1, we first present the advertized algorithm that runs in $O(\log n)$ rounds. Then, in Section 4.2 and Section 4.3, we explain how to simulate this algorithm in $O(\log\log n)$ rounds of the MPC model.

4.1 Basic $O(\log n)$-iteration Centralized Algorithm

We now provide a simple centralized algorithm for obtaining the described fractional matching and minimum vertex cover. We refer to this algorithm as Central.

Central: Centralized $O(\log n)$-round Fractional Matching and Vertex Cover:

- Initially, for each edge $e \in E$, set $x_e = 1/n$.
- Then, until each edge is frozen, in iteration t:

(A) Freeze each vertex v for which $y_v = \sum_{e \ni v} x_e \geq 1 - 2\varepsilon$ and freeze all its edges.

(B) For each active edge, set $x_e \leftarrow x_e/(1-\varepsilon)$.

- At the end, once all edges are frozen, output the set of values x_e as a fractional matching and the set of frozen vertices as a vertex cover.

Lemma 4.1. *For any constants ε such that $0 < \varepsilon \leq 1/10$, the algorithm Central terminates after $O(\log n)$ iterations, at which point all edges are frozen. Moreover, we have two properties:*

(A) The set of frozen vertices—i.e., those v for which $y_{v,t} = \sum_{e \ni v} x_e \geq 1 - 2\varepsilon$—is a vertex cover that has size within a $(2+5\varepsilon)$ factor of the minimum vertex cover.

(B) $\sum_{e \in E} x_e \geq |M^\star|/(2+5\varepsilon)$, that is, the computed fractional matching has size within $(2+5\varepsilon)$-factor of the maximum matching

Proof. We first prove the claim about vertex cover, and then about maximum matching.

Vertex cover: Let C be the vertex cover obtained by the algorithm. Every vertex added to C has weight at least $1-2\varepsilon$. Furthermore, an edge can be incident to at most 2 vertices of C. Let W_M be the weight of the fractional matching the algorithm constructs. Then, we have $|C| \leq 2W_M/(1-2\varepsilon) \leq 2(1+5\varepsilon)W_M$, for $\varepsilon \leq 1/10$. Note that the algorithm ensures that at every step $y_v \leq 1$. Hence, from the strong duality we have that the weight of fractional minimum vertex covers is at least W_M. Therefore, the minimum (integral) vertex cover has size at least W_M as well. This now implies that $|C|$ is a $2(1+5\varepsilon)$-approximate minimum vertex cover.

Maximum matching: Let $W_M^\star$ be the weight of a fractional maximum matching. Then, it holds $|M^\star| \leq W_M^\star \leq |C|$. From our analysis above and the last chain of inequalities we have $W_M \geq |M^\star|/(2(1+5\varepsilon))$. □

4.2 An Attempt for Simulation in $O(\log\log n)$ rounds of MPC

An Idealized MPC Simulation: Next, we explain an attempt toward simulating the algorithm Central in the MPC model. Once we discuss this, we will point out some shortcomings and then explain how we plan to adjust the algorithm to address these shortcomings.

The algorithm starts with every vertex and every edge being active. If not active, an edge/vertex is frozen. Throughout the algorithm, the minimum active fractional edge value increases and consequently, the degree of each vertex with respect to active edges decreases gradually. We break the simulation into phases, where the ith phase ensures to simulate enough of the algorithm until the minimum active fractional edge value is $1/\Delta^{-(0.9)^i}$, which implies that the active degree is at most $\Delta^{(0.9)^i}$. Hence, we finish within $O(\log\log n)$ phases. **Remark:** In our final implementation, the number of iteration one phase simulates is slightly different than presented here. However, that final implementation, that we precisely define in the sequel, follows the exact same behavior as presented here.

Let us focus on one phase. Suppose that G' is the remaining graph on the active edges, the minimum active fractional edge value is $1/d$, and thus G' has degree at most d. In this phase, we simulate the algorithm until the minimum active fractional edge value reaches $1/d^{0.9}$, which implies that the active degree is at most $d^{0.9}$.

We randomly partition the vertex-set of G', that consists only of active edges, among $m = \sqrt{d}$ machines; let G'_i be the graph given to machine i. In this way, each machine receives $O(n)$ edges w.h.p. Machine i for the next $\log_{1/(1-\varepsilon)} d/10$ rounds simulates the basic algorithm on G'_i. For that, in each round the machine which received a vertex v estimates $y_v = \sum_{e \ni v} x_e$ by $\tilde{y}_v$ defined as

$$\tilde{y}_v = m \cdot \sum_{e\ni v;\, e\in G'_i} x_e + \sum_{e\ni v;\, e\in G\setminus G'} x_e.$$

That is, $\tilde{y}_v$ is the summation of edge-values of G'-edges incident on v whose other endpoint is in the same machine, multiplied by m (to normalize for the partitioning), plus the value of all edges remaining from $G \setminus G'$, i.e., edges that were frozen before this phase. In each round and for every vertex v, if $\tilde{y}_v \geq 1-2\varepsilon$, then the machine freezes v and the edges incident to v. After this step, for any active edge $e \in G'_i$ the machine sets $x_e \leftarrow x_e \cdot 1/(1-\varepsilon)$. The phase ends after $\log_{1/(1-\varepsilon)} \Delta/10$ rounds. At the end, the round in which different vertices were frozen determines when the corresponding edges got frozen (if they did). So, it suffices to spread the information about the frozen vertices and the related timing to deduce the edge-values of all edges. Since per iteration each active edge increases by a factor of $1/(1-\varepsilon)$, after $\log_{1/(1-\varepsilon)} \Delta/10$ rounds, the minimum active edge value reaches $1/d^{0.9}$ and we are done with this phase.

The Issue with the Direct Simulation: Consider first the following wishful-thinking scenario. Assume for a moment that in *every iteration* it holds $|y_v - (1-2\varepsilon)| > |y_v - \tilde{y}_v|$, that is, y_v and $\tilde{y}_v$ are "on the same side" of the threshold. Then, the algorithm Central and the MPC simulation of it make the same decision on whether a vertex v gets frozen or not. Moreover, this happens in every iteration, as can be formalized by a simple induction. This in turn implies that the MPC algorithm performs the exact same computations as the Central algorithm and thus it provides the same approximation as Central. However, in general case, even if y_v and $\tilde{y}_v$ are almost equal, e.g., $|y_v - \tilde{y}_v| \ll \varepsilon$, it might happen that $y_v \geq 1-2\varepsilon$ and $\tilde{y}_v < 1-2\varepsilon$, resulting in the two algorithms making different decisions with respect to v. Furthermore, this situation could occur for many vertices simultaneously, and this deviation of the two algorithms might grow as we go through the round; these complicate the task of analyzing the behavior of the MPC algorithm.

Random Thresholding to the Rescue: Observe that if $|y_v - \tilde{y}_v|$ is small then there is only a "small range" of values of y_v around the threshold $1-2\varepsilon$ which could potentially lead to the two algorithms behaving differently with respect to v. Motivated by this observation, instead of having one fixed threshold throughout the whole algorithm, in each iteration t and for each vertex v the algorithm will uniformly at random choose a fresh threshold $\mathcal{T}_{v,t}$ from the interval $[1-4\varepsilon, 1-2\varepsilon]$. We call this algorithm Central-Rand, and state it below. Then, if v is not frozen until the tth iteration, v gets frozen by Central-Rand if $y_{v,t} \geq \mathcal{T}_{v,t}$ (and similarly, v get frozen by the MPC simulation if $\tilde{y}_{v,t} \geq \mathcal{T}_{v,t}$). In that case, if $|y_v - \tilde{y}_v| \ll \varepsilon$, then most of the time y_v would be far from the threshold and the two algorithms would behave similarly. We make this intuition formal in the next section by Lemma 4.4.

4.3 Our Actual Simulation in $O(\log\log n)$ rounds of MPC

We now present the modified Central-Rand algorithm with the random thresholding and then discuss how we simulate it in the MPC model.

Central-Rand: Centralized $O(\log n)$-round Fractional Matching and Vertex Cover with Random Thresholding:

- *Each vertex v chooses a list of thresholds $\mathcal{T}_{v,t}$ such that: the thresholds are chosen independently; each threshold is chosen uniformly at random from $[1-4\varepsilon, 1-2\varepsilon]$.*
- Initially, for each edge $e \in E$, set $x_e = 1/n$.
- Then, until each edge is frozen, in iteration t:

(A) Freeze each vertex v for which $y_{v,t} = \sum_{e\ni v} x_e \geq \mathcal{T}_{v,t}$ and freeze all its edges.

(B) For each active edge, set $x_e \leftarrow x_e/(1-\varepsilon)$.

- At the end, once all edges are frozen, output the set of values x_e as a fractional matching and the set of frozen vertices as a vertex cover.

Our Actual MPC Simulation: We now provide an MPC simulation of Central-Rand, that we will refer to by MPC-Simul, and discuss it below.

Our algorithm begins by selecting a collection of random thresholds $\mathcal{T}$. In the actual implementation, since these thresholds are chosen independently and each from the same interval, threshold $\mathcal{T}_{v,t}$ can be sampled when needed ("on the fly"). During the simulation, we maintain a vertex set $V' \subseteq V$ that consists of vertices that we consider for the rest of the simulation. The algorithm defines the initial weight of the edges to be $w_0 = (1-2\varepsilon)/n$. Also, it maintains variable d representing the upper-bound on the maximum degree in the remaining graph (in principle, the maximum degree can be smaller than d).

MPC-Simul is divided into phases. At the beginning of a phase, we consider a subgraph G' of $G[V']$ that consists only of the active edges. In the full version we prove that the maximum degree in G' is at most d. Also at the beginning of a phase, the algorithm defines y_v^{old} (see line (b)). This is part of the vertex-weight that remains the same throughout the execution of the phase. It corresponds to the sum of weights of the edges incident to v that were frozen in prior phases. Then, the vertex set V' is distributed across $m = \sqrt{d}$ machines. Each machines collects the induced graph of G' on the vertex set assigned to it. In the full version we prove that each of these induced graphs consists of $O(n)$ edges.

Each phase executes the steps under line (e), which simulates I iterations of Central-Rand. During a phase, we maintain the iteration-counter t. The value of t counts all the iterations since the beginning of the algorithm, and not only from the beginning of a phase. After this simulation is over, the weight x_e^{MPC} of each edge e is properly set/updated. For instance, if e was not assigned to any of the machines (i.e., its endpoints were assigned to distinct machines), then x_e^{MPC} was not changing during the simulation of Central-Rand in this phase even if both of its endpoints were active. To account for that, at line (g) the value x_e^{MPC} is set to $w_0 \frac{1}{(1-\varepsilon)^{t'}}$, where t' is the last iteration when both endpoints of e were active. To implement this step, each vertex will also keep a variable corresponding to the iteration when it was last active.

Every vertex v that has weight more than 1, i.e., $y_v^{MPC} > 1$, is along with its incident edges removed from the consideration, e.g., removed from V' at line (i), but v is added to the vertex cover that is reported at the end of the algorithm. Note that after the removal of such v, the edges incident to it are not considered anymore while computing y^{MPC} or $\tilde{y}$. This step ensures that throughout the algorithm the fractional matching on $G[V']$ will be valid. But it also ensures that all the edges that are in $G[V \setminus V']$, in particular those incident to v, will be covered by the final vertex cover.

MPC-Simul: MPC Simulation of algorithm Central-Rand:

(1) Each vertex v chooses a list of thresholds $\mathcal{T}_{v,t}$ such that: the thresholds are chosen independently; each threshold is chosen uniformly at random from $[1-4\varepsilon, 1-2\varepsilon]$.

(2) Init: $V' = V$; $\forall e \in E$, set $x_e^{MPC} = w_0 = \frac{1-2\varepsilon}{n}$; $d = n$; $t = 0$.

(3) While $d > \log^{20} n$:

  (a) Let G' be a graph on V' consisting only of the active edges of $G[V']$.

  (b) For each $v \in V'$, define $y_v^{old} = \sum_{e \ni v; e \in G[V'] \setminus G'} x_e^{MPC}$.

  (c) Set: # machines $m = \sqrt{d}$; # iterations $I = \frac{\log m}{10 \log 5}$.

  (d) Partition V' into m sets $V_1, \ldots, V_m$ by assigning each vertex to a machine independently and uniformly at random.

  (e) For each $i \in \{1, \ldots, m\}$ in parallel execute I iterations

    (A) For each $v \in V_i$ such that $\tilde{y}_{v,t} = m \cdot \sum_{e \ni v; e \in G'[V_i]} x_e^{MPC} + y_v^{old} \geq \mathcal{T}_{v,t}$: freeze v and freeze all its edges.

    (B) For each active edge of $G'[V_i]$, set $x_e^{MPC} \leftarrow \frac{x_e^{MPC}}{1-\varepsilon}$.

    (C) Increment the total iteration count: $t \leftarrow t+1$.

  (f) Update $d \leftarrow d(1-\varepsilon)^I$.

  (g) For every edge $e = \{u, v\}$: set $x_e^{MPC} = w_0 \frac{1}{(1-\varepsilon)^{t'}}$, where t' is the last iteration in which both u and v were active.

  (h) For each $v \in V'$ let $y_v^{MPC} = \sum_{e \ni v; e \in G[V']} x_e^{MPC}$.

  (i) For each $v \in V'$ such that $y_v^{MPC} > 1$: remove v from V'.

  (j) For each $v \in V'$ such that $y_v^{MPC} > 1-2\varepsilon$: freeze v and freeze all its edges.

(4) Directly simulate $\log_{1/(1-\varepsilon)} \log^{20} n$ iterations of Central-Rand.

(5) Output the vector x^{MPC} as a fractional matching and the set of frozen vertices as a vertex cover.

If some vertex has weight between $1-2\varepsilon$ and 1, it has sufficiently large fractional weight, so we simply freeze it (line (j)) before the next phase.

Once the upper-bound d becomes less than $\log^{20} n$, the algorithm exits from the main while loop, and the rest of the iterations needed to simulate Central-Rand are executed one by one. During this part of the simulation, MPC-Simul and Central-Rand behave identically.

4.4 The Main Technical Lemma

In this section, we show that $|y_v - \tilde{y}_v|$ remains small for most of the vertices (this claim is formalized in Lemma 4.8). Before we provide an outline of the analysis, we state some definition and describe the notation we use.

Definition 4.2 (Bad and good vertex). *We say that vertex is* bad *if it gets frozen in Central-Rand and not in MPC-Simul (or the other way around). Once bad, the vertex remains bad throughout the whole phase. If a vertex is not bad, we say it is* good.

Definition 4.3 (Local neighbor). *If a neighbor u of vertex v is in the given iteration of MPC-Simul on the same machine as v, then we say that u is a* local neighbor *of v.*

Notation: We use w_t to refer to the weight of active edge in the tth iteration. Let $N_A^{central}(v,t)$ (resp. $N_A^{local}(v,t)$) denote the active neighbors of v at the beginning of the tth iteration of the ideal (resp. MPC) algorithm. Similarly, we use $N^{local}(v,t)$ to denote the local neighbors of v in iteration t. If it is clear from the context which iteration we are referring to, sometimes we omit t from the notation. Throughout our proofs, we will be making claims of the following form $a = b \pm c$, which should be read as $a \in [b-c, b+c]$.

Analysis Outline: Recall that $\tilde{y}_{v,t}$ and $y_{v,t}$ represent the fractional weight of vertex v in the tth iteration of MPC-Simul and Central-Rand, respectively. From the definition, we have $y_{v,t} = y_{v,t-1} + \varepsilon w_{t-1} |N_A^{central}(v,t)|$, and similarly $\tilde{y}_{v,t} = \tilde{y}_{v,t-1} + \varepsilon w_{t-1} m |N_A^{local}(v,t)|$. To say that the algorithms stay close to each other, we upper-bound $|y_{v,t} - \tilde{y}_{v,t}|$ inductively as a function of t. Suppose that we already have an upper bound on $|y_{v,t-1} - \tilde{y}_{v,t-1}|$; we focus on upper-bounding the difference between $|N_A^{central}(v,t)|$ and $m|N_A^{local}(v,t)|$. There are two sources of difference between $|N_A^{central}(v,t)|$ and $m|N_A^{local}(v,t)|$:

(1) Some of the neighbors of v might be bad. Notice that this also implies that in general the set $N_A^{local}(v,t)$ might not even be a subset of $N_A^{central}(v,t)$.
(2) Even in the very first iteration (or more generally even if there is no bad vertex in $N_A^{local}(v,t)$), the set $N_A^{local}(v,t)$ is a random sample of $N_A^{central}(v,t)$ and hence $|N_A^{local}(v,t)|$ might deviate from its expectation $|N_A^{central}(v,t)|/m$.

Furthermore, in our analysis, we assume that at the beginning of each phase MPC-Simul and Central-Rand start from the same fractional matching. Namely, we compare MPC-Simul to the behavior of Central-Rand assuming that initially x equals x^{MPC}, for the value of x^{MPC} at the beginning of a given phase. Since we ensure that x^{MPC} is at the beginning of a phase always a valid fractional matching, Central-Rand in our approach will also maintain a valid fractional matching.

Also, we assume that the thresholds, i.e., $\mathcal{T}_{v,t}$ for each $v \in V$ and each iteration t, are the same for both MPC-Simul and Central-Rand. Note that the latter algorithm is only a hypothetical one, whose purpose is to compare our simulation to a process that constructs a fractional matching, so this assumption is made without loss of generality.

Analysis:

The following claim is a direct consequence of choosing the thresholds randomly at each iteration.

Lemma 4.4. *Consider the tth iteration of a phase. Let $|y_{v,t} - \tilde{y}_{v,t}| \le \sigma$ for every vertex v that is active in both Central-Rand and MPC-Simul. Then, v becomes bad in the tth iteration with probability at most ε/σ and independently of other vertices.*

Proof. If $|\tilde{y}_{v,t} - \mathcal{T}_{v,t}| > \sigma$, then the algorithms MPC-Simul and Central-Rand would behave the same with respect to vertex v. Since $\mathcal{T}_{v,t}$ is chosen uniformly at random within interval of size 2ε, MPC-Simul and Central-Rand would differ in iteration t with respect to v with probability at most $2\sigma/(2\varepsilon) = \sigma/\varepsilon$. Furthermore, as $\mathcal{T}_{v,t}$ is chosen independently of other vertices, v becomes bad independently of other vertices. □

There are two distinct steps where MPC-Simul directly or indirectly estimates y. The first one is computing $\tilde{y}$, which is used to deduce whether a vertex should be frozen or not. The second one corresponds to the actual weight that MPC-Simul assigns to the vertices. Namely, at the end of a phase, weight is assigned to each edge (line (g)) – for edge $e = \{u,v\}$, if u or v is frozen, then it is set $x_e^{MPC} = w_t$, where t is the iteration when the first of the two vertices got frozen; otherwise, $x_e^{MPC} = w_t$ for t being the most recent simulated iteration. Then, the weight of a vertex v, that we denote by y_v^{MPC}, is simply the sum of all x_e^{MPC} incident to v. This can be seen as an indirect estimate of y_v.

Our next goal is to understand how does the estimate $\tilde{y}_v$ and simulated vertex weight y_v^{MPC} relate to y_v. To that end, we define the notion to capture the difference in how the weights y_v and y_v^{MPC} are composed.

Definition 4.5 (Weight-difference). *We use $\text{diff}(v,t)$ to denote the total weight of the edges that contributed to the weight of $y_{v,t}$ and not to $y_{v,t}^{MPC}$, and the other way around. Formally, let $x_{e,t}^{MPC}$ be the updated weight of edge e in iteration t in MPC-Simul (updated in the sense as given by line (g) of the algorithm). Let $x_{e,t}$ be the weight of edge e in iteration t in Central-Rand. Then,*

$$\text{diff}(v,t) := \sum_{e \in N(v)} \left| x_{e,t} - x_{e,t}^{MPC} \right|.$$

Notice that $\left|y_{v,t} - y_{v,t}^{MPC}\right| \le \text{diff}(v,t)$. In general it might be the case that $\left|y_{v,t} - y_{v,t}^{MPC}\right| < \text{diff}(v,t)$. For instance, consider two edges e_1 and e_2 both incident to v. Assume that in Central-Rand e_1 is active, while e_2 is frozen. On the other hand, assume that in MPC-Simul it is the case that e_1 is frozen while e_2 active. So, these two edges alone do not make any difference in the change of the weight of $y_{v,t}$ and $y_{v,t}^{MPC}$ – their effect cancels out. However, their effect does not cancel each other in the definition of $\text{diff}(v,t)$.

As a first step, we state the following lemma that shows that y_v is close to y_v^{MPC} in the first iteration of some phase. Its proof is deferred to the full version.

Lemma 4.6. *Let iteration $t^\star$ be the first iteration of some phase, and let v be an active vertex by iteration $t^\star$. Then, w.h.p.*

$$|y_{v,t^\star} - \tilde{y}_{v,t^\star}| \le m^{-0.2}.$$

Furthermore, $\text{diff}(v,t^\star) = 0$ with certainty.

We now prove our main technical lemma, which quantifies the increase in the difference between y_v and its estimates $\tilde{y}_v$ and y_v^{MPC} over the course of one phase.

Lemma 4.7 (Evolution of weight-estimates). *Let v be an active vertex in iteration $t-1$ in both Central-Rand and MPC-Simul. Then, if $|y_{v,t-1} - \tilde{y}_{v,t-1}| \le \sigma$ and $\text{diff}(v,t) \le \sigma$, the following holds w.h.p.:*

- $|y_{v,t} - \tilde{y}_{v,t}| \le 4(\sigma + \varepsilon m^{-0.2})$, *and*
- $\text{diff}(v,t) \le 4(\sigma + \varepsilon m^{-0.2})$.

PROOF. We proceed by upper-bounding the effect of three different kinds of vertices on $|y_{v,t} - \tilde{y}_{v,t}|$: bad vertices prior to the tth iteration; vertices becoming bad in the tth iteration; and, the effect of the random partitioning. Observe that diff(v, t) is *not directly* affected by the random partitioning.

Old bad vertices.: Let $B_{v,t-1}$ be the set of bad vertices prior to the beginning of the tth iteration that are also local neighbors of v. The set $B_{v,t-1}$ accounts for the vertices $N_A^{local}(v, t-1) \setminus N_A^{central}(v, t-1)$, and for the local neighbors of v that are in $N_A^{central}(v, t-1)$ but not in $N_A^{local}(v, t-1)$. Since their weight was bounded by σ in the $(t-1)^{th}$, then their weight is bounded by $(1+\varepsilon)\sigma$ in the tth iteration. Hence, from iteration $t-1$ to iteration t, the effect of the old bad vertices increased by $\varepsilon\sigma$.

In a similar way, by defining $B_{v,t-1}$ to be the set of bad neighbors of v across *all* the machines, we get that from iteration $t-1$ to iteration t the effect of the old bad vertices on diff(v, t) increased by $\varepsilon\sigma$.

New bad vertices.: In addition to the bad vertices in $B_{v,t-1}$, there might be new bad vertices in the beginning of the tth iteration – the vertices of $N_A^{local}(v, t-1) \cap N_A^{central}(v, t-1)$ that are not in $N_A^{local}(v, t) \cap N_A^{central}(v, t)$. To bound the weight of those bad vertices, we first upper-bound the cardinality of $N_A^{local}(v, t-1) \cap N_A^{central}(v, t-1)$. For the sake of brevity, define

$$n_{v,t-1}^{local} := |N^{local}(v, t-1) \cap N_A^{central}(v, t-1)|$$

where, as a reminder, the set $N^{local}(v, t-1)$ refers to the local neighbors (both frozen and active) of v. We trivially have

$$|N_A^{local}(v, t-1) \cap N_A^{central}(v, t-1)| \le n_{v,t-1}^{local}.$$

Then, by Lemma 4.4, the number of new bad vertices is in expectation at most $n_{v,t-1}^{local}\sigma/\varepsilon$. We now proceed by providing a sharp concentration around this expected value. To that end, we provide an upper-bound on $n_{v,t-1}^{local}$ that holds w.h.p.

Observe that $N_A^{central}(v, t-1)$ is defined deterministically and independently of the MPC algorithm. Then, if $|N_A^{central}(v, t-1)| \ge m^{1.6}$, we have that w.h.p. $n_{v,t-1}^{local} \le (1+m^{-0.2})|N_A^{central}(v, t-1)|/m$. Otherwise, if $|N_A^{central}(v, t-1)| < m^{1.6}$, then w.h.p. $n_{v,t-1}^{local} \le 2m^{0.6}$. Therefore, for $\gamma := \max\{(1+m^{-0.2})|N_A^{central}(v, t-1)|, 2m^{1.6}\}$, we have the w.h.p.

$$m \cdot n_{v,t-1}^{local} \le \gamma.$$

Applying similar reasoning about $n_{v,t-1}^{local}\sigma/\varepsilon$, i.e., considering cases $n_{v,t-1}^{local}\sigma/\varepsilon \ge m^{0.6}$ and $n_{v,t-1}^{local}\sigma/\varepsilon < m^{0.6}$, we obtain that w.h.p. the number of new bad vertices is upper-bounded by $\max\{(1+m^{-0.2})n_{v,-1}^{local}\sigma/\varepsilon, 2m^{0.6}\}$. So, putting all together, we have that the weight coming from new bad vertices that affects the local estimate of $y_{v,t}$ is at most

$$\sigma_2 := \varepsilon w_{t-1} \cdot \max\{(1+m^{-0.2})\gamma\sigma/\varepsilon, 2m^{1.6}\}.$$

But now, using that $w_{t-1} \le m^{-1.8}$ and also that $|N_A^{central}(v, t-1)|w_{t-1} \le 1$ as v is a active vertex in CENTRAL-RAND, we derive $\sigma_2 \le 2(\sigma + \varepsilon m^{-0.2})$.

It remains to comment about the effect of new bad vertices on diff(v, t). Note that the expected number of new bad vertices affecting diff(v, t) is at most $|N_A^{central}(v, t-1)|\sigma/\varepsilon$. So, applying the same arguments as above, the weight of new bad vertices affects diff(v, t) by at most σ_2 w.h.p.

Effect of random partitioning.: Finally, we upper-bound the effect of the random partitioning on the estimate $\tilde{y}_{v,t}$. Similarly to our arguments given earlier, we have that w.h.p. the number of vertices of $N_A^{central}(v, t)$ that are local neighbors of v deviates from $|N_A^{central}(v, t)|/m$ by at most η defined as

$$\eta := \max\{m^{-0.2}|N_A^{central}(v, t)|, m^{1.6}\}/m.$$

The total weight of these vertices scaled by m is at most $\varepsilon w_{t-1} m\eta \le \varepsilon m^{-0.2}$.

Final step: Putting altogether, if

$$|y_{v,t-1} - \tilde{y}_{v,t-1}| \le \sigma$$

and

$$\left|y_{v,t-1} - y_{v,t-1}^{MPC}\right| \le \sigma,$$

then we have

$$\begin{aligned} |y_{v,t} - \tilde{y}_{v,t}| &\le (1+\varepsilon)\sigma + 2(\sigma + \varepsilon m^{-0.2}) + \varepsilon m^{-0.2} \\ &\le 4(\sigma + \varepsilon m^{-0.2}), \end{aligned}$$

and similarly

$$\text{diff}(v, t) \le (1+\varepsilon)\sigma + 2(\sigma + \varepsilon m^{-0.2}) \le 4(\sigma + \varepsilon m^{-0.2}),$$

as desired. □

Now, combining Lemma 4.6 and Lemma 4.7, it is not hard to show our main technical result.

Lemma 4.8. *Let v be an active vertex in iteration $t-1$ in both MPC-SIMUL and CENTRAL-RAND. If a phase consists of at most $I := (\log m)/(10 \log 5)$ iterations, then it holds $|y_{v,t} - \tilde{y}_{v,t}| \le m^{-0.1}$ and diff$(v, t) \le m^{-0.1}$ w.h.p.*

Acknowledgments

We thank anonymous reviewers for their valuable feedback. S.M. is grateful to his co-authors for the previous collaboration in [15] that was the starting point of this project. R.R. was supported by NSF award numbers CCF-1650733, CCF-1733808, CCF-1740751, IIS-1741137 and Israel Science Foundation Grant 1147/09. Most of the work on this paper has been carried out while C.K. was at the University of Warwick, where he was supported by the Centre for Discrete Mathematics and its Applications (DIMAP) and by EPSRC award EP/N011163/1. Part of this work has been carried out while S.M. was visiting MIT.

REFERENCES

[1] Kook Jin Ahn, Graham Cormode, Sudipto Guha, Andrew McGregor, and Anthony Wirth. 2015. Correlation Clustering in Data Streams. In *Proceedings of the 32Nd International Conference on International Conference on Machine Learning - Volume 37 (ICML'15)*. JMLR.org, 2237–2246. http://dl.acm.org/citation.cfm?id=3045118.3045356

[2] Kook Jin Ahn and Sudipto Guha. 2015. Access to Data and Number of Iterations: Dual Primal Algorithms for Maximum Matching under Resource Constraints. In *Proceedings of the 27th ACM on Symposium on Parallelism in Algorithms and Architectures, SPAA 2015, Portland, OR, USA, June 13–15, 2015.* 202–211. https://doi.org/10.1145/2755573.2755586

[3] Noga Alon, László Babai, and Alon Itai. 1986. A Fast and Simple Randomized Parallel Algorithm for the Maximal Independent Set Problem. *Journal of Algorithms* 7, 4 (1986), 567–583. https://doi.org/10.1016/0196-6774(86)90019-2

[4] Alexandr Andoni, Aleksandar Nikolov, Krzysztof Onak, and Grigory Yaroslavtsev. 2014. Parallel algorithms for geometric graph problems. In *Proceedings of the 46th ACM Symposium on Theory of Computing, STOC 2014, New York, NY, USA, May 31–June 3, 2014.* 574–583. https://doi.org/10.1145/2591796.2591805

[5] Sepehr Assadi. 2017. Simple Round Compression for Parallel Vertex Cover. *CoRR* abs/1709.04599 (September 2017). https://arxiv.org/abs/1709.04599

[6] Sepehr Assadi, MohammadHossein Bateni, Aaron Bernstein, Vahab S. Mirrokni, and Cliff Stein. 2017. Coresets Meet EDCS: Algorithms for Matching and Vertex Cover on Massive Graphs. *CoRR* abs/1711.03076 (2017). arXiv:1711.03076 http://arxiv.org/abs/1711.03076

[7] Sepehr Assadi and Sanjeev Khanna. 2017. Randomized Composable Coresets for Matching and Vertex Cover. In *Proceedings of the 29th ACM Symposium on Parallelism in Algorithms and Architectures, SPAA 2017, Washington DC, USA, July 24–26, 2017.* 3–12. https://doi.org/10.1145/3087556.3087581

[8] Leonid Barenboim, Michael Elkin, Seth Pettie, and Johannes Schneider. 2012. The locality of distributed symmetry breaking. In *Foundations of Computer Science (FOCS) 2012.* IEEE, 321–330.

[9] Paul Beame, Paraschos Koutris, and Dan Suciu. 2013. Communication steps for parallel query processing. In *Proceedings of the 32nd ACM SIGMOD-SIGACT-SIGART Symposium on Principles of Database Systems, PODS 2013, New York, NY, USA, June 22–27, 2013.* 273–284. https://doi.org/10.1145/2463664.2465224

[10] Florent Becker, Antonio Fernandez Anta, Ivan Rapaport, and Eric Reémila. 2015. Brief Announcement: A Hierarchy of Congested Clique Models, from Broadcast to Unicast. In *the Proc. of the Int'l Symp. on Princ. of Dist. Comp. (PODC) (PODC '15).* ACM, 167–169.

[11] Andrew Berns, James Hegeman, and Sriram V Pemmaraju. 2012. Super-fast distributed algorithms for metric facility location. In *the Pro. of the Int'l Colloquium on Automata, Languages and Programming (ICALP).* 428–439.

[12] Guy E Blelloch, Jeremy T Fineman, and Julian Shun. 2012. Greedy sequential maximal independent set and matching are parallel on average. In *Proceedings of the twenty-fourth annual ACM symposium on Parallelism in algorithms and architectures.* ACM, 308–317.

[13] Keren Censor-Hillel, Petteri Kaski, Janne H. Korhonen, Christoph Lenzen, Ami Paz, and Jukka Suomela. 2015. Algebraic Methods in the Congested Clique. In *the Proc. of the Int'l Symp. on Princ. of Dist. Comp. (PODC).* ACM, 143–152.

[14] Keren Censor-Hillel, Merav Parter, and Gregory Schwartzman. 2017. Derandomizing Local Distributed Algorithms under Bandwidth Restrictions. In *31 International Symposium on Distributed Computing.*

[15] Artur Czumaj, Jakub Łacki, Aleksander Mądry, Slobodan Mitrović, Krzysztof Onak, and Piotr Sankowski. 2018. Round Compression for Parallel Matching Algorithms. *STOC* (2018).

[16] Jeffrey Dean and Sanjay Ghemawat. 2004. MapReduce: Simplified Data Processing on Large Clusters. In *Proceedings of the 6th Conference on Symposium on Opearting Systems Design & Implementation, Volume 6 (OSDI'04).* USENIX Association, Berkeley, CA, USA, 10–10. http://dl.acm.org/citation.cfm?id=1251254.1251264

[17] Danny Dolev, Christoph Lenzen, and Shir Peled. 2012. "Tri, Tri Again": Finding Triangles and Small Subgraphs in a Distributed Setting. In *Distributed Computing.* Springer, 195–209.

[18] Andrew Drucker, Fabian Kuhn, and Rotem Oshman. 2014. On the Power of the Congested Clique Model. In *the Proc. of the Int'l Symp. on Princ. of Dist. Comp. (PODC).* ACM, 367–376.

[19] Manuela Fischer and Andreas Noever. 2018. Tight Analysis of Parallel Randomized Greedy MIS. In *Proceedings of the Twenty-Ninth Annual ACM-SIAM Symposium on Discrete Algorithms.* SIAM, 2152–2160.

[20] Mohsen Ghaffari. 2016. An Improved Distributed Algorithm for Maximal Independent Set. In *Pro. of ACM-SIAM Symp. on Disc. Alg. (SODA).*

[21] Mohsen Ghaffari. 2017. Distributed MIS via All-to-All Communication. In *Proceedings of the ACM Symposium on Principles of Distributed Computing.* ACM, 141–149.

[22] Mohsen Ghaffari and Merav Parter. 2016. MST in Log-Star Rounds of Congested Clique. In *the Proc. of the Int'l Symp. on Princ. of Dist. Comp. (PODC).*

[23] Michael T. Goodrich, Nodari Sitchinava, and Qin Zhang. 2011. Sorting, searching, and simulation in the MapReduce framework. In *International Symposium on Algorithms and Computation.* Springer, 374–383.

[24] James W. Hegeman, Gopal Pandurangan, Sriram V. Pemmaraju, Vivek B. Sardeshmukh, and Michele Scquizzato. 2015. Toward Optimal Bounds in the Congested Clique: Graph Connectivity and MST. In *the Proc. of the Int'l Symp. on Princ. of Dist. Comp. (PODC).* ACM, 91–100.

[25] James W Hegeman and Sriram V Pemmaraju. 2014. Lessons from the congested clique applied to MapReduce. In *the Proceedings of the International Colloquium on Structural Information and Communication Complexity.* Springer, 149–164.

[26] James W Hegeman, Sriram V Pemmaraju, and Vivek B Sardeshmukh. 2014. Near-constant-time distributed algorithms on a congested clique. In *Proc. of the Int'l Symp. on Dist. Comp. (DISC).* Springer, 514–530.

[27] Monika Henzinger, Sebastian Krinninger, and Danupon Nanongkai. 2016. A deterministic almost-tight distributed algorithm for approximating single-source shortest paths. In *Proceedings of the 48th Annual ACM SIGACT Symposium on Theory of Computing.* ACM, 489–498.

[28] Michael Isard, Mihai Budiu, Yuan Yu, Andrew Birrell, and Dennis Fetterly. 2007. Dryad: Distributed Data-parallel Programs from Sequential Building Blocks. *SIGOPS Operating Systems Review* 41, 3 (March 2007), 59–72. https://doi.org/10.1145/1272998.1273005

[29] Amos Israeli and Alon Itai. 1986. A Fast and Simple Randomized Parallel Algorithm for Maximal Matching. *Inform. Process. Lett.* 22, 2 (1986), 77–80. https://doi.org/10.1016/0020-0190(86)90144-4

[30] Amos Israeli and Yossi Shiloach. 1986. An Improved Parallel Algorithm for Maximal Matching. *Inform. Process. Lett.* 22, 2 (1986), 57–60. https://doi.org/10.1016/0020-0190(86)90141-9

[31] Tomasz Jurdziński and Krzysztof Nowicki. 2018. MST in O (1) Rounds of Congested Clique. In *Proceedings of the Twenty-Ninth Annual ACM-SIAM Symposium on Discrete Algorithms.* SIAM, 2620–2632.

[32] Howard J. Karloff, Siddharth Suri, and Sergei Vassilvitskii. 2010. A Model of Computation for MapReduce. In *Proceedings of the 21st Annual ACM-SIAM Symposium on Discrete Algorithms, SODA 2010, Austin, Texas, USA, January 17–19, 2010.* 938–948. https://doi.org/10.1137/1.9781611973075.76

[33] Janne H Korhonen. 2016. Deterministic MST Sparsification in the Congested Clique. *arXiv preprint arXiv:1605.02022* (2016).

[34] Silvio Lattanzi, Benjamin Moseley, Siddharth Suri, and Sergei Vassilvitskii. 2011. Filtering: a method for solving graph problems in MapReduce. In *Proceedings of the 23rd Annual ACM Symposium on Parallelism in Algorithms and Architectures, SPAA 2011, San Jose, CA, USA, June 4–6, 2011.* 85–94. https://doi.org/10.1145/1989493.1989505

[35] Christoph Lenzen. 2013. Optimal deterministic routing and sorting on the congested clique. In *the Proc. of the Int'l Symp. on Princ. of Dist. Comp. (PODC).* 42–50.

[36] Nathan Linial. 1987. Distributive graph algorithms Global solutions from local data. In *Proc. of the Symp. on Found. of Comp. Sci. (FOCS).* IEEE, 331–335.

[37] Zvi Lotker, Boaz Patt-Shamir, and Adi Rosén. 2009. Distributed approximate matching. *SIAM J. Comput.* 39, 2 (2009), 445–460.

[38] Zvi Lotker, Elan Pavlov, Boaz Patt-Shamir, and David Peleg. 2003. MST construction in O(log log n) communication rounds. In *the Proceedings of the Symposium on Parallel Algorithms and Architectures.* ACM, 94–100.

[39] Michael Luby. 1986. A Simple Parallel Algorithm for the Maximal Independent Set Problem. *SIAM J. Comput.* 15, 4 (1986), 1036–1053. https://doi.org/10.1137/0215074

[40] Andrew McGregor. 2005. Finding Graph Matchings in Data Streams. In *Approximation, Randomization and Combinatorial Optimization, Algorithms and Techniques, 8th International Workshop on Approximation Algorithms for Combinatorial Optimization Problems, APPROX 2005 and 9th InternationalWorkshop on Randomization and Computation, RANDOM 2005, Berkeley, CA, USA, August 22-24, 2005, Proceedings.* 170–181. https://doi.org/10.1007/11538462_15

[41] Danupon Nanongkai. 2014. Distributed Approximation Algorithms for Weighted Shortest Paths. In *Proc. of the Symp. on Theory of Comp. (STOC).*

[42] Boaz Patt-Shamir and Marat Teplitsky. 2011. The round complexity of distributed sorting. In *the Proc. of the Int'l Symp. on Princ. of Dist. Comp. (PODC).* 249–256.

[43] Tom White. 2012. *Hadoop: The Definitive Guide.* O'Reilly Media, Inc.

[44] Matei Zaharia, Mosharaf Chowdhury, Michael J. Franklin, Scott Shenker, and Ion Stoica. 2010. Spark: Cluster Computing with Working Sets. In *2nd USENIX Workshop on Hot Topics in Cloud Computing, HotCloud'10, Boston, MA, USA, June 22.* https://www.usenix.org/conference/hotcloud-10/spark-cluster-computing-working-sets

Distributed Spanner Approximation*†

Keren Censor-Hillel
Technion, Department of Computer Science
Haifa, Israel
ckeren@cs.technion.ac.il

Michal Dory
Technion, Department of Computer Science
Haifa, Israel
smichald@cs.technion.ac.il

ABSTRACT

We address the fundamental network design problem of constructing approximate minimum spanners. Our contributions are for the distributed setting, providing both algorithmic and hardness results.

Our main hardness result is that an α-approximation for the minimum directed k-spanner problem for $k \geq 5$ requires $\Omega(n/\sqrt{\alpha}\log n)$ rounds using deterministic algorithms or $\Omega(\sqrt{n}/\sqrt{\alpha}\log n)$ rounds using randomized ones, in the Congest model of distributed computing. Combined with the constant-round $O(n^{\epsilon})$-approximation algorithm in the Local model of [Barenboim, Elkin and Gavoille, 2016], as well as a polylog-round $(1+\epsilon)$-approximation algorithm in the Local model that we show here, our lower bounds for the Congest model imply a strict separation between the Local and Congest models. Notably, to the best of our knowledge, this is the first separation between these models for a *local approximation problem.*

Similarly, a separation between the directed and undirected cases is implied. We also prove a nearly-linear lower bound for the minimum weighted k-spanner problem for $k \geq 4$, and we show lower bounds for the weighted 2-spanner problem.

On the algorithmic side, apart from the aforementioned $(1+\epsilon)$-approximation algorithm for minimum k-spanners, our main contribution is a new distributed construction of minimum 2-spanners that uses only polynomial local computations. Our algorithm has a guaranteed approximation ratio of $O(\log(m/n))$ for a graph with n vertices and m edges, which matches the best known ratio for polynomial time sequential algorithms [Kortsarz and Peleg, 1994], and is tight if we restrict ourselves to polynomial local computations. Our approach allows us to extend our algorithm to work also for the directed, weighted, and client-server variants of the problem. It also provides a Congest algorithm for the minimum dominating set problem, with a *guaranteed* $O(\log\Delta)$ approximation ratio.

CCS CONCEPTS

• **Mathematics of computing → Graph algorithms; Approximation algorithms;** • **Theory of computation → Distributed computing models;**

KEYWORDS

approximation algorithms; distributed network design; spanners; hardness of approximation

ACM Reference Format:
Keren Censor-Hillel and Michal Dory. 2018. Distributed Spanner Approximation. In *PODC '18: ACM Symposium on Principles of Distributed Computing, July 23–27, 2018, Egham, United Kingdom.* ACM, New York, NY, USA, 10 pages. https://doi.org/10.1145/3212734.3212758

1 INTRODUCTION

A *k-spanner* of a graph G is a sparse subgraph of G that preserves distances up to a multiplicative factor of k. First introduced in the late 80's [53, 54], spanners have been central for numerous applications, such as synchronization [2, 3, 54], compact routing tables [4, 14, 55, 62], distance oracles [6, 59, 63], approximate shortest paths [27, 34], and more.

Due to the prominence of spanners for many distributed applications, it is vital to have distributed algorithms for constructing them. Indeed, there are many efficient distributed algorithms for finding sparse spanners in undirected graphs, which give a *global guarantee* on the size of the spanner. A prime example are algorithms that construct $(2k-1)$-spanners with $O(n^{1+1/k})$ edges, for a graph with n vertices [7, 18, 19, 30, 40], which is optimal in the worst case assuming Erdős's *girth conjecture* [35].

As opposed to finding spanners with the best worst-case sparsity, this paper focuses on the network design problem of approximating the *minimum* k-spanner, which is a fundamental optimization problem. This is particularly crucial for cases in which the worst-case sparsity is $\Theta(n^2)$ such as 2-spanners (complete bipartite graphs) or directed spanners. Spanner approximation is at the heart of a rich line of recent work in the sequential setting, presenting approximation algorithms [8, 16, 17, 22, 24], as well as hardness of approximation results [20, 33, 44].

There are only few distributed spanner approximation algorithms known to date. A distributed algorithm with an expected approximation ratio of $O(\log n)$ for the minimum 2-spanner problem is given in [22]. This was recently extended to $k > 2$, achieving an approximation ratio of $\widetilde{O}(\sqrt{n})$ for directed k-spanners [23], which matches the best approximation known in the sequential setting [8]. Yet, in the distributed setting, it is possible to obtain better approximations if local computation is not polynomially bounded. A *constant time* $O(n^{\epsilon})$-approximation algorithm for directed or undirected minimum k-spanner, which takes $exp(O(1/\epsilon))+O(k)$ rounds for any constant $\epsilon > 0$ and a positive integer k, is given in [5]. In addition, we show a polylogarithmic time $(1+\epsilon)$-approximation algorithm for these problems, following the framework of a recent algorithm for covering problems [39] (see Section 5). This approximation is much better than the best approximation that can be

*The full version of the paper is available at https://arxiv.org/abs/1802.03160.
†Supported in part by the Israel Science Foundation (grant 1696/14).

PODC '18, July 23–27, 2018, Egham, United Kingdom
© 2018 Association for Computing Machinery.
ACM ISBN 978-1-4503-5795-1/18/07...$15.00
https://doi.org/10.1145/3212734.3212758

acheived in the sequential setting, due to the hardness results of [20, 33]. All these algorithms work in the classic LOCAL model of distributed computing [50], where vertices exchange messages *of unbounded size* in synchronous rounds.

A natural question is whether we can obtain good approximations efficiently also in the CONGEST model [51], where the messages exchanged are bounded by $O(\log n)$ bits. In the undirected case, efficient constructions of $(2k-1)$-spanners with $O(n^{1+1/k})$ edges in the CONGEST model [7, 30] imply $O(n^{1/k})$-approximations, since any spanner of a connected graph has at least $n-1$ edges. However, for directed graphs there are no efficient algorithms in the CONGEST model.

Our contribution in this paper is twofold. We provide the first hardness of approximation results for minimum k-spanners in the distributed setting. Our main hardness result shows that there are *no* efficient approximation algorithms for the directed k-spanner problem for $k \geq 5$ in the CONGEST model. This explains why all the current approximation algorithms for the problem require large messages, and also creates a strict separation between the directed and undirected variants of the problem, as the latter admits efficient approximations in the CONGEST model. In addition, we provide new distributed algorithms for approximating the minimum k-spanner problem and several variants in the LOCAL model. Our main algorithmic contributaion is an algorithm for minimum 2-spanners that uses only polynomial local computations and *guarantees* an approximation ratio of $O(\log \frac{m}{n})$, which matches the best known approximation for polynomial sequential algorithms [45]. On the way to obtaining our results, we develop new techniques, both algorithmically and for obtaining our lower bounds, which can potentially find use in studying various related problems.

1.1 Our contributions

Hardness of approximation. We show several negative results implying hardness of approximating various spanner problems in both the LOCAL and CONGEST models. While there are many recent hardness of approximation results for spanner problems in the sequential setting [16, 20, 33, 44], to the best of our knowledge ours are the first for the distributed setting.

(I.) Directed k-spanner for $k \geq 5$ in the CONGEST model: Perhaps our main negative result is a proof for the hardness of approximating the directed k-spanner problem for $k \geq 5$ in the CONGEST model.

THEOREM 1.1. *Any (perhaps randomized) distributed α-approximation algorithm in the CONGEST model for the directed k-spanner problem for $k \geq 5$ takes $\Omega(\frac{\sqrt{n}}{\sqrt{\alpha}\cdot\log n})$ rounds, for $1 \leq \alpha \leq \frac{n}{100}$.*

When restricting attention to deterministic algorithms, we prove a stronger lower bound of $\widetilde{\Omega}(\frac{n}{\sqrt{\alpha}})$, for any $\alpha \leq \frac{n}{c}$ for a constant $c > 1$.

For example, this gives that a constant or a polylogarithmic approximation ratio for the directed k-spanner problem in the CONGEST model requires $\widetilde{\Omega}(\sqrt{n})$ rounds using randomized algorithms or $\widetilde{\Omega}(n)$ rounds using deterministic algorithms. Even an approximation ratio of only n^{ϵ} is hard for any $0 < \epsilon < 1$. Moreover, in the deterministic case, even an approximation ratio of $\frac{n}{c}$, for appropriate values of c, requires $\widetilde{\Omega}(\sqrt{n})$ rounds. This is to be contrasted with an approximation of n, which can be obtained without any communication by taking the entire graph, since any k-spanner has at least $n-1$ edges.

LOCAL vs. CONGEST. The major implication of the above is a strict separation between the LOCAL and CONGEST models, since the former admits a constant-round $O(n^{\epsilon})$-approximation algorithm [5][1] and a polylogarithmic $(1+\epsilon)$-approximation algorithm (see Section 5) for directed k-spanners. Such a separation was previously known only for *global problems* (problems that are subject to an $\Omega(D)$ lower bound, where D is the diameter of the graph), and for *local decision problems* (such as determining whether the graph contains a k-cycle). To the best of our knowledge, ours is the first separation for a *local approximation problem*.

Directed vs. undirected. Our lower bound also separates the undirected and directed k-spanner problems, since there are efficient algorithms in the CONGEST model for constructing $(2k-1)$-spanners with $O(n^{1+1/k})$ edges [30, 40] which imply an $O(n^{1/k})$-approximation. The best randomized algorithm for the task takes k rounds [30], and the best deterministic algorithm is a recent algorithm which takes $O(n^{1/2-1/k})$ rounds for a constant even k [40]. Achieving the same approximation for directed graphs necessitates $\widetilde{\Omega}(n^{1/2-1/2k})$ rounds using randomization, or $\widetilde{\Omega}(n^{1-1/2k})$ rounds using deterministic algorithms.

(II.) Weighted k-spanner for $k \geq 4$ in the CONGEST model: In addition to the above main result, we consider weighted k-spanners,[2] and show that any α-approximation for the weighted undirected k-spanner problem for $k \geq 4$ requires $\widetilde{\Omega}(\frac{n}{k})$ rounds, and that $\widetilde{\Omega}(n)$ rounds are needed for the weighted directed k-spanner problem.

Weighted vs. unweighted. As these lower bounds hold also for randomized algorithms, we obtain yet another separation, between the weighted and the unweighted variants of the problem, since the aforementioned k-round $(2k-1)$-spanner constructions imply an $O(n^{1/k})$ approximation for the unweighted case.

LOCAL vs. CONGEST. Since both the constant-round algorithm for approximating k-spanners within a factor of $O(n^{\epsilon})$ [5] and the $(1+\epsilon)$-approximation algorithm that we give in Section 5 are suitable for the weighted case, our hardness result for the weighted case implies the separation between the LOCAL and CONGEST models also when having weights. This holds also for the undirected weighted case.

(III.) Weighted 2-spanner in the LOCAL and CONGEST models: Finally, we show lower bounds for the weighted 2-spanner problem, which, in a nutshell, are obtained by a reduction that captures the intuition that approximating the minimum weight 2-spanner is at least as hard as approximating the minimum vertex cover (MVC). We emphasize that the reduction from the set cover problem to the unweighted 2-spanner problem given in [44] is inherently

[1] In [5], a constant time randomized algorithm for directed k-spanner is presented. However, the deterministic network decomposition presented in [5] gives a polylogarithmic deterministic approximation for directed k-spanner as well, which shows the separation also for the deterministic case.

[2] In this problem, the goal is to find a k-spanner of minimum cost. There is another variant of the weighted k-spanner problem, in which the weight of an edge represents a length. We emphasize that in our case all the edges have length 1.

sequential, by requiring the addition of a vertex that is connected to all other vertices in the graph, and hence is unsuitable for the distributed setting.

Our reduction implies that $\Omega(\frac{\log\Delta}{\log\log\Delta})$ or $\Omega(\sqrt{\frac{\log n}{\log\log n}})$ rounds are required for a logarithmic approximation ratio for weighted 2-spanner in the LOCAL model, by plugging in the lower bounds for MVC given in [47]. In addition, our reduction implies an $\widetilde{\Omega}(n^2)$ lower bound for an exact solution for weighted 2-spanner in the CONGEST model, by using the *near-quadratic* lower bound for exact MVC given recently in [12]. This is tight up to logarithmic factors since $O(n^2)$ rounds allow learning the entire graph topology and solving essentially all natural graph problems.

Distributed approximation algorithms. We show new distributed algorithms for approximating minimum k-spanners. Our main algorithmic contribution is a new algorithm for the minimum 2-spanner problem that uses only polynomial local computations. In addition, we show that if local computation is not polynomially bounded it is possible to achieve $(1+\epsilon)$-approximation for minimum k-spanners.

(I.) Distributed $(1+\epsilon)$-approximation of minimum k-spanners: In Section 5, we present $(1+\epsilon)$-approximation algorithms for spanner problems, following the framework of a recent algorithm for covering problems [39]. We show the following.

THEOREM 1.2. *There is a randomized algorithm with complexity $O(poly(\log n/\epsilon))$ in the LOCAL model that computes a $(1+\epsilon)$-approximation of the minimum k-spanner w.h.p, where k is a constant.*

The algorithm is quite general and can be adapted similarly to additional variants. Theorem 1.2 shows that although spanner problems are hard to approximate in the sequential setting, it is possible to achieve extremely strong approximations for them efficiently in the LOCAL model. This demonstrates the power of the LOCAL model. However, the algorithm is based on learning neighborhoods of polylogarithmic size and solving NP-complete problems (finding optimal spanners). It is desirable to design also algorithms that work with more realistic assumptions. We next focus on the 2-spanner problem and show a new algorithm that uses only polynomial local computations and uses the power of the LOCAL model only for learning neighborhoods of diameter 2.

(II.) Distributed approximation of minimum 2-spanners: If we restrict ourselves to polynomial local computations, the best algorithm for the minimum 2-spanner problem is the $O(\log n)$-round $O(\log n)$-approximation in expectation of Dinitz and Krauthgamer [22],[3] which solves even the more general problem of finding fault-tolerant spanners.

However, this still leaves several open questions regarding minimum 2-spanners. First, the best approximation to the problem in the sequential setting is $O(\log\frac{m}{n})$ where m is the number of edges in the graph. Can we achieve such approximation also in the distributed setting? Second, the approximation ratio holds only in expectation. Can we design an algorithm that *guarantees* the approximation ratio? Third, this algorithm requires learning neighborhoods of logarithmic radius, and hence a direct implementation of it in the CONGEST model is not efficient. Can we design a more efficient algorithm in the CONGEST model?

We design a new algorithm for the minimum 2-spanner problem, answering some of these questions. Our algorithm obtains an approximation ratio of $O(\log\frac{m}{n})$ *always*, within $O(\log n\log\Delta)$ rounds w.h.p,[4] where Δ is the maximum vertex degree, summarized as follows.

THEOREM 1.3. *There is a distributed algorithm for the minimum 2-spanner problem in the LOCAL model that guarantees an approximation ratio of $O(\log\frac{m}{n})$, and takes $O(\log n\log\Delta)$ rounds w.h.p.*

Our approximation ratio of $O(\log\frac{m}{n})$ matches that of the best approximation in the sequential setting up to a constant factor [45], and is tight if we restrict ourselves to polynomial local computations [44]. In addition, the approximation ratio of our algorithm is guaranteed, rather than only holding in expectation. This is crucial for the distributed setting since, as opposed to the sequential setting, running the algorithm several times and choosing the best solution completely blows up the complexity because learning the cost of the solution requires collecting global information. Note that although our algorithm can be converted into an algorithm with a *guaranteed* polylogarithmic time complexity and an approximation ratio that holds only in expectation, the opposite does not hold. Another feature of our algorithm is that it uses the power of the LOCAL model only for learning the 2-neighborhood of vertices. A direct implementation of our algorithm in the CONGEST model yields an overhead of $O(\Delta)$ rounds, which is efficient for small values of Δ. We address this issue further in Section 6.

(III.) Distributed approximation of additional 2-spanners: The techniques we develop for constructing and analyzing our spanner have the advantage of allowing us to easily extend our construction to the *directed, weighted* and *client-server* variants of the problem. We obtain the same approximation ratio for the directed case as in the undirected case, and for the weighted case we give an approximation ratio of $O(\log\Delta)$, both improving upon the $O(\log n)$ approximation in expectation of [22]. For the client-server 2-spanner case, which to the best of our knowledge ours is the first distributed approximation, we obtain an approximation ratio that matches that of the sequential algorithm [31].

(IV.) Distributed approximation of MDS:. Finally, our technique also gives an efficient algorithm for the minimum dominating set (MDS) problem, which obtains an approximation ratio of $O(\log\Delta)$ *always*. Our algorithm for MDS works even in the CONGEST model and takes $O(\log n\log\Delta)$ rounds w.h.p. The MDS problem has been studied extensively by the distributed computing community, with several efficient algorithms for MDS in the CONGEST obtaining an approximation ratio of $O(\log\Delta)$ in expectation [43, 47, 48]. To the best of our knowledge, our algorithm is the first that guarantees this approximation ratio always.

[3] In [22], a time complexity of $O(\log^2 n)$ rounds is claimed. However, the algorithm is based on sampling a certain decomposition $O(\log n)$ times independently, which takes $O(\log n)$ rounds each time. From the independence of the decompositions, the computations can be parallelized in the LOCAL model, achieving a time complexity of $O(\log n)$ rounds. See also [23].

[4] As standard in this setting, a high probability refers to a probability that is at least $1-\frac{1}{n^c}$ for a constant $c\geq 1$.

Roadmap: In Section 2, we present our hardness of approximation results for directed k-spanners in the CONGEST model. In Section 3, we provide hardness of approximation results for weighted 2-spanners. In Section 4, we present our algorithm for minimum 2-spanners. In Section 5, we show our $(1+\epsilon)$-approximation for minimum k-spanners. Finally, in Section 6, we discuss questions for future research. Full details and proofs appear in the full version [10].

1.2 Additional related work

Spanners have been studied extensively in the distributed setting, producing many efficient algorithms for finding sparse spanners in undirected graphs [7, 18, 19, 29, 30, 40]. These algorithms construct $(2k-1)$-spanners with $O(n^{1+1/k})$ edges for any fixed $k \geq 2$, with the fastest completing in k rounds [18, 30], which is tight [18]. Many additional works construct various non-multiplicative spanners in the distributed setting, such as [56] and the excellent overview within.

Many recent studies address spanner approximations in the sequential setting. The greedy algorithm of [45] achieves an approximation ratio of $O(\log \frac{m}{n})$ for the minimum 2-spanner problem. This was extended to the weighted, directed and client-server cases [31, 44]. Approximation algorithms for the directed k-spanner problem for $k > 2$ are given in [8, 9, 21, 24, 32], with the best approximation ratio of $O(\sqrt{n}\log n)$ for $k > 4$, and an approximation ratio of $\widetilde{O}(n^{1/3})$ for $k = 3, 4$ [8, 24]. These approximation ratios are matched by a recent distributed $O(k \log n)$-round algorithm, that uses only polynomial local computations [23]. Approximation algorithms are given also for pairwise spanners and distance preservers [16], for spanners with lowest maximum degree [15, 17, 23, 46], for fault-tolerant spanners [22, 24], and more.

Hardness of approximation results in the sequential setting give that for $k = 2$, no polynomial algorithm gives an approximation ratio better than $\Theta(\log n)$ [44], which shows that the sequential greedy algorithm is optimal. For $k > 2$, the problem is even harder. For any constant $\epsilon > 0$ and $k \geq 3$ there are no polynomial-time algorithms that approximate the k-spanner problem within a factor better than $2^{(\log^{1-\epsilon} n)/k}$ [20], or the directed k-spanner problem within a factor better than $2^{(\log^{1-\epsilon} n)}$ [33]. Similar results are known for additional variants [16, 33].

Spanner problems are closely related to covering problems such as set cover, minimum dominating set (MDS), and minimum vertex cover. Indeed, some of the ingredients of our algorithms borrow ideas from distributed and parallel algorithms for such problems. Our symmetry breaking scheme is inspired by the parallel algorithm for set cover of Rajagopalan and Vazirani [57], however, the general structure of this algorithm requires global coordination and hence is not suitable for the distributed setting. There are also several ideas inspired by the distributed MDS algorithm of Jia et al. [43], such as, rounding the densities and comparing densesties in 2-neighborhoods. However, [43] breaks the symmetry between the candidates in a different way which results in an approximation ratio of $O(\log \Delta)$ in expectation. The connection between spanners to set cover is used also in [9] where they show that covering the edges of a graph by stars is also useful for approximating the directed k-spanner problem for $k > 2$.

1.3 Preliminaries

Let $G = (V, E)$ be a connected undirected graph with n vertices and maximum degree Δ. Let $S \subseteq E$ be a subset of the edges, and let $k \geq 1$. We say that an edge $e = \{u, v\}$ is *covered* by S if there is a path of length at most k between u and v in S. A *k-spanner* of G is a subgraph of G that covers all the edges of G. A k-spanner of a subgraph $G' \subseteq G$ is a subgraph of G that covers all the edges of G'. For a directed graph, we say that a directed edge $e = (u, v)$ is covered by a subset of edges S, if S includes a *directed* path of length at most k from u to v, and define a k-spanner for a directed graph accordingly.

In the *minimum k-spanner* problem the input is a connected undirected graph $G = (V, E)$ and the goal is to find the minimum size k-spanner of G. The *directed k-spanner* problem is defined accordingly, with respect to directed graphs. In the *weighted k-spanner* problem each edge e has a non-negative weight $w(e)$ and the goal is to find the k-spanner of G having minimum cost, where the cost of a spanner H is $w(H) = \sum_{e \in H} w(e)$. In the *client-server k-spanner* problem, introduced in [31], the input is a connected undirected graph $G = (V, E)$ that its edges are divided to two types: clients C and servers S (there may be edges $e \in C \cap S$), and the goal it to find the minimum size k-spanner of C that has only edges of S.

In the distributed setting, the input for the k-spanner problem is the communication graph G itself. Each vertex initially knows only the identities of its neighbors, and needs to output a subset of its edges such that the union of all outputs is a k-spanner. The communication in the network is *bidirectional*, even when solving the directed k-spanner problem.

2 HARDNESS OF APPROXIMATION IN THE CONGEST MODEL

In this section, we give a high-level description of the construction that allows us to show that approximating the *directed* k-spanner problem in the CONGEST model is hard for $k \geq 5$. Full details appear in [10].

Our proof is by a reduction from 2-party communication problems, as has been proven fruitful for various lower bounds for the CONGEST model [1, 12, 26, 37, 42, 61]. The most common usage is of set-disjointness, although other 2-party communication problems have been used as well [11, 28, 36, 52]. The main idea is to construct a dense graph G having some edges depending on the inputs of the two players, Alice and Bob, such that G has a sparse k-spanner if and only if the inputs satisfy a certain boolean predicate. Hence, a distributed algorithm for approximating k-spanners would allow the two players to solve the 2-party communication problem. This yields a lower bound for approximating k-spanners, based on known lower bounds for the communication complexity of the 2-party problem.

The prime caveat in using this framework for approximation problems is that in the above examples a modification of a single input bit has a slight influence on the graph. For example, when showing a lower bound for computing the diameter, any bit of the input affects the distance between one pair of vertices [1, 37, 42]. This is sufficient when computing some global property of the graph. Indeed, the distance between a single pair of vertices can change the diameter of the graph. The challenge in designing a construction for approximating k-spanners is that now any single bit needs to affect drastically the size of the minimum k-spanner. In more detail, any k-spanner has at least $n-1$ edges and, hence, for a meaningful lower bound for an α-approximation, any input bit must affect at least $\Omega(\alpha n)$ edges.

We manage to overcome the above challenge by constructing a graph that captures this requirement and allows a reduction from set-disjointness. The main technical ingredient is a dense component in which many edges are affected by single input bits. This component resides in its entirety within the set of vertices that is simulated by a single player of the two, thus resulting in a non-symmetric graph construction. This is crucial for our proof, as otherwise the density of this component would imply a dense cut between the two sets of vertices simulated by the players, which in turn would nullify the achievable lower bound. For having this property, we believe that our construction may give rise to follow-up lower bound constructions for additional local approximation problems. Our graph construction is designed using several parameters, which allows us to show trade-offs between the time complexity of an algorithm and its approximation ratio, and gives lower bounds even for large values of α.

2.1 The construction

We describe a graph construction that allows us to provide a reduction from set disjointness. In the set disjointness problem there are two players, Alice and Bob, that receive the input strings $a = (a_1, ..., a_N)$ and $b = (b_1, ..., b_N)$, respectively. Their goal is to decide if their input strings represent disjoint subsets of $[N]$, that is, they need to decide if there is a bit $1 \le i \le N$ such that $a_i = b_i = 1$. Solving the set disjointness problem requires exchanging $\Omega(N)$ bits, even using randomized protocols [49, 58].

Our graph construction consists of two subgraphs. The first of them depends on the inputs of Alice and Bob, such that each bit of the inputs affects the distance between a pair of vertices in the graph. The second is a complete bipartite graph D that each of its sides is divided to ℓ blocks of size β. Each of the blocks is connected to one vertex outside of D. We connect the two subgraphs in such a way that each bit i of the inputs affects β^2 edges of D, which must be added to the spanner if and only if $a_i = b_i = 1$.

Let ℓ, β be positive integers. We construct a graph $G = G(\ell, \beta)$ according to the parameters ℓ and β. Later we plug-in different values of ℓ and β in order to obtain several trade-offs. The graph $G(\ell, \beta)$ is a directed graph, with $V = X_1 \cup X_2 \cup Y_1 \cup Y_2 \cup Y_3$, where $X_1 = \{x_i^1 | 1 \le i \le \ell\} \cup \{x_i^2 | 1 \le i \le \ell\}$, $Y_1 = \{y_i^1 | 1 \le i \le \ell\} \cup \{y_i^2 | 1 \le i \le \ell\}$, $X_2 = \{x_{ij} | 1 \le i \le \ell, 1 \le j \le \beta\}$, $Y_2 = \{y_{ij} | 1 \le i \le \ell, 1 \le j \le \beta\}$, and $Y_3 = \{y_i^3 | 1 \le i \le \ell\}$. See Figure 1 for an illustration.

The set of edges consists of a matching between X_1 and Y_1 that includes all the directed edges (x_i^1, y_i^1) and (x_i^2, y_i^2), for $1 \le i \le \ell$. In addition, there is a complete bipartite graph D between the vertices of X_2 and Y_2 that includes all the directed edges (x_{ij}, y_{rs}) for $1 \le i, r \le \ell, 1 \le j, s \le \beta$. For each vertex $x_{ij} \in X_2$ there is an edge (x_{ij}, x_i^1). For each vertex $y_{ij} \in Y_2$ there is an edge (y_i^3, y_{ij}). In addition, the graph includes the edges (y_i^2, y_i^3), for $1 \le i \le \ell$.

In addition, the two input strings a, b of length ℓ^2 bits, denoted by a_{ij}, b_{ij} for $1 \le i, j \le \ell$, affect G in the following way. The edge (x_i^1, x_j^2) is in G if and only if $a_{ij} = 0$, and the edge (y_i^1, y_j^2) is in G if and only if $b_{ij} = 0$.

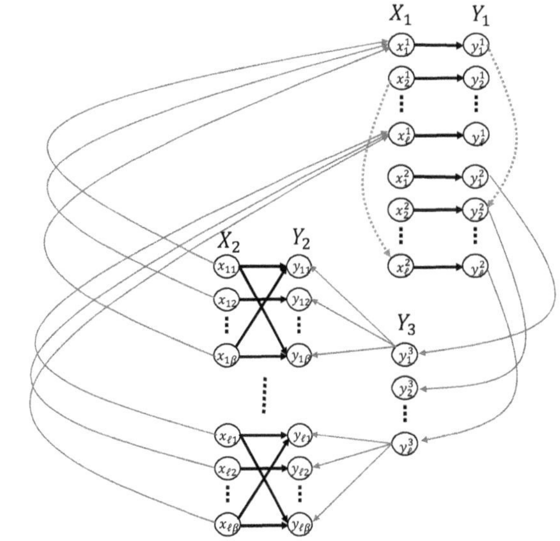

Figure 1: The graph G, with some of its edges omitted for clarity. On the left side there is a complete bipartite graph between X_2 and Y_2. The red dashed edges are examples of optional edges which depend on the input strings a and b. Note that these edges affect the distances between vertices in X_1 and Y_1. For example, the edge (y_1^1, y_2^2) creates a path of length 2 from x_1^1 to y_2^2.

Note that the number of vertices in G is $n = \Theta(\ell\beta)$, and that D consists of $(\ell\beta)^2 = \Theta(n^2)$ edges, and recall the goal of constructing a sparse k-spanner for G with $k \ge 5$. Since D is a dense subgraph, taking its edges to the spanner would be expensive. However, in order to avoid taking the edges of D to the spanner, the spanner must include a directed path of length at most k between every pair of vertices x_{ij}, y_{rs}, which does not include edges of D. The existence of such a path depends on the input strings in the following way.

Claim 2.1. *If one of the edges $(x_i^1, x_r^2), (y_i^1, y_r^2)$ is in G, there is a directed path of length 5 between the vertices x_{ij}, y_{rs} that does not contain edges of D. Otherwise, the only directed path from x_{ij} to y_{rs} is the path that consists of the edge (x_{ij}, y_{rs}).*

Proof. Note that any directed path from x_{ij} to y_{rs} that does not include the edges of D must begin with the edge (x_{ij}, x_i^1) and must end with the two edges $(y_r^2, y_r^3), (y_r^3, y_{rs})$. Hence, the existence of such a path depends on whether there is a directed path from x_i^1 to y_r^2. We show that there is a directed path of length 2 from x_i^1 to y_r^2 if at least one of the edges $(x_i^1, x_r^2), (y_i^1, y_r^2)$ is in G. Otherwise, there is no directed path of any length from x_i^1 to y_r^2.

Let P be a directed path from x_i^1 to y_r^2. The path P must cross the cut between X_1 to Y_1 either by the edge (x_i^1, y_i^1) or by the edge (x_r^2, y_r^2), since any path (of any length) from x_i^1 can only cross the cut through the edge (x_i^1, y_i^1) or by an edge of the form (x_j^2, y_j^2). However, if $j \neq r$, y_r^2 is not reachable from y_j^2. If P crosses by the edge (x_i^1, y_i^1) the only way to reach y_r^2 from y_i^1 is by the edge

(y_i^1, y_r^2). In the second case, the edge (x_i^1, x_r^2) must be the first edge in the path. This completes the proof. □

Using Claim 2.1 we can show that G has a sparse spanner if and only if the input strings a, b are disjoint.

Lemma 2.2. *Let $G = G(\ell, \beta)$ for $\beta \geq \ell$, let $k \geq 5$, and let $c = 7$. If the input strings a, b are disjoint, then there is a k-spanner of size at most $c\ell\beta$ for G. Otherwise, any k-spanner for G includes at least β^2 edges of D.*

Proof. If the input strings a, b are disjoint, then for every pair of indexes i, r at least one of the edges $(x_i^1, x_r^2), (y_i^1, y_r^2)$ is in G. Hence, by Claim 2.1, there is a directed path of length at most 5 between every two vertices x_{ij}, y_{rs}, which does not contain edges of D. This gives a 5-spanner of size at most $c\ell\beta$ edges for G by taking all the edges not in D, since there are at most $2\ell\beta + 2\ell^2 + 3\ell$ such edges, which is at most $c\ell\beta$ since $\ell \leq \beta$ and $c = 7$. This is also a k-spanner for any $k \geq 5$.

If the input strings are not disjoint, then there is a pair of indexes i, r such that neither of the edges $(x_i^1, x_r^2), (y_i^1, y_r^2)$ is in G. Hence, by Claim 2.1, there is no directed path between the vertices x_{ij}, y_{rs} except for the path that includes the edge (x_{ij}, y_{rs}). Therefore, we need to take all the edges (x_{ij}, y_{rs}) to the spanner for all values of j and s, which means adding β^2 edges of D to the spanner. □

Using Lemma 2.2, we get that if $\alpha \cdot c\ell\beta < \beta^2$, an α-approximation algorithm A for directed k-spanners for $k \geq 5$ can be used to solve set-disjointness. To solve set-disjointness, Alice and Bob simulate the algorithm A where Bob simulates all the vertices in Y_1 (note that the input string b affects only vertices in Y_1) and Alice simulates the rest of the vertices. To simulate a round of the algorithm, Alice and Bob send to each other all the messages going over the cut between them. Since Bob simulates only the vertices of Y_1 it results in a cut of size $\Theta(\ell)$. In addition, the inputs are of size $\Theta(\ell^2)$ bits, and the size of messages is $\Theta(\log n)$ bits. Since solving set-disjointness requires exchanging $\Omega(\ell^2)$ bits, the number of rounds required for A is $\Omega(\frac{\ell^2}{\ell \log n}) = \Omega(\frac{\ell}{\log n})$. Full analysis appears in [10].

To satisfy $\alpha \cdot c\ell\beta < \beta^2$, we choose $\beta^2 = \Theta(\alpha n)$ for an appropriate constant (the exact computation appears in [10]). Since the number of vertices in the graph is $n = \Theta(\ell\beta)$, we get $\ell = \Theta(n/\beta) = \Theta(\sqrt{n/\alpha})$, which completes the proof of Theorem 1.1.

Theorem 1.1. *Any (perhaps randomized) distributed α-approximation algorithm in the Congest model for the directed k-spanner problem for $k \geq 5$ takes $\Omega(\frac{\sqrt{n}}{\sqrt{\alpha} \cdot \log n})$ rounds, for $1 \leq \alpha \leq \frac{n}{100}$.*

2.2 The deterministic case

We next show that any *deterministic* algorithm solving the directed k-spanner problem for $k \geq 5$, requires $\Omega(\frac{n}{\sqrt{\alpha} \cdot \log n})$ rounds. The trick that allows a stronger lower bound is that we use a different problem from communication complexity, which we refer to as the *gap disjointness* problem. This problem is also mentioned in [36].

In the gap disjointness problem, Alice and Bob receive the input strings $a = (a_1, ..., a_N)$ and $b = (b_1, ..., b_N)$, respectively, and their goal is to distinguish whether their input strings are disjoint or are *far* from being disjoint. The inputs are far from being disjoint if there are at least $\frac{N}{12}$ indexes i, such that $a_i = b_i = 1$. If the inputs are neither disjoint nor far from being disjoint, any output of Alice and Bob is valid. The gap disjointness problem can be easily solved by randomized protocols exchanging $O(\log n)$ bits. However, solving the problem deterministically requires exchanging $\Omega(N)$ bits.

Lemma 2.3. *Solving the gap disjointness problem deterministically on input strings of size N requires exchanging $\Omega(N)$ bits.*

For a proof of Lemma 2.3, see example 5.5 in [49], where it is shown that approximating the size of the intersection $|a \cap b|$ requires exchanging $\Omega(N)$ bits. The proof relies only on showing that distinguishing between disjoint inputs and inputs with intersection of more than $\frac{N}{6}$ bits is difficult (note that any such inputs have intersection of size at least $\frac{N}{12}$). Hence, the exact same proof shows that solving gap disjointness requires exchanging $\Omega(N)$ bits using a deterministic protocol.

In order to use set disjointness for the proof of Theorem 1.1, it was necessary to devise a construction where each bit of the input affects many edges of the spanner, in order to argue that even if there is only one index i such that $a_i = b_i = 1$, then the players can correctly decide whether the inputs are disjoint by checking the size of the spanner. However, when we use gap disjointness, the players need to distinguish only between the case that the inputs are disjoint and the case that they are far from being disjoint, which allows much more flexibility and gives stronger lower bounds for the deterministic case. We believe that the flexibility of the gap-disjointness problem may be useful in showing additional strong lower bounds for approximation problems.

Lemma 2.4. *Let $G = G(\ell, \beta)$ for $1 \leq \beta \leq \ell$, let $k \geq 5$ and let $c = 7$. If the input strings a, b are disjoint, then there is a k-spanner of size at most $c\ell^2$. If the input strings are far from being disjoint, any k-spanner for G includes at least $\frac{\beta^2}{12}\ell^2$ edges of D.*

Proof. If the input strings are disjoint, taking all the edges not in D is a 5-spanner, as shown in the proof of Lemma 2.2. These are at most $2\ell\beta + 2\ell^2 + 3\ell$ edges not in D, which is at most $c\ell^2$ since $\beta \leq \ell$ and $c = 7$. This is also a k-spanner for any $k \geq 5$.

If the input strings are far from being disjoint then there are at least $\frac{\ell^2}{12}$ pairs (i, r) such that none of the edges $(x_i^1, x_r^2), (y_i^1, y_r^2)$ are in G. Hence, by Claim 2.1, there are at least $\frac{\ell^2}{12}$ pairs (i, r) such that there is no directed path between the vertices x_{ij}, y_{rs} except for the path that consists of the edge (x_{ij}, y_{rs}). For each such pair, we need to take all the directed edges (x_{ij}, y_{rs}) to the spanner for all the values of j and s, which means adding β^2 edges to the spanner. Summing over all the $\frac{\ell^2}{12}$ pairs, we get that any k-spanner must include at least $\frac{\beta^2}{12}\ell^2$ edges of D. □

According to Lemma 2.4, if $\alpha \cdot c\ell^2 < \frac{\beta^2}{12}\ell^2$, a deterministic α-approximation for directed k-spanners gives a deterministic protocol for gap disjointness. To satisfy this, we choose $\beta = \Theta(\sqrt{\alpha})$ for an appropriate constant, which gives a lower bound of $\Omega(\frac{\ell}{\log n}) = \Omega(\frac{n}{\beta \log n}) = \Omega(\frac{n}{\sqrt{\alpha} \log n})$ rounds. This completes the proof of Theorem 2.5. Full analysis appears in [10].

Theorem 2.5. *Any deterministic distributed α-approximation algorithm in the Congest model for the directed k-spanner problem* *for $k \geq 5$ takes $\Omega(\frac{n}{\sqrt{\alpha}\cdot\log n})$ rounds, for $1 \leq \alpha \leq \frac{n}{c'}$ for a constant* $c' > 1$.

2.3 The weighted case

In the full version, we extend our construction to the weighted case, showing that any approximation for the weighted k-spanner for $k \geq 4$ in the CONGEST model takes $\widetilde{\Omega}(n)$ rounds for directed graphs or $\widetilde{\Omega}(\frac{n}{k})$ for undirected graphs, even for randomized algorithms. In the weighted case, rather than guaranteeing that each input bit affects many edges of the spanner, we simply assign weight 0 to all the edges that are not in D and weight 1 to all the edges of D. Hence, taking even a single edge from D is very expensive if we can avoid it. This allows us to show a simpler construction, obtaining a stronger lower bound for the weighted case.

3 HARDNESS OF APPROXIMATION OF WEIGHTED 2-SPANNER

In the full version, we show that approximating the weighted 2-spanner problem is at least as hard as approximating the (unweighted) minimum vertex cover (MVC) problem. Here we give a high-level description of our reduction.

The main intuition is that in MVC the goal is to cover all the edges of the graph by vertices, where in the 2-spanner problem the goal is to cover all the edges by edges of the spanner. Hence, we would like to design a reduction where for every vertex v in a input graph G for MVC there is a corresponding edge e_v in a corresponding input graph G_S for minimum 2-spanner, where the edge e_v covers in G_S the same edges that v covers in G. We formalize this intuition and define the graph G_S as follows. For every vertex v in G, we add an edge $e_v = \{v_1, v_2\}$ to the graph G_S having weight 1, and we add additional two edges of weight 0 that cover e_v. For each edge e in G, we add 3 edges to G_S, one has weight 2 and the other have weight 0. (See Figure 2 for an illustration).

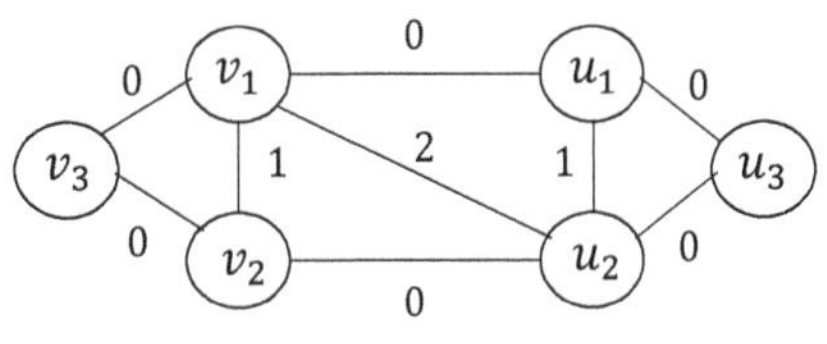

Figure 2: For each vertex $v \in G$, there is a corresponding triangle in G_S between the vertices v_1, v_2, v_3. The edge $\{v, u\} \in G$ has 3 corresponding edges in G_S: $\{v_1, u_1\}, \{v_2, u_2\}, \{v_1, u_2\}$. Note that if we add the edge $\{v_1, v_2\}$ or $\{u_1, u_2\}$ to the spanner, there is a path of length 2 that covers the edge $\{v_1, u_2\}$.

It holds that all the edges of weights 0 or 1 in G_S are covered by edges of weight 0. Hence, in order to find the minimum weight 2-spanner for G_S our goal is to cover all the edges having weight 2 optimally. We show that a vertex cover C in G gives a 2-spanner for G_S with cost $|C|$ by adding to the spanner all the edges of weight 0, and the edges $\{e_v | v \in C\}$. Similarly, we show that a 2-spanner H for G_S gives a vertex cover in G with size $w(H)$. To conclude, the cost of the minimum 2-spanner in G_S is exactly the size of the minimum vertex cover in G.

Since the reduction is local, an approximation algorithm for weighted 2-spanner in G_S can be simulated by the vertices in G, which gives an approximation algorithm for MVC. Therefore, known lower bounds for MVC translate directly to lower bounds for weighted 2-spanner. Our reduction therefore gives that $\Omega(\frac{\log \Delta}{\log\log \Delta})$ or $\Omega(\sqrt{\frac{\log n}{\log\log n}})$ rounds are required for a logarithmic approximation ratio for weighted 2-spanner in the LOCAL model, by plugging in the lower bounds for MVC given in [47]. In addition, $\widetilde{\Omega}(n^2)$ rounds are required for solving the problem *optimally* in the CONGEST model, using the lower bound for exact MVC given in [12].

4 DISTRIBUTED APPROXIMATION OF MINIMUM 2-SPANNERS

In this section we give a high-level overview of our minimum 2-spanner algorithm, full details and proofs appear in [10].

THEOREM 1.3. *There is a distributed algorithm for the minimum 2-spanner problem in the LOCAL model that guarantees an approximation ratio of $O(\log \frac{m}{n})$, and takes $O(\log n \log \Delta)$ rounds w.h.p.*

Our algorithm for approximating minimum 2-spanners is inspired by the sequential greedy algorithm of Kortsarz and Peleg [45], in which *dense stars* are added to the spanner one by one, obtaining an approximation ratio of $O(\log \frac{m}{n})$. A *star* is a subset of edges between a vertex v and *some* of its neighbors. The *density* of a star is the ratio between the number of edges *2-spanned* by the star and the size of the star, where an edge $e = \{u, v\}$ is *2-spanned* by a star S if S includes a path of length two between u and v. A roughly intuition for the greedy algorithm is that if S is a dense star then adding its edges to the spanner allows 2-spanning many edges by adding only a small number of edges to the spanner.

A direct implementation of this greedy approach in the distributed setting is highly expensive, since deciding upon the densest star inherently requires collecting global information. Moreover, one would like to leverage the ability of the distributed setting to add multiple stars to the spanner simultaneously. To address both sources of inefficiency, rather than computing the star that is the densest in the entire graph, we compute all the stars that are the densest in their local 2-neighborhood. While greatly speeding up the running time, adding all of these locally densest stars to the spanner is too extreme, and results in a poor approximation ratio. Instead, we consider these stars as *candidates* for being added to the spanner.

The key challenge is then to break symmetry among the candidates, while balancing the need to choose many stars in parallel (for a fast running time) with the need to bound the overlap in spanned edges among the candidates (for a small approximation ratio). We tackle this conflict by constructing a voting scheme for breaking symmetry by choosing among the stars based on a random permutation. Interestingly, our approach is inspired by a parallel algorithm for set cover [57]. We let each edge vote for the first candidate that 2-spans it according to the random permutation. A candidate that receives a number of votes which is at least $\frac{1}{8}$ of the edges it 2-spans is added to the spanner, and we continue this process iteratively.

Since we add to the spanner only stars receiving many votes, this approach guarantees that there is not too much overlap in the edges 2-spanned by different stars, which eventually culminates in a proof of an approximation ratio of $O(\log \frac{m}{n})$, which matches the one obtained by the greedy approach.

We next give the pseudo-code for each iteration, we need the following definitions. A *v-star* is a subset of edges between v and its neighbors. The *density* of a star S with respect to a subset of edges H, denoted by $\rho(S,H)$, equals $\frac{|C_S|}{|S|}$, where C_S is the set of edges of H *2-spanned* by the star S. The density of a vertex v with respect to H, denoted by $\rho(v,H)$, is the density of the densest v-star. The *rounded* density of a vertex v with respect to H, denoted by $\tilde{\rho}(v,H)$, is obtained by rounding $\rho(v,H)$ to the closest power of 2 that is greater than $\rho(v,H)$. The *full* v-star is the star that includes all the edges between v and its neighbors. The *2-neighborhood* of a vertex v consists of all the vertices at distance at most 2 from v.

In our algorithm, each vertex v maintains a set H_v that includes all the edges 2-spanned by the full v-star that are still not covered by the edges added to the spanner. The algorithm proceeds in iterations, where in each iteration the following is computed:

(1) Each vertex v computes its rounded density $\rho_v = \tilde{\rho}(v,H_v)$, and sends it to its 2-neighborhood.
(2) Each vertex v such that $\rho_v \geq \rho_u$ for each u in its 2-neighborhood and $\rho(v,H_v) \geq 1$ is a *candidate*. Let S_v be a v-star with density at least $\frac{\rho_v}{4}$ (The exact choice of S_v is described in [10]). Vertex v informs its neighbors about S_v. Let C_v be the edges of H_v 2-spanned by S_v.
(3) Each candidate v chooses a random number $r_v \in \{1,\dots,n^4\}$ and sends it to its neighbors.
(4) Each uncovered edge that is 2-spanned by at least one of the candidates, votes for the first candidate that 2-spans it according to the order of the values r_v.
(5) Each star S_v for which v receives at least $\frac{|C_v|}{8}$ votes from edges it 2-spans is added to the spanner.
(6) Each vertex v updates the set H_v in its 2-neighborhood by removing from it edges that are now covered.
(7) If the maximal density in the 2-neighborhood of v is at most 1, v adds to the spanner all the edges adjacent to it that are still not covered, and outputs the edges adjacent to it that were added to the spanner during the algorithm.

At the end of the algorithm all the edges are covered by spanner edges, since we add to the spanner edges that are not 2-spanned during the algorithm.

Since all the candidates have maximal rounded density in their 2-neighborhood, it follows that all the candidates that cover the same edge have the same rounded density, which is crucial in the analysis. In addition, rounding the densities guarantees that there are only $O(\log\Delta)$ possible values for the maximal rounded density, which allows us to show an efficient time complexity.

Each iteration takes constant number of rounds in the LOCAL model. For example, to calculate $\tilde{\rho}(v,H_v)$, each vertex v learns all the edges between its neighbors that are still uncovered, by having each vertex u send to its neighbors a list of its neighbors w such that the edges $\{u,w\}$ are still not covered.

We can compute the densest v-star in polynomial time as in the sequential algorithm (see Lemma 2.1 in [45]). This is the maximal density problem, that can be solved in polynomial time using flow techniques [38]. This allows us to compute the rounded density of a vertex. In [10] we explain how we choose the star S_v in polynomial time. Other computations in the algorithm are clearly polynomial.

4.1 The analysis

At a high level, to show the approximation ratio of $O(\log \frac{m}{n})$, we assign each edge $e \in E$ a value $cost(e)$ that depends on the density of the star that covers e in the algorithm, such that the sum of the costs of all edges is closely related both to the size of the spanner produced by the algorithm $|H|$ and to the size of a minimum 2-spanner $|H^*|$, by satisfying

$$|H| \leq 8\sum_{e\in E} cost(e) \leq O\left(\log\frac{m}{n}\right)|H^*|.$$

The left inequality is based on the fact the we add to the spanner only stars receiving many votes. To show the right inequity, we divide the edges to $O(\log \frac{m}{n})$ subsets according to their costs. For each subset E_i, we show that $\sum_{e\in E_i} cost(e) \leq O(|H_i^*|)$, where H_i^* is an optimal spanner for E_i. Since H^* is clearly a spanner for E_i, we get $\sum_{e\in E_i} cost(e) \leq O(|H^*|)$. Summing over all the $O(\log \frac{m}{n})$ subsets completes the proof. The approximation ratio analysis appears in [10].

A tricky obstacle lies in showing that our algorithm completes in $O(\log n \log \Delta)$ rounds w.h.p. In [43, 57], a potential function argument is given for analyzing the set cover and minimum dominating set problems that are addressed. We analyze our algorithm along a similar argument, but our algorithm necessitates a more intricate analysis. This is because, as opposed to the set cover case, there may be as many as 2^Δ different stars centered at each vertex, and a vertex may be required to add candidate stars multiple times during the execution of the algorithm. It turns out that an arbitrary choice for a candidate among all densest stars centered at a vertex is incapable of providing an efficient time complexity. To overcome this issue, we design a subtle mechanism for proposing a candidate star, and pair it with a proof that our algorithm indeed completes in the claimed number of rounds. The time analysis appears in [10].

4.2 Additional results

A compelling feature of our analysis is that it extends easily to the directed, weighted and client-server variants of the minimum 2-spanner problem. In addition, we show that our algorithm can be modified to give an efficient CONGEST algorithm for the minimum dominating set problem, *guaranteeing* an approximation ratio of $O(\log\Delta)$. The results appear in [10].

5 DISTRIBUTED $(1+\epsilon)$-APPROXIMATION FOR SPANNER PROBLEMS

In this section, we give a high-level overview of our distributed $(1+\epsilon)$-approximation algorithm for spanner problems, full details and proofs appear in [10]. The algorithm follows the framework of a recent algorithm for covering problems [39] (see Section 7).[5]

[5]The presentation of the framework in [39] is slightly different and goes through an intermediate *SLOCAL* model.

We start by describing a sequential $(1+\epsilon)$-approximation algorithm, and then explain how to implement it in the LOCAL model using network decomposition. During the algorithm we build a spanner H which is initialized to be empty. We need the following notation. For a given integer d, we denote by $B_d(v)$ the subgraph of all the vertices within distance at most d from v. For a vertex v and $d \geq 1$, let $g(v,d)$ be the size of an optimal spanner for all of the edges in $B_d(v)$ that are still not covered by edges added to H.

We process the vertices according to a given order $v_1, v_2, ..., v_n$. In step i, we look for the smallest radius r_i such that $g(v_i, r_i + 2k) \leq (1+\epsilon)g(v_i, r_i)$. Since an optimal spanner has size at most n^2, increasing the radius without the condition being met can only happen at most $r_i = O(\log n/\epsilon)$ times. We add to H an optimal spanner for all the uncovered edges in $B_{r_i+2k}(v_i)$, and mark all the edges covered by the new edges of H as covered.

Denote by E_i all the edges of $B_{r_i}(v_i)$ that are not covered before step i, and let H_i^* be the minimum set of edges in H^* that covers E_i, where H^* is an optimal spanner. From the choice of r_i, in step i we added to the spanner at most $(1+\epsilon)|H_i^*|$ edges. In addition, since all the edges of $B_{r_i+2k}(v_i)$ are covered after step i, it follows that E_i and E_j are at distance at least $2k+1$ for $i \neq j$. This shows that the subsets H_i^* are disjoint, and gives a $(1+\epsilon)$-approximation.

To implement the algorithm in the LOCAL model, the vertices invoke a network decomposition algorithm on the graph G^r, for a value of $r = O(\log n/\epsilon)$. This decomposes the graph into clusters of logarithmic diameter, colored by a logarithmic number of colors. We assign a vertex v the label (q_v, ID_v) where q_v is the color of the cluster of v and ID_v is the id of v. The lexicographic increasing order of the labels provides the order of the vertices. Now by increasing order of colors, the vertices of each color simulate the sequential algorithm for all the vertices in their cluster. They can do so, since the sequential algorithm depends only on r-neighborhoods of vertices, and every two vertices in the same r-neighborhood are neighbors in G^r, which means they are either in the same cluster or in two clusters with different colors. This guarantees that the algorithm can indeed be executed in parallel for vertices of the same color. The overall time complexity is $poly(\log n/\epsilon)$ rounds. For full details and proofs see [10].

The correctness of the algorithm relies only on the fact that the definition of k-spanners is local: an optimal spanner for $B_d(v)$ is contained in $B_{d+k}(v)$. Hence, the algorithm can be adapted similarly to the weighted, directed and client-server variants. In the weighted case the complexity is $O(poly(\log(nW)/\epsilon))$, where W is the ratio between the maximum and minimum positive weights of an edge.

6 DISCUSSION

While our results in this paper significantly advance the state-of-the-art in distributed approximation of minimum k-spanners, intriguing questions remain open.

First, the landscape of the trade-offs between the approximation ratio and the running time of distributed minimum k-spanner algorithms is yet to be fully mapped. In particular, an interesting question is to show a lower bound for approximating the undirected unweighted minimum k-spanner problem.

A curious question is whether our 2-spanner algorithm can be efficiently made to work in the CONGEST model. A direct implementation would yield an overhead of $O(\Delta)$ for the running time, for computing the densities of stars, and for sending the candidate stars. We emphasize that knowing the density of the neighborhood of vertices is crucial for additional algorithms, such as recent $(\Delta+1)$-coloring algorithms [13, 41]. Another interesting question is to design an efficient *deterministic* algorithm achieving the same approximation ratio.

For larger values of the stretch k, our lower bounds imply a strict separation between the LOCAL and CONGEST models for the number of rounds required for approximating directed minimum k-spanners. Such a separation was previously known only for *global problems* and for *local decision problems*. Interestingly, ours is the first separation for a *local approximation problem*. It is a central open question whether such separations hold also for *local symmetry breaking problems*.

Interestingly, our algorithms, as well as other distributed approximation algorithms for the minimum k-spanner in the LOCAL model, work also for directed graphs, achieving the same approximation ratio and round complexity. However, our hardness results create a strict separation between the undirected and directed variants in the CONGEST model. It will be interesting to show such separations for other problems. It is also interesting to study whether it is possible to design efficient algorithms for *roundtrip directed spanners* [60] in the distributed setting. In this problem, instead of preserving the distance between vertices, the goal is to preserve the roundtrip distance between vertices which is the sum $d(u,v)+d(v,u)$.

A compelling feature of our minimum 2-spanner algorithm is that it extends easily to additional variants, as well as to the MDS problem. Recently, we showed that the same approach also gives an efficient algorithm for the minimum 2-edge-connected spanning subgraph problem [25], which is a *global* covering problem. We believe that this approach may be useful for many additional local or global problems, especially in scenarios where it is important to *guarantee* the approximation.

Acknowledgment: We would like to thank Seri Khoury for fruitful discussions.

REFERENCES

[1] Amir Abboud, Keren Censor-Hillel, and Seri Khoury. 2016. Near-Linear Lower Bounds for Distributed Distance Computations, Even in Sparse Networks. In *Proceedings of the 30th International Symposium on Distributed Computing (DISC)*. 29–42.

[2] Baruch Awerbuch, Boaz Patt-Shamir, David Peleg, and Michael Saks. 1992. Adapting to asynchronous dynamic networks. In *Proceedings of the twenty-fourth annual ACM symposium on Theory of computing (STOC)*. 557–570.

[3] Baruch Awerbuch and David Peleg. 1990. Network synchronization with polylogarithmic overhead. In *Proceedings of the 31st Annual Symposium on Foundations of Computer Science (FOCS)*. 514–522.

[4] Baruch Awerbuch and David Peleg. 1992. Routing with polynomial communication-space trade-off. *SIAM Journal on Discrete Mathematics* 5, 2 (1992), 151–162.

[5] Leonid Barenboim, Michael Elkin, and Cyril Gavoille. 2016. A fast network-decomposition algorithm and its applications to constant-time distributed computation. *Theoretical Computer Science* (2016).

[6] Surender Baswana and Sandeep Sen. 2006. Approximate distance oracles for unweighted graphs in expected $O(n^2)$ time. *ACM Transactions on Algorithms (TALG)* 2, 4 (2006), 557–577.

[7] Surender Baswana and Sandeep Sen. 2007. A simple and linear time randomized algorithm for computing sparse spanners in weighted graphs. *Random Structures & Algorithms* 30, 4 (2007), 532–563.

[8] Piotr Berman, Arnab Bhattacharyya, Konstantin Makarychev, Sofya Raskhodnikova, and Grigory Yaroslavtsev. 2013. Approximation algorithms for spanner problems and directed steiner forest. *Information and Computation* 222 (2013), 93–107.

[9] Piotr Berman, Sofya Raskhodnikova, and Ge Ruan. 2010. Finding Sparser Directed Spanners. In *IARCS Annual Conference on Foundations of Software Technology and Theoretical Computer Science (FSTTCS)*. 424–435.

[10] Keren Censor-Hillel and Michal Dory. 2018. Distributed Spanner Approximation. *arXiv:1802.03160* (2018). https://arxiv.org/abs/1802.03160

[11] Keren Censor-Hillel, Telikepalli Kavitha, Ami Paz, and Amir Yehudayoff. 2016. Distributed construction of purely additive spanners. In *International Symposium on Distributed Computing (DISC)*. 129–142.

[12] Keren Censor-Hillel, Seri Khoury, and Ami Paz. 2017. Quadratic and Near-Quadratic Lower Bounds for the CONGEST Model. In *31st International Symposium on Distributed Computing, DISC 2017, October 16-20, 2017, Vienna, Austria*. 10:1–10:16. https://doi.org/10.4230/LIPIcs.DISC.2017.10

[13] Yi-Jun Chang, Wenzheng Li, and Seth Pettie. 2018. An Optimal Distributed (Δ+1)-Coloring Algorithm? *To appear in STOC 2018* (2018). arXiv:1711.01361

[14] Shiri Chechik. 2013. Compact routing schemes with improved stretch. In *Proceedings of the 2013 ACM symposium on Principles of distributed computing (PODC)*. 33–41.

[15] Eden Chlamtác and Michael Dinitz. 2014. Lowest Degree k-Spanner: Approximation and Hardness. In *Approximation, Randomization, and Combinatorial Optimization. Algorithms and Techniques (APPROX/RANDOM)*. 80–95.

[16] Eden Chlamtáč, Michael Dinitz, Guy Kortsarz, and Bundit Laekhanukit. 2017. Approximating spanners and directed steiner forest: Upper and lower bounds. In *Proceedings of the Twenty-Eighth Annual ACM-SIAM Symposium on Discrete Algorithms (SODA)*. 534–553.

[17] Eden Chlamtac, Michael Dinitz, and Robert Krauthgamer. 2012. Everywhere-sparse spanners via dense subgraphs. In *IEEE 53rd Annual Symposium on Foundations of Computer Science (FOCS)*. 758–767.

[18] Bilel Derbel, Cyril Gavoille, David Peleg, and Laurent Viennot. 2008. On the locality of distributed sparse spanner construction. In *Proceedings of the twenty-seventh ACM symposium on Principles of distributed computing (PODC)*. 273–282.

[19] Bilel Derbel, Mohamed Mosbah, and Akka Zemmari. 2010. Sublinear fully distributed partition with applications. *Theory of Computing Systems* 47, 2 (2010), 368–404.

[20] Michael Dinitz, Guy Kortsarz, and Ran Raz. 2016. Label cover instances with large girth and the hardness of approximating basic k-spanner. *ACM Transactions on Algorithms (TALG)* 12, 2 (2016), 25.

[21] Michael Dinitz and Robert Krauthgamer. 2011. Directed spanners via flow-based linear programs. In *Proceedings of the forty-third annual ACM symposium on Theory of computing (STOC)*. 323–332.

[22] Michael Dinitz and Robert Krauthgamer. 2011. Fault-tolerant spanners: better and simpler. In *Proceedings of the 30th annual ACM SIGACT-SIGOPS symposium on Principles of distributed computing (PODC)*. 169–178.

[23] Michael Dinitz and Yasamin Nazari. 2017. Distributed Distance-Bounded Network Design Through Distributed Convex Programming. In *21st International Conference on Principles of Distributed Systems, OPODIS 2017*. 5:1–5:19.

[24] Michael Dinitz and Zeyu Zhang. 2016. Approximating low-stretch spanners. In *Proceedings of the Twenty-Seventh Annual ACM-SIAM Symposium on Discrete Algorithms (SODA)*. 821–840.

[25] Michal Dory. 2018. Distributed Approximation of Minimum k-edge-connected Spanning Subgraphs. *To appear in PODC 2018* (2018). http://arxiv.org/abs/1805.07764

[26] Andrew Drucker, Fabian Kuhn, and Rotem Oshman. 2014. On the power of the congested clique model. In *Proceedings of the 2014 ACM symposium on Principles of distributed computing (PODC)*. 367–376.

[27] Michael Elkin. 2005. Computing almost shortest paths. *ACM Transactions on Algorithms (TALG)* 1, 2 (2005), 283–323.

[28] Michael Elkin. 2006. An Unconditional Lower Bound on the Time-Approximation Trade-off for the Distributed Minimum Spanning Tree Problem. *SIAM J. Comput.* 36, 2 (2006), 433–456. https://doi.org/10.1137/S0097539704441058

[29] Michael Elkin. 2007. A near-optimal distributed fully dynamic algorithm for maintaining sparse spanners. In *Proceedings of the twenty-sixth annual ACM symposium on Principles of distributed computing (PODC)*. 185–194.

[30] Michael Elkin and Ofer Neiman. 2017. Efficient algorithms for constructing very sparse spanners and emulators. In *Proceedings of the Twenty-Eighth Annual ACM-SIAM Symposium on Discrete Algorithms (SODA)*. 652–669.

[31] Michael Elkin and David Peleg. 2001. The Client-Server 2-Spanner Problem with Applications to Network Design. In *8th International Colloquium on Structural Information and Communication Complexity (SIROCCO)*. 117–132.

[32] Michael Elkin and David Peleg. 2005. Approximating k-spanner problems for $k > 2$. *Theoretical Computer Science* 337, 1 (2005), 249–277.

[33] Michael Elkin and David Peleg. 2007. The hardness of approximating spanner problems. *Theory of Computing Systems* 41, 4 (2007), 691–729.

[34] Michael Elkin and Jian Zhang. 2004. Efficient algorithms for constructing ($1+\epsilon$, β)-spanners in the distributed and streaming models. In *Proceedings of the twenty-third annual ACM symposium on Principles of distributed computing (PODC)*. 160–168.

[35] Paul Erdős. 1964. Extremal problems in graph theory. In *Theory Of Graphs And Its Applications, Proceedings of Symposium Smolenice*. Publ. House Czszechoslovak Acad. Sci., Prague, 29–36.

[36] Orr Fischer, Tzlil Gonen, and Rotem Oshman. 2017. Distributed Property Testing for Subgraph-Freeness Revisited. *CoRR* abs/1705.04033 (2017).

[37] Silvio Frischknecht, Stephan Holzer, and Roger Wattenhofer. 2012. Networks cannot compute their diameter in sublinear time. In *Proceedings of the twenty-third annual ACM-SIAM symposium on Discrete Algorithms (SODA)*. 1150–1162.

[38] Giorgio Gallo, Michael D Grigoriadis, and Robert E Tarjan. 1989. A fast parametric maximum flow algorithm and applications. *SIAM J. Comput.* 18, 1 (1989), 30–55.

[39] Mohsen Ghaffari, Fabian Kuhn, and Yannic Maus. 2017. On the complexity of local distributed graph problems. In *Proceedings of the 49th Annual ACM SIGACT Symposium on Theory of Computing (STOC)*. ACM, 784–797.

[40] Ofer Grossman and Merav Parter. 2017. Improved Deterministic Distributed Construction of Spanners. In *31st International Symposium on Distributed Computing, DISC 2017, October 16-20, 2017, Vienna, Austria*. 24:1–24:16. https://doi.org/10.4230/LIPIcs.DISC.2017.24

[41] David G Harris, Johannes Schneider, and Hsin-Hao Su. 2016. Distributed (Δ+1)-coloring in sublogarithmic rounds. In *Proceedings of the 48th Annual ACM SIGACT Symposium on Theory of Computing (STOC)*. 465–478.

[42] Stephan Holzer and Roger Wattenhofer. 2012. Optimal distributed all pairs shortest paths and applications. In *Proceedings of the 2012 ACM symposium on Principles of distributed computing (PODC)*. ACM, 355–364.

[43] Lujun Jia, Rajmohan Rajaraman, and Torsten Suel. 2002. An efficient distributed algorithm for constructing small dominating sets. *Distributed Computing* 15, 4 (2002), 193–205.

[44] Guy Kortsarz. 2001. On the hardness of approximating spanners. *Algorithmica* 30, 3 (2001), 432–450.

[45] Guy Kortsarz and David Peleg. 1994. Generating sparse 2-spanners. *Journal of Algorithms* 17, 2 (1994), 222–236.

[46] Guy Kortsarz and David Peleg. 1998. Generating low-degree 2-spanners. *SIAM J. Comput.* 27, 5 (1998), 1438–1456.

[47] Fabian Kuhn, Thomas Moscibroda, and Roger Wattenhofer. 2016. Local computation: Lower and upper bounds. *Journal of the ACM (JACM)* 63, 2 (2016), 17.

[48] Fabian Kuhn and Rogert Wattenhofer. 2003. Constant-time distributed dominating set approximation. In *Proceedings of the twenty-second annual symposium on Principles of distributed computing (PODC)*. 25–32.

[49] Eyal Kushilevitz and Noam Nisan. 1997. *Communication Complexity*. Cambridge University Press, New York, NY, USA.

[50] Nathan Linial. 1992. Locality in Distributed Graph Algorithms. *SIAM J. Comput.* 21, 1 (1992), 193–201. https://doi.org/10.1137/0221015

[51] David Peleg. 2000. *Distributed Computing: A Locality-Sensitive Approach*. SIAM.

[52] David Peleg and Vitaly Rubinovich. 2000. A Near-Tight Lower Bound on the Time Complexity of Distributed Minimum-Weight Spanning Tree Construction. *SIAM J. Comput.* 30, 5 (2000), 1427–1442. https://doi.org/10.1137/S0097539700369740

[53] David Peleg and Alejandro A Schäffer. 1989. Graph spanners. *Journal of graph theory* 13, 1 (1989), 99–116.

[54] David Peleg and Jeffrey D Ullman. 1989. An optimal synchronizer for the hypercube. *SIAM Journal on computing* 18, 4 (1989), 740–747.

[55] David Peleg and Eli Upfal. 1989. A trade-off between space and efficiency for routing tables. *Journal of the ACM (JACM)* 36, 3 (1989), 510–530.

[56] Seth Pettie. 2010. Distributed algorithms for ultrasparse spanners and linear size skeletons. *Distributed Computing* 22, 3 (2010), 147–166.

[57] Sridhar Rajagopalan and Vijay V Vazirani. 1998. Primal-dual RNC approximation algorithms for set cover and covering integer programs. *SIAM J. Comput.* 28, 2 (1998), 525–540.

[58] Alexander A. Razborov. 1992. On the distributional complexity of disjointness. *Theoretical Computer Science* 106, 2 (1992), 385–390.

[59] Liam Roditty, Mikkel Thorup, and Uri Zwick. 2005. Deterministic constructions of approximate distance oracles and spanners. In *International Colloquium on Automata, Languages, and Programming (ICALP)*. 261–272.

[60] Liam Roditty, Mikkel Thorup, and Uri Zwick. 2008. Roundtrip spanners and roundtrip routing in directed graphs. *ACM Transactions on Algorithms (TALG)* 4, 3 (2008), 29.

[61] Atish Das Sarma, Stephan Holzer, Liah Kor, Amos Korman, Danupon Nanongkai, Gopal Pandurangan, David Peleg, and Roger Wattenhofer. 2012. Distributed verification and hardness of distributed approximation. *SIAM J. Comput.* 41, 5 (2012), 1235–1265.

[62] Mikkel Thorup and Uri Zwick. 2001. Compact routing schemes. In *Proceedings of the thirteenth annual ACM symposium on Parallel algorithms and architectures (SPAA)*. 1–10.

[63] Mikkel Thorup and Uri Zwick. 2005. Approximate distance oracles. *Journal of the ACM (JACM)* 52, 1 (2005), 1–24.

Distributed Approximation of Minimum k-edge-connected Spanning Subgraphs*†

Michal Dory
Technion, Department of Computer Science
Haifa, Israel
smichald@cs.technion.ac.il

ABSTRACT

In the minimum k-edge-connected spanning subgraph (k-ECSS) problem the goal is to find the minimum weight subgraph resistant to up to $k-1$ edge failures. This is a central problem in network design, and a natural generalization of the minimum spanning tree (MST) problem. While the MST problem has been studied extensively by the distributed computing community, for $k \geq 2$ less is known in the distributed setting.

In this paper, we present fast randomized distributed approximation algorithms for k-ECSS in the CONGEST model. Our first contribution is an $\widetilde{O}(D + \sqrt{n})$-round $O(\log n)$-approximation for 2-ECSS, for a graph with n vertices and diameter D. The time complexity of our algorithm is almost tight and almost matches the time complexity of the MST problem. For larger constant values of k we give an $\widetilde{O}(n)$-round $O(\log n)$-approximation. Additionally, in the special case of *unweighted* 3-ECSS we show how to improve the time complexity to $O(D \log^3 n)$ rounds. All our results significantly improve the time complexity of previous algorithms.

CCS CONCEPTS

• **Mathematics of computing → Graph algorithms; Approximation algorithms;**

KEYWORDS

approximation algorithms; distributed network design; k-edge-connectivity

ACM Reference Format:
Michal Dory. 2018. Distributed Approximation of Minimum k-edge-connected Spanning Subgraphs. In *PODC '18: ACM Symposium on Principles of Distributed Computing, July 23–27, 2018, Egham, United Kingdom.* ACM, New York, NY, USA, 11 pages. https://doi.org/10.1145/3212734.3212760

1 INTRODUCTION

The edge-connectivity of a graph determines its resistance to edge failures, which is crucial for network reliability. In the minimum weight k-edge-connected[1] spanning subgraph (k-ECSS) problem the input is a k-edge-connected graph G, and the goal is to find the minimum weight k-ECSS of G. The minimum k-ECSS problem is widely studied in the sequential setting (see, e.g., [4, 10, 11, 16, 17, 22]). The unweighted version of the problem admits an $1 + \frac{1}{2k} + O(\frac{1}{k^2})$ approximation [10], and the weighted problem admits 2-approximations [17, 22]. Many additional related connectivity problems are studied in the sequential setting, see [21, 23] for surveys.

However, because of the distributed nature of networks, it is crucial to study the problem also from the distributed perspective. The 1-ECSS problem is just the minimum spanning tree (MST) problem, which is a central and well-studied problem in the distributed setting (see, e.g., [8, 9, 12, 13, 26, 29]). In the CONGEST model, there is an $O(D + \sqrt{n} \log^* n)$-round algorithm for the problem [26] for a graph with n vertices and diameter D, which is almost tight due to an $\Omega(D + \sqrt{\frac{n}{\log n}})$ lower bound [8, 31, 35]. Although an MST is a sparse low-cost backbone of a graph, even a single edge failure disconnects it and completely destroys its functionality. Hence, it is crucial to find low-cost backbones with higher connectivity.

Yet, for $k > 1$ less is known in the distributed setting. For *unweighted* 2-ECSS there is an $O(D)$-round 2-approximation [1], and an $O(n)$-round $\frac{3}{2}$-approximation [24]. For *unweighted* k-ECSS, there is an $O(k(D + \sqrt{n} \log^* n))$-round 2-approximation [37]. This algorithm is based on repeatedly finding maximal spanning forests in the graph, and removing their edges from the graph, which results in a k-ECSS with at most $k(n-1)$ edges. This guarantees a 2-approximation for the *unweighted* case, since any k-ECSS has at least $\frac{kn}{2}$ edges. However, this approach cannot extend to the weighted case, since in the weighted case even adding one redundant edge may be too expensive.

A natural question is whether it is possible to design efficient approximations also for *weighted* k-ECSS. For weighted 2-ECSS there are $O(n \log n)$-round [24] and $O(h_{MST} + \sqrt{n} \log^* n)$-round [1] 3-approximations, where h_{MST} is the height of the MST of the graph. Both these algorithms start by building an MST and then augment it to be 2-edge-connected. To do so, they use algorithms for the weighted *tree augmentation problem* (TAP), in which the goal is to augment the connectivity of a given spanning tree T to 2 by adding a minimum cost set of edges from the graph G to T. However, currently the best algorithm for solving weighted TAP takes $O(h)$ rounds [1], where h is the height of T. Since the algorithm for 2-ECSS augments an MST, it results in a time complexity that depends on h_{MST}, which can be $\Theta(n)$ in the worst case.

*The full version of the paper is available at http://arxiv.org/abs/1805.07764.
†Supported in part by the Israel Science Foundation (grant 1696/14).

PODC '18, July 23–27, 2018, Egham, United Kingdom

ACM ISBN 978-1-4503-5795-1/18/07...$15.00
https://doi.org/10.1145/3212734.3212760

[1]An undirected graph G is *k-edge-connected* if it remains connected after the removal of any $k-1$ edges.

To the best of our knowledge, the only distributed algorithm for weighted k-ECSS for $k > 2$ is an $O(knD)$-round $O(\log k)$-approximation algorithm [36] based on a primal-dual algorithm of Goemans et al. [16], that solves even the more general Steiner Network problem. If k is constant and D is small, the time complexity of [36] is close to linear, but in the worst case the time complexity is $\Omega(n^2)$, which is trivial in the distributed setting.[2]

In this paper, we address this fundamental topic, and present efficient distributed approximation algorithms for k-ECSS. Our algorithms work in the CONGEST model of distributed computing [30], in which vertices exchange messages of $O(\log n)$ bits in synchronous rounds.

1.1 Our contributions

Our first contribution is the first sublinear algorithm for weighted 2-ECSS.

THEOREM 1.1. *There is a distributed algorithm for weighted 2-ECSS in the* CONGEST *model that guarantees an approximation ratio of $O(\log n)$, and takes $O((D + \sqrt{n}) \log^2 n)$ rounds w.h.p.*

The time complexity of our algorithm improves upon the previos $O(h_{MST} + \sqrt{n} \log^* n)$-round algorithm [1], it almost matches the time complexity of the MST problem, and it is almost tight. Computing an α-approximation for weighted 2-ECSS requires $\Omega(D + \frac{\sqrt{n}}{\log n})$ rounds, for any polynomial function α [1].[3] We next consider the case $k > 2$, and show the following.

THEOREM 1.2. *There is a distributed algorithm for weighted k-ECSS in the* CONGEST *model with an expected approximation ratio of $O(k \log n)$, and time complexity of $O(k(D \log^3 n + n))$ rounds.*

This gives the first nearly-linear time algorithm for any constant k, and improves upon the previous $O(knD)$-round algorithm [36]. We also show that in the special case of *unweighted* 3-ECSS we can improve the time complexity of the algorithm to $O(D \log^3 n)$ rounds, which improves upon the previous $O(D + \sqrt{n} \log^* n)$-round algorithm [37].

THEOREM 1.3. *There is a distributed algorithm for unweighted 3-ECSS in the* CONGEST *model with an expected approximation ratio of $O(\log n)$, and time complexity of $O(D \log^3 n)$ rounds.*

Roadmap: In Section 2, we give a high-level overview of our algorithms. In Sections 3,4 and 5 we present our 2-ECSS, k-ECSS and 3-ECSS algorithms, respectively. Finally, in Section 6, we discuss questions for future research. Full details and proofs appear in the full version [7].

1.2 Additional related work

FT-MST: In the fault-tolerant MST problem the goal is to find a sparse subgraph of the input graph G that contains an MST of $G \setminus \{e\}$ for each edge e. This problem can be solved in $O(D + \sqrt{n} \log n)$ rounds using the distributed algorithm of Ghaffari and Parter [15]. One of the ingredients in [15] is a decomposition of the tree into segments that turns out to be useful also for our 2-ECSS algorithm. While an FT-MST and a minimum 2-ECSS are both low-cost 2-edge-connected spanning subgraphs, the main difference between the problems is that in the latter the goal is to minimize the *sum of costs* of edges in the solution. Hence, the total cost of a solution for minimum 2-ECSS may be much cheaper.

Cycle space sampling: The *cycle space sampling* technique introduced by Pritchard and Thurimella [33] allows to detect small cuts in a graph using connections between the cycles and cuts in a graph. They show an $O(D)$-round algorithm that assigns the edges of a graph short labels that allow to detect cuts of size 1 or 2 in $O(D)$ rounds. In particular, this gives an $O(D)$-round algorithm for verifying if a graph is 2-edge-connected or 3-edge-connected (for more details, see Section 5). We use this technique to show an efficient algorithm for the minimum *size* 3-ECSS.

Additional related problems: There are also other $O(D)$-round algorithms for verifying if a graph is 2-edge-connected [1, 32]. A natural approach for verifying if a graph is k-edge-connected is computing the size λ of a minimum cut in a graph. There are approximation and exact algorithms for the minimum cut problem in $\widetilde{O}(D + \sqrt{n})$ rounds [14, 28] and $\widetilde{O}((D + \sqrt{n})\lambda^4)$ rounds [28], respectively, and a lower bound of $\Omega(D + \frac{1}{\log n}\sqrt{\frac{n}{\alpha\lambda}})$ rounds for an α-approximation in a graph with diameter $D = O(\log n + \frac{1}{\lambda \log n}\sqrt{\frac{n}{\alpha\lambda}})$ [14] (note that if $\lambda = O(1)$ this lower bound becomes $\Omega(D)$). Another related problem studied in the distributed setting is the decomposition of a graph with large connectivity into many disjoint trees, while almost preserving the total connectivity through the trees [3].

Covering problems: We show that the minimum k-ECSS problem is closely related to the set cover problem. Some elements in our algorithms and analysis are inspired by the parallel set cover algorithm of Rajagopalan and Vazirani [34], and the minimum dominating set (MDS) algorithm of Jia et al. [18]. It is worth noting that our 2-ECSS algorithm *guarantees* the approximation ratio, where other distributed $O(\log n)$-approximations for set cover obtain approximations that hold in expectation or w.h.p [18, 25]. For this reason, we believe that our approach can be useful for additional local or global covering problems, particularly in scenarios where it is important to guarantee the approximation. We also used it in a recent algorithm for the minimum 2-spanner problem [2].

1.3 Preliminaries

Problem definition: An undirected graph G is *k-edge-connected* if it remains connected after the removal of any $k - 1$ edges. In the *minimum weight k-edge-connected spanning subgraph problem (k-ECSS)* the input is an undirected k-edge-connected graph G with n vertices and non-negative weights $w(e)$ on the edges. The goal is to find the minimum weight k-ECSS of G. We assume that the weights of the edges are integers and are polynomial in n. This guarantees that a weight can be represented in $O(\log n)$ bits. In *unweighted* k-ECSS the goal is to find the minimum *size* k-ECSS of G. It is equivalent to weighted k-ECSS where all the edges have unit-weight.

[2] All previous results use deterministic algorithms.

[3] The lower bound in [1] is for weighted TAP, however an α-approximation algorithm for weighted 2-ECSS gives an α-approximation algorithm for weighted TAP where we give to the edges of the input tree T weight 0. Hence, a lower bound for weighted TAP implies a lower bound for weighted 2-ECSS.

The distributed model: In the distributed CONGEST model, the input graph G to the problem is the communication network. Initially all the vertices know the ids of their neighbors and the weights of the edges adjacent to them, and at the end each vertex knows which of the edges adjacent to it are taken to the solution. In our algorithms, it would be convenient to say that the edges do some computations. When we say this, we mean that the endpoints of the edge simulate the computation.

During our algorithm it is useful to communicate over a BFS tree. We construct a BFS tree with root r in $O(D)$ rounds [30], where r is the vertex with minimum id. Using the BFS tree we can distribute ℓ different messages from vertices in the tree to all the vertices in the tree in $O(D+\ell)$ rounds using standard techniques [30]. We assume that vertices know the number of vertices n and the number of edges m in the algorithm, they can learn this information in $O(D)$ rounds by communication over the BFS tree. For a rooted tree T, we denote by $p(v)$ the parent of v in the tree, and we denote by $LCA(u, v)$ the lowest common ancestor of u and v.

2 TECHNICAL OVERVIEW

A natural approach for finding a minimum k-ECSS is to start with an empty subgraph H, and in iteration i for $1 \leq i \leq k$ augment its connectivity from $i-1$ to i. We define the problem Aug_k as follows. Given a k-edge-connected graph G and a $(k-1)$-edge-connected spanning subgraph H of G, the goal is to find a minimum weight set of edges A from G, such that $H \cup A$ is k-edge-connected. For a set of edges H, we define $w(H) = \sum_{e \in H} w(e)$. We next show the following.

Claim 2.1. *Assume that for $1 \leq i \leq k$, the algorithm A_i is an α_i-approximation algorithm for Aug_i that takes T_i rounds, then there is an $(\sum_{i=1}^{k} \alpha_i)$-approximation algorithm for k-ECSS that takes $\sum_{i=1}^{k} T_i$ rounds.*

PROOF. The algorithm for k-ECSS starts with an empty subgraph, and in iteration i uses the algorithm A_i to augment the connectivity from $i-1$ to i. Let H_i be the set of edges added to the augmentation in iteration i, and let $H = \bigcup_{i=1}^{k} H_i$ be the solution constructed. H is clearly k-edge-connected. The correctness follows from the fact that an optimal solution H^* for k-ECSS is a set of edges that augments the connectivity of any subgraph produced in the algorithm to k (and in particular to any $i \leq k$). Since the algorithm A_i is an α_i-approximation algorithm, this gives $w(H_i) \leq \alpha_i w(H^*)$. This shows that $w(H) = \sum_{i=1}^{k} w(H_i) \leq \sum_{i=1}^{k} \alpha_i w(H^*)$, as needed. The time complexity of the algorithm is $\sum_{i=1}^{k} T_i$ rounds. □

A set of edges C is a *cut* in a connected graph G if $G \setminus C$ is disconnected. Let H be a subgraph of a graph $G = (V, E)$, and let C be a cut in H.

Definition 2.1. *An edge $e \in E$* covers *the cut C if $(H \setminus C) \cup \{e\}$ is connected.*

Note that in a $(k-1)$-edge-connected graph H, the minimum cut is of size at least $k-1$. To solve Aug_k our goal is to find a minimum cost set of edges A that covers all the cuts of size $k-1$ in H. This is a special case of the set cover problem.

2.1 General framework of our algorithms

In order to solve k'-ECSS, we present an algorithm for Aug_k for any $k \leq k'$. In the algorithm we maintain a set of edges A that contains all the edges added to the augmentation. For an edge $e \notin H$, we denote by S_e the set of cuts of size $k-1$ of H that e covers. During the algorithm and analysis, we denote by C_e all the cuts in S_e that are still not covered by edges added to A.

Cost-effectiveness. The *cost-effectiveness* of an edge $e \notin H$ is $\rho(e) = \frac{|C_e|}{w(e)}$. The *rounded* cost-effectiveness of an edge e, denoted by $\tilde{\rho}(e)$, is obtained by rounding $\rho(e)$ to the closest power of 2 that is greater than $\rho(e)$. If $w(e) = 0$, the values $\rho(e)$ and $\tilde{\rho}(e)$ are defined to be ∞. Adding an edge with maximum value of cost-effectiveness to A allows to cover many cuts, while paying minimal cost. This suggests the following *sequential* greedy algorithm. At each step, we add to A the edge with maximum cost-effectiveness, and we continue until all the cuts of size $k-1$ are covered. This approach that is based on the classic greedy algorithm for set cover achieves an $O(\log n)$-approximation.

Symmetry breaking. Adding only one edge in each step gives an algorithm that is inherently sequential, and in order to obtain an efficient *distributed* algorithm we would like to add many edges to A in parallel. A naive approach could be to add all the edges with maximum cost-effectiveness to A simultaneously. However, then we may add too many edges to A and the approximation ratio is no longer guaranteed. To overcome this, we consider all the edges with maximum rounded cost-effectiveness as *candidates*, and then we break the symmetry between the candidates. After that, some of the candidates are added to A, and we proceed in iterations until all the cuts of size $k-1$ are covered. This gives us the general structure of the algorithm.

All our algorithms have this structure, but they differ in the symmetry breaking mechanism and by the implementation of the cost-effectiveness computation and other computations required. We next explain how we implement each of our algorithms.

3 2-ECSS

In this section, we give a high-level overview of our 2-ECSS algorithm, full details and proofs appear in [7]. We show the following.

THEOREM 1.1. *There is a distributed algorithm for weighted 2-ECSS in the CONGEST model that guarantees an approximation ratio of $O(\log n)$, and takes $O((D + \sqrt{n}) \log^2 n)$ rounds w.h.p.*

Our algorithm starts by building an MST, T, using the $O(D + \sqrt{n} \log^* n)$-round algorithm of Kutten and Peleg [26]. Then, it augments T to be 2-edge-connected using a new algorithm for weighted TAP. Although there is an algorithm with time complexity $\widetilde{O}(D + \sqrt{n})$ for *unweighted* TAP [1], this algorithm and its analysis rely heavily on the fact that the problem is unweighted, hence, giving an efficient algorithm for the weighted problem requires a different approach. Our algorithm for weighted TAP follows the framework described in Section 2.1, and exploits the simple structure of cuts of size 1 in the graph.

As explained in Section 2.1, in order to augment the connectivity of T to 2, our goal is to cover all the cuts of size 1 in T. Since a cut of size 1 is an edge, our goal is to cover all the tree edges. Let

$e = \{u, v\}$ be a non-tree edge in G, and let P_e be the unique path between u and v in T. Adding e to T creates a cycle that includes all the tree edges in P_e. Since removing an edge from a cycle does not disconnect a graph, it follows that e covers a tree edge t if and only if $t \in P_e$. Hence, the set S_e of all the cuts of size 1 covered by e consists of all the tree edges of P_e, and C_e are all the tree edges in P_e that are still not covered by edges added to the augmentation A. In each iteration, all the non-tree edges with maximum rounded cost-effectiveness are the candidates.

3.1 Symmetry breaking

In order to break the symmetry between the candidates, we suggest the following approach, inspired by a parallel algorithm for set cover [34]. We also used it recently in designing distributed algorithms for the 2-spanner and minimum dominating set (MDS) problems [2]. Each candidate chooses a random number, and each tree edge chooses the first candidate that covers it according to the random values. A candidate edge e that receives at least $\frac{|C_e|}{8}$ votes is added to A. Since we add to A only edges receiving many votes, this approach allows us to add small number of edges to A while covering many tree edges, and results in an $O(\log n)$-approximation. Our algorithm proceeds in iterations until all the tree edges are covered. The pseudo-code for each iteration is given below. Before the first iteration, we add to A all the non-tree edges with weight 0.

(1) Each non-tree edge $e \notin A$ computes its rounded cost-effectiveness $\tilde{\rho}(e)$.
(2) Each non-tree edge $e \notin A$ with maximum rounded cost-effectiveness is a *candidate*.
(3) Each candidate e chooses a random number $r_e \in \{1, ..., n^8\}$.
(4) Each uncovered tree-edge that is in the set C_e for at least one of the candidates e, votes for the first of these candidates, according to the order of the values r_e. If there is more than one candidate with the same minimum value, it votes for the one with minimum ID.
(5) Each candidate e which receives at least $\frac{|C_e|}{8}$ votes from edges in C_e is added to A.
(6) Each tree edge learns if it is covered by edges added to A. If all the tree edges are covered, the algorithm terminates, and the output is all the edges added to A during the algorithm.

3.2 Efficient implementation

A major difference between TAP and local covering problems like 2-spanner and MDS is that in the 2-spanner and MDS algorithms all the computations depend on a small local neighborhood around vertices, where TAP is a *global* problem, and the algorithm requires to do many global computations simultaneously. For example, during the algorithm each one of the non-tree edges needs to compute its cost-effectiveness and learn how many tree edges vote for it, and each one of the tree edges should vote for the first candidate that covers it. However, there may be $\Theta(n^2)$ non-tree edges, and $n-1$ tree edges, and in order to get an efficient algorithm we should be able to do these computations in parallel. To achieve this, we decompose the tree into segments with a relatively simple structure, following a decomposition used for solving the FT-MST problem [15]. We next describe the decomposition, and explain how we use it in our algorithm.

Overview of the decomposition. In [7], we show how to decompose the tree into segments satisfying nice properties. We follow the decomposition in [15] (see Section 4.3) with slight changes. The main difference is that in [15], the first step of the decomposition is to choose random edges. We observe that it is possible to choose edges deterministically using the MST algorithm of Kutten and Peleg [26] and obtain a similiar decomposition. This gives an $O(D + \sqrt{n} \log^* n)$-round *deterministic* algorithm compared to the $O(D + \sqrt{n} \log n)$-round algorithm in [15]. Using this decomposition combined with the FT-MST algorithm in [15] gives a deterministic algorithm for the FT-MST problem in $O(D + \sqrt{n} \log^* n)$ rounds, which matches the time complexity of computing an MST.

In the decomposition, the tree is decomposed into $O(\sqrt{n})$ *edge-disjoint* segments with diameter $O(\sqrt{n})$. Each segment S has a root r_S, which is an ancestor of all the vertices in the segment. The segment contains a main path between the vertex r_S and a descendant of it d_S and additional subtrees attached to this path that are not connected by an edge to other segments in the tree. We call the main path of S the *highway* of S, and we call d_S the *unique descendant* of the segment S. The vertices r_S and d_S can be a part of other segments (If $r_S \neq r$ it is a unique descendant of another segment, and both r_S and d_S can be roots of additional segments), but other vertices in the segment are not connected by an edge to any other vertex outside the segment. The id of the segment is the pair (r_S, d_S). See Figure 1 for an illustration.

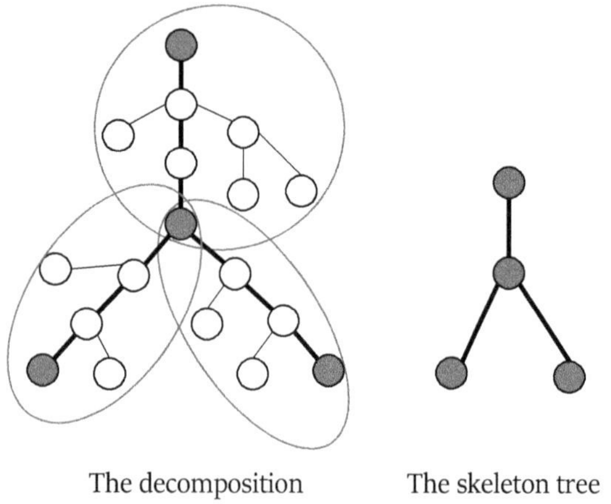

Figure 1: An illustration of the decomposition. The blue vertices are ancestors or unique descendants of segments, and the bold edges are highway edges. Note that the blue vertices can be a part of several segments, but other vertices are not connected by an edge to any vertex outside their segment. The edges of the skeleton tree correspond to highways in the original graph.

The relatively simple structure of the segments, and in particular the fact that r_S and d_S are the only vertices in S that are connected to other segments, will be very useful in our algorithm. The *skeleton tree* T_S is a virtual tree that its vertices are all the vertices that are either r_S or d_S for at least one segment S. The edges in T_S correspond to the highways of the segments, as follows. A vertex

v is a *parent* of the vertex $u \neq v$ in the skeleton tree if and only if $v = r_S$ and $u = d_S$ for some segment S. The time complexity for constructing the segments is $O(D + \sqrt{n}\log^* n)$ rounds. Let $P_{u,v}$ be the unique tree path between u and v. In [7], we show the following.

Claim 3.1. *In $O(D + \sqrt{n})$ rounds, the vertices learn the following information. All the vertices learn the id of their segment, and the complete structure of the skeleton tree. In addition, each vertex v in the segment S learns all the edges of the paths P_{v,r_S} and P_{v,d_S}.*

Claim 3.2. *Assume that each tree edge t and each segment S, have some information of $O(\log n)$ bits, denote them by m_t and m_S, respectively. In $O(D + \sqrt{n})$ rounds, the vertices learn the following information. Each vertex v in the segment S learns the values (t, m_t) for all the tree edges in the highway of S, and in the paths P_{v,r_S}, P_{v,d_S}. In addition, all the vertices learn all the values (S, m_S).*

Implementing the algorithm. We next explain how to implement our algorithm, full details appear in [7].

(I). Computing cost-effectiveness. For computing the cost-effectiveness of an edge $e = \{u, v\}$, the vertices u and v should learn how many tree edges in S_e are still not covered. We assume that at the beginning of the computation, each tree edge knows if it is covered. Later we explain how tree edges learn if they are covered at the end of each iteration. The key ingredient that allows efficient computations is that the path S_e consists of internal paths in the segments of v and u, as well as *highways* of other segments. For example, if u and v are in the same segment S, the unique path between them is contained in $P_{v,r_S} \cup P_{u,r_S}$. If u and v are in different segments, and their LCA is in another segment, S_e is composed of the 3 paths $P_{u,r_u}, P_{v,r_v}, P_{r_v,r_u}$ where r_v and r_u are the ancestors in the segments of v and u. Since both r_v and r_u are vertices in the skeleton tree, the path P_{r_v,r_u} corresponds to the path between r_v and r_u in the skeleton tree, where each edge of the skeleton tree is replaced by the corresponding highway. We give a full case analysis in [7].

Now, using Claims 3.1 and 3.2 where m_t indicates if the tree edge t is covered, and m_S is the number of uncovered tree edges in the *highway* of the segment S, we get the following. All the vertices know the complete structure of the skeleton tree, each vertex learns exactly which edges are not covered in the path P_{v,r_v} and how many tree edges are still not covered on the highway of each segment. Given this information, all the non-tree edges compute locally the cost-effectiveness of edges, the overall time complexity is $O(D + \sqrt{n})$ rounds.

(II). Learning the first candidate that covers a tree edge. Once all the non-tree edges computed the cost-effectiveness, computing the maximum rounded cost-effectiveness in the graph takes $O(D)$ rounds by communication over the BFS tree, and choosing random numbers is a completely local task. We next explain how all the tree edges learn which is the first candidate edge that covers them. A similar computation is done in [15] where they compute the minimum weight edges that cover each tree edge. The high-level idea is to classify the non-tree edges that cover a tree edge t according to 3 types: *short-range*, *mid-range* and *long-range*, which indicate if $e = \{u, v\}$ has 2, 1 or 0 endpoints in the segment of t. Then, each tree edge t learns which is the first candidate that covers it for each of these 3 types, the minimum of them is the first candidate that covers it. An important observation is that all the tree edges on the highway of a certain segment have the same first *long-range* candidate. The full description of the algorithm appears in [7]. In a similar way, at the end of each iteration each tree edge learns if it is covered (it can be seen as learning the *first* non-tree edge that covers t from the edges added to A).

(III). Computing the number of votes. To complete the description of the algorithm, we explain how each candidate learns how many tree edges vote for it. At this point of the algorithm, all the tree edges know which is the candidate they vote for. The computation is similar to the cost-effectiveness computation. Again, the tree edges that vote for $e = \{u, v\}$ are in the path S_e that consists of tree paths in the segments of v and u, as well as highways. A crucial observation is that if e covers a tree edge t that is not in the segments of v and u, this edge is necessarily an highway edge, and e is a *long-range* edge for it. Hence, t votes for e only if e is the first long-range candidate that covers the highway of t, and if the long-range candidate is the first candidate that covers t. We define m_t to be the candidate that t votes for, and $m_S = (e_S, n_S)$ where e_S is the first long-range candidate that covers the highway of S, and n_S is the number of edges of the highway that vote for e_S. Using Claim 3.2, all the vertices learn all the relevant values m_t, m_S which allows computing the number of votes.

To conclude, each iteration can be implemented in $O(D + \sqrt{n})$ rounds.

3.3 Approximation ratio analysis

In this section, we show that our algorithm for weighted TAP guarantees an $O(\log n)$-approximation. Some elements of our analysis have similar analogues in the classic analysis of the greedy set cover algorithm [5, 19, 27]. We also used similar ideas in a recent algorithm for the minimum 2-spanner problem [2].

Let A be the set of edges added to the augmentation by the algorithm. When the algorithm ends, all the tree edges are covered, hence $T \cup A$ is 2-edge-connected. We show that $w(A) \leq O(\log n)w(A^*)$, where A^* is an optimal augmentation.

To show the approximation ratio, we assign each edge $t \in T$ a value $cost(t)$ such that the sum of the costs of all edges is closely related both to $w(A)$ and $w(A^*)$, by satisfying

$$w(A) \leq 8 \sum_{t \in T} cost(t) \leq O(\log n)w(A^*),$$

which implies our claimed approximation ratio.

For a tree edge t, let i be the iteration in which t is first covered in the algorithm. The edge t may be covered by a candidate edge e that it votes for and is added to A at iteration i. In this case, we set $cost(t) = \frac{1}{\rho(e)}$, where $\rho(e)$ is the cost-effectiveness of the edge e at iteration i. Another option is that t is covered by other edges added to A at iteration i, or at the beginning of the algorithm since it is covered by an edge of weight 0. In these cases, we set $cost(t) = 0$. We first show the left inequality above.

Lemma 3.3. $w(A) \leq 8 \cdot \sum_{t \in T} cost(t)$.

Proof. Let e be an edge with non-zero weight that is added to A at iteration i, and let $\rho(e)$ be the cost-effectiveness of e at iteration

i. Recall that we add e to A since it gets at least $\frac{|C_e|}{8}$ votes from the tree edges it covers. Denote by $Votes(e)$ the set of tree edges that vote for e at iteration i. For each $t \in Votes(e)$, we defined $cost(t) = \frac{1}{\rho(e)}$, which gives,

$$\sum_{t \in Votes(e)} cost(t) \geq \frac{1}{\rho(e)} \cdot \frac{|C_e|}{8} = \frac{w(e)}{|C_e|} \cdot \frac{|C_e|}{8} = \frac{w(e)}{8}.$$

Hence, for each $e \in A$, $w(e) \leq 8 \cdot \sum_{t \in Votes(e)} cost(t)$ (for an edge with weight 0, this holds trivially). For each tree edge t, there is at most one edge $e \in A$ such that $t \in Votes(e)$, since t votes for at most one edge at the iteration in which it is covered. Hence, we get

$$w(A) = \sum_{e \in A} w(e) \leq 8 \cdot \sum_{e \in A} \sum_{t \in Votes(e)} cost(t) \leq 8 \cdot \sum_{t \in T} cost(t).$$

This completes the proof of Lemma 3.3. □

Lemma 3.4. $\sum_{t \in T} cost(t) \leq O(\log n) w(A^*)$.

Proof. Consider an edge $e \in A^*$ and let $(t_1, ..., t_\ell)$ be the sequence of tree edges covered by e according to the order in which they are covered in the algorithm. Assume first that $w(e) \neq 0$. The cost-effectiveness of e at the beginning of the iteration in which t_1 is covered is $\frac{\ell}{w(e)}$. All the candidates that cover t_1 have maximum rounded cost-effectiveness. In particular, the cost-effectiveness of the edge that covers t_1 is at least $\frac{\ell}{2w(e)}$. Hence, $cost(t_1) \leq \frac{2w(e)}{\ell}$. Similarly, the cost-effectiveness of e at the beginning of the iteration in which t_j is covered is at least $\frac{\ell-j+1}{w(e)}$, which gives $cost(t_j) \leq \frac{2w(e)}{\ell-j+1}$. This gives,

$$\sum_{j=1}^{\ell} cost(t_j) \leq 2w(e) \cdot \sum_{j=1}^{\ell} \frac{1}{\ell - j + 1} = O(\log \ell) w(e) = O(\log n) w(e).$$

The last equality is because the number of tree edges ℓ covered by e is at most n.

For an edge $e \in A^*$ such that $w(e) = 0$, note that $cost(t) = 0$ for all the edges covered by e, since they are all covered at the beginning of the algorithm without voting for any candidate. Hence, we get in this case $\sum_{j=1}^{\ell} cost(t_j) = 0 = O(\log n) w(e)$.

Recall that S_e is the set of tree edges covered by the edge e. Since A^* is an augmentation, every edge $t \in T$ is covered by at least one edge $e \in A^*$. Summing over all the edges in A^* we get,

$$\sum_{t \in T} cost(t) \leq \sum_{e \in A^*} \sum_{t \in S_e} cost(t) \leq O(\log n) \sum_{e \in A^*} w(e) = O(\log n) w(A^*).$$

This completes the proof. □

In conclusion, we get $w(A) \leq 8 \sum_{t \in T} cost(t) \leq O(\log n) w(A^*)$, which completes the proof of the $O(\log n)$-approximation ratio for weighted TAP, giving the following lemma.

Lemma 3.5. *The approximation ratio of the weighted TAP algorithm is* $O(\log n)$.

3.4 Time analysis

Finally, we show in [7] that the number of iterations is $O(\log^2 n)$ w.h.p.[4] The analysis is based on a potential function argument which is described in [18, 34] for the set cover and minimum dominating set problems. The potential function is defined as follows. Let $\tilde{\rho}$ be the maximum rounded cost-effectiveness at the beginning of iteration i. We define the potential function

$$\phi = \sum_{e : \tilde{\rho}(e) = \tilde{\rho}} |C_e|,$$

where C_e are the edges in S_e that are still not covered by A at the beginning of iteration i. The high-level idea is to show that if the value of $\tilde{\rho}$ does not change between iterations, the potential function ϕ decreases by a multiplicative factor between iterations in expectation. This shows that after $O(\log n)$ iterations the maximum rounded cost-effectiveness decreases w.h.p. Since the weights are polynomial and each non-tree edge covers at most $n-1$ tree edges, there are $O(\log n)$ possible values for rounded cost-effectiveness, which shows that the number of iterations is $O(\log^2 n)$ w.h.p.

Since each iteration takes $O(D+\sqrt{n})$ rounds, this gives an $O((D+\sqrt{n}) \log^2 n)$-round $O(\log n)$-approximation for weighted TAP and weighted 2-ECSS.

[4] As standard in this setting, a high probability refers to a probability that is at least $1 - \frac{1}{n^c}$ for a constant $c \geq 1$.

4 k-ECSS

In this section, we give a high-level overview of our k-ECSS algorithm, full details and proofs appear in [7]. We show the following.

Theorem 1.2. *There is a distributed algorithm for weighted k-ECSS in the Congest model with an expected approximation ratio of $O(k \log n)$, and time complexity of $O(k(D \log^3 n + n))$ rounds.*

The main obstacle in extending our 2-ECSS algorithm for larger values of k is the need to work with many different cuts in parallel. For the case $k = 2$, the cuts we needed to cover were represented by the tree edges. However, for larger values of k, we need to cover also cuts that contain several tree edges that may be far away from each other. Our goal is to design an algorithm for Aug_k that follows the framework described in Section 2.1, but it is not clear anymore how to compute the cost-effectiveness of edges efficiently, and how to break the symmetry between candidates.

Computing cost-effectiveness. In order to compute the cost-effectiveness of edges, we use the following observation. The minimum k-ECSS has $O(kn)$ edges which is $O(n)$ for a constant k. If we guarantee that the subgraph H constructed in our algorithm has $O(kn)$ edges, all the vertices can learn the complete structure of H in $O(kn)$ time during the algorithm, and then each one of the (possibly $\Theta(n^2)$) edges can compute its cost-effectiveness locally.

Symmetry breaking. The main challenge is to break the symmetry between candidates. Let $deg(C)$ be the number of candidates that cover a cut C. To cover C, it is enough to add only one of these candidates to A, and if each of them is added to A with probability $\frac{1}{deg(C)}$, then we add one candidate to cover C in expectation. Ideally, we would like that each edge would be added to A with probability that depends on the numbers $deg(C)$ of the cuts that it covers. A similar idea is used in the MDS algorithm of Jia et al. [18]. However, in our case, it is not clear how to compute these values efficiently.

In order to overcome this, we suggest the following "guessing" approach. Each candidate edge is added to A with probability p. At the first iteration where the maximum rounded cost-effectiveness equals some value $\tilde{\rho}$, we set $p = \frac{1}{m}$ where m is the number of edges. After $O(\log n)$ iterations we increase p by a factor of 2 and we continue in the same manner until $p = 1$. However, after each iteration, each candidate edge that was not added to A, computes its cost-effectiveness and remains a candidate only if its rounded cost-effectiveness is still $\tilde{\rho}$.

Approximation ratio analysis. The approximation ratio of the algorithm is $O(\log n)$ in expectation. The general proof idea is similar to the analysis in our 2-ECSS algorithm. We assign a cost to all the cuts of size $k-1$ in H, as follows. For each cut C, we define $cost(C) = 1/\tilde{\rho}(e)$ where e is an edge that covers C in the first iteration in which it is covered in the algorithm, and $cost(C) = 0$ if $\tilde{\rho}(e) = \infty$. Note that all the edges added to A in a specific iteration have the same rounded cost-effectiveness, hence $cost(C)$ is well-defined.

Our goal is to show that $w(A) \approx \sum_C cost(C) \le O(\log n)w(A^*)$, where A^* is an optimal augmentation. The proof of the right inequality follows the proof of Lemma 3.4 with slight changes, and is based on the fact that we always add edges with maximum rounded cost-effectiveness.

For the left inequality, we show that $E[w(A)] \le 6 \cdot E[\sum_C cost(C)]$. The proof is based on showing that we do not add too many candidates to cover the same cuts. The intuition is that for each value of $\tilde{\rho}$, the maximum degree of a cut decreases during the algorithm. At the beginning $deg(C) \le m$ for all cuts, however if there are cuts with degree close to m they would probably be covered in the first $O(\log n)$ iterations where $p = \frac{1}{m}$. Similarly, when we reach the phase that $p = \frac{1}{2^i}$, the maximum degree of a cut is at most 2^i w.h.p, and since each candidate is added to A with probability $p = \frac{1}{2^i}$ then we do not add too many candidates to cover the same cuts. The full analysis appears in [7].

Time analysis. The algorithm takes $O(\log^3 n)$ iterations: we change the value of p every $O(\log n)$ iterations, and we increase p at most $O(\log n)$ times for each value of $\tilde{\rho}$. In addition, there are $O(\log n)$ possible values for $\tilde{\rho}$ because the weights are polynomial and there are at most $\binom{n}{2}$ minimum cuts of size $k-1$ in H.[5] All the candidates can compute p since they know the value of $\tilde{\rho}$ in each iteration.

To guarantee that the number of edges added to A is indeed $O(n)$, which is crucial for the time analysis, we suggest the following approach. Instead of adding candidates to A with probability p, each candidate becomes an *active candidate* with probability p. Then, we add to A a maximal number of active candidates without creating cycles. We show that this guarantees that all the cuts covered by active candidates are indeed covered at the end of the iteration, and that $|A| \le n-1$. We emphasize that this is important for the time analysis, however the approximation ratio analysis works exactly the same even if we add all the active candidates to A. At each iteration, all the vertices learn all the edges added to A. Since the number of edges added is at most $n-1$ in the *whole* algorithm, and since each of the $O(\log^3 n)$ iterations requires global communication, we get a time complexity of $O(D\log^3 n + n)$ rounds, which results in an $O(D\log^3 n + n)$-round $O(\log n)$-approximation for Aug_k.

[5]This follows from the minimum cut algorithm of Karger [20], another proof is in [6].

To solve k-ECSS, we start with an empty subgraph and in step $1 \le i \le k$ augment its connectivity from $i-1$ to i using our algorithm for Aug_i. According to Claim 2.1, this gives an $O(k(D\log^3 n + n))$-round $O(k\log n)$-approximation for k-ECSS.

5 UNWEIGHTED 3-ECSS

In this section, we show how to improve the time complexity of our k-ECSS algorithm to $O(D\log^3 n)$ rounds for the special case of *unweighted* 3-ECSS, showing the following.

THEOREM 1.3. *There is a distributed algorithm for unweighted 3-ECSS in the* CONGEST *model with an expected approximation ratio of $O(\log n)$, and time complexity of $O(D\log^3 n)$ rounds.*

This section gives a high-level overview of the algorithm, full details and proofs appear in [7]. The bottleneck of our k-ECSS algorithm is the cost-effectiveness computation. In the special case of *unweighted* 3-ECSS we show how to compute it in $O(D)$ rounds for a graph with diameter D. The main tool in our algorithm is the beautiful *cycle space sampling* technique introduced by Pritchard and Thurimella [33]. In a nutshell, this technique assigns to the edges of a 2-edge-connected graph labels $\phi(e)$, such that two edges e and f define a cut of size 2 in the graph if and only if $\phi(e) = \phi(f)$. We show that using the labels we can understand the structure of cuts of size 2 in a graph, and compute how many cuts are covered by an edge in $O(D)$ rounds.

Definitions and general structure of the algorithm. We say that $\{e, f\}$ is a *cut pair* in a 2-edge-connected graph G if removing e and f from G disconnects it.

Our algorithm for unweighted 3-ECSS starts by computing a 2-edge-connected subgraph H, and then augments its connectivity. To build H, we use an $O(D)$-round 2-approximation algorithm for *unweighted* 2-ECSS [1]. This algorithm starts by building a BFS tree T, and then augments its connectivity to 2. In particular, the diameter of H is $O(D)$. For an edge $e \notin T$, we define S_e^1 to be all the *tree edges* in the unique tree path covered by e. We say that $e \notin H$ covers a cut pair $\{f, f'\}$ if $\{f, f'\}$ is not a cut pair in $H \cup \{e\}$. For an edge $e \notin H$, we define S_e^2 to be all the *cut pairs* covered by e. During the algorithm, we maintain a set of edges A that includes all the edges added to the augmentation, initially $A = \emptyset$. C_e are all the cut pairs in S_e^2 that are not covered by A. The cost-effectiveness of an edge $e \in H$ is defined as in Aug_i. However, since all the edges have unit-weight, $\rho(e) = |C_e|$.

Our algorithm for augmenting the connectivity of H from 2 to 3, follows our algorithm for Aug_k in Section 4. At the beginning, edges $e \notin H \cup A$ compute their cost-effectiveness and become candidates if they have maximum rounded cost-effectiveness. Candidates are added to A with probability p, and we continue iteratively until all cut pairs are covered. We choose the probability p as in Section 4. A difference from the algorithm for Aug_k is that now we just add all the active candidates to A. As explained in Section 4, this does not affect the approximation ratio analysis. The pseudo-code for iteration i is given below.

(1) Each edge $e \notin H \cup A$ computes its rounded cost-effectiveness $\tilde{\rho}(e)$.
(2) Each edge $e \notin H \cup A$ with maximum rounded cost-effectiveness is a *candidate*.
(3) Each candidate e is added to the augmentation with probability p_i.
(4) If all the cut pairs in H are covered by A, the algorithm terminates, and the output is all the edges of A.

The choice of the probability p_i and the approximation ratio analysis follow our algorithm for Aug_k and its analysis. The number of iterations is $O(\log^3 n)$ as explained in our Aug_k algorithm. Hence, our goal is to explain how to implement the algorithm efficiently. The computation in line 2 takes $O(D)$ rounds as before, and the computation in line 3 is completely local. We next show how to implement lines 1 and 4 efficiently using the cycle space sampling technique.

5.1 The cycle space sampling technique

In [7], we give an overview of the cycle space sampling technique. Here we present the main conclusions that we use in our algorithm. Let T be the BFS tree, and let e be a non-tree edge, we denote by Cyc_e the unique cycle in $T \cup \{e\}$. Note that $Cyc_e = S_e^1 \cup \{e\}$. We assign labels to the edges, as follows. Each non-tree edge e chooses a uniformly independent $O(\log n)$-bit string $\phi(e)$. This defines ϕ for all the non-tree edges, and can be computed locally by the non-tree edges. For a tree edge t, the label $\phi(t)$ is defined as follows: $\phi(t) = \bigoplus_{t \in Cyc_e} \phi(e) = \bigoplus_{t \in S_e^1} \phi(e)$. (Where $\bigoplus$ stands for addition of vectors modulo 2). In [33], it is shown that the following algorithm allows to compute the labels of the tree edges in $O(D)$ rounds (see Theorem 4.2). We scan the tree from the leaves to the root, and each vertex v computes the label of $\{v, p(v)\}$ according to the non-tree edges adjacent to it and the labels it receives from its children, as follows. $\phi(\{v, p(v)\}) = \bigoplus_{f \in \delta(v) \setminus \{v, p(v)\}} \phi(f)$, where $\delta(v)$ is the set of edges adjacent to v. The time complexity is $O(D)$ rounds for scanning the tree since it is a BFS tree. As we explain in [7], the following property holds w.h.p. See Figure 2 for an example.

Property 5.1. *For all the edges, $\phi(e) = \phi(f)$ if and only if $\{e, f\}$ is a cut pair.*

Lemma 5.1. *Property 5.1 holds w.h.p.*

5.2 Identifying cut pairs

Let G be a 2-edge-connected graph G, and let T be a spanning tree of it. Note that since T is connected, any cut pair has at least one tree edge. We next give a simple characterization of all the cut pairs in a graph based on the cycle space sampling technique. From the definition of labels, it is easy to see that if e and f are two tree edges that are covered by the same non-tree edges, then $\phi(e) = \phi(f)$, which by Lemma 5.1 shows that $\{e, f\}$ is a cut pair. Similarly, if e is a tree edge covered by the unique non-tree edge f, then $\phi(e) = \phi(f)$, and $\{e, f\}$ is a cut pair. In [7], we prove that these are the only cut pairs in the graph.

Claim 5.2. *The edges $\{e, f\}$ are a cut pair in a 2-edge connected graph G where e is a tree edge, if and only if one of the following holds.*

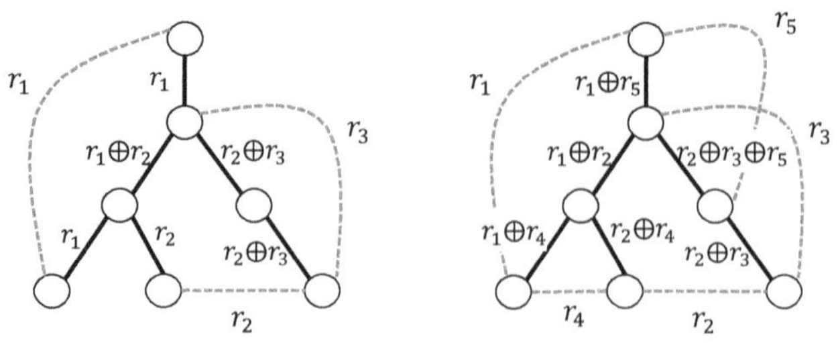

Figure 2: On the left there is a 2-edge-connected graph, with 3 non-tree edges with the labels r_1, r_2, r_3. The label of a tree edge e is the xor of labels of non-tree edges that cover it. The cut pairs are all the pairs of edges with the same label. On the right, there are 2 additional non-tree edges, and now all the labels of edges are unique and there are no cut pairs.

(1) e is a tree edge and f is the unique non-tree edge in G that covers it.
(2) e and f are tree edges covered by the exact same non-tree edges.

The next corollary follows from Claim 5.2.

Corollary 5.3. *Let H be a 2-edge-connected spanning subgraph of a graph G and let T be a spanning tree of H, an edge $e \notin H$ covers the cut pair $\{f, f'\}$ if an only if exactly one of f, f' is in S_e^1.*

Proof. Let $\{f, f'\}$ be a cut pair in H. If f and f' are two tree edges, they are covered by the exact same non-tree edges in H according to Claim 5.2. By the same claim, $\{f, f'\}$ is not a cut pair in $H \cup \{e\}$ if and only if they are not covered by the exact same non-tree edges in $H \cup \{e\}$. This happens if and only if e covers exactly one of f, f'.

If $\{f, f'\}$ has one tree edge, say f, then f' is the only non-tree edge that covers it in H according to Claim 5.2. By the same claim, $\{f, f'\}$ is not a cut pair in $H \cup \{e\}$ if and only if f' is not the only non-tree edge in $H \cup \{e\}$ that covers f. This happens if and only if e covers f. □

5.3 Implementing the algorithm

We next explain how to use the labels for computing the cost-effectiveness. First, we apply the $O(D)$-round algorithm for computing the labels on the graph $H \cup A$. We next assume that Property 5.1 holds, and show how to compute the cost-effectiveness. We later address the case that it does not happen, and show how it affects the algorithm.

For computing cost-effectiveness, we need the following definitions. Let t be a tree edge, we denote by $n_{\phi(t)}$ the number of edges in $H \cup A$ with the label $\phi(t)$. For an edge $e \notin H \cup A$, we denote by $n_{\phi(t),e}$ the number of edges in S_e^1 with label $\phi(t)$. Note that if $\{f, f'\}$ is a cut pair, then $\phi(f) = \phi(f')$, we say that $\phi(f)$ is the label of the cut. We next show the following.

Claim 5.4. *For an edge $e \notin H \cup A$, the number of cut pairs with label $\phi(t)$ covered by e is exactly $n_{\phi(t),e}(n_{\phi(t)} - n_{\phi(t),e})$.*

Proof. According to Corollary 5.3, the edge e covers a cut pair $\{f, f'\}$ if and only if exactly one of f, f' is in S_e^1. Hence, for a tree edge $f \in S_e^1$ with label $\phi(t)$, the edge e covers all the cut pairs of the form $\{f, f'\}$ where $\{f, f'\}$ is a cut pair and $f' \notin S_e^1$, there are $n_{\phi(t)} - n_{\phi(t),e}$ cuts of this form. Since there are $n_{\phi(t),e}$ edges in S_e^1 with label $\phi(t)$, the number of cut pairs with label $\phi(t)$ covered by e is exactly $n_{\phi(t),e}(n_{\phi(t)} - n_{\phi(t),e})$. □

According to Claim 5.4, if we sum the value $n_{\phi(t),e}(n_{\phi(t)} - n_{\phi(t),e})$ over all the labels $\phi(t)$ where $n_{\phi(t),e} \geq 1$ we get the number of cut pairs in $H \cup A$ covered by e, which is exactly $\rho(e) = |C_e|$. Therefore, to compute cost-effectiveness we need to explain how each edge $e \notin H \cup A$ learns all the relevant values $n_{\phi(t)}, n_{\phi(t),e}$. The high-level idea is:

(a). Each non-tree edge $e \in H$ learns the values $(t, \phi(t))$ for all the edges in S_e^1.
(b). Each tree edge t learns $n_{\phi(t)}$.
(c). Each edge $e \notin H \cup A$ learns all the values $(t, \phi(t), n_{\phi(t)})$ for all the edges in S_e^1.
(d). Each edge $e \notin H \cup A$ deduces all the relevant values $n_{\phi(t)}, n_{\phi(t),e}$.

Note that after step (c), each edge $e \notin H \cup A$ knows all the labels of edges in S_e^1, and all the relevant values $n_{\phi(t)}$. This allows computing $n_{\phi(t)}, n_{\phi(t),e}$. We next explain how to implement steps (a)-(c) in $O(D)$ rounds. Let m_t be a piece of information of $O(\log n)$ bits associated with the tree edge t. Then, all the vertices can learn in $O(D)$ rounds all the values (t, m_t) for the tree edges in the tree path between them to the root r, as follows. First, each vertex v sends to its children the message (t, m_t) for the tree edge $t = \{v, p(v)\}$. Then, it sends to them the message it receives from its parent in the previous round. After $O(D)$ rounds each vertex v knows all the values (t, m_t) for all the tree edges in the path $P_{r,v}$.

Let $e = \{u, v\}$ be a non-tree edge, the vertices v and u can learn all the values (t, m_t) for all the tree edges in S_e^1 by exchanging between them full information about the paths $P_{r,u}, P_{r,v}$ in $O(D)$ rounds. This allows them to compute their LCA, learn which edges are in S_e^1 and learn all the relevant values (t, m_t). Hence, step (a) can be easily computed in $O(D)$ rounds, and step (c) can be computed in $O(D)$ rounds after all the tree edges learn the values $n_{\phi(t)}$. We next explain how the tree edges learn the values $n_{\phi(t)}$ in step (b).

Let t be a tree edge with label $\phi(t)$. Since H is 2-edge-connected, there is at least one non-tree edge $e \in H$ that covers t. Let $n_{\phi(t),e}$ be the number of tree edges in $Cyc_e = S_e^1 \cup \{e\}$ with label $\phi(t)$. Then, the following holds.

Claim 5.5. *If $e \in H$ covers t, then $n_{\phi(t),e} = n_{\phi(t)}$.*

Proof. According to Property 5.1 (that holds w.h.p by Lemma 5.1), $\{f, f'\}$ is a cut pair in $H \cup A$ if and only if $\phi(f) = \phi(f')$. We consider two cases.

If t is covered by only one non-tree edge in $H \cup A$, this edge is necessarily e, and $\phi(t) = \phi(e)$ by the definition of labels. Note that the edge e is in a cut pair $\{e, f\}$ if and only if f is a tree edge that is covered only by e according to Claim 5.2. Since $\{e, f\}$ is a cut pair if and only if $\phi(e) = \phi(f)$, it follows that all the edges with label $\phi(t) = \phi(e)$ are in Cyc_e, which shows that $n_{\phi(t),e} = n_{\phi(t)}$.

If t is covered by at least two edges in $H \cup A$, then $\{t, f\}$ is a cut pair if and only if f is a tree edge covered by the exact same edges as t, according to Claim 5.2. In particular, e covers f. This shows that all the edges with label $\phi(t)$ are in $S_e^1 \subseteq Cyc_e$, which gives $n_{\phi(t),e} = n_{\phi(t)}$. □

Hence, to learn $n_{\phi(t)}$, it is enough to learn $n_{\phi(t),e}$ for an edge $e \in H$ that covers t. In addition, the edge e learns in step (a) the labels of all the tree edges in S_e^1, which allows it computing $n_{\phi(t),e}$. Note that exactly one of the endpoints of e, say u, is a descendant of t in T, and u can pass the information $n_{\phi(t),e}$ to t. In order that all the tree edges would learn the values $n_{\phi(t)}$ simultaneously we use a pipelined upcast over the BFS tree. Each leaf u sends to its parent the values $n_{\phi(t)}$ for all the tree edges above it in the tree where u knows the value $n_{\phi(t)}$. Each internal vertex sends to its parent these values based on the messages it receives from its children, and the values already known to it. We can pipeline the computations to get a time complexity of $O(D)$ rounds. This completes the description of the cost-effectiveness computation, and shows how to implement Line 1 of the algorithm in $O(D)$ rounds.

To complete the description of the algorithm, we need to explain how to verify if $H \cup A$ is 3-edge-connected in Line 4 of the algorithm in $O(D)$ rounds. To do so, we use again the algorithm for computing the labels. Now we apply it on the graph $H \cup A$ in Line 4 (after we added new edges to A in Line 3). We also compute for each tree edge the value $n_{\phi(t)}$ in $O(D)$ rounds as before.

Claim 5.6. *The graph $H \cup A$ is 3-edge connected if and only if $n_{\phi(t)} = 1$ for all the tree edges.*

Proof. According to Property 5.1, $\{e, f\}$ is a cut pair if and only if $\phi(e) = \phi(f)$. Hence, $n_{\phi(t)} = 1$ for all the tree edges, if and only if none of the tree edges is in a cut pair in $H \cup A$. Since any cut pair has at least one tree edge, this happens if and only if $H \cup A$ is 3-edge-connected. □

After each tree edge knows $n_{\phi(t)}$, we can check in $O(D)$ rounds if at least one of these values is greater than 1 by communication over the BFS tree. This completes the description of Line 4 of the algorithm. In [7] we show that although our algorithm assumes that Property 5.1 holds, which happens w.h.p, the algorithm always terminates after $O(\log^3 n)$ iterations, at the end $H \cup A$ is *guaranteed* to be 3-edge-connected, and the approximation ratio is still $O(\log n)$ in expectation. Since each iteration takes $O(D)$ rounds, this results in an $O(D \log^3 n)$-round $O(\log n)$-approximation for unweighted 3-ECSS.

Remarks. Our 3-ECSS algorithm works also for *weighted* 3-ECSS. However, in the weighted case our algorithm starts by computing an MST and not a BFS tree. Since the time complexity of the algorithm depends on the height of the tree, each iteration now takes $O(h_{MST})$ rounds instead of $O(D)$ rounds. Hence, the time complexity of the algorithm in the worst case is $O(n \log^3 n)$, which is worse than the algorithm in Section 4.

In our 2-ECSS algorithm, each non-tree edge needed to learn an $O(\log n)$-bit piece of information: how many tree edges vote for it or how many uncovered tree edges are in S_e. This allowed to parallelize the computations efficiently. Yet, in our 3-ECSS algorithm, non-tree edges need to learn *all* the labels of the tree edges in S_e^1. For this reason, achieving a sublinear algorithm for weighted 3-ECSS seems to be more involved.

A key observation that allows us to achieve $O(D \log^3 n)$-round algorithm for unweighted 3-ECSS is that for any cut pair $\{f, f'\}$ in H there is some non-tree edge $e \in H$ where $\{f, f'\} \subseteq Cyc_e$. For $k > 3$ this observation is not true anymore, which suggests that this problem may be harder.

6 DISCUSSION

In this paper, we provide efficient distributed algorithms for k-ECSS. While our results improve significantly the time complexity of previous algorithms, many intriguing questions remain open.

First, our algorithms obtain $O(\log n)$-approximations, and a natural question is whether it is possible to design efficient algorithms with a better approximation ratio. Our approach which is based on set cover allows us to parallelize the computations efficiently, however it cannot achieve an approximation better than $O(\log n)$. Another option is to try to convert sequential algorithms for k-ECSS to distributed ones. However, algorithms that obtain constant approximations in the sequential setting seem inherently sequential [16, 17, 22].

Second, we have presented a sublinear algorithm for *weighted* 2-ECSS. The k-ECSS problem seems to be more involved for $k > 2$, and it would be interesting to study whether sublinear algorithms exist also for $k > 2$, or alternatively prove that this problem is indeed harder. In addition, we showed here an $O(D \log^3 n)$-round algorithm for *unweighted* 3-ECSS. A natural question is whether algorithms with a similar time complexity exist also for $k > 3$.

Finally, all our algorithms are randomized, and it would be interesting to study whether it is possible to obtain also *deterministic* algorithms with a similar time complexity.

Acknowledgments: I would like to thank Keren Censor-Hillel for her guidance and support, and for many helpful comments. I am also grateful to Merav Parter for suggesting the connection between the FT-MST algorithm [15] and the 2-ECSS problem.

REFERENCES

[1] Keren Censor-Hillel and Michal Dory. 2017. Fast Distributed Approximation for TAP and 2-Edge-Connectivity. In *21st International Conference on Principles of Distributed Systems (OPODIS)*. 21:1–21:20.

[2] Keren Censor-Hillel and Michal Dory. 2018. Distributed Spanner Approximation. *To appear in PODC 2018* (2018). https://arxiv.org/abs/1802.03160

[3] Keren Censor-Hillel, Mohsen Ghaffari, and Fabian Kuhn. 2014. Distributed connectivity decomposition. In *Proceedings of the 2014 ACM symposium on Principles of distributed computing (PODC)*. ACM, 156–165.

[4] Joseph Cheriyan and Ramakrishna Thurimella. 2000. Approximating minimum-size k-connected spanning subgraphs via matching. *SIAM J. Comput.* 30, 2 (2000), 528–560.

[5] Vasek Chvatal. 1979. A greedy heuristic for the set-covering problem. *Mathematics of operations research* 4, 3 (1979), 233–235.

[6] Efim A Dinitz, Alexander V Karzanov, and Michael V Lomonosov. 1976. On the structure of the system of minimum edge cuts in a graph. *Issledovaniya po Diskretnoi Optimizatsii* (1976), 290–306.

[7] Michal Dory. 2018. Distributed Approximation of Minimum k-edge-connected Spanning Subgraphs. *arXiv:1805.07764* (2018). http://arxiv.org/abs/1805.07764

[8] Michael Elkin. 2006. An unconditional lower bound on the time-approximation trade-off for the distributed minimum spanning tree problem. *SIAM J. Comput.* 36, 2 (2006), 433–456.

[9] Michael Elkin. 2017. A Simple Deterministic Distributed MST Algorithm, with Near-Optimal Time and Message Complexities. In *Proceedings of the ACM Symposium on Principles of Distributed Computing (PODC)*. 157–163.

[10] Harold N Gabow and Suzanne R Gallagher. 2012. Iterated rounding algorithms for the smallest k-edge connected spanning subgraph. *SIAM J. Comput.* 41, 1 (2012), 61–103.

[11] Harold N Gabow, Michel X Goemans, Éva Tardos, and David P Williamson. 2009. Approximating the smallest k-edge connected spanning subgraph by LP-rounding. *Networks* 53, 4 (2009), 345–357.

[12] Robert G. Gallager, Pierre A. Humblet, and Philip M. Spira. 1983. A distributed algorithm for minimum-weight spanning trees. *ACM Transactions on Programming Languages and systems (TOPLAS)* 5, 1 (1983), 66–77.

[13] Juan A Garay, Shay Kutten, and David Peleg. 1998. A sublinear time distributed algorithm for minimum-weight spanning trees. *SIAM J. Comput.* 27, 1 (1998), 302–316.

[14] Mohsen Ghaffari and Fabian Kuhn. 2013. Distributed Minimum Cut Approximation. *CoRR* abs/1305.5520 (2013). arXiv:1305.5520 http://arxiv.org/abs/1305.5520

[15] Mohsen Ghaffari and Merav Parter. 2016. Near-Optimal Distributed Algorithms for Fault-Tolerant Tree Structures. In *Proceedings of the 28th ACM Symposium on Parallelism in Algorithms and Architectures (SPAA)*. ACM, 387–396.

[16] Michel X Goemans, Andrew V Goldberg, Serge A Plotkin, David B Shmoys, Eva Tardos, and David P Williamson. 1994. Improved Approximation Algorithms for Network Design Problems. In *SODA*, Vol. 94. 223–232.

[17] Kamal Jain. 2001. A factor 2 approximation algorithm for the generalized Steiner network problem. *Combinatorica* 21, 1 (2001), 39–60.

[18] Lujun Jia, Rajmohan Rajaraman, and Torsten Suel. 2002. An efficient distributed algorithm for constructing small dominating sets. *Distributed Computing* 15, 4 (2002), 193–205.

[19] David S Johnson. 1974. Approximation algorithms for combinatorial problems. *Journal of computer and system sciences* 9, 3 (1974), 256–278.

[20] David R. Karger. 1993. Global Min-cuts in RNC, and Other Ramifications of a Simple Min-Cut Algorithm. In *Proceedings of the Fourth Annual Symposium on Discrete Algorithms, (SODA)*. 21–30.

[21] Samir Khuller. 1996. Approximation algorithms for finding highly connected subgraphs. In *Approximation algorithms for NP-hard problems*. PWS Publishing Co., 236–265.

[22] Samir Khuller and Uzi Vishkin. 1994. Biconnectivity approximations and graph carvings. *Journal of the ACM (JACM)* 41, 2 (1994), 214–235.

[23] Guy Kortsarz and Zeev Nutov. 2010. Approximating minimum cost connectivity problems. In *Dagstuhl Seminar Proceedings*. Schloss Dagstuhl-Leibniz-Zentrum für Informatik.

[24] Sven O Krumke, Peter Merz, Tim Nonner, and Katharina Rupp. 2007. Distributed approximation algorithms for finding 2-edge-connected subgraphs. In *International Conference On Principles Of Distributed Systems (OPODIS)*. Springer, 159–173.

[25] Fabian Kuhn, Thomas Moscibroda, and Roger Wattenhofer. 2016. Local computation: Lower and upper bounds. *Journal of the ACM (JACM)* 63, 2 (2016), 17.

[26] Shay Kutten and David Peleg. 1998. Fast distributed construction of small k-dominating sets and applications. *Journal of Algorithms* 28, 1 (1998), 40–66.

[27] László Lovász. 1975. On the ratio of optimal integral and fractional covers. *Discrete mathematics* 13, 4 (1975), 383–390.

[28] Danupon Nanongkai and Hsin-Hao Su. 2014. Almost-tight distributed minimum cut algorithms. In *International Symposium on Distributed Computing (DISC)*. Springer, 439–453.

[29] Gopal Pandurangan, Peter Robinson, and Michele Scquizzato. 2017. A time- and message-optimal distributed algorithm for minimum spanning trees. In *Proceedings of the 49th Annual ACM SIGACT Symposium on Theory of Computing (STOC)*. ACM, 743–756.

[30] David Peleg. 2000. *Distributed Computing: A Locality-Sensitive Approach.* SIAM.

[31] David Peleg and Vitaly Rubinovich. 2000. A near-tight lower bound on the time complexity of distributed minimum-weight spanning tree construction. *SIAM J. Comput.* 30, 5 (2000), 1427–1442.

[32] David Pritchard. 2005. *Robust network computation.* Master's thesis. MIT.

[33] David Pritchard and Ramakrishna Thurimella. 2011. Fast computation of small cuts via cycle space sampling. *ACM Transactions on Algorithms (TALG)* 7, 4 (2011), 46.

[34] Sridhar Rajagopalan and Vijay V Vazirani. 1998. Primal-dual RNC approximation algorithms for set cover and covering integer programs. *SIAM J. Comput.* 28, 2 (1998), 525–540.

[35] Atish Das Sarma, Stephan Holzer, Liah Kor, Amos Korman, Danupon Nanongkai, Gopal Pandurangan, David Peleg, and Roger Wattenhofer. 2012. Distributed verification and hardness of distributed approximation. *SIAM J. Comput.* 41, 5 (2012), 1235–1265.

[36] Amir Shadeh. 2009. *Distributed primal-dual approximation algorithms for network design problems.* Master's thesis. Open University of Israel.

[37] Ramakrishna Thurimella. 1995. Sub-linear distributed algorithms for sparse certificates and biconnected components. In *Proceedings of the fourteenth annual ACM symposium on Principles of distributed computing (PODC)*. ACM, 28–37.

Brief Announcement: Distributed Minimum Vertex Coloring and Maximum Independent Set in Chordal Graphs*

Christian Konrad†
Department of Computer Science, University of Bristol
Bristol, United Kingdom
Christian.Konrad@bristol.ac.uk

Viktor Zamaraev‡
Department of Computer Science, Durham University
Durham, United Kingdom
Viktor.Zamaraev@durham.ac.uk

ABSTRACT

We give deterministic distributed $(1 + \epsilon)$-approximation algorithms for Minimum Vertex Coloring and Maximum Independent Set on chordal graphs in the LOCAL model. Our coloring algorithm runs in $O(\frac{1}{\epsilon} \log n)$ rounds, and our independent set algorithm has a runtime of $O(\frac{1}{\epsilon} \log(\frac{1}{\epsilon}) \log^* n)$ rounds. For coloring, existing lower bounds imply that the dependencies on $\frac{1}{\epsilon}$ and $\log n$ are best possible. For independent set, we prove that $\Omega(\frac{1}{\epsilon})$ rounds are necessary.

Both our algorithms make use of the tree decomposition of the input chordal graph. They iteratively peel off interval subgraphs, which are identified via the tree decomposition of the input graph, thereby partitioning the vertex set into $O(\log n)$ layers. For coloring, each interval graph is colored independently, which results in various coloring conflicts between the layers. These conflicts are then resolved in a separate phase, using the particular structure of our partitioning. For independent set, only the first $O(\log \frac{1}{\epsilon})$ layers are required as they already contain a large enough independent set. We develop a $(1 + \epsilon)$-approximation maximum independent set algorithm for interval graphs, which we then apply to those layers.

This work raises the question as to how useful tree decompositions are for distributed computing.

KEYWORDS

local model, approximation algorithms, minimum vertex coloring, maximum independent set, chordal graphs

ACM Reference Format:

Christian Konrad and Viktor Zamaraev. 2018. Brief Announcement: Distributed Minimum Vertex Coloring and Maximum Independent Set in Chordal Graphs. In *PODC '18: ACM Symposium on Principles of Distributed Computing, July 23–27, 2018, Egham, United Kingdom.* ACM, New York, NY, USA, 3 pages. https://doi.org/10.1145/3212734.3212787

1 INTRODUCTION

The LOCAL Model. In the LOCAL model of distributed computation, the input graph $G = (V, E)$ represents a communication network, where every network node hosts a computational entity. Nodes have unique IDs. A distributed algorithm is executed on all network nodes simultaneously and proceeds in discrete rounds. Initially, besides their own IDs, nodes only know their neighbors. Each round consists of a computation and a communication phase. In the computation phase, nodes are allowed to perform unlimited computations. In the communication phase, nodes can exchange individual messages of unbounded sizes with each of their neighbors. The runtime of the algorithm is the total number of communication rounds, and the objective is to design algorithms that run in as few rounds as possible. The output is typically distributed: For vertex colorings, it is required that upon termination of the algorithm, every node knows its own color, and for independent sets, every node knows whether it participates in the independent set.

Distributed Vertex Coloring. Vertex coloring problems have been studied in distributed computational models since more than 30 years. Given a graph $G = (V, E)$, a *(legal) c-coloring* of G is an assignment $\gamma : V \rightarrow [c]$ of at most c colors to the nodes of G such that every pair of adjacent nodes receives different colors. The algorithmic challenge lies in computing colorings with few colors. The *chromatic number* $\chi(G)$ is the smallest c such that there is a c-coloring of G. The MINIMUM VERTEX COLORING problem (MVC), one of the problems studied in this paper, asks to find a $\chi(G)$-coloring. This is a difficult task, even in the centralized setting: In general graphs, MVC is hard to approximate within a factor of $n^{1-\epsilon}$, for any $\epsilon > 0$ [22].

Most research papers on distributed vertex coloring address the problem of computing a $(\Delta + 1)$-coloring, where Δ is the maximum degree of the input graph. In the distributed setting, this is a non-trivial task, and a long line of research has culminated in the randomized algorithm of Chang et al. [7], which runs in $O(\log^* n + 2^{\sqrt{\log \log n}})$ rounds, and the deterministic algorithm of Fraigniaud et al. [10], which runs in $O(\sqrt{\Delta} \log^{2.5} \Delta + \log^* n)$ rounds.

Only very few research papers address the MVC problem in a distributed model itself. On general graphs, the best distributed algorithm computes a $O(\log n)$-approximation in $O(\log^2 n)$ rounds [2]. This algorithm uses exponential time computations, which due to the computational hardness of MVC is necessary unless $P = NP$. Barenboim et al. [4] gave a $O(n^{\epsilon})$-approximation algorithm that runs in $\exp O(1/\epsilon)$ rounds. Both the exponential time computations and the relatively large best known approximation factor of $O(\log n)$ on general graphs motivate the study of special graph classes. Besides results on graph classes with bounded chromatic number [3, 13, 14], the only graph class with unbounded chromatic number that has been addressed in the literature are *interval graphs*,

*A full version of this paper appears in [17].
†C. Konrad was supported by DIMAP and by EPSRC award EP/N011163/1.
‡V. Zamaraev was supported by EPSRC award EP/P020372/1.

PODC '18, July 23–27, 2018, Egham, United Kingdom

ACM ISBN 978-1-4503-5795-1/18/07.
https://doi.org/10.1145/3212734.3212787

which are the intersection graphs of intervals on the line. Halldórsson and Konrad gave a $(1+\epsilon)$-approximation algorithm for MVC on interval graphs that runs in $O(\frac{1}{\epsilon}\log^* n)$ rounds [16] (see also [15]). This work is the most relevant related work to our results.

Distributed Independent Sets. An *independent set* in a graph is a subset of pairwise non-adjacent nodes. In this paper we study the MAXIMUM INDEPENDENT SET problem (MIS) that asks to find an independent set of maximum size. Similar to MVC, the MIS problem is hard to approximate within a factor of $n^{1-\epsilon}$, for every $\epsilon > 0$ [22]. In the distributed setting, Luby [20] and independently Alon et al. [1] gave distributed $O(\log n)$ rounds maximal independent set algorithms more than 30 years ago. Improved results are possible for graphs with bounded maximum degree ([5, 11]) or on specific graph classes (e.g. [8, 21]). Using exponential time computations, a $(1+\epsilon)$-approximation to MIS can be computed in general graphs in $O(\frac{1}{\epsilon}\log n)$ rounds [6] (see also [12]). Deterministic distributed MIS algorithms may be inferior to randomized ones: It is known that every deterministic MIS $O(1)$-approximation algorithm on a path requires $\Omega(\log^* n)$ rounds [9, 18], while a simple randomized $O(1)$ rounds $O(1)$-approximation algorithm exists [9].

Chordal Graphs. In this paper, we study MVC and MIS on *chordal graphs*. A graph is chordal, if every cycle on at least four nodes contains a *chord*, i.e., an edge connecting two non-consecutive nodes of the cycle. Chordal graphs play an important role in graph theory and have many applications, for example in belief propagation in machine learning. They constitute a superclass of interval graphs and trees and an inportant subclass of perfect graphs. The key motivations for our work are as follows:

1. Minimum Vertex Colorings. Since the best known distributed MVC algorithm only gives a $O(\log n)$-approximation, we are interested in pinpointing graph structures that are difficult to handle. In this paper, we show that MVC and MIS can both be well solved on chordal graphs. A defining feature of a chordal graph is that it does not contain any induced cycles of lengths at least 4. This in turn implies that difficult instances for distributed coloring necessarily contain induced cycles of length at least 4.

Furthermore, as previously mentioned, MVC can be solved well on interval graphs in the distributed setting [16]. We are therefore interested in identifying more general graph classes that admit distributed $(1+\epsilon)$-approximation algorithms for MVC. Since trees are chordal, Linial's lower bound for coloring trees applies [19]. Linial proved that coloring trees with a constant number of colors requires $\Omega(\log n)$ rounds, which gives a $\Omega(\log n)$ lower bound for any constant factor approximation to MVC on chordal graphs. This separates the difficulties of MVC on chordal and interval graphs. Furthermore, it is proved in [16] that a $(1+\epsilon)$-approximation to MVC on interval graphs requires $\Omega(\frac{1}{\epsilon})$ rounds. Combined, we obtain a $\Omega(\frac{1}{\epsilon}+\log n)$ lower bound on the round complexity for approximating MVC on chordal graphs within a factor of $1+\epsilon$.

2. Tree Decompositions. Tree decompositions are a powerful algorithmic tool that allow for the design of (centralized) linear time algorithms for NP-hard problems on graphs of bounded treewidth. They have played however only a minor role in the design of distributed algorithms. A *tree decomposition* of a graph $G = (V, E)$ is identified by a set of bags $S_1, S_2, \ldots \subseteq V$ that are arranged in a forest $\mathcal{T}$ such that every adjacent pair of nodes $uv \in E$ is contained in at least one bag, and, for any $v \in V$, the set of bags that contain v induces a non-empty tree in $\mathcal{T}$, which we denote $\mathcal{T}(v)$. It is well known that a graph G is chordal if and only if it has a tree decomposition $\mathcal{T} = (C, \mathcal{E})$ whose set of vertices (i.e., bags) C is the family of maximal cliques of G. We call such a tree decomposition a *clique forest* of chordal graph G.

One potential reason for the limited success of tree decompositions in distributed computing is that even simple graphs, such as a ring on n nodes, require that many bags of their tree decompositions consist of nodes that are at distance $\Omega(n)$ in the original graph. For these graphs, it is thus impossible that nodes obtain coherent local views of a tree decomposition in $o(n)$ rounds.

Chordal graphs are well-suited for studying distributed algorithms that exploit the input graph's tree decomposition, since in a chordal graph each bag is a clique. Thus, every bag that contains a node $v \in V$ further only contains nodes that lie in v's neighborhood. We exploit this locality property and show that in the LOCAL model, nodes can indeed obtain coherent local views of a global tree decomposition.

2 NEW RESULTS

We give deterministic distributed $(1+\epsilon)$-approximation algorithms for MVC and MIS on chordal graphs in the LOCAL model. Our algorithm for MVC runs in $O(\frac{1}{\epsilon}\log n)$ rounds, and our algorithm for MIS has a runtime of $O(\frac{1}{\epsilon}\log(\frac{1}{\epsilon})\log^* n)$ rounds. For MVC, the dependencies of the runtime on $\log n$ and $\frac{1}{\epsilon}$ are best possible (though the existence of an algorithm with runtime $O(\frac{1}{\epsilon}+\log n)$ is not ruled out). For MIS, we prove that any, possibly randomized, $(1+\epsilon)$-approximation algorithm requires $\Omega(\frac{1}{\epsilon})$ rounds, even on paths.

We say that a path in a graph is *binary*, if all its vertices have degree at most 2 in the graph. We say that a binary path is *pendant*, if at least one of its end vertices has degree 1; and we say that it is *internal*, if all its vertices have degree 2.

2.1 Minimum Vertex Coloring

Our algorithm consists of the pruning, the coloring, and the color correction phases: In the pruning phase, the node set V is partitioned into at most $\lceil \log n \rceil$ *layers* $V_1, \ldots, V_{\lceil \log n \rceil}$ such that, for every $i \in [\lceil \log n \rceil]$, $G[V_i]$ constitutes an interval graph. In each step of the pruning phase, we remove every node $v \in U_i$ from the current graph $G[U_i]$ (we set $U_1 = V$ and hence $G[U_1] = G$) whose corresponding subtree $\mathcal{T}(v)$ in the clique forest $\mathcal{T}_i$ of $G[U_i]$ is a subpath of a pendant path or an internal path of diameter at least $3k$. The set of removed nodes, which we denoted by V_i, induces an interval graph. We prove that the clique forest $\mathcal{T}_{i+1}$ of the resulting graph $G[U_{i+1}]$, where $U_{i+1} = U_i \setminus V_i$, can be obtained by removing all pendant paths and all internal paths of diameter at least $3k$ from $\mathcal{T}_i$. We also show that the pruning process ends after at most $\lceil \log n \rceil$ iterations and thus creates at most $\lceil \log n \rceil$ layers.

In the coloring phase, each interval graph $G[V_i]$ is colored with at most $(1+1/k)\chi(G[V_i])+1$ colors. In the centralized setting, it would be easy to color these interval graphs optimally. However, since we implement the algorithm in the distributed setting, and an optimal coloring on interval graphs cannot be computed distributively in few rounds, we impose a weaker quality guarantee that can be achieved distributively. The colorings of different layers are computed independently from each other and do not give a coherent coloring of the entire input graph.

In the color correction phase, these incoherencies are corrected. To this end, the colors of $V_{\lceil \log n \rceil}$ remain unchanged and we correct the layers iteratively, starting with layer $\lceil \log n \rceil - 1$ and proceeding downwards to layer V_1. In a general step, for every path $\mathcal{P} \in \mathcal{L}_i$, we show that the nodes $W \subseteq V_i$ whose subtrees are subpaths of $\mathcal{P}$ form an interval graph together with those nodes in $\bigcup_{j \geq i+1} V_j$ that have coloring conflicts towards W. Notice that each path $\mathcal{P}$ connects to at most two bags (i.e., maximal cliques) in $\mathcal{T}_i$. The neighborhood of W thus consists of subsets of these (at most two) cliques, which implies that all conflicting nodes in $\bigcup_{j \geq i+1} V_j$ are included in these cliques as well. We then reuse a recoloring result previously proved by Halldórsson and Konrad [16], which shows that we can resolve all conflicts by changing the colors of those nodes in W that are at distance at most $k + 3$ from the (at most) two conflicting cliques.

Theorem 2.1. *For every $\epsilon \geq \frac{2}{\chi(G)}$, there is a deterministic $(1 + \epsilon)$-approximation algorithm for MVC on chordal graphs that runs in $O(\frac{1}{\epsilon} \log n)$ rounds in the LOCAL model.*

2.2 Maximum Independent Set

Our distributed MIS algorithm uses an adapted version of the peeling process used in our coloring algorithm. The key observation that allows us to obtain a runtime of $o(\log n)$ is the fact that the first $O(\log \frac{1}{\epsilon})$ layers computed by our peeling process already contain an independent set of large enough size. Our algorithm proceeds as follows: In each iteration $i = 1, \ldots, O(\frac{1}{\epsilon})$ of the peeling process, we remove all pendant paths and all internal paths of large enough diameter[1] (let $\mathcal{L}_i$ be the set of removed paths) from the clique forest $\mathcal{T}_i$ of the graph induced by the remaining nodes. Next, we compute large independent sets among the nodes whose trees are included in each path $\mathcal{P} \in \mathcal{L}_i$. If $\mathcal{P}$ has a large independence number[2] then we run our $(1 + \epsilon)$-approximation algorithm for interval graphs in $O(\frac{1}{\epsilon} \log^* n)$ rounds (which we design as an auxiliary tool for our main algorithm for chordal graphs). If $\mathcal{P}$ has small independence number we need to compute an optimal independent set in order to locally stay within a $(1 + \epsilon)$-approximation guarantee. This can be achieved using only $O(\frac{1}{\epsilon})$ rounds, since paths with small independence number necessarily have small diameter. The runtime is thus dominated by the product of the number of iterations $O(\log \frac{1}{\epsilon})$ and the $O(\frac{1}{\epsilon} \log^* n)$ runtime of our MIS algorithm for interval graphs.

Theorem 2.2. *For any $\epsilon \in (0, 1/2)$, there is a deterministic $(1 + \epsilon)$-approximation algorithm for MIS on chordal graphs that runs in $O(\frac{1}{\epsilon} \log(\frac{1}{\epsilon}) \log^* n)$ rounds in the LOCAL model.*

2.3 Lower Bound on the Complexity for MIS

Using an indistinguishability argument, we obtain a lower bound on the round complexity for MIS on paths.

Theorem 2.3. *For every $\epsilon > 0$ and n large enough, every randomized algorithm in the LOCAL model with expected approximation factor at most $1 + \epsilon$ for MIS requires $\Omega(\frac{1}{\epsilon})$ rounds.*

[1]The *diameter* of a path in the clique forest is the maximum distance in the graph between the nodes belonging to the bags of the path.

[2]The *independence number* of a path in the clique forest is the maximum number of pairwise non-adjacent nodes that belongs to the bags of the path.

REFERENCES

[1] Noga Alon, László Babai, and Alon Itai. 1986. A fast and simple randomized parallel algorithm for the maximal independent set problem. *Journal of Algorithms* 7, 4 (1986), 567 – 583. https://doi.org/10.1016/0196-6774(86)90019-2

[2] Leonid Barenboim. 2012. On the Locality of Some NP-complete Problems. In *Proceedings of the 39th International Colloquium Conference on Automata, Languages, and Programming - Volume Part II (ICALP'12)*. Springer-Verlag, Berlin, Heidelberg, 403–415. https://doi.org/10.1007/978-3-642-31585-5_37

[3] Leonid Barenboim and Michael Elkin. 2010. Sublogarithmic distributed MIS algorithm for sparse graphs using Nash-Williams decomposition. *Distributed Computing* 22, 5 (2010), 363–379.

[4] Leonid Barenboim, Michael Elkin, and Cyril Gavoille. 2015. A Fast Network-Decomposition Algorithm and Its Applications to Constant-Time Distributed Computation. In *Post-Proceedings of the 22Nd International Colloquium on Structural Information and Communication Complexity - Volume 9439 (SIROCCO 2015)*. Springer-Verlag New York, Inc., New York, NY, USA, 209–223. https://doi.org/10.1007/978-3-319-25258-2_15

[5] Leonid Barenboim, Michael Elkin, Seth Pettie, and Johannes Schneider. 2016. The Locality of Distributed Symmetry Breaking. *J. ACM* 63, 3, Article 20 (June 2016), 45 pages. https://doi.org/10.1145/2903137

[6] Marijke H.L. Bodlaender, Magnús M. Halldórsson, Christian Konrad, and Fabian Kuhn. 2016. Brief Announcement: Local Independent Set Approximation. In *Proceedings of the 2016 ACM Symposium on Principles of Distributed Computing (PODC '16)*. ACM, New York, NY, USA, 93–95. https://doi.org/10.1145/2933057.2933068

[7] Yi-Jun Chang, Wenzheng Li, and Seth Pettie. 2018. An Optimal Distributed ($\Delta + 1$)-Coloring Algorithm?, In Proceedings of the 50th Annual ACM SIGACT Symposium on Theory of Computing. *arXiv preprint https://arxiv.org/abs/1711.01361*.

[8] Richard Cole and Uzi Vishkin. 1986. Deterministic Coin Tossing with Applications to Optimal Parallel List Ranking. *Inf. Control* 70, 1 (July 1986), 32–53. https://doi.org/10.1016/S0019-9958(86)80023-7

[9] Andrzej Czygrinow, Michal Hańćkowiak, and Wojciech Wawrzyniak. 2008. Fast Distributed Approximations in Planar Graphs. In *Distributed Computing*, Gadi Taubenfeld (Ed.). Springer Berlin Heidelberg, Berlin, Heidelberg, 78–92.

[10] Pierre Fraigniaud, Marc Heinrich, and Adrian Kosowski. 2016. Local Conflict Coloring. In *IEEE 57th Annual Symposium on Foundations of Computer Science, FOCS 2016, 9-11 October 2016, Hyatt Regency, New Brunswick, New Jersey, USA*. 625–634.

[11] Mohsen Ghaffari. 2016. An Improved Distributed Algorithm for Maximal Independent Set. In *Proceedings of the Twenty-seventh Annual ACM-SIAM Symposium on Discrete Algorithms (SODA '16)*. Society for Industrial and Applied Mathematics, Philadelphia, PA, USA, 270–277. http://dl.acm.org/citation.cfm?id=2884435.2884455

[12] Mohsen Ghaffari, Fabian Kuhn, and Yannic Maus. 2017. On the Complexity of Local Distributed Graph Problems. In *Proceedings of the 49th Annual ACM SIGACT Symposium on Theory of Computing (STOC 2017)*. ACM, New York, NY, USA, 784–797. https://doi.org/10.1145/3055399.3055471

[13] Mohsen Ghaffari and Christina Lymouri. 2017. Simple and Near-Optimal Distributed Coloring for Sparse Graphs. In *Distributed Computing: 31th International Symposium, DISC 2017, Vienna, Austria, October 16-20, 2017. Proceedings.*

[14] Andrew V. Goldberg, Serge A. Plotkin, and Gregory E. Shannon. 1988. Parallel Symmetry-Breaking in Sparse Graphs. *SIAM J. Discrete Math.* 1, 4 (1988), 434–446. https://doi.org/10.1137/0401044

[15] Magnús M. Halldórsson and Christian Konrad. 2014. *Distributed Algorithms for Coloring Interval Graphs*. Springer, 454–468. https://doi.org/10.1007/978-3-662-45174-8_31

[16] Magnús M. Halldórsson and Christian Konrad. 2017. Improved Distributed Algorithms for Coloring Interval Graphs with Application to Multicoloring Trees. In *Post-Proceedings of the 24th International Colloquium on Structural Information and Communication Complexity (SIROCCO 2017)*.

[17] Christian Konrad and Viktor Zamaraev. 2018. Distributed Coloring and Independent Set in Chordal Graphs. *arXiv preprint https://arxiv.org/abs/1805.04544* (2018).

[18] Christoph Lenzen and Roger Wattenhofer. 2008. Leveraging Linial's Locality Limit. In *Distributed Computing*, Gadi Taubenfeld (Ed.). Springer Berlin Heidelberg, Berlin, Heidelberg, 394–407.

[19] Nathan Linial. 1992. Locality in Distributed Graph Algorithms. *SIAM J. Comput.* 21, 1 (Feb. 1992), 193–201. https://doi.org/10.1137/0221015

[20] Michael Luby. 1986. A Simple Parallel Algorithm for the Maximal Independent Set Problem. *SIAM J. Comput.* 15, 4 (1986), 1036–1053. https://doi.org/10.1137/0215074

[21] Johannes Schneider and Roger Wattenhofer. 2010. An optimal maximal independent set algorithm for bounded-independence graphs. *Distributed Computing* 22, 5 (01 Aug 2010), 349–361. https://doi.org/10.1007/s00446-010-0097-1

[22] David Zuckerman. 2007. Linear Degree Extractors and the Inapproximability of Max Clique and Chromatic Number. *Theory of Computing* 3, 1 (2007), 103–128.

Brief Announcement: Simple and Local Independent Set Approximation

Ravi B. Boppana
MIT
USA
rboppana@mit.edu

Magnús M. Halldórsson*
Reykjavik University
Iceland
mmh@ru.is

Dror Rawitz†
Bar-Ilan University
Israel
dror.rawitz@biu.ac.il

ABSTRACT

We bound the performance guarantees that follow from Turán-like bounds for unweighted and weighted independent sets in bounded-degree graphs. In particular, a randomized approach of Boppana forms a simple 1-round distributed algorithm, as well as a streaming and preemptive online algorithm. We show it gives a tight $(\Delta+1)/2$-approximation in unweighted graphs of maximum degree Δ, which is best possible for 1-round distributed algorithms. For weighted graphs, it gives only a $(\Delta+1)$-approximation, but a simple modification results in an asymptotic expected $0.529(\Delta+1)$-approximation.

CCS CONCEPTS

• **Theory of computation → Approximation algorithms analysis; Distributed algorithms;**

KEYWORDS

independent set, Turán bound, approximation algorithm, distributed algorithm

ACM Reference Format:
Ravi B. Boppana, Magnús M. Halldórsson, and Dror Rawitz. 2018. Brief Announcement: Simple and Local Independent Set Approximation. In *PODC '18: ACM Symposium on Principles of Distributed Computing, July 23–27, 2018, Egham, United Kingdom.* ACM, New York, NY, USA, 3 pages. https://doi.org/10.1145/3212734.3212793

1 INTRODUCTION

Independent sets are among the most fundamental graph structures. A classic result of Turán [20] says that every graph $G = (V, E)$ contains an independent set of size at least $\text{Turán}(G) \doteq n/(\bar{d}+1)$, where $n = |V|$ is the number of vertices and $\bar{d} = 2m/n$ is the average degree, where $m = |E|$. Turán's bound is tight for regular graphs, but for non-regular graphs an improved bound was given independently by Caro [10] and Wei [21]:

$$\alpha(G) \geq \text{CaroWei}(G) \doteq \sum_{v \in V} \frac{1}{d(v)+1}, \tag{1}$$

where $\alpha(G)$ is the cardinality of a maximum independent set in G and $d(v)$ is the degree of vertex $v \in V$.

There are numerous proofs of the Caro-Wei bound, some involving simple greedy algorithms. Arguably the simplest argument known is a probabilistic one:

Uniformly randomly permute the vertices, and output the set of vertices that precede all their neighbors in the permutation. (2)

Each node v precedes its neighbors with probability $1/(d(v)+1)$, so by linearity of expectation the expected size of the output matches exactly $\text{CaroWei}(G)$. This argument, which first appeared in the book of Alon and Spencer [3], is due to Boppana [9]. It clearly leads to a very simple local decision rule once the permutation is selected.

An alternative formulation of the algorithm is practical in certain contexts.

Each vertex v picks a random real number x_v from $[0, 1]$. The vertex joins the independent set if its random number is larger than that of its neighbors. (3)

It suffices to select the numbers with precision $1/n^3$, for which collisions are very unlikely. This leads to a fully *1-local* algorithm, in which each node decides whether to join the independent set after a single round of communication with its neighbors. The same $O(\log n)$ bits a node transmits go to all of its neighbors, which matches the Broadcast-CONGEST model of distributed algorithms. Furthermore, it is asynchronous. This is just about the simplest distributed algorithm one could hope for.

The simplicity of the approach allows for other applications. The basic algorithm works well with edge streams, storing only the permutation and the current solution as a bit-vector. The storage can be reduced with an ϵ-min-wise permutation, at a small cost in performance. This can also be viewed as a preemptive online algorithm, where edges can cause nodes to be kicked out of the solution but never reenter.

Our contribution. The main purpose of this essay is to analyze the performance guarantees of Boppana's algorithm on graphs of maximum degree Δ. We show that it achieves a tight $(\Delta+1)/2$-approximation, which then also gives a bound on the fidelity of the Caro-Wei bound. In terms of the average degree $\bar{d}$, the performance is at most $(\bar{d}+2)/1.657$. We also show that the Turán bound has strictly (but only slightly) worse performance than the Caro-Wei bound for bounded-degree graphs, or $(\Delta+1)/2 + 1/(8\Delta)$.

We then address the case of weighted graphs, and find that unchanged Boppana's algorithm gives only a $(\Delta+1)$-approximation. However, a slight modification yields an improved approximation which asymptotically approaches $0.529(\Delta+1)$.

---

*Supported by grants nos. 152679-05 and 174484-05 from the Icelandic Research Fund.
†Supported by the Israel Science Foundation (grant no. 497/14).

ACM ISBN 978-1-4503-5795-1/18/07.
https://doi.org/10.1145/3212734.3212793

Related work. Turán [20] showed that $\alpha(G) \geq \textsc{Turán}(G)$. Caro [10] and Wei [21] independently showed (in unpublished technical reports) that $\alpha(G) \geq \textsc{CaroWei}(G)$. The bound can also be seen to follow from an earlier work of Erdős [15], who showed that the bound is tight only for disjoint collections of cliques. Observe that $\textsc{CaroWei}(G) \geq \textsc{Turán}(G)$, for every graph G.

The best sequential approximation known is $\tilde{O}(\Delta/\log^2 \Delta)$ [5], which uses semi-definite programming. This matches the inapproximability result known, up to doubly-logarithmic factors, that holds assuming the Unique Games Conjecture [4]. The problem is known to be NP-hard to approximate within an $O(\Delta/\log^4 \Delta)$ factor [12]. For small values of Δ, a $(\Delta + 3)/5$-approximation [7] is achievable combinatorially, but requires extensive local search.

Most works on distributed algorithms have focused on finding maximal independent sets, rather than optimizing their size. Boppana's algorithm corresponds to the first of $O(\log n)$ rounds of Luby's maximal independent set algorithm (see also Alon et al. [2]). As for approximations, $n^{\Theta(1/k)}$-approximation is achievable and best possible in k rounds of the LOCAL model [8], while Ghaffary, Kuhn, and Maus [16] showed that $(1 + \epsilon)$-approximation is possible within poly-logarithmic number of rounds. These upper bounds necessarily assume unlimited computation.

Bar-Yehuda et al. [6] gave a randomized Δ-approximation algorithm for weighted independent sets using the local ratio technique that runs in time $O(\text{MIS} \cdot \log W)$ rounds in the CONGEST model, where MIS is the number of rounds needed to compute a maximal independent set and W is the ratio between the largest and smallest edge weight. This result is incomparable to ours, since only the time complexity is probabilistic, while the approximation factor is always at most Δ.

Alon [1] gave nearly tight bounds for testing independence properties; his lower bound carries over to distributed algorithms, as we shall see in Sec. 2.1. For matchings, which correspond to independent sets in line graphs, Kuhn et al. [19] showed that achieving any constant factor approximation requires $\Omega(\max(\log \Delta/\log\log \Delta, \sqrt{\log n/\log\log n}))$ rounds. Censor-Hillel, Khoury, and Paz [11] presented a nearly quadratic lower bound on the number of rounds for solving maximum independent set exacly in the CONGEST model.

Halldórsson and Konrad [18] gave a randomized one-round distributed algorithm where nodes broadcast only a single bit that yields an independent set of expected size at least $0.24 \cdot \textsc{CaroWei}(G)$ on every graph G.

Streaming algorithms (including Boppana's) achieving Turán-like bounds in graphs and hypergraphs were considered in [17], and streaming algorithms for approximating $\textsc{CaroWei}(G)$ were given recently by Cormode et al. [13].

Motivated by a packet forwarding application, Emek et al. [14] considered the online set packing problem that corresponds to maintaining strong independent sets of large weight in hypergraphs under edge additions. We give a tight bound on their method for the special case of graphs.

2 CARO-WEI-TURÁN BOUNDS

We examine here how well the Caro-Wei and the Turán bounds perform on (unweighted) bounded-degree and sparse graphs.

We say that a bound $B(G)$ has a performance ratio $f(\Delta)$ if, for all graphs G with $\Delta(G) = \Delta$ it holds that $\alpha(G) \geq B(G) \geq \frac{\alpha(G)}{f(\Delta)}$.

Theorem 2.1. *CaroWei has performance ratio $(\Delta + 1)/2$.*

Proof. Let G be a graph. Let $\textsc{opt}$ be an optimal independent set of size $\alpha = \alpha(G)$ and let $V' = V \setminus \textsc{opt}$. Let O_i, for $i = 1, 2, \ldots, \Delta$, denote the number of vertices in $\textsc{opt}$ of degree i. Our approach is to separate the contributions of the different O_is to the Caro-Wei bound. The nodes of high degree have a smaller direct contribution, but also have an indirect contribution in forcing more nodes to be in V'.

Let m_{OPT} be the number of edges with an endpoint in $\textsc{opt}$. Each such edge has the other endpoint in V', whereas nodes in V' are incident on at most Δ edges. Thus,

$$\textstyle\sum_{i=1}^{\Delta} i \cdot O_i = m_{\text{OPT}} \leq \Delta |V'| \,. \quad (4)$$

Applying (4), we then obtain

$$\begin{aligned}
\textsc{CaroWei}(G) &= \textstyle\sum_{i=1}^{\Delta} \frac{O_i}{i+1} + \sum_{v \in V'} \frac{1}{d(v)+1} \\
&\geq \textstyle\sum_{i=1}^{\Delta} \frac{O_i}{i+1} + \frac{|V'|}{\Delta+1} \\
&\geq \textstyle\frac{1}{\Delta+1} \sum_{i=1}^{\Delta} O_i \left(\frac{\Delta+1}{i+1} + \frac{i}{\Delta}\right) \\
&= \textstyle\frac{1}{\Delta+1} \sum_{i=1}^{\Delta} O_i \left(2 + \frac{\Delta-i}{i+1} - \frac{\Delta-i}{\Delta}\right) \\
&\geq \textstyle\frac{1}{\Delta+1} \sum_{i=1}^{\Delta} O_i \cdot 2 \\
&= \textstyle\frac{2}{\Delta+1} \alpha(G) \,,
\end{aligned}$$

obtaining the approximation upper bound claimed. Observe that the bound is tight only if the graph is regular.

To see that the ratio attained is no better than $(\Delta + 1)/2$, observe that in any regular graph, Boppana's algorithm achieves a solution of exactly $n/(\Delta + 1)$, while in bipartite regular graphs the optimal solution has size $n/2$. □

We also analyze the performance of the Caro-Wei bound in terms of the average degree $\overline{d} = 2m/n$.

Theorem 2.2. *The performance ratio of CaroWei is $(\overline{d} + 2)/1.657$.*

Recall Turán's theorem that $\alpha(G) \geq \textsc{Turán}(G) = \frac{n}{\overline{d}+1} = \frac{n^2}{2m+n}$. We find that the guarantee of the Turán bound is strictly weaker than that of Caro-Wei, yet asymptotically equivalent.

Theorem 2.3. *Turán has performance ratio $\frac{(2\Delta+1)^2}{8\Delta} = \frac{\Delta+1}{2} + \frac{1}{8\Delta}$.*

2.1 Limitations of Distributed Algorithms

We may assume that we are equipped with unique labels from a universe of N labels, where $N \geq \Delta \cdot n$. The nodes have knowledge of n, Δ and N, and have unlimited bandwidth and computational ability. The nodes have distinct ports for communication with their neighbors, but do not initially know their labels.

Our result for Boppana's algorithm is optimal for 1-round algorithms. Observe that the lower bounds below hold also for randomized algorithms.

Theorem 2.4. *Every 1-round distributed algorithm has performance ratio at least $(\Delta + 1)/2$, even on unweighted regular graphs.*

Proof. In a single round, each node can only learn the labels of their neighbors and their random bits. Consider the graph $G_1 = K_{\Delta+1}$, and G_2, which is any Δ-regular bipartite graph. Distributions over neighborhoods are identical. Hence, no 1-round algorithm can distinguish between these graphs. All nodes will join the independent set with the same probability, averaged over all possible labelings, since they share the same views. This probability can be at most $1/(\Delta+1)$, as otherwise the algorithm would produce incorrect answers on $K_{\Delta+1}$. The size of the solution is then at most $n/(\Delta+1)$, while on every Δ-regular bipartite graphs, the optimal solution contains $n/2$ nodes. □

It is not clear if better results can be obtained when using more rounds. A weaker lower bound holds even for nearly logarithmic number of rounds.

Theorem 2.5. *There are positive constants c_1 and c_2 such that the following holds: Every $c_1 \log_\Delta n$-round distributed algorithm has performance ratio at least $c_2\Delta/\log\Delta$.*

Proof. Alon [1] constructs a Δ-regular graph G_1 of girth $\Omega(\log n/\log\Delta)$ with independence number $O(n\log\Delta/\Delta)$, and notes that it is well known that there exists a bipartite Δ-regular graph G_2 of girth $\Omega(\log n/\log\Delta)$. The distributions over the k-neighborhoods of these graphs are identical, for $k = O(\log n/\log\Delta)$. Hence, no k-round distributed algorithm can distinguish between the two. □

3 WEIGHTED GRAPHS

In the weighted setting, each node v is assigned a positive integral weight $w(v)$ and the goal is to find an independent set I maximizing the $\sum_{v\in I} w(v)$. For a set $X \subseteq V$, denote $w(X) = \sum_{x\in X} w(x)$.

Boppana's algorithm can be applied unchanged to weighted graphs, producing a solution B of expected weight $\mathbb{E}[w(B)] = \sum_{v\in B} \frac{w(v)}{d(v)+1}$ by linearity of expectation. This immediately implies that $\mathbb{E}[w(B)] \geq w(V)/(\Delta+1)$, for a performance ratio at most $\Delta+1$. To see that this is also the best possible bound, consider the complete bipartite graphs $K_{N,N}$, where the nodes on one side have weight 1 and on the other side weight Q, for a parameter $Q \geq \Delta^2$. The expected weight of the algorithm solution is $(N+NQ)/(\Delta+1)$, while the optimal solution is of weight NQ. The performance ratio is then $(\Delta+1)/(1+1/Q)$, which goes to $\Delta+1$ as Q gets large.

We therefore turn our attention to modifications that take the weights into account. We consider now a variation, Max, previously considered in an online setting in [14].

> Each node v picks a random real number x_v uniformly from $[0,1]$. It broadcasts the values x_v and w_v to its neighbors, who compute from it $r_v = x_v^{1/w_v}$. As before, each node u joins the solution if its value r_u is the highest among its neighbors.

The only difference is the computation of r_v, which now depends on the weight w_v. Again the algorithm runs in a single round of Broadcast-CONGEST, with correctness following as before. The algorithm was previously shown in [14] to attain a Δ-approximation.

We obtain a tight bound, which does not have a nice closed expression.

Theorem 3.1. *The performance ratio $\rho(\Delta)$ of Max, as a function of Δ, is given by $\frac{1}{\rho(\Delta)} = \min_{x\in[0,1]} \left(x^2/(\Delta+x) + 1/(x\Delta+1)\right)$.*

If we focus on the asymptotics as Δ gets large, we can ignore the additive terms in the denominators, obtaining that

$$\frac{1}{\rho(\Delta)} \underset{\Delta\to\infty}{\to} \min_{x\in[0,1]} \left(\frac{x^2}{\Delta+1} + \frac{1}{x(\Delta+1)}\right) = \frac{\min_{x\in[0,1]}\left(x^2+1/x\right)}{\Delta+1}.$$

The derivative is of $g(x) = x^2 + 1/x$ is $\frac{dg(x)}{dx} = 2x - 1/x^2$. Hence, it is maximized when $x = 2^{-1/3}$ for a ratio of $\frac{2^{2/3}}{3}(\Delta+1) \sim 0.529(\Delta+1)$.

Theorem 3.2. *The asymptotic performance ratio of Max is $\frac{2^{2/3}}{3}(\Delta+1) \sim 0.529(\Delta+1)$.*

For $\Delta = 2$, we find that $1/\rho \sim 0.593$, or $\rho \sim 1.657 \sim 0.562(\Delta+1)$, which is about 6% larger than $0.529(\Delta+1)$, but 20% smaller than Δ. For $\Delta = 1$, the algorithm can be made optimal by preferring nodes with higher weight than their sole neighbor.

4 CONCLUSION

It is surprising that the best distributed approximations known of independent sets are obtained by the simplest algorithm. Repeating the algorithm on the remaining graph will certainly give a better solution – the challenge is to quantify the improvement.

REFERENCES

[1] Noga Alon. 2010. On Constant Time Approximation of Parameters of Bounded Degree Graphs. In *Property Testing - Current Research and Surveys*. 234–239.
[2] Noga Alon, László Babai, and Alon Itai. 1986. A Fast and Simple Randomized Parallel Algorithm for the Maximal Independent Set Problem. *J. Algorithms* 7, 4 (1986), 567–583.
[3] Noga Alon and Joel H Spencer. 2016. *The probabilistic method* (fourth ed.). John Wiley & Sons.
[4] Per Austrin, Subhash Khot, and Muli Safra. 2009. Inapproximability of vertex cover and independent set in bounded degree graphs. In *24th IEEE CCC*. 74–80.
[5] Nikhil Bansal, Anupam Gupta, and Guru Guruganesh. 2015. On the Lovász Theta function for Independent Sets in Sparse Graphs. In *47th ACM STOC*. 193–200.
[6] Reuven Bar-Yehuda, Keren Censor-Hillel, Mohsen Ghaffari, and Gregory Schwartzman. 2017. Distributed Approximation of Maximum Independent Set and Maximum Matching. In *36th ACM PODC*. 165–174.
[7] Piotr Berman and Toshihiro Fujito. 1999. On Approximation Properties of the Independent Set Problem for Low Degree Graphs. *Theory Comput. Syst.* 32, 2 (1999), 115–132.
[8] Marijke H.L. Bodlaender, Magnús M. Halldórsson, Christian Konrad, and Fabian Kuhn. 2016. Brief Announcement: Local Independent Set Approximation. In *35th ACM PODC*. 377–378.
[9] Ravi B. Boppana. 1987. Personal communication to Joel Spencer.
[10] Y. Caro. 1979. *New results on the independence number*. Technical Report. Tel Aviv Univ.
[11] Keren Censor-Hillel, Seri Khoury, and Ami Paz. 2017. Quadratic and Near-Quadratic Lower Bounds for the CONGEST Model. In *31st DISC*. 10:1–10:16.
[12] Siu On Chan. 2016. Approximation resistance from pairwise-independent subgroups. *J. ACM* 63, 3 (2016), 27.
[13] Graham Cormode, Jacques Dark, and Christian Konrad. 2017. *Independent Set Size Approximation in Graph Streams*. Technical Report arXiv:1702.08299. CoRR.
[14] Yuval Emek, Magnús M. Halldórsson, Yishay Mansour, Boaz Patt-Shamir, Jaikumar Radhakrishnan, and Dror Rawitz. 2012. Online set packing. *SIAM Journal of Computing* 41, 4 (2012), 728–746.
[15] Paul Erdős. 1970. On the graph theorem of Turán (in Hungarian). *Mat. Lapok* 21 (1970), 249–251.
[16] Mohsen Ghaffari, Fabian Kuhn, and Yannic Maus. 2017. On the complexity of local distributed graph problems. In *49th ACM STOC*. 784–797.
[17] Bjarni V. Halldórsson, Magnús M. Halldórsson, Elena Losievskaja, and Mario Szegedy. 2016. Streaming Algorithms for Independent Sets in Sparse Hypergraphs. *Algorithmica* 76 (2016), 490–501. Issue 2.
[18] Magnús M. Halldórsson and Christian Konrad. 2018. Computing Large Independent Sets in a Single Round. *Distributed Computing* 31, 1 (2018), 69–82.
[19] Fabian Kuhn, Thomas Moscibroda, and Roger Wattenhofer. 2016. Local Computation: Lower and Upper Bounds. *J. ACM* 63, 2, Article 17 (2016), 44 pages.
[20] P. Turán. 1941. On an extremal problem in graph theory (in Hungarian). *Mat. Fiz. Lapok* 48 (1941), 436–452.
[21] V.K. Wei. 1981. *A lower bound on the stability number of a simple graph*. Technical Report. Bell Laboratories.

Data Summarization and Distributed Computation

Graham Cormode

ABSTRACT

The notion of summarization is to provide a compact representation of data which approximately captures its essential characteristics. If such summaries can be created, they can lead to efficient distributed algorithms which exchange summaries in order to compute a desired function. In this talk, I'll describe recent efforts in this direction for problems inspired by machine learning: building graphical models over evolving, distributed training examples, and solving robust regression problems over large, distributed data sets.

ACM Reference Format:
Graham Cormode. 2018. Data Summarization and Distributed Computation. In *PODC '18: ACM Symposium on Principles of Distributed Computing, July 23–27, 2018, Egham, United Kingdom.* ACM, New York, NY, USA, 2 pages. https://doi.org/10.1145/3212734.3212795

Although we may have to deal with a very high volume of data, we can often work with only an approximate representation of it to perform a desired computation. For example, in building a predictive model, we need to extract a modest number of parameters from a large number of examples in order to define the model. This leads us to consider the notion of *data summarization*: trying to capture aspects of the inherent behaviour of the data in a compact form, without necessarily having full access to the entirety of the data or complete information about what questions will be asked of it.

A powerful and generic approach to building a data summary is to randomly sample parts of the dataset. This can be used to answer a large number of different questions, and in many cases the guarantees on the resulting accuracy can be expressed as a function of the size of the sample. Other approaches to summarization emerge from using transformations of the data, random projections, and rounding, amongst many others. In some cases, these techniques yield better accuracy/size tradeoffs than random sampling, or allow summarization when random sampling fails.

Data summarization is closely linked with distributed computation. A central question about a distributed computation surrounds the amount of communication and coordination needed between the different computational entities. Algorithms for data summarization can contribute to distributed computation, and yield improved bounds or new approaches to solving problems, particularly when an approximate solution can be acceptable. The structure of distributed computation can impose additional constraints: we would typically like summaries that can be applied to fragments of a data set, and be combined so that they summarize the union of their inputs.

PODC '18, July 23–27, 2018, Egham, United Kingdom

ACM ISBN 978-1-4503-5795-1/18/07.
https://doi.org/10.1145/3212734.3212795

This talk will give an overview of some recent work in data summarization with a distributed flavour, and their applications in data analysis.

Learning Graphical Models from a Distributed Stream [3]. A current challenge for distributed data management is to support the construction and maintenance of machine learning models over data that is large, multi-dimensional, and evolving. The need to scale to distributed, streaming data requires new models and algorithms. In this setting, as well as computational scalability and model accuracy, we also need to minimize the amount of communication between distributed processors, which is the chief component of latency. We consider Bayesian networks, the workhorse of graphical models, and describe a communication-efficient method for continuously learning and maintaining a Bayesian network model over data that is arriving as a distributed stream partitioned across multiple processors. This builds on prior work that has addressed the abstract problem of maintaining the count of a number of events in a distributed setting [2]. Adopting this primitive yields a strategy for maintaining model parameters that leads to an exponential reduction in communication when compared with baseline approaches to maintain the exact MLE (maximum likelihood estimation). Optimizing the parameter settings leads to further improvements in the communication cost, while providing similar prediction errors for the target distribution and for classification tasks as the baseline.

Deterministic Distributed Summaries for High-dimensional Regression [1]. Work on approximate linear algebra has led to efficient distributed and streaming algorithms for problems such as approximate matrix multiplication, low rank approximation, and regression, primarily for the Euclidean norm ℓ_2. In recent work, we study other ℓ_p norms, which are more robust for $p < 2$, and can be used to find outliers for $p > 2$. Unlike previous algorithms for such norms, we give algorithms that are (1) deterministic, (2) work simultaneously for every $p \geq 1$, including $p = \infty$, and (3) can be implemented in both distributed and streaming environments. We focus on ℓ_p-regression, and show the resulting distributed algorithms are accurate and communication-efficient.

SHORT BIOGRAPHY

Graham Cormode is a Professor in Computer Science at the University of Warwick in the UK, where he works on research topics in data management, privacy and big data analysis. Previously, he was a principal member of technical staff at AT&T Labs-Research. His work has attracted over 11,000 citations in the literature and has appeared in over 90 conference papers, 40 journal papers, and been awarded 30 US Patents. Cormode is the co-recipient of the 2017 Adams Prize for Mathematics for his work on Statistical Analysis of Big Data. He has also edited two books on applications of algorithms to different areas, and co-authored a third.

ACKNOWLEDGMENTS

The work of GC presented in this talk is supported in part by European Research Council grant ERC-2014-CoG 647557 and a Royal Society Wolfson Research Merit Award.

REFERENCES

[1] Graham Cormode, Charlie Dickens, and David Woodruff. Leveraging well-conditioned bases: Streaming and distributed summaries in minkowski p-norms. In *International Conference on Machine Learning*, 2018.

[2] Zengfeng Huang, Ke Yi, and Qin Zhang. Randomized algorithms for tracking distributed count, frequencies, and ranks. In *ACM Principles of Database Systems*, pages 295–306, 2012.

[3] Yu Zhang, Srikanta Tirthapura, and Graham Cormode. Learning graphical models from a distributed stream. In *IEEE International Conference on Data Engineering*, 2018.

The Convergence of Stochastic Gradient Descent in Asynchronous Shared Memory

Dan Alistarh
IST Austria
Klosterneuburg
dan.alistarh@ist.ac.at

Christopher De Sa
Cornell University
Ithaca, New York
cdesa@cs.cornell.edu

Nikola Konstantinov
IST Austria
Klosterneuburg
nikola.konstantinov@ist.ac.at

ABSTRACT

Stochastic Gradient Descent (SGD) is a fundamental algorithm in machine learning, representing the optimization backbone for training several classic models, from regression to neural networks. Given the recent practical focus on distributed machine learning, significant work has been dedicated to the convergence properties of this algorithm under the inconsistent and noisy updates arising from execution in a distributed environment. However, surprisingly, the convergence properties of this classic algorithm in the standard shared-memory model are still not well-understood.

In this work, we address this gap, and provide new convergence bounds for lock-free concurrent stochastic gradient descent, executing in the classic asynchronous shared memory model, against a strong adaptive adversary. Our results give improved upper and lower bounds on the "price of asynchrony" when executing the fundamental SGD algorithm in a concurrent setting. They show that this classic optimization tool can converge faster and with a wider range of parameters than previously known under asynchronous iterations. At the same time, we exhibit a fundamental trade-off between the maximum delay in the system and the rate at which SGD can converge, which governs the set of parameters under which this algorithm can still work efficiently.

CCS CONCEPTS

• **Mathematics of computing → Mathematical optimization**; • **Computing methodologies → Machine learning**; **Distributed algorithms**;

KEYWORDS

Shared Memory, Stochastic Gradient Descent, Distributed Optimization, Lower Bounds

ACM Reference Format:
Dan Alistarh, Christopher De Sa, and Nikola Konstantinov. 2018. The Convergence of Stochastic Gradient Descent in Asynchronous Shared Memory. In *PODC '18: ACM Symposium on Principles of Distributed Computing, July 23–27, 2018, Egham, United Kingdom.* ACM, New York, NY, USA, 9 pages. https://doi.org/10.1145/3212734.3212763

ACM ISBN 978-1-4503-5795-1/18/07...$15.00
https://doi.org/10.1145/3212734.3212763

1 INTRODUCTION

Background. The tremendous recent progress in machine learning can be explained in part through the availability of extremely vast amounts of data, but also through improved computational support for executing machine learning tasks at scale. Perhaps surprisingly, some of the main algorithms driving this progress are have been known in some form or another for a very long time. One such tool is the classic stochastic gradient descent (SGD) optimization algorithm [24], introduced by Robbins and Munro in the 1950s, variants of which are currently the tool of choice for optimization in a variety of settings, such as image classification and speech recognition via neural networks, but also in fundamental data processing tools such as regression.

In a nutshell, SGD works as follows. Given a d-dimensional function $f : \mathbb{R}^d \to \mathbb{R}$ which we want to minimize, we have access to stochastic gradients $\widetilde{g}(x)$ of this function at the point x, that is, random vectors with the property that $\mathbb{E}[\widetilde{g}(x)] = \nabla f(x)$. SGD then consists in the iteration

$$x_{t+1} = x_t - \alpha_t \widetilde{g}(x_t),$$

where x_t is a d-dimensional vector which we will henceforth call the *model*, encoding our current beliefs about the data, and α_t is the step size, which controls how "aggressive" updates should be.

A classic instance of this method, which we consider in this paper, is the following. We are given a large set of m data points $X_1, \ldots, X_m$, where to each point X_i, with $i \in \{1, 2, \ldots, m\}$, we associate a loss function $L_i(x)$, measuring the loss of any model x at the data point X_i (mapping the difference between the prediction of our model on X_i with the true label to a real value), and we wish to identify a model $x^\star$ which minimizes the average loss over the dataset, that is, minimize the function

$$f(x) = \frac{1}{m} \sum_{i=1}^{m} L_i(x).$$

This setting can be mapped to fundamental optimization tasks, such as linear regression over a given set of points, or training neural networks through backpropagation [25]. In both settings, we are given a large dataset, from which we pick a sample point uniformly at random in every iteration t. In every such iteration, a process reads the current version of the model x_t, computes the stochastic gradient $\widetilde{g}(x_t)$ of this model with respect to the current sample by examining the derivative of the loss function at the point, given its label, and updates the model's components correspondingly. Thus, the stochastic gradients $\widetilde{g}(x_t)$ correspond to the gradient of the model x_t taken at a uniformly random data point X_i. Indeed, since the data point at which we compute the gradient is chosen uniformly at random, we have

$$\mathbb{E}[\widetilde{g}(x)] = \frac{1}{m}\sum_{i=1}^{m} \nabla L_i(x) = \nabla f(x).$$

Parallel SGD. The ability to parallelize this process at extremely large scale, up to thousands of nodes, e.g. [11], has enabled researchers to approach new problems, and to reach super-human accuracy for several classic problems, e.g. [8, 14, 15, 28, 29]. The standard way to distribute SGD to multiple compute nodes is *data parallelism*: given n nodes, which we will abstract as parallel *processes*, we split the dataset into n partitions. Nodes process samples from their partitions in parallel, and synchronize by using a *shared model* x. In this paper, we will focus on the case where the nodes are *threads*, communicating through *asynchronous shared memory*.

In theory, data parallelism would allow the system to perform n times more iterations (and model updates) per unit of time. The catch is that threads will need to *synchronize* on the shared model, reducing scalability. In fact, early studies [16] proposed using *coarse-grained locking* to keep the process consistent to a sequential execution. As expected, coarse-grained locking leads to significant loss of performance.

In this context, a breakthrough by Niu et al. [23] proved the unintuitive result that SGD should be able to converge even *without coarse-grained synchronization* to maintain model consistency, under some technical conditions, including high sparsity of the gradient updates, and under the assumption that individual updates are applied via fetch-and-add synchronization operations. (This latter assumption appears necessary in general, since otherwise a delayed thread could completely obliterate all progress made up to some point, by overwriting the entire model, which resides in shared memory.) This work has sparked significant research on the convergence properties of asynchronous SGD, e.g. [10, 12, 18, 19, 26, 34], improving theoretical bounds and considering more general settings.

In a nutshell, these results show, under various delay models and analytic assumptions, that SGD can still converge if iterations are asynchronous, that is, they cannot be "serialized" in any meaningful way. At the same time, all known convergence upper bounds, e.g. [10, 18], have a linear dependence in $\tau_{\max}$, the maximum delay between the time where a gradient update is *generated* by any thread, and the point where the gradient is *applied* to the model.[1] This means that asynchronous SGD will take $\tau_{\max}$ times more iterations to converge, compared to the synchronous variant. Since $\tau_{\max}$ is technically only upper bounded by the *length of the execution*, this upper bound appears extremely harsh. It is therefore natural to ask if this dependency is inherent, or whether it can be improved, yielding superior convergence rates for this classical algorithm.

Contribution. In this paper, we address this problem. Our approach is to express data-parallel SGD in the classic asynchronous shared memory model, against a strong (adaptive) adversarial scheduler, which designs schedules to delay the algorithm from converging, with full knowledge of the algorithm and random coin flips. Under this formulation, our main results are as follows:

- We show that, under standard analytic assumptions, for convex objective functions f, there exists a simple variant of the classic SGD algorithm which still converges under this strong adversarial model.
- We prove that, under reasonable parameter settings, the convergence slowdown of SGD iterations due to asynchrony can be upper bounded by $\sqrt{\tau_{\max} n}$, where $\tau_{\max}$ is the *maximum* interval contention over all operations and n is the number of threads. This result shows for the first time that the runtime dependence need not be linear in $\tau_{\max}$, even against a strong adversary, and is our main technical contribution.
- We prove that, in general, the adversary can cause a convergence slowdown that is *linear* in $\tau_{\max}$, if the algorithm does not decrease the step size α_t to offset the influence of stale gradient updates. This shows for the first time that the adversary can consistently and significantly slow down convergence by inducing delays, and that decreasing the step size (which is done by our algorithm) is in fact *necessary* for good convergence under asynchrony.

In sum, our results give new and improved upper and lower bounds on the "price of asynchrony" when executing the fundamental SGD algorithm in a concurrent setting. They show that this classic optimization tool can converge faster and with a wider range of parameters than previously known, under asynchronous iterations. At the same time, we exhibit a simple yet fundamental trade-off between the maximum delay in the system and the convergence rate of SGD, which governs the set of parameters under which SGD can still work efficiently.

Techniques and Related Work. From the technical perspective, our results build upon martingale-based approaches for bounding the convergence of SGD, e.g. [9, 10]. These techniques complement the classic "regret" bounds for characterizing the convergence of SGD, e.g. [5]. We exploit martingale-based techniques in the asynchronous setting. To our knowledge, the only other work to employ such techniques for convex SGD is [10], whose results we significantly extend. Specifically, with respect to this reference, the main departures are that 1) we consider a more challenging adaptive adversarial model, as opposed to a stochastic scheduling model; 2) eliminate the requirement that gradients contain a single non-zero entry, thereby significantly expanding the applicability of the framework; 3) reduce the linear convergence dependency in $\tau_{\max}$ to one of the form $\sqrt{\tau_{\max} n}$; 4) prove lower bounds on the slowdown due to asynchrony.

There is an extremely vast literature studying the convergence properties of asynchronous optimization methods [10, 12, 17–19, 22, 23], as well as efficient parallel implementations, e.g. [27, 34], starting with seminal work by Bertsekas and Tsitsiklis [3]. A complete survey is beyond the scope of this paper, and we therefore focus on work that is directly related to ours. Reference [23] showed for the first time that, under strong analytical assumptions on sparsity and on the target loss function, asynchronous SGD can still converge, and that, moreover, the convergence rate can be similar to that of the baseline under further assumptions on the parameters. Agarwal and Duchi [1] showed that, under strong ordering assumptions, delayed gradient computation does not affect the convergence of SGD. Lian et al. [18] provided ergodic convergence rates for asynchronous SGD for *non-convex* objectives. Duchi et al. [12] considered

[1] In shared-memory parlance, $\tau_{\max}$ is upper bounded by the *interval contention*, where we define SGD iterations as individual operations. Intuitively, $\tau_{\max}$ is upper bounded by the number of iterations which can take steps between the start and end points of any fixed iteration.

a model similar to ours, and showed that the impact of any asynchrony on the rate at which the algorithm converges is negligible, under strong technical assumptions on the convex function f to be optimized, on the structure of its optimum, and on the sampling noise. Concurrent work [17, 22] provides significantly more general analyses of iterative processes under asynchrony, covering several important optimization algorithms. With the exception of [12], which makes strong technical assumptions, all previous results for asynchronous SGD had a linear dependence in the maximum delay $\tau_{\max}$. We improve this dependency in this work.

There exists significant work on mitigating the effects of asynchrony in applied settings, e.g. [20, 35, 36]. A subset of these works are designed for a distributed shared memory setting, where it may be possible to examine the "staleness" of an update immediately before applying it, and adjust hyperparameters accordingly, and validated empirically. By contrast, we consider an adversarial setting, where the scheduler actively attempts to thwart the algorithm's progress. Our lower bound applies to these works as well.

There has recently been significant work connecting machine learning and optimization with distributed computing. References [4, 7, 33] consider distributed SGD in a *Byzantine* adversarial setting, but in a message-passing system. In a series of papers [30, 32], Su and Vaidya have considered the problem of adding fault-tolerance to the problem of multi-agent optimization, as well as non-Bayesian optimization under asynchrony and crash failures [31].

2 MODEL

Asynchronous Shared Memory. We consider a standard asynchronous shared-memory model [2], in which n threads (or processes) $P_1, \ldots, P_n$, communicate through atomic memory locations called registers, on which they perform atomic operations such as read, write, compare&swap and fetch&add. In particular, the algorithm we consider employs atomic read and fetch&add operations, which are now standard in mass-produced multiprocessors. The fetch&add operation takes one argument, and returns the value of the register before the increment was performed, incrementing its value by the corresponding operand.

As is usual, we will assume a *sequentially consistent* memory model, in which once a thread returns from its invocation of a primitive (for example, a fetch&add), the value written by the thread is immediately applied to shared memory, and henceforth visible by other processors.

The Adversarial Scheduler. Threads follow an algorithm composed of shared-memory steps and local computation, including random coin flips. The order of process steps is controlled by an adversarial entity we call the *scheduler*. Time is measured in terms of the number of shared-memory steps scheduled by the adversary. The adversary may choose to crash a set of at most $n-1$ processes by not scheduling them for the rest of the execution. A process that is not crashed at a certain step is *correct*, and if it never crashes then it takes an infinite number of steps in the execution. In the following, we assume a standard *strong* adversarial scheduler, which can see the results of the threads' local coins when deciding the scheduling.

Contention Bound. In the following, fix a (concurrent) SGD iteration θ, and let $\rho(\theta)$ be the *interval contention* of the iteration θ, defined as the number of SGD iterations which can execute concurrently with θ. Let $\tau_{\max}$ be the upper bound over all these interval contention values, i.e. $\tau_{\max} = \max_\theta \rho(\theta)$. Let τ_{avg} be an upper bound on the *average* interval contention over all iterations during the (finite) execution of a program, i.e. $\tau_{avg} = 1/T \sum_{1 \leq \theta \leq T} \rho(\theta)$, where T is the total number of iterations of the algorithm. It is known that $\tau_{avg} \leq 2n$, where n is the number of threads [13].

3 BACKGROUND ON STOCHASTIC GRADIENT DESCENT

Stochastic gradient descent (SGD) is a standard method in optimization. Let $f : \mathbb{R}^d \to \mathbb{R}$ be a function which we want to minimize. We have access to stochastic gradients $\widetilde{g}$ of f, such that $\mathbb{E}[\widetilde{g}(x)] = \nabla f(x)$. SGD will start at a randomly chosen point x_0, and converge towards the minimum by iterating the procedure

$$x_{t+1} = x_t - \alpha_t \widetilde{g}(x_t), \tag{1}$$

where x_t is the current candidate, and α_t is a variable step-size parameter. Notably, this arises if we are given i.i.d. data points $X_1, \ldots, X_m$ generated from an unknown distribution D, and a loss function $\ell(X, \theta)$, which measures the loss of the model θ at data point X. We wish to find a model θ^* which minimizes $f(\theta) = \mathbb{E}_{X\sim D}[\ell(X, \theta)]$, the expected loss to the data.

Unless otherwise noted, we consider SGD for *convex optimization* and with a *constant learning rate*, that is $\alpha_t = \alpha$ for all t. We also make the following standard assumptions:

- The function f is strongly convex with parameter c, i.e. for all $x, y \in \mathbb{R}^d$:
$$(x-y)^T (\nabla f(x) - \nabla f(y)) \geq c\|x-y\|^2 \tag{2}$$
- The stochastic gradient $\widetilde{g}(x)$ is L-Lipschitz continuous in expectation for some $L > 0$, i.e. for all $x, y \in \mathbb{R}^d$:
$$\mathbb{E}(\|\widetilde{g}(x) - \widetilde{g}(y)\|) \leq L\|x-y\| \tag{3}$$
- The second moment of the stochastic gradients is bounded by some $M^2 > 0$, i.e. for all $x \in \mathbb{R}^d$:
$$\mathbb{E}\left(\|\widetilde{g}(x)\|^2\right) \leq M^2. \tag{4}$$

Classic approaches for analyzing the convergence of SGD attempt to bound the distance between the expected value of f at the average of the currently generated iterates and the optimal value of the function (e.g. Theorem 6.3 in [5]), showing that this distance decreases linearly with the number of iterations.

Here we consider a different approach that aims at estimating the probability that the algorithm has failed to converge to a success region around the optimal parameter value after T steps. To this end, we employ a martingale-based analysis of the algorithm, an approach that has recently become a popular tool for analyzing asynchronous optimization algorithms [6, 10]. Let x^* be the minimizer of the function f. Given an $\epsilon > 0$, we denote by

$$S = \{x \mid \|x - x^*\|^2 \leq \epsilon\}$$

the success region around this minimizer, to which we want to converge. Our analysis aims to bound the probability of the event F_T that $x_i \notin S$ for all $i \leq T$, i.e. the event that the algorithm has failed to hit the success region by time T.

An existing result of this type about the convergence of parallel SGD was derived in [10]. Under the non-standard additional assumption that each gradient update on the parameter value only effects a single entry of x_t (i.e., that the stochastic gradients contain a single non-zero entry),[2] one can obtain the following:

THEOREM 3.1 ([10]). *Consider the SGD algorithm under the assumptions above, run for T steps, with a success region* $S = \{x \mid \|x - x^*\|^2 \leq \epsilon\}$ *and with learning rate* $\alpha = \frac{c\epsilon\vartheta}{M^2}$ *for some constant* $\vartheta \in (0, 1)$. *Then the probability of the event* F_T *that* $x_i \notin S$ *for all* $i \leq T$ *is:*

$$\mathbb{P}(F_T) \leq \frac{M^2}{c^2\epsilon\vartheta T} \log\left(e\|x_0 - x^*\|^2\epsilon^{-1}\right). \quad (5)$$

Note that this bound also decreases linearly with the number of iterations.

4 LOCK-FREE SGD IN SHARED-MEMORY

A standard way of parallelizing the SGD algorithm is to have multiple parallel threads execute the procedure in Equation 1. We assume a lock-free setting, in which threads share the set of parameters (model) $X[d]$, which they can read and update entry-wise (through read and fetch&add operations) concurrently, without additional synchronization. Each thread executes the steps in Algorithm 1:

Input: Dataset D, dimension d, function f
Output: Minimizer X, initially $X = (0, 0, \ldots, 0)$
Data: Shared copy of the parameter array X, of dimension d
Data: Iteration counter C, learning rate α
procedure EpochSGD(T, α)
  for *each iteration* θ **do**
    if C.fetch&add(1) $\geq T$ **then return**
    for j *from* 1 *to* d **do** $v_\theta[j] \leftarrow X[j]$.read()
    $\widetilde{g}_\theta \leftarrow$ stochastic gradient at v_θ, so $\mathbb{E}(\widetilde{g}_\theta) = f(v_\theta)$
    for j *from* 1 *to* d **do**
      if $\widetilde{g}_\theta[j] \neq 0$ **then** $X[j]$.fetch&add($-\alpha\widetilde{g}_\theta[j]$)
    end
  end

Algorithm 1: SGD code for a single thread.

We emphasize that this modeling of the algorithm is standard: virtually all papers which analyze asynchronous SGD consider this formulation, e.g. [10, 12, 23]. Updates are assumed to occur via fetch&add, to avoid complete resets of the state by a delayed thread.

5 A SLOWDOWN LOWER BOUND VIA ADVERSARIAL DELAYS

Setup. We now provide a simple argument which yields a lower bound on the achievable speedup if the adversary can delay gradients by a large $\tau_{\max}$. This argument might also serve as a brisk hands-on introduction to SGD. We consider a standard setting, where two threads each have access to local gradient samples, and

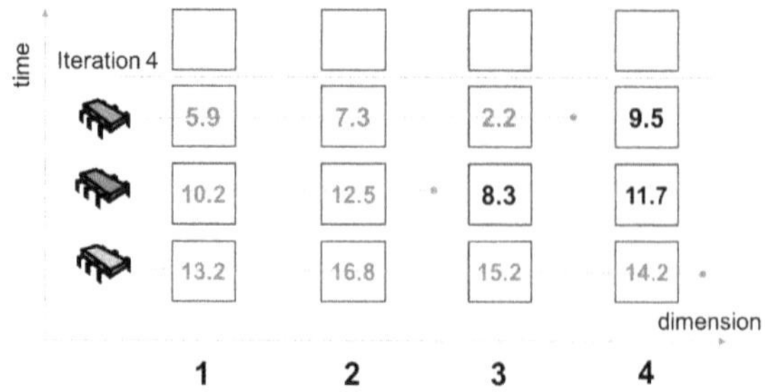

Figure 1: Algorithm modeling. The updates in red have been applied to shared memory, while the updates in black are still pending. The updates in black or red form x_t. The dot is the point where the thread has currently stopped updating. To obtain the value of v_t at the current time, we sum values in red on each column (i.e. all values up to the dot on the row).

share the model. Assume we are trying to minimize the (convex) objective function

$$f(x) = \frac{1}{2}x^2,$$

and have access to its noisy gradients

$$\widetilde{g}(x) = x - \tilde{u},$$

where $\tilde{u}$ is normally distributed noise with mean 0 and variance σ^2. Observe the minimum is at 0, and $\mathbb{E}[\widetilde{g}(x)] = \nabla f(x)$. Now if u_t is the stochastic gradient at time t, the SGD update is

$$x_{t+1} = x_t - \alpha\widetilde{g}(x_t) = (1 - \alpha)x_t + \alpha\tilde{u}_t.$$

Adversarial Strategy. Suppose that the adversary is executing the following strategy. First, both threads generate a gradient with respect to x_0. The first thread then executes for τ consecutive iterations, and then the second writes the state with a gradient from the initial value. Let us now analyze the rate at which this algorithm can converge.

Analysis. After the first thread runs, the output will be

$$x_\tau = (1 - \alpha)^\tau x_0 + \alpha \sum_{k=1}^{\tau} (1 - \alpha)^{\tau-k} \tilde{u}_{k-1}.$$

After the second thread merges in its stale gradient, which has the form $x_0 - \tilde{u}_\tau$, we have:

$$x_{\tau+1} = \left((1 - \alpha)^\tau - \alpha\right) x_0 + \alpha \sum_{k=1}^{\tau} (1 - \alpha)^{\tau-k} \tilde{u}_{k-1} + \alpha\tilde{u}_\tau.$$

The second term of this last expression will be a zero-mean Gaussian with a variance of

$$\overline{\sigma}^2 = \alpha^2 \sum_{k=1}^{\tau} (1 - \alpha)^{2\tau-2k}\sigma^2 + \alpha^2\sigma^2$$
$$= \alpha^2\sigma^2 \left(1 + \sum_{k=0}^{\tau-1} \left((1 - \alpha)^2\right)^k\right)$$

[2]Our analysis eliminates this assumption, a result which may be of independent interest.

$$= \alpha^2\sigma^2\left(1 + \frac{1-(1-\alpha)^{2\tau}}{1-(1-\alpha)^2}\right).$$

For a fixed α, if we choose τ large enough that $2(1-\alpha)^\tau \leq \alpha$, and suppose for simplicity that $\sigma = 0$, then we can get

$$\|x_{\tau+1}\| \geq \frac{\alpha}{2}\|x_0\|, \text{ versus } \|x_{\tau+1}\| = (1-\alpha)^\tau \|x_0\|$$

in the case with no adversary. To compare these rates, we take the logarithm, and obtain a slowdown factor of

$$\frac{\log\left((1-\alpha)^\tau\right)}{\log\left(\frac{\alpha}{2}\right)} = \tau\frac{\log(1-\alpha)}{\log(\alpha)-\log(2)} = \Omega(\tau),$$

which implies an $\Omega(\tau)$ factor slowdown is possible from a delay of τ. This shows that with a maximum delay $\tau_{\max} = \tau$, the adversary can achieve an asymptotic slowdown that is linear in τ. We conclude as follows.

Theorem 5.1. *Given an instance of the lock-free SGD Algorithm in 1 with fixed learning rate α, there exists an adversarial strategy with maximum delay $\tau_{\max} = O(\log(\alpha)/\log(1-\alpha))$ such that the algorithm converges $\tau_{\max}$ times slower than the sequential variant.*

6 CONVERGENCE UPPER BOUNDS IN ASYNCHRONOUS SHARED MEMORY

6.1 Preliminaries

Notation and Iteration Ordering. We now introduce some notation, and a few basic claims about the above concurrent process. First, we define an order on the above iterations, performed possibly by distinct threads, by the time at which the iteration performs its first `fetch&add` operation, on the first model component $X[1]$. (Here we are using the sequential consistency property of the memory model.) This ordering induces a useful total order between iterations: for any integer $t \geq 1$, iteration t is the tth iteration to complete its `fetch&add` on $X[1]$. We now note that all of these iterations up to iteration t must have completed their computation, but may not have completed *writing their updates* to X by the time when iteration $t+1$ starts. At most n of these iterations may be incomplete at any given time. We formalize this as follows.

Lemma 6.1. *Let iteration t be the tth iteration to update $X[1]$. This is a total order on the iterations. We say that an iteration is* incomplete *at a given point in the execution if it has performed its first update (on $X[1]$), but has not completed its last update (on $X[d]$). For any $t \geq 1$, at most n iterations with indices $\leq t$ can be incomplete.*

By assumption the maximal interval contention is bounded by $\tau_{\max}$. However, since at most n threads can run at the same time, it is intuitive that the average contention should be $O(n)$. We formalize this via the following:

Lemma 6.2. *Fix a parameter K, and an arbitrary time interval I during which exactly Kn consecutive SGD iterations start. We call an SGD iteration θ* bad *if more than Kn iterations start between its start time and end time. Otherwise, an SGD iteration is* good. *Then, the number of bad iterations which complete during I is less than n.*

Proof. Assume for contradiction that the number of bad iterations is n or larger. Then, there must exist a thread p which completes two of these bad iterations during this interval. Denote the second iteration by θ. Since the two iterations by p cannot be concurrent with each other, the maximum number of iterations which can be concurrent with θ (except itself) is at most $Kn-2$. Hence, θ cannot be bad, a contradiction. □

Inconsistent Views v_t and Accumulators x_t. Let $\widetilde{g}_t$ be the gradient vector which the corresponding thread executing iteration t wishes to add to X, and v_t be this thread's *view* of the model X when generating this gradient, composed out of the values the thread read for each entry. Importantly, we define the auxiliary (global) vector $x_t = \sum_{k=1}^{t}\widetilde{g}_k$, containing all of the updates which various *started* iterations wish to apply to the model X up to t. We note that the view v_t which iteration t uses to generate its gradient update can consist of a possibly inconsistent set of updates across the various components of X. However, at all times 1) all of these updates must be contained in x_t, in the sense that they feature in $\widetilde{g}_k$ for some $k \leq t$; and 2) if we denote by t' the highest iteration whose update is read by v_t, we must have that there can be at most $\ell(\theta)$ updates with indices $< t'$ which v_t sees as incomplete during its scan. This is illustrated in Figure 1.

SGD Convergence. We now analyze the convergence of SGD under this lock-free model. Following [10], we employ a martingale approach for proving convergence rates of SGD.

Given a probability space $(\Omega, \mathcal{F}, \mathbb{R})$, a real-valued stochastic process $W : \mathbb{N}\times\Omega \to \mathbb{R}$ is called a supermartingale if $\mathbb{E}(W_{t+1}|W_t, W_{t-1}, ..., W_0) \leq W_t$ for all $t \geq 0$.
Here we consider supermartingales of the form $W_t(x_t, ..., x_0)$, defined based on the state of the optimization algorithm. Intuitively, W_t represents our unhappiness about the state of the algorithm at time t. More precisely, we have the following:

Definition 6.1 ([10]). Given a stochastic optimization algorithm, a non-negative process $W_t : \mathbb{R}^{d\times t} \to \mathbb{R}$ is a rate supermartingale with horizon B, if two conditions hold. Firstly, it is a supermartingale, i.e. for all $x_t, ..., x_0$ and for all $t \leq B$:

$$\mathbb{E}\left(W_{t+1}\left(x_t - \alpha\widetilde{g}(x_t), x_t, ..., x_0\right)\right) \leq W_t\left(x_t, x_{t-1}, ..., x_0\right), \quad (6)$$

where expectation is taken with respect to the randomness at time t and conditional on the past. Secondly, for any time $T \leq B$ and any sequence $x_T, ..., x_0$, if the algorithm has not succeeded by time T (i.e. $x_t \notin S$ for all $t \leq T$), then:

$$W_T\left(x_T, x_{T-1}, ..., x_0\right) \geq T. \quad (7)$$

The main result in [10] shows how constructing such a supermartingale for an optimization algorithm can be used to obtain a bound on the probability that the algorithm has not visited the success region after a certain number of iterations. Under the considered stochastic scheduling model, the authors employ a parameter τ, that denotes the *worst-case expected delay* caused by the parallel updates. Under the additional assumption that the stochastic gradients contain a single non-zero entry, the following result is derived:

Theorem 6.3 ([10]). *Consider the SGD algorithm for optimizing a convex function f that satisfies the assumptions above and under the asynchronous model of [10], with a success region $S = \{x \mid \|x - x^*\|^2 \leq \epsilon\}$ and with learning rate $\alpha = \frac{c\epsilon\vartheta}{M^2+2LM\tau\sqrt{\epsilon}}$ for some constant $\vartheta \in (0,1)$. Then the probability of the event F_T that $x_i \notin S$ for all $i \leq T$ is:*

$$\mathbb{P}(F_T) \leq \frac{M^2 + 2LM\tau\sqrt{\epsilon}}{c^2\epsilon\vartheta T}\log\left(e\|x_0 - x^*\|^2\epsilon^{-1}\right). \quad (8)$$

Again, the bound decreases linearly with the number of iterations. However, there is an additive term that increases with τ. In particular, the bound on the failure probability is worse than in the sequential SGD case described previously.

6.2 Convergence Analysis

We now apply a martingale analysis similar to the one in [10] to obtain results about the rate of convergence of SGD under the Asynchronous Shared Memory model. We denote the maximum delay at time t by $\tau_t \geq 0$. We also assume that all τ_t are bounded by some maximum $\tau_{\max}$, i.e. $\tau_t \leq \tau_{\max}$ for all t.

Note that at any time t, the gradient is computed based on a view v_t that might be missing updates from only the last τ_t iterations. Therefore,

$$\begin{aligned}\|x_t - v_t\|_1 &\leq \sum_{k=1}^{\tau_t} \|x_{t-k+1} - x_{t-k}\|_1 \\ &\leq \sum_{k=1}^{t} \|x_{t-k+1} - x_{t-k}\|_1 \mathbf{1}_{\{\tau_t \geq k\}}\end{aligned}$$

Now since for any $x \in \mathbb{R}^d$, we have $\|x\|_2 \leq \|x\|_1 \leq \sqrt{d}\|x\|_2$, it follows that:

$$\|x_t - v_t\| \leq \sqrt{d} \sum_{k=1}^{t} \|x_{t-k+1} - x_{t-k}\| \mathbf{1}_{\{\tau_t \geq k\}} \tag{9}$$

For the subsequent analysis we will also need the following:

Lemma 6.4. *For any t:*

$$\sum_{m=1}^{\infty} \mathbf{1}_{\{\tau_{t+m} \geq m\}} = \sum_{m=1}^{\tau_{max}} \mathbf{1}_{\{\tau_{t+m} \geq m\}} \leq 2\sqrt{\tau_{max} n}. \tag{10}$$

Proof. By Lemma 6.2, we know that for any constant K and for any Kn consecutive steps $t+1, \ldots, t+Kn$, $\tau_{t+i} > Kn$ for at most n indexes. Hence,

$$\begin{aligned}\sum_{m=1}^{\tau_{\max}} \mathbf{1}_{\{\tau_{t+m} \geq m\}} &\leq Kn + \sum_{m=Kn+1}^{\tau_{\max}} \mathbf{1}_{\{\tau_{t+m} > Kn\}} \\ &\leq Kn + \left(\frac{\tau_{\max} - Kn}{Kn} + 1\right) n \\ &= \frac{\tau_{\max}}{K} + Kn.\end{aligned}$$

This holds for any positive K. The bound is minimized at $K = \sqrt{\frac{\tau_{\max}}{n}}$, which yields the result. □

Next, we obtain a bound on the probability that the algorithm has not visited a given success region $S = \{x \mid \|x - x^*\|^2 \leq \epsilon\}$. To this end, we show a result similar to the one in Theorem 1 in [10]. We will assume the existence of a rate supermartingale with respect to the underlying sequential SGD process that is Lipschitz in its first coordinate and show that this can be used to obtain a bound on the failure probability. The exact assumptions on W are as follows:

- W is a supermartingale with horizon B with respect to the sequential SGD process $x_{t+1} = x_t - \alpha\tilde{g}(x_t)$. Note that W need not be a supermartingale with respect to the lock-free SGD algorithm.
- For any $T > 0$, if $x_i \notin S$ for all $i \leq T$, then: $W_T(x_T, \ldots, x_0) \geq T$. Otherwise, we say that the algorithm *has succeeded* at time T.
- W is Lipschitz continuous in the current iterate with parameter H, i.e. for all t, u, v and any $x_{t-1}, \ldots, x_0$:

$$\|W_t(u, x_{t-1}, \ldots, x_0) - W_t(v, x_{t-1}, \ldots, x_0)\| \leq H\|u - v\|$$

Under these assumptions, we can prove our main technical claim, whose proof is deferred to the Appendix.

Theorem 6.5. *Assume that W is a rate supermartingale with horizon B for the sequential SGD algorithm and that W is H-Lipschitz in the first coordinate. Assume further that $\alpha^2 HLMC\sqrt{d} < 1$, where $C = 2\sqrt{\tau_{max} n}$. Then for any $T \leq B$, the probability that the lock-free SGD algorithm has not succeeded at time T (that is, the probability of the event F_T that $x_i \notin S$ for all $i \leq T$) is:*

$$\mathbb{P}(F_T) \leq \frac{\mathbb{E}(W_0(x_0))}{\left(1 - \alpha^2 HLMC\sqrt{d}\right) T}. \tag{11}$$

Proof. Consider a process defined by $V_0 = W_0$ and by:

$$\begin{aligned}V_t &= W_t - \alpha^2 HLMC\sqrt{d}t \\ &+ \alpha HL\sqrt{d} \sum_{k=1}^{t} \|x_{t-k+1} - x_{t-k}\| \sum_{m=k}^{\infty} \mathbf{1}_{\{\tau_{t-k+m} \geq m\}},\end{aligned} \tag{12}$$

whenever $x_i \notin S$ for all $0 \leq i \leq t$. Finally, if $x_i \in S$ for some $0 \leq i \leq t$, then define

$$V_t(x_t, \ldots, x_{u-1}, \ldots, x_0) = V_{u-1}(x_{u-1}, \ldots, x_0),$$

where u is the minimal index, such that $x_u \in S$. Assume that the algorithm has not succeeded at time t. Using the Lipschitzness of W:

$$\begin{aligned}V_{t+1} &= W_{t+1}(x_t - \alpha\tilde{g}(v_t), x_t, \ldots, x_0) \\ &\quad - \alpha^2 HLMC\sqrt{d}(t+1) \\ &\quad + \alpha HL\sqrt{d}\|x_{t+1} - x_t\| \sum_{m=1}^{\infty} \mathbf{1}_{\{\tau_{t+m} \geq m\}} \\ &\quad + \alpha HL\sqrt{d} \sum_{k=2}^{t+1} \|x_{t-k+2} - x_{t-k+1}\| \sum_{m=k}^{\infty} \mathbf{1}_{\{\tau_{t+1-k+m} \geq m\}} \\ &\leq W_{t+1}(x_t - \alpha\tilde{g}(x_t), \ldots, x_0) \\ &\quad + \alpha H\|\tilde{g}(x_t) - \tilde{g}(v_t)\| \\ &\quad - \alpha^2 HLMC\sqrt{d}(t+1) \\ &\quad + \alpha HL\sqrt{d}\|x_{t+1} - x_t\| \sum_{m=1}^{\infty} \mathbf{1}_{\{\tau_{t+m} \geq m\}} \\ &\quad + \alpha HL\sqrt{d} \sum_{k=1}^{t} \|x_{t-k+1} - x_{t-k}\| \sum_{m=k+1}^{\infty} \mathbf{1}_{\{\tau_{t-k+m} \geq m\}}\end{aligned}$$

Now we take expectation with respect to the gradient at time t and condition on the past (denoted by $\mathbb{E}_{t|.}$). Using the Lipschitzness of $\tilde{g}$ and the supermartingale property of W_t for the first step and the bound on the expected norm of the gradient and Lemma 6.4 for the second:

$$\mathbb{E}_{t|.}(V_{t+1}) \leq W_t(x_t, \ldots, x_0) + \alpha HL\|x_t - v_t\| - \alpha^2 HLMC\sqrt{d}t$$

$$+ \left(\alpha HL\sqrt{d}\mathbb{E}_{t|.}\left(\|\alpha\tilde{g}(v_t)\|\right)\sum_{m=1}^{\infty}\mathbf{1}_{\{\tau_{t+m}\geq m\}} - \alpha^2 HLMC\sqrt{d}\right)$$
$$+ \alpha HL\sqrt{d}\sum_{k=1}^{t}\|x_{t-k+1}-x_{t-k}\|\sum_{m=k+1}^{\infty}\mathbf{1}_{\{\tau_{t-k+m}\geq m\}}$$
$$\leq W_t - \alpha^2 HLMC\sqrt{d}t$$
$$+ \alpha HL\sqrt{d}\sum_{k=1}^{t}\|x_{t-k+1}-x_{t-k}\|\sum_{m=k}^{\infty}\mathbf{1}_{\{\tau_{t-k+m}\geq m\}}$$
$$+ \alpha HL\left(\|x_t - v_t\| - \sqrt{d}\sum_{k=1}^{t}\|x_{t-k+1}-x_{t-k}\|\mathbf{1}_{\{\tau_t\geq k\}}\right)$$
$$\leq V_t$$

This inequality also trivially holds in the case when the algorithm has succeeded at time t. Hence, the process V_t is a supermartingale for the lock-free SGD process.

Note also that if the algorithm has not succeeded at time T, then $W_T \geq T$ and hence:

$$V_T = W_T - \alpha^2 HLMC\sqrt{d}T$$
$$+ \alpha HL\sqrt{d}\sum_{k=1}^{T}\|x_{T-k+1}-x_{T-k}\|\sum_{m=k}^{\infty}\mathbf{1}_{\{\tau_{T-k+m}\geq m\}}$$
$$\geq W_T - \alpha^2 HLMC\sqrt{d}T \geq T\left(1-\alpha^2 HLMC\sqrt{d}\right) \geq 0$$

It follows that $V_t \geq 0$ for all t. We also have that $V_0 = W_0$. Now for any $T > 0$:

$$\mathbb{E}(W_0) = \mathbb{E}(V_0) \geq \mathbb{E}(V_T)$$
$$= \mathbb{E}(V_T|F_T)\mathbb{P}(F_T) + \mathbb{E}(V_T|\neg F_T)\mathbb{P}(\neg F_T)$$
$$\geq \mathbb{E}(V_T|F_T)\mathbb{P}(F_T)$$
$$= \mathbb{E}\Big(W_T - \alpha^2 HLMC\sqrt{d}T$$
$$+ \alpha HL\sqrt{d}\sum_{k=1}^{T}\|x_{T-k+1}-x_{T-k}\|\sum_{m=k}^{\infty}\mathbf{1}_{\{\tau_{T-k+m}\geq m\}}|F_T\Big)\mathbb{P}(F_T)$$
$$\geq \mathbb{E}\left(W_T - \alpha^2 HLMC\sqrt{d}T|F_T\right)\mathbb{P}(F_T)$$
$$= \left(\mathbb{E}(W_T|F_T) - \alpha^2 HLMC\sqrt{d}T\right)\mathbb{P}(F_T)$$
$$\geq \left(1-\alpha^2 HLMC\sqrt{d}\right)T\mathbb{P}(F_T).$$

We conclude that:

$$\mathbb{P}(F_T) \leq \frac{\mathbb{E}(W_0)}{\left(1-\alpha^2 HLMC\sqrt{d}\right)T}. \tag{13}$$

□

We now apply the result with a particular choice for the martingale W_t. We use the process proposed in [10] in the case of convex optimization, which they show is a rate supermartingale for the sequential SGD process. More precisely, we have the following:

Lemma 6.6 ([10]). *Define the piecewise logarithm function to be*

$$\text{plog}(x) = \begin{cases} \log(ex) & : x \geq 1 \\ x & : x \leq 1 \end{cases}$$

Define the process W_t by:

$$W_t(x_t,\ldots,x_0) = \frac{\epsilon}{2\alpha c\epsilon - \alpha^2 M^2}\text{plog}\left(\|x_t - x^*\|^2\epsilon^{-1}\right) + t.$$

If the algorithm has not succeeded by timestep t (i.e. $x_i \notin S$ for all $i \leq t$) and by $W_t = W_{u-1}$ whenever $x_i \in S$ for some $i \leq t$ and u is the minimal index with this property. Then W_t is a rate supermartingale for sequential SGD with horizon $B = \infty$. It is also H-Lipschitz in the first coordinate, with $H = 2\sqrt{\epsilon}\left(2\alpha c\epsilon - \alpha^2 M^2\right)^{-1}$, that is for any t, u, v and any sequence $x_{t-1},\ldots,x_0$:

$$\|W_t(u, x_{t-1},\ldots,x_0) - W_t(v, x_{t-1},\ldots,x_0)\| \leq H\|u-v\|.$$

Using this martingale in Theorem 6.5, we obtain the following result, whose proof is deferred to the Appendix:

Corollary 6.7. *Assume that we run the lock-free SGD algorithm under the Asynchronous Shared Memory model for minimizing a convex function f satisfying the listed assumptions. Set the learning rate to:*

$$\alpha = \frac{c\epsilon\vartheta}{M^2 + 2\sqrt{\epsilon}LMC\sqrt{d}} = \frac{c\epsilon\vartheta}{M^2 + 4\sqrt{\epsilon}LM\sqrt{\tau_{max}n}\sqrt{d}}, \tag{14}$$

for some constant $\vartheta \in (0,1]$. Then for any $T > 0$ the probability that $x_i \notin S$ for all $i \leq T$ is:

$$\mathbb{P}(F_T) \leq \frac{M^2 + 4\sqrt{\epsilon}LM\sqrt{\tau_{max}n}\sqrt{d}}{c^2\epsilon\vartheta T}\text{plog}\left(\frac{e\|x_0 - x^*\|^2}{\epsilon}\right). \tag{15}$$

Proof. Substituting and using the result from [10] that

$$\mathbb{E}(W_0(x_0)) \leq \frac{\epsilon}{2\alpha c\epsilon - \alpha^2 M^2}\text{plog}\left(\frac{e\|x_0 - x^*\|^2}{\epsilon}\right)$$

we obtain that:

$$\mathbb{P}(F_T) \leq \frac{\mathbb{E}(W_0)}{\left(1-\alpha^2 HLMC\sqrt{d}\right)T}$$
$$\leq \frac{\epsilon}{2\alpha c\epsilon - \alpha^2 M^2}\text{plog}\left(\frac{e\|x_0 - x^*\|^2}{\epsilon}\right)$$
$$\left(\left(1 - \alpha^2\frac{2\sqrt{\epsilon}}{2\alpha c\epsilon - \alpha^2 M^2}LMC\sqrt{d}\right)T\right)^{-1}$$
$$\leq \frac{\epsilon}{\left(2\alpha c\epsilon - \alpha^2\left(M^2 + 2\sqrt{\epsilon}LMC\sqrt{d}\right)\right)T}\text{plog}\left(\frac{e\|x_0 - x^*\|^2}{\epsilon}\right)$$

Substituting the suggested value for the learning rate:

$$\mathbb{P}(F_T) \leq \frac{\epsilon}{T}\Bigg(2c\epsilon\frac{c\epsilon\vartheta}{M^2 + 2\sqrt{\epsilon}LMC\sqrt{d}}$$
$$- \left(M^2 + 2\sqrt{\epsilon}LMC\sqrt{d}\right)\left(\frac{c\epsilon\vartheta}{M^2 + 2\sqrt{\epsilon}LMC\sqrt{d}}\right)^2\Bigg)^{-1}$$
$$\text{plog}\left(\frac{e\|x_0 - x^*\|^2}{\epsilon}\right)$$
$$= \frac{\epsilon\,\text{plog}\left(\frac{e\|x_0 - x^*\|^2}{\epsilon}\right)}{\left(\frac{2c^2\epsilon^2\vartheta}{M^2+2\sqrt{\epsilon}LMC\sqrt{d}} - \frac{c^2\epsilon^2\vartheta^2}{M^2+2\sqrt{\epsilon}LMC\sqrt{d}}\right)T}$$
$$\leq \frac{M^2 + 2\sqrt{\epsilon}LMC\sqrt{d}}{c^2\epsilon\vartheta T}\text{plog}\left(\frac{e\|x_0 - x^*\|^2}{\epsilon}\right)$$

$$= \frac{M^2 + 4\sqrt{\epsilon} LM\sqrt{\tau_{\max} n}\sqrt{d}}{c^2 \epsilon \vartheta T} \text{plog}\left(\frac{e\|x_0 - x^*\|^2}{\epsilon}\right).$$

□

Choosing $\vartheta = 1$ gives the smallest value for the upper bound under this setting. We can impose an arbitrary small learning rate by selecting a small ϑ, while still ensuring convergence.

7 ITERATED ALGORITHM WITH GUARANTEED CONVERGENCE

The procedure in Algorithm 1 has the property that, for an appropriately chosen stopping time T, it will eventually reach the "success" region, where the distance to the optimal parameter value falls below ϵ. However, due to asynchrony and adversarial updates, threads might perform updates which cause them to *leave* the success region: a delayed thread might apply stale gradients to the model, overwriting the progress.

We now present an extension of the algorithm which deals with this problem, and allows us to converge to a success region of radius ϵ around the optimum x^*, for any $\epsilon > 0$. The algorithm will run a series of *epochs*, each of which is a series of T SGD iterations, executed using the procedure in Algorithm 1. The only difference between epochs is that they are executed with an exponentially decreasing learning rate α. (We note that this epoch pattern is already used in many settings, such as neural network training.) The epochs share the model X, with the critical note that we require that a gradient update can only be applied to X in the same epoch when it was generated. This condition can be enforced either by maintaining an epoch counter, on which threads condition their update via double-compare-single-swap (DCAS), or by having a distinct model allocated for each epoch.

```
Input: Dataset D, dimension d, function f to minimize
Output: Minimizer X, initially X = (0, 0, . . . , 0)
Data: Learning rate α, iteration count T, gradient bound M
//At thread i:
procedure FullSGD(ε, α, n)
    for j from 0 to log(α2Mn/√ε) do
        EpochSGD(T, α)
        α ← α/2
    end
    //The last epoch:
    Execute EpochSGD(T, α), accumulating local gradients into
      Acc[i]
    r ← sum_{k=1}^{n}(Acc[k]) //Collect entrywise sum
    return r
```

Algorithm 2: Full SGD code for a single thread.

The only distinct epoch is the last, in which threads each aggregate the gradients they produced locally. At the end of the epoch, the threads will collect all local gradients locally. As we show in the Appendix, the model will be guaranteed to be close to optimal in expectation.

Corollary 7.1. *The* FullSGD *procedure given in Algorithm 2 guarantees that* $\mathbb{E}[\|r - x^\star\|] \leq \epsilon$ *after executing for* $O(T \log(\alpha 2Mn/\sqrt{\epsilon}))$ *iterations.*

Proof Sketch. The main idea behind the analysis is as follows. By Theorem 6.5, we know that, with high probability, there exists a time t in each epoch where the aggregated gradients x_t enter the success region, i.e. $\|x_t - x^*\|^2 \leq \epsilon$, for a fixed parameter ϵ. The algorithm will guarantee that the model will not leave the success region before the end of the last epoch. This is ensured via our choice of the learning rate.

Let us now focus on the last epoch. Fix an $\epsilon > 0$; we wish to prove that, $\|x_T - x^\star\|^2 \leq \epsilon$ at the end of this epoch, in expectation. We fix the success condition of EpochSGD such that that there exists an iteration t in the epoch such that $\|x_t - x^\star\| \leq \sqrt{\epsilon}/2$. We note that the adversary may attempt to schedule "stale" updates, generated earlier in the execution, to cause the algorithm to leave the success region. However, we notice that there can be at most $n-1$ gradients generated *before* time t, which have not been applied yet. Denote these gradients by $(G(v_{\theta_i}))_{i=1,\ldots,n-1}$.

Finally, we claim that, in expectation, the distance between the final model x_T and the optimum is upper bounded by

$$\begin{aligned} \|x_T - x^*\| \leq \|x_t + \alpha \sum_{i=1}^{n-1} G(v_{\theta_i}) - x^\star\| &\leq \|x_T - x^*\| + \alpha n M \\ &\leq \sqrt{\epsilon}/2 + \sqrt{\epsilon}/2 \\ &= \sqrt{\epsilon}. \end{aligned}$$

□

We can characterize the probability of success by reducing the target ϵ, and applying Markov's inequality.

8 DISCUSSION

Learning Rates versus Asynchronous Convergence. An immediate consequence of our lower bound in Theorem 5.1 is that the algorithm must either have a low initial learning rate, or lower the learning rate across multiple iterations (as in Algorithm 2) in order to be able to withstand adversarial delays. Otherwise, the adversary can always apply stale gradients generated at a far enough time in the past to nullify progress. An alternative approach, which we did not consider here, would be to introduce a "momentum" term by which the current model value is multiplied [20].

Lower Bounds versus Upper Bounds. The attentive reader might find it curious that our lower bound suggests a linear slowdown in $\tau_{\max}$, whereas our upper bound suggests that the slowdown is linear in $O(\sqrt{\tau_{\max} n})$. However, a close examination of the preconditions for these two results will reveal that they are in fact complementary: in the lower bound, given fixed learning rate α, the adversary needs to set a large delay $\tau_{\max} \geq (\log(\alpha/2))/\log(1-\alpha)$ in order to slow down convergence. At the same time, the upper bound in Theorem 6.5 requires that $2\alpha^2 HLM\sqrt{d\tau_{\max} n} < 1$, which is incompatible with the above condition. Specifically, our improved convergence bound shows that asynchronous SGD converges faster and for a wider range of parameters than previously known.

Why is Asynchronous SGD Fast in Practice? In a nutshell, Theorem 6.5 shows that the gap in convergence between asynchronous SGD and the sequential variant becomes negligible if $\alpha^2 HLMC\sqrt{d\tau_{\max} n} \ll 1$. Intuitively, this condition holds in practice since gradients are often sparse, meaning that d is low, the delay factors $\tau_{\max}$ and τ_{avg} are *not* set adversarially, and the learning rate α can be set by the user to be small enough to offset any increase in the other terms. In particular, $\tau_{\max}$ is limited by the staleness of updates in the write buffer at each core, which is well bounded in practice [21].

At the same time, it is important to note that, while we "sequentialize" iterations in our analysis, up to n iterations may happen in parallel at any time, reducing the wall-clock convergence time by up to a factor of n. Thus, the practical trade-off is between any slowdown caused by asynchrony, and the parallelism due to multiple computation threads.

ACKNOWLEDGMENTS

We would like to thank Martin Jaggi for useful discussions. This project has received funding from the European Union's Horizon 2020 research and innovation programme under the Marie Skłodowska-Curie Grant Agreement No. 665385.

REFERENCES

[1] Alekh Agarwal and John C Duchi. 2011. Distributed delayed stochastic optimization. In *Advances in Neural Information Processing Systems*. 873–881.
[2] Hagit Attiya and Jennifer Welch. 2004. *Distributed computing: fundamentals, simulations, and advanced topics*. Vol. 19. John Wiley & Sons.
[3] Dimitri P Bertsekas and John N Tsitsiklis. 1989. *Parallel and distributed computation: numerical methods*. Vol. 23. Prentice hall Englewood Cliffs, NJ.
[4] Peva Blanchard, El Mahdi El Mhamdi, Rachid Guerraoui, and Julien Stainer. 2017. Byzantine-tolerant machine learning. *Proceedings of NIPS 2017* (2017).
[5] Sébastien Bubeck et al. 2015. Convex optimization: Algorithms and complexity. *Foundations and Trends® in Machine Learning* 8, 3-4 (2015), 231–357.
[6] Sorathan Chaturapruek, John C Duchi, and Christopher Ré. 2015. Asynchronous stochastic convex optimization: the noise is in the noise and SGD don't care. In *Advances in Neural Information Processing Systems*. 1531–1539.
[7] Yudong Chen, Lili Su, and Jiaming Xu. 2017. Distributed Statistical Machine Learning in Adversarial Settings: Byzantine Gradient Descent. *Proc. ACM Meas. Anal. Comput. Syst.* 1, 2, Article 44 (Dec. 2017), 25 pages. https://doi.org/10.1145/3154503
[8] Trishul M Chilimbi, Yutaka Suzue, Johnson Apacible, and Karthik Kalyanaraman. 2014. Project Adam: Building an Efficient and Scalable Deep Learning Training System.. In *OSDI*, Vol. 14. 571–582.
[9] Christopher De Sa, Kunle Olukotun, and Christopher Ré. 2014. Global convergence of stochastic gradient descent for some non-convex matrix problems. *arXiv preprint arXiv:1411.1134* (2014).
[10] Christopher M De Sa, Ce Zhang, Kunle Olukotun, and Christopher Ré. 2015. Taming the Wild: A Unified Analysis of Hogwild-style Algorithms. In *Advances in Neural Information Processing Systems*. 2674–2682.
[11] Jeffrey Dean, Greg Corrado, Rajat Monga, Kai Chen, Matthieu Devin, Mark Mao, Andrew Senior, Paul Tucker, Ke Yang, Quoc V Le, et al. 2012. Large scale distributed deep networks. In *Advances in neural information processing systems*. 1223–1231.
[12] John C Duchi, Sorathan Chaturapruek, and Christopher Ré. 2015. Asynchronous stochastic convex optimization. *arXiv preprint arXiv:1508.00882* (2015).
[13] Joel Gibson and Vincent Gramoli. 2015. Why non-blocking operations should be selfish. In *International Symposium on Distributed Computing*. Springer, 200–214.
[14] Kaiming He, Xiangyu Zhang, Shaoqing Ren, and Jian Sun. 2016. Deep residual learning for image recognition. In *Proceedings of the IEEE conference on computer vision and pattern recognition*. 770–778.
[15] Alex Krizhevsky, Ilya Sutskever, and Geoffrey E Hinton. 2012. Imagenet classification with deep convolutional neural networks. In *Advances in neural information processing systems*. 1097–1105.
[16] John Langford, Alexander J Smola, and Martin Zinkevich. 2009. Slow learners are fast. *Advances in Neural Information Processing Systems* 22 (2009), 2331–2339.
[17] Rémi Leblond, Fabian Pederegosa, and Simon Lacoste-Julien. 2018. Improved asynchronous parallel optimization analysis for stochastic incremental methods. *arXiv preprint arXiv:1801.03749* (2018).
[18] Xiangru Lian, Yijun Huang, Yuncheng Li, and Ji Liu. 2015. Asynchronous parallel stochastic gradient for nonconvex optimization. In *Advances in Neural Information Processing Systems*. 2737–2745.
[19] Ji Liu and Stephen J Wright. 2015. Asynchronous stochastic coordinate descent: Parallelism and convergence properties. *SIAM Journal on Optimization* 25, 1 (2015), 351–376.
[20] Ioannis Mitliagkas, Ce Zhang, Stefan Hadjis, and Christopher Ré. 2016. Asynchrony begets momentum, with an application to deep learning. In *54th Annual Allerton Conference on Communication, Control, and Computing, Allerton 2016, Monticello, IL, USA, September 27-30, 2016*. IEEE, 997–1004. https://doi.org/10.1109/ALLERTON.2016.7852343
[21] Adam Morrison and Yehuda Afek. 2015. Temporally bounding TSO for fence-free asymmetric synchronization. In *ACM SIGPLAN Notices*, Vol. 50. ACM, 45–58.
[22] Lam M Nguyen, Phuong Ha Nguyen, Marten van Dijk, Peter Richtárik, Katya Scheinberg, and Martin Takáč. 2018. SGD and Hogwild! Convergence Without the Bounded Gradients Assumption. *arXiv preprint arXiv:1802.03801* (2018).
[23] Benjamin Recht, Christopher Re, Stephen Wright, and Feng Niu. 2011. Hogwild: A lock-free approach to parallelizing stochastic gradient descent. In *Advances in neural information processing systems*. 693–701.
[24] Herbert Robbins and Sutton Monro. 1951. A stochastic approximation method. *The Annals of Mathematical Statistics* (1951), 400–407.
[25] David E Rumelhart, Geoffrey E Hinton, and Ronald J Williams. 1986. Learning representations by back-propagating errors. *nature* 323, 6088 (1986), 533.
[26] C. M. De Sa, C. Zhang, K. Olukotun, and C. Re. 2015. Taming the wild: A unified analysis of hogwild-style algorihms. In *Advances in Neural Information Processing Systems*.
[27] Scott Sallinen, Nadathur Satish, Mikhail Smelyanskiy, Samantika S Sury, and Christopher Ré. 2016. High performance parallel stochastic gradient descent in shared memory. In *Parallel and Distributed Processing Symposium, 2016 IEEE International*. IEEE, 873–882.
[28] F. Seide, H. Fu, L. G. Jasha, and D. Yu. 2014. 1-bit stochastic gradient descent and application to data-parallel distributed training of speech dnns. *Interspeech* (2014).
[29] David Silver, Aja Huang, Chris J Maddison, Arthur Guez, Laurent Sifre, George Van Den Driessche, Julian Schrittwieser, Ioannis Antonoglou, Veda Panneershelvam, Marc Lanctot, et al. 2016. Mastering the game of Go with deep neural networks and tree search. *nature* 529, 7587 (2016), 484–489.
[30] Lili Su and Nitin Vaidya. 2016. Multi-agent optimization in the presence of byzantine adversaries: fundamental limits. In *American Control Conference (ACC), 2016*. IEEE, 7183–7188.
[31] Lili Su and Nitin H Vaidya. 2016. Asynchronous non-bayesian learning in the presence of crash failures. In *International Symposium on Stabilization, Safety, and Security of Distributed Systems*. Springer, 352–367.
[32] Lili Su and Nitin H Vaidya. 2016. Fault-tolerant multi-agent optimization: optimal iterative distributed algorithms. In *Proceedings of the 2016 ACM Symposium on Principles of Distributed Computing*. ACM, 425–434.
[33] Zhixiong Yang and Waheed U Bajwa. 2017. ByRDiE: Byzantine-resilient distributed coordinate descent for decentralized learning. *arXiv preprint arXiv:1708.08155* (2017).
[34] Jian Zhang, Ioannis Mitliagkas, and Christopher Ré. 2017. YellowFin and the Art of Momentum Tuning. *arXiv preprint arXiv:1706.03471* (2017).
[35] Wei Zhang, Suyog Gupta, Xiangru Lian, and Ji Liu. 2016. Staleness-aware async-SGD for distributed deep learning. In *Proceedings of the Twenty-Fifth International Joint Conference on Artificial Intelligence*. AAAI Press, 2350–2356.
[36] Shuxin Zheng, Qi Meng, Taifeng Wang, Wei Chen, Nenghai Yu, Zhi-Ming Ma, and Tie-Yan Liu. 2017. Asynchronous Stochastic Gradient Descent with Delay Compensation. In *International Conference on Machine Learning*. 4120–4129.

Optimal Gossip Algorithms for Exact and Approximate Quantile Computations

Bernhard Haeupler*
CMU
haeupler@cs.cmu.edu

Jeet Mohapatra
MIT
jeetmo@mit.edu

Hsin-Hao Su
UNC Charlotte
hsinhaosu@uncc.edu

ABSTRACT

This paper gives drastically faster gossip algorithms to compute exact and approximate quantiles.

Gossip algorithms, which allow each node to contact a uniformly random other node in each round, have been intensely studied and been adopted in many applications due to their fast convergence and their robustness to failures. Kempe et al. [24] gave gossip algorithms to compute important aggregate statistics if every node is given a value. In particular, they gave a beautiful $O(\log n + \log \frac{1}{\epsilon})$ round algorithm to ϵ-approximate the sum of all values and an $O(\log^2 n)$ round algorithm to compute the exact ϕ-quantile, i.e., the $\lceil \phi n \rceil$ smallest value.

We give an quadratically faster and in fact optimal gossip algorithm for the exact ϕ-quantile problem which runs in $O(\log n)$ rounds. We furthermore show that one can achieve an exponential speedup if one allows for an ϵ-approximation. In particular, we give an $O(\log \log n + \log \frac{1}{\epsilon})$ round gossip algorithm which computes a value of rank between ϕn and $(\phi + \epsilon)n$ at every node. Our algorithms are extremely simple and very robust - they can be operated with the same running times even if every transmission fails with a, potentially different, constant probability. We also give a matching $\Omega(\log \log n + \log \frac{1}{\epsilon})$ lower bound which shows that our algorithm is optimal for all values of ϵ.

ACM Reference Format:
Bernhard Haeupler, Jeet Mohapatra, and Hsin-Hao Su. 2018. Optimal Gossip Algorithms for Exact and Approximate Quantile Computations. In *PODC '18: ACM Symposium on Principles of Distributed Computing, July 23–27, 2018, Egham, United Kingdom.* ACM, New York, NY, USA, 10 pages. https://doi.org/10.1145/3212734.3212770

1 INTRODUCTION

Today, due to the vast amount of data and advances in connectivity between computers, distributed data processing has become increasingly important. In distributed systems, data is stored across different nodes. When one requires some aggregate properties of the data, such as, sums, ranks, quantiles, or other statistics, nodes must communicate in order to compute these properties. Aggregating data in an efficient and reliable way is a central topic in distributed systems such as P2P networks and sensor networks [27, 39, 40].

We consider uniform gossip protocols, which are often very practical due to their fast convergence, their simplicity, and their stability under stress and disruptions. In uniform gossiping protocols, computation proceeds in synchronized rounds. In each round, each node chooses to **pull** or **push**. In a push a node chooses a message, which is delivered to a uniformly random other node. In a pull each node receives a message from a random node. The message size is typically restricted to $O(\log n)$ bits. The (time) complexity of an algorithm is measured by the number rounds executed. One typically wants algorithms that succeed with high probability, i.e., with probability at least $1 - 1/\text{poly}(n)$.

In this paper, we study the quantile computation problem. In the **exact ϕ-quantile problem** each node v is given a distinct[1] $O(\log n)$ bit value x_v and wants to compute the $\lceil \phi n \rceil$ smallest value overall. In the **ϵ-approximate ϕ-quantile problem** each node wants to compute a value whose rank is between $(\phi + \epsilon)n$ and $(\phi - \epsilon)n$.

Previously, Kempe et al. [24] gave a beautiful and simple $O(\log n + \log \frac{1}{\epsilon})$ round gossip algorithm to approximate the sum of all values up to a $(1 \pm \epsilon)$ factor. They also showed how to use this algorithm to solve the exact ϕ-quantile problem in $O(\log^2 n)$ rounds with high probability.

The main result of this paper is a quadratically faster gossip algorithm for the ϕ-quantile problem. The $O(\log n)$ round complexity of our algorithm means that the exact ϕ-quantile can be computed as fast as broadcasting a single message.

Theorem 1.1. *For any $\phi \in [0, 1]$ there is a uniform gossip algorithm which solves the exact ϕ-quantile problem in $O(\log n)$ rounds with high probability using $O(\log n)$ bit messages.*

Clearly the running time of this algorithm is optimal as $\Omega(\log n)$ rounds are known to be necessary to even just broadcast to each node the ϕ-quantile value, after it has been identified.

Equally interestingly we show that one achieve even faster algorithms if one considers the approximate ϕ-quantile problem. While a $O(\frac{1}{\epsilon^2} \log n)$ round algorithm for an ϵ-approximation follows from simple sampling and a $O(\log n)$ round algorithm computing the median up to a $\pm O(\sqrt{\frac{\log n}{n}})$ (but not general quantiles) was given by Doerr et al. [7], no approximation algorithm for the quantile problem with a sub-logarithmic round complexity was known prior

*Supported in part by NSF grants CCF-1527110, CCF-1618280 and NSF CAREER award CCF-1750808.

PODC '18, July 23–27, 2018, Egham, United Kingdom

ACM ISBN 978-1-4503-5795-1/18/07...$15.00
https://doi.org/10.1145/3212734.3212770

[1]The assumption of distinct values is without loss of generality and made for simplicity as one can always break ties consistently, e.g., according to the ID of the node where the value started.

to this work. We give an $O(\log\log n + \log(1/\epsilon))$ round algorithm for ϵ-approximating any ϕ-quantile which, for arbitrarily good constant approximations, is exponentially faster than our optimal exact algorithm:

Theorem 1.2. *For any constant or non-constant $\epsilon(n) > 0$ and any $\phi \in [0, 1]$, there exists a uniform gossip algorithm that solves the ϵ-approximate ϕ quantile problem in $O(\log\log n + \log \frac{1}{\epsilon(n)})$ rounds with high probability using $O(\log n)$ bit messages.*

We also give a $\Omega(\log \frac{1}{\epsilon})$ and a $\Omega(\log\log n)$ lower bound for the ϵ-approximate ϕ-quantile problem, which shows that our algorithm is optimal for essentially any value of ϵ.

Theorem 1.3. *For any $\frac{10\log n}{n} < \epsilon < 1/8$ and $\phi \in [0, 1]$, any gossip algorithm that uses less than $\frac{1}{2}\log\log n$ or less than $\log_4 \frac{8}{\epsilon}$ round fails to solve the ϵ-approximate ϕ-quantile problem with probability at least 1/3. This remains true even for unlimited message sizes.*

We furthermore show that our algorithms can be made **robust to random failures**, i.e., the same round complexities apply even if nodes fail with some constant probability. We remark that a small caveat of excluding an $\exp(-t)$ fraction of nodes after a running time of t rounds is necessary and indeed optimal given that this is the expected fraction of nodes which will not have participated in any successful push or pull after t rounds.

Theorem 1.4. *Suppose in every round every node fails with a, potentially different, probability bounded by some constant $\mu < 1$. For any $\phi \in [0, 1]$ there is a gossip algorithm that solves the ϕ quantile problem in $O(\log n)$ rounds. For any t and any $\epsilon(n) > 0$, there furthermore exists a gossip algorithm that solves the ϵ-approximate ϕ-quantile problem in $O(\log\log n + \log \frac{1}{\epsilon(n)} + t)$ rounds for all but $\frac{n}{2^t}$ nodes, with high probability.*

Despite being extremely fast and robust our algorithms remain very simple. In fact they do little more than repeatedly sampling two or three nodes, requesting their current value and selecting the largest, smallest, or median value. Given that in many cases an ϵ-approximation is more than sufficient we expect this algorithm to easily find applications in areas like sensor networks and distributed database systems. For instance, suppose that a sensor network consisting of thousands of devices is spread across an object to monitor and control the temperature. Say the top and bottom 10%-quantiles need special attention. By computing the 90%- and 10%-quantile, each node can determine whether it lies in the range. It is unlikely that such a computation needs to be exact. In fact, for any $0 < \epsilon < 1$, running $O(1/\epsilon)$ approximate quantile computations suffices for each node to determine its own quantile/rank up to an additive ϵ. The fact that this can be done in $O(\log\log n)$ rounds further demonstrates the power of approximations as there is not even a $o(n)$ algorithm known[2] which allows each node to compute its quantile/rank exactly.

Corollary 1.5. *For any constant or non-constant $\epsilon > 0$ and given that each node has a value there is a gossip algorithm that allows every node to approximate the quantile of its value up to an additive ϵ in $\frac{1}{\epsilon} \cdot O(\log\log n + \log \frac{1}{\epsilon})$ rounds with high probability using $O(\log n)$ bit messages.*

[2]The trivial algorithm which broadcasts the maximum value n times requires $O(n \log n)$ rounds. Using network coding gossip [18] one can improve this to $O(n)$ rounds. It is likely that computing the exact rank at each node cannot be done faster.

Technical Summary. While computing exact quantiles seems to be a very different problem from the approximate problem at first we achieve our exact algorithm by first designing an extremely efficient solution to the ϵ-approximate quantile problem running in $O(\log\log n + \log \frac{1}{\epsilon})$ rounds. This algorithm is in some sense based on sampling and inherently is not able to work for the exact quantile problem or too small ϵ itself, as it might randomly discard the target value in its first iteration. However, we show that the algorithm does work for ϵ larger than some polynomial in n. This allows us to bootstrap this algorithm and repeatedly remove a polynomial fraction of values within $O(\log n)$ rounds until, after a constant number of such iterations, only the target value persists. Overall this leads to an $O(\log\log n + \log \frac{1}{\epsilon})$ algorithm for the ϵ-approximate ϕ-quantile problem which works for ϵ values that can be any function of n. This actually generalizes the $O(\log n)$ algorithm for the exact ϕ-quantile problem, too, given that the $\frac{1}{2n}$-approximate ϕ-quantile problem is accurate enough to compute exact ranks and quantiles.

Next we outline an, indeed very simple, intuition of why a time complexity of $O(\log\log n + \log \frac{1}{\epsilon})$ is conceivable for the quantile computation problem: Suppose we sample $\Theta(\log n/\epsilon^2)$ many values uniformly and independently at random. With high probability the ϕ-quantile of the sampled values is an ϵ-approximation to the ϕ-quantile in the original data. Since each node can sample t node values (with replacement) in t rounds, one immediately get an $O(\log n/\epsilon^2)$ round algorithm that uses $O(\log n)$ bit messages.

Using larger message sizes, it is possible to reduce the number of rounds. Consider the following *doubling algorithm*: Each node v maintains a set S_v such that initially $S_v = \{x_v\}$. In each round, let $t(v)$ be the node contacted by v. Node v updates S_v by setting $S_v \leftarrow S_v \cup S_{t(v)}$. Since the set size essentially doubles each round, after $\log O(\log n/\epsilon^2) = O(\log\log n + \log \frac{1}{\epsilon})$ rounds, we have sampled $\Omega(\log n/\epsilon^2)$ values uniformly, albeit not quite independently, at random. A careful analysis shows that indeed a $O(\log\log n + \log \frac{1}{\epsilon})$ running time can be achieved using messages of size $\Theta(\log^2 n/\epsilon^2)$ bits.

Our first approach for reducing the message sizes tried to utilize the quantile approximation sketches from the streaming algorithm community (see related work). We managed to reduce the message complexity to $O(\frac{1}{\epsilon} \cdot \log n \cdot (\log\log n + \log(1/\epsilon)))$ by adopting the compactor ideas from these streaming sketches. A write-up of this might be of independent interest and can be found in the full version. Unfortunately even if one could losslesly port the state-of-the-art compactors scheme from [21] into this setting, the $\Omega(\frac{1}{\epsilon}\log\log(1/\delta))$ for getting ϵ-approximate quantile sketches with probability $1-\delta$ suggests that one cannot achieve a $o(\log n \log\log n)$ message size this way, even if ϵ is a constant. In contrast to most other distributed models of computation gossip algorithms furthermore do not allow to easily shift extra factors in the message size over to the round complexity. In fact, we did not manage to devise any $o(\log n)$ round gossip algorithm based on sketching which adheres to the standard $O(\log n)$ bound on message sizes.

Instead of sticking to the centralized mentality where each node tries to gather information to compute the answer, consider the following 3-TOURNAMENT mechanism. In each iteration, each node uniformly samples three values (in three rounds) and assign its value to the middle one[3]. Intuitively nodes close to the median should have a higher probability of surviving and being replicated. Indeed, we show that the number of nodes that have values that are ϵ close to the median grows exponentially for the first $O(\log \frac{1}{\epsilon})$ iterations. After that, the number of nodes with values more than ϵn away from the median decreases double exponentially. For sufficiently large ϵ this simple 3-TOURNAMENT algorithm gives an approximation of the the median in $O(\log \frac{1}{\epsilon} + \log\log n)$ iterations. In general, if we want to approximate the ϕ-quantile, we shift the $[\phi - \epsilon, \phi + \epsilon]$ quantiles to the quantiles around the median by the following 2-TOURNAMENT mechanism. If $\phi < 1/2$, each node samples two values and assign its value to the higher one. The case for $\phi > 1/2$ is symmetric. Intuitively this process makes it more likely for nodes with higher/smaller values to survive. Indeed, we show that with a bit of extra care in the last iterations, $O(\log \frac{1}{\epsilon})$ invocations suffice to shift the values around the ϕ-quantile to almost exactly the median, at which point one can apply the median approximation algorithm.

Finally, our lower bound comes from the fact that if one chooses $\Theta(\epsilon n)$ nodes and either gives them a very large or a very small value, then knowing which of the two cases occurred is crucial for computing any ϵ-approximate quantiles. However, initially only these $\Theta(\epsilon n)$ nodes have such information. We show that it takes $\Omega(\log\log n + \log \frac{1}{\epsilon})$ rounds to spread the information from these nodes to every node, regardless of the message size.

Related Work. The randomized gossip-based algorithms dates back to Demers et al. [6]. The initial studies are on the spreading of a single message [14, 22, 32], where Karp et al. [22] showed that $O(\log n)$ round and $O(n \log\log n)$ total messages is sufficient to spread a single message w.h.p. Kempe et al. [24] studied gossip-based algorithms for the quantile computation problem as well as other aggregation problems such as computing the sum and the average. Kempe et al. developed $O(\log n)$ rounds algorithm to compute the sum and average w.h.p. Later, efforts have been made to reduce the total messages to $O(n \log\log n)$ for computing the sum and the average [4, 23]. Using the ability to sample and count, Kempe et al. implemented the classic randomized selection algorithm [12, 19] in $O(\log^2 n)$ rounds. Doerr et al. [7] considered gossip algorithms for the problem of achieving a stabilizing consensus algorithm under adversarial node failures. They analyze the median rule, i.e., sample three values and keep the middle value, in this setting and show that $O(\log n)$ rounds suffice to converge to an $\pm O(\sqrt{\frac{\log n}{n}})$-approximate median even if $O(\sqrt{n})$ adversarial node failures occur. Similar gossip dynamics were also studied in [10] which considers randomly corrupted (binary) messages.

The exact quantile computation is also known as the selection problem, where the goal is to select the k'th smallest element. The problem has been studied extensively in both centralized and distributed settings. Blum et al. [3] gave a deterministic linear time algorithm for the problem in the centralized setting. In the distributed setting, Kuhn et al. [25] gave an optimal algorithm for the selection problem that runs in $O(D \log_D n)$ rounds in the CONGEST model, where D is the diameter of the graph. Many works have been focused on the communication complexity aspect (i.e. the total message size sent by each node) of the problem [16, 30, 31, 34–38]. Most of them are for complete graphs or stars. Others studied specific class of graphs such as two nodes connected by an edge [5, 33], rings, meshes, and complete binary trees [13].

The quantile computation problem has also been studied extensively in the streaming algorithm literature [1, 2, 11, 15, 17, 20, 21, 26, 28, 29], where the goal is to approximate ϕ-quantile using a small space complexity when the data comes in a single stream.

[3]Such gossip dynamics have also been analyzed in [7] for the setting of adversarial node failures and in [10] for the setting of random message corruptions.

2 THE TOURNAMENT ALGORITHMS

In this section, we present our algorithm for the ϵ-approximate quantile computation problem for sufficiently large ϵ. For convenience, we use $a \pm b$ to denote the interval $[a - b, a + b]$.

Theorem 2.1. *For any constant or non-constant $\epsilon(n) = \Omega(1/n^{0.096})$ and any $\phi \in [0, 1]$, there exists a uniform gossip algorithm that solves the ϵ-approximate ϕ quantile problem in $O(\log\log n + \log \frac{1}{\epsilon(n)})$ rounds with high probability using $O(\log n)$ bit messages.*

The algorithm is divided into two phases. In the first phase, each node adjusts its value so that the quantiles around the ϕ-quantile will become the median quantiles approximately. In the second phase, we show how to compute the approximate median.

2.1 Phase I: Shifting the Target Quantiles to Approximate Medians

Algorithm 1 2-TOURNAMENT(v)

```
h_0 ← (1 − (φ + ε))
i ← 0, T = 1/2 − ε.
while h_i > T do
    h_{i+1} ← h_i^2
    δ ← min(1, (h_i − T)/(h_i − h_{i+1}))
    With probability δ do
        Select two nodes t_1(v) and t_2(v) randomly
        x_v ← min(x_{t_1(v)}, x_{t_2(v)})
    Otherwise do
        Select a node t_1(v) randomly
        x_v ← x_{t_1(v)}
    i ← i + 1
end while
```

Let L_i, M_i, and H_i denote the nodes whose quantiles lie in $[0, \phi - \epsilon)$, $[\phi - \epsilon, \phi + \epsilon]$, and $(\phi + \epsilon, 1]$ respectively at the end of iteration i, and L_0, M_0, and H_0 be the nodes with those quantiles in the beginning. We run the 2-TOURNAMENT algorithm (Algorithm 1) until the iteration t such that $h_t \leq T$, where $T = 1/2 - \epsilon$. The goal is to show that by the end of iteration t, the size of $|L_t|$ and $|H_t|$ are $(1/2 - \Omega(\epsilon)) \cdot n$ so that an approximate median lies in M_t, which consists of our target quantiles.

Let $h_0 = 1 - (\phi + \epsilon)$ and $l_0 = \phi - \epsilon$. We first consider the case where $h_0 \geq l_0$ and the other case is symmetric. Initially, we have $\frac{|H_0|}{n} \in h_0 \pm 1/n$. Let $h_{i+1} = h_i^2$ for $i \geq 1$. We will show that $t = O(\log(1/\epsilon))$ and $\frac{|H_i|}{n}$ concentrates around h_i for iteration $1 \leq i \leq t-1$ and in the end we have $\frac{|H_t|}{n} \in T \pm \frac{\epsilon}{2}$.

The algorithm ends when h_i decreases below T. The lemma below bounds the number of iterations needed for this to happen. It can be shown that since h_i squares in each iteration, the quantity $(1 - h_i)$ roughly grows by a constant factor in each iteration. Since initially $(1-h_0) \geq \epsilon$, $O(\log(1/\epsilon))$ iterations suffice for h_i to decrease below T. The missing proofs of the lemmas in this section can be found in the full version.

Lemma 2.2. *Let t denote the number of iterations in Algorithm 1, $t \leq \log_{7/4}(4/\epsilon) + 2$.*

Proof. The algorithm ends when $h_t \leq 1/2 - \epsilon$. The highest possible value for h_0 is $1 - \epsilon$. We show that $h_i \leq 1 - \left(\frac{7}{4}\right)^i \cdot \epsilon$ provided that $1 - \left(\frac{7}{4}\right)^{i-1} \cdot \epsilon \geq 3/4$.

Suppose by induction that $h_{i-1} \leq 1 - \left(\frac{7}{4}\right)^{i-1} \cdot \epsilon$. We have

$$\begin{aligned} h_i &= h_{i-1}^2 \\ &\leq \left(1 - \left(\frac{7}{4}\right)^{i-1} \cdot \epsilon\right)^2 \\ &= 1 - \left(\frac{7}{4}\right)^{i-1} \cdot \epsilon \cdot \left(2 - \left(\frac{7}{4}\right)^{i-1} \cdot \epsilon\right) \\ &\leq 1 - \left(\frac{7}{4}\right)^{i-1} \cdot \epsilon \cdot \left(2 - \frac{1}{4}\right) \leq 1 - \left(\frac{7}{4}\right)^{i} \cdot \epsilon \qquad 1 - \left(\frac{7}{4}\right)^{i-1} \cdot \epsilon \geq 3/4 \end{aligned}$$

Therefore, after $i_0 = \log_{7/4}(4/\epsilon)$ iterations we have, $h_{i_0} \leq 1 - (\frac{7}{4})^i \cdot \epsilon \leq 1 - \frac{1}{4} = \frac{3}{4}$. Since $h_{i_0+2} \leq (\frac{3}{4})^4 < \frac{1}{2} - \epsilon$ for $\epsilon < 1/8$, it must be the case $t \leq i_0 + 2 = O(\log(1/\epsilon))$. □

Note that Line 7 and Line 8 are executed with probability 1 during the first $t - 1$ iterations. We show the following.

Lemma 2.3. *For iteration $1 \leq i < t-1$, $\mathbb{E}[\frac{|H_{i+1}|}{n} \mid H_i] = \frac{|H_i|^2}{n^2}$.*

Proof.

$$\begin{aligned} \mathbb{E}\left[\frac{|H_{i+1}|}{n} \mid H_i\right] &= \frac{1}{n}\sum_{v \in V} \Pr(x_{t_1(v)} \in H_i \wedge x_{t_2(v)} \in H_i) \\ &= \frac{1}{n}\sum_{v \in V} \left(\frac{|H_i|}{n}\right)^2 = \left(\frac{|H_i|^2}{n^2}\right) \end{aligned}$$ □

Therefore, for $1 \leq i \leq t-1$, if $\frac{|H_i|}{n} \sim h_i$ ($\sim$ means they are close), then $\frac{|H_{i+1}|}{n} \sim h_{i+1}$ if $\frac{|H_{i+1}|}{n}$ concentrates around its expectation, since $h_{i+1} = h_i^2$.

In the last iteration, we truncate the probability of doing the tournament by doing it with only probability δ for each node, so that ideally we hope to have $\mathbb{E}[\frac{|H_t|}{n}|H_{t-1}] = T$. However, since δ is calculated with respect to h_{t-1} instead of the actual $\frac{|H_{t-1}|}{n}$, we need the following lemma to bound the deviated expectation. In the next lemma, we show that if $\frac{|H_{t-1}|}{n} \sim h_{t-1}$, then indeed we have $\mathbb{E}[\frac{|H_t|}{n}|H_{t-1}] \sim T$.

Lemma 2.4. *Suppose that $(1-\epsilon'')h_{t-1} \leq \frac{|H_{t-1}|}{n} \leq (1+\epsilon'')h_{t-1}$ for some $0 < \epsilon'' < 1$. We have $T - 3\epsilon'' \leq \mathbb{E}\left[\frac{|H_t|}{n} \mid H_{t-1}\right] \leq T + 3\epsilon''$.*

In the end, we hope that $\frac{|H_t|}{n}$ deviates from T by at most $\epsilon/2$. To achieve this, we show that in each iteration $1 \leq i \leq t-1$, $\frac{|H_i|}{n}$ deviates from its expectation, $\frac{|H_{i-1}|^2}{n^2}$, by at most a $(1 \pm \epsilon')$ factor, where $\epsilon' = \epsilon/2^{t+4}$ is an error control parameter that is much less than ϵ. Note that $\frac{|H_{i-1}|^2}{n^2}$ is already deviated from $h_{i-1}^2 = h_i$ to some degree. The next lemma bounds the cumulative deviation of $\frac{|H_i|}{n}$ from h_i. Note that ϵ' has to be large enough in order guarantee that $\frac{|H_i|}{n}$ lies in the $(1 \pm \epsilon') \cdot \frac{|H_{i-1}|^2}{n^2}$ range. This also implies ϵ has to be large enough.

Lemma 2.5. *Let $\epsilon = \Omega(1/n^{1/4.47})$ and $\epsilon' = \frac{\epsilon}{2^{t+4}}$. W.h.p. for iteration $0 \leq i < t$, we have $\frac{|H_i|}{n} \in (1 \pm \epsilon')^{2^{i+1}-1} \cdot h_i$.*

Combining Lemma 2.4 for the deviation on the last round and Lemma 2.5 for the deviation on first $t-1$ rounds, the following lemma summarizes the final deviation.

Lemma 2.6. *Let $\epsilon = \Omega(1/n^{1/4.47})$. At the end of the algorithm, w.h.p. $T - \frac{\epsilon}{2} \leq \frac{|H_t|}{n} \leq T + \frac{\epsilon}{2}$.*

Proof. Let $\epsilon' = \frac{\epsilon}{2^{t+4}}$. By Lemma 2.5, we have $\frac{|H_{t-1}|}{n} \in (1 \pm \epsilon')^{2^t-1} \cdot h_{t-1}$ w.h.p.

Note that $(1+\epsilon')^{2^t-1} \leq 1 + 2(2^t-1)\epsilon' \leq 1 + 2^{t+1}\epsilon'$, since $(1+a)^b \leq 1 + 2ab$ provided $0 < ab \leq 1/2$ and we have $(2^t-1)\epsilon' \leq \epsilon/16 \leq 1/2$. Similarly, $(1-\epsilon')^{2^t-1} \geq 1 - 2^{t+1}\epsilon'$. Therefore, we can let $\epsilon'' = 2^{t+1}\epsilon'$ and apply Lemma 2.4 to conclude that

$$T - 3 \cdot 2^{t+1}\epsilon' \leq T - 3\epsilon'' \leq \mathbb{E}\left[\frac{|H_t|}{n} \mid H_{t-1}\right] \leq T - 3\epsilon'' \leq T + 3 \cdot 2^{t+1}\epsilon'$$

Since $\frac{|H_{t-1}|}{n} = \Omega(1)$ (by Lemma 2.5) and $\epsilon' = \epsilon/2^{t+4} = \Omega(\sqrt{\log n/n})$. we can apply Chernoff Bound to show w.h.p. $|H_t| \in (1 \pm \epsilon)\mathbb{E}[|H_t| \mid H_{t-1}]$. Thus,

$$\begin{aligned} (1-\epsilon')(T - 3 \cdot 2^{t+1}\epsilon') \leq \frac{|H_t|}{n} &\leq (1+\epsilon')(T + 3 \cdot 2^{t+1}\epsilon') \\ T - 4 \cdot 2^{t+1}\epsilon' \leq \frac{|H_t|}{n} &\leq T + 4 \cdot 2^{t+1}\epsilon' \\ T - \frac{\epsilon}{2} \leq \frac{|H_t|}{n} &\leq T + \frac{\epsilon}{2} \qquad \epsilon' = \epsilon/(2^{t+4}) \end{aligned}$$ □

Initially, $\frac{|M_0|}{n} \geq 2\epsilon$. In a similar vein, we show that that $\frac{|M_t|}{n}$ does not decreases much from 2ϵ.

Lemma 2.7. *Let $\epsilon = \Omega(1/n^{1/4.47})$. At the end of the algorithm, w.h.p. $\frac{|M_t|}{n} \geq \frac{7\epsilon}{4}$.*

The following lemma shows that at the end of Algorithm 1, the problem has been reduced to finding the approximate median.

Lemma 2.8. *Let $\epsilon = \Omega(1/n^{1/4.47})$. At the end of iteration t of Algorithm 1, w.h.p. any ϕ'-quantile where $\phi' \in [\frac{1}{2} - \frac{\epsilon}{4}, \frac{1}{2} + \frac{\epsilon}{4}]$ must be in M_t.*

Proof. Since $\frac{1}{2} - \frac{3\epsilon}{2} \le \frac{|H_t|}{n} \le \frac{1}{2} - \frac{\epsilon}{2}$ and $\frac{|M_t|}{n} \ge \frac{7\epsilon}{4}$ by Lemma 2.5 and Lemma 2.7, we have $\frac{|M_t|}{n} + \frac{|H_t|}{n} \ge \frac{1}{2} + \frac{\epsilon}{4}$. Combined with the fact that $\frac{|H_t|}{n} \le \frac{1}{2} - \frac{\epsilon}{2}$, we conclude that any ϕ'-quantile where $\phi' \in [\frac{1}{2} - \frac{\epsilon}{4}, \frac{1}{2} + \frac{\epsilon}{4}]$ must be in M_t. □

2.2 Phase II: Approximating the Median

Let L_i, M_i, and H_i denote the nodes whose quantiles lie in $[0, \frac{1}{2} - \epsilon)$, $[\frac{1}{2} - \epsilon, \frac{1}{2} + \epsilon]$, and $(\frac{1}{2} - \epsilon, 1]$ respectively at the end of iteration i, and L_0, M_0, and H_0 be the nodes with those quantiles in the beginning. Note that L_i and H_i are the nodes whose values are not our targets. We will show the quantities of $\frac{|L_i|}{n}$ and $\frac{|H_i|}{n}$ decrease in each iteration as our 3-TOURNAMENT algorithm (Algorithm 2) makes progress.

Initially, $l_0 = h_0 = \frac{1}{2} - \epsilon$. Let $h_{i+1} = 3h_i^2 - 2h_i^3$ and $l_{i+1} = 3l_i^2 - 2l_i^3$ for $i \ge 0$, we will show that $\frac{|L_i|}{n}$ and $\frac{|H_i|}{n}$ concentrate around l_i and h_i. Note that h_i and l_i roughly square in each iteration. Once they decrease below a constant after the first $O(\log(1/\epsilon))$ iterations, they decrease double exponentially in each iteration. The tournaments end when l_i and h_i decrease below $T = 1/n^{1/3}$.

Algorithm 2 3-TOURNAMENT(v)

1: $h_0, l_0 \leftarrow \frac{1}{2} - \epsilon$
2: $i \leftarrow 0, T = 1/n^{1/3}$.
3: **while** $l_i > T$ **do**
4: $\quad h_{i+1} \leftarrow 3h_i^2 - 2h_i^3, l_{i+1} \leftarrow 3l_i^2 - 2l_i^3$
5: $\quad$ Select three nodes $t_1(v), t_2(v), t_3(v)$ randomly.
6: $\quad x_v \leftarrow median(x_{t_1(v)}, x_{t_2(v)}, x_{t_3(v)})$.
7: **end while**
8: Sample $K = O(1)$ nodes uniformly at random and output the median value of these nodes.

Lemma 2.9. *Let t denote the number of iterations in Algorithm 2. We have $t \le \log_{11/8}(\frac{1}{4\epsilon}) + \log_2 \log_4 n = O(\log(1/\epsilon) + \log\log n)$.*

Proof. Suppose that $(\frac{11}{8})^{i-1}\epsilon \le 1/4$, we will show that $l_i \le 1/2 - (\frac{11}{8})^i\epsilon$. First, $l_0 = 1/2 - \epsilon$. Suppose by induction that $l_{i-1} \le 1/2 - (\frac{11}{8})^{i-1}\epsilon$. We have:

$$\begin{aligned} l_i &= 3l_{i-1}^2 - 2l_{i-1}^3 \\ &= 3\left(\frac{1}{2} - \left(\frac{11}{8}\right)^{i-1} \cdot \epsilon\right)^2 - 2\left(\frac{1}{2} - \left(\frac{11}{8}\right)^{i-1} \cdot \epsilon\right)^3 \\ &= \frac{1}{2} - \frac{3}{2}\left(\frac{11}{8}\right)^{i-1} \cdot \epsilon + 2\left(\left(\frac{11}{8}\right)^{i-1} \cdot \epsilon\right)^3 \\ &\le \frac{1}{2} - \frac{3}{2}\left(\frac{11}{8}\right)^{i-1} \cdot \epsilon + \frac{1}{8}\left(\left(\frac{11}{8} \cdot \epsilon\right)^{i-1}\right) \\ &= \frac{1}{2} - \left(\frac{11}{8}\right)^{i} \cdot \epsilon \end{aligned}$$

Therefore, after $i_0 = \log_{11/8}(\frac{1}{4\epsilon})$ iterations, we have $l_i \le \frac{1}{2} - \left(\frac{11}{8}\right)^{i_0} \epsilon \le \frac{1}{2} - \frac{1}{4} = \frac{1}{4}$.

Suppose that $i_1 = \log_2 \log_4 n$, we have

$$\begin{aligned} l_{i_0+i_1} &\le 3l_{i_0+i_1-1}^2 \le 3^{i_1} l_{i_0}^{2^{i_1}} \le 3^{i_1} \cdot \left(\frac{1}{4}\right)^{2^{i_1}} \\ &\le (\log_4 n)^{\log_2 3} \cdot \left(\frac{1}{4}\right)^{\log_4 n} = \frac{(\log_4 n)^{\log_2 3}}{n} \le n^{2/3} \end{aligned}$$

Therefore, $t \le i_0 + i_1 = \log_{11/8}(\frac{1}{4\epsilon}) + \log_2 \log_4 n = O(\log(1/\epsilon) + \log\log n)$. □

Lemma 2.10. *For each iteration $0 \le i < t$, $\mathbb{E}[\frac{|L_{i+1}|}{n} \mid L_i] = 3(\frac{|L_i|}{n})^2 - 2(\frac{|L_i|}{n})^3$ and $\mathbb{E}[\frac{|H_{i+1}|}{n} \mid H_i] = 3(\frac{|H_i|}{n})^2 - 2(\frac{|H_i|}{n})^3$.*

Proof. We will show the proof for $\mathbb{E}[\frac{|L_{i+1}|}{n} | L_i]$, since $\mathbb{E}[\frac{|H_{i+1}|}{n} \mid H_i]$ is the same. Note that a node v is in L_{i+1} if and only if at least 2 of $t_1(v), t_2(v), t_3(v)$ are in L_i. Therefore,

$$\begin{aligned} \mathbb{E}\left[\frac{|L_{i+1}|}{n} \mid L_i\right] &= \frac{1}{n}\sum_{v \in V}\left(\left(\frac{|L_i|}{n}\right)^3 + 3\left(\frac{|L_i|}{n}\right)^2\left(1 - \frac{|L_i|}{n}\right)\right) \\ &= 3\left(\frac{|L_i|}{n}\right)^2 - 2\left(\frac{|L_i|}{n}\right)^3 \end{aligned}$$ □

The following lemma shows the probabilities that $\frac{|L_i|}{n}$ and $\frac{|H_i|}{n}$ deviate from their expectation by a $(1 + \epsilon')$ factor are polynomially small in n, provided ϵ' is sufficiently large. We cap the quantity at T for the purpose of applying concentration inequalities.

Lemma 2.11. *Let $\epsilon' = \Omega(\frac{(\log n)^{1/2}}{n^{1/3}})$, w.h.p. for each iteration $0 \le i <= t$, $\frac{|H_i|}{n} \le (1+\epsilon') \cdot \max(T, \mathbb{E}[\frac{|H_i|}{n} \mid H_{i-1}])$ and $\frac{|L_i|}{n} \le (1+\epsilon') \cdot \max(T, \mathbb{E}[\frac{|L_i|}{n} \mid L_{i-1}])$.*

Proof. In each iteration, since each node set its value independently, by Chernoff Bound (see Lemma A.2), we have

$$\begin{aligned} &\Pr\left(\frac{|L_i|}{n} \le (1+\epsilon') \cdot \max(T, \frac{\mathbb{E}[|L_i| \mid L_{i-1}]}{n})\right) \\ &\le \exp(-\Omega(\epsilon'^2 \max(n \cdot T, \mathbb{E}[|L_i| \mid L_{i-1}]))) \\ &= \exp(-\Omega(\epsilon'^2 n^{2/3})) = 1/\text{poly}(n) \end{aligned}$$

The proof for $|H_i|$ is the same. □

Then we bound the cumulative deviation of $\frac{|H_i|}{n}$ from h_i and the cumulative deviation of $\frac{|L_i|}{n}$ from l_i.

Lemma 2.12. *Let $\epsilon' = \Omega(\frac{\log n^{1/2}}{n^{1/3}})$. W.h.p. for each iteration $0 \le i <= t$, $\frac{|L_i|}{n} \le \max((1+\epsilon')^{\frac{3^i-1}{2}} \cdot l_i, (1+\epsilon')T)$ and $\frac{|H_i|}{n} \le \max((1+\epsilon')^{\frac{3^i-1}{2}} \cdot h_{i+1}, (1+\epsilon')T)$.*

Proof. We only show the proof for $|L_i|$ and we will prove by induction. Initially, $\frac{|L_0|}{n} \le l_0$. Suppose that $\frac{|L_i|}{n} \le \max((1+\epsilon')^{\frac{3^i-1}{2}} \cdot l_{i+1}, (1+\epsilon')T)$ is true.

By Lemma 2.11, we have w.h.p., $\frac{|L_{i+1}|}{n} \le (1+\epsilon') \cdot \max(\frac{\mathbb{E}[|L_{i+1}||L_i]}{n}, T)$. If $\frac{\mathbb{E}[|L_{i+1}||L_i]}{n} \le T$, then we are done, since $\frac{|L_{i+1}|}{n} \le (1+\epsilon') \cdot \frac{\mathbb{E}[|L_{i+1}||L_i]}{n} = (1+\epsilon') \cdot T$. Also, if $\frac{|L_i|}{n} \ge (1+\epsilon')T$, then $\frac{\mathbb{E}[|L_{i+1}||L_i]}{n} \le 3 \cdot \frac{|L_i|^2}{n^2} \le \frac{|L_i|}{n} \cdot O(\frac{1}{n^{2/3}}) \le T$.

Otherwise, if $\frac{|L_i|}{n} > (1+\epsilon')T$ then it must be the case that $\frac{|L_i|}{n} \le (1+\epsilon')^{\frac{3^i-1}{2}} \cdot l_{i+1}$ by induction hypothesis. Therefore,

$$\begin{aligned}\frac{|L_{i+1}|}{n} &\le (1+\epsilon') \cdot \frac{\mathbb{E}[|L_i| \mid L_{i-1}]}{n} \\ &\le (1+\epsilon') \cdot 3\left(\frac{|L_i|}{n}\right)^2 - 2\left(\frac{|L_i|}{n}\right)^3 \\ &\le (1+\epsilon') \cdot \left(3\left((1+\epsilon')^{\frac{3^i-1}{2}} \cdot l_i\right)^2 - 2\left((1+\epsilon')^{\frac{3^i-1}{2}} \cdot l_i\right)^3\right) \\ &\le (1+\epsilon') \cdot \left(\left((1+\epsilon')^{\frac{3^{i+1}-3}{2}}\right) \cdot \left(3 \cdot l_i^2 - 2 \cdot l_i^3\right)\right) \\ &= \left((1+\epsilon')^{\frac{3^{i+1}-1}{2}}\right) \cdot l_{i+1} \qquad \square\end{aligned}$$

Now, by setting ϵ' roughly equal to $1/3^t \sim \epsilon^{3.45}/(\log_4 n)^{1.59}$, we can bound the final deviations of $\frac{|H_i|}{n}$ and $\frac{|L_i|}{n}$ from T by a factor of 2 w.h.p.

Lemma 2.13. *Let* $\epsilon = \Omega(\frac{\log^{0.61} n}{n^{0.096}})$ *and* $\epsilon' = \epsilon^{3.45}/(\log_4 n)^{1.59}$, *then* $\frac{|L_t|}{n} \le 2T$ *and* $\frac{|H_t|}{n} \le 2T$ *w.h.p.*

Proof. First, $\epsilon' = \Omega(\frac{\epsilon^{3.45}}{\log^{1.59} n}) = \Omega(\frac{\log^{1/2} n}{n^{1/3}})$. By Lemma 2.12, w.h.p. we have either $\frac{|L_t|}{n} \le (1+\epsilon') \cdot T$ or $\frac{|L_t|}{n} \le (1+\epsilon')^{\frac{3^t-1}{2}} \cdot l_t$. If it is the former, then we are done since $\frac{|L_t|}{n} \le (1+\epsilon') \cdot T \le 2T$. Otherwise, we have

$$\begin{aligned}\frac{|L_t|}{n} &\le \left((1+\epsilon')^{\frac{3^t-1}{2}}\right) \cdot T \\ &\le \left(1 + 2 \cdot \epsilon' \cdot \frac{3^t-1}{2}\right) \cdot T \qquad (1+x)^n \le 1+2nx \text{ for } nx \le \tfrac{1}{2} \\ &\le \left(1 + \epsilon' \cdot 3^{\log_{11/8}(\frac{1}{4\epsilon}) + \log_2 \log_4 n}\right) \cdot T \\ &\le \left(1 + \epsilon' \cdot \left(\frac{1}{4\epsilon}\right)^{\log_{11/8} 3} \cdot \log_4^{\log_2 3} n\right) \cdot T \\ &\le 2 \cdot T \qquad \epsilon' = \epsilon^{3.45}/(\log_4 n)^{1.59} \qquad \square\end{aligned}$$

Finally, we show that when $\frac{|L_t|}{n}$ and $\frac{|H_t|}{n}$ are $O(1/n^{2/3})$, if we sample a constant number of values randomly and output the median of them, then w.h.p. the median is in M_t.

Lemma 2.14. *W.h.p. every node outputs a quantile in* $[\frac{1}{2}-\epsilon, \frac{1}{2}+\epsilon]$.

Proof. By Corollary 2.13, w.h.p. at the end of iteration t, $\frac{|L_t|}{n} \le 2/n^{2/3}$ and $\frac{|H_t|}{n} \le 2/n^{2/3}$. The algorithm outputs a quantile in $[\frac{1}{2}-\epsilon, \frac{1}{2}+\epsilon]$ if there are less than $K/2$ nodes in L_t are sampled and less than $K/2$ nodes in H_t are sampled.

The probability that at least $K/2$ nodes in $|L_t|$ are sampled is at most

$$\binom{K}{K/2} \cdot \left(\frac{2}{n^{2/3}}\right)^{K/2} \le \left(\frac{eK}{\frac{K}{2}}\right)^{K/2} \cdot \left(\frac{2}{n^{2/3}}\right)^{K/2} \le \left(\frac{4e}{n^{2/3}}\right)^{K/2}$$

Similarly, the probability that at least $K/2$ nodes in $|H_t|$ are sampled is also at most $\left(\frac{4e}{n^{2/3}}\right)^{K/2}$. By an union bound, the probability that less than $K/2$ nodes in L_t are sampled and less than $K/2$ nodes in H_t are sample is at least $1 - 2 \cdot \left(\frac{4e}{n^{2/3}}\right)^{K/2} = 1 - 1/\text{poly}(n)$. $\square$

Theorem 2.1 follows from Lemma 2.8 and Lemma 2.14.

3 EXACT QUANTILE COMPUTATION

To fill the gap of approximating the ϕ-quantile with ϵ error for $\epsilon = O(1/n^{0.096})$, we show that the exact quantile computation can be done in $O(\log n)$ rounds using $O(\log n)$ message size. Since we are to compute the exact quantile ϕ, we can assume that $k_0 \stackrel{\text{def}}{=} \phi \cdot n$ is an integer. The problem is to compute a value whose rank is k_0. Again, w.l.o.g. we assume that every node has a distinct value initially.

Algorithm 3 Exact Quantile Computation

```
1: k_0 ← φ · n
2: for i = 1, 2, ..., 25 do
3:   Each node v computes an ε/2-approximate of the (k_{i-1}/n − ε/2)-
     quantile and an ε/2-approximate of the (k_{i-1}/n + ε/2)-quantile
     with ε = n^{-0.05}/2.
4:   Each node learns the max and the min of these approximates
     of all nodes.
5:   Compute the rank of min among the original x_v's and denote
     it by R.
6:   Each node v set x_v ← ∞ if x_v ∉ [min, max]. Call these
     nodes valueless, otherwise valued.
7:   Let m_i be the smallest power of 2 that is larger than
     (n^{0.99}/2)/(# valued nodes). Each valued node makes m_i co-
     pies of its value and distribute them to valueless nodes so
     that there are at least n^{0.99}/2 valued nodes. (For convenience,
     we let the duplicated values to have smaller ranks than the
     original one.)
8:   Set k_i ← m_i · (k_{i-1} − R + 1).
9: end for
10: Every node outputs an (ε/3)-approximate (k_25/n − ε/2)-quantile.
```

The following is a detailed implementation of each step.

Step 3: Since $\epsilon = n^{-0.05}/2$, we can $\frac{\epsilon}{2}$-approximate the quantiles in $O(\log n)$ rounds by Theorem 2.1.

Step 4: The maximum (the minimum) can be computed by having each node forwarding the maximum (the minimum) value it has ever received. Since it takes $O(\log n)$ rounds to spread a message by [14, 32], this step can be done in $O(\log n)$ rounds.

Step 5: The rank of the minimum can be computed by performing a counting. The nodes whose x_v values are less than or equal to the minimum will be assigned 1. Otherwise they are assigned 0. By Kempe et al. [24], the sum can be aggregated in $O(\log n)$ rounds w.h.p.

Step 7: Consider the following process for distributing the values. Initially, every valued node v generates a token with weight equal to m_i, the targeted number of copies. We denote the token by a value-weight pair (x_v, m_i). Recall that m_i is a power of 2 and it can be computed by counting the number of valued nodes in $O(\log n)$ rounds. The goal is to split and distribute the tokens so that every node has at most one token of weight 1 in the end.

The process consists of $O(\log n)$ phases and each phase uses $O(1)$ rounds. Suppose that node v holds tokens $(x_1, w_1), (x_2, w_2), \ldots (x_m, w_m)$ at the beginning of a phase. For each token (x_i, w_i), if $w_i \neq 1$, v splits (x_i, w_i) into two tokens $(x_i, w_i/2)$ and push each one to a node randomly. If $w_i = 1$, then the token remains at v. Note that when two tokens of the same value are on the same node, they do not merge.

First note $\lg m_i = O(\log n)$ phases are needed to split to tokens into tokens of weight 1. Now, we show that it takes constant number of rounds to implement one phase.

Let $N(v, i)$ denote the number of tokens at v at the end i'th phase. Let $N = \max_{v,i} N(v, i)$. It takes N rounds to implement one phase. The value of $N(v, i)$ can be bounded by following calculation. Since at any phase, there cannot be more than $n^{0.99}$ tokens and each token appears at a node chosen uniformly at random, we have

$$\Pr(N(v,i) \geq 100K) \leq \binom{n^{0.99}}{100K} \cdot \frac{1}{n^{100K}} \leq \left(\frac{n^{0.99}}{n}\right)^{100K} = (1/n)^K.$$

By taking an union bound over each v and i, we conclude that $N < 100K$ w.h.p. Therefore, w.h.p. each phase can be implemented in $200K = O(1)$ rounds. At the end of $O(\log n)$ phase, every node has at most $100K$ tokens of weight 1 w.h.p.

Next, in the subsequent phases, if a node holds more than one token, then it will push every token except one to a random node (one random node per token). We say a token succeeded at the end of the phase if it was pushed to a node without any other tokens. Consider a token, the probability a token did not succeed in a phase is at most $n^{0.99}/n = 1/n^{0.01}$, since there are at most $n^{0.99}$ nodes with tokens at the end of the phase.

Therefore, after $100K$ phases, the probability that a token did not succeed is at most $1/n^{0.01 \cdot 100K} = 1/n^K$. By a union bound over the tokens, we conclude that w.h.p. all tokens succeeded. Moreover, again, each phase can be implemented using $100K$ rounds. Therefore, we can split and distribute the tokens in $O(\log n)$ rounds. Each original token is duplicated with exactly m_i copies. Then, those nodes holding a token set its value to the value of the token. Nodes without a token will remain valueless.

Correctness: Let ans be the answer (the value whose initial rank is k_0). Let $M_i = \prod_{j=1}^{i} m_i$ denote the number of copies of each value from the beginning. We show by induction that the values whose ranks lying in $(k_i - M_i, k_i]$ are ans after iteration i. Initially, $M_0 = 1$, the statement trivially holds.

Suppose that at the end of iteration $i-1$, the values whose ranks lying in $(k_{i-1} - M_i, k_{i-1}]$ are ans. After Step 6 in iteration i, the rank of ans is exactly $k_{i-1} - R + 1$. Since every value is duplicated to have m_i copies after Step 7, the rank of ans becomes $k_i = m_i \cdot (k_{i-1} - R + 1)$ (Recall that we let the original value to have a larger rank than the duplicated values). Since the values whose ranks lying in $(k_{i-1} - M_{i-1}, k_{i-1}]$ were ans at the end of iteration $i-1$ and ans $\in$ [min, max], it must be the case that every value in this range is duplicated with m_i copies. Therefore, all values whose ranks lying in $(k_i - m_i \cdot M_{i-1}, k_i] = (k_i - M_i, k_i]$ are ans after iteration i.

Next, we show that after 25 iterations, $M_{25} \geq \epsilon n$. Suppose that $M_{i-1} \leq \epsilon n$. The number of valueless node after Step 6 is at most $2\epsilon n + 2M_{i-1} \leq 4\epsilon n$. The $2\epsilon n$ comes from the fact that at most $2\epsilon n$ values can lie in the range (min, max). The $2M_{i-1}$ term is because at most M_{i-1} values are equal to min and max. Therefore, $m_i \geq (n^{0.99}/2)/(4\epsilon n) = (n^{0.04}/4)$ and $M_i \geq (n^{0.04}/4) \cdot M_{i-1}$.

Therefore, $M_{25} \geq \min(\epsilon n, (n^{0.04}/4)^{25}) = \epsilon n$. Now the the values of the items whose ranks are in the range of $(k_{25} - \epsilon n, k_{25}]$ must be ans. We then compute a quantile in $(\frac{k_{25}}{n} - \epsilon, \frac{k_{25}}{n}]$ using our $\epsilon/3$-approximate quantile computation algorithm to approximate the $(\frac{k_{25}}{n} - \frac{\epsilon}{2})$-quantile in $O(\log n)$ rounds.

4 A LOWER BOUND

We show that it takes at least $\Omega(\log(1/\epsilon) + \log\log n)$ rounds to approximate the ϕ-quantile up to ϵ error w.h.p.

Theorem 1.4. *Suppose in every round every node fails with a, potentially different, probability bounded by some constant $\mu < 1$. For any $\phi \in [0, 1]$ there is a gossip algorithm that solves the ϕ quantile problem in $O(\log n)$ rounds. For any t and any $\epsilon(n) > 0$, there furthermore exists a gossip algorithm that solves the ϵ-approximate ϕ-quantile problem in $O(\log\log n + \log \frac{1}{\epsilon(n)} + t)$ rounds for all but $\frac{n}{2^t}$ nodes, with high probability.*

Proof. Consider the following two scenarios. The first is when each node is associated with a distinct value from $\{1, 2, \ldots, n\}$. The second is when each node is associated with a distinct value from $\{1 + \lfloor 2\epsilon n \rfloor, \ldots, n + \lfloor 2\epsilon n \rfloor\}$.

A node is able to distinguish between these cases only if it recieves an value from $S \stackrel{\text{def}}{=} \{1, 2, \ldots, \lfloor 2\epsilon n \rfloor\} \cup \{n+1, n+2, \ldots, n + \lfloor 2\epsilon n \rfloor\}$. Otherwise, it can only output a value whose quantile is in $[1/2 - \epsilon, 1/2 + \epsilon]$ with probability 1/2, since the difference of the ϕ-quantile in both scenarios is at least $\lfloor 2\epsilon n \rfloor \geq \epsilon n$.

Call a node *good* if it ever received a value from S, and *bad* otherwise. Note that a bad node cannot outputs a correct answer with probability more than 1/2. Initially there are at most $2 \cdot \lfloor 2\epsilon n \rfloor \leq 4\epsilon n$ good nodes. We will show that with probability $1 - 1/n$ there exists at least one bad node at the end of round t.

Let $X_0 = 2 \cdot \lfloor 2\epsilon n \rfloor$ and let X_i denote the number of good nodes at the end of round i. Given a bad node v, it can become good if it pulls from a good node or some good node pushes to it. Let Y_v denote the event that v pulls from a good node, we have $\Pr(Y_v \mid X_i) = X_i/n$. Also, the pushes from the good nodes can only generate another at most X_i good nodes. Therefore,

$$\mathbb{E}[X_{i+1} \mid X_i] \leq 2X_i + \mathbb{E}\left[\sum_{v \in B_i} Y_v\right] \leq 3X_i$$

$$\text{since } \mathbb{E}[\textstyle\sum_{v \in B_i} Y_v \mid X_i] \leq X_i$$

By Chernoff Bound, we have $\Pr(\sum_{v \in B_i} Y_v > 2X_i \mid X_i) \leq e^{-X_i/2} \leq e^{-5\log n} \leq 1/n^5$, since $X_i \geq X_0 \geq 10 \log n$. Therefore, with probability at least $1 - 1/n^5$, $X_{i+1} \leq 4X_i$. By taking a union bound over such events for the first $t' = \log_4(8/\epsilon)$ rounds, we conclude with probability at least $1 - 1/n^4$, $X_{t'} \leq (4\epsilon n)4^{t'} \leq n/2$.

Let t_0 be the last round such that $X_{t_0} \leq n/2$. Define $Z_i = |B_i|/n$. A node v remains in B_i if it did not pull from a good node **and** it was not pushed from any good nodes. Denote the event by W_v, we have $\Pr(W_v \mid B_i) \geq Z_i \cdot (1 - \frac{1}{n})^{n-1} \geq Z_i \cdot e^{-1}$. Therefore,

$$\mathbb{E}[|B_{i+1}| \mid B_i] = \mathbb{E}\left[\sum_{v \in B_i} W_v \mid B_i\right] \geq \left(\sum_{v \in B_i} Z_i \cdot e^{-1}\right) = |B_i| \cdot Z_i \cdot e^{-1}$$

Note that the events $\{W_v\}_{v \in B_i}$ are negatively dependent [8] (the number of empty bins in the balls into bins problem). Suppose that $Z_i \cdot |B_i| \geq 60e \log n$. By Chernoff Bound,

$$\Pr(|B_{i+1}| \leq |B_i| \cdot Z_i/(2e) \mid B_i) \leq e^{-Z_i \cdot |B_i|/(12e)} \leq 1/n^5$$

Therefore, $\Pr(Z_{i+1} \leq Z_i^2/(2e) \mid Z_i) \leq 1/n^5$. Suppose that $t_1 = O(n)$. We can take an union bound over the subsequent t_1 rounds to show that with probability at least $1 - 1/n^4$, $Z_{i+1} \geq Z_i^2/(2e)$ holds for these rounds, as long as $Z^2_{t_0+t_1} \geq (60 \log n)/n$.

Let $z_{t_0} = 1/2$ and $z_{i+1} = z_i^2/(2e)$. If $z^2_{t_0+t_1} \geq (60 \log n)/n$, with probability at least $1 - 1/n^4$, we have $Z_{t_0+t_1} \geq z_{t_0+t_1}$. Let $t_1 = \frac{1}{2} \lg \log n$, by definition of z_i, we have

$$\begin{aligned}
z_{t_0+t_1} &= \left(\frac{1}{2e}\right)^{t_1} \cdot z_{t_0}^{2^{t_1}} \\
&\geq \left(\frac{1}{2e}\right)^{t_1+2^{t_1}} && z_{t_0} = 1/2 \geq 1/(2e) \\
&= \left(\frac{1}{2e}\right)^{(\lg \log n)/2 + \sqrt{\log n}} \\
&\geq \left(\frac{1}{2e}\right)^{2\sqrt{\log n}} && \text{for sufficiently large } n
\end{aligned}$$

Since $(2e)^{-2\sqrt{\log n}} = \Omega((\log n)/n)$, $z_{t_0+t_1} \geq 2^{-2\sqrt{\log n}} \geq (60 \log n)/n$ for sufficiently large n. Therefore, with probability at least $1 - 1/n^4$, $Z_{t_0+t_1} > 0$.

Since with probability $1-1/n^4$, $t_0 \geq \log_4 8/\epsilon$. By taking an union bound over these two events, we conclude with probability at most $2/n^4$, all nodes are good by the end of round $t_0 + t_1$.

Therefore, the probability that every node computes a correct output at the end of round $t_0 + t_1$ is at most $1/2 + 2/n^4$. □

5 ROBUSTNESS

In this section, we show that our algorithm is robust against failures. We consider the following model of failures: Let $0 < \mu < 1$ be a constant. Every node v in every round i is associated with a probability $0 \leq p_{v,i} \leq \mu$. Note that $p_{v,i}$ is pre-determined before the execution of the algorithm. During the execution of round i, each node v fails with probability $p_{v,i}$ to perform its operation (which may be either push or pull). We show how to modify the algorithm and the analysis for the tournament algorithms and the exact quantile computation algorithms in the following.

5.1 The Tournament Algorithms

First consider the 2-TOURNAMENT algorithm. Initially, every node is *good*. Consider node v, instead of only pulling from 2 neighbors each iteration, now pull from $\Theta(\frac{1}{1-\mu} \cdot \log(\frac{1}{1-\mu}))$ neighbors. We say a pull is *good* if the node performing the pull operation did not fail **and** it pulls from a node who is good at the end of iteration $i - 1$. A node remains good at the end of iteration i if there are at least two good pulls. Then, v uses the first two good pulls to execute the tournament procedure. Also, note that in the last iteration, we let a good node to have probability of δ to do the two tournament using the first two good pulls and probability $1 - \delta$ to set the value equal to the first good pull. We show that the good nodes always consists of a constant fraction of nodes.

Lemma 5.1. *For $0 \leq i \leq t - 1$, w.h.p. at the end of each iteration i of 2-TOURNAMENT, there are at least $n/2$ good nodes if every node pulls from $k = \Theta(\frac{1}{1-\mu} \cdot \log(\frac{1}{1-\mu}))$ other nodes.*

Proof. We will prove by induction. Initially, every node is good. Suppose that there are at least $n/2$ good nodes at the end of iteration $i - 1$. During iteration i, a node with more than $k - 2$ bad pulls will become bad at the end of iteration i.

Let $k = \frac{4}{1-\mu} \log \frac{4}{1-\mu} + 1$. The probability that there are at least $k - 1$ bad pulls is at most:

$$\begin{aligned}
\binom{k}{k-1} \cdot \left(1 - \frac{(1-\mu)}{2}\right)^{k-1} &\leq k \cdot e^{-\frac{(1-\mu)}{2} \cdot (k-1)} \\
&\leq \left(\frac{4}{1-\mu} \log \frac{4}{1-\mu} + 1\right) \cdot \left(\frac{1-\mu}{4}\right)^2 \\
&\leq 1/e + 1/16 \leq 0.44 \\
& \qquad x \log(1/x) \text{ maximized at } 1/e
\end{aligned}$$

Therefore, the expected number of bad nodes is at most $0.44n$ for iteration $1 \leq i \leq t - 1$. Since each node becomes bad independently of other nodes, by Chernoff Bound, w.h.p. there are at most $0.5n$ bad nodes at the end of iteration i. □

At the end of iteration $t - 1$, there are at least $n/2$ good nodes w.h.p. The expected number of bad nodes at the end of iteration t is at most $\sum_{v \in V} \delta \cdot 0.44 + (1 - \delta)/2 \leq 0.5n$. By Chernoff Bound again, we can conclude that w.h.p. there are at least $n/3$ good nodes.

We can also modify the process in the same way for the 3-TOURNAMENT algorithm. That is, in each iteration each node pulls from $\Theta(\frac{1}{1-\mu} \log \frac{1}{1-\mu})$ other nodes. If there are less than 3 good pulls, then the node becomes bad. Otherwise, it uses the first 3 good pulls to do the tournament procedure. We can show similarly that there are at most a constant fraction bad nodes in each iteration.

Consider a node v in the modified processes. Suppose that v is good in iteration i, then v must have at least two (or three) good pulls. Note that the probability that v pulls from a particular good node, conditioned v is good at the end of iteration, is uniform among all nodes that are good at the end of iteration $i - 1$.

Let V_i denote the set of good nodes and $n_i = |V_i|$. Given any subset of good nodes $S \subseteq V_{i-1}$, the probability of choosing a node in $|S|$ is therefore $|S|/n_i$. Therefore, we can replace $\frac{|L_i|}{n}$, $\frac{|H_i|}{n}$, and $\frac{|M_i|}{n}$ in our proofs in the previous section with $\frac{|L_i|}{n_i}$, $\frac{|H_i|}{n_i}$, and $\frac{|M_i|}{n_i}$ and observe that all the statements hold. Note that $n_i \geq n/3 = \Omega(n)$ for $0 \leq i \leq t$ w.h.p. Thus, all the concentration inequalities also hold.

In the last step of Algorithm 2, all nodes pulls from $\Theta(\frac{K}{1-\mu} \log \frac{K}{1-\mu})$ nodes. If there are K good pulls, then each node outputs the median directly. Otherwise, it becomes bad and outputs nothing. We can similarly show that there are at least constant fraction of good nodes. Therefore, at least a constant fraction of nodes output a correct answer and all the others output nothing. Note that we can use additional $O(t)$ rounds of pulling from valueless nodes to have all but $\frac{n}{2^t}$ nodes learn a correct answer.

5.2 Exact Quantile Computation

Consider Algorithm 3. We know Step 3 (Section 5.1), Step 4 [9], and Step 5 [24] tolerate such failures with a constant factor delay on the running time.

The only step that remains to discuss is Step 7. We run the same algorithm described. Initially each valued node v generates a token (x_v, m_i). In the first $O(\log n)$ phases, each node tries to split every token whose weight is larger than 1 into two tokens with halved weight, and push one of them to a random node. If the push succeed, the token has been pushed is considered a *new token* and the one with halved weight remaining at the same node is considered as the *old one*. If the push fails, then we will merge them back to the original one.

We will show that at the end of $O(\log n)$ phase, each node holds at most $O(1)$ tokens and their weights are 1. In each subsequent phases, if a node has more than one tokens, then it will push every token except one to a random neighbor. We argue that after $O(\log n)$ phases, every node contains exactly one token.

First, we show that the number of tokens at each node is bounded by a constant w.h.p. so that each phase can be implemented in $O(1)$ rounds. Recall that $N(v, i)$ is the number of tokens at v at the end of i'th phase. Suppose the total number of phases is $C \log n$ for some constant $C > 0$. For a token (except the one that is initially at v) to be at node i, it must be the case that it was pushed to i during one of the phase. Note that at any phase, there are at most $n^{0.99}$ tokens. By taking an union bound over all possible set of tokens of size $200K$ and all possible combinations of phases on when each of the token was pushed to i, we have

$$\Pr(N(v,i) \geq 200K + 1) \leq \binom{n^{0.99}}{200K} \cdot (C \log n)^{200K} \cdot \frac{1}{n^{200K}}$$
$$\leq \left(\frac{Cn^{0.99} \log n}{n}\right)^{200K} \leq 1/n^K.$$

Next, we show that for a token (x_v, m_i), it takes $O(\log n)$ rounds to split into tokens of weight 1 w.h.p. Let $T_v(i)$ denote the set of all v's tokens with weight at least 2 at the end of Phase i. Let $\Phi(i) = \sum_{(x_v,w) \in T_v(i)} w^2$ be a potential function. Consider a token $(x_v, w) \in T_v(i)$, since with probability at most μ it fails to split, the expected contribution of the token to the $\Phi(i + 1)$ is at most:

$$\mu w^2 + (1-\mu) 2 \cdot (w/2)^2 = \left(1 - \frac{1-\mu}{2}\right) \cdot w^2$$

Therefore, $\mathbb{E}[\Phi(i + 1) \mid \Phi(i)] \leq (1 - (1 - \mu)/2) \cdot \Phi(i)$. Since $\Phi(0) \leq n$, after $t = \frac{2K}{1-\mu} \log n$ rounds, we have

$$\mathbb{E}[\Phi(t)] \leq \left(1 - \frac{1-\mu}{2}\right)^{\frac{2K}{1-\mu} \log n} \cdot n \leq e^{-K \log n} \cdot n \leq 1/n^{K-1}$$

Since $\Phi(t)$ must be an integer, we conclude that with probability at least $1 - 1/n^{K-1}$, $\Phi(t) = 0$ by Markov's inequality. Therefore, after t rounds w.h.p. every token of value v has weight 1. We can further take an union over all tokens to show that it holds for all tokens w.h.p.

Therefore, w.h.p. the weight of all tokens are 1 at the end of $O(\log n)$ round. In the subsequent phases, the probability a token fail to be pushed to a node without any other tokens is at most $\mu + n^{0.99}/n = O(1)$. Therefore, the probability a token fails in the all of the next $O(\log n)$ phases is at most $1/\text{poly}(n)$. Thus, w.h.p. after $O(\log n)$ phases, every node has at most one token. Since each phase can be implemented using $O(1)$ rounds, we conclude that Step 7 can be done in $O(\log n)$ rounds in our failure model.

ACKNOWLEDGEMENT

We thank Lewis Tseng and the anonymous reviewers for helpful suggestions and comments. We also thank Frederik Mallmann-Trenn for pointing out [7] to us.

REFERENCES

[1] Pankaj K. Agarwal, Graham Cormode, Zengfeng Huang, Jeff M. Phillips, Zhewei Wei, and Ke Yi. 2013. Mergeable Summaries. *ACM Trans. Database Syst.* 38, 4, Article 26 (2013), 28 pages.

[2] Khaled Alsabti, Sanjay Ranka, and Vineet Singh. 1997. A One-Pass Algorithm for Accurately Estimating Quantiles for Disk-Resident Data. In *Proc. 23rd Int'l Conference on Very Large Data Bases (VLDB).* 346–355.

[3] Manuel Blum, Robert W. Floyd, Vaughan Pratt, Ronald L. Rivest, and Robert E. Tarjan. 1973. Time Bounds for Selection. *J. Comput. Syst. Sci.* 7, 4 (1973), 448–461.

[4] Jen-Yeu Chen and Gopal Pandurangan. 2012. Almost-Optimal Gossip-Based Aggregate Computation. *SIAM J. Comput.* 41, 3 (2012), 455–483.

[5] Francis Chin and H. F. Ting. 1987. An improved algorithm for finding the median distributively. *Algorithmica* 2, 1 (1987), 235–249.

[6] Alan Demers, Dan Greene, Carl Hauser, Wes Irish, John Larson, Scott Shenker, Howard Sturgis, Dan Swinehart, and Doug Terry. 1987. Epidemic Algorithms for Replicated Database Maintenance. In *Proc. 6th ACM Symposium on Principles of Distributed Computing (PODC).* 1–12.

[7] Benjamin Doerr, Leslie Ann Goldberg, Lorenz Minder, Thomas Sauerwald, and Christian Scheideler. 2011. Stabilizing Consensus with the Power of Two Choices. In *Proc. 23rd Annual ACM Symposium on Parallelism in Algorithms and Architectures (SPAA).* 149–158.

[8] Devdatt Dubhashi and Desh Ranjan. 1998. Balls and bins: A study in negative dependence. *Random Structures & Algorithms* 13, 2 (1998), 99–124.

[9] R. Elsässer and T. Sauerwald. 2009. On the Runtime and Robustness of Randomized Broadcasting. *Theor. Comput. Sci.* 410, 36 (2009), 3414–3427.

[10] Ofer Feinerman, Bernhard Haeupler, and Amos Korman. 2017. Breathe before speaking: efficient information dissemination despite noisy, limited and anonymous communication. *Distributed Computing* 30, 5 (2017), 339–355.

[11] David Felber and Rafail Ostrovsky. 2015. A Randomized Online Quantile Summary in $O((1/\epsilon)\log(1/\epsilon))$ Words. In *Approximation, Randomization, and Combinatorial Optimization. Algorithms and Techniques, APPROX/RANDOM.* 775–785.

[12] Robert W. Floyd and Ronald L. Rivest. 1975. Expected Time Bounds for Selection. *Commun. ACM* 18, 3 (1975), 165–172.

[13] Greg N. Frederickson. 1983. Tradeoffs for Selection in Distributed Networks (Preliminary Version). In *Proc. 2nd ACM Symposium on Principles of Distributed Computing (PODC).* 154–160.

[14] A.M. Frieze and G.R. Grimmett. 1985. The shortest-path problem for graphs with random arc-lengths. *Discrete Applied Mathematics* 10, 1 (1985), 57 – 77.

[15] Michael Greenwald and Sanjeev Khanna. 2001. Space-efficient Online Computation of Quantile Summaries. *SIGMOD Rec.* 30, 2 (2001), 58–66.

[16] Michael B. Greenwald and Sanjeev Khanna. 2004. Power-conserving Computation of Order-statistics over Sensor Networks. In *Proc. of the 23rd ACM Symposium on Principles of Database Systems (PODS).* 275–285.

[17] Sudipto Guha and Andrew McGregor. 2009. Stream Order and Order Statistics: Quantile Estimation in Random-Order Streams. *SIAM J. Comput.* 38, 5 (2009), 2044–2059.

[18] Bernhard Haeupler. 2016. Analyzing Network Coding (Gossip) Made Easy. *J. ACM* (2016), 26:1–26:22. https://doi.org/10.1145/2629696

[19] C. A. R. Hoare. 1961. Algorithm 63 (PARTITION) and Algorithm 65 (FIND). *Commun. ACM* 4, 7 (1961), 321–322.

[20] Regant Y. S. Hung and Hingfung F. Ting. 2010. An $\Omega((1/\epsilon)\log(1/\epsilon))$ Space Lower Bound for Finding ϵ-approximate Quantiles in a Data Stream. In *Proc. 4th International Conference on Frontiers in Algorithmics (FAW).* 89–100.

[21] Z. Karnin, K. Lang, and E. Liberty. 2016. Optimal Quantile Approximation in Streams. In *Proc. 57th IEEE Annual Symposium on Foundations of Computer Science*

(FOCS). 71–78.
[22] R. Karp, C. Schindelhauer, S. Shenker, and B. Vocking. 2000. Randomized rumor spreading. In *Proc. 41st IEEE Symposium on Foundations of Computer Science (FOCS)*. 565–574.
[23] Srinivas Kashyap, Supratim Deb, K. V. M. Naidu, Rajeev Rastogi, and Anand Srinivasan. 2006. Efficient Gossip-based Aggregate Computation. In *Proc. of the 25th ACM Symposium on Principles of Database Systems (PODS)*. 308–317.
[24] David Kempe, Alin Dobra, and Johannes Gehrke. 2003. Gossip-Based Computation of Aggregate Information. In *Proc. 44th IEEE Symposium on Foundations of Computer Science (FOCS 2003)*. 482–491.
[25] Fabian Kuhn, Thomas Locher, and Rogert Wattenhofer. 2007. Tight Bounds for Distributed Selection. In *Proc. of 19th Annual ACM Symposium on Parallel Algorithms and Architectures (SPAA)*. 145–153.
[26] Qiang Ma, S. Muthukrishnan, and Mark Sandler. 2013. Frugal Streaming for Estimating Quantiles. In *Space-Efficient Data Structures, Streams, and Algorithms: Papers in Honor of J. Ian Munro on the Occasion of His 66th Birthday*. 77–96.
[27] Samuel Madden, Michael J. Franklin, Joseph M. Hellerstein, and Wei Hong. 2002. TAG: A Tiny AGgregation Service for Ad-hoc Sensor Networks. *SIGOPS Oper. Syst. Rev.* 36, SI (Dec. 2002), 131–146.
[28] Gurmeet Singh Manku, Sridhar Rajagopalan, and Bruce G. Lindsay. 1999. Random Sampling Techniques for Space Efficient Online Computation of Order Statistics of Large Datasets. *SIGMOD Rec.* 28, 2 (1999), 251–262.
[29] J.I. Munro and M.S. Paterson. 1980. Selection and sorting with limited storage. *Theoretical Computer Science* 12, 3 (1980), 315 – 323.
[30] A. Negro, N. Santoro, and J. Urrutia. 1997. Efficient distributed selection with bounded messages. *IEEE Transactions on Parallel and Distributed Systems* 8, 4 (1997), 397–401.
[31] Boaz Patt-Shamir. 2007. A Note on Efficient Aggregate Queries in Sensor Networks. *Theor. Comput. Sci.* 370, 1-3 (Feb. 2007), 254–264.
[32] Boris Pittel. 1987. On Spreading a Rumor. *SIAM J. Appl. Math.* 47, 1 (1987), 213–223.
[33] Michael Rodeh. 1982. Finding the median distributively. *J. Comput. System Sci.* 24, 2 (1982), 162–166.
[34] Doron Rotem, Nicola Santoro, and Jeffrey B. Sidney. 1986. Shout echo selection in distributed files. *Networks* 16, 1 (1986), 77–86. https://doi.org/10.1002/net.3230160108
[35] Nicola Santoro, Michael Scheutzow, and Jeffrey B. Sidney. 1988. On the expected complexity of distributed selection. *J. Parallel and Distrib. Comput.* 5, 2 (1988), 194 – 203.
[36] Nicola Santoro, Jeffrey B. Sidney, and Stuart J. Sidney. 1992. A distributed selection algorithm and its expected communication complexity. *Theoretical Computer Science* 100, 1 (1992), 185 – 204. https://doi.org/10.1016/0304-3975(92)90368-P
[37] N. Santoro and E. Suen. 1989. Reduction techniques for selection in distributed files. *IEEE Trans. Comput.* 38, 6 (1989), 891–896.
[38] Liuba Shrira, Nissim Francez, and Michael Rodeh. 1983. Distributed K-selection: From a Sequential to a Distributed Algorithm. In *Proceedings of 2nd ACM Symposium on Principles of Distributed Computing (PODC)*. 143–153.
[39] Nisheeth Shrivastava, Chiranjeeb Buragohain, Divyakant Agrawal, and Subhash Suri. 2004. Medians and Beyond: New Aggregation Techniques for Sensor Networks. In *Proceedings of the 2nd International Conference on Embedded Networked Sensor Systems (SenSys '04)*. ACM, New York, NY, USA, 239–249. https://doi.org/10.1145/1031495.1031524
[40] Yong Yao and Johannes Gehrke. 2002. The Cougar Approach to In-network Query Processing in Sensor Networks. *SIGMOD Rec.* 31, 3 (2002), 9–18.

A TOOLS

Lemma A.1. (Chernoff Bound) *Let* $X_1, \dots, X_n$ *be indicator variables such that* $\Pr(X_i = 1) = p$. *Let* $X = \sum_{i=1}^{n} X_i$. *Then, for* $\delta > 0$:

$$\Pr(X \geq (1+\delta)\mathbb{E}[X]) < \left[\frac{e^{\delta}}{(1+\delta)^{(1+\delta)}}\right]^{\mathbb{E}[X]}$$

$$\Pr(X \leq (1-\delta)\mathbb{E}[X]) < \left[\frac{e^{\delta}}{(1-\delta)^{(1-\delta)}}\right]^{\mathbb{E}[X]}$$

The two bounds above imply that for $0 < \delta < 1$, *we have:*

$$\Pr(X \geq (1+\delta)\mathbb{E}[X]) < e^{-\delta^2 \mathbb{E}[X]/3}$$

$$\Pr(X \leq (1-\delta)\mathbb{E}[X]) < e^{-\delta^2 \mathbb{E}[X]/2}.$$

Lemma A.2. *Suppose that for any* $\delta > 0$,

$$\Pr(X > (1+\delta)np) \leq \left[\frac{e^{\delta}}{(1+\delta)^{(1+\delta)}}\right]^{np}$$

then for any $M \geq np$ *and* $0 < \delta < 1$,

$$\Pr(X > np + \delta M) \leq \left[\frac{e^{\delta}}{(1+\delta)^{(1+\delta)}}\right]^{M} \leq e^{-\delta^2 M/3}$$

Proof. Without loss of generality, assume $M = tnp$ for some $t \geq 1$, we have

$$\begin{aligned} &\Pr(X > np + \delta M) \\ &\leq \left[\frac{e^{t\delta}}{(1+t\delta)^{(1+t\delta)}}\right]^{np} \\ &= \left[\frac{e^{\delta}}{(1+t\delta)^{(1+t\delta)/t}}\right]^{M} \\ &\leq \left[\frac{e^{\delta}}{(1+\delta)^{(1+\delta)}}\right]^{M} \qquad (*) \\ &\leq e^{-\delta^2 M/3} \qquad \frac{e^{\delta}}{(1+\delta)^{(1+\delta)}} \leq e^{-\delta^2/3} \text{ for } 0 < \delta < 1 \end{aligned}$$

Inequality (*) follows if $(1+t\delta)^{(1+t\delta)/t} \geq (1+\delta)^{(1+\delta)}$, or equivalently, $((1+t\delta)/t)\ln(1+t\delta) \geq (1+\delta)\ln(1+\delta)$. Letting $f(t) = ((1+t\delta)/t)\ln(1+t\delta) - (1+\delta)\ln(1+\delta)$, we have $f'(t) = \frac{1}{t^2}(\delta t - \ln(1+\delta t)) \geq 0$ for $t > 0$. Since $f(1) = 0$ and $f'(t) \geq 0$ for $t > 0$, we must have $f(t) \geq 0$ for $t \geq 1$. □

On Local Distributed Sampling and Counting*

Weiming Feng
State Key Laboratory for Novel Software Technology
Nanjing University, China
fengwm@smail.nju.edu.cn

Yitong Yin
State Key Laboratory for Novel Software Technology
Nanjing University, China
yinyt@nju.edu.cn

ABSTRACT

In classic distributed graph problems, each instance on a graph specifies a space of feasible solutions (e.g. all proper $(\Delta + 1)$-list-colorings of the graph), and the task of distributed algorithm is to construct a feasible solution using local information.

We study distributed sampling and counting problems, in which each instance specifies a joint distribution of feasible solutions. The task of distributed algorithm is to sample from this joint distribution, or to locally measure the volume of the probability space via the marginal probabilities. The latter task is also known as inference, which is a local counterpart of counting.

For self-reducible classes of instances, the following equivalences are established in the LOCAL model up to polylogarithmic factors:

- For all joint distributions, approximate inference and approximate sampling are computationally equivalent.
- For all joint distributions defined by local constraints, exact sampling is reducible to either one of the above tasks.
- If further, sequentially constructing a feasible solution is trivial locally, then all above tasks are easy if and only if the joint distribution exhibits strong spatial mixing.

Combining with the state of the arts of strong spatial mixing, we obtain efficient sampling algorithms in the LOCAL model for various important sampling problems, including: an $O(\sqrt{\Delta}\log^3 n)$-round algorithm for exact sampling matchings in graphs with maximum degree Δ, and an $O(\log^3 n)$-round algorithm for sampling according to the hardcore model (weighted independent sets) in the uniqueness regime, which along with the $\Omega(\text{diam})$ lower bound in [3] for sampling according to the hardcore model in the non-uniqueness regime, gives the first computational phase transition for distributed sampling.

CCS CONCEPTS

• **Theory of computation → Design and analysis of algorithms**; **Distributed algorithms**; • **Mathematics of computing →** *Gibbs sampling*;

KEYWORDS

distributed graph algorithms; local computation; sampling algorithms; Gibbs distribution; strong spatial mixing

ACM Reference Format:
Weiming Feng and Yitong Yin. 2018. On Local Distributed Sampling and Counting. In *PODC '18: ACM Symposium on Principles of Distributed Computing, July 23–27, 2018, Egham, United Kingdom.* ACM, New York, NY, USA, 10 pages. https://doi.org/10.1145/3212734.3212757

1 INTRODUCTION

In local computation, classic distributed graph problems are formulated in such a way that each instance $\mathcal{I}$ on a graph $G = (V, E)$ specifies a set $\Omega_{\mathcal{I}}$ of feasible solutions $\boldsymbol{y} = (y_v)_{v \in V}$, and the goal of the distributed algorithm is to construct a feasible solution $\boldsymbol{y} \in \Omega_{\mathcal{I}}$ by outputting y_v at each node $v \in V$. As a paradigm, we consider the list-coloring problem, where each instance $\mathcal{I}$ gives a graph $G = (V, E)$ with each node $v \in V$ associated with a list L_v of available colors. Then the set $\Omega_{\mathcal{I}}$ contains all proper list-colorings $\boldsymbol{y}$ with $y_v \in L_v$ for every $v \in V$, satisfying $y_u \neq y_v$ for all edges $uv \in E$.

Alternatively, we can consider the set of feasible solutions $\Omega_{\mathcal{I}}$ as the sample space of a probability distribution and imagine that each instance $\mathcal{I}$ specifies a joint distribution $\mu_{\mathcal{I}}$ of feasible solutions $\boldsymbol{y} = (y_v)_{v \in V} \in \Omega_{\mathcal{I}}$. A distributed graph problem is then given by a class of joint distributions $\mu_{\mathcal{I}}$ indexed by instances $\mathcal{I}$. (In the paradigm of list-coloring problem, we may take each $\mu_{\mathcal{I}}$ as the uniform distribution over all proper list-colorings of instance $\mathcal{I}$.) To each class of joint distributions of this form, there correspond a number of naturally defined problems.

- Construction: Exhibit a feasible solution $\boldsymbol{y} = (y_v)_{v \in V}$ satisfying $\mu_{\mathcal{I}}(\boldsymbol{y}) > 0$, where each node $v \in V$ outputs y_v. This is the task for classic distributed graph problems. (e.g. Construct a proper list-coloring of instance $\mathcal{I}$.)
- Sampling: Generate a random solution $Y = (Y_v)_{v \in V}$ distributed according to $\mu_{\mathcal{I}}$, where each node $v \in V$ outputs Y_v. (e.g. Generate uniformly a proper list-coloring of instance $\mathcal{I}$ at random.)
- Inference (Counting): Each node calculates the marginal probabilities of the random variable Y_v being specific values, where the random vector $Y = (Y_v)_{v \in V}$ is drawn from $\mu_{\mathcal{I}}$. (e.g. Each node $v \in V$ calculates the probabilities of v being assigned specific colors in a uniform random proper list-coloring of instance $\mathcal{I}$.)

We choose the inference problem as a local version of counting, as the marginal probabilities are typical local knowledges regarding the volume of probability space. A more standard global definition of counting is to estimate the number of feasible solutions $|\Omega_{\mathcal{I}}|$ (or the total weights if the joint distribution $\mu_{\mathcal{I}}$ is non-uniform), which

*This research is supported by the National Key R&D Program of China 2018YFB1003202 and the National Science Foundation of China under Grant Nos. 61722207 and 61672275.

PODC '18, July 23–27, 2018, Egham, United Kingdom

ACM ISBN 978-1-4503-5795-1/18/07...$15.00
https://doi.org/10.1145/3212734.3212757

is unsuitable to study for local computation because it computes a global information. However, it is well known that for self-reducible problems, such global information can be decomposed via the chain rule into the marginal probabilities computed by inference problems [10]. Furthermore, the inference problem itself is especially well-motivated by distributed machine learning [16].

Previous studies in local computation were focused on the complexity of constructing a feasible solution. The studies of sampling problems in local computation were started very recently [2–4]. Several fundamental questions regarding the local complexities of sampling and counting need to be answered.

Question 1: *What is the relation between sampling and counting in local computation?*

It is well known that for self-reducible problems, approximate counting and approximate sampling are inter-reducible on polynomial-time Turing machines [11]. A natural question is whether this is true for local computation. To see the nontriviality of the question, recall that the generic reduction from sampling to counting has to be sequential because the procedure is fully-adaptive: Each individual variable is sampled according to the marginal distribution conditioning on the outcomes of previous samplings. To understand the relation between counting and sampling in local computation, one has to answer the following question first: "How much non-adaptively can we sample a random vector $Y = (Y_i)$ by accessing to marginal distributions of individual variables Y_i?" which by itself is a fundamental question with a broader background.

Question 2: *What are the roles of approximation in sampling and counting in local computation?*

Due to the pioneering works of Valiant [21] and Stockmeyer [20], on Turing machines exact counting can be much harder then approximate counting. Similar phenomena occur for local computation: Due to a straightforward information-theoretical argument, exact inference is impossible to compute locally unless for joint distributions with zero long-range correlation.

For sampling, a celebrated result of Jerrum, Valiant, and Vazirani [11] shows that on polynomial-time Turing machines, for self-reducible problems, approximate sampling can be boosted into exact sampling via a rejection sampling procedure (the JVV sampler), such that the algorithm succeeds with high probability (with certifiable failures) and conditioning on success the output is distributed precisely according to the joint distribution $\mu_{\mathcal{I}}$ specified by the instance $\mathcal{I}$. Our question is whether there is a distributed variant of the JVV sampler. Answering this question also involves investigating a fundamental problem: "Can rejection sampling be made local?" Considering that the rejection sampling as a basic Monte Carlo method has been studied for more than half a century, this is certainly worth studying in local computation.

Question 3: *What makes a sampling or counting problem solvable by local computations?*

Finally, we want to characterize the easiness of sampling and counting in local computation by the properties of joint distributions. For sampling and counting on polynomial-time Turing machines, a phase transition of computational complexity is witnessed at the threshold for the decay of correlation (strong spatial mixing) [18, 22]. We wonder whether similar computational phase transitions exist for local computation.

1.1 Our results

We study the local complexities of self-reducible sampling and counting problems, and provide answers to above fundamental questions.

We formulate distributed sampling and inference (counting) problems by classes of joint distributions of solutions. Besides general joint distributions, we focus on the joint distributions with following properties naturally arising from local computation:

- (⋆) Joint distributions defined by local constraints. These are the counterparts of locally checkable labelings (LCL) in the world of sampling and counting. In our paper, these joint distributions are called local Gibbs distributions (Definition 2.3).
- (⋆⋆) Joint distributions for which constructing a feasible solution is trivial for a sequential local oblivious procedure. For example, this includes distributions over $(\Delta + 1)$-list-colorings, but not the distributions over Δ-list-colorings. The property is related to the ergodicity of the local dynamics on feasible solutions. In our paper, joint distributions of this property are called locally admissible (Definition 2.5).

Main results: For self-reducible classes of instances, we show the followings hold for sampling and inference (counting) in the LOCAL model:

- Approximate inference and approximate sampling are inter-reducible, in a sense that if one of the tasks is tractable in the LOCAL model so is the other one (Theorem 3.2 and Theorem 3.3), where an approximate problem is tractable in the LOCAL model if the problem is solvable for any n and $\delta > 0$, where n is the number of nodes and δ is the approximation error, within time complexity poly$(\log n, \log \frac{1}{\delta})$.
- If property (⋆) is satisfied, then approximate inference, approximate sampling, and exact sampling are all inter-reducible. With the above results, this is proved by a distributed JVV sampler that successfully terminates within polylog(n) rounds with high probability, and conditioning on success, returns a solution distributed precisely as the desired distribution (Theorem 4.2).
- If further, property (⋆⋆) is satisfied, then all above tasks are easy if and only if the joint distribution exhibits certain degrees of strong spatial mixing (Theorem 5.2 and Corollary 5.4), a decay of correlation property which is critically related to the computational complexity of approximate counting [18, 22].

Minor results: As by-products of above results, we obtain two boosting lemmas:

- If property (⋆) is satisfied, then approximate inference with bounded additive (total variation) error can be boosted to with bounded multiplicative error (Lemma 4.1).
- If further, property (⋆⋆) is satisfied, then strong spatial mixing in total variation distance implies strong spatial mixing with decay in multiplicative error (Corollary 5.3).
  This explains why so far the known strong spatial mixing results for several major problems (e.g. independent sets,

matchings, and graph colorings) were all proved in this stronger form with decay in multiplicative error [1, 5, 6, 22].

Interestingly, the second boosting result states a proposition in probability theory, which seems unrelated to distributed algorithms, but is proved by us via local computation.

Applications in the LOCAL model: The main results in above together with the state of the arts of strong spatial mixing [1, 6, 12, 19, 22], imply the following exact sampling algorithms for various important sampling problems and statistical physics models:

- An $O(\sqrt{\Delta}\log^3 n)$-round algorithm for exact sampling matchings in graphs with maximum degree Δ.
- An $O(\log^3 n)$-round exact sampling according to the hardcore model (weighted independent sets) in the uniqueness regime, which along with the $\Omega(\text{diam})$ lower bound in a previous work [3] for sampling according to the hardcore model in the non-uniqueness regime, gives the first *computational phase transition* for distributed sampling and counting.
- $O(\log^3 n)$-round exact sampling algorithms for sampling according to various anti-ferromagnetic models, including: anti-ferromagnetic 2-spin model in the uniqueness regime, weighted hypergraph matchings in the uniqueness regime, proper q-colorings of triangle-free graphs when $q \ge \alpha\Delta$ where $\alpha > \alpha^*$ and $\alpha^* \approx 1.763$ is the positive root of the euqation $x = e^{1/x}$.

2 MODELS AND DEFINITIONS

The LOCAL Model: In the LOCAL model [14, 17], the network is a simple, undirected graph $G = (V, E)$. Initially, each node $v \in V$ receives a local input and an arbitrary long random bit string sampled independently at v. For a LOCAL algorithm with time complexity t, each node $v \in V$ gathers all information within radius t from v, including the topology of the graph, the inputs and random bits of the nodes within that radius, and performs an arbitrary local computation with the information to compute an output.

Joint Distributions: Let V be a set of size $n = |V|$ and Σ an *alphabet* of size $q = |\Sigma| \le \text{poly}(n)$. Let $\Omega = \Sigma^V$ be the *sample space.* Each $\sigma \in \Sigma^V$ is called a *configuration.* For $S \subseteq V$, we use σ_S or $\sigma(S)$ to denote the restriction of σ on subset S.

Let μ be a distribution over Σ^V, called a *joint distribution*, because each $Y \sim \mu$ is a random vector $Y = (Y_v)_{v\in V}$ consisting of n jointly distributed random variables. For $R \subseteq V$, let μ_R denote the *marginal distribution* over Σ^R induced by μ on subset R. In particular, when $R = \{v\}$ for some $v \in V$, we write $\mu_v = \mu_{\{v\}}$. A configuration $\sigma \in \Sigma^V$ is *feasible* with respect to μ if $\mu(\sigma) > 0$. A configuration $\tau \in \Sigma^\Lambda$ on a subset $\Lambda \subseteq V$ is feasible with respect to μ if there is a $\sigma \in \Sigma^V$ such that $\mu(\sigma) > 0$ and $\sigma_\Lambda = \tau$. Given a feasible configuration $\tau \in \Sigma^\Lambda$ on a subset $\Lambda \subseteq V$, we use μ^τ to denote the distribution over Σ^V induced by μ conditioning on τ. The conditional marginal distributions μ_R^τ and μ_v^τ are accordingly defined.

Suppose that μ and ν are two distributions over the same sample space Ω. The *total variation distance* between μ and ν, denoted by $d_{\text{TV}}(\mu, \nu)$, is defined as: $d_{\text{TV}}(\mu, \nu) \triangleq \frac{1}{2}\|\mu - \nu\|_1 = \max_{A\subseteq\Omega} |\mu(A) - \nu(A)|$.

Distributed Graph Problems: We reformulate the notion of *distributed graph problems* in [8] by classes of joint distributions.

Definition 2.1 (distributed graph problems). A distributed graph problem is given by a class of joint distributions $\mathfrak{M} = \{\mu_{(G,\boldsymbol{x})}\}$, indexed by labeled graphs $(G, \boldsymbol{x})$, where $G = (V, E)$ is a simple, undirected graph and $\boldsymbol{x} = (x_v)_{v\in V}$ is a $|V|$-dimensional vector. Each $\mu_{(G,\boldsymbol{x})}$ is a joint distribution over Σ^V, where $\Sigma = \Sigma_{(G,\boldsymbol{x})}$ is an alphabet of size $q = |\Sigma| \le \text{poly}(|V|)$.

The class of distributions $\mathfrak{M}$ is *translation-invariant,* which means that if the labeled graphs $(G, \boldsymbol{x})$ and $(\tilde{G}, \tilde{\boldsymbol{x}})$ are isomorphic under bijection ϕ on vertices, then $\mu_{(G,\boldsymbol{x})} \in \mathfrak{M}$ is well-defined if and only if $\mu_{(\tilde{G},\tilde{\boldsymbol{x}})}$ is, and the distributions $\mu_{(G,\boldsymbol{x})}$ and $\mu_{(\tilde{G},\tilde{\boldsymbol{x}})}$ are identical under bijection ϕ.

Initially, each node $v \in V$ knows x_v. For classic distributed graph problems, the nodes need to construct a feasible $\boldsymbol{y}$ that $\mu_{(G,\boldsymbol{x})}(\boldsymbol{y}) > 0$, where each node $v \in V$ outputs y_v.

Remark 2.1. *In [8], a distributed graph problem is defined by a relation $\mathcal{T}$ that contains all satisfying tuples $(G, \boldsymbol{x}, \boldsymbol{y})$ instead of as a class of distributions $\mathfrak{M} = \{\mu_{(G,\boldsymbol{x})}\}$ over $\boldsymbol{y}$. The two definitions are equivalent: Given a relation $\mathcal{T}$, for any $(G, \boldsymbol{x})$, $\mu_{(G,\boldsymbol{x})}$ is just a positive distribution over all feasible solutions $\boldsymbol{y}$ satisfying $(G, \boldsymbol{x}, \boldsymbol{y}) \in \mathcal{T}$ (e.g. the uniform distribution over feasible solutions); and conversely, given $\mathfrak{M} = \{\mu_{(G,\boldsymbol{x})}\}$, the relation $\mathcal{T}$ can be constructed as $\mathcal{T} = \{(G, \boldsymbol{x}, \boldsymbol{y}) \mid \mu_{(G,\boldsymbol{x})}(\boldsymbol{y}) > 0\}$.*

Distributed Sampling and Counting: A distributed sampling or counting problem is also given by a class of joint distributions $\mathfrak{M} = \{\mu_{(G,\boldsymbol{x})}\}$ as defined in Definition 2.1.

Definition 2.2 (instances for distributed sampling/counting). Let $\mathfrak{M} = \{\mu_{(G,\boldsymbol{x})}\}$ be a class of joint distributions as defined in Definition 2.1. An instance for distributed sampling/counting is a tuple $(G, \boldsymbol{x}, \tau)$, where $(G, \boldsymbol{x})$ specifies a joint distribution $\mu = \mu_{(G,\boldsymbol{x})}$ over Σ^V, and $\tau \in \Sigma^\Lambda$ is an arbitrary configuration on a subset $\Lambda \subseteq V$ that is feasible with respect to μ. We call the distribution μ^τ the *target distribution.*

Given an instance $(G, \boldsymbol{x}, \tau)$ where τ is specified on the subset $\Lambda \subseteq V$, initially each node $v \in V$ knows x_v, and also τ_v if $v \in \Lambda$. We assume that x_v includes a unique ID for v, a global polynomial upper bound of $n = |V|$, and a global upper bound on errors if approximation is involved.

Remark 2.2. *The reason to include an arbitrary partially specified configuration τ into the problem instance, is to explicitly enforce the* self-reducibility, *a property that is essential to problems such as sampling and counting [11].*[1] *For example, consider μ as the uniform distribution over all proper $(\Delta + 1)$-colorings of G. For any proper $(\Delta + 1)$-coloring τ of vertices in a subset $\Lambda \subseteq V$, μ^τ is the uniform distribution over all proper $(\Delta + 1)$-colorings of G consistent with τ. This equivalently specifies a uniform distribution over list-colorings*

[1] Alternatively, one may enforce the self-reducibility implicitly by assuming it as a property of the class of joint distributions $\mathfrak{M} = \{\mu_{(G,\boldsymbol{x})}\}$: For every $\mu_{(G,\boldsymbol{x})} \in \mathfrak{M}$ where $G = (V, E)$, for any feasible configuration $\tau \in \Sigma^\Lambda$ on a subset $\Lambda \subseteq V$, there exists a $\mu_{(G',\boldsymbol{x}')} \in \mathfrak{M}$ such that $G' = (V, E')$ is a subgraph of G with identical vertex set and $\mu^\tau_{(G,\boldsymbol{x})} = \mu_{(G',\boldsymbol{x}')}$, where the new instance $(G', \boldsymbol{x}')$ can be constructed locally from $(G, \boldsymbol{x})$, providing τ_v to each node $v \in \Lambda$. This alternative formulation of self-reducibility is equivalent to the one we used above.

of the subgraph $G[V \setminus \Lambda]$ induced by subset $V \setminus \Lambda$, where each node $v \in V$ holds a list of available colors $L_v = [q] \setminus \{\tau_u \mid uv \in E\}$.

We assume that the time complexity of a distributed algorithm is fixed. Upon termination the algorithm either successfully returns or fails. We assume that the algorithm succeeds with high probability, and all failures are *locally certifiable.* Upon termination, each node $v \in V$ besides the regular output explicitly outputs a random bit F_v indicating whether the algorithm fails locally at v, and it is guaranteed that $\sum_{v \in V} \mathbb{E}[F_v] = O(\frac{1}{n})$. This is a well accepted notion of the Las Vegas algorithms for local computation [7].

The goal of *distributed sampling* is to draw a random sample according to the target distribution μ^τ given by the instance $(G, \boldsymbol{x}, \tau)$.

Exact sampling: Given any instance $(G, \boldsymbol{x}, \tau)$, the nodes need to sample a random $Y = (Y_v)_{v \in V}$ upon successful termination, where each node $v \in V$ outputs Y_v or fails, such that conditioning on that no one fails the distribution of Y is precisely μ^τ.

Approximate sampling: Given any instance $(G, \boldsymbol{x}, \tau)$, for any $\delta > 0$, the nodes need to output a random $Y = (Y_v)_{v \in V}$ upon successful termination, such that conditioning on success the distribution $\hat{\mu}$ of Y satisfies $d_{\mathrm{TV}}(\hat{\mu}, \mu^\tau) \le \delta$.

We use the *distributed inference* to represent counting in distributed settings. Here, the goal is to estimate the marginal distribution μ_v^τ for each node $v \in V$, where μ_v^τ is the target distribution given by the instance $(G, \boldsymbol{x}, \tau)$. Due to an information-theoretical argument, exact inference with local information is impossible for joint distributions with nonzero long-range correlations. Hence we focus on approximate inference.

Approximate inference: Given any instance $(G, \boldsymbol{x}, \tau)$, for any $\delta > 0$, each node $v \in V$ needs to output a marginal distribution $\hat{\mu}_v$ over Σ, which is a vector $\hat{\mu}_v \in [0,1]^\Sigma$ and $\|\hat{\mu}\|_1 = 1$, satisfying that $d_{\mathrm{TV}}(\hat{\mu}_v, \mu_v^\tau) \le \delta$.

A more accurate approximate inference with bounded multiplicative error is discussed in Section 4.1.

Joint Distributions Defined by Local Constraints: We use the Gibbs distributions defined by the *weighted constraint satisfaction problems (CSPs)*, also known as the *factor graphs* [13], to model joint distributions characterized by local constraints.

Definition 2.3 (local Gibbs distributions). A *Gibbs distribution* μ is specified by a tuple $(G, \Sigma, \mathcal{F})$, where $G = (V, E)$ is an undirected graph, Σ is an alphabet of size $q = |\Sigma|$ bounded in polynomial of $n = |V|$, and $\mathcal{F}$ is a collection of *constraints* (also called *factors*). A constraint $(f, S) \in \mathcal{F}$ consists of a nonnegative-valued function $f : \Sigma^S \to \mathbb{R}_{\ge 0}$ defined on the *scope* $S \subseteq V$.

For each configuration $\sigma \in \Sigma^V$, $w(\sigma) = \prod_{(f,S) \in \mathcal{F}} f(\sigma_S)$ is the weight assigned to σ. The Gibbs distribution μ over all configurations in Σ^V is defined proportional to the weights $\mu(\sigma) = \frac{w(\sigma)}{Z}$, where the normalizing factor $Z = \sum_{\sigma \in \Sigma^V} w(\sigma)$ is known as the *partition function*, which can be seen as a function of the specification $(G, \Sigma, \mathcal{F})$ of the distribution μ.

A Gibbs distribution specified by $(G, \Sigma, \mathcal{F})$ is *local* if for any constraint $(f, S) \in \mathcal{F}$, the diameter of the scope S in graph G is bounded as $\max_{u,v \in S} \mathrm{dist}_G(u, v) = O(1)$.

The local Gibbs distributions are the counterparts of the LCL problems [14] in the world of distributed sampling/counting. Just as that the LCL problems are the distributed graph problems that are defined by local constraints, the local Gibbs distributions are the joint distributions that are defined by local factors.

An important property of Gibbs distribution is the *spatial Markovian* property, also known as conditional independence, which is stated formally by the following proposition.

PROPOSITION 2.4 (CONDITIONAL INDEPENDENCE). *Let μ be a Gibbs distribution specified by $(G, \Sigma, \mathcal{F})$, where $G = (V, E)$. Let $H = (V, F)$ denote the hypergraph with vertices V and hyperedges $F = \{S \mid (f, S) \in \mathcal{F}\}$. Suppose that $A, B, C \subset V$ are disjoint nonempty subsets and C is a vertex separator whose removal disconnects A and B in H. For a random vector $Y \in \Sigma^V$ distributed according to μ, Y_A and Y_B are conditionally independent given that Y_C is arbitrarily and feasibly fixed. Formally, for any $\sigma_C \in \Sigma^C$ that is feasible with respect to μ, any $\sigma_A \in \Sigma^A$ and $\sigma_B \in \Sigma^B$, it holds that*

$$\begin{aligned}&\Pr_{Y \sim \mu}[Y_A = \sigma_A \wedge Y_B = \sigma_B \mid Y_C = \sigma_C]\\ &= \Pr_{Y \sim \mu}[Y_A = \sigma_A \mid Y_C = \sigma_C] \Pr_{Y \sim \mu}[Y_B = \sigma_B \mid Y_C = \sigma_C].\end{aligned}$$

We also consider a restrictive class of Gibbs distributions, with the following property.

Definition 2.5 (locally admissible). Let μ be a Gibbs distribution specified by $(G, \Sigma, \mathcal{F})$ where $G = (V, E)$. Let $\Lambda \subseteq V$ be a subset. A configuration $\sigma \in \Sigma^\Lambda$ on a subset $\Lambda \subseteq V$ is *locally feasible* if σ itself does not violate any constraint onsite, i.e. $\prod_{(f,S) \in \mathcal{F}, S \subseteq \Lambda} f(\sigma_S) > 0$.

A Gibbs distribution μ is said to be *locally admissible* if $\forall \Lambda \subseteq V$, $\forall \sigma \in \Sigma^\Lambda$, σ is feasible $\iff$ σ is locally feasible.

REMARK 2.3. *The locally admissible, local Gibbs distributions represent the LCL problems that can be solved by sequential local oblivious algorithms. For any class of locally admissible, local Gibbs distributions $\mathfrak{M} = \{\mu_{(G,\boldsymbol{x})}\}$, the problem of constructing a $\boldsymbol{y}$ that is feasible with respect to $\mu_{(G,\boldsymbol{x})}$, can always be solved by a sequential local oblivious algorithm on any vertex ordering, i.e. the problem is in* SLOCAL($O(1)$).

3 FROM SEQUENTIAL TO PARALLEL FOR DISTRIBUTED SAMPLING

In this section, we establishes the computational equivalence (up to polylogarithmic factor) between approximate inference and approximate sampling in the LOCAL model. The results in this section holds for general classes of joint distributions $\mathfrak{M} = \{\mu_{(G,\boldsymbol{x})}\}$.

A key step is to first resolve the problems sequentially with bounded locality. The sequential local mode (SLOCAL) is introduced in a recent breakthrough [8]. An important property of the SLOCAL model is that any SLOCAL algorithm with locality r can be transformed into a LOCAL algorithm with time complexity $O(r)$ multiplying the cost for network decomposition [15]. We restate this in the following lemma in a slightly more refined way, in order to cover more general problems such as distributed sampling.

LEMMA 3.1 (GHAFFARI, KUHN, MAUS [8]). *Let $\mathcal{A}$ be a k-pass SLOCAL algorithm. Given any instance I on graph $G = (V, E)$ with $n = |V|$, any ordering π of nodes in V, $\mathcal{A}$ scans all nodes in the same ordering π by k passes with locality $r_i(n)$ in the i-th pass. $\mathcal{A}$ returns a random vector $Y = (Y_v)_{v \in V}$, where each node $v \in V$ outputs Y_v, such that Y follows the distribution $\hat{\mu}_{I,\pi}$.*

Then there is a LOCAL *algorithm* $\mathcal{B}$ *which given any instance* I *on graph* $G = (V, E)$ *with* $n = |V|$, *outputs within time complexity* $O(kr(n)\log^2 n)$ *a pair* (Y_v, F_v) *at each node* $v \in V$, *where* $r(n) = \max_{1 \le i \le k} r_i(n)$ *and* F_v *is a Boolean random variable indicating whether the algorithm fails locally at* v, *satisfying that* $\sum_{v \in V} \mathbb{E}[F_v] < \frac{1}{n^2}$ *and conditioning on that* $F_v = 0$ *for all nodes* $v \in V$, *the distribution of* $Y = (Y_v)_{v \in V}$ *is precisely* $\hat{\mu}_{I,\pi}$ *for some ordering* π *of nodes in* V.

Lemma 3.1 is proved in a similar way as Theorem 1.6 in [8]. Algorithm $\mathcal{B}$ first computes an $(O(\log n), O(\log n))$-network decomposition on power graph $G^{r(n)+1}$. Then $\mathcal{B}$ simulates $\mathcal{A}$ with k epochs, each having $O(r(n)\log^2 n)$ rounds. In the i-th epoch, $\mathcal{B}$ simulates the i-th pass of $\mathcal{A}$ according to the unique ordering of nodes provided by network decomposition.

With this lemma, the standard sequential sampler by progressively sampling according to the marginal distributions, can be transformed to a LOCAL algorithm for approximate sampling.

Theorem 3.2. *For any class of joint distributions* $\mathfrak{M} = \{\mu_{(G,\boldsymbol{x})}\}$, *if there is a* LOCAL *algorithm for approximate inference (within arbitrary total variation error* $\delta > 0$*) with time complexity at most* $t(n, \delta)$, *then there is a* LOCAL *algorithm for approximate sampling (within arbitrary total variation error* $\delta > 0$*) with time complexity* $O\left(t\left(n, \frac{\delta}{n}\right)\log^2 n\right)$.

On the other hand, the reduction from approximate inference to approximate sampling in the LOCAL model can be done by averaging over all local random choices.

Theorem 3.3. *For any class of joint distributions* $\mathfrak{M} = \{\mu_{(G,\boldsymbol{x})}\}$, *if there is a* LOCAL *algorithm for approximate sampling (within arbitrary total variation error* $\delta > 0$*) with time complexity at most* $t(n, \delta)$, *then there is a* LOCAL *algorithm for approximate inference (within total variation error* $\delta + \epsilon_0$*) with time complexity at most* $t(n, \delta)$, *where* $\epsilon_0 \ge \sum_{v \in V} \mathbb{E}[F_v]$ *is the probability that the approximate sampling algorithm fails.*

4 LOCAL SELF-REDUCTIONS

It is well-known that on Turing machines, for self-reducible problems the accuracy of approximate counting can be boosted and approximate counting implies exact sampling (the Jerrum-Valiant-Vazirani sampler) [11].

In this section, we give two boosting results for local distributed counting and sampling:

- a *local boosting* for approximate inference which transforms approximate inference with bounded total variation error to the one with bounded multiplicative error;
- a *distributed JVV sampler* which uses approximate inference to achieve exact sampling via the *local rejection sampling*.

Both results utilizes *local self-reductions*, the self-reductions with bounded locality. The correctness of such reductions relies on the spatial Markovian (conditional independence) property of local Gibbs distributions.

4.1 The Boosting Lemma

We consider approximate inference with a stronger accuracy guarantee. The *multiplicative error function* err $(\cdot, \cdot)$ is defined as follows: for any two distributions μ and $\hat{\mu}$ over the same sample space Σ,

$$\text{err}\,(\mu, \hat{\mu}) \triangleq \max_{x \in \Sigma} |\ln \mu(x) - \ln \hat{\mu}(x)|, \tag{1}$$

with the convention that $0/0 = 1$ and $\ln 0 - \ln 0 = \ln(0/0) = 0$.

Approximate inference (with multiplicative error ϵ): For any instance $(G, \boldsymbol{x}, \tau)$, any $0 < \epsilon < 1$, each node v returns a marginal distribution $\hat{\mu}_v$, such that err $(\hat{\mu}_v, \mu_v^\tau) \le \epsilon$.

For sufficiently small $\epsilon > 0$, the condition err $(\hat{\mu}_v, \mu_v^\tau) \le \epsilon$ implies $1 - \epsilon \approx e^{-\epsilon} \le \frac{\hat{\mu}_v(c)}{\mu_v^\tau(c)} \le e^{\epsilon} \approx 1 + \epsilon$ for any $c \in \Sigma$, which gives a more accurate approximation than the bounded total variation error.

The boosting lemma stated below says that for local Gibbs distributions, approximate inference with total variation error can be boosted into that with multiplicative error.

Lemma 4.1 (boosting lemma). *For any class of local Gibbs distributions* $\mathfrak{M} = \{\mu_{(G,\boldsymbol{x})}\}$, *if there is a* LOCAL *algorithm for approximate inference (within arbitrary total variation error* $\delta > 0$*) with time complexity at most* $t(n, \delta)$, *then there is a* LOCAL *algorithm for approximate inference (within arbitrary multiplicative error* $0 < \epsilon < 1$*) with time complexity* $O(t(n, \frac{\epsilon}{5qn}))$, *where* $q = |\Sigma| \le \text{poly}(n)$ *is the size of the alphabet.*

Proof. Let $\mathcal{A}_\delta^+$ denote the LOCAL algorithm for approximate inference with arbitrary total variation error $\delta > 0$ whose time complexity is $t(n, \delta)$. We construct a LOCAL algorithm $\mathcal{A}_\epsilon^\times$ for approximate inference with arbitrary multiplicative error $0 < \epsilon < 1$.

Let $(G, \boldsymbol{x}, \tau)$ be an instance, where $G = (V, E)$. The joint distribution $\mu = \mu_{(G,\boldsymbol{x})}$ is a Gibbs distribution given by $(G, \Sigma, \mathcal{F})$, where $q = |\Sigma|$. Since the Gibbs distribution is local, we assume that there is an $\ell = O(1)$ such that $\forall (f, S) \in \mathcal{F} : \max_{u,v \in S} \text{dist}_G(u, v) \le \ell$.

Algorithm $\mathcal{A}_\epsilon^\times$: Let $v \in V$. We assume $v \notin \Lambda$, otherwise the inference problem is trivial. Let $\delta = \frac{\epsilon}{5qn}$ and $t = t(n, \frac{\epsilon}{5qn})$ be the time complexity of the LOCAL algorithm A_δ^+. Node v collects all information up to distance $2t + \ell$ and simulates the following algorithm locally.

Recall that $B_r(v)$ denotes the r-ball centered at v in G. We define

$$\Gamma = B_{t+\ell}(v) \setminus (B_t(v) \cup \Lambda).$$

Let $v_1, v_2, \ldots, v_m$, where $m = |\Gamma|$, be vertices in Γ enumerated in the increasing order of their unique IDs. A sequence of configurations $\tau_i \in \Sigma^{\Lambda_i}$ on subsets Λ_i, $0 \le i \le m$, is constructed as follows:

- Initially, let $\Lambda_0 = \Lambda$ and $\tau_0 = \tau$.
- For $i = 1, 2, \ldots, m$, let $\Lambda_i = \Lambda_{i-1} \cup \{v_i\}$, and the configurations $\tau_i \in \Sigma^{\Lambda_i}$ is constructed such that τ_i is consistent with τ_{i-1} over Λ_{i-1}, and $\tau_i(v_i) = c_i$ for the $c_i \in \Sigma$ that maximizes the marginal probability $\hat{\mu}_{v_i}^{\tau_{i-1}}(c_i)$ where $\hat{\mu}_{v_i}^{\tau_{i-1}}$ is the marginal distribution returned by $\mathcal{A}_\delta^+$ at node v_i on the instance $(G, \boldsymbol{x}, \tau_{i-1})$.

Finally, the marginal distribution $\mu_v^{\tau_m}$ is returned. Due to the conditional independence guaranteed by Proposition 2.4, $\mu_v^{\tau_m}$ is fully determined by the information in $B_{t+\ell}(v)$. Specifically, denoted $B = B_{t+\ell}(v)$, and define C to be the set of all configurations $\sigma \in \Sigma^B$ consistent with τ_m over $B \cap \Lambda_m$, i.e.

$$C = \{\sigma \in \Sigma^B \mid \forall u \in B \cap (\Gamma \cup \Lambda) : \sigma_u = \tau_m(u)\}.$$

Then for every $c \in \Sigma$, the marginal probability $\mu_v^{\tau_m}(c)$ is computed as

$$\mu_v^{\tau_m}(c) = \frac{\sum_{\sigma \in C: \sigma_v = c} w_B(\sigma)}{\sum_{\sigma \in C} w_B(\sigma)},$$

where $w_B(\sigma) = \prod_{(f,S) \in \mathcal{F}: S \subseteq B} f(\sigma_S)$. This finishes the definition of Algorithm $\mathcal{A}_\epsilon^\times$.

We then show that τ_m is feasible with respect to μ, so the marginal distribution $\mu_v^{\tau_m}$ is well-defined. Furthermore, it holds that

$$\forall c \in \Sigma: \quad e^{-\epsilon} \mu_v^{\tau}(c) \leq \mu_v^{\tau_m}(c) \leq e^{\epsilon} \mu_v^{\tau}(c), \tag{2}$$

which proves the Theorem.

For the sequence of configurations $\tau_i \in \Sigma^{\Lambda_i}$ on subsets Λ_i, $0 \leq i \leq m$, constructed in Algorithm $\mathcal{A}_\epsilon^\times$, for every $c \in \Sigma$, let $\tau_i^c \in \Sigma^{\Lambda_i \cup \{v\}}$ denote the configuration on $\Lambda_i \cup \{v\}$ such that τ_i^c is consistent with τ_i over Λ_i and $\tau_i^c(v) = c$.

Claim. *If τ_0^c is feasible with respect to μ, then all τ_i^c are feasible with respect to μ.*

Proof. We prove this by induction on i. For $i = 0$, the claim holds trivially. For general i, suppose that τ_{i-1}^c is feasible. Then τ_{i-1} must be feasible in the first place because τ_{i-1}^c extends τ_{i-1}. The two configurations τ_{i-1}^c and τ_{i-1} differ only at vertex v and $\mathrm{dist}_G(v, v_{i-1}) > t$, where $t = t(n, \frac{\epsilon}{5qn})$, Algorithm $\mathcal{A}_\delta^+$ will output the same marginal distribution $\hat{\mu}_{v_{i-1}}^{\tau_{i-1}}$ at node v_{i-1} on the instances $(G, \boldsymbol{x}, \tau_{i-1}^c)$ and $(G, \boldsymbol{x}, \tau_{i-1})$, such that $d_{\mathrm{TV}}\left(\hat{\mu}_{v_{i-1}}^{\tau_{i-1}}, \mu_{v_i}^{\tau_{i-1}^c}\right) \leq \frac{\epsilon}{5qn}$ and $d_{\mathrm{TV}}\left(\hat{\mu}_{v_{i-1}}^{\tau_{i-1}}, \mu_{v_i}^{\tau_{i-1}}\right) \leq \frac{\epsilon}{5qn}$. By triangle inequality,

$$d_{\mathrm{TV}}\left(\mu_{v_i}^{\tau_{i-1}^c}, \mu_{v_i}^{\tau_{i-1}}\right) \leq \frac{2\epsilon}{5nq}. \tag{3}$$

Recall that τ_i is constructed from τ_{i-1} in such a way that $\tau_i(v_i) = c_i$ for the $c_i \in \Sigma$ that maximizes the marginal probability $\hat{\mu}_{v_i}^{\tau_{i-1}}(c_i)$, and $q = |\Sigma|$. Therefore, we have

$$\mu_{v_i}^{\tau_{i-1}}(\tau_i(v_i)) \geq \frac{1}{q} - \frac{\epsilon}{5nq}. \tag{4}$$

Note that $\mu_{\Lambda_i \cup \{v\}}(\tau_i^c) = \mu_{\Lambda_{i-1} \cup \{v\}}(\tau_{i-1}^c) \cdot \mu_{v_i}^{\tau_{i-1}^c}(c_i)$, where $c_i = \tau_i(v_i)$. By induction hypothesis τ_{i-1}^c is feasible, then it holds that $\mu_{\Lambda_{i-1} \cup \{v\}}(\tau_{i-1}^c) > 0$. Combining with (3) and (4), we have

$$\mu_{v_i}^{\tau_{i-1}^c}(c_i) \geq \mu_{v_i}^{\tau_{i-1}}(c_i) - \frac{2\epsilon}{5nq} \geq \frac{1}{q} - \frac{3\epsilon}{5nq} > 0,$$

which implies that $\mu_{\Lambda_i \cup \{v\}}(\tau_i^c) > 0$ and τ_i^c is feasible with respect to μ. The claim is proved. □

Recall that $\tau_0 = \tau$ for a feasible $\tau \in \Sigma^\Lambda$. There must exist $c \in \Sigma$ such that τ_0^c is feasible, which according to above claim implies that all τ_i^c are feasible, and hence in particular, τ_m^c is feasible, which means τ_m is feasible in the first place since τ_m^c extends τ_m.

Consider each $c \in \Sigma$ that $\mu_v^\tau(c) > 0$. For such $c \in \Sigma$, τ_0^c must be feasible since $\tau_0 = \tau$, which according to above claim implies that τ_0^c is feasible. Denote that $c_i = \tau_i(v_i)$ for $0 \leq i \leq m$. Apply the chain rule in two different orders of vertices, we have

$$\mu_{\Lambda \cup \{v\}}^{\tau}(\tau_m^c) = \left(\prod_{i=1}^{m} \mu_{v_i}^{\tau_{i-1}}(c_i)\right) \mu_v^{\tau_m}(c),$$

$$\text{and} \quad \mu_{\Lambda \cup \{v\}}^{\tau}(\tau_m^c) = \mu_v^{\tau}(c) \left(\prod_{i=1}^{m} \mu_{v_i}^{\tau_{i-1}^c}(c_i)\right).$$

Solving the above equations gives us

$$\mu_v^{\tau_m}(c) = \left(\prod_{i=1}^{m} \frac{\mu_{v_i}^{\tau_{i-1}^c}(c_i)}{\mu_{v_i}^{\tau_{i-1}}(c_i)}\right) \mu_v^{\tau}(c).$$

For each $1 \leq i \leq m$, by (3) and (4), it holds that

$$e^{-\epsilon/n} \leq 1 - \frac{2\epsilon}{5n - \epsilon} \leq \frac{\mu_{v_i}^{\tau_{i-1}^c}(c_i)}{\mu_{v_i}^{\tau_{i-1}}(c_i)} \leq 1 + \frac{2\epsilon}{5n - \epsilon} \leq e^{\epsilon/n}.$$

Since $m = |\Lambda| \leq n$, we have $e^{-\epsilon} \leq \frac{\mu_v^{\tau_m}(c)}{\mu_v^{\tau}(c)} \leq e^{\epsilon}$.

For those $c \in \Sigma$ that $\mu_v^\tau(c) = 0$, it holds that τ_0^c is infeasible. It must hold that $\mu_v^{\tau_m}(c) = 0$, since if otherwise $\mu_v^{\tau_m}(c) > 0$, then τ_m^c is feasible, contradicting that τ_0^c is infeasible since τ_m^c extends τ_0^c. □

4.2 Distributed JVV Sampler

The Jerrum-Valiant-Vazirani (JVV) sampler [11] is a general global reduction from exact sampling to approximate counting for self-reducible problems via rejection sampling. Here we give a local distributed JVV sampler by realizing a local rejection sampling.

Theorem 4.2. *For a class of local Gibbs distributions $\mathfrak{M} = \{\mu_{(G,\boldsymbol{x})}\}$, if there is a LOCAL algorithm for approximate inference (with total variation error $\leq 1/5qn^4$) with time complexity at most $t(n)$, where $q = |\Sigma| \leq \mathrm{poly}(n)$ is the size of the alphabet, then there is a LOCAL algorithm for exact sampling with time complexity $O(t(n) \log^2 n)$.*

By the boosting lemma (Lemma 4.1), the algorithm for approximate inference with total variation error in the assumption of Theorem 4.2 can be boosted to an approximate inference algorithm with multiplicative error $1/n^3$ and time complexity $O(t(n))$. Theorem 4.2 is then a consequence of the following proposition.

Proposition 4.3. *For a class of local Gibbs distributions $\mathfrak{M} = \{\mu_{(G,\boldsymbol{x})}\}$, if there is a LOCAL algorithm for approximate inference (with multiplicative error $\leq 1/n^3$) with time complexity at most $t(n)$, then there is a LOCAL algorithm for exact sampling with time complexity $O(t(n) \log^2 n)$.*

Let $\mathcal{A}$ be the LOCAL algorithm for approximate inference with multiplicative error $1/n^3$ and time complexity at most $t = t(n)$. We construct an SLOCAL algorithm called local-JVV for exact sampling with time complexity $O(t)$. For convenience, the local-JVV algorithm is presented as a multi-pass SLOCAL algorithm with the ability of writing nearby nodes' internal memories. It was observed in [8] that these variations will not substantially change the power of SLOCAL algorithms.

The following lemma holds for SLOCAL algorithms.

Lemma 4.4 (Observation 2.1 in [8]). *Any SLOCAL algorithm $\mathcal{A}$ with locality R in which each node v can write into the local memory S_u of other nodes u within its radius $r \leq R$ can be transformed into an SLOCAL algorithm $\mathcal{B}$ with locality $r + R$ in which v writes only in its own memory S_v.*

Let $(G, \boldsymbol{x}, \tau)$ be an instance, where $G = (V, E)$. The joint distribution $\mu = \mu_{(G,\boldsymbol{x})}$ is a Gibbs distribution given by $(G, \Sigma, \mathcal{F})$, where $q = |\Sigma|$. Since the Gibbs distribution is local, we assume that there is an $\ell = O(1)$ such that $\forall (f, S) \in \mathcal{F} : \max_{u,v \in S} \mathrm{dist}_G(u, v) \leq \ell$.

The $\tau \in \Sigma^\Lambda$ is an arbitrary feasible configuration on an arbitrary subset $\Lambda \subseteq V$. The distribution μ^τ is the target distribution that we want to sample from.

4.2.1 The local-JVV algorithm. The local-JVV algorithm is an SLOCAL algorithm for the *local rejection sampling*: Upon termination, the algorithm returns a $(Y, F') = ((Y_v)_{v \in V}, (F'_v)_{v \in V})$, where each node $v \in V$ outputs Y_v and F'_v, such that $Y \in \Sigma^V$ is a random configuration, and each $F'_v \in \{0, 1\}$ indicates that the algorithm fails (rejects) locally at node v.

The SLOCAL algorithm consists of three passes. In each pass, the algorithm scans the nodes in the same ordering $\pi = v_1, v_2, \ldots, v_n$ provided to the algorithm by an adversary.

In the first pass, a configuration $\sigma_0 \in \Sigma^V$ that is feasible with respect to the target distribution μ^τ, called the *ground state*, is constructed by the following procedure:

- Initially, $\sigma_0 \in \Sigma^\Lambda$ and $\sigma_0 = \tau$. Then σ_0 is updated at each step.
- In the i-th step, simulate the algorithm $\mathcal{A}$ at node v_i within radius $t = t(n)$ on the instance $(G, \boldsymbol{x}, \sigma_0)$, which returns a marginal distribution $\hat{\mu}_{v_i}^{\sigma_0}$. Pick an arbitrary $c_i \in \Sigma$ with $\hat{\mu}_{v_i}^{\sigma_0}(c_i) > 0$, and extend the current σ_0 further onto v_i by setting $\sigma_0(v_i) \leftarrow c_i$.

In the second pass, a random configurations $Y \in \Sigma^V$ is generated independently by the following procedure:

- Initially, $Y \in \Sigma^\Lambda$ and $Y = \tau$. Then Y is randomly updated at each step.
- In the i-th step, simulate the algorithm $\mathcal{A}$ at node v_i on the instance $(G, \boldsymbol{x}, Y)$, which returns a marginal distribution $\hat{\mu}_{v_i}^{Y}$. Sample a random $Y_i \in \Sigma$ independently according to $\hat{\mu}_{v_i}^{Y}$, and extend the current Y further onto v_i by setting $Y(v_i) \leftarrow Y_i$.

Let $\hat{\mu}^\tau$ be the distribution of $Y \in \Sigma^V$ generated as above. It closely approximates the μ^τ.

CLAIM 4.5. *For any $\sigma \in \Sigma^V$, it holds that $e^{-1/n^2} \le \frac{\hat{\mu}^\tau(\sigma)}{\mu^\tau(\sigma)} \le e^{1/n^2}$.*

The proof of Claim 4.5 appears in the full version of this paper.

REMARK. *It is easy to verify that the configuration $\sigma_0 \in \Sigma^V$ constructed in the first pass satisfies $\hat{\mu}^\tau(\sigma_0) > 0$. By Claim 4.5, it holds that $\mu^\tau(\sigma_0) > 0$. Thus σ_0 is a feasible configuration with respect to the target distribution μ^τ.*

In the third pass, each node v_i carefully computes a probability q_{v_i}, and uses q_{v_i} to independently sample a random $F'_{v_i} \in \{0, 1\}$ indicating the local failure at v_i.

- Initially, let $\sigma_0 \in \Sigma^V$ be the ground state constructed in the first pass.
- A sequence of configurations $\sigma_1, \sigma_2, \ldots, \sigma_n \in \Sigma^V$ is constructed, where $\sigma_n = Y$ is the configuration randomly generated in the second pass, such that the following invariants hold for all $0 \le i \le n$:

$$\sigma_i \text{ is feasible with respect to } \mu^\tau; \tag{5}$$

$$\forall 1 \le j \le i: \quad \sigma_i(v_j) = Y(v_j); \tag{6}$$

$$\sigma_i \text{ and } \sigma_{i-1} \text{ differ only over the } t\text{-ball } B_t(v_i). \tag{7}$$

The invariants hold trivially for σ_0. In the i-th step, assume the above invariants for σ_{i-1}. Construct a $\sigma_i \in \Sigma^V$ satisfying these invariants by enumerating all configurations $\sigma' \in \Sigma^B$ over the t-ball $B = B_t(v_i)$ and trying replacing the assignment of $\sigma_{i-1}(B)$ with σ'. The following claim guarantees the existence of such $\sigma_i \in \Sigma^V$.

CLAIM 4.6. *Assume that $\sigma_{i-1} \in \Sigma^V$ is feasible with respect to μ^τ and $\sigma_{i-1}(v_j) = Y(v_j)$ for all $1 \le j \le i-1$. There exists a $\sigma_i \in \Sigma^V$ satisfying (5), (6) and (7).*

Assuming this claim, the algorithm can always find a good σ_i and verify the invariants within bounded radius from v_i. Specifically, assuming the invariants for σ_{i-1}, invariant (7) holds trivially by the construction of σ_i, invariant (6) can be verified at v_i within radius t, and invariant (5) can be verified within radius $t + \ell$ due to the conditional independence property stated in Proposition 2.4. Formally, one can check the feasibility of σ_i by testing whether $\forall v \in B_t(v_i) \cap \Lambda$: $\sigma_i(v) = \tau(v)$ and $\prod_{\substack{(S,f) \in \mathcal{F} \\ S \subseteq B_{t+\ell}(v_i)}} f(\sigma_i(S)) > 0$.

Once a good σ_i is found, node v_i updates the internal states of all nodes in $B_t(v_i)$ to update the current configuration to σ_i.

Node v_i computes the value of

$$q_{v_i} = q_{v_i}(Y) \triangleq \frac{\hat{\mu}^\tau(\sigma_{i-1}) w(\sigma_i)}{\hat{\mu}^\tau(\sigma_i) w(\sigma_{i-1})} e^{-3/n^2}, \tag{8}$$

where $\hat{\mu}^\tau$ stands for the distribution of the random configuration Y generated in the second pass, and $w(\cdot)$ is the weight for the Gibbs distribution defined in Definition 2.3.

CLAIM 4.7. *The q_{v_i} defined in (8) can be computed at v_i within radius $3t+\ell = O(t)$ and it always holds that $e^{-5/n^2} \le q_{v_i} \le 1$.*

- At last, v_i samples a random $F'_{v_i} \in \{0, 1\}$ such that $F'_{v_i} = 0$ with probability q_{v_i}.

Finally, each node v_i returns a pair (Y_{v_i}, F'_{v_i}) where $Y = (Y_{v_i})_{1 \le i \le n}$ is the random configuration sampled in the second pass and the algorithm fails locally at v_i if $F'_{v_i} = 1$.

The Pseudocode for local-JVV algorithm is given in Algorithm 1.

4.2.2 Proofs of Claim 4.6 and Claim 4.7.

PROOF OF CLAIM 4.6. Assume that $\sigma_{i-1} \in \Sigma^V$ is feasible with respect to μ^τ and $\sigma_{i-1}(v_j) = Y(v_j)$ for all $1 \le j \le i-1$. We show that there exists a $\sigma_i \in \Sigma^V$ satisfying (5), (6), and (7). Define set of nodes $\Gamma = \{v_j \in V \mid v_j \notin B_t(v) \text{ or } j \le i-1\} \cup \Lambda$. Let $\tau_1 = \sigma_{i-1}(\Gamma)$ and $\tau_2 = Y(\Gamma)$ be two configurations on subset Γ. By assumption and Claim 4.5, σ_{i-1} and Y are feasible, so τ_1 and τ_2 are also feasible and $\sigma_{i-1}(\Lambda) = Y(\Lambda) = \tau$.

The marginal distributions returned by $\mathcal{A}$ at node v_i on the two instances $(G, \boldsymbol{x}, \tau_1)$ and $(G, \boldsymbol{x}, \tau_2)$ are identical, because τ_1 and τ_2 agree with each other over $B_t(v_i)$. We denote this marginal distribution as $\hat{\mu}_{v_i}^{\tau_1} = \hat{\mu}_{v_i}^{\tau_2}$, which is an approximation of the marginal distributions $\mu_{v_i}^{\tau_1}, \mu_{v_i}^{\tau_2}$ with multiplicative error $1/n^3$. It holds that

$$e^{1/n^3} \cdot \mu_{v_i}^{\tau_1}(Y(v_i)) \ge \hat{\mu}_{v_i}^{\tau_1}(Y(v_i)) \ge e^{-1/n^3} \cdot \mu_{v_i}^{\tau_2}(Y(v_i)) > 0.$$

where the last inequality is due to that Y is feasible.

This shows that $\mu_{v_i}^{\tau_1}(Y(v_i)) > 0$, which means there exists a feasible configuration $\sigma \in \Sigma^V$ such that $\sigma(\Gamma) = \tau_1 = \sigma_{i-1}(\Gamma)$ and

Algorithm 1: Pseudocode for local-JVV algorithm

Input: A problem instance $(G, \boldsymbol{x}, \tau)$ and an ordering of nodes $\pi = v_1, v_2, \ldots, v_n$ provided by an adversary.

First Pass:
- Initialize $\sigma_0 = \tau \in \Sigma^{\Lambda}$;
- **for** *i = 1 through n* **do**
  - Simulate algorithm $\mathcal{A}$ at node v_i within radius $t(n)$ on instance $(G, \boldsymbol{x}, \sigma_0)$ to obtain the output marginal distribution $\hat{\mu}_{v_i}^{\sigma_0}$;
  - Pick an arbitrary $c_i \in \Sigma$ with $\hat{\mu}_{v_i}^{\sigma_0}(c_i) > 0$;
  - Extend σ_0 further on v_i by setting $\sigma_0(v_i) \leftarrow c_i$;
- Each node $v \in V$ outputs $\sigma_0(v)$.

Second Pass:
- Initialize $Y = \tau \in \Sigma^{\Lambda}$;
- **for** *i = 1 through n* **do**
  - Simulate algorithm $\mathcal{A}$ at node v_i within radius $t(n)$ on instance $(G, \boldsymbol{x}, Y)$ to obtain the output marginal distribution $\hat{\mu}_{v_i}^{Y}$;
  - Sample a random $Y_i \in \Sigma$ independently according to the distribution $\hat{\mu}_{v_i}^{Y}$;
  - Extend Y further on v_i by setting $Y(v_i) \leftarrow Y_i$;
- Each node $v \in V$ outputs Y_v.

Third Pass:
- Let σ_0 and Y be the output configurations of the first and the second passes;
- **for** *i = 1 through n* **do**
  - Enumerate all configurations $\sigma' \in \Sigma^{B_t(v_i)}$ over the t-ball $B_t(v_i)$ to find a configuration
    $$\sigma_i(v) = \begin{cases} \sigma_{i-1}(v) & \text{if } v \notin B_t(v_i) \\ \sigma'(v) & \text{if } v \in B_t(v_i) \end{cases}$$
    such that following three local conditions hold:
    - $\forall 1 \le j \le i, v_j \in B_t(v_i) : \sigma_i(v_j) = Y(v_j)$,
    - $\forall v \in B_t(v_i) \cap \Lambda : \sigma_i(v) = \tau(v)$,
    - $\prod_{\substack{(S,f)\in\mathcal{F} \\ S\subseteq B_{t+\ell}(v_i)}} f(\sigma_i(S)) > 0$;
  - Compute the value of $q_{v_i} = \frac{\hat{\mu}^{\tau}(\sigma_{i-1})w(\sigma_i)}{\hat{\mu}^{\tau}(\sigma_i)w(\sigma_{i-1})} \mathrm{e}^{-3/n^2}$ by Equations (9) and (10);
  - Sample a random $F'_{v_i} \in \{0, 1\}$ independently such that $F'_{v_i} = 0$ with probability q_{v_i};
  - Write $\sigma_i(v)$ into the internal states of all nodes v in the t-ball $B_t(v_i)$ to update the configuration σ_{i-1} into σ_i.
- Each node $v \in V$ outputs F'_v;

Output: Each node $v \in V$ outputs the pair (Y_v, F'_v);

$\sigma(v_i) = Y(v_i)$. Such σ is the σ_i we want. It can be easily verified that it satisfies the invariants (5), (6) and (7). □

Proof of Claim 4.7. Recall that the value of q_{v_i} is defined as $q_{v_i} = \frac{\hat{\mu}^{\tau}(\sigma_{i-1})w(\sigma_i)}{\hat{\mu}^{\tau}(\sigma_i)w(\sigma_{i-1})} \mathrm{e}^{-3/n^2}$. Due to Claim 4.6, every σ_i is feasible with respect to μ^{τ}, so $w(\sigma_i) > 0$ and moreover by Claim 4.5, we have $\hat{\mu}^{\tau}(\sigma_i) > 0$. The ratio q_{v_i} is well-defined.

Consider the configurations $\sigma_0, \sigma_1, \ldots, \sigma_n \in \Sigma^V$ constructed in the third pass of the local-JVV algorithm. For each σ_i, we define a sequence of configurations $\sigma_i^0, \sigma_i^1, \ldots, \sigma_i^n$, where $\sigma_i^0 = \tau$ and $\sigma_i^n = \sigma_i$. Let σ_i^j denote the Y^j when $Y = \sigma_i$, where Y^j denotes the partially specified random configuration Y constructed in the j-th step in the second pass of the the local-JVV algorithm. Namely, σ_i^j is a partially specified configuration on subset $S_j = \Lambda \cup \{v_1, v_2, \ldots, v_j\}$ such that $\sigma_i^j = \sigma_i(S_j)$. We have

$$\frac{\hat{\mu}^{\tau}(\sigma_{i-1})}{\hat{\mu}^{\tau}(\sigma_i)} = \prod_{j=1}^{n} \frac{\hat{\mu}_{v_j}^{\sigma_{i-1}^{j-1}}(\sigma_{i-1}(v_j))}{\hat{\mu}_{v_j}^{\sigma_i^{j-1}}(\sigma_i(v_j))}.$$

Note that the two configurations σ_i and σ_{i-1} differ only on the t-ball $B_t(v_i)$. Therefore, for all σ_i and σ_{i-1} agree with each other over $B_t(v_k)$ for any $v_k \notin B_{2t}(v_i)$. The two instances $(G, \boldsymbol{x}, \sigma_{i-1}^{k-1})$ and $(G, \boldsymbol{x}, \sigma_i^{k-1})$ are indistinguishable to the t-local approximate inference algorithm $\mathcal{A}$, thus $\hat{\mu}_{v_k}^{\sigma_{i-1}^{k-1}}(\sigma_{i-1}(v_k)) = \hat{\mu}_{v_k}^{\sigma_i^{k-1}}(\sigma_i(v_k))$, which means

$$\frac{\hat{\mu}^{\tau}(\sigma_{i-1})}{\hat{\mu}^{\tau}(\sigma_i)} = \prod_{v_j \in B_{2t}(v_i)} \frac{\hat{\mu}_{v_j}^{\sigma_{i-1}^{j-1}}(\sigma_{i-1}(v_j))}{\hat{\mu}_{v_j}^{\sigma_i^{j-1}}(\sigma_i(v_j))}, \tag{9}$$

where each marginal probability $\hat{\mu}_{v_j}^{\cdot}(\cdot)$ can be computed by the local algorithm $\mathcal{A}$ at node v_j within radius t.

On the other hand, since the two configurations σ_i and σ_{i-1} differ only on nodes in $B_t(v_i)$, by the definition of the weight $w(\cdot)$ in Definition 2.3, we have

$$\frac{w(\sigma_i)}{w(\sigma_{i-1})} = \prod_{\substack{(S,f)\in\mathcal{F} \\ S\subseteq B_{t+\ell}(v_i)}} \frac{f(\sigma_i(S))}{f(\sigma_{i-1}(S))}. \tag{10}$$

Equations (9) and (10) imply that the quantity q_{v_i} can be computed at node v_i by gathering all information up to distance $3t + \ell$.

For the Gibbs distribution μ, it always holds that $\frac{\mu^{\tau}(\sigma_{i-1})w(\sigma_i)}{\mu^{\tau}(\sigma_i)w(\sigma_{i-1})} = 1$ since the measure μ is defined proportional to the weights $w(\cdot)$. Due to Claim 4.5, we have

$$\mathrm{e}^{-2/n^2} \le \frac{\hat{\mu}^{\tau}(\sigma_{i-1})w(\sigma_i)}{\hat{\mu}^{\tau}(\sigma_i)w(\sigma_{i-1})} \le \mathrm{e}^{2/n^2},$$

which implies $\mathrm{e}^{-5/n^2} \le q_{v_i}(\sigma) \le \mathrm{e}^{-1/n^2} \le 1$. □

4.2.3 Proof of Proposition 4.3.

The correctness of the local-JVV algorithm is guaranteed by the following lemma.

Lemma 4.8. *On any ordering of nodes, the local-JVV algorithm fails with probability at most $\sum_{i=1}^{n} \mathbb{E}[F'_{v_i}] = 1 - O(1/n)$ and conditioning on that $F'_{v_i} = 0$ for all v_i, the $Y \in \Sigma^V$ randomly sampled by the algorithm follows precisely the target distribution μ^{τ}.*

Proof. Let $\mathcal{G}$ denote the event that the local-JVV algorithm succeeds, i.e. $F'_{v_i} = 0$ for all v_i. Recall that for any $\sigma \in \Sigma^V$,

$$\Pr[F'_{v_i} = 1 \mid Y = \sigma] = q_{v_i}(\sigma),$$

where $q_{v_i}(\sigma) = q_{v_i}(Y)\big|_{Y=\sigma}$ is as defined in (8). Due to Claim 4.7, for any $\sigma \in \Sigma^V$, $\Pr[\mathcal{G} \mid Y = \sigma] = \prod_{i=1}^{n} q_{v_i}(\sigma) \ge \mathrm{e}^{-5/n} = 1 - O\left(\frac{1}{n}\right)$. This proves that the algorithm succeeds with probability $\Pr[\mathcal{G}] = 1 - O\left(\frac{1}{n}\right)$.

Next, we show that $\Pr[Y = \sigma \mid \mathcal{G}] = \mu^\tau(\sigma)$ for any $\sigma \in \Sigma^V$, which proves the lemma.

For any $\sigma \in \Sigma^V$ that $\mu^\tau(\sigma) = 0$, by Claim 4.5, we have $\hat{\mu}^\tau(\sigma) = \Pr[Y = \sigma] = 0$, therefore $\Pr[Y = \sigma \mid \mathcal{G}] = 0$.

For any $\sigma \in \Sigma^V$ that $\mu^\tau(\sigma) > 0$, by Claim 4.5, we have $\hat{\mu}^\tau(\sigma) = \Pr[Y = \sigma] > 0$. The probability that the algorithm succeeds and outputs $Y = \sigma$ is given by

$$\begin{aligned}\Pr[Y = \sigma \wedge \mathcal{G}] &= \hat{\mu}^\tau(\sigma)\Pr[\mathcal{G} \mid Y = \sigma] = \hat{\mu}^\tau(\sigma)\prod_{i=1}^{n} q_{v_i}(\sigma)\\ &= \hat{\mu}^\tau(\sigma)\prod_{i=1}^{n}\left(\frac{\hat{\mu}^\tau(\sigma_{i-1})w(\sigma_i)}{\hat{\mu}^\tau(\sigma_i)w(\sigma_{i-1})}\mathrm{e}^{-3/n^2}\right)\Bigg|_{\sigma_n = Y = \sigma}\\ &= \left(\frac{\hat{\mu}^\tau(\sigma_0)}{w(\sigma_0)}\cdot \mathrm{e}^{-3/n}\right)w(\sigma).\end{aligned}$$

Note that the factor $\left(\frac{\hat{\mu}^\tau(\sigma_0)}{w(\sigma_0)}\cdot \mathrm{e}^{-3/n}\right)$ is independent of σ. Therefore,

$$\begin{aligned}\Pr[Y = \sigma \mid \mathcal{G}] &= \frac{\Pr[Y = \sigma \wedge \mathcal{G}]}{\sum_{\sigma' : \mu^\tau(\sigma') > 0}\Pr[Y = \sigma' \wedge \mathcal{G}]}\\ &= \frac{w(\sigma)}{\sum_{\sigma' : \mu^\tau(\sigma') > 0} w(\sigma')} = \mu^\tau(\sigma).\end{aligned}$$

□

Finally, we are going to prove Proposition 4.3. It can be easily verified that the local-JVV algorithm has locality $O(t)$ where $t = t(n)$ is the time complexity of the LOCAL algorithm $\mathcal{A}$.

We apply Lemma 4.4 and Lemma 3.1 to transform the local-JVV algorithm defined in the SLOCAL model to a LOCAL algorithm. Due to Lemma 3.1, upon successful termination, the LOCAL algorithm preserves the distribution of the output (Y, F') of the SLOCAL algorithm on some ordering of nodes, where $Y = (Y_v)_{v \in V}$ is the randomly sampled configuration and $F' = (F'_v)_{v \in V}$ is the vector of random indicators for local failures generated in the final pass of the local-JVV algorithm. The transformation to the LOCAL model will introduce another random failure $F''_v \in \{0, 1\}$ to each node v which is independent of (Y, F'), where $F''_v = 1$ indicates the failure at node v caused by the network decomposition and $\sum_{v \in V}\mathbb{E}[F''_v] = O(1/n^2)$. We combine the two failures and define $F_v = F'_v \vee F''_v$ to indicate the failure of the LOCAL algorithm at node v. Clearly,

$$\sum_{v \in V}\mathbb{E}[F_v] \le \sum_{v \in V}\mathbb{E}[F'_v] + \sum_{v \in V}\mathbb{E}[F''_v] = O\left(\frac{1}{n}\right).$$

Furthermore, since $(F''_v)_{v \in V}$ is independent of (Y, F'), it still holds that conditioning on that $F_v = 0$ for all nodes $v \in V$, the distribution of Y is precisely the target distribution.

5 APPROXIMATE INFERENCE AND STRONG SPATIAL MIXING

In this section, we explore the intrinsic relation between distributed sampling/counting problems and decays of correlation in joint distributions. The main result in this section holds for locally admissible, local Gibbs distributions.

An important decay of correlation property for joint distributions is the *strong spatial mixing*. We adopt the definition of strong spatial mixing in [22] into our context.

Definition 5.1 (strong spatial mixing). Let $\delta_n : \mathbb{N} \to \mathbb{R}_{\ge 0}$ be a sequence of non-increasing functions. A class of joint distributions $\mathfrak{M} = \{\mu_{(G,\boldsymbol{x})}\}$ is said to exhibit *strong spatial mixing* with rate $\delta_n(\cdot)$ if for every distribution $\mu_{(G,\boldsymbol{x})} \in \mathfrak{M}$ over Σ^V, where $G = (V, E)$ and $n = |V|$, for every $v \in V, \Lambda \subseteq V$, and any two feasible configurations $\sigma, \tau \in \Sigma^\Lambda$,

$$d_{\mathrm{TV}}(\mu_v^\sigma, \mu_v^\tau) \le \delta_n(\mathrm{dist}_G(v, D)), \tag{11}$$

where $D \subseteq \Lambda$ is the subset on which σ and τ differ.

In particular, the strong spatial mixing is said to be *with exponential decay at rate* α, for some $0 < \alpha < 1$, if the mixing rate $\delta_\cdot(\cdot)$ is in the form $\delta_n(t) = \mathrm{poly}(n)\cdot\alpha^t$.

The strong spatial mixing is intrinsically related to the approximate inference in the LOCAL model. In fact, the strong spatial mixing can be thought as a weaker form of approximate inference in the LOCAL model, where every node knows the graph G and distribution μ but not the partially specified feasible configuration τ. Therefore, it is quite natural that the approximate inference always implies strong spatial mixing. Meanwhile, the converse also holds for locally admissible, local Gibbs distributions.

THEOREM 5.2. *For any class of joint distributions $\mathfrak{M} = \{\mu_{(G,\boldsymbol{x})}\}$, if there is a LOCAL algorithm for approximate inference (within arbitrary total variation error $\delta > 0$) with time complexity at most $t(n, \delta)$, then $\mathfrak{M}$ exhibits strong spatial mixing with rate $\delta_n(t) = 2\min\{\delta \mid t(n, \delta) \le t - 1\}$.*

Conversely, for any class of locally admissible, local Gibbs distributions $\mathfrak{M} = \{\mu_{(G,\boldsymbol{x})}\}$, if $\mathfrak{M}$ exhibits strong spatial mixing with rate $\delta_n(t)$, then there is a LOCAL algorithm for approximate inference (within arbitrary total variation error $\delta > 0$) with time complexity $t(n, \delta) = \min\{t \mid \delta_n(t) \le \delta\} + O(1)$.

The strong spatial mixing defined in Definition 5.1 measures the decay of correlation in terms of total variation distance. If we replace the total variation distance $d_{\mathrm{TV}}(\cdot,\cdot)$ in (11) with the multiplicative error function err $(\cdot,\cdot)$ defined in (1), we have an even stronger form of strong spatial mixing, namely the one with decay in multiplicative error. Several well-known strong spatial mixing results for important classes of Gibbs distributions (e.g. independent sets, matchings, and graph colorings) were actually established in this stronger form [1, 5, 6, 22]. Here we see this is not a coincidence. Combing Theorem 5.2 with the boosting lemma (Lemma 4.1), we have the following corollary.

COROLLARY 5.3. *A class of locally admissible, local Gibbs distributions $\mathfrak{M}$ exhibits strong spatial mixing with exponential decay at rate α in total variation distance, if and only if it exhibits strong spatial mixing with exponential decay at rate α in multiplicative error.*

Interestingly, the corollary gives a result in probability theory proved by local computation.

Combining Theorem 5.2 with the distributed JVV sampler (Theorem 4.2), we have the followings.

COROLLARY 5.4. *For any class of locally admissible, local Gibbs distributions $\mathfrak{M} = \{\mu_{(G,\boldsymbol{x})}\}$, if $\mathfrak{M}$ exhibits strong spatial mixing with exponential decay at rate α for some $\alpha < 1$, then there is a LOCAL algorithm for exact sampling with time complexity $O(\frac{1}{1-\alpha}\log^3 n)$.*

Combining with the state-of-the-arts for strong spatial mixing in [1, 6, 12, 19, 22], the corollary gives us the following LOCAL algorithm for exact sampling:

- an $O(\sqrt{\Delta}\log^3 n)$-round algorithm for sampling matchings in graphs with maximum degree Δ due to the strong spatial mixing of matchings with exponential decay at rate $1 - \Omega(1/\sqrt{\Delta})$ [1];
- an $O(\log^3 n)$-round algorithm for sampling independent sets in graphs with max-degree $\Delta \leq 5$, or more generally, for sampling according to the hardcore model (weighted independent sets) with fugacity λ up to the uniqueness threshold (where $\lambda < \lambda_c(\Delta) \triangleq (\Delta-1)^{(\Delta-1)}/(\Delta-2)^{\Delta}$), due to the strong spatial mixing of the model up to the uniqueness threshold [22];
- an $O(\log^3 n)$-round algorithm for sampling q-colorings of triangle-free graphs when $q \geq \alpha\Delta$ for $\alpha > \alpha^*$ where $\alpha^* \approx 1.763\ldots$ satisfies $\alpha^* = \exp(\frac{1}{\alpha^*})$, due to the strong spatial mixing proved in [6];
- an $O(\log^3 n)$-round algorithm for sampling according to the anti-ferromagnetic 2-spin model in the interior of the uniqueness regime, due to the strong spatial mixing of the model in the uniqueness regime [12];
- an $O(\log^3 n)$-round algorithm for sampling weighted hypergraph matchings up to the uniqueness threshold (when the weight $\lambda < \lambda_c(r,\Delta) \triangleq \frac{(\Delta-1)^{(\Delta-1)}}{(r-1)(\Delta-2)^{\Delta}}$, where r is the rank of the hypergraph), due to the strong spatial mixing of the model up to the uniqueness threshold [19].

The definitions of these models are given in the referred papers. All these joint distributions are either locally admissible, local Gibbs distributions, or in the case of edge models (e.g. graph/hypergraph matchings) can be represented as such joint distributions through dualities of graphs/hypergraphs, which preserve the distances.

For lower bounds, the long-range correlation established in a previous work ([3], Theorem 5.3) implies an $\Omega(\text{diam})$ lower bound for approximate sampling according to the hardcore model with fugacity λ in the non-uniqueness regime (where $\lambda > \lambda_c(\Delta)$). Along with the $O(\log^3 n)$ upper bound for exact sampling according to the hardcore model in the uniqueness regime obtained above, we discover for the first time a computational phase transition for local distributed sampling and counting, at the same critical threshold for the computational phase transition discovered for sampling and counting on polynomial-time Turing machines [18, 22].

6 CONCLUSION

We study the complexities of sampling and counting in the LOCAL model, where the counting is represented by a local variant, namely the inference problem. We found that for self-reducible problems, the well known generic relations between sampling and counting on classic polynomial-time Turing machines hold similarly for local computation. Meanwhile, the tractability of these problems by local computation is captured by a decay of correlation property known as the strong spatial mixing.

Perhaps a lesson we could learn from this research is that it is helpful to model local computation problems as joint distributions, and hence studying the complexities of these problems is reduced to studying the discrepancies between such problem-specified joint distributions and the distributions that can be generated by local algorithms. This new approach for local computation seems to have much potential.

Several open problems are worth investigating. First, can we make the LOCAL algorithms in this paper use bounded-size messages and bounded local computation? Such efficient distributed algorithms would necessarily improve the state of the arts of sampling and approximate counting on polynomial-time Turing machines. Second, how should we classify complexities of sampling and counting in local computation, and does there exist a complexity hierarchy? Third, the distributed JVV sampler given in this paper terminates in a fixed number of rounds with bounded locally certifiable failure. Can we make this algorithm Las Vegas, in a sense that the time complexity of the algorithm may be random but once it terminates the algorithm always outputs precisely according to the correct distribution, and still being local? This requires a strategy for non-biased local resampling, which is far from being well understood. So far, it was only discovered for the Lovász-local-lemma-based sampler for restrictive problems under strict conditions [9].

REFERENCES

[1] Mohsen Bayati, David Gamarnik, Dimitriy Katz, Chandra Nair, and Prasad Tetali. 2007. Simple deterministic approximation algorithms for counting matchings. In *STOC'07*.

[2] Weiming Feng, Thomas P Hayes, and Yitong Yin. 2018. Distributed Symmetry Breaking in Sampling (Optimal Distributed Randomly Coloring with Fewer Colors). *arXiv preprint arXiv:1802.06953* (2018).

[3] Weiming Feng, Yuxin Sun, and Yitong Yin. 2017. What Can be Sampled Locally?. In *PODC'17*.

[4] Manuela Fischer and Mohsen Ghaffari. 2018. A Simple Parallel and Distributed Sampling Technique: Local Glauber Dynamics. *arXiv preprint arXiv:1802.06676* (2018).

[5] David Gamarnik and Dmitriy Katz. 2007. Correlation decay and deterministic FPTAS for counting list-colorings of a graph. In *SODA'07*.

[6] David Gamarnik, Dmitriy Katz, and Sidhant Misra. 2013. Strong spatial mixing of list coloring of graphs. *Random Structures & Algorithms* (2013).

[7] Mohsen Ghaffari, David G Harris, and Fabian Kuhn. 2017. On Derandomizing Local Distributed Algorithms. *arXiv preprint arXiv:1711.02194* (2017).

[8] Mohsen Ghaffari, Fabian Kuhn, and Yannic Maus. 2017. On the Complexity of Local Distributed Graph Problems. In *STOC'17*.

[9] Heng Guo, Mark Jerrum, and Jingcheng Liu. 2017. Uniform Sampling through the Lovász Local Lemma. In *STOC'17*.

[10] Mark Jerrum. 2003. *Counting, Sampling and Integrating: Algorithms and Complexity*. Birkh auser Basel.

[11] M R Jerrum, L G Valiant, and V V Vazirani. 1986. Random generation of combinatorial structures from a uniform distribution. *Theor. Comput. Sci.* 43 (1986), 169–188.

[12] Liang Li, Pinyan Lu, and Yitong Yin. 2013. Correlation decay up to uniqueness in spin systems. In *SODA'13*.

[13] Marc Mezard and Andrea Montanari. 2009. *Information, physics, and computation*. Oxford University Press.

[14] Moni Naor and Larry Stockmeyer. 1995. What can be computed locally? *SIAM Journal on Computing (SICOMP)* 24, 6 (1995), 1259–1277.

[15] Alessandro Panconesi and Aravind Srinivasan. 1996. On the complexity of distributed network decomposition. *Journal of Algorithms* 20, 2 (1996), 356–374.

[16] Mark A Paskin and Carlos E Guestrin. 2004. Robust probabilistic inference in distributed systems. In *UAI'04*.

[17] David Peleg. 2000. *Distributed computing: a locality-sensitive approach*. SIAM.

[18] Allan Sly. 2010. Computational transition at the uniqueness threshold. In *FOCS'10*.

[19] Renjie Song, Yitong Yin, and Jinman Zhao. 2016. Counting Hypergraph Matchings up to Uniqueness Threshold. In *RANDOM'16*.

[20] Larry J. Stockmeyer. 1983. The Complexity of Approximate Counting. In *STOC'83*.

[21] Leslie G. Valiant. 1979. The Complexity of Computing the Permanent. *Theor. Comput. Sci.* 8 (1979), 189–201.

[22] Dror Weitz. 2006. Counting independent sets up to the tree threshold. In *STOC'06*.

A Deterministic Distributed Algorithm for Exact Weighted All-Pairs Shortest Paths in $\tilde{O}(n^{3/2})$ Rounds

Udit Agarwal*
Dept. of Computer Science,
University of Texas at Austin
Austin, TX, USA
udit@cs.utexas.edu

Vijaya Ramachandran*
Dept. of Computer Science,
University of Texas at Austin
Austin, TX, USA
vlr@cs.utexas.edu

Valerie King†
Dept. of Computer Science,
University of Victoria
Victoria, BC, Canada
val@uvic.ca

Matteo Pontecorvi
Nokia Bell Labs
Nozay, Île-de-France, France
matteo.pontecorvi@nokia.com

ABSTRACT

We present a deterministic distributed algorithm to compute all-pairs shortest paths (APSP) in an edge-weighted directed or undirected graph. Our algorithm runs in $\tilde{O}(n^{3/2})$ rounds in the Congest model, where n is the number of nodes in the graph. This is the first $o(n^2)$ rounds deterministic distributed algorithm for the weighted APSP problem. Our algorithm is fairly simple and incorporates a deterministic distributed algorithm we develop for computing a 'blocker set' [14], which has been used earlier in sequential dynamic computation of APSP.

CCS CONCEPTS

• **Theory of computation → Shortest paths; Distributed algorithms;**

KEYWORDS

Shortest paths; Distributed Algorithms; Blocker set; CONGEST Model

ACM Reference Format:
Udit Agarwal, Vijaya Ramachandran, Valerie King, and Matteo Pontecorvi. 2018. A Deterministic Distributed Algorithm for Exact Weighted All-Pairs Shortest Paths in $\tilde{O}(n^{3/2})$ Rounds. In *PODC '18: ACM Symposium on Principles of Distributed Computing, July 23–27, 2018, Egham, United Kingdom.* ACM, New York, NY, USA, 7 pages. https://doi.org/10.1145/3212734.3212773

*This work was supported by NSF Grant CCF-1320675.
†This work was supported by an NSERC Discovery Grant and the Simons Institute.

ACM ISBN 978-1-4503-5795-1/18/07...$15.00
https://doi.org/10.1145/3212734.3212773

1 INTRODUCTION

The design of distributed algorithms for various network (or graph) problems such as shortest paths [3, 13, 17, 18] and minimum spanning tree [7, 8, 15, 21] is a well-studied area of research. The most widely considered model for studying distributed algorithms is the Congest model [19] (also see [3, 9, 12, 13, 17, 18]), described in more detail below. In this paper we consider the problem of computing all pairs shortest paths (APSP) in a weighted directed (or undirected) graph in this model.

The problem of computing all pairs shortest paths (APSP) in distributed networks is a very fundamental problem, and there has been a considerable line of work for the Congest model as described below in Section 1.2. However, for a weighted graph no deterministic algorithm was known in this model other than a trivial method that runs in n^2 rounds. In this paper we present the first algorithm for this problem in the Congest model that computes weighted APSP deterministically in less than n^2 rounds. Our algorithm computes APSP deterministically in $O(n^{3/2} \cdot \sqrt{\log n})$ rounds in this model in both directed and undirected graphs.

Our distributed APSP algorithm is quite simple and we give an overview in Section 2. It uses the notion of a blocker set introduced by King [14] in the context of sequential fully dynamic APSP computation. Our deterministic distributed algorithm for computing a blocker set is the most nontrivial component of our algorithm, and is described in Section 3.

1.1 The Congest Model

In the Congest model [19], there are n independent processors interconnected in a network. We refer to these processors as nodes. These nodes are connected in the network by bounded-bandwidth links which we refer to as edges. The network is modeled by a graph $G = (V, E)$ where V is the set of processors and E is the set of edges or links between these processors. Here $|V| = n$ and $|E| = m$.

Each node is assigned a unique ID between 1 and $poly(n)$ and has infinite computational power. Each node has limited topological knowledge and only knows about its incident edges. For the weighted APSP problem we consider, each edge has a positive integer weight bounded by $poly(n)$. Also if the edges are directed, the corresponding communication channels are bidirectional and hence the communication network can be represented by the underlying undirected graph U_G of G (this model is also used in [10, 13, 22]).

The computation proceeds in rounds. In each round each processor can send a message of size $O(\log n)$ along edges incident to it, and it receives the messages sent to it in the previous round. The model allows a node to send different message along different edges though we do not need this feature in our algorithm. The performance of an algorithm in the CONGEST model is measured by its round complexity, which is the worst-case number of rounds of distributed communication. Hence the goal is to minimize the round complexity of an algorithm.

1.2 Prior Work

Unweighted APSP. For APSP in unweighted undirected graphs, $O(n)$-round algorithms were given independently in [12, 20]. An improved $n + O(D)$-round algorithm was then given in [17], where D is the diameter of the undirected graph. Although this latter result was claimed only for undirected graphs, the algorithm in [17] is also a correct $O(n)$-round APSP algorithm for directed unweighted graphs. The message complexity of directed unweighted APSP was reduced to $mn + O(m)$ in a recent algorithm [22] that runs in $\min\{2n, n + O(D)\}$rounds (where D is now the directed diameter of the graph). A lower bound of $\Omega(n/\log n)$ for the number of rounds needed to compute the diameter of the graph in the CONGEST model is given in [6].

Weighted APSP. While unweighted APSP is well-understood in the CONGEST model much remains to be done in the weighted case. For deterministic algorithms, weighted SSSP for a single source can be computed in n rounds using the classic Bellman-Ford algorithm [2, 5], and this leads to a simple deterministic weighted APSP algorithm that runs in $O(n^2)$ rounds. Nothing better was known for the number of rounds for deterministic weighted APSP until our current results.

Exact Randomized APSP Algorithms. Even with randomization, nothing better than n^2 rounds was known for exact weighted APSP until recently, when Elkin [3] gave a randomized weighted APSP algorithm that runs in $\tilde{O}(n^{5/3})$ rounds and this was further improved to $\tilde{O}(n^{5/4})$ rounds in Huang et al. [13]. Both of these results hold with high probability in n.

Deterministic Approximation Algorithms for APSP. There are deterministic algorithms for approximating weighted all pairs shortest path problem, and these run in $\tilde{O}(n)$ rounds for both directed [16] and undirected graphs [4, 11, 16].

2 OVERVIEW OF THE APSP ALGORITHM

Let $G = (V, E)$ be an edge-weighted graph (directed or undirected) with weight function w and with $|V| = n$ and $|E| = m$. The CONGEST model assumes that every message is of $O(\log n)$-bit size, which restricts $w(e)$ to be an $O(\log n)$ size integer value. However, outside of this restriction imposed by the CONGEST model, our algorithm works for arbitrary edge-weights (even negative edge-weights as long as there is no negative-weight cycle). Given a path p we will use *weight* or *distance* to denote the sum of the weights of the edges on the path and *length* (or sometimes *hops*) to denote the number of edges on the path. We denote the shortest path distance from a vertex x to a vertex y in G by $\delta(x, y)$. In the following we will assume that G is directed, but the same algorithm works for undirected graphs as well.

An h-hop SSSP tree for G rooted at a vertex r is a tree of height h where the weight of the path from r to a vertex v in the tree is the shortest path distance in G among all paths that have at most h edges. In the case of multiple paths with the same distance from r to v we assume that v chooses the parent vertex with minimum id as its parent in the h-hop SSSP tree. We denote the hop-length of the path from root r to v in this tree by $h_r(v)$. We will use $h = \sqrt{n \cdot \log n}$ in our algorithm.

Our overall APSP algorithm is given in Algorithm 1. In Step 1 an h-hop SSSP tree and the associated SSSP distances, $\delta_h(r, v)$, are computed at vertex v for each root $r \in V$.

Step 2 computes a *blocker set* Q of $q = O((n \log n)/h)$ nodes for the collection of h-hop SSSP trees constructed in Step 1. This step is described in detail in the next section, where we describe a distributed implementation of King's sequential method [14]. Our method computes the blocker set Q in $O(nh + (n^2 \log n)/h)$ rounds. We now give the definition of a blocker set for a collection of rooted h-hop trees.

Definition 2.1 (**Blocker Set** *[14]).* Let H be a collection of rooted h-hop trees in a graph $G = (V, E)$. A set $Q \subseteq V$ is a *blocker set* for H if every root to leaf path of length h in every tree in H contains a vertex in Q. Each vertex in Q is called a *blocker vertex* for H.

In Step 3 of Algorithm 1 we compute $\delta(c, v)$ for each $c \in Q$ and for all $v \in V$. In Step 4 each blocker vertex c broadcasts all of the $\delta_h(v, c)$ values it computed in Step 1. Finally, in Step 5 each node v computes $\delta(u, v)$ for each $u \in V$ using the values it computed or received in the earlier steps. More specifically, v computes $\delta(u, v)$ as:

$$\delta(u, v) = \min \left\{ \delta_h(u, v), \min_{c \in Q} (\delta_h(u, c) + \delta(c, v)) \right\} \quad (1)$$

LEMMA 2.2. *The $\delta(u, v)$ values computed at each v in Step 5 of Algorithm 1 are the correct shortest path distances.*

PROOF. Fix vertices u, v and consider a shortest path p from u to v. If p has at most h edges then $w(p) = \delta_h(u, v)$ and this value is directly computed at v in Step 1. Otherwise by the property of the blocker set Q we know that there is a vertex $c \in Q$ which lies along p within the h-hop SSSP tree rooted at u that is constructed in Step 1. Let p_1 be the portion of p from u to c and let p_2 be the portion from c to v. So $w(p_1) = \delta_h(u, c)$, $w(p_2) = \delta(c, v)$ and $w(p) = w(p_1) + w(p_2)$.

The value $\delta_h(u, c)$ is received by v in the broadcast step for center c in Step 4. The value $\delta(c, v)$ is computed at v when SSSP with root c is computed in Step 3. Hence v has the information needed to compute $\delta(u, v)$ in Step 5 for each u using Equation 1. □

We now bound the number of rounds needed for each step in Algorithm 1 (other than Step 2). For this we first state bounds for some simple primitives that will be used to execute these steps.

LEMMA 2.3. *Given a source $s \in V$, using the Bellman-Ford algorithm:*

Algorithm 1 Main Algorithm

1: **for each** $v \in V$ in sequence: compute an h-hop SSSP rooted at v by computing at each $x \in V$ the h-hop shortest path distances $\delta_h(v, x)$, the parent pointer in the SSSP tree, and the hop-length $h_v(x)$ in T_v.
2: Compute a blocker set Q of size $\Theta((n \log n)/h)$ for the h-hop SSSP trees computed in Step 1 using Algorithm 2.
3: **for each** $c \in Q$ in sequence: compute SSSP with root c and $\delta(c, v)$ at each $v \in V$
4: **for each** $c \in Q$ in sequence: broadcast to all other nodes c's ID and the $\delta_h(v, c)$ values it computed for each v in Step 1.
5: **Local step at each node:** At each v compute $\delta(u, v)$ values for each $u \in V$ by using equation 1 with $\delta_h(u, v)$ from Step 1, the $\delta(c, v)$ values from Step 3, and the $\delta_h(u, c)$ values received in Step 4.

(a) *the shortest path distance $\delta(s, v)$ can be computed at each $v \in V$ in n rounds.*
(b) *the h-hop shortest path distance $\delta_h(s, v)$, the hop length $h_s(v)$, and parent pointer in the h-hop SSSP tree rooted at s can be computed at each $v \in V$ in h rounds.*

LEMMA 2.4. *A node v can broadcast k local values to all other nodes reachable from it deterministically in $O(n + k)$ rounds.*

PROOF. We construct a BFS tree rooted at v in at most n rounds and then we pipeline the broadcast of the k values. The root v sends the i-th value to all its children in round i for $1 \le i \le k$. In a general round, each node x that received a value in the previous round sends that value to all its children. It is readily seen that the i-th value reaches all nodes at hop-length d from v in the BFS tree in round $i + d - 1$, and this is the only value that node x receives in this round. □

LEMMA 2.5. *All $v \in V$ can broadcast a local value to every other node they can reach in $O(n)$ rounds deterministically.*

PROOF. This broadcast can be done in $O(n)$ rounds in many ways, for example by piggy-backing on an $O(n)$ round unweighted APSP algorithm [17, 22] (and also [12, 20] for undirected graphs) where now each message contains the value sent by source s in addition to the current shortest path distance estimate for source s. □

LEMMA 2.6. *Algorithm 1 runs in $O(n \cdot h + (n^2/h) \cdot \log n)$ rounds assuming Step 2 can be implemented to run within this bound.*

PROOF. Let the size of the blocker set be $q = \frac{n}{h} \cdot \log n$. Using part (b) of Lemma 2.3, Step 1 can be computed in $O(n \cdot h)$ rounds by computing the n h-hop SSSP trees in sequence. Step 3 can be computed in $O(n \cdot q) = O((n^2/h) \cdot \log n)$ rounds by part (a) of Lemma 2.3. Step 4 can be computed in $O(n \cdot q) = O((n^2/h) \cdot \log n)$ rounds by Lemma 2.4 (using $k = n$). Finally, Step 5 involves only local computation and no communication. This establishes the lemma. □

In the next section we give a deterministic algorithm to compute Step 2 in $O(n \cdot h + (n^2/h) \cdot \log n)$ rounds, which leads to our main theorem (by using $h = \sqrt{n \cdot \log n}$).

THEOREM 2.7. *Algorithm 1 is a deterministic distributed algorithm for weighted APSP in directed or undirected graphs that runs in $O(n^{3/2} \cdot \sqrt{\log n})$ rounds in the CONGEST model.*

3 COMPUTING A BLOCKER SET DETERMINISTICALLY

The simplest method to find a blocker set is to chose the vertices randomly. An early use of this method for path problems in graphs was in Ullman and Yannakakis [23] where a random set of $O(\sqrt{n} \cdot \log n)$ distinguished nodes was picked. It is readily seen that some vertex in this set will intersect any path of $O(\sqrt{n})$ vertices in the graph (and so this set would serve as a blocker set of size $O((n \log n)/h)$for our algorithm if $h = \sqrt{n}$). Using this observation an improved randomized parallel algorithm (in the PRAM model) was given in [23] to compute the transitive closure. Since then this method of using random sampling to choose a suitable blocker set has been used extensively in parallel and dynamic computation of transitive closure and shortest paths, and more recently, in distributed computation of APSP [13].

It is not clear if the above simple randomized strategy can be derandomized in its full generality. However, for our purposes a blocker set only needs to intersect all paths in the set of hop trees we construct in Step 1 of Algorithm 1. For this, a deterministic sequential algorithm for computing a blocker set was given in King [14] in order to compute fully dynamic APSP. This algorithm computes a blocker set of size $O((n/h) \ln p)$ for a collection F of h-hop trees with a total of p leaves across all trees (and hence p root to leaf paths) in an n-node graph. In our setting $p \le n^2$ since we have n trees and each tree could have up to n leaves.

King's sequential blocker set algorithm uses the following simple observation: Given a collection of p paths each with exactly h nodes from an underlying set V of n nodes, there must exist a vertex that is contained in at least ph/n paths. The algorithm adds one such vertex v to the blocker set, removes all paths that are covered by this vertex and repeats this process until no path remains in the collection. The number of paths is reduced from p to at most $(1 - h/n) \cdot p$ when the blocker vertex v is removed, hence after $O((n/h) \ln p)$ removals of vertices, all paths are removed. Since p is at most n^2 the size of the blocker set is $O((n \log n)/h)$. King's sequential algorithm for finding a blocker set runs in $O(n^2 \log n)$ deterministic time (a correction to the bound given in King [14]).

We now describe our distributed algorithm to compute a blocker set. As in King [14], for each vertex v in a tree T_x in the collection of trees H we define:

- $score_x(v)$ is the number of leaves at depth h in T_x that are in the subtree rooted at v in T_x;
- $score(v) = \sum_x score_x(v)$.

Thus, $score(v)$ is the number of root-to-leaf paths of length h in the collection of trees H that contain vertex v. Initially, our distributed algorithm computes all $score_x(v)$ and $score(v)$ for all vertices $v \in V$

Algorithm 2 COMPUTE-BLOCKER

Input: set H of all h-hop trees T_x; Output: set Q

1: **Initialization [lines 2-6]:**
2: Run Algorithm 3 to compute scores for all $v \in V$
3: For each T_x compute the ancestors of each vertex v in T_x in $Anc_x(v)$ using Algorithm 4
4: **for** each $v \in V$ **do**
5:     **Local Step:** $score(v) \leftarrow \sum_{x \in V} score_x(v)$
6:     broadcast $score(v)$ to all nodes in V (using Lemma 2.5)
7: **Add blocker vertices to blocker set Q [lines 8-12]:**
8: **while** there is a node c with $score(c) > 0$ **do**
9:     **for** each $v \in V$ **do**
10:         **Local Step:** select the node c with max score as next vertex in Q
11:         Run Algorithms 5 and 6 to update $score_x(v)$ for each $x \in V$ and $score(v)$
12:         broadcast $score(v)$ to all nodes in V and receive $score(x)$ from all other nodes x

and all h-hop trees T_x in $O(n \cdot h)$ rounds using Algorithm 3. Then through an all-to-all broadcast of $score(v)$ to all other nodes for all v, all nodes identify the vertex c with maximum score as the next blocker vertex to be removed from the trees and added to the blocker set Q. (In case there are multiple vertices with the maximum score the algorithm chooses the vertex of minimum id having this maximum score. This ensures that all vertices will locally choose the same vertex as the next blocker vertex once they have received the scores of all vertices.) We repeat this process until all scores are zeroed out. By the discussion above (and as observed in [14]) we will identify all the vertices in Q in $O((n \cdot \log n)/h)$ repeats of this process.

What remains is to obtain an $O(n)$ round procedure to update the *score* and $score_x$ values at all nodes each time a vertex c is removed so that we have the correct values at each node for each tree when the leaves covered by c are removed from the tree.

If a vertex v is a descendant of the removed vertex c in T_x then all paths in T_x that pass through v are removed when c is removed and hence $score_x(v)$ needs to go down to zero for each such tree T_x where v is a descendant of the chosen blocker node c. In order to faciliate an $O(n)$-round computation of these updated $score_x$ values in each tree at all nodes that are descendants of c, we initially precompute at every node v a list $Anc_x(v)$ all of its ancestors in each tree T_x. This is computed in $O(n \cdot h)$ rounds using Algorithm 4. Thereafter, each time a new blocker vertex c is selected to be removed from the trees and added to Q, it is a local computation at each node v to determine which of the $Anc_x(v)$ sets at v contain c and to zero out $score_x(v)$ for each such x.

The other type of vertices whose scores change after a vertex c is removed are the ancestors of c in each tree. If v is an ancestor of c in T_x then after c is removed $score_x(v)$ needs to be reduced by $score_x(c)$ (i.e., c's score before it was removed and added to Q) since these paths no longer need to be covered by v. For these ancestor updates we give an $O(n)$-round algorithm that runs after the addition of each new blocker node to Q and correctly updates the scores for these ancestors in every tree (Algorithm 6). These algorithms together give the overall deterministic algorithm (Algorithm 2) for the computation of the blocker set Q in $O(n \cdot h + (n^2 \log n)/h)$ rounds.

We now give the details of our algorithms. Recall that we use the Bellman-Ford algorithm for Step 1 in Algorithm 1. Hence after that step, for each tree T_s rooted at s every node v in the tree knows its shortest path distance from s, $\delta(s, v)$, its hop length $h_s(v)$ and its parent node in T_s. We also determine for each node its children in T_s. We can compute this in one round for each T_s by have each node send its child status to its parent. Thus after n rounds all nodes know all their children in every tree T_s.

3.1 The Blocker Set Algorithm

Algorithm 2 gives our distributed deterministic method to compute a blocker set. It uses a collection of helper algorithms that are described in the next section. This blocker set algorithm is at the heart of our main algorithm (Algorithm 1, Step 2) for computing the exact weighted APSP.

Step 2 of Algorithm 2 executes Algorithm 3 to compute all the initial scores at all nodes v. Step 3 involves running Algorithm 4 for pre-computing ancestors of each node in every T_x. Step 5 is a local computation (no communication) where all nodes v compute their total score by summing up the scores for all trees T_x to which they belong. And in Step 6, each node v broadcasts its score value to all other nodes.

The while loop in Steps 8-12 of Algorithm 2 runs as long as there is a node with positive score. In Step 10, the node with maximum score is selected as the vertex c to be added to Q (and if there are multiple nodes with the maximum score, then among them the node with the minimum ID is selected, so that the same node is selected locally at every vertex). In Step 11, after blocker vertex c is selected, each node v checks whether it is a descendant of c in each T_x and if so update its score for that tree using Algorithm 5. This is followed by an execution of Algorithm 6 which updates the scores at each node v for each tree T_x in which v is an ancestor of c. Then in Step 12, all the nodes broadcast their score to all other nodes so that they can all select the next vertex to be added to Q. This leads to the following lemma, assuming the results shown in the next section.

LEMMA 3.1. *Algorithm 2 correctly computes the blocker set Q in $O(n \cdot h + n \cdot |Q|)$ rounds.*

Algorithm 3 Compute Initial scores for a node v in T_x

1: **Initialization [Local Step]:** **if** $h_x(v) = h$ **then** $score_x(v) \leftarrow 1$ **else** $score_x(v) \leftarrow 0$
2: **In round** $r > 0$:
3: **send:** **if** $r = h - h_x(v) + 1$ **then** send $\langle score_x(v) \rangle$ to $parent_x(v)$

4: **receive [lines 5-9]:**
5: **if** $r = h - h_x(v)$ **then**
6: let I be the set of incoming messages to v
7: **for each** $M \in I$ **do**
8: let $M = \langle score^- \rangle$ and let the sender be w
9: **if** w is a child of v in T_x **then** $score_x(v) \leftarrow score_x(v) + score^-$

Proof. Step 2 runs in $O(n \cdot h)$ rounds (by Lemma 3.2) and so does Step 3 (see Lemma 3.3 below). Step 5 is a local computation and the broadcast in Step 6 runs in $O(n)$ rounds by Lemma 2.5.

The while loop starting in Step 8 runs for $|Q|$ iterations since a new blocker vertex is added to Q in each iteration. In each iteration, Step 10 is a local computation as is the execution of Algorithm 5 in Step 11. Algorithm 6 in Step 11 runs in $O(n)$ rounds (Lemma 3.6). The all-to-all broadcast in Step 12 is the same as the initial all-to-all broadcast in Step 6 and runs in $O(n)$ rounds. Hence each iteration of the while loop runs in $O(n)$ rounds giving the desired bound. □

3.2 Algorithms for Computing and Updating Scores

In this section we give the details of our algorithms for computing initial scores (Algorithm 3) and for updating these scores values once a blocker vertex c is selected and added to the blocker set Q (Algorithms 4-6).

Algorithm 3 gives the procedure for computing the initial scores for a node v in a tree T_x. In Step 1 each leaf node at depth h initializes its score for T_x to 1 and all other nodes set their initial score to 0. In a general round $r > 0$, nodes with $h_x(v) = h + 1 - r$ send out their scores to their parents and nodes with $h_x(v) = h - r$ will receive all the scores from its children in T_x and set its score equal to the sum of these received scores (Steps 5-9).

Lemma 3.2. *Algorithm 3 computes the initial scores for every node v in T_x in $O(h)$ rounds.*

Proof. The leaves at depth h correctly initialize their score to 1 locally in Step 1. Since we only consider paths of length h from the root x to a leaf, it is readily seen that a node v that is $h_x(v)$ hops away from x in T_x will receive scores from its children in round $h - h_x(v)$ and thus will have the correct $score_x(v)$ value to send in Step 3. □

For every $x \in V$, every node $v \in T_x$ will run this algorithm to compute their score in T_x. Since every run of Algorithm 3 for a given x takes h rounds, all the initial scores can be computed in $O(n \cdot h)$ rounds.

Algorithm 4 describes our algorithm for precomputing the ancestors of each node v in a tree T_x of height h. In round 1, every node v sends its ID to its children in T_x as described in Step 5. And in a general round r, v sends the ID of the ancestor that it received in round $r - 1$ (Steps 7-8). If a node v receives the ID of an ancestor y, then it immediately adds it to its ancestor set, $Anc_x(v)$ (Steps 10-11).

Algorithm 4 Ancestors (v, x): Algorithm for computing ancestors of node v in T_x at round r

1: **Initialization [Local Step]:** $Anc_x(v) \leftarrow \phi$
2: **In round** $r > 0$:
3: **send [lines 4-8]:**
4: **if** $r = 1$ **then**
5: send $\langle v \rangle$ to v's children in T_x
6: **else**
7: let $\langle y \rangle$ be the message v received in round $r - 1$
8: send $\langle y \rangle$ to v's children in T_x
9: **receive [lines 10-11]:**
10: let $\langle y \rangle$ be the message v received in this round
11: add y to $Anc_x(v)$

Algorithm 5 Algorithm for updating scores at v when v is a descendant of new blocker node c

Input: blocker vertex c added to Q.
There is no communication in this algorithm, it is entirely a **local computation** at v.
1: **if** $score(v) \neq 0$ **then**
2: **for each** $x \in V$ **do**
3: **if** $c \in Anc_x(v)$ **then**
4: $score(v) \leftarrow score(v) - score_x(v)$
5: $score_x(v) \leftarrow 0$

Lemma 3.3. *For a tree T_x of height h rooted at vertex x, Algorithm 4 correctly computes the set of ancestors for all nodes v in T_x in $O(h)$ rounds.*

Proof. We show that all nodes v correctly computes all their ancestors in T_x in the set $Anc_x(v)$ using induction on round r. We show that by round r, every node v has added all its ancestors that are at most r hops away from v.

If $r = 1$, then v's parent in T_x (say y) would have send out its *ID* to v in Step 5 and v would have added it to $Anc_x(v)$ in Step 11.

Assume that every node v has already added all ancestors in the set $Anc_x(v)$ that are at most $r - 1$ hops away from v.

Let u be the ancestor of v in T_x that is exactly r hops away from v. Then by induction, $u \in Anc_x(y)$ since u is exactly $r - 1$ hops away from y and thus y must have send u's *ID* to v in round r in Step 8 and hence v would have added u to its set $Anc_x(v)$ in round r in Step 11. □

Once we have pre-computed the $Anc_x(v)$ sets for all vertices v and all trees T_x using Algorithm 4, updating the scores at each node for all trees in which it is a descendant of the newly chosen blocker node c becomes a purely local computation. Algorithm 5 describes the algorithm at node v that updates its scores after a vertex c is added as a blocker node to Q. At node v for each given T_x, v checks if $c \in Anc_x(v)$ and if so update its score values in Steps 4-5.

Lemma 3.4. *Given a blocker vertex c, Algorithm 5 correctly updates the scores of all nodes v such that v is a descendant of c in some tree T_x.*

Algorithm 6 Pipelined Algorithm for updating scores at v for all trees T_x in which v is an ancestor of newly chosen blocker node c

Input: current blocker set Q, newly chosen blocker node c

1: **Send [lines 2-3]: (only for** c**)**
2: **Local Step at** c: create a list $list_c$ and **for each** $x \in V$ **do** add an entry $Z = \langle x, score_x(c)\rangle$ to $list_c$ if $score_x(c) \neq 0$; then set $score_x(c)$ to 0 for each $x \in V$ and set $score(c)$ to 0
3: **Round** i: let $Z = \langle x, score_x(c)\rangle$ be the i-th entry in $list_c$; send $\langle Z\rangle$ to c's parent in T_x
4: **In round** $r > 0$: **(for vertices** $v \in V - Q - \{c\}$**)**
5: **send [lines 6-8]:**
6: **if** v received a message in round $r - 1$ **then**
7:     let that message be $\langle Z\rangle = \langle x, score_x(c)\rangle$.
8:     **if** $v \neq x$ **then** send $\langle Z\rangle$ to v's parent in T_x
9: **receive [lines 10-11]:**
10: **if** v receives a message M of the form $\langle x, score_x(c)\rangle$ **then**
11:     $score_x(v) \leftarrow score_x(v) - score_x(c)$; $score(v) \leftarrow score(v) - score_x(c)$

Proof. Fix a vertex v and a tree T_x such that v is a descendant of c in T_x. By Lemma 3.3 $c \in Anc_x(v)$, and thus v will correctly update its score values in Steps 4-5. □

We now move to the last remaining part of the blocker set algorithm: our method to correctly update scores at ancestors of the newly chosen blocker node c in each T_x. Recall that if v is an ancestor of c in T_x we need to subtract $score_x(c)$ from $score_x(v)$. Here, in contrast to Algorithms 4 and 5 for nodes that are descendants of c in a tree, we do not precompute anything. Instead we give an $O(n)$-round method in Algorithm 6 to correctly update scores for each vertex for all trees in which that vertex is an ancestor of c.

Before we describe Algorithm 6 we establish the following lemma, which is key to our $O(n)$-round method.

Lemma 3.5. *Fix a vertex c. For each root vertex $x \in V - \{c\}$, let $\pi_{x,c}$ be the path from x to c in the h-hop SSSP tree T_x. Let $T = \cup_{x \in V-\{c\}} \{e \mid e$ lies on $\pi_{x,c}\}$, i.e., T is the set of edges that lie on some $\pi_{x,c}$. Then T is an in-tree rooted at c.*

Proof. If not, there exists some $x, y \in V - \{c\}$ such that $\pi_{x,c}$ and $\pi_{y,c}$ coincide first at some vertex z and the subpaths in $\pi_{x,c}$ and $\pi_{y,c}$ from z to c are different.

Consider the first vertex z' at which these two paths coincide after diverging from z (such a vertex exists since the two paths meet at c). Let the subpath from z to z' in $\pi_{x,c}$ be $\pi^1_{z,z'}$ and the corresponding subpath in $\pi_{y,c}$ be $\pi^2_{z,z'}$. Similarly let $\pi_{x,z}$ be the subpath of $\pi_{x,c}$ from x to z and let $\pi_{y,z}$ be the subpath of $\pi_{y,c}$ from y to z.

Clearly both $\pi^1_{z,z'}$ and $\pi^2_{z,z'}$ have equal weight (otherwise one of $\pi_{x,c}$ or $\pi_{y,c}$ cannot be a shortest path). Thus the path $\pi_{x,z} \circ \pi^2_{z,z'}$ is also a shortest path.

Let (a, z') be the last edge on the path $\pi^1_{z,z'}$ and (b, z') be the last edge on the path $\pi^2_{z,z'}$. Nodes a and b must be different by our choice of vertex z'. Since the path $\pi_{x,z'}$ has (a, z') as the last edge and we break ties using the IDs of the vertices, hence $ID(a) < ID(b)$. But then the shortest path $\pi_{y,z'}$ must also have chosen (a, z') as the last edge and hence $\pi_{y,z} \circ \pi^1_{z,z'}$ must be the subpath of path $\pi_{y,c}$, resulting in a contradiction. □

Lemma 3.5 allows us to re-cast the task for ancestor nodes to the following (where we use the notation in the statement of Lemma 3.5): the new blocker node c needs to send $score_x(c)$ to all nodes on $\pi_{x,c}$ for each tree T_x. Recall that in the Congest model for directed graphs the graph edges are bi-directional. Hence this task can be accomplished by having c send out $score_x(c)$ for each tree T_x (other than T_c) in $n - 1$ rounds, one score per round (in no particular order) along the parent edge for T_x. Each message $\langle x, score_x(c)\rangle$ will move along edges in $\pi_{x,c}$ (in reverse order) along parent edges in T_x from c to x. Consider any node v. In general it will be an ancestor of c in some subset of the $n - 1$ trees T_x. But the characterization in Lemma 3.5 establishes that the incoming edge to v in all of these trees is the same edge (u, v) and this is the unique edge on the path from c to v in tree T (T is defined in the statement of Lemma 3.5). In fact, the messages for all of the trees in which v is an ancestor of c will traverse exactly the same path from c to v. Hence, for the messages sent out by c for the different trees in $n - 1$ different rounds (one for each tree other than T_c), if each vertex simply forwards any message $\langle x, score_x(c)\rangle$ it receives to its parent in tree T_x all messages will be pipelined to all ancestors in $n - 1 + h$ rounds. This is what is done in Algorithm 6, whose steps we describe below, for completeness.

Step 2 of Algorithm 6 is local computation at the new blocker vertex c where for each T_x to which c belongs, c adds an entry $\langle x, score_x(c)\rangle$ to a local list $list_c$. In round i, c sends the i-th entry in its list, say $\langle y, score_y(c)\rangle$, to its parent in T_y. For node v other than c, in a general round $r > 0$, if v receives a message for some $x \in V$ it updates its score value for x (Steps 10-11) and then forwards this message to its parent in T_x in round $r + 1$ (Step 6-8).

Lemma 3.6. *Given a new blocker vertex c, Algorithm 6 correctly updates the scores of all nodes v in every tree T_x in which v is an ancestor of c in $O(n + h)$ rounds.*

Proof. Correctness of Algorithm 6 was argued above. For the number of rounds, c sends out it last message in round $n - 1$, and if $\pi_{v,c}$ has length k then v receives all messages sent to it by round $n - 1 + k$. Since we only have h-hop trees $k \leq h$ for all nodes, and the lemma follows. □

4 CONCLUSION

We have presented a new distributed algorithm for the exact computation of weighted all pairs shortest paths in both directed and undirected graphs. This algorithm runs in $O(n^{3/2} \cdot \sqrt{\log n})$ rounds and is the first $o(n^2)$-round deterministic algorithm for this problem in the CONGEST model. At the heart of our algorithm is a deterministic algorithm for computing blocker set. Our blocker set construction may have applications in other distributed algorithms that need to identify a relatively small set of vertices that intersect all paths in a set of paths with the same (relatively long) length.

The main open question left by our work is to improve the bound on the number of rounds for deterministic weighted APSP. In the unweighted case APSP can be computed in $O(n)$ rounds [12, 17, 20, 22], and weighted APSP can be computed in $\tilde{O}(n^{5/4})$ rounds [13] w.h.p. with randomization. In this paper we give the first $o(n^2)$ rounds deterministic algorithm for weighted APSP. Also very recently in [1], the first two authors presented a new pipelined algorithm for Step 1 of our Algorithm 1 that runs in $O(n\sqrt{h})$ rounds (improved from $O(nh)$ that we have here). This, together with some changes to the blocker set algorithm in Step 2, gives an $\tilde{O}(n^{4/3})$ rounds deterministic algorithm for APSP in the Congest model. This leaves open the question of whether we can match the current randomized bound with a deterministic algorithm, and whether we can improve the bound for the number of rounds to below $n^{5/4}$ either deterministic or randomized.

REFERENCES

[1] Udit Agarwal and Vijaya Ramachandran. 2018. A Faster Deterministic Distributed Algorithm for Weighted APSP Through Pipelining. (2018). Manuscript.

[2] Richard Bellman. 1958. On a routing problem. *Quarterly of applied mathematics* 16, 1 (1958), 87–90.

[3] Michael Elkin. 2017. Distributed exact shortest paths in sublinear time. In *Proc. STOC*. ACM, 757–770.

[4] Michael Elkin and Ofer Neiman. 2016. Hopsets with constant hopbound, and applications to approximate shortest paths. In *Proc. FOCS*. IEEE, 128–137.

[5] Lester R Ford Jr. 1956. *Network flow theory*. Technical Report. RAND CORP SANTA MONICA CA.

[6] Silvio Frischknecht, Stephan Holzer, and Roger Wattenhofer. 2012. Networks Cannot Compute Their Diameter in Sublinear Time. In *SODA '12*. 1150–1162.

[7] Robert G. Gallager, Pierre A. Humblet, and Philip M. Spira. 1983. A distributed algorithm for minimum-weight spanning trees. *ACM Trans. Prog. Lang. Syst.* 5, 1 (1983), 66–77.

[8] Juan A Garay, Shay Kutten, and David Peleg. 1998. A sublinear time distributed algorithm for minimum-weight spanning trees. *SIAM J. Comp.* 27, 1 (1998), 302–316.

[9] Mohsen Ghaffari. 2015. Near-optimal scheduling of distributed algorithms. In *Proc. PODC*. ACM, 3–12.

[10] Mohsen Ghaffari and Jason Li. 2017. Improved Distributed Algorithms for Exact Shortest Paths. *arXiv preprint arXiv:1712.09121* (2017).

[11] Monika Henzinger, Sebastian Krinninger, and Danupon Nanongkai. 2016. A deterministic almost-tight distributed algorithm for approximating single-source shortest paths. In *Proc. STOC*. ACM, 489–498.

[12] Stephan Holzer and Roger Wattenhofer. 2012. Optimal Distributed All Pairs Shortest Paths and Applications. In *PODC '12*. 355–364.

[13] Chien-Chung Huang, Danupon Na Nongkai, and Thatchaphol Saranurak. 2017. Distributed Exact Weighted All-Pairs Shortest Paths in $\tilde{O}(n^{5/4})$ Rounds. In *Proc. FOCS*. IEEE, 168–179.

[14] Valerie King. 1999. Fully dynamic algorithms for maintaining all-pairs shortest paths and transitive closure in digraphs. In *Proc. FOCS*. IEEE, 81–89.

[15] Shay Kutten and David Peleg. 1998. Fast distributed construction of smallk-dominating sets and applications. *J. Algorithms* 28, 1 (1998), 40–66.

[16] Christoph Lenzen and Boaz Patt-Shamir. 2015. Fast partial distance estimation and applications. In *Proc. PODC*. ACM, 153–162.

[17] Christoph Lenzen and David Peleg. 2013. Efficient distributed source detection with limited bandwidth. In *Proc. PODC*. ACM, 375–382.

[18] Danupon Nanongkai. 2014. Distributed approximation algorithms for weighted shortest paths. In *Proc. STOC*. ACM, 565–573.

[19] David Peleg. 2000. Distributed computing: A Locality-sensitive Approach. *SIAM Monographs on discrete mathematics and applications* 5 (2000).

[20] David Peleg, Liam Roditty, and Elad Tal. 2012. Distributed algorithms for network diameter and girth. In *Proc. ICALP*. Springer, 660–672.

[21] David Peleg and Vitaly Rubinovich. 1999. A near-tight lower bound on the time complexity of distributed mst construction. In *Proc. FOCS*. IEEE, 253–261.

[22] Matteo Pontecorvi and Vijaya Ramachandran. 2018. Distributed algorithms for directed betweenness centrality and all pairs shortest paths. *arXiv preprint arXiv:1805.08124* (2018).

[23] Jeffrey D Ullman and Mihalis Yannakakis. 1991. High-probability parallel transitive-closure algorithms. *SIAM J. Comp.* 20, 1 (1991), 100–125.

Near-Optimal Distributed Routing with Low Memory

Extended Abstract

Michael Elkin*
Department of Computer Science, Ben-Gurion University of the Negev
Beer Sheva, Israel
elkinm@cs.bgu.ac.il

Ofer Neiman†
Department of Computer Science, Ben-Gurion University of the Negev
Beer Sheva, Israel
neimano@cs.bgu.ac.il

ABSTRACT

Distributed *routing* is one of the most central and fundamental problems in the area of Distributed Graph Algorithms. It was extensively studied for almost thirty years. Nevertheless, the currently existing solutions for this problem require either prohibitively large construction (aka preprocessing) time, or prohibitively large memory usage either during the construction or during the routing phase, and suffer from suboptimal labels and tables' sizes.

We devise a distributed routing scheme that enjoys the best of all worlds. Specifically, its construction time and memory requirements during the construction phase are near-optimal, and so is also the tradeoff between the sizes of routing tables and labels on the one hand, and the stretch on the other.

On the way to this result, we also improve upon existing solutions for the distributed exact *tree* routing problem. Previous solutions require $\Omega(\sqrt{n})$ memory, and provide tables and labels of size $O(\log n)$ and $O(\log^2 n)$, respectively.

Our solution, on the other hand, requires just $O(\log n)$ memory, and has tables of size $O(1)$, and labels of size $O(\log n)$. These bounds match the bounds of the best-known centralized solution.

CCS CONCEPTS

• **Theory of computation** → **Routing and network design problems**; *Distributed algorithms*;

KEYWORDS

Compact Routing; CONGEST

ACM Reference Format:
Michael Elkin and Ofer Neiman. 2018. Near-Optimal Distributed Routing with Low Memory: Extended Abstract. In *PODC '18: ACM Symposium on Principles of Distributed Computing, July 23–27, 2018, Egham, United Kingdom.* ACM, New York, NY, USA, 10 pages. https://doi.org/10.1145/3212734.3212761

*This research was supported by the ISF grant No. (724/15).
†Supported in part by ISF grant 1817/17, and by BSF Grant 2015813.

PODC '18, July 23–27, 2018, Egham, United Kingdom

ACM ISBN 978-1-4503-5795-1/18/07...$15.00
https://doi.org/10.1145/3212734.3212761

1 INTRODUCTION

A network is represented as a weighted undirected n-vertex graph $G = (V, E)$. A routing scheme has two main phases: the preprocessing phase, and the routing phase. In the preprocessing phase, each vertex is assigned a routing table and a routing label.[1] In the routing phase, a vertex u gets a message M with a short header $Header(M)$ and with a destination label $Label(v)$ of a vertex v, and based on its routing table $Table(u)$, on $Label(v)$, and on $Header(M)$, the vertex u decides to which neighbor $x \in \Gamma(u)$ to forward the message M, and which header to attach to the message. The *stretch* of a routing scheme is the worst-case ratio between the length of a path on which a message M travels, and the graph distance between the message's origin and destination.

Due to its both theoretical and practical appeal, routing is a central problem in distributed graph algorithms [1, 3, 5–7, 13, 20, 23]. A landmark routing scheme was devised by Thorup and Zwick in [23]. For an integer $k \geq 1$, the stretch of their scheme is $4k - 5$, the tables are of size $\tilde{O}(n^{1/k})$, the labels are of size $O(k \log n)$, and the headers are of size $O(\log n)$. Chechik [5] improved this result, and devised a scheme with stretch $3.68k$, and other parameters like in [23].

An active thread of research [3, 4, 10, 14, 15] focuses on efficient implementation of the *preprocessing* phase of routing in the distributed CONGEST model (see Section 2 for a definition of the model), i.e., computing compact tables and short labels that allow for future low-stretch routing. This problem was raised in a seminal paper by Awerbuch, Bar-Noy, Linial and Peleg [3], who devised a routing scheme with stretch $2^{O(k)}$, overall memory requirement $\tilde{O}(n^{1+1/k})$,[2] individual memory requirement for a vertex v of $\tilde{O}(\deg(v) + n^{1/k})$, and construction time $\tilde{O}(n^{1+1/k})$ (in the CONGEST model). The "individual memory requirement" parameter encapsulates the routing tables and labels, and the memory used while computing the tables and labels.

Lenzen and Patt-Shamir [15] devised a distributed routing scheme (based on [23]) with stretch $4k - 3 + o(1)$, tables of size $\tilde{O}(n^{1/k})$, labels of size $O(k \log n)$, individual memory requirement of $\tilde{O}(n^{1/k})$, and construction time $\tilde{O}(S + n^{1/k})$, where S is the *shortest-path diameter* of the input graph G, i.e., the maximum number of hops in a shortest path between a pair of vertices in G. Though S is often

[1] In this paper we only consider *labeled* or *name-dependent* routing, in which vertices are assigned labels by the scheme. There is also a large body of literature on name-independent routing schemes; cf. [2] and the references therein. However, a lower bound [14] shows that constructing a name-independent routing scheme with stretch ρ requires $\tilde{\Omega}(n/\rho^2)$ time in the CONGEST model.

[2] $\tilde{O}(f(n))$-notation hides polylogarithmic in $f(n)$ factors.

much smaller than n, it is desirable to evaluate complexity measures of distributed algorithms in terms of n and D, where D is the *hop-diameter* of G, defined as the maximum distance between a pair of vertices u, v in the underlying unweighted graph of G. Typically, we have $D \ll S \ll n$, and it is always the case that $D \leq S \leq n$. (See Peleg's book [19] for a comprehensive discussion.)

Lenzen and Patt-Shamir [14] also devised a routing scheme with tables of size $\tilde{O}(n^{1/2+1/k})$, labels of size $O(\log n \cdot \log k)$, stretch at most $O(k \log k)$, and construction time of $\tilde{O}(n^{1/2+1/k} + D) \cdot \log \Lambda$ rounds, where Λ is the ratio between the largest to the smallest distance in the graph. They (based on [21]) also showed a lower bound of $\tilde{\Omega}(D + \sqrt{n})$ on the time required to construct a routing scheme. In a follow-up paper, [15] showed how to improve the stretch of the above scheme to $O(k)$. The main drawback of this result is the prohibitively large size of the routing tables. (The individual memory requirement is consequently prohibitively large as well.) They also exhibited a different tradeoff, that overcame the issue of large routing tables. They devised an algorithm that produced routing tables of size $\tilde{O}(n^{1/k})$, labels of size $O(k \log^2 n)$ and stretch $4k - 3 + o(1)$, albeit with sub-optimal running time $\tilde{O}(\min\{(nD)^{1/2} n^{1/k}, n^{2/3} + D\}) \cdot \log \Lambda$, and no guarantee on the individual memory requirement during the preprocessing phase.[3] In [10], the current authors improved the bounds of [14, 15]. In the current state-of-the-art scheme [10], the stretch is $4k - 5 + o(1)$, the tables and labels are of the same size as in [14, 15] (i.e., $\tilde{O}(n^{1/k})$ and $O(k \log^2 n)$, respectively), the construction time is $O((n^{1/2+1/k} + D) \cdot \min\{(\log n)^{O(k)}, 2^{\tilde{O}(\sqrt{\log n})}\} \cdot \log \Lambda$. (A similar, though slightly weaker, result was independently achieved by [17].) Still there is no meaningful guarantee on the individual memory requirement in the preprocessing phase. In the last three results the table size is larger by a factor of $\approx \log n$ than Thorup-Zwick's sequential construction (this is hidden by the $\tilde{O}$ notation). See Table 1 for a concise summary of existing bounds, and a comparison with our new results.

To summarize, all currently existing distributed routing algorithms with nearly-optimal running time $\approx D + n^{1/2+1/k}$ suffer from three issues. First, they provide no meaningful guarantee on individual memory requirement on vertices in the preprocessing phase; second, their tables and labels sizes are roughly $O(\log n)$ off from the respective tables and labels' sizes of Thorup-Zwick's sequential construction [23]; and third, their preprocessing time depends at least linearly on $\log \Lambda$.

We note that the quest to design routing schemes with small tables and labels is typically justified by inherent storage limitations of vertices that run the scheme. This justification is however inconsistent with allowing vertices to use a very large memory (much larger than the eventual size of routing tables and labels) during the preprocessing stage.

We devise an algorithm that addresses all these issues. Most importantly, the individual memory requirement in our algorithm is at most $\tilde{O}(n^{1/k})$, i.e., it is within polylogarithmic factor of the size of routing tables and labels (together), which is an obvious lower bound on the individual memory usage. Previous solutions used at least $\tilde{O}(n^{1/2})$ memory. In particular, for large k we can have polylogarithmic individual memory requirement and construction time $O((n^{1/2} + D) \cdot n^{\epsilon})$, for an arbitrarily small constant $\epsilon > 0$. We can also reduce the running time to $(n^{1/2+1/k} + D) \cdot \min\{(\log n)^{O(\max\{k, \log\log n\})}, 2^{\tilde{O}(\sqrt{\log n})}\}$, while the individual memory increases slightly to $\max\{\tilde{O}(n^{1/k}), 2^{\tilde{O}(\sqrt{\log n})}\}$.

The stretch of our scheme is $4k - 5 + o(1)$, i.e., almost matching the stretch $4k - 5$ of [23]. The sizes of tables and labels match the respective sizes of Thorup-Zwick's construction, i.e., they are $\tilde{O}(n^{1/k})$ and $O(k \log n)$, respectively. Note that as $1 \leq k = O(\log n)$, our label size is polynomially better than the previous bound $O(k \log^2 n)$. For constant k, the improvement is quadratic. In the opposite end of the spectrum, when $k = \log n$, our label size is $O(\log^2 n)$, instead of the previous $O(\log^3 n)$, but then our table size is polynomially better than the previous bound.

Finally, our construction time $(n^{\frac{1}{2}+\frac{1}{k}} + D) \cdot (\log n)^{O(\max\{k, \log\log n\})}$ is independent of Λ.[4]

Distributed Tree Routing: An important ingredient in the existing distributed routing schemes [10, 15, 17] for general graphs, and in our new routing scheme, is a distributed tree routing scheme. Thorup and Zwick [23] showed that with routing tables of size $O(1)$ and labels of size $O(\log n)$, one can have an *exact* (i.e., no stretch) tree routing. [10, 15] showed that in $\tilde{O}(D + \sqrt{n})$ time, one can construct exact tree routing with tables and labels of size $O(\log n)$ and $O(\log^2 n)$, respectively, i.e., there is an overhead of $\log n$ in both parameters with respect to Thorup-Zwick's centralized construction. In addition, both these solutions require $\tilde{O}(\sqrt{n})$ memory per vertex. (In this problem, one is given a graph G of hop-diameter D, and a spanning tree T of G. One then wishes to compute a tree routing scheme for T, using the fact that D is typically much smaller than the hop-diameter of T.) In this paper we significantly improve this result, and devise an $\tilde{O}(D + \sqrt{n})$-time algorithm that constructs tree-routing tables and labels of sizes that match the sequential construction of Thorup and Zwick, i.e., of sizes $O(1)$ (instead of $O(\log n)$) and $O(\log n)$ (instead of $O(\log^2 n)$), respectively. Even more importantly, our algorithm requires only $O(\log n)$ (instead of $\tilde{O}(\sqrt{n})$) individual memory in each vertex. See Table 2 for a concise comparison.

Reference	# of Rounds	Table size	Label size	Memory per vertex
[10, 15]	$\tilde{O}(D + \sqrt{n})$	$O(\log n)$	$O(\log^2 n)$	$\tilde{O}(\sqrt{n})$
[23]	NA	$O(1)$	$O(\log n)$	NA
This paper	$\tilde{O}(D + \sqrt{n})$	$O(1)$	$O(\log n)$	$O(\log n)$

Table 2: Comparison of distributed compact exact tree-routing schemes for graphs with n vertices and hop-diameter D.

1.1 Technical Overview

The basic approach in previously-existing distributed routing schemes [9, 14, 15, 17] that have construction time $\approx D + \sqrt{n}$ is to sample a set V' of $\approx \sqrt{n}$ vertices, and to build a "virtual" graph $G' = (V', E', \omega')$ on them. The edge set E' consists of pairs $u', v' \in V'$, such that

[3]The paper [15] claimed label size $O(k \log n)$, but in [16] it was communicated to us that the actual size is $O(k \log^2 n)$.

[4]We assume that edge weights can be sent in a single message, which we believe is a natural assumption. If one does care about the bit complexity, in our solution the construction time is proportional to $\log_n \log \Lambda$, as opposed to $\Omega(\log \Lambda)$ in all previous solutions. See Section 2 for further discussion.

Reference	Number of Rounds	Table size	Label size	Stretch	Memory per vertex
[3]	$O(n^{1+\frac{1}{k}})$	$\tilde{O}(n^{1/k})$	$O(k \log n)$	$2 \cdot 3^k - 1$	$\tilde{O}(\deg(v)+n^{\frac{1}{k}})$
[23]	NA	$\tilde{O}(n^{1/k})$	$O(k \log n)$	$4k - 5$	NA
[5]	NA	$\tilde{O}(n^{1/k})$	$O(k \log n)$	$3.68k$	NA
[14, 15]	$\tilde{O}(n^{\frac{1}{2}+\frac{1}{4k}} + D)$	$\tilde{O}(n^{\frac{1}{2}+\frac{1}{4k}})$	$O(\log n)$	$6k - 1 + o(1)$	$\tilde{O}(n^{\frac{1}{2}+\frac{1}{4k}})$
[15]	$\tilde{O}(S + n^{\frac{1}{k}})$	$\tilde{O}(n^{1/k})$	$O(k \log n)$	$4k - 3$	$O(n^{\frac{1}{k}} \cdot \log n)$
	$\tilde{O}(\min\{(nD)^{\frac{1}{2}} \cdot n^{\frac{1}{k}}, n^{\frac{2}{3}+\frac{2}{3k}} + D\})$	$\tilde{O}(n^{1/k})$	$O(k \log^2 n)$	$4k - 3 + o(1)$	$\tilde{O}(n^{\frac{1}{2}})$
[17]	$(n^{\frac{1}{2}+\frac{1}{k}} + D) \cdot 2^{\tilde{O}(\sqrt{\log n})}$	$\tilde{O}(n^{1/k})$	$O(k \log^2 n)$	$4k - 3 + o(1)$	$\tilde{O}(n^{\frac{1}{2}})$
[10]	$(n^{\frac{1}{2}+\frac{1}{k}} + D) \cdot \min\{(\log n)^{O(k)}, 2^{\tilde{O}(\sqrt{\log n})}\}$	$\tilde{O}(n^{1/k})$	$O(k \log^2 n)$	$4k - 5 + o(1)$	$\tilde{O}(n^{\frac{1}{2}})$
This paper	$(n^{\frac{1}{2}+\frac{1}{k}} + D) \cdot (\log n)^{O(\max\{k, \log\log n\})}$	$\tilde{O}(n^{1/k})$	$O(k \log n)$	$4k - 5 + o(1)$	$\tilde{O}(n^{\frac{1}{k}})$
	$(n^{\frac{1}{2}+\frac{1}{k}} + D) \cdot 2^{\tilde{O}(\sqrt{\log n})}$	$\tilde{O}(n^{1/k})$	$O(k \log n)$	$4k - 5 + o(1)$	$\max\{\tilde{O}(n^{1/k}), 2^{\tilde{O}(\sqrt{\log n})}\}$

Table 1: Comparison of distributed compact routing schemes for graphs with n vertices, hop-diameter D, and shortest path diameter S. By setting $k = \epsilon \log n / \log\log n$, for a small constant $\epsilon > 0$, in the penultimate line one obtains *polylogarithmic* memory requirement, and construction time $(n^{1/2} + D) \cdot n^{O(\epsilon)}$.

there exists a u'-v' path in G with $c\sqrt{n} \cdot \log n$ edges, for some fixed sufficiently large constant c. Such a path is said to be $c\sqrt{n} \cdot \log n$-bounded. The weight function $\omega'(u', v')$ is set to be the length of the shortest u'-v' $c\sqrt{n} \cdot \log n$-bounded path in G.

One then constructs a (β, ϵ)-hopset $G'' = (V', E'', \omega'')$ for G', for a positive integer *hop-bound* parameter β, and a positive parameter ϵ, i.e., a sparse graph that satisfies for every $x', y' \in V'$,

$$d_{G'}(x', y') \leq d^{(\beta)}_{G' \cup G''}(x', y') \leq (1 + \epsilon) d_{G'}(x', y') ,$$

where $d^{(\beta)}_{G'}(x, 'y')$ stands for the β-bounded distance between x' and y' in G', i.e., the length of the shortest β-bounded path between them. One then uses $G' \cup G''$ to build an efficient routing scheme for the vertices of V', and then extends this partial routing scheme to the entire set V. (We remark that this entire approach was originated in Nanongkai's seminal paper [18] on distributed approximate shortest paths.)

The computations of the virtual graph G' and the hopset G'' in [9, 14, 15, 17, 18] are quite costly in terms of local memory. In particular, they require each of the virtual vertices $v' \in V'$ to store up to $|V'| - 1 = \Omega(\sqrt{n})$ virtual edges (of E') incident on them. This alone makes the memory requirements of these distributed routing schemes $\Omega(\sqrt{n})$.

To overcome this issue, we use a novel hopset construction from our companion paper [12]. This hopset construction, like the construction of exact hopsets from [8], has the nice property that a hopset G'' for G' can be constructed without ever fully constructing the virtual graph G' itself. Instead, only those edges of G' that are really required for constructing the hopset G'' are computed. Moreover, the hopset G'' itself has a small *arboricity*[5] $\tilde{O}(n^{1/k})$, and thus every vertex $v' \in V'$ needs only to store its $\tilde{O}(n^{1/k})$ parents in the trees of the arboricity decomposition to which it belongs.

Note, however, that even once the hopset G'' of G' is constructed, one still needs the virtual graph G' itself to compute the routing scheme for it. This computation involves Bellman-Ford explorations to hop-depth β (the hop-bound of the hopset G'') in $G' \cup G''$. On the other hand, we cannot store the entire virtual graph G', as it would require some vertices to store $\Omega(\sqrt{n})$ pieces of information.

To resolve this hurdle, we compute only those edges of G' that are required for running these Bellman-Ford explorations *on the fly*, i.e., during these explorations, and as a result we never store (or even compute) the virtual graph G' in its entirety.

Finally, we outline our improved distributed *tree* routing scheme. Previously-existing schemes [9, 15] partitioned the tree T for which one builds the routing scheme into $|V'|$ subtrees $T(v')$, rooted at v', for every $v' \in V'$. This partition also induces a virtual tree T' on V'. The schemes of [9, 15] constructed a separate tree-routing scheme for T', and separate tree-routing schemes for each of the subtrees $\{T(v') \mid v' \in V'\}$. Constructing a tree routing scheme for T' involved broadcasting the entire virtual tree, storing it in local memory of all virtual vertices, and computing the scheme locally. This resulted in prohibitively high memory usage. Also, the combination of these routing schemes into a single tree-routing scheme for the original tree T increased the labels' and tables' sizes from $O(1)$ and $O(\log n)$, respectively, to $O(\log n)$ and $O(\log^2 n)$, respectively.

In the current paper we never construct a separate routing scheme for the virtual tree T'. Instead we implement the original Thorup-Zwick tree routing scheme. We use the partition $\{T(v') \mid v' \in V'\}$ of T to conduct local computations in the subtrees. We then incorporate the results of these local computations into a global routing scheme for the original tree T by applying pointer jumping ideas, which involve broadcasts and convergecasts of information associated with vertices of V'. This new approach enables us to achieve labels' and tables' sizes $O(1)$ and $O(\log n)$, respectively, matching the centralized bounds of Thorup and Zwick [23]. Even more importantly, it enables us to implement tree routing using logarithmic individual memory, as we never store the virtual tree T'. This resolves the last obstacle on our way to a low-memory distributed routing scheme for general graphs. We believe that the technique that we developed for the tree-routing problem will be found useful for other problems in which available memory is limited.

[5]The *arboricity* of a graph $G = (V, E)$ is the minimum number of forests needed to cover the edge set E of G. This collection of forests will be referred to as *arboricity forest decomposition*.

1.2 Structure of the Paper

In Section 3 we describe our tree-routing scheme. Our low-memory routing scheme for general graphs is described in Section 4.

2 PRELIMINARIES

Distributed Models. In the CONGEST model of computation, every vertex of an n-vertex weighted graph $G = (V, E)$ hosts a processor, and the processors communicate with one another in discrete rounds, via short (of size $O(\log n)$ bits) messages. In the CONGEST RAM variant of the CONGEST model, which we introduce here and in the companion paper [11], each message is allowed to contain an identity of a vertex, an edge weight, a distance in the graph, or anything else of no larger (up to a fixed constant factor) size. The local computation is assumed to require zero time, and we are interested in algorithms that run for as few rounds as possible. A parameter of interest is the *hop-diameter* D of the graph, which is the diameter of G viewed as an unweighted graph. The following lemma formalizes the broadcast ability of a distributed network (see, e.g., [19]).

Lemma 1. *Suppose every $v \in V$ holds m_v messages, each of $O(1)$ words, for a total of $M = \sum_{v \in V} m_v$. Then all vertices can receive all the messages within $O(M + D)$ rounds.*

Hopsets. Let $G = (V, E)$ be a weighted undirected graph. Let d_G denote the shortest path metric on G. For an integer t and $u, v \in V$, the *t-bounded distance* $d_G^{(t)}(u, v)$, is the length of the shortest path between u, v that contains at most t edges, aka hops (note that $d_G^{(t)}$ is not a metric). A *(β, ϵ)-hopset* H with weight function ω_H is a set of edges such that for any $u, v \in V$,

$$d_G(u,v) \leq d^{(\beta)}_{G \cup H}(u,v) \leq (1+\epsilon) \cdot d_G(u,v),$$

i.e., every pair has an approximate shortest path containing at most β hops in $G \cup H$.

Path recovery mechanism. Bearing in mind the current applications of hopsets to approximate shortest paths and routing schemes, our path recovery mechanism enables the vertices on paths implementing hopset edges to compute distances to a certain set of roots (which correspond to the sources of shortest paths we would like to compute, or to the roots of trees in which routing is conducted). We say that a hopset H has a *path-recovery mechanism*, if every edge $e \in H$ corresponds to a path $P(e)$ with $\omega(P(e)) = \omega_H(e)$ in G, and also the following property holds. Suppose we are given a collection of root vertices $R \subseteq V$, so that each hopset edge $e = (x, y)$ is associated with a subset of them $R(e) \subseteq R$, and has approximate distance $\hat{d}(x, z)$ from x to each $z \in R(e)$ (and also the approximate distance from y, since e knows its own weight). Then there exists a *protocol* that enables one to inform each $v \in V$ on $R(v) = \bigcup_{e \,:\, v \in P(e)} R(e)$, and also to compute the approximate distances to all roots in $R(v)$. The approximate distance $\hat{d}(v, z)$ to $z \in R(v)$ is bounded by $d_{P(e)}(v, x) + \hat{d}(x, z)$. In addition, v will know of a *parent*, a neighbor in some path $P(e)$, so that $v \in P(e)$, implementing $\hat{d}(v, z)$. The running time of this protocol is $\tilde{O}(|H| \cdot C + D) \cdot \beta$, where $C = \max_{v \in V} |R(v)|$, and the required memory per vertex is proportional to that required by the hopset construction.

A *virtual graph* is a graph $G' = (V', E')$ such that $V' \subseteq V$ and $d_G(u, v) \leq d_{G'}(u, v)$ for every $u, v \in V'$. (In our setting the edges of E' correspond to $\tilde{O}(n/|V'|)$-bounded distances in G.) The following theorem is shown in [11].

Theorem 1. *Let $G = (V, E)$ be any weighted graph on n vertices with hop-diameter D, given an integer $\kappa > 1$, and parameters $0 < \rho < 1$, $0 < \epsilon < 1/5$, and a virtual graph $G' = (V', E')$ embedded in G on $|V'| = \Theta(\sqrt{n})$ vertices, where E' corresponds to $B = \tilde{O}(\sqrt{n})$-bounded distances in G. Then there is a distributed algorithm in the CONGEST model that runs in $\tilde{O}(n^{(1+\rho)/2} + D) \cdot \beta$ rounds, that computes a (β, ϵ)-hopset H with a path-recovery mechanism, of size at most $O(n^{(1+1/\kappa)/2})$, where*

$$\beta = O\left(\frac{(\log \kappa + 1/\rho) \cdot \log n}{\epsilon}\right)^{\log \kappa + 1/\rho + 1},$$

and both the arboricity of H and the internal memory per vertex are bounded by $\tilde{O}(n^{\rho/2})$.

Bellman-Ford algorithm. The classical Bellman-Ford is an algorithm to compute single source shortest paths in a graph. Given a root $u \in V$, every vertex $v \in V$ holds a distance estimate $b_u(v)$. Initially, $b_u(u) = 0$ and all other estimates are ∞. The algorithm is executed in iterations. In every iteration v communicates $b_u(v)$ to its neighbors, and updates $b_u(v)$ according to the messages it received from its neighbors and the edge weights to those neighbors. The following lemma argues that given a bounded arboricity hopset, one can efficiently compute approximate shortest paths with low memory for each vertex. (Its proof appears also in [11]. We provide full details for the sake of completeness.)

Lemma 2. *Let $G'' = (V', E' \cup H)$ be a virtual graph on m vertices embedded in an n-vertex graph $G = (V, E)$ of hop-diameter D, such that edges in E' correspond to B-bounded distances in G, and H has arboricity α. Then one can compute distances from a given root vertex (or set), that are at most those given by β iterations of Bellman-Ford in G'' (and no less than those in G) in the CONGEST model, within $O((m \cdot \alpha + B + D) \cdot \beta \cdot \log n)$ rounds, so that every vertex requires only $O(\alpha + \log n)$ memory.*

Proof. To implement a single iteration of the Bellman-Ford exploration, every vertex $v \in V'$ which holds a current distance estimate $b(v)$ will need to communicate it to its neighbors in G''. First it will initiate an exploration in G for B rounds. In each round, every vertex $u \in V$ will forward the smallest value it received so far. This guarantees that if $\{v, x\} \in E'$, then x will receive a value at most $b(v) + \omega'(v, x)$ (where ω' is the edge weight of $\{v, x\}$ in E').

Next we have to handle the edges of H. Recall that every $v \in V'$ knows of at most α such edges incident on it. Let T be a spanning tree of G with hop-depth D. Every $v \in V'$ will broadcast via T its current distance estimate to the entire graph, and will also send all the existing edges of H incident on it that v knows about. All vertices $w \in V'$ that know of a hopset edge $\{v, w\}$ (or that learn about it from v's message) will update their value accordingly. Since there are $O(m \cdot \alpha)$ messages, by Lemma 1 this can be done in $O(m \cdot \alpha + D)$ rounds. In order to guarantee small internal memory, each v selects at random a number from $\{1, 2, \ldots, m \cdot \alpha\}$ for each message it sends, as a round to start its broadcast (clearly this increases the number of rounds by at most $m \cdot \alpha$); Since each message of v will reach every vertex of T at most once, the probability that some $u \in V$ receives t messages in a single round is at most $\binom{m \cdot \alpha}{t} \cdot 1/(m \cdot \alpha)^t \leq (e/t)^t$, thus with high probability no vertex will receive more than $O(\log n)$ messages each round (recall there are n vertices in T). By increasing the number of rounds by a factor of $O(\log n)$, whp there will be no congestion. The total number of rounds required is thus $O(m \cdot \alpha + B + D) \cdot \beta \cdot \log n$, and every vertex stores only the hopset edges, its distance estimate, and the $O(\log n)$ messages it needs to deliver at each round. □

To adapt our algorithm to the standard CONGEST model (i.e., with messages of size $O(\log n)$, rather than messages that can contain $O(1)$ edge weights and Identity numbers), we round all edge weights to the closest power of $(1 + \epsilon)$. As a result, each edge weight can now be represented with $O(\log\log \Lambda + \log 1/\epsilon)$ bits, and so the overhead for implementing our algorithm in this model is $O\left(\frac{\log\log\Lambda + \log 1/\epsilon}{\log n}\right)$. (The effect of this rounding on approximation guarantee of the hopset is minor; ϵ is rescaled by a constant factor, and as a result constants hidden by O-notation in other parameters grow.) This is in contrast to previous solutions [9, 15, 17], whose running time is at least linear in $\log \Lambda$.

3 DISTRIBUTED TREE ROUTING WITH SMALL MEMORY

In this section we present our exact compact routing scheme for trees that can be efficiently computed in a distributed manner, whose tables' and labels' sizes matches the best known sequential construction, while using small internal memory. In previous constructions of distributed routing schemes for trees [10, 17], the internal memory was as high as $\Omega(\sqrt{n})$, and it was also somewhat inefficient: the label size is $O(\log^2 n)$ and the routing tables are of size $O(\log n)$. Compare this to the classical [23] tree routing, which has label size $O(\log n)$ and routing tables of size $O(1)$.

We select a set $U \subseteq V$, such that each vertex is sampled to U independently with probability $q \leq 1/\sqrt{n}$ (the parameter q will be chosen later). Fix a tree T on vertices $V(T) \subseteq V$ with root z. The vertices $U(T) = (U \cap V(T)) \cup \{z\}$ induce a partition of T into subtrees, by removing the edges from each vertex in $U(T) \setminus \{z\}$ to its parent. Each of the $|U(T)|$ subtrees is rooted in a vertex of $U(T)$. Denote by T_w the subtree rooted at w. We call the trees T_w the *local* trees, and T is the global tree. We also consider T', the virtual tree on the vertices of $U(T)$, which is rooted at z, and contains an edge (x, y) if the T-parent of y lies in T_x. It is not hard to see (e.g., [10]) that whp the depth of each T_w is $\tilde{O}(1/q)$ and that $|U| \leq O(qn)$.

In both [10, 17], routing schemes were created for each T_w, and also a routing scheme for the virtual tree T'. This computation required large internal memory, since z had to locally compute the scheme for T'. The inefficiency in the size was due to the fact that when routing in T', traveling over a virtual edge (x, y), one has to route in T_x from x to the parent of y. This requires storing additional routing information for this subtree, increasing both label and table size. We overcome this issue by storing routing information only with respect to the actual tree T, while applying pointer jumping techniques and using broadcasts for the virtual tree T' to quickly compute the full labels.

Before describing our approach, let us briefly recall the Thorup-Zwick construction of tree routing. The idea is to assign to every (non-leaf) vertex $x \in T$ its *heavy child*, which is the child whose subtree has maximal size. Note that the subtree of any non-heavy child of x contains at most 1/2 of the vertices that the tree rooted at x contains. For this reason, any path from the root z to some $y \in T$ contains at most $\log n$ non-heavy edges. They also conduct a DFS search in T that assigns to each y the DFS entry and exit times for its subtree. The label of y is these entry and exit times, and also the names of the non-heavy edges on the z to y path. The routing table y stores consists of its DFS times, the name of the heavy child, and the name of the parent of y in the tree. The routing towards a target v in the tree is done as follows. At any intermediate vertex $y \in T$, if v is not in the subtree rooted at y (can be checked via the DFS times) then y forwards to its parent. If v is in the subtree, y inspects v's label to see if an edge (y, x) is written there. If this is the case, it forwards the message to x. Otherwise it forwards the message to its heavy child.

Now we show how to implement this scheme in a distributed manner, and with $O(\log n)$ internal memory. Our algorithm is composed of several stages, in these stages we compute the subtree sizes (to infer heavy children), the light edges on the path to the root, and the DFS entry and exit times. Each stage has three steps, first we compute the appropriate information for each local tree T_w, and then use pointer jumping to aggregate the local pieces and create a structure for the global tree T, but only for the vertices in $U(T)$. The last step uses each local tree to send the global information to all T, inside each T_w in parallel.

3.1 Stage 1: Computing Subtree Sizes

Computing local subtree sizes. Initially every vertex $y \in T$ only knows that it is in T and its parent $p(y)$. We begin by informing each vertex in which local tree T_w it lies. Every $w \in U(T)$ sends a message about itself to the vertices of T_w, by sending it to its children. Every vertex (in $V(T) \setminus U(T)$) receiving this message infers it is in T_w, and forwards the message to its own children. Note that this message will arrive to every vertex $x \in U(T)$ who is a child of w in the virtual tree T' (but x will not forward this message to its children), so x will know its (virtual) parent $p'(x)$ in T'.

In order to compute the local subtree sizes, for each $w \in U(T)$, every vertex in T_w sends to its parent the size of the subtree of T_w rooted at it, beginning with the leaves. Every vertex that received messages from all its children, sums up the values, adds 1, and sends this to its own parent. This can be done in parallel for all trees T_w for $w \in U(T)$, and will take $\tilde{O}(1/q)$ (the bound on the height of each T_w) rounds. When this stage concludes, every $x \in U(T)$ knows $|T_x|$.

Computing global subtree sizes. For each $x \in U(T)$, its subtree size is exactly the sum of sizes of subtrees T_w for $w \in U(T)$ that are descendants of x in T'. Note that computing these values from the leaves of T' up will not be efficient, since every message on a virtual edge may require $O(D)$ rounds, and the depth of T' may be as large as qn (which will be approximately $\sqrt{n}$), and thus will result in $O(D\sqrt{n})$ rounds. To alleviate this issue, we use the following "pointer jumping" idea. For a vertex v in the virtual tree T', and a positive integer h, we say that a vertex u is an *h-ancestor* of v, if u lies on the unique $v - z$ path in T' with h hops (virtual edges) from v. Denote by $a_i(x)$ the 2^i-ancestor of x (in particular, $a_0(x)$ is $p'(x)$). We run Algorithm 1 to compute the sizes. (By broadcast we mean using the BFS tree of G to send the messages to every vertex of the graph.)

Algorithm 1 `Global subtree sizes`

for $x \in U(T)$ **do**
  $a_0(x) = p'(x)$; (for the root $a_0(z) = \perp$);
  $s_0(x) = |T_x|$;
end for
for $i = 0, 1, \ldots, \log n - 1$ **do**
  for $x \in U(T)$ **do**
    Broadcast $s_i(x)$ and $a_i(x)$;
    $a_{i+1}(x) = a_i(a_i(x))$;
    $s_{i+1}(x) \leftarrow s_i(x)$;
    for every $w \in U(T)$ such that $x = a_i(w)$ **do**
      Increase $s_{i+1}(x)$ by $s_i(w)$;
    end for
  end for
end for

When the algorithm concludes, denote $s_x = s_{\log n}(x)$. It is not hard to verify that the ancestors $a_i(x)$ are computed correctly.

Claim 3. *For every $x \in U(T)$ we have that s_x is the size of the subtree of T rooted at x.*

Proof. Denote by $T_i(x)$ the maximal subtree (of T) rooted at x that contains at most 2^i vertices of $U(T)$ on any root-leaf path. Clearly $T_{\log n}(x)$ is the subtree of T rooted at x. We prove by induction on i, that $s_i(x) = |T_i(x)|$. The base case $i = 0$ holds by the initial setup, since $T_x = T_0(x)$ is indeed the maximal subtree containing a single vertex of $U(T)$ (the vertex x itself) on any root-leaf path. For $i \geq 0$, at the beginning of the i-th round, each $w \in U(T)$ that has $x = a_i(w)$, holds $s_i(w) = |T_i(w)|$ (by the inductive assumption). Observe that these w are exactly the children of vertices in $T_i(x)$ that lie outside $T_i(x)$, so the size of $T_{i+1}(x)$ is equal to the sum of these $|T_i(w)|$ together with $|T_i(x)|$. The algorithm ensures $s_{i+1}(x)$ is updated accordingly. □

As there are $O(|U(T)|) \leq \tilde{O}(qn)$ messages sent each iteration for $\log n$ iterations, by Lemma 1 it will take $\tilde{O}(qn + D)$ rounds to implement this algorithm. Each vertex $x \in U(T)$ stores $\{a_i(x)\}_{i=0,1,\ldots,\log n}$ for future use, which requires only $O(\log n)$ memory words.

In order to compute s_y, the size of the subtree of T rooted at y, for all $y \in T$, every $x \in U(T)$ informs its parent in T, $p(x)$, on s_x. Then $p(x)$ updates its size by adding s_x. Once again, for every $w \in U(T)$ in parallel, the leaves of T_w send to their parents their current size. This time, some of these leaves and internal vertices could be parents of vertices in $U(T)$, so these sizes are the actual subtree size in T. In $\tilde{O}(1/q)$ rounds, every vertex $y \in T$ will know s_y. By informing these values to the parents, every vertex can infer who is its heavy child.

3.2 Stage 2: Computing the light edges on the path to the root

Light edges in the local trees. For $y \in T$, its label contains the collection of edges $\{(u, v)\}$ that are on the z to y path in T, such that v is not the heavy child of u. These are the light edges. As noted above, there can be at most $\log n$ such edges on this path. If $y \in T_x$ for some $x \in U(T)$, we start by computing the list of light edges on the path from x to y. We execute Algorithm 2, where $b = \tilde{O}(1/q)$ is the maximal height of a local tree. Note that every vertex $u \in T_x$ will update the lists for all its children, in particular, every (virtual) child w of x in T' will have a list $L(w)$ that contains all the light edges on the path in T from x to w. Also observe that u does not need to store any information about its non-heavy children, just to send them the message $L(u)$ to which they will append the appropriate edge. This stage clearly runs in $\tilde{O}(1/q)$ rounds, the maximum height of any local tree.

Algorithm 2 `Local light edges`

for every $u \in T$ **do**
  $L(u) = \perp$;
end for
for every $x \in U(T)$ in parallel **do**
  $L(x) = \emptyset$;
  for $j = 1, 2, \ldots, b$ **do**
    for every $u \in T_x$ of height j, with heavy child v and other children $v_1, \ldots, v_r$ **do**
      $L(v) = L(u)$;
      for $i = 1, \ldots, r$ **do**
        $L(v) = L(u) \cup \{(u, v)\}$;
      end for
    end for
  end for
end for

Light edges in the global tree. We again apply pointer jumping to compute all the light edges. The following Algorithm 3 computes this for vertices $x \in U(T)$. The value $L_i(x)$ denote the list of edges x has just before the i-th iteration of the algorithm, and the final list will be $L_{\log n}(x)$.

Algorithm 3 `Global light edges`

for $x \in U(T)$ **do**
  $L_0(x) = L(x)$;
end for
for $i = 0, 1, \ldots, \log n - 1$ **do**
  for $x \in U(T)$ **do**
    Broadcast $L_i(x)$;
    $L_{i+1}(x) \leftarrow L_i(a_i(x)) \cup L_i(x)$;
  end for
end for

Claim 4. *For every $x \in U(T)$, $L_{\log n}(x)$ contains all the light edges in the path from x to z in T.*

Proof. We prove by induction on i that for every $x \in U(T)$, $L_i(x)$ is the set of light edges on the path in T from $a_i(x)$ to x. The base case holds by the initial setup $L_0(x) = L(x)$, which is correct by Algorithm 2. The induction step follows by the value set for L_{i+1}, and by the induction hypothesis on x and $a_i(x)$ (since the set of light edges on the path from x to $a_{i+1}(x)$ is equal to the union of those on the path from x to $a_i(x)$, and those on the path from $a_i(x)$ to $a_i(a_i(x)) = a_{i+1}(x)$). □

Since every list has size $O(\log n)$, it will take $\tilde{O}(qn + D)$ rounds to implement this stage. It remains to update the lists for all $y \in T$. In another $\tilde{O}(1/q)$ rounds, each $x \in U(T)$ sends its updated list $L_{\log n}(x)$ to every vertex $y \in T_x$, and they update their list by appending $L_{\log n}(x)$. This is the correct list, since the light edges on the z to y path are exactly those on the z to x path, together with the light edges $L(y)$ in the local tree T_x.

3.3 Stage 3: DFS entry and exit times for Distributed Tree Routing

Here we complete our distributed tree routing algorithm and present the third stage, which is computing the DFS entry and exit times.

Local DFS.. First, for every $x \in U(T)$ we conduct a "parallel" DFS in T_x to assign local DFS range for each $u \in T_x$.

Initially, x holds the range $[1, s_x]$, and it assigns ranges to its children according to the sizes of their respective subtrees in T (recall that s_x is the size of the subtree of T rooted at x) in parallel. In the next round, each child assigns a range to its own children, and so on.

We remark that a vertex y does not need memory proportional to its degree in order to inform its children $y_1, \dots, y_r$ on their appropriate ranges, the details on this are deferred to the full version.

Note that the children of x in T' will receive these messages as well, i.e., if w is a child of x in T', it will receive a range of size s_w (but will not forward it on). The number of rounds is once again $\tilde{O}(1/q)$.

Global DFS.. In this stage we need to shift each DFS range so that they will correspond to a DFS on the entire tree T. Observe that for the root z, each vertex in T_z has the correct range (since the subtree sizes used in the local DFS correspond to the global tree T). Consider some $w \in U(T)$ which is a child of z in T'. Then in the parallel DFS on T_z, w received (from its parent in T) a range of size s_w, say $[q_w + 1, q_w + s_w]$, so it needs to "shift" the range of each vertex in T_w by q_w, in order to agree with the DFS search of the root z. We say that z induces a q_w shift for w. In fact, every vertex $x \in U(T)$ is informed about its range, say $[q_x + 1, q_x + s_x]$, from its parent. For the root z, $q_z = 0$. In general, observe that such a vertex x, that on the path from x to z has $z = w_0, w_1, \dots, w_b = x$ vertices of $U(T)$, will need to shift its range $[1, s_x]$ by $\sum_{i=0}^{b} q_{w_i}$. The following Algorithm 4, using pointer jumping, will incur the appropriate shifts efficiently.

It can be shown by induction on i, that before the i-th round, $q_i(x)$ is the DFS range shift induced by the first 2^i ancestors of x in T'. This algorithm takes $O(qn + D)$ rounds. When the algorithm concludes, each $x \in U(T)$ in parallel informs all the vertices in T_x on the required shift $q_{\log n}(x)$, which takes $\tilde{O}(1/q)$ rounds.

Algorithm 4 `Global DFS`

```
for x ∈ U(T) do
    q_0(x) = q_x;
end for
for i = 0,1,...,log n − 1 do
    for x ∈ U(T) do
        Broadcast q_x;
        q_{i+1}(x) ← q_i(x) + q_i(a_i(x));
    end for
end for
```

3.4 Conclusion of Distributed Tree Routing

Choice of parameter q. If one desires a routing scheme for a single tree, just take $q = 1/\sqrt{n}$, so the running time will be $\tilde{O}(\sqrt{n} + D)$. If we desire to compute a routing scheme in parallel for multiple trees, but have the guarantee that every $v \in V$ belongs to at most s trees, (this is the case when we apply the tree-routing scheme for routing in general graphs), then pick $q = 1/\sqrt{sn}$, and a random start time for each tree, sampled uniformly from $\{1, \dots, O(\sqrt{sn} \cdot \log n)\}$. Using an argument as in [10], we obtain whp running time $\tilde{O}(\sqrt{sn} + D)$ (rather than the naive $\tilde{O}(s \cdot \sqrt{n} + D)$). We conclude with formally describing our result.

Theorem 2. *For any tree T on n vertices, lying in a network with hop-diameter D, there exists a distributed randomized algorithm in the CONGEST model, that whp runs in $\tilde{O}(\sqrt{n} + D)$ rounds, and computes an exact tree routing scheme with label size $O(\log n)$ and routing tables of size $O(1)$, such that every vertex uses only $O(\log n)$ words of memory throughout the computation.*

In addition, given a network with n vertices and a set of trees so that each vertex is contained in at most s trees, one can compute an exact tree routing scheme as above for all trees in parallel, within $\tilde{O}(\sqrt{sn} + D)$ rounds, while using memory $O(s \cdot \log n)$ at each vertex.

4 DISTRIBUTED ROUTING IN GENERAL GRAPHS

In this section we use the hopsets of [11] with their path-recovery mechanism, combined with our novel distributed tree routing, and design a compact routing scheme that can be efficiently computed in a distributed manner with low memory throughout the computation. Let $G = (V, E)$ be a weighted graph with n vertices and hop-diameter D. Fix a parameter $k > 1$.

We briefly sketch the approach of [10] and the current improvement allowing low memory and improved bounds. First construct the Thorup-Zwick hierarchy $V = A_0 \supseteq A_1 \supseteq \dots \supseteq A_k = \emptyset$, where each vertex in A_{i-1} is sampled to A_i independently with probability $n^{-1/k}$. Then the cluster $C(v) = \{u \in V : d_G(u, v) < d_G(u, A_{i+1})\}$ for $v \in A_i \setminus A_{i+1}$ can be viewed as tree rooted at v. Computing this cluster is done by a limited Dijkstra exploration from v, i.e., only vertices in $C(v)$ continue the exploration of v. Routing from x to y is done by finding an appropriate cluster $C(v)$ containing both x, y, and routing in that tree. Whenever $i < k/2$ these trees have whp depth $\tilde{O}(\sqrt{n})$, so they can be easily computed in a distributed manner within $\tilde{O}(n^{1/2+1/k})$ rounds. The main issue is computing the clusters for $i \geq k/2$.

The method of [10] was to work with a virtual graph G', whose vertices are $V' = A_{k/2}$, and whose edges correspond to $B = c \cdot \sqrt{n}\log n$-bounded distances in G between the vertices of V'. Then a hopset is computed for this virtual graph, which enables the computation of Bellman-Ford explorations in only $O(\beta) \approx (\log n)^{O(k)}$ rounds. The fact that β-bounded distances can suffer $1+\epsilon$ stretch creates additional complications; one needs to define *approximate clusters*, and make sure that these approximate clusters correspond to actual trees in G. Finally, since the trees corresponding to $C(v)$ for the high level vertices $v \in A_i$, $i \geq k/2$ can have large depth, one needs to adapt the Thorup-Zwick routing scheme for trees [23]. In both [10, 17] this adaptation significantly increased both the table and label size, and required large memory.

Our improved result has two main ingredients. First, we do not explicitly construct G'; In both [10, 17], computing the weights of edges in G' was a rather expensive step, and required large memory and induced factor depending logarithmically on the aspect ratio to the running time. In addition, only approximate values were obtained. We observe that not all the edges of G' are required for the algorithm, and thus we do not compute G' at all. Instead, we conduct the explorations in G' by implementing in each iteration of Bellman-Ford a B-bounded search in G, which not only saves memory and running time, but also simplifies the analysis, since now there is no error in the edge weights of G'. Second, our new tree-routing scheme has both improved label and routing table size, and can be computed with small memory. For more details see Section 3. Our main result is

Theorem 3. *Let $G = (V,E)$ be a weighted graph with n vertices and hop-diameter D, and let $k > 1$ be a parameter. Then there exists a routing scheme with stretch at most $4k-5+o(1)$, labels of size $O(k\log n)$ and routing tables of size $\tilde{O}(n^{1/k})$, that can be computed in a distributed manner within $(n^{1/2+1/k}+D)\cdot(\log n)^{O(\max\{k,\log\log n\})}$ rounds, such that every vertex has memory of size $\tilde{O}(n^{1/k})$.*

Alternatively, whenever $k \geq \sqrt{\log n/\log\log n}$, the number of rounds can be made $(n^{1/2+1/k}+D)\cdot 2^{\tilde{O}(\sqrt{\log n})}$ with memory $2^{\tilde{O}(\sqrt{\log n})}$ at each vertex.

In particular, whenever $k = \delta\log n/\log\log n$ for a small constant δ, we get $(\sqrt{n}+D)\cdot n^{O(\delta)}$ rounds with polylog(n) memory per vertex.

Construction of Routing Scheme. Let $G = (V,E)$ be a weighted graph, fix $k > 1$. We describe a scheme with stretch $4k-3+o(1)$, the improvement to $4k-5+o(1)$ is done as in [10, 23] (while paying a small polylogarithmic factor in the table size). Sample a collection of sets $V = A_0 \supseteq A_1 \cdots \supseteq A_k = \emptyset$, where for each $0 < i < k$, each vertex in A_{i-1} is chosen independently to be in A_i with probability $n^{-1/k}$. A point $z \in A_i$ is called an i-pivot of v if $d_G(v,z) = d_G(v,A_i)$. The cluster of a vertex $u \in A_i \setminus A_{i+1}$ is defined as

$$C(u) = \{v \in V \ : \ d_G(u,v) < d_G(v,A_{i+1})\}\ . \tag{1}$$

It was shown in [22] that

Claim 5. *With high probability, each vertex is contained in at most $4n^{1/k}\log n$ clusters.*

We recall a few definitions from [10]. For each $v \in V$ and $0 \leq i \leq k-1$, a point $\hat{z} \in A_i$ is called an *approximate i-pivot* of v if

$$d_G(v,\hat{z}) \leq (1+\epsilon)d_G(v,A_i)\ . \tag{2}$$

Define

$$C_\epsilon(u) = \{v \in V \ : \ d_G(u,v) < \frac{d_G(v,A_{i+1})}{1+\epsilon}\}. \tag{3}$$

The approximate cluster $\tilde{C}(u)$ will be any set that satisfies the following:

$$C_{6\epsilon}(u) \subseteq \tilde{C}(u) \subseteq C(u)\ . \tag{4}$$

It was shown in [10] that once we obtain approximate clusters as trees of G and provide an exact routing scheme for these trees, it implies a routing scheme for G with stretch $4k-5+o(1)$ whenever $\epsilon \leq 1/(48k^4)$. Concretely, the routing table for x will be the tables for the at most $4n^{1/k}\log n$ trees containing it, and its label will be the collection of labels needed for tree routing in the at most k trees corresponding to its approximate pivots. So the table size is $O(n^{1/k}\log n)$ and the label size is $O(k\log n)$. It remains to show how to efficiently compute approximate clusters as trees of G, and the approximate pivots.

Let $h(u,v)$ denote the number of vertices on the shortest path from u to v in G, and set $B = 4\sqrt{n}\cdot\ln n$. The following were also shown in [10] to hold with high probability.[6]

Claim 6. *For any $u,v \in V$ with $h(u,v) \geq B$, there exists a vertex of $A_{k/2}$ on the shortest path between them.*

Claim 7. *For any $0 \leq i < k-1$, $v \in A_i \setminus A_{i+1}$ and $u \in C(v)$, it holds that $h(u,v) \leq 4n^{(i+1)/k}\ln n$.*

In particular, for $i < k/2$ we can find $C(v)$ (the "exact" cluster) for $v \in A_i \setminus A_{i+1}$ by a simple limited Bellman-Ford exploration from all such v for $4n^{(i+1)/k}\ln n \leq \tilde{O}(\sqrt{n})$ rounds. By Claim 5, the congestion induced at each $u \in V$ by the merit of being a part of many clusters is only $4n^{1/k}\ln n$, so the total number of rounds required is $\tilde{O}(n^{1/2+1/k})$, and each vertex needs to store at most $4n^{1/k}\ln n$ words (the clusters containing it). Finally, note that these clusters indeed correspond to trees, since every vertex $u \in C(v)$ can store as a parent the vertex who last updated the distance estimate u has for v.

From now on we consider the high levels, where $i \geq k/2$. Define $G' = (V',E')$ as a virtual graph where $V' = A_{k/2}$, and E' corresponds to B-bounded distances in G. Observe that Claim 6 implies that $d_{G'}(v,v') = d_G(v,v')$ for any $v,v' \in V'$ (because any shortest path in G has a vertex of V' among any B consecutive vertices on that path). First, we compute a (β,ϵ)-hopset H for the virtual graph G' as in Theorem 1, with parameters $\kappa = \log n$, ϵ and $\rho = 1/\kappa$. We thus get $\beta = (\log n)^{O(\max\{k,\log\log n\})}$ (since $\epsilon \geq \Omega(1/\log^4 n)$). Note that the graph G' is implicit. Since $|A_{k/2}| = \Theta(\sqrt{n})$ whp, the number of rounds required to compute H is at most $(n^{1/2+1/k}+D)\cdot\beta$, and the size of the hopset is $O(n^{1/2})$. The arboricity and memory required per vertex is $\tilde{O}(n^{1/k})$, and it has a path-recovery mechanism. (If one desires the second assertion of the Theorem 3, pick $\rho = \sqrt{\log\log n/\log n}$.)

[6] For the sake of simplicity we will assume k is even, for odd k we can slightly improve the running time by a factor of $n^{1/(2k)}$.

Approximate Pivots. To compute the approximate pivots, conduct β iterations of Bellman-Ford in $G'' = G' \cup H$ rooted in A_{i+1}, using low memory as in Lemma 2. Since H is a (β, ϵ)-hopset, each $v \in V'$ has a value $\hat{d}(v, A_{i+1}) \in [d_G(v, A_{i+1}), (1+\epsilon) \cdot d_G(v, A_{i+1})]$. We perform another B-bounded exploration in G, where initially every vertex $v \in V'$ sends its current estimate $\hat{d}(v, A_{i+1})$, and in every step every vertex forwards the smallest value it has heard so far. We claim that every $u \in V$ will learn of an approximate $(i+1)$-pivot $\hat{z} \in A_{i+1}$. To see this, let z be the $(i+1)$-pivot of u. If $h(u,z) \le B$ then u will hear z's message in the last B-bounded exploration. Otherwise, by Claim 6 there exists a vertex $v \in V'$ on the shortest path from u to z within B hops from u. In the final exploration to range B, v will communicate $\hat{d}(v, A_{i+1})$ on the path towards u, thus u will have a value at most

$$\begin{aligned}\hat{d}(u, A_{i+1}) &\le d_G^{(B)}(u,v) + \hat{d}(v, A_{i+1}) \\ &\le d_G(u,v) + (1+\epsilon) d_G(v, A_{i+1}) \\ &\le (1+\epsilon) d_G(u, A_{i+1}) ,\end{aligned}$$

where the last inequality used that $d_G(u,v) + d_G(v, A_{i+1}) = d_G(u, A_{i+1})$, which follows since v lies on the shortest path from u to the nearest vertex of A_{i+1}. We conclude that no matter which $\hat{z}$ is the approximate pivot of u, the distance estimate u has for it cannot be larger than $(1+\epsilon) d_G(u, A_{i+1})$. Computing the approximate pivots takes whp $\tilde{O}(n^{(1+\rho)/2} + D) \cdot \beta$ rounds (recall by Theorem 1 we have $\alpha = \tilde{O}(n^{\rho/2})$).

Approximate Clusters. Fix some $i \ge k/2$, and for each $v \in A_i \setminus A_{i+1}$ we conduct a *limited* Bellman-Ford exploration in $G'' = G' \cup H$ for β iterations rooted at v, as in Lemma 2. The limit means that any vertex $u \in V'$ receiving a message originated at v, will forward it to its neighbors iff the current distance estimate is strictly less than $\hat{d}(u, A_{i+1})/(1+\epsilon)^2$. We need to avoid congestion at intermediate vertices during the B-bounded exploration in G described in Lemma 2, so these vertices will also need to implement some sort of limitation. Concretely, vertices $u \in V \setminus V'$ will forward v's message iff their current estimate is strictly less than $\hat{d}(u, A_{i+1})/(1+\epsilon)$. The exploration over edges of H is done as before, where Claim 5 guarantees every vertex participates in at most $4n^{1/k} \ln n$ clusters (we will soon show that the approximate clusters are indeed contained in the clusters). This increases the number of rounds required for executing a Bellman-Ford iteration over the edges of E' from $\tilde{O}(n^{1/2})$ to $\tilde{O}(n^{1/2+1/k})$. However, the number of rounds for executing a Bellman-Ford iteration over the edges of H increases only by a constant factor, since in every iteration each $v \in V'$ broadcasts a single distance estimate for each cluster containing it, and $\alpha = \tilde{O}(n^{1/k})$ messages with identities of opposite endpoints of its outgoing hopset edges – but these are the same hopset edges for all clusters. Thus the number of rounds required is at most $\tilde{O}(n^{1/2+1/k} + D) \cdot \beta$. Also the memory each vertex uses for this computation is bounded by $\tilde{O}(n^{1/k})$ (which is essentially the number of clusters containing the vertex).

The exploration rooted at v induces a virtual tree (rooted at v). For every edge $(x,y) \in E'$ on this tree, we add all the vertices in G on the B-bounded path from x to y. This can be done via an acknowledgement message from y back to x on this path, and every vertex updates its parent accordingly. For every hopset edge $e = (x,y) \in H$ of the tree, we use the path-recovery mechanism in order to notify all vertices $u \in P(e)$ (recall $P(e)$ is the path in G implementing the edge e) to join the tree with root v, and also compute their approximate distance $\hat{d}(u,v)$ to v and the corresponding parent. If the computed distance satisfies $\hat{d}(u,v) < b_v(u)$, then u updates $b_v(u) \leftarrow \hat{d}(u,v)$, where $b_v(u)$ is the current distance estimate that u keeps concerning its distance to v. Also, u updates its parent. By Claim 5, any vertex in V is contained in at most $\tilde{O}(n^{1/k})$ clusters, and Claim 8 below will show that the approximate clusters are contained in clusters. So every vertex $u \in V$ may be a part of at most $C = \tilde{O}(n^{1/k})$ different trees. We get that the number of rounds required to implement the path-recovery protocol is $\tilde{O}((|H| \cdot C + D) \cdot \beta) = \tilde{O}(n^{1/2+1/k} + D) \cdot \beta$.

Finally, we perform another limited B iterations of Bellman-Ford in G, where every vertex x in the tree of v has initial value $b_v(x)$, and every vertex $u \in V$ will forward in each iteration the smallest estimate it heard so far, but iff it is strictly less than $\hat{d}(u, A_{i+1})/(1+\epsilon)$. In that case it will also join the approximate cluster of v, and will update its parent as its neighbor in G whose message caused u to last update its distance estimate to v.

Observe that the same vertex may join a tree more than once, due to several edges in $E' \cup H$ whose path contain it. In such a case the vertex will have as a parent the vertex which minimize the estimated distance to the root. Since every vertex has a single parent, we will have that the approximate cluster of v, $\tilde{C}(v)$, is indeed a tree. It remains to prove (4), which is done in the next two claims. Recall $b_v(u)$ is the distance estimate u has to v in the exploration rooted at v.

Claim 8. *For any $v \in V'$, $\tilde{C}(v) \subseteq C(v)$.*

Proof. Consider any $u \in \tilde{C}(v)$. If it is the case that $u \in V$ joined the approximate cluster by the exploration rooted at v, either by being in V' or on a B-bounded path in G that implements an edge of E', then it must satisfy $b_v(u) < \hat{d}(u, A_{i+1})/(1+\epsilon)$. Now,

$$d_G(u,v) \le b_v(u) < \hat{d}(u, A_{i+1})/(1+\epsilon) \overset{(5)}{\le} d_G(u, A_{i+1}) ,$$

so indeed $u \in C(v)$. The other case is that u is part of a hopset edge (x,y) that was added to the virtual tree. Since y joins the approximate cluster, it must satisfy $b_v(y) < \hat{d}(y, A_{i+1})/(1+\epsilon)^2$. Recall that the weight of the hopset edge $w_H(x,y)$ is the weight of the path P from x to y in G that u lies on, hence $d_P(x,u) + d_P(u,y) = w_H(x,y)$. It follows that

$$\begin{aligned} d_G(u, A_{i+1}) &\overset{(5)}{\ge} \frac{\hat{d}(u, A_{i+1})}{1+\epsilon} \ge \frac{d_G(u, A_{i+1})}{1+\epsilon} \\ &\ge \frac{d_G(y, A_{i+1}) - d_G(u,y)}{1+\epsilon} \\ &\overset{(5)}{\ge} \frac{\hat{d}(y, A_{i+1})}{(1+\epsilon)^2} - \frac{d_P(u,y)}{1+\epsilon} > b_v(y) - d_P(u,y) \\ &= b_v(x) + w_H(x,y) - d_P(u,y) = b_v(x) + d_P(x,u) \\ &\ge b_v(u) \ge d_G(u,v) ,\end{aligned}$$

where in the penultimate inequality we used the fact that u knows $d_P(x,u)$ so could have updated its distance estimate to v as $b_v(x) + d_P(x,u)$ (note it may have used a smaller estimate). Thus $u \in C(v)$, as required. □

Claim 9. *For any* $v \in V'$, $C_{6\epsilon}(v) \subseteq \tilde{C}(v)$.

Proof. Let $u \in C_{6\epsilon}(v)$, we would like to show that $u \in \tilde{C}(v)$. Consider the shortest path P from u to v in G, then by Claim 6 there is a vertex $u' \in V'$ on P that is within B hops from u. Notice that

$$\begin{aligned} d_G(v,u') &= d_G(v,u) - d_G(u,u') \le \frac{d_G(u,A_{i+1}) - d_G(u,u')}{1+6\epsilon} \\ &\le \frac{d_G(u',A_{i+1})}{1+6\epsilon} . \end{aligned} \tag{5}$$

We will show that the limited exploration originated at v will reach u', and in the final depth B exploration it will reach u and include it in $\tilde{C}(v)$. Since H is a (β,ϵ)-hopset, there is a path P' in G'' from v to u' that contains at most β edges, so that

$$d_{P'}(v,u') \le (1+\epsilon)d_{G'}(v,u') = (1+\epsilon)d_G(v,u') . \tag{6}$$

Let $z \in P'$ be any vertex on P' that lies t hops from v, then after t steps of Bellman-Ford exploration from v we have that

$$\begin{aligned} b_z(v) &= d_{P'}(v,z) = d_{P'}(v,u') - d_{P'}(z,u') \\ &\overset{(6)}{\le} (1+\epsilon)d_G(v,u') - d_G(z,u') \\ &\overset{(5)}{\le} \frac{(1+\epsilon)d_G(u',A_{i+1})}{1+6\epsilon} - d_G(z,u') \\ &\le \frac{d_G(u',A_{i+1}) - d_G(z,u')}{1+4\epsilon} < \frac{d_G(z,A_{i+1})}{(1+\epsilon)^2} \le \frac{\hat{d}(z,A_{i+1})}{(1+\epsilon)^2} , \end{aligned}$$

where we used that $\epsilon < 1/5$. We conclude that z satisfies the limit condition for the exploration rooted at v, and forwards the message of v onwards. In particular, $b_v(u') \le d_{P'}(v,u') \le (1+\epsilon)d_G(v,u')$. In the final phase we make a Bellman-Ford exploration for B rounds in G from each vertex that received v's message. Thus u' will start such an exploration with distance estimate $b_v(u')$. Consider the subpath $Q \subseteq P$ from u' to u, we have to show that every vertex on this path forwards the message of v, that is, that it satisfies the limit condition. Let $y \in Q$ be such a vertex, since this is a shortest path in G we have

$$\begin{aligned} b_v(y) &\le b_v(u') + d_Q(u',y) \le (1+\epsilon)d_G(v,u') + d_G(u',y) \\ &\le (1+\epsilon)d_G(v,y) = (1+\epsilon)(d_G(v,u) - d_G(y,u)) \\ &\overset{(3)}{\le} \frac{(1+\epsilon)d_G(u,A_{i+1})}{1+6\epsilon} - d_G(y,u) \\ &\le \frac{d_G(u,A_{i+1}) - d_G(y,u)}{1+4\epsilon} \\ &\le \frac{d_G(y,A_{i+1})}{1+4\epsilon} < \frac{\hat{d}(y,A_{i+1})}{1+\epsilon} , \end{aligned}$$

as required. □

ACKNOWLEDGEMENTS

We are grateful to an anonymous reviewer for his helpful comments about the path-recovery mechanism.

REFERENCES

[1] Ittai Abraham, Cyril Gavoille, and Dahlia Malkhi. 2004. Routing with Improved Communication-Space Trade-Off. In *Distributed Computing, 18th International Conference, DISC 2004, Amsterdam, The Netherlands, October 4-7, 2004, Proceedings.* 305–319. https://doi.org/10.1007/978-3-540-30186-8_22

[2] Ittai Abraham, Cyril Gavoille, Dahlia Malkhi, Noam Nisan, and Mikkel Thorup. 2008. Compact Name-independent Routing with Minimum Stretch. *ACM Trans. Algorithms* 4, 3, Article 37 (July 2008), 12 pages. https://doi.org/10.1145/1367064.1367077

[3] Baruch Awerbuch, Amotz Bar-Noy, Nathan Linial, and David Peleg. 1990. Improved Routing Strategies with Succinct Tables. *J. Algorithms* 11, 3 (Sept. 1990), 307–341. https://doi.org/10.1016/0196-6774(90)90017-9

[4] B. Awerbuch and D. Peleg. 1992. Routing with polynomial communication-space tradeoff. *SIAM J. Discrete Mathematics* 5 (1992), 151–162.

[5] Shiri Chechik. 2013. Compact routing schemes with improved stretch. In *ACM Symposium on Principles of Distributed Computing, PODC '13, Montreal, QC, Canada, July 22-24, 2013.* 33–41. https://doi.org/10.1145/2484239.2484268

[6] Lenore Cowen. 2001. Compact Routing with Minimum Stretch. *J. Algorithms* 38, 1 (2001), 170–183. https://doi.org/10.1006/jagm.2000.1134

[7] Tamar Eilam, Cyril Gavoille, and David Peleg. 2003. Compact routing schemes with low stretch factor. *J. Algorithms* 46, 2 (2003), 97–114. https://doi.org/10.1016/S0196-6774(03)00002-6

[8] Michael Elkin. 2017. Distributed Exact Shortest Paths in Sublinear Time. In *Proceedings of the 49th Annual ACM SIGACT Symposium on Theory of Computing (STOC 2017).* ACM, New York, NY, USA, 757–770. https://doi.org/10.1145/3055399.3055452

[9] Michael Elkin and Ofer Neiman. 2016. Hopsets with Constant Hopbound, and Applications to Approximate Shortest Paths. In *IEEE 57th Annual Symposium on Foundations of Computer Science, FOCS 2016, 9-11 October 2016, Hyatt Regency, New Brunswick, New Jersey, USA.* 128–137. https://doi.org/10.1109/FOCS.2016.22

[10] Michael Elkin and Ofer Neiman. 2016. On Efficient Distributed Construction of Near Optimal Routing Schemes: Extended Abstract. In *Proceedings of the 2016 ACM Symposium on Principles of Distributed Computing (PODC '16).* ACM, New York, NY, USA, 235–244. https://doi.org/10.1145/2933057.2933098

[11] Michael Elkin and Ofer Neiman. 2017. Linear-Size Hopsets with Small Hopbound, and Constant-Hopbound Hopsets in RNC. To be published.

[12] Michael Elkin and Ofer Neiman. 2017. Linear-Size Hopsets with Small Hopbound, and Distributed Routing with Low Memory. *CoRR* abs/1704.08468 (2017). http://arxiv.org/abs/1704.08468

[13] Cyril Gavoille and David Peleg. 2003. Compact and localized distributed data structures. *Distributed Computing* 16, 2-3 (2003), 111–120. https://doi.org/10.1007/s00446-002-0073-5

[14] Christoph Lenzen and Boaz Patt-Shamir. 2013. Fast routing table construction using small messages. In *Symposium on Theory of Computing Conference, STOC'13, Palo Alto, CA, USA, June 1-4, 2013.* 381–390. https://doi.org/10.1145/2488608.2488656

[15] Christoph Lenzen and Boaz Patt-Shamir. 2015. Fast Partial Distance Estimation and Applications. In *Proceedings of the 2015 ACM Symposium on Principles of Distributed Computing, PODC 2015, Donostia-San Sebastián, Spain, July 21 - 23, 2015.* 153–162. https://doi.org/10.1145/2767386.2767398

[16] Christoph Lenzen and Boaz Patt-Shamir. 2016. Personal communication.

[17] Christoph Lenzen, Boaz Patt-Shamir, and David Peleg. 2016. Distributed Distance Computation and Routing with Small Messages. manuscript.

[18] Danupon Nanongkai. 2014. Distributed approximation algorithms for weighted shortest paths. In *Symposium on Theory of Computing, STOC 2014, New York, NY, USA, May 31 - June 03, 2014.* 565–573. https://doi.org/10.1145/2591796.2591850

[19] David Peleg. 2000. *Distributed Computing: A Locality-sensitive Approach.* Society for Industrial and Applied Mathematics, Philadelphia, PA, USA.

[20] David Peleg and Eli Upfal. 1989. A trade-off between space and efficiency for routing tables. *J. ACM* 36, 3 (1989), 510–530. https://doi.org/10.1145/65950.65953

[21] Atish Das Sarma, Stephan Holzer, Liah Kor, Amos Korman, Danupon Nanongkai, Gopal Pandurangan, David Peleg, and Roger Wattenhofer. 2012. Distributed Verification and Hardness of Distributed Approximation. *SIAM J. Comput.* 41, 5 (2012), 1235–1265. https://doi.org/10.1137/11085178X

[22] M. Thorup and U. Zwick. 2001. Approximate Distance Oracles. In *Proc. of the 33rd ACM Symp. on Theory of Computing.* 183–192.

[23] Mikkel Thorup and Uri Zwick. 2001. Compact Routing Schemes. In *Proceedings of the Thirteenth Annual ACM Symposium on Parallel Algorithms and Architectures (SPAA '01).* ACM, New York, NY, USA, 1–10. https://doi.org/10.1145/378580.378581

Fair Leader Election for Rational Agents in Asynchronous Rings and Networks

Assaf Yifrach
Tel-Aviv University
Tel-Aviv, Israel
asafyi@gmail.com

Yishay Mansour
Tel-Aviv University & Google Research
Tel-Aviv, Israel
mansour.yishay@gmail.com

ABSTRACT

We study a game theoretic model where a coalition of processors might collude to bias the outcome of the protocol, where we assume that the processors always prefer any legitimate outcome over a non-legitimate one. We show that the problems of Fair Leader Election and Fair Coin Toss are equivalent, and focus on Fair Leader Election.

Our main focus is on a directed asynchronous ring of n processors, where we investigate the protocol proposed by Abraham et al. [4] and studied in Afek et al. [5]. We show that in general the protocol is resilient only to sub-linear size coalitions. Specifically, we show that $\Omega(\sqrt{n \log n})$ randomly located processors or $\Omega(\sqrt[3]{n})$ adversarially located processors can force any outcome. We complement this by showing that the protocol is resilient to any adversarial coalition of size $O(\sqrt[4]{n})$. We propose a modification to the protocol, and show that it is resilient to every coalition of size $\Theta(\sqrt{n})$, by exhibiting both an attack and a resilience result.

For every $k \geq 1$, we define a family of graphs $\mathcal{G}_k$ that can be simulated by trees where each node in the tree simulates at most k processors. We show that for every graph in $\mathcal{G}_k$, there is no fair leader election protocol that is resilient to coalitions of size k. Our result generalizes a previous result of Abraham et al. [4] that states that for every graph, there is no fair leader election protocol which is resilient to coalitions of size $\lceil \frac{n}{2} \rceil$.

KEYWORDS

Fair leader election; Rational distributed agents; Fair coin toss; Asynchronous unidirectional ring

ACM Reference Format:

Assaf Yifrach and Yishay Mansour. 2018. Fair Leader Election for Rational Agents in Asynchronous Rings and Networks. In *PODC '18: ACM Symposium on Principles of Distributed Computing, July 23–27, 2018, Egham, United Kingdom.* ACM, New York, NY, USA, 10 pages. https://doi.org/10.1145/3212734.3212767

Supported in part by a grant from the Israel Science Foundation.

ACM ISBN 978-1-4503-5795-1/18/07...$15.00
https://doi.org/10.1145/3212734.3212767

1 INTRODUCTION

One of the most fundamental tasks in distributed computing is fault tolerance, the ability to overcome malicious or abnormal behavior of processors. Fault tolerance is essential to make distributed systems viable, and enables them to operate at large scale and in unsecured environments. Different models of fault tolerance assume different assumptions about faulty processors. For example, some model assume that faulty processors are Byzantine, i.e., they can behave in an arbitrary malicious way. As another example, some models assume that faulty processors are fail-stop, i.e., they execute the protocol normally until an arbitrary point and then they stop responding. In both cases, the only objective of faulty processors is to fail the protocol.

In this paper, we study protocols that are tolerant to a third type of faulty processors, *rational agents*. We assume the processors are selfish. Given a protocol, each processor (which is a rational agent) has its own utility function over the possible outcomes of the protocol. A processor deviates from the protocol (i.e., cheats by running another protocol) if deviating increases its expected utility.

Later, we explain what reasonable assumptions can be made about the processors' utility functions.

At a high level we would like to design protocols which are resilient to such deviations. This line of research has been active for over a decade (see, [1, 2, 4–6, 13, 19, 22]).

Following this research, we look for solutions (i.e., resilient protocols) in terms of game-theory. Specifically, we look for a protocol that is a strong-k-Nash-equilibria. That is, a protocol for which there is no coalition (any subset of the processors) of up to k processors, that can increase the expected utility of each of its members by deviating cooperatively. Where deviating cooperatively means running another protocol instead of the prescribed protocol. As in strong-k-Nash-equilibria, such a coalition assumes that all of the processors outside the coalition play honestly, i.e., execute the protocol honestly. In other words, two coalitions cannot deviate in parallel. If a protocol is a strong-k-Nash-equilibria for every set of utility functions, then we ssay it is *k-resilient.*

We explain and motivate our setting using an example. Consider the problem of designing a leader election protocol for rational agents. The main issue is that some processors might want to get elected as a leader in order to gain additional privileges. A natural solution would be a *Fair* Leader Election protocol, which is a leader election protocol that elects each processor with equal probability. One simple protocol, assuming that the n ids of the processors are $[1, n]$, is to let each processor select a random value in $[n]$ and broadcast it. Each processor, after receiving all the random values, can sum the values up (modulus n) and the result would be the id of the elected leader. This simple protocol selects a leader uniformly, assuming all the processors follow it precisely. However, in an asynchronous network even a single deviating processor can control the output and select the leader. A single processor can cheat by waiting for the random values of all the other processors to arrive before selecting its own value. Note that this simple protocol is applicable also in message-passing networks, because one can implement broadcast over the network.

The weakness of that simple protocol was already observed by Abraham et al. [4], who suggested a methodology to overcome it in a unidirectional ring network. They named their protocol A-LEAD^{uni}. The main idea in A-LEAD^{uni} is to use buffering in order to delay the flow of the messages along the ring and thus limit the effect of malicious processors. They showed that A-LEAD^{uni} is a strong-1-Nash-equilibria, thus, is overcoming a single malicious processor. They claimed that their protocol is $(\frac{n}{2}-1)$-resilient, i.e., resilient to **every** coalition of size $k \leq \frac{1}{2}n - 1$, however, it is true only for coalitions that are located **consecutively** along the ring.

Later, Afek et al. [5] simplified A-LEAD^{uni}, and decomposed it into useful intuitive building blocks.

The main thrust of this paper is studying the resilience of A-LEAD^{uni} and improving it.

In our model, we assume the *solution preference* assumption, i.e., that processors always prefer a selection of any leader over a failure of the protocol. This assumption is reasonable in various settings. For example, processors might be able to cheat only during the leader election, which is usually a preliminary step, but not during the main computation. In such case, leaving the system in an erroneous state at the termination of the leader election step, fails also the main computation and thus prevents them from benefiting from its results.

The solution preference assumption has two benefits. First, we can hope for non-trivial resilience results. In a unidirectional ring, two processors can disconnect the ring and thus fail every reasonable protocol, however due to the solution preference, a failure is the worst possible outcome in terms of utility, so they want to avoid it. Therefore, we can still hope for k-resilient protocols with $k > 2$. Second, the solution preference assumption allows processors to "punish" deviating processors. If a processor detects a deviation, then it aborts the protocol by terminating with an invalid output and therefore no processor gets elected. Since all processors know this threatening behavior, a coalition wishes to bias the output by deviating from the protocol without getting detected.

In our setting, malicious processors would like to bias the leader election as much as possible. Our main notion of resilience measures how much the malicious processors can influence the outcome of the leader election. At a high level, in our attacks, the malicious processors almost determine the elected processor. In our resilience results, we prove that the malicious processors might be able to increase the probability of a processor to get elected only by a negligible amount.

Our Contributions: Our primary focus is to find a function $k = k(n)$ as large as possible, such that there exists a k-resilient leader election protocol for an asynchronous unidirectional ring. From the other direction, while considering other topologies of asynchronous networks, we want to find a function $k = k(n)$ as small as possible, such that there **does not exist** a k-resilient fair leader election protocol. In-existence of a k-resilient protocol is called an impossibility claim.

Abraham et al. [4] presented a uniform leader election protocol for a unidirectional ring, named A-LEAD^{uni}, and showed that it is resilient to coalitions of size $k < \frac{1}{2}n$ that are located **consecutively** along the ring (for completeness, we also give a resilience proof of this result in the full paper [28]). For a general asynchronous network, in particular for a unidirectional ring, Abraham et al. showed that there is no k-resilient protocol for every $k \geq \frac{1}{2}n$.

Our main contributions are:

- We give an almost tight resilience analysis for A-LEAD^{uni}, for generally located coalitions. First, we show that it is **not** resilient to a randomly located coalition of size $k = \Theta(\sqrt{n\log(n)})$ with high probability (in the full paper). Then, we also show that this protocol is **not** resilient to $k = 2\sqrt[3]{n}$ carefully located (i.e., worst case) processors (Section 4). Next, we prove that A-LEAD^{uni} is k-resilient for $k = O(\sqrt[4]{n})$ (Section 5).
- We improve A-LEAD^{uni} by introducing a new protocol PhaseAsyncLead, a $\Theta(\sqrt{n})$-resilient fair leader election protocol for a unidirectional ring. We exhibit both an attack with $\Theta(\sqrt{n})$ malicious processors, and prove that PhaseAsyncLead is k-resilient for $k = O(\sqrt{n})$.
- We generalize a previous impossibility result from [4], by showing that there is no k-resilient fair leader election protocol for every asynchronous k-simulated tree. A k-simulated tree is a network that can be simulated by a tree network, where each processor in the tree simulates at most k processors. This generalizes the previous impossibility result because any graph is a $\lceil\frac{1}{2}n\rceil$-simulated tree. Also, it strictly improves the previous result because some graphs are k-simulated trees for $k \ll \frac{1}{2}n$ (for example, trees are 1-simulated trees).
- Unsurprisingly, we show that Fair Coin Toss and Fair Leader Election are equivalent. Essentially, Fair Coin Toss requires the ability to toss a fair binary coin, while fair leader election requires the ability to toss $\log_2(n)$ binary coins. In order to implement leader election using $log(n)$ coin tosses, we assume the ability to run independent coin tosses. We include the details only in the full paper.

Our Techniques: The main idea in our attacks on A-LEAD^{uni} is rushing the information. Namely, the attacking processors reduce the number of messages traversing the ring by not generating their own random value. This allows them to acquire quickly all the information that is required to influence the outcome of the protocol.

The main observation in our resilience proof for A-LEAD^{uni} is that all of the processors must be "k^2-synchronized" during the execution, or else a deviation is detected by the honest processors which abort. In this context, "m-synchronized" means that at every point in time during the execution, every two processors have sent the same number of messages up to a difference of $O(m)$.

Another observation used for our resilience proof for A-LEAD^{uni} is that the information required for a processor p in the coalition in order to bias the output is initially located far away. If the coalition is small enough, then by the time the information reaches p, it is already too late for it to bias the output. This is because p is committed to what it will send in the future, because the honest processors validate the contents of all its future messages (honest processors abort if p does not send the expected messages). For this reason p cannot manipulate the output calculated by its honest successor, so in particular the coalition cannot bias the outcome.

Our main idea in the design of PhaseAsyncLead is forcing processors to be more synchronized, specifically, "k - synchronized" instead of "k^2-synchronized". As a side effect of the synchronization enforcement in our improved protocol, small amounts of information might travel quickly, so the technique used for the previous resilience proof does not apply (as required far away information can now travel quickly). In order to cope with that problem, we use a random function that forces any malicious processor to obtain a lot of information before being able to bias the output. We show that due to "k-synchronization", in order to get that amount of information, a processor must send a lot of messages. However, by the time it sends so many messages, it has already committed to all of its outgoing messages that might affect the output (i.e., all of its future messages that might affect the output are validated by other processors as before).

Related Work: Most of our work focuses the fundamental problem of leader election on a ring. Standard algorithms, which are not fault tolerant were studied in [12, 16, 24]. These classical works, elect the processor with the maximal (or minimal) id as the leader.

Fault tolerance in distributed systems under classic assumptions of Byzantine faults and fail-stop faults has been studied extensively. For examples refer to the following surveys [14, 27]. Fault models that combine both Byzantine, and rational processors, where studied in [2, 3, 7, 22].

There is a variety of game-theoretic approaches to distributed computing. A discussion about the basic definitions and a brief survey can be found in [1]. A well studied problem in the intersection of game-theoretic and distributed computing is secret sharing and multi-party computation [2, 15, 17–21]. Recall that our main procedure is a sub-protocol that performs secret sharing.

Fair leader election, fair coin toss and fair consensus (which is similar to fair coin toss) were explored in various models. For example, Afek et al. [6] study a variety of fairness problems in synchronous networks, Clement et al. [13] study fair consensus in the Gossip model, and finally, maybe the most studied problem is coin-toss in the synchronous full-information model [8–11, 25, 26, 29]. Our usage of a non-constructive random function in PhaseAsyncLead is inspired by the randomized non-constructive approach suggested by [9].

2 MODEL

We use an asynchronous version of the LOCAL computation model (see, [23]). That is, the processors are nodes on a communication graph $G = (V, E)$ and they communicate by sending messages of unlimited size along the edges. Messages are guaranteed to arrive uncorrupted in a FIFO order. Processors are allowed to perform computations and send messages only upon wake up, or upon receiving a message. Additionally, each processor may perform local randomization. Equivalently, each processor has an infinite *random string* as input and it operates deterministically. Each processor has a unique *id* which it cannot modify. The set of *ids*, V, is known to the processors, therefore w.l.o.g we may assume that $V = [n] := \{1, \dots, n\}$. When a processor receives a message, it may send zero or more messages and afterwards it may also select some *output* and terminate. The *output* may be any value, including $\perp$ which denotes *abort*. The messages are delivered asynchronously along the links by some oblivious message schedule which does not depend on the messages' values.

A ***strategy*** of a processor is a (deterministic) function that defines its behavior. Upon waking-up or receiving an incoming message, the strategy decides what messages to send and whether or not to terminate. The decision is based on everything known to the processor until that time: Its *id*, its random string and its history (all the messages it has received). A **protocol** is a vector of n strategies - a strategy for each processor in V. A ***symmetric protocol***, is a protocol that provides the same strategy to all the processors. In game-theoretic terms, the processors are the players and a protocol is a strategy profile.

Given an execution e of a protocol, define $outcome(e) = o$ (for some $o \in V$) if all processors terminate with $output = o$. We call such an outcome $o \in V$, *valid*. Otherwise, if either some processor never terminates, or some processor i terminates with $output_i = \perp$, or some processors i and j terminate with $output_i \neq output_j$, then we have $outcome(e) = \texttt{FAIL}$. Notice that the *output* of each processor is determined *locally*, while the *outcome* of an execution is a function of all the individual outputs so is therefore determined *globally*.

The solution preference assumption might seem problematic due to this definition of outcome. At first glance, one might think that a cheater could "force" all processors to agree on its preferred outcome by always terminating with its most preferred output. If all players know this behavior, since they prefer any valid outcome over a failure, then they will aline with the cheater. However, it is not the case because the strategy of each honest (non-cheating) agent is predetermined. That is, the agents do not have any side-channel to discuss threats. As a motivating reasoning, the technician installs the program on each computer and it is never modified.

A **fair leader election** (FLE) protocol P elects a leader uniformly. Formally, P is a symmetric protocol that assigns a strategy S to every processor such that for every message schedule

$$\forall j \in V : Pr(outcome(e) = j) = \frac{1}{n},$$

where the probability is over the local randomization of the processors.

In order to define a game, we assume that each processor maximizes their expected utility, which is only a function of the outcome. More, we assume that each processor is rational, i.e., it has a higher utility for valid outcomes. Formally,

Definition 2.1. *A* **rational utility** *of a processor p is a function $u_p : [n] \cup \{\texttt{FAIL}\} \to [0, 1]$, such that $u_p(\texttt{FAIL}) = 0$.*

The motivation for the definition is that each processor, including the deviating processors, would prefer any legitimate outcome (in V) over any other outcome (which will result in FAIL), i.e., we assume the solution preference assumption. Notice that any processor can force $outcome(e) = \texttt{FAIL}$ by aborting (terminating with $output = \perp$). So if we had $u_p(\texttt{FAIL}) > u_p(i)$ for some $i \in [n]$ then whenever p sees that the output is going to be i, it would simply abort instead. Intuitively, processors would like to promote their preferred leader while having the protocol succeed.

We start by defining a deviation of a coalition.

Definition 2.2. *(Adversarial Deviation) Let P be a symmetric protocol that assigns the strategy S to every processor. Let $C \subset V$ be a subset of k processors. An adversarial deviation of C from P is a protocol P', in which every processor $i \notin C$ executes S and every processor $i \in C$ executes an arbitrary strategy P'_i. The processors in C are called adversaries and the processors not in C (i.e., in $V \backslash C$) are called honest.*

Concisely, a protocol is ϵ-k-***resilient*** if no coalition of size k can increase the expected utility of each of its members by at least ϵ by an adversarial deviation (note that this is an ϵ-k-Strong Nash equilibria). A protocol is *k-resilient* if it is ϵ-k-*resilient* for $\epsilon = 0$. Formally,

Definition 2.3. *A protocol P is ϵ-k-**resilient** if, for every oblivious messages schedule, for every rational utilities, for every coalition C of size k, and for every adversarial deviation $D = (P_{V-C}, P'_C)$ of the coalition C using P', there exists $p \in C$ such that,*

$$E_D[u_p] \leq E_P[u_p] + \epsilon$$

For a unidirectional ring, which is the focus of this paper, all message schedules are equivalent because each processor has only one incoming FIFO link. For a general scenario, the above definition implies that the adversaries may choose any oblivious schedule. But the selection of the schedule may not depend on the inputs or on the processors' randomization.

To simplify the proofs, rather than considering the expected utility of each adversary, we consider the change in probabilities of valid outcomes. An FLE protocol P with is ϵ-k-*unbiased* if for every adversarial deviation D of size k:

$$\forall j \in V : Pr_D(outcome(e) = j) \leq \frac{1}{n} + \epsilon$$

The following lemma shows the equivalence of resilience and unbias.

Lemma 2.4. *If an FLE protocol P is ϵ-k-resilient then it is ϵ-k-unbiased. If an FLE protocol is ϵ-k-unbiased then it is $(n\epsilon)$-k-resilient.*

Proof. Let P be an ϵ-k-*resilient* FLE protocol ans C be an adversarial coalition of size k. Assign the following rational utility to every processor $p \in C$ we have $u_p(j) := \mathbb{1}_{[j=j_0]}$ and for $p \notin C$ we have $u_p(j) := \mathbb{1}_{[j=p]}$. (We can select any utility for $p \notin C$ and the same proof holds.) Let D be an adversarial deviation from P for C. Then by resilience we get, for $p \in C$, $E_D[u_p] \leq E_P[u_p] + \epsilon = \frac{1}{n} + \epsilon$, but $E_D[u_p] = Pr_D(outcome = j_0)$, so $Pr_D(outcome = j_0) \leq \frac{1}{n} + \epsilon$. Therefore P is ϵ-k-*unbiased*.

For the other direction, let P be an ϵ-k-*unbiased* FLE protocol. Fix a processor p and let u_p be its rational utility. Let D be an adversarial deviation of size k. Since P is unbiased, we get $\forall j \in [n]$: $Pr_D(outcome = j) \leq \frac{1}{n} + \epsilon$. So, $E_D[u_p] = \sum_{j \in [n]} Pr_D(outcome = j)u_p(j) \leq \sum_{j \in [n]}(\frac{1}{n} + \epsilon)u_p(j) =$
$\sum_{j \in [n]} Pr_P(outcome = j)u_p(j) + \sum_{j \in [n]} \epsilon u_p(j) \leq E_P[u_p] + \epsilon n$. Therefore P is $(n\epsilon)$-k-*resilient.* □

3 A RESILIENT FAIR LEADER ELECTION PROTOCOL FOR AN ASYNCHRONOUS UNIDIRECTIONAL RING

We present A-LEAD^{uni}, the asynchronous unidirectional ring FLE protocol of [4, 5]. The protocol relies on a *secret sharing* sub-protocol. First, we describe the protocol without specifying the implementation of the secret sharing sub-protocol. Then we present its implementation.

Each processor i, selects a secret $d_i \in [n]$ uniformly. Then, using a secret sharing sub-protocol, all processors share the secret values $\{d_i\}_{i=1}^n$ with each other, such that each processor i gets the values $\hat{d}_{i,1}, \hat{d}_{i,2}, \ldots \hat{d}_{i,n}$ where $\hat{d}_{i,j} = d_j$ for all j. Then, each processor i validates locally that $\hat{d}_{i,i} = d_i$. If $\hat{d}_{i,i} \neq d_i$ then it aborts by terminating with $output_i = \perp$. Finally, each processor i terminates with $output_i = \sum_{j=1}^n \hat{d}_{i,j} \pmod{n}$.

It remains to define the secret sharing sub-protocol. For didactic reasons, first consider the following non-resilient secret-sharing sub-protocol as in [4]: Each processor j sends its secret d_j, and then forwards $n-1$ messages (receives and sends immediately). If all processors execute this sub-protocol honestly, then each processor receives every secret exactly once. Using the scheme defined above with this secret sharing sub-protocol is not resilient even to a single adversary (a coalition of size $k = 1$). An adversary could wait to receive $n-1$ values before sending its first message and then select its secret value to control the total sum $\sum_{i=1}^n d_i \pmod{n}$. (The pseudo-code can be found in the full paper.)

Ideally, we want every processor to "commit" to its secret value before knowing any other secret value. In order to force processors to "commit" to their values, the processors delay every incoming message for one round. W.l.o.g., define processor 1 to be the *origin* processor, and define it to be the only processor which wakes up spontaneously. Let the rest of the processors be *normal* processors. We specify different functionality for the *origin* processor and for the *normal* processors.

Algorithm: Secret sharing for A-LEAD^{uni}, shares the values $\{d_i\}_{i=1}^n$

1. *Strategy for a normal processor i*: Initially, store d_i in a buffer. For the following n incoming messages, upon receiving a new message m, send the value which is currently in the buffer and then store m in the buffer.
2. *Strategy for origin*: Initially (upon wake-up) send d_1 and then forward (receive and send immediately) $n-1$ incoming messages.

The artificial delay in the secret sharing defined above forces every processor to give away its secret value before it gets to know the other secret values. Furthermore, this delay limits the communication of the adversaries. Two adversaries that are separated by l consecutive honest processors need to send $l+1$ messages in order to transfer information.

Definition 3.1 (*honest segment*). *Given an adversarial coalition $C = \{a_1, \ldots, a_k\} \subseteq V$, where there is no adversary a_i between a_j*

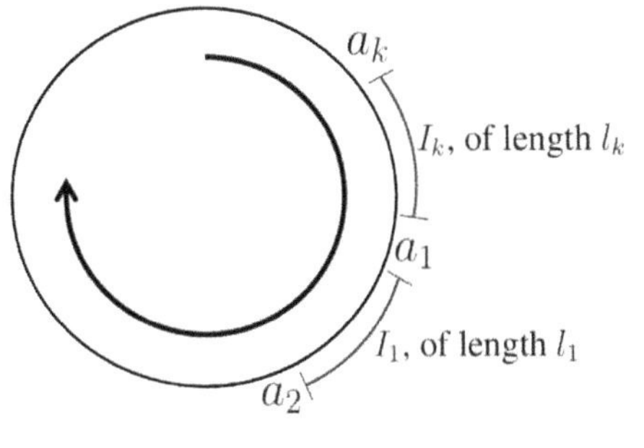

Figure 1: The adversaries locations on the ring.

and a_{j+1}, a maximal set of consecutive honest processors is called an honest segment. Denote by $I_j \subseteq V$ the honest segment between a_j and a_{j+1}, and let l_j be its length. (See Figure 1.)

Definition 3.2. *An adversary a_i with non-trivial segment $l_i \geq 1$ is called an exposed adversary.*

By the definition of *outcome*, an execution of an adversarial deviation from A-LEAD^{uni} might have *outcome* = FAIL for three reasons. First, the execution might run forever because some exposed adversary sends less than n messages. Second, two honest processors might calculate different outputs. Third, an honest processor h might abort by terminating with *output* $= \perp$ if its nth incoming message is invalid, i.e., $\hat{d}_{h,h} \neq d_h$. We characterize these reasons in the following lemma.

Lemma 3.3. *For every adversarial deviation from* A-LEAD^{uni}*, an execution succeeds (outcome $\neq$* FAIL*) if and only if the following conditions hold:*

(1) Every exposed adversary sends n messages.
(2) The sums of all the outgoing messages of the exposed adversaries, are identical modulo n.
(3) For every adversary a_j, its last l_j messages are the secret values of the honest processors in I_j, in the appropriate order.

Note that in order to bias the output, the adversaries do not necessarily need to send the same set of messages. They only need to comply to conditions 1 and 3 while controlling the sum of their outgoing messages (in addition to condition 2). In our attacks we show this is indeed possible. Note that condition 1 implies that every honest processor sends n messages and therefore all the honest processors terminate.

Lemma 3.4. *For every $a_j \in C$, if the last l_j outgoing messages of a_j are the secret values of I_j in the appropriate order, then the calculated sum of every processor in I_j is the sum of the outgoing messages of a_j.*

Proof. Assume that the last l_j messages of a_j are the random values of I_j in the appropriate order. Since I_j is continuous, it is enough to show that every two consecutive processors in I_j calculate the same sum.
Let b, c be two consecutive processors in I_j where c is the successor of b. Let $[m_1, m_2, ..., m_n]$ be the incoming messages of b. Since b is honest, the incoming messages of c are $[r, m_1, ..., m_{n-1}]$ where r is the random value of b. Since the last l_j messages of a_j are the random values of I_j, the last message that b receives, m_n, is its random value r. Therefore, b and c received the same list of messages up to a permutation, in particular their calculated sums in e are equal. □

Lemma 3.5. *Let e be an execution of P. Let $a_j \in C$. The last l_j messages of a_j are the random values of I_j in the appropriate order, if and only if all the processors in I_j pass validation.*

Proof. Denote $I_j = (h_1, h_2, ..., h_{l_j})$ the honest processors along I_j, denote $(m_{l_j}, ..., m_2, m_1)$ the last l_j messages of a_j in the order they are sent. The last message that h_1 receives is a_j's last outgoing message, m_1. Since h_1 is honest, the last message that h_2 receives is m_2 etc. So every processor in I_j receives its random value as the last message if and only if the last l_j messages of a_j are the random values of I_j in the appropriate order.
We conclude because a processor passes validation if and only if its last incoming message is its random value. □

Lemma 3.3. *For every adversarial deviation from* A-LEAD^{uni}*, an execution succeeds (outcome $\neq$* FAIL*) if and only if the following conditions hold:*

(1) Every exposed adversary sends n messages.
(2) The sums of all the outgoing messages of the exposed adversaries, are identical modulo n.
(3) For every adversary a_j, its last l_j messages are the secret values of the honest processors in I_j, in the appropriate order.

Proof. ($\Rightarrow$)Let e be an execution of P. Assume that either 1 or 2 does not hold. If 1 does not hold, then let a_i, a_j be two such adversaries with different sum of outgoing messages S_i, S_j. Let b_i, b_j be their successors, they are honest because $l_i > 0$ and $l_j > 0$. So b_i elects $L[S_i]$ and b_j elects $L[S_j]$. There are two different outputs, and therefore *outcome* = FAIL.
If 2 does not hold, then one of the processors in I_j fails validation by Lemma 3.5, it aborts and therefore *outcome* = FAIL.

($\Leftarrow$)Let e be an execution of P. Assume that 1 and 2 hold. Since 2 holds, all processors pass validation, therefore they all output a valid value in $[n]$ (*output* $\neq \perp$). So it is enough to show that all the honest processors calculate the same sum. Let $h_i \in I_i, h_j \in I_j$ be two honest processors. Since 2 holds, from Lemma 3.4 the sum that h_i calculates is the sum of outgoing messages of a_i, similarly for h_j. Since 1 holds, these two sums are equal, so h_i and h_j calculate the same sum. Therefore all the honest processor terminate with the same output. □

Remark. Originally, in the model defined in [4], the *ids* are unknown prior to the execution, so the protocol begins with a wake-up phase, in which processors exchange *ids* and select an orientation for the ring. Clearly, our attacks still hold for the original protocol, since the adversarial processors can behave honestly during this initial phase. We are unsure how to extend our resilience proofs to handle this case. The worry is that adversaries can abuse the wake-up phase in order to transfer information.

Remark. There exist general commitment schemes in other research areas, but they do not fit in our model. Since we assume unlimited computation power, generic computation-based cryptographic commitment schemes such as one-way functions are useless in our model.

4 ADVERSARIAL ATTACKS ON A-LEAD^{uni}

In this section we describe the adversarial attacks on A-LEAD^{uni}. First, we show that a coalition of size $k = \sqrt{n}$ located at equal distances **can control the outcome**. Namely, for any $w \in [n]$ they can force $outcome = w$. Second, we show that, with high probability, a coalition of $O(\sqrt{n \log n})$ randomly located processors can control the outcome. Third, we show that an adversarially located coalition of size $O(\sqrt[3]{n})$ can also control the outcome.

The case of equally spaced coalition of size $k = \sqrt{n}$ follows from the following.

Lemma 4.1. *For every coalition $C \subsetneq V$ such that every honest segment I_j is of length $l_j \leq k-1$, the adversaries can control the outcome. I.e., for every $w \in [n]$, there exists an adversarial deviation D from* A-LEAD^{uni} *such that for every execution e of D: $outcome(e) = w$.*

Proof. We show that the adversaries can comply to conditions 1 and 3 of Lemma 3.3 while controlling the sum of outgoing messages of every adversary. The main idea is that adversaries never select a secret value for themselves. Moreover, instead of buffering every incoming message, the adversaries just *forward every incoming message immediately*. This way, after $n-k$ rounds, every adversary sent only $n-k$ messages and knows all the secret values of all the $n-k$ honest processors.

Each adversary a_j can control the sum of its outgoing messages while complying to conditions 1 and 3 of Lemma 3.3: It sends a message M (we explain later how to choose M), then it sends $k-l_j-1$ times 0, and finally it sends its last l_j secret value messages of the honest processors in I_j, as expected. Since the total sum is $\Gamma = \sum_{i \notin C} d_i + M + 0 \cdot (k - l_j - 1) + \sum_{i \in I_j} d_i \pmod{n}$, adversary a_j can control this sum by selecting M properly, i.e., for $M = w - \sum_{i \notin C} d_i - \sum_{i \in I_j} d_i \pmod{n}$ we have $\Gamma = w$. □

From the above lemma we deduce the following theorem.

Theorem 4.2. A-LEAD^{uni} *is **not** ϵ-k-resilient for every $k \geq \sqrt{n}$, $\epsilon < 1 - \frac{1}{n}$.*

Proof. Let C be a coalition of size $k \geq \sqrt{n}$ located at equal distances along the ring (equal distances means $|l_i - l_j| \leq 1$). Every honest segment I_j, is of length $l_j < \frac{n-k}{k} + 1 = \frac{n}{k} \leq \sqrt{n} \leq k$. So, $l_j \leq k-1$. Therefore the condition for Lemma 4.1 holds and the adversaries can control the outcome, i.e., $Pr(outcome = 1) = 1 = \frac{1}{n} + (1 - \frac{1}{n})$. Therefore A-LEAD^{uni} is not *ϵ-k-unbiased* for $\epsilon < 1 - \frac{1}{n}$, and, by Lemma 2.4, it is not *ϵ-k-resilient* for $\epsilon < 1 - \frac{1}{n}$. □

Notice that Lemma 4.1 requires only $l_j \leq k-1$ for all j. Unsurprisingly, $k = \Theta(\sqrt{n \log n})$ *randomly* located adversaries, with high probability, will comply to this requirement (an explicit calculation is included in the full paper). Therefore, A-LEAD^{uni} is not resilient against $k = \Theta(\sqrt{n \log n})$ randomly located adversaries. In the full paper we also show a similar attack for $k = \Theta(\sqrt{n \log n})$ randomly located adversaries that do not even know their distances $\{l_j\}$ and the exact number of adversaries k.

Next, we improve the attack from Lemma 4.1 and show that $k = \Theta(\sqrt[3]{n})$ adversaries can control the outcome. The key observation from Lemma 4.1 is that the adversaries do not need to select a secret value for themselves so they can transfer the secret values of the honest processors faster than expected. Notice that when the adversaries do not send their values, they have k extra messages they are allowed to send. In the new attack, the adversaries leverage these extra messages to "push" information faster along the ring.

Technically, we locate the k adversaries having the following distances $l_i = (k+1-i)(k-1)$. For simplicity, one can think that $n = k + (k-1)\sum_{i=1}^{k} i = \frac{1}{2}k^3 + \Theta(k^2)$. However, we prove the attack works for general k and n such that $k \geq 2\sqrt[3]{n}$. We show that a coalition, with such distances, can control the output.

Algorithm: Cubic Attack, strategy for adversary a_i, for electing w.
(1) Transfer (receive and send immediately) $n-k-l_i$ incoming messages. Denote with m_j the jth message that was received. (2) Send $k-1$ messages with the value 0. (3) Wait to receive l_i more incoming messages, to get a total of $n-k$ messages (only receive, do not send them). (4) Send the message $M = w - \sum_{j=1}^{n-k} m_j \pmod{n}$. (5) Send the following messages, one after the other, $m_{n-k-l_i+1}, \ldots, m_{n-k}$

See an explicit pseudo-code in the full paper.

Theorem 4.3 (Cubic Attack). A-LEAD^{uni} *is **not** ϵ-k-unbiased for every $\epsilon < 1 - \frac{1}{n}$ and $k \geq 2\sqrt[3]{n}$.*

For simplicity, assume that the origin is honest. Recall we assumed the distances are $\forall i : l_i = (k+1-i)(k-1)$. In this section, we relax this requirement to $l_k \leq k-1, \forall i < k : l_i \leq l_{i+1} + k - 1$.

Assume we have $k' > 2\sqrt[3]{n}$ adversaries, calculation shows that for every $n > 4$: $\sum_{i=1}^{k'-1}(k'-1)i = (k'-1)\frac{k'(k'+1)}{2} \geq n - k'$. Let $k \leq k'$ be the minimal integer such that $\sum_{i=1}^{k-1}(k-1)i \geq n-k$. Let $(l_i)_{i=1}^{k}$ be integers such that $\forall i : l_i \leq l_{i+1} + k - 1$ and $l_k \leq k-1$. Locate k adversaries along the ring within distances $(l_i)_{i=1}^{k}$ where l_i denotes the distance between a_i and a_{i+1}. Locate the rest of the $k'-k$ adversaries arbitrarily and define them to behave honestly.

Lemma 4.4. *All adversaries terminate.*

Proof. Since $l_1 = max_i(l_i)$, for $n-k-l_1$ rounds all the adversaries behave like pipes. So after $n-k-l_1$ rounds, for every i, a_i received and sent $n-k-l_1$ messages.
Then, a_1 begins step 2. It sends $k-1$ zeros. So a_2 received $n-k-l_1+k-1 \geq n-k-l_2$ messages. Then a_2 begins step 2. Now a_2 sends $k-1$ zeros, therefore a_3 begins step 2 and so on. Until a_k completes step 2.
After completing step 2, a_k sent $n-k-l_k+k-1 \geq n-k$ messages. Therefore, a_1 receives a total of at least $n-k$ messages, so it completes waiting in step 3, performs steps 4-5 and terminates. Then, a_2 receives $n \geq n-k$ messages, so it completes as well and then a_3 completes and so on. □

Let $I_i = \{a_i + 1, ..., a_i + l_i\}$ be an honest segment. Denote the reversed series of the secret values of the segment $secret(I_i) = (d_{a_i+l_i}, ... d_{a_i+1})$.

Lemma 4.5. *In the Cubic Attack, the first $n - k$ incoming messages of each adversary processor a_i are the secret values of the honest processors according to their order along the ring, that is $secret(I_{i-1})$, $secret(I_{i-2})$, $secret(I_{i-3})$, ..., $secret(I_i)$*

Proof. For each adversary a_i, the first l_{i-1} incoming messages of a_i are $secret(I_{i-1})$. Its following l_{i-2} incoming messages are the first l_{i-2} outgoing messages of a_{i-1} which are the first l_{i-2} incoming messages of a_{i-1}, which are $secret(I_{i-2})$ and so on. So the first $n - k = \sum_{j=1}^{k} l_{i-j \pmod k}$ incoming messages of a_i are $secret(I_{i-1})$, $secret(I_{i-2})$, $secret(I_{i-3})$,..., $secret(I_i)$. □

Notice that we implicitly used the fact that each adversary a_i transfers its first $n - k - l_i$ incoming messages. A careful proof by explicit induction uses it.

Theorem 4.3 (Cubic Attack). *A-LEAD^{uni} is **not** ϵ-k-unbiased for every $\epsilon < 1 - \frac{1}{n}$ and $k \geq 2\sqrt[3]{n}$.*

Proof. Consider the adversarial deviation described above. By Lemma 4.4, it is enough to show that all the honest processors terminate with $output = t$. Therefore, by Lemma 3.3, it is enough to show that for each adversary a_i, the last l_i outgoing messages of a_i are the secret values of its honest segment I_i, and that the total sum of its outgoing messages is t.
By Lemma 4.5, the first $n-k$ incoming messages of a_i are $secret(I_{i-1})$, $secret(I_{i-2})$, $secret(I_{i-3})$,..., $secret(I_i)$. In particular, the last l_i of them $m_{n-k-l_i+1}, \ldots, m_{n-k}$ are $secret(I_i)$. So the last l_i outgoing messages of a_i are the secret value of I_i as required.
More, let us calculate the sum of outgoing messages of a_i. By definition, the sum is $\sum_{j=1}^{n-k-l_i} m_j + (t-S) + \sum_{j=n-k-l_i+1}^{n-k} m_j = t - S + S = t$ as required. □

Corollary 4.6. *A-LEAD^{uni} is **not** ϵ-k-resilient for every $0 \leq \epsilon \leq 1 - \frac{1}{n}, k \geq 2\sqrt[3]{n}$*

Finally, we conjecture that A-LEAD^{uni} is *k-resilient* for $k = \Omega(\sqrt[3]{n})$:

Conjecture 4.7. *There exists a constant $\alpha > \frac{1}{8}$, such that for every large enough n, A-LEAD^{uni} is k-resilient for every $k \leq \alpha\sqrt[3]{n}$.*

5 RESILIENCE RESULTS FOR A-LEAD^{uni}

In this section, we outline a proof that shows A-LEAD^{uni} is ϵ-k-*resilient* for $\epsilon = n^{-\Omega(\sqrt[4]{n})}$ and $k = O(\sqrt[4]{n})$. (See a complete proof in the full paper.) For simplicity, assume the *origin* is an adversary, which changes the resilience bound by only 1. Our main resilience result for A-LEAD^{uni} is:

Theorem 5.1. *For every n, A-LEAD^{uni} is ϵ-k-resilient for all $k \leq k_0 := \frac{1}{4}\sqrt[4]{n}$ and $\epsilon \geq n^3 n^{-k_0}$.*

The proof of Theorem 5.1 is in the full paper. Here we provide the intuition for three observations that are the main ingredients in the proof. Let $C = (a_1, ..., a_k)$, where $a_i \in [n]$ be an adversarial coalition of size k. For every adversarial coalition there exists an honest segment of length at least $\frac{n-k}{k} > 60k^3$. W.l.o.g. assume that a_1 precedes that honest segment of length $l_1 \geq 60k^3$.

The first observation is that at every time point, the total number of messages sent by two adversaries a_i and a_j is similar. We show that from the outgoing messages of every adversary, it should be possible to recover $n - k$ secret values of the honest processors in order to pass all the validations. Since an adversary sends only a total of n messages, then it can send up to k spare messages - otherwise some adversary a_i will not be able to send the last l_i messages correctly. From this, we deduce that at every time point t, an adversary cannot send $2k$ messages more than it has received by time t. This implies that all adversaries are approximately synchronized, i.e., the difference between the total number of messages sent by a_i and a_j at any time is at most $2k^2$.

The second observation is that a_1 needs to send at least $n - l_1$ messages before it can obtain any information about d_{h_1}, where h_1 is the honest successor of a_1. In order for information about d_{h_1} reach a_2, a_1 must send at least l_1 messages. Then, in order for that information to travel from a_i to a_{i+1} for every i, the adversary a_1 must send at least $l_i - 4k^2$ more messages. Overall, a_1 sends at least $n - 4k^3$ messages before any information about d_{h_1} reaches a_1. From the selection of a_1 we have $l_1 > 60k^3$, so $n - 4k^3 > n - 60k^3 > n - l_i$ and the observation is complete.

The third observation, which is a direct result of Lemma 3.3, is that when the adversary a_1 sends its $(n - l_1)^{th}$ outgoing message it commits to all of its outgoing messages, since its last l_1 outgoing messages are predetermined to be the secret values of I_1.

Combining the last two observations, we see that the only outgoing message of a_1 which depends on d_{h_1} is its last message, which must be d_{h_1}, therefore the sum of its outgoing messages distributes uniformly. So the output calculated by h_1 is distributes uniformly.

We conjecture that this resilience result is not tight. In the proof, we utilize a synchronization lemma, which states that all processors are synchronized up to $2k^2$ messages. While this lemma is tight (processors indeed might be out of synchronization of order $\Theta(k^2)$), it cannot happen repeatedly in practice. However, we applied this lemma repeatedly in a conservative manner.

6 PHASEASYNCLEAD - A NEW ϵ-$\Theta(\sqrt{n})$-RESILIENT FAIR LEADER ELECTION PROTOCOL

In this section, we present PhaseAsyncLead , a new FLE protocol, which is based on A-LEAD^{uni} and show that it is resilient to $k = O(\sqrt{n})$ adversaries. Our new protocol improves upon A-LEAD^{uni}, for which $k = O(\sqrt[3]{n})$ adversaries can control its outcome (Section 4).

As discussed before, A-LEAD^{uni} simulates "rounds". In every round, each processor in its turn receives a data value and then sends the data value it received in the previous round. Let $Sent_i^t$ be the number of messages a processor i sent until time t. Without adversaries, in A-LEAD^{uni} we have for every time t, $|Sent_i^t - Sent_j^t| \leq 1$. This means that all processors are "*synchronized*". The cubic attack utilizes the asynchronous nature of the network to take the honest processors out of synchronization. Specifically, in the cubic attack there exist an adversary a_i and a time t, such that $|Sent_i^t - Sent_1^t| = \Omega(k^2)$ and the honest processors do not notice any deviation. The key observation that makes the attack possible is that this gap $|Sent_i^t - Sent_1^t|$ is larger than the longest honest segment I_1, therefore the adversary a_1 learns all the data values before committing, i.e., before sending $n - l_1$ messages.

We modify the protocol A-LEAD^{uni} by adding a "phase validation" mechanism that keeps all processors better synchronized. That is, we enforce the following property: for every processor i and time t, $|Sent_i^t - Sent_1^t| = O(k)$.

The "phase validation" mechanism works as follows: Each processor i selects a secret **validation value** $v_i \in [m]$ uniformly (define $m = 2n^2$). In round i, processor i is the current round *validator*, and send v_i. All the other processors transfer the validation value v_i along the ring without delay. Then, the round's validator validates that the validation value it receives is indeed the same one it selected.

The random secret values in A-LEAD^{uni} are denoted by $\{d_i\}_{i=1}^n$, and we call them **data values.** The *output* in A-LEAD^{uni} is defined to be $\sum_{i=1}^n d_i \pmod n$. Recall the point of commitment of adversary a_j: when an adversary a_j sends its $n - l_j$ outgoing message. After the point of commitment, the adversary a_j is obligated to send the data values of the honest segment I_j and therefore cannot affect its outgoing messages anymore. In A-LEAD^{uni}, as seen in Theorem 5.1, there exists an adversary that cannot find out the sum of the data values, $S := \sum_{h \notin C} d_h \pmod n$, before sending too many messages. Therefore, it commits to its outgoing messages before being able to bias the output.

In PhaseAsyncLead every processor receives alternately a message from the original protocol A-LEAD^{uni}, carrying a data value, and a message from the phase validation mechanism, carrying a validation value. Therefore, each processor treats all the odd incoming messages (first, third, etc.) as **data messages** and all the even incoming messages (second, fourth, etc.) as **validation messages**.

While the phase validation mechanism described above keeps all the processors synchronized, adding it to A-LEAD^{uni} makes it non-resilient even to $k = 4$ adversaries. The adversaries can abuse the validation messages to share partial sums of $S = \sum_{h \notin C} d_h \pmod n$ quickly and thus control the outcome. We give a full explanation of such an attack in the full paper. We solve this problem by substituting the "sum" function with a random function f, so adversaries cannot calculate useful partial information about the input.

The resilience proof of PhaseAsyncLead relies on the disability of adversaries to transfer enough information before committing. Due to the difficulty in separating information about data values from information about validation values, we apply f not only on the data values, but also on some of the validation values. We choose the inputs to f such that an adversary commits to them before being able to bias f by manipulating them. After sending $n - l_i$ data messages, a_i is committed to all of its outgoing data messages, however it could still manipulate its last l_i outgoing validation messages. Therefore, we apply f only on the first $n - l$ validation messages where $l \leq \frac{n}{k} \leq \max_j\{l_j\} = l_{j_0}$ (later we also lower bound l). This way, a_{j_0} is committed to all of its outgoing messages that affect the output after sending only $n - l$ messages. Intuitively, after $n - l$ rounds an adversary can collect $(n - l)$ honest validation values and information about $(n - l + 2k)$ data values, since it can abuse k validation values to collect information about data values. We want this to be less than all the information that goes into f. The total information that goes into f is $(n-l)+(n-k)$, so we want $(n-l)+(n-l+2k) < (n-l)+(n-k)$, therefore we need $l > 3k$. Combining this inequality with $l \leq \frac{n}{k}$ we deduce that we need $k = O(\sqrt{n})$ and then we select $l = \Theta(\sqrt{n})$. To conclude, we define $f: [n]^n \times [m]^{n-l} \to [n]$ to be a fixed random function and the output calculated by processor i is $output_i = f(\hat{d}_{i,1}, \hat{d}_{i,2}, \ldots, \hat{d}_{i,n}, \hat{v}_{i,1}, \hat{v}_{i,2}, \ldots \hat{v}_{i,n-l})$.

We define $l := \lceil 10\sqrt{n} \rceil$, because then for $k < \frac{1}{10}\sqrt{n}$ there exists an honest segment of length at least l. Assume w.l.o.g that $l_1 \geq l$, i.e., a_1 precedes a long segment. So as soon as a_1 sends $n - l$ messages, it is committed to the output.

Recall that A-LEAD^{uni} is composed from a scheme that relies on secret sharing sub-protocol that shares $\{d_i\}_{i=1}^n$. PhaseAsyncLead is composed of a similar scheme which relies on a stronger secret sharing sub-protocol: Each processor i, selects secrets $d_i \in [n]$ and $v_i \in [m]$ uniformly. Then, using a secret sharing sub-protocol, all processors share the data values and the validation values $\{d_i\}_{i=1}^n, \{v_i\}_{i=1}^n$ with each other, such that each processor i gets the values $\hat{d}_{i,1}$ and $\hat{d}_{i,2}, \ldots \hat{d}_{i,n}, \hat{v}_{i,1}, \hat{v}_{i,2}, \ldots \hat{v}_{i,n}$ where $\hat{v}_{i,j} = v_j$ and $\hat{d}_{i,j} = d_j$ for all j. Then, each processor i validates locally its identities, i.e., if $\hat{d}_{i,i} \neq d_i$ or $\hat{v}_{i,i} \neq v_i$ then it aborts by terminating with $output_i = \perp$. Finally, each processor i terminates with $output_i = f(\hat{d}_{i,1}, \hat{d}_{i,2}, \ldots, \hat{d}_{i,n}, \hat{v}_{i,1}, \hat{v}_{i,2}, \ldots \hat{v}_{i,n-l})$.

As in A-LEAD^{uni}, processor 1 is called *origin* and the rest of the processors are called *normal* processors. For notation simplicity, we assume the processors are located in an ascending order along the ring $1, \ldots, n$, however, our protocol and resilience proof can be modified to cope with generally located processors.

Algorithm: Secret sharing for PhaseAsyncLead , shares the values $\{d_i\}_{i=1}^n$ and $\{v_i\}_{i=1}^n$

Code for a ***normal*** **processor** i:
Initially, $\hat{d}_{i,i} := d_i$
for $j = 1$ **to** n **do**
  Wait to receive a data message $\hat{d}_{i,i-j \pmod n}$ and then send the previous data message $\hat{d}_{i,i-j+1 \pmod n}$.
  if $j \neq i$ **then**
    wait for an incoming validation message $\hat{v}_{i,j}$ and forward it immediately.
  else
    perform validation by sending v_i and waiting to receive it.
Code for ***origin***:
Initially, $\hat{d}_{1,1} := d_1$
for $j = 1$ **to** n **do**
  Send $\hat{d}_{1,n-j+2 \pmod n}$ and then wait to receive a data message $\hat{d}_{1,n-j+1 \pmod n}$
  if $j \neq 1$ **then**
    forward an incoming validation message $\hat{v}_{1,j}$
  else
    perform validation by sending v_1 and waiting to receive it.
send the last incoming data message $\hat{d}_{1,n-j \pmod n}$

Next, is our main result.

Theorem 6.1. *With exponentially high probability over randomizing f,* PhaseAsyncLead *is ϵ-k-unbiased for every $\epsilon \geq n^{-\sqrt{n}}, k \leq \frac{1}{10}\sqrt{n}$*

This result is asymptotically tight because with high probability over selecting f, it is not ϵ-k-*resilient* for $k = \sqrt{n} + 3$ because the rushing attack demonstrated in Lemma 4.1 works for PhaseAsyncLead as well: While rushing data messages and handling validation messages honestly, within $n-k$ rounds, each adversary knows all the data values, and the first $n-l < n-k$ validation values. Then, each adversary can control at least 3 entries in the input of f. Thus, for a random f, with high probability every adversary a_j can control the output of its segment I_j almost for every input.

6.1 Proof outline

As in Section 5, we perform the following simplifications w.l.o.g: Consider only deterministic deviations and notice the message schedule has no impact over the calculations. We show that with high probability over f, $Pr(outcome = 1) < \frac{1}{n} + \epsilon$.

For deviations from PhaseAsyncLead , the input space is $\chi := [n]^{n-k} \times [m]^{n-k}$ (recall that $m := 2n^2$). For a deviation D, denote by $NoFail^D$ the inputs for which every honest processor h terminate with a valid output, $output_h \neq \bot$, i.e., inputs for every honest processor h, $\hat{d}_{h,h} = d_h$ and $\hat{v}_{h,h} = v_h$.

For every processor b, for every integer $1 \leq i \leq 2n$, denote by $send(b,i)$ the event that b sends its ith outgoing message. For every honest processor h, denote by $s(h) = send(h, 2h)$ the event that h sends its validation message as the validator. Denote by $r(h) = send(h-1, 2h)$ the event that its predecessor, $h-1$, sends a message which is interpreted by h as $\hat{v}_{h,h}$ (so is expected to be equal to v_h). Define the event $nr := send(a_1, 2(n-l))$ be the point of commitment of a_1. Notice that after the event nr occurs, a_1 is committed, i.e., it already sent all the messages that affect the output as it is calculated by processors in I_1, except for the data values of I_1 which are predetermined anyway.

We write $\alpha \rightsquigarrow \beta$ if the event α happens before the event β for every message schedule (this is an intuitive definition, in the full proof we give an equivalent, however more useful definition for this notation).

Given a deviation, an input and an event α, denote by $data(\alpha)$ its value. An honest processor is **unvalidated** if $data(s(h))$ is not used to calculate $data(r(h))$ - for example, it holds when $s(h) \not\rightsquigarrow r(h)$. I.e., when $r(h)$ might happen before $s(h)$ (in the full proof we give an equivalent definition for this notation as well).

Proof outline for Theorem 6.1. In this proof, we call an adversarial deviation a "***deviation***". For each deviation, we partition the inputs space χ into three disjoint sets: $\chi = \chi_1^D \cup \chi_2^D \cup \chi_3^D$.

Intuitively, the first set χ_1^D, contains inputs for which the adversaries break synchronization severely before the event nr occurs. Denote $M_0 = 2(n-l+4k+2)$. In an honest execution (no adversaries), we have the following linear order over the events $s(1) \rightsquigarrow s(2) \rightsquigarrow \ldots \rightsquigarrow s(n-l) \rightsquigarrow nr \rightsquigarrow s(n-l+1) \rightsquigarrow \ldots \rightsquigarrow s(\frac{1}{2}M_0) \rightsquigarrow send(a_i, M_0) \ldots \rightsquigarrow s(n)$. Given a deviation, we say the synchronization is **broken severely** by an input, if there exists an adversary a_i for which $send(a_i, M_0) \rightsquigarrow nr$. Next, we analyze the validation mechanism and show that when the linear order noted above does not hold, honest processors tend to be unvalidated. Leveraging these insights, we show that for inputs that break synchronization severely, there are at least $k+1$ unvalidated honest processors. When an unvalidated processor is the round's validator, the adversaries "guess" the validation value because $data(r(h))$ is calculated independently of $data(s(h))$. From that, we deduce that $Pr(NoFail^D \mid \chi_1^D) \leq \frac{1}{n}$. Note that while the existence of a single unvalidated processor is enough for the explanation above, in the full proof we need $k+1$ of them due to deeper reasons.

The second set, χ_2^D, contains inputs for which the first $2(n-l)$ outgoing messages of a_1 are not informative enough. For such inputs the adversaries are unlikely to reconstruct correctly the data values and the validation values in order for all the validations to succeed (namely, they need the following equalities to hold $\hat{d}_{i,i} = d_i$ and $\hat{v}_{i,i} = v_i$) and therefore the honest processors are likely to abort. More specifically, we get $Pr(NoFail^D \mid \chi_2^D) \leq \frac{1}{n}$.

The set χ_3^D includes the rest of the inputs.

Notice that a deviation is defined by $2nk$ decision functions, that each receives a history (a list of incoming messages) and returns a list (possibly empty) of messages to send.

We partition all the deterministic deviations into equivalence classes $[\cdot]_\approx$ according the first M_0 decision functions of each adversary. Intuitively, two deviations are equivalent if their behavior during the first $\frac{1}{2}M_0$ rounds is identical.

Next, we see that the behavior of the deviation over inputs in χ_3^D until the point of commitment nr is determined by the equivalence class of D. From that we deduce that $Pr(outcome = 1 \mid \chi_3^D) > \frac{1}{n} + \epsilon$ implies a bias property over the class $[D]_\approx$. Since f is random and since the first $2(n-l)$ outgoing messages of a_1 have many different options (by definition $\chi_3^D \cap \chi_2^D = \emptyset$, so they are "informative"), we deduce that the probability for that bias property to hold is low, by using a Hoeffding's concentration inequality. Then, applying a union bound over the equivalence classes we get that for a random f it is likely that all classes do not have that bias property, which implies that $Pr(outcome = 1 \mid \chi_3^D) < \frac{1}{n} + \epsilon$ for every deviation D.

From the law of total probability over $\{\chi_i^D\}_i$ we get that for every D: $Pr(outcome = 1) \leq \frac{1}{n} + \epsilon$. □

Full details and and proofs for PhaseAsyncLead are available in the full paper.

7 RESILIENCE IMPOSSIBILITY FOR GRAPHS WHICH ARE SIMULATED BY TREES

Abraham et al. [4] proved that for any graph there is no ϵ-k-*resilient* FLE protocol for $k \geq \frac{1}{2}n$. In this section we generalize the result to graphs that can be simulated by a tree, where each node in the tree simulates at most k processors. This is a generalization since every graph can be simulated by a tree of size 2, where each node in the tree simulates at most $\lceil \frac{1}{2}n \rceil$ processors.

Definition 7.1. *(k-simulated tree) An undirected graph $G = (V, E)$ is a k-**simulated tree**, if there exists a tree $T = (V_T, E_T)$ and a graph homomorphism $f : V \to V_T$ from G to T such that*

(1) For all $v \in V_T$, $|f^{-1}(v)| \leq k$

(2) For all $v \in V_T$, $f^{-1}(v)$ is connected in G.

Note that requiring f to be a homomorphism means $\{(f(x), f(y)) \mid (x, y) \in E\} \subseteq E_T$. The mapping f can be viewed as a partition of the vertices of G to sets of size at most k, such that each part is connected and the induced graph over the partition constitutes a tree.

We show (in the full paper) that for any such graph, there exists a coalition of size at most k (which is mapped to a single vertex in the simulating tree) that can bias the outcome.

THEOREM 7.2. *For every k-simulated tree, there is no ϵ-k-resilient FLE protocol for every $\epsilon \leq \frac{1}{n}$.*

8 CONCLUSION

We analyzed A-LEAD^{uni} and showed that is resilient to $\Theta(\sqrt[4]{n})$ adversaries, and that it is not resilient to $\Theta(\sqrt[3]{n})$ adversaries. In the construction of the $\Theta(\sqrt[3]{n})$ adversaries attack, we locate the adversaries at increasing distances, to optimize the ability of adversaries to rush the information forward. In the resilience proof, we utilized a synchronization lemma, which states that at any time, different adversaries send a similar number of messages. The exact resilience of the A-LEAD^{uni} remains as an open problem, and we conjecture that A-LEAD^{uni} is actually resilient to $\Theta(\sqrt[3]{n})$ adversaries.

In order to enforce synchronization in A-LEAD^{uni}, we modified it by adding a validated synchronization mechanism and used a random function to calculate the output, instead of a sum. The synchronization mechanism forces all the adversaries to send the same amount of messages at every time point. Namely, it provides an improved synchronization lemma. The random function prevents the adversaries from compressing the information required to bias the output. So it prevents them from utilizing the synchronization mechanism to cheat by calculating partial sums.

We give a tight resilience $\Theta(\sqrt{n})$ bound for our modified protocol, PhaseAsyncLead . While the attack is similar to the previous simpler attack (with $\Theta(\sqrt{n})$ adversaries), our resilience proof is involved. Interestingly, most of the resilience proof focuses on the improved synchronization lemma.

We successfully analyzed the resilience of specific protocols, however, the optimal resilience bound is still an open problem. The only general lower bound for a ring is $\frac{n}{2}$ adversaries [4]. We derived an algorithm that can overcome $\Theta(\sqrt{n})$ adversaries. Closing this large gap, either by improving the general lower bound or by composing a better protocol, would be of great interest.

Our model assumes that the set of *ids* is known to all the processors prior to the execution of the protocol, however in other models they are not known. The obvious solution is adding a renaming phase. However, it raises a potentially significant problem. The problem is that some honest segments might complete the renaming phase, and enter the leader lection protocol, before others. In such a case, adversarial processors might leverage the renaming phase in order to transfer information about the execution of the actual leader election protocol. This requires extending our resilience proofs to consider also a renaming phase, which is very plausible but leave it as an open problem.

REFERENCES

[1] Ittai Abraham, Lorenzo Alvisi, and Joseph Y Halpern. Distributed computing meets game theory: combining insights from two fields. *Acm Sigact News*, 42(2):69–76, 2011.

[2] Ittai Abraham, Danny Dolev, Rica Gonen, and Joe Halpern. Distributed computing meets game theory: robust mechanisms for rational secret sharing and multiparty computation. In *Proceedings of the twenty-fifth annual ACM symposium on Principles of distributed computing*, pages 53–62. ACM, 2006.

[3] Ittai Abraham, Danny Dolev, and Joseph Y Halpern. Lower bounds on implementing robust and resilient mediators. In *Theory of Cryptography Conference*, pages 302–319. Springer, 2008.

[4] Ittai Abraham, Danny Dolev, and Joseph Y Halpern. Distributed protocols for leader election: A game-theoretic perspective. In *International Symposium on Distributed Computing*, pages 61–75. Springer, 2013.

[5] Yehuda Afek, Yehonatan Ginzberg, Shir Landau Feibish, and Moshe Sulamy. Distributed computing building blocks for rational agents. In *Proceedings of the 2014 ACM symposium on Principles of distributed computing*, pages 406–415. ACM, 2014.

[6] Yehuda Afek, Shaked Rafaeli, and Moshe Sulamy. Cheating by duplication: Equilibrium requires global knowledge. *arXiv preprint arXiv:1711.04728*, 2017.

[7] Amitanand S Aiyer, Lorenzo Alvisi, Allen Clement, Mike Dahlin, Jean-Philippe Martin, and Carl Porth. Bar fault tolerance for cooperative services. In *ACM SIGOPS operating systems review*, volume 39, pages 45–58. ACM, 2005.

[8] Miklós Ajtai and Nathan Linial. The influence of large coalitions. *Combinatorica*, 13(2):129–145, 1993.

[9] Noga Alon and Moni Naor. Coin-flipping games immune against linear-sized coalitions. *SIAM Journal on Computing*, 22(2):403–417, 1993.

[10] Michael Ben-Or and Nathan Linial. Collective coin flipping. *randomness and computation*, 5:91–115, 1990.

[11] Ravi B Boppana and Babu O Narayanan. Perfect-information leader election with optimal resilience. *SIAM Journal on Computing*, 29(4):1304–1320, 2000.

[12] Ernest Chang and Rosemary Roberts. An improved algorithm for decentralized extrema-finding in circular configurations of processes. *Communications of the ACM*, 22(5):281–283, 1979.

[13] Andrea Clementi, Luciano Gualà, Guido Proietti, and Giacomo Scornavacca. Rational fair consensus in the gossip model. In *Parallel and Distributed Processing Symposium (IPDPS), 2017 IEEE International*, pages 163–171. IEEE, 2017.

[14] Miguel Correia, Giuliana Santos Veronese, Nuno Ferreira Neves, and Paulo Verissimo. Byzantine consensus in asynchronous message-passing systems: a survey. *International Journal of Critical Computer-Based Systems*, 2(2):141–161, 2011.

[15] Varsha Dani, Mahnush Movahedi, Yamel Rodriguez, and Jared Saia. Scalable rational secret sharing. In *Proceedings of the 30th annual ACM SIGACT-SIGOPS symposium on Principles of distributed computing*, pages 187–196. ACM, 2011.

[16] Danny Dolev, Maria Klawe, and Michael Rodeh. An o (n log n) unidirectional distributed algorithm for extrema finding in a circle. *Journal of Algorithms*, 3(3):245–260, 1982.

[17] Georg Fuchsbauer, Jonathan Katz, and David Naccache. Efficient rational secret sharing in standard communication networks. In *Theory of Cryptography Conference*, pages 419–436. Springer, 2010.

[18] S Dov Gordon and Jonathan Katz. Rational secret sharing, revisited. In *International Conference on Security and Cryptography for Networks*, pages 229–241. Springer, 2006.

[19] Joseph Halpern and Vanessa Teague. Rational secret sharing and multiparty computation. In *Proceedings of the thirty-sixth annual ACM symposium on Theory of computing*, pages 623–632. ACM, 2004.

[20] Gillat Kol and Moni Naor. Games for exchanging information. In *Proceedings of the fortieth annual ACM symposium on Theory of computing*, pages 423–432. ACM, 2008.

[21] Anna Lysyanskaya and Nikos Triandopoulos. Rationality and adversarial behavior in multi-party computation. In *Annual International Cryptology Conference*, pages 180–197. Springer, 2006.

[22] Thomas Moscibroda, Stefan Schmid, and Rogert Wattenhofer. When selfish meets evil: Byzantine players in a virus inoculation game. In *Proceedings of the twenty-fifth annual ACM symposium on Principles of distributed computing*, pages 35–44. ACM, 2006.

[23] David Peleg. *Distributed Computing: A Locality-sensitive Approach*. SIAM, 2000.

[24] Gary L Peterson. An o (n log n) unidirectional algorithm for the circular extrema problem. *ACM Transactions on Programming Languages and Systems (TOPLAS)*, 4(4):758–762, 1982.

[25] Alexander Russell and David Zuckerman. Perfect information leader election in log* n+ o (1) rounds. *Journal of Computer and System Sciences*, 63(4):612–626, 2001.

[26] Michael Saks. A robust noncryptographic protocol for collective coin flipping. *SIAM Journal on Discrete Mathematics*, 2(2):240–244, 1989.

[27] Arif Sari and Murat Akkaya. Fault tolerance mechanisms in distributed systems. *International Journal of Communications, Network and System Sciences*, 8(12):471, 2015.

[28] Assaf Yifrach and Yishay Mansour. Fair leader election for rational agents in asynchronous rings and networks. *arXiv preprint arXiv:1805.04778*, 2018.

[29] David Zuckerman. Randomness-optimal sampling, extractors, and constructive leader election. In *Proceedings of the twenty-eighth annual ACM symposium on Theory of computing*, pages 286–295. ACM, 1996.

Leader Election in Well-Connected Graphs*

Seth Gilbert
National University of Singapore
seth.gilbert@comp.nus.edu.sg

Peter Robinson†
McMaster University
peter.robinson@mcmaster.ca

Suman Sourav‡
National University of Singapore
sourav@comp.nus.edu.sg

ABSTRACT

In this paper, we look at the problem of randomized leader election in synchronous distributed networks with a special focus on the message complexity. We provide an algorithm that solves the implicit version of leader election (where non-leader nodes need not be aware of the identity of the leader) in any general network with $O(\sqrt{n}\log^{7/2} n \cdot t_{mix})$ messages and in $O(t_{mix}\log^2 n)$ time, where n is the number of nodes and t_{mix} refers to the mixing time of a random walk in the network graph G. For several classes of well-connected networks (that have a large conductance or alternatively small mixing times e.g. expanders, hypercubes, etc), the above result implies extremely efficient (sublinear running time and messages) leader election algorithms. Correspondingly, we show that any substantial improvement is not possible over our algorithm, by presenting an almost matching lower bound for randomized leader election. We show that $\Omega(\sqrt{n}/\phi^{3/4})$ messages are needed for any leader election algorithm that succeeds with probability at least $1 - o(1)$, where ϕ refers to the conductance of a graph. To the best of our knowledge, this is the first work that shows a dependence between the time and message complexity to solve leader election and the connectivity of the graph G, which is often characterized by the graph's conductance ϕ. Apart from the $\Omega(m)$ bound in [23] (where m denotes the number of edges of the graph), this work also provides one of the first non-trivial lower bounds for leader election in general networks.

KEYWORDS

Leader Election; Conductance; Mixing time; Random Walks

ACM Reference Format:

Seth Gilbert, Peter Robinson, and Suman Sourav. 2018. Leader Election in Well-Connected Graphs. In *PODC '18: ACM Symposium on Principles of Distributed Computing, July 23–27, 2018, Egham, United Kingdom.* ACM, New York, NY, USA, 10 pages. https://doi.org/10.1145/3212734.3212754

*A full version of the paper is available in [17]. Authors are listed alphabetically.

†Peter Robinson acknowledges the support of the Natural Sciences and Engineering Research Council of Canada (NSERC).

‡This author is the corresponding author. This research was supported by AcRF Tier 1 grant T1 251RES1719 (Adaptive Data Structures: Concurrent, Cache-Efficient, Distributed).

PODC '18, July 23–27, 2018, Egham, United Kingdom

ACM ISBN 978-1-4503-5795-1/18/07...$15.00
https://doi.org/10.1145/3212734.3212754

1 INTRODUCTION

Leader election is one of the most classical and fundamental problem in the field of distributed computing having applications in numerous problems relating to synchronization, resource allocation, reliable replication, load balancing, job scheduling (in master slave environment), crash recovery, membership maintenance etc. Computing a leader can be thought of as a form of symmetry breaking, where exactly one special node or process (denoted as leader) is chosen to take some critical decisions.

Loosely speaking, the problem of leader election requires a set of nodes in a distributed network to elect a unique leader among themselves, i.e., exactly one node must output the decision that it is the leader. There are two well known variants of this problem (cf. [3, 26]), the explicit variant where at the end of the election process all the nodes are required to be aware of the identity of the leader and the implicit variant where the non-leader nodes need not be aware of the identity of the leader.

Often, the implicit variant is sufficient for many practical applications, e.g. its original application for token generation in token ring environments [25] etc. This variant also allows us to clearly distinguish between the two aspects of explicit leader election and costs associated to each of them, i.e. electing a leader (implicitly) as compared to broadcasting the unique id of the leader to all the other nodes. Clearly, any solution for the explicit variant of leader election also solves the implicit variant. However, it is to be noted that any solution for the implicit leader election could solve explicit leader election by broadcasting the identity of the leader to all the nodes. In this paper, we mainly focus on the implicit variant of leader election on a network without edge or link failures.

Compared to deterministic solutions that provide absolute guarantees for the election of a unique leader, randomized solutions guarantees unique leader election with high probability. However, this weakened assumption is still sufficient for many practical applications. With an acceptable error probability, randomization can result in a significant reduction in time and message complexities. This is highly advantageous for large scale distributed systems (e.g. P2P systems, overlay and sensor networks [32, 33, 37]), where scalability is an important issue. Furthermore, in anonymous networks, a randomized solution is often possible by randomly assigning unique identifiers to nodes (as done herein) whereas a corresponding deterministic solution is impossible (see [2]).

This paper focuses on studying the message complexity of implicit leader election in synchronous distributed networks. Here, we show the relationship between the graph connectivity (which is characterized by the graph's conductance ϕ) with the time and number of messages required for leader election. We provide an algorithm that solves implicit leader election in any general network with $\tilde{O}(\sqrt{n} \cdot t_{mix})$ messages and in $\tilde{O}(t_{mix})$ time, where n is the number of nodes and t_{mix} refers to the mixing time of a random walk in the network graph G.[1] Correspondingly, we show that $\Omega(\sqrt{n}/(\phi)^{3/4})$ messages are needed for any leader election algorithm that succeeds with high probability. We also show that the knowledge of the network size n is critical to achieve the said message and time complexities, but surprisingly, knowledge of other graph properties, such as the conductance, mixing time, or diameter is not needed.

Computing Model. We model the network as a connected, undirected graph $G = (V, E)$ with $|V| = n$ nodes and $|E| = m$ edges where nodes communicate over the graph edges. We assume synchronous communication that follows the standard $\mathcal{CONGEST}$ model [30]. In each round, each node can perform some local computation which can involve accessing a private source of randomness. Additionally, each node u is allowed to send a message of size $O(\log n)$ bits through each edge (u, v) incident on u. Nodes do not have predefined ids and there are no node or link failures.

Port Numbering Model. We assume that the nodes know the network size n and wake up simultaneously at the beginning of the execution. Also, nodes are anonymous in the sense that they do not have unique IDs. [2] Each node chooses an id uniformly at random from within the range $[1, n^4]$.[3] Each node u with degree $|d_u|$ has ports $1, \ldots, d_u$, over which it can send messages across undirected links to its neighbors; that is, each neighbor of u is the endpoint of exactly 1 of u's ports. Nodes only know the port numbers of connections and are unaware of their neighbors' identities. We do not assume these mappings to be symmetric: in particular, it can happen that u is connected to v via port number i, whereas v is connected to u via port number $j \neq i$.

Randomized Implicit Leader Election. Every node of a given distributed network has a flag variable (or a boolean variable) initialized to 0 and, after the process of election, w.h.p., only one node, called the leader, sets its flag variable to 1. An algorithm $\mathcal{A}$ solves leader election in T rounds, if within T rounds nodes elect a unique leader w.h.p. (exactly one node raises its flag and all other nodes still have their flag variable set to 0), and no nodes send any more messages after T rounds.

Results. In this paper, we present both upper and lower bounds for the problem of implicit leader election in general networks. We provide an algorithm that solves implicit leader election in any general network with $O(\sqrt{n}\log^{7/2} n \cdot t_{mix})$ messages and in $O(t_{mix}\log^2 n)$ time, where n is the number of nodes and t_{mix} refers to the mixing time of a random walk in the network graph G. If larger message sizes of $O(\log^3 n)$ is allowed, the message and time complexity reduces to $O(\sqrt{n}\log^{3/2} n \cdot t_{mix})$ and $O(t_{mix})$ respectively. This implies significantly faster and efficient solutions (that are sub-linear in terms of message complexity) for leader election in several important classes of well-connected graphs that have a large conductance or alternatively a small mixing time. For e.g., to solve implicit leader election, in expander graphs (see [19] for applications) that have a mixing time of $O(\log n)$, it takes only $O(\log^3 n)$ time and $O(\sqrt{n}\log^{9/2} n)$ messages; in hypercube graphs, that have a mixing time of $O(\log n \log\log n)$, it takes only $O(\log^3 n \log\log n)$ time and $O(\sqrt{n}\log^{9/2} n \log\log n)$ messages. The algorithm can also be used for solving the explicit variant of leader election by adding a broadcasting procedure, wherein the leader broadcasts its identity to all other nodes. For well connected graphs, this breaks the $\Omega(m)$ lower bound given in [23] (where m denotes the number of edges of the graph) and nearly matches with the $\Omega(\sqrt{n})$ lower bound for clique graphs [24] (as cliques have constant conductance).

Correspondingly, we show that $\Omega(\sqrt{n}/(\phi)^{3/4})$ messages are needed for any leader election algorithm that succeeds with probability at least $1 - o(1)$. This nearly matches with the upper bound as we know that $\Theta(1/\phi) \leqslant t_{mix} \leqslant \Theta(1/\phi^2)$ from [34].

With similar analysis, we also provide lower bounds for other graph problems like broadcast and spanning tree construction in terms of the graph's conductance. Our lower bounds also apply for the $\mathcal{LOCAL}$ model [30], where there are no restrictions on the message size. Other than the $\Omega(m)$ bound in [23], to the best of our knowledge, this is the first non-trivial lower bound for randomized leader election in general networks. Also, ours is one of the first results to show the dependence of the time and message complexity to solve leader election on the connectivity of the graph G, which is often characterized by the graph's conductance ϕ.

Additionally, we show that the knowledge of the network size n is critical for our algorithm to succeed by giving a lower bound of $\Omega(m)$ for all graphs if n is not known. However surprisingly, the knowledge of other graph properties, like the conductance, mixing time, or diameter is not needed.

Prior Works. Leader election, a fundamental paradigm in the theory of distributed computing has been widely studied. The problem of leader election was first stated by Gérard Le Lann in [25] in the context of token ring networks, and thereafter has been extensively studied for various types of networks, scenarios and communication models. For particular types of networks topologies like token rings, mesh, torus, hypercubes and cliques the problem of leader election has been well-studied resulting in specialized algorithms and lower bounds in terms of both, time and message complexities (e.g. [1, 9, 11, 13, 22, 24, 26, 30, 31, 36] and references therein). In a seminal paper Gallager, Humblet and Spira [15], provided a deterministic solution for general graphs by finding the minimum spanning tree of the graph in $O(n \log n)$ time and exchanging a total of $O(m \log n)$ messages. Thereafter, Awerbuch [4] provided an $O(n)$ round deterministic algorithm with a message complexity of $O(m + n \log n)$ messages, where m refers to the total number of edges in the graph. Peleg [29] provided an $O(D)$ time optimal algorithm for leader election with a message complexity of $O(mD)$, where D refers to the diameter of the graph. In [23], an algorithm is given that requires only $O(m)$ messages though it could take arbitrary (albeit finite) time.

There also exists significant amount of literature (see [8, 12, 18, 35] and references therein) that provides a solution for leader election on fault prone networks, with possible node or link failures.

The best known bounds for general graphs are as follows. In [23] Kutten et al. show that $\Omega(m)$ is the lower bound on messages and $\Omega(D)$ is the lower bound on time for any implicit leader election algorithm. Unlike the deterministic case where an algorithm cannot be simultaneously time and message optimal (e.g. in a cycle any $O(n)$ time deterministic algorithm requires at least $\Omega(n \log n)$ messages even when nodes know n [14]), they show that for the randomized case simultaneous optimality can be achieved in certain

[1] Throughout the paper, we use the $\tilde{O}$ notation to hide $\log n$ factors.
[2] Our lower bound holds even if nodes start with unique IDs.
[3] This range guarantees that the chosen values are unique with high probability [26] (Chapter 4, page 72).

cases. In particular, they give an algorithm that takes $O(m)$ messages (not time optimal), an algorithm that, w.h.p., takes $O(m \log \log n)$ messages and $O(D)$ time (almost simultaneously optimal).

In [24], Kutten et al. show that in terms of message complexity, there exists a gap between the implicit and the explicit variants of leader election. For the explicit variant, all nodes needs to be informed of the identity of the leader, and as such $\Omega(n)$ messages is the obvious lower bound for all graphs. However, for the implicit version they provide a sub-linear bound algorithm on complete networks that runs in $O(1)$ rounds and (w.h.p.) uses only $O(\sqrt{n} \log^{3/2} n)$ messages to elect a unique leader (w.h.p.). They extend this algorithm to solve leader election on any connected graph G in $O(t_{mix})$ time and $O(t_{mix} \cdot \sqrt{n} \log^{3/2} n)$ messages, where t_{mix} is the mixing time of a random walk on G.

A key difference, however, was that they assume that every node in the graph knows the mixing time of the graph, which significantly simplifies the problem. An important challenge addressed by our algorithm is (effectively) estimating when a collection of random walks is well-enough mixed. While there is a recent result in [27] that shows how nodes can quickly estimate the mixing time of the graph, their algorithm requires $\Omega(m)$ messages and hence cannot be used for the purpose of achieving a small message complexity, where m is the total number of edges in the graph.

2 PRELIMINARIES

In this section, we describe some basic definitions and concepts that we make use of throughout the paper. First, we give a brief overview and the definition of graph conductance. Next, we describe some basic notation for random walks on a graph G including its mixing time, and state the relationship between the mixing time and the conductance of G.

Conductance, in general, is a characterization of the bottleneck in communication of a graph. The notion of graph conductance was introduced by Sinclair [20]. For a given graph $G = (V, E)$, a subset of nodes $U \subseteq V$ and cut $\mathcal{K} = (U, V \setminus U)$, we define $E_{\mathcal{K}}$ to be the subset of edges across the cut $\mathcal{K}$, and the volume $\text{Vol}(U) = \sum_{v \in U} d_v$, where d_v refers to the degree of node v. The cut-conductance is defined as $\phi_{\mathcal{K}} = |E_{\mathcal{K}}| / \min\{\text{Vol}(U), \text{Vol}(V \setminus U)\}$. The conductance of the graph G is defined as the minimum of the cut-conductances across all possible cuts $\tilde{\mathcal{K}}$, i.e., $\phi(G) = \min\{\phi_{\mathcal{K}} \mid \mathcal{K} \in \tilde{\mathcal{K}}\}$. We write ϕ instead of $\phi(G)$, when graph G is clear from the context.

For a random walk on $G(V, E)$, we define a node set $V = \{v_1, \ldots, v_n\}$ and an $n \times n$ transition matrix P of G. Each position of the form $P[i, i]$ in the transition matrix has an entry $p_{v_i, v_i} = 1/2$, else if $i \neq j$ then $P[i, j]$ has an entry $p_{v_i, v_j} = 1/2d_{v_i}$ if there is an edge $(v_i, v_j) \in E$, otherwise $p_{v_i, v_j} = 0$. At a particular step, the entry p_{v_i, v_j} gives the probability of a random walk moving from node v_i to node v_j. This exactly corresponds to a *lazy* random walk wherein a random walk either stays in the current node with probability $1/2$; otherwise moves to a neighbor with probability $1/2d_{v_i}$. The probability distribution π_t determined by P represents the position of a random walk after t steps. If some node v_i starts a random walk, the initial distribution π_0 of the walk is an n-dimensional vector having all zeros except at index i where it is 1. After the node v_i has chosen to forward the random walk token, either to itself or to a random neighbor, the distribution of the walk (after 1 step) is given by $\pi_1 = P\pi_0$ and in general we have $\pi_t = P^t \pi_0$. For any connected graph G, the distribution will eventually converge to the stationary distribution $\pi_* = (q_1, \ldots, q_n)$, which has entries $q_i = d_{v_i}/(2|E|)$ and satisfies $\pi_* = P\pi_*$.

The mixing time of an n-node graph G, $t_{mix}(G)$ is defined as the minimum t such that, for each starting distribution π_0, $\| P\pi_t - \pi_* \|_\infty \leqslant \frac{1}{2n}$, where $\| \cdot \|_\infty$ denotes the usual maximum norm on a vector. We simply write t_{mix} instead of $t_{mix}(G)$, when graph G is clear from the context.

Note that, the connectedness of a graph G (determined by its conductance ϕ) and the mixing time of a random walk on G are closely related. Better connectivity implies fast mixing and vice versa. There is a well known result that formally relates the graph conductance ϕ to the mixing time (see [34]) as follows

$$\Theta(1/\phi) \leqslant t_{mix} \leqslant \Theta(1/\phi^2) \qquad (1)$$

3 A LEADER ELECTION ALGORITHM FOR WELL-CONNECTED NETWORKS

In this section, we provide an algorithm that solves implicit leader election for any given graph G with time complexity of $\tilde{O}(t_{mix})$ and more importantly, with $\tilde{O}(\sqrt{n}\, t_{mix})$ message complexity.

The proposed algorithm, in its initial phase is similar to the algorithms given in [16, 24] where the initial objective is to reduce the number of competing nodes (contenders), while also ensuring that there exists at least one contender (w.h.p.). For this purpose, each node v in the network graph G, elects itself as a contender with a probability of $c_1 \log(n)/n$, where c_1 is a sufficiently large constant. As such, the probability of no node electing itself as a contender is $(1 - \frac{c_1 \log n}{n})^n \approx \exp(-c_1 \log n) = n^{-c_1}$; thus, implying that w.h.p. the number of contenders is nonzero.

Now, imagine a scenario in which each of these contenders contacts a set of nodes, which we refer to as the contender's target set. If the target set is large enough (say, $n/2 + 1$), then for any two contenders we can say that there would be common/intersecting node that would have communicated with both contenders. Thereafter, the contenders can communicate via this intersecting node. If all contenders have a sufficiently large target set then all contenders would be able to communicate with one another. We design our algorithm based on this idea.

First, we determine the minimum size of the target set needed to guarantee an intersection w.h.p. between the target sets of any two contenders. It can be easily shown with the birthday paradox argument that if any two contender nodes u and v contact $O(\sqrt{n \log n})$ random nodes, then w.h.p. there is at least one node w that was chosen by both u and v. By the definition of mixing time, if a random walk has taken at least t_{mix} steps, then (for all practical purposes) its end point can be considered as a random node. Therefore, each contender node can find $O(\sqrt{n \log n})$ random nodes by performing $O(\sqrt{n \log n})$ independent random walks in parallel. The random walks essentially function as mechanisms for selecting/sampling "random" nodes, where the guarantee is if the length of the walk is long enough, the choice is close to uniform. We might as well think of the random walks as a black box that return a collection of random nodes. However, as nodes are not aware of the mixing time, this technique cannot be used directly to obtain random nodes.

Without knowledge of the mixing time, it is difficult (if not impossible) to obtain a set of nodes that are chosen uniformly at random by using random walks. Therefore, the major challenge reduces to correctly obtaining a set of possibly non-random nodes (as random walks might be of length less than the mixing time) that satisfy the required properties that we had hoped to achieve from a uniformly random chosen target set. One difficulty here lies in determining the ideal length of the random walks of each contender without the knowledge of the mixing time. To deal with this, we use a guess and double strategy where in each iteration nodes guess a length for the random walk, perform random walks of the chosen length, determine based on some criteria if the length is sufficient; if not the next iteration begins with double the previous estimate.

The critical part is to determine the criterion for which we can consider the length of the random walks to be sufficient. A natural solution would be to check if there are enough intersections in the target set (with target sets of other contenders). For e.g., if the target set of each contender had an intersection with target sets of all other contenders, all of them can communicate via the intersecting node(s). However, then we would require the knowledge of the exact number of contenders to determine termination, which is difficult to obtain with certainty. In fact, we show that an intersection with greater than half of the contenders is sufficient and obtainable.

Given such a criterion, it creates another challenge, as it might be the case that all the random walks do not terminate in the same round. For e.g., consider the case where a large number of contenders belong to the same locality of the graph and as a result they contact each other quickly, via their random walks. However, a few of the contenders are slightly far off from this locality. In this case, the target set of the locally placed contenders would belong to the same locality (and not nearly randomly spread). As such, it would be difficult for the far flung contenders to make contact with any of the locally placed contender's target sets, requiring much longer lengths of random walks than the mixing time. For this case, we would also need to guarantee that the random walks that terminate early are still easily discoverable.

To deal with the above challenges, we provide a twofold stopping criterion: first, we want to ensure that the end points of the random walks of a contender intersect with the random walks of at least half of the total number of contenders; second, we would also like to ensure that the end points of these random walks are sufficiently spread out, such that other random walks do not spend too much time discovering them. Another crucial part to consider, is the congestion that might be caused by the information carried along the random walks.

Basically, the given randomized leader election algorithm can be divided into three major parts. First, a node makes a probabilistic decision determining its candidature, i.e., whether or not it becomes a contender. Then, in the second part, contenders guess and double length of random walks until it satisfies some required properties. Lastly, based on information retrieved from random walks, a node elects itself as the leader if it satisfies a certain winning condition.

We provide the following contender lemma which restricts the total number of possible contenders. The missing proofs can be found in the full version of the paper [17].

LEMMA 1. *(Contender Lemma) With high probability the number of contenders is in the range* $[\frac{3}{4}c_1 \log n, \frac{5}{4}c_1 \log n]$, *where* c_1 *is a sufficiently large constant.*

Each contender node u creates $c_2\sqrt{n \log n}$ tokens and starts $c_2\sqrt{n \log n}$ random walks of length t_u in parallel, where c_2 is a constant > 2. Each random walk is represented by a token $\langle u, t_u \rangle$ (of $O(\log n)$ bits), where u represents the node's id, and t_u represents the length of the random walk. At each step of the random walk t_u is decremented by 1, until it finally becomes 0. We define *proxies* of node u as the nodes where the random walks generated by u complete t_u steps, where t_u is either u's current or final guess of the length of the random walk. Two contender nodes are said to be *adjacent* if they share at least one proxy.

The algorithm guarantees the following properties at the end of the execution:

Intersection Property: A contender u satisfies the intersection property iff u is adjacent to at least $\geqslant \frac{3}{4}c_1 \log n$ of the other contender nodes. Using Lemma 1, we see that any node which satisfies the intersection property is adjacent to more than half of the total number of contenders (as $\frac{3}{4}c_1 \log n \geqslant \frac{1}{2}\left(\frac{5}{4}c_1 \log n\right)$) w.h.p.

Distinctness Property: We say that a contender node u satisfies the distinctness property if $\geqslant \frac{c_2}{2}\sqrt{n \log n}$ of its proxies are distinct. For a particular guess of t_u, a proxy p_u of a random walk belonging to u is called a distinct proxy only if p_u is the end node of exactly one random walk belonging to u (among the $c_2\sqrt{n \log n}$ many random walks belonging to u).

In the $\mathcal{CONGEST}$ model, due to the restriction on the message size, it is impossible to perform too many walks in parallel along an edge. We solve this issue by sending only one token and the count of tokens that need to be sent by a particular contender which is still $O(\log n)$, and not all the tokens themselves. Similarly, our algorithm also requires some id information (set of ids of other contenders) to be sent along the random walk. We note that the maximum possible number of contenders is $\leqslant \frac{5}{4}c_1 \log n$ w.h.p. (c.f. Lemma 1). In the worst case, an intermediate node might have to deal with $O(\log n)$ messages of $O(\log^2 n)$ size each, introducing a maximum possible delay of $O(\log^2 n)$ rounds. To account for this delay, in the algorithm, we define $T = \frac{25}{16}c_1 t_u \log^2 n$, and use this upper bound estimate to keep the execution of the algorithm in synchrony. We relegate the formal details of handling congestion to the proof of Lemma 12.

Algorithm 1 Leader Election: Initialization

1: Each node generates a random id in the range $[1, \ldots, n^4]$.
2: Each node designates itself a contender with probability $c_1(\log n/n)$.
3: Each contender begins the protocol by executing a Random Walk Phase of length $O(1)$.
4: Any node that is not a contender declares itself as non-leader.

Consider contender nodes that are yet to satisfy the intersection and distinctness properties as active nodes; consequently nodes that have already satisfied the said properties are considered inactive. That is, all nodes that will not double their estimate of t_u are considered as inactive. Note that, all the active nodes are synchronous and for all inactive nodes, the distance to their respective proxies is less than the current estimate of T (of the active nodes).

Algorithm 2 Leader Election: Random Walk Phase of length t_u of contender u.

1: Each contender u initiates $c_2\sqrt{n \log n}$ parallel random walks of length t_u for time $T = O(t_u \log^2 n)$.
2: When a random walk completes, the last node in the random walk is called a **proxy of** u.
3: Node u then performs three synchronized rounds of information exchange with its proxies, each taking time $T = O(t_u \log^2 n)$:
Round 1. Each proxy sends back its id, a Boolean d determined by distinctness, and the set I_1, which contains the ids of the other contenders for which it is also a proxy.
Round 2. u sends set I_2 to its proxies, which is the union of the I_1 sets received in round 1.
Round 3. Proxies send back set I_3: the union of the I_2 sets received.
4: Contender u decides to stop if the *Intersection Property* and the *Distinctness Property* are met for the set I_2.
5: Let I_4 be the union of all I_3 sets received by u. If u decides to stop, has the largest id in set I_4, and it has not previously received any *winner* messages, then it designates itself as the leader and sends its proxies a *winner* message.
6: The first time a proxy receives a *winner* message, it sends it to all its contenders.
7: The first time a contender receives a *winner* message, it sends it to all its proxies and appends it to all future messages.
8: At the end of the random walk phase, a contender that has not decided to stop waits $2T$ time (for *winner* messages to propagate) and then begins a new Random Walk Phase of length $2t_u$.
9: Any contender that has stopped and is not a leader, declares itself as non-leader.

Observation 2. *All inactive contender nodes satisfy both the intersection and the distinctness properties.*

Lemma 3. *For any active contender node y, after the iteration where $t_y = c_3 t_{mix}$ ($c_3 \geqslant 1$), w.h.p. y satisfies both the intersection and distinctness properties. In fact, y has intersecting proxies with all of the other contenders (both active and inactive).*

Proof. Consider a set Y consisting of all active contenders and a set X of all the inactive contenders (contenders that decided not to double their estimate after some previous epoch). We prove the lemma using the following claims.

Claim 4. *Each contender node in Y is adjacent to (has intersecting proxies with) all the other contender nodes, w.h.p.*

Proof. For a contender node $y \in Y$, when $t_y = c_3 t_{mix}$ ($c_3 \geqslant 1$), y has $c_2\sqrt{n \log n}$ random proxies by running $c_2\sqrt{n \log n}$ independent random walks of length $= c_3 t_{mix}$ (proxies are random by the definition of mixing time). For any contender node $x \in X$, since x satisfies the distinctness property, it has at least $\frac{c_2}{2}\sqrt{n \log n}$ distinct proxies. The probability of non-intersection between this set of $\frac{c_2}{2}\sqrt{n \log n}$ distinct proxies and the set $c_2\sqrt{n \log n}$ random proxies is given by a birthday-paradox argument to be $\left(1 - \frac{(c_2/2)\sqrt{n \log n}}{n}\right)^{c_2\sqrt{n \log n}} = \exp\left(-\frac{(c_2)^2}{2} \log n\right) = O(1/n^{\Omega(1)})$. The statement is true for all pairs of nodes in (Y, X) by taking a simple union bound. Thus, with high probability, each contender node in Y has at least one common/intersecting proxy with any contender node in X.

Now, consider two different contenders $y_1, y_2 \in Y$, each of which has a set of $c_2\sqrt{n \log n}$ random proxies. Using similar arguments as above it can be easily shown that each contender node in Y has at least one common/intersecting proxy with every other contender node in Y, w.h.p.

This implies that each contender in Y has intersecting proxies with all the other contenders, both in X and Y, and is thus adjacent to all the other contenders. □

Claim 5. *Each contender node y in Y satisfies the distinctness property, w.h.p., when $t_y = c_3 t_{mix}$, where c_3 is a constant $\geqslant 1$.*

The proof of the above claim can be found in [17]. □

The time complexity of the algorithm, is determined by the following lemma.

Lemma 6 (Safety Lemma). *In $O(t_{mix} \log^2 n)$ time, w.h.p. all contender nodes satisfy both the intersection and the distinctness properties. Consequently, for the given algorithm, every node eventually stops, no later than $O(t_{mix} \log^2 n)$ time.*

Proof. Each contender u in parallel, runs several random walks till it satisfies the intersection and distinctness properties. u begins with an initial estimate of 1 and doubles each time till the above condition is not satisfied. This is the standard guess and double strategy and this does not increase the overall complexity by more than a constant factor of the maximum estimate. From Observation 2 and Lemma 3, we see that all contender nodes satisfy both the conditions w.h.p. when $t_u = c_3 t_{mix}$ ($c_3 \geqslant 1$). Since the algorithm runs an upper-bound of t_u, i.e. $T = O(t_u \log^2 n)$ to avoid congestion, the time required to satisfy both the intersection and distinctness property is $O(T) = O(t_{mix} \log^2 n)$. □

Lemma 7 (At least one leader). *After the iteration where the active nodes estimate $t_u = c_3 t_{mix}$, where c_3 is a constant $\geqslant 1$, if no node has elected itself as leader in any of the earlier rounds, at least one contender node elects itself as the leader.*

Proof. Consider the iteration i, where the active nodes estimate $t_u = c_3 t_{mix}$ ($c_3 \geqslant 1$). We look at the contender node with the highest id, say v_h. In iteration i, v_h can either be inactive or active depending on whether it has stopped. (If v_h is inactive, we look at the iteration j ($j < i$) in which v_h became inactive). We show that for either case, if no other node has elected itself as the leader in any of the earlier rounds then v_h becomes leader.

Suppose that v_h becomes inactive in iteration j where ($j < i$) and no other node has elected itself as the leader in any of the earlier iterations. By Observation 2, v_h satisfies both the intersection and the distinctness properties. Alternatively, it could be that v_h is active until iteration i, where the active nodes estimate $t_u = c_3 t_{mix}$. Also in that case, Lemma 3 says that v_h satisfies the intersection and the distinctness properties. For either case, since v_h has the highest id among the contender nodes, satisfies both the distinctness and the intersection properties and none of the other nodes has elected itself as the leader in any of the earlier rounds (implying that v_h has not received a *winner* message), v_h satisfies all the required conditions and becomes leader. □

LEMMA 8 (AT MOST ONE LEADER). *After the completion of the algorithm, at most one contender node elects itself as the leader.*

We prove the lemma by combining the following two claims:

CLAIM 9. *Two different nodes cannot elect themselves as the leader in an iteration of the algorithm.*

PROOF. Suppose two nodes u and v elect themselves as the leader in the same iteration of the algorithm. We know by the description of the algorithm that any node that becomes the leader would first need to satisfy both the intersection and the distinctness properties. Therefore, both contenders u and v would have at least $\frac{c_2}{2}\sqrt{n \log n}$ distinct proxies and would be adjacent to $> \frac{3}{4}c_1 \log n$, i.e., more than half of the contenders. Recall that the sets I_2 of u and v (denoted by $I_2(u)$ resp. $I_2(v)$) contain the ids of their adjacent contenders. Let w be a contender whose id is in the intersection of $I_2(u)$ and $I_2(v)$. As both u and v are adjacent to more than half of the contenders, there must be at least one such node w.

Without loss of generality, assume that the id of u is larger than the id of w. Since $w \in ID_2(u)$, some proxy p_1 of u must have also been a proxy of w in this iteration. Similarly, since $w \in ID_2(v)$, some proxy p_2 of v must have also been a proxy of w in this iteration. Then, by the description of the algorithm w would obtain the ids of both u and v in the set $I_2(w)$, which it then disseminated to all its proxies. The proxies p_1 and p_2 both get this information $I_2(w)$ (of ids of u and v) which is then forwarded to u and v respectively as sets $I_3(p_1)$ and $I_3(p_2)$ respectively. This means that v must have known about u while checking the winning condition and hence it knows that its id was not maximal, a contradiction. □

CLAIM 10. *If a node elects itself as the leader in some iteration i, no other node can elect itself as the leader in any subsequent iteration.*

PROOF SKETCH. Suppose two nodes u and v elect themselves as the leader and suppose that u does so in iteration i whereas v does so in iteration $j > i$. For this case we show that when iteration $i + 1$ begins, more than half of the contender nodes are aware that some node u has become the leader. If any other contender node v satisfies both, the intersection and the distinctness properties, then it must have interacted with at least one of the nodes that is aware of the existence of a leader and thereby also becomes aware of the leader. This means that v must have known about the existence of a leader by receiving a *winner* message (either directly or indirectly), leading to a contradiction. □

This completes the proof of Lemma 8.

Combining Lemma 7 and Lemma 8, we obtain the following lemma that determines the correctness of the algorithm.

LEMMA 11 (UNIQUE LEADER LEMMA). *With high probability and in $O(t_{mix} \log^2 n)$ time, exactly one contender becomes the leader.*

LEMMA 12 (MESSAGE COMPLEXITY LEMMA). *The total number of messages sent by the above algorithm is at most $O(\sqrt{n} \log^{7/2} n \cdot t_{mix})$ w.h.p. If larger message size of $O(\log^3 n)$ is allowed the total number of messages comes down to $O(\sqrt{n} \log^{3/2} n \cdot t_{mix})$.*

PROOF. To calculate the message complexity, we look at the various messages that are sent by the algorithm. Considering Algorithm 2, we observe that all the information is sent only along the random walks. The messages that are sent include the random walk tokens, the sets I_1, I_2 and I_3, the Boolean d and the *winner* messages. In each phase (iteration), the maximum number of steps taken by any of these messages is proportional to the estimate of the length of the random walk t_u. The maximum possible estimate is $O(t_{mix})$ (c.f. Lemma 6) and as this estimate is chosen in a guess-and-double style which only increases the overall complexity to a constant factor of the maximum guess for a successful trial, the overall number of steps taken throughout the algorithm (without accounting for congestion) by any of these messages is $O(t_{mix})$ as well.

Individually, the Boolean d and the *winner* messages are of $O(1)$ bits and the random walk tokens are of $O(\log n)$ bits. Since the ids of the contenders are of $O(\log n)$ bits and number of contenders is $\leqslant \frac{5}{4}c_1 \log n$ (c.f. Lemma 1), the sets I_1, I_2 and I_3 can be of size $O(\log^2 n)$ as they can contain the ids of $O(\log n)$ other contenders. This implies that an intermediate node might receive up to $O(\log n)$ many $O(\log^2 n)$ sized messages.

First, consider the case where $O(\log^3 n)$ message sizes are allowed to be sent over an edge. Each contender node ($O(\log n)$ many) initiates a total of $O(\sqrt{n \log n})$ messages which backtracks after reaching the proxies taking a total of $O(t_{mix})$ steps. Additionally, the *winner* message also takes only $O(t_{mix})$ many steps. As there would be no congestion, the message complexity here would be $O(\log n) \times O(\sqrt{n \log n}) \times O(t_{mix})$ w.h.p. , which equals $O(\sqrt{n} \log^{3/2} n \cdot t_{mix})$.

Now, we consider the standard $\mathcal{CONGEST}$ model where message sizes are restricted to $O(\log n)$. Firstly, during the execution of the random walk, a contender node u does not send $O(\sqrt{n \log n})$ different tokens for each random walk, but rather sends only one token along with a count of tokens that need to be sent in a particular path. For multiple instances of the variable d originating from different proxies of the same contender, only the summation value is sent (which is $O(\log n)$). Multiple messages coming from either the same or different nodes could possibly lead to congestion. For messages that have the same destination, we send only one distinct copy of id information over a particular edge (i.e. we use a filtering and forwarding technique wherein if an intermediate node has sent the information to a particular destination once it does not send the same information again to that destination). For messages having different destinations, there is a possibility that $O(\log n)$ many messages of $O(\log^2 n)$ size could arrive at a particular intermediate node. Larger sized messages of $O(\log^2 n)$ bits would have to be broken down into $O(\log n)$ sized messages, i.e. we can assume that each $O(\log n)$ sized message contains the information of the id of a node and some additional $O(1)$ bits. The maximum delay possible here an at intermediate node is $O(\log^2 n)$. We note that we use the variable $T = O(t_{mix} \log^2 n)$ in the algorithm to deal with this possible delay. Hence, the number of messages sent in the worst case is $O(\log n) \times c_2\sqrt{n \log n} \times t_{mix} \times O(\log^2 n)$ w.h.p. , which equals $O(\sqrt{n} \log^{7/2} n \cdot t_{mix})$. □

We conclude with the following theorem that combines the results of all the previous lemmas.

THEOREM 13. *For any graph G that has a mixing time of* t_{mix}*, there exists an implicit leader election algorithm that succeeds w.h.p. in* $O(t_{mix}\log^2 n)$ *time and has a message complexity of* $O(\sqrt{n}\log^{7/2} n \cdot t_{mix})$*, assuming that nodes know n.*

After finding the leader we can use the well known push-pull broadcast [21] to disseminate the id of the leader to all the other nodes to obtain a solution for the explicit variant of leader election.

COROLLARY 14. *For any graph G that has a conductance of* ϕ *and a mixing time of* t_{mix}*, there exists an explicit leader election algorithm that succeeds w.h.p. in* $O(t_{mix}\log^2 n)$ *time and has a message complexity of* $O(\sqrt{n}\log^{7/2} n \cdot t_{mix} + n\frac{\log n}{\phi})$*, assuming that nodes know n and there are no failures.*

4 LOWER BOUNDS

In this section, we show the lower bound for implicit leader election by showing that there exists a class of graphs with conductance ϕ on which any leader election algorithm that succeeds with probability $1-o(1)$ requires $\Omega\left(\sqrt{n}/\phi^{3/4}\right)$ messages in expectation. We also give a corollary that bounds the total number of messages required by other graph problems like broadcast and spanning tree construction.

THEOREM 15. *Suppose there is a randomized leader election algorithm that succeeds with probability* $1-o(1)$ *in n-node networks where each node has a unique ID and knows the network size n. Then, for every* α*, where* $\frac{1}{n^2} < \alpha < \frac{1}{12^2}$*, there exists a graph G of* $\Theta(n)$ *nodes and conductance* $\phi = \Theta(\alpha)$ *such that the algorithm requires* $\Omega\left(\sqrt{n}/\phi^{3/4}\right)$ *messages in expectation.*

Throughout the proof of Theorem 15, we assume that nodes start *without* unique ids. However, since nodes have knowledge of the network size n, it is straightforward to generate unique IDs with high probability. Hence we can use the same reduction as [10] (Sec. 3, paragraph "Unique IDs vs Anonymous") to remove this assumption and show that our result holds even when nodes are equipped with unique ids.

We first describe the construction of the graph G that we use to prove the message complexity lower bound. For any given n and α such that $(1/n^2) < \alpha < (1/12^2)$, we create the graph G that has a total number of n nodes and a conductance $\phi = \Theta(\alpha)$. In this regard, we also define a parameter $\epsilon = \log(1/\alpha)/2\log n$. We first construct a super-node graph $\mathcal{GS}$ with $N = \lfloor n^{1-\epsilon} \rfloor$ super-nodes, and later derive the graph G from $\mathcal{GS}$. The graph $\mathcal{GS}$ is created as a random regular graph (as in [7],[6]) where each super-node has a degree 4. See Figure 1. For the purpose of analysis, since it does not change our bounds, we assume that both $n^{1-\epsilon}$ and n^{ϵ} are integers.
Say $V(\mathcal{GS}) = \{s_1, s_2, \ldots s_{n^{1-\epsilon}}\}$ and $E(\mathcal{GS}) = \{e_1, \ldots, e_{4n^{1-\epsilon}}\}$ be the vertex set and the edge set of the graph $\mathcal{GS}$. To create the graph G from $\mathcal{GS}$, each super-node s_i is replaced with a clique C_i of $\lceil n^{\epsilon} \rceil$ nodes. For each edge e_i of $\mathcal{GS}$, that exists between two super-nodes say s_j and s_k, a corresponding edge e_i' is created in the graph G between a (previously unchosen) node chosen randomly from the clique C_j and a (previously unchosen) node chosen randomly from the clique C_k. As each super-node has exactly 4 edges connected

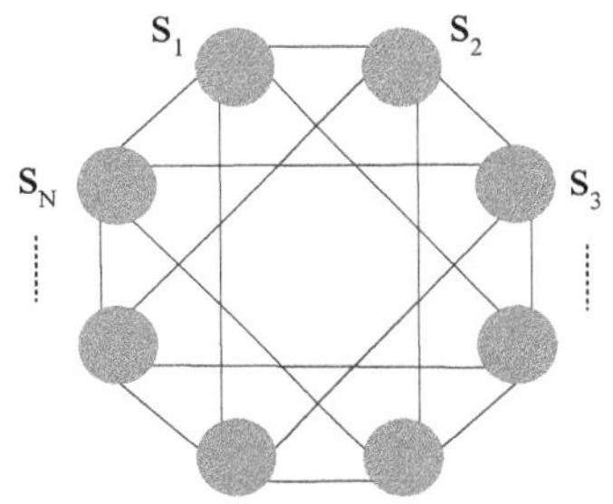

Figure 1: A random 4-regular super-node graph $\mathcal{GS}$ with $N = n^{1-\epsilon}$ super-nodes.

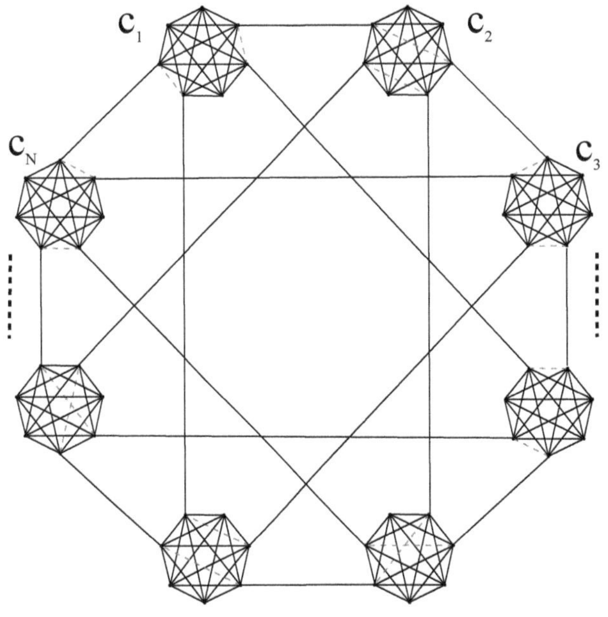

Figure 2: Graph G constructed from $\mathcal{GS}$, where each super-node is replaced by a clique of size n^{ϵ}. The red dashed lines indicate the edges of the cliques that are removed to maintain uniform node degree.

to it, for each clique there would exist 4 such chosen nodes (called external-edged nodes). An edge between any two nodes belonging to the same clique is called an intra-clique edge, whereas an edge between nodes belonging to different cliques is called an *inter-clique edge.* To maintain uniform node degrees of exactly n^{ϵ}, two intra-clique edges are removed, one from between any two of the external-edged nodes, and the other from between the remaining two external-edged nodes. See Figure 2. Thus, in any clique of the graph G there would be two types of nodes, $n^{\epsilon} - 4$ nodes with only intra-clique edges called internal-edged nodes and 4 nodes with both intra-clique edges and one inter-clique edge called external-edged nodes.

LEMMA 16. *The conductance of the graph G is* $\phi = \Theta(\alpha) = \Theta(1/n^{2\epsilon})$ *with high probability.*

Based on the construction of G, there exists a one to one mapping between the nodes of the super-node graph $\mathcal{GS}$ and the cliques in the graph G. We define the *clique communication graph* $\mathcal{CG}$ as a graph whose vertex set is equivalent to the vertex set of the super-node graph $\mathcal{GS}$, which we simply call *cliques*. An edge exists in $\mathcal{CG}$ from clique C_1 to C_2 iff a message is sent on the inter-clique edge from some node in C_1 to a node in C_2. Note that the edge set of $\mathcal{CG}$ can grow over the course of the algorithm. For the purpose of our analysis, we only keep track of the first message sent on an inter-clique edges and so we treat $\mathcal{CG}$ as a simple graph.

We show our proposed lower bound through a contradiction. Let $M := o(n^{(1-\epsilon)/2})$ and suppose there exists an algorithm that solves implicit leader election on the graph G by sending at most $Mn^{2\epsilon}$ messages in expectation. Note that for this construction of G, this implies that $Mn^{2\epsilon} = o(\sqrt{n}/(\phi)^{3/4})$, as $\phi = \Theta(1/n^{2\epsilon})$ and $M := o(n^{(1-\epsilon)/2})$. We now leverage this assumed upper bound on the expected message complexity to show that distinct parts of the network, where nodes might be initiating the exploration of their neighborhoods, are likely to never communicate.

In more detail, we proceed as follows: First, we show that by sending at most $Mn^{2\epsilon}$ many messages, the algorithm is likely to find at most $O(M)$ inter-clique edges. Given the fact that only inter-clique edges can be used for communicating in the clique communication graph $\mathcal{CG}$, we show that the random variables representing the states of the resulting connected components (in $\mathcal{CG}$) are nearly independent of one another. We leverage this "near independence" to show that the algorithm is likely to elect either no leader or more than one leader with constant probability (similarly to identically distributed and fully independent indicator random variables), thus resulting in a contradiction.

We formalize the above overview in the remainder of this section. The following lemma quantifies the number of messages required to find the very first inter-clique edge of a clique.

Lemma 17. *If a node in a clique C sends a message over an inter-clique edge, then it follows that the nodes in C have sent at least $\Omega(n^{2\epsilon})$ messages in expectation.*

Proof. Recall from the construction of the super-node graph $\mathcal{GS}$ that we have assigned the inter-clique ports uniformly at random among all available ports of C. Any clique C has a total of $n^{2\epsilon}$ ports out of which only 4 ports belong to inter-clique edges. Also, the nodes are unaware of their neighbors' identities, and in particular, the four nodes containing inter-clique port are unaware of this fact. First, we see that if a clique C sends more than $n^{2\epsilon}/2$ messages before sending its first inter-clique message,[4] the lemma is vacuously true. Otherwise, it holds that, at any point before sending the first inter-clique edge, there are at least $n^{2\epsilon}/2$ ports among the nodes in C over which no message has been sent yet, and each of them is equally likely to connect to an inter-clique edge. Thus, the probability that a message is sent over its first inter-clique edges is at most $4/(n^{2\epsilon} - \frac{n^{2\epsilon}}{2}) = 8/n^{2\epsilon}$.

Therefore, in expectation the number of messages sent by any clique C before sending its first inter-clique message would be at least $n^{2\epsilon}/8$ which is $\Omega(n^{2\epsilon})$. □

[4]We slightly abuse notation by saying a clique C sends a message when, in fact, some node in C performs the sending action.

Using Lemma 17 along with the fact that the algorithm under consideration can send at most $Mn^{1-\epsilon}$ messages, we obtain the following result about the size of the edge set of $\mathcal{CG}$:

Lemma 18. *With probability $1 - o(1)$, the clique communication graph $\mathcal{CG}$ contains at most $O(M)$ edges.*

Spontaneous Cliques. Since we consider randomized algorithms, we assume that each node is equipped with a random bit string of infinite length. If a clique C does not have any incoming edges in $\mathcal{CG}$ throughout the execution, i.e., it does not receive any messages from nodes in other cliques, then the actions and the state transitions of its nodes depend exclusively on the supplied random bit strings. In particular, inspecting these random bit strings, we can determine whether nodes in C will send messages across any inter-clique edges of C. This motivates us to call C *spontaneous*, if some node in C eventually sends an outgoing message assuming that no node ever receives an incoming message (as per its initial random string). (In practice, it may not actually send an outgoing message because it may receive a message first from some node in another clique.) We use the notation $P(C)$ to denote the *connected component* of a clique C in $\mathcal{CG}$ and note that $P(C)$ can grow over time.

Disjoint Components. We define Disj to be the event where, at any point in the algorithm's execution, each connected component in $\mathcal{CG}$ contains at most one spontaneous clique, and each non-singleton connected component contains exactly one. This, we show is in fact likely to occur.

Lemma 19. *Event* Disj *occurs with probability* $1 - o(1)$.

So far, we have shown that connected components are likely to remain disjoint throughout the execution. However, we cannot directly argue that this implies a small probability of electing a leader, since the conditioning on event Disj restricts the evolution of a given connected component, as we explain in more detail below.

We view the execution of the algorithm as a sequence of *steps* performed by cliques, where a step involves either an update to a clique's state (defined below) or the sending of a message. Note that a *step* here is different from a round as there may be simultaneous actions at cliques happening in the same round, but we can consider an arbitrary order on such simultaneous events for analysis.

We define the state of clique C in $\mathcal{CG}$ as (1) *empty*, if C is not spontaneous, or (2) consisting of the local states of the nodes that are part of the connected component in $\mathcal{CG}$. In this notation, sending a message between two nodes in the same clique corresponds to a local update to the clique's state.

Formally, we use the notation $S(C, t)$ to denote the *state of clique C after t steps* and define $S(t)$ to be the *collective state of all the cliques after t steps*. By inspecting $S(C, t)$, we can derive whether there is a leader in one of the cliques of the connected component of C in $\mathcal{CG}$. We define an indicator random variable $Y(C, t)$ such that $Y(C, t) = 1$ if and only if clique C is spontaneous and has a leader in its connected component after step t; we simply write $Y(C)$ when t is clear from the context or not important. By symmetry, all cliques are identical, and hence are equally likely to be spontaneous and also equally likely to be in a connected component with a leader. We define s as the probability of C being spontaneous and p as the probability of the spontaneous clique C having a leader, i.e, $p = \Pr[Y(C) = 1 \mid C \text{ is spontaneous}]$. It follows that $\Pr[Y(C)=1] = sp$.

For the rest of the proof, we assume that all connected components remain disjoint throughout the execution (see Lemma 19). Note that under this assumption, the Ys are *not* necessarily independent. For example, the knowledge that $Y(C') = 1$, for some clique C', might imply that the connected component of C' has a certain minimum size, which in turn limits the ways in which the connected component of C can expand in the next step.

Let κ be a collection of states after step t for all the cliques and suppose that κ represents a state in which Disj holds; formally, the event $S(t) = \kappa$ has nonzero probability conditioned on Disj. We use the notation $\kappa(C)$ to refer to the state of C in the collection of states κ. If the clique nodes eventual states were completely independent, then we would have $\Pr[S(t) = \kappa] = \prod_{C \in \mathcal{CG}} \Pr[(S(C,t) = \kappa(C)]$. As argued above, the conditioning on Disj can introduce dependencies between the event that some clique transits to a given state and the state of some other cliques and thus we cannot assume that the equality holds. However, we prove that any possible dependency due to event Disj, cannot decrease the probability of $S(t) = \kappa$, which is sufficient for our purposes:

Lemma 20. *Let κ be a collection of the clique states after step t that has positive probability of occurring conditioned on* Disj. *Then, it holds that*

$$\Pr[S(t) = \kappa] \geqslant \prod_{C \in \mathcal{CG}} \Pr[S(C,t) = \kappa(C)]. \qquad (2)$$

At this point, we have shown that, conditioned on the connected components remaining disjoint, the state of the individual connected components is *almost* independent. In particular, we have shown that the probability of collectively being in any specific disjoint state is at least as large as the product of the individual probabilities. Throughout, we are conditioning on the connected components being disjoint.

To complete the proof, we need three further steps. First, we need to relate the states of the cliques to whether or not a given clique has elected a leader. Then, we need to relate this almost independent process to a collection of independent random variables that are easier to analyze. Finally, we show that with constant probability the algorithm elects zero or more than one leaders.

Leadership. We want to analyze the probability of a given set of outcomes in terms of leader election. Recall that $Y(C)$ is an indicator random variable for the event where clique C is spontaneous and there is a leader elected in C. Let Z be a vector of desired outcomes for these indicator random variables, i.e., for each clique C consider whether $Y(C) = Z_C$. Let $L(C)$ be the set of states for C compatible with the outcomes Z_C, i.e., where component C does or does not elect a leader as specified by $L(C)$. Let L be the product of all the $L(C)$ subspaces, i.e., L is exactly the set of states compatible with Z for all C. Let S be the state of the algorithm when it stops sending messages. In the following lemma, we show that the probability of being in one of the states compatible with Z can be decomposed into the probabilities of the individual indicator random variables. (If the connected components were really independent, it would be exact equality, rather than $\geqslant$.)

Lemma 21. $\Pr[Y = Z] \geqslant \prod_{C \in \mathcal{CG}} \Pr[Y(C) = Z_C]$.

Independent variables. Recall that $\Pr[Y(C) = 1] = sp$, where s is the probability that C is spontaneous and p is the probability that a clique elects a leader if it is spontaneous. (And by symmetry, these are all identical.) We define a new set of *independent* indicator random variables $X(C)$ where $\Pr[X(C) = 1] = sp$. The previous lemma immediately implies the following:

Lemma 22. $\Pr[\sum_C Y(C) > k] \geqslant \Pr[\sum_C X(C) > k]$, *for any given integer k.*

We use this relationship among $X(C)$ and $Y(C)$ to obtain a lower bound on the following probability:

Lemma 23. $ps \geqslant 1/n^{1-\epsilon}$

More than one leader. We now analyze the probability that there is more than one leader, showing that this occurs with constant probability. This concludes our proof, as it indicates that the algorithm fails to elect exactly one leader with constant probability.

Lemma 24. $\Pr[\sum_C Y(C) > 1] > \Omega(1)$

Proof. We assume from Lemma 23 that $ps > 1/n^{1-\epsilon}$. We know from Lemma 22 that $\Pr[\sum_C Y(C) > 1] \geqslant \Pr[\sum_C X(C) > 1]$. So we are going to analyze the probability that $\sum_C X(C) > 1$. And this is a straightforward analysis of independent random variables.

The probability that all the $X(C)$ are 0 is at most:

$$(1 - ps)^{n^{1-\epsilon}} \leqslant (1 - 1/n^{1-\epsilon})^{n^{1-\epsilon}} \leqslant 1/e\,.$$

(This relies on the fact that $ps \geqslant 1/n^{1-\epsilon}$.)

We can also analyze the probability that there is exactly one C where $X(C) = 1$. Specifically, this occurs with probability:

$$n^{1-\epsilon} ps(1 - ps)^{n^{1-\epsilon}-1}\,.$$

This is maximized when $ps = 1/n^{1-\epsilon}$, so we conclude that

$$\Pr\left[\sum_C X(C) = 1\right] \leqslant n^{1-\epsilon}(1/n^{1-\epsilon})(1 - 1/n^{1-\epsilon})^{n^{1-\epsilon}-1} \leqslant 1/e + o(1).$$

Finally, then, we conclude that $\Pr[\sum_C X(C) > 1] \geqslant 1 - 2/e - o(1)$. That is, with at least constant probability there is more than one $X(C) = 1$, and hence $\Pr[\sum_C (Y(C)) > 1] \geqslant \Omega(1)$. With constant probability, the algorithm elects more than one leader. □

Lastly, we give the following corollary that shows the dependence of any broadcast or spanning tree construction algorithm with the graph conductance ϕ.

Corollary 25. *Suppose that there is a randomized broadcast algorithm (or a spanning tree construction algorithm) that succeeds with probability $1 - o(1)$. Then, for every α, where $(1/n^2) < \alpha < (1/12^2)$, there exists a graph G of $\Theta(n)$ nodes and conductance $\phi = \Theta(\alpha)$ such that the algorithm requires $\Omega\left(n/\sqrt{\phi}\right)$ messages in expectation.*

5 THE CRITICAL KNOWLEDGE OF THE NETWORK SIZE

In this section, we show that the knowledge of the network size n is critical for our algorithm to succeed by giving a message complexity lower bound of $\Omega(m)$ for all graphs if n is not known.

In [23], Kutten et al. show a message complexity lower bound of $\Omega(m)$ in expectation for implicit leader election in general graphs even when the number of nodes in the network n and the diameter of the network D are known. Here, we show that this lower bound applies only to graphs that are not well connected or where nodes are not aware of the value of n. This lower bound fails for the case of well-connected graphs for the case where n is known (as shown by our algorithm). However, we would like to point out that the knowledge of n is critical for our algorithm to succeed.

Consider any 2-connected graph G_0 of n nodes, where nodes do not know the value of n and a range $Z = [1, n^4]$ of ID's. G_0 can have many instantiations, depending upon the node ID assignment and the port number mapping. An ID assignment is a function $\varphi : V(G_0) \mapsto Z$. A port mapping for node v is a mapping $P_v : [1, deg_v] \mapsto \Gamma(v)$ (namely, v's neighbors). A port mapping for the graph G_0 is $P = \langle P_{v_1}, \ldots, P_{v_n} \rangle$. Every choice of φ and P yields a concrete graph $G_{\varphi,P}$.

THEOREM 26. *Let $\mathcal{R}$ be any implicit leader election algorithm that succeeds with probability at least $1 - \beta$, for some constant $\beta \leqslant 3/56$. If n is not known to the nodes, for any 2-connected graph G_0 of n nodes and m edges, there exists an id assignment and a port mapping, for which the expected number of messages used by $\mathcal{R}$ on G is $\Omega(m)$.*

6 CONCLUSION

In this paper we show that implicit leader election can be achieved in sub-linear message complexity for sufficiently well-connected graphs. This shows that the major communication cost for the explicit variant of the leader election comes from broadcasting the leader information to all the nodes rather than the process of electing a leader.

The model used here, where nodes only have local knowledge is referred to as the clean network model in [30] and is also otherwise referred to as the KT_0 model [5, 28]. We believe that our bounds can be extended to the KT_1 model, where nodes are aware of the identities of their neighbors.

Also, we observe that that there exists a possible gap of $O(1/\phi^{5/4})$ between the upper and the lower bounds shown here. It remains an interesting open problem to see if this gap can be reduced further.

REFERENCES

[1] Yehuda Afek and Eli Gafni. 1985. Time and Message Bounds for Election in Synchronous and Asynchronous Complete Networks. In *Proceedings of the Fourth Annual ACM Symposium on Principles of Distributed Computing (PODC '85)*. ACM, New York, NY, USA, 186–195.

[2] Dana Angluin. 1980. Local and Global Properties in Networks of Processors (Extended Abstract). In *Proceedings of the Twelfth Annual ACM Symposium on Theory of Computing (STOC '80)*. ACM, New York, NY, USA, 82–93.

[3] Hagit Attiya and Jennifer Welch. 2004. *Distributed Computing: Fundamentals, Simulations and Advanced Topics*. John Wiley Interscience.

[4] B. Awerbuch. 1987. Optimal Distributed Algorithms for Minimum Weight Spanning Tree, Counting, Leader Election, and Related Problems. In *Proceedings of the Nineteenth Annual ACM Symposium on Theory of Computing (STOC '87)*. ACM, New York, NY, USA, 230–240.

[5] Baruch Awerbuch, Oded Goldreich, David Peleg, and Ronen Vainish. 1990. A Trade-Off between Information and Communication in Broadcast Protocols. *J. ACM* 37, 2 (1990), 238–256.

[6] B. Bollobás. 1988. The Isoperimetric Number of Random Regular Graphs. *European Journal of Combinatorics* 9, 3 (1988), 241 – 244.

[7] B. Bollobás. 2001. *Random Graphs*. Cambridge University Press.

[8] Jacob Brunekreef, Joost-Pieter Katoen, Ron Koymans, and Sjouke Mauw. 1996. Design and analysis of dynamic leader election protocols in broadcast networks. *Distributed Computing* 9, 4 (01 Feb 1996), 157.

[9] Ernest Chang and Rosemary Roberts. 1979. An Improved Algorithm for Decentralized Extrema-finding in Circular Configurations of Processes. *Commun. ACM* 22, 5 (May 1979), 281–283.

[10] S. Chatterjee, G. Pandurangan, and P. Robinson. 2018. The Complexity of Leader Election: A Chasm at Diameter Two. In *Proceedings of the 19th International Conference on Distributed Computing and Networking (ICDCN '18)*. ACM, New York, NY, USA, Article 13, 10 pages.

[11] Danny Dolev, Maria Klawe, and Michael Rodeh. 1982. An O(n log n) unidirectional distributed algorithm for extrema finding in a circle. *Journal of Algorithms* 3, 3 (1982), 245 – 260.

[12] C. Fetzer and F. Cristian. 1999. A highly available local leader election service. *IEEE Transactions on Software Engineering* 25, 5 (1999), 603–618.

[13] Paola Flocchini and Bernard Mans. 1996. Optimal Elections in Labeled Hypercubes. *J. Parallel and Distrib. Comput.* 33, 1 (1996), 76 – 83.

[14] Greg N. Frederickson and Nancy A. Lynch. 1987. Electing a Leader in a Synchronous Ring. *J. ACM* 34, 1 (Jan. 1987), 98–115.

[15] R. G. Gallager, P. A. Humblet, and P. M. Spira. 1983. A Distributed Algorithm for Minimum-Weight Spanning Trees. *ACM Trans. Program. Lang. Syst.* 5, 1 (Jan. 1983), 66–77.

[16] Seth Gilbert and Dariusz R. Kowalski. 2010. Distributed Agreement with Optimal Communication Complexity. In *Proceedings of the Twenty-first Annual ACM-SIAM Symposium on Discrete Algorithms (SODA '10)*. 965–977.

[17] Seth Gilbert, Peter Robinson, and Suman Sourav. 2018. Leader Election in Well-Connected Graphs. *To appear in ArXiv e-prints* (2018).

[18] Indranil Gupta, Robbert van Renesse, and Kenneth P. Birman. 2000. A Probabilistically Correct Leader Election Protocol for Large Groups. In *Distributed Computing*, Maurice Herlihy (Ed.). Springer Berlin Heidelberg, 89–103.

[19] Shlomo Hoory, Nathan Linial, and Avi Wigderson. 2006. Expander Graphs and Their Applications. *Bull. Amer. Math. Soc.* 43, 04 (2006), 439–562.

[20] Mark Jerrum and Alistair Sinclair. 1988. Conductance and the Rapid Mixing Property for Markov Chains: The Approximation of Permanent Resolved. In *Proceedings of the 20th Annual ACM Symposium on Theory of Computing (STOC '88)*. ACM, New York, NY, USA, 235–244.

[21] R. Karp, C. Schindelhauer, S. Shenker, and B. Vocking. 2000. Randomized Rumor Spreading. In *Proceedings of the 41st Annual Symposium on Foundations of Computer Science (FOCS '00)*. IEEE Computer Society, Washington, DC, USA, 565–.

[22] E. Korach, S. Moran, and S. Zaks. 1987. The Optimality of Distributive Constructions of Min Weight and Degree Restricted Spanning Trees in a Complete Network of Processors. *SIAM J. Comput.* 16, 2 (1987), 231–236.

[23] Shay Kutten, Gopal Pandurangan, David Peleg, Peter Robinson, and Amitabh Trehan. 2015. On the Complexity of Universal Leader Election. *J. ACM* 62, 1, Article 7 (March 2015), 27 pages.

[24] Shay Kutten, Gopal Pandurangan, David Peleg, Peter Robinson, and Amitabh Trehan. 2015. Sublinear Bounds for Randomized Leader Election. *Theor. Comput. Sci.* 561, PB (Jan. 2015), 134–143.

[25] Gérard Le Lann. 1977. Distributed Systems - Towards a Formal Approach. In *IFIP Congress*. 155–160.

[26] Nancy A. Lynch. 1996. *Distributed Algorithms*. Morgan Kaufmann Publishers Inc., San Francisco, CA, USA.

[27] Anisur Rahaman Molla and Gopal Pandurangan. 2017. Distributed Computation of Mixing Time. In *Proceedings of the 18th International Conference on Distributed Computing and Networking (ICDCN '17)*. ACM, Article 5, 4 pages.

[28] Gopal Pandurangan, Peter Robinson, and Michele Scquizzato. 2017. A Time- and Message-optimal Distributed Algorithm for Minimum Spanning Trees. In *Proceedings of the 49th Annual ACM SIGACT Symposium on Theory of Computing (STOC 2017)*. ACM, New York, NY, USA, 743–756.

[29] David Peleg. 1990. Time-optimal Leader Election in General Networks. *J. Parallel Distrib. Comput.* 8, 1 (Jan. 1990), 96–99.

[30] D. Peleg. 2000. *Distributed Computing: A Locality-Sensitive Approach*. Society for Industrial and Applied Mathematics.

[31] Murali Krishna Ramanathan, Ronaldo A. Ferreira, Suresh Jagannathan, Ananth Grama, and Wojciech Szpankowski. 2007. Randomized leader election. *Distributed Computing* 19, 5 (01 Apr 2007), 403–418.

[32] Sylvia Ratnasamy, Paul Francis, Mark Handley, Richard Karp, and Scott Shenker. 2001. A Scalable Content-addressable Network. *SIGCOMM Comput. Commun. Rev.* 31, 4 (Aug. 2001), 161–172.

[33] Antony I. T. Rowstron and Peter Druschel. 2001. Pastry: Scalable, Decentralized Object Location, and Routing for Large-Scale Peer-to-Peer Systems. In *Proceedings of the IFIP/ACM International Conference on Distributed Systems Platforms*. Springer-Verlag, London, UK, UK, 329–350.

[34] A. Sinclair. 1993. *Algorithms for Random Generation and Counting*. Birkhauser, Boston, MA, USA.

[35] G. Singh. 1996. Leader election in the presence of link failures. *IEEE Transactions on Parallel and Distributed Systems* 7, 3 (Mar 1996), 231–236.

[36] Paul M.B. Vitányi. 1984. Distributed Elections in an Archimedean Ring of Processors. In *Proceedings of the Sixteenth Annual ACM Symposium on Theory of Computing (STOC '84)*. ACM, New York, NY, USA, 542–547.

[37] B. Y. Zhao, Ling Huang, J. Stribling, S. C. Rhea, A. D. Joseph, and J. D. Kubiatowicz. 2006. Tapestry: A Resilient Global-scale Overlay for Service Deployment. *IEEE J.Sel. A. Commun.* 22, 1 (Sept. 2006), 41–53.

Brief Announcement: Beeping a Time-Optimal Leader Election*

Fabien Dufoulon
LRI, Université Paris-Sud, CNRS,
Université Paris-Saclay
Orsay, France
dufoulon@lri.fr

Janna Burman
LRI, Université Paris-Sud, CNRS,
Université Paris-Saclay
Orsay, France
burman@lri.fr

Joffroy Beauquier
LRI, Université Paris-Sud, CNRS,
Université Paris-Saclay
Orsay, France
beauquier@lri.fr

ABSTRACT

The *beeping model* is an extremely restrictive broadcast communication model that relies only on carrier sensing. In this model, we solve the *deterministic leader election* problem with an asymptotically optimal round complexity. Using this result, we obtain an asymptotically optimal *randomized leader election* algorithm for anonymous networks, as well as improved algorithms for symmetry-breaking and communication primitives. The techniques that we introduce give a new insight as to how local constraints on the exchangeable messages can result in efficient algorithms, when dealing with the beeping model.

CCS CONCEPTS

• **Theory of computation** → **Distributed computing models**; **Distributed algorithms**; *Design and analysis of algorithms*;

KEYWORDS

distributed algorithms; leader election; beeping model; time complexity; deterministic algorithms

ACM Reference Format:

Fabien Dufoulon, Janna Burman, and Joffroy Beauquier. 2018. Brief Announcement: Beeping a Time-Optimal Leader Election. In *PODC '18: ACM Symposium on Principles of Distributed Computing, July 23–27, 2018, Egham, United Kingdom.* ACM, New York, NY, USA, 3 pages. https://doi.org/10.1145/3212734.3212779

1 INTRODUCTION

Wireless networks with severe restrictions on communication capabilities are an increasingly prevalent subject of study, e.g., [4, 5, 9]. In order to represent these networks, Cornejo and Kuhn [4] introduced a convenient formal framework, the *discrete beeping model*. In this model, time is divided into synchronous rounds, and in each round a node can either listen or transmit a unary signal (*beep*) to all its neighbors. The possibility to directly transmit a beep to a node is defined by a *static communication graph*, of unknown (to nodes) *size n* and *diameter D*. As a beep is merely a detectable burst of energy, a listening node does not receive the *identifiers* (integers from $\{1, \ldots, N\}$ where $N = n^c$ for a constant $c > 1$) of its beeping neighbors. Even more critically, a beeping node receives no feedback, while a silent (listening) one can only detect that either at least one of its neighbors beeped or that all of them were silent.

Beeps are an extremely limited form of communication, making it difficult to coordinate nodes effectively. Amongst the fundamental coordination problems, *leader election* (LE) has received a lot of attention. A prime concern is the design of time-efficient *uniform* solutions, i.e., not requiring any knowledge on the graph topology or on the parameters n and D (or even on their upper bounds). Indeed, it is unrealistic to assume that upper bounds on these parameters are always available, especially when considering dynamic networks. Amongst existing solutions for LE in the beeping model, the more difficult (for design) deterministic case has received less attention. However, this case is useful whenever a random behavior is inappropriate or deterministic guarantees are required.

Related Work. A time complexity lower bound (for LE) of $\Omega(D + \log n)$ (for both deterministic and randomized solutions) is established in [9]. Probabilistic solutions are given in [5, 9], solving LE in $O(D + \log n) \cdot O(\log^2 \log n)$ rounds w.h.p.[1], or in $O(D + \log n)$ rounds in expectation. As for deterministic LE, Förster et al. [8] give the first algorithm in the beeping model, with an $O(D \cdot \log n)$ round complexity. This algorithm is uniform in both n and D. The round complexities of different LE algorithms, including those presented here, are compared below in Table 1.

Amongst the extensive leader election literature in other models, [2] is particularly relevant here. It proposes an $O(D + \log n)$ time deterministic LE algorithm in the $\mathcal{ECONGEST}$ model (limited to messages of $O(1)$ size). $\mathcal{ECONGEST}$ is much stronger than the beeping model. A node can easily learn its local topology and has direct links to communicate with its neighbors, whereas the absence of such links in the beeping model causes interference and makes directed messages (with known sender and receiver) unachievable or plainly inefficient. Nevertheless, we show how this difficulty can be overcome in an efficient way. Note that known transformers can simulate $\mathcal{ECONGEST}$, but with a prohibitive multiplicative factor of $O(\Delta^4)$ [1] (where Δ is the *maximum degree*).

Table 1: LE algorithms in the beeping model

Ref	Round complexity	Safety (see Sect. 2)
[9]	$O(D + \log n) \cdot O(\log^2 \log n)$ w.h.p.	w.h.p.
[8]	$O(D \cdot \log n)$: deterministic time	Deterministic
[5]	$O(D + \log n)$ expected time	w.h.p.
Here	$O(D + \log n)$: deterministic time	Deterministic
Here	$O(D + \log n)$ w.h.p.	w.h.p.

*The full version of the paper is available in [7].

[1] with high probability: with probability at least $1 - n^{-\theta(1)}$

PODC '18, July 23–27, 2018, Egham, United Kingdom

ACM ISBN 978-1-4503-5795-1/18/07.
https://doi.org/10.1145/3212734.3212779

Contributions. We propose a deterministic and completely uniform (in n and D) leader election algorithm with an $O(D + \log n)$ asymptotically optimal round complexity. By independently sampling $\theta(\log n)$ bits to create unique identifiers w.h.p. and using this algorithm, we obtain a uniform (in D only) randomized leader election algorithm which takes $O(D + \log n)$ rounds w.h.p. and works in anonymous networks. Both solutions are the first to achieve time-optimality for these guarantees in the beeping model, outperforming all previous deterministic and randomized results. Furthermore, using the proposed deterministic LE algorithm, we propose the first asymptotically time-optimal (of $O(\log n)$ rounds) Maximal Independent Set (MIS) and 5-coloring algorithms for trees in the beeping model (leveraging the fact that given a leader in a tree network, it is simple to compute a 2-coloring). Deterministic LE can also be used to solve k-source *multi-broadcast* for general graphs in $O(min\{k, \log n\} \cdot D + k \log \frac{nM}{k})$ rounds (for messages in $\{1, \ldots, M\}$). This latter result improves on previous solutions [6] when the number of sources is sublogarithmic ($k < \log n$).
Below, we only present the deterministic LE algorithm. The details of other algorithms based on it appear in [7].

2 DEFINITIONS

The α-encoding [2] of an integer $i \in \mathbb{N}^{>0}$ is a (binary) word obtained from the binary representation *bin* of i. By definition, $\alpha(i) = 1^{|bin|} \parallel 0 \parallel bin$ (where $\parallel$ denotes word concatenation). In the proposed algorithm, instead of identifiers, nodes compare their α-encodings (α-id), to ensure it is performed uniformly (in n). A word x is *well-formed* if there exists an integer i such that $x = \alpha(i)$.

In the *leader election* (LE) problem, each node has a boolean variable, corresponding to a *leader* or a *non-leader* state. During an execution, there is never more than one leader (*safety* property). Initially, all nodes are non-leaders. Every execution *terminates*, and at the termination there is exactly one leader [2]. Now we give auxiliary definitions. First, we define *eventual leader election*, where the algorithm terminates but no node is aware of when. Then, we define *explicit* leader election (when nodes have unique identifiers): the algorithm terminates and nodes know when this happens, together with the identifier of the unique leader at the termination.

3 LEADER ELECTION ALGORITHMS

The approaches developed to solve leader election in $\mathcal{ECONGEST}$ do not work in the beeping model. Although they can be adapted using a general transformer, doing so is too costly in most communication graph topologies (see Related Work). To solve the strongest version of LE, explicit leader election, we proceed in two steps. First, we design a uniform algorithm for eventual leader election, in Sect. 3.1. Then, in Sect. 3.2, we combine this algorithm with a specially designed uniform termination detection component to obtain a uniform explicit leader election algorithm.

3.1 Uniform Eventual Leader Election

The algorithm (Algorithm 1) is described first (Sect. 3.1.1). Then, in Sect. 3.1.2, k-balanced messages are presented. They are used to allow constant-size *communication phases* composed of rounds and dedicated to the communication of (large) messages respecting local constraints. A detailed description of the communication phases (of Algorithm 1, line 6) is given in Sect. 3.1.3.

Algorithm 1 Uniform Eventual Leader Election Algorithm

1: **IN:** *id*: identifier ; **OUT:** *leader*: boolean, *leaderId*: identifier
2: $candidate := true$, $Z := \epsilon$ ▷ ϵ is the empty word
3: $leaderId := \epsilon$, $leader := false$, $suspicious := false$
4: **for** diffusion phase p ; p++ **do**
5: // *First, a communication phase with c rounds.*
6: Communicate (Z, *suspicious*) to all neighboring nodes.
7: Use received (Z, *suspicious*) pairs to update Z, *candidate* and *suspicious* (using the described rules).
8: **if** not *candidate* **then** $leader := false$
9: **else if** $Z = \alpha(id)$ **then** $leader := true$
10: **if** Z is well-formed **then** $leaderId := \alpha^{-1}(Z)$

3.1.1 Description. All nodes aim to spread their identifiers to the whole network (*information diffusion algorithm*). They start out as *candidates*, with two variables: Z and *suspicious*. The boolean *suspicious* is initialized to $false$, and the word Z to the empty word ϵ. The former represents whether a node removed bits in the last phase. Z represents the prefix of an α-id, and most of the time, the highest prefix the node is aware of. A prefix Z_u is said to be *higher* than a prefix Z_v, if Z_v is a proper prefix of Z_u, or if $Z_u > Z_v$, i.e., for the first differing bit, Z_u has 1 and Z_v has 0, even if $|Z_u| < |Z_v|$.

Nodes execute *diffusion phases* (of c rounds) synchronously. A diffusion phase consists of one *communication phase* of $c = O(1)$ rounds (line 6), used to send Z and *suspicious* to all neighbors. The communication phase is described in detail in Sect. 3.1.3. In the same phase, each node receives (Z, *suspicious*) pairs from its neighbors, but does not know which node sent which message, nor how many nodes sent any of these messages (*multiplicity*).
After the communication phase, any node v checks if Z_v is a *locally higher prefix*, using the received pairs. More precisely, in line 7, the set of predicates given below is evaluated on the set of the received (Z, *suspicious*) pairs, in the given order of priority, and the appropriate update is done. If any of the predicates in rules 1 to 5 is true, Z_v is not a locally higher prefix. Therefore, v becomes a *follower* (i.e., *candidate* is set to $false$, and v never becomes leader, line 8). If any of the predicates in rules 1 and 2 is true, *suspicious* is set to *true* for the next phase.

(1) If there is a suspicious neighbor u, s.t. Z_u is a proper prefix of Z_v, remove $min\{|Z_v| - |Z_u|, 3\}$ letters from Z_v's end.
(2) If $Z_v = (z \parallel 0 \parallel w)$ with $w \neq \epsilon$ and there exists a neighbor u with $Z_u = (z \parallel 1 \parallel y)$, delete $|w|$ letters from the end of Z_v.
(3) If $Z_v = (z \parallel 0)$ and there exists a neighbor u with $Z_u = (z \parallel 1 \parallel y)$, then change Z_v to $(z \parallel 1)$.
(4) If there exists a neighbor u with $Z_u = (Z_v \parallel 1 \parallel w)$ then append 1 to Z_v.
(5) If there exists a neighbor u with $Z_u = (Z_v \parallel 0 \parallel w)$ then append 0 to Z_v.
(6) Otherwise, append a bit from the α-id to Z_v.

[2]We use the classical definitions of the system where a *configuration* is a vector of nodes' states, an *execution* is a sequence of configurations of the rounds' ends, and at the *termination* there is a *terminal configuration* that is repeated indefinitely.

Additional local computations in lines 8-10 conclude a diffusion phase. Once a candidate's Z_v variable is well-formed (once $id(v) = \alpha^{-1}(Z_v)$), this node becomes a leader. However, it can become a follower in later rounds. The 6 rules described above are adopted from [2] and adapted here to the beeping model. Thus by [2] the described information diffusion process satisfies Lemma 3.1 below and is used to obtain Theorem 3.2.

LEMMA 3.1. *Let u and v be two neighboring nodes. Then,* $||Z_u| - |Z_v|| \leq 6$. *Moreover, assume w.l.o.g. that* $|Z_u| \leq |Z_v|$, *then* Z_u *and* Z_v *are identical, except in at most 6 bits: from the* $|Z_u|$*th bit (possibly included) to the* $|Z_v|$*th bit. Note that if the* $|Z_u|$*th bit differs in* Z_u *and* Z_v, *then* $||Z_u| - |Z_v|| < 6$.

THEOREM 3.2. *Uniform Eventual Leader Election is solved by Algorithm 1 in* $O(D + \log n)$ *rounds (in the beeping model).*

3.1.2 Balanced messages. A basic design technique called the multi-slot design pattern [3] allows to communicate constant-size messages without the sender's identifier nor multiplicity, given a synchronous start. It works in communication phases of M rounds, if at most M different messages (in $\{1, \ldots, M\}$) are allowed. Beeping in the jth round of a phase is equivalent to sending the message j. However, receivers cannot detect which (and how many) nodes sent that message. Clearly, this design technique cannot be used alone to directly send Z values, as these values are in $\{1, \ldots, N\}$, and communication phases would be $O(N)$ rounds long. But this technique can be adapted to send the values of a locally constrained (k-balanced) variable. A variable var is said to be k-balanced if it satisfies the *k-balancing property*, that is, if the difference between neighboring var values is at most k (for every node v and neighboring node u, $|var_u - var_v| \leq k$).

If one wishes to communicate k-balanced messages, then it is enough to transmit, for a message m, the *remainder* $r = m \mod(1 + 2k)$, using the previous technique, with phases of $M = 1 + 2k$ rounds (where k is known a priori to all nodes). Then, the receiver, knowing both its own remainder, the sender's remainder and the fact that the messages are k-balanced, can deduce the originally sent message (but does not know if multiple nodes sent this message). Specifically, let v be the receiver and u the sender. Node v deduces the original message m_u from the received remainder message r_u by $m_u = m_v + r_u - r_v - \lfloor \frac{r_u - r_v}{k+1} \rfloor M$.
The $-\lfloor \frac{r_u - r_v}{k+1} \rfloor M$ factor deals with the fact that some lower (than m_v) messages m_u result in a high remainder r_u, and some higher messages m_u in a low remainder r_u, due to the modulo operation. Consider the example depicted in Fig. 1 for $k = 2$.

Received remainder r_u =	'0'	'1'	'2'	'3'	'4'
$m_u - m_v = (r_u - r_v) - \lfloor \frac{r_u - r_v}{k+1} \rfloor M$	-1	v	+1	+2	-2
Decoded message m_u =	18	19	20	21	17

Figure 1: Communication of 2-balanced messages.

3.1.3 Designing constant-size communication phases. In this section, we show that by applying the balanced messages approach, using only $O(1)$ beeping rounds, a node can deduce its neighbors' Z values (and whether some of them are suspicious), even though there are $O(N)$ different possible values for Z.

From Lemma 3.1, we know that $|Z|$ is a 6-balanced variable. Moreover, two neighboring nodes have similar Z values, which differ only in (at most 6 of) the last bits. Therefore, if a node can learn the last 6 bits of a neighboring Z value, and their exact positions, then it can fill up the empty bits (in more significant positions) using the bits from its own Z variable. For that, one could use two consecutive communication subphases: the first communicates the *position* of the last bit (which is $|Z|$, a 6-balanced variable) in a subphase with 13 rounds, and the second communicates an *ending* message with the last 6 bits (using a message from $\{1, \ldots, 2^6\}$, encoding all possible 6 letters combinations), in a subphase with 64 rounds. However, this does not work in the beeping model because one needs to know, for every ending message, the corresponding position of the last bit (thus the corresponding position message). Fortunately, as the message space is constant-size in both of these communication subphases, the Cartesian product of both message spaces is also constant-size. This allows to associate position and ending messages, using $O(1)$ rounds, even in the beeping model. Consequently, communication phases of 832 rounds (for messages in $\{1, .., 13\} \times \{1, \ldots, 2^6\}$) are needed to communicate enough information for a node to deduce all neighboring Z values, using the balanced messages approach.

On top of that, nodes also need to communicate the boolean *suspicious*. For this reason, the message space is adapted to $\{1, .., 13\} \times \{1, \ldots, 2^6\} \times \{false, true\}$. This results in communication phases (introduced in Algorithm 1, Sect. 3.1.1) of length $c = 1664$ rounds, which although large, is still $O(1)$ size.

3.2 Explicit Leader Election

Being often used as a primitive, the LE algorithm must be uniform and detect termination (e.g., so that it can be composed with other algorithms). Since classical approaches are not suited to the beeping model, we propose an explicit leader election algorithm using a different termination detection approach. This approach uses modified overlay networks [8], allowing a node to detect if and when it is the last remaining candidate in the network. These overlays only connect nodes with the same (well-formed) Z value. Multiple overlays are grown simultaneously, and the one rooted in the highest id node eliminates all other overlays, until it covers the network. When it has done so, it detects termination. Due to the lack of space, we refer to an extended version [7] for this algorithm.

REFERENCES

[1] J. Beauquier, J. Burman, F. Dufoulon, and S. Kutten. 2018. Fast Beeping Protocols for Deterministic MIS and (Δ+1)-Coloring in Sparse Graphs. In *IEEE INFOCOM*.
[2] A. Casteigts, Y. Métivier, J.M. Robson, and A. Zemmari. 2016. Deterministic Leader Election in $O(D + \log n)$ Time with Messages of Size $O(1)$. In *DISC*. 16–28.
[3] A. Casteigts, Y. Métivier, J. M. Robson, and A. Zemmari. 2016. Design Patterns in Beeping Algorithms. In *OPODIS*. 15:1–15:16.
[4] A. Cornejo and F. Kuhn. 2010. Deploying Wireless Networks with Beeps. In *DISC*. 148–162.
[5] A. Czumaj and P. Davies. 2016. Brief Announcement: Optimal Leader Election in Multi-Hop Radio Networks. In *PODC*. 47–49.
[6] A. Czumaj and P. Davies. 2016. Communicating with Beeps. In *OPODIS*. 1–16.
[7] F. Dufoulon, J. Burman, and J. Beauquier. 2018. *Beeping a Deterministic Time-Optimal Leader Election.* Research Report. https://hal.archives-ouvertes.fr/hal-01794711
[8] K.-T. Förster, J. Seidel, and R. Wattenhofer. 2014. Deterministic Leader Election in Multi-hop Beeping Networks. In *DISC*. 212–226.
[9] M. Ghaffari and B. Haeupler. 2013. Near Optimal Leader Election in Multi-hop Radio Networks. In *SODA*. 748–766.

Brief Announcement: Graph Exploration Using Constant-Size Memory and Storage

Naoki Kitamura
Nagoya Institute of Technology
Nagoya, Aichi
ktmr522@yahoo.co.jp

Kazuki Kakizawa
Nagoya Institute of Technology
Nagoya, Aichi
kezawa0612@gmail.com

Yuya Kawabata
Nagoya Institute of Technology
Nagoya, Aichi
29414043@stn.nitech.ac.jp

Taisuke Izumi
Nagoya Institute of Technology
Nagoya, Aichi
t-izumi@nitech.ac.jp

ABSTRACT

We consider the exploration problem in undirected graphs without node labels, which requires that a mobile agent initially placed at an arbitrary node visits all nodes and terminates. We assume that both of the agent and nodes are equipped with little memory, and the algorithm cannot use any initial knowledge on the topology of the graph. In this paper, we propose a new deterministic polynomial-time exploration (more precisely, depth-first search) algorithm which can be implemented using only $O(1)$-bit memory of the agent and $O(1)$-bit storage for each node. To the best of our knowledge, this is the first polynomial-time exploration algorithm achieving both sublogarithmic memory and sublogarithmic storage. The technical ingredient of our algorithm consists of the idea from the recent progress on small-space DFS algorithms by Asano et al. [ISAAC2014] and Elmasry et al. [STACS2015], and a new distributed backtrack algorithm for DFS paths. The algorithm also includes a new compact (i.e., using $O(1)$-bit storage) s-t path maintenance mechanism, which may be of independent interest.

CCS CONCEPTS

• **Mathematics of computing** → **Graph algorithms**; • **Theory of computation** → *Distributed algorithms*;

KEYWORDS

graph exploration, depth-first search, space complexity

ACM Reference Format:
Naoki Kitamura, Kazuki Kakizawa, Yuya Kawabata, and Taisuke Izumi. 2018. Brief Announcement: Graph Exploration Using Constant-Size Memory and Storage. In *PODC '18: ACM Symposium on Principles of Distributed Computing, July 23–27, 2018, Egham, United Kingdom.* ACM, New York, NY, USA, 3 pages. https://doi.org/10.1145/3212734.3212780

ACM ISBN 978-1-4503-5795-1/18/07.
https://doi.org/10.1145/3212734.3212780

1 INTRODUCTION

1.1 Background and Our Result

The graph exploration problem is one of the fundamental problems in both distributed and centralized contexts, which requires an agent to visit all the nodes in the graph. It does not have only several practical applications such as mobile robots and web crawlers, but also receives much attention in relation to the complexity theory of small-space computability: The problem of deciding s-t connectivity is definitely a subproblem of graph exploration and it is a key problem of capturing the hardness of space-bounded computation. In this paper, we focus on the space-complexity matter of graph exploration in distributed settings. A standard setting is the exploration of *unlabelled* graphs, where each node has no unique IDs, and each neighbor is identified by *local port numbers* assigned to the edges incident to each node. The agent has a limited amount of persistent memory, and does not have any knowledge on the network topology. It starts the exploration from an arbitrary node, and has to go back to the initial node after visiting all other nodes. The model we consider in this paper equips each node also with persistent memory (to distinguish the agent memory, we call it *storage* or *whiteboard*), which can be read and written by the agent visiting there. Obviously, this model has two measures of space complexity, that is, memory size and storage size (per node). That fact derives several natural questions: For some specific problem, can we trade one of those costs to the other one? Or is it possible to solve some problem achieving the low-space complexity in both senses? For the graph exploration problem, the $O(\log n)$-bit space restriction on memory or storage is recognized as the state-of-the-art borderline. Solving the graph exploration problem using $O(\log n)$-bit storage is rather easy. The classical DFS algorithm can be implemented on the agent-based system even if the agent is oblivious (i.e., no persistent memory). The case of $O(\log n)$-bit memory space is more complicated, but it is surprisingly possible. The seminal Reingold's undirected s-t connectivity algorithm achieves graph exploration using only $O(\log n)$-bit memory and no storage [5]. The optimality of this algorithm in no-storage cases is also shown by Fraigniaud et al. [4]. However, in fully-sublogarithmic cases (i.e., the memory and the storage are both sublogarithmic), the feasibility of polynomial-time graph exploration is still unclear. One of the closest results for this question is the pebble-based algorithm proposed by Disser et al. [2], which is a graph exploration algorithm using $O(\log\log n)$ distinct pebbles. The k-pebble model is one of the restricted versions of the memory-storage model, where each agent has k distinguished pebbles, and can put and pick-up each pebble on any node for leaving some information there. Since $\Omega(k)$-bit memory and storage is sufficient to implement k-pebble systems in the memory-storage model, the algorithm by Disser et al. achieves $O(\log\log n)$-bit memory and storage. Unfortunately, the running time of this algorithm can become super-polynomial of n ($O(n^{\log\log n})$ steps), and thus the existence of the algorithm achieving all of three properties – polynomial-running time, sublogarithmic memory, and sublogarithmic storage – is still an open problem.

The main contribution of this paper is to answer positively this question in a very strong sense. More precisely, we present an extremely-simple deterministic polynomial-time graph exploration algorithm only using $O(1)$-bit memory and storage. While many of known algorithms are based on complicated techniques such as *universal exploration sequences*, the approach of our algorithm is just a simulation of the depth-first search. The key ingredient of our algorithm consists of the recent progress on small-space (centralized) DFS algorithms by Asano et al. [1], and Elmasry et al. [3], as well as a new distributed backtrack algorithm for DFS paths. It includes a novel compact (i.e., using $O(1)$-bit storage) s-t path maintenance mechanism called *R-path*, which may be of independent interest. The total running time of our algorithm is $O(mn)$ steps.

2 MODEL

Throughout this paper, we denote by $[a, b]$ the set of integers at least a and at most b. The graph exploration problem is considered on a simple undirected connected graph with port numbering $G = (V, E, \Pi)$, where V is the set of nodes, $E \subseteq V \times V$ is the set of edges, and Π is the set of port-numbering functions (explained later). Let n and m be the numbers of nodes and edges respectively. Let $E(v)$ be the set of edges incident to node v, and $\Delta(v)$ be the degree of node $v \in V$. We assume that the graph is anonymous, i.e., the vertices of the graph are unlabeled and thus cannot be identified by the agent. However, for introducing and analyzing our algorithm, we refer each node as a value in $[1, n]$. For navigating the agent locally, we introduce *local port numbers*. The edges incident to a vertex v have distinct labels in $[1, \Delta(v)]$. The port numbering function $\pi_v : E(v) \to [1, \Delta(v)]$ defines the port number assigned to each edge incident to v. The set Π consists of the port-numbering functions for all nodes in V. Let $N(v)$ be the set of nodes that are adjacent to v. Since $E(v)$ and $N(v)$ has one-to-one correspondence, we often treat π_v as a function from $N(v)$. That is, for any $u \in N(v)$, $\pi_v(u)$ represents the v's port number of edge (v, u). Furthermore, we also denote the inverse function of $\pi_v(u)$ (on $N(v)$) by π_v^{-1} (i.e., $\pi_v^{-1} : [1, \Delta(v)] \to N(v)$). Note that an edge (u, v) has two port numbers, once at u and one at v, and thus they can be different, i.e., $\pi_v(u) \neq \pi_u(v)$ may hold for some $(u, v) \in E$. Each node $v \in V$ has a storage called *whiteboard* $b(v)$, which is a persistent memory keeping information even after the agent leaves (that is, the agent can refer that information when it comes back). The execution of the agent follows discrete time steps. In each step, the agent observes the degree of the current vertex v and the port number of the edge from which it entered v, and then performs local computation. The computation outputs the information left to the current node and the port number $x \in [1, \Delta(v)]$ indicating the destination of the next movement. Finally, the step finishes with the movement to $\pi_v^{-1}(x)$. It is guaranteed that the movement at a step finishes by the beginning of the next step. The node where the agent currently stays is referred as v_{cur}, and the port number from which the agent comes to v_{cur} is referred as π_{in}. Note that the "current step" implied by notations v_{cur} and π_{in} depends on the context.

The agent is a deterministic state machine moving on the nodes in G along edges. Agent has an $O(1)$-bit memory (i.e., a constant number of states). The behavior of the agent is formally specified by a deterministic function $A : Q \times \mathcal{B} \times \mathbb{N} \to Q \times \mathcal{B} \times \mathbb{N}$, where Q is the set of agent states, $\mathcal{B}$ is the set of possible values written to each whiteboard. The input triple of A means the current agent state, the contents of the whiteboard where the agent stays, and the port number of the edges from which the agent comes to the current node. The triple of A's output represents the state of the agent, the value written to the whiteboard, and the port number to which the agent goes out at the next movement. If the agent does not move, A returns zero as the port number. In addition, the port number zero is also inputted to A initially.

Note that our algorithms can use $\omega(1)$-size working (i.e., non-persistent) memory in the local computation at each step. That assumption is crucial because the agent must handle port numbers, which cannot be stored only with $O(1)$ bits. It should be also noted that while any local computation performed in the proposed algorithm is implementable on the turing machine of only using $O(\log n)$ bits.

3 LEX-DFS ALGORITHM

3.1 Overview of $O(n)$-bit Centralized Lex-DFS

This section provides the high-level view of our small-space Lex-DFS algorithm, called DLDFS. The fundamental structure of DLDFS follows the (centralized) Lex-DFS algorithm using only $O(n)$-bit memory space (more precisely, it manages labels of $O(1)$ bits per one node) proposed concurrently by Asano et al. [1] and Elmasry et al. [3]. Hence we first review their algorithm(s) briefly, and then explain how to adopt it in the agent-based system.

Let r be the node where the agent starts the exploration. The technical challenge of $O(n)$-bit Lex-DFS is to identify the parent node *par(v)* in backtracking at node v. In the forward phase, the algorithm behaves completely same as the naive Lex-DFS algorithm. All visited nodes are marked by the sign of "already visited", and in each iteration the algorithm checks if there exists an unvisited neighbor of the current node or not. If it is found, the algorithm chooses the unvisited neighbor with the minimum port number as the next node. When no unvisited neighbor exists, the algorithm performs the backtrack to the parent node in the Lex-DFS tree $T_{G,r}$ with root r. The solution by Asano et al. is to keep only the set of nodes contained in the path from the root r to the current node in $T_{G,r}$. In the naive implementation of Lex-DFS it corresponds to the set of nodes stored in the stack. The set of nodes is managed by marking the nodes using one-bit flags. We call those marked nodes *in-stack nodes*. The following lemma shown in [1] states that the path in $T_{G,r}$ from r (i.e., the order of in-stack nodes) can be recovered only from the information of the set of in-stack nodes.

LEMMA 3.1 (ASANO ET AL. [1], ELMASRY ET AL. [3]). *Let $G = (V, E, \Pi)$ and $r \in V$ be any instance of Lex-DFS, and $P_u = v_0, v_1, \cdots, v_k$ be the path from r to u in $T_{G,r}$ ($r = v_0$ and $u = v_k$). Then, for any $i \in [0, k-1]$, $\pi_{v_i}(v_{i+1}) = \min\{\pi_{v_i}(v_j) \mid j \in [i+1, k], v_j \in N(v_i)\}$ holds.*

The lemma above implies that the following process correctly traverses P_u: The traversal starts from the root node. Consider the situation where $v_0, v_1, \cdots, v_{i-1}$ are already traversed and the algorithm at the current node v_i is finding the next node v_{i+1}. Assume that all traversed nodes are colored by black, and $v_{i+1}, v_{i+2}, \cdots v_k$ are colored by white. Then the algorithm can identify v_{i+1} locally because it is the non-black in-stack neighbor with the minimum port number. After changing the color of v_i to black, the algorithm visits v_{i+1}. Iterating this process the algorithm completely traverses the sequence P_u and can identify $par(u)$ (when it finds u, the current node is $par(u)$).

3.2 Distributed Implementation

Almost all parts of the $O(n)$-bit Lex-DFS algorithm shown above is easy to implement in the agent-based system. The forwarding part is trivial: Each node manages two variables color and visited in its local whiteboard. The backtrack part is more complicated, but except for the matter how we can make the agent go back to the root node for traversing in-stack nodes, the identification of $par(v_{\mathrm{cur}})$ is straightforward. Assume that the agent must perform the backtrack at a node u, and P_u be the path in $T_{G,r}$ from r to u. If the agent can go back to the root r, it moves along P_u with changing the colors of the nodes in P_u from white to black. Eventually it gets to the node u. Then the port number π_{in} indicates the way to the parent of u in $T_{G,r}$. The agent moves to $\pi_u^{-1}(\pi_{\mathrm{in}})$ with excluding u from the set of in-stack nodes (by changing the value of color to none), and the backtrack finishes. You may think that for future invocation of the backtrack process, the agent must recolor in-stack nodes by white. Fortunately, such an recoloring is not necessary because it suffices to swap the role of black and white.

The remaining problem is how to implement the mechanism of making the agent move to r. To resolve it, we newly introduce a new distributed date structure called *R-path*, which is explained in the next section.

4 R-PATH DATA STRUCTURE

An instance X of *R-path* maintains a traversable path connecting an arbitrary *source node* (the root node in our use) to a *target node*. The important features of *R-path* are twofold: We can dynamically update the location of the target node, and $O(1)$-bit memory and storage suffice to implement it.

4.1 Compact Encoding of Path

The main idea for saving space is that R-path maintains the set of in-path nodes constituting a "minimal" path from the source node to the target node, where the minimality means that the subgraph induced by P forms a path graph. This feature guarantees that any node in P has at most two neighbors in P. To traverse the maintained path correctly, we further add one-bit information by variable direction, which indicates the backward in-path neighbor (i.e., the neighbor closer to the source node). Precisely, the value "Backward > Forward" (resp. "Backward < Forward") of variable direction implies that the port number of the backward neighbor is greater (resp. smaller) than that of the forward one. Supported by this information, the agent can perform backward and forward movement in the path correctly.

4.2 Installing R-path in the Lex-DFS algorithm

It is not difficult to apply the R-path structure for obtaining our space-efficient Lex-DFS algorithm. In running the Lex-DFS algorithm explained in Section 3, the agent manages the s-t path for $s = r$ and $t = v_{\mathrm{cur}}$ using R-path structure. When it must go back to the root in the process of backtrack, it suffices to update target node, and thus the remaining matter is resolved.

The running time of updating of target node and moving root node depends on the number of edges incident to in-path nodes. In the worst-case, the maintained s-t path can contain $\Theta(n)$ nodes. The computation cost at each in-path node is bounded by $O(m)$ (i.e., the sum of the degrees of in-path nodes). In the main routine of our Lex-DFS algorithm, updating of target node and moving root node will be invoked $\Theta(n)$ times respectively. Thus the total cost brought by the R-path subroutine is $O(mn)$ steps. Except for that, the time complexity of the main routine is the same as the naive Lex-DFS algorithm, that is, $O(m)$ steps. Consequently we have the following theorem.

THEOREM 4.1. *There exists an agent-based Lex-DFS algorithm using a constant-space memory and storage, which runs in $O(mn)$ steps.*

5 CONCLUSION AND FUTURE DIRECTIONS

In this paper, we proposed a small-space Lex-DFS algorithm which consumes only a constant-size memory and storages. This is the first polynomial-time graph exploration algorithm with fully-sublogarithmic space complexity. Finally, our results raise up several interesting open problems: (1) Is it possible to construct a faster DFS algorithm running in $o(mn)$ steps with keeping the same space usage? (2) Can we have any time-complexity lower bound in this settings? (3) Is there a graph exploration algorithm for oblivious agents using $O(1)$-bit storages? (4) Can we adopt our technique for solving any collaborative tasks by multiple agents?

REFERENCES

[1] Tetsuo Asano, Taisuke Izumi, Masashi Kiyomi, Matsuo Konagaya, Hirotaka Ono, Yota Otachi, Pascal Schweitzer, Jun Tarui, and Ryuhei Uehara. 2014. Depth-First Search Using $O(n)$ Bits.. In *Proc. of 25th International Symposium on Algorithms and Computation (ISAAC)*. 553–564.

[2] Yann Disser, Jan Hackfeld, and Max Klimm. 2016. Undirected Graph Exploration with Θ (Log Log N) Pebbles. In *Proc. of 27th Annual ACM-SIAM Symposium on Discrete Algorithms (SODA)*. 25–39.

[3] Amr Elmasry, Torben Hagerup, and Frank Kammer. 2015. Space-efficient Basic Graph Algorithms. In *Proc. of 32nd International Symposium on Theoretical Aspects of Computer Science (STACS 2015)*, Vol. 30. 288–301.

[4] Pierre Fraigniaud, David Ilcinkas, Guy Peer, Andrzej Pelc, and David Peleg. 2005. Graph exploration by a finite automaton. *Theoretical Computer Science* 345 (2005), 331–344.

[5] Omer Reingold. 2008. Undirected connectivity in log-space. *Journal of the ACM (JACM)* 55 (2008), 17.

Atomic Cross-Chain Swaps

Maurice Herlihy
Computer Science Department
Brown University
Providence, Rhode Island
maurice.herlihy@gmail.com

ABSTRACT

An *atomic cross-chain swap* is a distributed coordination task where multiple parties exchange assets across multiple blockchains, for example, trading bitcoin for ether.

An *atomic* swap protocol guarantees (1) if all parties conform to the protocol, then all swaps take place, (2) if some coalition deviates from the protocol, then no conforming party ends up worse off, and (3) no coalition has an incentive to deviate from the protocol.

A cross-chain swap is modeled as a directed graph $\mathcal{D}$, whose vertexes are parties and whose arcs are proposed asset transfers. For any pair $(\mathcal{D}, L)$, where $\mathcal{D} = (V, A)$ is a strongly-connected directed graph and $L \subset V$ a feedback vertex set for $\mathcal{D}$, we give an atomic cross-chain swap protocol for $\mathcal{D}$, using a form of hashed timelock contracts, where the vertexes in L generate the hashlocked secrets. We show that no such protocol is possible if $\mathcal{D}$ is not strongly connected, or if $\mathcal{D}$ is strongly connected but L is not a feedback vertex set. The protocol has time complexity $O(diam(\mathcal{D}))$ and space complexity (bits stored on all blockchains) $O(|A|^2)$.

ACM Reference Format:
Maurice Herlihy. 2018. Atomic Cross-Chain Swaps. In *PODC '18: ACM Symposium on Principles of Distributed Computing, July 23–27, 2018, Egham, United Kingdom.* ACM, New York, NY, USA, 10 pages. https://doi.org/10.1145/3212734.3212736

1 MOTIVATION

Carol wants to sell her Cadillac for bitcoins. Alice is willing to buy Carol's Cadillac, but she wants to pay in an "alt-coin" cryptocurrency. Fortunately, Bob is willing to trade alt-coins for bitcoins. Alice, Bob, and Carol need to arrange a three-way swap: Alice will transfer her alt-coins to Bob, Bob will transfer his bitcoins to Carol, and Carol will transfer title of her Cadillac to Alice[1]. Of course, no one trusts anyone else. How can we devise a protocol that ensures that if all parties behave rationally, in his or her own self-interest, then all assets are exchanged, but if some parties behave irrationally, then no rational party will end up worse off?

In many blockchains, assets are transferred under the control of so-called *smart contracts* (or just *contracts*), scripts published on the blockchain that establish and enforce conditions necessary to transfer an asset from one party to another. For example, let $H(\cdot)$ be a cryptographic hash function. Alice might place her alt-coins in escrow by publishing on the alt-coin blockchain a smart contract with *hashlock* h and *timelock* t. Hashlock h means that if Bob sends the contract a value s, called a *secret*, such that $h = H(s)$, then the contract irrevocably transfers ownership of those alt-coins from Alice to Bob. Timelock t means that if Bob fails to produce that secret before time t elapses, then the escrowed alt-coins are refunded to Alice.

Here is a simple protocol for Alice, Bob, and Carol's three-way swap, illustrated in Figures 1 and 2. Let Δ be enough time for one party to publish a smart contract on any of the blockchains, or to change a contract's state, and for the other party to detect the change.

- Alice creates a secret s, $h = H(s)$, and publishes a contract on the alt-coin blockchain with hashlock h and timelock 6Δ in the future, to transfer her alt-coins to Bob.
- When Bob confirms that Alice's contract has been published on the alt-coin blockchain, he publishes a contract on the Bitcoin blockchain with the same hashlock h but with timelock 5Δ in the future, to transfer his bitcoins to Carol.
- When Carol confirms that Bob's contract has been published on the Bitcoin blockchain, she publishes a contract on the automobile title blockchain with the same hashlock h, but with timeout 4Δ in the future, to transfer her Cadillac's title to Alice.
- When Alice confirms that Carol's contract has been published on the title blockchain, she sends s to Carol's contract, acquiring the title and revealing s to Carol.
- Carol then sends s to Bob's contract, acquiring the bitcoins and revealing s to Bob.
- Bob sends s to Alice's contract, acquiring the alt-coins and completing the swap.

What could go wrong? If any party halts while contracts are being deployed, then all contracts eventually time out and trigger refunds. If any party halts while contracts are being triggered, then only that party ends up worse off. For example, if Carol halts without triggering her contract, then Alice gets the Cadillac and Bob gets a refund, so Carol's misbehavior harms only herself.

The order in which contracts are deployed matters. If Carol were to post her contract with Alice before Bob posts his contract with Carol, then Alice could take ownership of the Cadillac without paying Carol.

Timelock values matter. If Carol's contract with Bob were to expire at the same time as Bob's contract with Alice, then Carol could reveal s to collect Bob's bitcoins at the very last moment, leaving Bob no time to collect his alt-coins from Alice.

[1] Naturally, they live in a state that records automobile titles in a blockchain.

ACM ISBN 978-1-4503-5795-1/18/07.
https://doi.org/10.1145/3212734.3212736

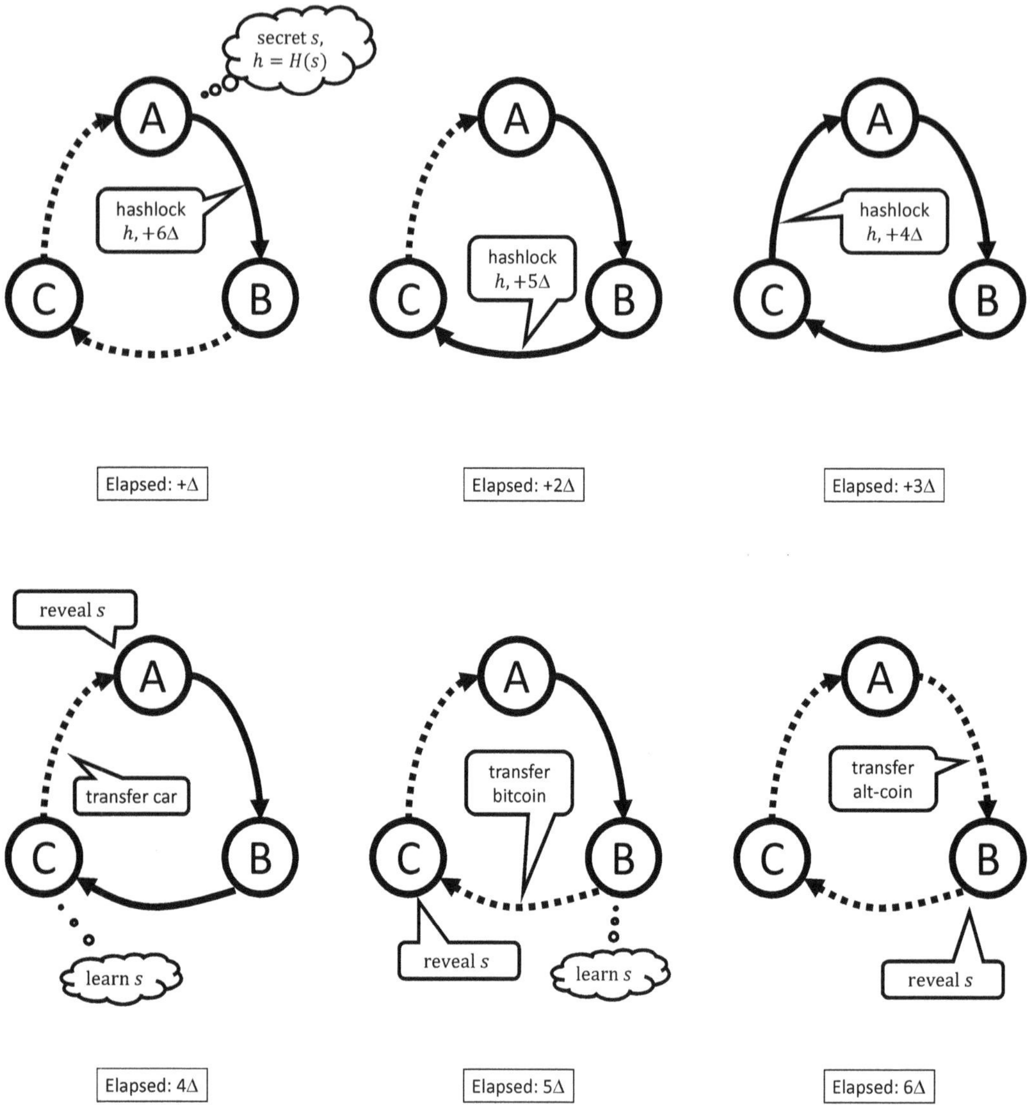

Figure 2: Atomic cross-chain swap: triggering arcs

What if parties behave irrationally? If Alice (irrationally) reveals s before the first phase completes, then Bob can take Alice's alt-coins, and perhaps Carol can take Bob's bitcoins, but Alice will not get her Cadillac, so only she is worse off.

A *atomic swap protocol* guarantees (1) if all parties conform to the protocol, then all swaps take place, (2) if some parties deviate from the protocol, then no conforming party ends up worse off[2], and (3) no coalition has an incentive to deviate from the protocol. Alice, Bob, and Carol's swapping adventure suggests broader questions: when are atomic cross-chain swaps possible, how can we implement them, and what do they cost?

[2]Other than the inconvenience of having assets temporarily locked up.

While swapping digital assets is the immediate motivation for this study, atomic cross-chain swap protocols have other possible applications. *Sharding* [7] splits one blockchain into many for better load-balancing and scalability. Most of the time, activities on different shards proceed independently. When they cannot, an atomic swap protocol can coordinate needed cross-chain updates. In a decentralized distributed system, *upgrades* from one software version to another, or from one data schema to another, could benefit from atomic cross-chain swaps. An atomic swap protocol can be thought of as a trust-free, Byzantine-hardened form of *distributed commitment* [26]. An atomic cross-chain swap is a special case of a *distributed atomic transaction* [25], although not all atomic transactions can be expressed as cross-chain swaps.

Cross-chain swaps are well-known to the blockchain community [4, 6, 9, 20, 21, 27], but to our knowledge, this is the first systematic analysis of the theory underlying such protocols. We make the following contributions. A cross-chain swap is modeled as a directed graph (digraph) $\mathcal{D}$, whose vertexes are parties and whose arcs are proposed asset transfers. For any pair $(\mathcal{D}, L)$, where $\mathcal{D} = (V, A)$ is a *strongly-connected* digraph and $L \subset V$ a *feedback vertex set* for $\mathcal{D}$, we give an atomic cross-chain swap protocol using a form of hashed timelock contracts, where the vertexes in L, called *leaders*, generate the hashlocked secrets. (Vertexes that are not leaders are *followers*.) We also show that no such protocol is possible if $\mathcal{D}$ is not strongly connected, or if $\mathcal{D}$ is strongly connected but the set of leaders L is not a feedback vertex set. The protocol has time complexity $O(diam(\mathcal{D}))$ and communication complexity (bits published on blockchains) $O(|A| \cdot |L|)$.

2 MODEL

2.1 Digraphs

A *directed graph* (or *digraph*) $\mathcal{D}$ is a pair (V, A), where V is a finite set of *vertexes*, and A is a finite set of ordered pairs of distinct vertexes called *arcs*. We use $V(\mathcal{D})$ for $\mathcal{D}$'s set of vertexes, and $A(\mathcal{D})$ for its set of arcs. An arc (u, v) has *head* u and *tail* v. An arc *leaves* its head and *enters* its tail. An arc (u, v) *enters* a set of vertexes $W \subseteq V$ if $u \notin W$ and $v \in W$, and similarly for leaving.

A digraph C is a *subdigraph* of $\mathcal{D}$ if $V(C) \subseteq V(\mathcal{D}), A(C) \subseteq A(\mathcal{D})$ and every arc in $A(C)$ has both its head and tail in $V(C)$.

A *path* p in $\mathcal{D}$ is a sequence of vertexes $(u_0, \ldots, u_\ell)$ such that $u_0, \ldots, u_{\ell-1}$ are distinct. Path p has *length* ℓ, denoted by $|p|$. If v is a vertex, and $(u_0, \ldots, u_\ell)$ a path that does not include the arc (v, u_0), then $v + p$ denotes the path $(v, u_0, \ldots, u_\ell)$. For vertexes u, v, $D(u, v)$ is the length of the longest path from u to v in $\mathcal{D}$.

A path $(u_0, \ldots, u_\ell)$ is a *cycle* if $u_0 = u_\ell$. A digraph is *acycli*c if it has no cycles. Vertex v is *reachable* from vertex u if there path from u to v. $\mathcal{D}$'s *diameter* $diam(\mathcal{D})$ is the length of the lon path from any vertex to any other. $\mathcal{D}$ is *connected* if its underly graph is connected, and *strongly connected* if, for every pair of distinct vertexes in $\mathcal{D}$, u is reachable from v and v is reach from u. A *feedback vertex set* is a subset of V whose deletion le $\mathcal{D}$ acyclic.

The *transpose* $\mathcal{D}^T$ is the digraph obtained from $\mathcal{D}$ by rever all arcs. If $\mathcal{D}$ is strongly connected, so is $\mathcal{D}^T$, and any feedb vertex set for $\mathcal{D}$ is also a feedback vertex set for $\mathcal{D}^T$.

2.2 Blockchains and Smart Contracts

For our purposes, a *blockchain* is a distributed service that all clients to publish transactions to a publicly-readable, tamper-p distributed ledger. Our analysis is independent of the partic blockchain algorithm. We assume a timing model where there is a known duration Δ long enough for one party to publish a contract to a blockchain, and for a second party to confirm that the contract has been published.

The owner of an asset (such as a unit of cryptocurrency or an automobile title) can create a smart contract to transfer ownership of that asset to a *counterparty* if specified conditions are met. A contract is *published* when its creator places it on a blockchain ledger. Once a contract is published, it is irrevocable: neither the contract's creator nor any other party can remove the contract nor tamper with its terms.

A *rational* party acts in its own self-interest, deviating from a protocol only if it is profitable to do so. Rational parties can collude with one another to disadvantage other parties. An *irrational* party may deviate from a protocol even if it is not profitable to do so. Parties may behave irrationally out of spite, because they were hacked, or because they profit in ways not foreseen by the protocol designers.

Blockchain protocols typically require parties to have public and private keys. We use $sig(x, v)$ to denote the result of v using its private key to sign x.

3 SWAP DIGRAPHS AND GAMES

A cross-chain swap is given by a digraph $\mathcal{D} = (V, A)$, where each vertex in V represents a party, and each arc in A represents a proposed asset transfer from the arc's head to its tail via a shared blockchain. (We assume without loss of generality that $\mathcal{D}$ is connected, because a disconnected digraph can be treated as multiple swaps.) Henceforth, we use *party* and *vertex*, *blockchain* and *arc*, interchangeably, depending on whether we emphasize roles or digraph structure.

In the terminology of game theory, a swap $\mathcal{D}$ is a *cooperative game*, organized so that if all parties follow the protocol, each transfer on each arc happens. Each possible outcome is given by a subdigraph $\mathcal{E} = (V, A')$ of $\mathcal{D}$. If a proposed transfer $(u, v) \in A$ is also in $(u, v) \in A'$, then that transfer happened. For short, we say arc (u, v) was *triggered*.

A protocol is a *strategy* for playing a game: a set of rules that determines which step a party takes at any stage of a game. To model real-world situations where multiple parties are secretly controlled by a single adversary, the swap game is *cooperative*:

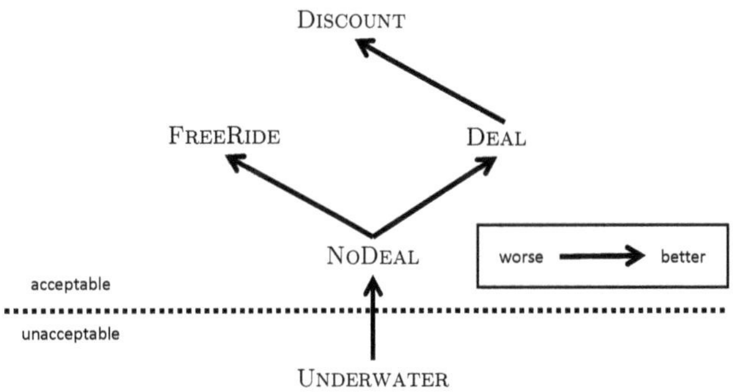

Figure 3: Partial order of protocol outcomes

Here are the outcomes for a party v, organized into classes, For brevity, each class has a shorthand name.

- The party acquires assets without paying: at least one arc entering v is triggered, but no arc leaving v is triggered (FREERIDE).

- The party acquires assets while paying less than expected: all arcs entering v are triggered, but at least one arc leaving v is not triggered (DISCOUNT).
- The party swaps assets as expected: all arcs entering and leaving v are triggered (DEAL).
- No assets change hands: no arc entering or leaving v is triggered (NODEAL).
- The party pays without acquiring all expected assets: at least one arc entering v is not triggered, and at least one arc leaving v is triggered (UNDERWATER).

Payoffs for a coalition $C \subset V$ are defined by replacing v with C in the definitions above.

The protocol design incorporates certain conservative assumptions about parties' preferences. The protocol's preferred outcome is for all conforming parties to end with outcome DEAL. In the presence of failures or deviation, however, it is acceptable for conforming parties to end with outcome NODEAL, the *status quo*, rendering them no worse off. Furthermore, each party is assumed to prefer DEAL to NODEAL, because otherwise it would not have agreed to the swap in the first place. It follows that each party prefers any FREERIDE outcome to NODEAL, because it acquires additional assets "for free", without relinquishing any assets of its own. Similarly, each party prefers any DISCOUNT outcome to DEAL, since that party acquires the same assets in both outcomes, but relinquishes fewer in DISCOUNT outcomes. For these reasons, DEAL, NODEAL, DISCOUNT, and FREERIDE are all considered acceptable outcomes for conforming parties if the protocol execution is unable to complete because of failures or adversarial behavior.

We consider the remaining UNDERWATER outcomes to be unacceptable to conforming parties. It is possible that in some idiosyncratic cases, a party may actually prefer particular UNDERWATER outcomes to NODEAL. For example, a party with three entering arcs and one leaving arc may be be willing to relinquish its asset in return for acquiring only two out of three of the entering arcs' assets. We leave the design of protocols that make such fine distinctions to future work.

Definition 3.1. A swap protocol $\mathbb{P}$ is *uniform* if it satisfies:

- If all parties follow $\mathbb{P}$, they all finish with payoff DEAL.
- If any coalition cooperatively deviates from $\mathbb{P}$, no conforming party finishes with payoff UNDERWATER.

A uniform protocol is not useful if rational parties will not follow it. A swap protocol is a *strong Nash equilibrium strategy* if no coalition improves its payoff when its members cooperatively deviate from that protocol.

Definition 3.2. A swap protocol $\mathbb{P}$ is *atomic* if it is both uniform and a strong Nash equilibrium strategy.

This definition formalizes the notion that if all parties are rational, all swaps happen, but if some parties are irrational, the rational parties will never end up worse off. Recall that a *conforming* party follows the protocol, while a *deviating* party does not.

LEMMA 3.3. *If $\mathcal{D}$ is strongly connected, then any uniform swap protocol $\mathbb{P}$ is atomic.*

PROOF. If a deviating coalition $C \subset V$ achieves a better payoff than DEAL, then that payoff is either in FREERIDE or DISCOUNT. It follows that some arc that enters C is triggered, and some arc that leaves C is untriggered. Moreover, if any arc that enters C is untriggered, then all arcs that leave C are untriggered.

A conforming party $v \notin C$ cannot end up UNDERWATER, so if an arc entering v is untriggered, then every arc leaving v must be untriggered, and if an arc leaving v is triggered, then every arc entering v must be triggered.

Let (c, v) be an untriggered arc leaving C. Since v is conforming, every arc leaving v is untriggered. Because $\mathcal{D}$ is strongly connected, there is a path $(v, v_0), (v_1, v_2), \ldots, (v_k, c_0)$ where each $v_i \notin C$, and $c_0 \in C$. By a simple inductive argument, each arc in this path is untriggered, so the arc (v_k, c_0) that enters C is untriggered, so *every* arc leaving C must be untriggered, and some arc entering C must be triggered.

Let (v, c) be a triggered arc entering C. Since v is conforming, every arc entering v is triggered. Because $\mathcal{D}$ is strongly connected, there is a path $(c_1, v_0), (v_0, v_1), \ldots, (v_k, c)$ where each $v_i \notin C$, and $c_1 \in C$. By a simple inductive argument, each arc in this path is triggered, so the arc (c_1, v_0) leaving C is triggered, contradicting the fact that every arc leaving C is untriggered. □

LEMMA 3.4. *If $\mathcal{D}$ is not strongly connected, then no uniform swap protocol is atomic.*

PROOF. Because $\mathcal{D}$ is not strongly connected, it contains vertexes x, y such that y is reachable from x, but not vice-versa. Let Y be the set of vertexes reachable from y, and X the rest: $X = V \setminus Y$. X is non-empty because it contains x. Because y is reachable from x, there is at least one arc from X to Y, but no arcs from Y to X.

Coalition X can improve its payoff by triggering all arcs between vertexes in X, but no arcs from X to Y, yielding payoff FREERIDE for X, since it triggers strictly fewer arcs leaving X, without affecting any arcs entering X. In fact, the payoff for each individual vertex in X is either the same or better than DEAL. □

We have just proved:

THEOREM 3.5. *A uniform swap protocol for $\mathcal{D}$ is atomic if and only if $\mathcal{D}$ is strongly connected.*

Informally, if $\mathcal{D}$ is not strongly connected, then rational parties will deviate from any uniform protocol. In practice, such a swap would never be proposed, because the parties in X would never agree to a swap with the free riders in Y. Henceforth, $\mathcal{D}$ is assumed strongly connected.

We remark that Theorem 3.5 relies on the implicit technical assumption that all value transfers are explicitly represented on some blockchain. This theorem would be falsified, for example, if Carol responds to learning Alice's secret by sending a large drone to drop her Cadillac in the middle of Alice's driveway, without ever recording that transfer in a shared blockchain. We will assume that if swaps have off-chain consequences, as they typically do, that those consequences are explicitly recorded in the form of blockchain updates.

```
contract Swap{
  Asset asset;                /* asset to be transferred or refunded */
  Digraph digraph;            /* swap digraph */
  address[] leaders;          /* leaders */
  address party;              /* transfer asset from */
  address counterparty;       /* transfer asset to */
  uint[] timelock;            /* vector of timelocks */
  uint[] hashlock;            /* vector of hashlocks */
  bool[] unlocked;            /* which hashlocks unlocked? */
  uint   start;               /* protocol starting time */
  /* constructor */
  function Swap(Asset _asset; /* asset to be transferred or refunded */
                Digraph _digraph;      /* swap digraph */
                address[] _leaders;    /* leaders */
                address _party;        /* transfer asset from */
                address _counterparty; /* transfer asset to */
                uint[]  _timelock;     /* vector of timelocks */
                uint[]  _hashlock;     /* vector of hashlocks */
                uint    _start         /* protocol starting time */
                ){
    asset = _asset;                                  /* copy */
    party = _party; counterparty = _counterparty;    /* copy */
    timelock = _timelock; hashlock = _hashlock;      /* copy */
    unlocked = [false, ..., false];                  /* all unlocked */
  }
```

Figure 4: Swap contract (part one)

4 AN ATOMIC SWAP PROTOCOL

4.1 Hashlocks and Hashkeys

In a simple two-party swap, each party publishes a contract that assumes temporary control of that party's asset. This *hashed timelock contract* [5] stores a pair (h, t), and ensures that if the contract receives the matching secret s, $h = H(s)$, before time t has elapsed, then the contract is *triggered*, irrevocably transferring ownership of the asset to the counterparty. If the contract does not receive the matching secret before time t has elapsed, then the asset is *refunded* to the original owner. For multi-party cross-chain swaps, we will need to extend these notions in several ways.

In the three-way swap recounted earlier, each arc had a single hashlock and a single timeout. Timeouts were assigned so that the timeout on each arc entering a follower v was later by at least Δ than the timeout on each arc leaving v. This gap ensures that if any arc leaving v is triggered, then v has time to trigger every entering arc.

If a swap digraph has only one leader, $\hat{v}$, then the subdigraph of its followers is acyclic. As in our three-way swap example, the hashlock on arc (u, v) can be given timeout $(diam(\mathcal{D}) + D(v, \hat{v}) + 1) \cdot \Delta$, where $D(v, \hat{v})$ is the length of the longest path from v to the unique leader $\hat{v}$. (See left-hand side of Figure 6.)

This formula does not work if a swap digraph has more than one leader, because the subdigraph of any leader's followers has a cycle, and it is not possible to assign timeouts across a cycle in a way that guarantees a gap of at least Δ between entering and leaving arcs. (See right-hand side of Figure 6.)

Instead, for general digraphs, we must replace timed hashlocks with a more general mechanism, one that assigns different timeouts to different paths. Pick a set $L = \{v_0, \dots, v_\ell\}$ of vertexes, called *leaders*, forming a feedback vertex set for $\mathcal{D}$. Each leader v_i generates a secret s_i and hashlock value $h_i = H(s_i)$, yielding a *hashlock vector* $(h_0, \dots, h_\ell)$, which is assigned to every arc.

A *hashkey* for h on arc (u, v) is a triple (s, p, σ), where s is the secret $h = H(s)$, p is a path $(u_0, \dots, u_k)$ in $\mathcal{D}$ where $u_0 = v$ and u_k is the leader who generated s, and

$$\sigma = sig(\cdots sig(s, u_k), \dots, u_0),$$

the result of having each party in the path sign s. A hashkey (s, p, σ) *times out* at time $(diam(\mathcal{D}) + |p|) \cdot \Delta$ after the start of the protocol. That hashkey *unlocks* h on (u, v) if it is presented before it times out. An arc is *triggered* when all of its hashlocks are unlocked. A hashlock has *timed out* on an arc when all of its hashkeys on that arc have timed out. Figure 7 shows partial hashkeys for a two-leader swap digraph.

```
function unlock (int i, uint s, Path path, Sig sig) {
    require (msg.sender == counterparty); /* only from counterparty */
    if (now < start + (diam(digraph) + |path|) * Δ /* hashkey still valid? */
        && hashlock[i] == H(s)                /* secret correct? */
        && isPath(path, digraph, leader[i], counterparty) /* path valid? */
        && verifySigs(sig, s, path) { /* signatures valid? */
      unlocked[i] = true;
    }
  }
  function refund () {
    require (msg.sender == party); /* only from party */
    if (any hashlock unlocked and timed out) {
      transfer asset to party;
      halt;
    }
  }
  function claim () {
    require (msg.sender == counterparty); /* only from counterparty */
    if (every hashlock unlocked) {
      transfer asset to counterparty;
      halt;
    }
  }
}
```

Figure 5: Swap contract (part two)

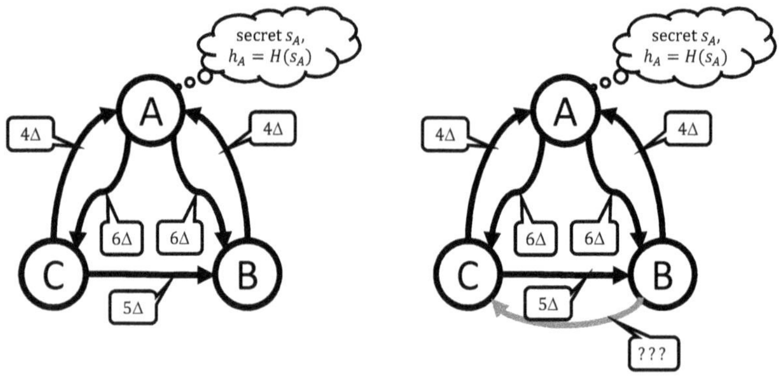

Figure 6: *A* is the leader, *B* and *C* followers. Timeouts can be assigned when the follower subdigraph is acyclic (left) but not when it is cyclic (right)

4.2 Market Clearing

For simplicity, assume the swap digraph is constructed by a (possibly centralized) market-clearing service, which perhaps communicates with the parties through its own blockchain. The clearing service is not a trusted party, because the parties can check the consistency of the clearing service's responses.

Each party creates a secret s and matching hashlock $h = H(s)$. It sends the clearing service its hashlock, along with an offer characterizing the swaps it is willing to make. The service combines these offers, and publishes a swap digraph $\mathcal{D} = (V, A)$, a vector $L \subset V$ of *leaders* forming a feedback vertex set, a vector of those leaders' hashlocks $h_0, \ldots, h_\ell$, and a *starting time* T, at least Δ in the future.

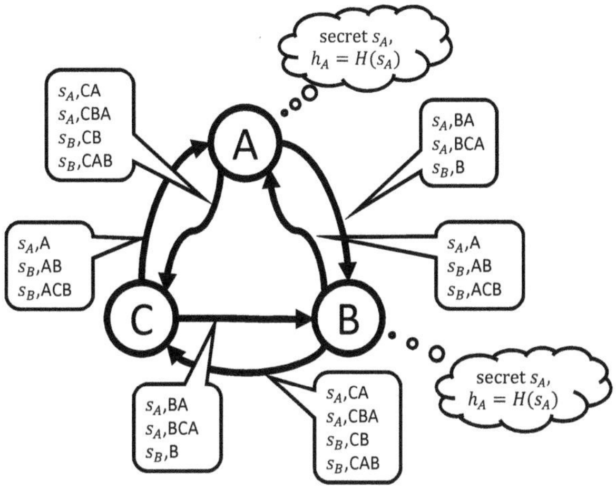

Figure 7: Hashkey paths for arcs of two-leader digraph

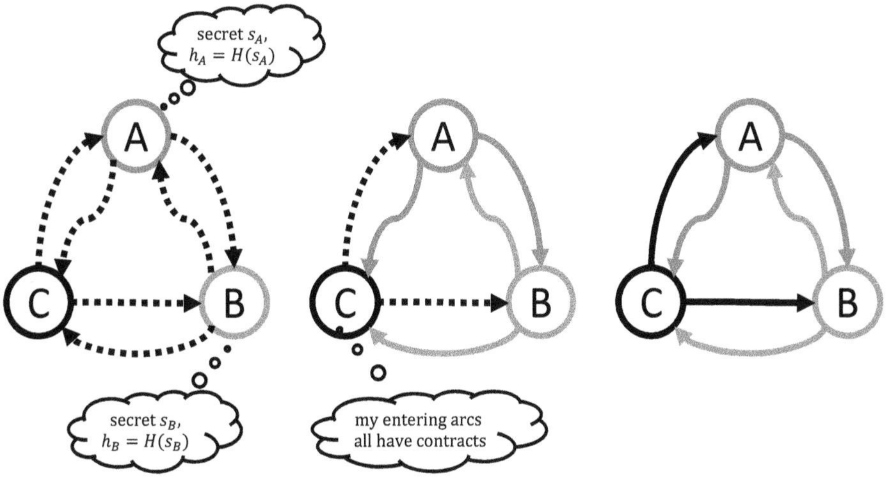

Figure 8: Concurrent contract propagation for two-leader digraph

If all parties conform to the protocol, all contracts will be triggered before $T + 2 \cdot diam(\mathcal{D}) \cdot \Delta$, but if some parties deviate, the conforming parties' assets will be refunded by then.

4.3 Contracts

Figures 4 and 5 show pseudocode[3] for a hashed timelock swap contract. A smart contract resembles an object in an object-oriented programming language, providing *long-lived state* (Lines 2-9), a *constructor* to initialize that state (Lines 12-25), and one or more *functions* to manage that state (Lines 26-48).

The contract's long-lived state records the asset to be transferred or refunded (Line 2), the digraph $\mathcal{D}$ (Line 3), the digraph's set of leaders (Line 4), the party transferring the asset (Line 5), the counterparty receiving the asset (Line 6), a vector of timelocks (Line 7), a vector of hashlocks (Line 8), and a Boolean unlocked vector marking which hashlocks have been unlocked (Line 9).

When the contract is initialized, its constructor copies the fields provided into the contract's long-lived state (Lines 21-23) and sets each entry in unlocked to *false* (Line 24).

The unlock() function (Line 26), callable only by the counterparty (Line 27), takes an index i, a secret s_i, a path p, and the signature sig. The hashlock h_i is unlocked if

- the current time is less than $T + (diam(\mathcal{D}) + |p|) \cdot \Delta$ (Line 28),
- $h_i = H(s_i)$ (Line 29),
- p is a path in $\mathcal{D}$ from the counterparty to the leader who generated s_i (Line 30), and
- the signature is the result of signing s_i by the parties in p (Line 31)

The refund() function (Line 35), callable only by the party, refunds the asset to the party if any unlocked hashlock has timed out. The claim() function (Line 42), callable only by the counterparty

[3] This pseudocode is based loosely on the popular Solidity programming language for smart contracts [24].

(Line 36), transfers the asset to the counterparty if all hashlocks have been unlocked.

4.4 Pebble Games

We analyze the protocol using two variations on a simple pebble game. We are given a strongly-connected digraph $\mathcal{D} = (V, A)$, and a vertex feedback set $L \subset V$ of *leaders*.

In the *lazy* pebble game, start by placing pebbles on the arcs leaving each leader. Place new pebbles on the arcs leaving vertex v when there is a pebble on *every* arc entering v.

In the *eager* pebble game, start by placing a single pebble on one vertex z. Place new pebbles on the arcs leaving v when there is a pebble on *any* arc entering v. Both games continue until no more pebbles can be placed.

Lemma 4.1. *In the lazy game, every arc in $\mathcal{D}$ eventually has a pebble.*

Proof. Suppose by way of contradiction, the game stops in a state where an arc (u, v) has no pebble. There must be a pebble-free arc (u', u) entering u, because otherwise the game would have placed a pebble on (u, v). Continuing in this way, build a longer and longer pebble-free path until it becomes a pebble-free cycle. But leaders form a feedback vertex set, so every cycle in $\mathcal{D}$ includes a leader, and the arcs leaving that leader have pebbles placed in the first step. □

Lemma 4.2. *In the eager game, every arc in $\mathcal{D}$ eventually has a pebble.*

Proof. Suppose by way of contradiction, the game stops in a state where an arc (u, v) has no pebble. Because $\mathcal{G}$ is strongly connected, there is a path from z to v. Since z has a pebble and v does not, there is an arc (w, w') on that path where w has a pebble but w' does not, so w' will get a pebble in the next step, contradicting the hypothesis that the game has stopped. □

Suppose there is a worst-case delay Δ between when the last pebble is placed on any arc entering v, and when the last pebble is placed on any arc leaving v.

Lemma 4.3. *In both pebble games, every arc will have a pebble in time at most $diam(\mathcal{D}) \cdot \Delta$ from when the game started.*

Proof. For the lazy game, it is enough to show that in each interval of time Δ, the longest pebble-free path shrinks by one. At any time after the first step, let $a_0, \ldots, a_k$ be a pebble-free path of maximal length. That path cannot be a cycle, because then it would include a leader, who would have placed a pebble on a_0 in the first step. It follows that every arc entering the head of a_0 must have a pebble, because otherwise we could construct a longer pebble-free path. By hypothesis, within time Δ, a_0 will have a pebble, and the path will have shrunk by one.

For the eager game, it is enough to observe that in each interval of time Δ, for every vertex v, the number of unpebbled vertexes in every path from z to w shrinks by one. Because $\mathcal{D}$ is strongly connected, such a path always exists. □

Corollary 4.4. *Under the stated timing assumptions, for both games, every arc has a pebble within time $diam(\mathcal{D}) \cdot \Delta$.*

4.5 The Protocol

There are two phases. In Phase One, instances of the Swap contract (Figures 4 and 5) are propagated through $\mathcal{D}$, starting at the leaders. Each time a party observes that a contract has been published on an entering arc, it verifies that contract is a correct swap contract, and abandons the protocol otherwise.

Here is the Phase-One protocol for leaders:

(1) Publish a contract on every arc leaving the leader, then
(2) wait until contracts have been published on all arcs entering the leader.

Here is the protocol for followers:

(1) wait until correct contracts have been published on all arcs entering the vertex, then
(2) publish a contract on every arc leaving the vertex.

Figure 7 shows how contracts are propagated in a swap digraph with two leaders.

In Phase Two, the parties disseminate secrets via hashkeys. While contracts propagate in the direction of the arcs, from party to counterparty, hashkeys propagate in the opposite direction, from counterparty to party. Informally, each party is motivated to trigger the contracts on entering arcs to acquire the assets controlled by those contracts.

We now trace how the secret s_i generated by leader v_i is propagated. At the start of the phase, v_i calls $\mathsf{unlock}(s_i, v_i, sig(s_i, v_i))$ at each entering arc's contract (here, the function's arguments are the hashkey, and v_i is a degenerate path). The first time any other party v observes that hashlock h_i on a leaving arc's contract has been unlocked by a call to $\mathsf{unlock}(s_i, p, \sigma)$, it calls $\mathsf{unlock}(s_i, v+p, sig(\sigma, v))$ at each entering arc's contract. The propagation of s_i is complete when h_i has either timed out or has been unlocked on all arcs.

Lemma 4.5. *If all parties conform to the protocol, then every arc has a contract within time $diam(\mathcal{D}) \cdot \Delta$ of when the protocol started.*

Proof. Phase One is an instance of the lazy pebble game on $\mathcal{D}$, so the claim follows from Lemmas 4.1 and 4.3. □

Lemma 4.6. *If all parties conform to the protocol, then every arc's contract is triggered within time $2 \cdot diam(\mathcal{D}) \cdot \Delta$ of when the protocol started.*

Proof. Each secret's dissemination is an instance of the eager pebble games on $\mathcal{D}^T$, the transpose digraph. The secrets are disseminated in parallel. □

Theorem 4.7. *If all parties conform to the protocol, then every contract is triggered within time $2 \cdot diam(\mathcal{D}) \cdot \Delta$ of when the protocol started.*

The deadline $2 \cdot diam(\mathcal{D}) \cdot \Delta$ bounds the time assets can be held in escrow when things go wrong. In practice, one would expect actual running times to be shorter.

There is a simple optimization that ensures that Phase Two completes in constant time when all parties conform to the protocol. We use a shared blockchain, perhaps that of the market-clearing service, as a broadcast medium. Each leader v_i publishes its secret s_i on the shared blockchain, and each follower monitors that blockchain, triggering its entering arcs when it learns the secret. (Logically, we create an arc from each follower directly to that leader.) Unfortunately, while this broadcasting blockchain can "short-circuit" the Phase Two protocol, it cannot replace it, because a deviating leader might refrain from publishing the secret on that blockchain, but publish it on others. (Miller *et al.* [18] propose a similar optimization for the Lightning network.)

Lemma 4.8. *If hashlock h times out on any arc entering a conforming v, then h must have timed out on every arc leaving v.*

Proof. Suppose h was triggered on (v, w) by hashkey (s, p, σ). If v does not appear in p, then $v + p$ is a path from v to the leader, and v can immediately trigger h on (u, v) using the hashkey $(s, v + p, sig(\sigma, v))$, which has not timed out. If v appears in p, then v has already received (and signed) a hashkey that triggers h on (u, v). □

Theorem 4.9. *No conforming party ends up* Underwater.

Proof. Assume by way of contradiction that some conforming party v ends up Underwater: a leaving arc (v, w) has a triggered contract, but an entering arc (u, v) does not and will not.

First, arc (u, v) must have a contract. Suppose v is a leader. Since (v, w) has been triggered, v has revealed its secret through a hashkey. But a leader issues hashkeys in Phase Two only after a contract has been published on every entering arc during Phase One. Suppose instead v is a follower. Since (v, w) has been triggered, one of the arcs leaving v has a contract. But in Phase One, a follower publishes a contract on a leaving arc only after contracts have been published on all of its incoming arcs.

Since (u, v) has a contract, one of that arc's hashlocks must have timed out. By Lemma 4.8, the arc (v, w) must also have timed out, a contradiction. □

Theorem 4.10. *For $\mathcal{D} = (V, A)$ with leaders $L \subset V$, the space complexity, measured as the number of bits stored on all blockchains, is $O(|A|^2)$.*

Proof. There are $|A|$ contracts, one on each arc, each with a copy of the digraph $\mathcal{D}$, which requires $O(|A|)$ storage. □

Finally, any atomic cross-chain swap protocol using hashed timelocks must assign secrets to a feedback vertex set.

Lemma 4.11. *In any uniform hashed timelock swap protocol, no follower v can publish a contract on an arc leaving v before contracts have been published on all arcs entering v.*

Proof. If follower v has has a contract on arc (v, w) but no contract on arc (u, v), then the parties other than v could collude to trigger the contract on (v, w), while refusing to publish a contract on (u, v), leaving v Underwater. □

Theorem 4.12. *In any uniform swap protocol based on hashed timelocks, the set L of leaders is a feedback vertex set in $\mathcal{D}$.*

Proof. Suppose, instead, there is a uniform swap protocol where the leaders do not form a vertex feedback set.

At any step in the protocol, the *waits-for* digraph W is the subdigraph of $\mathcal{D}^T$ where (v, u) is an arc of W if (u, v) has no published contract. Informally, Lemma 4.11 implies that v must be waiting for u to publish a contract on (u, v) before u can publish any contracts on its own outgoing arcs. In the initial state, if $\mathcal{D} \setminus L$ contains a cycle, so does W. At each protocol step, a follower v can publish a contract on a leaving arc only if v has indegree zero in the current waits-for digraph. But no vertex on a cycle in the waits-for digraph will ever have indegree zero, a contradiction. □

4.6 Single-Leader Digraphs

As noted, in the common special case where a swap digraph needs only one leader, we can replace hashkeys with simple timeouts, reducing message sizes and eliminating the need for digital signatures. In the following, let $\mathcal{D}$ be a swap digraph with a single leader $\hat{v}$ with hashlock h.

Lemma 4.13. *If each arc (u, v) has timeout $(diam(\mathcal{D}) + D(v, \hat{v}) + 1) \cdot \Delta$, then for every conforming $v \neq \hat{v}$, the timeout on each arc (u, v) is later by at least Δ than the timeout on each arc (v, w).*

Proof. Let p be the longest path from w to the leader $\hat{v}$. Because the subdigraph of followers is acyclic, $v + p$ is a path of length $D(w, \hat{v}) + 1$ from v to $\hat{v}$, so $D(v, \hat{v}) \geq D(w, \hat{v}) + 1$. □

Lemma 4.14. *For a single-leader digraph using timeouts, if hashlock h times out on any arc entering a conforming v, then h must have timed out on every arc leaving v.*

Proof. By Lemma 4.14, once h is triggered on (v, w), v has time at least Δ to trigger (u, v). □

From this point on, the bounds on running time and proofs of safety for the single-leader-using-timeouts protocol are essentially the same as for the general protocol.

5 REMARKS

We have seen that single-leader swap digraphs do not require hashkeys and digital signatures, only timeouts. Is there a way to reduce the use of digital signatures in the general case?

Finding a minimal feedback vertex set for $\mathcal{D}$ is NP-complete [15], although there exists an efficient 2-approximation [3].

The protocol is easily extended to a model where there may be more than one arc from one vertex to another, so-called *directed multi-graphs* [2], reflecting the situation where Alice wants to transfer assets on distinct blockchains to Bob.

The swap protocol is still vulnerable to a weak denial-of-service attack where an adversarial party repeatedly proposes an attractive swap, and then fails to complete the protocol, triggering refunds, but temporarily rendering assets inaccessible. We leave for future work the question whether one could require parties to post bonds, and following a failed swap. examine the blockchains to determine who was at fault (by failing to execute an enabled transition).

An interesting open problem is the extent to which this swap protocol can be modified to provide better privacy, analogous to the way the Bolt network [12] improves on Lightning.

As noted, some parties may be willing to accept certain Underwater outcomes rejected by the swap protocol presented here. Future work might investigate protocols where parties are endowed with customized objective functions to provide finer-grained control which outcomes are acceptable.

The swap protocol can be made recurrent by having the leaders distribute the next round's hashlocks in Phase Two of the previous round. If swaps are recurrent, then it would be useful to conduct swaps *off-chain* as much as possible, similar to the way that Lightning [22] and Raiden [19] networks support off-chain transactions for bitcoin and ERC20 tokens.

One limitation of the swap protocol presented here is the assumption that the swap digraph, its leaders, and their hashlocks are common knowledge among the participants. Future work might address constructing and propagating this information dynamically.

6 RELATED WORK

The use of hashed timelock contracts for two-party cross-chain swaps is believed to have emerged from an on-line discussion forum in 2016 [4, 20]. There is open-source code [6, 9, 21] for two-party cross-chain swap protocols between selected currencies, and proposals for applications using swaps [27].

Off-chain payment networks [8, 12, 19, 22] circumvent the scalability limits of existing blockchains by conducting multiple transactions off the blockchain, eventually resolving final balances through a single on-chain transaction. The Revive network [16] rebalances off-chain networks in a way that ensures that compliant parties do not end up worse off. These algorithms also use hashed timelock contracts, but they address a different set of problems.

Multi-party swaps arise when matching kidney donors and recipients. A transplant recipient with an incompatible donor can swap donors to ensure that each recipient obtains a compatible organ. A number of algorithms [1, 10, 13] have been proposed for matching donors and recipients. Shapley and Scarf [23] consider the circumstances under which certain kinds of swap markets have strong equilibriums. Kaplan [14] describes a polynomial-time algorithm that given a set of proposed swaps, constructs a swap digraph if one exists. These papers and many others focus on "the clearing problem", roughly analogous to constructing a swap digraph, but not on how to execute those swaps on blockchains.

The *fair exchange* problem [11, 17] is a precursor to the atomic cross-chain swap problem. Alice has a digital asset Bob wants, and vice-versa, and at the end of the protocol, either Alice and Bob have exchanged assets, or they both keep their assets. In the absence of blockchains, trusted, or semi-trusted third parties are required, but roles of those trusted parties can be minimized in clever ways.

A *atomic cross-chain transaction* is a distributed task where a *sequence* of exchanges occurs at each blockchain. An atomic cross-chain swap is an atomic cross-chain transaction, but not vice-versa, because not all transactions can be expressed as swaps. In our original example, Alice could not borrow bitcoins from Bob to pay Carol, because then Alice would have to execute two steps in sequence (borrow, then spend) instead of executing a single swap. A better understanding of atomic cross-chain transactions is the subject of future work.

REFERENCES

[1] David J. Abraham, Avrim Blum, and Tuomas Sandholm. 2007. Clearing Algorithms for Barter Exchange Markets: Enabling Nationwide Kidney Exchanges. In *Proceedings of the 8th ACM Conference on Electronic Commerce (EC '07)*. ACM, New York, NY, USA, 295–304. https://doi.org/10.1145/1250910.1250954

[2] J. Bang-Jensen and G. Gutin. 2001. *Digraphs: Theory, Algorithms, and Applications.* Springer. https://books.google.com/books?id=d3gpAQAAMAAJ

[3] Ann Becker and Dan Geiger. 1996. Optimization of Pearl's method of conditioning and greedy-like approximation algorithms for the vertex feedback set problem. *Artificial Intelligence* 83, 1 (1996), 167 – 188. https://doi.org/10.1016/0004-3702(95)00004-6

[4] bitcoinwiki. [n. d.]. Atomic cross-chain trading. https://en.bitcoin.it/wiki/Atomic_cross-chain_trading. As of 9 January 2018.

[5] bitcoinwiki. [n. d.]. Hashed Timelock Contracts. Retrieved 8 January 2018 from https://en.bitcoin.it/wiki/Hashed_Timelock_Contracts

[6] Sean Bowe and Daira Hopwood. [n. d.]. Hashed Time-Locked Contract transactions. Retrieved 9 January 2018 from https://github.com/bitcoin/bips/blob/master/bip-0199.mediawiki

[7] Vitalik Buterin. [n. d.]. On sharding blockchains. Retrieved 8 January 2018 from https://github.com/ethereum/wiki/wiki/Sharding-FAQ

[8] Christian Decker and Roger Wattenhofer. 2015. A Fast and Scalable Payment Network with Bitcoin Duplex Micropayment Channels. In *Stabilization, Safety, and Security of Distributed Systems*, Andrzej Pelc and Alexander A. Schwarzmann (Eds.). Springer International Publishing, Cham, 3–18.

[9] DeCred. [n. d.]. Decred cross-chain atomic swapping. Retrieved 8 January 2018 from https://github.com/decred/atomicswap

[10] John P. Dickerson, David F. Manlove, Benjamin Plaut, Tuomas Sandholm, and James Trimble. 2016. Position-Indexed Formulations for Kidney Exchange. *CoRR* abs/1606.01623 (2016). arXiv:1606.01623 http://arxiv.org/abs/1606.01623

[11] Matthew K. Franklin and Gene Tsudik. 1998. Secure Group Barter: Multi-party Fair Exchange with Semi-Trusted Neutral Parties. In *Financial Cryptography.*

[12] Matthew Green and Ian Miers. 2016. Bolt: Anonymous Payment Channels for Decentralized Currencies. Cryptology ePrint Archive, Report 2016/701. https://eprint.iacr.org/2016/701.

[13] Zhipeng Jia, Pingzhong Tang, Ruosong Wang, and Hanrui Zhang. 2017. Efficient Near-optimal Algorithms for Barter Exchange. In *Proceedings of the 16th Conference on Autonomous Agents and MultiAgent Systems (AAMAS '17)*. International Foundation for Autonomous Agents and Multiagent Systems, Richland, SC, 362–370. http://dl.acm.org/citation.cfm?id=3091125.3091181

[14] Randy M. Kaplan. 2011. An improved algorithm for multi-way trading for exchange and barter. *Electronic Commerce Research and Applications* 10, 1 (2011), 67 – 74. https://doi.org/10.1016/j.elerap.2010.08.001 Special Section: Service Innovation in E-Commerce.

[15] Richard M. Karp. 1972. Reducibility Among Combinatorial Problems. In *Proceedings of a symposium on the Complexity of Computer Computations, held March 20-22, 1972, at the IBM Thomas J. Watson Research Center, Yorktown Heights, New York.* 85–103. http://www.cs.berkeley.edu/~luca/cs172/karp.pdf

[16] Rami Khalil and Arthur Gervais. 2017. Revive: Rebalancing Off-Blockchain Payment Networks. In *Proceedings of the 2017 ACM SIGSAC Conference on Computer and Communications Security (CCS '17)*. ACM, New York, NY, USA, 439–453. https://doi.org/10.1145/3133956.3134033

[17] Silvio Micali. 2003. Simple and Fast Optimistic Protocols for Fair Electronic Exchange. In *Proceedings of the Twenty-second Annual Symposium on Principles of Distributed Computing (PODC '03)*. ACM, New York, NY, USA, 12–19. https://doi.org/10.1145/872035.872038

[18] Andrew Miller, Iddo Bentov, Ranjit Kumaresan, and Patrick McCorry. 2017. Sprites: Payment Channels that Go Faster than Lightning. *CoRR* abs/1702.05812 (2017). arXiv:1702.05812 http://arxiv.org/abs/1702.05812

[19] Raiden Network. [n. d.]. What is the Raiden Network? Retrieved 26 January 2018 from https://raiden.network/101.html

[20] T. Nolan. [n. d.]. Atomic swaps using cut and choose. Retrieved 9 January 2018 from https://bitcointalk.org/index.php?topic=1364951

[21] The Komodo Organization. [n. d.]. The BarterDEX Whitepaper: A Decentralized, Open-Source Cryptocurrency Exchange, Powered by Atomic-Swap Technology. Retrieved 9 January 2018 from https://supernet.org/en/technology/whitepapers/BarterDEX-Whitepaper-v0.4.pdf

[22] J. Poon and T. Dryja. 2016. The Bitcoin Lightning Network: Scalable Off-Chain Instant Payments. https://lightning.network/lightning-network-paper.pdf As of 29 December 2017.

[23] Lloyd Shapley and Herbert Scarf. 1974. On cores and indivisibility. *Journal of Mathematical Economics* 1, 1 (1974), 23–37. https://EconPapers.repec.org/RePEc:eee:mateco:v:1:y:1974:i:1:p:23-37

[24] Solidity documentation. [n. d.]. http://solidity.readthedocs.io/en/latest/index.html.

[25] Gerhard Weikum and Gottfried Vossen. 2001. *Transactional Information Systems: Theory, Algorithms, and the Practice of Concurrency Control and Recovery.* Morgan Kaufmann Publishers Inc., San Francisco, CA, USA.

[26] Wikipedia. [n. d.]. Two-phase commit protocol. Retrieved 18 May 2018 from https://en.wikipedia.org/wiki/Two-phase_commit_protocol

[27] G. Zyskind, C. Kisagun, and C. FromKnecht. [n. d.]. Enigma Catalyst: a machine-based investing platform and infrastructure for crypto-assets. https://www.enigma.co/enigma_catalyst.pdf. As of 25 January 2018.

Interactive Distributed Proofs

Gillat Kol
Princeton University
Princeton, NJ, USA
gillat.kol@gmail.coml

Rotem Oshman
Tel-Aviv University
Tel-Aviv, Israel
roshman@tau.ac.il

Raghuvansh R. Saxena
Princeton University
Princeton, NJ, USA
rrsaxena@princeton.edu

ABSTRACT

Interactive proof systems allow a resource-bounded *verifier* to decide an intractable language (or compute a hard function) by communicating with a powerful but untrusted *prover*. Such systems guarantee that the prover can only convince the verifier of true statements. In the context of centralized computation, a celebrated result shows that interactive proofs are extremely powerful, allowing polynomial-time verifiers to decide any language in PSPACE.

In this work we initiate the study of *interactive distributed proofs*: a network of nodes interacts with a single untrusted prover, who sees the entire network graph, to decide whether the graph satisfies some property. We focus on the communication cost of the protocol – the number of bits the nodes must exchange with the prover and each other. Our model can also be viewed as a generalization of the various models of "distributed NP" (proof labeling schemes, etc.) which received significant attention recently: while these models only allow the prover to present each network node with a string of advice, our model allows for back-and-forth interaction. We prove both upper and lower bounds for the new model. We show that for some problems, interaction can exponentially decrease the communication cost compared to a non-interactive prover, but on the other hand, some problems retain non-trivial cost even with interaction.

CCS CONCEPTS

• **Theory of computation → Interactive computation; Interactive proof systems; Distributed algorithms;**

ACM Reference Format:
Gillat Kol, Rotem Oshman, and Raghuvansh R. Saxena. 2018. Interactive Distributed Proofs. In *PODC '18: ACM Symposium on Principles of Distributed Computing, July 23–27, 2018, Egham, United Kingdom.* ACM, New York, NY, USA, 10 pages. https://doi.org/10.1145/3212734.3212772

1 INTRODUCTION

Prover-assisted computation has received significant attention from the distributed computing community [4, 10–14, 17, 20–23, 25, 26]. In this "distributed NP" setting, a powerful prover attempts to convince a set of nodes communicating over a network graph G that the graph and their inputs satisfy some property, by giving each node a short proof (usually called "advice" or "label") of this fact. The nodes then communicate briefly and decide whether to accept or reject the proof given to them; the proof is accepted iff *all* nodes accept it.

Several notions of "distributed NP" have been considered in the literature. All assume that the prover knows the entire graph topology and input, while each node sees only local information and a small part of the proof. Some problems, such as checking bipartiteness, admit very short proofs [23], but some problems essentially require the prover to give each node the entire network graph [17, 23].

One motivation for "distributed NP" is certifying the correctness of a distributed algorithm; for example, a distributed spanning tree algorithm might store, at each node, some additional information beyond the tree pointers, so that the nodes can efficiently verify that the output of the algorithm is indeed a spanning tree. In this scenario we do not have a physical prover that is a separate entity from the network – the advice is computed by the nodes themselves when they run the distributed algorithm. However, another reason to consider distributed NP is *actual* prover-assisted computation, with a powerful prover that has *more* resources than the nodes.

The setting involving a "live" powerful prover is more relevant today than ever, due to the rise of the internet, cloud-based computation, and data-intensive applications. Cloud computing allows computationally limited devices to *delegate* their costly computation to a cloud with tremendous computational power. Interactive proof systems can thus allow devices that do not trust their cloud service (as it may be malicious, motivated by self-interest, or simply buggy) to verify the correctness of the computation performed. In the same manner, interactive distributed proofs can allow central entities holding massive amounts of data (Facebook knowing the topology of a social network, 23andMe and other genetic companies having large graphs describing gene propagation, etc.) to convince their clients of some truth about the network. (For example, if the graph has good expansion, this means that small communities do not tend to segregate.)

With this motivation in mind, in this work we initiate the study of *interactive distributed proofs*, a distributed analogue of the interactive proof systems that are well-studied in complexity theory. Instead of merely having the prover give the network nodes a proof and "disappear", we allow the nodes to engage in a brief *interaction* with the prover, spanning multiple (but typically constant) rounds. We ask whether such interaction can help reduce the proof size for problems that are intractable in "distributed NP".

We follow the usual complexity-theoretic nomenclature, where the prover is called *Merlin* (because of its unbounded power) and the verifier is called *Arthur* (the mortal, with bounded resources). For example, a *distributed Arthur-Merlin protocol*, or a dAM-protocol for short, proceeds as follows: first, each network node v sends

PODC '18, July 23–27, 2018, Egham, United Kingdom

ACM ISBN 978-1-4503-5795-1/18/07...$15.00
https://doi.org/10.1145/3212734.3212772

the prover some independent random bits, R_v (a "challenge").[1] The prover responds by giving each node v a response M_v. The node then examines the responses received by itself and its immediate neighbors, $\{M_u \mid u \in N(v)\}$, together with its input and randomness R_v, and decides whether to accept or reject. The protocol accepts if and only if all nodes accept. Similarly, a dMAM protocol (*distributed Merlin-Arthur-Merlin protocol*) will start with the prover giving each node a message. This is followed by each node responding with some random bits (challenge), and the prover replying to the challenge with a second message to each node.

An interactive protocol is *correct* if for any YES-instance (i.e., any graph and input satisfying the property we are interested in), there exists a prover that has probability at least 2/3 of causing all nodes to accept; and on the other hand, for any NO-instance, no prover has probability more than 1/3 of causing all nodes to accept. The complexity measure we are interested in is the total amount of communication between any individual node and the prover. For upper bounds, we include the random bits sent to the prover in the cost; for our lower bound we do not charge for them. Unlike the complexity-theoretic setting, but in keeping with typical distributed models, the network nodes and the prover are computationally unbounded.

We note that interaction lends tremendous power to verifiers in the computational complexity setting [2, 24, 27]: adding interaction allows the verifier to decide all languages in PSPACE [24, 27], which is widely believed to be *much* larger than NP. Interactive proofs were also considered in the communication complexity setting, where it is assumed that the two communicating parties may consult a prover that knows both of their inputs [1, 18, 19]. Unfortunately, proving lower bounds in the interactive communication-complexity setting is very difficult, and for Arthur-Merlin protocols only certain restricted lower bounds are known [16].

1.1 Our Contributions

In this paper we make some first steps towards understanding the role of interaction in distributed proofs. We define interactive distributed proof systems and give positive and negative results regarding their power.

1.1.1 The Graph Symmetry Problem (Section 3). In the Graph Symmetry Problem, Sym, studied in [17], the network must decide whether the network graph has a non-trivial automorphism (see Section 2 for a formal definition). It is shown in [17] that Sym requires proofs of length $\Theta(n^2)$ at each node in the NP setting; we show that interaction is very useful for this problem.

dMAM *protocol (Section 3.1).* We give a dMAM interactive protocol in which the communication between each network node and the prover is $O(\log n)$ bits. In our protocol, the prover first "commits" to a function ρ (that is supposedly an automorphism of the graph) by giving each node its image under ρ. The next two rounds are devoted to verifying that ρ is a permutation and that ρ "respects" the edges of the graph. We show that this verification can be done with low communication using distributed linear hashing. We mention that our approach crucially utilizes the interaction, as the seed for the hash *must* be selected by the verifiers after the prover is already committed to ρ.

Theorem 1.1. $\mathsf{Sym} \in \mathsf{dMAM}[O(\log n)]$.

Exponential separation of distributed NP and distributed AM (Section 3.3). The Symmetry problem can be modified to yield an exponential separation between distributed NP and AM: if we restrict the automorphism to a *fixed* one instead of asking whether there *exists* an automorphism, we can eliminate the first round, where the prover commits to the automorphism. We call the restricted problem DSym, and observe that it is still subject to the quadratic lower bound from [17], therefore yielding:

Theorem 1.2 (informal statement). $\mathsf{DSym} \in \mathsf{dAM}[O(\log n)]$, *but any "distributed NP" scheme requires advice of length* $\Omega(n^2)$.

An interesting open problem is whether this is the largest possible gap between distributed NP and AM.

dMAM *protocol (Section 3.2).* While for restricted versions of Symmetry our dMAM protocol implies a dAM protocol with the same cost, it is unclear if this is achievable in the general case. However, we are able to show a dAM protocol for Symmetry with nearly linear cost.

Theorem 1.3. $\mathsf{Sym} \in \mathsf{dAM}[O(n \log n)]$.

We mention that in the computational complexity setting, it is known that $AM[k] = AM[2]$ for any constant k, meaning that round reduction is always possible. The same is not known for our model, and an intriguing open problem is devising general round reduction theorems.

Lower bound (Section 3.4). In [17], an $\Omega(n^2)$ lower bound for Symmetry is proven by essentially reducing from the nondeterministic two-party communication complexity of the Equality function.[2] A lower bound of $\Omega(n^2/\log(n))$ for Non-3-Colorability is proven by reduction from Set Disjointness. Unfortunately, the strategy of reducing from a hard 2-party communication complexity problem is not available to us here: proving any explicit non-trivial lower bound for two-party Arthur-Merlin communication complexity is a long-standing open problem (see for example [16]).

Instead, we leverage the distributed nature of the problem: the fact that each node can only see a small part of the input and the prover's response. We show a lower bound of $\Omega(\log \log n)$ on Arthur-Merlin interactive protocols for Symmetry, even if the nodes share an unbounded amount of randomness with the prover and with each other. (Sharing unbounded randomness with the prover amounts to allowing the nodes to send the prover messages of unbounded length "for free".) We note that such bounds cannot be obtained by simple counting arguments, as the prover's message to each of the nodes may depend on the random challenges communicated by *all* nodes.

Theorem 1.4. *If* $\mathsf{Sym} \in \mathsf{dAM}[f(n)]$, *then* $f(n) = \Omega(\log \log n)$.

We develop a framework for proving lower bounds like the one in Theorem 1.4, using a packing argument: we show how to associate

[1] We note that the restriction to challenges that are purely random is not significant if the verifiers do not have randomness hidden from the prover: the prover can see each node's input, so we can *simulate* more complicated challenges by asking the prover to compute the challenge using the node's randomness and input.

[2] The proof in [17] is not stated as a reduction, and it re-proves the hardness of Equality, but it can easily be transformed into a formal reduction from Equality.

the execution of a protocol of length L on a graph G with an $f(L)$-dimensional vector (in our case, $f(L) = 2^{2^{O(L)}}$). We prove that if the protocol is correct, then it must be able to differentiate between the different graphs, in the sense that the vectors associated with different graphs must be "far apart". Since it is not possible to pack too many "far apart" vectors into $[0, 1]^{f(L)}$, but the set of possible graphs is large, a lower bound on L is obtained. We mention that part of our argument is general and also holds for properties other than Sym. Adapting the full proof to other graph properties, and closing the gap between our dAM upper and lower bounds for Symmetry, remain interesting challenges.

1.1.2 The Graph Non-Isomorphism Problem (Section 4). Finally, we turn our attention to the famous Graph Non-Isomorphism (GNI) problem, which is in some sense the poster child for classical interactive and zero-knowledge proofs. It seems that the "standard" protocol for GNI cannot be adapted to the distributed setting (see section 4 for discussion). Instead, we develop a distributed version of the beautiful Goldwasser-Sipser protocol for GNI. This protocol was developed in [15] in the context of proving that interactive proofs do not require the verifier to have private randomness which is hidden from the prover. We show that with a few rounds of interaction (Arthur-Merlin-Arthur-Merlin), the Goldwasser-Sipser protocol can be made distributed, and obtain an $O(n \log n)$ protocol for GNI.

Theorem 1.5. $\mathsf{GNI} \in \mathsf{dAMAM}[O(n \log n)]$.

Our main technical contribution here is a type of distributed hash function that we call *distributed almost pairwise-independent hash.* The Goldwasser-Sipser protocol crucially relies on the use of a pairwise-independent hash function with a short seed length, but the seed length is too long for us ($\Theta(n^2)$ bits), and it is not possible to "break" the seed into small parts and give each node one part without ruining the linearity of the hash[3]. Instead, we show that the requirement of pairwise-independence can be relaxed into *almost* pairwise-independence, and for the weaker requirement we construct a distributed hash function where the seed *can* be distributed, with each node contributing a small part.

We mention that it can be shown that the distributed GNI problem requires $\Omega(n^2)$ bits of advice without interaction, using an argument similar to the one used in [17] to prove the $\Omega(n^2)$ lower bound for Symmetry.

1.2 Related Work

There is a large body of work on various notions for "distributed NP" and their relative expressive power, e.g., [6, 8, 9, 20–23, 25, 26]; we refer to the excellent surveys [7, 28] for a comprehensive overview. For lack of space, we mention here only the most directly relevant work.

Our protocols rely on the spanning-tree construction from [23], which uses advice of length $\Theta(\log n)$.

Our lower bound construction for Symmetry is inspired by the dumbbell construction from [17].

In [4], a notion of *randomized proof-labeling schemes* (RPLS) is introduced, where the prover can give advice of unbounded length to each node, and the nodes then send each other randomized messages and decide whether to accept or reject. It is shown in [4] that any problem has an RPLS of exponentially-smaller length compared to the deterministic length required. However, this result is not applicable to our setting, because we do charge the prover for its communication with the nodes; the scheme from [4] increases the advice length by a factor corresponding to the maximum degree, i.e., up to linear.

In [3], the authors equip the verifiers with *alternating* Turing Machines, and classify decision tasks based on the levels of alternation (exists/forall) required. Alternation can be viewed as a type of interaction with two provers: one prover trying to convince the verifiers of the "exists" statement, and the other of its negation, a "for all" statement. However, in [3] there is no randomization, and the provers *compete* with each other. In contrast, here we have a single prover, and the interaction is randomized.

2 PRELIMINARIES

2.1 Notation

We let $N_G(u)$ denote the neighborhood of node u in graph G, including node u itself. We omit the subscript G when the graph is clear from the context. We let $\mathcal{G}(V)$ denote the set of all graphs on vertices V. We sometimes give each graph node an input from some domain $\mathcal{I}$; let $\mathcal{I}(V)$ denote the set of all assignments of inputs from $\mathcal{I}$ to the nodes in V.

When we work with a graph $G = (V, E)$ on n vertices, we use $\{0, 1\}^{m \times V}$ to denote the set of n-vectors where each coordinate is in $\{0, 1\}^m$, and the coordinates are indexed by V. We let $x_v \in \{0, 1\}^m$ denote the coordinate corresponding to v in $x \in \{0, 1\}^{m \times V}$; and for a subset $S = \{v_1, \ldots, v_k\} \subseteq V$, we let x_S denote the vector $x_{v_1} \ldots x_{v_k}$ corresponding to nodes in S. For example, if a prover's response to all nodes in the graph is $M \in \{0, 1\}^{m \times V}$, then a specific node v's response is written M_v, and the responses given to v's neighbors, including v, are $M_{N_G(v)}$.

We often conflate a set $S \subseteq X$ with its *characteristic vector* $\chi : X \to \{0, 1\}$, where $\chi_x = 1$ iff $x \in S$. We abuse notation by using the same letter to denote both the set and its characteristic vector.

2.2 Interactive Distributed Proofs

We define here one-round Arthur-Merlin proofs, the class dAM, somewhat informally.

Definition 1 (1-Round Arthur-Merlin Protocol, Informal). *In a 1-round Arthur-Merlin protocol of length ℓ, each vertex v sends the prover a uniformly random challenge $r_v \in \{0, 1\}^\ell$. The prover P sends back a response $M_v \in \{0, 1\}^\ell$, which is a function of the graph G, the input I, and the random challenges $\{r_v \mid v \in V\}$.*

The protocol specifies a decision function out_v *for each $v \in V$, which takes node v's neighborhood and input, the random challenges of node v and its neighbors, and the response issued to node v and its neighbors, and outputs a Boolean value. We denote:*

- $\mathrm{out}_v^\Pi(G, I, r, M) = \mathrm{out}_v^\Pi(N_G(v), I(v), r_{N_G(v)}, M_{N_G(v)})$, *the decision value at node v when the graph is G, the input is I, the random challenge is r and the prover's response is M;*
- $\Pi(P, G, I, v)$, *the random variable representing v's decision when it interacts with a prover P.*

[3]Recall that our protocols for Symmetry exploit the linearity of the hash to compute the hash value in a distributed manner.

We remark that our upper bounds do not need the nodes to see the randomness of their neighbors, $r_{N_G(v)}$, only their own randomness r_v. Our lower bound does give $r_{N_G(v)}$ to each node v.

Definition 2 (The class dAM[ℓ]). *A language $\mathcal{L} \subseteq \mathcal{G}(V) \times \mathcal{I}(V)$ is in the class* dAM[ℓ], *for $\ell \in \mathbb{N}$, if there is a protocol Π of length ℓ satisfying:*

$$(G, I) \in \mathcal{L} \implies \exists P, \Pr(\text{all nodes accept}) > 2/3$$
$$(G, I) \notin \mathcal{L} \implies \forall P, \Pr(\text{all nodes accept}) < 1/3.$$

Sometimes we are interested in "pure graph properties", where there is no input other than the network graph. In this case we omit the input I from all our notation.

In Section 3.1 we give a *Merlin-Arthur-Merlin* (dMAM) protocol. Here, the prover goes first, and gives each node v a response M_v^1. The nodes then send a random challenge r_v, and the prover sends back a second response M_v^2. Finally, each node outputs a decision, depending on its input, and the randomness and responses of itself and its neighbors. Our correctness requirement is the same as for dAM.

We assume for simplicity that we have a fixed set of nodes V, known in advance to all the participants. However, our upper bounds generalize in a straightforward manner to the case where we have some polynomially-large namespace N, and we draw n nodes from N.

Describing interactive protocols. When we specify an interactive protocol, we specify two types of interaction: messages sent by the prover to the nodes, and messages sent by the nodes to the prover. Messages from nodes to the prover are indicated by $\boldsymbol{v \rightarrow P}$, followed by the contents of the message. Here, v is the identifier of the sending node.

For convenience, we use two types of prover responses:

- *Broadcast* messages, where the prover is required to provide all nodes with the same value, and the nodes verify that indeed they all got the same value. This type of message is indicated by $\boldsymbol{P \rightarrow v}$ **(Broadcast)**, followed by the contents of the message. We assume implicitly that each node compares the response it received to the responses its neighbors received, and rejects if some neighbor received a different response.
- *Unicast* messages, where the prover can give a different value to each node. This type of message is indicated by $\boldsymbol{P \rightarrow v}$ **(Unicast)**, followed again by the contents.

2.3 Problem Definitions

We consider the following problems:

Definition 3 (Graph Symmetry). *The language* Sym *is the set of all symmetric graphs, that is, graphs that have a non-trivial automorphism.*

(A permutation $\rho : V \rightarrow V$ is an *automorphism* of $G = (V, E)$ if for every $u, v \in V$ we have $\{u, v\} \in E$ iff $\{\rho(u), \rho(v)\} \in E$. A *non-trivial* automorphism is an automorphism that is not the identity function.)

We formulate a distributed version of Graph Non-Isomorphism, as follows:

Definition 4 (Graph Non-Isomorphism). *The language* GNI *is the set of all pairs of graphs (G_0, G_1) such that G_0 is not isomorphic to G_1.*

Here, the network graph is the graph G_0, and the second graph G_1 is given as inputs to the nodes, with each node v receiving its neighborhood $N_{G_1}(v)$. An alternative definition, which our algorithm also solves, is the following: we have only one graph, the network graph G. Each node in the graph is marked with an input from $\{0, 1, \perp\}$, and the goal is to determine whether the subgraph induced by the nodes marked 0 is not isomorphic to the subgraph induced by the nodes marked 1. The version we formulated in Definition 4 is a little stronger than this second version, because it does not allow nodes to communicate over the edges of the second graph G_1.

3 INTERACTIVE DISTRIBUTED PROOFS FOR THE SYMMETRY PROBLEM

3.1 An $O(\log n)$-Bit dMAM Protocol

Recall that Sym is the class of all graphs that have a non-trivial automorphism. To verify that $G \in$ Sym, we ask the prover to provide a non-trivial automorphism $\rho : V \rightarrow V$ of the graph, by giving each node $v \in V$ its image $\rho(v)$ under the automorphism. We then *verify* that ρ is indeed a non-trivial automorphism, that is, ρ is not the identity function, and ρ is an automorphism of G.

Verifying that ρ is not the identity function is easy: we ask the prover to broadcast (i.e., tell all the nodes) a node $v \in V$ such that $\rho(v) \neq v$, and node v then checks that indeed $\rho(v) \neq v$.

To check that ρ is an automorphism of G we use the *adjacency matrix* of G, a matrix A_G whose rows and columns are indexed by nodes $v \in V$, and where $A_G(u, v) = 1$ iff $\{u, v\} \in E$. Intuitively, ρ is an automorphism of G iff when we permute the rows and columns of A_G according to ρ, we get the same matrix we started with: $(u, v) \in E$ iff $(\rho(u), \rho(v)) \in E$. Let $\rho(A_G)$ denote the ρ-permuted version of A_G, where the v-th row is replaced by the $\rho(v)$-th row for each $v \in V$, and similarly for the columns.

No single node of G knows the entire adjacency matrix A_G, but each node v knows its row in A_G. Moreover, since v sees all the images $\rho(u)$ of its neighbors $u \in N_G(v)$, it can compute row $\rho(v)$ of the ρ-permuted matrix, $\rho(A_G)$. We exploit this to check whether $A_G = \rho(A_G)$.

3.1.1 The Permuted Adjacency Matrix. For a vector $r \in \{0, 1\}^n$, we denote by $[i, r]$ the $n \times n$ boolean matrix where the i-th row is r, and the rest of the matrix is 0. This is a convenient representation: for any $n \times n$ boolean matrix A, if the rows of A are $r_1, \ldots, r_n \in \{0, 1\}^n$, then $A = \sum_{i=1}^{n} [i, r_i]$. In particular, for a graph G, the adjacency matrix of G can be written as $A_G = \sum_{v \in V} [v, N(v)]$, where here we think of the neighborhood $N(v)$ as represented by a vector $N(v) \in \{0, 1\}^V$ (with self-loops for all vertices).

Given a function $\rho : V \rightarrow V$ and a subset $S \subseteq V$, let $\rho(S) = \{\rho(s) \mid s \in S\}$. Equivalently, when S is represented as the characteristic vector $S \in \{0, 1\}^V$, then $\rho(S)$ is the characteristic vector where $\rho(S)_v = 1$ iff there exists u such that $\rho(u) = v$ and $S_u = 1$.

Our protocol requires the prover to commit to an automorphism of G. To verify that the prover-provided mapping is an automorphism, we rely on the following observation:

Observation 1. A permutation $\rho : V \to V$ is an automorphism of G iff for all $v \in V$ we have $N(\rho(v)) = \rho(N(v))$.

Proof. By definition, ρ is an automorphism iff for every $u, v \in V$, it holds that $u \in N(v)$ iff $\rho(u) \in N(\rho(v))$. Since ρ is a permutation, this is equivalent to saying that for every $u, v \in V$, $\rho^{-1}(u) \in N(v)$ iff $u \in N(\rho(v))$, that is, $\rho(N(v)) = N(\rho(v))$. □

As a corollary, we can show:

Lemma 3.1. *Let $\rho : V \to V$ be a function such that $\sum_{v \in V}[v, N(v)] = \sum_{v \in V}[\rho(v), \rho(N(v))]$. Then ρ is an automorphism of G.*

Proof. First, we prove that ρ is a permutation on V. Assume for contradiction that ρ is not a permutation. In this case, there exists a $v^* \in V$ such that v^* is not in the range of ρ, *i.e.*, $\rho(v) \neq v^*$ for any $v \in V$. Thus, in the sum $\sum_{v \in V}[v, N(v)]$, the row corresponding to v^* is non-zero, as $N(v^*)_{v^*} = 1$. On the other hand, the row corresponding to v^* in the sum $\sum_{v \in V}[\rho(v), \rho(N(v))]$ is the all zero row, a contradiction.

Having established that ρ is a permutation on V, it is easy to see that ρ is an automorphism of G: for each $u \in V$, the row corresponding to $\rho(u)$ in the sum $\sum_{v \in V}[v, N(v)]$ is $N(\rho(u))$, and in the sum $\sum_{v \in V}[\rho(v), \rho(N(u))]$ the row corresponding to $\rho(u)$ is $\rho(N(u))$. Therefore these two rows must be equal for every $u \in V$. By Observation 1, this means that ρ is an automorphism of G. □

We see that to check if ρ is an automorphism, it suffices to verify that $\sum_{v \in V}[v, N(v)] = \sum_{v \in V}[\rho(v), \rho(N(v))]$. However, we can not afford to have nodes send their entire rows, because this would require $O(n)$ bits per node in the worst case. Instead, we use *linear hash functions* to hash the rows of A_G and $\rho(A_G)$, sum up the hashes for the rows of each matrix, and verify that the sums are equal.

3.1.2 Hashing the Adjacency Matrix. A linear hash function allows us to hash a composite object, $x_1 + x_2$, by hashing its building blocks, x_1 and x_2; in our case, we can hash the entire adjacency matrix by having each node hash its own row.

A small linear hash function family is known to exist:

Theorem 3.2. *Let $m, p \in \mathbb{N}$, where p is prime. There exists a family $\mathcal{H}$ of functions $h : \{0,1\}^m \to \{0, \ldots, p-1\}$ of size $|\mathcal{H}| = p$ such that for $x, x' \in \{0,1\}^m$, we have the following properties:*

*(1) **Linearity:** $h(x + x') = h(x) + h(x')$.*

*(2) **Small collision probability:** If $x \neq x'$ then*

$$\Pr_{h \in \mathcal{H}}\left(h(x) = h(x')\right) \leq \frac{m}{p}.$$

Note that in (1) above, the sum on the right-hand is modulo p, and the sum on the left-hand side is defined as $x + x' = (x_1 + x'_1 \ (mod\ p), \ldots, x_m + x'_m \ (mod\ p))$.

We always use Theorem 3.2 to hash $n \times n$ boolean matrices, so we always take $m = n^2$. Note that since $|\mathcal{H}| = p$, picking a random hash function from $\mathcal{H}$ only requires $O(\log p)$ random bits.

Unless stated otherwise, let $\mathcal{H}$ be the hash function family given by Theorem 3.2, for some prime $p \in [10n^3, 100n^3]$. (Such a prime exists by Bertrand's Postulate / Chebyshev's Theorem.) Picking a random hash function from $\mathcal{H}$ only requires $O(\log n)$ random bits ("the seed").

3.1.3 The Protocol. Now we are ready to describe our dMAM protocol for Symmetry; see the formal description in Protocol 1. As a building-block, we use the spanning tree proof labeling scheme from [23], and the prover helps the nodes "sum their hash values up the tree".

In the first round, the prover presents each node $v \in V$ with: the value $\rho_v \in V$, the parent $t_v \in V$ of v in the spanning tree, the root $r \in V$ of the tree, and v's distance $d_v \in [n]$ from the root, in (what the prover claims is) a spanning tree rooted at a node r such that $\rho_r \neq r$.

The nodes verify that indeed they received a spanning tree, in the standard way [23], and that they agree on the root of the tree. The root r verifies that $\rho_r \neq r$, to ensure that the claimed automorphism is not trivial.

Let $\rho : V \to V$ be defined by $\rho(v) = \rho_v$ (where ρ_v is the value the prover gave to v). Next, we want to verify that $\sum_{v \in V}[v, N(v)] = \sum_{v \in V}[\rho(v), \rho(N(v))]$, by having the nodes agree on a hash function and apply it to both sides. However, the hash function needs to be random, and all nodes need to know it; since the nodes do not have shared randomness, we use the prover to "simulate" it. The root of the tree selects a random hash function $h_i \in \mathcal{H}$ and sends its index to the prover; the prover then gives h_i to all the nodes, and they verify that they all received the same h_i. The prover also assists the nodes in applying the linear hash function "up the tree": to each node v, if T_v is the subtree rooted at v (in the spanning tree the prover provided), the prover gives v two values $a_v, b_v \in [p]$, which it claims are the two hash values:

$$a_v = h_i\Big(\sum_{u \in T_v}[u, N(u)]\Big), \qquad b_v = h_i\Big(\sum_{u \in T_v}[\rho(u), \rho(N(u))]\Big). \quad (1)$$

To verify that the prover computed the hash correctly, each node sums its children's hash values and adds the hash of its neighborhood, and verifies that the sum matches the value it got from the prover.

In Protocol 1, each of the nodes exchanges a total of $O(\log n)$ bits with the prover. The rest of this subsection is devoted to proving the correctness of the protocol.

Lemma 3.3. *Suppose that all vertices in the graph decided to accept. Then, $a_r = h_i\left(\sum_{v \in V}[v, N(v)]\right)$ and $b_r = h_i\left(\sum_{v \in V}[\rho(v), \rho(N(v))]\right)$.*

Proof. Due to Line 1, there is an edge between v and t_v for all $v \neq r$. Let T be the subgraph formed by these edges. Then T is a spanning tree rooted at r; this part is standard, so we omit the proof.

We show by induction on the height of node v in T that $a_v = \sum_{u \in T_v} h_i([u, N(u)])$, and $b_v = \sum_{u \in T_v} h_i([\rho(u), \rho(N(u))])$.

The base case is immediate: leaves have no children, so their verification step (Line 3) verifies the claim. As for the step, suppose that the claim holds for all children of v: for each $u \in C(v)$, $a_u = \sum_{w \in T_u} h_i([w, N(w)])$, and similarly for b_u. Then in v's verification

Protocol 1 A dMAM protocol for Sym

$P \rightarrow v$ (Broadcast): The prover sends a vertex r (claimed spanning tree root).

$P \rightarrow v$ (Unicast): The prover sends:
the identifier ρ_v (claimed image under the automorphism);
the identifier t_v (claimed parent);
and a number $d_v \in [n]$ (claimed distance from the root).

$v \rightarrow P$: Each node sends a random index $i_v \in [|\mathcal{H}|]$.

$P \rightarrow v$ (Broadcast): The prover sends an index $i \in [|\mathcal{H}|]$ (claimed hash index sent by the root).

$P \rightarrow v$ (Unicast): The prover sends hash values $a_v, b_v \in [p]$.

The verification procedure:

1: If $v \neq r$, verify that $t_v \in N(v)$ and $d_{t_v} = d_v - 1$.
If $v = r$, verify that $d_v = 0$.

2: Let $C(v) = \{u \in N(v) \mid t_u = v\}$.

3: v verifies that

$$a_v = h_i([v, N(v)]) + \sum_{u \in C(v)} a_u,$$

$$b_v = h_i([\rho_v, N_\rho(v)]) + \sum_{u \in C(v)} b_u.$$

Here, $N_\rho(v)$ is the vector whose v^{th} coordinate is 1 iff there exists $c \in C(v)$ such that $\rho_c = v$.

4: If $v = r$, verify that $a_r = b_r$, $\rho_r \neq r$, and $i = i_r$.

step, it verifies that

$$\begin{aligned} a_v &= h_i([v, N(v)]) + \sum_{u \in C(v)} a_u \\ &= h_i([v, N(v)]) + \sum_{u \in C(v)} \sum_{w \in T_u} h_i([w, N(w)]) \\ &= \sum_{w \in T_v} h_i([w, N(w)]) = h_i\left(\sum_{w \in T_v} [w, N(w)]\right), \end{aligned}$$

where the last step is by linearity of h_i. The verification for b_v is similar. □

THEOREM 3.4. *Algorithm 1 satisfies the followings:*

$$G \text{ is symmetric} \implies \exists P, \Pr(\text{all nodes accept}) > 2/3$$
$$G \text{ is not symmetric} \implies \forall P, \Pr(\text{all nodes accept}) < 1/3.$$

PROOF. Consider first the case where G is symmetric, and let ρ be a non-trivial automorphism of G. Let $r \in V$ be some vertex such that $\rho(r) \neq r$. An "honest" prover can convince all nodes to accept, by specifying:

- Any spanning tree T rooted at r. The prover gives each vertex v its image under ρ, its parent in T, its distance from r, and the name of r.
- After receiving the random indices from each vertex, the prover responds with the index $i = i_r$ sent by the root. It then gives each vertex v the values a_v, b_v computed according to (1).

It is easy to verify that these responses pass the verification procedure.

Now suppose that G is *not* symmetric, and fix a prover P. We show that the probability that P convinces all nodes to accept is less than $1/3$. Specifically, we show that for any choice of root r_0, if the prover specifies r_0 as the root, then the probability it can convince all nodes to accept is less than $1/3$;

To that end, consider a fixed root $r_0 \in V$. By Lemma 3.3, if all vertices decided to accept we have

$$a_{r_0} = h_i\left(\sum_{v \in V} [v, N(v)]\right) \quad \text{and} \quad b_{r_0} = h_i\left(\sum_{v \in V} [\rho(v), \rho(N(v))]\right).$$

If G is not symmetric, then in particular, the mapping ρ provided by the prover in the first round is not a non-trivial automorphism. We know that ρ is not the identity mapping, because $\rho(r_0) \neq r_0$ (otherwise the root rejects). Therefore, it is not an automorphism, and by Theorem 3.1, we must have $\sum_{v \in V}[v, N(v)] \neq \sum_{v \in V}[\rho(v), \rho(N(v))]$. However, the root only accepts if $a_{r_0} = b_{r_0}$. Due to Theorem 3.2 and by the selection of the parameters of $\mathcal{H}$, it holds that if $\sum_{v \in V}[v, N(v)] \neq \sum_{v \in V}[\rho(v), \rho(N(v))]$, then the probability of the event $a_{r_0} = b_{r_0}$ is at most $1/3$. The reason is that the hash indices i_v were sent to the prover after the prover already committed to r and ρ_v. Therefore, $i = i_r$ is a random hash index that is only known to the prover after the prover is already committed to the values $\sum_{v \in V}[v, N(v)]$ and $\sum_{v \in V}[\rho(v), \rho(N(v))]$. □

3.2 An $O(n \log n)$-Bit dAM Protocol

Let us now leverage the ideas from the previous section to obtain a dAM protocol for Symmetry. The prover in dAM has more power than it does in dMAM: in dAM, we cannot force the prover to *commit* to the permutation ρ before the random challenge is issued. To deal with the extra difficulty, our dAM protocol is longer, and uses $O(n \log n)$ bits. We use the extra bits first, we ask the prover to give each vertex v the full automorphism $\rho : V \rightarrow V$, not just its own value $\rho(v)$. Second, we use a much longer hash, to make the probability of collision so small that we can union-bound over all possible mappings $V \rightarrow V$.

Other than these two changes, the protocol is similar to the dMAM protocol, but the random challenge is now issued before the prover provides the spanning tree and the permutation (see formal description in Protocol 2). The protocol uses the hash function family given by Theorem 3.2 for some prime $p \in [10n^{n+2}, 100n^{n+2}]$. Picking a random hash function from $\mathcal{H}$ requires $O(n \log n)$ random bits.

In Protocol 2, each of the nodes exchanges $O(n \log n)$ bits with the prover. The rest of this subsection is devoted to proving the correctness of the protocol.

Observe that Lemma 3.3 continues to hold: its correctness does not depend on when the random challenge i_r is issued, whether it is before or after the prover specifies the spanning tree and the permutation.

THEOREM 3.5. *Algorithm 2 satisfies the followings:*

$$G \text{ is symmetric} \implies \exists P, \Pr(\text{all nodes accept}) > 2/3$$
$$G \text{ is not symmetric} \implies \forall P, \Pr(\text{all nodes accept}) < 1/3.$$

PROOF. If G is symmetric, an honest prover can convince all nodes to accept, much the same as it did in the dMAM protocol.

Protocol 2 A dAM protocol for Sym

$v \to P$: Each node sends a random index $i_v \in [|\mathcal{H}|]$.
$P \to v$ (Broadcast): a permutation $\rho : V \to V$, an index $i \in [|\mathcal{H}|]$ and a vertex $r \in V$.
$P \to v$ (Unicast): an identifier $t_v \in V$, a number $d_v \in [n]$, and two hash values $a_v, b_v \in [p]$.
The verification procedure:

1: If $v \neq r$, verify that $t_v \in N(v)$ and $d_{t_v} = d_v - 1$.
If $v = r$, verify that $d_v = 0$.
2: Let $C(v) = \{u \in N(v) \mid t_u = v\}$.
3: v verifies that

$$a_v = h_i([v, N(v)]) + \sum_{u \in C(v)} a_u,$$

$$b_v = h_i([\rho(v), \rho(N(v))]) + \sum_{u \in C(v)} b_u.$$

4: If $v = r$, verify that $a_r = b_r$ and $\rho(r) \neq r$ and $i = i_r$.

Suppose that G is not symmetric, and fix a root r_0. Since G is not symmetric, by Lemma 3.1, for any mapping $\sigma : V \to V$ that is not the identity, we have $\sum_{v \in V}[v, N(v)] \neq \sum_{v \in V}[\sigma(v), \sigma(N(v))]$. However, by Lemma 3.3, the root only accepts if

$$h_i\left(\sum_{v \in V}[v, N(v)]\right) = h_i\left(\sum_{v \in V}[\rho(v), \rho(N(v))]\right).$$

We show that for a random $h_i \in \mathcal{H}$, the probability that there *exists* a mapping $\sigma : V \to V$ that is not the identity and will make the verifiers accept is small:

$$\Pr_{h_i \in \mathcal{H}}\left(\exists \sigma : h_i\left(\sum_{v \in V}[v, N(v)]\right) = h_i\left(\sum_{v \in V}[\sigma(v), \sigma(N(v))]\right)\right) < \frac{1}{3}.$$

Since by Line 4, $\rho(r) \neq r$, thus ρ is not the identity, it follows that the prover can only convince all nodes to accept with probability less than 1/3.

Consider a specific mapping $\sigma : V \to V$ that is not the identity. By universality,

$$\Pr_{h_i \in \mathcal{H}}\left(h_i\left(\sum_{v \in V}[v, N(v)]\right) = h_i\left(\sum_{v \in V}[\sigma(v), \sigma(N(v))]\right)\right) \leq \frac{1}{3n^n}.$$

A union bound across all n^n mappings yields the claim. □

3.3 An Exponential Separation between Distributed NP and Distributed AM

In the previous sections, we gave a dMAM protocol for Symmetry using $O(\log n)$ bits, and an dAM protocol using $O(n \log n)$ bits. Symmetry is known to require $\Omega(n^2)$ bits with no interaction [17] even in the relatively powerful Locally Checkable Proof model. We now define a simple variant, which we call *Dumbbell Symmetry*, for which we can give an $O(\log n)$-bit AM protocol. The variant is still subject to the $\Omega(n^2)$ lower bound from [17], so this shows an exponential separation between one-round distributed interactive proofs and LCPs. In fact, the definition of Dumbbell Symmetry is directly inspired by the lower bound of [17]: it is the Symmetry problem, but restricted to symmetric dumbbell graphs with a fixed isomorphism mapping one side of the dumbbell to the other.

For the sake of concreteness, let us restrict attention to the case of LCPs with local horizon 1, that is, each node sees only the advice of itself and its immediate neighborhood. (Extending to any constant local horizon, even one which is not known in advance, is easy.)

Theorem 3.6. *There is a language* DSym *of $O(n)$-vertex graphs, which is in* dAM$[O(\log n)]$, *but does not have a Locally Checkable Proof with local horizon 1 and length $\Omega(n^2)$.*

Definition 5 (Dumbbell Symmetry). *The language* DSym *is the set of $(2n + 2r + 1)$-vertex graphs $G = (\{0, \ldots, 2n + 2r\}, E)$ which have the following structure:*

- *Let F_0, F_1 be the subgraphs induced by G on vertices $\{0, \ldots, n-1\}$ and $\{n, \ldots, 2n-1\}$, respectively. Then the mapping $\sigma'(x) = x + n$ is an isomorphism from F_0 to F_1.*
- *The subgraphs F_0, F_1 are connected to each other by a path using the remaining vertices,*

$$0 - (2n) - (2n + 1) - \ldots - \ldots (2n + 2r) - n.$$

- *G contains no edges other than the internal edges of F_0, F_1 and the path.*

In [17] it is shown that DSym requires $\Omega(n^2)$ bits for Locally Checkable Proofs, even if each node can see the advice of its entire r-neighborhood.

We next show that DSym can be decided by a dAM protocol using $O(\log n)$ bits. By definition of DSym, we have $G \in$ DSym iff all the following conditions hold:

(1) The following mapping is an automorphism of G:

$$\sigma(x) = \begin{cases} x + n & \text{if } x \in \{0, \ldots, n-1\}, \\ x - n & \text{if } x \in \{n, \ldots, 2n-1\}, \\ 2n + 2r - (x - 2n) & \text{if } x \in \{2n, \ldots, 2n + r\}, \\ 2n + (2n + 2r - x) & \text{if } x \in \{2n + r + 1, \ldots, 2n + 2r\}. \end{cases}$$

(the bottom two cases map $2n \to 2n{+}2r, 2n{+}1 \to 2n{+}2r{-}1, \ldots$)

(2) The path $0 - (2n) - (2n + 1) - \ldots - \ldots (2n + 2r) - n$ is present in G.

(3) G contains no edges other than the internal edges in $\{0, \ldots, n-1\}$ and in $\{n, \ldots, 2n-1\}$, and the path edges.

The second and third conditions can be verified locally without the prover's assistance: each path node verifies that it indeed has edges to both its neighbors on the path, and all nodes verify that they have no edges that are not path edges or internal to $\{0, \ldots, n-1\}$ or to $\{n, \ldots, 2n-1\}$. To verify the first condition, we use Protocol 1 from Section 3.1, but now the prover does not need to commit up-front to the mapping ρ, because we need only consider one specific automorphism, σ. This eliminates the first Merlin round, and yields an Arthur-Merlin protocol for DSym.

3.4 Lower Bound

In this section we show a lower bound of $\Omega(\log \log n)$ on the communication cost of every dAM protocol for Sym. For our lower bound, we require a large family $\mathcal{F}$ of graphs on vertices $\{1, \ldots, n\}$, with the property that all graphs in $\mathcal{F}$ are asymmetric (i.e., they have no non-trivial automorphisms), and no two graphs in $\mathcal{F}$ are isomorphic to each other. It is known that for sufficiently large n, there is such a class $\mathcal{F}$ of size $\Omega(2^{n^2}/n!) = \Omega(2^{n^2 - n \log n}) = \Omega(2^{n^2})$.

Our lower bound for the Symmetry problem uses a graph family $\mathcal{G}$ which is similar to the family used for the Symmetry lower bound in [17]. Each graph in $G \in \mathcal{G}$ is defined by $G = G(F_A, F_B)$, where $F_A, F_B \in \mathcal{F}$ are not necessarily distinct. We fix three disjoint sets: $V_A = \{u_1^A, \ldots, u_n^A\}$, $V_B = \{u_1^B, \ldots, u_n^B\}$, and a *bridge*, consisting of two nodes $x_A, x_B \notin V_A \cup V_B$. We also fix two nodes $v_A \in V_A, v_B \in V_B$. The nodes x_A, x_B are referred to as *bridge nodes*.

Each graph $G = G(F_A, F_B) \in \mathcal{G}$ is defined as follows: on the nodes in V_A and V_B respectively, we construct copies of F_A, F_B (resp.) by replacing node i of V_A (resp. V_B) with u_i^A (resp. u_i^B). We also add edges $\{v_A, x_A\}, \{x_A, x_B\}, \{x_B, v_B\}$. This yields a "dumbbell graph", with copies of F_A and F_B on either side, connected by a short "bridge". Crucially, $G(F_A, F_B)$ has a non-trivial automorphism iff $F_A = F_B$.

Fix a dAM protocol Π, and let L be the maximum length of the prover's response to any node. We prove the lower bound in two steps. First we show that any dAM protocol can be transformed into what we call a *simple* protocol, where the two bridge nodes always expect to get the same message, and their decision whether to accept or reject is based only on this (shared) message and the randomness. This makes it easier to focus on the view of these bridge nodes. Then we show that the distribution of the message the bridge nodes receive must "encapsulate" all the information about the two sides F_A and F_B of the graph. This distribution, which can be represented as a $d = 2^{2^{O(L)}}$-dimensional vector, must be "far apart" for different graphs $G(F_A, F_B)$. Since it is not possible to pack too many "far apart" vectors into $[0,1]^{2^{2^{O(L)}}}$, but the class $\mathcal{G}$ does contain many different graphs ($|\mathcal{G}| = 2^{\Omega(n^2)}$), we get that L must be at least $\Omega(\log \log n)$.

We begin by defining *simple protocols*, where we restrict the output function for the bridge nodes, so that they only accept if they both receive the same response from the prover. In this definition and the rest of this section, we implicitly assume that all graphs are from the family $\mathcal{G}$.

Definition 6 (Simple protocols). *A* dAM *protocol* Π *is said to be* simple *if there exist* $f_{x_A}, f_{x_B} : \{0,1\}^L \times \{0,1\}^L \to \{0,1\}$ *such that*

(1) For all graphs G, challenges R and responses M,

$$\mathrm{out}_{x_A}(G, R, M) = 1 \Leftrightarrow \left[f_{x_A}(R_{N(x_A)}, M_{x_A}) = 1 \text{ and } M_{x_A} = M_{x_B} \right].$$

(2) Similarly for x_B.

We use the short-hand notation $f_{x_A}(R, M)$ for $f_{x_A}(R_{N(x_A)}, M_{x_A})$. It is not hard to see that any dAM[1] protocol for the class $\mathcal{G}$ can be transformed into a simple protocol at little extra cost:

Lemma 3.7. *If a graph property* $\mathcal{P}$ *is decided by a* 1*-round distributed AM protocol* Π *with length L, then there exists a simple* 1*-round distributed AM protocol* Π' *that decides* $\mathcal{P}$ *for* $\mathcal{G}$ *and has length* $4L$.

In Π', we "ask" the prover to give each bridge node $4L$ bits, comprising the four responses it would have given nodes v_A, x_A, x_B, v_B under Π. Nodes v_A, x_A, x_B, v_B verify that the prover gave them the same response, extract their part of the response (i.e., the L bits they expected to receive under Π), and apply their decision function from Π.

From now on we restrict attention to simple protocols, and we focus on the view of the two bridge nodes, x_A and x_B. We claim that for graphs of the form $G(F, F)$, the distribution of messages these nodes receive must capture everything there is to know about F: intuitively, if there exist $F_1 \neq F_2 \in \mathcal{F}$ such that x_A and x_B receive similar responses on $G(F_1, F_1)$ and on $G(F_2, F_2)$, then the adversary can convince all nodes to accept the graph $G(F_1, F_2)$, which is not symmetric. Let us now formalize this intuition.

Define $\mathcal{M}_A(F, r)$ to be the set of responses m to bridge node x_A, such that when the challenge is r and the graph is $G = G(F, F)$, the response m can be extended into a response M for all nodes of V_A and x_A that makes them accept. That is, $m \in \mathcal{M}_A(F, r)$ iff there exists $M \in \{0,1\}^{L \times V_A \cup \{x_A\}}$ with $M_{x_A} = m$, such that (a) for each $v \in V_A$ we have $\mathrm{out}_v(G, r, M) = 1$, and (b) $f_{x_A}(r, M) = 1$. Similarly, let $\mathcal{M}_B(F, r)$ be the set of responses m to x_B, such that on challenge r and the graph is $G(F, F)$, the response m can be extended into a response M that causes all nodes in $V_B \cup \{x_B\}$ to accept.

In a graph $G(F_A, F_B)$, for a given challenge r and response M, the decisions of nodes in $V_A \cup \{x_A\}$ whether to accept or reject does not depend on F_B, and similarly for $V_B \cup \{x_B\}$ and F_A. Therefore we get:

Lemma 3.8. *For any* $F, F' \in \mathcal{F}$ *and random challenge r, we have:* $m \in \mathcal{M}_A(F, r) \cap \mathcal{M}_B(F', r)$ *iff there is a prover response M with* $M_{x_A} = M_{x_B} = m$*, such that* $\mathrm{out}_v(G(F, F'), r, M) = 1$ *for all* $v \in V$.

Because of this behavior, the prover's probability to convince all nodes to accept is exactly characterized by the probability that the challenge it received has $\mathcal{M}_A(F_A, r) \cap \mathcal{M}_B(F_B, r) \neq \emptyset$:

Lemma 3.9. *For any* $G(F_A, F_B) \in \mathcal{G}$,

$$\max_P \left(\Pr_r(\forall v : \Pi(G, P, v) = 1) \right) = \Pr_r\left(\mathcal{M}_A(F_A, r) \cap \mathcal{M}_B(F_B, r)\right).$$

From the correctness of Π, together with Lemma 3.9 above, we get:

Corollary 3.10. *For any* $F_A, F_B \in \mathcal{F}$*, if* $F_A = F_B$*, then*

$$\Pr_r\left(\mathcal{M}_A(F_A, r) \cap \mathcal{M}_B(F_B, r)\right) \geq 2/3.$$

On the other hand, if $F_A \neq F_B$*, then*

$$\Pr_r\left(\mathcal{M}_A(F_A, r) \cap \mathcal{M}_B(F_B, r)\right) \leq 1/3.$$

Now let $\mu_A(F_A)$ be the distribution of $\mathcal{M}_A(F_A, r)$, where the challenge r is uniformly random. From the previous corollary, for any $F_1, F_2 \in \mathcal{F}$, there is an event — having a non-empty intersection with $\mathcal{M}_B(F_1, r)$ — that has large probability under $\mu_A(F_1)$, but small probability under $\mu_A(F_2)$. Therefore the distributions are *far apart*:

Lemma 3.11. *For any two* $F_1, F_2 \in \mathcal{F}$*, if* $F_1 \neq F_2$*, then* $\|\mu_A(F_1) - \mu_A(F_2)\|_1 \geq 2/3$.

Here, $\|\cdot\|_1$ is the L_1 norm, $\|x\|_1 = \sum_{i=1}^N |x_i|$, where N is the dimension of x. It is known that if η_1, η_2 are two distributions on some domain Ω, and there exists an event $Q \subseteq \Omega$ such that $|\eta_1(Q) - \eta_2(Q)| \geq p$, then $\|\eta_1 - \eta_2\|_1 \geq 2p$.

Finally, the following standard argument shows that it is not possible to pack too many distributions that are far apart in L_1-distance into a domain of small size:

Lemma 3.12. *Fix $d \in \mathbb{N}$, and let $\mathcal{U}$ be a set of distributions on the domain $[d]$ such that for all $\mu \neq \eta \in \mathcal{U}$, we have $\|\mu - \eta\| > 1/2$. Then $|\mathcal{U}| < 5^d$.*

Proof. We represent each distribution in $\mathcal{U}$ as a vector in $[0,1]^d$. For a distribution $\mu \in \mathcal{U} \subseteq [0,1]^d$ and a radius $r \in [0,1]$, define an open ball

$$B(\mu, r) = \left\{ x \in [0,1]^d \mid \|\mu - \eta\|_1 < r \right\}.$$

Then we must have $B(\mu, 1/4) \cap B(\eta, 1/4) = \emptyset$ for any $\mu \neq \eta \in \mathcal{U}$: suppose not, and let $x \in B(\mu, 1/4) \cap B(\eta, 1/4)$. Then by the triangle inequality,

$$\|\mu - \eta\|_1 \leq \|\mu - x\|_1 + \|x - \eta\|_1 \leq 1/4 + 1/4 = 1/2.$$

This contradicts our assumption about $\mathcal{U}$.

Now let $B(\vec{0}, 5/4)$ be the open ball

$$B(\vec{0}, 5/4) = \left\{ x \in [0,1]^d \mid \|x\|_1 < 5/4 \right\}.$$

(Here, $\vec{0}$ is the d-dimensional zero vector.)

Since each $\mu \in \mathcal{U}$ is a distribution, it has $\|\mu\|_1 = 1$, and therefore $B(\mu, 1/4) \subseteq B(\vec{0}, 5/4)$: if $x \in B(\mu, 1/4)$, then $\|\mu - x\|_1 < 1/4$, and hence $\|x\|_1 \leq \|\mu\| + 1/4 < 5/4$.

So, we have shown that the set $\mathcal{U}$ induces $|\mathcal{U}|$ mutually-disjoint balls of radius $1/4$, and all are contained within the ball $B(\vec{0}, 5/4)$. The d-dimensional volume (for natural $d \geq 1$) of the ball $B(x, r)$ with respect to L_1 is given by

$$\mathrm{vol}\left(B(x, r)\right) = \frac{(4r)^d}{(d+1)!}.$$

Therefore,

$$|\mathcal{U}| \leq \frac{\mathrm{vol}\left(B(\vec{0}, 5/4)\right)}{\mathrm{vol}\left(B(\vec{0}, 1/4)\right)} = \frac{\frac{(4 \cdot \frac{5}{4})^d}{(d+1)!}}{\frac{(4 \cdot \frac{1}{4})^d}{(d+1)!}} = 5^d.$$

□

Now we can put all the ingredients together to prove the main theorem:

Proof of Theorem 1.4. Fix a simple protocol Π of length L, and let $\mathcal{U} = \{\mathcal{M}_A(F) \mid F \in \mathcal{F}\}$ be the set of distributions that Π induces for the different graphs in $\mathcal{F}$. Each $\mu \in \mathcal{U}$ is a distribution on *sets* of prover's responses to node x_A, so the domain of the distribution in $\mathcal{U}$ has size at most 2^{2^L}.

By Lemma 3.11, for any two $F \neq F' \in \mathcal{F}$ we must have $\|\mathcal{M}_A(F) - \mathcal{M}_A(F')\|_1 \geq 2/3$. In particular, no two distributions in $\mathcal{U}$ are the same, so $|\mathcal{U}| = |\mathcal{F}|$. By Lemma 3.12, we have $|\mathcal{U}| < 5^{2^{2^L}}$. On the other hand, the number of graphs in $\mathcal{F}$ is $2^{\Omega(n^2)}$, and therefore we must have $L = \Omega(\log \log n)$. □

4 INTERACTIVE DISTRIBUTED PROOFS FOR GRAPH NON-ISOMORPHISM

The "standard" GNI protocol. We first attempt to explain why the standard "pepsi vs. cola" protocol for the Graph Non-Isomorphism problem in the centralized setting cannot be adapted to the distributed setting. Recall that in the "pepsi vs. cola" protocol for GNI, the verifier's input is a pair of graphs (G_0, G_1) ("pepsi and cola") on the same vertex set V. The prover claims that G_0 is not isomorphic to G_1. The verifier tests the prover by subjecting it to a "blind taste test": it chooses a random bit $a \in \{0,1\}$, scrambles the graph G_a by applying a random permutation σ to it, and sends $\sigma(G_a)$ to the prover. If pepsi and cola are not "the same drink with a different name" – that is, if G_0 and G_1 are not isomorphic – then the prover can tell which scrambled graph was sent to it, $\sigma(G_0)$ or $\sigma(G_1)$, because no permutation will turn one graph into the other. It responds to the verifier with a bit b, and the prover accepts iff $a = b$. If G_0 *is* isomorphic to G_1, however, the prover has only probability $1/2$ of guessing which graph was presented to it.

Now consider, for example, the following distributed version of GNI (described in subsection 2.3): in addition to getting its neighbor set $N \subseteq V$ in network graph G over which the nodes communicate, each node is given two additional subsets of N as inputs, denoted N_0 and N_1. These sets naturally define two subgraphs G_0 and G_1 of G. We ask the nodes whether G_0 and G_1 are not isomorphic.

Unfortunately, developing a distributed version of the "pepsi vs. cola" GNI protocol seems like a non-starter: in a distributed interactive proof, each network node only sees a small part of the graph, and the nodes have no shared randomness. Even if the nodes *did* have shared randomness, it seems impossible for the nodes to apply a permutation to the entire graph without enlisting the prover's assistance; but asking the prover for help would reveal which graph the nodes chose to scramble, thus "removing the blindfold" and allowing the prover to always succeed.

The Goldwasser-Sipser GNI protocol. Finally, we describe our dAMAM protocol for the GNI problem. This protocol is a distributed version of the Goldwasser-Sipser protocol for GNI [15]. The protocol from [15] is based on the following fact: fix graphs G_0 and G_1, and consider the set S of graphs which are isomorphic to *either* G_0 *or* G_1 (or both). If G_0, G_1 are not isomorphic, then applying any permutation σ to G_0 yields a different graph than we would get if we apply σ to G_1. Intuitively (but incorrectly – see below), since there are $n!$ permutations, then:

1. if G_0 and G_1 are isomorphic, we should have $|S| = n!$; but
2. if G_0 and G_1 are not isomorphic, then we should have $|S| = 2n!$, as each permutation of G_0 yields a graph that is not a permutation of G_1.

Thus, to tell whether $(G_0, G_1) \in \mathsf{GNI}$, the verifier *estimates* the size of S: it challenges the prover with a pairwise-independent hash function $h : \{0,1\}^{n^2} \rightarrow \{0,1\}^L$ (for large enough L), and a random value $r \in \{0,1\}^L$. The prover is supposed to respond with a graph $G \in S$ which is in the pre-image of r under h, that is, $h(G) = r$. The probability that there *exists* such a graph G is proportional to the size of S, so there is a gap between the acceptance probability when $(G_0, G_1) \in \mathsf{GNI}$ compared to when $(G_0, G_1) \in \mathsf{GNI}$.

Specifying a graph on n vertices requires $\Theta(n^2)$ bits. However, the prover is supposed to respond with a graph G that is isomorphic to either G_0 or G_1. Thus, it specifies G by giving a permutation σ and a bit $b \in \{0,1\}$, with the implicit understanding that $G = \sigma(G_b)$. The verifier then checks that $h(\sigma(G_b)) = r$.

As we mentioned, it is not really true that if $(G_0, G_1) \in \mathsf{GNI}$ then $|S| = 2n!$, and if $(G_0, G_1) \notin \mathsf{GNI}$ then $|S| = n!$: if one of the graphs is *symmetric*, applying different permutations to it could yield the same result, reducing the size of S. This is fixed cleverly in [15] by changing the definition of S: in addition to the graph G_b, the prover is asked to provide an automorphism of G_b, to "compensate" for symmetries (if there are any). With this new definition of S, it is indeed true that if $(G_0, G_1) \in \mathsf{GNI}$ then $|S| = 2n!$. To simplify the presentation here, we avoid this issue altogether, and restrict attention to asymmetric graphs. To solve the unrestricted GNI problem, we utilize the dAM protocol for Symmetry constructed in Section 3.2.

A distributed GNI protocol. To develop a distributed version of Goldwasser-Sipser, after the prover specifies σ and b, the nodes enlist the prover's help in verifying that $h(\sigma(G_b)) = r$. This requires an additional Arthur-Merlin exchange.

The main difficulty is that in [15], the hash function h is pairwise-independent (PI); this is needed to ensure that the size of the image $h(S)$ is proportional to the true size of S. Unfortunately, PI hash functions require a long random seed [29]. (The family from Theorem 3.2, which we used for Symmetry, is not PI.) We could try to "break up" the seed and have each node send a small part of it to the prover, but we could not find a way to do this that also allowed the nodes to later *verify* that the prover computed the hash correctly.

Instead, we relax the pairwise-independence requirement, and use *ε-almost pairwise-independence* (ε-API) [5, 29]. if the hash is from n bits to m bits, we only require that for each $x_1 \neq x_2 \in \{0,1\}^n$ and $y_1, y_2 \in \{0,1\}^m$, we have

(1) $\Pr_{h \in \mathcal{H}}(h(x_1) = y_1 \wedge h(x_2) = y_2) \leq (1+\epsilon)/2^{2m}$.
(2) $\Pr_{h \in \mathcal{H}}(h(x_1) = y_1) = 1/2^m$.

When we plug in an ε-API hash function h in the GNI protocol, the size of the image $h(S)$ is distorted, but not by too much. We show that we can still recover good success probability for the verifiers.

We give a construction for a distributed ε-API hash, which can be computed "up a spanning tree" in a recursive manner. Each node of the tree has a small part of the input to be hashed, and a short private seed that is not known to the other nodes. The hash for a subtree T_v of node v with children $u_1, \ldots, u_c$ is computed by taking the "partial hashes" $h(T_{u_1}), \ldots, h(T_{u_c})$ sent up by the children of v, and applying a local operation, $h(T_v) = f(h(T_{u_1}), \ldots, h(T_{u_c}), I(v))$, where $I(v)$ is the input of v. Our construction has the useful property that a claimed hash value can be efficiently verified by the nodes with the assistance of the prover.

We use this hash in our GNI protocol: each node v sends the prover its seed, and the prover must respond with the hash value $h(\sigma(G_b)|_{T_v})$. Here, $\sigma(G_b)|_{T_v}$ denotes the "partial adjacency matrix" $\sum_{u \in T_v}[u, \sigma(N(u))]$, which includes only rows corresponding to nodes in v's subtree. Node v verifies that the hash was computed correctly by checking that indeed $h(T_v) = f(h(T_{u_1}), \ldots, h(T_{u_c}), I(v))$. At the root r, we have $\sigma(G_b)|_{T_r} = \sigma(G_b)$, so the hash is complete; the root then verifies that indeed $h(\sigma(G_b)) = r$.

REFERENCES

[1] Scott Aaronson and Avi Wigderson. Algebrization: A new barrier in complexity theory. *ACM Transactions on Computation Theory (TOCT)*, 1(1):2, 2009.
[2] László Babai and Shlomo Moran. Arthur-merlin games: a randomized proof system, and a hierarchy of complexity classes. *Journal of Computer and System Sciences*, 36(2):254–276, 1988.
[3] Alkida Balliu, Gianlorenzo D'Angelo, Pierre Fraigniaud, and Dennis Olivetti. What can be verified locally? In *STACS*, volume 66, pages 8:1–8:13, 2017.
[4] Mor Baruch, Pierre Fraigniaud, and Boaz Patt-Shamir. Randomized proof-labeling schemes. In *ACM Symposium on Principles of Distributed Computing (PODC)*, pages 315–324. ACM, 2015.
[5] Jürgen Bierbrauer, Thomas Johansson, Gregory Kabatianskii, and Ben Smeets. On families of hash functions via geometric codes and concatenation. In *Annual International Cryptology Conference*, pages 331–342. Springer, 1993.
[6] Keren Censor-Hillel, Ami Paz, and Mor Perry. Approximate proof-labeling schemes. In *International Colloquium on Structural Information and Communication Complexity*, pages 71–89. Springer, 2017.
[7] Laurent Feuilloley and Pierre Fraigniaud. Survey of distributed decision. *Bulletin of the (EATCS)*, 119, 2016.
[8] Laurent Feuilloley and Pierre Fraigniaud. Error-sensitive proof-labeling schemes. In *Symposium on Distributed Computing (DISC)*, pages 16:1–16:15, 2017.
[9] Laurent Feuilloley, Pierre Fraigniaud, and Juho Hirvonen. A hierarchy of local decision. In *43rd International Colloquium on Automata, Languages, and Programming, (ICALP)*, pages 118:1–118:15, 2016.
[10] Pierre Fraigniaud, Mika Göös, Amos Korman, Merav Parter, and David Peleg. Randomized distributed decision. *Distributed Computing*, 27(6):419–434, 2014.
[11] Pierre Fraigniaud, Mika Göös, Amos Korman, and Jukka Suomela. What can be decided locally without identifiers? In *ACM symposium on Principles of distributed computing (PODC)*, pages 157–165. ACM, 2013.
[12] Pierre Fraigniaud, Magnús M Halldórsson, and Amos Korman. On the impact of identifiers on local decision. In *International Conference On Principles Of Distributed Systems*, pages 224–238. Springer, 2012.
[13] Pierre Fraigniaud, Amos Korman, and David Peleg. Local distributed decision. In *Foundations of Computer Science (FOCS)*, pages 708–717. IEEE, 2011.
[14] Pierre Fraigniaud, Amos Korman, and David Peleg. Towards a complexity theory for local distributed computing. *Journal of the ACM (JACM)*, 60(5):35, 2013.
[15] Shafi Goldwasser and Michael Sipser. Private coins versus public coins in interactive proof systems. *Advances in Computing Research*, 5:73–90, 1989.
[16] Mika Göös, Toniann Pitassi, and Thomas Watson. Zero-information protocols and unambiguity in arthur-merlin communication. *Algorithmica*, 76(3):684–719, 2016.
[17] Mika Göös and Jukka Suomela. Locally checkable proofs in distributed computing. *Theory of Computing*, 12(1):1–33, 2016.
[18] Hartmut Klauck. Rectangle size bounds and threshold covers in communication complexity. In *Conference on Computational Complexity (CCC)*, pages 118–134. IEEE, 2003.
[19] Hartmut Klauck. On arthur merlin games in communication complexity. In *Conference on Computational Complexity (CCC)*, pages 189–199. IEEE, 2011.
[20] Liah Kor, Amos Korman, and David Peleg. Tight bounds for distributed minimum-weight spanning tree verification. *Theory of Computing Systems*, 53(2):318–340, 2013.
[21] Janne H Korhonen and Jukka Suomela. Towards a complexity theory for the congested clique. In *Symposium on Distributed Computing (DISC)*, pages 55:1–55:3, 2017.
[22] Amos Korman and Shay Kutten. Distributed verification of minimum spanning trees. *Distributed Computing*, 20(4):253–266, 2007.
[23] Amos Korman, Shay Kutten, and David Peleg. Proof labeling schemes. *Distributed Computing*, 22:215–233, 2010.
[24] Carsten Lund, Lance Fortnow, Howard Karloff, and Noam Nisan. Algebraic methods for interactive proof systems. *J. ACM*, 39(4):859–868, October 1992.
[25] Boaz Patt-Shamir and Mor Perry. Proof-labeling schemes: broadcast, unicast and in between. In *International Symposium on Stabilization, Safety, and Security of Distributed Systems*, pages 1–17. Springer, 2017.
[26] Atish Das Sarma, Stephan Holzer, Liah Kor, Amos Korman, Danupon Nanongkai, Gopal Pandurangan, David Peleg, and Roger Wattenhofer. Distributed verification and hardness of distributed approximation. *SIAM Journal on Computing*, 41(5):1235–1265, 2012.
[27] Adi Shamir. IP= PSPACE. *Journal of the ACM (JACM)*, 39(4):869–877, 1992.
[28] Jukka Suomela. Survey of local algorithms. *ACM Computing Surveys (CSUR)*, 45(2):24, 2013.
[29] Salil P Vadhan. Pseudorandomness. *Foundations and Trends in Theoretical Computer Science*, 7(1–3):1–336, 2012.

Brief Announcement: Asynchronous Secure Distributed Computing with Transferrable Non-equivocation Revisited

Rishabh Bhadauria and Ashish Choudhury*
International Institute of Information Technology Bangalore, India
rishabh.bhadauria@iiitb.org,ashish.choudhury@iiitb.ac.in

ABSTRACT

In this paper, we consider two fundamental problems in secure distributed computing, namely *Asynchronous Byzantine Agreement* (ABA) and *Asynchronous Secure Multi-party Computation* (ASMPC). Our focus is on the *honest majority* setting, involving a set of n mutually distrusting parties, t of which can be under the control of a *computationally bounded* Byzantine adversary Adv, where $t < n/2$. It is well known that in the cryptographic setting where the parties have access to a *public-key infrastructure* (PKI) set-up and are connected by pair-wise channels, both ABA and ASMPC requires $t < n/3$. However, Clement et al. (PODC 2012) and Backes et al. (PODC 2014) showed that it is possible to design computationally-secure ABA and ASMPC protocols respectively, even with $t < n/2$, provided the parties are available with a *transferrable non-equivocation* mechanism. Non-equivocation is a message authentication mechanism, which prevents a corrupt sender from sending conflicting messages to different parties. The transferability of the mechanism enables a receiver to verifiably transfer any authenticated statement to other parties, on behalf of the sender. In this paper, we revisit the work of Clement et al. and Backes et al. and show the following:

- If $n \leq 3t$, then it is impossible to achieve the traditional notion of *validity* by any ABA protocol, which demands that if the inputs of *all honest* parties are same, say x, then all honest parties should output x at the end of the protocol. Moreover, this holds even if the parties are equipped with a transferrable non-equivocation mechanism.
- The input phase of the ASMPC protocol of Backes et al (and hence the overall ASMPC protocol) may never terminate for the honest parties. The input phase runs an asynchronous primitive called *Agreement on a Common Subset* (ACS), which allows the honest parties to agree upon a common subset of $n - t$ parties who provide their inputs for the computation. The ACS primitive runs n parallel instances of an ABA protocol, where the ith instance is to decide whether the ith party has provided its input. We show that since the underlying ABA instances does not satisfy the validity condition, the ACS primitive may never terminate for the honest parties; this results in the honest parties waiting indefinitely to identify the set of $n - t$ input providers.

*The authors would like to thank Infosys foundation for financial support.

PODC '18, July 23–27, 2018, Egham, United Kingdom

ACM ISBN 978-1-4503-5795-1/18/07.
https://doi.org/10.1145/3212734.3212777

ACM Reference Format:
Rishabh Bhadauria and Ashish Choudhury. 2018. Brief Announcement: Asynchronous Secure Distributed Computing with Transferrable Non-equivocation Revisited. In *PODC '18: ACM Symposium on Principles of Distributed Computing, July 23–27, 2018, Egham, United Kingdom.* ACM, New York, NY, USA, 3 pages. https://doi.org/10.1145/3212734.3212777

1 INTRODUCTION

Byzantine Agreement (BA) [16] and *Secure Multi-party Computation* (MPC) [5, 7, 13, 17, 18] are fundamental problems in secure distributed computing. Consider a set of n mutually distrusting parties $\mathcal{P} = \{P_1, \ldots, P_n\}$, where t parties can be corrupted by a *Byzantine* adversary Adv and behave in any arbitrary fashion during the execution of a protocol. In a BA protocol, each P_i has some private bit b_i and the goal is to achieve the following: **(a) Agreement**: All *honest* parties (namely the parties which are not under the control of Adv) should output a common bit b; **(b) Byz-Validity**: If the inputs of *all honest* parties are the same, then all honest parties should output this common bit. That is, if $b_i = b_j$ holds for every *honest* P_i, P_j, then $b = b_i$ should hold. In an MPC protocol, each P_i has a private input x_i from some finite field $\mathbb{F}$ and the goal is to let the parties jointly and securely compute any publicly known function $f : \mathbb{F}^n \rightarrow \mathbb{F}$, such that the following conditions are satisfied: **(a) Correctness**: the honest parties correctly obtain $y = f(x_1, \ldots, x_n)$, irrespective of the behaviour of Adv; **(b) Privacy**: by participating in the protocol, Adv does not learn any "additional information", beyond what can be inferred by the inputs of the corrupt parties and the function output y. BA and MPC have been widely studied in varieties of settings (see [1, 6, 12, 15] and their references).

We consider the *asynchronous* variants of BA and SMPC, called ABA and ASMPC respectively. In the asynchronous communication setting, there are no known upper bounds on the message delivery and the messages can be arbitrarily delayed; the only guarantee is that the messages of the honest parties will reach to their destinations eventually. Hence, the parties cannot distinguish between a *slow, but honest* sender (whose messages are delayed arbitrarily) and a *corrupt* sender (who does not send messages at all). As a result, at each step of an asynchronous protocol, a party can afford to receive messages from only $n - t$ parties to avoid endless wait. But in this process, the messages from t potentially slow honest parties get ignored. For ABA and ASMPC we require an additional **Termination** property, which demands that the honest parties eventually terminate with a high probability (From [11], any *deterministic* ABA protocol must have non-terminating executions, where the honest parties do not terminate, even if there is a single crash failure. A common approach to circumvent this impossibility result is to consider randomized ABA protocols [1] and hope that honest parties terminate with a high probability).

ABA and ASMPC with a Strict Honest Majority. We consider the *computational* setting, where the computing power of Adv is restricted to probabilistic polynomial time. It is well known that if the parties have access to a public-key infrastructure (PKI) set-up and if the parties are connected by point-to-point channels, then ABA and ASMPC is possible iff $t < n/3$ [14]. In [9], it is show how to design computationally-secure ABA protocols, even with $t < n/2$, assuming that the parties are available with an additional *transferrable non-equivocation* mechanism. Informally, non-equivocation is a message authentication mechanism, which prevents a corrupt sender from sending conflicting messages to different parties. The transferability of the mechanism further enables a receiver to verifiably transfer any authenticated statement to other parties, on behalf of the sender. Such a primitive can be deployed by combining digital signatures, along with tamper-proof hardware. In [2] it is shown that one can even design a computationally-secure AMPC protocol with $t < n/2$, assuming the existence of a transferrable non-equivocation mechanism. Even though the deployment of non-equivocation mechanism significantly improves the *resilience* of ABA and ASMPC protocols (from $t < n/3$ to $t < n/2$), we report some fundamental limitations in the protocols of [2, 9]. Specifically, we show that the ABA protocol of [9] (and in general any ABA protocol with $n \leq 3t$ and transferrable non-equivocation mechanism) may not satisfy the Byz-Validity property. As a consequence, when the ABA protocol is used in the ASMPC protocol of [2], it leads to non-termination for the honest parties.

2 WEAKER NOTION OF VALIDITY FOR NON-EQUIVOCATION BASED ABA WITH $t < n/2$

In [9], the authors presented a general compiler, which takes as input *any* crash-tolerant agreement protocol tolerating t crash failures and outputs an ABA protocol tolerating Adv, provided the parties have access to a transferrable non-equivocation mechanism. We note that in the crash-failure model, upto t out of the n parties may crash and stop functioning at any stage of a protocol; however as long such parties are alive, they behave like an honest party and correctly follow the protocol instructions. On a very high level, the deployment of the transferrable non-equivocation mechanism enforces the t Byzantine corrupt parties to behave like t crash failures. We note that the validity requirement of any asynchronous *crash-tolerant* agreement protocol (which we call **Crash-Validity**) is different from Byz-Validity and requires that if the input b_i of *all* parties (including the crashed parties) are the same, then all honest parties should output this common bit. For the *binary* domain where the inputs of the parties are bits, this is equivalent to saying that final output bit should be the input of *one* of the parties, possibly including a crashed node [1]. The compiler of [9] ensures that the compiled protocol achieves exactly the *same* properties as the input crash-tolerant agreement protocol. Specifically, the compiled protocol satisfies the crash-validity condition, instead of Byz-validity. As a result, the resultant protocol does not satisfy the definition of ABA. In fact, we argue that for any $n \leq 3t$, it is impossible to achieve Byz-Validity, even in the presence of a non-equivocation mechanism.

THEOREM 2.1. *If $n \leq 3t$, then it is impossible to design any computationally-secure ABA protocol tolerating* Adv *which satisfies* **Byz-Validity**, *even in the presence of a transferrable non-equivocation mechanism.*

PROOF: Let $n = 3t$. We prove the theorem for $\mathcal{P} = \{P_1, P_2, P_3\}$, assuming $n = 3$ and $t = 1$. By using a standard player-partitioning technique [1, 15], the proof can be carried over for the case when $n = 3t$ by creating three disjoint partitions of the n parties, each of size t, with Adv controlling one of three partitions and where the parties in each partition "emulates" the role of one of the parties in our impossibility proof for $n = 3$. Let Π^3_{ABA} be an ABA protocol for $\mathcal{P} = \{P_1, P_2, P_3\}$ with $t = 1$, satisfying the termination, Byz-Validity and agreement conditions. We consider two executions of Π^3_{ABA}, where in the second execution, either the Byz-Validity or agreement condition is violated with a *non-zero* probability, which is a contradiction.

- **Execution** E_1: Here P_1 and P_2 are honest and participates with inputs $b_1 = 0$ and $b_2 = 1$ and randomness r_1 and r_2 respectively. Party P_3 is under the control of Adv and crashes at the beginning of the protocol and sends no messages throughout E_1. Let τ_1 denote the transcript of P_1, namely the messages sent and received by P_1. Both P_1 and P_2 terminate, say by time t, with a common output, say 1.
- **Execution** E_2: Here P_1, P_3 are honest, with inputs $b_1 = b_3 = 0$ and randomness r_1 and r_3 respectively. Party P_2 is under the control of Adv. The messages from P_3 to P_1 are delayed till time t. Moreover, P_2 behaves as if its input $b_2 = 1$ and randomness is r_2 and sends messages to P_1 till time t, which are consistent with transcript τ_1 as per execution E_1. Furthermore, P_2 does not send any messages to P_3 and ignores every message received from P_3. Now the view of P_1 is exactly the same as in E_1 and hence it outputs 1. Since Π^3_{ABA} is an ABA protocol, as per the agreement condition, P_3 should also eventually output 1, but this is a violation of the Byz-Validity condition. On the other hand, if P_3 outputs 0 (to satisfy Byz-Validity), then this violates the agreement condition, as P_1 has output 1.

For the above adversarial strategy to work, P_1 should participate in E_2 with the same randomness as in E_1. The probability p of this event may be exponentially small in the size of randomness space, but it is *non-zero*. Hence with probability p, either the agreement or Byz-Validity property will be violated for P_3. We note that the above proof strategy is similar to the one used in [10] to show the impossibility of authenticated ABA with Byz-Validity and $n \leq 3t$ in the partially synchronous setting; the same proof strategy works even in the presence of transferrable non-equivocation. □

3 NON-TERMINATION OF THE ASMPC PROTOCOL OF [2]

In [2], an ASMPC protocol with $n = 2t + 1$ is presented, assuming that the parties have access to a transferrable non-equivocation mechanism (apart from a PKI setup). In the protocol, it is assumed that the function $f : \mathbb{F}^n \rightarrow \mathbb{F}$ is expressed by a publicly known arithmetic circuit over $\mathbb{F}$, with party P_i holding the private input $x_i \in \mathbb{F}$. The protocol consists of two stages, an *input* stage where each party verifiably secret-shares its input and a *computation* stage, where the the parties "securely evaluate" the circuit in a shared fashion. We focus only on the input stage and show that it may never terminate for the honest parties. The goal of the input stage is to allow each P_i acts a *dealer* and t-*share* its input x_i by invoking an instance Sh of *asynchronous verifiable secret sharing* (AVSS) [3, 4, 6, 8]. Informally, the Sh protocol allows a designated *dealer* $\mathsf{D} \in \mathcal{P}$ to t-share its private input $v \in \mathbb{F}$ among $\mathcal{P}$, by selecting a random polynomial of degree at most t over $\mathbb{F}$, say $f(\cdot)$, with $f(0) = v$ and each P_i holding a *share* $f(\alpha_i)$ of s, where $\alpha_1, \ldots, \alpha_n$ are publicly known non-zero distinct elements from $\mathbb{F}$. The verifiability ensures that the value v of even a potentially *corrupt* D is shared through a t-degree polynomial; moreover, if D is honest then Adv knowing at most t shares learns no information about v. In [2], an AVSS protocol Sh is presented with $n = 2t + 1$, assuming the parties have access to a transferrable non-equivocation mechanism. The *termination* properties of Sh ensure the following, provided all *honest* parties (including D) participate in the Sh protocol: (a) If D of the Sh instance is *honest*, then the Sh instance eventually terminates for all honest parties; (b) If D of the Sh instance is *corrupt* and the Sh instance terminates for some honest party, then the Sh instance eventually terminates for every other honest party.

Let Sh_i denote the instance of Sh invoked by P_i as a D to share x_i. Due to the asynchrony, the parties can afford to wait for only $n - t$ "input providers", whose Sh instances will eventually terminate for every honest party. This is because, a corrupt P_i may never invoke the corresponding instance Sh_i. To agree on a common subset of $n - t$ input providers, the parties execute an instance of *agreement on a common subset* (ACS) protocol [4, 6]. The idea behind the ACS protocol (Fig 1) is to execute n independent instances of an ABA protocol, where the ith instance is to decide whether Sh_i eventually terminates for every honest party.

CODE FOR THE PARTY P_i — Every party in $\mathcal{P}$ executes this code:

(1) For each $P_j \in \mathcal{P}$ such that the sharing instance Sh_j has terminated, participate in ABA_j with input 1. Here ABA_j denotes the instance of an ABA protocol executed to decide if Sh_j eventually terminates for every (honest) party.
(2) Upon terminating $n - t$ instances of ABA protocol with output 1, enter input 0 to all other instances of ABA, for which you have not entered a value yet.
(3) Upon terminating $\mathsf{ABA}_1, \ldots, \mathsf{ABA}_n$, let your $\mathcal{S}_i$ be the set of all indices j for which ABA_j had output 1.
(4) Output the set of parties corresponding to the indices in $\mathcal{S}_i$ and terminate.

Figure 1: ACS Protocol for the agreement on a common subset of $n - t$ input providers.

In [4, 6], it is proved that if the underlying ABA protocol satisfies the termination, agreement and Byz-Validy conditions, then ACS terminates for each honest party, with a common set of $n - t$ input providers. However, as proved in the previous section, for any $n \leq 3t$, it is impossible to design an ABA protocol satisfying Byz-Validity condition, even in the presence of a transferrable non-equivocation mechanism. As a consequence of this, we show an adversary strategy which ensures that the ACS protocol does not terminate for any honest party. Let $n = 3t$ and without loss of generality, let $P_1, \ldots, P_{2t}$ be the honest parties and $P_{2t+1}, \ldots, P_n$ be under the control of Adv. The instances $\mathsf{Sh}_1, \ldots, \mathsf{Sh}_{2t}$ eventually terminates for each honest party (follows from the termination property of Sh) and hence $P_1, \ldots, P_{2t}$ participates in the ABA instances $\mathsf{ABA}_1, \ldots, \mathsf{ABA}_{2t}$ with input 1. The adversary strategy is as follows: it does not invoke the instances $\mathsf{Sh}_{2t+1}, \ldots, \mathsf{Sh}_n$ and hence *no* party terminates these Sh instances. As a consequence, no honest party participates in the ABA instances $\mathsf{ABA}_{2t+1}, \ldots, \mathsf{ABA}_n$ and hence these ABA instances never terminate. The adversary further ensures that $P_{2t+1}, \ldots, P_n$ participates in the ABA instances $\mathsf{ABA}_1, \ldots, \mathsf{ABA}_{2t}$ with input 0. Hence, the overall scenario is the following: in the ABA instances $\mathsf{ABA}_1, \ldots, \mathsf{ABA}_{2t}$, the honest parties participate with input 1, while the corrupt parties participate with input 0; on the other hand, no party (including the honest parties) participates in remaining ABA instances $\mathsf{ABA}_{2t+1}, \ldots, \mathsf{ABA}_n$. Since the ABA instances does not satisfy Byz-Validity, it may happen that the honest parties output 0 in the ABA instances $\mathsf{ABA}_1, \ldots, \mathsf{ABA}_{2t}$, even though all honest parties participated in these ABA instances with input 1. As a consequence, the honest parties will not participate in the ABA instances $\mathsf{ABA}_{2t+1}, \ldots, \mathsf{ABA}_n$ and hence would not terminate the ACS protocol. We are currently working on fixing the above problem to ensure that the input phase eventually terminates for each honest party.

REFERENCES

[1] H. Attiya and J. Welch. *Distributed computing: fundamentals, simulations, and advanced topics*, volume 19. John Wiley & Sons, 2004.
[2] M. Backes, F. Bendun, A. Choudhury, and A. Kate. Asynchronous MPC with a Strict Honest Majority Using Non-equivocation. In *PODC*, pages 10–19. ACM, 2014.
[3] Z. Beerliová-Trubíniová and M. Hirt. Simple and Efficient Perfectly-Secure Asynchronous MPC. In *ASIACRYPT*, volume 4833 of *Lecture Notes in Computer Science*, pages 376–392. Springer Verlag, 2007.
[4] M. Ben-Or, R. Canetti, and O. Goldreich. Asynchronous Secure Computation. In *STOC*, pages 52–61. ACM, 1993.
[5] M. Ben-Or, S. Goldwasser, and A. Wigderson. Completeness Theorems for Non-Cryptographic Fault-Tolerant Distributed Computation (Extended Abstract). In *STOC*, pages 1–10. ACM, 1988.
[6] R. Canetti. *Studies in Secure Multiparty Computation and Applications*. PhD thesis, Weizmann Institute, Israel, 1995.
[7] D. Chaum, C. Crépeau, and I. Damgård. Multiparty Unconditionally Secure Protocols (Extended Abstract). In *STOC*, pages 11–19. ACM, 1988.
[8] A. Choudhury, M. Hirt, and A. Patra. Asynchronous Multiparty Computation with Linear Communication Complexity. In *DISC*, volume 8205 of *Lecture Notes in Computer Science*, pages 388–402. Springer, 2013.
[9] A. Clement, F. Junqueira, A. Kate, and R. Rodrigues. On the (Limited) Power of Non-equivocation. In *PODC*, pages 301–308. ACM, 2012.
[10] C. Dwork, N. Lynch, and L. Stockmeyer. Consensus in the Presence of Partial Synchrony. *J. ACM*, 35(2), 1988.
[11] M. J. Fischer, N. A. Lynch, and M. Paterson. Impossibility of Distributed Consensus with One Faulty Process. *J. ACM*, 32(2):374–382, 1985.
[12] Matthias Fitzi. *Generalized communication and security models in Byzantine agreement*. PhD thesis, ETH Zurich, 2002.
[13] O. Goldreich, S. Micali, and A. Wigderson. How to Play any Mental Game or A Completeness Theorem for Protocols with Honest Majority. In *STOC*, pages 218–229. ACM, 1987.
[14] M. Hirt, J. B. Nielsen, and B. Przydatek. Cryptographic Asynchronous Multi-party Computation with Optimal Resilience (Extended Abstract). In *EUROCRYPT*, volume 3494 of *Lecture Notes in Computer Science*, pages 322–340. Springer, 2005.
[15] Nancy A Lynch. *Distributed algorithms*. Morgan Kaufmann, 1996.
[16] M. Pease, R. Shostak, and L. Lamport. Reaching Agreement in the Presence of Faults. *J. ACM*, 27(2):228–234, 1980.
[17] T. Rabin and M. Ben-Or. Verifiable Secret Sharing and Multiparty Protocols with Honest Majority (Extended Abstract). In *STOC*, pages 73–85. ACM, 1989.
[18] A. C. Yao. Protocols for Secure Computations (Extended Abstract). In *FOCS*, pages 160–164. IEEE Computer Society, 1982.

Brief Announcement: Sustainable Blockchains through Proof of eXercise

Ali Shoker*
HASLab, INESC TEC & Minho University
ali.shoker@inesctec.pt

ABSTRACT

Cryptocurrency and blockchain technologies are recently gaining wide adoption since the introduction of Bitcoin, being distributed, authority-free, and secure. Proof of Work (PoW) is at the heart of blockchain's security, asset generation, and maintenance. Although simple and secure, a hash-based PoW like Bitcoin's puzzle is often referred to as "useless", and the used intensive computations are considered "waste" of energy. A myriad of *Proof of "something"* alternatives have been proposed to mitigate energy consumption; however, they either introduced new security threats and limitations, or the "work" remained far from being really "useful". In this work, we introduce *Proof of eXercise* (PoX): a sustainable alternative to PoW where an *eXercise* is a real world matrix-based scientific computation problem. We provide a novel study of the properties of Bitcoin's PoW, the challenges of a more "rational" solution as PoX, and we suggest a comprehensive approach for PoX.

CCS CONCEPTS

• **Security and privacy → Distributed systems security**; Cryptography; • **Social and professional topics → Centralization / decentralization**; *Sustainability*; • **Applied computing → Digital cash**; **Physical sciences and engineering**; **Computational biology**; • **Software and its engineering → Distributed systems organizing principles**; • **Theory of computation →** *Theory of database privacy and security*; • **Computer systems organization →** *Peer-to-peer architectures*;

KEYWORDS

Blockchain, Cryptocurrency, Bitcoin, Security, Sustainablity

ACM Reference Format:
Ali Shoker. 2018. Brief Announcement: Sustainable Blockchains through Proof of eXercise. In *PODC '18: ACM Symposium on Principles of Distributed Computing, July 23–27, 2018, Egham, United Kingdom.* ACM, New York, NY, USA, 3 pages. https://doi.org/10.1145/3212734.3212781

*The research leading to these results has received funding from the European Union's Horizon 2020 - The EU Framework Programme for Research and Innovation 2014-2020, under grant agreement No. 732505. Project "TEC4Growth - Pervasive Intelligence, Enhancers and Proofs of Concept with Industrial Impact/NORTE-01-0145-FEDER-000020" is financed by the North Portugal Regional Operational Programme (NORTE 2020), under the PORTUGAL 2020 Partnership Agreement, and through the European Regional Development Fund (ERDF).

PODC '18, July 23–27, 2018, Egham, United Kingdom

ACM ISBN 978-1-4503-5795-1/18/07.
https://doi.org/10.1145/3212734.3212781

1 INTRODUCTION

Blockchains and cryptocurrenies are increasingly drawing the attention of business, industry, and academia [4, 8, 9, 14, 15, 28]. The concept is based on using cryptographic tamper-proof public ledger, called *blockchain*, to protect the generation and transfer of "digital" money in a fully distributed peer-to-peer (P2P) fashion. The goals of cyrptocurrenices are mainly to avoid central authorities (like banks), reduce transaction delays and fees, and preserve the real value of money by backing the currency with some "work", done through *mining*. At the heart of blockchain, mining maintains the security and correctness of the system and generates (a.k.a., mines) money as a reward for the miner's work, namely, adding new blocks (of *transactions*) to the blockchain, and verifying the protocol's invariants [25]. Being a critical part of these systems, the "work" is made credible through providing a tamper-proof Proof of Work (PoW)—whose properties are discussed further in [2].

Problem. In blockchain protocols that are based on PoW (or similar Proof-of-Something variants), the "work" a miner must do is to solve a cryptographic puzzle: find a random $n \in \mathbb{N}$ such that given the last seen block header B_h, the following inequation holds:

$$H_{B_h}(n) = \text{SHA-256}^2(B_h \mid n) \leq \tau$$

where H is a SHA-256 [30] hashing function that once applied twi to the concatenation of B_h with the nonce n, returns a positive integer not greater than a predefined target τ, known as *difficulty* [29]. This puzzle together with n represent the PoW and live forever in the blockchain (together with the block), allowing for future verifications. Since SHA-256 is random, the best strategy for the solver is to start with an initial n and keep incrementing it with a set-and-test loop until the puzzle is solved. Unfortunately, this is a very computation-hungry process that manifests in very high energy consumption. Recent studies have shown that the annual electricity consumption of Bitcoin system is almost equivalent to that of entire countries like Ireland, Portugal, and Denmark [10, 12, 21]. This raised the voices referring to Bitcoin's hash-based puzzle as "useless" work; whereas, Bitcoin proponents consider this a legitimate price for maintaining the system. We argue that the work can be more *rational* if the puzzle itself is useful, rather than being random.

Current approaches. Three directions are being followed to reduce the "wasted" energy. The first, e.g., *Proof of Stake* (PoS) [18], is based on Game Theory where creating new blocks is based on *coin age*: a function of coin balance and earning time. The proposal is often criticized that coin age accumulates even when the node is not connected to the network, and being non-democratic solution – biased to wealthy peers. Other variants like Delegated Proof-of-Stake [19] and Proof of Stake Velocity [26] tried to address each issue aside, leaving the other open and inducing new limitations or security threats [27]; whereas, Proof of Activity (PoA) [6] is a hybrid solution of PoS and PoW, where computation is still considered wasted on a useless nonce. The second direction—usually adopted by academics—is to use Byzantine Fault Tolerance approaches in permissioned blockchains; these are rather not scalable in public settings [28]. The third approach, like ours, is to simply replace the puzzle with a more useful real world problem. However, the usefullness of work in current proposals is questionable and do not address a wide range of real interesting problems. For instance, Primecoin [17] suggested finding prime numbers instead of a random useless nonce; Permacoin [20] tried to use have the miners to invest on the system's storage and memory through *Proof of Retrievability*; while PieceWork [24] tried to outsource work like spam deterrence and Denial of Service defense.

Proposed approach. We introduce *Proof of eXercise* (PoX), an approach to rationalize mining in cryptocurrencies – focusing on Bitcoin – through solving a real eXercise: a scientific computation matrix-based problem. The choice behind matrix-based problems is two-fold: (1) matrices have interesting composability properties that help in tuning difficulty, collaborative verification, and *pool-mining* (see later); and (2) matrix-based problems span a wide range of useful real world problems, being a principle abstraction for most scientific computation problems, among them: DNA and RNA sequencing and data comparison [1, 7], protein structure analysis, image comparison, object superposition, surface matching [3, 11], collaborative-filtering recommendation, data mining [16], computational geometry [13], face detection, and many others [16, 23].

In the following, we overview the Proof of eXercise approach, and we present it as a potential promising approach to make PoW-based blockchains sustainable—that requries further research in the future. A more detailed study on the proprties of PoW, the challenges and details of PoX can be found in the extended version [2].

2 PROOF OF EXERCISE (POX)

We propose Proof of eXercise (PoX), an approach to replace the hash-based puzzle with solving a matrix-based scientific computation problems [22, 23]. To identify the challenges of PoX and address them, we need baseline properties to compare against. Since we are unaware of such a comprehensive study, we found it intuitive to first analyze the properties of Bitcoin's PoW first, then address the PoX challenges and potential solutions, and finally present our solution. Given the submission limits, we only convey the latter contribution and we urge the reader to read the first two in the extended paper [2]. For better presentation, we explain the approach through referring the steps in the PoX workflow in Figure 1.

Task proposals. Consider an employer E having a scientific problem, a.k.a., an eXercise X, that requires computing a matrix product. E stores X in a highly available database XDB (step 1), and gets the corresponding credentials and hash digest H(X)—Figure 1, step 2. For simplicity, assume that XDB is an external paid DB service. Then, E creates an eXercise Transaction XT (step 3) that comprises the PoX version, H(X), meta-data about X, e.g., "type:matrix product; Proof of Hardness: OK; dimension: 1 Billion, etc". Then, it deposits a credit (in Bitcoins) for a tolerated period of time after which E can give up (i.e., E is only interested in the solution before that

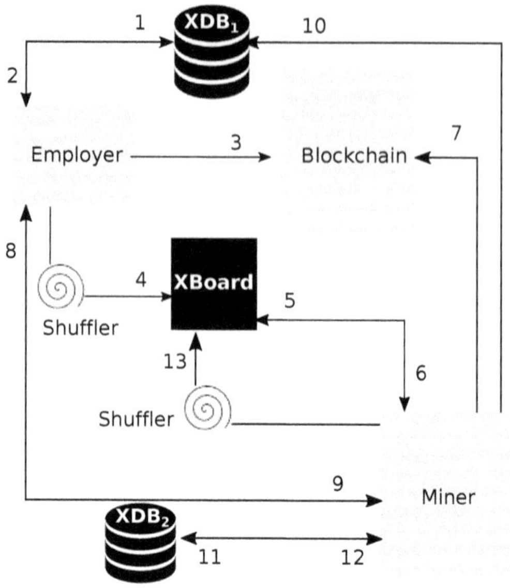

Figure 1: The workflow of PoX without verification. Verification occurs in a similar manner to the steps from 5 through 13 on a verified instance. Refer to Section 2 for more details.

time expires). This guarantees the availability and correctness of X, otherwise the miner may lose (part of) his work. This credit may only be claimed once the eXercise X is solved and verified or the tolerated time has expired. After that, E computes a hash digest H(XT) and submits it to a shuffling service that shuffles H(XT) several times to make it impossible to relate H(XT) to E, and thus prevent collude (step 4). The shuffling service then publishes SH(XT), i.e., the shuffled H(XT), to the eXercise Board (XBoard). Only SH(XT)s that were published for a predefined time may be selected by miners to avoid forks in XBoard – that requires expensive handling as in Bitcoin—since delays are not critical at this level.

eXercise bidding and mining. On the other side, a miner M collects a set of (paid) transactions to be committed and added to the blockchain. To do so, M needs to solve an eXercise chosen from the XBoard and provide a corresponding PoX (step 5). To prevent collude, M gets assigned an eXercise X in a random way, e.g., through matching the hash of block header $H(B_h)$ to the eXercises in XBoard. (Matching can succeed via a pre-defined size of a matching string, or using the hash of $H(B_h)$ and hash digests in XBoard in a similar scheme to Bitcoin's difficulty.) At this stage (step 7), M promises to solve X in the eXercise Transaction XT' through creating a Deal Transaction (DT) that contains: PoX version, SH(XT'), and $H(B_h)$; and then deposits a credit (in Bitcoin's) for a defined period of time – sufficiently long enough – to guarantee its commitment to solve the assigned eXercise. In a similar way to the employer E, the miner M can claim the credit in case the eXercise X is incorrect or became unaccessible. Once the DT is issued, the shuffling service uncovers the onion such that M and E know each other. Consequently, E unveils the meta-data of the eXercise in XT' and gives the credentials of X in the XDB to start working on it (step 9).

PoX Audit. Once the miner M finds Y', i.e., the solution of X, it follows the same process of the eXercise proposing above, making it available for verifiers, called Auditors. In particular, M stores Y' in highly available store, e.g., XDB, and gets a corresponding hash digest H(Y') and access credentials (steps 11 and 12); it creates a corresponding Verify eXercise Transaction (VXT') which is similar to XT, but without requiring a credit this time since M has already deposited a credit through Deal Transaction above. The auditor submits the VXT' to a shuffling service which publishes SH(VXT') – a shuffled version of VXT' to be verified (step 13). Again, this is required to remove any bias in verification. Auditors follow the same bidding procedure as well to choose a random solution Y" to verify, retrieve access details from M and E after the SH(VXT') onion is unshielded, and start auditing Y" through a fast probabilistic verification scheme: an auditor chooses a random number of indices in the matrix to compute; auditing the same eXercise by a sufficient number of auditors will prevent the miner from cheating, as described in more details in the extended version [2].

If the verification *Passed*, the auditor submits a Passed Report through creating an Audit Transaction (AT) that includes the (random) *verification instance* this auditor used for its report, otherwise a Failed Report is submitted. The verification instance is also stored in XDB, and is made available for future audits (within a predefined time frame). Auditors have no interest in submitting false reports since they are at the risk of being caught by other honest auditors in case the same verification instance is repeated. To the contrary, malicious auditors may try submit Failed Reports to compromise the system. This can be prevented by having auditors deposit a credit as a guarantee against false reports – only in the case of submitting Failed Reports.

Committing the block. Once M notices a pre-defined number of Audit Transactions with Passed Reports, it collects the references of all XT, DT, VXT, and AT transactions together with H(X) and H(Y'), and attaches them as a PoX to the block header, that is confirmed by now and can thus safely be added to the blockchain. Finally, all credit deposits are claimed using the PoX of the confirmed block, and the stored matrix in XDB can be removed. (Contrary to Bitcoin, there is no need to verify all the blockchain history since a suffcient number of auditors guarantees the correct PoX correctness with a high probability.) Recall that this verification scheme is important to reduce the overhead of repeated verification of the entire blockchain as well as the data storage and availability costs – which are expensive in the case of PoX.

3 CONCLUSIONS

We introduced Proof of eXercise (PoX): a new proof of work for cryptocurrencies, where the work is a real matrix-based scientific computation problem. Our work shows that the complexity of designing and implementing PoX is much higher than PoW, and therefore, as long as no cheaper alternatives that do not sacrifice the genuine properties of PoW are proposed, it is wise to explore the feasibility of PoX by studying individual scientific computation use-cases, and discussing potential extensions, e.g., as those based on computational complexity [5]. Otherwise, one may opt to stick to cheaper Proof of Stake [6, 18, 19, 26] methods as long as the limitations and constrains are tolerated. Finally, an empirical evaluation that compares the difficulty levels of PoW versus PoX matrices (e.g., dimension, sparseness, etc.) is an interesting future work.

REFERENCES

[1] Amir Abboud, Virginia Vassilevska Williams, and Oren Weimann. 2014. Consequences of faster alignment of sequences. In *International Colloquium on Automata, Languages, and Programming*. Springer, 39–51.

[2] Ali Shoker. 2017. Sustainable Blockchain through Proof of eXercise. In *The 16th IEEE International Symposium on Network Computing and Applications (NCA'17)*. IEEE Computer Society.

[3] Helmut Alt and Michael Godau. 1995. Computing the Fréchet distance between two polygonal curves. *International Journal of Computational Geometry & Applications* 5, 01n02 (1995), 75–91.

[4] Angel.co. [n. d.]. Blockchains Startups. https://angel.co/blockchains. Accessed: 2017-09-15.

[5] Marshall Ball, Alon Rosen, Manuel Sabin, and Prashant Nalini Vasudevan. 2017. Proofs of Useful Work. (2017).

[6] Iddo Bentov, Charles Lee, Alex Mizrahi, and Meni Rosenfeld. 2014. Proof of Activity: Extending Bitcoin's Proof of Work via Proof of Stake [Extended Abstract] y. *ACM SIGMETRICS Performance Evaluation Review* 42, 3 (2014), 34–37.

[7] Philip Bille. 2005. A survey on tree edit distance and related problems. *Theoretical computer science* 337, 1 (2005), 217–239.

[8] Vitalik Buterin. 2014. A next-generation smart contract and decentralized application platform. *white paper* (2014).

[9] Intel Corporation. [n. d.]. Intel Software Guard Extensions (Intel SGX) SDK. https://software.intel.com/en-us/sgx-sdk. Accessed: 2017-08-29.

[10] Sebastiaan Deetman. [n. d.]. Bitcoin Could Consume as Much Electricity as Denmark by 2020. https://motherboard.vice.com/en_us/article/aek3za/bitcoin-could-consume-as-much-electricity-as-denmark-by-2020. Accessed: 2017-09-05.

[11] Michel Marie Deza and Elena Deza. 2009. Encyclopedia of distances. In *Encyclopedia of Distances*. Springer, 1–583.

[12] Digiconomist. 2018. Bitcoin Energy Consumption. https://digiconomist.net/bitcoin-energy-consumption.

[13] Anka Gajentaan and Mark H Overmars. 1995. On a class of O (n2) problems in computational geometry. *Computational geometry* 5, 3 (1995), 165–185.

[14] IBM. [n. d.]. Hyperledger Fabric. https://www.ibm.com/blockchain/hyperledger.html. Accessed: 2017-09-15.

[15] Bitmain Technologies Inc. [n. d.]. Antminer Hardware. https://shop.bitmain.com/main.htm?lang=en. Accessed: 2017-09-15.

[16] Maja Kabiljo and Aleksandar Ilic. [n. d.]. Recommending items to more than a billion people. https://code.facebook.com/posts/861999383875667/recommending-items-to-more-than-a-billion-people/. Accessed: 2017-08-29.

[17] Sunny King. 2013. Primecoin: Cryptocurrency with prime number proof-of-work. *July 7th* (2013).

[18] Sunny King and Scott Nadal. 2012. Ppcoin: Peer-to-peer crypto-currency with proof-of-stake. *self-published paper, August* 19 (2012).

[19] Daniel Larimer. 2014. Delegated Proof-of-Stake (DPOS). *Bitshare whitepaper* (2014). https://bitshares.org/technology/delegated-proof-of-stake-consensus/

[20] Andrew Miller, Ari Juels, Elaine Shi, Bryan Parno, and Jonathan Katz. 2014. Permacoin: Repurposing bitcoin work for data preservation. In *Security and Privacy (SP), 2014 IEEE Symposium on*. IEEE, 475–490.

[21] Karl J O'Dwyer and David Malone. 2014. Bitcoin mining and its energy footprint. (2014).

[22] University of California. [n. d.]. BOINC projects. http://boinc.berkeley.edu/projects.php. Accessed: 2017-08-29.

[23] University of Zurich. [n. d.]. The Center for Theoretical Astrophysics & Cosmology Program. http://www.ctac.uzh.ch/research/index.html. Accessed: 2017-09-9.

[24] Ittay Eyal Philip Daian, Emin GÃijn Sirer and Ari Juels. 2017. PieceWork: Generalized Outsourcing Control for Proofs of Work. In *BITCOIN Workshop*. Springer.

[25] Bitcoin Project. [n. d.]. Bitcoin documentation. https://bitcoin.org/en/developer-reference. Accessed: 2017-08-29.

[26] Larry Ren. 2014. Proof of stake velocity: Building the social currency of the digital age. (2014).

[27] Florian Tschorsch and Björn Scheuermann. 2016. Bitcoin and beyond: A technical survey on decentralized digital currencies. *IEEE Communications Surveys & Tutorials* 18, 3 (2016), 2084–2123.

[28] Marko Vukolić. 2015. The quest for scalable blockchain fabric: Proof-of-work vs. BFT replication. In *International Workshop on Open Problems in Network Security*. Springer, 112–125.

[29] Bitcoin Wiki. [n. d.]. Difficulty. https://en.bitcoin.it/wiki/Difficulty. Accessed: 2017-09-06.

[30] Bitcoin Wiki. [n. d.]. SHA-256. https://en.bitcoin.it/wiki/SHA-256. Accessed: 2017-09-06.

Brief Announcement: Partially Replicated Causally Consistent Shared Memory*†

Zhuolun Xiang
University of Illinois at Urbana-Champaign
Illinois, USA
xiangzhuolun@gmail.com

Nitin H. Vaidya
University of Illinois at Urbana-Champaign
Illinois, USA
nhv@illinois.edu

ABSTRACT

Distributed shared memory systems maintain multiple replicas of the shared memory registers. Maintaining causal consistency in such systems has received significant attention in the past. However, much of the previous literature focuses on *full* replication wherein each replica stores a copy of all the registers in the shared memory. In this paper, we investigate causal consistency in partially replicated systems, wherein each replica may store only a subset of the shared data. To achieve causal consistency, it is necessary to ensure that, before an update is performed at any given replica, all causally preceding updates must also be performed. Achieving this goal requires some mechanism to track causal dependencies. In the context of full replication, this goal is often achieved using vector timestamps, with the number of vector elements being equal to the number of replicas. Building on the past work, this paper makes two key contributions:

- For a family of algorithms for maintaining causal consistency, we present necessary conditions on the metadata (which we refer as a *timestamp*) that must be maintained by each replica.
- We present an algorithm for achieving causal consistency using a timestamp that matches one of the necessary conditions referred above, thus showing that the condition is necessary and sufficient both.

CCS CONCEPTS

• **Theory of computation → Shared memory algorithms**;

KEYWORDS

distributed shared memory, causal consistency, partial replication, timestamps, lower bounds

ACM Reference Format:
Zhuolun Xiang and Nitin H. Vaidya. 2018. Brief Announcement: Partially Replicated Causally Consistent Shared Memory. In *PODC '18: ACM Symposium on Principles of Distributed Computing, July 23–27, 2018, Egham, United Kingdom.* ACM, New York, NY, USA, Article 4, 3 pages. https://doi.org/10.1145/3212734.3212790

1 INTRODUCTION

The focus of this work is on causal consistency in a *partially replicated* distributed shared memory (DSM) system that provides the abstraction of shared read/write registers.

This brief announcement focuses on the *peer-to-peer* architecture, where each peer has a *client* that performs read/write operations to the shared memory and a *replica* that helps implement the shared memory abstraction. Extensions to client-server architecture can be found in the full version [6]. We focus on the case when each replica is *partial* and may store a copy of just a subset of the shared registers. *Full replication* is obtained as a special case when each replica stores a copy of each shared register.

For *full replication*, it suffices to use a vector timestamp [4] of length equal to the number of replicas [3] to achieve causal consistency. Several researchers have observed that *partial replication* requires larger amount of metadata to track causal dependencies [1, 2]. Thus, partial replication yields a trade-off between flexibility of replication of the shared registers, and the overhead of the metadata for tracking causality. A goal of our work is to characterize this trade-off. Intuitively, in our solution, each replica maintains an *edge-indexed vector timestamp* which keeps counters for a subset of edges in a *"share graph"* that characterizes how registers are shared among the replicas. We show that our timestamp is *optimal* in the sense that the subset of share graph edges tracked is necessary for correctness (Theorem 1). Later in Section 3 we present a lower bound for the size of the timestamp space, which matches upper bound achieved by our algorithm in some special cases.

1.1 Preliminaries

We assume an asynchronous system. There are R peers, and hence there are R replicas, numbered 1 through R. Replica i stores copies of a subset of shared registers named X_i. In practice, set X_i for replica i may change dynamically, however, we consider the *static* case in this paper. The client invokes *read* or *write* operations on a shared register stored at the local replica, and waits for a response from the replica. The replicas communicate using reliable point-to-point message-passing channels.

1.2 Algorithm Prototype

We consider causally consistent shared memory that is implemented using an algorithm based on the prototype below, where the structure of the timestamp, how to update the timestamp, and predicate $\mathcal{J}$ are not specified. The choice of the timestamp must ensure that

*This research is supported in part by National Science Foundation award 1409416, and Toyota InfoTechnology Center. Any opinions, findings, and conclusions or recommendations expressed here are those of the authors and do not necessarily reflect the views of the funding agencies or the U.S. government.
†A full version of the paper is available in [6].

ACM ISBN 978-1-4503-5795-1/18/07.
https://doi.org/10.1145/3212734.3212790

the timestamp contains adequate information to be able to achieve causal consistency.

> **Replica prototype:** Replica i maintains timestamp τ_i that is suitably initialized.
> (1) When replica i receives a *read*(x) request from the client, replica i responds with the value of the local copy of register x.
> (2) When replica i receives a *write*(x, v) request from the client, replica i performs the following operations atomically:
> (i) write v into the local copy of register x,
> (ii) update timestamp τ_i as $\tau_i := advance(i, \tau_i, x, v)$,
> (iii) send $update(i, \tau_i, x, v)$ message to each other replica $k \in V$ such that $x \in X_k$,
> (iv) return *ack* to the client.
> (3) When replica i receives a message $update(k, \tau_k, x, v)$, it adds $update(k, \tau_k, x, v)$ to a local data structure named $pending_i$.
> (4) For any $update(k, \tau_k, x, v) \in pending_i$, when predicate $\mathcal{J}(i, \tau_i, k, \tau_k)$ evaluates True, replica i performs the following operations atomically:
> (i) writes value v to its local copy of register x,
> (ii) updates its timestamp as $\tau_i := merge(i, \tau_i, k, \tau_k)$,
> (iii) removes $update(k, \tau_k, x, v)$ from $pending_i$.

Notation for updates: We will use short labels, such as u or u_1, to represent an update. When all operations in step 2, or all operations in step 4 have been performed, we say that $update(i, \tau, x, v)$ has been *applied at* replica i. The replica i is said to *issue an update* when step 2 is performed.

1.3 Replica-centric Causal Consistency

The causal consistency model addressed in our work is inspired by replicated shared memory systems such as Lazy Replication [3]. We refer to this model as the *replica-centric* causal consistency model.

Definition 1 (Happened-before relation $\hookrightarrow$ for updates). *Given updates u_1 and u_2, $u_1 \hookrightarrow u_2$ if and only if at least one of the following conditions is true:*

- *(i) u_1 is applied at a replica sometime before the same replica issues u_2,*
- *(ii) There exists an update u_3 such that $u_1 \hookrightarrow u_3$ and $u_3 \hookrightarrow u_2$.*

Intuitively, an update issued by replica i is considered causally dependent on any updates that were previously applied at that replica, regardless of whether the previously updated registers were read by the client or not. We define *replica-centric* causal consistency more formally now using relation $\hookrightarrow$.

Definition 2. *Replica-centric causal consistency is achieved if the following two properties are satisfied:*

- **Safety:** *If an update u_1 for register $x \in X_i$ has been applied at a replica i, then there* must not exist *update u_2 for some register in X_i such that (i) $u_2 \hookrightarrow u_1$, and (ii) replica i has not yet applied u_2.*
- **Liveness:** *Any update u issued by a replica i for a register $x \in X_i$ will eventually be applied at each replica j such that $x \in X_j$.*

For two important reasons, we consider the replica-centric causal consistency in this paper. (i) First, the lower bounds on timestamp size presented in Section 3 for the replica-centric causal consistency is also a lower bound for the client-centric causal consistency. (ii) Second, in practice, the replica-centric approach is convenient, since it only uses a single timestamp per replica (as compared to, for instance, a timestamp per register per replica). Many practical systems, including Lazy Replication [3] and SwiftCloud [7], in fact, conform to the replica-centric view.

2 TIMESTAMPS FOR REPLICA-CENTRIC CAUSAL CONSISTENCY

In this section, we identify a necessary and sufficient condition on the timestamp τ_i maintained by each replica i in the prototype in order to achieve the replica-centric causal consistency. Intuitively, our condition identifies a subset of directed edges in the share graph that are *necessary and sufficient* to "keep track" of for each replica in order to achieve replica-centric causal consistency.

Hélary and Milani [2] introduced the notion of a *share graph* to represent a partially replicated system. We define $X_{ij} = X_i \cap X_j$, the set of registers stored at replicas i and j both. In the following, e_{ij} is a directed edge from i to j.

Definition 3 (**Share Graph [2]**). *Share graph is defined as a directed graph $G = (V, E)$, where $V = \{1, 2, \cdots, R\}$, and vertex $i \in V$ represents replica i. There exist directed edges e_{ij} and e_{ji} in E if and only if $X_{ij} \neq \emptyset$.*

For a replica i, and directed edge e_{jk} (from j to k), Definition 4 defines an (i, e_{jk})-loop.

Definition 4 (**(i, e_{jk})-loop**). *Given replica i and edge e_{jk} ($j \neq i \neq k$) in share graph G, consider a simple loop of the form $(i,\ l_1,\ l_2, \cdots, l_s = k,\ j = r_1,\ r_2, \cdots, r_t,\ i)$, where $s \geq 1$ and $t \geq 1$. Define $i = r_{t+1}$. The simple loop is said to be an (i, e_{jk})-loop provided that:*

(i) $X_{jk} - \left(\cup_{1 \leq p \leq s-1} X_{l_p}\right) \neq \emptyset$,

(ii) $X_{jr_2} - \left(\cup_{1 \leq p \leq s-1} X_{l_p}\right) \neq \emptyset$, *and*

(iii) for $2 \leq q \leq t$, $X_{r_q r_{q+1}} - \left(\cup_{1 \leq p \leq s} X_{l_p}\right) \neq \emptyset$.

To help present the necessary condition in Section 2.1, we now define a *timestamp graph.* Intuitively, timestamp graph G_i consists of directed edges that are *necessary and sufficient* for replica i to keep track of in its timestamp, as we will show later in this section.

Definition 5 (**Timestamp graph G_i of replica i**). *Given share graph $G = (V, E)$, timestamp graph of replica i is defined as a directed graph $G_i = (V_i, E_i)$, where*

$$\begin{aligned} E_i =& \{e_{ij} \mid e_{ij} \in E\} \cup \{e_{ji} \mid e_{ji} \in E\} \cup \\ & \{e_{jk} \mid \exists\, (i, e_{jk})\text{-loop in } G,\ j \neq i \neq k,\ e_{jk} \in E\} \\ V_i =& \{u, v \mid e_{uv} \in E_i\} \end{aligned}$$

Thus, E_i consists of all directed edges incident at i, and each edge $e_{jk} \in E$ such that an (i, e_{jk})-loop exists. Note that timestamp edges are not necessarily bidirectional.

2.1 A Necessary Condition for Timestamps

In order to achieve replica-centric causal consistency, the timestamp maintained by each replica must contain adequate information, as shown in Theorem 1.

THEOREM 1 (INFORMAL). *Consider a shared memory system that implements replica-centric causal consistency using an algorithm conforming with the prototype in Section 1.2. Any replica i's timestamp has to be dependent on the updates performed on edge e_{jk} for each $e_{jk} \in E_i$.*

Formal statement of the above theorem can be found in [6]. In Section 2.2 we present an algorithm that uses timestamps precisely satisfy the necessary condition above, proving that the necessary condition in Theorem 1 is sufficient as well.

2.2 Sufficiency of Tracking Edges in Timestamp Graph

The algorithm uses an *edge-indexed* vector timestamp. In particular, replica i's timestamp τ_i is a vector of length $|E_i|$ with its elements being indexed using edges in E_i. Recall that timestamp graph edges sets E_i and E_j may be distinct for distinct replicas i and j. Therefore, the timestamps maintained by different replicas may have different sizes, and indexed by different edges. Despite this non-uniformity, the timestamps suffice to implement replica-centric causal consistency.

Proposed algorithm: Since the algorithm conforms to prototype in Section 1.2, it suffices to describe the timestamp structure, *advance* and *merge* functions, and predicate $\mathcal{J}$ for each replica i.

- Timestamp maintained by replica i: Each replica i maintains a vector timestamp τ_i that is indexed by the edges in E_i. For edge $e_{jk} \in E_i$, $\tau_i[e_{jk}]$ is an integer, initialized to 0.
- Function *advance*(i, τ_i, x, v) returns vector T_i (indexed by edges in E_i) defined as follows. For each $e_{jk} \in E_i$:
$$T_i[e_{jk}] := \begin{cases} \tau_i[e_{jk}] + 1, & \text{if } j = i \text{ and } x \in X_{ik}, \\ \tau_i[e_{jk}], & \text{otherwise} \end{cases}$$
Observe that *advance*(i, τ_i, x, v) increments elements of τ_i corresponding to edges from i to only those replicas that also store register x.
- Function *merge*(i, τ_i, k, τ_k) returns following vector T_i (indexed by edges in E_i):
$$T_i[e] := \begin{cases} \max(\tau_i[e], \tau_k[e]), & \text{for each edge } e \in E_i \cap E_k, \\ \tau_i[e], & \text{for each edge } e \in E_i - E_k \end{cases}$$
- For $k \neq i$, predicate $\mathcal{J}(i, \tau_i, k, \tau_k) = True$ if and only if $\tau_i[e_{ki}] = \tau_k[e_{ki}] - 1$ and $\tau_i[e_{ji}] \geq \tau_k[e_{ji}]$, for each $e_{ji} \in E_i \cap E_k$, $j \neq k$.

The full version [6] presents several optimizations that can reduce the timestamps sizes in practice.

3 LOWER BOUND ON TIMESTAMP SIZE

In this section, we present a lower bound (in bits) on the size of the timestamps for the restricted case where timestamps are assigned as a function of the *causal past* of a replica.

DEFINITION 6 (**Causal past**[5]). *Causal past S of a replica that has applied updates in set U consists of updates in*
$$S = U \cup \{u' \mid u \in U,\ u' \hookrightarrow u\}$$

Recall that $G = (V, E)$ denotes the share graph. For $e_{jk} \in E$, let $S|_{e_{jk}}$ denote the set of updates in S that are issued by replica j on registers in X_{jk}. For $e_{jk} \notin E$, define $S|_{e_{jk}} = \emptyset$ for convenience.

DEFINITION 7 (CONFLICT). *Given share graph $G = (V, E)$, and two possible causal pasts S_1, S_2 of replica i from executions where each replica issues up to m updates, we say that S_1 and S_2 conflict if following conditions hold:*

(1) $\forall e \in E$, $S_1|_e \neq \emptyset \neq S_2|_e$, and

(2) $\exists e \in E$ such that $S_1|_e \subset S_2|_e$, where $e = e_{ij}$ or $e = e_{ji}$ or $\exists$ a simple loop $(i, l_1, \cdots, l_s, r_1, \cdots, r_t, i = r_{t+1}) \in G$ where $e = e_{r_1 l_s}$ such that

(1) $S_1|_{e_{r_p l_q}} = S_2|_{e_{r_p l_q}}$ for $1 \leq p \leq t+1, 1 \leq q \leq s$ and $e_{r_p l_q} \neq e_{r_1 l_s}$, and

(2) $S_x|_{e_{r_p r_{p+1}}} - \bigcup_{1 \leq q \leq s} S_x|_{e_{r_p l_q}} \neq \emptyset$ for $1 \leq p \leq t$ and $x = 1, 2$

LEMMA 1. *Consider two possible causal pasts S_1, S_2 of replica i. If S_1 and S_2 conflict, then distinct timestamps must be assigned to them for ensuring the safety and liveness properties in Definition 2.*

For replica i, we define a **conflict graph** H_i with vertex set equal to the set of all possible causal pasts of replica i. An edge is added between any two causal pasts of replica i that conflict. Then, the *chromatic number* for the conflict graph is a lower bound on timestamp space size. Therefore, we have the following theorem.

THEOREM 2. *Consider a shared memory system that implements replica-centric causal consistency using an algorithm conforming with the prototype in Section 1.2. Let $\chi(H_i)$ denote the chromatic number of conflict graph H_i. Then, for partial replication, the timestamp space size for any replica i is lower bounded by $\chi(H_i)$.*

Implication: It can be shown that when the share graph is a tree, a cycle of n replicas, or a clique representing full replication, the above theorem implies a lower bound on the timestamp size that is *tight* due to the fact that our algorithm also uses timestamp of the same size.

Summary: This work investigates partially replicated causally consistent shared memory systems. We present some necessary conditions and an algorithm that achieves replica-centric causal consistency in a partially replicated system.

REFERENCES

[1] Tyler Crain and Marc Shapiro. 2015. Designing a causally consistent protocol for geo-distributed partial replication. In *Proceedings of the First Workshop on Principles and Practice of Consistency for Distributed Data*. ACM.

[2] Jean-Michel Hélary and Alessia Milani. 2006. About the efficiency of partial replication to implement distributed shared memory. In *International Conference on Parallel Processing*. IEEE.

[3] Rivka Ladin, Barbara Liskov, Liuba Shrira, and Sanjay Ghemawat. 1992. Providing high availability using lazy replication. *ACM Transactions on Computer Systems (TOCS)* (1992).

[4] Friedemann Mattern. 1988. Virtual Time and Global States of Distributed Systems. In *Workshop on Parallel and Distributed Algorithms*.

[5] Giovanna Melideo. 2001. *Tracking Causality in Distributed Computations*. Ph.D. Dissertation.

[6] Zhuolun Xiang and Nitin H Vaidya. 2017. Lower Bounds and Algorithm for Partially Replicated Causally Consistent Shared Memory. *arXiv preprint arXiv:1703.05424* (2017).

[7] Marek Zawirski, Annette Bieniusa, Valter Balegas, Sérgio Duarte, Carlos Baquero, Marc Shapiro, and Nuno Preguiça. 2013. SwiftCloud: Fault-tolerant geo-replication integrated all the way to the client machine. *arXiv preprint arXiv:1310.3107* (2013).

Brief Announcement: Optimal Record and Replay under Causal Consistency*

Russell L. Jones
University of Illinois at Urbana-Champaign
rjones27@illinois.edu

Muhammad S. Khan
University of Illinois at Urbana-Champaign
mskhan6@illinois.edu

Nitin H. Vaidya
University of Illinois at Urbana-Champaign
nhv@illinois.edu

ABSTRACT

We investigate the minimum record needed to replay executions of processes that share causally consistent memory. For a version of causal consistency, we identify optimal records under both offline and online recording setting. Under the offline setting, a central authority has information about every process' view of the execution and can decide what information to record for each process. Under the online setting, each process has to decide on the record at runtime as the operations are observed.

CCS CONCEPTS

• **Theory of computation** → **Shared memory algorithms**;

ACM Reference Format:

Russell L. Jones, Muhammad S. Khan, and Nitin H. Vaidya. 2018. Brief Announcement: Optimal Record and Replay under Causal Consistency. In *PODC '18: ACM Symposium on Principles of Distributed Computing, July 23–27, 2018, Egham, United Kingdom.* ACM, New York, NY, USA, 3 pages. https://doi.org/10.1145/3212734.3212789

1 INTRODUCTION

In this paper, we explore *Record and Replay* (RnR) of multi-process applications where processes communicate via shared memory. Record and replay mechanisms aim to allow parallel program debugging to proceed as follows. The programmer runs the program, and potentially observes incorrect behavior. The programmer then reruns the program, while more closely watching the program state, and attempts to discover where a program bug may have occurred. However, even when a parallel program is re-executed with the same input, different executions of the program may proceed differently, due to non-determinism introduced by the uncertainty in the delays incurred in performing various operations. Thus, the observed bug may not re-occur during rerun, making it quite difficult to discover the cause of the original problem. Record and Replay (RnR) aims to solve this problem by creating a *record* during the original execution, and using it during replay to guarantee that the rerun produces the same outcome as the original execution. In other words, while the original execution may be non-deterministic, the replay using the record eliminates the non-determinism as desired.

This work is motivated by the trade-off between the consistency model for shared memory and the amount of information that must be recorded to facilitate a replay. A stronger consistency model imposes more constraints on the execution, resulting in a smaller space of allowed executions. Intuitively, a stronger consistency model should require a smaller record to resolve the non-determinism during replay. In the full paper [4] we present a concrete example execution to illustrate that this intuition is indeed correct. In prior work, Netzer [7] identified the minimum record necessary for RnR under the *sequential consistency* model. The computer architecture research community has also investigated RnR systems under various consistency models (e.g., [6], [1], [2]). However, to the best of our knowledge, only Netzer's work [7] has addressed identification of minimum record for RnR.

This paper builds on Netzer's work to address the minimum record for correct replay under *causal consistency*. Whether a certain record is necessary and sufficient for replay depends on several factors, as discussed in the full paper [4]. We describe the RnR model for this work in Section 4.

*This research is supported in part by National Science Foundation award 1409416, and Toyota InfoTechnology Center. Any opinions, findings, and conclusions or recommendations expressed here are those of the authors and do not necessarily reflect the views of the funding agencies or the U.S. government.

PODC '18, July 23–27, 2018, Egham, United Kingdom

ACM ISBN 978-1-4503-5795-1/18/07.
https://doi.org/10.1145/3212734.3212789

2 PRELIMINARIES

A *relation* R on a set O is a set of tuples (a, b) such that $a, b \in O$. We use the notation $a <_R b$ if $(a, b) \in R$. We denote $a \leq_R b$ if either $a <_R b$ or $a = b$. An irreflexive, antisymmetric, and transitive relation is called a *partial order*. A partial order R on a set O is a *total order* if for any $a, b \in O$, either $a <_R b$ or $b <_R a$. A partial order can be represented by a directed acyclic graph which is closed under transitivity. For two partial orders A and B on a set O, we say that A *respects* B if $B \subseteq A$. We use the notation $A \mid O'$ to restrict the partial order A on set O to a subset $O' \subseteq O$. $\widehat{A}$ denotes the (unique) transitive reduction of A and $a \lessdot_A b$ denotes $(a, b) \in \widehat{A}$. We use $A \cup B$ to denote the union, with the transitive closure, of A and B, and $A \uplus B$ to denote the disjoint union of A and B. For example, consider two partial orders A and B on the set $\{a, b\}$, given by $A = \{(a, b)\}$ and $B = \{(b, a)\}$. Then, $A \cup B = \{(a, b), (b, a), (a, a), (b, b)\}$ while $A \uplus B = \{(a, b), (b, a)\}$. Observe that union and disjoint union of two partial orders may not be a partial order, as the previous example shows.

We borrow some notation by Steinke and Nutt [8] for shared memory formalism. The shared memory consists of a set of variables X and supports two operations, read and write. We use w for writes, r for reads, and o when the operation can be either read or write. We use a subscript for process identifier or leave it blank if it is unspecified. Formally, an *operation* is a 4-tuple (op, i, x, id) where op is r for read and w for write, i is the unique identifier of the process that performed the operation, x is the (shared) variable on which the operation was performed, and id is the unique identifier of the operation. This notation allows for wild-card entries, e.g. $(\mathrm{w}, i, *, *)$ is the set of all writes executed by process i. Observe that we do not specify the values in the notation. We assume that each write operation writes a unique value[1]. The values read by read operations may vary between executions, but each read operation reads a value written by some write.

All operations in $(*, i, *, *)$ are totally ordered. We denote this total order by $PO(i)$. The *program order* is given by $PO = \cup_i PO(i)$. We assume that the program order PO is fixed. Formally, a shared memory *system* is a set of processes P, a set of operations O, a program order PO on O, a set of shared variables X, and a shared memory Π. An execution is the result of processes running their programs on a shared memory system where each read operation returns a value written by some write operation.

Definition 2.1 (Writes-to). Given an execution, a write operation w writes-to a read operation r, denoted $w \mapsto r$, if w and r are on the same variable and r returns the value written by w.

3 SHARED MEMORY CONSISTENCY

For an execution, a *view* V on a set of operations $O' \subseteq O$ is a total order on O' such that each read $r \in O'$ returns the last value written to the corresponding variable in V. Reasoning about allowed executions under a shared memory consistency model relies on existence of some collection of views $\mathcal{V}$ that satisfy some properties, depending on the shared memory consistency model. We say that $\mathcal{V}$ *explains* the execution under the consistency model. For example, causal consistency requires existence of per-process views that satisfy causality, which is the union (with the transitive closure) of the writes-to relation and the program order. Formally, we use the definition by Steinke and Nutt [8].

Definition 3.1 (Write-read-write Order [Steinke and Nutt [8]]). Given an execution with a writes-to relation $\mapsto$, two writes, $w^1 \in (\mathrm{w}, *, *, *)$ and $w^2 \in (\mathrm{w}, *, *, *)$, are ordered by *write-read-write order*, $(w^1, w^2) \in WO$, if there exists a read operation $r \in (\mathrm{r}, *, *, *)$ such that $w^1 \mapsto r <_{PO} w^2$.

Definition 3.2 (Causal Consistency [Steinke and Nutt [8]]). An execution is causally consistent if there exists a set of views $\mathcal{V} = \{V_i\}_{i \in P}$ such that, for every process i,

- V_i is a view on the set of operations $(*, i, *, *) \cup (\mathrm{w}, *, *, *)$, and
- V_i respects $WO \cup \big(PO|(*, i, *, *) \cup (\mathrm{w}, *, *, *)\big)$.

A shared memory Π is *causally consistent* if every execution run on Π is causally consistent.

Note that, by definition, each view V_i already respects the writes-to relation restricted to $(*, i, *, *) \cup (\mathrm{w}, *, *, *)$. Note also that read operations are only observed by the processes that perform them while write operations are observed by every process. We work with a version of causal consistency which we call *strong causal consistency*. This model is motivated by an implementation of causal consistency via lazy replication [5]. Ladin et. al. [5] use vector timestamps to ensure that a write operation w_i from process i is only committed locally when all write operations in w_i's history, as summarized by w_i's vector timestamp, have been observed. Formally, we define strong causal consistency as follows.

Definition 3.3 (Strong Causal Order). Given a set of views $\mathcal{V} = \{V_i\}_{i \in P}$, two writes, $w^1 \in (\mathrm{w}, *, *, *)$ and $w_i^2 \in (\mathrm{w}, i, *, *)$, are ordered by *strong causal order*, $(w^1, w_i^2) \in SCO(\mathcal{V})$, if $(w^1, w_i^2) \in V_i$.

Definition 3.4 (Strong Causal Consistency). An execution is *strongly causal consistent* if there exists a set of views $\mathcal{V} = \{V_i\}_{i \in P}$ such that, for every process i,

- V_i is a view on the set of operations $(*, i, *, *) \cup (\mathrm{w}, *, *, *)$, and
- V_i respects $SCO(\mathcal{V}) \cup \big(PO|(*, i, *, *) \cup (\mathrm{w}, *, *, *)\big)$.

A shared memory Π is *strongly causally consistent* if every execution run on Π is strongly causally consistent.

Observe that strong causal consistency does not violate the write-read-write order and thus it is at least as strong as causal consistency. In fact, it is strictly stronger than causal consistency, as shown in the full paper [4]. In this work we focus on optimal record for strong causal consistency.

4 RNR MODEL

For replaying executions, we assume that the per-process views are provided to the RnR system. The RnR system uses the views to determine the record. In case of online recording, the views are provided to the RnR system incrementally, as and when new operations occur that affect the views. Now let us illustrate how this requirement may be implemented in practice. Consider a shared memory implementation wherein each process has a copy of the shared variable and the shared memory is implemented via message passing. Then the shared memory adds a write operation to a process i's view when the local copy of the corresponding variable is updated at process i. Similarly a read by process i is added to process i's view when the local copy is read.

The RnR system will record some edges from each view (i.e. on each process) and the replay execution is only allowed views that enforce these records. Note that we do not place any restriction on how the record is enforced. We assume that any set of views can explain the replay as long as it extends the record and is consistent under the shared memory consistency model. Formally, given a set of views $\mathcal{V} = \{V_i\}_{i \in P}$, $\mathcal{R} = \{R_i\}_{i \in P}$ is a *record* of $\mathcal{V}$ if each $R_i \subseteq V_i$. An execution is a *replay* of $\mathcal{R}$ if there exists a set of views $\mathcal{V}' = \{V_i'\}_{i \in P}$ that explain the execution under the consistency model and each V_i' respects R_i. We say that $\mathcal{V}'$ *certifies* the replay to be valid for $\mathcal{R}$. A record $\mathcal{R}$ of a set of views $\mathcal{V}$ is *good* if, for any replay of $\mathcal{R}$, under the same consistency model, any set of views $\mathcal{V}' = \{V_i'\}_{i \in P}$ that certifies the replay to be valid for $\mathcal{R}$ must have $V_i' = V_i$ for all $i \in P$ (i.e. only $\mathcal{V}$ certifies the replay to be valid for $\mathcal{R}$). Note that for each record, there exists at least one replay, specifically the original execution.

5 OPTIMAL RECORD FOR STRONG CAUSAL CONSISTENCY

Offline Record

In this section we consider offline record for strong causal consistency. In this case the entire set of per-process views $\mathcal{V} = \{V_i\}_{i \in P}$

[1]The unique write values have a one-to-one correspondence with the unique identifiers of the respective write operations.

are made available to the RnR system. The RnR system determines the record that must be saved. We first present what edges do not need to be recorded. Consider a process i. Since PO is fixed and independent of executions the RnR system does not have to record these edges in V_i as they are guaranteed by the consistency model. Now consider two write operations $w^1 \in (\mathrm{w}, *, *, *)$ and $w_j^2 \in (\mathrm{w}, j, *, *)$, for $j \neq i$, such that $(w^1, w_j^2) \in SCO(\mathcal{V})$. If process j correctly orders the two operations (w^1, w_j^2) in the replay, then this edge will be guaranteed by the consistency model, due to strong causal order, and process i does not need to record it. Such edges are captured by the following definition.

Definition 5.1. Given a set of views $\mathcal{V} = \{V_i\}_{i \in P}$, the relation $SCO_i(\mathcal{V})$, for a process $i \in P$, is defined as follows. Two writes, $w^1 \in (\mathrm{w}, *, *, *)$ and $w_j^2 \in (\mathrm{w}, j, *, *)$, are ordered $(w^1, w_j^2) \in SCO_i(\mathcal{V})$, if $(w^1, w_j^2) \in SCO(\mathcal{V})$ and $j \neq i$.

The following set of edges also do not need to be recorded.

Definition 5.2. Given a set of views $\mathcal{V} = \{V_i\}_{i \in P}$, the relation $B_i(\mathcal{V})$, for a process $i \in P$, is defined as follows. Two writes, $w_i^1 \in (\mathrm{w}, i, *, *)$ and $w_j^2 \in (\mathrm{w}, j, *, *)$ such that $i \neq j$, are ordered $(w_i^1, w_j^2) \in B_i(\mathcal{V})$ if $(w_i^1, w_j^2) \in V_i$ and there exists a process $k \neq i, j$ such that $(w_i^1, w_j^2) \in V_k$.

In any set of views $\mathcal{V}'$ that explain a replay of $\mathcal{R}$, setting $(w_j^2, w_i^1) \in V_i'$ will create an $SCO(\mathcal{V}')$ edge (w_j^2, w_i^1) which will conflict with V_k'. Theorems 5.3 and 5.4 show that the record $\mathcal{R} = \{R_i\}_{i \in P}$ such that $R_i = \widehat{V}_i \setminus (SCO_i(\mathcal{V}) \cup PO \cup B_i(\mathcal{V}))$ is both sufficient and necessary for a correct replay under strong causal consistency.

THEOREM 5.3. *Given a set of views $\mathcal{V} = \{V_i\}_{i \in P}$ that explain a strongly causal consistent execution. For each process $i \in P$, let $R_i = \widehat{V}_i \setminus (SCO_i(\mathcal{V}) \cup PO \cup B_i(\mathcal{V}))$. Then, $\mathcal{R} = \{R_i\}_{i \in P}$ is a good record of $\mathcal{V}$.*

THEOREM 5.4. *Given a set of views $\mathcal{V} = \{V_i\}_{i \in P}$ that explain a strongly causal consistent execution. For any good record $\mathcal{R} = \{R_i\}_{i \in P}$ of $\mathcal{V}$, for any process $i \in P$ and any two operations $o^1, o^2 \in (*, i, *, *) \cup (\mathrm{w}, *, *, *)$, if $(o^1, o^2) \in \widehat{V}_i \setminus PO \cup SCO_i(\mathcal{V}) \cup B_i(\mathcal{V})$, then $(o^1, o^2) \in R_i$.*

Online Record

In the online setting each process has a fixed set of read and write operations $(*, i, *, *)$ that it executes in their local order $PO(i)$ by communicating with the shared memory. Executing an operation may take arbitrarily long and the process may spend arbitrarily long time to execute the next operation but each process only executes one operation at a time. Via the shared memory, a process i *observes* its own operations and write operations from other processes one at a time. The order in which these operations are observed give rise to the view V_i. More formally, the execution proceeds in time steps. At each time step in the execution, a unique[2] process i observes an operation from $(*, i, *, *) \cup (\mathrm{w}, *, *, *)$ and adds it to its view V_i.

The online record algorithm proceeds as follows. Suppose process i wants to record $(o^1, o^2) \in V_i$. Then, process i must record (o^1, o^2) at the time when it observes o^2. In the online setting, process i has limited information about views of other processes at any given time in the execution. How much does process i know? We assume that, at most, process i has access to the history of other processes brought with the observed operation. More precisely, at any time in the execution, if process i is *aware* that $(o^1, o^2) \in V_j$, for some process $j \neq i$, then process i must have already observed $o_j^3 \in (*, j, *, *)$ such that $o^1 <_{V_j} o^2 \leq_{V_j} o_j^3$. As discussed in Section 4, the recording proceeds without information about the internal workings of the shared memory. However, we assume that the RnR system is aware of the shared memory guarantees. More precisely, for strong causal consistency, we assume that any process i can check if $(o^1, o^2) \in SCO(\mathcal{V})$ and also if $(o^1, o^2) \in PO$. For a given execution $\mathcal{V} = \{V_i\}_{i \in P}$, we say that a record $\mathcal{R} = \{R_i\}_{i \in P}$ is an *online record* of $\mathcal{V}$ if $\mathcal{R}$ can be recorded in this manner.

Theorems 5.5 and 5.6 state that for each process i, $R_i = \widehat{V}_i \setminus (SCO_i(\mathcal{V}) \cup PO)$ is both sufficient and necessary in the online setting.

THEOREM 5.5. *Given a set of views $\mathcal{V} = \{V_i\}_{i \in P}$ that explain a strongly causal consistent execution. For each process $i \in P$, let $R_i = \widehat{V}_i \setminus (SCO_i(\mathcal{V}) \cup PO)$. Then, $\mathcal{R} = \{R_i\}_{i \in P}$ is a good* ***online*** *record of $\mathcal{V}$.*

THEOREM 5.6. *Given a set of views $\mathcal{V} = \{V_i\}_{i \in P}$ that explain a strongly causal consistent execution. For any good* ***online*** *record $\mathcal{R} = \{R_i\}_{i \in P}$ of $\mathcal{V}$, for any process $i \in P$ and any two operations $o^1, o^2 \in (*, i, *, *) \cup (\mathrm{w}, *, *, *)$, if $(o^1, o^2) \in \widehat{V}_i \setminus PO \cup SCO_i(\mathcal{V})$, then $(o^1, o^2) \in R_i$.*

6 SUMMARY

In this brief announcement we have stated our results for the optimal record for RnR under strong causal consistency. The full paper [4] contains more details and proofs. The optimal record for causal consistency is still an open problem.

REFERENCES

[1] George W. Dunlap, Dominic G. Lucchetti, Michael A. Fetterman, and Peter M. Chen. 2008. Execution Replay of Multiprocessor Virtual Machines. In *Proceedings of the Fourth ACM SIGPLAN/SIGOPS International Conference on Virtual Execution Environments (VEE '08)*. ACM, New York, NY, USA, 121–130. https://doi.org/10.1145/1346256.1346273

[2] Nima Honarmand and Josep Torrellas. 2014. RelaxReplay: Record and Replay for Relaxed-consistency Multiprocessors. *SIGARCH Comput. Archit. News* 42, 1 (Feb. 2014), 223–238. https://doi.org/10.1145/2654822.2541979

[3] Russell Llewellyn Jones. 2016. *Record and Replay under Relaxed Consistency.* Master's thesis. University of Illinois at Urbana-Champaign. http://hdl.handle.net/2142/92729

[4] Russell L. Jones, Muhammad S. Khan, and Nitin H. Vaidya. 2018. Optimal Record and Replay under Causal Consistency. In *arXiv: to be submitted.*

[5] Rivka Ladin, Barbara Liskov, Liuba Shrira, and Sanjay Ghemawat. 1992. Providing High Availability Using Lazy Replication. *ACM Trans. Comput. Syst.* 10, 4 (Nov. 1992), 360–391. https://doi.org/10.1145/138873.138877

[6] Dongyoon Lee, Benjamin Wester, Kaushik Veeraraghavan, Satish Narayanasamy, Peter M. Chen, and Jason Flinn. 2010. Respec: Efficient Online Multiprocessor Replayvia Speculation and External Determinism. *SIGPLAN Not.* 45, 3 (March 2010), 77–90. https://doi.org/10.1145/1735971.1736031

[7] Robert H. B. Netzer. 1993. Optimal Tracing and Replay for Debugging Shared-memory Parallel Programs. *SIGPLAN Not.* 28, 12 (Dec. 1993), 1–11. https://doi.org/10.1145/174267.174268

[8] Robert C. Steinke and Gary J. Nutt. 2004. A Unified Theory of Shared Memory Consistency. *J. ACM* 51, 5 (Sept. 2004), 800–849. https://doi.org/10.1145/1017460.1017464

[2] Uniqueness of the process makes the model simpler. If more than one process observes an operation at a given time step, we can separate this into multiple time steps ordered by the process identifiers.

Brief Announcement: MUSIC: Multi-Site Entry Consistency for Geo-Distributed Services

Bharath Balasubramanian
ATT Labs Research
bharathb@research.att.com

Richard Schlichting
ATT Labs Research
rick.schlichting@gmail.com

Pamela Zave
Princeton University
pamela@pamelazave.com

ABSTRACT

Geo-distributed services that are executed across multiple sites at a global scale are increasingly prevalent, and are at the core of the control plane tasked with managing the Virtual Network Functions (VNFs) of next-generation network infrastructure. A key building block of any replicated service of this type is logically shared state, an abstraction that is often implemented by having multiple copies of each data element and using one of any number of distributed protocols to enforce consistency with guarantees ranging from eventual to causal to sequential consistency. These solutions fail to meet the real needs of geo-distributed services found in a VNF control plane (and elsewhere), which are to provide guarantees strong enough to be useful, yet still efficiently implementable in a global network with larger latencies and a wider range of failure modes. Here, we propose a new solution to state consistency based on extending *entry consistency*, a paradigm originally developed for failure-free multi-processor systems, for use in geo-distributed services with failures. We outline the challenges associated with state consistency in such services, and describe a data-store called MUSIC (MUlti-SIte entry Consistency) that combines an eventually consistent key-value store with locking primitives to implement entry-consistent semantics.

ACM Reference format:
Bharath Balasubramanian, Richard Schlichting, and Pamela Zave. 2018. Brief Announcement: MUSIC: Multi-Site Entry Consistency for Geo-Distributed Services. In *Proceedings of ACM Symposium on Principles of Distributed Computing, July 23–27, 2018, Egham, UK., (PODC '18)*, 3 pages.
DOI: http://dx.doi.org/10.1145/3212734.3212782

1 MOTIVATION AND OVERVIEW

Network Service Providers are currently transitioning from infrastructures based on hardware appliances to virtualized infrastructures that use Virtual Network Functions (VNFs) to reduce costs and enhance flexibility. These new infrastructures are global, with VNFs being deployed worldwide in sites ranging from customer premises, cell towers, and central offices to full-fledged data centers. Managing such a geo-distributed infrastructure is challenging, and requires that the *VNF control plane* itself be distributed on a global scale. This control plane is a platform consisting of various software components that manage the design, deployment, and execution of VNFs on the virtualized infrastructure, and is exemplified by the Open Network Automation Platform (ONAP) [1].

This paper focuses on simplifying the complexity of these platform components, and in particular, on the consistency requirements for shared state across *geo-distributed services* that are executed in multiple sites connected by wide-area networks. As an example, consider the *VNF homing service* in ONAP, which uses optimization techniques to find suitable sites on which to deploy complex VNFs [2]. The location or "home" of a VNF is chosen based on application contraints and hardware requirements. For reliability, availability, and quick response this service is replicated across multiple sites around the world, and a VNF homing request (with constraints) is typically submitted to the closest replica. Homing itself is a multi-step process that can take on the order of seconds, involving communication with several resource databases and execution of optimization algorithms. To maintain the appropriate semantics, such a system must ensure that: (i) at most one replica is working on an incomplete deployment request, and (ii) in case of replica failure, another replica can take over and continue an incomplete deployment request from the last known state.

Realizing these constraints requires logically shared state for consistent decision-making among replicas. This state—often implemented by having copies of data on different machines—is typically based on the use of technologies such as a database or key-value store [3, 4], a coordination service and its underlying state primitives built on Paxos [5], and/or a paradigm such as state machine replication (SMR) [6]. Associated with a given solution are consistency guarantees, examples of which include eventual consistency [7], causal consistency [8] and sequential consistency [9]. In general, each type of consistency represents a given point in the spectrum of trade-offs between the strength of the guarantees and the efficiency of the implementation.

Our experience is that most common solutions for maintaining logical state consistency are not well suited to the geo-distributed services found in a VNF control plane and elsewhere. The fundamental issue is that they fail to provide guarantees that are strong enough to be useful, yet can still be implemented efficiently in a global network with its larger latencies and wider range of failure modes, including partitioned behaviors. Our contention is that a new solution is needed that addresses the fundamental trade-off between consistency guarantees and efficiency in a different way, one that is more aligned with the needs of a geo-distributed service.

Here, we propose a state-consistency solution for geo-distributed services based on *entry consistency*. As originally defined [10], entry consistency specifies that data shared among multiple processors becomes consistent at a processor only when it acquires a synchronization object (e.g., lock) that guards the data, and only the data known to be guarded by the acquired object is guaranteed to be consistent. For geo-distributed services the semantics of entry

PODC '18, July 23–27, 2018, Egham, UK.

978-1-4503-5795-1/18/07..
DOI: http://dx.doi.org/10.1145/3212734.3212782

consistency must be extended, most importantly to account for failures. Our claim is that entry consistency is an effective and elegant abstraction of the state consistency needed for geo-distributed services. For example, in the homing service, the details and progress of each request can be maintained in an entry-consistent store. A service replica must acquire the lock for a homing request before working on it, which ensures exclusive access and atomic progress updates. If the lock holder for a request fails and another replica takes over, it is guaranteed to see the latest version of request state.

We realize this approach through a key-value store called MUSIC (MUlti-SIte entry Consistency), that combines an eventually consistent data store with locking primitives to implement entry-consistent semantics. Our core contributions have been to address the following intertwined key challenges, in the following ways:

Failure semantics. The original definition of entry consistency does not consider failures, yet node and network failures are sure to affect geo-distributed services. We define the semantics of an entry consistent store for geo-distributed services that incorporates failures of store replicas, failures of service replicas (clients of the store), and failures of network connections between replica pairs. Further, we formally model these semantics in Alloy [11].

Imperfect failure detection. It is difficult in geo-distributed services to distinguish between a failed node and one that is slow or unreachable. When we preempt a lock holder on suspicion of failure, we face the possibility that the lock holder is still alive and will attempt to modify state that is now locked for another client. Guaranteeing entry consistency in such scenarios presents challenges that go beyond current solutions for fault-tolerant lock services [12, 13]. These challenges are addressed directly with a new algorithm that has been formally verified by model-checking with the Alloy Analyzer [14].

Performance and availability. Synchronization objects of the type needed for entry consistency are typically built using consensus protocols that involve multiple rounds of communication across a quorum of replicas [13]. Higher latencies and network partitions make these protocols difficult to implement in wide-area networks [15]. We restrict the use of consensus to entries/exits of critical sections; during a critical section there can be thousands of reads and writes implemented by single-round quorum operations.

2 ENTRY CONSISTENCY FOR GEO-DISTRIBUTED SERVICES

Our system model assumes a distributed system of nodes that communicate using messages. To overcome the impossibility of distributed consensus in asynchronous systems [16], like most practical systems, we assume partial synchrony [17, 18] to achieve consensus, where there are sufficient periods of communication synchrony with an upper bound on message delay. Nodes can suffer crash failures [19], which implies that a node cannot distinguish between a failed node and one that is slow to respond and/or unable to communicate. The latter is relatively common in geo-distributed systems where failures in communication links [20, 21] can render a node partitioned from some subset of other nodes in the system.

Our model of an entry-consistent store is based on a replicated key-value store, where reads and writes to the key value (shared state) by a client are controlled using locks. In this key-value store, the semantics of replication is that a key has a single correct value determined by the rule "last write wins", based on the time-stamp associated with each write. The entry-consistent store provides the following properties:

Locking. To read or write to a set of keys, a client first acquires a lock to the keys, and the lock holder is guaranteed a consistent version that reflects the most recent updates to the keys. There can only be one lock holder for each key in the set, and no other client can acquire a lock to a key in the set until the current lock holder releases its lock. Granting of a lock is fair.

Critical operations. On acquiring a lock, the lock holder enters a *critical section.* When the lock holder performs reads and writes to the locked keys—called *critical operations*—other writers are excluded and the operations are sequentially consistent so that all reads and writes are totally ordered.

Failures. Critical operations must succeed on at least a quorum of replicas that are alive and reachable. If a client detects failure of a store replica during an operation, it can retry the operation using another store replica. If a lock-holding client fails in a critical section the entry-consistent store forcibly releases the lock and grants it to the next client in line. If there was an incomplete *criticalPut* operation in progress at the time of the forced release, it is either completed or completely aborted (the choice of which is nondeterministic). After a forced release, even if failure detection was wrong and the former lock holder is still alive, its attempts to perform critical operations will fail.

Note that entry consistency in multi-processor systems [10, 22] is focused only on the first property above. Since failures are not considered in these systems, the third property is irrelevant and the second property is taken for granted, i.e., the processor that owns the lock writes to its local cache, which is always assumed to be propagated reliably to other processors.

MUSIC implements an entry-consistent data store with these semantics, along with a collection of operations and an API oriented around locks and critical sections. Figure 1 summarizes these operations and highlights how they can be used to build a MUSIC critical section. To illustrate further, we outline two production use cases from the ONAP VNF control plane: VNF homing (from above) and service orchestration.

VNF homing: A job scheduler with consistent failover. The VNF homing use case presented above is an example of the job-scheduler paradigm where workers (homing service replicas) vie for jobs (requests). Previous systems that support this design pattern use distributed agreement on *each update to shared state* [23–25]. For example, [25] maintains all state in Zookeeper [5], where each write uses for distributed consensus. In contrast, MUSIC is carefully tailored for multiple sites and restricts distributed consensus to critical section entry and exit, with updates to the shared state done using single-round quorum operations. Specifically, this use-case can easily be realized using the operations from Figure 1, as follows. First, a new homing request is entered into MUSIC using a *createPut* with a unique key/id for this job. Next, a service replica vying for the right to handle this request attempts to acquire the appropriate lock using the sequence *createLockRef* and *acquireLock* over the job id. On successfully entering the critical section, the service replica does the actual work, while regularly updating the job state

Core MUSIC Operations necessary for entry consistency	
createPut (key)	Creates the key in the MUSIC store and a queue associated with it to maintain lock requests for the key **[local write]**
lockRef = createLockRef (key)	Returns a lockRef to the key, which is a unique monotonically increasing identifier that is good for one critical section only. The lockRef is pushed into the queue for the key. **[single paxos write]**
result = acquireLock (lockRef):	Returns true only to the lockRef at the top of the queue for the key. During normal operation **[local read]**, on failure-detected transfer (rare) **[single quorum read + write]**
criticalPut (key, lockRef, value)	Enabled only for the current lock holder of the key, this updates the value of the key at a quorum of MUSIC replicas. **[local read + single quorum write]**
value = criticalGet (key, lockRef)	Enabled only for the current lock holder of the key, this returns the latest the value of the key from a quorum of MUSIC replicas. **[local read+ single quorum read]**
releaseLock (lockRef)	Removes the lockRef from the queue for the key. **[local read + single paxos write]**
Supplementary MUSIC Operations for practical use-cases	
value = get (key)	Returns value of the key at the local MUSIC replica.
put (non-critical-key, value)	Updates value of the key at local MUSIC replica. Only enabled for keys on which no critical operations will be attempted.

```
//Example of a MUSIC critical section
createPut(key);
lockRef = createLockRef (key);
while (acquireLock (lockRef) != true)
    skip;
//critical section
v1 = criticalGet(lockRef, key);
v1`= v1+1;
criticalPut(lockRef, key, v1`);
releaseLock(lockRef);

//Example of non critical
  MUSIC operations
v1 = get(non-critical-key);
v1`=v1+1;
put(non-critical-key, v1`);
```

Figure 1: MUSIC operations and an implementation of a critical section.

by using *criticalPut*. The lock to the job is released upon critical section exit using *releaseLock*.

Service orchestration: Active replication with mixed consistency. While the ONAP homing service described above finds suitable sites to deploy VNFs, the ONAP master service orchestrator (MSO) is responsible for the actual instantiation, release, and subsequent migration and relocation of these VNFs [26]. MSO is deployed in active-active mode, where multiple service replicas process orchestration requests. However, since the underlying cloud and network resources are shared, the replicas need strongly consistent shared state to prevent duplicate allocation of physical resources. MSO's data model consists of over forty tables (shared state), of which only ten read/write information related to resource consumption. To achieve good performance without compromising correctness, these ten tables can be replicated with entry consistency, while the other tables can be replicated with high-performance eventual consistency. So reads and writes to any row among these ten tables can be done in a MUSIC critical section using the *criticalGet* and *criticalPut* operations, while the MUSIC *get* and *put* operations (that do not require locking) are sufficient for the other tables. Other solutions for mixed consistency [27, 28] often require rigorous static checking or complicated runtime conflict resolution protocols.

REFERENCES

[1] "Open network automation platform (onap)." https://www.onap.org/.
[2] "Onap homing and allocation service." https://wiki.onap.org/pages/viewpage.action?pageId=16005528.
[3] A. Lakshman and P. Malik, "Cassandra: a decentralized structured storage system," *ACM SIGOPS Operating Systems Review*, vol. 44, no. 2, pp. 35–40, 2010.
[4] K. Chodorow and M. Dirolf, *MongoDB: The Definitive Guide*. O'Reilly Media, Inc., 1st ed., 2010.
[5] P. Hunt, M. Konar, F. P. Junqueira, and B. Reed, "Zookeeper: Wait-free coordination for internet-scale systems," in *USENIX Annual Technical Conference*, vol. 8, p. 9, 2010.
[6] F. B. Schneider, "Implementing fault-tolerant services using the state machine approach: A tutorial," *ACM Comput. Surv.*, vol. 22, pp. 299–319, Dec. 1990.
[7] G. DeCandia, D. Hastorun, M. Jampani, G. Kakulapati, A. Lakshman, A. Pilchin, S. Sivasubramanian, P. Vosshall, and W. Vogels, "Dynamo: amazon's highly available key-value store," in *ACM SIGOPS Operating Systems Review*, vol. 41, pp. 205–220, ACM, 2007.
[8] W. Lloyd, M. J. Freedman, M. Kaminsky, and D. G. Andersen, "Don't settle for eventual: scalable causal consistency for wide-area storage with cops," in *Proceedings of the 23rd ACM Symposium on Operating Systems Principles (SOSP)*, pp. 401–416, ACM, 2011.
[9] L. Lamport, "How to make a multiprocessor computer that correctly executes multiprocess programs," *IEEE Trans. Comput.*, vol. 28, pp. 690–691, Sept. 1979.
[10] B. N. Bershad, M. J. Zekauskas, and W. A. Sawdon, "The midway distributed shared memory system," in *Digest of Papers. Compcon Spring*, pp. 528–537, Feb 1993.
[11] D. Jackson, *Software Abstractions: Logic, Language, and Analysis*. MIT Press, 2006, 2012.
[12] M. Burrows, "The chubby lock service for loosely-coupled distributed systems," in *Proceedings of the 7th Symposium on Operating Systems Design and Implementation(OSDI)*, pp. 335–350, 2006.
[13] T. D. Chandra, R. Griesemer, and J. Redstone, "Paxos made live: an engineering perspective," in *Proceedings of the 26th Annual ACM Symposium on Principles of Distributed Computing (PODC)*, pp. 398–407, ACM, 2007.
[14] "Alloy." http://alloytools.org.
[15] K. Lev-Ari, E. Bortnikov, I. Keidar, and A. Shraer, "Modular composition of coordination services," in *USENIX Annual Technical Conference (ATC)*, 2016.
[16] M. J. Fischer, N. A. Lynch, and M. S. Paterson, "Impossibility of distributed consensus with one faulty process," *J. ACM*, vol. 32, pp. 374–382, Apr. 1985.
[17] D. Dolev, C. Dwork, and L. Stockmeyer, "On the minimal synchronism needed for distributed consensus," *J. ACM*, vol. 34, pp. 77–97, Jan. 1987.
[18] C. Dwork, N. Lynch, and L. Stockmeyer, "Consensus in the presence of partial synchrony," *J. ACM*, vol. 35, pp. 288–323, Apr. 1988.
[19] N. A. Lynch, *Distributed Algorithms*. San Francisco, CA, USA: Morgan Kaufmann Publishers Inc., 1996.
[20] "The network is reliable: An informal survey of real-world communications failures." http://www.bailis.org/papers/partitions-queue2014.pdf.
[21] P. Deutsch, "The eight fallacies of distributed computing," *URL: http://today.java.net/jag/Fallacies. html*, 2004.
[22] L. Iftode, J. P. Singh, and K. Li, "Scope consistency: A bridge between release consistency and entry consistency," in *Proceedings of the Eighth Annual ACM Symposium on Parallel Algorithms and Architectures*, SPAA '96, (New York, NY, USA), pp. 277–287, ACM, 1996.
[23] D. E. Bakken and R. D. Schlichting, "Supporting fault-tolerant parallel programming in linda," *IEEE Transactions on Parallel and Distributed Systems*, vol. 6, pp. 287–302, Mar 1995.
[24] A. N. Bessani, E. P. Alchieri, M. Correia, and J. S. Fraga, "Depspace: A byzantine fault-tolerant coordination service," in *Proceedings of the 3rd ACM SIGOPS/EuroSys European Conference on Computer Systems 2008*, Eurosys '08, (New York, NY, USA), pp. 163–176, ACM, 2008.
[25] T. Distler, C. Bahn, A. Bessani, F. Fischer, and F. Junqueira, "Extensible distributed coordination," in *Proceedings of the Tenth European Conference on Computer Systems*, EuroSys '15, (New York, NY, USA), pp. 10:1–10:16, ACM, 2015.
[26] "Onap service orchestrator." https://wiki.onap.org/pages/viewpage.action?pageId=1015834.
[27] C. Li, D. Porto, A. Clement, J. Gehrke, N. Preguiça, and R. Rodrigues, "Making geo-replicated systems fast as possible, consistent when necessary," in *Proceedings of the 10th USENIX Symposium on Operating Systems Design and Implementation (OSDI)*, pp. 265–278, USENIX, 2012.
[28] V. Balegas, S. Duarte, C. Ferreira, R. Rodrigues, N. Preguiça, M. Najafzadeh, and M. Shapiro, "Putting consistency back into eventual consistency," in *Proceedings of the 10th European Conference on Computer Systems (EuroSys)*, pp. 6:1–6:16, 2015.

Silence

Guy Goren
Viterbi Faculty of Electrical Engineering, Technion
Haifa, Israel
sgoren@campus.technion.ac.il

Yoram Moses
Viterbi Faculty of Electrical Engineering, Technion
Haifa, Israel
moses@ee.technion.ac.il

ABSTRACT

The cost of communication is a substantial factor affecting the scalability of many distributed applications. Every message sent can incur a cost in storage, computation, energy and bandwidth. Consequently, reducing the communication costs of distributed applications is highly desirable. The best way to reduce message costs is by communicating without sending any messages whatsoever. This paper initiates a rigorous investigation into the use of silence in synchronous settings, in which processes can fail. We formalize sufficient conditions for information transfer using silence, as well as necessary conditions for particular cases of interest. This allows us to identify message patterns that enable communication through silence. In particular, a pattern called a *silent choir* is identified, and shown to be central to information transfer via silence in failure-prone systems. The power of the new framework is demonstrated on the *atomic commitment* problem (AC). A complete characterization of the tradeoff between message complexity and round complexity in the synchronous model with crash failures is provided, in terms of lower bounds and matching protocols. In particular, a new message-optimal AC protocol is designed using silence, in which processes decide in 3 rounds in the common case. This significantly improves on the best previously known message-optimal AC protocol, in which decisions were performed in $\Theta(n)$ rounds.

And in the naked light I saw
Ten thousand people, maybe more
People talking without speaking
...
And no one dared
Disturb the sound of silence

Paul Simon, 1964

CCS CONCEPTS

• **Theory of computation → Distributed computing models**; **Distributed algorithms**; • **Computing methodologies → Reasoning about belief and knowledge**; **Distributed algorithms**; *Multi-agent systems*; • **Networks →** *Network protocol design*;

The work of the first author was supported in part by a grant from the Technion Hiroshi Fujiwara cyber security research center and the Israel cyber bureau. Yoram Moses is the Israel Pollak academic chair at the Technion.

PODC '18, July 23–27, 2018, Egham, United Kingdom

ACM ISBN 978-1-4503-5795-1/18/07...$15.00
https://doi.org/10.1145/3212734.3212768

KEYWORDS

Silent information exchange; null messages; silent choir; atomic commitment; consensus; optimality; fault-tolerance; knowledge.

ACM Reference Format:
Guy Goren and Yoram Moses. 2018. Silence. In *PODC '18: ACM Symposium on Principles of Distributed Computing, July 23–27, 2018, Egham, United Kingdom.* ACM, New York, NY, USA, 10 pages. https://doi.org/10.1145/3212734.3212768

1 INTRODUCTION

The cost of communication is a substantial factor limiting the scalability of many distributed applications (see, e.g. [20, 21, 25, 27, 29]). Indeed, sending a message imposes costs in storage, computation, energy and bandwidth. Consequently, reducing the communication costs of distributed applications is highly desirable. The best way to reduce these costs is by communicating without sending any messages whatsoever. In reliable synchronous systems processes can exchange information in silence, effectively "*sending a message by not sending a message*," to use a term from [22]. In fault-prone systems, however, using silence in this way is considerably more subtle. Roughly speaking, in a reliable system in which messages from j to i are guaranteed to be delivered within Δ time units, if j sends no message to i at time t, then i is able to detect this fact at time $t + \Delta$. This, in turn, can be used to pass information from j to i. In a setting in which j may fail, however, it is possible for i not to receive j's message because j failed in some way.

Given the value of reducing communication costs and the power of silence to do so, efficient protocols for a variety of tasks of interest make effective, albeit implicit, use of silence (see, e.g., [1, 2, 4, 9, 15, 18, 26]). There is no clear theory underlying this use of silence, however. This paper initiates a rigorous investigation into the use of silence in synchronous settings in which processes can fail. We formalize sufficient conditions for information transfer using silence, as well as necessary conditions for particular cases of interest. This allows us to identify message patterns that enable silent communication.

Using the proposed framework, we consider the *atomic commitment* problem (AC) in synchronous systems with crash failures [5, 12] as a case study. A silence-based analysis provides new lower bounds on the efficiency of AC protocols that are optimal in the common case. The conditions identified for using silence are then used to provide protocols that match the lower bounds. In some cases, the new protocols significantly improve the state-of-the-art.

The main contributions of this paper are:

- Simple rules for silent information transfer in the presence of failures are provided and formalized.
- The *Silent Choir* Theorem, which precisely captures the communication patterns required for silence to convey information about the initial values, is proven. In failure-prone systems, a silent choir plays the role that null messages play in reliable systems, facilitating communication via silence.

- Using a silence-based analysis, lower bounds are established on the number of messages needed for AC protocols to decide in D rounds in the common case, for any given $D \geq 1$.
- Silent information transfer rules are used to design protocols that prove these bounds to be tight, thereby completely characterizing the tradeoff between the message complexity and round complexity of AC. For the most interesting case of message-optimal AC, we present the STEALTH protocol, which reduces the decision times from $\Theta(n)$ to $\Theta(1)$ rounds (in fact, from $n + 2f$ to 3).

This paper is organized as follows. The next section introduces our model of computation, and formal definitions of indistinguishability, knowledge and AC. Section 3 formalizes how silence can be used to convey information in fault-prone synchronous message-passing systems. In Section 4 lower bounds and upper bounds for optimal AC in the common case are established. Finally, concluding remarks are discussed in Section 5.

2 DEFINITIONS AND PRELIMINARY RESULTS

2.1 Atomic Commitment

In the atomic commitment problem [5, 12, 15, 16], each process j starts out with a binary initial value $v_j \in \{0, 1\}$. Processes need to decide among two actions, commit or abort. All runs of an AC protocol are required to satisfy the following conditions:

ATOMIC COMMITMENT:

Decision: Every correct process must eventually decide either commit or abort,

Agreement: All processes that decide make the same decision,

Commit Validity: A process can decide commit only if all initial values are 1, and

Abort Validity: A process can decide abort only if some initial value is 0, or if some process failed.

The AC problem is motivated by distributed databases, in which the processes are involved in performing a joint transaction. An initial value of 0 can correspond to a vote to abort the transaction, while 1 is a vote to commit the transaction. Typically, processes enter the AC protocol with a vote to commit, and failures in runs of AC are rare. We call a run in which all initial values are 1 and no failures occur, a *nice* run. As first advocated by [12], it is sensible to seek AC protocols that are optimized for the common case, i.e., for nice runs. Natural parameters to optimize are the number of messages sent in nice runs, and the number of rounds required for decision, and for halting. We call an AC protocol that sends the fewest possible messages in nice runs *message optimal*, and one that decides the soonest *round optimal*. In a recent paper [15], Guerraoui and Wang present a message-optimal AC protocol. It uses $n + f - 1$ messages in nice runs (for a system with n processes and up to f crash failures). But this message efficiency seems to come at a cost in terms of decision time: processes decide in nice runs only at the end of $n + 2f$ rounds. This raises an interesting open problem of identifying the tradeoff between message complexity and decision time, for AC protocols in the common case.

2.2 Model of Computation

We consider the standard synchronous message-passing model with benign crash failures. We assume a set $\mathbb{P} = \{0, 1, \ldots, n-1\}$ of $n > 2$ processes. Each pair of processes is connected by a two-way communication link, and for each message the receiver knows the identity of the sender. All processes share a discrete global clock that starts at time 0 and advances by increments of one. Communication in the system proceeds in a sequence of *rounds*, with round $m + 1$ taking place between time m and time $m + 1$, for $m \geq 0$. A message sent at time m (i.e., in round $m + 1$) from a process i to j will reach j by time $m + 1$, i.e., the end of round $m + 1$. In every round, each process performs local computations, sends a set of messages to other processes, and finally receives messages sent to it by other processes during the same round. A faulty process in a given execution fails by *crashing* in some round $m \geq 1$. In this case, the process behaves correctly in the first $m - 1$ rounds and it performs no actions and sends no messages from round $m + 1$ on. During its crashing round m, the process sends messages to an arbitrary subset among the processes to whom the protocol prescribes that it send messages in round m. It does not take any decisions at the end of its crashing round (i.e., at time m). As is customary in agreement problems such as Consensus, we shall assume that each process i starts at time 0 in some *initial state*, which can be assumed for simplicity in this paper to consist of its *initial value* $v_i \in \{0, 1\}$.

At any given time $m \geq 0$, a process is in a well-defined ***local state***. For simplicity, we assume that the local state of a process i consists of its initial value v_i, the current time m, and the sequence of the actions that i has performed (including the messages it has sent and received) up to that time. In particular, its local state at time 0 has the form $(v_i, 0, \{\})$. We will also assume that once a process has crashed, its local state becomes $\perp$. A ***protocol*** describes what messages a process sends and what decisions it takes, as a deterministic function of its local state.

We will consider the design of protocols that are required to withstand up to f crashes. Thus, given $1 \leq f < n$, we denote by γ^f the model described above in which it is guaranteed that no more than f processes fail in any given run. We assume that a protocol $\mathcal{P}$ has access to the values of n and f, typically passed to $\mathcal{P}$ as parameters.

A ***run*** is a description of a (possibly infinite) execution of the system. We call a set of runs R a ***system***. We will be interested in systems of the form $R_{\mathcal{P}} = R(\mathcal{P}, \gamma^f)$ consisting of all runs of a given protocol $\mathcal{P}$ in which no more than f processes fail. Observe that a protocol $\mathcal{P}$ solves AC in the model γ^f if and only if every run of $R_{\mathcal{P}}$ satisfies the Decision, Agreement and two Validity conditions described above. Given a run r and a time m, we denote the local state of process i at time m in run r by $r_i(m)$. Notice that a process i can be in the same local state in different runs of the same protocol. Since the current time m is represented in the local state $r_i(m)$, however, $r(m) = r'(m')$ can hold only if $m = m'$.

2.3 Indistinguishability and Knowledge

We shall say that two runs r and r' are *indistinguishable* to process i at time m if $r_i(m) = r'_i(m)$. We denote this by $r \approx_i^m r'$. Notice that since we assume that processes follow deterministic protocols, if $r \approx_i^m r'$ then process i is guaranteed to perform the same actions at time m in both r and r'. Problem specifications typically impose restrictions on actions, based on properties of the run. Moreover, since the actions that a process performs are a function of its local state, the restrictions can depend on properties of other runs as well.

For example, the Agreement condition in AC implies that a process i cannot decide to commit at time m in a run r if there is an indistinguishable run $r' \approx_i^m r$ in which some process decides abort. Similarly, by Commit Validity a process i can not commit if there is a run r' that is indistinguishable from r (to i at time m) in which one of the initial values is 0. Similarly, by Abort Validity i can not abort at time m if there exists a nice run $r' \approx_i^m r$ (i.e., all initial values are 1 and no failure occurs in r'). These examples illustrate how indistinguishability can inhibit actions — performing an action can be prohibited because of what may be true at indistinguishable runs.

Rather than considering when actions are prohibited, we can choose to consider what is required in order for an action to be allowed by the specification. To this end, we can view Commit Validity as implying that process i is allowed to perform commit at time m in r only if all initial values are 1 in every run $r' \approx_i^m r$. This is much stronger than stating that all values are 1 only in the run r itself, of course. Roughly speaking, the stronger statement is true because at time m process i cannot tell whether it is in r or in any of the runs $r' \approx_i^m r$. When this condition holds, we say that i *knows* that all values are 1. Generally, it will be convenient to define the dual of indistinguishability, i.e., what is true at all indistinguishable runs, as what the process knows. More formally, following in the spirit of [13, 19], we proceed to define knowledge in our distributed systems as follows.[1]

We shall focus on knowledge of facts that correspond to properties of runs. We call these *facts about the run*, and denote them by φ, ψ, etc. In particular, facts such as "$v_j = 1$" (j's initial value is 1), "*j is faulty*" (in the current run), and "*j decides* commit" (in the current run), are all examples of facts about the run.

Definition 1 (Knowledge). *Fix a system R, a run $r \in R$, a process i and a fact φ. We say that $K_i\varphi$ (which we read as "process i **knows** φ") holds at time m in r iff φ is true of all runs $r' \in R$ such that $r' \approx_i^m r$.*

Notice that knowledge is defined with respect to a given system R. Often, the system is clear from context and is not stated explicitly. Definition 1 immediately implies the so-called *Knowledge property*: If $K_i\varphi$ holds at (any) time m in r, then r satisfies φ.

We use Boolean operators such as $\neg$ (Not), $\wedge$ (And), and $\vee$ (Or) freely in the sequel. While the basic facts φ, ψ, etc. of interest are properties of the run, knowledge can change over time. Thus, for example, $K_i(v_j = 0)$ may be false at time m in a run r and true at time $m+1$, based perhaps on messages that i does or does not receive in round $m + 1$.

A recent paper [28] provides an essential connection between knowledge and action in distributed protocols called the ***knowledge of preconditions principle*** (KoP). It states that whatever must be true when a particular action is performed by a process i must be known by i when the action is performed. This is one way of capturing the role of indistinguishability discussed above. More formally, we say that a fact φ is a ***necessary condition*** for an action α in a system R if for all runs $r \in R$ and times m, if α is performed at time m in r then φ must be true at time m in r. For deterministic protocols in synchronous models such as γ^f, the KoP can be stated as follows:

[1] We introduce just enough of the theory of knowledge to support the analysis performed in this paper. For more details, see [13].

Theorem 1 (KoP, [28]). *Fix a protocol $\mathcal{P}$ for γ^f, let $i \in \mathbb{P}$ and let α be an action of i in $R_{\mathcal{P}}$. If φ is a necessary condition for α in $R_{\mathcal{P}}$ then $K_i\varphi$ is a necessary condition for α in $R_{\mathcal{P}}$.*

We denote the fact that all initial values are 1 by `all[1]`. Since `all[1]` is a necessary condition for performing commit in AC, Theorem 1 immediately implies the following, which will be useful in our analysis of AC in Section 4:

Corollary 1 (Hadzilacos [16]). *When a process i commits in a run of an AC protocol, it must know* `all[1]` *(in particular, $K_i(v_j = 1)$ must hold for every process j).*

Hadzilacos [16] is a very elegant paper that was the first to apply knowledge theory to the study of commitment problems.

3 SILENCE IN THE PRESENCE OF CRASHES

In a reliable setting, we can intuitively describe information transfer via silence as follows (we formalize the rules **S1—S3** in Section 3.1):

S1. Silent inference from a reliable source: Suppose that a process j is guaranteed to send i a message at time t in case some condition φ of interest *is false*. If, by time $t + \Delta$, process i has not received a message that j sent to i at time t, then i can infer that φ holds.

In fact, extensive use of silence can achieve an even greater effect. Suppose that the proper operation of a synchronous system depends on the truth of local conditions φ_j, for different processes j. In this case, all nodes of the system can be informed that all conditions hold simply if no process reports a violation of its local condition. Effectively, this achieves a (silent) broadcast from each process to all processes, at no cost.

Notice that silence can be informative only in case there are alternative circumstances (e.g., when φ does not hold) under which a message would be received by i. Thus, in a precise sense, the use of silence can serve to shift the communication costs among scenarios. This can be especially useful for optimizing the behavior of protocols in cases of interest. Most popular is optimization for the common case (often referred to as *fast path/slow path* protocols) in which a protocol is designed to be very efficient in the common case, at the expense of being less efficient in uncommon cases. In **S1**, the ability to convey information by silence depends on a reliability assumption, since if j may fail by crashing, for example, then it would be possible for i not to hear from j even if φ is untrue. The information conveyed by a null message in this case can be described by:

S2. Silent inference from an unreliable source: Suppose that a process j is guaranteed to send i a message at time t in case some condition φ of interest *does not* hold and it is not faulty. If, by time $t + \Delta$, process i has not received a message that j sent to i at time t, then i can infer that at least one of the following is true: (i) φ holds, or (ii) a failure has occurred.

In particular, if j sends messages to i over a reliable communication link, then (ii) reduces to process j being faulty. Despite the fact that i may fall short of inferring that φ holds when it does not hear from j, the information that it does obtain may still be very useful. In many problems having to do with fault-tolerance, the specification depends on whether failures occur. Thus, for example, in the original *atomic commit* problem [12, 15], deciding to abort is allowed if one of the initial values is 0, or if a failure occurs. In *Byzantine agreement* [30] and *weak agreement* [23], deciding on a default value is allowed in case of a failure. But this is not true in general. In the popular *consensus* problem, for example, the Validity condition is independent of whether failures occur [8], thus rendering conditional knowledge as provided by **S2** insufficient. As we will see, there are circumstances under which silence can provide unconditional information even in the face of failures.

For ease of exposition, our investigation will focus on synchronous message-passing systems, in which processes communicate in rounds, and a message sent in a particular round is received by the end of the round. Moreover, we will consider settings in which only processes may fail, and there is an *a priori* bound of f on the number of processes that can fail. One way to infer unconditional information in such settings is captured by:

S3. Silent inference with bounded failures: Assume that at most f processes can fail, and let S be a set of at least $f + 1$ processes. Moreover, suppose that every process $j \in S$ is guaranteed to send i a message no later than round m in case φ *does not* hold and j is not faulty. If i hears from no process in S by time m, then i can infer that φ holds.

S3 is used, for example, by Amdur *et al.* [1], who consider message-efficient solutions to Byzantine agreement. In order to prove to all processes that the original sender completed the first round, their protocol has the sender send messages to a set B of f processes in the second round. In the third round, a member of B sends no messages if it received the sender's second round message. This implies, in particular, that the sender did not fail in the first round. A member of B does send third round messages to everyone in case it did not hear from the sender in the second round. The set $S = \{\text{sender}\} \cup B$ satisfies the above rule, and allows all processes to infer the fact φ = *"the sender completed the first round successfully"* based on silence in the third round.

The rules **S1**-**S3** provide sufficient conditions for silent information transfer. As we will show, both **S2** and **S3** can be used to facilitate the design and analysis of efficient fault-tolerant protocols. Moreover, **S3** is in a precise sense also a necessary condition for inferring particular facts of interest from silence. This, in turn, will allow us to obtain simple and intuitive proofs of lower bounds and matching optimal protocols.

3.1 Silent Broadcast

There are several ways to formally state the rules **S1**—**S3**; we will state them in a form that will be most convenient to use in the sequel. It is natural to capture the fact that process i infers that φ holds using the knowledge terminology. Moreover, in a synchronous setting, not sending a message at a given point is a choice just like performing an action. In **S1**, process j is assumed not to send a message in case φ holds. Thus, by the knowledge of preconditions principle (Theorem 1), j must know φ to make this choice. We say that a protocol guarantees a property if this property is true in all runs of the protocol. We can thus formalize **S1** as follows:

Lemma 1. *Let R be a synchronous system with reliable communication in which process j reliably follows a protocol $\mathcal{P}$. Let φ be a fact about runs in R and assume that $\mathcal{P}$ guarantees that if $\neg K_j\varphi$ at time $m-1$ then j sends a message to i in round m. If i does not receive a message from j in round m of a run $r \in R$ then $K_i\varphi$ holds at time m in r.*

Proof. Fix $r \in R$ and assume that i does not receive a message from j in round m of r. Moreover, choose an arbitrary run $r' \in R$ such that $r' \approx_i^m r$. By Definition 1 it suffices to show that r' satisfies φ. By assumption, i has the same local state at time m in both runs, and so it does not receive a message from j in round m of r'. Since R is synchronous and communication is assumed to be reliable, it follows that j did not send a message to i in round m of r'. Process j is assumed to reliably follow the protocol $\mathcal{P}$. Hence, by assumption, $K_j\varphi$ must be true at time $m-1$ in r', or else it would have sent a message to i. By the knowledge property it follows that φ holds at time $m-1$ in r'. Moreover, since φ is a fact about runs, r' satisfies φ, and we are done. □

S2 considers information gained by silence in systems in which processes can fail, such as the context γ^f. In this case, i might not receive a message from j due to a failure, rather than because of information that j has at the beginning of the round. We thus obtain a weaker variant of Lemma 1, formalizing **S2**:

Lemma 2. *Let φ be a fact about runs in the system $R_{\mathcal{P}} = R(\mathcal{P}, \gamma^f)$, and fix $i, j \in \mathbb{P}$ and a time $m > 0$. Moreover, assume that $\mathcal{P}$ guarantees that if $\neg K_j\varphi$ at time $m-1$ then j sends a message to i in round m. If i does not receive a round m message from j in a run $r \in R_{\mathcal{P}}$ then $K_i(\varphi \vee j$ is faulty$)$ holds at time m in r.*

Proof. The proof is very similar to that of Lemma 1. Fix $r \in R$ and assume that i does not receive a message from j in round m of r. Moreover, choose an arbitrary run $r' \in R$ such that $r' \approx_i^m r$. By Definition 1 we need to show that r' satisfies $(\varphi \vee j$ is faulty$)$. By assumption, i has the same local state at time m in both runs, and so it does not receive a message from j in round m of r'. However, since in $R_{\mathcal{P}}$ the protocol $\mathcal{P}$ is applied in the unreliable context γ^f, there are two possible reasons for this. One is that j fails in r' before it has a chance to send i a message in round m, in which case j is faulty in r'. The other one is that j reliably follows $\mathcal{P}$ at time $m-1$, in which case by assumption, $K_j\varphi$ must be true at time $m-1$ in r' (implying φ is true in r'), or else it would have sent a message to i. It follows that $(\varphi \vee j$ is faulty$)$ must be true in r', and we are done. □

Clearly, the knowledge that is obtained by silence in γ^f, as captured by Lemma 2, is contingent, and hence quite a bit weaker than what can be guaranteed in the more reliable setting of Lemma 1. As mentioned in the Introduction, there are problems in which such weaker knowledge may be sufficient. A closer inspection shows, however, that it is possible to obtain unqualified knowledge even in fault-tolerant settings such as the context γ^f. The key to this is the fact that even when any single process may be faulty, a process is often guaranteed that a set of processes must contain a nonfaulty process. In this case, we can use Lemma 2 to obtain the following formalization of **S3**:

Corollary 2. *Let $R_{\mathcal{P}} = R(\mathcal{P}, \gamma^f)$, let φ be a fact about runs in $R_{\mathcal{P}}$, fix a process $i \in \mathbb{P}$ and a set $|S| > f$ of processes. Moreover, assume that for all $j \in S$ the protocol $\mathcal{P}$ guarantees that if $\neg K_j\varphi$ at time $m-1 \geq 0$ then j sends a message to i in round m. If, in some run $r \in R_{\mathcal{P}}$, process i does not receive a round m message from any process in S, then $K_i\varphi$ holds at time m in r.*

Proof. Under the assumptions of the claim, choose a run $r' \approx_i^m r$ in $R_{\mathcal{P}}$. It suffices to show that φ is true in r'. Since $|S| > f$ there must be a process $h \in S$ that is correct in r'. Lemma 2 implies that

($\varphi \vee h$ is faulty) is true in r'. But since h is not faulty in r' we obtain that φ holds in r', as required. □

Corollary 2 shows how a set $|S| > f$ of processes can inform a specific process i of a fact φ by not sending messages to i. In fact, with no extra cost the set S can be silent to all processes in a round m of interest, thereby informing everyone that φ holds. We call this a ***silent broadcast***.

3.2 The Silent Choir Theorem

The rule **S3** and its formalization in Corollary 2 show that a protocol can orchestrate information transfer through silence by first informing (perhaps directly) a large enough set of processes about the fact of interest. We now show that, in a precise sense, this is indeed necessary. Intuitively, transferring information through silence requires enough processes to be mum to ensure that at least one of them is correct. We will call this the *Silent Choir Theorem*. The direct information transfer in the reliable case (**S1**) is a particular instance of this, because a choir of one suffices when there are no failures. While the sufficient conditions of Section 3.1 apply rather broadly to general facts φ about runs, to prove necessary conditions we need to restrict attention to certain *primitive* facts. This is because knowledge of a composite fact such as conjunction $\varphi = \psi_1 \wedge \psi_2$, for example, can be obtained by separately learning about each of its components. Intuitively, a primitive fact is a fact that is local to a process j and whose truth is not determined by the local states of the other processes. For ease of exposition, our analysis will exclusively consider a single primitive fact, the fact $v_j = 1$ stating that j's local value is 1. Knowledge about initial values plays an important role in many problems, including consensus [8, 11] and AC.

Our treatment will make use of message chains. Given processes $i, i' \in \mathbb{P}$ and times $m, m' \geq 0$, we say that ***there is a message chain from*** (i, m) ***to*** (i', m') ***in a run*** r, and write $(i, m) \rightsquigarrow_r (i', m')$, if either (a) $i = i'$ and $m \leq m'$, or if (b) there exist processes $i = j_0, j_1, \ldots, j_\ell = i'$ and times $m \leq t_0 < t_1, \ldots, < t_\ell \leq m'$ such that for all $0 \leq k < \ell$, a message from j_k to j_{k+1} is sent in r at time t_k. Such a message chain is said to have ***length*** ℓ. (Notice that $m \leq t_0$, so the first message in the chain may be sent after time m.) We say that there is a message chain from i to j in r if $(i, 0) \rightsquigarrow_r (j, m)$ for some time $m \geq 0$.

Recall that in γ^f process j's initial value is not known to processes $i \neq j$ at the start. Clearly, one way in which process i can come to know that $v_j = 1$ is by direct communication, i.e., via a message chain from j to i. Alternatively, i can learn this fact using silence. The ways by which a process i can come to know that $v_j = 1$ in γ^f are characterized by the following theorem.

Theorem 2 (Silent Choir). *Let $r \in R(\mathcal{P}, \gamma^f)$, denote by $\mathbb{F}^r$ the set of faulty processes in r, and define $S_j^r(t) \triangleq \{h \in \mathbb{P} \colon (j, 0) \rightsquigarrow_r (h, t)\}$. If $K_i(v_j = 1)$ holds at time m in r and r does not contain a message chain from j to i, then $m > 0$ and $|\mathbb{F}^r \cup S_j^r(m-1)| > f$.*

Proof. Let i, j, r and m satisfy the assumptions. If there is a message chain from j to i in r, then we are done. So assume that no such message chain exists. Let r' be a run in which v_i is the same as in r and $v_j = 0$. Clearly, $r \approx_i^0 r'$ and so $\neg K_i(v_j = 1)$ at time 0 in r. It follows that $m > 0$. Roughly speaking, $S_j^r(t)$ is the set of processes that could have learned v_j by time t, via a message chain from j. We will establish that $|\mathbb{F}^r \cup S_j^r(m-1)| > f$ by proving the contraposition; i.e., that if $|\mathbb{F}^r \cup S_j^r(m-1)| \leq f$ then i does not know that $v_j = 1$ at time m. Intuitively, the claim will follow because if $|\mathbb{F}^r \cup S_j^r(m-1)| \leq f$ then i would consider it possible at time m that $v_j = 0$ and j crashed initially, and that everyone who may have noticed its value crashed without informing anyone. More formally, for every $h \in S_j^r(m-1)$, define k_h to be the round in r in which h first receives a message completing a message chain from j. Consider a run r' of $\mathcal{P}$ in which $v_j = 0$ and all other initial values are the same as in r. Every process $h \in S_j^r(m-1)$ crashes in round $k_h + 1$ of r' without sending any messages. (In particular, j crashes initially.) The faulty processes in r' are those in $\mathbb{F}^r \cup S_j^r(m-1)$. By assumption, their number does not exceed f, and so r' is a run of $\mathcal{P}$ in γ^f.

We now prove by induction on ℓ in the range $0 \leq \ell \leq m-1$ that for all $z \in \mathbb{P}$, if $z \notin S_j^r(m-1)$ or $z \in S_j^r(m-1)$ but $\ell < k_z$, then $r_z(\ell) = r_z'(\ell)$, and z sends the same messages and performs the same actions in round $\ell+1$ of both runs. Recall that $j \in S_j^r(m-1)$ and $k_j = 0$. For $\ell = 0$ we have that $r_z(0) = r_z'(0)$ for all $z \neq j$ since by choice of r' all initial values other than v_j are the same in both runs. Since $\mathcal{P}$ is deterministic, all processes other than j send the same messages and perform the same actions in round 1. Let $0 < \ell \leq m-1$, and assume that the inductive claim holds for $\ell - 1$. Suppose that either $z \notin S_j^r(m-1)$ or both $z \in S_j^r(m-1)$ and $\ell < k_z$. Then by definition of $S_j^r(m-1)$ and k_z it follows that in round ℓ of r process z receives no messages from a process $y \in S_j^r(m-1)$ for which $k_y < \ell - 1$. Consequently, z receives the same set of messages in round ℓ of both runs. Since $r_z(\ell-1) = r_z'(\ell-1)$ by the inductive hypothesis, it follows that $r_z(\ell) = r_z'(\ell)$. Again, since $\mathcal{P}$ is deterministic, z will send the same messages and perform the same actions in round $\ell + 1$ of both runs. This completes the inductive argument.

The inductive claim implies, in particular, that all $z \notin S_j^r(m-1)$ send the same messages in round m of both runs r and r'. Notice that $i \notin S_j^r(m-1)$ by assumption, and i receives no messages from processes in $S_j^r(m-1)$ in round m of the original run r. It follows that i receives the same set of messages in round m of both runs. Since $i \notin S_j^r(m-1)$ we also have that $r_i(m-1) = r_i'(m-1)$, and so we obtain that $r_i(m) = r_i'(m)$. In other words, the two runs are indistinguishable to i at time m. By construction, $v_j \neq 1$ in r', and so $K_i(v_j = 1)$ does *not* hold at time m in r. The claim follows. □

By Theorem 2, any run in which a process learns about initial values without an explicit message chain must contain a silent choir. Indeed, it is possible to identify a silent choir in the message-optimal AC protocol of [15], as well as in message-optimal protocols for Byzantine agreementf [1, 18] and for failure discovery [17].

4 EFFICIENT PROTOCOLS FOR ATOMIC COMMITMENT

Guerraoui and Wang [15] present state-of-the-art protocols for AC optimized for nice runs in a variety of models and point out that there is a tradeoff between time and messages in their protocols. For γ^f they present three different protocols. In nice runs of their most message-efficient protocol, $n + f - 1$ messages are sent, and processes decide after $n + 2f$ rounds. In nice runs of their fastest protocol, decisions are obtained within two rounds, and $2n^2 - 2n$ messages are sent.

4.1 Lower Bounds on AC in the Common Case

We are now ready to apply the formalism of Section 3 to the analysis of AC protocols that are efficient in the common case. Our first goal is to show that silence must be used in message-optimal AC protocols. To do so, we start by proving a useful combinatorial property relating message chains and message complexity:

Lemma 3. *Let $k > 0$, and assume that the run r contains, for every process $j \in \mathbb{P}$, message chains to at least k other processes. Then at least $n + k - 1$ messages are sent in r.*

Proof. First notice that every process $i \in \mathbb{P}$ must send at least one message in r, since it has message chains to other processes. Define the ***rank*** of a process $i \in \mathbb{P}$ to be the length of the longest message chain from $(i, 0)$ in the run r. If there is a process with rank $\geq n + k - 1$ we are done. Otherwise let h be a process with minimal rank, and let M be the set of messages on chains that start at h. Clearly $|M| \geq k$, because r contains message chains from h to at least k other processes. Moreover, every $j \neq h$ must send at least one message that is not in M, since otherwise j's rank would be strictly smaller than that of h. Thus, at least $n - 1 + |M| \geq n + k - 1$ messages must be sent in r, as claimed. □

The message-optimal AC protocol for γ^f presented in [15], which we shall refer to as the *GW protocol*, sends $n + f - 1$ messages in nice runs. This can be used to prove

Corollary 3. *Message-optimal AC protocols in γ^f must make use of silence when $f < n - 1$.*

Proof. Every process i commits in a nice run r, and by Corollary 1 i must know that $v_j = 1$, for all j, when it commits. Theorem 2 implies that if silence is not used in r, then there must be a message chain from j to i. The conditions of Lemma 3 thus hold in r for $k = n - 1$, implying that a nice run must send at least $2n - 2 > n + f - 1$ messages. The claim follows. □

Recall that the common case in this setting consists of nice runs, i.e., runs where all initial values are 1, and no failures occur. Corollary 1 captures a basic property of AC protocols: A committing process must know that all initial values are 1. The Silent Choir Theorem and the KoP can be used to show the following property, which will be key to our lower bound proofs:

Lemma 4. *When a process i commits in a run of an AC protocol, it must know, for every $j \in \mathbb{P}$, that there is a message chain from j to some correct process in the current run.*

Proof. Assume that i commits in the run r of $\mathcal{P}$. By Theorem 1, it suffices to show that if i commits in r then r contains a message chain from j to some correct process, for every $j \in \mathbb{P}$. Fix $j \in \mathbb{P}$. Since $f < n$, there must be at least one correct process in r; denote it by h. Given that i commits in r, we have by Agreement that h commits in r. Let us denote by m the decision time of h. By Corollary 1 we have that $K_h(v_j = 1)$ holds when h commits. If there is a message chain from j to h in r we are done, since h is the desired correct process. Otherwise, Theorem 2 states that $|\mathbb{F}^r \cup S_j^r(m-1)| > f$. Thus, $S_j^r(m-1)$ contains a correct process and there is a message chain from j to a correct process in r. □

We are now in a position to state and prove a set of lower bounds on the tradeoff between the decision time and number of messages sent in nice runs of AC protocols.

Theorem 3. *Let $\mathcal{P}$ be an AC protocol for γ^f, let D be the number of rounds at the end of which decision is reached in its nice runs, and let M be the number of messages sent in nice rounds. Then D and M satisfy the following constraints:*

(a) If $D = 1$ then $f = 1$ and $M \geq n^2 - n$;
(b) If $D = 2$ then $M \geq fn$; and
(c) If $D \geq 3$ then $M \geq n + f - 1$.[2]

Proof. Throughout the proof, r will denote a nice run of an AC protocol $\mathcal{P}$. Consider part (a), in which $\mathcal{P}$ decides in $D = 1$ round. Charron-Bost and Schiper established in [7] that if $f > 1$ then $D \geq 2$. Since by definition $f \geq 1$, it follows that if $D = 1$ then $f = 1$. In addition, given that $D = 1$ all processes commit at time $m = 1$ in r. Thus, by Corollary 1, the fact $K_i(v_j = 1)$ must hold at time $m = 1$ in r for all $i, j \in \mathbb{P}$. Since no message chains among distinct processes exist in r at time $m - 1 = 0$, using the notation of the Silent Choir Theorem (2) we have that $S_j^r(m-1) = \emptyset$ for all $j \in \mathbb{P}$. By Theorem 2 we thus obtain that r must construct a message chain between every pair of processes $i \neq j \in \mathbb{P}$ in the first round. It follows that $M \geq n(n-1) = n^2 - n$ messages are sent in r, as claimed. For part (b), it suffices to show that if $D = 2$ then every process must send at least f messages in r. Let $\mathcal{P}$ be an AC protocol with $D = 2$, let $i \in \mathbb{P}$, and denote by T the set of processes to which i sends messages in the nice run r. Assume, by way of contradiction, that $|T| < f$. Consider a run r' of $\mathcal{P}$ in which i crashes after deciding, without sending any messages after the second round. Moreover, every process $h \in T$ fails in the second round without sending messages to any process except possibly to i (to whom h sends iff it does in r). The run r' is a run of $\mathcal{P}$ in γ^f because it contains $|T| + 1 \leq f$ failures. The run r' contains no message chain from i itself to a correct process. Moreover, $r' \approx_i^2 r$ by construction, and therefore when it commits in r, process i does not know that the run contains a message chain from itself to a correct process. This contradicts Lemma 4. For part (c) we now prove that $M \geq n + f - 1$. This will follow by Lemma 3 once we show that the run r must contain, for every process $j \in \mathbb{P}$, message chains from j to at least f other processes. Fix a process j. If r contains message chains from j to all other processes then we are done, since $f \leq n - 1$. Otherwise, let i be a process to whom there is no message chain from j in r. Since r is nice, all processes commit in r. Denote by m the time at which i commits. Given that there is no message chain from j to i in r, Theorem 2 implies that $|\mathbb{F}^r \cup S_j^r(m-1)| > f$, where $S_j^r(m-1)$ is the set of processes to whom a message chain from j is completed by time $m - 1$ in r. Since r is nice we have that $\mathbb{F}^r = \emptyset$, and so $|S_j^r(m-1)| > f$. Finally, as $j \in |S_j^r(m-1)|$, there must be message chains from j to at least f other processes in r. The claim follows. □

Next we turn to prove that the bounds of Theorem 3 are tight by providing matching upper bounds.

[2] We prove that $M \geq n + f - 1$ for completeness. It was proved for the case of $f = n - 1$ by Dwork and Skeen in [12], and appears for general f in Guerraoui and Wang [15], with some details of the proof omitted.

4.2 Upper Bounds on AC in the Common Case

Recall that we consider the set of processes to be $\mathbb{P} = \{0, 1, \ldots, n-1\}$. Roughly speaking, the message-optimal GW protocol spends $n+f-1$ rounds creating a long chain of $n + f - 1$ messages sent in cyclic order from process 1 through $n - 1$ and then continuing to $0, \ldots, f$. It then runs a consensus protocol for another f rounds starting at time $n + f$ to decide among the actions commit and abort. In our terminology, the first process to know that $v_j = 1$ for all j is process 0. The processes $0, 1, \ldots, f$ form the silent choir: They must inform the processes in case the chain is broken. At time $n + f$, if a process is not informed of a problem, it knows that all initial values are 1.

Using the terminology of Theorem 3, the GW protocol decides in $D = n+2f$ rounds. Dwork and Skeen's message-optimal protocol for the case $f = n - 1$ decides in $D = 2n + 1$ rounds [12]. There is a very large gap between these decision times and the lower bound of $D \geq 3$ established in Theorem 3(c). We now present the Stealth protocol, a message-optimal AC protocol that decides in $D = 3$ rounds. We will then proceed to present two additional Pareto optimal protocols, deciding in $D = 2$ rounds for the case of $f > 1$ and in $D = 1$ round when $f = 1$, respectively. Together, these three protocols prove that the bounds in Theorem 3 are all tight, and completely characterize the tradeoff between time and message complexities in the common case for AC protocols.[3] Full descriptions of all protocols in this section appear in Appendices A.1 – A.3, and their proofs of correctness can be found in the full version [14].

Stealth: an AC protocol with $D = 3$ and $M = n + f - 1$.

Fast Path: In the first round, all processes that have value 1 send a message to process 0. If process 0 hears from all processes, it sends messages to processes $1, 2, \ldots, f$ in the second round. In case all these messages are indeed sent, no messages are sent in the third round. A process that receives no message in the third round performs commit at time 3. Finally, if such a process receives no messages in the fourth round, it halts at time 4.

Slow Path: The slow path in Stealth operates as follows. Any member of the choir that did not receive its second round message (or $n-1$ first-round messages in the case of process 0) broadcasts (i.e., sends all processes) an "error" message in the third round. Any process that receives error messages in the third round broadcasts a clarification request message "huh?" in the fourth round. Finally, if any "huh?" message is sent in the fourth round, then the processes run an $f - 1$ crash-tolerant consensus for f rounds starting in the fifth round. The variant of consensus used by Stealth has the property that if a correct process starts with value 1 then the final decision is 1. For details, see Appendix A.1. A process votes 1 (in favor of committing) in the consensus protocol if it received no message in the third round, or if it is in the choir and received its second round message. It votes 0 (in favor of aborting) otherwise. Processes that participate in the consensus protocol halt when their role in the consensus protocol ends. In the worst case, the last process halts in Stealth at time $f + 5$. ♣

[3] Guerraoui and Wang present a protocol called 1NBAC in [15] in which processes decide in the second round in nice runs, but do so after the sending phase of the second round, and before receiving second-round messages. 1NBAC requires $2n^2 - 2n$ messages in nice runs. In Appendix B we prove a lower bound of $n^2 + fn - n$ messages for their model, and present a matching protocol that proves that the bound is tight.

In nice runs, the Stealth protocol constructs a silent choir for the fact that all values are 1 in round 2, and uses round 3 to allow the choir to perform a silent broadcast of this fact to all processes. Interestingly, it uses silence in an additional manner: Round 4 performs a silent broadcast from all processes to all processes. This does not require a silent choir because it makes use of the rule **S2**: a null message from j informs i that j is either active and has committed, or has crashed without deciding. The next protocol also uses two rounds of silence in a similar manner.

D2: an AC protocol with $D = 2$ and $M = fn$.

Fast Path: In the first round, every process j with $v_j = 1$ sends messages to the f processes $j + 1, j + 2, \ldots, j + f$ (wrapping around mod n). A process that sent messages and received all f possible messages in the first round remains silent in the second round. A process that receives no messages in the second round performs commit at time 2. Finally, if such a process receives no messages in the third round, it halts at time 3.

Slow Path: The slow path is similar in spirit to that of Stealth, starting one round earlier. A process j such that $v_j = 0$, or that does not receive first-round messages from all of its f predecessors $j - 1, j - 2, \ldots, j - f \pmod n$ broadcasts an "error" message in the second round. In the third round, a process that (sent or) received an "error" message in the second round broadcasts a message listing all processes whose values it knows to be 1. All processes that do not halt at time 3 participate in a consensus protocol as in Stealth, that starts in the fourth round. In this case, a process enters the consensus protocol with value 1 iff it knows that all initial values were 1. ♣

Our third protocol treats the boundary case of $f = 1$. Rather than two silent rounds, only the latter one, corresponding to **S2**, is needed in nice runs:

D1f1: an AC protocol with $D = 1$ and $M = n^2 - n$ for $f = 1$.

Fast Path: In the first round, every process j with $v_j = 1$ sends messages to all other processes. A process with value 1 that receives messages from all processes in the first round performs commit at time 1. Finally, if such a process receives no messages in the second round, it halts at time 2.

Slow Path: For the slow path, a process j with $v_j = 1$ that does not receive messages from everyone in the first round broadcasts a "huh?" message in the second round. A committed process that receives such a message in the second round, responds in the third round with an "`all[1]`" message to the requesting process j. Finally, a process that did not commit at time 1 will perform commit at time 3 if it received an "`all[1]`" message in the second round, and will perform abort otherwise. All processes halt at time 3 (possibly after deciding at time 3) and send no messages in the fourth round. ♣

5 DISCUSSION

In the well-known story *Silver Blaze*, Sherlock Holmes is able to conclude that a victim's dog was familiar with the murderer, based on the fact that the dog was silent when the criminal entered [10]. In that example, Conan Doyle crisply illustrates how crucial knowledge can be gained by observing silence. The focus of our investigation has been on the use of silence in distributed protocols. A variety of protocols in the literature make implicit use of silence (e.g., [6, 9, 24]). In network protocols, periodically sending *Keep-alive* messages is commonly used to inform a peer that a node is active. The absence of such messages allows the peer to discover that a failure has occurred [31].

As has been elucidated by [22], synchronous channels allow processes to send null messages by not sending a message. In a precise sense, our analysis considers what information can be passed using null messages. This becomes especially interesting in systems with failures, since the absence of a message in such settings can be caused by a failure, rather than by deliberate silence. In the presence of a bounded number of crash failures, we identified the notion of a silent choir as an essential component of information transfer by silence. We showed that the only way that a process j can inform another process i of j's initial value without an explicit message chain between them is by constructing a silent choir (Theorem 2). Indeed, in a variety of message-optimal protocols it is possible to identify silent choirs. These include [15] for Atomic Commitment, [1, 18] for Byzantine Agreement, and [17] for the failure discovery problem. The silent choir is a valuable tool for a protocol designer. By directly constructing silent choirs, we were able to reduce the number of rounds for message-optimal AC protocols from $n + 2f$ to 3 in the Stealth protocol, and to design a protocol (D2) that is message optimal among round-optimal AC protocols in Section 4.2. Since silent choirs are necessary in some cases, they can also serve in theoretical analyses. In Theorem 3, we used the necessity of silent choirs to obtain a complete characterization of the tradeoff between decision times and communication costs for AC protocols.

A notion of potential causality for reliable synchronous systems based on allowing null messages in message chains was defined in [3]. Defining a similar notion for fault-prone systems by using silent choirs rather than null messages is an interesting topic for further investigation.

While our investigation focused on the synchronous round-based model γ^f in which processes fail by crashing and the network is fully connected, it applies to more general synchronous systems. In particular, the rules **S2** and **S3** and their formalizations, as well as the Silent Choir Theorem, hold with minor modifications even in the presence of Byzantine failures. The use of silence, and more generally the topic of how information can be gleaned from actions that are *not* performed by processes in a system, is an exciting topic that deserves further investigation in the future.

REFERENCES

[1] Eugene S Amdur, Samuel M Weber, and Vassos Hadzilacos. 1992. On the message complexity of binary byzantine agreement under crash failures. *Distributed Computing* 5, 4 (1992), 175–186.

[2] Amotz Bar-Noy and Danny Dolev. 1991. Consensus algorithms with one-bit messages. *Distributed Computing* 4, 3 (1991), 105–110.

[3] Ido Ben-Zvi and Yoram Moses. 2014. Beyond Lamport's Happened-before: On Time Bounds and the Ordering of Events in Distributed Systems. *Journal of the ACM (JACM)* 61, 2 (2014), 13.

[4] Arthur J. Bernstein. 1985. A loosely coupled distributed system for reliably storing data. *IEEE Transactions on Software Engineering* 5 (1985), 446–454.

[5] P.A. Bernstein, V. Hadzilacos, and N. Goodman. 1987. *Concurrency control and recovery in database systems.*

[6] Armando Castaneda, Yannai A Gonczarowski, and Yoram Moses. 2014. Unbeatable consensus. In *Proceedings of DISC.* Springer, 91–106.

[7] Bernadette Charron-Bost and André Schiper. 2004. Uniform consensus is harder than consensus. *Journal of Algorithms* 51, 1 (2004), 15–37.

[8] Danny Dolev, Cynthia Dwork, and Larry J. Stockmeyer. 1983. On the Minimal Synchronism Needed for Distributed Consensus. In *24th FOCS.* 393–402.

[9] Danny Dolev and H. Raymond Strong. 1983. Authenticated algorithms for Byzantine agreement. *SIAM J. Comput.* 12, 4 (1983), 656–666.

[10] Arthur Conan Doyle and Sidney Paget. 1892. *The adventure of silver blaze.* Mary McLaughlin and M. Einisman for the Scotland Yard Bookstore.

[11] C. Dwork and Y. Moses. 1990. Knowledge and common knowledge in a Byzantine environment: crash failures. 88, 2 (1990), 156–186.

[12] Cynthia Dwork and Dale Skeen. 1983. The inherent cost of nonblocking commitment. In *Proceedings of the second annual ACM symposium on Principles of distributed computing.* ACM, 1–11.

[13] R. Fagin, J. Y. Halpern, Y. Moses, and M. Y. Vardi. 2003. *Reasoning about Knowledge.* MIT Press, Cambridge, Mass.

[14] Guy Goren and Yoram Moses. 2018. Silence. In *arXiv:1805.07954.*

[15] Rachid Guerraoui and Jingjing Wang. 2017. How fast can a distributed transaction commit?. In *Proceedings of the 36th ACM SIGMOD-SIGACT-SIGAI Symposium on Principles of Database Systems.* ACM, 107–122.

[16] Vassos Hadzilacos. 1987. A knowledge-theoretic analysis of atomic commitment protocols. In *Proceedings of the sixth ACM SIGACT-SIGMOD-SIGART symposium on Principles of database systems.* ACM, 129–134.

[17] Vassos Hadzilacos and Joseph Y Halpern. 1993. The failure discovery problem. *Mathematical systems theory* 26, 1 (1993), 103–129.

[18] Vassos Hadzilacos and Joseph Y Halpern. 1993. Message-optimal protocols for Byzantine agreement. *Mathematical Systems Theory* 26, 1 (1993), 41–102.

[19] J. Y. Halpern and Y. Moses. 1990. Knowledge and Common Knowledge in a Distributed Environment. 37, 3 (1990), 549–587. A preliminary version appeared in *Proc. 3rd ACM PODC,* 1984.

[20] Patrick Hunt, Mahadev Konar, Flavio Paiva Junqueira, and Benjamin Reed. 2010. ZooKeeper: Wait-free Coordination for Internet-scale Systems.. In *USENIX annual technical conference,* Vol. 8. Boston, MA, USA.

[21] Prasad Jogalekar and Murray Woodside. 2000. Evaluating the scalability of distributed systems. *IEEE Transactions on parallel and distributed systems* 11, 6 (2000), 589–603.

[22] Leslie Lamport. 1984. Using time instead of timeout for fault-tolerant distributed systems. *ACM Transactions on Programming Languages and Systems (TOPLAS)* 6, 2 (1984), 254–280.

[23] L. Lamport and M. J. Fischer. 1982. *Byzantine generals and transactions commit protocols.* Technical Report Opus 62. SRI International, Menlo Park, Calif.

[24] Christoph Lenzen and Joel Rybicki. 2016. Near-optimal self-stabilising counting and firing squads. In *International Symposium on Stabilization, Safety, and Security of Distributed Systems.* Springer, 263–280.

[25] Kfir Lev-Ari, Edward Bortnikov, Idit Keidar, and Alexander Shraer. 2016. Modular Composition of Coordination Services.. In *USENIX Annual Technical Conference.* 251–264.

[26] Barbara Liskov. 1993. Practical uses of synchronized clocks in distributed systems. *Distributed Computing* 6, 4 (1993), 211–219.

[27] Shengyun Liu, Paolo Viotti, Christian Cachin, Vivien Quéma, and Marko Vukolic. 2016. XFT: Practical Fault Tolerance beyond Crashes.. In *OSDI.* 485–500.

[28] Yoram Moses. 2015. Relating Knowledge and Coordinated Action: The Knowledge of Preconditions Principle. *Proceedings of TARK 2015, arXiv:1606.07525* (2015).

[29] Satoshi Nakamoto. 2008. Bitcoin: A peer-to-peer electronic cash system.

[30] M. Pease, R. Shostak, and L. Lamport. 1980. Reaching agreement in the presence of faults. 27, 2 (1980), 228–234.

[31] Richard Price, Peter Tiňo, and Georgios Theodoropoulos. 2012. Still alive: Extending keep-alive intervals in P2P overlay networks. *Mobile Networks and Applications* 17, 3 (2012), 378–394.

A DESCRIPTIONS OF THE PROTOCOLS

Recall that the goal is to optimize AC for the common-case, i.e., for nice runs. Therefore, in order to capture the essence of silence and simplify the protocols, improvements regarding the uncommon cases, when runs are not nice, are left out. In some not "nice" runs the Stealth and D2 protocols make use of a consensus variant that we denote by B.1.Consensus. This stands for a consensus process that is "*biased to 1,*" which means that if some correct process $i \in \mathbb{P}$ starts the consensus phase with value 1, then the processes will necessarily decide 1.

A.1 The STEALTH Protocol

The STEALTH protocol, sketched in Section 4.2, is presented in Figure 1. It reaches the lower bound of Theorem 3(c). That is, for $f > 1$, STEALTH is round optimal among message-optimal AC protocols with $M = n + f - 1$ and $D = 3$. The protocol is also optimal in bits as well as in messages. Each message sent in STEALTH consists of a single bit. Both all[1], '$\overline{err}$' and 'huh?' can be represented by '1' as they are the only messages that might appear in rounds 2, 3 and 4 respectively.

round 1
$\forall i \in \mathbb{P}$:
  if $v_i = 1$ **then** send '1' to process 0
round 2
Process 0:
  if received '1' from all **then** send all[1] to processes $\{0, 1, 2, \ldots, f\}$
  % processes $\{0, 1, 2, \ldots, f\}$ form the silent choir in STEALTH.
round 3
Processes $\{0, 1, 2, \ldots, f\}$:
  if received no message from process 0 in round 2 **then** send '$\overline{err}$' to all
round 4
$\forall i \in \mathbb{P}$:
  if did not receive any '$\overline{err}$' **then** commit
  else send 'huh?' to all
round 5
$\forall i \in \mathbb{P}$:
  if no 'huh?' message received **then** halt
  else *% this can take up to f rounds*
    $\hat{v}_i \leftarrow \begin{cases} 1 & \text{if received all[1] or performed commit} \\ 0 & \text{otherwise} \end{cases};$
    dec ← B.1.Consensus($f - 1$, $\hat{v}_i$);
    if haven't performed commit **then**
      commit **if** dec = 1,
      abort **if** dec = 0

Figure 1: The STEALTH protocol. Not all processes participate in all rounds.

Two possible runs of STEALTH are illustrated in Figures 2 and 3. Figure 2 depicts the protocol's nice run, and it goes as follows: in **round 1** all processes send 1 to process 0; in **round 2** process 0 sends all[1] to processes 1, 2, .., f; in **round 3** all processes are quiet; at time 3 all processes decide 1 (at the end of three rounds of communication); and at time 4 (after another silent round) all processes halt.

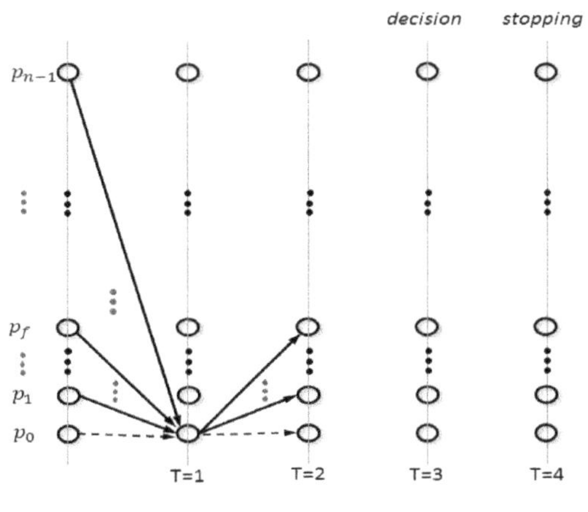

Figure 2: The nice run of STEALTH (all vote 1 and no failures).

Figure 3 depicts an example of a complicated run that is not nice. It goes as follows: in **round 1** all processes send 1 to process 0; in **round 2** process 0 tries to send all[1] to processes 1, 2, .., f but crashes. some receive it and some not; in **round 3** processes from $\{1, 2, .., f\}$ that didn't receive all[1], send $\overline{err}$ to all, the rest are quiet; in **round 4** all processes that received $\overline{err}$ send 'huh?' to all (asking for help); in **round 5** the living processes start B.1.Consensus, a process that knows all[1] starts with 1 (green smiley), the rest start with 0 (red smiley). In this case, in which the run is not nice, round 5 initiates a consensus protocol, which can take up to f additional rounds to complete.

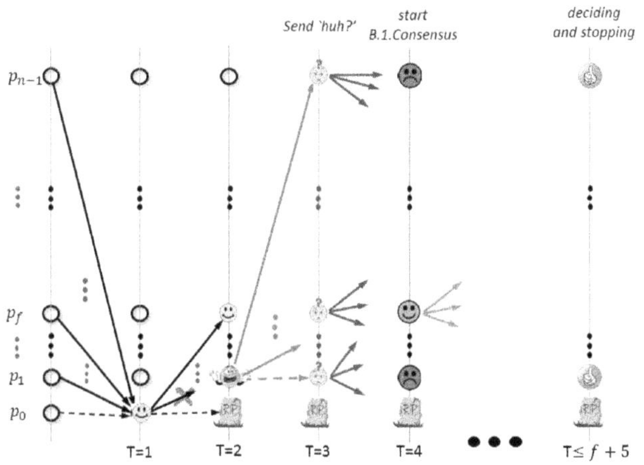

Figure 3: A run of STEALTH with failures.

A.2 The D2 Protocol

The protocol in Figure 4 commits at time 2 in nice runs and uses only nf messages to do so. Its proof of correctness can be found in the full version [14].

$\forall i \in \mathbb{P}$:
round 1
  if $v_i = 1$ **then** send '1' to $\{i, i + 1, \ldots, i + f\}$ mod n;
  % processes $\{i, i + 1, \ldots, i + f\}$ form a silent choir for "$v_i = 1$".
round 2
  if received fewer than $f + 1$ messages of '1' **then** send '$\overline{err}$' to all;
round 3
  if did not receive '$\overline{err}$' in previous round **then** commit;
  else send to all the id's of processes from whom 1 was received in round 1;
round 4
  if did not receive any messages in round 3 **then** halt;
  else *% this can take up to f rounds*
    $\hat{v}_i \leftarrow \begin{cases} 1 & \text{if received all id's } \{0, 1, \ldots, n-1\} \text{ or commited} \\ 0 & \text{otherwise} \end{cases};$
    dec ← B.1.Consensus($f - 1$, $\hat{v}_i$);
    if haven't performed commit **then**
      commit **if** dec = 1,
      abort **if** dec = 0

Figure 4: Round-optimal protocol D2: decides in $D = 2$ rounds with $M = nf$ messages in nice runs.

A.3 The D1f1 Protocol

In the special case of a single possible failure protocol D1f1 is presented in Figure 5. Its proof of correctness can be found in the full version [14].

```
∀i ∈ ℙ:
round 1
        if v_i = 1 then send '1' to all;
round 2
        if v_i = 1 and received '1' from all in previous round then commit;
        else send 'huh?' to all;
round 3
        if performed commit and did not receive any 'huh?' in previous round
          then halt;
        else if performed commit and received 'huh?' from j in previous round
          then send all[1] to j;
round 4
        if received all[1] in previous round then commit; halt;
        else abort; halt;
```

Figure 5: The protocol D1f1 for $f = 1$, which decides at time $D = 1$ in nice runs.

B COMMITTING IN MID-ROUND

Charron-Bost and Schiper [7] showed that no AC protocol tolerating $f > 1$ commits in $D = 1$ round in nice runs of γ^f. Nevertheless, Guerraoui and Wang present in [15] an AC protocol called 1NBAC that is claimed to commit after one round of communication in nice runs. The source of the discrepancy is that Guerraoui and Wang assume a slightly different model than the standard synchronous model γ^f. In their model, processes can decide on a value in mid-round. In particular, in nice runs of 1NBAC, the processes commit after sending their second-round messages and before receiving any second-round message. In the spirit of γ^f, they assume that if a process has completed the sending phase, then all of the messages that it has sent will be delivered. We denote their model by $\tilde{\gamma}^f$. All of the protocols that we have presented solve AC within the stated complexity in $\tilde{\gamma}^f$. For completeness we now present lower and upper bounds for deciding before time 2 in $\tilde{\gamma}^f$.

The following lemma forms the basis of the analysis,

Lemma 5. *Assume that $f > 1$, let r be a nice run of an AC protocol in $\tilde{\gamma}^f$, and let $i \in \mathbb{P}$ be a process that decides before time 2 in r. Then (a) i receives a first-round message from every process in r, and (b) i sends at least f round-two messages before it commits.*

Proof. Let r and i satisfy the assumptions in the claim's statement. In particular, i commits in r at time 1, perhaps after sending some messages in round two. By Corollary 1, process i needs to know that all initial values were 1 when it commits. If i does not receive a round one message from some process $j \neq i$, then there is a run r' in which $v_j = 0$, everyone else starts with 1, and j crashes before sending any messages. Clearly r' is a legal run, $r_i(1) = r'_i(1)$, and so i does not know that $v_j = 1$ at time 1 in r. This establishes (a).

To prove (b), fix, in addition, a process j. Since $f > 1$ and i has no information about failures at time 1 in r, i considers it possible that j crashed without sending round one messages to anyone other than i and that, in addition, i itself will crash immediately after committing.

Recall from Lemma 4 that when i commits, it must know that there is a message chain in the run from j to at least one correct process, with respect to every $j \in \mathbb{P}$. If i is the only process who has heard from j in round one and it crashes immediately after committing, then the only way that there will be a message chain from j to a correct process is if i sends round-two messages to at least $f - 1$ processes other than j before it commits. Since $f > 1$ by assumption, i must send at least one message in round two before committing. Let j' be a process to whom i sends a round-two message before committing in r. The same argument as we have made w.r.t. j (ensuring a message chain from j' to a correct process), yields that i must send round-two messages to at least $f - 1$ processes other than j'. Since i also sends a round-two message to j', it follows that i must send at least f round two messages before committing, establishing claim (b). □

Lemma 5 states that every process that commits before time 2 in a nice run must receive at least $n - 1$ messages in the first round and send at least f messages in the second. Thus, we get:

Corollary 4. *For $f > 1$, no AC protocol in context $\tilde{\gamma}^f$ can commit in a nice run without sending round-two messages.*

Moreover, using Lemma 5 and the fact that every round-one message is received by a unique process, and every round-two message is sent by a unique process, we obtain:

Corollary 5. *Let $\mathcal{P}$ be an AC protocol in $\tilde{\gamma}^f$, in which all processes commit before time 2 in every nice run. Then at least $M \geq n^2 + (f-1)n$ messages are sent in nice runs of $\mathcal{P}$.*

The bound of $M \geq n^2 + (f-1)n$ is smaller than the upper bound of $2n^2 - 2n$ presented by the 1NBAC of [15]. The protocol 1.5D in Figure 6 decides at the same time as 1NBAC and uses only $M = n^2 + (f-1)n$ messages, establishing that the bound is tight. As in Stealth, all messages of the *1.5D* protocol consist of a single bit. The only non-trivial message is 'huh?', which is implemented using at most one bit by being quiet to $\{i+1, \ldots, i+f\} \bmod n$, and sending 1 to the rest.

```
∀i ∈ ℙ:
round 1
        if v_i = 1 then send '1' to all;
round 2
        if received '1' from all in previous round
                then send all[1] to {i + 1, ..., i + f} mod n; commit;
        else send 'huh?' to all;
round 3
        if did not receive any 'huh?' in previous round then halt;
        else      % this can take up to f rounds

                    v̂_i ← { 1  if received all[1] or performed commit
                           { 0  otherwise                              };

                    dec ← B.1.Consensus(f − 1, v̂_i);
                    if haven't performed commit then
                            commit   if dec = 1,
                            abort    if dec = 0
```

Figure 6: Message-optimal AC Protocol *1.5D* for $\tilde{\gamma}^f$ deciding before time 2.

Almost-Surely Terminating Asynchronous Byzantine Agreement Revisited*

Laasya Bangalore[†]
International Institute of Information Technology Bangalore, India
b.laasya@iiitb.org

Ashish Choudhury[‡]
International Institute of Information Technology Bangalore, India
ashish.choudhury@iiitb.ac.in

Arpita Patra[§]
Indian Institute of Science Bangalore, India
arpita@iisc.ac.in

ABSTRACT

The problem of Byzantine Agreement (BA) is of interest to both distributed computing and cryptography community. Following well-known results from the distributed computing literature, BA problem in the *asynchronous* network setting encounters inevitable non-termination issues. The impasse is overcome via randomization that allows construction of BA protocols in two flavours of termination guarantee – with overwhelming probability and with probability one. The latter type termed as *almost-surely terminating* BAs are the focus of this paper. An eluding problem in the domain of almost-surely terminating BAs is achieving a constant expected running time. Our work makes progress in this direction.

In a setting with n parties and an adversary with unbounded computing power controlling at most t parties in Byzantine fashion, we present two asynchronous almost-surely terminating BA protocols:

- With the *optimal resilience* of $t < \frac{n}{3}$, our first protocol runs for expected $O(n)$ time. The existing protocols in the same setting either runs for expected $O(n^2)$ time (Abraham et al, PODC 2008) or requires exponential computing power from the honest parties (Wang, CoRR 2015). In terms of communication complexity, our construction outperforms all the known constructions that offer almost-surely terminating feature.
- With the resilience of $t < \frac{n}{3+\epsilon}$ for any $\epsilon > 0$, our second protocol runs for expected $O(\frac{1}{\epsilon})$ time. The expected running time of our protocol turns constant when ϵ is a constant fraction. The known constructions with constant expected running time either require ϵ to be at least 1 (Feldman-Micali, STOC 1988), implying $t < n/4$, or calls for exponential computing power from the honest parties (Wang, CoRR 2015).

We follow the traditional route of building BA via common coin protocol that in turn reduces to *asynchronous verifiable secret-sharing* (AVSS). Our constructions are built on a variant of AVSS that is termed as *shunning*. A shunning AVSS fails to offer the properties of AVSS when the corrupt parties strike, but allows the honest parties to *locally* detect and shun a set of corrupt parties for any future communication. Our shunning AVSS with $t < n/3$ and $t < \frac{n}{3+\epsilon}$ guarantee $\Omega(n)$ and respectively $\Omega(\epsilon t^2)$ conflicts to be revealed when failure occurs. Turning this shunning AVSS to a common coin protocol constitutes another contribution of our paper.

KEYWORDS

Distributed Computing; Byzantine Agreement; Secret Sharing

ACM Reference Format:
Laasya Bangalore, Ashish Choudhury, and Arpita Patra. 2018. Almost-Surely Terminating Asynchronous Byzantine Agreement Revisited. In *PODC '18: ACM Symposium on Principles of Distributed Computing, July 23–27, 2018, Egham, United Kingdom.* ACM, New York, NY, USA, 10 pages. https://doi.org/10.1145/3212734.3212735

*The full version of this extended abstract is accessible at [3].

†Financial support from Infosys foundation and Microsoft Research India acknowledged.
‡Financial support from Infosys foundation acknowledged.
§The author would like to acknowledge the financial support by SERB Women Excellence Award from Science and Engineering Research Board of India and INSPIRE Faculty Fellowship from Department of Science & Technology, India.

PODC '18, July 23–27, 2018, Egham, United Kingdom

ACM ISBN 978-1-4503-5795-1/18/07...$15.00
https://doi.org/10.1145/3212734.3212735

1 INTRODUCTION

Byzantine Agreement (BA) [20] is a fundamental problem in secure distributed computing. Informally, a BA protocol allows a set of n parties, each holding a private bit, to agree on a common bit, tolerating a *computationally unbounded* adversary who can corrupt any t parties in a *Byzantine* fashion. In the literature, BA has been studied in two prominent network settings – synchronous and asynchronous. In the synchronous setting, it is assumed that the delay of messages over the channels of the network is bounded by a *known constant.* In contrast, in the asynchronous setting, the channels may have arbitrary delays and may deliver messages in any arbitrary order, with the only restriction that every sent message is eventually delivered. To model the worst case, the adversary is allowed to control the scheduling of messages in the network. While the BA problem has been investigated extensively in the *synchronous* setting (see [2, 15, 17] and their references), the progress for the asynchronous setting that models real-world networks like the Internet more appropriately, has been rather slow. The primary difficulty in designing a distributed protocol in the latter setting comes from the fact that it is impossible for an honest party to distinguish between a slow but honest sender (whose messages are delayed) and a corrupt sender (who did not send any message). Hence, at any stage of an asynchronous protocol, a party cannot wait to receive messages from all the n parties (to avoid endless waiting) and the communication from t (potentially slow but honest) parties may have to be ignored.

The condition $t < n/3$ is necessary and sufficient for asynchronous BA (ABA) [20]. An ABA protocol designed with exactly $n = 3t + 1$ parties is thus termed as *optimally-resilient*. From [14], any ABA protocol must have non-terminating runs, where some honest party(ies) may not terminate at all. Use of randomization helps circumvent this impasse [5, 7, 21], leading to two types of constructions. The first kind, known as $(1 - \lambda)$-terminating ABA [9, 10, 19], allow the honest parties to terminate with probability at least $(1 - \lambda)$, for some λ that is non-zero yet negligible. The second kind, referred to as *almost-surely terminating* ABA protocols [1], ensure turning the probability of the occurrence of a non-terminating execution to asymptotically zero, making the honest parties terminate with probability 1. Our focus in this paper is the latter kind of ABA. The historical constructions [5, 7] in this domain require an exponential expected running time (ERT) (and therefore require exponential expected communication as well as computation complexity). The work of [13] reduces the ERT to a constant at the expense of non-optimal resilience of $t < n/4$. The state-of-the-art constitutes the works of [1] and [22]. The former presents the first construction that offers optimal resilience and polynomial ($O(n^2)$, to be specific) ERT simultaneously. The latter reduces the ERT to $O(n)$ at the expense of requiring exponential computation from the honest parties. A side result in the same paper makes the ERT $O(1/\epsilon)$ while decreasing the resilience to $t < \frac{n}{3+\epsilon}$ for any $\epsilon > 0$. Since then constructing an optimally-resilient, polynomial computation complexity ABA with a constant ERT remains an eluding problem. Our work, elaborated below, makes progress in this direction.

Our Results. We present two almost-surely terminating polynomial time ABA protocols. With $t < \frac{n}{3}$, our first protocol has $O(n)$ ERT, improving the ERT of [1] by a factor of n. With $t < \frac{n}{3+\epsilon}$ for any $\epsilon > 0$, our second protocol has ERT $O(\frac{1}{\epsilon})$. The ERT becomes a constant when ϵ is a constant fraction. Previously, constant ERT was achieved either with $\epsilon \geq 1$ (implying $t < n/4$) [13] or at the cost of exponential computing power from honest parties [22]. In terms of expected communication, both our constructions outperform all the known constructions in their respective settings. Our results put in the context of relevant existing results are presented in Table 1, where $\mathbb{F}$ denotes a finite field over which computations are done.

Our Approach. Most ABA protocols follow the blueprint of [5, 7, 21] by reducing ABA to the design of a *common coin* (CC) protocol, which allows the parties to output common randomness with a certain success probability. The success probability that inversely impacts the running time of the ABA is desired to be a constant fraction, for an ABA protocol to have a constant expected running time. [13] showed how to implement CC with a constant success probability using an *asynchronous verifiable secret sharing* (AVSS) scheme. AVSS is a two phase protocol (Sharing and Reconstruction) carried out among n parties with a designated party called *dealer* D in the presence of an adversary who can corrupt up to any t parties including the dealer. The goal is to let D share a secret s, among the n parties during the sharing phase in a way that would later allow for a unique reconstruction of s in the reconstruction phase, irrespective of whether D is honest or corrupt (correctness), while preserving the secrecy of s until the reconstruction phase, if D is honest (privacy).

[13] shows a perfect (no error) AVSS protocol with $t < n/4$ and turns it into an almost-surely terminating ABA with the same resilience. AVSS protocols with $t < n/3$ and with λ probability of non-termination are proposed in [10, 19] and are used for building $(1 - \lambda)$-terminating ABA with a constant expected running time. The work of [1] introduces a weaker form of AVSS called *shunning asynchronous verifiable secret sharing* (SAVSS) with just $t < n/3$ that suffices to construct an almost-surely terminating ABA. An SAVSS fails to offer the correctness property of AVSS when the corrupt parties strike, but allows some honest party to locally detect and shun at least one corrupt party for all future communication. Importantly, the SAVSS scheme *always* terminates. Building on the SAVSS scheme, [1] designs a *shunning common coin* (SCC) protocol. Being a shunning variant of CC, it ensures that either the properties of CC are satisfied or at least one local fault detection occurs along with eventual termination guarantee. Since there are $O(n^2)$ pairs of honest and corrupt parties, there may be $O(n^2)$ 'failed' (but terminating) SAVSS instances (where the correctness is violated) before hitting a correct SAVSS instance. Consequently, a correct CC instance may take $O(n^2)$ 'failed' SCC instances to run, making the ABA protocol of [1] run for $O(n^2)$ expected running time. [22] boosts the fault detection capability of their SAVSS and SCC by a factor of $\Omega(n)$ to come up with an ABA protocol with $O(n)$ expected running time, but at the expense of exponential computation complexity.

At the heart of our ABA lies a new SAVSS that catches asymptotically the same number of local faults as [22] while requiring only polynomial computation complexity. But we get this at the cost of having a termination guarantee that is weaker than the prior SAVSS. Namely, there may not be a termination guarantee at all, but in this case, our protocol helps *all* the honest parties to shun $\Omega(t)$ corrupt parties. This leads to a weaker form of SCC that inherits the same termination property. We then turn this weak SCC to one that always terminates by running a constant number of weak SCC instances. The novelty lies in interleaving these weak SCC instances and combining their outputs in a subtle way to achieve a constant fraction success probability. Interestingly, we show that 3 instances are sufficient to achieve an SCC with a success probability of $\frac{1}{4}$. Lastly, we note that our protocol improves over the expected communication complexity of the SAVSS schemes of [1, 22] and is conceptually simpler than the construction of [1] that is built on top of yet another primitive called *moderated weak SVSS* (MW-SVSS). We now elaborate on our SAVSS with $t < n/3$.

High Level Overview of Our SAVSS. Our starting point is the MW-SVSS of [1], based on the idea of sharing the secret by embedding it in a t-degree symmetric bivariate polynomial $F(x, y)$, where each party P_i receives $f_i(x) = F(x, i)$. The parties then exchange common values with each other to identify a set of $n - t$ parties referred as $\mathcal{V}$, such that each $P_i \in \mathcal{V}$ is confirmed by a set of $n - t$ parties, $\mathcal{V}_i$, about the receipt of consistent polynomials i.e. $f_i(j) = f_j(i)$ holds for each $P_j \in \mathcal{V}_i$. In the reconstruction phase, the polynomial of every P_i from $\mathcal{V}$ is reconstructed from the values produced by

Table 1: Comparison of our results with existing results for almost-surely terminating ABA protocols.

Reference	Resilience	ERT (R)	Expected Communication Complexity	Computation Complexity (in n)
[13]	$n > 4t$	$O(1)$	$O(n^6 \log n \log \lvert\mathbb{F}\rvert)$	Polynomial
[1]	$n > 3t$	$O(n^2)$	$O(n^{10} \log \lvert\mathbb{F}\rvert)$	Polynomial
[22]	$n > 3t$	$O(n)$	$O(n^7 \log \lvert\mathbb{F}\rvert)$	Exponential
[22]	$n > (3+\epsilon)t, \epsilon > 0$	$O(1/\epsilon)$	$O(n^7 \log \lvert\mathbb{F}\rvert)$	Exponential
This paper	$n > 3t$	$O(n)$	$O(n^6 \log \lvert\mathbb{F}\rvert)$	Polynomial
This paper	$n > (3+\epsilon)t, \epsilon > 0$	$O(1/\epsilon)$	$O(n^6 \log \lvert\mathbb{F}\rvert)$	Polynomial

any $n - t - t = n - 2t$ parties in $\mathcal{V}_i$. For a guaranteed termination, $n - 2t$ is the maximum number of values that can be waited for in the asynchronous setting. This construction fails to be an SAVSS, satisfying only a weaker notion of MW-SVSS due to the following: for a *corrupt* D and a *corrupt* P_i from $\mathcal{V}$, an incorrect polynomial of P_i may get reconstructed leading to the violation of correctness, while none of the corrupt parties are shunned. When at least one of D or P_i is *honest*, then either $f_i(x)$ is correctly reconstructed or the honest party between D and P_i can shun the corrupt P_j from $\mathcal{V}_i$ that contributes an incorrect value of $f_i(x)$. We turn this construction to an SAVSS that fails to guarantee correctness at the cost of *locally* catching $\Omega(n)$ faults (irrespective of D) and fails to offer termination at the cost of *globally* shunning $\Omega(n)$ corrupt parties.

While the sharing phase remains to be almost the same, except for the construction of $\mathcal{V}$, we bring the following modifications in the reconstruction phase. First, $n - t - \frac{t}{2}$ values (instead of $n - 2t$ values) are taken into account for reconstructing a polynomial. The protocol will not terminate if some $t/2 + 1$ corrupt parties from one of the $\mathcal{V}_i$ sets do not respond. But *all* the honest parties can keep a tab and shun the non-responsive parties for all future instances. This is the guarantee we promised when termination is not met. Second, the reconstruction of a polynomial is made robust against at most $t/4$ faulty values. This is achieved via Reed-Solomon (RS) error-correction [18] (see the next section for the formal details) that allows error correction of upto $t/4$ values when at least $n - t - t/2$ values of a t-degree polynomial are received and indeed up to $t/4$ values are faulty, provided $n = 3t + 1$. More than $t/4$ parties in some $\mathcal{V}_i$ must contribute incorrect values for P_i's polynomial to be reconstructed incorrectly, leading to the breach of correctness. But some honest parties will be able to locally identify those parties who contributed incorrectly and shun them. This is the guarantee we promised when correctness fails. We note that this guarantee is achieved, even if *both* D as well as P_i are corrupt. This is due to our modified construction of $\mathcal{V}$; we defer the details to Section 3.

Other Related Work. In this work, we consider pair-wise secure channel model, where the parties are assumed to be connected by pair-wise private and authentic channels and the adversary cannot read the messages exchanged between the honest parties; the adversary can only control message scheduling, without preventing the messages of honest parties from being delivered indefinitely. In [6, 11, 16], BA protocols in the full-information model are presented, where the adversary can even listen the communication happening between any pair of honest parties. In [8], computationally-secure ABA protocols are presented, assuming a computationally bounded adversary and a public-key infrastructure set-up.

2 PRELIMINARIES

We assume a set of n parties $\mathcal{P} = \{P_1, \ldots, P_n\}$, connected by pair-wise private and authentic channels. A *computationally unbounded* adversary A can corrupt any $t < n/3$ parties during the execution of a protocol and force the parties under its control (called corrupted parties) to behave in any arbitrary manner during the protocol execution. For simplicity, we assume the adversary is *static*, who decides the set of corrupted parties at the beginning of the execution of a protocol. However, our protocols remain secure even against a more powerful *adaptive* adversary, who decides the set of corrupt parties during the run time, depending upon the values seen so far during the execution of a protocol. For simplicity, we assume $n = 3t + 1$, so that $t = \Theta(n)$. In our protocols, all computation and communication are done over a finite field $\mathbb{F}$, where $|\mathbb{F}| > 2n$.

The communication channels are asynchronous allowing arbitrary, but a finite delay (the messages sent by the honest parties reach their destinations eventually). The order of the message delivery is decided by a *scheduler*, controlled by A. The scheduler can only schedule the messages exchanged between the honest parties, without having access to the "contents" of these messages. A protocol execution is considered as a sequence of *atomic steps*, where a single party is *active* in each such step. A party is activated when it receives a message, after which it performs an internal computation and then possibly sends messages on its outgoing channels. The order of the atomic steps is controlled by A. At the beginning of a protocol, each party will be in a special *start* state. A party is said to *terminate/complete* a protocol if it reaches a *halt* state, after which it does not perform any further computation. A protocol execution is said to be complete if all the honest parties terminate the computation. We measure the running time of a protocol following [9].

In our protocols, each P_i maintains a local "block" set $\mathcal{B}_i$ for all protocol instances and a "wait" set $\mathcal{W}_i$, which are initialized to $\emptyset$. It is to be noted that P_i maintains a *single* local set $\mathcal{B}_i$, where as a *separate* set $\mathcal{W}_i$ is maintained for each SAVSS protocol instance. P_i includes P_j in $\mathcal{B}_i$ if during some protocol instance, x is expected from P_j, but instead $x' \neq x$ is received. An *honest* P_i is said to be in *local conflict* with P_j when $P_j \in \mathcal{B}_i$. P_i includes P_j in $\mathcal{W}_i$ corresponding to some SAVSS protocol instance, if during that instance, P_i is expecting some communication from P_j. While a party taking entry in $\mathcal{B}_i$ remains part of it until the end of the execution of the ABA protocol, any entry in a wait list is temporary and removed as and when the expected communication is received. Until the receipt of the desired communication from a party in $\mathcal{W}_i$, party P_i suspends (saves yet does not use) its future communication.

Definition 2.1 (Shunning Asynchronous Verifiable Secret Sharing (SAVSS)). Let (Sh, Rec) be a pair of protocols for the n parties in $\mathcal{P}$, each maintaining a local $\mathcal{B}_i$ and $\mathcal{W}_i$ set, and for a special party *dealer* $\mathsf{D} \in \mathcal{P}$ that has a private input $s \in \mathbb{F}$ for Sh. (Sh, Rec) is an SAVSS scheme if the following hold for every possible A.

- **Termination**: **(a)**: If D is *honest* and all honest parties participate in Sh, then each honest party eventually terminates Sh. **(b)**: If some honest party terminates Sh, then every honest party eventually terminates Sh. **(c)**: If all honest parties participate in Rec, then *one* of the following holds: **(c.i)**: All honest parties eventually terminate Rec; or **(c.ii)**: Some corrupt parties are included in the $\mathcal{W}$ sets of some honest parties.
- **Correctness**: If the honest parties terminate Rec, then there is a unique value $\bar{s}$ where $\bar{s} = s$ for an honest D and $\bar{s} \in \mathbb{F} \cup \{\perp\}$ for a corrupt D, such that *one* of the following holds: **(a)**: All honest parties output $\bar{s}$ at the end of Rec; or **(b)**: Some corrupt parties are included in the $\mathcal{B}$ sets of some honest parties.
- **Privacy**: If D is *honest*, then the view of A during Sh is independent of s.

Definition 2.2 (Weak Shunning Common Coin (WSCC)). Let Π be a protocol for the n parties, each maintaining a local $\mathcal{B}_i$ and $\mathcal{W}_i$ set, where each party has some local random input and a possible binary output. Then Π is said to be a (p_0, p_1)-weak shunning common coin (WSCC) protocol, if the following hold for every possible A – **Correctness**: If all the honest parties obtain their output, then one of the following holds: **(a)**: For every value $\sigma \in \{0, 1\}$, with probability at least p_σ, all honest parties output σ; or **(b)**: Some corrupt parties are included in the $\mathcal{B}$ sets of some honest parties.

Definition 2.3 (Shunning Common Coin (SCC)). A protocol Π is a p-shunning common coin (SCC) if it is a (p, p)-WSCC and additionally satisfies the following termination guarantee for every possible A – **Termination**: If all honest parties participate in Π, then all honest parties eventually terminate Π.

We stress that we do not explicitly define any termination property for WSCC; the parties may continue running the protocol, even after obtaining output. Our WSCC will be used as a blackbox to design our SCC protocol. And the termination of our SCC ensures that all the underlying instances of WSCC also terminate.

Definition 2.4 (Almost-Surely Terminating Asynchronous Byzantine Agreement (ABA)). Let Π be a protocol for the parties in $\mathcal{P}$, where each P_i has a binary input x_i and a binary output σ_i. Then, Π is said to be an almost-surely terminating ABA protocol, if the following hold for every possible A – **(a) Termination**: If all honest parties participate, then with probability one, all honest parties eventually terminate Π. **(b) Agreement**: $\sigma_i = \sigma_j$ holds for every honest P_i and P_j. **(c) Validity**: If all honest parties have the same input $x \in \{0, 1\}$, then $\sigma_i = x$ holds for every honest P_i.

Existing Tools and Primitives. In our protocols, we use univariate and bivariate polynomials over $\mathbb{F}$. A t-degree univariate polynomial is of the form $f(x) = a_0 + a_1x + \ldots + a_tx^t$, where each $a_i \in \mathbb{F}$. A t-degree symmetric bivariate polynomial is of the form $F(x, y) = \sum_{i=0}^{i=t} \sum_{j=0}^{j=t} r_{ij}x^iy^j$, where $r_{ij} = r_{ji}$ for $i, j = 1, \ldots, t$ and each $r_{ij} \in \mathbb{F}$. We use the following property of Reed-Solomon (RS) codes. Let $f(x)$ be an arbitrary unknown t-degree polynomial and let $\mathcal{K} = \{(i_1, v_{i_1}), \ldots, (i_N, v_{i_N})\}$ be a set of N points such that at most c of them do not lie on $f(x)$ i.e. $v_{i_k} \neq f(i_k)$ holds for c pairs. RS decoding algorithm RS-Dec$(t, c, \mathcal{K})$ allows correct reconstruction of the polynomial $f(x)$ from $\mathcal{K}$ if and only if $N \geq t + 1 + 2c$ [18].

We use the *asynchronous reliable broadcast* protocol of Bracha with $n = 3t + 1$ [7], which allows a *sender* $\mathsf{S} \in \mathcal{P}$ to identically send some message m to all the parties in $\mathcal{P}$. It ensures that: (a) if S is *honest*, then every honest party eventually terminates the protocol with output m; (b) if S is *corrupt* and some honest party terminates with output $m^\star$, then every other honest party eventually terminates with output $m^\star$. The protocol has communication complexity of $O(n^2)$ bits over point-to-point channels to broadcast a single bit message. We use the term P_i *broadcasts m* to mean that P_i acts as S and invokes an instance of Bracha's protocol to broadcast m. Similarly, the term P_j *receives m from the broadcast of* P_i means that P_j (as a receiver) completes the execution of P_i's broadcast (namely the instance of broadcast protocol where P_i is S), with m as output.

3 SAVSS PROTOCOL WITH $n = 3t + 1$

D hides its secret s in the constant term of a t-degree symmetric bivariate polynomial $F(x, y)$ and gives the ith t-degree univariate polynomial $f_i(x) = F(x, i)$ to each P_i. For an honest D, every pair of *honest* parties P_i, P_j should be "pair-wise consistent" and $f_i(j) = f_j(i)$ should hold. So each P_i is designated as a "guard" to verify the pair-wise consistency of $f_i(x)$ with $n - t$ parties P_j, who are considered as "sub-guards" for P_i. Each P_i, P_j privately exchanges the common value of $f_i(x)$ and $f_j(x)$ and then publicly announce the status of consistency check. The goal is then to identify if D has given t-degree univariate polynomials to at least $n - t$ guards, say $\mathcal{V}$, such that each guard P_i in $\mathcal{V}$ has further verified the pair-wise consistency of its polynomial $f_i(x)$ with at least $n - t$ sub-guards, denoted by $\mathcal{V}_i$. Moreover, for every guard P_i in $\mathcal{V}$, every sub-guard in $\mathcal{V}_i$ should be from $\mathcal{V}$, implying that sub-guard P_j of *any* guard is itself a guard. To ensure that all parties identify the same $\mathcal{V}$ and sub-guard lists, D is assigned the task of identifying $\mathcal{V}$ and the sub-guard lists and broadcast the same. The parties terminate the sharing phase, if D broadcasts a legitimate $\mathcal{V}$ and sub-guard lists. If D is *honest*, then the set of honest parties always constitute a candidate $\mathcal{V}$ and hence the sharing phase always terminates for an honest D.

During the reconstruction phase, the goal is to reconstruct back t-degree univariate polynomials of *all* the guards in $\mathcal{V}$ and using them, interpolate the t-degree bivariate polynomial committed by D. Due to asynchrony, the parties cannot afford for *each* guard in $\mathcal{V}$ to reveal its univariate polynomial. Instead, the univariate polynomial of each guard P_j is reconstructed using the points held by the sub-guards P_k in $\mathcal{V}_j$ who are asked to publicly reveal their respective univariate polynomial $f_k(x)$. We wait for $n - t - \frac{t}{2} = \frac{3t}{2} + 1$ sub-guards in $\mathcal{V}_j$ to respond. Then using the $\frac{3t}{2} + 1$ revealed $f_j(k)$ values, we try to error-correct $\frac{t}{4}$ errors and interpolate back $f_j(x)$. When at most $\frac{t}{4}$ sub-guards out of the $\frac{3t}{2} + 1$ sub-guards produce incorrect polynomials, the reconstructed polynomial $f_j(x)$ is correct. Otherwise, at least $\frac{t}{4} + 1$ *corrupt* sub-guards P_k who produced wrong polynomials and are also guards will be identified locally as corrupt by at least one *honest* sub-guard P_l in $\mathcal{V}_k$. The reconstruction phase may not terminate if less than $\frac{3t}{2}+1$ parties from $\mathcal{V}_j$ participate for some guard P_j. But this will lead to communication from at least $\frac{t}{2}+1$ corrupt sub-guards in $\mathcal{V}_j$ being marked as "pending" by *all* honest parties. As a consequence, in any subsequent SAVSS instance, there will be at most $\frac{t}{2}-1$ corrupt participants, resulting in at least $\frac{3t}{2}+1$ *honest* sub-guards in each sub-guard list. So the adversary can neither disrupt the correctness nor fail termination of any further SAVSS reconstruction instance.

The sharing and reconstruction protocols are presented in Fig 1. Each instance of SAVSS is associated with a unique id sid $\in \mathbb{N}$. All messages communicated during the SAVSS instance sid are tagged with this id. However, we skip tagging every message explicitly with id for simplicity. In the sharing phase, once $\mathcal{V}$ is agreed upon, then the parties locally populate their respective $\mathcal{W}$ sets, anticipating the values they expect from the various guards and sub-guards during the reconstruction phase. At the beginning of each instance of the SAVSS, a corresponding *memory management* protocol SAVSS-MM is invoked (Fig 1), according to which each party locally decides whether to process a received message as per the SAVSS, delay it temporarily or block it permanently. The SAVSS-MM protocol for id sid examines the messages produced by the various sub-guards during the reconstruction phase and accordingly the $\mathcal{W}$ and $\mathcal{B}$ lists of the parties are updated. We stress that the parties keep executing SAVSS-MM with id sid, even after terminating the (Sh, Rec) protocols with id sid. This ensures that if some message is pending from a party in instance sid, then its communication is ignored by the SAVSS-MM protocol in any future instance sid′ > sid. This will be useful in our WSCC protocol to ensure global shunning of at least $\frac{t}{2}+1$ corrupt parties, if any Rec instance fails to terminate in WSCC. Due to space constraints, we only state the following theorem and refer to [3] for the formal proof.

THEOREM 3.1. *For every* sid $\in \mathbb{N}$, *the pair of protocols* (Sh, Rec) *with id* sid *is an SAVSS scheme. The* Sh *and* Rec *protocols have a communication complexity of* $O(n^4 \log|\mathbb{F}|)$ *bits each.*

4 WEAK SHUNNING COMMON COIN (WSCC) PROTOCOL WITH $n = 3t + 1$

Our WSCC protocol WSCC has two main stages. In the first stage, each party attaches itself with a uniform random value that is unknown to all including itself and simultaneously ensures that a "sufficiently large" number of parties do the same. In the second stage, the secret values are revealed and a bit is output taking these opened values into account. The first stage is implemented by making each party act as a dealer to run n instances of Sh and share n random values from $\mathbb{F}$, one for each party. Each party P_i *attaches* itself, with the secrets meant for it, to a set of at least $t+1$ dealers C_i whose Sh instances it terminates. Then each P_i decides whether there exists a sufficiently large set of parties H_i, such that the set C_j has been identified for each P_j in H_i. Once this is done, the next stage is to reconstruct the values attached to the parties in H_i, based on which each party in H_i is *associated* with a uniformly random value. The transition from stage one to stage two is locally marked by setting a local Boolean variable $\texttt{Flag}_i$ by each P_i. Party P_i then decides its outcome based on the values associated to the parties in H_i.

The SCC protocol of [1] ensures that either all honest parties output the same coin with probability at least $\frac{1}{4}$ or one of the Rec instances fail and *at least one* local conflict occurs. However, the SCC protocol *always* terminates, as their underlying Rec instances *always* terminate. We depart from the protocol of [1] in several ways. First, when Rec instance fails and the correctness of common coin is disturbed, at least $\frac{t}{4}+1$ local conflicts, instead of just one, are guaranteed to occur, allowing a faster convergence to a correct instance. This directly carries over from the correctness of the underlying SAVSS protocol. Second, the parties may not be able to compute their outcome always, owing to the fact that some underlying Rec instance may not terminate, in contrast to guaranteed termination of the SCC of [1]. In this case, we ensure that at least $\frac{t}{2}+1$ corrupt parties are shunned by *all* honest parties. This guarantee ensures that in any subsequent invocation of WSCC, there can be at most $\frac{t}{2}-1$ corrupt parties participating, who can never prevent the honest parties from computing their outcome. Ensuring the above, however, needs an additional step in the existing SCC protocol and a clever memory management protocol WSCC-MM. Specifically, we do it in two steps. First, by using a "watch-list mechanism" and applying a stricter condition for attaching a party's shared value, we ensure that *at least* $t+1$ honest parties shun at least $\frac{t}{2}+1$ corrupt parties when some Rec instance contributing its secret to some honest party's output does not terminate. Next, our WSCC-MM ensures that *all* honest parties shun those $\frac{t}{2}+1$ corrupt parties from participating in any subsequent instance of WSCC. The details follow.

Let Sh_{jk} denote the Sh instance with P_j as a dealer to share a secret for P_k and let Rec_{jk} denote the corresponding Rec instance. Each party P_i maintains a local dynamic watch-list $\mathcal{T}_i$, to keep track of instances Sh_{jk} that terminate for P_i. The goal to is to keep their corresponding Rec instances under surveillance so that P_i shuns at least $\frac{t}{2}+1$ corrupt parties in case Rec instance of some Sh instance from $\mathcal{T}_i$ does not terminate. Now to ensure that not just P_i alone but at least a set of $t+1$ honest parties shun the same set of corrupt parties, the condition for inclusion in C_i and attaching a value is made stricter. Namely, P_i adds P_j to C_i if at least $n-t$ parties confirm that Sh_{jk} for all $k = 1, \ldots, n$ terminates for them and is present in their respective $\mathcal{T}$ sets. Now to ensure that *every* honest party in $\mathcal{P}$ (and not just $t+1$ honest parties) shuns these corrupt parties, we do the following. As part of the memory management protocol WSCC-MM, a party P_i "approves" a party P_j *locally* by broadcasting OK signal only when P_j clears all pending messages as a part of all the Rec instances corresponding to $\mathcal{T}_i$ which is *freezed* at the time of setting $\texttt{Flag}_i$. Finally, P_i approves P_j *globally* and allows it to participate in any subsequent WSCC instance, if at least $n-t$ parties broadcast OK message for P_j during WSCC-MM. As a consequence of these steps, any instance Rec_{jk} that contributes to the attached value of some honest party is watched by at least $t+1$ honest parties. These parties will shun and never broadcast OK signal for the shunned $\frac{t}{2}+1$ corrupt parties when the Rec_{jk} instance does not terminate. So these corrupt parties are never approved globally by any of the honest parties. Consequently, these corrupt parties are shunned for all subsequent WSCC invocations.

Due to asynchrony, the sets H_i and H_j might be different for P_i and P_j. To ensure that *all* honest parties participate in the Rec

Figure 1: SAVSS with $n = 3t + 1$ and id sid.

Protocol $\mathsf{Sh}(\mathsf{D}, \mathcal{P}, s)$

Distribution by D – D selects a random, t-degree symmetric bivariate polynomial $F(x, y)$ with $F(0, 0) = s$ and sends $f_i(x) = F(x, i)$ to each $P_i \in \mathcal{P}$.

Pair-wise consistency check – Each party $P_i \in \mathcal{P}$ (including D), executes the following code:

- Wait until a t-degree polynomial $\widehat{f}_i(x)$ is received from D.
- For $j = 1, \ldots, n$, send $\widehat{f}_i(j)$ to party P_j. Then broadcast the message sent.
- If $\widehat{f}_{ji}$ is received from P_j and sent is received from the broadcast of P_j, such that $\widehat{f}_{ji} = \widehat{f}_i(j)$, then broadcast (ok, P_j).

Construction of $\mathcal{V}$ – The following code is executed only by D:

- Find sets $\mathcal{V} \subseteq \mathcal{P}$ and $\mathcal{V}_i \subseteq \mathcal{P}$, for every $P_i \in \mathcal{V}$, such that: $|\mathcal{V}| \geq n - t, |\mathcal{V} \cap \mathcal{V}_i| \geq n - t$ and for every $P_i \in \mathcal{V}$ and $P_j \in \mathcal{V}_i$, (ok, P_j) and sent is received from the broadcast of P_i and P_j respectively.
- Redefine $\mathcal{V}$ as $\mathcal{V} = \mathcal{V} \cap (\bigcup_{P_j \in \mathcal{V}} \mathcal{V}_j)$ and $\mathcal{V}_i = \mathcal{V} \cap \mathcal{V}_i$. Broadcast the redefined $\mathcal{V}$ and $\mathcal{V}_i$ sets.

Verifying $\mathcal{V}$ and populating $\mathcal{W}$ sets – Each $P_i \in \mathcal{P}$ (including D) executes the following code:

- Wait to receive $\mathcal{V}$ and $\mathcal{V}_j$ corresponding to each $P_j \in \mathcal{V}$ from the broadcast of D. On receiving check if $\mathcal{V} = \bigcup_{P_j \in \mathcal{V}} \mathcal{V}_j$ and $|\mathcal{V} \cap \mathcal{V}_j| \geq n - t$ holds for every $P_j \in \mathcal{V}$. *Accept* $\mathcal{V}$ if for each $P_j \in \mathcal{V}$ and each $P_k \in \mathcal{V}_j$, the message (ok, P_k) and sent is received from the broadcast of P_j and P_k respectively.
- Wait until $\mathcal{V}$ is accepted. Then populate $\mathcal{W}_{(i,\mathsf{sid})}$, initialized to $\emptyset$ as follows and terminate:
  - If P_i = D, then add $(P_j, P_k, f_j(k))$ to $\mathcal{W}_{(i,\mathsf{sid})}$ for each $P_j \in \mathcal{V}$ and each $P_k \in \mathcal{V}_j$. This is interpreted as D expects P_k to reveal $f_j(k)$ as a sub-guard for the guard P_j during Rec.
  - If $P_i \in \mathcal{V}$, then add the following triplets to $\mathcal{W}_{(i,\mathsf{sid})}$:
    - $(P_i, P_j, \widehat{f}_i(j))$ for each $P_j \in \mathcal{V}_i$. This is interpreted as P_i (as a guard), expects P_j to reveal $\widehat{f}_i(j)$ (as a sub-guard) during Rec.
    - $(P_i, P_j, \widehat{f}_i(j))$ for all P_j such that $P_j \notin \mathcal{V}_i$, $P_j \in \mathcal{V}$ and $P_i \in \mathcal{V}_j$. This is interpreted as P_i (as a sub-guard), expects P_j to reveal $\widehat{f}_i(j)$ (as a sub-guard of some guard) during Rec.
  - Else add the triplet $(P_j, P_k, \star)$ to $\mathcal{W}_{(i,\mathsf{sid})}$ for each $P_j \in \mathcal{V}$ and each $P_k \in \mathcal{V}_j$. This is interpreted as P_i expects P_k to reveal some value from $\mathbb{F}$ as a sub-guard for the guard P_j during Rec.

Protocol $\mathsf{Rec}(\mathsf{D}, \mathcal{P}, s)$

Making the polynomials public — Each $P_i \in \mathcal{V}$ broadcasts the t-degree polynomial $\widehat{f}_i(x)$.

Reconstructing the polynomials of guards: The following code is executed by every party $P_i \in \mathcal{P}$:

- For each $P_j \in \mathcal{V}$, initialize $\mathcal{K}_j$ to $\emptyset$. Add $(k, \widehat{f}_k(j))$ to $\mathcal{K}_j$, if a t-degree polynomial $\widehat{f}_k(x)$ is received from the broadcast of $P_k \in \mathcal{V}_j$.
- Wait until $|\mathcal{K}_j| \geq n - t - \frac{t}{2} = \frac{3}{2}t + 1$ for each $P_j \in \mathcal{V}$ and then execute RS-Dec$(t, \frac{t}{4}, \mathcal{K}_j)$. If for some $P_j \in \mathcal{V}$, RS-Dec$(t, \frac{t}{4}, \mathcal{K}_j)$ does not output a t-degree polynomial, then output $\perp$ and terminate.
- Else let $\bar{f}_j(x)$ denote the t-degree polynomial obtained by RS-Dec$(t, \frac{t}{4}, \mathcal{K}_j)$. If there exists a t-degree symmetric bivariate polynomial $\overline{F}(x, y)$, such that $\overline{F}(x, j) = \bar{f}_j(x)$ holds for each $P_j \in \mathcal{V}$, then output $\bar{s} = \overline{F}(0, 0)$ and terminate. Else output $\perp$ and terminate.

Protocol SAVSS-MM(D)

The following code is executed by each $P_i \in \mathcal{P}$:

Initialization: Initialize $\mathcal{W}_{(i,\mathsf{sid})}$ and $\mathcal{B}_i$ to $\emptyset$. The set $\mathcal{B}_i$ is initialized by P_i only once (when sid = 0) and dynamically updated during the instances of SAVSS-MM. The set $\mathcal{W}_{(i,\mathsf{sid})}$ is initialized in and maintained for the SAVSS instance with id sid only.

Blocking messages: If $P_j \in \mathcal{B}_i$, discard any message received from P_j during (Sh, Rec) with id sid.

Filtering messages: If $P_j \notin \mathcal{B}_i$, then any message received from P_j during the SAVSS instance with id sid is processed as follows:

1. If a t-degree $\widehat{f}_k(x)$ is received from the broadcast of $P_k \in \mathcal{V}$ during Rec with id sid such that $(P_j, P_k, val) \in \mathcal{W}_{(i,\mathsf{sid})}$, then:
   - If $val = \star$, remove (P_j, P_k, x) from $\mathcal{W}_{(i,\mathsf{sid})}$ and forward $\widehat{f}_k(x)$ to the SAVSS instance sid;
   - If $val \neq \star$ and $\widehat{f}_k(j) = val$, then do the same as above;
   - If $val \neq \star$ and $\widehat{f}_k(j) \neq val$, add P_k to $\mathcal{B}_i$.
2. Else forward the received message to the SAVSS instance sid.

instances, required to reconstruct the attached values of the parties in H_i and H_j, every honest party keeps participating in WSCC, even after obtaining its output. This is crucial as there is no guarantee of termination of a Rec instance, if only a strict subset of honest parties participate in the Rec instance. This is why there is no termination condition imposed on WSCC. Protocol WSCC and WSCC-MM are formally presented in Fig 2. We note that our protocol has different probabilities of outputting 0 and 1. Yet, our SCC that uses WSCC as a subprotocol outputs both possible bits with the same probability of $\frac{1}{4}$, a property achieved traditionally by the existing common coins.

Each instance of WSCC is identified by a unique id (sid, r), where $\text{sid} \in \mathbb{N}$ and $\text{r} \in \{1, 2, 3\}$. Looking ahead, in our SCC protocol SCC with id sid, three parallel instances of WSCC are executed and we will associate the ids (sid, 1), (sid, 2) and (sid, 3) to these WSCC instances. Inside the WSCC protocol, each $P_i \in \mathcal{P}$ acts as a D and invokes an instance of Sh on the behalf of every party $P_j \in \mathcal{P}$. These Sh (and the corresponding Rec and SAVSS-MM) instances will be associated with id of the form[1] $(\text{sid}, \text{r}, P_i, P_j)$; accordingly, the corresponding $\mathcal{W}$ sets for each P_k will be of the form $\mathcal{W}_{(k, \text{sid}, \text{r}, P_i, P_j)}$. Also, we add additional technicalities in WSCC to ensure proper working of the watch-list mechanism discussed earlier, which is very crucial for the termination of our SCC that uses WSCC as a sub-protocol. An instance of WSCC-MM accompany each instance of WSCC, according to which each party locally decides whether to process a received message as per the WSCC protocol, delay it temporarily or block it permanently. Due to space constraints, we only state the following theorem and refer to [3] for the formal proof.

THEOREM 4.1. *For any id* (sid, r) *with* $\text{sid} \in \mathbb{N}$ *and* $\text{r} \in \{1, 2, 3\}$, *protocol* WSCC *with id* (sid, r) *is a* (0.139, 0.63)*-WSCC scheme with communication complexity of* $O(n^6 \log |\mathbb{F}|)$ *bits.*

5 THE SHUNNING COMMON COIN (SCC) PROTOCOL WITH $n = 3t + 1$

Here we present our SCC protocol SCC. In SCC, the parties execute three parallel instances of WSCC and it is guaranteed that each party obtains its output in at least two WSCC instances, based on which it decides its outcome for SCC and terminates. Note that different parties may end up using different pairs of WSCC instances to decide their outcome for SCC. Despite this, we ensure that the output of SCC for all honest parties is the same with a probability of at least 0.25. It is precisely to achieve this property for which the parties need to consider the outcome of two WSCC instances. The intuition behind the guaranteed output delivery in two out of the three WSCC instances is as follows: if there is an WSCC instance for which no honest party obtains its output, then the corresponding WSCC-MM protocol ensures that communication from at least $\frac{t}{2} + 1$ corrupt parties are ignored by all the honest parties in the remaining WSCC instances. As a consequence, there can be at most $\frac{t}{2} - 1$ corrupt parties participating in the remaining WSCC instances. And these many corrupt parties are not sufficient to prevent output delivery in the remaining WSCC instances.

[1]Recall that during the description of Sh, Rec and SAVSS-MM, we used ids of the form sid; the additional components r, P_i and P_j are brought out here to distinguish the various instances of Sh, Rec and SAVSS-MM invoked inside WSCC.

There might be a problem if a P_j terminates SCC (and the underlying WSCC instances) *immediately* after obtaining its output in two WSCC instances. This is because a different party, say P_i, may be still in the process of obtaining its outcome in two WSCC instances. And the participation of *all* honest parties is required for the output delivery in every WSCC instance. This is because output delivery in WSCC instances depend upon the termination of the underlying Rec instances, which is not guaranteed if only a strict subset of honest parties participate in the Rec instances. To deal with this problem, as soon as an honest P_j obtains its output from two WSCC instances, it broadcasts the identity of these WSCC instances, along with the corresponding H_j and S_j sets and then terminates SCC. Every party P_i who has not yet obtained its output from two WSCC instances check if the broadcasted H_j and S_j sets are subset of its own $\mathcal{G}_i$ and $\mathcal{S}_i$ sets respectively, which eventually happens (see [3] for a proof of this). As a result, P_i can now decide its outcome for the WSCC instances based on the received H_j sets, instead of basing them on H_i sets (a similar idea is also used in the SCC protocol of [22] to ensure guaranteed termination). Protocol SCC is presented in Fig 3. Each instance of SCC is identified by a unique id $\text{sid} \in \mathbb{N}$. Inside SCC, there are three invocations of the WSCC protocol with ids of the form (sid, r), where $\text{r} \in \{1, 2, 3\}$. The properties of SCC are stated in the following theorem, whose proof is available in [3].

THEOREM 5.1. *For every* $\text{sid} \in \mathbb{N}$, *protocol* SCC *is a* $\frac{1}{4}$*-SCC scheme, with communication complexity of* $O(n^6 \log |\mathbb{F}|)$ *bits.*

6 ALMOST-SURELY TERMINATING ABA

The design of our ABA protocol ABA from SCC is exactly the same as that of [1, 22]. We first recall a voting protocol called Vote from [9], which will be used in our ABA protocol. Informally, the voting protocol does "whatever can be done deterministically" to reach agreement. In a voting protocol, every party has a single bit as input. The protocol tries to find out whether there is a detectable majority for some value among the inputs of the parties. In the protocol, each party's output can have *five* different forms:

(1) For $\sigma \in \{0, 1\}$, the output $(\sigma, 2)$ stands for "overwhelming majority for σ";
(2) For $\sigma \in \{0, 1\}$, the output $(\sigma, 1)$ stands for "distinct majority for σ";
(3) The output $(\Lambda, 0)$ stands for "non-distinct majority".

The voting protocol ensures the following properties:

(1) If each honest party has the same input σ, then each honest party outputs $(\sigma, 2)$;
(2) If some honest party outputs $(\sigma, 2)$, then every other honest party outputs either $(\sigma, 2)$ or $(\sigma, 1)$;
(3) If some honest party outputs $(\sigma, 1)$ and no honest party outputs $(\sigma, 2)$ then each honest party outputs $(\sigma, 1)$ or $(\Lambda, 0)$.

We refer to [3, 19] for the description of Vote and its properties. Given protocol SCC and Vote, we design our ABA protocol called ABA for a single bit (Fig 4), following [1, 22]. The protocol is based on the idea of [9], which uses CC and Vote for several rounds to decide the outcome. In our case, we replace the CC protocol by our SCC protocol. In the protocol, during each iteration, every party computes a "modified input" value. In the first iteration, the

Figure 2: WSCC with $n = 3t + 1$ and id (sid, r).

WSCC(sid, r)

Each $P_i \in \mathcal{P}$ executes the following code:

1. For $1 \le j \le n$, choose a random secret $s_{ij} \in_R \mathbb{F}$ on the behalf of P_j and as a D, invoke an instance $\mathsf{Sh}(P_i, \mathcal{P}, s_{ij})$ of Sh with id $(\mathsf{sid}, \mathsf{r}, P_i, P_j)$. Denote this invocation by Sh_{ij}. Participate in the invocations Sh_{jk} for every $P_j, P_k \in \mathcal{P}$.
2. Broadcast $(\texttt{Completed}, (\mathsf{sid}, \mathsf{r}, P_j, P_k))$ and add $(\mathsf{sid}, \mathsf{r}, P_j, P_k)$ to $\mathcal{T}_{(i,\mathsf{sid},\mathsf{r})}$, initialized to $\emptyset$, on terminating Sh_{jk}.
3. Initialize a set $\mathcal{C}_i$ to $\emptyset$. Add party P_j to $\mathcal{C}_i$, if the following two conditions are satisfied for all $1 \le k \le n$:
   - Sh_{jk} has terminated and
   - The message $(\texttt{Completed}, (\mathsf{sid}, \mathsf{r}, P_j, P_k))$ is received from the broadcast of $n - t$ parties.

   Wait until $|\mathcal{C}_i| \ge t + 1$. Then, assign $C_i = \mathcal{C}_i$ and broadcast the message $(\texttt{Attach}, C_i, P_i)$. We say that that the values $\{s_{ji} | P_j \in C_i\}$ represent the *secrets attached to party* P_i.
4. *Accept* P_j and include it in the set $\mathcal{G}_i$, if the message $(\texttt{Attach}, C_j, P_j)$ is received from the broadcast of P_j and $C_j \subseteq \mathcal{C}_i$ holds. Wait until $|\mathcal{G}_i| \ge n - t$. Then, let $G_i = \mathcal{G}_i$ and broadcast the message $(\mathsf{Ready}, P_i, G_i)$.
5. Consider P_j to be *supportive* and include it in the set $\mathcal{S}_i$, if P_i receives the message $(\mathsf{Ready}, P_j, G_j)$ from the broadcast of P_j and each party in G_j is accepted (i.e. $G_j \subseteq \mathcal{G}_i$). Wait until $|\mathcal{S}_i| \ge n - t$. Then, set $\texttt{Flag}_i = 1$ (initialized to 0). Let S_i and H_i denote the contents of $\mathcal{S}_i$ and $\mathcal{G}_i$ respectively, when $\texttt{Flag}_i$ becomes 1.
6. Wait until $\texttt{Flag}_i = 1$. Then reconstruct the secrets attached to all the accepted parties. That is, for each $P_j \in C_k$ such that $P_k \in \mathcal{G}_i$, start participating in the instances $\mathsf{Rec}(P_j, \mathcal{P}, s_{jk})$. Denote this instance of Rec as Rec_{jk} and let r_{jk} be the corresponding output. (Some parties may be included in $\mathcal{G}_i$ after $\texttt{Flag}_i$ is set to 1. In that case, immediately start participating in the corresponding Rec instances.) In addition, stop executing step 2. That is, only keep participating in any Sh instance which has not yet terminated, after setting $\texttt{Flag}_i$ to one. But upon terminating these Sh instances, do not include these Sh instances to $\mathcal{T}_i$ and do not broadcast any $\texttt{Completed}$ message
7. Let $u \stackrel{def}{=} \lceil 2.22n \rceil$. For every $P_k \in \mathcal{G}_i$, define v_k, the *value associated with* P_k, to be the sum modulo u of all the secrets attached to P_k. That is, $v_k \stackrel{def}{=} \left(\sum_{P_j \in C_k} r_{jk}\right) \mod u$.
8. Wait until the values associated will all the parties in H_i are computed. If there exists a party $P_k \in H_i$ where $v_k = 0$, then output 0. Else, output 1. [a]

WSCC-MM(sid, r)

Each $P_i \in \mathcal{P}$ executes the following code:

Initialization: Initialize the set $\mathcal{T}_{(i,\mathsf{sid},\mathsf{r})}$ to $\emptyset$ and the set $\mathcal{A}_{(i,\mathsf{sid},\mathsf{r})}$ to $\emptyset$ at the beginning of WSCC instance with id (sid, r).

Permanently blocking: If $P_j \in \mathcal{B}_i$, then all the messages received from P_j during the WSCC instance with id (sid, r) are discarded.

Filtering messages:

- If r = 1, then forward every message received from P_j during the WSCC instance with id (sid, r) to the underlying WSCC protocol.
- If r > 1, then any message received from P_j during the WSCC instance with id (sid, r) is processed as follows:
  - If $P_j \in \mathcal{A}_{(i,\mathsf{sid},\mathsf{r}')}$ for all $\mathsf{r}' < \mathsf{r}$, then forward the message to the WSCC instance with id (sid, r).
  - Else, delay it.

Identifying pending messages from the current WSCC instance:

- If $\texttt{Flag}_i = 1$, then broadcast the message (OK, P_j) if the following conditions hold:
  - $P_j \notin \mathcal{B}_i$ and
  - For every SAVSS instance $(\mathsf{sid}, \mathsf{r}, P_k, P_l) \in \mathcal{T}_{(i,\mathsf{sid},\mathsf{r})}$, there exists no triplet of the form $(\star, P_j, \star)$ in the set $\mathcal{W}_{(i,\mathsf{sid},\mathsf{r},P_k,P_l)}$.
- If $n - t$ parties broadcast (OK, P_j), then add P_j to $\mathcal{A}_{(i,\mathsf{sid},\mathsf{r})}$.

[a] Party P_i keeps executing the protocol even if it obtains its output. Note that the step for computing the output will be executed at most once, as the set H_i gets fixed, once $\texttt{Flag}_i$ is set to 1.

modified input of a party P_i is its private input bit (for the ABA protocol) x_i. In each iteration, the parties execute an instance of the protocol Vote and SCC *sequentially*, that is, a party participates in the instance of SCC, only after terminating the instance of Vote. If a party outputs $(\sigma, 1)$ in the instance of the Vote protocol, implying that it finds a "distinct majority" for the value σ, then the party sets its modified input for the next iteration to σ, irrespective of the value which is going to be output in the instance of SCC; otherwise, the party sets its modified input for the next iteration to be the output of the SCC protocol, which is invoked by all the parties

Figure 3: Protocol SCC(sid): the shunning common coin protocol with $n = 3t + 1$ and id sid.

Each $P_i \in \mathcal{P}$ executes the following code:

1. Invoke WSCC(sid, r) for r = 1, 2, 3. Denote the instance WSCC(sid, r) as WSCC_r and let $C_{\mathsf{sid,r},i}, \mathcal{C}_{\mathsf{sid,r},i}, \mathcal{G}_{\mathsf{sid,r},i}, G_{\mathsf{sid,r},i}, \mathcal{S}_{\mathsf{sid,r},i}, S_{\mathsf{sid,r},i}$ and $H_{\mathsf{sid,r},i}$ denote the $C_i, \mathcal{C}_i, \mathcal{G}_i, G_i, \mathcal{S}_i, S_i$ and H_i sets respectively, built during WSCC_r. // See protocol WSCC in Section 4 for the notations.
2. If output is obtained during WSCC_r, include (sid, r) to the decision set $\mathsf{DS}_{(i,\mathsf{sid})}$, initialized to $\emptyset$.
3. If $|\mathsf{DS}_{(i,\mathsf{sid})}| \geq 2$ then do the following, followed by terminating $\mathsf{WSCC}_1, \mathsf{WSCC}_2, \mathsf{WSCC}_3$, along with the underlying WSCC-MM, SAVSS-MM instances, followed by terminating SCC:
   - Broadcast (Terminate, P_i, $\mathsf{DS}_{(i,\mathsf{sid})}$, $\{(S_{\mathsf{sid,r},i}, H_{\mathsf{sid,r},i})\}_{(\mathsf{sid,r}) \in \mathsf{DS}_{(i,\mathsf{sid})}}$).
   - Output 0 if 0 is computed as the output during WSCC_r for any $(\mathsf{sid,r}) \in \mathsf{DS}_{(i,\mathsf{sid})}$, else output 1.
4. If (Terminate, P_j, $\mathsf{DS}_{(j,\mathsf{sid})}$, $\{(S_{\mathsf{sid,r},j}, H_{\mathsf{sid,r},j})\}_{(\mathsf{sid,r}) \in \mathsf{DS}_{(j,\mathsf{sid})}}$) is received from the broadcast of some party P_j, then do the following:

   a Check if all the following holds:
   - $|\mathsf{DS}_{(j,\mathsf{sid})}| \geq 2$;
   - For every $(\mathsf{sid,r}) \in \mathsf{DS}_{(j,\mathsf{sid})}$, the condition $S_{\mathsf{sid,r},j} \subseteq \mathcal{S}_{\mathsf{sid,r},i}$ and $H_{\mathsf{sid,r},j} \subseteq \mathcal{G}_{\mathsf{sid,r},i}$ holds;
   - For every $(\mathsf{sid,r}) \in \mathsf{DS}_{(j,\mathsf{sid})}$, the associated value v_k of every $P_k \in H_{\mathsf{sid,r},j}$ is computed during WSCC_r. // See WSCC in Section 4 for the meaning of associated values.

   b If all the above holds then do the following, followed by terminating $\mathsf{WSCC}_1, \mathsf{WSCC}_2, \mathsf{WSCC}_3$, along with the underlying WSCC-MM, SAVSS-MM instances, followed by terminating SCC.
   - For every $(\mathsf{sid,r}) \in \mathsf{DS}_{(j,\mathsf{sid})}$ where output is not yet obtained in WSCC_r, compute the output of WSCC_r as follows: If there exists a party $P_k \in H_{\mathsf{sid,r},j}$ whose associated value $v_k = 0$, then set 0 as the output of WSCC_r. Else, set 1 as the output of WSCC_r.
   - Output 0 if 0 is the output during WSCC_r for any $(\mathsf{sid,r}) \in \mathsf{DS}_{(j,\mathsf{sid})}$, else output 1.

in each iteration, irrespective of whether the output of the SCC protocol is used or not by the parties for setting the modified inputs for the next iteration. Once a party outputs $(\sigma, 2)$ in an instance of the Vote protocol, implying that it finds an "overwhelming majority" for the value σ, then it broadcasts σ. Finally, once a party receives σ from the broadcast of $t + 1$ parties, it outputs σ and terminates. The properties of ABA are stated in the theorem below and the proof appears in [3].

THEOREM 6.1. *Let $n = 3t + 1$. Then protocol* ABA *is an almost-surely terminating ABA protocol for a single bit with expected communication complexity of $O(n^7 \log |\mathbb{F}|)$ bits and expected running time of* $\mathsf{R} = O(n)$.

7 VARIANTS OF OUR ABA PROTOCOL

7.1 Agreement on $t + 1$ Bits Simultaneously

We show how to modify the protocol ABA to allow agreement on $t + 1$ bits simultaneously, without affecting its running time or communication complexity. So in the amortized sense, agreement on a single bit involves an expected communication complexity of $O(n^6 \log |\mathbb{F}|)$ bits. We first discuss how we can modify WSCC to obtain a multi-valued WSCC protocol MWSCC, which allows the parties to obtain $t + 1$ independent common coins, instead of a single common coin. Before doing that, we discuss a well known randomness-extraction technique, used in MWSCC.

Information-Theoretic Randomness Extraction [4, 12, 19]. Let $a_1, \ldots, a_N \in \mathbb{F}$, such that *at least* K out of these N values are selected uniformly at random from $\mathbb{F}$; however, the exact identities of those K values are unknown. The goal is to compute K values from $a_1, \ldots, a_N$, say $b_1, \ldots, b_K$, each of which is uniformly distributed over $\mathbb{F}$. This is achieved as follows: let $f(x)$ be the polynomial of degree at most $N - 1$, such that $f(i) = a_{i+1}$, for $i = 0, \ldots, N - 1$. Then set $b_1 = f(N), \ldots, b_K = f(N + K - 1)$ (note that, we require $|\mathbb{F}| \geq N + K$ to make the technique work; in our protocols, N, K and $|\mathbb{F}|$ will be such that this relationship holds). The elements $b_1, \ldots, b_K$ are uniformly distributed over $\mathbb{F}$, as there exists a one-to-one mapping between $b_1, \ldots, b_K$ and the K random elements in the vector $(a_1, \ldots, a_N)$. We call this algorithm as Extrand and invoke it as $(b_1, \ldots, b_K) = \mathsf{Extrand}(a_1, \ldots, a_N)$.

From WSCC **to** MWSCC: The idea behind extending WSCC to MWSCC is based on a technique of [19]. Each party P_i now ensures that its C_i set is $2t + 1$ instead of $t + 1$. We note that this eventually happens for each *honest* P_i, as there are at least $2t + 1$ Sh instances, invoked by the honest dealers, which eventually terminates for P_i. This modification ensures that there are at least $t + 1$ honest parties in the set C_i, who share truly random and unknown values on the behalf of P_i. This implies that at least $t + 1$ truly random values from $\mathbb{F}$ are *attached* to P_i. Now let $\{s_{ji}\}_{P_j \in C_i}$ denote the secrets attached to P_i. And let $\{r_{ji}\}_{P_j \in C_i}$ denote the corresponding values, which are later reconstructed. If $\{r_{ji}\}_{P_j \in C_i} \neq \{s_{ji}\}_{P_j \in C_i}$, then at least $\frac{t}{4} + 1$ local faults occur. On the other hand, consider the case when $\{r_{ji}\}_{P_j \in C_i} = \{s_{ji}\}_{P_j \in C_i}$. As at least $t + 1$ values in the set $\{r_{ji}\}_{P_j \in C_i}$ are truly random, it follows from the properties of Extrand that if we set $(V_{i1}, \ldots, V_{i(t+1)}) = \mathsf{Extrand}(\{r_{ji}\}_{P_j \in C_i})$, with N and K being $2t + 1$ and $t + 1$ respectively, then the values $V_{i1}, \ldots, V_{i(t+1)}$ will be truly random values from $\mathbb{F}$. This further implies that if we set $v_{ik} \stackrel{def}{=} V_{ik} \bmod u$ for $k = 1, \ldots, t + 1$,

Figure 4: Almost-surely terminating ABA protocol for a single bit with $n = 3t + 1$.

ABA

Each $P_i \in \mathcal{P}$ executes the following code:

1. Set sid $= 0$ and $v_i = x_i$, where $x_i \in \{0, 1\}$ is the input bit for party P_i.
2. Repeat until terminating: (each iteration is considered as a round)
   a. Set sid $=$ sid $+ 1$. Participate in Vote(sid) with input v_{sid} and wait for its termination. Let $(y_{\text{sid}}, m_{\text{sid}})$ denote the output of Vote(sid).
   b. Invoke SCC(sid) and wait until its termination. Let c_{sid} denote the output of SCC(sid).
   c. Consider the following cases:
      i. If $m_{\text{sid}} = 2$, then set $v_{\text{sid}+1} = y_{\text{sid}}$ and broadcast the message (`Terminate with` v_{sid}). Participate in only one more instance of Vote protocol and only one more instance of SCC.
      ii. If $m_{\text{sid}} = 1$, then set $v_{\text{sid}+1} = y_{\text{sid}}$.
      iii. Else, set $v_{\text{sid}+1} = c_{\text{sid}}$
   d. Upon receiving the message (`Terminate with` σ) for some value $\sigma \in \{0, 1\}$ from the broadcast of $t + 1$ different parties, output σ and terminate the protocol.

then the $t + 1$ values $v_{i1}, \ldots, v_{i(t+1)}$ will be uniformly distributed over $[0, \ldots u - 1]$. These $t + 1$ values are now considered as the $t + 1$ values *associated* with P_i. This way, instead of associating one random value in the range $[0, \ldots, u - 1]$ with P_i, the parties now associate $t + 1$ random values. Now the decision rule to decide the final outcome of MWSCC is extended for the case of $t + 1$ bits, by applying $t + 1$ times the decision rule used in WSCC.

Next, using MWSCC, we extend SCC to MSCC to output $t + 1$ shunning common coins, which is further used to design MABA to reach agreement on $t + 1$ bits simultaneously; see [3] for details.

7.2 Almost-surely Terminating ABA with a Constant Expected Running Time

The expected running time of our ABA protocol can be reduced to $O(\frac{1}{\epsilon})$ for $n \geq (3 + \epsilon)t$ where $\epsilon > 0$. This improvement is due to a modified SAVSS scheme, comprising of (CSh, CRec). While CSh is the same as Sh, the following modification is made in Rec to get CRec: all RS decoding procedures are invoked as RS-Dec(t, $\frac{2n-5t-2}{4}$, $\mathcal{K}_j$); hence the parameter c is changed from $\frac{t}{4}$ to $\frac{2n-5t-2}{4}$. Notice that $N = |\mathcal{K}_j| = n - t - \frac{t}{2}$ is automatically changed from $\frac{3t}{2} + 1$ to $\frac{3t}{2} + \epsilon t$. This is because now $n \geq (3+\epsilon)t$, instead of $n = 3t+1$. In [3], we show that due to the above modification, at least $\frac{\epsilon t^2}{4}(1+2\epsilon)$ local conflicts occur in CRec if correctness is violated. Using (CSh, CRec), we design ConstMWSCC, which is further used to design a protocol ConstMSCC, which ensures that at least $\frac{\epsilon t^2}{4}(1 + 2\epsilon)$ local conflicts occur, whenever the common randomness property for the honest parties is violated with probability more than $\frac{3}{4}$. Finally, we extend MABA to ConstMABA, where the parties invoke ConstMSCC in each iteration and use the output of ConstMSCC to update their values. There can be at most $\frac{8}{\epsilon}$ iterations where the updated values of all honest parties will be different with probability more than $\frac{3}{4}$. From this, we can infer that ConstMABA protocol will run for at least $\frac{8}{\epsilon}$ iterations in the worst case. For the more details, see [3].

Acknowledgement: We would like to thank the anonymous referees of PODC 2018 for their helpful comments.

REFERENCES

[1] I. Abraham, D. Dolev, and J. Y. Halpern. 2008. An Almost-surely Terminating Polynomial Protocol for Asynchronous Byzantine Agreement with Optimal Resilience. In *PODC*. ACM, 405–414.

[2] H. Attiya and J. Welch. 2004. *Distributed Computing: Fundamentals, Simulations, and Advanced Topics*. Vol. 19. John Wiley & Sons.

[3] L. Bangalore, A. Choudhury, and A. Patra. 2018. Almost-Surely Terminating Asynchronous Byzantine Agreement Revisited. Cryptology ePrint Archive, Report 2018/394.

[4] Z. Beerliová-Trubíniová and M. Hirt. 2008. Perfectly-Secure MPC with Linear Communication Complexity. In *TCC (Lecture Notes in Computer Science)*, Vol. 4948. Springer Verlag, 213–230.

[5] M. Ben-Or. 1983. Another Advantage of Free Choice (Extended Abstract): Completely Asynchronous Agreement Protocols. In *PODC*. ACM, 27–30.

[6] M. Ben-Or, E. Pavlov, and V. Vaikuntanathan. 2006. Byzantine Agreement in the Full-Information Model in $O(\log n)$ Rounds. In *STOC*. ACM, 179–186.

[7] G. Bracha. 1984. An Asynchronous [(n-1)/3]-Resilient Consensus Protocol. In *PODC*. ACM, 154–162.

[8] C. Cachin, K. Kursawe, and V. Shoup. 2005. Random Oracles in Constantinople: Practical Asynchronous Byzantine Agreement Using Cryptography. *J. Cryptology* 18, 3 (2005), 219–246.

[9] R. Canetti. 1995. *Studies in Secure Multiparty Computation and Applications*. Ph.D. Dissertation. Weizmann Institute, Israel.

[10] R. Canetti and T. Rabin. 1993. Fast Asynchronous Byzantine Agreement with Optimal Resilience. In *STOC*. ACM, 42–51.

[11] B. Chor and B. A. Coan. 1985. A Simple and Efficient Randomized Byzantine Agreement Algorithm. *IEEE Trans. Software Eng.* 11, 6 (1985), 531–539.

[12] I. Damgård and J. B. Nielsen. 2007. Scalable and Unconditionally Secure Multiparty Computation. In *CRYPTO (Lecture Notes in Computer Science)*, Vol. 4622. Springer Verlag, 572–590.

[13] P. Feldman and S. Micali. 1988. Optimal Algorithms for Byzantine Agreement. In *STOC*. ACM, 148–161.

[14] M. J. Fischer, N. A. Lynch, and M. Paterson. 1985. Impossibility of Distributed Consensus with One Faulty Process. *J. ACM* 32, 2 (1985), 374–382.

[15] M. Fitzi. 2002. *Generalized Communication and Security Models in Byzantine Agreement*. Ph.D. Dissertation. ETH Zurich.

[16] V. King and J. Saia. 2016. Byzantine Agreement in Expected Polynomial Time. *J. ACM* 63, 2 (2016), 13:1–13:21.

[17] Nancy A Lynch. 1996. *Distributed algorithms*. Morgan Kaufmann.

[18] F. J. MacWilliams and N. J. A. Sloane. 1978. *The Theory of Error Correcting Codes*. North-Holland Publishing Company.

[19] A. Patra, A. Choudhury, and C. Pandu Rangan. 2014. Asynchronous Byzantine Agreement with Optimal Resilience. *Distributed Computing* 27, 2 (2014), 111–146.

[20] M. Pease, R. Shostak, and L. Lamport. 1980. Reaching Agreement in the Presence of Faults. *Journal of the ACM (JACM)* 27, 2 (1980), 228–234.

[21] M. O. Rabin. 1983. Randomized Byzantine Generals. In *FOCS*. IEEE, 403–409.

[22] C. Wang. 2015. Asynchronous Byzantine Agreement with Optimal Resilience and Linear Complexity. *CoRR* abs/1507.06165 (2015).

Nearly-Tight Analysis for 2-Choice and 3-Majority Consensus Dynamics

Extended Abstract*

Mohsen Ghaffari
ETH Zürich
Zürich, Switzerland
ghaffari@inf.ethz.ch

Johannes Lengler
ETH Zürich
Zürich, Switzerland
johannes.lengler@inf.ethz.ch

ABSTRACT

We present improved analyses for two of the well-studied randomized dynamics of stabilizing consensus, namely 2-choice and 3-majority. The resulting bounds are tight up to logarithmic factors. In the latter case, this answers an open question of Becchetti et al. [SODA'16].

Consider a distributed system of n nodes, each initially holding an opinion in $\{1, 2, \ldots, k\}$. The system should converge to a setting where all (non-corrupted) nodes hold the same opinion. This consensus opinion should be valid, meaning that it should be among the initially supported opinions, and the (fast) convergence should happen even in the presence of a malicious adversary who can corrupt a bounded number of nodes per round and in particular modify their opinions.

Two of the well-studied distributed algorithms for this problem work as follows: In both of these dynamics, each node gathers the opinion of three nodes and sets its new opinion equal to the majority of this set. In the 2-choice dynamics, the three nodes are the node itself and two random nodes and ties are broken towards the node's own opinion. In the 3-majority dynamics, the three nodes are selected at random and ties are broken randomly.

Becchetti et al. [SODA'16] showed that the 3-majority dynamics converges to consensus in $O((k^2\sqrt{\log n}+k\log n)(k+\log n))$ rounds, even in the presence of a limited adversary, for k bounded by some polynomial of n. We prove that, even with a stronger adversary, the convergence happens within $O(k \log n)$ rounds, both for 3-majority and 2-choice. For 3-majority, this bound is known to be optimal for $k = \tilde{O}(\sqrt{n})$. More generally, we prove that 3-majority converges always in $\tilde{O}(n^{2/3})$ time, improving on a $\tilde{O}(n^{3/4})$ upper bound of Berenbrink et al. [PODC'17].

CCS CONCEPTS

• Theory of computation → Distributed algorithms; • Mathematics of computing → Probabilistic algorithms; Stochastic processes;

*The full version of the paper is available at https://arxiv.org/abs/1705.05583.

PODC '18, July 23–27, 2018, Egham, United Kingdom

ACM ISBN 978-1-4503-5795-1/18/07...$15.00
https://doi.org/10.1145/3212734.3212738

KEYWORDS

Probabilistic Dynamics, Consensus, 2-Choice Dynamics, 3-Majority Dynamics

ACM Reference Format:
Mohsen Ghaffari and Johannes Lengler. 2018. Nearly-Tight Analysis for 2-Choice and 3-Majority Consensus Dynamics: Extended Abstract. In *PODC '18: ACM Symposium on Principles of Distributed Computing, July 23–27, 2018, Egham, United Kingdom.* ACM, New York, NY, USA, 9 pages. https://doi.org/10.1145/3212734.3212738

1 INTRODUCTION AND RELATED WORK

In this paper, we provide a new and tighter analysis for the convergence time of two well-known consensus dynamics, namely 2-choice [7, 13] and 3-majority [5, 6]. Both are simple probabilistic processes which allow a distributed system to converge to consensus on one of the opinions held by one of the nodes in the system, even in the presence of a byzantine adversary with some limited power. Other than much previous work, we do not assume that there is an initial plurality opinion with a head start. We go directly into the dynamics, referring to [6] for a nice discussion about the motivations and applications of this type of dynamics in distributed systems.

The 2-Choice and the 3-Majority Dynamics. Consider a distributed system of n nodes, each initially holding an opinion in $\{1, 2, \ldots, k\}$. Communications happen in the classical GOSSIP model, with synchronous rounds. Per round, each node v takes three opinions: for 2-choice, it takes its own opinion and pulls the opinion of two other nodes chosen independently and uniformly at random. For 3-majority, it pulls the opinion of three nodes chosen independently and uniformly at random. Then, node v updates its opinion to the majority of the set of three opinions. For 3-majority ties are broken randomly, while for 2-choice ties are broken towards the node's own opinion. I.e., for 2-choice any node v that holds opinion i will keep its own opinion, unless both of the randomly pulled nodes hold the same opinion $j \neq i$, in which case v switches to opinion j. The 2-choice process has also been called *two-sample voting* [10]. Note that the 3-majority process can also be described as a 2-choice process where in case of a tie between the two opinions node v does not keep its own opinion, but rather switches to the opinion of a third random node.

A key desirable property of these simple dynamics is that they converge to a *consensus* setting where all nodes support the same opinion. Indeed, the convergence happens even in the presence of an F*-bounded adversary*, who can corrupt F nodes per round, for a reasonably small F, modifying their opinions to arbitrary *valid* opinions in $\{1, 2, \ldots, k\}$ or even to some *non-valid* opinions not in $\{1, 2, \ldots, k\}$. In this case, almost all nodes converge to consensus, modulo those corrupted, and the consensus is on a valid opinion. The main question of interest in analyzing the processes is to characterize the convergence time to consensus.

1.1 Prior Analysis and Our Contribution

Prior Analysis. Results of Doerr et al. [11] showed for 2-choice that in the binary case $k = 2$, the convergence happens within $O(\log n)$ rounds with high probability[1], even for an $F = O(\sqrt{n})$-bounded adversary. We remark that their analysis was formulated for the 3-median dynamics, where each node updates its value to the median of its own and two random opinions, but for $k = 2$ this dynamics is equivalent both to the 2-choice dynamics. Their time complexity for the convergence is tight both for 2-choice and for 3-majority. For 3-majority, Becchetti et al. [5] proved more generally that for some initial configurations and $k \leq (n/\log n)^{1/4}$ the convergence time is $\Omega(k \log n)$, even without an adversary.

Becchetti et al. [6] proved that 3-majority converges in at most $O((k^2\sqrt{\log n} + k \log n)(k + \log n))$ rounds. This convergence happens even despite an $F = O(\sqrt{n}/(k^{2.5} \log n))$-bounded adversary. They left improving this upper bound on the convergence time as an open question. Indeed, see the future work section of [6, Section 5], where Bechetti et al. express their strong belief that the $\Omega(k^3)$ behavior in this convergence-time is not tight, and where they discuss the obstacles in improving the bound using their analysis. For larger k, the best bound for 3-majority is due to Berenbrink et al. [7], who showed an $\tilde{O}(n^{3/4})$ bound for any k (without an adversary). They also showed that no comparable, strongly sublinear bound for 2-choice can hold for large k. Specifically they proved a lower bound of $\Omega(n/\log n)$ for 2-choice if every opinion is initially supported by $O(\log n)$ nodes. Our main result gives improvements both for the regime of small k (for 2-choice and 3-majority) and for the regime of large k (for 3-majority).

Main Result

THEOREM 1.1. *For both 2-choice with $k = O(\sqrt{n/\log n})$ and 3-majority with $k = O(n^{1/3}/\sqrt{\log n})$, the convergence time is $O(k \log n)$ rounds, with high probability. This bound still holds in the presence of an $F = O(\sqrt{n}/k^{1.5})$-bounded adversary. For the 3-majority process without adversary, for arbitrary k the convergence time is $O(n^{2/3} \log^{3/2} n)$ with high probability.*

For small k, our bound matches the aforementioned lower bound of Bechetti et al. [5], which is proven for 3-majority and up to $k = \tilde{O}(n^{1/4})$, and answers the main open question of Becchetti et al. [6], even for an adversary that is stronger than in [6]. For large k, our result improves the bound $\tilde{O}(n^{3/4})$ by Berenbrink et al. [7].

1.2 Other Related Work

We refer the interested reader to [6] and [7], which cover all the related work for the 2-choice and the 3-majority dynamics. [6] also provides some motivation for these dynamics, and gives connections to the well-studied *consensus* problem in various distributed settings. Here we only mention briefly some directly related work.

There is another regime of interest for consensus dynamics, where one assumes that at the beginning one of the opinions is much stronger than the others, and then desires that the convergence happens to this plurality opinion. Generally, the type of technical challenges in analyzing that regime is quite different, as indicated and discussed by Becchetti et al. [6]. Elsässer et al. have shown ([13] for 2-choice, [14] for 3-majority) that the convergence time in that regime is $O(k \log n)$ rounds if $k = O(n^{\epsilon})$, assuming an initial gap of at least $\Omega(\sqrt{n \log n})$ nodes between the plurality opinion and the others. Similar results were obtained by Bechetti et al. [5]. The heart of the technical challenge in our work, and also that of [6], is actually in the regime where there is no such gap at the beginning and all opinions start with the same or almost the same amount of support.

Two other closely resembling simple probabilistic dynamics for consensus have been studied in the literature. One is the *3-state* dynamics, which is used and analyzed for binary consensus where $k = 2$, in the population-protocols model where per round exactly one chosen pair of nodes interact [3, 18]. Another related dynamics is the *3-median* dynamics where per round, each node updates its opinion to the median of the sampled set of size three. This is studied by Doerr et al. [11] for general k. However, we note that this dynamic is mainly of interest in settings with no adversary; it is known that this dynamics may converge to an invalid opinion – i.e. an opinion introduced by adversary and not supported by the non-corrupted nodes initially – even with a very weak adversary where $F = \text{poly} \log n$, see [6, Section 2].

Finally, we note that over the past decade, there has been extensive interest in developing and analyzing simple probabilistic dynamics for distributed system. In particular, a great number of various simple probabilistic distributed dynamics have been studied in somewhat similar settings, either in the uniform gossip model, the gossip model on graphs, or the population-protocols model. These are motivated by a wide range of application domains spanning chemical reaction networks, biological settings, social networks, and peer-to-peer networks. It is well beyond the scope of this paper to provide an exhaustive coverage of all of these work. Merely as a random sample of some recent work, we mention [1, 2, 4, 8, 16].

2 ANALYSIS INTUITION AND OUTLINE

For simplicity, when providing the analysis, we first discard the adversary. The analysis is presented in a format that allows us to easily incorporate the adversary's effect, as we explain in Section 4.1, without changing the asymptotic bounds. In particular, the effect of the adversary, who can change the opinion of at most $F = \epsilon\sqrt{n}/k^{1.5}$ nodes per round, for a small constant $\epsilon > 0$, will be weaker than the random deviations that we take into account in our analysis.

2.1 Intuition Based on a First-Order Analysis

We first explain in this subsection what would happen if deviations from the variance could be completely neglected. Consider the 2-choice protocol. For each $i \in \{1, 2, \ldots, k\}$, let p_i denote the fraction of nodes who hold opinion i. Then, in one round, we expect the

[1] *With high probability* or *whp* means that for every constant $c > 0$ and sufficiently large n the probability is at least $1 - n^{-c}$. The hidden constants in $O(.)$ notation may depend on c.

following change:

$$\mathbb{E}[p_i^{\text{new}}] = p_i + (\sum_{j\neq i} p_j)p_i^2 - p_i(\sum_{j\neq i} p_j^2).$$

Here, the second term indicates the expected fraction of nodes of opinion $j \neq i$, summed up over all j, who sample two nodes of opinion i and thus join opinion i. The third term indicates the expected fraction of nodes of opinion i who sample two nodes of another opinion $j \neq i$, summed up over all j, and thus migrate to opinion j. Using notation $\Sigma_2 = \sum_j p_j^2$ and the fact that $\sum_j p_j = 1$, we now rewrite this expected change in a more convenient format:

$$\mathbb{E}[p_i^{\text{new}}] = p_i(1 + p_i - \Sigma_2). \tag{1}$$

A similar calculation shows that (1) also holds for 3-majority.

The hardest regime for the analysis is when most opinions are close to the maximum size opinion. Once an opinion is by a constant factor weaker than the plurality opinion, it will be rather easy to show that this weak opinion will die out soon. So consider the hard case that all the opinions have almost the same size, i.e., where we have $p_i = \Theta(1/k)$ for all $i \in \{1, 2, \ldots, k\}$.

Consider two opinions i and j, and without loss of generality suppose that $p_i \geq p_j$. Define $g_{ij} = (p_i - p_j)/p_j$. That is, $p_i/p_j = 1 + g_{ij}$. Then, without variance we would have

$$\begin{aligned} 1 + g_{ij}^{\text{new}} &= \frac{p_i^{\text{new}}}{p_j^{\text{new}}} \approx \frac{p_i}{p_j} \cdot \frac{1 + p_i - \Sigma_2}{1 + p_j - \Sigma_2} = (1 + g_{ij})(1 + \frac{p_i - p_j}{1 + p_j - \Sigma_2}) \\ &\geq (1 + g_{ij})(1 + g_{ij} \cdot \frac{p_j}{2}). \end{aligned} \tag{2}$$

This implies that g_{ij} grows like $g_{ij}^{\text{new}} \gtrapprox g_{ij}(1+p_j/2)$. For illustration, suppose that we start with a minimal non-zero difference between p_i and p_j, which implies that at the beginning $g_{ij} \geq 1/n$. We note that this initial difference will not be sufficient once we bring back the deviations into our analysis. But for now, this simplistic assumption gives an instructive intuition. If $g_{ij} \geq 1/n$, so long as p_j does not drop below $\Theta(1/k)$, per round this gap parameter g_{ij} would grow by at least a factor of $(1 + \Omega(1/k))$ by (2). Hence, if that continues for more than $\Theta(k \log n)$ rounds, it would imply $g_{ij} \geq n^3$, which due to the integrability considerations, would mean $p_j = 0$. This means that after $O(k \log n)$ rounds, opinion j is out of the race.

If we could prove some analysis resembling the above for every pair of opinions, we would be done. That is, if one could show that a similar gap shows up between any pair of opinions, i.e. at least one of the two opinions drops to 0, then effectively all but one opinion are out of the race. But of course, (2) is only an approximation, and the actual changes will deviate from this mean-field calculation. Moreover, if g_{ij} is small then the change will be far from concentrated, so it is not true that the deviations are negligible in all the rounds. On the contrary, we will sometimes need to argue that some anti-concentration type phenomena happen and the support of different opinions get some minimal difference, due to the variances. Thus, analyzing opinions that are very close to each other in size is quite non-trivial, and requires much care due to the likely deviations from the expected behavior.

2.2 Analysis Outline

The above discussions provide some intuition for how the process evolves. We next describe the high-level outline of how we turn this intuition into an analysis.

Throughout, when talking about a round t, we use $p_1, p_2, \ldots p_k$ to denote the fraction of nodes of opinions $1, 2, \ldots k$, respectively, at time t. For the sake of simplicity, we do not express the fact that these fractions change with time t explicitly in our notations. When needed, we will use superscripts to indicate the time to which these parameters correspond. Sometimes, when talking about a given interval of time, we use the superscript *new* — for instance by writing p_i^{new} — to indicate the values at the end of the interval.

Large k. Berenbrink et al. [7] showed for 3-majority that for any $k \geq 1$, whp[2] after $O(n/k \cdot \log n)$ rounds the number of remaining opinions is at most k. With this result, our statement for small k immediately implies the statement for large k: for $k_0 := n^{1/3}/\sqrt{\log n}$ it takes $O(n^{2/3} \log^{3/2} n)$ to reduce the number of opinions to at most k_0 by [7], and $O(k_0 \log n) = o(n^{2/3})$ further rounds to reach consensus.[3] So henceforth, we will restrict ourselves to the case of small k. Moreover, in the regime of small k the analysis for 2-choice and 3-majority will be almost identical. We concentrate our exposition on 2-choice, and explain the changes for 3-majority on page 8.

Super-Weak, Weak, and Strong Opinions. We call an opinion i *super-weak* if its support is $p_i \leq 1/(10k)$. Even summed up over all opinions, the super-weak opinions can take only a $1/10$ fraction of the nodes. Thus, at least a $9/10$ fraction of the support is on *not-super-weak* opinions. Furthermore, we call an opinion i *weak* in a given round if $p_i \leq p_{\max}/5$. Here, $p_{\max} = \max_i p_i$ in that round. If $p_i \geq p_{\max}/5$, we call opinion i a *strong* opinion in that round.

We will see that super-weak opinions remain super-weak, whp. Moreover, weak opinions are also effectively out of the race, because as we shall prove, weak opinions remain weak, whp. Moreover, each weak opinion becomes super-weak at some point and thus falls completely out of the race. Our core attention will be on *strong* opinions.

Lemma 2.1. ***(Property (P1))*** *Whp, super-weak opinions remain super-weak, and weak opinions remain weak.*

Epochs of the Analysis. We break time into *epochs* of variable length, each made of an interval of consecutive rounds. This is done in a way that at all times during the ith epoch, the number of opinions that are not super-weak is at most $\lfloor k(5/6)^{i-1} \rfloor$.

Let us consider the ith epoch, and let $\kappa = \lfloor k(5/6)^{i-1} \rfloor$. Suppose that $\kappa \geq 2$. Notice that at the beginning of this epoch, we have $p_{\max} = \max_i p_i \geq 0.9/\kappa$. This is because there are at most κ opinions which are not super-weak, and these opinions have at least a $9/10$ fraction of nodes in total. If at any time during the epoch, we reach a setting where $p_{\max} = \max_i p_i \geq 1.5/\kappa$, then we say that the *end-of-time* has arrived for this epoch. Note that this does not mean that the epoch ends immediately, but we will show that the epoch ends shortly afterwards.

[2] They defined "whp" as probability $\geq 1 - 1/n$, but their proof also implies the form that we use.

[3] We cannot choose larger k_0 since in our result for small k assumes $k = O(n^{1/3}/\sqrt{\log n})$.

It will be easy to show that once the end-of-time arrives, within at most $O(\kappa \log n)$ additional rounds, only $5\kappa/6$ opinions remain which are not super-weak, and hence, the next epoch begins. The most interesting regime of the analysis is before the *end-of-time.*

We will show that whp within $O(\kappa \log n)$ rounds from the beginning of the epoch the end-of-time arrives. Once we have that, we can infer that this epoch takes at most $O(\kappa \log n)$ rounds overall, including the period before the end-of-time and the period after that. Hence, thanks to the geometric decay of κ throughout different epochs, even summed over all epochs, the time complexity is $O(k \log n)$. This is until we reach a setting where $\kappa = 1$ and only one not-super-weak opinion remains. This single opinion must have at least $9/10$ fraction of the support, as the super-weak opinions can in total have at most $1/10$ fraction of the support. It follows from [13] that whp the majority opinion will get everyone's support within $O(\log n)$ additional rounds.

Phases of an Epoch. The most interesting part of the analysis of each epoch is showing that the *end-of-time* arrives soon. Concretely, we prove that starting in an epoch where only κ not-super-weak opinions exist, we get to the end-of-time where $p_{\max} = \max_i p_i \geq 1.5/\kappa$, within $O(\kappa \log n)$ rounds. We break this period of time into *phases.* We define each *phase* to consist of $\delta\kappa$ consecutive rounds, for a desirably small constant $\delta > 0$. The phase ends prematurely if the end-of-time of the current epoch arrives. The length of a phase is chosen so that the change in the supports of the opinions during one phase is small. Let us explain. So long as we are within this epoch and the end-of-time has not arrived, we have $\max_i p_i \leq 1.5/\kappa$. As such, the expected fraction of nodes that change their opinion during one round is at most $\sum_j p_j^2 \leq \max_i p_i \leq 1.5/\kappa$, and we will show that a similar upper bound holds also whp. Hence, even over all the $\delta\kappa$ rounds of this phase, we expect at most a $3\delta \ll 1$ fraction of nodes to change their opinions. If δ is a small enough constant, the change during the phase is relatively small. In some sense, this gives us sufficient *smoothness* during the phase, which allows us to ignore some smaller-order effects.

Seven Key Properties In Analyzing Phases and Epochs. We will establish six key properties, aside from the property (P1) stated above, for the analysis of each epoch. Properties (P2) to (P5) are about the period of the epoch before the end-of-time. Hence, during properties (P2) to (P5), we may assume that the end-of-time has not arrived yet and we have $\sum_i p_i \leq 1.5/\kappa$. All properties below focus on strong opinions. Notice that during this time, $p_{\max} \in [0.9/\kappa, 1.5/\kappa]$ and thus each strong opinion i has $p_i \in [0.18/\kappa, 1.5/\kappa]$. Properties (P6) and (P7) handle how the end-of-time arrives and we exit this epoch.

For properties (P2) to (P5), we use a key auxiliary definition, which captures the gap between the size of two (strong) opinions. For two strong opinions p_i and p_j, recall that $g_{ij} = (p_i - p_j)/p_j$ and $g_{ji} = (p_j - p_i)/p_i$, or equivalently $1 + g_{ij} = p_i/p_j$. In the most interesting regime of the analysis, $p_i/p_j \approx 1$, we effectively think of g_{ij} as the second-order term in p_i/p_j.

For all following lemmas, we assume that $n \geq n_0$ for a sufficiently large constant $n_0 \geq 2$.

Lemma 2.2. ***(Property (P2))*** *Consider two fixed strong opinions i and j. For any desirably large constant $C_1 > 0$, by the end of the phase* $\Pr[\max\{g_{ij}, g_{ji}\} \geq C_1/\sqrt{n/\kappa}] \geq C_2$, *for a constant $C_2 > 0$ that depends on C_1, unless the end-of-time arrives.*[4]

Lemma 2.3. ***(Property (P3))*** *Consider two fixed strong opinions i and j, and suppose that at the start of the phase, $p_i \geq p_j$ and $g_{ij} = x/\sqrt{n/\kappa}$, with $C_1 \leq x \leq \sqrt{n/\kappa}$ for a desirably large constant $C_1 > 0$. Let g_{ij}^{new} be the gap parameter at the end of the phase. Then* $\Pr[g_{ij}^{new} \geq (1+\delta/100)\cdot g_{ij}] \geq 1-\exp(-C_3x^2)$, *where C_3 is a constant that depends on C_1, unless the end-of-time arrives.*

Lemma 2.4. ***(Property (P4))*** *For every two fixed strong opinions i and j and every constant $C_5 \geq 0$, whp after $O(\log n)$ phases we have* $\max\{g_{ij}, g_{ji}\} \geq C_5\sqrt{\log n}/\sqrt{n/\kappa}$, *unless the end-of-time arrives.*

Lemma 2.5. ***(Property (P5))*** *Consider two fixed strong opinions i and j, and suppose that at the start of the phase, $p_i \geq p_j$ and $g_{ij} \geq C_5\sqrt{\log n}/\sqrt{n/\kappa}$, for a desirably large constant $C_5 > 0$. Then, by the end of the phase, whp $g_{ij}^{new} \geq g_{ij} \cdot (1 + \delta/100)$, unless the end-of-time arrives.*

Lemma 2.6. ***(Property (P6))*** *Consider the ith epoch where at most $\kappa = \lfloor k(5/6)^{i-1} \rfloor \geq 2$ not-super-weak opinions exist at the beginning. Whp, within $O(\kappa \log n)$ rounds, the end-of-time arrives, i.e. we have $p_{\max} = \max_j p_j \geq 1.5/\kappa$.*

Lemma 2.7. ***(Property (P7))*** *Consider the ith epoch, which starts with at most $\kappa = \lfloor k(5/6)^{i-1} \rfloor$ not-super-weak opinions. Suppose that in some round the end-of-time of the ith epoch arrives, i.e,* $\max_j p_j \geq 1.5/\kappa$. *Then, within $O(\kappa \log n)$ additional rounds, whp, at most $5\kappa/6$ not-super-weak opinions remain and thus, the next epoch begins.*

We still assume that there is no adversary, and add the adversary later in Section 4.1. Without adversary, Lemma 2.7 implies the desired runtime bound, because we can iteratively apply Lemma 2.7 until we reach $\kappa < 2$. Since κ drops exponentially, this takes in total only $O(k \log n)$ rounds if the $O(\kappa \log n)$ bound holds in each application of Lemma 2.7 (which is true whp by a union bound). Once $\kappa < 2$ is reached, there is at most $\lfloor \kappa \rfloor = 1$ opinion left which is not-super-weak. By definition of super-weak, this opinion will have at least $9/10$ of the support, it is known from [13] that whp the remaining opinions are swallowed by the majority in $O(\log n)$ rounds. Altogether, whp the algorithm terminates after $O(k \log n)$ rounds, as desired.

Proof Types. Let us discuss the type of arguments that goes into proving these seven properties. Properties (P1) and (P7) will be established using standard concentration arguments. Properties (P2), (P3), and (P5) will require the most care and effort. Proofs of (P3) and (P5) are very close, and they are stated separately merely for convenience. These three properties are established by closely analyzing the behavior during one phase, and showing rather tight concentration for the process. We will need the per-round analysis

[4]Formally, this "unless" formulation simply denotes "or", i.e., Pr[end-of-time arrives *or* $\max\{g_{ij}, g_{ji}\} \geq C_1/\sqrt{n/\kappa}] \geq C_2$. However, we do believe that this way of formulating is beneficial and we advise the reader to just ignore the part about the end-of-time since the very purpose of our analysis is to show that the end-of-time arrives soon. But note that "unless" does not indicate conditional probabilities. In this paper we never condition on future events, like the event that the end-of-time does not arrives in the current phase. Rather, we always only(!) condition on the history of the process.

to be sharp modulo the third-order term. The proof of (P2) is similar, but we need anti-concentration instead of concentration. We obtain this by showing that the deviations within a phase follow approximatively a Gaussian distribution. Property (P4) is much less complex, particularly because it does not deal with the specifics of our dynamic directly; it will be established using arguments that are somewhat standard for the so-called *explosive processes*, where one wishes to prove that a dynamics polarizes to one side or the other. Finally, property (P6) is a rather straightforward consequence of properties (P4) and (P5).

3 DETAILS OF THE ANALYSIS: PROVING THE SEVEN PROPERTIES

The proofs of properties (P1), (P4), (P6), and (P7) are simpler and omitted due to space limitations. Here, we discuss the proof of property (P5), which is one of the main ingredients of the analysis. We will present the proof in a format that can be easily extended to property (P3), which we present later in Section 3.2. Property (P2) also fits the same framework, and the proof of (P5) will provide the reader with the key tools for proving (P2), but details are omitted as well.

3.1 Proof of Lemma 2.5

In property (P5), we focus on one phase, which is made of $\delta\kappa$ rounds (unless the end-of-time arrives), for a constant $\delta > 0$ that will be chosen desirably small. By definition of end-of-time, throughout the phase $p_{\max} = \max_i p_i \leq 1.5/\kappa$.

We start with some preparatory analysis of the first-order (expectation-based) trajectory and a proof outline. Then, we present a coloring scheme that allows us to track how far off the process goes from its first-order trajectory. Then, we bound the components of this coloring and thus prove bounds on these deviations from the expectations. At the end, we put the first-order analysis together with the bounds on the deviations to complete the proof.

Preparations and Proof Outline. To prove the lemma, we fix two opinions i and j and we closely examine the changes of their support during the $\delta\kappa$ rounds of the phase. We will not monitor the changes in the other opinions, except that we assume $p_{\max} \leq 1.5/\kappa$ in all rounds during this phase. This is because otherwise the end-of-time arrives, in which case we are done. Focusing on two strong opinions i and j, let us call nodes who support opinion i *blue* and nodes who support opinion j *red*.

Let us start with the first round of the phase. During this round, we have the following expected behavior. The two populations of *blue* and *red* will have only a small change. We expect $p_i\Sigma_2$ fraction of nodes to migrate out of the blue region, and p_i^2 fraction of nodes to migrate into the blue region. Similarly, we expect $p_j\Sigma_2$ fraction of nodes to migrate out of the red region, and p_j^2 fraction of nodes to migrate into the red region. Notice that all of these terms are of the order $\Theta(1/\kappa^2)$. Since i and j are strong, we have $p_i, p_j \in [0.18/\kappa, 1.5/\kappa]$, in particular $p_i, p_j \in \Theta(1/\kappa)$. Therefore, in relative terms, the expected changes are in the order of $\Theta(1/\kappa)$.

Our main analysis focuses on g_{ij}, which is the second-order term in the ratio p_i/p_j, since $p_i/p_j = 1 + g_{ij}$. In this regard, at least in expectation, the outwards migrations are proportional to the current population (with a Σ_2 factor) and thus, the outwards migrations will not skew the ratio p_i/p_j. On the other hand, the inwards migrations favor the blue region slightly, as the blue region is slightly bigger. Hence, we expect that the blue region grows slightly faster. Concretely, in expectation, by the end of round, $\mathbb{E}[p_i^{\text{new}}] \approx p_i(1 + p_i - \Sigma_2)$ and $\mathbb{E}[p_j^{\text{new}}] \approx p_j(1 + p_j - \Sigma_2)$. If the changes were sharply concentrated around these means, the ratio p_i/p_j would grow by a factor of $(1 + p_i - \Sigma_2)/(1 + p_j - \Sigma_2) \geq 1 + \frac{1}{2}(p_i - p_j) \geq 1 + 0.09g_{ij}/\kappa$, since $p_i - p_j = g_{ij}p_j$. That would be at least a $1 + 0.09/\kappa$ growth in g_{ij}. If this behavior continues over the next $\delta\kappa$ rounds, during this phase, g_{ij} sees a growth by a factor of at least $(1 + 0.09/\kappa)^{\delta\kappa} \geq 1 + \delta/30$. Of course, the whole challenge is that concentration is not strong enough to let such a growth reliably occur every round.

Let us check the deviations in the blue population. In the above calculation based on expectations, we said that we expect $p_i\Sigma_2 n$ nodes to migrate out of the blue region and $p_i^2 n$ nodes to migrate into the blue region. Note that both of these are at most $(1.5/\kappa)^2 n$, because $\Sigma_2 \leq p_{\max} \leq 1.5/\kappa$. Clearly, we will have some deviation around these mean. In particular, Chernoff bounds tell us that whp the actual number of nodes that move in/out deviates from its expectation by at most an additive $\pm C_6\sqrt{n \log n/\kappa^2}$, for some constant $C_6 > 0$. In relative terms compared to p_i, this is at most a $\pm C_7\sqrt{\log n/n}$ additive deviation for the change in the value of p_i, because $p_i \in [0.18/\kappa, 1.5/\kappa]$. In other words, whp, $p_i^{\text{new}} \in \mathbb{E}[p_i^{\text{new}}] \pm p_i \cdot C_7\sqrt{\log n/n}$. That is, for some constant $C_8 > 0$, whp,

$$p_i^{\text{new}} \in p_i(1 + p_i - \Sigma_2) \cdot (1 \pm C_8\sqrt{\log n/n}).$$

This deviation term $(1 \pm C_8\sqrt{\log n/n})$ may look tolerable for one round. However, we cannot afford to use this worst case bound in each round, as then over the whole phase the deviation from the expected behavior could be a factor of $(1 \pm C_8\sqrt{\log n/n})^{\delta\kappa} \approx (1 \pm C_8\delta\kappa\sqrt{\log n/n})$. Notice that we are working on a parameter $p_i/p_j = 1 + g_{ij}$, which itself is quite close to 1; it can be as small as $1 + C_5\sqrt{\log n}/\sqrt{n/\kappa}$. The analysis is mainly on the second order term of the change of p_i/p_j during the phase. Hence, even though we may be able to afford deviation factors up to $(1 \pm O(\sqrt{\kappa}) \cdot \sqrt{\log n/n})$, we certainly cannot afford the $(1 \pm C_8\delta\kappa\sqrt{\log n/n})$ deviation term that would come from worst-case analysis per round. Notice that the difference is roughly a $\sqrt{k}$ factor in the second-order term. This is what we need to put up a fight for! Essentially, we need to do the per-round analysis of p_i/p_j in a manner that is tight within the third-order term.

The saving grace is that the worst-case per round additive deviations are essentially independent, modulo a smaller effect that we can control. Intuitively, there is no reason that all the $\delta\kappa$ of these deviations terms should go in the same direction, as the above analysis assumed. We will provide an analysis that formalizes this. Very roughly speaking, we show that the overall deviation in terms of the number of nodes (not in terms of fractions) is approximately the sum of $\delta\kappa$ zero-mean Gaussians, each with variance at most $O(n(1.5/\kappa)^2)$. This sum is itself a Gaussian of zero-mean and a $\delta\kappa$ factor higher variance. When expressed relative to p_i, this is at most a deviation factor of $\left(1 \pm O(\sqrt{\kappa}\sqrt{\log n/n})\right)$, whp. This deviation is within our tolerable range.

A Coloring Scheme to Track Deviations in One Phase. To formalize the above intuition and track the deviations from the expected behavior, we use a certain coloring of the nodes. For instance, nodes of opinion i will be colored *clear blue, light blue,* or *extra-light blue.* In particular, the majority of supporters of opinion i will be *clear blue* nodes, a minority will be *light blue,* and an even much smaller minority will be *extra-light blue.* In a nutshell, the number of clear blue nodes will be exactly the number that we would get from the expectation. The light blue nodes capture the second order term, and its number will be given by the sum of *independent* random variables. Finally, the extra-light blue nodes will capture the error that we make with the light blue nodes by assuming independence. We will need to follow the population of *blue* nodes sharply, and the population of *light blues* up to a constant factor, but for the *extra-light blue* we can afford to be much more coarse and use only a simple upper bound. We will perform a similar coloring for nodes of opinion j, coloring them with *red, light red,* or *extra-light red.*

We now formally describe the blue coloring scheme. We start with the very first round of the phase. As mentioned before, we expect the fraction of nodes of opinion i to go from p_i to $p_i + p_i^2 - p_i\Sigma_2$. At the end of the round, we will color exactly $p_i + p_i^2 - p_i\Sigma_2$ fraction of nodes *clear blue.* Of course this may be less than or more than the actual number of nodes of opinion i, due to the deviations. If we actually have more nodes of opinion i than we colored blue, we will color the left over nodes as *positive-charge light blue* nodes. If we have less nodes in opinion i than we colored blue, then we color a number of the clear blues equal to the excess as *negative-charge light blue* nodes. Hence, as of now, the supporters of opinion i have two colorings: a *clear blue* color, the number of which is exactly $p_i + p_i^2 - p_i\Sigma_2$, and a minority of nodes who have color *light blue.* These light blue nodes may have a positive or negative charge. These charges indicate whether we are above or below the expectation. In the case of negative charge, a node may have both a clear blue color and a negative-charge light blue color. Still, when we talk of nodes with color clear blue, it includes these and it is a population of size exactly equal to $p_i + p_i^2 - p_i\Sigma_2$ fraction of nodes.

We next define how we proceed with the coloring scheme for an arbitrary round t during the phase. At the beginning of round t, we have a body of q_i clear blue nodes, some (minority of) light blue nodes of positive or negative charge, and possibly some (even fewer) extra-light blue nodes. To define clear blue and light blue nodes, we pretend for a moment that at the beginning of round t the set of nodes which support opinion i would be exactly the set S of clear blue nodes. Then after this round, this would yield some set S' of blue nodes. In expectation $\mathbb{E}[|S'|] = q_i + q_i^2 - q_i\Sigma_2$ and this will be our guide for defining the clear blue nodes, that is, we color exactly $q_i + q_i^2 - q_i\Sigma_2$ nodes clear blue. Then, as in the first round we give $||S'| - |S||$ nodes a light-blue color, where the charge is given by the sign of $|S'| - |S|$. Furthermore, we simplify the charges so that at any time we either only have positive charge light blues, or negative charge light blues. That is, if we still have a body of positive charge light blue nodes but $|S'| < |S|$ then we first cancel the positive charge light blues before we start introducing negative charge light blues, and vice versa.

Of course, it is not true that at the beginning of the round S is exactly the set of nodes of opinion i, and we capture the difference by *extra-light blue* nodes. Formally, consider a node v of an opinion $\ell \neq i$ that joins opinion i because v sampled two nodes of opinion i. Then we color node v *extra-light blue* if one or two of these sampled opinion-i nodes were *light blue* or *extra-light blue*, and we say that v is a hiring of those (extra)-light blue node(s). Node v will remain *extra-light* permanently in our coloring scheme, throughout the phase. As we will see, the fraction of such extra-light nodes is very small, small enough so that we may almost ignore them, only using some coarse upper bound. There are so few that we do not even bother to distinguish between positive and negative charges for them. For intuition, we provide a rough calculation now, the formal argument will come later.

In expectation, a light blue node u of opinion i cause a hiring of at most $2p_{\max} \leq 3/\kappa$ other nodes per round. These hired nodes become *permanent extra-light* hirings of u. Even over all the $\delta\kappa$ rounds, this is an expected hiring of at most $3\delta\kappa/\kappa = 3\delta \ll 1$ extra-light blue nodes for node u. These *extra-light* blue nodes, who were hired by u, can have hirings of their own, but we will show nevertheless that the population of extra-light nodes is at most a $10\delta \ll 1$ factor of the light blue nodes. For now, let us first focus on the light blue nodes.

Bounding Light Blue Nodes. In the first round, the number of light blues is simply the deviation of the move out/in of the initial blue nodes from the expectation. The number of nodes that move in/out of blue in one round is given by the difference of two binomial distributions where the means exactly cancel each other, the two means being at most $n(1.5/\kappa)^2$. We call such a distribution an *almost-Gaussian distribution.* That is, an almost-Gaussian distribution with variance σ^2 is the difference $X-Y$ of two Poisson-binomial distributions X and Y which have identical means $\mathbb{E}[X] = \mathbb{E}[Y] = \sigma^2$. We note that the name is justified because the sum of two almost-Gaussians with variances σ_1^2 and σ_2^2 is again almost-Gaussian with variance $\sigma_1^2+\sigma_2^2$, and by the Chernoff bounds an almost-Gaussian distributed random variable X with variance σ^2 satisfies the tail bound $\Pr[|X| \geq C\sigma] \leq 4e^{-\min\{C^2,C\sigma\}/3}$ for all $C \geq 0$ (Lemma 5.1), which is somewhat similar to the tail of a Gaussian if C is not too large. In particular, we will frequently use that whp $|X| = O(\sigma\sqrt{\log n})$ if $\sigma^2 = \Omega(\log n)$, and that whp $|X| = O(\sigma \log n)$ in all cases.

In the second round, we again have some new deviation from the expectation. As a consequence, the number of light blue nodes changes according to an almost-Gaussian distribution with variance at most $n(1.5/\kappa)^2$. Crucially, by our definition of light blues nodes, this change is *independent* of the number of light-blue nodes after the first round. Similarly, in each next round, the number of light-blue nodes changes according to an almost-Gaussian with variance at most $n(1.5/\kappa)^2$, and these binomials are independent of the previous rounds. Altogether, even in the last round $r = \delta\kappa$, the variance is at most $\delta n\kappa(1.5/\kappa)^2 < 3n/\kappa$. That is, in the last round, the number of light-blue nodes is at most $C_6\sqrt{n\log n/\kappa}$, whp. This number of nodes translates to $\pm C_6\sqrt{\log n/(\kappa n)}$ fraction of nodes. As i is a strong opinion and thus we have $p_i = \Theta(1/\kappa)$, in relative terms compared to p_i, this is a deviation factor of $(1 \pm C_7\sqrt{\kappa \log n/n})$ from the expectation, for some constant $C_7 > 0$.

Bounding Extra-Light Blue Nodes. We now bound the number of extra-light blue nodes. Consider a light blue node u in a round r of this phase. We count the number of nodes who join opinion i because of direct or indirect chains of meetings with two opinion-i nodes, that end in the light blue node u in round r. If a node v joined opinion i in round r, because of meeting two nodes of opinion i one of which was u, then we consider v as recruited by node u in round r. Moreover, if later on, any node switches to opinion i because of meeting node v, or one of the recruits of v, those are counted as recruitment of v and thus, indirectly, as recruitment of u. Therefore, they are also taken into account when we examine the effect of u being a light blue node in round r.

In round r, the number of direct recruitment of u to opinion i is a binomial distribution with expectation at most $n \cdot 1/n \cdot p_i \leq p_{\max} \leq 1.5/\kappa$. Each recruited node v, which becomes an extra-light node, may have its own direct recruitment. Over all the rounds, that is a binomial distribution with expectation at most $\delta\kappa p_{\max} \leq 3\delta \ll 1$. Similarly, any recruited extra-light node may recruit further nodes, according to a binomial distribution with expectation at most $\delta\kappa p_{\max} \leq 3\delta \ll 1$. Hence, the overall number of extra-light blues created because of u being a light-blue node in round r is at most the size of a simple Galton-Watson branching process [17]. In this process, first the root gives birth to a binomially distributed number of children with expectation at most $p_{\max}$, and from that point on, each node gives birth to a binomially distributed number of children with expectation at most $3\delta \ll 1$. It is simple and well-known that in this regime of each node creating strictly less than one off-spring in expectation, the process dies out and moreover, the size of the whole tree has an exponentially decaying probability tail. Concretely, in our case, the probability that the size of the tree exceeds $3tp_{\max}$ decays exponentially with t. Therefore, since the sum of random variables with exponentially decaying tail has a Chernoff-like concentration (see e.g., [11, Lemma 7]), if we let s^r be the fraction of light blue nodes in round r, we can conclude that whp, the fraction of extra-light blue nodes is at most $\sum_r |s^r| \cdot 4p_{\max} + O(\log n)$. Now, we bound the sum $\sum_r |s^r|$. In particular, we bound $\max_r |s^r|$ using Etemadi's inequality [15].

Theorem 3.1 (Etemadi's Inequality [15]). *Let X_N for $N = 1, 2, 3, \ldots$ be a sequence of independent random variables, though not necessarily having identical distributions. For each L, define $S_L = \sum_{\ell=1}^{L} X_\ell$. For all $x > 0$, we have*

$$\Pr\Big[\max_{1\leq \ell \leq N} |S_\ell| \geq x\Big] \leq 3 \max_{1\leq \ell\leq N} \Pr\Big[|S_\ell| \geq x/3\Big].$$

Recall that the fraction of light-blue nodes s^r in round r is the sum of r independent almost-Gaussians, each with variance at most $n(1.5/\kappa)^2 \leq 3n/\kappa^2$. In the context of Etemadi's inequality, think of each of these almost-Gaussians as one of the summands X_ℓ. Then Etemadi's inequality shows that $\Pr[\max_r |s^r| \geq x]$ is at most 3 times the probability that an almost-Gaussian with variance at most $\delta\kappa \cdot 3n/\kappa^2$ exceeds $x/3$. Thus, whp $|s^r| \leq 3C_6\sqrt{n\log n/\kappa}$ for all rounds r. Hence $\sum_r |s^r| \leq 3C_6\delta\kappa\sqrt{n\log n/\kappa} \leq C_{10}\delta\sqrt{\kappa n\log n}$. Therefore, whp the total number of extra-light blues is at most $4p_{\max} \cdot C_{10}\delta\sqrt{\kappa n\log n} + O(\log n) \ll C_{11}\delta\sqrt{n\log n/\kappa}$, for some constant C_{11}. By choosing constant δ sufficiently small, we can make this desirably smaller than our bound of $C_6\sqrt{n\log n/\kappa}$ on the number of light-blue nodes. Thus extra-light blues are negligible compared to the blue nodes.

Putting Things Together. In the above, we provided arguments that bound the number of light blue and extra-light blue nodes. We can now say that the number of nodes of opinion i at the end of the phase is within a factor of $(1 \pm C_{12}\sqrt{\kappa\log n/n})$ of its expectation, for some constant $C_{12} > 0$. This expectation is captured by the number of the clear blue nodes. To finish the analysis, we now go back to analyzing this expectation. In the first round, the number of blue nodes is set to $p_i(1 + p_i - \Sigma_2)$ and the number of red nodes is set to $p_j(1 + p_j - \Sigma_2)$. This is a growth of $\frac{(1+p_i-\Sigma_2)}{(1+p_j-\Sigma_2)} \geq 1 + \frac{p_i-p_j}{1+p_j-\Sigma_2} \geq 1 + \frac{1}{2}(p_i - p_j)$ factor in the ratio p_i/p_j. Similarly, per round, the expectations (captured by clear blue nodes) grow at least by a factor $1+\frac{1}{2}(p_i^t - p_j^t)$, where p_i^t and p_j^t indicate the fraction of clear blue and clear red nodes of round t. Since these numbers are deterministic by definition of clear blue and clear red nodes, it is easy to verify that for all t, we have $1 + \frac{1}{2}(p_i^t - p_j^t) \geq 1 + \frac{1}{2}(p_i - p_j)$. Hence, at least in terms of the clear blue populations, we expect p_i/p_j to grow by a factor of at least $(1 + \frac{1}{2}(p_i - p_j))^{\delta\kappa} \geq 1 + \delta g_{ij}/30$. As argued above, the actual denominator and numerator may each be up to a factor of $(1 \pm C_{12}\sqrt{\kappa\log n/n})$ off from these expectations. Hence we can conclude that whp, by the end of the phase, we have

$$1 + g_{ij}^{\text{new}} \geq (1 + g_{ij})(1 + \tfrac{\delta}{30} g_{ij}) \cdot (1 - 3C_{12}\frac{\sqrt{\log n}}{\sqrt{n/\kappa}}).$$

Since we started with the assumption that $g_{ij} \geq C_5\sqrt{\log n}/\sqrt{n/\kappa}$, for a desirably large constant $C_5 > 0$, we can assume that $3C_{12} \leq \delta C_5/60$, which allows us to infer $g_{ij}^{\text{new}} \geq g_{ij}(1 + \delta/100)$. This concludes the proof.

3.2 Proof of Lemma 2.3

As stated before, the proof is quite close to that of Lemma 2.5. We only mention the differences. In proving Lemma 2.5, we needed a high probability guarantee. We thus said that the number of light-blue nodes at the end of the phase, which has an almost-Gaussian distribution with variance at most $3n\delta/\kappa$, cannot be more than $\pm C_6\sqrt{n\log n/\kappa}$, whp. Here, we cannot afford to throw in this $\sqrt{\log n}$ factor for a high probability guarantee. However, fixing a small constant $0 < \delta' < 1$ and using Chernoff bounds for almost-Gaussians (Lemma 5.1), the probability that the number exceeds $\pm C_7 x\delta'\sqrt{n/\kappa}$ is at most $\exp(-C_{13}\min\{x^2\delta'^2, x\delta'\sqrt{n/\kappa}\}) = \exp(-C_{13}x^2\delta'^2)$ for some constant $C_{13} > 0$ that is independent of δ'. Similarly, using Etemadi's inequality as before, we get that the probability that the number of light blue nodes ever exceeds $\pm 3C_7 x\delta'\sqrt{n/\kappa}$ is at most $\exp(-C_{14}x^2\delta'^2)$, and we can bound the number of extra-light blue nodes as before. Note that if the *number* of light blue nodes is within $\pm C_7 x\delta'\sqrt{n/\kappa}$, then the deviation *factors* are bounded by $(1 \pm C_{15}x\delta'/\sqrt{n/\kappa}) = (1 \pm C_{15}\delta' g_{ij})$. Hence, with probability at least $1 - \exp(-C_{14}x^2\delta'^2)$, we have $1 + g_{ij}^{\text{new}} \geq (1 + g_{ij})(1 + \delta/30 \cdot g_{ij}) \cdot (1 \pm C_{15}\delta' g_{ij})$. Since we may choose δ' arbitrarily, in particular smaller than $\delta/(200C_{15})$, we can conclude that with probability at least $1 - \exp(-C_{14}x^2\delta'^2)$, we have $g_{ij}^{\text{new}} \geq (1 + \delta/100)g_{ij}$.

4 ADAPTATION FOR 3-MAJORITY

Compared to 2-choice, the 3-majority consensus dynamics has the same first order dynamics [7], but the variances are higher. However, our analysis builds on *comparisons between variances*, and all variances are scaled up by the same factors. Therefore the proof still goes through. Here we list the most important changes, skipping the details.

- The variances increase by a factor of κ. In particular, the variance of the number of blue vertices (of a strong opinion) is $\Theta(n/\kappa)$ instead of $\Theta(n/\kappa^2)$. So for example, we expect the number of light blue vertices after the first round of an epoch to be of order $\sqrt{n/\kappa}$ instead of $\sqrt{n/\kappa^2}$. Similarly, for each phase the variance of the number of blue vertices is $\Theta(n)$ instead of $\Theta(n/\kappa)$, and we expect the deviations to be of order $\sqrt{n}$ instead $\sqrt{n/\kappa}$.
  More formally, the factors $1/\sqrt{n/k}$ in Lemmas 2.2, 2.3, 2.4, and 2.5 need to be replaced by $1/\sqrt{n}$.
- For Lemma 2.1 we need that weak opinions remain weak. Thus we need that if $g_{ij} = \Omega(1)$ is sufficiently large, the expected gain of g_{ij} in each round dominates the deviation. The gain is $\Omega(1/\kappa)$, while the standard deviation of g_{ij} is $O(\sqrt{\kappa/n})$ (instead of $O(1/\sqrt{n})$). Thus we need $1/\kappa \gg \sqrt{\kappa/n}$, or $\kappa \ll n^{1/3}$, where an additional logarithmic factor is needed to ensure whp.
- For the proof we need to adapt our definition of extra-light blue nodes. We say that a light-blue node u recruits an extra-light blue node v if v changes its opinion to blue in a round in which it saw *u and another blue node.* If a node u changes an opinion due to a light-blue node in a tie, then we color u clear blue or light blue. In this way, the number of extra-light blue nodes is the same as in our analysis, and can be treated analogously.
- The treatment of light-blue nodes becomes slightly more complicated: let x_{i-1} and x_i be the number of light blue vertices in round $i-1$ and i, respectively. Then in our proof we use that x_i equals x_{i-1} plus the deviation from mean of the number of clear blue nodes in round i (which may be positive or negative). For 3-majority, the term x_{i-1} must yet be replaced by a binomially distributed random variable Z, so the variations of Z cause additional variance in x_i. However, Z is binomially distributed with expectation x_{i-1}, so it can be handled with Azuma's inequality. Since the variance of Z is strictly dominated by the variance in the clear blue vertices, the additional terms are negligible.

4.1 Bringing Back the Adversary to The Analysis

For any valid opinion, we will show that the impact of an F-bounded adversary, for $F = \varepsilon\sqrt{n}/k^{1.5}$ where ε is a desirably small constant, is at most as strong as the random deviations that we took into account in our analysis. For non-valid opinions, which are introduced to the system by the adversary, we group all these non-valid opinions as one opinion $i = k + 1$. Clearly, this can not increase our chances of converging to a valid opinion, it can only strengthen the non-valid opinions. Despite that, we show that this single non-valid opinion is super-weak and remains super-weak at all times.

First, in the case of the adversary's influence on valid opinion, this can only impact proofs of properties (P1), (P2), (P3), (P5), and (P7). This is because properties (P4) and (P6) do not deal with the dynamics directly, and merely rely on the other properties. Let us now examine these potentially impacted properties.

In proof of property (P1), for each opinion, we took into account a deviation of size at most $O(\sqrt{n \log n/k^2})$. The adversary's influence is $F = \varepsilon\sqrt{n}/k^{1.5} = o(\sqrt{n \log n/k^2})$. Hence, in this case, the adversary's impact is at most a second-order term in the deviations, and thus, since we anyways did not rely on the constant in the deviations, the proof goes through as before. The effect in property (P7) is similar, it is much smaller than the deviations that are already taken into account, and thus the analysis remains the same. Notice that in the case of (P1) and (P7), there is even some slack and we could have tolerated an even larger F. The bottleneck on that appears in properties (P2), (P3), (P5).

The adversary's effect in (P2), (P3), (P5) is similar. Recall that all three of these are about one phase, which is made of δk rounds. During these rounds, the adversary can increase the number of nodes of one opinion by at most $\delta kF \leq \epsilon\delta\sqrt{n/k}$. For instance, in the case of opinion i, we consider these as a small increase in the number of light blue nodes. As argued before, the number of extra-light blue nodes created because of these light blue nodes is at most $10\epsilon\delta^2\sqrt{n/k}$. Hence, overall, the effect of the adversary is increasing the number of light blue or extra light blue nodes by $\pm 2\epsilon\delta\sqrt{n/k}$. In terms of fraction of nodes, this is at most $2\epsilon\delta/\sqrt{nk}$. Choosing ε a small enough constant, this is much smaller than the overall deviation $C_7 x/\sqrt{\kappa n}$ taken into account in proving (P3), the $C_7\sqrt{\log n}/\sqrt{\kappa n}$ deviation taken into account in proving $C_7 x/\sqrt{\kappa n}$, and the $C_{17}/\sqrt{\kappa n}$ taken into account in proving (P2). Hence, in all of these, the adversary's impact is far below the deviations that we took into account, and therefore, the analysis remains effectively the same.

5 TECHNICAL TOOLS

Since we frequently use the Chernoff bound for almost-Gaussian distributed random variables, we give a brief derivation.

LEMMA 5.1 (CHERNOFF BOUND FOR DIFFERENCE OF POISSON-BINOMIALS). *Let $X_1, \ldots, X_n, Y_1, \ldots, Y_m$ be independent random variables (not necessarily i.i.d.) that take values in $[0,1]$. Let $X = \sum_{i=1}^{n} X_i$ and $Y = \sum_{i=1}^{m} Y_i$, and assume that $\mathbb{E}[X] = \mathbb{E}[Y] =: \mu$. Then for all $C > 0$,*

$$\Pr(|X - Y| \geq 2C\sqrt{\mu}) \leq 4e^{-\min\{C^2, C\sqrt{\mu}\}/3}.$$

PROOF. The formulation follows immediately from the standard Chernoff bound [12] by a union bound over the two events $|X-\mu| \geq C\sqrt{\mu}$ and $|Y-\mu| \geq C\sqrt{\mu}$. □

REFERENCES

[1] Dan Alistarh, James Aspnes, David Eisenstat, Rati Gelashvili, and Ronald L Rivest. 2017. Time-space trade-offs in population protocols. In *Proc. of ACM-SIAM Symp. on Disc. Alg. (SODA)*. 2560–2579.

[2] Dan Alistarh, Rati Gelashvili, and Milan Vojnović. 2015. Fast and exact majority in population protocols. In *the Proc. of the Int'l Symp. on Princ. of Dist. Comp. (PODC)*. 47–56.

[3] Dana Angluin, James Aspnes, and David Eisenstat. 2008. A simple population protocol for fast robust approximate majority. *Distributed Computing* 21, 2 (2008), 87–102.

[4] Luca Becchetti, Andrea Clementi, Emanuele Natale, Francesco Pasquale, and Riccardo Silvestri. 2015. Plurality consensus in the gossip model. In *Proc. of ACM-SIAM Symp. on Disc. Alg. (SODA)*. Society for Industrial and Applied Mathematics, 371–390.

[5] Luca Becchetti, Andrea Clementi, Emanuele Natale, Francesco Pasquale, Riccardo Silvestri, and Luca Trevisan. 2014. Simple dynamics for plurality consensus. In *the Proc. of the Symp. on Parallel Algorithms and Architectures (SPAA)*. 247–256.

[6] Luca Becchetti, Andrea Clementi, Emanuele Natale, Francesco Pasquale, and Luca Trevisan. 2016. Stabilizing consensus with many opinions. In *Proc. of ACM-SIAM Symp. on Disc. Alg. (SODA)*. 620–635.

[7] Petra Berenbrink, Andrea Clementi, Robert Elsässer, Peter Kling, Frederik Mallmann-Trenn, and Emanuele Natale. 2017. Ignore or comply? on breaking symmetry in consensus. *arXiv preprint arXiv:1702.04921* (2017).

[8] Petra Berenbrink, Tom Friedetzky, George Giakkoupis, and Peter Kling. 2016. Efficient plurality consensus, or: The benefits of cleaning up from time to time. In *the Proc. of the Int'l Colloquium on Automata, Languages and Programming (ICALP)*.

[9] Patrick Billingsley. 2013. *Convergence of probability measures*. John Wiley & Sons.

[10] Colin Cooper, Robert Elsässer, and Tomasz Radzik. 2014. The power of two choices in distributed voting. In *International Colloquium on Automata, Languages, and Programming*. Springer, 435–446.

[11] Benjamin Doerr, Leslie Ann Goldberg, Lorenz Minder, Thomas Sauerwald, and Christian Scheideler. 2011. Stabilizing consensus with the power of two choices. In *the Proc. of the Symp. on Parallel Algorithms and Architectures (SPAA)*. 149–158.

[12] Devdatt P Dubhashi and Alessandro Panconesi. 2009. *Concentration of measure for the analysis of randomized algorithms*. Cambridge University Press.

[13] Robert Elsässer, Tom Friedetzky, Dominik Kaaser, Frederik Mallmann-Trenn, and Horst Trinker. 2016. Efficient k-party voting with two choices. *ArXiv e-prints* (2016).

[14] Robert Elsässer, Tom Friedetzky, Dominik Kaaser, Frederik Mallmann-Trenn, and Horst Trinker. 2016. Rapid Asynchronous Plurality Consensus. *arXiv preprint arXiv:1602.04667* (2016).

[15] Nasrollah Etemadi. 1985. On some classical results in probability theory. *Sankhyā: The Indian Journal of Statistics, Series A* (1985), 215–221.

[16] Mohsen Ghaffari and Merav Parter. 2016. A polylogarithmic gossip algorithm for plurality consensus. In *the Proc. of the Int'l Symp. on Princ. of Dist. Comp. (PODC)*. 117–126.

[17] Theodore E Harris. 2002. *The theory of branching processes*. Courier Corporation.

[18] Etienne Perron, Dinkar Vasudevan, and Milan Vojnovic. 2009. Using three states for binary consensus on complete graphs. In *INFOCOM 2009, IEEE*. 2527–2535.

Sublinear Message Bounds for Randomized Agreement

John Augustine*
Department of Computer Science and Engineering, Indian Institute of Technology at Madras
Chennai, Tamil Nadu, India
augustine@iitm.ac.in

Anisur Rahaman Molla†
School of Computer Sciences, National Institute of Science Education and Research Bhubaneswar
Khurda, Odisha, India
molla@niser.ac.in

Gopal Pandurangan‡
Department of Computer Science, University of Houston
Houston, Texas, USA
gopalpandurangan@gmail.com

ABSTRACT

This paper focuses on understanding the message complexity of *randomized* agreement in synchronous distributed networks. We focus on the so-called *implicit agreement* problem where each node starts with an input value (0 or 1) and at the end *one or more* nodes should decide on a common input value which should be equal to some node's input value (there can be undecided nodes). Implicit agreement is a generalization of the fundamental agreement and leader election problems.

We present *sublinear* (in n, where n is the number of nodes) algorithms and lower bounds on the message complexity of implicit agreement in fully-connected (i.e., complete) networks. Specifically our main results are:

(1) We show that for any implicit agreement algorithm that succeeds with probability at least $1-\epsilon$, for some suitably small constant $\epsilon > 0$, needs at least $\Omega(n^{0.5})$ messages with constant probability. This bound holds regardless of the number of rounds used and applies to both LOCAL and CONGEST models. This lower bound is essentially tight for complete networks, as there exists a randomized agreement algorithm that uses only $\tilde{O}(n^{0.5})$ messages[1] with high probability[2] and runs in $O(1)$ rounds and succeeds with high probability. Both the upper and lower bounds assume that nodes have access to (only) *private* coins.

(2) In contrast to the above bounds, if nodes have access to an unbiased *global (shared)* coin, we present a randomized algorithm which, with high probability, achieves implicit agreement, and uses $\tilde{O}(n^{0.4})$ messages in expectation and runs in $O(1)$ rounds (deterministically). This algorithm works in the CONGEST model as well. Our result shows the power of a global coin in significantly improving (by a polynomial factor) the message complexity of agreement. As another contrast, we show that the same benefit *does not apply to leader election*, i.e., even with access to a global coin, $\Omega(n^{0.5})$ messages (in expectation) are needed for any *leader election* algorithm that succeeds with probability at least $1-\epsilon$, for a small constant $\epsilon > 0$.

(3) We extend our results to a natural generalization of agreement called as *subset agreement* where a given (non-empty) *subset* of nodes should agree on a common value. We show that subset agreement on a subset of size k nodes can be accomplished by a randomized algorithm that succeeds with high probability, and uses (in expecation) $\tilde{O}(\min\{kn^{0.5}, n\})$ (using only private coins) and $\tilde{O}(\min\{kn^{0.4}, n\})$ messages (using global coin) respectively.

We view our results as a step towards understanding the complexity of randomized agreement in distributed networks, in particular, message complexity with or without shared randomness.

CCS CONCEPTS

• **Theory of computation** → *Design and analysis of algorithms*; *Models of computation*; • **Networks** → *Network algorithms*;

KEYWORDS

Distributed Algorithm, Randomized Algorithm, Agreement, Leader Election, Global Coin, Shared Randomness

ACM Reference Format:
John Augustine, Anisur Rahaman Molla, and Gopal Pandurangan. 2018. Sublinear Message Bounds for Randomized Agreement. In *PODC '18: ACM Symposium on Principles of Distributed Computing, July 23–27, 2018, Egham, United Kingdom.* ACM, New York, NY, USA, 10 pages. https://doi.org/10.1145/3212734.3212751

1 INTRODUCTION

Agreement is a fundamental problem in distributed computing and, along with its variants, it has been extensively studied for the last four decades. In this paper, we focus on a basic question in solving agreement in (synchronous) distributed networks: *What is the minimum number of messages required to solve agreement?* In the classical (binary) agreement problem, we have n nodes each starting with an input value (0 or 1) and the goal of agreement is to guarantee the following two conditions: (1) *All* nodes should agree (decide) on the same input value (*consensus condition*) and (2) the

*Research supported in part by an Extra-Mural Research Grant (file number EMR/2016/003016) funded by the Science and Engineering Research Board, Department of Science and Technology, Government of India.
†Supported by DST Inspire Faculty Research grant (grant number DST/INSPIRE/04/2015/002801).
‡Supported, in part, by NSF grants CCF-1527867, CCF-1540512, IIS-1633720, CCF-BSF-1717075, and BSF award 2016419.
[1]The notations $\tilde{O}$ and $\tilde{\Omega}$ hide polylog(n) factors.
[2]Throughout,"with high probability" or "whp" in short means with probability at least $1 - 1/n^c$ for some constant $c \geq 1$.

ACM ISBN 978-1-4503-5795-1/18/07...$15.00
https://doi.org/10.1145/3212734.3212751

common value should be the input value of some node (*validity condition*). If there are no failures, the above problem is easy to solve. For example, in a fully-connected (i.e., complete) network with all good nodes, the following simple algorithm takes only 1 round: each node broadcasts its value to all other nodes and then all nodes take the majority value to be consensus value (if it is a tie, then they can all choose, say, 1). However, this easy solution, though optimal in the number of rounds, requires $\Theta(n^2)$ messages.[3]

The problem becomes much more difficult to solve when there are *faults or Byzantine failures*; these have been extensively investigated and continue to be investigated with a long history (e.g., see [5, 18] or the more recent results discussed below). In the vast majority of the works in the literature (under various settings and assumptions), the focus is mainly on the time complexity, i.e., the number of rounds needed for agreement. The message complexity has also been investigated, but somewhat less number of results have focused on this aspect. To be concrete, let's focus on the Byzantine agreement problem (on fully-connected networks) which was first defined in early 80's by a landmark paper by Pease, Shostak, and Lamport [23] and has since been studied extensively. In the Byzantine setting, a subset of the nodes can be Byzantine, i.e., can behave maliciously (including crashing) and can deviate arbitrarily from the behaviour of the protocol executed by the good nodes and try to foil the good nodes reaching agreement. In the Byzantine setting, condition (1) should hold for all honest nodes, i.e., all honest nodes should agree on a common value (condition 2 also holds). Byzantine agreement can be considered as a "flagship" problem in distributed computing, as it gives a building block of creating reliable distributed systems that can operate under failures and malicious nodes. Its importance can be seen from the widespread and continued application in many domains, e.g., sensor networks [27], grid computing [4], peer-to-peer networks [26] and cloud computing [28]. However, despite intensive research, there has still not been a practical solution to the Byzantine agreement problem for large networks. A main reason for this is the *large message complexity* of currently known protocols; this has been suggested by many systems papers [2, 3, 9, 19, 29]. Till recently, the best known protocols had quadratic message complexity, i.e., $\Theta(n^2)$, where n is the number of participants (nodes) in the network.

In a breakthrough result, King and Saia [12] presented the first Byzantine agreement algorithm in *synchronous complete networks* that *breaks* the quadratic message barrier. They presented an algorithm where *each* processor sends only $\tilde{O}(\sqrt{n})$ messages, and thus the total message complexity is bounded by $\tilde{O}(n^{1.5})$. Their algorithm is *randomized Monte Carlo* (succeeds with high probability) and works even under an adaptive adversary which can control up to 1/3 of the processors (but assumes private channels). This is essentially the best message complexity known for Byzantine agreement. However, no non-trivial message lower bound is known for Byzantine agreement. In particular, Saia and King raise the open question whether each processor needs to send at least $\tilde{\Omega}(\sqrt{n})$ to solve Byzantine agreement. Also, it is not known if one needs $\tilde{\Omega}(n^{1.5})$ (total) message complexity. In fact, a tight *message complexity* of solving just agreement (even with no Byzantine nodes) is still not fully understood in the *randomized* setting (cf. Section 1.3); this is especially true for the variants of the agreement problem addressed here (discussed below). Understanding the message complexity of randomized agreement in the *fault-free* setting will help shed light in the more challenging Byzantine setting; in particular, the lower bounds in the fault-free setting also apply for the Byzantine setting. This is one main motivation for this work.

Another main motivation for this work is understanding the significance of a key resource in randomized agreement, namely, the use of *private* versus *global (shared)* coins. Protocols that use private coins only, assume that all nodes have access to private (unbiased) coin tosses that are not visible to other nodes. On the other hand, protocols that use global coins assume that all nodes have access to a shared coin. For example, one of the first randomized protocols for Byzantine agreement by Rabin [25] (see the protocol's description in [21]) uses an unbiased global coin to achieve Byzantine agreement in (expected) constant number of rounds in a complete network; however, this protocol takes $\Theta(n^2)$ messages. Many other randomized protocols have been designed since then that uses private coins. One of the earliest protocols by Ben-Or [6] also uses *private coins*, but this also takes $\Theta(n^2)$ messages (and also exponential time to finish if there is a linear number of Byzantine nodes). There has been a lot of work on "coin flipping" protocols (see e.g., [7] and the references therein) where the goal is to generate a *common coin* despite the presence of Byzantine nodes. Common coin (see e.g., [8, 10] for a definition) is a somewhat weaker notion than a global coin where it is sufficient for the value to be the same across all (honest) nodes with only constant probability and both 0 and 1 values should occur with constant probability. Common coins are a fundamental primitive that enables implementation of randomized byzantine agreement (among other protocols), e.g., it is sufficient for implementing Rabin's protocol [8]. However, almost all the work till now has focused on reducing the time complexity of coin flipping and not the message complexity. All these protocols have $\Theta(n^2)$ message complexity (except for the work of King and Saia [12] discussed earlier which has $\tilde{O}(n^{1.5})$ message complexity). Hence a fundamental question is understanding the message complexity of coin flipping as well as the communication (message) cost of using global coin verses private coins.

In this paper, motivated by understanding the message complexity of randomized agreement, we introduce and study the notions of *implicit agreement* and *subset agreement* which generalize the agreement problem. Intuitively, an "implicit" agreement doesn't require all the participants to agree on a value, rather it is enough if a non-empty subset of them agree. Formally we define implicit agreement on an n node-network as follows.

Definition 1.1 (Implicit Agreement). *Suppose initially each node has an input value in* $\{0, 1\}$. *An* implicit agreement *holds when the final state of all the nodes is either* $\{0, \perp\}$ *or* $\{1, \perp\}$ *and at least one node has state other than* $\perp$ *(which should be the input value of some node), where* $\perp$ *denotes the 'undecided' state. In other words, all the decided nodes must agree on the* same value which is an initial input value of some node *and there must be* at least one decided node *in the network.*

[3] Our results (cf. Section 1.1) implies that this problem can be solved optimally with regards to both time and message complexity by a randomized algorithm that uses $O(n)$ messages with high probability and runs in $O(1)$ rounds.

We study the implicit agreement problem in a fully-connected (complete) n-node distributed network. Implicit agreement is a generalization of the agreement problem. The flexibility of the implicit agreement lies in the fact that all the nodes need not agree or do not need to know the agreed value. Therefore, in principle, the agreement can be fulfilled with much less communication. In particular, *sublinear* message bounds are possible, unlike the case of the usual agreement when *all* nodes need to agree (this requires at least n messages). Implicit agreement is also interesting in understanding lower bounds for agreement in the faulty setting (either crash failures or Byzantine nodes) where we don't care about the values output by the "bad" nodes. Thus, clearly, lower bounds for implicit agreement apply for full agreement in the faulty setting as well. Implicit agreement also generalizes the fundamental *leader election* problem, or, in other words, leader election can be considered as a special case of implicit agreement. We note that if there is *exactly one decided* node, then the problem is equivalent to *implicit leader election* problem which has been studied extensively for over three decades, see e.g., [5, 16–18] and the references therein (see also Section 1.3). The decider node will be the leader. However, in comparison to the leader election problem, the implicit agreement has the flexibility of multiple nodes deciding (and hence presumably easier), however, the challenging part is that all the deciding nodes must decide on the same value (which should be the input value of some node as well). In this paper, we also fully characterize the message complexity of (implicit) leader election vis-a-vis implicit agreement.

We also consider a natural generalization of implicit agreement called *subset agreement* which can also be independent interest and useful in applications. For example, consider a large network such as the Internet, and an (a priori) unknown subset of nodes want to agree on a common value; the subset size can be much smaller than the network size.

Definition 1.2 (Subset Agreement). *Initially each node has a value in* $\{0, 1\}$, *the* subset agreement *is an agreement by a (specified) non-empty subset* $S \subseteq V$ *of nodes. We assume that each node knows whether it belongs to* S *or not, but doesn't know the identities of other nodes in the subset. The agreement on* S *holds when the final state of all the nodes in* S *is "decided" and the deciding value of all of them is either* 0 *or* 1 *(which should be the input value of some node in the network).*

Note that subset agreement is the same as traditional agreement if the subset includes all the nodes. We study sublinear message bounds for subset agreement.

1.1 Our Contributions

We present *sublinear* (in n, where n is the number of nodes) algorithms and lower bounds on the message complexity of implicit agreement and subset agreement in fully-connected (i.e., complete) networks. Specifically our main results are:

(1) We show that for any implicit agreement algorithm that succeeds with probability at least $1 - \epsilon$, for some suitably small constant $\epsilon > 0$, needs at least $\Omega(n^{0.5})$ messages with constant probability. (Note that this implies that $\Omega(n^{0.5})$ messages are needed in expectation as well.) This lower bound is essentially tight for complete networks, as there exists a randomized algorithm for implicit agreement that uses only $\tilde{O}(n^{0.5})$ messages with high probability[4] and runs in $O(1)$ rounds and succeeds with high probability.[5] Both the upper and lower bounds assume that nodes have access to (only) *private* coins.

(2) In contrast to the above bounds, if nodes have access to an unbiased *global (shared)* coin, we present a randomized algorithm for implicit agreement which succeeds with high probability, and that uses $\tilde{O}(n^{0.4})$ messages (in expectation)[6] and runs in $O(1)$ rounds (deterministically). Our result shows the power of a global coin in significantly improving (by a polynomial factor) the message complexity of implicit agreement. As another contrast, we show that the same benefit *does not apply to leader election*, i.e., even with access to a global coin, $\Omega(n^{0.5})$ messages are needed for any *leader election* algorithm that succeeds with probability at least ϵ, for a fixed constant $0 < \epsilon < 1$. Our results show that agreement is a strictly easier problem (with respect to message complexity) than leader election under access to global coin.

(3) We show that subset agreement on a subset of size k nodes can be accomplished by randomized algorithm, which succeeds with high probability, and uses (in expectation) $\tilde{O}(\min\{kn^{0.5}, n\})$ messages (with access to private coins only) and $\tilde{O}(\min\{kn^{0.4}, n\})$ messages (with access to global coin). We note that these bounds are sublinear in n when $k = o(\sqrt{n})$ and $k = o(n^{0.6})$ respectively.

For our algorithms, we assume that the communication is synchronous and follows the standard CONGEST model [24], where a node can send in each round at most one message of size $O(\log n)$ bits on a single edge. We do not however assume that the nodes have unique IDs, hence the algorithms in this paper apply also for *anonymous* networks. We assume that all nodes wake up simultaneously at the beginning of the execution. (Additional details on our distributed computation model are given in Section 1.2.) Our lower bounds hold *regardless of the number of rounds* even in the LOCAL model [24], where there is no restriction on the number of bits that can be sent on each edge in each round.

We view our results as a step towards understanding the complexity of randomized agreement in distributed networks, in particular, message complexity with or without shared randomness. Our work raises many interesting open problems which we discuss in Section 6.

1.2 Distributed Computing Model

The distributed computing model we consider is similar to the models of [1, 11, 13–15], with the main addition of giving processors access to a *private* unbiased coin. For our algorithm of Section 3, we also allow processors access to a *global (shared)* unbiased coin. Also, we do not assume unique identities; however, we show that our lower bounds hold regardless of whether we have unique identities or not. We consider a network of n nodes, represented as

[4] Throughout, "with high probability" or "whp" in short means with probability at least $1 - 1/n^c$ for some constant $c \geq 1$.
[5] It can be shown that, if no randomness is allowed, i.e., for deterministic algorithms, $\Omega(n)$ is a (tight) lower bound on the message complexity of implicit agreement.
[6] The message complexity bound also holds with probability at least $1 - 1/n^{1/5}$.

an undirected complete (fully-connected) graph $G = (V, E)$. Each node runs an instance of a distributed algorithm. The computation advances in synchronous rounds where, in every round, nodes can send messages, receive messages that were sent in the same round by neighbors in G, and perform some local computation. Messages are the only means of communication; in particular, nodes cannot access the coin flips of other nodes, and do not share any memory. Throughout this paper, we assume that all nodes are awake initially and simultaneously start executing the algorithm.

We note that initially nodes have knowledge only of themselves, in other words we assume the *clean network model* — also called the *KT0 model* [24] which is standard and most commonly used. On the other hand, if one assumes the *KT1 model*, where nodes have an initial knowledge of the IDs of their neighbors, then leader election (and hence implicit agreement) is trivial, since the minimum ID node can become the leader. (However, subset agreement is still not trivial if nodes in the subset don't know each other, as assumed here.)

1.3 Other Related Work

We focus only on those works that are closely related to the work here, in particular, agreement and leader election in the *fault-free* setting. The work of Kutten et al. [17, 22] considers the (implicit) leader election in complete networks and showed that, *contrary to deterministic setting* (which has been studied extensively see e.g., [17] and the references therein), randomization allows one to obtain *sublinear* message bounds. In particular, they demonstrated that, for randomized algorithms, the seemingly obvious lower bound of $\Omega(n)$ messages for a complete graph does not hold. Specifically, it presented an algorithm that executes in $O(1)$ time and uses only $O(\sqrt{n}\log^{3/2} n)$ messages to elect a leader in a complete graph. They also showed an almost matching lower bound for randomized leader election, by showing that $\Omega(\sqrt{n})$ messages are needed for any leader election algorithm that succeeds with probability at least $1/e+\epsilon$, for any small constant $\epsilon > 0$. The subsequent work of Kutten et al. [16] studied (implicit) leader election in general networks and showed that $\Theta(m)$ (m is the number of edges) and $\Theta(D)$ (D is the network diameter) are tight bounds on the message and time complexity of randomized leader election in *general* networks.

The present work is inspired by the works of [16, 17] and studies the randomized complexity of (implicit) agreement. It is clear that an algorithm for leader election also solves implicit agreement, but since agreement is weaker, a natural question is whether the $\Omega(\sqrt{n})$ message lower bound for leader election also applies for agreement. We show that it indeed does, although the proof for the agreement is different and more involved (the main reason being that the agreement problem has inputs, unlike, leader election). This motivates us to consider agreement with global coins where we show that the $\Omega(\sqrt{n})$ lower bound can be beaten by a polynomial factor: we can obtain a $\tilde{O}(n^{0.4})$ messages algorithm. This is in contrast to leader election where we show that having access shared coins *does not* help: the $\Omega(\sqrt{n})$ lower bound still holds. This proof closely builds on the lower bound proof of [17].

To the best of our knowledge, the subset agreement problem has not been studied before.

2 LOWER BOUND FOR IMPLICIT AGREEMENT

In this section, we show that any algorithm for implicit agreement - even randomized - will, with constant probability, require $\Omega(\sqrt{n})$ messages to be sent in order to achieve implicit agreement with probability at least $1 - \epsilon$ for a sufficiently small $\epsilon > 0$. Kutten *et al.* [17] show that leader election requires $\Omega(\sqrt{n})$ messages, but our proof is different because, under leader election, all nodes essentially start in identical configurations. In our implicit agreement problem, however, the nodes start with initial values and our lower bound argument takes that into account and shows that no algorithm can exploit those initial values in order to reach agreement with fewer messages.

Consider a randomized algorithm $\mathcal{A}$ to achieve implicit agreement with probability $1 - \epsilon$. For the sake of contradiction, let us assume that $\mathcal{A}$ sends at most $o(\sqrt{n})$ messages with probability at least $1 - o(1)$. $\mathcal{A}$ can be randomized in the sense that each node individually has access to a source of uniform and independent random bits. We will show that $\mathcal{A}$ must have an error probability that is at least a constant, so for the sake of contradiction, assume that the probability with which $\mathcal{A}$ does not reach implicit agreement is at most $o(1)$. For now, we will assume that the nodes are anonymous, so $\mathcal{A}$ does not have access to unique node identifiers or any other identifying feature pertaining to individual nodes.

Recall also that the network model is the $KT0$ variant, so a node u, at least at the start of the protocol, will not know which incident edge leads to some neighbour v. In fact, for the purpose of showing this lower bound, we assume that for every node, the neighbor sequence (as we enumerate from port 1 to port $n - 1$) is a uniformly random permutation independent of all other nodes' permutations.

Given any $p \in [0, 1]$, let C_p denote the (random) starting configuration wherein each node is independently assigned an initial value of 1 with probability p, or 0 with probability $1 - p$. Let G_p be the (random) directed graph on the n nodes with an edge from u to v iff u sent a message to v and the message was sent before v sent any message to u as $\mathcal{A}$ executed from the starting configuration C_p. We now show that with probability at least $1 - \epsilon$, G_p is a forest comprising trees that are directed away from their respective root.

Lemma 2.1. *With probability at least $1 - \epsilon'$ for some arbitrarily small but constant $\epsilon' > 0$, the graph G_p for all $p \in [0, 1]$ is a forest in which each tree contains exactly one node (called its root) with zero in-edges and, furthermore, all tree edges are oriented away from the root.*

Proof. Recall that the number of messages passed by $\mathcal{A}$ is at most $o(\sqrt{n})$ with probability at least $1 - o(1)$. Therefore, with probability at least $1 - o(1)$, we can apply the condition that the number of nodes that participate in any form of communication (either sending or receiving) is at most $o(\sqrt{n})$. Recall also that each message is sent to a random node. Therefore, the probability that none of those $o(\sqrt{n})$ messages is targeted towards either a node that has sent messages or a node that has already received some message is at least $\left(1 - o(\sqrt{n})/n\right)^{o(\sqrt{n})} \geq 1 - o(1)$. Removing the conditioning, we get the probability that all components in G_p are rooted and oriented trees is again at least $1 - \epsilon'$ for some fixed $\epsilon' > 0$. □

Thus, for the rest of the argument, we apply the condition that for all $p \in [0, 1]$, G_p is a forest as described in Lemma 2.1. We say that a tree is a deciding tree if there is at least one deciding node within that tree.

LEMMA 2.2. *For every value of $p \in [0, 1]$, the probability that there are at least two deciding trees is at least a constant.*

PROOF. Since $\mathcal{A}$ reaches agreement with probability at least $1-\epsilon$, the probability that no tree decides is at most ϵ.

For all values of p, the probability that there is at most one deciding tree is at most a suitable constant c bounded away from 1. Otherwise there exists a p value for which, with probability at least c, exactly one tree decides. Then, quite easily, the root of that deciding tree can be made a leader. This yields a leader election protocol that succeeds with probability at least c, which will contradict Theorem 3 from [17] when c is a sufficiently large constant strictly less than $1 - \epsilon$.

Adding up all these possibilities, we are still left with a probability of at least a constant $q < 1 - \epsilon - c$ with which there must be two or mode deciding trees. □

Now that we know that the there are at least two deciding trees with constant probability, we show that these trees reach opposing decisions with probability also bounded from below by a constant, thereby leading to a contradiction that $\mathcal{A}$ reaches agreement with high probability.

LEMMA 2.3. *There exists a value $p^* \in [0, 1]$ such that the probability that there are at least two deciding trees in G_{p^*} with opposing decisions is at least a constant.*

PROOF. We can define the *probabilistic valency* of p with respect to $\mathcal{A}$, denoted V_p, as the probability that $\mathcal{A}$ will terminate with a decision value 1 under the initial configuration C_p. Thus, the probabilistic valencies of $p = 0$ and $p = 1$ are 0 and 1, respectively. It is easy to see that V_p is a continuous function of $p \in [0, 1]$ as infinitesimally small changes to p can only result in infinitesimally small changes to V_p. This is true because infinitesimally small changes to p will only result in infinitesimally small changes to C_p, and since the algorithm's behaviour is based on the initial configuration (which does not change much), V_p will also only change infinitesimally. This continuity in V_p implies that for every $x \in [0, 1]$, there is a p such that $V_p = x$.

We prove this lemma under the condition that there are at least two deciding trees and that these two trees do not interact with each other. We have seen that enforcing this conditioning requires a probability of q bounded away from 0. An important implication here is that, despite this conditioning, the probabilities of the two decision values must both be bounded from below by a constant. For the sake of contradiction, let us suppose (without loss of generality) that the algorithm decides 1 with probability at most $o(1)$ under this conditioning. Let us fix p such that $V_p = 1 - q/2$. Then, the probability that it decides 1 without the conditioning will be at most $q(o(1)) + (1 - q) < 1 - q/2$, a contradiction.

Now consider two deciding trees T_1 and T_2. For simplicity, let us assume that the decision outcome of T_1 is (say) 0; this occurs with some constant probability. We now reason that the probability that the decision outcome of T_2 is 1 will be at least a constant. This is true because the random input values for T_2 were all chosen independent of the input values for T_1. Thus, the two trees can decide contradictory values with probability at least a constant. □

Thus, we have shown that when the nodes are anonymous and the number of messages sent is at most $o(\sqrt{n})$, implicit agreement is not reached with probability at least a constant. To generalize to the case where nodes do have IDs, we simply assume that the adversary provides ID's chosen uniformly at random from, say, $[1, n^4]$. Let $\mathcal{A}^*$ be an algorithm that exploits these unique IDs.

Notice however, that the execution of $\mathcal{A}^*$ that exploits the adversarially generated random IDs is essentially akin to the execution of $\mathcal{A}^*$ in the anonymous setting in which each node first generates a random number between $[1, n^4]$ and then uses that random number as their IDs. The only difference is that multiple nodes may generate the same random number, thereby inheriting the same ID, but this is an event whose probability is at most $1/n$, so when we condition on these random numbers being distinct, the two executions are probabilistically identical, so any lower bound on the execution without adversarially generated IDs will extend to the case where nodes have unique IDs provided by the adversary. Thus,

THEOREM 2.4. *Suppose $\mathcal{A}$ is an algorithm that solves implicit agreement with probability at least $1 - \epsilon$ for some sufficiently small constant $\epsilon > 0$ in a network of n nodes with unique IDs. Then, with probability at least a constant, the message complexity of $\mathcal{A}$ is at least $\Omega(\sqrt{n})$.*

Optimal Message Complexity Algorithm: Kutten et al. [17, 22] present an algorithm that solves the leader election with high probability and uses $\tilde{O}(\sqrt{n})$ messages. Their algorithm immediately solves the implicit agreement problem as the leader decides on its own value. The following theorem on implicit agreement follows from their leader election result (Theorem 1, [17]).

THEOREM 2.5. *With high probability, implicit agreement can be solved in $O(1)$ rounds and using at most $O(\sqrt{n}\log^{3/2} n)$ messages with high probability on a complete n-node network.*

3 IMPLICIT AGREEMENT USING A GLOBAL COIN

Let us now consider the case where the nodes have access to an unbiased global coin through which they can generate common random bits. The shared random bits are oblivious to the adversary, but it knows the algorithm. With the knowledge of the algorithm, the adversary determines the initial distribution of the $0 - 1$ values over the n nodes. We study the implicit agreement problem under this additional assumption of shared random bits. We design a randomized algorithm which solves the implicit agreement problem with high probability in $O(1)$ communication rounds and incurs expected $O(n^{0.4}\log^{8/5} n)$ messages. Note that our algorithm is correct, i.e., achieves agreement, with probability at least $1 - 1/n$; however the message bound holds in expectation and also with probability at least $1 - 1/n^c$, for some constant $c > 0$, and the time bound of $O(1)$ is deterministic.

High-level idea of the algorithm. We first select a smaller set of nodes which will be responsible for the agreement. This is done by choosing a random set of *candidate nodes* of size $O(\log n)$. For this, every node selects itself with probability $O(\log n/n)$ to become a *candidate node.* The candidate nodes are responsible for the agreement. Next, each candidate node v samples another $O(\log n)$ random nodes from the network and gets their (input) values (0 or 1). Let x_v be the number of 1s among $O(\log n)$ sampled values. Each candidate node v computes $p(v)$ as the fraction of 1s it receives, i.e., $p(v) = x_v/\log n$. We show that with high probability $p(v) \in [\ell, \ell + 5/\sqrt{\log n}]$ for any candidate node v, where $\ell \in [0, (1 - 5/\sqrt{\log n})]$. In other words, all the $p(v)$ values belong to a strip (an interval in [0, 1])) of length $5/\sqrt{\log n}$ (follows from the Lemma 3.1). Let us denote the strip by δ. We abuse the notation by referring to the length of the strip by δ also. The candidate nodes then use the global coin and draw a random real number, say r, in the interval [0, 1]. Notice that the value r is same for the candidates nodes as they use same random bits (from the global coin). One simple way to generate a random (real) number[7] in the interval [0, 1] from the random bit string is as follows. Suppose the random bit string is S. Then the random number is the converted decimal number of 0.S (in binary).[8] Then the candidate nodes decide on '0' if $p(v)$ is on the left of r; otherwise, they decide on '1'. The only case where the agreement could be wrong is when the random number r falls within the strip δ and the probability of that case is δ (note that this depends on the input values which is not under the control of the algorithm). The probability that the random number r doesn't fall in the strip δ is $(1 - \delta)$. Therefore, with probability $(1 - 5/\sqrt{\log n})$, the real number r is either on the left or on the right side of all the $p(v)$ values in the line [0, 1]. That is with probability $(1 - 5/\sqrt{\log n})$, all the candidate nodes decide on the same value and hence, the implicit agreement is satisfied. The message complexity of the algorithm is $O(\log^2 n)$ as the size of the candidate nodes is $O(\log n)$ and each candidate node contacts $O(\log n)$ random nodes. Thus, although this uses only polylogarithmic messages in total, the success probability is not high as required, i.e., it is not with probability $> (1 - 1/n)$.

Note that in the above algorithm if we increase the number of sampled nodes by each candidate node then the strip length δ will be smaller and hence the probability that the random number r will fall in the strip is smaller. That is, the probability of success increases if the number of samples is large. However, this doesn't help much as the number of samples counts towards the message complexity.

We now discuss how to achieve high probability of success. Recall that when the random number r falls inside the strip δ, then some candidate nodes may decide on 0 and some on 1 (based on left or right of r) and hence the agreement could be invalid. To get rid of this, we put some candidate nodes in undecided state, say to those nodes v for which $|p(v) - r| \leq 4\delta$. But then the issue is how the undecided (candidate) nodes know that there is at least one decided node (which is needed to satisfy implicit agreement). If there is no decided node, then the candidate nodes have to repeat the process until there is at least one decided node. Therefore, the intuition is to add a verification phase through which the undecided nodes make sure that there is some decided node (if any) and they stop; otherwise all the candidate nodes repeat the process by generating another random number using the shared random bits. Later we see that the bulk of the communication (among the decided and undecided nodes) is in the verification phase. The main idea to keep the messages low and yet achieve the high success probability is by allowing the decided nodes to communicate less (i.e., $o(\sqrt{n})$) messages and the undecided nodes to communicate more (i.e., $\omega(\sqrt{n})$) messages. Since most of the nodes will be decided nodes this reduces the overall communication. Let us now describe the improved algorithm step by step (see Algorithm 1 for pseudocode).

Let us use parameters in the algorithm and later in the analysis, we declare the appropriate value of the parameters by optimizing the message complexity bound.

In the first round, each node elects itself with probability $2 \log n/n$ to become a *candidate node.* Hence, the size of the candidate node set is $\Theta(\log n)$ with high probability. (Note that modulo choosing this candidate set, the algorithm is Las Vegas.) Similar to the simpler algorithm, the elected candidate nodes are responsible for the agreement. In the next round, each candidate node v samples another f random nodes from the network and gets their values– 0 or 1. Then each candidate node v computes $p(v)$ as the fraction of 1s it receives among the f samples. It will be shown that, with high probability, all the $p(v)$ values belong to the strip of length $\delta = \sqrt{24 \log n/f}$. Now we iterate the following steps until the agreement succeeds. The candidate nodes generate a common random real number, say r, in the interval [0, 1], using the global coin. All the candidate nodes v locally check if the difference $|p(v) - r|$ is more than 4δ. For the nodes whose difference is more than 4δ, they become *decided* nodes; otherwise, they become *undecided* nodes. Then, all the deciding nodes decide on 0 if their $p(v)$ is on the left side of r in the line segment [0, 1]; otherwise, they decide on 1. Then the algorithm performs a verification to make sure that there exists at least one decided node. If there exists at least one decided node, then the algorithm stops; otherwise it repeats the iteration.

In the verification phase, each undecided node tries to check if there is at least one decided node; if so, it can safely terminate. In this phase, all the decided nodes (if there are any) sample $2n^{1/2-\gamma}\sqrt{\log n}$ random nodes (where γ is a suitably chosen parameter that will be fixed in the analysis to optimize the message complexity) from the n nodes and send them the message ⟨*decided, deciding_value*⟩. Similarly, in parallel, all the undecided nodes (if there are any) sample $2n^{1/2+\gamma}\sqrt{\log n}$ random nodes and send them the message ⟨*undecided*⟩. Then it can be shown that for any pair of decided and undecided nodes, with high probability, there is at least *one common node* in their randomly sampled set. The common neighbor informs the undecided node about the existence of the decided node. Therefore, if there is any decided node, the undecided node knows the existence of the decided node(s) and their decided value. Thus the agreement is solved with all the candidate nodes (decided and

[7]For simplicity in the argument, we will assume a real number; however, we only need to sample $O(\log n)$ random bits from the shared coin to get a high-enough precision that is sufficient for the analysis. The error introduced due to this can be made $O(1/n^a)$ for any large constant $a > 0$, which does not change our analysis.

[8]Say, $S = 10011$, then the number in the interval [0, 1] would be 0.10011 (in binary) which converts to 0.59375 in decimal.

undecided) having the agreed value. Below we show all the above claims formally.

Algorithm 1 IMPLICIT-AGREEMENT-WITH-GLOBAL-COIN

Input: A complete n node anonymous network where each node receives a value in $\{0, 1\}$ given by an adversary. The nodes have access to an unbiased global coin which is oblivious to the adversary.

Output: Implicit agreement.

Each node elects itself as a candidate node with probability $\frac{2 \log n}{n}$.
Each candidate node v randomly samples $n^{\frac{2}{5}} \log^{\frac{3}{5}} n$ adjacent edges and contacts the nodes (at the other end of these sampled edges including itself) to know their $0-1$ values. Let x_v = number of 1s among the values received by v.
Each candidate node v computes the fraction $p(v) = \frac{x_v}{n^{2/5} \log^{3/5} n}$. Then $p(v)$ will be a point in the line segment $[0, 1]$.
for $i = 1, 2, \ldots$ **do**
    Each candidate node uses the global coin to generate a random number r in $[0, 1]$. Note that r is the same for all the candidate nodes.
    A candidate node v is a deciding node if $|p(v) - r| > 4\delta$, where $\delta = \sqrt{24}(\log n/n)^{1/5}$. Otherwise v is an undecided node. All the deciding nodes decide on 0 if $p(v)$ is on the left of r; otherwise, they decide on 1.
    ▷ **Verification Phase:**
    All the decided nodes sample $2n^{2/5} \log^{3/5} n$ random nodes and send them the message ⟨*decided*, *deciding_value*⟩. Similarly all the undecided nodes sample $2n^{3/5} \log^{2/5} n$ random nodes and send them the message ⟨*undecided*⟩.
    If a node w receives message from both decided and undecided node (at least one from each category), w informs all the undecided nodes (from whom it has received) the message ⟨*decided*, *deciding_value*⟩.
    if an undecided node hears about at least one decided node **then**
        Stop and exit from the 'for-loop'.
    end if
end for
All the candidate nodes (both decided and undecided) know the *deciding_value*.

Let us first show that if the number of random samples is f, then the strip length is $O(\sqrt{\log n/f})$ whp.

LEMMA 3.1. *Suppose the values $\{0, 1\}$ are distributed arbitrarily over the n-nodes. Let f be the number of random samples drawn by each candidate node. Then the $p(v)$ value of all the candidate nodes v belong to a strip of length $\delta = \sqrt{24 \log n/f}$ with high probability.*

PROOF. Each candidate node samples f nodes from the set of n nodes uniformly and independently at random. Consider an arbitrary but fixed candidate node v. Let $X_1, \ldots, X_f$ be the $0-1$ random variable corresponding to the f random samples by the node v. Notice that each X_i is independent and identically distributed $0-1$ random variable. Hence, the expected value $E(X_i)$ is same for all X_i, say $E(X_i) = \mu$. By the definition of $p(v)$, $p(v) = (\sum_{i=1}^{f} X_i)/f$. Now we use the following (ϵ, α)-approximation result for μ.

LEMMA 3.2 (THEOREM 11.1, [20]). *Let $X_1, X_2, \ldots, X_m$ be independent and identically distributed indicator random variables, with $\mu = E[X_i]$. If $m \geq (3 \ln(2/\alpha))/\epsilon^2 \mu$, then*

$$\Pr\left(\left|\frac{1}{m}\sum_{i=1}^{m} X_i - \mu\right| \geq \epsilon\mu\right) \leq \alpha$$

Therefore, we get $\Pr(|p(v) - \mu| \geq \epsilon\mu) \leq \alpha$, where the number of samples f should be larger than $(3\ln(2/\alpha))/\epsilon^2\mu$. Let us choose $f = (3\ln(2/\alpha))/\epsilon^2\mu$ and $\alpha = 2/n^2$. Then $p(v) \in (\mu - \epsilon\mu, \mu + \epsilon\mu)$ with probability at least $(1 - 2/n^2)$. That is, with high probability, $p(v)$ belongs to the strip of length $2\epsilon\mu$. Now we have,

$$f = (3\ln(n^2))/\epsilon^2\mu = (6\ln(n))/\epsilon^2\mu$$
$$\Rightarrow \epsilon = \sqrt{6\ln(n)/f\mu}$$
$$\Rightarrow 2\epsilon\mu = \sqrt{24\ln(n)\mu/f} \leq \sqrt{24\ln(n)/f}, \qquad [\text{since } \mu \leq 1]$$

Therefore, the strip length is at most $\sqrt{24\ln(n)/f}$ with high probability. Since v is an arbitrary node, the same is true for all the candidate nodes. Moreover, $\sqrt{24\ln(n)/f} < \sqrt{24\log n/f}$, as $\ln(x) < \log(x)$[9]. Hence the lemma.

□

CLAIM 3.3. *Suppose v is a decided node and u is an undecided node. If v samples $2n^{1/2-\gamma}\sqrt{\log n}$ random nodes and u samples $2n^{1/2+\gamma}\sqrt{\log n}$ random nodes for any $\gamma > 0$, then, with high probability, there is at least one common node in their sampled set.*

PROOF. Let A be the set of random nodes sampled by v and similarly the set B sampled by u. Then $|A| = 2n^{1/2-\gamma}\sqrt{\log n}$ and $|B| = 2n^{1/2+\gamma}\sqrt{\log n}$. The probability that any node will be in A is $|A|/n$, since A is chosen uniformly at random over n nodes. Therefore, the probability that a particular node of B will not be in A is $(1 - |A|/n)$. Hence the probability that no node of B will be in A, i.e., $\Pr[A \cap B = \emptyset]$ is $(1 - |A|/n)^{|B|}$. It gives,

$$\left(1 - \frac{2n^{1/2-\gamma}\sqrt{\log n}}{n}\right)^{2n^{1/2+\gamma}\sqrt{\log n}} \leq \exp(-4\log n) = \frac{1}{n^4}.$$

That is $\Pr[A \cap B \neq \emptyset] > (1 - 1/n^4)$. In other words, with high probability, there is a common member in the sampled set of v and u. □

LEMMA 3.4. *For any pair of decided and undecided nodes, with high probability there is at least one common node in their random sampled set.*

PROOF. The proof follows from the above Claim 3.3 and by taking a union bound over all the candidate nodes. Recall that there is at most $O(\log n)$ candidate nodes. □

Now let us calculate the message complexity by putting the appropriate value of the parameters.

---

[9] $\log(x)$ is the logarithmic function with base 2 and $\ln(x)$ is the natural logarithmic function, i.e., with base e.

Lemma 3.5. *The message complexity of the Algorithm 1 is $O(n^{\frac{2}{5}}\log^{\frac{8}{5}} n)$ in expectation and also holds with probability at least $(1 - 1/n^{\frac{1}{5}})$.*

Proof. In the first phase, every candidate node contacts f nodes to compute $p(v)$. So the messages cost in this part of the algorithm is $O(f \log n)$ as size of the candidate nodes is $O(\log n)$. In the second phase (i.e., the verification phase), all the decided nodes sample $2n^{1/2-\gamma}\sqrt{\log n}$ nodes. There could be at most $O(\log n)$ decided nodes (say, all the candidate nodes). The undecided nodes sample $2n^{1/2+\gamma}\sqrt{\log n}$. Similarly there could be at most $O(\log n)$ undecided nodes. The probability of the event that there exist undecided nodes is 4δ which is $4\sqrt{24\log n/f}$. Hence the message cost of the verification part in a single iteration is $O(\log n(2n^{1/2-\gamma}\sqrt{\log n} + (4\sqrt{24\log n/f})\cdot(2n^{1/2+\gamma}\sqrt{\log n})))$. We might have to repeat the process from the verification phase if there is no decided node. The probability that there is no decided node in one iteration is at most 4δ. This implies the probability that there is at least one decided node in one iteration is at least $(1 - 4\delta)$. Since the iterations are independent, the number of repetitions to get high probability of success is at most $1/(1 - 4\delta) = O(1)$, since $\delta = 1/n^{1/5}$. Thus, the verification phase is repeated at most $O(1)$ times. Hence, to achieve agreement with high probability of success, the total number of messages used by the Algorithm 1 is:

$$O\left(f\log n + 2n^{(\frac{1}{2}-\gamma}\log^{3/2} n + 8\log^2 n(\sqrt{24/f})n^{\frac{1}{2}+\gamma}\right)$$

$$= O\left(f\log n + n^{\frac{1}{2}-\gamma}\log^{3/2} n + \frac{n^{\frac{1}{2}+\gamma}}{\sqrt{f}}\log^2 n\right)$$

By optimizing the above quantity for the parameters γ and f, we get:

$$\gamma = \frac{1}{10} - \frac{1}{5}\log_n(\sqrt{\log n}) \quad \text{and} \quad f = n^{\frac{2}{5}}\log^{\frac{3}{5}} n.$$

Furthermore, the above value of γ and f gives the precise value of the following quantities.

- The strip length: $\delta = \sqrt{24\log n/f} = \sqrt{24}(\log n/n)^{1/5}$, (cf. Lemma 3.1).
- In the verification phase, number of sampled nodes by the decided nodes: $2n^{1/2-\gamma}\sqrt{\log n} = 2n^{2/5}\log^{3/5} n$.
- In the verification phase, number of sampled nodes by the undecided nodes: $2n^{1/2+\gamma}\sqrt{\log n} = 2n^{3/5}\log^{2/5} n$.

Since each undecided node sends $O(n^{3/5}\log^{2/5} n)$ messages (which is $\omega(n^{\frac{2}{5}}\log^{\frac{8}{5}} n)$) and the probability that there exist undecided nodes is $4\sqrt{24\log n/f} \leq n^{-\frac{1}{5}}$, the message complexity of the Algorithm 1 is $O(n^{\frac{2}{5}}\log^{\frac{8}{5}} n)$ with probability at least $(1 - n^{-\frac{1}{5}})$. The same message bound also holds in expectation, since the verification phase is repeated $O(1)$ times. □

Correctness of the Agreement. Finally we claim that the Algorithm 1 outputs valid and correct implicit agreement. All the decided nodes agree on the same value. The size of the candidate node set is $\Theta(\log n)$ with high probability. If all the values in the initial distribution are 0 (or 1 respectively) then $p(v)$ of all the candidate nodes will be 0 (or 1 respectively) and they all agree on the same $p(v)$ value with high probability. Moreover, if the generated random number r (using the global coin) doesn't fall in the $p(v)$-strip of length 4δ, then all the candidate nodes make a decision and the value of the decision is same. The reason is: if r is outside of the strip then the $p(v)$ for all candidate nodes v are in one side of r in the $[0, 1]$ line, i.e., either all are in the left or all are in the right side of r. The agreed value is valid as it must be from the input values.

Let us now analyze the time complexity of the algorithm.

Lemma 3.6. *The time complexity of the Algorithm 1 is $O(1)$ with high probability.*

Proof. Every node tosses a coin with probability $2\log n/n$ to become a candidate node. Hence, with high probability $O(\log n)$ candidate nodes are elected (easy to show using standard Chernoff bound.This is done locally. Each candidate node contacts $O(\log n)$ random nodes in parallel to compute the $p(v)$ value. This is one time communication and hence takes 1 round. Then algorithm repeats the Step 5, until there is at least one deciding node. This happens when the distance of all the candidate nodes from the random point r is less than 4δ. The probability of this event is at most 4δ. Therefore, the failure probability of the algorithm (i.e., there is no deciding node) is at most 4δ which is $4\sqrt{24}(\log n/n)^{1/5}$, as $\delta = \sqrt{24}(\log n/n)^{1/5}$. Hence there must be one success in $O(1)$ repetitions with high probability. Moreover, inside each repetition, the algorithm takes $O(1)$ rounds as the deciding nodes and undecided nodes sample f nodes in parallel by one time communication. All other computations are done locally. Hence the time complexity is $O(1)$ rounds with high probability. □

Therefore, by combining the above Lemma 3.5 and Lemma 3.6, we get the following main result of this section.

Theorem 3.7. *Consider a complete n-node network and CONGEST communication model. There is a randomized algorithm which, with the help of global coin, solves implicit agreement with high probability in $O(1)$ rounds and uses $O(n^{\frac{2}{5}}\log^{\frac{8}{5}} n)$ messages in expectation.*

4 SUBSET AGREEMENT

Suppose a subset S of k nodes (among the n nodes in a complete network) want to accomplish agreement. The nodes in S do not know each other. Further, assume that the size of S is unknown to the nodes. Then one can solve the subset agreement easily using the implicit agreement algorithms in Section 2 and 3. All the k nodes in S act as candidate nodes and run the rest of the implicit agreement algorithm. Since the message complexity of the implicit agreement algorithm is dominated by $O(C \cdot f)$, where C is the number of candidate nodes and f is the number of random samples drawn by the candidate nodes, the message complexity of the subset agreement algorithms are $\tilde{O}(k\sqrt{n})$ in the case of accessing private coins only, and $\tilde{O}(kn^{0.4})$ in the case of accessing global coin. Moreover, the algorithms finish in $O(1)$ communication rounds.

However notice that, when $k \geq \Omega(\sqrt{n})$ (for the private coins) or when $k \geq \Omega(n^{0.6})$ (for global coin), the above message bounds are more than $\Omega(n)$ which is worse than a simple $O(n)$ message complexity algorithm that solves full (explicit) agreement (i.e., $k = n$) over all the n-nodes. Full agreement can be solved using $O(n)$ messages in $O(1)$ rounds by simply solving implicit agreement (or leader election) and the deciding nodes (or the leader) broadcasting the agreed value to all nodes. This is better if $k \geq \sqrt{n}$.

We combine both the above approaches as follows, assuming we know k (which we discuss later). First compute a leader in S using $O((k \log^{3/2} n)/\sqrt{n})$ messages and $O(1)$ rounds, see [17] (or, see below the leader election algorithm and the analysis). Then the leader notifies its decided_value to all the n nodes in the next round, which takes $O(n)$ messages. Therefore, if the size of the set S, i.e., k is known to the nodes of S then the subset agreement problem can be solved with message complexity $O(\min\{kM, n\})$, where M is the message complexity of the implicit agreement algorithm. In fact, it is sufficient if the nodes in S know whether k is less than or greater than $\sqrt{n}$ (less or greater than $n^{0.6}$ for the global coin case).

Let us now discuss an approach to check if the value of k is smaller or larger than $\sqrt{n}$ using $O(k \log^{3/2} n)$ messages. The similar technique can be used to check whether $k \leq$ or $> n^{0.6}$. Each node in S *elects* itself with probability $(\log n)/\sqrt{n}$. Then using linearity of expectation and a Chernoff bound, it can be shown that $\Theta((k \log n)/\sqrt{n})$ nodes are elected with high probability. Each elected node again samples another $O(\sqrt{n \log n})$ random referee nodes and sends them its ID. Then it can be shown in the similar way to the proof of Claim 3.3 that any two elected nodes have one common referee with high probability. This implies that any elected node has at least one common referee among all the other elected nodes. In the next round, each referee node sends back the *count* of the IDs to the elected nodes from where it received the IDs. Then it is easy to see that: if the elected nodes get back $\Omega(\log n)$ count, then $k \geq \Omega(\sqrt{n})$; else if the count is $o(\log n)$, then $k \leq o(\sqrt{n})$. Thus the elected nodes can distinguish whether the size of S is $o(\sqrt{n})$ or $\Omega(\sqrt{n})$. With this knowledg (i.e., whether k is $\Omega(n^{0.5})$ or not) the nodes in S can run either the $O(kM)$ message complexity algorithm (if $k \leq o(\sqrt{n})$), or the linear message complexity algorithm (if $k \geq \Omega(\sqrt{n})$). The message complexity of this size estimation approach is $\Theta((k \log n)/\sqrt{n}) \cdot O(\sqrt{n \log n})$, which is $O(k \log^{3/2} n)$.

There is still a small issue with the above idea: only the elected nodes of S may know about the value of k and not all the nodes in S are elected. So how do the non-elected nodes also know the condition that $k \leq o(\sqrt{n})$, so that all the nodes in S can run the implicit agreement algorithm (as a candidate node)? Note that when $k \geq \Omega(\sqrt{n})$, the non-elected nodes do not need to know the condition as the algorithm sends the decided_value to all the n nodes (explicit agreement) in the next round. When $k \leq o(\sqrt{n})$, all the nodes in S wait for some constant number rounds i.e., until the run time of algorithm when $k \geq \Omega(\sqrt{n})$. If the non-elected nodes receive any message (decided_value) by that time, then it's understood that $k \geq \Omega(\sqrt{n})$ (that's when all the n nodes received the agreement value). Otherwise, if the non-elected nodes do not hear anything by that time, it indicates that $k \leq o(\sqrt{n})$ and all the nodes in S will start executing the implicit agreement algorithm in the next round onwards.

Then we get the two corollaries of the two theorems– (Theorem 2.5) for agreement without global coin i.e., with private coins only and (Theorem 3.7) for agreement with global coin.

Theorem 4.1 (Subset Agreement with Private Coin Only). *Consider a complete n-node network $G(V, E)$ and a subset $S \subseteq V$ of size k. There is a randomized algorithm which solves the subset agreement over S with high probability in $O(1)$ rounds and uses $\min\{\tilde{O}(k\sqrt{n}), O(n)\}$ messages in expectation.*

Theorem 4.2 (Subset Agreement with Global Coin). *Consider a complete n-node network $G(V, E)$ and a subset $S \subseteq V$ of size k. There is a randomized algorithm which, with the help of global coin, solves the subset agreement over S with high probability and finishes in $O(1)$ rounds and uses $\min\{\tilde{O}(kn^{0.4}), O(n)\}$ messages in expectation.*

5 LEADER ELECTION USING A GLOBAL COIN

Let us first define the (implicit) leader election problem in a general network, while in this section, we consider the problem is a complete network. Given a n-node network, the (implicit) leader election is defined as follows.

Definition 5.1 (Implicit Leader Election, [17]). *Let every node in the network maintains its status, that can take value in $\{\bot$, Non-elected, Elected$\}$. Initially each node starts with status $= \bot$. An implicit leader election satisfies when the final status of exactly one node is Elected and all other nodes have status Non-elected. In other words, the elected leader (exactly one) knows that it's the leader and all other nodes know they are not leader.*

We show an $\Omega(\sqrt{n})$ lower bound on the message complexity of the leader election problem using shared random bits. There is a $\tilde{O}(\sqrt{n})$ message complexity algorithm which computes a leader in a complete network without shared random bits [17]. The lower bound result demonstrates that having global coin doesn't help to achieve a better message complexity algorithm for the leader election problem compared to what can be acheived using private coins. This results shows that agreement is a strictly easier problem than leader election under access to global coins. More preciselyly, we show that any algorithm $\mathcal{A}$ which computes a leader with probability ϵ, for a fixed constant $0 < \epsilon < 1$, must incur $\Omega(\sqrt{n})$ messages in a complete network. The message size could be arbitrarily large. That is, the result holds in both *LOCAL* and *CONGEST* models. Kutten et al. [17] showed a $\Omega(\sqrt{n})$ lower bound on the leader election problem without the global coin. We adapt the proof framework from there and show the same lower bound holds on the number of messages when using shared random bits. The model assumes that all the processors have an access to an unbiased global coin through which they can generate common random bits. Further, all processors run the same algorithm. We show the lower bound result by first assuming the nodes are anonymous. Then it can be easily extended (using standard method) to the non-anonymous case where each node has unique identifiers. The main result is presented in Theorem 5.2. We defer the detailed proof to the full version.

Theorem 5.2. *Consider any algorithm $\mathcal{A}$ that has an access to an unbiased random coin and sends at most $f(n)$ messages (of arbitrary size) with high probability in a complete network of n nodes. If $\mathcal{A}$ solves leader election with probability at least ϵ, for some large enough constant $0 < \epsilon < 1$, then $f(n) \in \Omega(\sqrt{n})$. This holds even if nodes are equipped with unique identifiers (chosen by an adversary).*

Remark 5.3. *We like to mention that the above theorem is tight with respect to the number of messages and success probability of* *electing a leader. Notice that a naive randomized algorithm (where each node chooses to become leader with probability $1/n$ and then terminates) computes a leader with zero message cost, but the success probability is $\binom{n}{1}(1/n)(1-1/n)^{n-1} \approx 1/e$. Moreover, there is an algorithm which succeeds with large constant probability but incurs $\Omega(\sqrt{n})$ messages [17]. This implies that there is a sudden jump in the message complexity when breaking the $1/e$ barrier in success probability.*

6 CONCLUSION

We studied the role played by randomization in the message complexity of randomized agreement. Some open questions raised by our work: (1) Is our upper bound of $\tilde{O}(n^{0.4})$ tight (up to polylog factors) for agreement with a global coin? Can we show a lower bound on agreement with global coins? (2) Can we show an agreement algorithm that works with a *common coin* which is weaker than a (unbiased) global coin assumed here? (3) Can we improve our upper bounds for subset agreement and show lower bounds? (4) Can we extend our results for general graphs? (5) Finally, what are the message bounds for agreement and leader election in the presence of Byzantine nodes?

REFERENCES

[1] Y. Afek and E. Gafni. 1991. Time and Message Bounds for Election in Synchronous and Asynchronous Complete Networks. *SIAM J. Comput.* 20, 2 (1991), 376–394. https://doi.org/10.1137/0220023 arXiv:http://epubs.siam.org/doi/pdf/10.1137/0220023

[2] A. Agbaria and R. Friedman. 2003. Overcoming Byzantine Failures Using Checkpointing. *University of Illinois at Urbana-Champaign Coordinated Science Laboratory technical report no. UILU-ENG- 03-2228 (CRHC-03-14)* (2003).

[3] Yair Amir, Claudiu Danilov, Jonathan Kirsch, John Lane, Danny Dolev, Cristina Nita-Rotaru, Josh Olsen, and David John Zage. 2006. Scaling Byzantine Fault-Tolerant Replication toWide Area Networks. In *Proc. of International Conference on Dependable Systems and Networks (DSN).* 105–114.

[4] D. P. Anderson and J. Kubiatowicz. 2002. The worldwide computer. *Scientific American* 286, 3 (2002), 28–35.

[5] Hagit Attiya and Jennifer Welch. 2004. *Distributed Computing: Fundamentals, Simulations and Advanced Topics (2nd edition).* John Wiley Interscience.

[6] Michael Ben-Or. 1983. Another Advantage of Free Choice: Completely Asynchronous Agreement Protocols. In *Proc. of the Second Annual ACM SIGACT-SIGOPS Symposium on Principles of Distributed Computing (PODC).* 27–30.

[7] Michael Ben-Or and Nathan Linial. 1989. Collective Coin Flipping. *Advances in Computing Research* 5 (1989), 91–115.

[8] Michael Ben-Or, Elan Pavlov, and Vinod Vaikuntanathan. 2006. Byzantine agreement in the full-information model in O(log n) rounds. In *Proc. of the 38th Annual ACM Symposium on Theory of Computing (STOC).* 179–186.

[9] Miguel Castro and Barbara Liskov. 2002. Practical byzantine fault tolerance and proactive recovery. *ACM Trans. Comput. Syst.* 20, 4 (2002), 398–461.

[10] Pesech Feldman and Silvio Micali. 1997. An Optimal Probabilistic Protocol for Synchronous Byzantine Agreement. *SIAM J. Comput.* 26, 4 (1997), 873–933.

[11] P Humblet. 1984. Electing a leader in a clique in $O(n \log n)$ messages. (1984). Intern. Memo., Laboratory for Information and Decision Systems, M.I.T., Cambridge, Mass.

[12] Valerie King and Jared Saia. 2011. Breaking the $O(n^2)$ bit barrier: Scalable byzantine agreement with an adaptive adversary. *J. ACM* 58, Article 18 (July 2011), 24 pages. Issue 4.

[13] E. Korach, S. Kutten, and S. Moran. 1990. A modular technique for the design of efficient distributed leader finding algorithms. *ACM Trans. Program. Lang. Syst.* 12, 1 (Jan. 1990), 84–101. https://doi.org/10.1145/77606.77610

[14] E. Korach, S. Moran, and S. Zaks. 1987. The Optimality of Distributive Constructions of Minimum Weight and Degree Restricted Spanning Trees in a Complete Network of Processors. *SIAM J. Comput.* 16, 2 (1987), 231–236. https://doi.org/10.1137/0216019 arXiv:http://epubs.siam.org/doi/pdf/10.1137/0216019

[15] E. Korach, S. Moran, and S. Zaks. 1989. Optimal lower bounds for some distributed algorithms for a complete network of processors. *Theor. Comput. Sci.* 64, 1 (1989), 125 – 132. https://doi.org/10.1016/0304-3975(89)90103-5

[16] Shay Kutten, Gopal Pandurangan, David Peleg, Peter Robinson, and Amitabh Trehan. 2015. On the Complexity of Universal Leader Election. *J. ACM* 62, 1 (2015), 7:1–7:27.

[17] Shay Kutten, Gopal Pandurangan, David Peleg, Peter Robinson, and Amitabh Trehan. 2015. Sublinear bounds for randomized leader election. *Theor. Comput. Sci.* 561 (2015), 134–143.

[18] Nancy Lynch. 1996. *Distributed Algorithms.* Morgan Kaufman Publishers, Inc., San Francisco, USA.

[19] Dahlia Malkhi and Michael K. Reiter. 1997. Unreliable Intrusion Detection in Distributed Computations. In *Proc.of the 10th Computer Security Foundations Workshop (CSFW).* 116–125.

[20] Michael Mitzenmacher and Eli Upfal. 2017. *Probability and Computing: Randomization and Probabilistic Techniques in Algorithms and Data Analysis* (second ed.). Cambridge University Press.

[21] Rajeev Motwani and Prabhakar Raghavan. 1995. *Randomized Algorithms.* Cambridge University Press.

[22] Gopal Pandurangan. 2018. *Distributed Network Algorithms.* http://sites.google.com/site/gopalpandurangan/dnabook.pdf

[23] Marshall C. Pease, Robert E. Shostak, and Leslie Lamport. 1980. Reaching Agreement in the Presence of Faults. *J. ACM* 27, 2 (1980), 228–234.

[24] David Peleg. 2000. *Distributed Computing: A Locality-Sensitive Approach.* SIAM, Philadelphia.

[25] Michael O. Rabin. 1983. Randomized Byzantine Generals. In *Proc. of the 24th Annual Symposium on Foundations of Computer Science (FOCS).* 403–409.

[26] Sean C. Rhea, Patrick R. Eaton, Dennis Geels, Hakim Weatherspoon, Ben Y. Zhao, and John Kubiatowicz. 2003. Pond: The OceanStore Prototype. In *Proc. of the FAST '03 Conference on File and Storage Technologies.* 1–14.

[27] Elaine Shi and Adrian Perrig. 2004. Designing secure sensor networks. *IEEE Wireless Commun.* 11, 6 (2004), 38–43.

[28] Alex Wright. 2009. Contemporary approaches to fault tolerance. *Commun. ACM* 52, 7 (2009), 13–15.

[29] Hiroyuki Yoshino, Naohiro Hayashibara, Tomoya Enokido, and Makoto Takizawa. 2005. Byzantine Agreement Protocol using Hierarchical Groups. In *Proc.of the 11th International Conference on Parallel and Distributed Systems (ICPADS).* 64–70.

Tight Bounds for Asymptotic and Approximate Consensus

Matthias Függer
CNRS, LSV, ENS Paris-Saclay, Inria
mfuegger@lsv.fr

Thomas Nowak
Université Paris-Sud
thomas.nowak@lri.fr

Manfred Schwarz
ECS, TU Wien
mschwarz@ecs.tuwien.ac.at

ABSTRACT

We study the performance of asymptotic and approximate consensus algorithms under harsh environmental conditions. The asymptotic consensus problem requires a set of agents to repeatedly set their outputs such that the outputs converge to a common value within the convex hull of initial values. This problem, and the related approximate consensus problem, are fundamental building blocks in distributed systems where exact consensus among agents is not required or possible, e.g., man-made distributed control systems, and have applications in the analysis of natural distributed systems, such as flocking and opinion dynamics. We prove tight lower bounds on the contraction rates of asymptotic consensus algorithms in dynamic networks, from which we deduce bounds on the time complexity of approximate consensus algorithms. In particular, the obtained bounds show optimality of asymptotic and approximate consensus algorithms presented in [Charron-Bost et al., ICALP'16] for certain dynamic networks, including the weakest dynamic network model in which asymptotic and approximate consensus are solvable. As a corollary we also obtain asymptotically tight bounds for asymptotic consensus in the classical asynchronous model with crashes.

Central to our lower bound proofs is an extended notion of valency, the set of reachable limits of an asymptotic consensus algorithm starting from a given configuration. We further relate topological properties of valencies to the solvability of exact consensus, shedding some light on the relation of these three fundamental problems in dynamic networks.

CCS CONCEPTS

• **Theory of computation → Distributed algorithms;**

KEYWORDS

asymptotic consensus; approximate consensus; lower bounds; dynamic networks

ACM Reference Format:
Matthias Függer, Thomas Nowak, and Manfred Schwarz. 2018. Tight Bounds for Asymptotic and Approximate Consensus. In *PODC '18: ACM Symposium on Principles of Distributed Computing, July 23–27, 2018, Egham, United Kingdom.* ACM, New York, NY, USA, 10 pages. https://doi.org/10.1145/3212734.3212762

ACM ISBN 978-1-4503-5795-1/18/07.
https://doi.org/10.1145/3212734.3212762

1 INTRODUCTION

In the *asymptotic consensus* problem a set of agents, each starting from an initial value in $\mathbb{R}^d$, update their values such that all agents' values converge to a common value within the convex hull of initial values. The problem is closely related to the *approximate consensus* problem, in which agents have to irrevocably decide on values that lie within a predefined distance $\varepsilon > 0$ of each other. The latter is weaker than the *exact consensus* problem in which agents need to decide on the same value. Both the asymptotic and the approximate consensus problems have not only a variety of applications in the design of man-made control systems like sensor fusion [4], clock synchronization [21], formation control [15], rendezvous in space [22], or load balancing [13], but also for analyzing natural systems like flocking [31], firefly synchronization [26], or opinion dynamics [20]. These problems often have to be solved under harsh environmental restrictions in which exact consensus is not achievable, or too costly to achieve: with limited computational power and local storage, under restricted communication abilities, and in presence of communication uncertainty.

In this work we study the performance of asymptotic and approximate consensus algorithms under such harsh conditions. Specifically, we study algorithms in a *network model* $\mathcal{N}$ with round-based computation and a dynamic communication topology whose *directed* communication graphs are chosen each round from a predefined set $\mathcal{N}$ of communication graphs. While this model naturally captures highly unstable communication topologies, we later on show that it also allows to assess performance within classical, more stable, distributed fault models.

Solvability and Algorithms. In previous work [8], Charron-Bost et al. showed that asymptotic consensus is solvable precisely within *rooted network models* in which all communication graphs contain rooted spanning trees. These rooted spanning trees need not have any edges in common and can change from one round to the next.

An interesting special case of rooted network models are network models whose graphs are *non-split,* that is, any two agents have a common incoming neighbor. Their prominent role is motivated by two properties: (i) They occur as communication graphs in benign classical distributed failure models. For example, in synchronous systems with crashes, in asynchronous systems with a minority of crashes, and synchronous systems with send omissions. (ii) In [8], Charron-Bost et al. showed that non-split graphs also play a central role in arbitrary rooted network models: they showed that any product of $n-1$ rooted graphs with n nodes is non-split, allowing to transform asymptotic consensus algorithms for non-split network models into their *amortized* variants for rooted models.

Interestingly, solvability in any rooted network model is already provided by deceptively simple algorithms [8]: so-called *averaging* or *convex combination* algorithms, in which agents repeatedly broadcast their current value, and update it to some weighted average of the values they received in this round. One instance, presented by Charron-Bost et al. [9] is the *midpoint algorithm*, in which agents update their value to the midpoint of the set of received values, i.e., the average of the smallest and the largest of the received values.

Regarding time complexity, for dimension $d = 1$, the amortized midpoint algorithm was shown to have a contraction rate (of the range of reachable values; see Section 3 for a formal definition) of $\sqrt[n-1]{1/2}$ in arbitrary rooted network models with n agents, and the midpoint algorithm of $\frac{1}{2}$ in non-split network models [9]. The latter is *optimal* for "memoryless" averaging algorithms, which only depend on the values received in the current round [9].

A natural question is whether *non-averaging or non-memoryless algorithms*, i.e., algorithms that (i) do not necessarily set their output values to within the convex hull of previously received values or (ii) whose output is a function not only of the previously received values, allow faster contraction rates. In the context of classical failure models, deriving lower bounds independent of such assumptions, is a long-standing open problem raised by Dolev et al. in [14]. As an example for (i), consider the algorithm where each agent sends an equal fraction of its current output value to all out-neighbors and sets its output to the sum of values received in the current round. Note that the algorithm is not a convex combination algorithm as its output may lie outside the convex hull of the values of its in-neighbors. However, it solves asymptotic consensus algorithm for a fixed directed communication graph. Other examples of algorithms that violate (i) and (ii) are from control theory, where the usage of overshooting fast second-order controllers is common; see, e.g., [3].

Contribution. We prove asymptotically tight lower bounds on the contraction rate of any asymptotic consensus algorithm regardless of the structure of the algorithm: algorithms can be full-information and agents can set their outputs outside the convex hull of received values. This, e.g., includes using higher-order filters in contrast to the 0-order filters of averaging algorithms. In particular, the following lower bounds hold for a network model $\mathcal{N}$ with n agents: If exact consensus is solvable in $\mathcal{N}$, an optimal contraction rate of 0 can be achieved. Otherwise:

In a system with $n = 2$ agents, the contraction rate is lower bounded by 1/3 (Theorem 4.1). This is tight [9].

For an arbitrary communication graph G, we define the set $\mathrm{deaf}(G) = \{F_1, \ldots, F_n\}$, where F_i is derived from G by making agent i *deaf* in F_i, i.e., removing the incoming edges of i in G. In a system with $n \geq 3$ agents, if $\mathcal{N}$ contains $\mathrm{deaf}(G)$, then the contraction rate is lower bounded by 1/2 (Theorem 5.1). This is tight in non-split network models because of the midpoint algorithm [9].

We then show that if $\mathcal{N}$ contains certain rooted graphs Ψ, the contraction rate is lower bounded by $\sqrt[n-2]{1/2}$ (Theorem 6.1). This is asymptotically tight in rooted network models because of the amortized midpoint algorithm [9]. Specifically, this proves optimality of the amortized midpoint algorithm for the *weakest*, i.e., largest, network model in which asymptotic and approximate consensus is solvable: the set of all directed rooted communication graphs.

For arbitrary network models we show that in a system with $n \geq 3$ agents, any asymptotic consensus algorithm must have a contraction rate of at least $1/(D + 1)$, where D, the so-called α-diameter of $\mathcal{N}$, i.e., the smallest value which allows a connection of any pair of communication graphs in $\mathcal{N}$ via an indistinguishability chain of length at most D (Theorem 7.4).

We demonstrate how to apply the above mentioned bound to obtain new lower bounds on contraction rates for classical failure models as an immediate corollary. Specifically, we consider asynchronous message passing system of size n with up to $f < n/2$ crashes. For such systems, *algorithms operating in asynchronous rounds* are widely used [10, 14, 24]: each agent waits for $n - f$ messages corresponding to the current round, updates its state based on the received messages and its previous state, and broadcasts the next round's messages.

We show that no algorithm operating in asynchronous rounds can achieve a contraction rate better than $\frac{1}{\lceil n/f \rceil + 1}$ (Theorem 8.2). This shows that the asynchronous algorithms for systems of size $n > 5f$ with up to f Byzantine failures by Dolev et al. [14] and for systems of size $n > 2f$ with up to f crashes by Fekete [18] have asymptotically optimal contraction rates for round-based algorithms.

We then present an algorithm for $n > f$ that does *not operate in asynchronous rounds* and achieves a contraction rate of 0, demonstrating a large gap between round-based and non round-based algorithms for asymptotic consensus.

Table 1 summarizes lower and upper bounds. Central to the proofs is the concept of the *valency of a configuration* of an asymptotic consensus algorithm, defined as the set of limits reachable from this configuration. By studying the changes in valency along executions, we infer bounds on the contraction rate.

We extend the above results on contraction rates to derive new lower bounds on the decision time of any approximate consensus algorithm: Let $\Delta > 0$ be the largest distance between initial values. For $n = 2$ we obtain $\lceil \log_3 \frac{\Delta}{\varepsilon} \rceil$ (Theorem 9.1). For $n \geq 3$ and models that include $\mathrm{deaf}(G)$ for a communication graph G, we show $\lceil \log_2 \frac{\Delta}{\varepsilon} \rceil$ (Theorem 9.2), and for $n \geq 4$ and models that include certain Ψ graphs, we obtain $(n-2)\lceil \log_2 \frac{\Delta}{\varepsilon} \rceil$ (Theorem 9.3). For arbitrary network models in which exact consensus is not solvable, we show $\log_{D+1} \frac{\Delta}{\varepsilon n}$ (Theorem 9.4). Again, deciding versions of the asymptotic consensus algorithms from [9] have matching time complexities; showing optimality of these algorithms also for solving approximate consensus.

Related work. The problem of asymptotic consensus in dynamic networks has been extensively studied in distributed computing and control theory, see, e.g., [2, 5, 6, 11, 16, 27]. The question of guaranteed convergence rates and decision times of the corresponding approximate consensus problems, naturally arise in this context. Algorithms with convergence times exponential in the number of agents have been proposed, e.g., in [6].

Olshevsky and Tsitsiklis [30], proposed an algorithm with polynomial convergence time in bidirectional networks with certain stability assumptions on the occurring communication graphs. The bounds on convergence times were later on refined in [28]. Chazelle [11] proposed an averaging algorithm with polynomial convergence time, which works in any bidirectional connected network model.

To speed up convergence times, algorithms where agents set their output based on values that have been received in rounds

agents	network model			asynchronous + f crashes	
	general non-split	non-split with α-diameter D	general rooted	round-based alg. $0 < f < \frac{n}{2}$	arbitrary alg. $0 < f < n$
$n = 2$	$\frac{1}{3}^*$	0 or $\frac{1}{3}^*$	$\frac{1}{3}^*$	N/A	
$n \geq 3$	$\frac{1}{2}^*$	0 or $\left[\frac{1}{D+1}^*, \frac{1}{2}\right]$	$\left[\sqrt[n-2]{\frac{1}{2}}^*, \sqrt[n-1]{\frac{1}{2}}\right]$	$\left[\frac{1}{\lceil n/f \rceil + 1}^*, \frac{1}{\lceil n/f \rceil - 1}\right]$	0^*

Table 1: Summary of lower and upper bounds on contraction rates. New bounds proved in this work are marked with an *. The three left columns are worst-case contraction rates for the case the network model is (i) a general non-split, (ii) a non-split network model with α-diameter D, and (iii) a general rooted network model. For (ii) contraction rates are 0 iff exact consensus is solvable. The right two columns summarize the bounds for the classical model of an asynchronous system with crashes.

prior to the previous round have also been considered in literature: Olshevsky [29] proposed a linear convergence time algorithm that uses messages from two rounds, however, being restricted to fixed bidirectional communication graphs. In [32], a linear convergence time algorithm for a possibly non-bidirectional fixed topology was proposed. It requires storing all received values. In previous work [9], Charron-Bost et al. presented the midpoint algorithm, which has constant convergence time in non-split network models and the amortized midpoint algorithm with linear convergence time in rooted network models.

To the best of our knowledge, the only lower bound on convergence rate in dynamic networks has been shown in [7]: the authors proved that the convergence rate of a specific averaging algorithm in a non-split network model with n agents is at least $1 - \frac{1}{n}$.

In the context of classical distributed computing failure scenarios, Dolev et al. [14] studied the related approximate consensus problem: they considered fully-connected synchronous distributed systems with up to f Byzantine agents, and its asynchronous variant. The two presented algorithms require $n \geq 3f + 1$ for the synchronous and $n \geq 5f + 1$ for the asynchronous distributed system, the first of which is optimal in terms of resilience [19]. The latter result was improved to $n \geq 3f+1$ in [1]. Both papers also address the question of optimal contraction rate in such systems. Since, however, in synchronous systems with $n \geq 3f + 1$ exact consensus is solvable, leading to a contraction rate of 0, the authors consider bounds for round-by-round contraction rates. In [14] they showed that the achieved round-by-round contraction rate of $\frac{1}{2}$ is actually tight for a certain class of algorithms that repeatedly set their output to the image of a so-called cautious function applied to the multiset of received values. A lower bound for arbitrary algorithms, however, remained an open problem. In higher dimensions, i.e, for any $d \geq 1$, Mendes et al. [25] proposed algorithms with convergence time of $d \cdot \lceil \log_2 \frac{\sqrt{d}\Delta}{\varepsilon} \rceil$ under the optimal resiliency condition $n \geq f \cdot (d + 2) + 1$.

Fekete [17] also studied round-by-round contraction rates for several failure scenarios, again, all in which exact consensus is solvable. He proved asymptotically tight lower bounds for synchronous distributed systems in presence of crashes, omission, and Byzantine agents. The bounds hold for approximate consensus algorithms that potentially take into account information from all previous rounds. In [18], Fekete presented an algorithm for asynchronous message-passing systems with minority of crashes, also proving a tight lower bound on the contraction rate of any algorithm operating in asynchronous rounds for such systems.

2 DYNAMIC SYSTEM MODEL

We consider a set $[n] = \{1, \ldots, n\}$ of n agents (also classically called processes). We assume a distributed, round-based computational model in the spirit of the Heard-Of model [10]. Computation proceeds in *rounds*: In every round, each agent sends its state to its outgoing neighbors, receives messages from its incoming neighbors, and finally updates its state according to a deterministic local algorithm, i.e., a transition function that maps the collection of incoming messages to a new state. Rounds are communication closed in the sense that no agent receives messages in round t that are sent in a round different from t.

Communications that occur in a round are modeled by a *directed graph* with a node for each agent. Since an agent can obviously communicate with itself instantaneously, every communication graph contains a self-loop at each node. In the following, we use the *product* of two communication graphs G and H, denoted $G \circ H$, which is the directed graph with an edge from i to j if there exists k such that (i, k) and (k, j) are two edges in G and H, respectively.

We fix a nonempty set of communication graphs $\mathcal{N}$ which determines the *network model*. To fully model dynamic networks in which topology may change continually and unpredictably, the communication graph at each round is chosen arbitrarily among $\mathcal{N}$. Thus we form the infinite sequences of graphs in $\mathcal{N}$ which we call *communication patterns in* $\mathcal{N}$. In each communication pattern, the communication graph at round t is denoted by G_t, and $\mathrm{In}_i(t) = \mathrm{In}_i(G_t)$ and $\mathrm{Out}_i(t) = \mathrm{Out}_i(G_t)$ are the sets of incoming and outgoing neighbors (in-neighbors and out-neighbors for short) of agent i in G_t.

Let us fix an algorithm $\mathcal{A}$; a *configuration* is a collection of n agent states, one per agent. We assume that all agents pick their initial state from the same set of states. Obviously the picks can be different for different agents. Since agents are deterministic, given some configuration C and some communication graph G, the algorithm $\mathcal{A}$ uniquely determines a new configuration, which we simply denote $G.C$ if no confusion can arise. Then the *execution* E *of* $\mathcal{A}$ from the initial configuration C_0 and with the communication pattern $\left(G_t\right)_{t \geq 1}$ is the sequence $C_0, G_1, \ldots, C_{t-1}, G_t, C_t, \ldots$ of alternating configurations and communication graphs such that for each round t, $C_t = G_t.C_{t-1}$. The set of executions with communication patterns in $\mathcal{N}$, denoted $\mathcal{E}_{\mathcal{A}}^{\mathcal{N}}$, with the distance $\mathrm{dist}(E, E') = 1/2^{\theta}$, where θ is the first index at which E and E' differ, is a compact metric space (e.g., see [23]).

Finally, any configuration that occurs in some execution with a communication pattern in $\mathcal{N}$ is said to be *reachable from C_0 by $\mathcal{A}$ in $\mathcal{N}$*. In the sequel, the algorithm and the network model are omitted if no confusion can arise.

2.1 Asymptotic Consensus

We assume that the local state of agent i includes a variable y^i in Euclidean d-space, and we let $y_E^i(t) \in \mathbb{R}^d$ denote the value of y^i at the end of round t in execution E. Then we let $y_E(t) = \left(y_E^1(t), \ldots, y_E^n(t)\right)$. We write

$$\operatorname{diam}(A) = \sup_{x,y \in A} \|x - y\|$$

for the diameter of $A \subseteq \mathbb{R}^d$ and $\Delta(y(t)) = \operatorname{diam}\{y^1(t), \ldots, y^n(t)\}$ for the diameter of the set of values in round t.

We say an algorithm *solves the asymptotic consensus problem* in a network model $\mathcal{N}$ if the following holds for every execution E with a communication pattern in $\mathcal{N}$:

- *Convergence.* Each sequence $\left(y_E^i(t)\right)_{t \geq 0}$ converges.
- *Agreement.* If $y_E^i(t)$ and $y_E^j(t)$ converge, then they have a common limit.
- *Validity.* If $y_E^i(t)$ converges, then its limit is in the convex hull of the initial values $y_E^1(0), \ldots, y_E^n(0)$.

Observe that the *consensus function* defined by $y^* : E \in (\mathcal{E}, \operatorname{dist}) \mapsto y_E^* \in (\mathbb{R}^d, \|.\|)$, where y_E^* denotes the common limit of the n sequences $\left(y_E^i(t)\right)_{t \geq 0}$, is a priori not continuous. And indeed, there exist asymptotic consensus algorithms whose consensus functions are not continuous.

3 VALENCY AND CONTRACTION RATE

We now extend the notion of valency for a consensus algorithm to asymptotic consensus algorithms. We fix an asymptotic consensus algorithm $\mathcal{A}$ that solves d-dimensional asymptotic consensus in a certain network model $\mathcal{N}$ with $n \geq 2$ agents. Let C be a configuration reachable by $\mathcal{A}$ in $\mathcal{N}$. Then we define the *valency* of C by $Y^*_{\mathcal{N},\mathcal{A}}(C) = \{y_E^* \in \mathbb{R}^d \mid C \text{ occurs in } E \in \mathcal{E}_{\mathcal{A}}^{\mathcal{N}}\}$.

If the algorithm $\mathcal{A}$ is clear from the context, we skip it from the subscript. Observe that if $\mathcal{A}$ is a convex combination algorithm, then the valency of a configuration C is a compact set of $\mathbb{R}^d$ since the consensus function is continuous and the set of executions in which C occurs is a compact set. Set $\delta_{\mathcal{N}}(C) = \operatorname{diam}(Y^*_{\mathcal{N}}(C))$ the diameter of the set of reachable limits starting from configuration C.

We have $\delta_{\mathcal{N}}(C_t) \to 0$ in any execution $E = G_0, C_1, G_1, C_2, \ldots$ by Convergence and Agreement. To study the speed of convergence, we introduce the *contraction rate* of algorithm $\mathcal{A}$ in network model $\mathcal{N}$ as

$$\sup_{E \in \mathcal{E}_{\mathcal{A}}^{\mathcal{N}}} \limsup_{t \to \infty} \sqrt[t]{\delta_{\mathcal{N}}(C_t)}$$

where $E = C_0, G_1, C_1, G_2, \ldots$ In particular, any algorithm that guarantees $\delta_{\mathcal{N}}(C_t) \leq \gamma^t \delta_{\mathcal{N}}(C_0)$ for all $t \geq 0$ has a contraction rate of at most γ.

We obtain the following for subsets of network models:

Lemma 3.1. *Let $\mathcal{N}, \mathcal{N}'$ be two network models with $\mathcal{N}' \subseteq \mathcal{N}$. If $\mathcal{A}$ is an algorithm that solves asymptotic consensus in $\mathcal{N}$, then (i) it also solves asymptotic consensus in $\mathcal{N}'$, (ii) for every configuration C reachable by $\mathcal{A}$ in $\mathcal{N}'$, we have $Y^*_{\mathcal{N}'}(C) \subseteq Y^*_{\mathcal{N}}(C)$, (iii) $\delta_{\mathcal{N}'}(C) \leq \delta_{\mathcal{N}}(C)$, and (iv) the contraction rate in $\mathcal{N}'$ is less or equal to the contraction rate in $\mathcal{N}$.*

Proof. Statements (i), (ii), and (iii) immediately follow from the definition of valency. It remains to show statement (iv). From $\mathcal{E}_{\mathcal{A}}^{\mathcal{N}'} \subseteq \mathcal{E}_{\mathcal{A}}^{\mathcal{N}}$ and (iii), we deduce

$$\sup_{E \in \mathcal{E}_{\mathcal{A}}^{\mathcal{N}'}} \limsup_{t \to \infty} \sqrt[t]{\delta_{\mathcal{N}'}(C_t)} \leq \sup_{E \in \mathcal{E}_{\mathcal{A}}^{\mathcal{N}}} \limsup_{t \to \infty} \sqrt[t]{\delta_{\mathcal{N}}(C_t)} \ ,$$

which concludes the proof. □

We establish two branching properties of valency of configurations in execution trees.

Lemma 3.2. *Let C be a configuration reachable by algorithm $\mathcal{A}$ in network model $\mathcal{N}$. Then*

$$Y^*_{\mathcal{N}}(C) = \bigcup_{G \in \mathcal{N}} Y^*_{\mathcal{N}}(G.C) \ .$$

Proof. First let $y^* \in Y^*_{\mathcal{N}}(C)$. By definition of $Y^*_{\mathcal{N}}(C)$, there exists an execution $E = C_0, G_1, C_1, G_2, \ldots$ in $\mathcal{E}_{\mathcal{A}}^{\mathcal{N}}$ and a $t \geq 0$ such that $y^* = y_E^*$ and $C = C_t$. Set $G = G_{t+1}$. Hence we have $C_{t+1} = G.C$. But this shows that $y^* \in Y^*_{\mathcal{N}}(G.C)$ since $G.C$ occurs in execution E whose limit is y^*. This shows inclusion of the left-hand side in the right-hand side.

Now let $G \in \mathcal{N}$ and $y^* \in Y^*_{\mathcal{N}}(G.C)$. Then there is an execution $E = C_0, G_1, C_1, G_2, \ldots$ in $\mathcal{E}_{\mathcal{A}}^{\mathcal{N}}$ and a $t \geq 0$ such that $y^* = y_E^*$ and $G.C = C_t$. Since C is a reachable configuration, there exists an execution $E' = C'_0, G'_1, C'_1, G'_2, \ldots$ in $\mathcal{E}_{\mathcal{A}}^{\mathcal{N}}$ and an $s \geq 0$ such that $C'_s = C$. Then the sequence

$$E'' = C'_0, G'_1, \ldots, C'_s, G, C_t, G_{t+1}, \ldots$$

is an execution in $\mathcal{E}_{\mathcal{A}}^{\mathcal{N}}$ with $y^*_{E''} = y_E^* = y^*$. Hence $y^* \in Y^*_{\mathcal{N}}(C)$ because C occurs in E''. This shows inclusion of the right-hand side in the left-hand side and concludes the proof. □

Lemma 3.3. *Let C be a configuration reachable by algorithm $\mathcal{A}$ in network model $\mathcal{N}$. Then there exist $G, H \in \mathcal{N}$ such that*

$$\operatorname{diam}\left(Y^*_{\mathcal{N}}(C)\right) = \operatorname{diam}\left(Y^*_{\mathcal{N}}(G.C) \cup Y^*_{\mathcal{N}}(H.C)\right) \ .$$

Proof. Set $Y = Y^*_{\mathcal{N}}(C)$, and $Y_G = Y^*_{\mathcal{N}}(G.C)$ for $G \in \mathcal{N}$. By Lemma 3.2 it is $Y = \bigcup_{G \in \mathcal{N}} Y_G$, which means that every sequence of pairs of points in Y whose distances converge to $\operatorname{diam}(Y)$ includes an infinite subsequence in some product $Y_G \times Y_H$ because there are only finitely many. Thus $\operatorname{diam}(Y) \leq \operatorname{diam}(Y_G \cup Y_H)$. The other inequality follows from $Y_G \cup Y_H \subseteq Y$. □

Two configurations C and C' are called *indistinguishable for agent i*, denoted $C \sim_i C'$, if i is in the same state in C and in C'.

As an immediate consequence of the above definition, we obtain:

Lemma 3.4. *Let C and C' be two reachable configurations, and let G and G' be communication graphs in $\mathcal{N}$. If some agent i has the same in-neighbors in G and G' and if $C \sim_j C'$ for each of i's in-neighbors j, then $G.C \sim_i G'.C'$.*

An agent i is said to be *deaf in a communication graph* G if i has a unique in-neighbor in G, namely i itself. We are now in position to relate valencies of successor configurations.

LEMMA 3.5. *If agent i has the same in-neighbors in two communication graphs G and G' in $\mathcal{N}$, and if there exists a communication graph in $\mathcal{N}$ in which i is deaf and $C \sim_j C'$ for the in-neighbors j of i, then $Y^*_{\mathcal{N}}(G.C) \cap Y^*_{\mathcal{N}}(G'.C') \neq \emptyset$.*

PROOF. From Lemma 3.4, we have $G.C \sim_i G'.C'$.

Let D_i be a communication graph in $\mathcal{N}$ in which the agent i is deaf. Then we consider an execution E in which C occurs at some round $t_0 - 1$, G is the communication graph at round t_0, and from there on all communication graphs are equal to D_i. Analogously, let E' be an execution identical to E except that the communication graph at round t_0 is G' instead of G. By inductive application of Lemma 3.4, we show that for all $t \geq t_0$, we have $C_t \sim_i C'_t$. In particular, we obtain $y^i_E(t) = y^i_{E'}(t)$. Thus $y^*_E = y^*_{E'}$, which shows that $Y^*_{\mathcal{N}}(G.C)$ and $Y^*_{\mathcal{N}}(G'.C')$ intersect. □

From Lemma 3.5 we determine the valency of any initial configuration when the network model contains certain communication graphs. If every agent is deaf in some communication graph of the network model $\mathcal{N}$, then the next lemma shows that the diameter of the valency of any initial configuration is equal to the diameter of the set of its initial values.

LEMMA 3.6. *If, for every agent i, there is a communication graph in $\mathcal{N}$ in which i is deaf, then each initial configuration C_0 satisfies $\delta_{\mathcal{N}}(C_0) = \Delta(y(0))$. In particular, there is an initial configuration for which $\delta_{\mathcal{N}}(C_0) > 0$.*

PROOF. Since $Y^*_{\mathcal{N}}(C_0)$ is a subset of the convex hull of the set of points $\{y^1(0), \ldots, y^n(0)\}$ by the Validity property of asymptotic consensus and since the diameter of the convex hull of the set $\{y^1(0), \ldots, y^n(0)\}$ is equal to $\Delta(y(0))$, we have the inequality $\delta_{\mathcal{N}}(C_0) \leq \Delta(y(0))$.

To show the converse inequality, let i and j be two agents such that $\|y^i(0) - y^j(0)\| = \Delta(y(0))$. Let E be the execution with initial configuration C_0 and a constant communication graph in which agent i is deaf. Now consider $C^{(i)}_0$, an initial configuration such that all initial values are set to $y^i(0)$, and the execution $E^{(i)}$ from $C^{(i)}_0$ with the same communication pattern as in E.

By a repeated application of Lemma 3.4, we see that at each round t, we have $C_t \sim_i C^{(i)}_t$. Hence, $y^*_E = y^*_{E^{(i)}}$.

From the Validity condition, we deduce that $y^*(E^{(i)}) = y^i(0)$. It then follows that $y^i(0) \in Y^*_{\mathcal{N}}(C_0)$. By a similar argument, we see $y^j(0) \in Y^*_{\mathcal{N}}(C_0)$. Hence

$$\delta_{\mathcal{N}}(C_0) \geq \|y^i(0) - y^j(0)\| = \Delta(y(0)) ,$$

which concludes the proof. □

4 TIGHT BOUND FOR TWO AGENTS

In this section, we prove a lower bound of 1/3 on the contraction rate of algorithms that solve asymptotic consensus in the network model of all rooted (and here also non-split) communication graphs with two agents. Combined with Algorithm 1, which achieves this lower bound [9], we have indeed identified a tight bound on the contraction rate for $n = 2$. Moreover, the algorithm also shows that the lower bound is achieved by a simple convex combination algorithm.

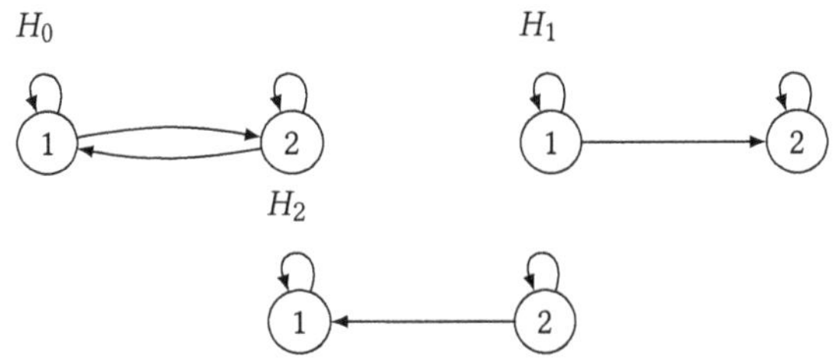

Figure 1: The rooted communication graphs H_0, H_1, and H_2 for $n = 2$

Algorithm 1 Algorithm with contraction rate 1/3 for $n = 2$

Initialization:
1: $y^i \in \mathbb{R}$
In round $t \geq 1$ do:
2: send y^i to other agent
3: **if** y^j was received from other agent **then**
4: $y^i \leftarrow y^i/3 + 2y^j/3$
5: **end if**

A straightforward analysis of Algorithm 1 shows that its contraction rate is equal to 1/3.

Note that for $n = 2$, there are 3 possible rooted communication graphs that may occur, all of which are non-split; see Figure 1: (i) H_0 in which all messages are received, (ii) H_1 in which agent 2 receives agent 1's message but not vice versa, and (iii) H_2 in which agent 1 receives agent 2's message but not vice versa.

THEOREM 4.1. *The contraction rate of any asymptotic consensus algorithm for $n = 2$ agents in a network model that includes the three graphs H_0, H_1, and H_2 is greater or equal to 1/3.*

PROOF. We show the stronger statement that for every initial configuration C_0 there is an execution $E = C_0, G_1, C_1, G_2, \ldots$ starting from C_0 such that

$$\delta_{\mathcal{N}}(C_t) \geq \frac{1}{3^t} \cdot \delta_{\mathcal{N}}(C_0) \tag{1}$$

for $t \geq 0$. This, applied to an initial configuration with $\delta_{\mathcal{N}}(C_0) > 0$, which exists by Lemma 3.6, then shows the theorem.

Note that it suffices to show (1) for the specific network model $\mathcal{N}' = \{H_0, H_1, H_2\}$ shown in Figure 1 because $\delta_{\mathcal{N}}(C_t) \geq \delta_{\mathcal{N}'}(C_t)$ by Lemma 3.1 and $\delta_{\mathcal{N}'}(C_0) = \delta_{\mathcal{N}}(C_0)$ by Lemma 3.6 whenever $\mathcal{N} \supseteq \mathcal{N}'$. We hence suppose $\mathcal{N} = \mathcal{N}'$ in the rest of the proof.

The proof is by inductive construction of an execution $E = C_0, G_1, C_1, G_2, \ldots$ whose configurations C_t satisfy (1). Equation (1) is trivial for $t = 0$.

Now assume $t \geq 0$ and that Equation (1) holds for t. There are three possible successor configurations of C_t, one for each of the communication graphs H_0, H_1, and H_2 in $\mathcal{N}'$. Set $C^k_{t+1} = H_k.C_t$. Further let $Y = Y^*_{\mathcal{N}'}(C_t)$, and $Y_k = Y^*_{\mathcal{N}'}(C^k_{t+1})$.

We will show that there is some $\hat{k} \in \{0,1,2\}$ with $\text{diam}(Y_{\hat{k}}) \geq \text{diam}(Y)/3$. We then define $G_{t+1} = H_{\hat{k}}$ and $C_{t+1} = C^{\hat{k}}_{t+1}$. By the induction hypothesis, we then have

$$\delta_{N'}(C_{t+1}) \geq \delta_{N'}(C_t)/3 \geq \delta_{N'}(C_0)/3^{t+1} \ ,$$

i.e., Equation (1) holds for $t+1$.

Assume by contradiction that $\text{diam}(Y_k) < \text{diam}(Y)/3$ for all $k \in \{0,1,2\}$. From Lemma 3.2 we have $Y = Y_0 \cup Y_1 \cup Y_2$. Noting that agent 1 is deaf in H_1 and agent 2 has the same incoming edges as in H_0, and that agent 2 is deaf in H_2 and agent 1 has the same incoming edges as in H_0, we obtain from Lemma 3.5 that

$$Y_0 \cap Y_1 \neq \emptyset \quad \text{and} \quad Y_0 \cap Y_2 \neq \emptyset \ .$$

The sets Y_0 and Y_1 intersecting means

$$\text{diam}(Y_0 \cup Y_1) \leq \text{diam}(Y_0) + \text{diam}(Y_1) < \frac{2}{3}\,\text{diam}(Y) \ .$$

Further, the sets $Y_0 \cup Y_1$ and Y_2 intersecting means

$$\begin{aligned}\text{diam}(Y) &= \text{diam}(Y_0 \cup Y_1 \cup Y_2) \\ &\leq \text{diam}(Y_0 \cup Y_1) + \text{diam}(Y_2) < \text{diam}(Y) \ ,\end{aligned}$$

a contradiction. This concludes the proof. □

5 TIGHT BOUND FOR NON-SPLIT MODEL: CONTRACTION IN PRESENCE OF DEAF GRAPHS

In this section, we prove a lower bound of 1/2 on the contraction rate of asymptotic consensus algorithms for $n \geq 3$ agents, in a network model that includes graphs derived from a communication graph G, where agents are made deaf in the derived graphs. As a special case this includes the network model of all non-split communication graphs. Charron-Bost et al. [9] presented the midpoint algorithm (given in Algorithm 2) for dimension one with contraction rate 1/2 for non-split communication graphs. Together this shows tightness of our lower bound in dimension one.

Algorithm 2 Midpoint algorithm

Initialization:
$y^i \in \mathbb{R}$
In round $t \geq 1$ **do:**
send y^i to all agents
$m^i \leftarrow \min\left\{y^j \mid j \in \text{In}_i(t)\right\}$
$M^i \leftarrow \max\left\{y^j \mid j \in \text{In}_i(t)\right\}$
$y^i \leftarrow (m^i + M^i)/2$

Let G be an arbitrary communication graph. Consider a system with $n \geq 3$ agents, and the n communication graphs $F_1, \ldots, F_n$ where F_i is obtained by making i deaf in G, i.e., by removing all the edges towards i except the self-loop (i,i): let $\text{deaf}(G) = \{F_1, \ldots, F_n\}$ with $F_i = G \setminus \left\{(j,i) \ : \ j \in [n] \setminus \{i\}\right\}$.

With a proof similar to that of Theorem 4.1 but noting that the valencies of all pairs of successor configurations intersect, we get:

Theorem 5.1. *The contraction rate of any asymptotic consensus algorithm for $n \geq 3$ agents in a network model that includes* deaf(G) *is greater or equal to* $1/2$.

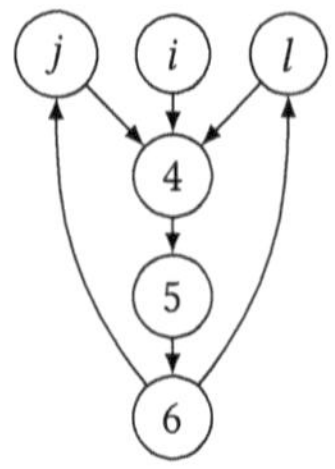

Figure 2: Rooted communication graph Ψ_i for $n = 6$

Note that the network model $\text{deaf}(K_n)$, where K_n is the complete digraph on n nodes, is a subset of the network model that contains all non-split communication graphs. Hence the lower bound holds and, since Algorithm 2 is applicable, a tight bound follows. In fact, it would even be sufficient to reduce $\text{deaf}(G)$ to the graphs F_i, F_j, F_l for three agents $i, j, l \in [n]$.

6 TIGHT BOUND FOR ROOTED MODEL: CONTRACTION IN PRESENCE OF Ψ GRAPHS

We next prove a lower bound of $\sqrt[n-2]{1/2}$ on the contraction rate of asymptotic consensus algorithms for $n \geq 4$ agents.

For $i \in \{1,2,3\}$, let Ψ_i (see Figure 2) be the communication graph where agents $4 \leq j \leq n-1$ form a path with edges from j to $j+1$, agents $\{1,2,3\} \setminus i$ have n as their in-neighbor and 4 as their out-neighbor, and i has 4 as its out-neighbor. For $i \in \{1,2,3\}$, let σ_i be the sequence of graphs Ψ_i of length $n-2$.

First observe that any communication pattern arising from the concatenation of σ_i sequences necessarily is a communication pattern of the network model of Ψ_i graphs, which are rooted. The analysis of the set of these communication patterns necessitates a generalization of our system model: generalizing from sets of allowed graphs to arbitrary sets of allowed communication patterns.

Theorem 6.1. *The contraction rate of any asymptotic consensus algorithm in a network model including the Ψ graphs is greater or equal to* $\sqrt[n-2]{1/2}$.

From [9] we have that the amortized midpoint algorithm guarantees a contraction of $\sqrt[n-1]{1/2}$ for rooted network models. Theorem 6.1 shows that this is asymptotically optimal.

6.1 From Network Models to Sequences

To prove Theorem 6.1, we generalize the system model from Section 2 and some of the basic lemmas we proved for the specific case of network models.. While we previously allowed the adversary to choose any sequence of communication graphs from the network model, we next consider more general properties on graph sequences, including safety and liveness properties.

A *property* is a set of communication patterns. A *snapshot* is a pair $S = (C, \pi)$ where C is a configuration, i.e., a collection of states of the agents, and π is a finite sequence of communication graphs. Given a snapshot $S = (C, \pi)$ and a communication graph G, define $G.S = (G.C, \pi \cdot G)$ where $\pi \cdot G$ is the addition of G to the end of π. We extend this definition to a finite sequence σ of communication graphs. We write $S \sim_i S'$ if agent i has the same local state in both S and S'.

A *trace* of an algorithm $\mathcal{A}$ in a property $\mathcal{P}$ is an infinite sequence $T = (S_0, S_1, \dots)$ of snapshots such that there exists a communication pattern $P \in \mathcal{P}$ with $S_t = G_t.S_{t-1}$ for all $t \geq 1$. We denote by $\mathcal{T}_{\mathcal{A}}^{\mathcal{P}}$ the set of all traces of $\mathcal{A}$ in $\mathcal{P}$. If $\mathcal{A}$ solves asymptotic consensus in $\mathcal{P}$, then we write y_T^* for the common limit of the agents' values in trace $T \in \mathcal{T}_{\mathcal{A}}^{\mathcal{P}}$.

We define the valency of snapshots and the contraction rate of an algorithm in $\mathcal{P}$ analogously to the case of network models as

$$Y_{\mathcal{P}}^*(S) = \left\{ y_T^* \in \mathbb{R}^d \mid S \text{ occurs in } T \in \mathcal{T}_{\mathcal{A}}^{\mathcal{P}} \right\}$$

and the contraction rate as

$$\sup_{T \in \mathcal{T}_{\mathcal{A}}^{\mathcal{P}}} \limsup_{t \to \infty} \sqrt[t]{\delta_{\mathcal{P}}(S_t)}$$

where $\delta_{\mathcal{P}}(S_t) = \operatorname{diam}\left(Y_{\mathcal{P}}^*(S_t)\right)$.

Lemma 6.2. *Let $\mathcal{P}, \mathcal{P}'$ be two properties with $\mathcal{P}' \subseteq \mathcal{P}$. If $\mathcal{A}$ is an algorithm that solves asymptotic consensus in $\mathcal{P}$, then (i) it also solves asymptotic consensus in $\mathcal{P}'$, (ii) for every snapshot S reachable by $\mathcal{A}$ in $\mathcal{P}'$, we have $Y_{\mathcal{P}'}^*(S) \subseteq Y_{\mathcal{P}}^*(S)$, (iii) $\delta_{\mathcal{P}'}(S) \leq \delta_{\mathcal{P}}(S)$, and (iv) the contraction rate in $\mathcal{P}'$ is less or equal to the contraction rate in $\mathcal{P}$.*

For a snapshot $S = (C, \pi)$ reachable by algorithm $\mathcal{A}$ in property $\mathcal{P}$, we define $\Sigma(S)$ to be the set of communication graphs G such that $\pi \cdot G$ is a prefix of a communication pattern in $\mathcal{P}$.

Lemma 6.3. *Let S be a snapshot reachable by algorithm $\mathcal{A}$ in property $\mathcal{P}$. Then*

$$Y_{\mathcal{P}}^*(S) = \bigcup_{G \in \Sigma(S)} Y_{\mathcal{P}}^*(G.S) \ .$$

Lemma 6.4. *Let S be a configuration reachable by algorithm $\mathcal{A}$ in property $\mathcal{P}$. Then there exist $G, H \in \Sigma(S)$ such that*

$$\operatorname{diam}\left(Y_{\mathcal{P}}^*(S)\right) = \operatorname{diam}\left(Y_{\mathcal{P}}^*(G.S) \cup Y_{\mathcal{P}}^*(H.S)\right) \ .$$

Lemma 6.5. *Let $S = (C, \pi)$ and $S' = (C', \pi')$ be two snapshots with $S \sim_i S'$. If there exist sequences of communication graphs α and α' such that $\pi \cdot \alpha \in \mathcal{P}$, $\pi' \cdot \alpha' \in \mathcal{P}$ and i is deaf in all communication graphs in α and α', then $Y_{\mathcal{P}}^*(S) \cap Y_{\mathcal{P}}^*(S') \neq \emptyset$.*

Lemma 6.6. *Let $\Delta \geq 0$. If there exist agents $i \neq j$ and communication patterns $P_i, P_j \in \mathcal{P}$ such that agent i is deaf in P_i and agent j is deaf in P_j, then there is an initial snapshot S_0 with $\delta_{\mathcal{P}}(S_0) = \Delta$. In particular, there is an initial snapshot for which $\delta_{\mathcal{P}}(S_0) > 0$.*

6.2 Proof of Theorem 6.1

Lemma 6.7. *For $i, j, \ell \in \{1, 2, 3\}$ with $\ell \neq i, j : \sigma_i.C_t \sim_\ell \sigma_j.C_t$.*

Proof. We inductively show the following stronger statement. Let σ_i^k be the sequence of graphs Ψ_i of length $k \in [n-2]$. For agents $i, j, \ell \in \{1, 2, 3\}$ with $\ell \neq i, j$, and $m \in \{k+3, \dots, n\}$, we have $\sigma_i^k.C_t \sim_{\ell,m} \sigma_j^k.C_t$.

Observe that agents ℓ and $\{4, \dots, n\}$ have the same in-neighbors in Ψ_i and Ψ_j. The base case ($k = 1$) follows from the observation and Lemma 3.4. For the inductive step ($k \mapsto k+1$), observe that agent ℓ and $\{k+4, \dots, n\}$ have only incoming edges from agents ℓ and $\{k+3, \dots, n\}$. From the hypothesis and Lemma 3.4, the inductive step follows. □

Let property $\mathcal{P}_{\text{seq}}$ contain any communication pattern arising from the concatenation of σ_i sequences defined at the start of the section and property $\mathcal{P}$ contain all communication patterns generated by rooted graphs. We show the stronger statement that for every initial snapshot S_0 there is a trace $T = S_0, S_1, \dots$ starting at S_0 such that

$$\delta_{\mathcal{P}}(S_t) \geq \frac{1}{2^{\lceil \frac{t}{n-2} \rceil}} \delta_{\mathcal{P}}(S_0) \tag{2}$$

for all $t \geq 0$. It suffices to show (2) for $\mathcal{P}_{\text{seq}}$ because $\delta_{\mathcal{P}}(S_t) \geq \delta_{\mathcal{P}_{\text{seq}}}(S_t)$ by Lemma 6.2 and $\delta_{\mathcal{P}_{\text{seq}}}(S_0) = \delta_{\mathcal{P}}(S_0)$ by Lemma 6.6 whenever $\mathcal{P} \supseteq \mathcal{P}_{\text{seq}}$. We hence suppose $\mathcal{P} = \mathcal{P}_{\text{seq}}$ in the rest of the proof. The proof is by inductive construction of a trace $T = S_0, S_1, \dots$ whose snapshots S_t satisfy (2). This, applied to an initial snapshot with $\delta_{\mathcal{P}}(S_0) > 0$, which exists by Lemma 6.6, then shows the theorem.

The base case ($t = 0$) is trivially fulfilled.

For the inductive step ($t = (n-2)k \mapsto t \leq (n-2)(k+1)$) assume that Equation (2) holds for $t = (n-2)k$. First observe that, by construction of any $P \in \mathcal{P}$, there are three possible successor patterns until round $t + n - 2$: $\sigma_1, \sigma_2, \sigma_3$. We thus have, $Y_{\mathcal{P}}^*(S_t) = Y_{\mathcal{P}}^*(S_{t+1}^1) \cup Y_{\mathcal{P}}^*(S_{t+1}^2) \cup Y_{\mathcal{P}}^*(S_{t+1}^3) = \dots = Y_{\mathcal{P}}^*(S_{t+n-2}^1) \cup Y_{\mathcal{P}}^*(S_{t+n-2}^2) \cup Y_{\mathcal{P}}^*(S_{t+n-2}^3)$, where $S_{t+n-2}^u = \sigma_u.S_t$ for agent $u \in \{1, 2, 3\}$.

Abbreviate $Y = Y_{\mathcal{P}}^*(S_t)$ and $Y_u = Y_{\mathcal{P}}^*(S_{t+n-2}^u)$. We will show that there exists a $\hat{u} \in \{1, 2, 3\}$ with

$$\operatorname{diam}(Y_{\hat{u}}) \geq \operatorname{diam}(Y)/2 \ . \tag{3}$$

We then define $S_{t+n-2} = S_{t+n-2}^{\hat{u}}$. By (3) and the induction hypothesis, we then have

$$\delta_{\mathcal{P}'}(S_{t+n-2}) = \dots = \delta_{\mathcal{P}'}(S_{t+1}) \geq \frac{\delta_{\mathcal{P}'}(S_t)}{2} \geq \frac{1}{2^{\lceil \frac{t}{n-2} \rceil + 1}} \delta_{\mathcal{P}'}(S_0) \ ,$$

i.e., Equation (2) holds up to round $t + n - 2$.

Assume by contradiction that for all $u \in \{1, 2, 3\}$ $\operatorname{diam}(Y_u) < \operatorname{diam}(Y)/2$. Since $n \geq 3$ and, by Lemma 6.7, $(C_t, \pi.\sigma_i) \sim_\ell (C_t, \pi.\sigma_j)$ together with the fact that $\pi.\sigma_i.\sigma_\ell^\omega \in \mathcal{P}_{\text{seq}}$ and $\pi.\sigma_j.\sigma_\ell^\omega \in \mathcal{P}_{\text{seq}}$ we can apply Lemma 6.5 which shows that, for any pair $i, j \in \{1, 2, 3\}$ we have

$$Y_i \cap Y_j \neq \emptyset \ .$$

By Lemma 6.4, there exist $u, u' \in \{1, 2, 3\}$ such that $\operatorname{diam}(Y_u \cup Y_{u'}) = \operatorname{diam}(Y)$. In particular, we can choose $i = u$ and $j = u'$, which implies that

$$\begin{aligned} \operatorname{diam}(Y) &= \operatorname{diam}(Y_u \cup Y_{u'}) \leq \operatorname{diam}(Y_u) + \operatorname{diam}(Y_{u'}) \\ &< \operatorname{diam}(Y) \end{aligned}$$

which is a contradiction and concludes the proof.

7 RELATION TO EXACT CONSENSUS AND GENERALIZED BOUNDS

In [12], Coulouma et al. characterized the network models in which exact consensus is solvable. In [8], Charron-Bost et al. showed that asymptotic consensus is solvable in a significantly broader class: it is solvable if and only if a network model is rooted. In this section we aim to shed light on the deeper relation between these two problems by studying valencies and convergence rates. Our main results are a characterization of the topological structure of valencies with respect to solvability of exact consensus (Theorem 7.2) and nontrivial lower bounds on the contraction rates whenever exact consensus is not solvable (Theorem 7.4 and Corollary 7.5).

We start with recalling some definitions from Coulouma et al. [12]. In the following, we denote by $R(G)$ the set of roots of a communication graph G, i.e., the set of agents that have a directed path to all other agents in G. For a set $S \subseteq [n]$, let $\mathrm{In}_S(G) = \bigcup_{j \in S} \mathrm{In}_j(G)$. The set $\mathrm{Out}_S(G)$ is defined analogously.

Definition 7.1 (Definition 4.7 in [12]). Let $\mathcal{N}$ be a network model. Given $G, H, K \in \mathcal{N}$, we define $G\alpha_{\mathcal{N},K}H$ if $\mathrm{In}_{R(K)}(G) = \mathrm{In}_{R(K)}(H)$. The relation $\alpha^*_{\mathcal{N}}$ is the transitive closure of the union of the relations $\alpha_{\mathcal{N},K}$ where K varies in $\mathcal{N}$.

The following theorem is a characterization of network models in which exact consensus is solvable by the topological structure of valencies of asymptotic consensus algorithms. Of course, having to decide in a discrete set of value for exact consensus, valencies should be disconnected. However, the theorem shows that this condition is actually already sufficient to solve exact consensus.

Theorem 7.2. *Let $\mathcal{N}$ be a network model. Exact consensus is solvable in $\mathcal{N}$ if and only if there exists an asymptotic consensus algorithm $\mathcal{A}$ for $\mathcal{N}$ such that $Y^*_{\mathcal{N}',\mathcal{A}}(C_0)$ is either a singleton or disconnected for all network models $\mathcal{N}' \subseteq \mathcal{N}$ and all initial configurations C_0 of $\mathcal{A}$.*

We next introduce the *α-diameter* of a network model $\mathcal{N}$, which we will then (see Theorem 7.4 and Corollary 7.5) show to be directly linked to a nontrivial lower bound on the contraction rate in $\mathcal{N}$ if exact consensus is not solvable in $\mathcal{N}$. Note, that in case exact consensus is solvable in $\mathcal{N}$, the optimal contraction rate always is 0, obtained by a reduction argument to exact consensus.

Definition 7.3. Let $\mathcal{N}$ be a network model. The *α-diameter* of $\mathcal{N}$ is the smallest $D \geq 1$ such that for all $G, H \in \mathcal{N}$ there exist communication graphs $H_0, \dots, H_q \in \mathcal{N}$ and $K_1, \dots, K_q \in \mathcal{N}$ with $q \leq D$ such that $G = H_0$, $H = H_q$, and $H_{r-1}\alpha_{\mathcal{N},K_r}H_r$ for all $r \in [q]$. In case it does not exists we set $D = \infty$.

Observe, that for the network model $\{H_0, H_1, H_2\}$ from Theorem 4.1, it is $D = 2$. Further, for network model $\mathrm{deaf}(G)$, where G is an arbitrary communication graph G, we have $D = 1$. The following theorem and corollary thus generalize Theorems 4.1 and 5.1 to arbitrary network models in which exact consensus is not solvable.

Theorem 7.4. *Let $\mathcal{N}$ be a network model in which exact consensus is not solvable. The contraction rate of any asymptotic consensus algorithm in $\mathcal{N}$ is greater or equal to $1/(D+1)$ where D is the α-diameter of $\mathcal{N}$.*

Direct application of Theorem 7.4 to a network model $\mathcal{N}$ in which exact consensus is not solvable may yield a trivial bound of 0 in case its α-diameter is ∞. Indeed, we can, however, use Lemma 3.1 to derive a strictly positive bound for any $\mathcal{N}$ in which exact consensus is not solvable:

Corollary 7.5. *Let $\mathcal{N}$ be a network model in which exact consensus is not solvable. The contraction rate of any asymptotic consensus algorithm in $\mathcal{N}$ is greater or equal to $1/(D+1)$ where D is the smallest α-diameter of $\mathcal{N}' \subseteq \mathcal{N}$ in which exact consensus is not solvable.*

Proof. Set $\mathcal{N}' \subseteq \mathcal{N}$ equal to the network model with the smallest α-diameter in which exact consensus is not solvable. Applying Theorem 7.4 to $\mathcal{N}'$, and Lemma 3.1 (iv) to $\mathcal{N}'$ and $\mathcal{N}$ yields the corollary. □

8 TIGHT BOUNDS FOR ASYNCHRONOUS SYSTEMS WITH CRASHES: THE PRICE OF ROUNDS

In this section we show that Corollary 7.5 provides a tool to clearly separate time complexities of algorithms that operate in rounds to general algorithms in the classical static fault model of asynchronous message passing systems with crashes. Our result applies to algorithms without any restriction: we do not make assumptions on the nature of the functions used by the agents, and agents are not required to be memoryless.

We start with recalling and adapting notation for the classical asynchronous message passing systems. We consider a distributed system where agents perform receive-compute-broadcast steps. An agent may crash, i.e., stop making steps. Crashes can be unclean: the final broadcast message may be received by a proper subset of correct, i.e., non crashed, agents, only. Since an agent that crashes stops to make steps, we require Convergence, Validity, and Agreement of asymptotic consensus to hold only for the set of correct agents. Analogously, the consensus function y^*, and thus the valencies, are restricted to correct agents only. Further, we apply the standard convention of measuring time in asynchronous systems, by normalizing to the longest end-to-end message delay from a broadcast to the respective receive in an execution.

8.1 Round-based Algorithms

An algorithm is said to operate in rounds if each agent waits for $n - f$ messages corresponding to the current round, updates its state based on the received messages and its previous state, and broadcasts the next round's messages. Indeed algorithms that operate in rounds are widely used in asynchronous systems; see, e.g., [10, 14, 24].

We next show that Corollary 7.5 can be applied to obtain new asymptotically tight bounds for round-based algorithms. Specifically, we prove a lower bound for asynchronous systems of size $n \geq 3$ with up to $f < n/2$ crashes whose agents operate in rounds.

Let us construct the following network model: Denote by $\mathcal{G}_n$ the set of communication graphs with n nodes and let

$$\mathcal{N}_A = \left\{ G \in \mathcal{G}_n \mid \forall i \in [n]\colon |\mathrm{In}_i(G)| \geq n - f \right\} ,$$

for some $f < n/2$.

Lemma 8.1. *The α-diameter of $\mathcal{N}_A$ is at most $\lceil n/f \rceil$.*

Proof. Let $G, H \in \mathcal{N}_A$. Setting $q = \lceil n/f \rceil$, we choose the communication graphs H_r and K_r defined by

$$\mathrm{In}_i(H_r) = \begin{cases} \mathrm{In}_i(G) & \text{if } 1 \leq i \leq rf \\ \mathrm{In}_i(H) & \text{if } rf + 1 \leq i \leq n \end{cases}$$

and

$$\mathrm{In}_i(K_r) = [n] \setminus \{ i \mid (r-1)f + 1 \leq i \leq rf \}$$

Clearly, it is $H_0 = G$ and $H_q = H$. Since we can write $R(K_r) = [n] \setminus \{i \mid (r-1)f + 1 \leq i \leq rf\}$ and $\text{In}_i(H_{r-1}) = \text{In}_i(H_r)$ for all $i \in K_r$, we also have $H_{r-1}\alpha_{\mathcal{N}_A,K_r}H_r$. Noting $H_r \in \mathcal{N}_A$ and $K_r \in \mathcal{N}_A$, this concludes the proof. □

From Lemma 8.1 and Corollary 7.5 we immediately obtain the lower bound:

THEOREM 8.2. *The contraction rate for any asymptotic consensus algorithm for $n \geq 3$ agents and at most $f < n/2$ crashes that operates in rounds is greater or equal to $\frac{1}{\lceil n/f \rceil + 1}$.*

Note that the contraction rate in Theorem 8.2 is with respect to rounds. However, we can easily construct an execution where a single round requires $1+\varepsilon$ time for arbitrarily small $\varepsilon > 0$: we assign all messages that are delivered according to the communication graph of the respective round, delay 1, and all others delay $1 + \varepsilon$. Theorem 8.2 thus also holds for a contraction rate with respect to time.

8.2 General Algorithms

We next show that there is an algorithm that does not operate in rounds that ensures that all agents' outputs are equal by time $f + 1$. This gives a contraction rate of 0.

The following algorithm *MinRelay* is inspired by the exact consensus algorithm for synchronous systems with crash faults (see, e.g,. [24]), and is based on a non-terminating reliable broadcast protocol: Initially, at time 0, each agent i sets S^i to the set containing only its initial value, and broadcasts S^i. Whenever an agent i receives a set $S \neq S^i$, it sets $S^i \leftarrow S^i \cup S$, $y^i \leftarrow \min(S^i)$, and broadcasts S^i.

THEOREM 8.3. *The MinRelay algorithm solves asymptotic consensus in asynchronous message passing systems with up to $f < n$ crashes. Specifically, all correct agents' sets S^i, and thus y^i, are equal by time $f + 1$, and the algorithm's contraction rate is 0.*

9 APPROXIMATE CONSENSUS

Alternatively to asymptotic consensus, one may also consider the *approximate consensus* problem, in which convergence is replaced by a decision in a finite number of rounds and where agreement should be achieved with an arbitrarily small error tolerance (see, e.g., [24]). Formally, the local state of i is augmented with a variable d^i initialized to $\perp$. Agent i is allowed to set d^i to some value $v \neq \perp$ only once, in which case we say that *i decides v*. In addition to the initial values $y^i(0)$, agents initially receive the error tolerance ε and an upper bound Δ on the maximum distance of initial values. An algorithm *solves approximate consensus* in $\mathcal{N}$ if for all $\varepsilon > 0$ and all Δ, each execution E with a communication pattern in $\mathcal{N}$ with initial diameter at most Δ satisfies:

- *Termination.* Each agent eventually decides.
- *ε-Agreement.* If agents i and j decide v and v', then we have $\|v - v'\| \leq \varepsilon$.
- *Validity.* If agent i decides v, then v is in the convex hull of initial values $y^1_E(0), \ldots, y^n_E(0)$.

The above two problems are clearly closely related. However, the ε-Agreement condition does not preclude the decisions of a given agent, as a function of the error tolerance parameter ε, to diverge, i.e., a priori may lead to unstable decisions with respect to this parameter.

We next extend our lower bounds on the contraction rate of asymptotic consensus to lower bounds on the decision time of approximate consensus. In particular, we show optimality of the decision times of the algorithms presented by Charron-Bost et al. [9]: For $n = 2$, running Algorithm 1 and deciding y^i after $\lceil \log_3 \frac{\Delta}{\varepsilon} \rceil$ rounds is optimal (Theorem 9.1). For $n \geq 3$ and the network model of all non-split graphs, running the midpoint algorithm and deciding after $\lceil \log_2 \frac{\Delta}{\varepsilon} \rceil$ rounds is optimal (Theorem 9.2). For $n \geq 4$ and the weakest network model of all rooted graphs, running the amortized midpoint algorithm and deciding after $(n-1)\lceil \log_2 \frac{\Delta}{\varepsilon} \rceil$ rounds is optimal within a multiplicative term of at most $\frac{n-1}{n-2}$ (Theorem 9.3).

We start with the case of two agents in Theorem 9.1. The proof is by reducing asymptotic consensus to approximate consensus, arriving at a contradiction with Theorem 4.1 for too fast approximate consensus algorithms.

THEOREM 9.1. *Let $\Delta > 0$ and $\varepsilon > 0$. In a network model of $n = 2$ agents that includes the three communication graphs H_0, H_1, and H_2, all approximate consensus algorithms have an execution with initial diameter $\Delta(y(0)) \leq \Delta$ and decision time greater or equal to $\log_3 \frac{\Delta}{\varepsilon}$.*

PROOF. Assume to the contrary that algorithm $\mathcal{A}$ solves approximate consensus in some network model $\mathcal{N} \supseteq \{H_0, H_1, H_2\}$ that decides in $T < \log_3 \frac{\Delta}{\varepsilon}$ rounds for all vectors of initial values $y(0)$ with $\Delta(y(0)) \leq \Delta$ and some $\varepsilon > 0$.

Choose any $y(0)$ with $\Delta(y(0)) = \Delta$. Define algorithm $\tilde{\mathcal{A}}$ by running algorithm $\mathcal{A}$, updating y to the agents' decision values in round T, and then running Algorithm 1 with the initial values $y^i(T) = d^i$ from round $T + 1$ on. Because Algorithm 1 is an asymptotic consensus algorithm and the decision values $y(T)$ of $\mathcal{A}$ satisfy the Validity condition of approximate consensus, algorithm $\tilde{\mathcal{A}}$ is an asymptotic consensus algorithm.

Let C_0 be an initial configuration of $\tilde{\mathcal{A}}$ with initial values $y(0)$. By the proof of Theorem 4.1, namely (1), there is an execution $E = C_0, G_1, C_1, G_2, \ldots$ starting from C_0 such that

$$\delta_{\mathcal{N}}(C_T) \geq \frac{1}{3^T} \cdot \delta_{\mathcal{N}}(C_0) \ .$$

We have $\delta_{\mathcal{N}}(C_0) = \Delta(y(0)) = \Delta$ by Lemma 3.6 and $\delta_{\mathcal{N}}(C_T) \leq \Delta(y(T)) \leq \varepsilon$ by Validity of Algorithm 1 and ε-Agreement of algorithm $\mathcal{A}$. But this means $T \geq \log_3 \frac{\Delta}{\varepsilon}$, a contradiction. □

With a similar proof, we also get the lower bound for approximate consensus with $n \geq 3$ agents:

THEOREM 9.2. *Let $\Delta > 0$ and $\varepsilon > 0$. In a network model of $n \geq 3$ agents that includes the communication graphs* deaf(G), *all approximate consensus algorithms have an execution with initial diameter $\Delta(y(0)) \leq \Delta$ and decision time greater or equal to $\log_2 \frac{\Delta}{\varepsilon}$.*

Analogously, for network models with rooted Ψ graphs, using (2), we obtain:

THEOREM 9.3. *Let $\Delta > 0$ and $\varepsilon > 0$. In a network model of $n \geq 4$ agents that includes the Ψ communication graphs, all approximate consensus algorithms have an execution with initial diameter $\Delta(y(0)) \leq \Delta$ and decision time greater or equal to $(n-2)\log_2 \frac{\Delta}{\varepsilon}$.*

In case the network model does not include any of the above graphs, we obtain the following general bound on the termination time:

THEOREM 9.4. *Let $\Delta > 0$ and $\varepsilon > 0$. In a network model in which exact consensus is not solvable, all approximate consensus algorithms have an execution with initial diameter $\Delta(y(0)) \leq \Delta$ and decision time greater or equal to $\log_{D+1} \frac{\Delta}{\varepsilon n}$, where D is the α-diameter of the network model.*

From Theorem 9.4 and the fact that $\mathcal{N}' \subseteq \mathcal{N}$ implies $\mathcal{E}' \subseteq \mathcal{E}$ for the corresponding sets of executions of algorithm $\mathcal{A}$, we get:

COROLLARY 9.5. *Let $\Delta > 0$ and $\varepsilon > 0$. In a network model in which exact consensus is not solvable, all approximate consensus algorithms have an execution with initial diameter $\Delta(y(0)) \leq \Delta$ and decision time greater or equal to $\log_{D+1} \frac{\Delta}{\varepsilon n}$, where D is the smallest α-diameter of a network model $\mathcal{N}' \subseteq \mathcal{N}$ in which exact consensus is not solvable.*

10 CONCLUSIONS

We introduced the notion of valency for asymptotic consensus algorithms, generalizing the concept of valency from exact consensus algorithms. Based on the study of valency diameters along executions we proved lower bounds on the contraction rates of asymptotic consensus algorithm in arbitrary network models: In particular, together with previously published averaging algorithms in [9], we showed tight bounds for the network model containing all non-split graphs, and the weakest network model in which asymptotic consensus is solvable, the network model of all rooted graphs. Furthermore we obtained a general lower bound of $1/(D+1)$ for any network model in which exact consensus is not solvable; here D denotes the newly introduced α-diameter of the network model. Interestingly, this result also immediately provides new tight lower bounds on classical static failure models, as exemplified in the case of asynchronous message-passing systems with crashes and shows a fundamental discrepancy in performance between round-based and general algorithms. We finally demonstrated how to obtain corresponding results for approximate consensus algorithms.

ACKNOWLEDGMENTS

We would like to thank Bernadette Charron-Bost for the many fruitful discussions and her valuable input, which greatly helped improve the paper. The research was partially funded by the Austrian Science Fund (FWF) projects SIC (P26436) and ADynNet (P28182), and by the CNRS project PEPS DEMO.

REFERENCES

[1] Ittai Abraham, Yonatan Amit, and Danny Dolev. 2004. Optimal resilience asynchronous approximate agreement. In *Proceedings of the 8th International Conference On Principles Of Distributed Systems (OPODIS 2004)*, Teruo Higashino (Ed.). Springer, Heidelberg, 229–239.

[2] David Angeli and Pierre-Alexandre Bliman. 2006. Stability of leaderless discrete-time multi-agent systems. *Mathematics of Control, Signals, and Systems* 18, 4 (2006), 293–322.

[3] Karl Johan Aström and Richard M. Murray. 2008. *Feedback Systems: An Introduction for Scientists and Engineers.* Princeton University Press, Princeton.

[4] J. A. Benediktsson and P. H. Swain. 1992. Consensus theoretic classification methods. *IEEE Transactions on Systems, Man, and Cybernetics* 22, 4 (1992), 688–704.

[5] Pierre-Alexandre Bliman, Angelia Nedic, and Asuman E. Ozdaglar. 2008. Rate of convergence for consensus with delays. In *Proceedings of the 47th IEEE Conference on Decision and Control, and the European Control Conference (CDC-ECC 2008).* IEEE, New York, 2226–2231.

[6] Ming Cao, A. Stephen Morse, and Brian D. O. Anderson. 2008. Reaching a consensus in a dynamically changing environment: convergence rates, measurement delays, and asynchronous events. *SIAM Journal on Control and Optimization* 47, 2 (2008), 601–623.

[7] Ming Cao, Daniel A. Spielman, and A. Stephen Morse. 2005. A lower bound on convergence of a distributed network consensus algorithm. In *Proceedings of the 44th IEEE Conference on Decision and Control, and the European Control Conference (CDC-ECC 2005)*, Hannes Frey, Xu Li, and Stefan Rührup (Eds.). IEEE, New York, 2356–2361.

[8] Bernadette Charron-Bost, Matthias Függer, and Thomas Nowak. 2015. Approximate consensus in highly dynamic networks: the role of averaging algorithms. In *Proceedings of the 42nd International Colloquium on Automata, Languages, and Programming (ICALP 2015)*, Magnús M. Halldórsson, Kazuo Iwama, Naoki Kobayashi, and Bettina Speckmann (Eds.). Springer, Heidelberg, 528–539.

[9] Bernadette Charron-Bost, Matthias Függer, and Thomas Nowak. 2016. Fast, robust, quantizable approximate consensus. In *Proceedings of the 43rd International Colloquium on Automata, Languages, and Programming (ICALP 2016)*, Ioannis Chatzigiannakis, Michael Mitzenmacher, Yuval Rabani, and Davide Sangiorgi (Eds.). Schloss Dagstuhl–Leibniz-Zentrum fuer Informatik, Dagstuhl, 137:1–137:14.

[10] Bernadette Charron-Bost and André Schiper. 2009. The Heard-Of model: computing in distributed systems with benign faults. *Distributed Computing* 22, 1 (2009), 49–71.

[11] Bernard Chazelle. 2011. The total s-energy of a multiagent system. *SIAM Journal on Control and Optimization* 49, 4 (2011), 1680–1706.

[12] Étienne Coulouma, Emmanuel Godard, and Joseph Peters. 2015. A characterization of oblivious message adversaries for which consensus is solvable. *Theoretical Computer Science* 584 (2015), 80–90.

[13] George Cybenko. 1989. Dynamic load balancing for distributed memory multiprocessors. *J. Parallel and Distrib. Comput.* 7, 2 (1989), 279–301.

[14] Danny Dolev, Nancy A. Lynch, Shlomit S. Pinter, Eugene W. Stark, and William E. Weihl. 1986. Reaching approximate agreement in the presence of faults. *J. ACM* 33, 2 (1986), 499–516.

[15] Magnus Egerstedt and Xiaoming Hu. 2001. Formation constrained multi-agent control. *IEEE Transactions on Robotics and Automation* 17, 6 (2001), 947–951.

[16] Seyed Rasoul Etesami and Tamer Başar. 2016. Convergence time for unbiased quantized consensus. *IEEE Trans. Automat. Control* 61, 2 (2016), 443–455.

[17] Alan D. Fekete. 1990. Asymptotically optimal algorithms for approximate agreement. *Distributed Computing* 4, 1 (1990), 9–29.

[18] Alan D. Fekete. 1994. Asynchronous approximate agreement. *Information and Computation* 115, 1 (1994), 95–124.

[19] Michael J Fischer, Nancy A Lynch, and Michael Merritt. 1986. Easy impossibility proofs for distributed consensus problems. *Distributed Computing* 1, 1 (1986), 26–39.

[20] Rainer Hegselmann and Ulrich Krause. 2002. Opinion dynamics and bounded confidence models, analysis, and simulation. *Journal of Artificial Societies and Social Simulation* 5, 3 (2002), 1–33.

[21] Qun Li and Daniela Rus. 2006. Global clock synchronization in sensor networks. *IEEE Trans. Comput.* 55, 2 (2006), 214–226.

[22] J. Lin, A.S. Morse, and B.D.O. Anderson. 2005. The multi-agent rendezvous problem. In *Cooperative Control: A Post-Workshop Volume, 2003 Block Island Workshop on Cooperative Control*, Vijay Kumar, Naomi Leonard, and A. Stephen Morse (Eds.). Springer, Heidelberg, 257–289.

[23] Ronit Lubitch and Shlomo Moran. 1995. Closed schedulers: a novel technique for analyzing asynchronous protocols. *Distributed Computing* 8, 4 (1995), 203–210.

[24] Nancy A. Lynch. 1996. *Distributed Algorithms.* Morgan Kaufmann, San Francisco.

[25] Hammurabi Mendes, Maurice Herlihy, Nitin Vaidya, and Vijay K Garg. 2015. Multidimensional agreement in Byzantine systems. *Distributed Computing* 28, 6 (2015), 423–441.

[26] Renato E. Mirollo and Steven H. Strogatz. 1990. Synchronization of pulse-coupled biological oscillators. *SIAM J. Appl. Math.* 50, 6 (1990), 1645–1662.

[27] Luc Moreau. 2005. Stability of multiagent systems with time-dependent communication links. *IEEE Trans. Automat. Control* 50, 2 (2005), 169–182.

[28] Angelia Nedic, Alexander Olshevsky, Asuman E. Ozdaglar, and John N. Tsitsiklis. 2009. On distributed averaging algorithms and quantization effects. *IEEE Trans. Automat. Control* 54, 11 (2009), 2506–2517.

[29] Alex Olshevsky. 2015. Linear time average consensus on fixed graphs. *IFAC-PapersOnLine* 48, 22 (2015), 94–99.

[30] Alex Olshevsky and John N. Tsitsiklis. 2011. Convergence speed in distributed consensus and averaging. *SIAM Rev.* 53, 4 (2011), 747–772.

[31] Tamás Vicsek, András Czirók, Eshel Ben-Jacob, Inon Cohen, and Ofer Shochet. 1995. Novel type of phase transition in a system of self-driven particles. *Physical Review Letters* 75, 6 (1995), 1226–1229.

[32] Y. Yuan, G.-B. Stan, L. Shi, M. Barahona, and J. Goncalves. 2013. Decentralized minimum-time consensus. *Automatica* 49, 5 (2013), 1227–1235.

Barriers due to Congestion and Two Ways to Deal With Them

Keren Censor-Hillel
Department of Computer Science, Technion
ckeren@cs.technion.ac.il

ABSTRACT

Restricting the bandwidth in models of distributed graph computations naturally introduces challenges that arise due to communication bottlenecks. In this talk, I will survey techniques for proving lower bounds on the complexity of fundamental graph problems under limited bandwidth. For some problems, allowing relaxed solutions can significantly reduce the required amount of communication, enabling efficient computations. Two successful approaches for overcoming provable barriers, namely, approximations and testing, will be exemplified and discussed in the context of distributed computing.

CCS CONCEPTS

• **Theory of computation → Approximation algorithms analysis; Distributed algorithms;**

KEYWORDS

Distributed Graph Algorithms, Limited Bandwidth, Lower bounds, Approximations, Testing

ACM Reference Format:
Keren Censor-Hillel. 2018. Barriers due to Congestion and Two Ways to Deal With Them. In *PODC '18: ACM Symposium on Principles of Distributed Computing, July 23–27, 2018, Egham, United Kingdom.* ACM, New York, NY, USA, 1 page. https://doi.org/10.1145/3212734.3212797

ACKNOWLEDGEMENT:

Keren Censor-Hillel's research has received funding from the European Research Council (ERC) under the European Unions Horizon 2020 research and innovation programme (grant agreement No 755839). Keren Censor-Hillel's research is also supported by the Israel Science Foundation, grant 1696/14.

ACM ISBN 978-1-4503-5795-1/18/07.
https://doi.org/10.1145/3212734.3212797

BIO

Keren Censor-Hillel is an associate professor in the Department of Computer Science at the Technion. She completed her Ph.D. dissertation at the Technion in 2010, for which she received the Principles of Distributed Computing Doctoral Dissertation Award. Afterward, she was a Simons Postdoctoral Fellow in the Computer Science and Artificial Intelligence Lab at MIT. She is a recipient of an Alon Fellowship awarded by the Israeli Academy of Science in 2013 and a Krill Prize awarded by the Wolf Foundation in 2016. She was recently awarded an ERC Starting Grant. Her research focuses on the theory of distributed computing.

Sublinear-Time Quantum Computation of the Diameter in CONGEST Networks

François Le Gall
Graduate School of Informatics, Kyoto University
Kyoto, Japan
legall@i.kyoto-u.ac.jp

Frédéric Magniez
IRIF, Univ. Paris Diderot, CNRS
Paris, France
magniez@irif.fr

ABSTRACT

The computation of the diameter is one of the most central problems in distributed computation. In the standard CONGEST model, in which two adjacent nodes can exchange $O(\log n)$ bits per round (here n denotes the number of nodes of the network), it is known that exact computation of the diameter requires $\tilde{\Omega}(n)$ rounds, even in networks with constant diameter. In this paper we investigate quantum distributed algorithms for this problem in the quantum CONGEST model, where two adjacent nodes can exchange $O(\log n)$ *quantum* bits per round. Our main result is a $\tilde{O}(\sqrt{nD})$-round quantum distributed algorithm for exact diameter computation, where D denotes the diameter. This shows a separation between the computational power of quantum and classical algorithms in the CONGEST model. We also show an unconditional lower bound $\tilde{\Omega}(\sqrt{n})$ on the round complexity of any quantum algorithm computing the diameter, and furthermore show a tight lower bound $\tilde{\Omega}(\sqrt{nD})$ for any distributed quantum algorithm in which each node can use only poly$(\log n)$ quantum bits of memory.

CCS CONCEPTS

• **Theory of computation** → **Quantum computation theory**; **Distributed algorithms**;

KEYWORDS

distributed algorithms, quantum computation, CONGEST model, graph algorithms

ACM Reference Format:

François Le Gall and Frédéric Magniez. 2018. Sublinear-Time Quantum Computation of the Diameter in CONGEST Networks. In *PODC '18: ACM Symposium on Principles of Distributed Computing, July 23–27, 2018, Egham, United Kingdom.* ACM, New York, NY, USA, 10 pages. https://doi.org/10.1145/3212734.3212744

1 INTRODUCTION

Diameter computation in CONGEST networks. The computation of the diameter is one of the most fundamental problems in distributed computing. In CONGEST networks, in which communication between nodes occurs with round-based synchrony and each channel has only $O(\log n)$-bit bandwidth, where n denotes the number of nodes of the network, the diameter can be computed in $O(n)$ rounds [15, 24]. A matching lower bound $\tilde{\Omega}(n)$ has been first shown by Frischknecht et al. [12],[1] which also holds for sparse networks [2] and even for deciding whether the network has diameter 2 or diameter 3 [15]. The latter result immediately implies (see also [2, 6]) that any distributed algorithm that computes a $(3/2-\varepsilon)$-approximation of the diameter, for any constant $\varepsilon > 0$, requires $\tilde{\Omega}(n)$ rounds.

If larger approximation ratios are allowed, however, sublinear-time[2] approximation algorithms can be constructed. First note that a 2-approximation of the diameter can trivially be computed in $O(D)$ rounds, where D denotes the diameter of the graph, by computing the eccentricity of any node. Much more interestingly, Lenzen and Peleg constructed a $O(\sqrt{n}\log n + D)$-round 3/2-approximation algorithm [21], which was improved by Holzer et al. to $O(\sqrt{n\log n}+D)$ rounds [14].

Quantum distributed computing. While it is well known that quantum communication can offer significant advantages over classical communication in several settings such as two-party communication complexity (see, e.g., [7, 9, 28]), there are relatively few results directly relevant to distributed network computation. One first evidence of the potential of quantum distributed computing was the design of exact quantum protocols for leader election [27]. Gavoille et al. [13] then considered quantum distributed computing in the LOCAL model, and showed that for several fundamental problems, allowing quantum communication does not lead to any significant advantage. The power of distributed network computation in the CONGEST model has recently been investigated by Elkin et al. [11]. In this model the nodes can use quantum processing and communicate using quantum bits (qubits): each edge of the network corresponds to a quantum channel (e.g., an optical fiber if qubits are implemented using photons) of bandwidth $O(\log n)$ qubits. The main conclusions reached in that paper were that for many fundamental problems in distributed computing, such as computing minimum spanning trees or minimum cuts, quantum communication does not, again, offer significant advantages over classical communication. The main technical contribution of [11] was the introduction of techniques to prove lower bound for quantum distributed computation, which is significantly more challenging than proving lower bounds in the classical setting due to several specific properties of quantum information, such as quantum non-locality

PODC '18, July 23–27, 2018, Egham, United Kingdom

ACM ISBN 978-1-4503-5795-1/18/07...$15.00
https://doi.org/10.1145/3212734.3212744

[1]In this paper the notation $\tilde{O}(\cdot)$ suppresses poly$(\log n)$ factors, and the notation $\tilde{\Omega}(\cdot)$ suppresses $\frac{1}{\mathrm{poly}(\log n)}$ factors.

[2]As usual when discussing algorithms in the CONGEST model, the *time complexity* of an algorithm refers to its round complexity. A sublinear-time algorithm means a $O(n^{1-\delta})$-round algorithm for some constant $\delta > 0$.

Problem	Classical	Quantum	
Exact computation	$O(n)$ [15, 24]	$O(\sqrt{nD})$	Th. 1.1
Exact computation	$\tilde{\Omega}(n)$ [12]	$\tilde{\Omega}(\sqrt{n}+D)$ $\tilde{\Omega}(\sqrt{nD/s}+D)$	Th. 1.2 Th. 1.3
$\frac{3}{2}$-approximation	$\tilde{O}(\sqrt{n}+D)$ [14, 21]	$\tilde{O}(\sqrt[3]{nD}+D)$	Th. 1.4
$(\frac{3}{2}-\varepsilon)$-approximation	$\tilde{\Omega}(n)$ [2, 6, 15]	$\tilde{\Omega}(\sqrt{n}+D)$	Th. 1.2

Table 1: Our results on the quantum round complexity of computing/approximating the diameter, and the corresponding known classical results. In this table n denotes the number of nodes in the network, D denotes the diameter and s denotes the quantum memory used by each node.

and the impossibility of "copying" quantum information. A pressing open question is to understand for which important problems in distributed computing quantum communication can help.

Our results. In this work we consider quantum distributed network computation in the CONGEST model, and especially investigate the complexity of computing the diameter. Our main contributions are for the exact computation of the diameter. We present the first quantum distributed algorithm that overcomes classical algorithms for this task:

Theorem 1.1. *There exists a $\tilde{O}(\sqrt{nD})$-round quantum distributed algorithm, in which each node uses $O((\log n)^2)$ qubits of memory, that computes with probability at least $1-1/poly(n)$ the diameter of the network, where n denotes the number of nodes of the network and D denotes the diameter.*

Theorem 1.1 shows in particular that if the diameter is small (constant or at most polylogarithmic in n), then it can be computed in $\tilde{O}(\sqrt{n})$ time in the quantum setting. Moreover, whenever the diameter is $O(n^{1-\delta})$ for some constant $\delta > 0$, it can be computed in sublinear time. This significantly contrasts with the classical setting, where even distinguishing if the diameter is 2 or 3 requires $\tilde{\Omega}(n)$ time [15], as already mentioned. Note that our quantum algorithm uses only $O((\log n)^2)$ space, i.e., each node only needs to keep $O((\log n)^2)$ qubits of memory at any step of the computation. This low space complexity is especially appealing due to the technological challenges to construct large-scale quantum memory.

A natural question is whether the upper bounds of Theorem 1.1 can further be improved. We first show the following lower bound by adapting the argument from prior works that lead to the classical lower bound [15].

Theorem 1.2. *Any quantum distributed algorithm that decides, with probability at least 2/3, whether the diameter of the network is at most 2 or at least 3 requires $\tilde{\Omega}(\sqrt{n})$ rounds.*

Note that this result holds even for quantum algorithms with an arbitrary amount of memory. Theorem 1.2 shows that the upper bound of Theorem 1.1 is tight for networks with small diameter. A similar argument can actually be used to derive a $\tilde{\Omega}(\sqrt{n})$ lower bound for any quantum algorithm that decides if the diameter is at most d or at least $d+1$ for larger values of d, but for large diameters this does not match the upper bound of Theorem 1.1. We succeed in proving another lower bound, which matches the upper bound of Theorem 1.1 for large diameters, under the assumption that the nodes in the distributed quantum algorithm use only small space. This is one of the main technical contributions of the paper.

Theorem 1.3. *Any quantum distributed algorithm, in which each node uses at most s qubits of memory, computing with probability at least 2/3 the diameter of the network requires $\tilde{\Omega}(\sqrt{nD/s})$ rounds.*

Observe that Theorems 1.1 and 1.3 together completely (up to possible polylogarithmic factor) settle the complexity of distributed quantum exact computation of the diameter with small quantum memory. While the memory restriction in the lower bound is a significant assumption, we believe that Theorem 1.3 is still a fairly general result since most known quantum communication protocols (e.g., protocols used to show the superiority of quantum communication in the model of communication complexity) use only a polylogarithmic amount of quantum memory. We actually conjecture that the upper bound of Theorem 1.1 is tight even without any restriction on the size of quantum memory used by the nodes.

We then consider approximation algorithms and show that the round complexity can be further decreased if we are only interested in computing a 3/2-approximation of the diameter.

Theorem 1.4. *There exists a $\tilde{O}(\sqrt[3]{nD}+D)$-round quantum distributed algorithm that computes with probability at least $1-1/poly(n)$ a 3/2-approximation of the diameter of the network.*

Whenever the diameter is small, this quantum approximation algorithm again provides a significant improvement over the best known classical algorithms [14, 21] already mentioned. The quantum algorithm of Theorem 1.4 actually consists of two phases, one classical and one quantum. The quantum phase still has polylogarithmic memory per node.

Our results are summarized in Table 1.

2 PRELIMINARIES

We assume that the reader is familiar with the basic notions of quantum computation and refer to, e.g., [23] for a good introduction. A quantum state will be written using the ket notation such as $|\psi\rangle$. A quantum register means a set of quantum bits (qubits). When the system has several identified registers, we indicate them as a subscript. For instance $|i\rangle_R|j\rangle_Q$, means that register R is in state $|i\rangle$, and register Q in state $|j\rangle$. Of course those could be entangled and in superposition. Then we write $|\psi\rangle = \sum_{i,j} \alpha_{ij}|i\rangle_R|j\rangle_Q$.

In this paper we will use the term *CNOT copy* to refer to the unitary operation on $2m$ qubits (for some integer m) that maps the state $|u\rangle|v\rangle$ to the state $|u\rangle|u \oplus v\rangle$ for any binary strings $u, v \in \{0,1\}^m$, where $u \oplus v$ is the bitwise XOR operation on u and v. This quantum operation can be implemented by applying m Controlled NOT gates. In particular it maps the state $|u\rangle|0\rangle$, for any binary string u, to the state $|u\rangle|u\rangle$, and thus corresponds to a classical copy.

For any integer M, we denote by $[M]$ the set $\{1, 2, \ldots, M\}$. For an undirected graph $G = (V, E)$, we write $d(u, v)$ the distance between $u, v \in V$, i.e., the minimum length of a path between u and v in G. The *eccentricity* of $u \in V$, denoted $\mathrm{ecc}(u)$, is the maximum distance of u to any other node $v \in V$. Then the *diameter* D is simply the maximum eccentricity among all nodes $u \in V$. Finally, the Breath First Search tree from u on G is denoted by $\mathsf{BFS}(u)$ and the Depth First Search tree is denoted $\mathsf{DFS}(u)$.

2.1 Quantum CONGEST networks

In this paper we consider the CONGEST communication model. The graph $G = (V, E)$ represents the topology of the network, executions proceed with round-based synchrony and each node can transfer one message of bw qubits to each adjacent node per round. Initially the nodes of the network do not share any entanglement. In this paper all the networks are undirected and unweighted. Unless explicitly mentioned, the bandwidth bw will always be $\mathrm{bw} = O(\log n)$, where $n = |V|$. The only exception is the results in Section 6.1, and in particular Theorem 6.1, where the bandwidth will be kept as a parameter. All links and nodes (corresponding to the edges and vertices of G, respectively) are reliable and suffer no faults. Each node has a distinct identifier. Initially, each node knows nothing about the topology of the network except the set of edges incident to itself and the value n.

We write $|\psi\rangle_v$ to denote a state in the memory space of node v. When such a state is entangled, we use the tensor product notation. For instance $\frac{1}{\sqrt{M}} \sum_{i\in[M]} \bigotimes_{v\in V} |i\rangle_v$ denotes a uniform superposition over integers in $[M]$ distributed over all nodes of V (i.e., each node is synchronized with the same value, in superposition).

When discussing the space complexity of quantum distributed algorithms, the memory refers to the number of qubits each node uses in its workspace. We assume for simplicity that each node performs unitary operations and measures its register only at the very end of the algorithm.[3]

2.2 Two-party communication complexity

Let X, Y and Z be three finite sets. Consider two players, usually called Alice and Bob, and assume that Alice receives as input an element $x \in X$, while Bob receives an element $y \in Y$. In the model of communication complexity, first introduced in the classical two-party setting by Yao [29], the players want to compute a function $f : X \times Y \to Z$ by running a protocol such that, at the end of the protocol, both Alice and Bob obtain $f(x, y)$, and they want to minimize the communication. In the quantum communication model, introduced by Yao [30], the players are allowed to communicate with qubits. More precisely, the quantum communication complexity of a quantum protocol is the maximum (over all inputs) number of qubits that the protocol sends. The quantum communication complexity of f is the minimum communication complexity of any quantum protocol that computes f with probability at least 2/3.

For any integer $n \geq 1$, the disjointness function $\mathrm{DISJ}_k : \{0,1\}^k \times \{0,1\}^k \to \{0,1\}$ is the function such that $\mathrm{DISJ}_k(x, y) = 0$ if and only if there exists an index $i \in \{1, \ldots, k\}$ such that $x_i = y_i = 1$. It is well known that its (randomized) classical communication complexity is $\Theta(k)$ bits [18, 25]. Its quantum communication complexity is $\Theta(\sqrt{k})$ qubits [1, 8, 16, 26]. Recently Braverman et al. [5] proved the following lower bound for quantum protocol with limited interaction, i.e., when only a bounded number of messages can be exchanged between Alice and Bob, which significantly improved the previous bound from [17]

THEOREM 2.1 ([5]). *The r-message quantum communication complexity of DISJ_k is $\tilde{\Omega}(k/r + r)$.*

This result shows in particular that any $O(\sqrt{k})$-qubit quantum protocol for DISJ_k requires $\tilde{\Omega}(\sqrt{k})$ messages, i.e., $\tilde{\Omega}(\sqrt{k})$ rounds of interaction between Alice and Bob.

2.3 Quantum generic search

We now review the general framework of quantum generic search in the centralized model (see for instance [22] for a more thorough treatment). In this framework, we are given a set of items X and we are looking for a marked item $x \in M$, for some unknown subset $M \subseteq X$. We have two main black-box unitary operators, and their inverses, available to design a quantum search procedure. The first one, Setup, is the quantum analogue of a random sampling. The second one, Checking, is a quantum checking procedure.

It will be convenient to assume the existence of a third procedure, Initialization, that performs some global initialization: the procedure is applied only once at the beginning of the algorithm and its output is later used in order to implement Setup and Checking.

We identify a specific register $|\cdot\rangle_I$ that we call *internal*, which is the core of the algorithm. Its size is polylogarithmic in all parameters. It is used to encode the element we are looking for, to perform basic operations such as arithmetic operations (e.g., counting), and also to control the application of other unitary matrices. The quantum algorithm uses two additional registers to represent additional information created by the procedures Initialization and Setup.

The framework thus assumes that the following three quantum procedures are given (as black-boxes).

Initialization: Creates an initial state $|0\rangle_I|\mathrm{init}\rangle$ with some possible precomputed information $|\mathrm{init}\rangle$ and a distinguished element $0 \in X$, usually a long enough bit string of 0s.

Setup: Produces a superposition from the initial state:

$$|0\rangle_I|\mathrm{init}\rangle \mapsto \sum_{x\in X} \alpha_x |x\rangle_I |\mathrm{data}(x)\rangle |\mathrm{init}\rangle,$$

where the α_x's are arbitrary amplitudes and data(x) represents some information depending on x.

Checking: Performs the transformation

$$|x, 0\rangle_I |\mathrm{data}(x)\rangle |\mathrm{init}\rangle \mapsto |x, b_x\rangle_I |\mathrm{data}(x)\rangle |\mathrm{init}\rangle,$$

where $b_x = 1$ if $x \in M$ and $b_x = 0$ otherwise.

[3]More general models, such as models allowing intermediate measurements and models that allow nodes to use both a quantum memory and a classical memory, can naturally be considered as well. We prefer not introducing such models in this paper since the precise definition (and in particular the relation between the classical part and the quantum part), which can for instance be proposed similarly to [19], would be fairly technical. We just mention that under natural "hybrid" models allowing both classical and quantum parts, the lower bound of Theorem 1.3 would hold for any quantum algorithm that uses s qubits of quantum memory, independently to the quantity of classical memory used, since the difficulty only comes from the quantum memory. A very simple example is the straightforward generalization of our model that allows a first classical phase with unbounded classical memory and then a quantum phase using only s qubits of memory per node.

Note that the procedures Initialization and Checking are often described as deterministic or randomized (i.e., classical) procedures. They can then been quantized using standard techniques: one first transforms it to a reversible map using standard techniques [3], with potentially additional garbage whose size is of the same order as the initial memory space.

Define $P_M = \sum_{x \in M} |\alpha_x|^2$, the probability to observe a marked element when measuring Register I after one application of Setup on the initial state. Classically one could iterate $\Theta(1/P_M)$ time this process in order to get at least one marked element with high probability. Amplitude amplification explains how to get a marked element using simply $\Theta(1/\sqrt{P_M})$ iterations of Setup and Checking.

Theorem 2.2 (Amplitude amplification [4]). *Let $\varepsilon > 0$ and assume that either $P_M = 0$ or $P_M \geq \varepsilon$ holds. Then, for any $\delta > 0$, there is a quantum algorithm that can decide if $M = \emptyset$ with success probability at least $1 - \delta$ using one unitary operator* Initialization, *$O(\sqrt{\log(1/\delta)/\varepsilon})$ unitary operators* Setup *and* Checking, *their inverse, and $O(\sqrt{\log(1/\delta)/\varepsilon})$ other basic operations (independent of M) on the internal register.*

More precisely, an observation of the internal register when the algorithm declares that $M \neq \emptyset$, outputs a random $x \in M$ with probability $|\alpha_x|^2/P_M$.

2.4 Distributed quantum optimization

Let us first explain how to derive a generic quantum procedure for optimization problems in the centralized model. Indeed, a well known application of amplitude amplification is optimization, such as minimum finding [10]. We are now given a procedure Evaluation instead of Checking, which evaluates the (unknown) function we want to maximize.

Evaluation: Performs the transformation

$$|x, 0\rangle_I |\text{data}(x)\rangle |\text{init}\rangle \mapsto |x, f(x)\rangle_I |\text{data}(x)\rangle |\text{init}\rangle,$$

where $f : X \to \mathbb{Z}$ is the function we want to maximize.

Define the probability P_{opt} to observe an element where f takes a maximum value when measuring Register I after one application of Setup on the initial state as

$$P_{\text{opt}} = \sum_{x: f(x) \text{ is maximal}} |\alpha_x|^2.$$

A standard application of amplitude amplification shows how to maximize f using $\Theta(1/\sqrt{P_{\text{opt}}})$ iterations of Setup and Evaluation. We state this result as follows.

Corollary 2.3 (Quantum optimization). *Let $\varepsilon > 0$ be such that $P_{\text{opt}} \geq \varepsilon$. Then, for any $\delta > 0$, there is a quantum algorithm that can find, with probability at least $1 - \delta$, some element x such that $f(x)$ is maximum, using one unitary operator* Initialization, *$O(\sqrt{\log(1/\delta)/\varepsilon})$ unitary operators* Setup *and* Evaluation, *and their inverses, and $O(\sqrt{\log(1/\delta)/\varepsilon})$ other basic operations (independent of f) on the internal register.*

Proof. The proof uses standard applications of Theorem 2.2 such as in [10]. We give the main lines of the reduction:

(1) Start with some fixed $a \in X$;
(2) Use amplitude amplification of Theorem 2.2 with $\varepsilon' = 1/2$ and $\delta' = \delta$ to find $b > a$;
(3) If an element is found, then set $a = b$ and go to (2);
(4) Else if $\varepsilon' > \varepsilon$, then set $\varepsilon' = \varepsilon'/2$ and go to (2);
(5) Output a and stop.

The expected number of iterations, that is of jumps to Step (2), can be shown to be $O(\log(1/\varepsilon))$, with an expected number of applications of unitary maps and of other basic operations in $O(\sqrt{\log(1/\delta)/\varepsilon})$ using similar arguments to [10] for minimum finding. In order to get the claimed worst case bounds, one just need to abort the computation when too much resources have been used and to output the current value of a. □

We now explain how to implement quantum optimization in the distributed model. In the distributed setting, the internal register I and therefore the control of the algorithm itself are simply centralized by a leader node. The two other registers $|\text{data}(x)\rangle$ and $|\text{init}\rangle$, however, can be distributed among all the nodes of the network, and implementing Procedures Setup and Evaluation thus generally requires communication through the network. As stated in Corollary 2.3, besides calls to Setup and Evaluation and their inverses, all the other operations performed in quantum optimization are done exclusively on the internal register I, and then can be implemented locally (i.e., without communication) by the chosen leader node. The round complexity of distributed quantum optimization thus depends on the round complexity of Procedures Setup and Evaluation. The precise statement follows.

Theorem 2.4 (Distributed quantum optimization). *Let $G = (V, E)$ be a distributed network with a predefined node* leader $\in V$. *Assume that* Initialization *can be implemented within T_0 rounds and using s memory per node in the quantum CONGEST model, and that unitary operators* Setup *and* Evaluation *and their inverses can be implemented within T rounds and using s memory per node. Assume that $s = \Omega(\log |X|)$.*

Let $\varepsilon > 0$ be such that $P_{\text{opt}} \geq \varepsilon$. Then, for any $\delta > 0$, the node leader *can find, with probability at least $1 - \delta$, some element x such that $f(x)$ is maximum, in $T_0 + O(\sqrt{\log(1/\delta)/\varepsilon}) \times T$ rounds. This quantum algorithm uses $O(s \times \log(1/\varepsilon))$ memory per node.*

Proof. The round complexity follows immediately from Corollary 2.3. Let us now analyze the amount of memory needed for the node leader. Since measurements in the procedure described in Corollary 2.3 are only performed at the end of the computation, all outcomes of amplitude amplification in Line (2) are recorded in the procedure, leading to an additional term $O(\log |X| \times \log(1/\varepsilon))$ in the memory size. The total amount of memory needed for the implementation is thus $O(s + \log |X| \times \log(1/\varepsilon)) = O(s \times \log(1/\varepsilon))$ qubits for leader and $O(s)$ qubits for the other nodes. □

3 FIRST ALGORITHM : EXACT COMPUTATION OF THE DIAMETER

Let $G = (V, E)$ denote the network we consider. We write $n = |V|$ and use D to denote its diameter. We assume that the network G has elected a node leader $\in V$, and computed its eccentricity ecc(leader). This can be done using standard methods in $O(D)$ classical rounds and $O(\log n)$ memory space per node. In addition, our

> **In ecc(leader) = $O(D)$ rounds:**
> (1) First, only leader is activated, it declares itself as its own parent, and sends a message through all its edges in order to activate its neighbors for the next round.
> (2) When a message reaches node v from node u:
> - If v was already activated, then v ignores the message.
> - Else v becomes activated, it sets its parent to u and sends, through all its edges, its distance to leader in order to activate its neighbors for the next round.

Figure 1: Construction of BFS(leader) in Proposition 3.1.

algorithm will use a Breadth First Search tree rooted at leader (denoted BFS(leader)), which can be computed efficiently as described in the following proposition.

Proposition 3.1. *There is a classical procedure that allocates to each node $v \in V$ its parent on* BFS(leader) *and its distance to* leader *in $O(D)$ rounds and $O(\log n)$ memory space per node.*

Proof. The procedure is the classical procedure described in Figure 1 that performs a Breadth First Search tree from leader. This procedure has complexity $O(D)$ and can be implemented with $O(\log n)$ bits of memory per node. □

Our quantum algorithm will compute the diameter, i.e., the maximum eccentricity among all nodes, using quantum optimization. In Section 3.1, we first give a simpler quantum algorithm that computes the diameter in $O(\sqrt{n}D)$ rounds. In Section 3.2 we then give our $O(\sqrt{nD})$-round quantum algorithm.

3.1 A simpler quantum algorithm

We apply the framework of Section 2.4 with $X = V$ and the function $f : V \to \mathbb{Z}$ defined for all $u \in V$ as

$$f(u) = \mathrm{ecc}(u) \qquad (1)$$

Obviously, maximizing f gives the diameter of the network.

Procedure Initialization is the classical procedure of Proposition 3.1. This means that $|\mathrm{init}\rangle$ represents the classical information computed by this classical procedure: this is a quantum register shared by all the nodes of the network, in which the part owned by each node contains its parent on BFS(leader) and its distance to leader.

For any $u_0 \in V$, the quantum state $|\mathrm{data}(u_0)\rangle$ used in the quantum algorithm is defined as $|\mathrm{data}(u_0)\rangle = \bigotimes_{v\in V} |u_0\rangle_v$. We set $\alpha_{u_0} = 1/\sqrt{n}$ for all $u_0 \in V$, and thus have $P_{\mathrm{opt}} \geq 1/n$. We first observe that Procedure Setup can be implemented efficiently.

Proposition 3.2. *The procedure* Setup *can be implemented in $O(D)$ rounds and using $O(\log n)$ memory space per node.*

Proof. The node leader first prepares the quantum state

$$\frac{1}{\sqrt{n}} \sum_{u_0 \in V} |u_0\rangle_{\mathrm{leader}}.$$

Then this state is simply broadcast using CNOT copies to all nodes of the network along BFS(leader), which takes d rounds. The resulting state is

$$\frac{1}{\sqrt{n}} \sum_{u_0 \in V} |u_0\rangle_{\mathrm{leader}} \bigotimes_{v\in V} |u_0\rangle_v = \frac{1}{\sqrt{n}} \sum_{u_0 \in V} |u_0\rangle_{\mathrm{leader}} |\mathrm{data}(u_0)\rangle,$$

as required. □

We now observe that Procedure Evaluation can also be implemented efficiently.

Proposition 3.3. *The procedure* Evaluation *for the function f defined in* (1) *can be implemented in $O(D)$ rounds and using $O(\log n)$ memory space.*

Proof. Consider the following problem: all the nodes of the network receive as input u_0, for some fixed $u_0 \in V$, and the goal is for node leader to output $\mathrm{ecc}(u_0)$. There is a straightforward $O(D)$-round classical algorithm solving this problem using $O(\log n)$ bits of memory per node: node u_0 starts building a Breadth First Search tree rooted at u_0, the nodes use this tree to compute their distance to u_0, and finally $\mathrm{ecc}(u_0)$ is transmitted to the node leader. Note that this algorithm is precisely a procedure to compute $f(u_0)$ when the nodes initially share the classical information contained in $|\mathrm{data}(u_0)\rangle$ (i.e., the nodes all know u_0). As mentioned in Section 2.3, this procedure can then been quantized using standard techniques in order to obtain a quantum algorithm that performs the transformation

$$|u_0, 0\rangle_I |\mathrm{data}(u_0)\rangle |\mathrm{init}\rangle \mapsto |u_0, f(u_0)\rangle_I |\mathrm{data}(u_0)\rangle |\mathrm{init}\rangle,$$

with the same round and space complexities. □

We are now ready to analyze the overall complexity of our algorithm. We apply Theorem 2.4 to maximize the function f defined in (1). Propositions 3.1, 3.2 and 3.3, along with the lower bound $P_{\mathrm{opt}} \geq 1/n$, show that this quantum algorithm uses $O(\sqrt{n}D)$ rounds and $O((\log n)^2)$ memory per node for any constant error probability δ.

3.2 The final quantum algorithm

We now show how to reduce the complexity to $O(\sqrt{nD})$. The key idea is to modify the function to be maximized, in order to increase P_{opt} when d is large. Before defining the new function, let us introduce some definitions.

We take some integer d such that $d \leq D \leq 2d$. Since $\mathrm{ecc}(v) \leq D \leq 2 \times \mathrm{ecc}(v)$ for any node $v \in V$, this will concretely be done by choosing $d = \mathrm{ecc}(\mathrm{leader})$. Similarly to [24], we introduce the following numbering on the vertices of G via a Depth-First-Search traversal of BFS(leader).

Definition 3.4 (DFS-*numbering*). The DFS(leader)-*number* of $v \in V$, denoted by $\tau(v)$, is the length of the path to reach v from leader on a DFS-traversal of BFS(leader). In particular $\tau(\mathrm{leader}) = 0$.

We now use the DFS-numbering to define sets of vertices.

Definition 3.5. For any $u \in V$, define $S(u) = \{v \in V : \tau(v) \in [\tau(u), \tau(u) + 2d \mod 2n]\}$. Let $\mathcal{S}$ be the collection of subsets $S(u)$ for all $u \in V$.

We following lemma, which will be crucial for our analysis, shows that $\mathcal{S}$ covers well the set V.

Lemma 3.6. *Fix any $v \in V$, and take some $u_0 \in V$ uniformly at random. Then $\Pr[v \in S(u_0)] \geq \frac{d}{2n}$.*

Proof. Consider a sequential execution π of DFS(leader) on BFS(leader). We now consider π as a circle by attaching its extremities. Observe that each top-down move to some node v at step t causes the numbering $\tau(v) = t$. In addition, since BFS(leader) has depth d, any segment of π with m_d top-down moves and m_u bottom-up ones must satisfy $|m_d - m_u| \leq d$.

Thus for any vertex $v \in V$, consider the part of π of length $2d$ ending in a top-down move to v. It must contain at least $\lceil d/2 \rceil$ top-down moves to some vertices $u_1, \ldots, u_{\lceil d/2 \rceil}$. Therefore $v \in S(u_i)$, for $i = 1, \ldots, \lceil d/2 \rceil$, and we conclude that $\Pr[v \in S(u_0)] \geq \frac{d}{2n}$. □

The function we will now optimize is the function $f\colon V \to \mathbb{Z}$ defined as

$$f(u) = \max_{v \in S(u)} (\mathrm{ecc}(v)) \qquad (2)$$

for any $u \in V$. Obviously, maximizing f gives the diameter of the network. We optimize this function via the distributed quantum optimization procedure of Section 2.4. We set X, α_x, $|\mathrm{init}\rangle$ and $|\mathrm{data}(x)\rangle$ exactly as in Section 3.1. Lemma 3.6 immediately implies that $P_{\mathrm{opt}} \geq d/2n$.

The procedures Initialization and Setup are the same as in Section 3.1. The procedure Evaluation, however, is different since the function to evaluate is not the same. We describe the new procedure, which is based on a refinement of the deterministic distributed algorithm for diameter in [24], in the next proposition. The proof of this proposition is postponed to Section 3.3.

Proposition 3.7. *The procedure* Evaluation *for the function f defined in (2) can be implemented in $O(D)$ rounds and using $O(\log n)$ memory space.*

We are now ready to analyze the overall complexity of our algorithm and prove Theorem 1.1.

Proof of Theorem 1.1. We apply Theorem 2.4 to maximize the function f defined in (2). Propositions 3.1, 3.2 and 3.7, along with the lower bound $P_{\mathrm{opt}} \geq d/2n$, show that this quantum algorithm uses $O(\sqrt{nD})$ rounds and $O((\log n)^2)$ memory per node for any constant error probability δ. □

3.3 The evaluation procedure

We prove Proposition 3.7 by describing the Procedure Evaluation for the function f defined in (2). Remember that this procedure should, for any $u_0 \in V$ given as input to all the nodes of the network, enable the node leader to output $f(u_0) = \max_{v \in S(u_0)}(\mathrm{ecc}(v))$. Remember also that we are assuming the each node $v \in V$ knows its parent on BFS(leader) and its distance to leader (this information was computed in Procedure Initialization).

The procedure Evaluation is described in Figure 2. (The procedure is described as a classical procedure. As mentioned in Section 2.3 and in the proof of Proposition 3.3, it can then been quantized using standard techniques.)

The main idea is simple: each node $v \in S(u_0)$ starts a process in order to globally compute its eccentricity. This will be done in parallel, and the main difficulty is to avoid congestions. We achieve this goal by refining techniques used in the deterministic distributed

Step 1. The network performs sequentially $2d$ steps of a Depth First Search traversal on BFS(leader) starting at u_0 (if it reaches the end of the DFS, it starts again from leader). Let us write S the nodes visited by the process, and for each $v \in S$, let $\tau'(v)$ to be the index of the round they are reached (for the first time) by the traversal.

Step 2. Each node $v \in V$ implements the following process during $6d$ rounds:

(1) Set $t_v = -1$ and $d_v = 0$.

(2) If $v \in S$ and only at round $2\tau'(v)$:
  Broadcast message $(\tau'(v), 0)$ along all edges (v, w).

(3) At each round:
  (a) Disregards all messages of type (τ', δ) with $\tau' \leq t_v$.
  (b) Keep at most one of the remaining messages of type (τ', δ) with $\tau' > t_v$.
  (In fact they are all equal according to Lemma 3.10.)
  If one message has been kept then:
    Set $t_v = \tau'$ and $d_v = \max(d_v, \delta)$.
    Broadcast message $(\tau', \delta + 1)$ along all edges (v, w) of G.

Step 3. Each node $v \in V$ sends its current value d_v to leader. In order to avoid congestions, the transmission is done bottom up on BFS(leader), and at each node only the maximum of received values is transmitted.

Step 4. Node leader computes the maximum of all received values.

Step 5. Revert steps 3 to 1, in order to clean all registers.

Figure 2: The procedure Evaluation.

algorithm from [24]. As in [24], we coordinate the starts of all the processes so that messages initiated by nodes $v \in S(u_0)$ arrive in the same order as their DFS(leader)-numbers. Therefore, there is no congestion, and messages to disregard are easily identified, even with a local memory of logarithmic size for each node.

A difference with [24] is that we do not use the DFS(leader)-number $\tau(v)$, which is too costly to compute, but instead the quantity $\tau'(v) = \tau(v) - \tau(u_0)$, which is much easier to compute, to coordinate the starts of the process. More precisely, node $v \in S(u_0)$ starts its process at round $2\tau'(v)$, see Step 2(2) of the algorithm.

Another difference is that each node v in Step 2 of the algorithm only keeps in memory the maximum of their previously computed distances. Nodes receive at each round messages of the form (τ', δ) that they either disregard or broadcast after incrementing δ. This message has been initiated at round τ' by the node $u \in S$ such that $\tau' = \tau'(u)$ in Step 2(2). The number δ is the number of rounds this message took to reach v for the first time, i.e., $\delta = d(u, v)$. The value t_v is used to decide which messages can be disregarded. The value d_v represents the maximum distance $d(u, v)$ over all the nodes u processed so far.

The procedure Evaluation can be implemented in $O(D)$ rounds and using $O(\log n)$ space per node since at any time each node only needs to keep one message (τ', δ), in addition to t_v and d_v, in memory. The correctness follows from the following three lemmas, which together show that the procedure computes the maximum of $\mathrm{ecc}(v)$ over all $v \in S(u_0)$.

LEMMA 3.8. *At Step 1, the computed set S satisfies $S = S(u_0)$. Furthermore, for every nodes $v, w \in S$, if $\tau'(v) < \tau'(w)$ then $d(v,w) \leq \tau'(w) - \tau'(v)$.*

PROOF. First observe that at Step 1, $\tau'(v) = \tau(v) - \tau(u_0)$, for all $v \in S(u_0)$. Therefore, the computed set S satisfies $S = S(u_0)$. Then the rest of the statement is a direct consequence of [24, Property 1] which was stated for the DFS(leader)-numbering τ, and therefore remains valid for τ since $\tau'(v) = \tau(v) - \tau(u_0)$, for all $v \in S(u_0)$. □

LEMMA 3.9. *Let r_1 be the first round that a message of type $(\tau'_1, *)$ reaches a given node v, and similarly for r_2 and τ'_2. Then $r_2 - r_1 \geq \tau'_2 - \tau'_1$. In particular, if $\tau'_1 < \tau'_2$ then $r_1 < r_2$.*

PROOF. Let z_1, z_2 be such that $\tau'_i = \tau'(z_i)$, for $i = 1, 2$. This is the first time that a message from z_i reaches v, therefore $r_i = 2\tau'(z_i) + d(z_i, v)$. In addition, by the triangle inequality, we also have that $d(z_1, v) - d(z_2, v) \leq d(z_1, z_2)$. Thus

$$d(z_1, z_2) \geq d(z_1, v) - d(z_2, v) = r_1 - r_2 + 2(\tau'(z_2) - \tau'(z_1)).$$

Since $\tau'(z_1) < \tau'(z_2)$, then by Lemma 3.8 we also have that

$$d(z_1, z_2) \leq \tau'(z_2) - \tau'(z_1).$$

Therefore we get

$$r_2 - r_1 \geq \tau'(z_2) - \tau'(z_1) > 0,$$

which proves the lemma. □

LEMMA 3.10. *At Step 3b, all remaining messages are identical.*

PROOF. Assume by contradiction that at least two messages (τ'_1, δ_1) and (τ'_2, δ_2) remain such that either $\tau'_1 \neq \tau'_2$ or $\delta_1 \neq \delta_2$. By construction of our algorithm, they are the first messages of types $(\tau'_1, *)$ and $(\tau'_2, *)$ reaching v.

If $\tau'_1 \neq \tau'_2$, by Lemma 3.9, those messages cannot arrive at the same round, which contradicts the fact they both arrive at the current round.

If $\tau'_1 = \tau'_2$, but $\delta_1 \neq \delta_2$, we get another contradiction. Indeed, those messages come from the same vertex u such that $\tau'(u) = \tau'_1$, and reach v at the same round for the first time. Thus they must satisfy $\delta_1 = \delta_2$. □

4 SECOND ALGORITHM: 3/2-APPROXIMATION OF THE DIAMETER

The framework for distributed quantum optimization we developed in this paper, and in particular its application to find vertices of maximum eccentricities presented in Section 3, can be used as well to design fast quantum approximation algorithms for the diameter. In this section we show how to apply our framework to speed up the 3/2 classical approximation algorithm designed in [14], which computes a value $\bar{D}$ such that $\bar{D} \leq D \leq 3\bar{D}/2$, and prove Theorem 1.4.

Our quantum algorithm for 3/2-approximation is described in Figure 3. In the description of the algorithm, $s \in [n]$ is an integer parameter that will be set later.

This quantum algorithm is exactly the same as Algorithm 1 in [14], except for the second part: in [14] the maximum eccentricity was computed classically in $O(s + D)$ rounds by computing a BFS tree for each vertex in R. We thus omit the details about the implementation of the first part and the proof of correctness of the whole algorithm (which can be found in [14]). Let us nevertheless point out that this first part requires a polynomial amount of (classical) memory. The quantum procedure for the second part we describe below, however, will only require a polylogarithmic amount of memory.

Preparation in $\tilde{O}(n/s + D)$ rounds. This part is the same as Steps 1 to 5 of Algorithm 1 in [14]:

(1) Each vertex joins a set S with probability $(\log n)/s$. If more than $(n(\log n)^2/s)$ vertices join S, then abort.
(2) Each vertex $v \in V$ computes the closest node in S to v, which is denoted $p(v)$. Compute a node $w \in V$ maximizing the distance $d(w, p(w))$.
(3) Compute a BFS tree from w. The s closest nodes to w in the tree join a set R.

Quantum optimization $\tilde{O}(\sqrt{sD} + D)$ rounds. Compute the maximum eccentricity of the vertices in R.

Output. Return the maximum computed eccentricity.

Figure 3: Our quantum algorithm computing a 3/2-approximation of the diameter.

The quantum procedure for the second part is essentially the same as the quantum algorithm presented in Section 3, which computed the maximum eccentricity of all the nodes in V (i.e., the diameter of the network). The difference is that this time we do the optimization only on the vertices in R: the function to optimize the function of Equation (2) restricted to the domain $R \subseteq V$. By replacing node leader by node w, and replacing "mod $2n$" by "mod $2s$" in Definition 3.5, we obtain $P_{\text{opt}} \geq d/2s$ instead $P_{\text{opt}} \geq d/2n$ since R is defined as the set of the s closest nodes to w. By additionally modifying the procedure Setup so that it distributes the state $\frac{1}{\sqrt{s}} \sum_{u_0 \in R} \bigotimes_{v \in V} |u_0\rangle_v$ instead of $\frac{1}{\sqrt{n}} \sum_{u_0 \in V} \bigotimes_{v \in V} |u_0\rangle_v$, Theorem 2.4 implies that the maximum eccentricity of the vertices in R can be computed with high probability in $\tilde{O}(\sqrt{sD} + D)$ rounds and using $O((\log n)^2)$ qubits of memory per node.

The overall round complexity of our algorithm is $\tilde{O}(n/s + \sqrt{ns} + D)$. Choosing $s = \Theta(n^{2/3}D^{-1/3})$ gives complexity $\tilde{O}(\sqrt[3]{nD} + D)$, as claimed in Theorem 1.4.

5 LOWER BOUND: TIGHT BOUND FOR SMALL DIAMETER

In this section we show that the connection established in prior works (in particular in [2, 6, 12, 15]) between the round complexity of computing the diameter and the two-party communication complexity of the disjointness function still holds in the quantum setting. We then use this connection to prove Theorem 1.2.

In the following we will use the notation $G = (U, V, E)$ to denote a bipartite graph whose partition has parts U and V: it will always be implicitly assumed that the sets U and V are disjoint, and that each edge in E has an endpoint in U and its other endpoint in V. We will use $\Delta(G)$ to denote the largest distance between one vertex in U and one vertex of V. We will use $\mathcal{E}(U)$ to denote the set of all pairs of elements in U and $\mathcal{E}(V)$ to denote the set of all pairs of elements in V.

All the recent lower bounds on the classical round complexity of computing or approximating the diameter rely on the notion of reduction introduced in the next definition.

Definition 5.1. Let b, k, d_1 and d_2 be four functions from $\mathbb{N}$ to $\mathbb{N}$. A (b, k, d_1, d_2)-reduction from disjointness to diameter computation is a family of triples $\{(G_n, g_n, h_n)\}_{n\geq 1}$ such that, for each $n \geq 1$, $G_n = (U_n, V_n, E_n)$ is a bipartite graph with $|U_n \cup V_n| = n$ and $|E_n| = b$, g_n is a function from $\{0,1\}^k$ to $\mathcal{E}(U_n)$ and h_n is a function from $\{0,1\}^k$ to $\mathcal{E}(V_n)$ satisfying the following two conditions for any $x, y \in \{0,1\}^k$:

(i) if $\mathrm{DISJ}_k(x, y) = 1$ then $\Delta(G_n(x, y)) \leq d_1$,
(ii) if $\mathrm{DISJ}_k(x, y) = 0$ then $\Delta(G_n(x, y)) \geq d_2$,

where $G_n(x, y)$ denotes the bipartite graph obtained from G_n by adding an edge $\{w, w'\}$ for each $\{w, w'\} \in g_n(x) \cup h_n(y)$.

In particular we will use in this paper the following two constructions from prior works.

Theorem 5.2 ([15]). *There exists a $(\Theta(n), \Theta(n^2), 2, 3)$-reduction from disjointness to diameter computation.*

Theorem 5.3 ([2]). *There exists a $(\Theta(\log n), \Theta(n), 4, 5)$-reduction from disjointness to diameter computation.*

An easy argument, used in all these prior works mentioned above, shows that the existence of a (b, k, d_1, d_2)-reduction from disjointness to diameter computation implies a $\tilde{\Omega}(k/b)$ lower bound on the round complexity of any classical distributed algorithm that decides whether the diameter of the network is at most d_1 or at least d_2. The main technical contribution of this section is the following quantum version of this argument, which is proved using the recent result from [5] on the message-bounded quantum communication complexity of disjointness presented in Section 2.2.

Theorem 5.4. *Assume that there exists a (b, k, d_1, d_2)-reduction from disjointness to diameter computation. Then any quantum distributed algorithm that decides, with high probability, whether the diameter of the network is at most d_1 or at least d_2 requires $\tilde{\Omega}(\sqrt{k/b})$ rounds.*

Proof. Assume that there exists an r-round quantum algorithm $\mathcal{A}$ that decides if the diameter of a network is at most d_1 or at least d_2. We will use this algorithm to construct a protocol that computes the disjointness function DISJ_k in the two-party quantum communication complexity setting. Let $x \in \{0,1\}^k$ and $y \in \{0,1\}^k$ be Alice's input and Bob's input, respectively.

The protocol works as follows. First note that Alice and Bob can jointly construct the graph $G_n(x, y)$: Alice can construct the subgraph induced by U_n (which depends on x), while Bob can construct the subgraph induced by V_n (which depends on y). Alice and Bob will thus simply simulate the computation of $\mathcal{A}$ on $G_n(x, y)$. To do this, they only need to exchange messages corresponding to the communication occurring along the b edges of $G_n(x, y)$ at each round of Algorithm $\mathcal{A}$. This can be done by replacing one round of communication in $\mathcal{A}$ by two messages of $O(b \log n)$ qubits (one from Alice to Bob, and the other from Bob to Alice). At the end of simulation Alice and Bob obtain the result of the computation by $\mathcal{A}$ on $G_n(x, y)$. From our assumption on $\mathcal{A}$, this enables them to decide if the diameter of $G_n(x, y)$ is at most d_1 or at least d_2, and thus to compute $\mathrm{DISJ}_k(x, y)$. The whole simulation uses $2r$ messages and a total number of $O(rb \log n)$ qubits of communication. From Theorem 2.1, we conclude that $rb = \tilde{\Omega}\left(\frac{k}{r} + r\right)$, which implies $r = \tilde{\Omega}(\sqrt{k/b})$. □

Theorem 1.2 directly follows by combining Theorem 5.2 and Theorem 5.4.

6 LOWER BOUND: CASE OF LARGE DIAMETER

In this section we prove Theorem 1.3. We first prove in Section 6.1 a general simulation result that will be crucial for our analysis, and then give the proof of Theorem 1.3 in Section 6.2.

6.1 Simulation argument

For any $d \geq 1$, let us introduce the following network $\mathcal{G}_d$. The network consists of two nodes A and B connected by a path of length $d+1$, corresponding to d intermediate nodes $P_1, \ldots, P_d$. The total number of nodes is thus $d+2$, and the number of edges is $d+1$. Each edge of $\mathcal{G}_d$ is a quantum channel of bandwidth bw qubits. The construction is illustrated in Figure 4.

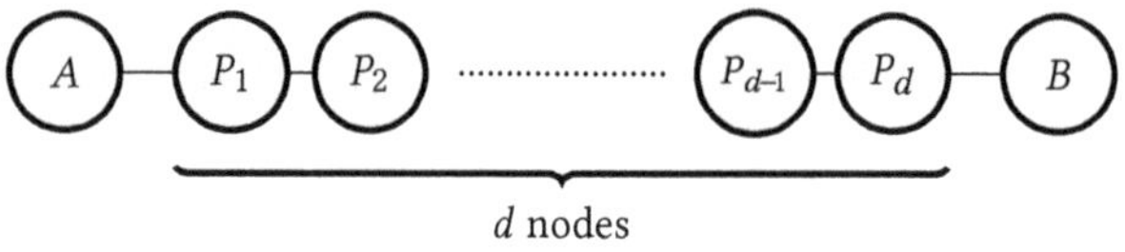

Figure 4: The graph $\mathcal{G}_d$.

Let X, Y be two finite sets, and let f be a function from $X \times Y$ to $\{0,1\}$. Consider the following computation problem over the network $\mathcal{G}_d$: node A receives an input $x \in X$ and node B receives an input $y \in Y$. The goal is for Alice and Bob to compute the value $f(x, y)$. Note that the intermediate nodes $P_1, \ldots, P_d$ do not receive any input. The following theorem relates the round complexity of this problem to the two-party communication complexity of f.

Theorem 6.1. *Let d and r be any positive integers, and f be any Boolean function. If there exists an r-round quantum distributed algorithm, in which each intermediate node uses at most s qubits of memory, that computes function f with probability p over $\mathcal{G}_d$, then there exists a $O(r/d)$-message two-party quantum protocol computing f with probability p using $O(r(\mathrm{bw} + s))$ qubits of communication.*

Proof. Consider any r-round quantum algorithm $\mathcal{A}$ computing function f over $\mathcal{G}_d$ in which each intermediate node uses s qubits of internal memory. For notational convenience, we will use P_0 and P_{d+1} to refer to nodes A and B, respectively. For any $i \in \{0, 1, \ldots, d+1\}$, let R_i denote the quantum register representing the memory of node P_i. Note that if $1 \leq i \leq d$ then R_i consists of at most s qubits, which we assume (without loss of generality) are initially in the all-zero quantum state. The registers R_0 and R_{d+1}

contain the input x and y, respectively, in addition to qubits initially in the all-zero quantum state.

For simplify notations, we will make the following assumption: at each round $t \in \{1, \ldots, r\}$ of the algorithm $\mathcal{A}$, if t is odd then messages are sent only from the left to the right (i.e, from P_i to P_{i+1} for each $i \in \{0, \ldots, d\}$), and if t is even then messages are sent only from the right to the left (i.e, from P_i to P_{i-1} for each $i \in \{1, \ldots, d+1\}$). This can be done without loss of generality since any algorithm can be converted into an algorithm satisfying this assumption by increasing the round complexity only by a factor 2. Without loss of generality, again, we can also assume that Algorithm $\mathcal{A}$ proceeds as follows (see the full version of the present paper [20] for an illustration for $d = 2$ and $r = 8$):

- Each node P_i, for $i \in \{0, \ldots, d\}$, initially owns one additional b-qubit quantum register T_i containing the all-zero quantum state.
- At the first round, for each $i \in \{0, \ldots, d\}$, node P_i performs a unitary operator on $(\mathsf{R}_i, \mathsf{T}_i)$, and then sends T_i to P_{i+1}. (Note that the contents of the register T_i can be — and will in general be — modified by the unitary operator.) Node P_{d+1} does nothing.
- At round number $t \in \{2, \ldots, r\}$ with t even, for each $i \in \{1, \ldots, d+1\}$ node P_i, who just received register T_{i-1} from P_{i-1} at the previous round, performs a unitary operator on $(\mathsf{R}_i, \mathsf{T}_{i-1})$, and then sends T_{i-1} to P_{i-1}. Node P_0 does nothing.
- At round number $t \in \{3, \ldots, r\}$ with t odd, for each $i \in \{0, \ldots, d\}$ node P_i, who just received register T_i from P_{i+1} at the previous round, performs a unitary operator on $(\mathsf{R}_i, \mathsf{T}_i)$, and then sends T_i to P_{i+1}. Node P_{d+1} does nothing.
- After round number r (the last round of communication), each node performs a unitary operator on its registers, then measures them and decides its output depending of the outcome of the measurement.

The registers $R_0, \ldots, R_{d+1}$ will be called the private registers (since they do not move during the execution of the protocol), while the registers $T_0, \ldots, T_d$ will be called the message registers.

We now describe a $O(r/d)$-message protocol $\mathcal{P}$ that computes f in the standard model of communication complexity, where Alice and Bob receive as input x and y, respectively. The idea is that Alice and Bob jointly simulate the computation of $\mathcal{A}$. The crucial observation is that, due to the time needed for a message from A to reach B in the network $\mathcal{G}_d$, the simulation can be done by dividing the computation into $O(r/d)$ areas, each of width d, and doing the simulation area per area. Each area will be simulated by one of the players, who will then send to the other player only the $O(d)$ registers that are needed to simulate the next area. The details of the simulation are as follows (see [20] for an illustration).

Note that Alice can create the initial state of register R_0, which depends only on x, and Bob can create the initial state R_{d+1}, which depends only on y. For simplicity we will assume that r is an even multiple of d, but the description can be readily adjusted for any value of r. For each s from 1 to r/d, Alice and Bob do the following:

- If s is odd then this is Bob's turn. Bob first simulates the computation of P_i in $\mathcal{A}$ up to step $t = (s-1)d + i - 1$, for each $i \in \{2, \ldots, d+1\}$. For each odd $i \in \{2, \ldots, d+1\}$, Bob then sends to Alice the message register of P_i. Bob then proceeds with the simulation and simulates the computation of P_i in $\mathcal{A}$ up to step $t = (s-1)d + i$, this time for each $i \in \{1, \ldots, d\}$. For any even $i \in \{1, \ldots, d\}$, Bob sends to Alice the message register of P_i. Finally, Bob sends to Alice the private register of P_i for each $i \in \{1, \ldots, d\}$. Note that all the communication from Bob to Alice can be concatenated into one message of $O(d(\mathrm{bw} + s))$ qubits.
- If s is even then this is Alice's turn. Alice first simulates the computation of P_i in $\mathcal{A}$ up to step $t = sd - i$, for each $i \in \{0, \ldots, d-1\}$. For any odd $i \in \{0, \ldots, d-1\}$, Alice then sends to Bob the message register of P_i. Alice then proceeds with the simulation and simulates the computation of P_i in $\mathcal{A}$ up to step $t = sd - i + 1$, this time for each $i \in \{1, \ldots, d\}$. For any even $i \in \{1, \ldots, d\}$, Alice sends to Bob the message register of P_i. Finally, Alice sends to Bob the private register of P_i for each $i \in \{1, \ldots, d\}$. Note that all the communication from Alice to Bob can be concatenated into one message of $O(d(\mathrm{bw} + s))$ qubits.

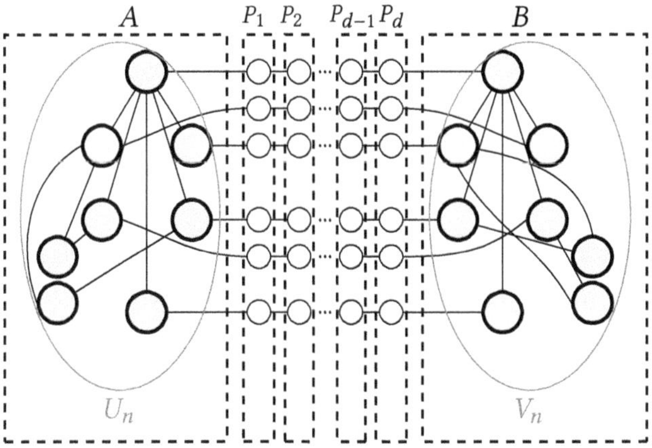

Figure 5: Example of graph $G'_n(x, y)$. Here $b = 6$: there are 6 edges between U_n and V_n in $G_n(x, y)$, and each of these edges is replaced by a path of length $d + 1$ in $G'_n(x, y)$.

After all those steps, Alice has received all the messages needed to complete the computation done by node A in Algorithm $\mathcal{A}$. She completes the computation, decides her output (as done by node A in $\mathcal{A}$), and sends it to Bob.

Protocol $\mathcal{P}$ uses $O(r/d)$ messages and simulates Algorithm $\mathcal{A}$, i.e., computes the function f. Its communication complexity is $O(r/d \times d(\mathrm{bw} + s)) = O(r(\mathrm{bw} + s))$ qubits. □

6.2 Proof of Theorem 1.3

We are now ready to give the proof of Theorem 1.3.

Proof of Theorem 1.3. Let $\{G_n\}_{n \geq 1}$ be the family of graphs that realizes the (b, k, d_1, d_2)-reduction from disjointness to diameter computation of Theorem 5.3. This means that we have $b = \Theta(\log n)$, $k = \Theta(n)$, $d_1 = 4$ and $d_2 = 5$. We will use below the same notations as in Definition 5.1.

Let d be any positive integer such that $d \leq n$. Assume that there exists an r-round quantum algorithm $\mathcal{A}$ that decides if the diameter of a network is at most $d + d_1$ or at least $d + d_2$. For any $k \geq 0$, we will use this algorithm to construct an r-round algorithm that computes the disjointness function DISJ_k in the model described in Section 6.1 with $d+2$ players $A, P_1, \ldots, P_d, B$ and bandwidth $\mathrm{bw} = \Theta(b \log n)$. Let $x \in \{0,1\}^k$ and $y \in \{0,1\}^k$ be the inputs of nodes A and B, respectively.

Consider the bipartite graph $G_n(x, y)$, which has b edges between U_n and V_n. We modify this graph to obtain a new graph $G'_n(x, y)$ by replacing each of these b edges by a path of length $d+1$ corresponding to d new nodes (see Figure 5 for an illustration). Note that $G'_n(x, y)$ contains $n' = n + bd$ nodes, i.e., the quantity n does not correspond anymore to the size of the network considered. This point can nevertheless be ignored since $b = \Theta(\log n)$ in our construction, which implies $n' = \Theta(n \log n)$, and since we ignore logarithmic terms in our lower bound.

The protocol works as follows. First note that the players can jointly construct the graph $G'_n(x, y)$: A can construct the subgraph induced by U_n, B can construct the subgraph induced by V_n, and the intermediate nodes can naturally be partitioned in d vertical layers constructed by $P_1, \ldots, P_d$ (see Figure 5). Nodes $A, P_1, \ldots, P_d, B$ will thus simply simulate the computation of $\mathcal{A}$ on $G'_n(x, y)$ in r rounds. At the end of simulation A and B obtain the result of the computation by $\mathcal{A}$ on $G'_n(x, y)$. From our assumption on $\mathcal{A}$, this enables them to decide whether the diameter of the network is at most $d + d_1$ or at least $d + d_2$ in r rounds and with at most s qubits of memory per node, and thus to compute $\mathrm{DISJ}_k(x, y)$ with the same complexity. Theorem 6.1 therefore implies the existence of a two-party quantum protocol for DISJ_k with $O(r/d)$ rounds and total quantum communication complexity $O(r(b \log n + s))$. From Theorem 2.1, we conclude that

$$r(b \log n + s) = \tilde{\Omega}\left(\frac{k}{r/d} + r/d\right),$$

which implies $r = \tilde{\Omega}(\sqrt{kd/(b+s)})$. The statement of Theorem 1.3 directly follows, since $b = \Theta(\log n)$ and $k = \Theta(n)$. □

ACKNOWLEDGMENTS

The authors are grateful to Rahul Jain, Ashwin Nayak and Dave Touchette for helpful discussions, and to the anonymous referees for valuable comments and suggestions. FLG was partially supported by the JSPS KAKENHI grants No. 16H01705 and No. 16H05853. FM was partially supported by the ERA-NET Cofund in Quantum Technologies project QuantAlgo and the French ANR Blanc project RDAM.

REFERENCES

[1] Scott Aaronson and Andris Ambainis. 2005. Quantum Search of Spatial Regions. *Theory of Computing* 1, 1 (2005), 47–79.

[2] Amir Abboud, Keren Censor-Hillel, and Seri Khoury. 2016. Near-Linear Lower Bounds for Distributed Distance Computations, Even in Sparse Networks. In *Proceedings of the 30th International Symposium on Distributed Computing (DISC 2016)*. 29–42.

[3] Charles H. Bennett. 1989. Time/Space Trade-Offs for Reversible Computation. *SIAM J. Comput.* 18, 4 (1989), 766–776.

[4] Gilles Brassard, Peter Høyer, and Alain Tapp. 1998. Quantum counting. In *Proceedings of the 25th International Colloquium on Automata, Languages and Programming (ICALP 1998)*. 820–831.

[5] Mark Braverman, Ankit Garg, Young Kun-Ko, Jieming Mao, and Dave Touchette. 2015. Near-Optimal Bounds on Bounded-Round Quantum Communication Complexity of Disjointness. In *Proceedings of the 56th Annual IEEE Symposium on Foundations of Computer Science (FOCS 2015)*. 773–791.

[6] Karl Bringmann and Sebastian Krinninger. 2017. A Note on Hardness of Diameter Approximation. In *Proceedings of the 31st International Symposium on Distributed Computing (DISC 2017)*. 44:1–44:3.

[7] Anne Broadbent and Alain Tapp. 2008. Can quantum mechanics help distributed computing? *SIGACT News* 39, 3 (2008), 67–76.

[8] Harry Buhrman, Richard Cleve, and Avi Wigderson. 1998. Quantum vs. Classical Communication and Computation. In *Proceedings of the 30th ACM Symposium on the Theory of Computing (STOC 1998)*. 63–68.

[9] Vasil S. Denchev and Gopal Pandurangan. 2008. Distributed quantum computing: a new frontier in distributed systems or science fiction? *SIGACT News* 39, 3 (2008), 77–95.

[10] Christoph Dürr, Mark Heiligman, Peter Høyer, and Mehdi Mhalla. 2006. Quantum Query Complexity of Some Graph Problems. *SIAM J. Comput.* 35, 6 (2006), 1310–1328.

[11] Michael Elkin, Hartmut Klauck, Danupon Nanongkai, and Gopal Pandurangan. 2014. Can quantum communication speed up distributed computation? In *Proceedings of the 2014 ACM Symposium on Principles of Distributed Computing (PODC 2014)*. 166–175.

[12] Silvio Frischknecht, Stephan Holzer, and Roger Wattenhofer. 2012. Networks cannot compute their diameter in sublinear time. In *Proceedings of the 23rd Annual ACM-SIAM Symposium on Discrete Algorithms (SODA 2012)*. 1150–1162.

[13] Cyril Gavoille, Adrian Kosowski, and Marcin Markiewicz. 2009. What Can Be Observed Locally? In *Proceedings of the 23rd International Symposium on Distributed Computing (DISC 2009)*. 243–257.

[14] Stephan Holzer, David Peleg, Liam Roditty, and Roger Wattenhofer. 2014. Distributed 3/2-Approximation of the Diameter. In *Proceedings of the 28th International Symposium on Distributed Computing (DISC 2014)*. 562–564.

[15] Stephan Holzer and Roger Wattenhofer. 2012. Optimal Distributed All Pairs Shortest Paths and Applications. In *Proceedings of the 2012 ACM Symposium on Principles of Distributed Computing (PODC 2012)*. 355–364.

[16] Peter Høyer and Ronald de Wolf. 2002. Improved Quantum Communication Complexity Bounds for Disjointness and Equality. In *Proceedings of the 19th Annual Symposium on Theoretical Aspects of Computer Science (STACS 2002)*. 299–310.

[17] Rahul Jain, Jaikumar Radhakrishnan, and Pranab Sen. 2003. A Lower Bound for the Bounded Round Quantum Communication Complexity of Set Disjointness. In *Proceedings of the 44th Annual IEEE Symposium on Foundations of Computer Science (FOCS 2003)*. 220–229.

[18] Bala Kalyanasundaram and Georg Schnitger. 1992. The Probabilistic Communication Complexity of Set Intersection. *SIAM Journal on Discrete Mathematics* 5, 4 (1992), 545–557.

[19] François Le Gall. 2009. Exponential Separation of Quantum and Classical Online Space Complexity. *Theory of Computing Systems* 45, 2 (2009), 188–202.

[20] François Le Gall and Frédéric Magniez. 2018. Sublinear-Time Quantum Computation of the Diameter in CONGEST Networks. ArXiv: 1804.02917.

[21] Christoph Lenzen and David Peleg. 2013. Efficient Distributed Source Detection with Limited Bandwidth. In *Proceedings of the 2013 ACM Symposium on Principles of Distributed Computing (PODC 2013)*. 375–382.

[22] Frédéric Magniez, Ashwin Nayak, Jérémie Roland, and Miklos Santha. 2011. Search via Quantum Walk. *SIAM J. Comput.* 40, 1 (2011), 142–164.

[23] Michael A. Nielsen and Isaac L. Chuang. 2011. *Quantum Computation and Quantum Information*. Cambridge University Press.

[24] David Peleg, Liam Roditty, and Elad Tal. 2012. Distributed Algorithms for Network Diameter and Girth. In *Proceedings of the 39th International Colloquium on Automata, Languages, and Programming (ICALP 2012)*. 660–672.

[25] Alexander A. Razborov. 1992. On the Distributional Complexity of Disjointness. *Theoretical Computer Science* 106, 2 (1992), 385–390.

[26] Alexander A. Razborov. 2003. Quantum communication complexity of symmetric predicates. *Izvestiya of the Russian Academy of Science: Mathematics* 67, 1 (2003), 159–176.

[27] Seiichiro Tani, Hirotada Kobayashi, and Keiji Matsumoto. 2012. Exact Quantum Algorithms for the Leader Election Problem. *ACM Transactions on Computation Theory* 4, 1 (2012), 1:1–1:24.

[28] Ronald de Wolf. 2002. Quantum communication and complexity. *Theoretical Computer Science* 287, 1 (2002), 337–353.

[29] Andrew C. Yao. 1979. Some complexity questions related to distributive computing (preliminary report). In *Proceedings of the 11th Annual ACM Symposium on Theory of Computing (STOC 1979)*. 209–213.

[30] Andrew C. Yao. 1993. Quantum circuit complexity. In *Proceedings of the 34th Annual IEEE Symposium on Foundations of Computer Science (FOCS 1993)*. 352–361.

Property Testing of Planarity in the CONGEST model

Regular paper

Reut Levi
Weizmann Institute of Science
reut.levi@weizmann.ac.il

Moti Medina
Ben Gurion University of the Negev
medinamo@bgu.ac.il

Dana Ron*
Tel Aviv University
danaron@tau.ac.il

ABSTRACT

We give a distributed algorithm in the CONGEST model for property testing of planarity with one-sided error in general (unbounded-degree) graphs. Following Censor-Hillel et al. (DISC 2016), who recently initiated the study of property testing in the distributed setting, our algorithm gives the following guarantee: For a graph $G = (V, E)$ and a distance parameter ϵ, if G is planar, then every node outputs accept, and if G is ϵ-far from being planar (i.e., more than $\epsilon \cdot |E|$ edges need to be removed in order to make G planar), then with probability $1 - 1/\text{poly}(n)$ at least one node outputs reject. The algorithm runs in $O(\log |V| \cdot \text{poly}(1/\epsilon))$ rounds, and we show that this result is tight in terms of the dependence on $|V|$.

Our algorithm combines several techniques of graph partitioning and local verification of planar embeddings. Furthermore, we show how a main subroutine in our algorithm can be applied to derive additional results for property testing of cycle-freeness and bipartiteness, as well as the construction of spanners, in minor-free (unweighted) graphs.

CCS CONCEPTS

• **Theory of computation → Distributed algorithms**; *Distributed computing models*; *Graph algorithms analysis*;

KEYWORDS

Distributed algorithms; Congest; Distributed property testing; Planarity testing

ACM Reference Format:

Reut Levi, Moti Medina, and Dana Ron. 2018. Property Testing of Planarity in the CONGEST model: Regular paper. In *PODC '18: ACM Symposium on Principles of Distributed Computing, July 23–27, 2018, Egham, United Kingdom.* ACM, New York, NY, USA, 10 pages. https://doi.org/10.1145/3212734.3212748

1 INTRODUCTION

Planarity is an important and well studied property of graphs. In the setting of centralized algorithms, there are several algorithms that run in linear time for deciding whether a graph is planar (e.g., [4, 31, 32]). In the context of distributed algorithms in the CONGEST [37] (and even LOCAL [36]) model, the number of rounds must be at least linear in the diameter of the graph (for any deterministic or randomized one-sided error algorithm). One begging question is whether there exists an algorithm (in the CONGEST model) for deciding planarity whose round complexity matches (or is not too far) from this lower bound.[1] Another question is whether there exists a natural relaxation of this decision problem, which allows to obtain round complexity that does not depend on the diameter.

In this work we address the latter question, by considering the relaxation of *property testing* in the distributed setting. In all that follows, unless explicitly stated otherwise, when we refer to distributed algorithms, we mean in the CONGEST model. Following Censor-Hillel et al. [6], who recently initiated the study of distributed property testing, we require the following from the algorithm. Let $G = (V, E)$ be a graph over n nodes and m edges. If G is planar, then all nodes should output accept, while if G is ϵ-far from being planar (i.e., more than $\epsilon \cdot m$ edges should be removed in order to make G planar), then at least one node should output reject. The algorithm is allowed a bounded error probability, where if it errs only on graphs that are ϵ-far from being planar, then it is said to have *one-sided error.* [2]

Our main result is a distributed one-sided error property testing algorithm for planarity that runs in $O(\log(n)\text{poly}(1/\epsilon))$ rounds and succeeds with probability $1-1/\text{poly}(n)$. We also show that $\Omega(\log n)$ rounds are necessary for any such algorithm and constant ϵ (even if the algorithm is allowed a constant error probability), implying that our result is tight up to the dependence on ϵ.

In the context of (centralized) property testing, there is a line of work on two-sided error testing of planarity in bounded-degree graphs [3, 30, 35]. The best known algorithm [35] performs a quasi-polynomial number of queries, i.e., $d^{O(\log^2(1/\epsilon))}$, where d is the degree bound (and succeeds with high constant probability). There is no known sublinear testing algorithm for unbounded-degree graphs and there is no known one-sided error testing algorithm, even for bounded-degree graphs. Note that in contrast, in the distributed setting we are able to obtain an optimal (in terms of the dependence on n) algorithm that has one-sided error and works for unbounded-degree graphs.

*This research was partially supported by the Israel Science Foundation grant No. 671/13.

PODC '18, July 23–27, 2018, Egham, United Kingdom

ACM ISBN 978-1-4503-5795-1/18/07...$15.00
https://doi.org/10.1145/3212734.3212748

[1] We note that Ghaffari and Haeupler [22] consider a different, but related question of finding a planar embedding of a planar graph. They give a distributed algorithm for this problem using $O(D \cdot \min\{\log n, D\})$ rounds (where D is the diameter and n is the number of nodes).

[2] Observe that if the algorithm has one-sided error and a constant error probability, then its error probability can be reduced to δ, for a given parameter δ, at a multiplicative cost of $\log(1/\delta)$ in the number of rounds. We are able to obtain error probability $1/\text{poly}(n)$ without this extra cost.

In addition to our main result, we show that under the promise that G is planar (and more generally, minor-free[3] for any fixed minor), we can use our techniques to obtain other distributed property testing algorithms as well as an algorithm for the construction of spanners.[4]

In the next two subsections we discuss our results in more detail.

1.1 A high-level description of our algorithm for testing planarity

The algorithm works in two stages. The goal of the first stage (which is deterministic) is to partition the nodes of G into parts for which the following holds: (1) Each part is connected and has diameter poly$(1/\epsilon)$; (2) The total number of edges between parts is at most $\epsilon m/2$. In the course of this stage, some node(s) may obtain evidence that the graph is not planar, and output reject. This evidence is in the form of messages received that are not consistent with the execution of the algorithm on any planar graph. Conditioned on this stage completing successfully, if G is ϵ-far from being planar, then the subgraph induced by at least one of the parts in the partition is $(\epsilon/2)$-far from being planar. The goal of the second stage is to search for evidence in each part to non-planarity, by exploiting the fact that the diameter of each part is small.

We next give some more details about each stage of the algorithm. Before doing so we recall several notions and basic facts. A *forest decomposition* of a graph is a partition of its edges into forests. The *arboricity* of a graph is the minimum number of forests into which its edges can be partitioned. Any planar graph has arboricity at most 3, and if we perform any sequence of contractions of edges on a planar graph, then we obtain a planar graph.

The first stage. The first stage consists of $t = O(\log(1/\epsilon))$ phases.

At the start of phase i, the nodes are partitioned into k_i parts, denoted $P_i^1, \ldots, P_i^{k_i}$ where each part is connected and has diameter at most 4^{i-1}. Let us denote this partition by $\mathcal{P}_i$. In the initial partition, $\mathcal{P}_1$, each part simply consists of a single node. For each phase, let $\mathcal{G}_i$ denote the auxiliary weighted graph that results from contracting each part P_i^j into a single node, which we denote by $v(P_i^j)$. The weight of an edge $(v(P_i^j), v(P_i^{j'}))$ is the number of edges in G with one endpoint in P_i^j and the other in $P_i^{j'}$.

Each phase starts by emulating the (deterministic distributed) forest decomposition algorithm of Barenboim and Elkin [2] on $\mathcal{G}_i$ (ignoring the weights). This algorithm works in $O(\log(n))$ rounds and gives the following guarantee. If $\mathcal{G}_i$ has arboricity at most α, then the algorithm provides a forest decomposition into at most 3α forests. On the other hand, if the algorithm fails in defining such a decomposition, then at least one node (in $\mathcal{G}_i$ and hence in G) has evidence that $\mathcal{G}_i$ has arboricity greater than α.

Following the above *forest decomposition step*, the algorithm executes a *merging step* (based on the clustering method of Czygrinow, Hańćkowiak, and Wawrzyniak [10]). In this step, parts of $\mathcal{P}_i$ are merged, thus creating $\mathcal{P}_{i+1}$. This merging procedure satisfies the following: (1) The maximum diameter of the parts in $\mathcal{P}_{i+1}$ is at most a constant factor larger than the maximum diameter of the parts in $\mathcal{P}_i$; (2) The number of edges in G between parts in $\mathcal{P}_{i+1}$ (the total weight of edges in $\mathcal{G}_{i+1}$) is a constant fraction of the number of edges between parts in $\mathcal{P}_i$ (the total weight of edges in $\mathcal{G}_i$). The latter crucially relies on the bounded arboricity of $\mathcal{G}_i$, which is ensured by the forest decomposition step.

Thus, the following central feature of (the first stage of) our algorithm emerges. Though we do not have a promise that the underlying graph is planar (indeed, it may be far from being planar), we are able to build on algorithms that work under the promise that the graph is planar. Namely, in each phase we verify that $\mathcal{G}_i$ has bounded arboricity, by running an algorithm that works under the promise that the underlying graph has bounded arboricity. Failure of this algorithm is detected by at least one node in the graph. On the other hand, if this algorithm succeeds, then we are ensured that we shall make the desired progress in the transformation from $\mathcal{G}_i$ to $\mathcal{G}_{i+1}$ (in terms of the decrease in the total weight of edges).

The second stage. Assume the first stage completed successfully (where this always holds if G is planar), and let $\mathcal{P} = (P^1, \ldots, P^k)$ be the final partition of the nodes (i.e., $\mathcal{P} = \mathcal{P}_t$). Recall that the subgraph induced by each part is connected, and has diameter poly$(1/\epsilon)$. Furthermore, the first stage ensures the following for each part P^j: (1) There is a designated *root* vertex in P^j, denoted r^j, where each node in P^j knows the identity of r^j; (2) There is an underlying spanning tree in P^j, rooted at r^j, where each node in P^j knows which of its incident edges is also incident to its parent in the tree, and which edges are incident to its children.

The second stage consists of two steps. In the first step, the (deterministic distributed) planar embedding algorithm of Ghaffari and Haeupler [22] is emulated on the subgraph induced by each part P^j, denoted G^j. The planar embedding algorithm works under the promise that G^j is planar, and when it completes, each node in G^j has a circular ordering over its incident edges that corresponds to a planar embedding (what is known as a *combinatorial embedding*). Since the diameter of each part is poly$(1/\epsilon)$, the number of rounds performed by this algorithm is poly$(1/\epsilon)$. If this step fails in determining an ordering for all nodes (in the aforementioned number of rounds), then this constitutes evidence that G^j is not planar. However, it is possible that an ordering is determined though G^j is not planar.

Hence, the second step in this stage is aimed at detecting non-planarity of some G^j. More precisely, as noted previously, if G is ϵ-far from being planar, then at least one G^j is $(\epsilon/2)$-far from being planar. Using the ordering of edges incident to each node in G^j together with a BFS tree rooted at r^j, denoted T_B^j (which can be constructed in poly$(1/\epsilon)$ rounds), we define a certain condition on each of the non-tree edges of T_B^j. We show that if G^j is far from being planar, then there are relatively many non-tree edges in G^j that violate this condition, while if G^j is planar, then no non-tree edge violates this condition. Furthermore, given a violating edge, it is possible to detect violation in poly$(1/\epsilon)$ rounds. Hence, by sampling $\Theta(\log(n)/\epsilon)$ non-tree edges in each G^j and running the

---

[3]Recall that a graph H is a *minor* of a graph G if H is isomorphic to a graph that can be obtained by zero or more edge contractions on a subgraph of G. We say that a graph G is H-*minor free* (or *excludes* H *as a minor*) if H is not a minor of G. We say that G is "minor-free" if it is H-minor free for some fixed H of constant size.

[4]A spanner of a graph G is a (sparse) subgraph of G that maintains distances up to a multiplicative factor, s, which is called the *stretch* factor, and the spanner is referred to as an s-spanner.

detection procedure on each, a violation is detected with probability $1 - 1/\text{poly}(1/n)$.

We note that, as shown in [13, 14], the algorithm of Elkin and Neiman [12] can be adapted to obtain with high probability a partition of the nodes into parts of diameter $O(\log(n)/\epsilon)$ such that the number of edges between parts is at most ϵm. Replacing Stage I in our algorithm with this procedure (and running Stage II on each part), results in a testing algorithm that runs in $O(\log^2(n)\text{poly}(1/\epsilon))$ (while our algorithm runs in $O(\log(n)\text{poly}(1/\epsilon))$ rounds).

1.2 Implications and applications for minor-free graphs

Suppose we have a promise that G is planar, or more generally, minor-free for any constant size minor. In such a case, the first stage of our algorithm always ensures that the nodes of G are partitioned into parts with diameter $\text{poly}(1/\epsilon)$ such that the number of edges between parts is at most $\epsilon m/2$. Such a partition can be used for testing properties such as cycle-freeness and bipartiteness (and more generally, hereditary properties that can be tested in a number of rounds that is linear (or even polynomial) in the diameter). Thus, for cycle-freeness and bipartiteness we obtain a *deterministic* testing algorithm that runs in $O(\log(n)\text{poly}(1/\epsilon))$ rounds. Such a partition can also be used to obtain $\text{poly}(1/\epsilon)$-spanners (for unweighted graphs) (deterministically) in $O(\log(n)\text{poly}(1/\epsilon))$ rounds.

We also show how to modify the partition algorithm so as to obtain a tradeoff between the round-complexity and the success probability of the algorithm. More precisely, with probability at least $1 - \delta$, the modified algorithm gives the same guarantee as above for the partition in $O(\log(1/\epsilon)(\log^*(n) + \log(1/\delta)))$ rounds. The complexity of the testing algorithms and spanner construction algorithm are improved accordingly (see Corollaries 16 and 17, respectively). Finally, if constant success probability suffices, then it is possibly to remove the dependence on n completely.

The testing results can be compared with the $\Omega(\log n)$ lower bound of Censor-Hillel et al. [6] for distributed testing of these properties on general (bounded-degree) graphs (with constant success probability). The spanner result can be compared to the recent result of Elkin and Neiman [12]. They provide a k-round distributed algorithm for general (unweighted) graphs that with probability $1-\delta$ constructs a $(2k-1)$-spanner with $O(n^{1+1/k}/\delta)$ edges. In order to obtain an *ultra-sparse spanner*, namely, a spanner of size $n(1+o(1))$ (with probability $1 - o(1)$), it is necessary to set $k = \omega(\log n)$. In our context, of minor-free graphs, we can obtain an ultra-sparse spanner deterministically for any $\epsilon = o(1)$, which allows to construct ultra-sparse spanners with stretch s for any $s = \omega(1)$.

1.3 Related work

Distributed Property Testing. As noted previously, the study of distributed property testing was initiated by Censor-Hillel et al. [6]. In particular, they designed and analyzed distributed property testing algorithms for: triangle-freeness, cycle-freeness, and bipartiteness. As noted previously, they also proved a logarithmic lower bound for the latter two properties. Fraigniaud et al. [21] studied distributed property testing of excluded subgraphs of size 4 and 5.

Since the appearance of the above papers, there was a fruitful line of research in distributed property testing for various properties, mainly focusing on properties of whether a graph excludes a sub-graph, e.g., triangle-freeness, cycle-freeness, subgraphs of constant size, tree-freeness, clique freeness [13, 14, 17–20]. In [16] the problem of testing the conductance of the input graph was studied, and a two-sided error tester is given.

Brakerski and Patt-Shamir [5] considered a related problem in the distributed setting. They show how to find a subset of vertices that is ϵ-close to being a clique if there is a subset that is ϵ^3-close to being a clique.

Distributed Algorithms with a promise in the CONGEST model. There is a large variety of distributed algorithms that work under a promise that the graph is planar (similarly, excludes a fixed minor, has bounded arboricity, and more). See e.g. [1, 2, 22–25, 27–29, 33, 34].

Centralized Property Testing. Most works in property testing on H-minor freeness (and related properties) focus on two-sided error testers. The problem of testing general H-minor freeness was studied by Benjamini, Schramm and Shapira in [3]. They showed that every minor-closed property of bounded degree graphs is testable with two-sided error with query complexity which is independent of the size of the graph. Subsequent work [30, 35] improved the dependence on the proximity parameter, ϵ. Yoshida and Ito [38] provided a tester with two-sided error for outerplanarity whose query complexity is $\text{poly}(1/\epsilon)$. Eden et al. [11] studied tolerant testing of bounded arboricity in the general graph model and showed almost tight bounds in terms of the dependence on n and m.

Czumaj et al. [8] studied property testing of H-minor freeness with one-sided error. They proved that for H which is a forest, H-minor freeness can be tested in query complexity which is independent on n. For any H that contains a cycle they showed a lower bound of $\Omega(\sqrt{n})$ queries. They also provided almost matching upper bounds for any H which is a simple cycle. Recently, Fichtenberger et al. [15] provided a $\tilde{O}(n^{2/3})$-query tester for outerplanarity, and other properties that can be characterized by forbidden minors, with one-sided error.

Czumaj et al. [9] studied testing bipartitness under the promise the input graph is planar. While in general, the query complexity of testing bipartitness is $\Omega(\sqrt{n})$, even for bounded degree graphs, they showed that under the promise of planarity, bipartiteness can be tested in time which is independent of n, even if the maximum degree is unbounded.

2 THE ALGORITHM FOR TESTING PLANARITY

In this section we establish the following theorem.

THEOREM 1. *There exists a distributed one-sided error property testing algorithm for planarity that runs in $O(\log(n) \cdot \text{poly}(1/\epsilon))$ rounds in the* CONGEST *model.*

As noted in the introduction (Section 1.1), our algorithm works in two stages: a *Partition stage* and a *Planarity testing stage*. In what follows we describe and analyze each in detail, where we refer to the first as Stage I and the second as Stage II.

2.1 A detailed description and analysis of Stage I

Recall from the description in the introduction (Section 1.1) that Stage I consists of $t = O(\log(1/\epsilon))$ phases. Each phase is associated with a partition of the nodes, where in the initial partition each node is a singleton part, and in general, each part is connected. We denote by $\mathcal{P}_i = (P_i^1, \ldots, P_i^{k_i})$ the partition associated with Phase i. Each partition $\mathcal{P}_i$ defines an auxiliary weighted graph, denoted $\mathcal{G}_i$. Each part P_i^j corresponds to a node in $\mathcal{G}_i$, denoted $\mathrm{v}(P_i^j)$, and the weight of an edge $(\mathrm{v}(P_i^j), \mathrm{v}(P_i^{j'}))$ is the number of edges with one endpoint in P_i^j and the other in $P_i^{j'}$. Each part in $\mathcal{P}_{i+1}$ is a union of several parts in $\mathcal{P}_i$.

Each phase consists of two steps: A *forest decomposition step* and a *merging step*. We first describe these steps in terms of the auxiliary graphs $\{\mathcal{G}_i\}_{i=1}^{t+1}$ (so that each part P_i^j is viewed as a single node, which may be denoted by v or u rather than $\mathrm{v}(P_i^j)$). We then explain how they are emulated on G.

Sending message up and down trees. Both in G and in the auxiliary graphs $\{\mathcal{G}_i\}_{i=1}^{t+1}$, we consider distributing information on trees (where each node knows which of its incident edges is incident to its parent in the tree and which of these edges are incident to its children). For such a tree T, let $r(T)$ denote its root. When we say that $r(T)$ sends a message *down the tree*, we mean that $r(T)$ sends the message to its children in T and they send it to their children, and so on, until the message reaches all nodes in T. In some cases the message may be augmented/modifed as it goes down the tree. When we say that the a node $v \in T$ sends a message *up the tree*, we mean that v sends the message to its parent in T, which in turn send it to its parent, and so on, until it reaches the root $r(T)$. Here too a message may be modified as it goes up the tree. In particular, if several nodes simultaneously send different messages up the tree, then this may cause congestion, and we explain how this is addressed whenever it arises.

2.1.1 The forest decomposition step on $\mathcal{G}_i$. This step correspond to the forest decomposition algorithm of Barenboim and Elkin [2]. Their algorithm works under the promise that the underlying graph $\mathcal{G}_i$ has arboricity at most α where in our case α is set to 3 (the bound on the arboricity of planar graphs). The algorithm ignores the weights on the edges of $\mathcal{G}_i$, and proceeds as follows. Initially all nodes in $\mathcal{G}_i$ are *active*. For $s = \Theta(\log n)$ rounds, each active node u does the following. If u has at most 3α active neighbors (in the current round), then u sends a message to all its neighbors that it becomes *inactive* in the next round. As shown in [2] (and is not hard to verify), if $\mathcal{G}_i$ has arboricity at most α, then in each round a constant fraction of the nodes become inactive. Since the number of rounds is $\Theta(\log n)$ (and the number of nodes in $\mathcal{G}_i$ is at most n), if $\mathcal{G}_i$ has arboricity at most α, all the nodes are inactive by the termination of the algorithm. In other words, if some node remains active after s rounds, then this serves as evidence that $\mathcal{G}_i$ has arboricity larger than α.

If the process terminates successfully (i.e., all nodes become inactive), then it is possible to define a forest decomposition into at most 3α forests. That is, it is possible to orient the edges of $\mathcal{G}_i$ so that each node in $\mathcal{G}_i$ has at most 3α outgoing edges, one to each of its parents in the different forests (where no cycles are formed). Specifically, consider a node u that becomes inactive in round ℓ, and let $\mathrm{v}_1, \ldots, \mathrm{v}_d$, for $d \leq 3\alpha$, be its active neighbors at the start of round ℓ. For each v_q such that v_q remains active in round $\ell + 1$, we orient the edge $\{\mathrm{u}, \mathrm{v}_q\}$ from u to v_q. For each v_q such that v_q also becomes inactive in round ℓ, we orient the edge $\{\mathrm{u}, \mathrm{v}_q\}$ from the node with the smaller id to the node with the larger id (so that no directed cycles are formed). We emphasize that each node knows the orientation of its incident edges.

2.1.2 The merging step: from $\mathcal{G}_i$ to $\mathcal{G}_{i+1}$. Assuming the forest decomposition step completed successfully (and hence each node in $\mathcal{G}_i$ has at most 3α outgoing edges pointing to its parents in the forest decomposition), the merging step consists of the following sub-steps. Sub-step 2 is as in [10].

(1) Each node u in $\mathcal{G}_i$ selects its outgoing edge (u, v) that has the highest weight. Let $\mathcal{F}_i$ denote the forest induced by the selected edges.
(2) Select a set of "shallow" subtrees of $\mathcal{F}_i$, denoted $\mathcal{T}_i$, as follows:
   (a) Obtain a coloring χ of $\mathcal{F}_i$ using colors in $\{1, 2, 3\}$ by running the distributed algorithm of Cole and Vishkin [7], and Goldberg, Plotkin and Shannon [26].
   (b) Mark the edges of $\mathcal{F}_i$ according to the rules defined next (where if a node marks an incident edge, it notifies the other endpoint).
      - For each node u such that $\chi(\mathrm{u}) = 1$, u marks its outgoing edge (assuming such exists) if the weight of this edge is greater or equal to the sum of the weights of all its incoming edges. Otherwise, u marks all its incoming edges.
      - For each node u such that $\chi(\mathrm{u}) = 2$, u marks its outgoing edge if the other endpoint is colored 3 and the weight of this edge is greater or equal to the sum of the weights of all its incoming edges whose other endpoint is colored 3. Otherwise it marks all these incoming edges.
   (c) Let $\mathcal{T}_i$ be the set of subtrees induced by the marked edges.
(3) For each subtree $T \in \mathcal{T}_i$, let $w_0(T)$ denote the total weight of edges that go from an even level in T up to an odd level (referred to as "even edges"), and let $w_1(T)$ denote the total weight of the remaining edges in T (referred to as "odd edges"). The root of T, denoted $r(T)$, obtains $w_0(T)$ and $w_1(T)$ (by sending a message down the tree so that each node learns its level, and receiving message sent up the tree in which weights of even/odd edges are summed). If $w_0(T) \geq w_1(T)$, then $r(T)$ sends the message '0' down the tree, and otherwise it sends '1'.
(4) If the message sent down the tree is '0', then all even edges are contracted, and otherwise all odd edges are contracted.

Observe that each node in $\mathcal{G}_{i+1}$ corresponds to a star subgraph in $\mathcal{G}_i$.

Let $w(\mathcal{G}_i)$ denote the total weight of edges in $\mathcal{G}_i$ (and similarly define $w(\mathcal{F}_i)$ and $w(\mathcal{T}_i)$).

Claim 1. *The merging step runs in $O(\log^* n)$ rounds (on $\mathcal{G}_i$) and* $w(\mathcal{G}_{i+1}) \leq \left(1 - \frac{1}{12\alpha}\right) \cdot w(\mathcal{G}_i)$.

Proof. First observe that by the definition of $\mathcal{F}_i$ (in Sub-step 1), $w(\mathcal{F}_i) \geq w(\mathcal{G}_i)/3\alpha$. By [7], the number of rounds performed in Sub-step 2a is $O(\log^* n)$ (and hence $O(\log^* n)$ bounds the number of rounds performed in all of Sub-step 2). By the analysis presented in [10, Section 2], $w(\mathcal{T}_i) \geq w(\mathcal{F}_i)/2$, and the height of each tree T in $\mathcal{T}_i$ is at most 10. Therefore, Sub-step 3 runs in a constant number of rounds (and the same is true of Sub-step 4). Finally, by the choice of which edges to contract (in Sub-step 3), the weight of the contracted edges is at least $w(\mathcal{T}_i)/2$. The claim follows. □

2.1.3 Successful completion of Stage I. Before turning to the emulation of Stage I on G, we introduce one definition and two claims, whose correctness does not depends on the details of the emulation.

Definition 2. *We say that Stage I* completes successfully *if the forest decomposition step in each phase terminates with no remaining active node.*

Claim 3. *If G is planar, then Stage I always completes successfully. If G is ϵ-far from being planar, then either Stage I does not complete successfully, or $w(\mathcal{G}_{t+1}) \leq \epsilon m/2$.*

Proof. The first part of the claim follows immediately from the fact that the arboricity of planar graphs is at most 3 and that any minor of a planar graph is planar. The second part of the claim follows from the fact that $w(\mathcal{G}_1) = m$, Claim 1, and the setting of the number of phases $t = \Theta(\log(1/\epsilon))$. □

Claim 4. *For each phase i and part P_i^j, the subgraph induced by P_i^j is connected and has diameter at most 4^i.*

Proof. We prove the claim by induction on i. The claim trivially holds for $i = 1$. To establish the induction step, consider a single merging step in which the nodes $v(P_i^{j_1}), \ldots, v(P_i^{j_s})$ in $\mathcal{G}_i$ all merge with $v(P_i^{j_0})$ (that is, the edges $\left\{\left(v(P_i^{j_q}), v(P_i^{j_0})\right)\right\}_{q=1}^{s}$ were contracted). Clearly, the subgraph induced by $\bigcup_{q=0}^{s} P_i^{j_q}$ (which corresponds to a part in $\mathcal{P}_{i+1}$) is connected. As for the diameter of this subgraph, by the induction hypothesis, it is at most $3 \cdot 4^i + 2 \leq 4^{i+1}$. □

Conditioned on Stage I completing successfully, let $\mathcal{P} = (P^1, \ldots, P^k)$ denote the final partition (i.e., $\mathcal{P} = \mathcal{P}_{t+1}$). For each $j \in [k]$, let $G^j = G(P^j)$ denote the subgraph induced by P^j. As a corollary of Claim 4 we get:

Corollary 5. *Each G^j is connected and has diameter* poly$(1/\epsilon)$.

2.1.4 Preliminaries for the emulation. For each phase $i \in [t]$ and part $P_i^j \in \mathcal{P}_i$, let G_i^j denote the subgraph induced by P_i^j. We say that a node $u \in P_i^j$ is a *boundary* node, if at least one of its neighbors belongs to a part $P_i^{j'}$ for $j' \neq j$.

In Section 2.1.6 we establish the following lemma.

Lemma 6. *For every $i \in [t]$ and every $P_i^j \in \mathcal{P}_i$, there is a unique root node $r_i^j \in P_i^j$, such that each node in P_i^j knows the identity of r_i^j. Furthermore, there is a spanning tree of G_i^j, rooted at r_i^j and denoted T_i^j, for which the following holds. Each node u in G_i^j knows which of its incident edges is incident to its parent in T_i^j and which of these edges is incident to its children.*

2.1.5 Emulating the forest decomposition step. We assume that at the start of each phase i, the conditions in Lemma 6 hold. We refer to each round in the forest decomposition algorithm described in Section 2.1.1 (on $\mathcal{G}_i$) as a *super-round.* In the forest decomposition step of each phase i, we have $s = O(\log n)$ super-rounds in which each active node $v(P_i^j)$ in $\mathcal{G}_i$ needs to determine if it is still active in the next super-round and to send a corresponding message to its neighbors. Each super-round is emulated by several rounds (on G), as described next.

The root of P_i^j, r_i^j, plays the role of $v(P_i^j)$ as follows. For each super-round ℓ, at the start of which $v(P_i^j)$ is active, if r_i^j determines in the course of this super-round that $v(P_i^j)$ should remain active in the next super-round $(\ell + 1)$, then it sends a message ('Active', r_i^j) down the tree T_i^j. Each boundary node in P_i^j also sends this message to its neighbors outside of P_i^j. The process by which r_i^j determines in super-round ℓ whether $v(P_i^j)$ remains active or not is defined as follows (where this process is also executed one super-round after $v(P_i^j)$ becomes inactive so that r_i^j can learn which neighbors of $v(P_i^j)$ also became inactive in super-round ℓ).

At the beginning of each super-round ℓ, each boundary node u in P_i^j that received in the previous super-round messages of the form ('Active', $r_i^{j'}$) for $j' \neq j$, does the following. If u received more than 3α such messages with *distinct* root ids, then it sends a message 'Active' up the tree (meaning that $v(P_i^j)$ should remain active since it has more than 3α active neighbors). Otherwise, for each $r_i^{j'}$ such that u received a message ('Active', $r_i^{j'}$), u sends a message ('Active', $r_i^{j'}$, x) to its parent, where x indicates how many messages ('Active', $r_i^{j'}$) it received. These messages go up the tree, where if a node u receives the message 'Active', then this is the single message it passes on. If u did not receive 'Active' but it received more than 3α messages ('Active', $r_i^{j'}$, x) with distinct root ids, then it also sends 'Active' up the tree. Otherwise, for each $r_i^{j'}$, let the messages u received with this root id be ('Active', $r_i^{j'}$, x_1), ..., ('Active', $r_i^{j'}$, x_q). Then u sends its parent a message $\left(\text{'Active'}, r_i^{j'}, \sum_{p=1}^{q} x_p\right)$. Finally, if r_i^j received the message 'Active' or if it received more than 3α messages with distinct root ids, then r_i^j determines that $v(P_i^j)$ remains active in the next super-round. Otherwise, it determines that $v(P_i^j)$ becomes inactive. In the latter case, not only that the out-edges of $v(P_i^j)$ can be determined by r_i^j, their weights can be determined as well (this is the role of the third parameter in the messages going up the tree).

The total number of rounds (on G) sufficient for emulating a single super-round on $\mathcal{G}_i$ is hence upper bounded by the maximum diameter of parts in $\mathcal{P}_i$, which by Claim 4 is poly$(1/\epsilon)$ (times 3α, which is a constant).

If after all $O(\log(n))$ super rounds there is some r_i^j such that $v(P_i^j)$ is still active, then r_i^j outputs reject (implying that Stage I did not complete successfully).

2.1.6 Emulating the merging step. In this subsection we explain how to emulate all sub-steps in the merging step, and establish Lemma 6 by induction on i. The base of the induction, $i = 1$ is trivial, since in $\mathcal{P}_1$ each node belongs to a singleton part, and in one round each node learns the identity of all its neighbors.

Determining the heaviest out-edge (Sub-step 1). For a part P_i^j, consider the super-round ℓ in the forest decomposition algorithm in which $v(P_i^j)$ becomes inactive. By the end of this super-round, r_i^j obtained the ids of the roots, $r_i^{j'_1}, \ldots, r_i^{j'_q}$ where $q \leq 3\alpha$, such that $v(P_i^{j'_1}), \ldots, v(P_i^{j'_q})$ are the active neighbors of $v(P_i^j)$ in $\mathcal{G}_i$ at the start of super-round ℓ. Furthermore, for each of the corresponding parts $P_i^{j'_p}$, the root r_i^j obtained the number of edges between P_i^j and $P_i^{j'_p}$, so that it knows the weight of $(v(P_i^j), v(P_i^{j'_p}))$ in $\mathcal{G}_i$.

It remains to determine which of these edges is an outgoing edge of $v(P_i^j)$. If ℓ is not the final round, then in the next round, r_i^j learns which of nodes $v(P_i^{j'_1}), \ldots, v(P_i^{j'_q})$ remained active in round $\ell + 1$. For each such node $v(P_i^{j'_p})$, the edge $(v(P_i^j), v(P_i^{j'_p}))$ is an outgoing edge of $v(P_i^j)$, and for each $v(P_i^{j'_p})$ that also became inactive in super-round ℓ, the direction of the edge is determined by the ids of r_i^j and $r_i^{j'_p}$. If ℓ is the last round, then either some node in $\mathcal{G}_i$ remained active, causing the corresponding root node in G to reject, or all nodes in $\mathcal{G}_i$ became inactive, so that edge directions are determined by root ids.

For the sake of the following sub-steps, it will be convenient to designate, for each selected outgoing edge $(v(P_i^j), v(P_i^{j'}))$, a single edge (u, v) in G such that $u \in P_i^j$ and $v \in P_i^{j'}$. To this end, let $(v(P_i^j), v(P_i^{h(i,j)}))$ be the heaviest outgoing edge of $v(P_i^j)$. The root, r_i^j send a message with the id of $r_i^{h(i,j)}$ down the tree. Each node $u \in P_i^j$ that has a neighbor in $P_i^{h(i,j)}$) sends its id up the tree, where if a node receives more than one "candidate" node id from its children, then it sends the minimum id among them. In this manner, r_i^j obtains the id of a single node $u_i^j \in P_i^j$ that has a neighbor, v_i^j, in $P_i^{h(i,j)}$, and it can notify u_i^j that it "in charge" of of the outgoing edge of P_i^j (by sending an appropriate message down the tree).

Selecting (marking) shallow subtrees (Sub-step 2). In order to emulate this sub-step it is first necessary to emulate the coloring algorithm of Cole and Vishkin [7], and Goldberg, Plotkin and Shannon [26]. The important observation is that in this algorithm, whenever a node $v(P_i^j)$ in $\mathcal{F}_i$ sends a message to its children in $\mathcal{F}_i$ (where a message is always of size $O(\log n)$ bits), it sends the same message. Hence, this can be emulated by simply sending (broadcasting) this message from r_i^j down the tree T_i^j. Once the message reaches the boundary nodes of P_i^j they also send it to their neighbors in G, and the message can go up the trees of the parts corresponding to the children of $v(P_i^j)$. Sending a message from $v(P_i^j)$ to its parent in $\mathcal{F}_i$ is similar (and even simpler, since there is a single parent).

In order to emulate the marking of edges, each root r_i^j needs to gather information regarding the number of edges between P_i^j and parts $P_i^{j'}$ such that $j = h(i, j')$, for the different color classes. This information can be easily gathered by sending appropriate messages up the tree, and summing edge counts that correspond to the same color.

Deciding if to contract even or odd edges in each tree (Sub-step 3). The emulation of this part is also simple. For each tree $T \in \mathcal{T}_i$, first messages should be sent down T, so that each $v(P_i^j)$ can learn its level. Each such message from $v(P_i^j)$ to its children in T, $v(P_i^{j_1}), \ldots, v(P_i^{j_q})$ is emulated by sending a message down T_i^j from r_i^j, and then up the trees $T_i^{j_p}$. In a similar manner messages are sent up the tree T, summing up the weights of even and odd edges, and then the bit '0' or '1' is sent down T.

Contracting edges (Sub-step 4). Once a root r_i^j corresponding to a node $v(P_i^j)$ learns that the edge $(v(P_i^j), v(P_i^{h(i,j)}))$ should be contracted, it sends a message down the tree T_i^j notifying all nodes that $r_i^{h(i,j)}$ is their new root. When this message reaches u_i^j (the node in charge of the edge $(v(P_i^j), v(P_i^{h(i,j)})))$, it makes v_i^j (its neighbor in $P_i^{h(i,j)}$) its parent, and sends a message up T_i^j that each edge on the path to r_i^j should flip its orientation. The induction step for Lemma 6, follows.

Emulation cost. The total number of rounds (on G) sufficient for emulating the merging step (from $\mathcal{G}_i$ to $\mathcal{G}_{i+1}$) is hence upper bounded by $O(\log^*(n))$ (by Claim 1) times the maximum diameter of parts in $\mathcal{P}_i$, which by Claim 4 is poly$(1/\epsilon)$.

2.2 A detailed description and analysis of Stage II

Assume Stage I completes successfully. By Claim 3, this always holds when G is planar, and by the definition of planarity, each subgraph G^j is planar. On the other hand, if G is ϵ-far from being planar, then by Claim 3, at least one subgraph G^{j*} is $(\epsilon/2)$-far from being planar. That is, if for each $j \in [k]$ we let $m(G^j)$ denote the number of edges in G^j, then the number of edges that need to be removed from G^{j*} in order to make it planar is at least $(\epsilon/2)m(G^{j*})$.

2.2.1 Preliminary preprocessing rounds. Stage II begins with several preliminary rounds of *basic information gathering*, where we build on Corollary 5 and Lemma 6. Specifically, we use the fact that each G^j is connected, has diameter poly$(1/\epsilon)$ and has a designated root node, r^j, that is known to all nodes in G^j.

- In the first poly$(1/\epsilon)$ rounds, for each $j \in [k]$, the nodes in each G^j construct a BFS tree, rooted at r^j and denoted T_B^j. This is done simply as follows. The root r^j sends a message $(r^j, r^j, 0)$ to all its neighbors (indicating that it belongs to level 0 in the BFS tree rooted at r^j). Once a node u in G^j receives a message (r^j, v, s) from a neighbor v, u notifies v that it is v's child in the tree, and sends a message $(r^j, u, s+1)$ to all its neighbors (this is of course done only once, upon receiving this first such message). When this process terminates, each node in G^j knows which of its incident edges is incident to its parent in T_B^j, which edges are incident to its children in T_B^j, and which are edges in G^j that do not belong to T_B^j (which we refer to as *non-tree edges*). Each edge in G^j is assigned to its higher-level endpoint (breaking ties by ids in the case of edges with both endpoints in the same level).

- In the next poly$(1/\epsilon)$ rounds, for each $j \in [k]$, the root r^j obtains the number of nodes $n(G^j)$ in G^j and the number of edges, $m(G^j)$. This is done simply by sending the corresponding information up the tree T_B^j. Namely, to obtain $n(G^j)$, each node sends its parent the number of nodes in its subtree (once it obtains the number of nodes in the subtrees of its children). Similarly, to obtain $m(G^j)$, each node sends its parent the number of edges assigned to nodes in its subtree. Once $n(G^j)$ and $m(G^j)$ are computed by r^j, it can broadcast them (down T_B^j) to all nodes in G^j (in another poly$(1/\epsilon)$ rounds).

2.2.2 Planarity testing within each G^j. If $m(G^j) > 3n(G^j) - 6$, then r^j rejects. Otherwise, the distributed planar embedding algorithm of Ghaffari and Haeupler [22] is executed on G^j. Recall that if G^j is planar, then this algorithm computes for each node a circular (clockwise) ordering of its incident edges (known as a *combinatorial embedding*), such that there exists a planar (geometric) embedding of G^j that is consistent with all edge orderings. If some node v does not obtain an ordering of its incident edges in G^j (within the allotted number of rounds: $O(D(G^j) + \min(\log(n(G^j)), D(G^j))$ where $D(G^j)$ is the diameter of G^j)), then it rejects.

Otherwise, using this ordering, together with the BFS tree T_B^j, each node in G^j associates a label with each of its incident edges that are incident to its children in T_B^j. Specifically, r^j arbitrarily labels one of its incident edges e by '1', and the remaining edges are labeled consecutively according to their order with respect to e. For each other node v in the tree, if the circular clockwise order of its incident edges is $(v,u), (v,w_1), \ldots, (v,w_s)$ where u is its parent and $w_1, \ldots, w_s$ are its children, then u labels each edge (u, w_j) by j.

This labeling of edges is then used to induce a labeling on the vertices of G^j in the natural manner: the label of a node u, denoted $\ell(u)$ is the concatenation of the labels of the edges on the path in T_B^j from r^j down to the node. This labeling can be computed in poly$(1/\epsilon)$ rounds, by distributing the label information down the tree, starting from r^j. This labeling of nodes defines a lexicographic order on the nodes.[5]

We now introduce a central notion regarding non-tree edges and prove two claims relating to this notion.

Definition 7. *Let (u,v) and (u',v') be two edges where $\ell(u) < \ell(v)$, $\ell(u') < \ell(v')$ and $\ell(u) < \ell(u')$. We say that (u,v) and (u',v')* intersect *if $\ell(u) < \ell(u') < \ell(v) < \ell(v')$. We say that a non-tree edge (u,v) is a* violating *edge, if there exists at least one non-tree edge (u',v') such that (u,v) and (u',v') intersect.*

Claim 8. *If G^j does not contain any violating edge, then it is planar.*

Proof. Consider the following (geometric) embedding of G^j. We put the nodes of G^j on a line (say, in equal distances), ordered according to the lexicographic ordering of their labels. Observe first that we can draw all tree edges as curves above the line, without any two crossing. This is true because tree edges cannot intersect. Using the non intersection of non-tree edges, we draw these edges below the line, as non crossing curves. □

As a corollary of Claim 8 we get:

Corollary 9. *If G^j is γ-far from planarity, then there exist at least $\gamma \cdot m(G^j)$ violating edges in G^j.*

Claim 10. *If G^j is planar, then there are no violating edges in G^j.*

Proof. Consider a planar embedding of G^j that is consistent with the ordering O on the edges incident to each node in G^j as computed by the algorithm of Ghaffari and Haeupler. For each non-tree edge (u,v) (where without loss of generality $\ell(u) < \ell(v)$), consider the simple cycle, denoted $C(u,v)$, that (u,v) forms with the tree edges. That is, if y is the least common ancestor of u and v, then this cycle consists of the tree path from y to u, the tree path from y to v, and the edge (u,v). Since the planar embedding is consistent with O, all vertices x such that $\ell(u) < \ell(x) < \ell(y)$ must be drawn inside the cycle, and all other vertices must be drawn outside the cycle, or vice versa. But this implies that there is no non-tree edge (u',v') that intersects (u,v), or else (u',v') would cross some edge in $C(u,v)$, in contradiction to the planarity of the embedding. □

Given Claims 8 and 10, the algorithm proceeds as follows. First r^j broadcasts the labels of $s = \Theta(\log n/\epsilon)$ non-tree edges G^j that are selected uniformly, independently, at random. Such a selection can be performed in $\log n \cdot$poly$(1/\epsilon)$ rounds. In particular, each node can decide independently for each of the non-tree edges assigned to it whether it is selected (by flipping a coin with bias $\Theta((\log n/\epsilon)/\tilde{m}^j)$ for each of these edges, where $\tilde{m}^j$ is the total number of non-tree edges in G^j). The selected edges (i.e., pairs of node labels) are sent up the tree, where if the number of selected edges is significantly larger than the expected number, then the algorithm fails (this happens with probability $1/\text{poly}(n)$). Once r^j obtained such a sample of non-tree edges, it broadcasts the labels of these edges to all nodes in the tree. Each node in the tree can now check whether any of the non-tree edges assigned to it intersects any one of the sampled edges, and reject based on such an intersection.

We have thus completed establishing Theorem 1.

3 A LOWER BOUND

Recall that for a fixed graph H, H is a *minor* of a graph G if H is isomorphic to a graph that can be obtained by zero or more edge contractions on a subgraph of G. We say that a graph G is *H-minor free* (or *excludes H as a minor*) if H is not a minor of G. For a family $\mathcal{H}$ of (constant-size) graphs, we say that a graph G is *$\mathcal{H}$-minor free* if it is H-minor free for every $H \in \mathcal{H}$. In particular, planar graphs are $\{K_{3,3}, K_5\}$-minor free.

In this section we establish the following theorem, which extends a result of Censor-Hillel et al. [6, Theorem 7.3] for K_3-minor freeness (cycle-freeness).[6]

[5] That is, for two (different) nodes u and v, let $\ell(u) = \sigma_1, \ldots, \sigma_p$ and $\ell(v) = \tau_1, \ldots, \tau_q$, where without loss of generality, $p \leq q$ (and for $u = r^j$ we have $p = 0$). Let i be the maximum index such that $\sigma_1, \ldots, \sigma_i = \tau_1, \ldots, \tau_i$, where if no such index exists, then $i = 0$. If $i = p$, then $\ell(u) < \ell(v)$. Otherwise, $\ell(u) < \ell(v)$ if $\sigma_{i+1} < \tau_{i+1}$, and $\ell(u) > \ell(v)$ otherwise.

[6] To be precise, the graphs in the lower-bound construction of Censor-Hillel have a constant degree, while the graphs in our lower bound construction do not necessarily

Theorem 2. *Let $\mathcal{H}$ be a fixed family of constant-size graphs where at least one $H \in \mathcal{H}$ contains a cycle. Any distributed one-sided error algorithm for testing $\mathcal{H}$-minor freeness must run in $\Omega(\log n)$ rounds (for constant ϵ).*

Our proof of Theorem 2 is very similar to the proof of Theorem 7.3 in [6]. We also build on a lower bound proof of Czumaj et al. [8] for one-sided error testing of minor-freeness. Similarly to [6], we use the probabilistic method to establish that for any constant k and any number of nodes n, there exist graphs G over n nodes for which the following hold: (1) G is ϵ-far from being K_k-minor free for $\epsilon = \epsilon(k)$; (2) G contains no cycles of length $\log(n)/c$ for a sufficiently large constant $c = c(k)$. Theorem 2 directly follows by setting k to be the minimum size of $H \in \mathcal{H}$ that contains a cycle and observing that for any one-sided error algorithm that runs in less than $\log(n)/c$ rounds, when executed on G, all nodes must accept.

In order to construct such graphs, we first select a graph $\widetilde{G}$ distributed according to $\mathcal{G}(n,p)$ for $p = \Theta(1/n)$, and prove that it is far from being K_k-free with high probability. We then show that by removing a relatively small number of edges, the resulting graph, G, has no short cycles, and remains far from being K_k-free. The next claim is similar to [8, Claim 6.2] and its proof can be found in the full version of this paper.

Claim 11. *Let $\widetilde{G}$ be a graph selected according to $\mathcal{G}(n,p)$ for $p = 1000k^2/n$. With probability $1-2^{\Omega(n)}$, the graph $\widetilde{G}$ has at most $2000k^2n$ edges and is ϵ-far from K_k-minor freeness for $\epsilon = 1/(50k^2)$.*

The next claim uses the same argument as in [6, Lemma 7.7].

Claim 12. *Let $\widetilde{G}$ be as defined in Claim 11 and let G be a graph resulting from $\widetilde{G}$ by removing a single edge from each cycle in $\widetilde{G}$ whose length is less than $\log(n)/c(k)$, where $c(k) = \Theta(\log k)$. With probability at least $1/2 - 2^{-\Omega(n)}$, the graph G is ϵ-far from K_k-minor freeness for $\epsilon = 1/(100k^2)$.*

Proof. Let S be a fixed set of ℓ nodes. The probability (over the choice of G) that there is a cycle over S is at most $\ell! \cdot p^\ell$. Therefore, the expected number of cycles of length at most ℓ is upper bounded by $\binom{n}{\ell} \cdot \ell! \cdot p^\ell < (1000k^2)^\ell$, and with probability at least $1/2$ it is at most twice this number. If we set $\ell = \log(n)/\log(1000k^2)$ then by Claim 11 and a union bound over all "bad" events, Claim 12 follows. □

4 A PARTITIONING ALGORITHM FOR MINOR-FREE GRAPHS AND APPLICATIONS

In what follows, when we use the term "a distributed partitioning algorithm", we mean an algorithm that gives the following guarantee. Upon completion, there is a partition $\mathcal{P} = (P^1, \ldots, P^k)$ of the nodes such that for each $j \in [k]$, the subgraph induced by P^j is connected, and there is a designated node $r^j \in P^j$ such that all nodes in P^j know the id of r^j. We first note that Stage I of our testing algorithm (described in Section 2.1) implies the next theorem.

have a constant degree. However, we can easily modify the construction so that the graphs have a constant degree, in the same manner as in [6, Theorem 7.3].

Theorem 3. *There exists a deterministic distributed partitioning algorithm in the CONGEST model for which the following holds. For an edge-cut parameter $\epsilon \in (0,1)$, the algorithm runs in $O(\text{poly}(1/\epsilon)\log n)$ rounds, the diameter of each part is $\text{poly}(1/\epsilon)$, and if G is minor-free, then the total number of edges between parts is at most ϵn.*

We show that by modifying the algorithm referred to in Theorem 3, we obtain a tradeoff between the round complexity and the success probability, as stated next.

Theorem 4. *There exists a distributed partitioning algorithm in the CONGEST model for which the following holds. For an edge-cut parameter $\epsilon \in (0,1)$ and a confidence parameter $\delta \in (0,1)$, the algorithm runs in $O(\text{poly}(1/\epsilon)(\log(1/\delta) + \log^* n))$ rounds, the diameter of each part is $\text{poly}(1/\epsilon)$, and if G is minor-free, then with probability at least $1-\delta$, the total number of edges between parts is at most ϵn.*

Remark 1. *If one is willing to settle for constant success probability (i.e., constant δ), then the round complexity of Theorem 4 can be improved to be only $\text{poly}(1/\epsilon)$.*

In what follows we prove Theorem 4.

Recall that in the algorithm for testing planarity described in Section 2, the source of the dependence on $\log(n)$ in the round complexity was due to the forest decomposition step in each phase of the partition stage. This step served to verify that each $\mathcal{G}_i$ has constant arboricity, as well as to allow for each node in $\mathcal{G}_i$ to select its heaviest outgoing edge in the corresponding forest decomposition (when the arboricity is bounded as required).

If however, there is a promise that G is H-minor free, for any fixed H of constant size h, then the arboricity of every $\mathcal{G}_i$ is upper bounded by a constant $c(h)$. Therefore, there is no need to perform this arboricity verification step. Furthermore, as we show below, instead of selecting the heaviest outgoing edge in a forest decomposition, it suffices to select a random incident edge, where the probability to select an edge is a function of its weight.

As discussed above, the algorithm referred to in Theorem 4 is a modified version of Stage I of the planarity testing algorithm. It too runs in $\log(1/\epsilon)$ phases, where in Phase i it coarsens the partition $\mathcal{P}_i$ and obtains the partition $\mathcal{P}_{i+1}$ (initially, $\mathcal{P}_1$ is the partition into singleton parts). The first difference is that the forest decomposition step is not executed. The second difference is in the choice of an incident edge for each node in $\mathcal{G}_i$. We next describe how the choice of an incident edge is performed as well as the merge decision. In Section 4.1 we explain how this choice and decision are emulated on G. Once a decision to merge is made, the emulation of the merge is performed as described in Section 2.1.6.

Recall that the algorithm in Section 2.1.2, which runs on $\mathcal{G}_i$, consists of 4 Sub-steps. Sub-step 1 is the only sub-step that is modified: Instead of selecting the heaviest out-going edge, each node in $\mathcal{G}_i$ randomly selects an edge as described next. The resulting graph, i.e., the graph induced on the selected edges, is guaranteed to be a directed pseudo-forest: the edge selected by each node is its only out-edge, and if an edge is selected by both endpoints then it is oriented as the out-edge of the node of lower id. We note that for Sub-steps 2a and 2b we only rely on the fact that $\mathcal{F}_i$ is a directed pseudo-forest. In order to show that the marking process in Sub-step 2b results in a graph which is a forest we prove Claim 15. This claim is required for the correctness of Sub-step 3 of the algorithm.

Edge Selection. Let α be the arboricity of $\mathcal{G}_i$ (which is a constant since G is minor-free). Each node in $\mathcal{G}_i$ draws one of its incident edges with probability that is proportional to its weight. Namely, for a node $\mathrm{u} \in \mathcal{G}_i$ and an edge (u,v), the probability that u draws (u,v) is $\frac{w(\mathrm{u},\mathrm{v})}{w(\mathrm{v})}$ where $w(\mathrm{v}) = \sum_{(\mathrm{y},\mathrm{v})\in E(\mathcal{G}_i)} w(\mathrm{y},\mathrm{v})$. This is repeated $s = \Theta(\log(1/\delta))$ times, and then each node selects the edge of maximum weight over the s trials. We call this *weighted-edge selection.*

We prove the following lemma.

Lemma 13. *With probability at least $1-\delta$, the total weight of the edges selected in $\mathcal{G}_i$ is at least $\frac{w(\mathcal{G}_i)}{16\alpha}$.*

Proof. Consider a forest decomposition of $\mathcal{G}_i$ into α forests. Orient the edges from children to parents so that the out-degree of each node is at most α. Let $w_{\mathrm{out}}(\mathrm{v})$ denote the weight of the out-going edges incident to v. Observe that $w(\mathcal{G}_i) = \sum_{\mathrm{v}\in V(\mathcal{G}_i)} w_{\mathrm{out}}(\mathrm{v}) = \frac{1}{2}\sum_{\mathrm{v}\in V(\mathcal{G}_i)} w(\mathrm{v})$. Let U denote the set of nodes, v, such that $w_{\mathrm{out}}(\mathrm{v}) \geq w(\mathrm{v})/4$. Then,

$$\begin{aligned}\sum_{\mathrm{v}\in U} w_{\mathrm{out}}(\mathrm{v}) &= \sum_{\mathrm{v}\in V} w_{\mathrm{out}}(\mathrm{v}) - \sum_{\mathrm{v}\notin U} w_{\mathrm{out}}(\mathrm{v}) \\ &\geq w(\mathcal{G}_i) - \sum_{\mathrm{v}\notin U} w(\mathrm{v})/4 \ \geq\ w(\mathcal{G}_i)/2\,. \qquad (1)\end{aligned}$$

Let $\mathrm{v}\in U$ and $i\in[s]$. Define $w(\mathrm{v},i)$ to be the weight of the edge that v drew in trial i. Then $\mathrm{Ex}[w(\mathrm{v},i)] \geq w_{\mathrm{out}}(\mathrm{v})/(4\alpha)$. To verify this, observe that with probability at least $1/4$, v draws one of its out-edges, and conditioned on that, with probability at least $1/\alpha$, the heaviest out-edge is drawn. By linearity of expectation and Equation (1), for each trial $i\in[s]$, $\mathrm{Ex}\left[\sum_{\mathrm{v}\in U} w(\mathrm{v},i)\right] \geq w(\mathcal{G}_i)/(8\alpha)$. We claim that for every $i\in[s]$, with probability at least $1-1/(16\alpha-1)$, $\sum_{\mathrm{v}\in U} w(\mathrm{v},i) \geq w(\mathcal{G}_i)/(16\alpha)$. Assume otherwise and obtain a contradiction:

$$\mathrm{Ex}\left[\sum_{\mathrm{v}\in U} w(\mathrm{v},i)\right] < \frac{w(\mathcal{G}_i)}{16\alpha-1} + \left(1-\frac{1}{16\alpha-1}\right)\frac{w(\mathcal{G}_i)}{16\alpha} = \frac{w(\mathcal{G}_i)}{8\alpha}\,.$$

Thus, the probability that in all s trials we get that $\sum_{\mathrm{v}\in U} w(\mathrm{v},i) < w(\mathcal{G}_i)/(16\alpha)$ is at most $(1/(16\alpha-1))^s$. Since $s=\Theta(\log(1/\delta))$, we obtain that with probability at least $1-\delta$, there exists a trial $i\in[s]$ such that $\sum_{\mathrm{v}\in U} w(\mathrm{v},i) \geq w(\mathcal{G}_i)/(16\alpha)$. From the fact that $\sum_{\mathrm{v}\in U}\max_i(w(\mathrm{v},i)) \geq \max_i\left(\sum_{\mathrm{v}\in U} w(\mathrm{v},i)\right)$, we obtain the desired result. □

Claim 14. *With probability at least $1-\delta$, $w(\mathcal{G}_{i+1}) \leq \left(1-\frac{1}{64\alpha}\right)\cdot w(\mathcal{G}_i)$.*

Proof. The proof follows from Lemma 13 and the same analysis as in Claim 1. □

Claim 15. *For an input graph that is a directed pseudo-forest, the graph resulting from the marking process in Sub-step 2b is a tree.*

Proof. We first note that given a directed pseudo-forest, the only cycle that might exist in the graph has to be a directed cycle. Assume towards contradiction that there exists a directed cycle in the marked graph. We claim that it must contain a node that is colored by 1. To verify this, observe that any vertex that is colored by 2, cannot have a marked outgoing edge and a marked incoming edge, such that for both edges, the other endpoint is colored by 3. But since every node that is colored by 1 can only have either out-going edges or in-going edges, we reach a contradiction. □

4.1 Emulation of the weighted-edge selection

In what follows, when we say that an edge $(u,v)\in E(G)$ is incident to a part P_i^j, we mean that $u\in P_i^j$ and $v\in P_i^{j'}$ for $j'\neq j$. In order to draw an edge incident to $\mathrm{v}(P_i^j)$ in $\mathcal{G}_i$ with probability proportional to its weight (i.e., emulate the drawing of edges in the weighted-edge selection), we run a procedure for uniformly selecting an edge in G incident to P_i^j. If the selected edge in G is (u,v) where $v\in P_i^{j'}$, then the corresponding drawn edge in $\mathcal{G}_i$ is $(\mathrm{v}(P_i^j),\mathrm{v}(P_i^{j'}))$.

This uniform selection is implemented as follows. First, each node sends a message to all its neighbors with the id of the root of its part. Following this round, each node u on the boundary of P_i^j, knows the set of incident edges (u,v) such that $v\notin P_i^j$. We denote this set by $E_{i,\mathrm{out}}(u)$ and let $d_{i,\mathrm{out}}(u) = |E_{i,\mathrm{out}}(u)|$. Provided with this information, u selects, uniformly at random, one edge $e\in E_{i,\mathrm{out}}(u)$ and sends its parent (in the tree T_i^j) the message $(e, d_{i,\mathrm{out}}(u))$. In each consecutive round, if a node v received the messages $(e_1,d_1),\ldots,(e_s,d_s)$ from its children, then it does the following. It sets $d=\sum_{p=1}^{s} d_p$, and selects one of the edges e_p with probability d_p/d. It then sends the message (e_p,d) to its parent. For the sake of consistency of the description, r_i^j sends messages to itself. At the end of this process (after $\mathrm{poly}(1/\epsilon)$ rounds), r_i^j has a single edge, denoted $e_i^j = (u_i^j, v_i^j)$ for $u_i^j\in P_i^j$ and $v_i^j\in P_i^{j'}$, that is uniformly distributed among the edges incident to P_i^j.

Theorem 4 now follows from Claim 14, and the fact that the total cost of the weighted-edge selection is linear in the diameter of the parts P_i^j, which is $\mathrm{poly}(1/\epsilon)$, times the number of repetitions which is $O(\log(1/\delta))$.

4.2 Applications of the partitioning algorithm for minor-free graphs

As a corollary of Theorems 3 and 4 we get the following.

Corollary 16. *There is a deterministic algorithm and a randomized algorithm in the CONGEST model for testing the following properties on minor-free graphs: cycle-freeness and bipartiteness. The deterministic algorithm runs in $O(\mathrm{poly}(1/\epsilon)\log n)$ rounds. The randomized algorithm has one-sided error, runs in $O(\mathrm{poly}(1/\epsilon)(\log(1/\delta+\log^* n))$ rounds and has success probability $1-\delta$.*

We note that similar statements can be derived for any hereditary property that can either be verified or (property) tested in a number of rounds that is polynomial in the diameter.

Proof. For both properties, first the algorithm of Theorem 3 or Theorem 4 is run with the edge-cut parameter set to slightly below ϵ (the distance parameter for property testing). Let $\mathcal{P} = (P^1,\ldots,P^k)$ be the resulting partition, and let G^j denote the subgraph induced by P^j. By both theorems, if G is ϵ-far from having the property in question, then (with probability 1 or with probability $1 - \delta$) at least one subgraph G^j does not have the property (while if G has the property, then every G^j has the property). Therefore, it suffices to verify the property on each G^j. To this end, an algorithm for finding a BFS tree is executed on each G^j. If the case of cycle freeness, each node now checks whether it has any incident non-tree edges in G^j, and in the case of bipartiteness it checks whether there is any such edge that closes an odd-length cycle. □

The proof of the following corollary is similar.

Corollary 17. *There is a deterministic algorithm and a randomized algorithm in the* CONGEST *model that, given* $\epsilon \in (0, 1)$, *construct an* $O(\text{poly}(1/\epsilon))$*-spanner of any unweighted, minor-free graph. The spanner has* $(1 + O(\epsilon))n$ *edges with probability* 1 *in the deterministic algorithm, and with probability* $1 - \delta$ *in the randomized algorithm. The round complexity of the deterministic algorithm is* $O(\text{poly}(1/\epsilon) \log n)$ *and of the randomized algorithm is* $O(\text{poly}(1/\epsilon)(\log(1/\delta) + \log^* n))$.

Acknowledgements

We would like to thank Mohsen Ghaffari and Merav Parter for helpful information. We would also like to thank the anonymous PODC reviewers for their helpful comments.

REFERENCES

[1] Saeed Akhoondian Amiri, Stefan Schmid, and Sebastian Siebertz. 2016. A local constant factor MDS approximation for bounded genus graphs. In *Proceedings of the 2016 ACM Symposium on Principles of Distributed Computing (PODC)*. ACM, 227–233.

[2] Leonid Barenboim and Michael Elkin. 2010. Sublogarithmic distributed MIS algorithm for sparse graphs using Nash-Williams decomposition. *Distributed Computing* 22, 5-6 (2010), 363–379. https://doi.org/10.1007/s00446-009-0088-2

[3] Itai Benjamini, Oded Schramm, and Asaf Shapira. 2008. Every minor-closed property of sparse graphs is testable. In *Proceedings of the 40th Annual ACM Symposium on the Theory of Computing (STOC)*. 393–402. https://doi.org/10.1145/1374376.1374433

[4] John M. Boyer and Wendy J. Myrvoid. 2004. On the cutting edge: simplified $O(n)$ planrity by edge addition. *Journal of Graph Algorithms and Applications* 8, 3 (2004), 241–273.

[5] Zvika Brakerski and Boaz Patt-Shamir. 2011. Distributed discovery of large near-cliques. *Distributed Computing* 24, 2 (2011), 79–89.

[6] Keren Censor-Hillel, Eldar Fischer, Gregory Schwartzman, and Yadu Vasudev. 2016. Fast Distributed Algorithms for Testing Graph Properties. In *Proceedings of the 30th International Symposium on Distributed Computing (DISC)*. 43–56. https://doi.org/10.1007/978-3-662-53426-7_4

[7] Richard Cole and Uzi Vishkin. 1986. Deterministic coin tossing with applications to optimal parallel list ranking. *Information and Control* 70, 1 (1986), 32–53.

[8] Artur Czumaj, Oded Goldreich, Dana Ron, C. Seshadhri, Asaf Shapira, and Christian Sohler. 2014. Finding Cycles and Trees in Sublinear Time. *Random Structures and Algorithms* 45, 2 (2014), 139–184.

[9] Artur Czumaj, Morteza Monemizadeh, Krzysztof Onak, and Christian Sohler. 2011. Planar Graphs: Random Walks and Bipartiteness Testing. (2011), 423–432.

[10] Andrzej Czygrinow, Michal Hańćkowiak, and Wojciech Wawrzyniak. 2008. Fast Distributed Approximations in Planar Graphs. In *Proceedings of the 22nd International Symposium on Distributed Computing (DISC)*. 78–92.

[11] Talya Eden, Reut Levi, and Dana Ron. 2018. Testing bounded arboricity. In *Proceedings of the 29th Annual ACM-SIAM Symposium on Discrete Algorithms, (SODA)*. 2081–2092. https://doi.org/10.1137/1.9781611975031.136

[12] Michael Elkin and Ofer Neiman. 2017. Efficient algorithms for constructing very sparse spanners and emulators. In *Proceedings of the 28th Annual ACM-SIAM Symposium on Discrete Algorithms, (SODA)*. Society for Industrial and Applied Mathematics, 652–669.

[13] Guy Even, Orr Fischer, Pierre Fraigniaud, Tzlil Gonen, Reut Levi, Moti Medina, Pedro Montealegre, Dennis Olivetti, Rotem Oshman, Ivan Rapaport, and Ioan Todinca. 2017. Three Notes on Distributed Property Testing. In *Proceedings of the 41st International Symposium on Distributed Computing (DISC)*. 15:1–15:30. https://doi.org/10.4230/LIPIcs.DISC.2017.15

[14] Guy Even, Reut Levi, and Moti Medina. 2017. Faster and Simpler Distributed Algorithms for Testing and Correcting Graph Properties in the CONGEST-Model. *CoRR* abs/1705.04898 (2017). http://arxiv.org/abs/1705.04898

[15] Hendrik Fichtenberger, Reut Levi, Yadu Vasudev, and Maximilian Wötzel. 2017. On Testing Minor-Freeness in Bounded Degree Graphs With One-Sided Error. *CoRR* abs/1707.06126 (2017). arXiv:1707.06126 http://arxiv.org/abs/1707.06126

[16] Hendrik Fichtenberger and Yadu Vasudev. 2017. Distributed Testing of Conductance. *arXiv preprint arXiv:1705.08174* (2017).

[17] Orr Fischer, Shay Gershtein, and Rotem Oshman. 2017. On the Multiparty Communication Complexity of Testing Triangle-Freeness. In *Proceedings of the 2017 ACM Symposium on Principles of Distributed Computing (PODC)*. ACM, 111–120.

[18] Orr Fischer, Tzlil Gonen, and Rotem Oshman. 2017. Distributed Property Testing for Subgraph-Freeness Revisited. *CoRR* abs/1705.04033 (2017). http://arxiv.org/abs/1705.04033

[19] Pierre Fraigniaud, Pedro Montealegre, Dennis Olivetti, Ivan Rapaport, and Ioan Todinca. 2017. Distributed Subgraph Detection. *CoRR* abs/1706.03996 (2017). http://arxiv.org/abs/1706.03996

[20] Pierre Fraigniaud and Dennis Olivetti. 2017. Distributed Detection of Cycles. In *Proceedings of the 29th ACM Symposium on Parallelism in Algorithms and Architectures*. ACM, 153–162.

[21] Pierre Fraigniaud, Ivan Rapaport, Ville Salo, and Ioan Todinca. 2016. Distributed Testing of Excluded Subgraphs. In *Proceedings of the 30th International Symposium on Distributed Computing (DISC) (LNCS)*, Vol. 9888. Springer, 342–356.

[22] Mohsen Ghaffari and Bernhard Haeupler. 2016. Distributed algorithms for planar networks I: Planar embedding. In *Proceedings of the 2016 ACM Symposium on Principles of Distributed Computing (PODC)*. 29–38.

[23] Mohsen Ghaffari and Bernhard Haeupler. 2016. Distributed Algorithms for Planar Networks II: Low-Congestion Shortcuts, MST, and Min-Cut. 202–219. https://doi.org/10.1137/1.9781611974331.ch16

[24] Mohsen Ghaffari and Christiana Lymouri. 2017. Simple and Near-Optimal Distributed Coloring for Sparse Graphs. In *Proceedings of the 41st International Symposium on Distributed Computing (DISC)*.

[25] Mohsen Ghaffari and Merav Parter. 2017. Near-Optimal Distributed DFS in Planar Graphs. 21:1–21:16.

[26] Andrew V Goldberg, Serge A Plotkin, and Gregory E Shannon. 1988. Parallel Symmetry-Breaking in Sparse Graphs. *SIAM Journal on Discrete Mathematics* 1, 4 (1988), 434.

[27] Bernhard Haeupler, Taisuke Izumi, and Goran Zuzic. 2016. Low-congestion shortcuts without embedding. In *Proceedings of the 2016 ACM Symposium on Principles of Distributed Computing (PODC)*. ACM, 451–460.

[28] Bernhard Haeupler, Taisuke Izumi, and Goran Zuzic. 2016. Near-optimal low-congestion shortcuts on bounded parameter graphs. In *Proceedings of the 30th International Symposium on Distributed Computing (DISC)*. Springer, 158–172.

[29] Bernhard Haeupler, Jason Li, and Goran Zuzic. 2018. Minor Excluded Network Families Admit Fast Distributed Algorithms. *arXiv preprint arXiv:1801.06237* (2018).

[30] Avinatan Hassidim, Jonathan A. Kelner, Huy N. Nguyen, and Krzysztof Onak. 2009. Local Graph Partitions for Approximation and Testing. In *Proceedings of the 50th Annual IEEE Symposium on Foundations of Computer Science (FOCS)*. 22–31. https://doi.org/10.1109/FOCS.2009.77

[31] John Hopcroft and Robert E. Tarjan. 1974. Efficient planarity testing. *J. ACM* 21, 4 (1974), 549–568.

[32] Abraham Lempel, Shimon Even, and Israel Cederbaum. 1967. An algorithm for planarity testing of graphs. *Theory of Graphs, International Syposium, Rome, July 1966* (1967).

[33] Christoph Lenzen, Yvonne-Anne Pignolet, and Roger Wattenhofer. 2013. Distributed minimum dominating set approximations in restricted families of graphs. *Distributed computing* 26, 2 (2013), 119–137.

[34] Christoph Lenzen and Roger Wattenhofer. 2010. Minimum Dominating Set Approximation in Graphs of Bounded Arboricity. In *Proceedings of the 24th International Symposium on Distributed Computing (DISC)*. 510–524. https://doi.org/10.1007/978-3-642-15763-9_48

[35] Reut Levi and Dana Ron. 2015. A Quasi-Polynomial Time Partition Oracle for Graphs with an Excluded Minor. *ACM Trans. Algorithms* 11, 3 (2015), 24:1–24:13. https://doi.org/10.1145/2629508

[36] Nathan Linial. 1992. Locality in distributed graph algorithms. *SIAM J. Comput.* 21, 1 (1992), 193–201.

[37] David Peleg. 2000. Distributed computing. *SIAM Monographs on discrete mathematics and applications* 5 (2000).

[38] Yuichi Yoshida and Hiro Ito. 2015. Testing Outerplanarity of Bounded Degree Graphs. *Algorithmica* 73, 1 (2015), 1–20. https://doi.org/10.1007/s00453-014-9897-1

Congested Clique Algorithms for the Minimum Cut Problem

Mohsen Ghaffari
ETH Zurich
ghaffari@inf.ethz.ch

Krzysztof Nowicki*
University of Wroclaw
knowicki@cs.uni.wroc.pl

ABSTRACT

We provide three different approaches to the minimum cut problem in the Congested Clique model of distributed computing. In this model, n nodes of the graph, each of which knows its own edges, can communicate in synchronous rounds; per round each node can send B-bits to each other node, where typically $B = O(\log n)$. At the end, each node should know its own part of the output, e.g., which side of the cut it is on.

- Our first algorithm is an $O(1)$ round algorithm that finds a $1 + o(1)$ approximation of the minimum cut. If the min-cut size is $\tilde{O}(n^{1/3})$, the algorithm finds an exact min-cut. This algorithm combines Karger's random sampling and his contraction algorithm; Nagamochi–Ibaraki–Nishizeki–Poljak's k–connectivity certificates; and Ahn–Guha–McGregor's algorithm for finding those certificates in the streaming model. To get an efficient implementation, we provide an algorithm that can solve simultaneously polynomially many instances of the MST problem in $O(1)$ rounds.
- Our second algorithm is an $O(\log^3 n)$ round exact algorithm, based on the Karger-Stein approach. Its time complexity improves when larger messages are allowed. To implement this algorithm we present a general method to perform divide and conquer algorithms in the Congested Clique model.
- Our third algorithm is an $O(\log^2 n)$ round exact algorithm based on Karger's state of the art sequential exact min-cut algorithm, which works via tree-packing.

CCS CONCEPTS

• **Theory of computation → Distributed algorithms**;

KEYWORDS

Congested Clique; Minimum Cut; Approximation Algorithms

ACM Reference Format:
Mohsen Ghaffari and Krzysztof Nowicki. 2018. Congested Clique Algorithms for the Minimum Cut Problem. In *PODC '18: ACM Symposium on Principles of Distributed Computing, July 23–27, 2018, Egham, United Kingdom.* ACM, New York, NY, USA, 10 pages. https://doi.org/10.1145/3212734.3212750

*The second author's work was supported by the National Science Centre, Poland grant 2017/25/B/ST6/02010.

PODC '18, July 23–27, 2018, Egham, United Kingdom
© 2018 Association for Computing Machinery.
ACM ISBN 978-1-4503-5795-1/18/07...$15.00
https://doi.org/10.1145/3212734.3212750

1 INTRODUCTION

In the Congested Clique model of distributed computing, which was introduced by Lotker et al. [LPSPP05], n nodes of the graph, each of which knows its own edges, can communicate in synchronous rounds. Per round each node can send B-bits to each other node, where typically $B = O(\log n)$. At the end, each node should know its own part of the output, e.g., when talking about the minimum cut problem, the node should know which side of the cut it is on. The main complexity measure in this model is the number of rounds until the algorithm terminates.

The congested clique model has received extensive attention over the past few years, espcially for various graph algorithms [PST11, DLP12, BHP12, Len13a, DKO14a, Nan14, HPS14, HP14, CHKK+15, HPP+15b, BKKL17, Gal16, CLT18, Gha16, GGK+18, Gha17]. The motivations for the study of this model are as follows: As argued in [LPSPP05, GP16], the Congested Clique model can be viewed as a theoretical model for overlay networks. Moreover, it is tightly related to the models of Modern Parallel Computation (MPC) [RVW16, KSV10, HP14], which are theoretical abstractions of practical frameworks such as MapReduce [DG08]. The connection to the MPC model is made even more concrete in the simultaneous work of Ghaffari et al.[GGK+18], which shows algorithms that work in both of the MPC and Congested Clique models and improve the state of the art for local problems such as maximal independent set, maximum matching approximation, and minimum vertex cover. From slightly more theoretical point of view, it may be considered as a variant of the number–in–hand multi–party communication model [PVZ12, DKO14b].

MST in the Congested Clique **Model**: The central problem in the study of Congested Clique model has been the Minimum Spanning Tree problem. In particular, the first paper [LPSPP05] on the Congested Clique model provided an $O(\log\log n)$ round deterministic algorithm for MST.

For about a decade, there was no progress on this problem. Then came the randomized algorithm of Hegeman et al. [HPP+15a] which improved the round complexity to $O(\log\log\log n)$. This result builds on the work of Ahn et al. [AGM12] which introduced *linear sketching* based techniques for graph problems in the streaming model. Consequently, the round complexity for MST in Congested Clique was improved to $O(\log^* n)$ rounds by Ghaffari and Parter [GP16]. Very recently, Jurdziński and Nowicki [JN18] settled the round complexity, by presenting an $O(1)$-round randomized MST algorithm.

How this paper continues that line of work: In this paper, we continue studies of the MST problem. We show that one can solve polynomially many instances of the MST problem in $O(1)$ rounds of Congested Clique. Moreover, simultaneous MST computations allows us to find the exact minimum cut in graphs with small cut size and approximations of minimum cut in graphs of higher connectivity. Thus, this paper may be considered as continuation of the results in the aforementioned line of work, in two ways. The first is that we consider the minimum cut problem which is a natural extension of the basic connectivity problem. The second is that we provide an algorithm that solves MST efficiently enough to allow us to solve polynomially many instances of it in $O(1)$ rounds of Congested Clique, simultaneously.

Moreover, our studies shed more light on what can be done in the Congested Clique model in $O(1)$ rounds. The overall goal is to develop better understanding of what kind of problems are easy in multi-party communication model, and which properties of the problems may be the cause of hardness. In particular, we show that in three cases, $O(1)$ rounds suffice for computing an exact minimum cut: (A) if we consider graphs with bounded size minimum cut, or (B) if we allow polynomially large message sizes, or (C) if we are fine with a $(1 + o(1))$-approximate solutions.

1.1 The minimum cut problem and the related work

In this paper, we study the minimum cut (min-cut) problem, which is a central and well-studied problem in graph algorithms. The problem is defined as follows: for a given graph $G = (V, E)$, we have to find a partition of nodes into two disjoint sets $V_1, V_2 = V \setminus V_1$ such that a set of edges E' that have exactly one endpoint in V_1 and exactly one endpoint in V_2 is as small as possible. Here, finding a $(1 + \epsilon)$ approximation to the exact solution is defined as finding a division of V into two disjoint sets $V_1', V_2' = V \setminus V_1'$ such that set of edges E'' between them is at most $(1 + \epsilon)$ times larger than E'.

The size of the min-cut is the smallest number of edges which one has to remove in order to make the graph disconnected. Therefore, the value of the min-cut can be viewed as a good indicator of both reliability and communication bottlenecks in the network. In particular, networks with small cuts may easily get disconnected because of link failures. Moreover, a small cut might lead to a high congestion on the links across the cut, if a large number of messages (or large amount of information) should be passed from one side of the cut to the other side.

In in this paper, we explain how to bring some of the techniques for the min-cut problem from the sequential model to the Congested Clique model. The traditional approach to the problem was to use max flow algorithms [FF56, EFS56, FF10], as summarized in section 1.3 of [KS96]. The 1990s witnessed a rapid development of new approaches to the problem: The first was based on a matroid characterization of the min-cut [Gab91]. Then there were three results, which we use in this paper – the first of them is Karger's random sampling technique [Kar94]; the second is the Karger–Stein algorithm [KS96], which is based on Karger's contraction algorithm [Kar93]; and the third is the state of the art algorithm for finding the min-cut in nearly linear time [Kar00], which combines random sampling and tree packing techniques.

The min-cut problem has also been studied in models of distributed computing: Ghaffari and Kuhn [MK13] provide an approximation algorithm for the min-cut in the CONGEST model. The result was improved by Nanongkai and Su [NS14]. Both results use different approaches, and none of them translate to an $O(1)$-round Congested Clique algorithm with a good approximation ratio.

In the models that are closely related to Congested Clique, there are two results which are relevant to the content of this paper. The first is [LMSV11], which provides an $O(1)$ round MapReduce algorithm for min-cut. This algorithm can be translated into Congested Clique algorithm, but would require larger messages. The algorithm we present gives better tradeoff between the message size and the number of rounds. The second is the paper [adHM98] which provides an implementation of Karger–Stein algorithm in $O(\log^4 n)$ rounds[1] of the BSP model, which translates into an $O(\log^4 n)$ round algorithm in the Congested Clique.

1.2 Our results

We provide three approaches to the min-cut problem in the Congested Clique model.

First Result: Our first result is an $O(1)$ round algorithm that finds an exact min-cut in graphs wit min-cut size at most $\tilde{O}(n^{1/3})$ and a $(1 + o(1))$ approximation in general graphs. More precisely, we prove the following theorem:

Theorem 1.1. *It is possible to find a* $1+O\left(\frac{\log^{17/6} n}{n^{1/6}}\right)$ *approximation of the min-cut in* $O(1)$ *rounds of* Congested Clique.

We provide the proof of Theorem 1.1 in Section 3. On a high level, the main part of this algorithm is an $O(1)$ round algorithm that finds an exact solution to the problem, when the min-cut is sufficiently small. In a nutshell, we simulate in parallel $\tilde{\Theta}(n^{2/3})$ instances of Karger's contraction algorithm[Kar93]. We stop each of these contraction process when it has $\tilde{\Theta}(n^{2/3})$ contracted nodes. Then, we find certificate of c–connectivity for all contracted graphs, in parallel, for $c \in \tilde{O}(n^{1/3})$. The graph certificates were introduced simultaneously by [NI92] and [NP89]. Moreover, they were used in algorithms for cut approximation in the semi-streaming model [AGM12]. We use the same concept, but we are able to implement the certificates for all $\tilde{\Theta}(n^{2/3})$ contracted graphs in parallel. Having the exact algorithm for graphs with bounded value of the min-cut, we can combine it with Karger's sampling technique [Kar94] to get a $1 + o(1)$ approximation to the min-cut in $O(1)$ rounds of Congested Clique in general graphs.

Second Result: Our second result is to provide an $O(\log^3 n)$ round Congested Clique model implementation of the sequential algorithm of Karger and Stein [KS96] for computing a min-cut. In our implementation, we use the fact that a single instance of the Congested Clique model can simulate a large number of smaller instances. This allows us to obtain an $O(\log n)$ round implementation of certain classes of divide and conquer algorithms. Karger–Stein algorithm is in this class, however it still require $O(\log^2 n)$ repetitions to get the answer with high probability. In particular we provide two theorems. The first is about the Congested Clique model with messages of size $O(\log n)$.

Theorem 1.2. *It is possible to implement Karger–Stein algorithm in* Congested Clique, *so that it requires* $O(\log^3 n)$ *rounds.*

The second theorem generalizes the above to provide a tradeoff between message size and round complexity, as follows:

Theorem 1.3. *We can find a min-cut of a graph in* Congested Clique *with* $O(d \log n)$ *message size,*

[1] The authors provide an $O(\log^5 n)$ round algorithm, but in conclusions they claim that an $O(1)$-round connectivity algorithm would remove one $\log n$ factor from the complexity.

- *in* $O\left(\frac{\log^3 n}{d}\right)$ *rounds for* $d \in O(\log^2 n)$
- *in* $O\left(\log_{d'} n\right)$ *rounds for* $d' = \frac{d}{\log^2 n}$ *and* $d \in \Omega(\log^2 n)$.

We provide the proof of Theorem 1.3 in Section 4. Theorem 1.2 is just special case of Theorem 1.3 for $d \in O(1)$.

Third Result: Our third algorithm is based on the state of the art sequential algorithm for min-cut, also by Karger[Kar00], which works via tree packing. This algorithm allows us to get a better time complexity for the exact version of the problem, but it relies on tree–packing, for which we do not know an $o(\log^2 n)$ round implementation, even if we allow larger messages. This result is described by Theorem 1.4, which is proven in Section 5.

THEOREM 1.4. *It is possible to find a min-cut of a graph in* $O(\log^2 n)$ *rounds of* Congested Clique.

2 MODEL

Here, we formally define the Congested Clique model, which is in a sense a multi-party communication model of computing. In this model, we have n players (aka, parties / nodes) with unique identifiers from the set $\{1, 2, \ldots, n\}$. We have synchronous rounds of communication and the main complexity measure is the number of rounds that the algorithm needs to complete the execution. Each round consist of two stages – in the first stage, each node performs some local computation; in the second stage, each pair of nodes exchange B bit messages. Often, we require $B \in O(\log n)$. However, it is also common to analyze the algorithm's performance when the message size B is larger.

Graph problems in the Congested Clique model are usually defined in the following way:

- each player corresponds to a single node of an input graph $G = (V, E)$, and knows all the edges incident to this node in the graph G;
- the goal is to compute some function $f(G)$ of the input graph;
- as a result of the algorithm, each node should know its own part of $f(G)$.

We comment that even though this is the usual way of defining the input for the Congested Clique, for some subproblem along the way to our final algorithm, instead of identifying each player with a specific node of the graph, we will assign to each player a particular set of edges from the graph.

3 MINIMUM CUT APPROXIMATION IN $\tilde{O}(1)$ ROUNDS

In this section, we present the proof of Theorem 1.1. In particular, we show that it is possible to find a $1 + o(1)$ approximation of the min-cut in $O(1)$ rounds of Congested Clique. On the top level, the algorithm is based on Karger's sampling method [Kar94] which brings down the connectivity in a controlled way, and his contraction algorithm [Kar93]which, as we explain, is especially suitable for graphs of small min-cut. In particular, we provide a contraction based exact algorithm for graphs with the min-cut of size $\tilde{O}(n^{1/3})$. Combined with sampling approach, this yields a $1 + o(1)$ approximation algorithm for general graphs.

Our exact algorithm for graphs with a small min-cut is based on an observation from [KS96]: In a rough sense, the method uses a sequence of contractions along randomly chosen edges, where in each contraction the two endpoints of the chosen edge are unified, until the number of remaining nodes reaches a desirably small threshold. Then it finds the min-cut on this remaining graph using a different approach which is suitable for graphs with a small number of nodes. A similar idea was used in the paper [LMSV11]. Here, we provide an alternative way of simulating several contraction sequences, and a different approach to the min-cut problem on smaller instances which allow us to find the exact min-cut in Congested Clique in $O(1)$ rounds, as summarized by Lemma 3.1 below:

Lemma 3.1. *There exists an algorithm which for any n node graph G and for any* $c \in O\left(\frac{n^{1/3}}{\log^{14/3} n}\right)$, *can verify whether G is c–connected in* $O(1)$ *rounds of the* Congested Clique. *If the graph G is not c–connected, the algorithm provides the exact min-cut of G. The algorithm may be executed for* $\Theta(\log n)$ *instances simultaneously.*

The above lemma is the main technical part of our algorithm stated in Theorem 1.1. In subsection 3.1 below, we explain how we transform general graphs to those with small min-cut, so that we can use Lemma 3.1. Then, in Subsections 3.2 to 3.4, we provide the proof of Lemma 3.1.

3.1 Karger's sampling approach

In this subsection we provide a proof of Theorem 1.1, under the assumption that Lemma 3.1 is correct. In order to do so, we rely on Karger's sampling method. Here, we will consider only graphs which are c–connected for some $c \in O\left(\frac{n^{1/3}}{\log^{14/3} n}\right)$, because for graphs that are not c–connected, we can find an exact min-cut by Lemma 3.1.

Random Edge-Sampling Notation: For any given graph G, we use the notation $G(p)$ to denote a random subgraph sampled from G, where we add each edge of G in $G(p)$ randomly and independently with probability p.

Lemma 3.2. *[Kar94] Let G be any graph with min-cut* λ *and let* $p = \frac{2(d+2)(\ln n)}{\epsilon^2 \lambda}$. *Then, with probability* $1 - O(1/n^d)$, *each cut in* $G(p)$ *has value within a* $(1 \pm \epsilon)$ *of its expected value.*

Lemma 3.2 allows us to find a $1 + \tilde{O}\left(1/n^{1/6}\right)$ approximation to the min-cut, in graphs that are c–connected for $c \in \Omega\left(\frac{n^{1/3}}{\log^{14/3} n}\right)$. In particular if we sample G, which has a min-cut of size λ, with probability $p = \frac{n^{1/3}\Theta(\log n))}{\lambda \log^{11/3} n}$, by Lemma 3.2 we know that $G(p)$ has a min-cut of size $O\left(\frac{n^{1/3}}{\log^{14/3} n}\right)$ and more importantly, a min-cut of $G(p)$ corresponds to a $\left(1 + O\left(\frac{\log^{17/6} n}{n^{1/6}}\right)\right)$-approximate min-cut of G, with high probability.

Let us consider a sequence of probabilities $p_i = 1/2^i$, for $i \in \{1, 2, \ldots, \Theta(\log n)\}$. Among them, there exists a probability p^*, such that $p \leq p^* < 2p$. If we use the algorithm provided by Lemma 3.1 on $G(p^*)$, with sufficiently large constant c, we can find the min-cut of $G(p^*)$ in $O(1)$ rounds of Congested Clique. By Lemma 3.2, this min-cut corresponds to a $\left(1 + O\left(\frac{\log^{17/6} n}{n^{1/6}}\right)\right)$-approximate min-cut of G. Moreover, we can execute the algorithm provided by Lemma 3.1, simultaneously for all $G(p_i)$ in $O(1)$ rounds. This allows us to find the min-cut of $G(p^*)$ even though we do not know the value of p^* beforehand.

3.2 Karger's contraction algorithm

Starting with this subsection, in the remaining part of Section 3, we provide a proof of Lemma 3.1. In particular, in this subsection, we describe Karger's contraction algorithm [Kar93], which is the base of our exact algorithm for graphs with small min-cut. On a high level, we use this contraction algorithm in the Congested Clique model because it allows us to reduce the size of the input graph (i.e., effectively its number of nodes) significantly. This helps in the Congested Clique model because, with such a reduced graph, intuitively, each single player can gather a larger amount of information about each node of a graph. In particular, if we can gather $\tilde{\Theta}(c)$ bits of information per node, then we can verify c-connectivity of the graph, and find the min-cut for graphs, which are not c−connected, using an approach from [AGM12].

Karger's Random Contraction Algorithm: In this algorithm we execute a sequence of random edge contractions. As a result of contracting edge $e = \{u, v\}$, we replace nodes u and v with a single node w, remove all edges incident to u and v, and for each removed edge $\{t, u\}$ or $\{t, v\}$, we introduce a new edge $\{t, w\}$. We note that latter might lead lead to the introduction of parallel edges.

Let consider graph G and some fixed min-cut of G. Suppose the γ denotes the min-cut size. The algorithm uses the following property: if G' is a result of contracting a single edge of G, then the min-cut of G' is not smaller than γ. Also, if we select an edge uniformly at random, the probability of selecting a edge from the min-cut in consideration is no larger than $\frac{2}{n}$, for an n node graph. Therefore, if we randomly select the order of contracting edges, after $n - 2$ contractions, with probability $\Omega\left(\prod_{i=3}^{n}(1 - (2/i))\right) = \Omega(1/n^2)$, we did not contract any edge from the min-cut in consideration. Thus, the min-cut of graph after all contractions, the edges between the two remaining nodes corresponds to the min-cut of the input graph with probability $\Omega(1/n^2)$. Therefore, if we repeat the whole contraction process $\Theta(n^2 \log n)$ times, with high probability, after at least one contraction sequence, we have found a cut which corresponds to the min-cut of the input graph. For our purposes, we use a slightly more detailed analysis from [KS96], which provides the following Lemma:

Lemma 3.3. *[KS96] A particular min-cut (A, B) survives contraction to k vertices with probability at least $\binom{k}{2}/\binom{n}{2} = \Omega(k^2/n^2)$.*

In Lemma 3.3, the phrase 'cut survives' indicates that, during the contraction process, we do not contract any edge from this cut. Therefore Lemma 3.3 provides that we can reduce one min-cut problem to $\Theta(n^2/k^2 \log n)$ problems of size k, and with high probability the min-cut of one of those smaller problems corresponds to the min-cut of G. Therefore, an efficient algorithm for graphs of size k will give us an efficient algorithm for the graph of size n.

In order to get an $O(1)$ round algorithm in the Congested Clique model, we have to go one step further and execute all contraction processes and compute the min-cut for all small sub-problems simultaneously. This idea was also used by [LMSV11]. However, we provide a different approach to executing contraction sequences in parallel and to finding the min-cut in reduced sub-problems, which is suitable for the Congested Clique model.

Simulating Contractions using MST computations: In order to simulate many contractions, we can use an MST algorithm. In particular, suppose that we want to simulate a contraction sequence, such that after all contractions there are only k remaining nodes. To simulate this contraction process, it is enough to assign to each edge a weight uniformly at random, say from $\{1, \ldots, n^{10}\}$, and compute the MST on this weighted graph. The weights of different edges are chosen independently. This range $\{1, \ldots, n^{10}\}$ is large enough that ensures that, with high probability, no two edges have the same weight. We get the following property from this MST for random weights: removing the $k - 1$ heaviest edges from this MST splits the MST into k connected components, such that each connected component corresponds to one contracted node, in the contraction process down to k components.

Let us elaborate further on this. To understand the connection between MST and random contractions, consider a contraction sequence such that we contract edges from the lightest to the heaviest. This corresponds to executing Kruskal's MST algorithm [Kru56] on a graph with those weights. Also, the last $k - 1$ edges to contract are the heaviest edges in the MST, therefore by removing the $k - 1$ heaviest edges from this MST we get a division of nodes which corresponds to the nodes of a graph after $n - k$ contractions.

This relation between MST and a sequence of random contractions allows us to efficiently simulate many contraction sequences by solving many MST problems, simultaneously. We describe details in the subsection 3.3. Then, we use an approach based on *linear sketching* to find min-cuts (as long as they are sufficiently small) on the contracted graphs. This approach is described in subsection 3.4. We note that this linear sketching method was first introduced in the streaming model algorithms by Ahn et al.[AGM12].

3.3 Simultaneous MST computations

In this subsection we discuss simultaneous MST computations in the Congested Clique model. Simultaneouss MST computations is a crucial part of our approximate min-cut algorithm. Additionally, we find the question of solving many MST instances simultaneously, in $O(1)$ rounds of Congested Clique, to be interesting on its own.

Before going to our algorithm for simultaneous MST computations, we recall Lenzen's routing procedure for the Congested Clique model[Len13b]; we use this procedure in several places.

Lemma 3.4. *[Len13b] Suppose that each player is given a set of $O(n)$ messages, each with a fixed destination. Moreover, each player is the destination of $O(n)$ messages from the other players. Then, it is possible to deliver all messages in $O(1)$ rounds of the* Congested Clique.

Having this helper routing subroutine, we are now ready to discuss our MST algorithm. The rest of this subsection is dedicated to proving the following theorem:

Theorem 3.5. *It is possible to solve $O(n^{1-\epsilon})$ independent instances of the MST problem in $O(\epsilon^{-1})$ rounds of* Congested Clique.

High-level Roadmap: On the top level, to prove Theorem 3.5, we use two key Lemmas: (1) Lemma 3.6, which says that we can reduce each instance of MST in general graphs to a sequence of $O(\epsilon^{-1})$

instances of MST problem on sparse graphs, each having at most $\tilde{O}(n^{1+\varepsilon/3})$ edges, and (2) Lemma 3.10, which allows us to solve all these instances of MST on sparse graphs simultaneously.

3.3.1 Sparsifying MST via KKT in Congested Clique. In this part of subsection 3.3, our goal is to prove that each instance of MST may be reduced to several significantly sparser instances. Moreover, this reduction can be executed for all $O(n^{1-\epsilon})$ instances of MST in parallel. More precisely, we show the following.

Lemma 3.6. *Given a set of $O(n^{1-\epsilon})$ instances of MST, we can reduce each of them into $O(\epsilon^{-1})$ instances of MST executed in a sequence, such that each of them has $\tilde{O}(n^{1+\epsilon/3})$ edges, w.h.p..*

Toward proving Lemma 3.6, the first building block we use is sampling technique from Karger, Klein, and Tarjan [KKT95]; in the rest of the paper, we refer to this as *KKT sampling*. The idea is to randomly select some sparser subgraph, find its minimum spanning forest F and use it to filter the set of remaining edges of the original graph, that is, to quickly discard many of the edges of the original graph that cannot be in the MST. If an edge e is the heaviest edge in some cycle in $F \cup \{e\}$, then, edge e can not be in the MST of the input graph. Such an edge is called F–heavy. All edges which are not F–heavy are called F-light. The following key lemma characterizes the expected number of light edges for a randomly sampled subgraph:

Lemma 3.7. *[KKT95] Let $G = (V, E, w)$ be an n node weighted undirected graph and let $0 < p < 1$. Let $G_0 = (V, E_0, w)$ be a random subgraph of G obtained by choosing every edge, independently, with probability p. Let F be an MST of G_0. Then, the expected number of edges of G that are F-light is at most n/p.*

The main idea, allowing simultaneous MST computations, is to sparsify all instances to the point where the total number of edges in all instances is $O(n^2)$. We cannot use a naive implementation of the KKT sampling for many simultaneous MST computations, because that would require each node to know the partial forest F for each MST. However, we will use a message efficient sampling implementation for the Congested Clique which was provided by Pemmaraju and Sardeshmukh [PS16].

Component–wise sketches: *Component–wise* sketches are based on *linear sketches* [AGM12]. For our purpose, it is enough to say that each component-wise sketch is a randomized data structure, which for a component allows to randomly select one outgoing edge. Here we use implementation providing, that its size is $O(\log^4 n)$ bits [HPP+15a]. Moreover, we can build component-wise sketch for $C = C_1 \cup C_2$, using component-wise sketches for C_1 and C_2. Furthermore, knowing $\Theta(c \log n)$ component-wise sketches, for each node of a graph, allows to find c–connectivity certificates. In order to compute sketches for some set of components:

- each node v computes component–wise sketch as it is separate component $\{v\}$
- for each component C we gather sketches from $v \in C$, and merge them to get a sketch for C

In particular we will use the following result regarding computing multiple sets of component-wise sketches for many division into components simultaneously.

Lemma 3.8. *Suppose that we have set of x divisions into components, and each is known by a separate commander node. Let γ, an arbitrary positive integer, be the number of sets of component–wise sketches we have to compute. Suppose that the total number of components in all divisions is k, and*

- *$k\gamma \log^4 n \in O(n \log n)$, i.e. we can store all component–wise sketches,*
- *$x\gamma \log^4 n \in O(n \log n)$, i.e. each node can send its sketches.*

Then, we can compute γ sets of component-wise sketches, using $O(\log_{\frac{n}{(\gamma \log^3 n)}} n)$ rounds of Congested Clique.

Proof. Let us assume that some fixed commander node knows the division into components. Our goal is to compute γ sets of sketches for components in this division. Since the size of the result may be $\Theta(n\gamma \log^4 n)$ bits, we may need $\Theta(\gamma \log^3 n)$ nodes just to store the result. Therefore, we assign $\Theta(\gamma \log^3 n)$ auxiliary nodes for each instance.

We start with a single message from the commander node, to all other nodes. In this message, the commander informs each node to which auxiliary node should send computed sketches. Then, commander node announces the division into components to all auxiliary nodes. Then, each auxiliary node, based on the division into components, merges received sketches. At this point, for any component which had all sketches gathered in a single node, we already know a component-wise sketch. For remaining components, we can organize auxiliary nodes having partial sketches for a single component into tree of degree $\frac{n \log n}{\gamma \log^4 n}$, and compute component-wise sketch using this tree in $O(\log_{\frac{n}{(\gamma \log^3 n)}} n)$ rounds. □

Efficient KKT sampling in the Congested Clique: The implementation of KKT sampling provided in [PS16] is based on linear sketches. Here, we present a slightly modified version, which can be executed efficiently for many instances simultaneously.

Lemma 3.9. *[PS16] Let $G = (V, E, w)$ be an n node weighted undirected graph, and let $0 < p < 1$. Let $G_0 = (V, E_0, w)$ be a random subgraph of G obtained by choosing every edge, independently, with probability p. Let F be an MST of G_0. Then, we can find set of $\tilde{O}(n/p)$ edges, such that it contains all edges of G, which are F-light, w.h.p.. It takes $O(\max(1, \log_{\tilde{\Theta}(n/p)} n))$ rounds, and each node has to send $\tilde{O}(1/p)$ sketches, $\tilde{O}(1/p)$ auxiliary nodes have to send/receive $O(n)$ messages. This procedure can be executed for $O(np/\operatorname{poly}\log n)$ instances of MST simultaneously.*

Proof. Let us consider Borůvka's algorithm executed on F. This algorithm is executed in phases. We start i-th phase, with some non maximal spanning forest F_{i-1} of the input graph F. In each phase we merge some of the connected components of F_{i-1}. To merge components, we use set of edges E_i such that each of them is a minimum weight outgoing edge for some component in F_{i-1}. In particular to construct F_i it is enough to add to F_{i-1} all edges which do not violate cycle property in $F_{i-1} \cup E_i$.

Let $C_1^i, C_2^i \dots$ be the connected components of F_i, and e_j^i be the minimum weight outgoing edge of C_j^i in F. Then, Pemmaraju–Sardeshmukh show that in order to find F-light edges, it is enough, for each component C_j^i to sample $O(\log^5 n/p)$ outgoing edges, out of edges lighter than e_j^i.

In order to find those edges in the Congested Clique, we select $\Theta(\log n)$ commander nodes. Each of them computes F_i for one i, therefore all values e_j^i are known. Next, each commander node sends value e_j^i to all nodes in the component C_j^i. Then, all nodes are able to compute proper set of $O(\log^5 n/p)$ sketches. By Lemma 3.8, we can combine them into component–wise sketches, which we use to execute sampling. Additionally, the number of sketches to compute by a single node is such that Lemma 3.8 allows us to gather component–wise sketches for $O(np/\operatorname{poly}\log n)$ instances simultaneously. □

If we set $p = n^{-\epsilon/3}$, then by Lemma 3.9 we can reduce a single MST instance to two instances, the first with $\tilde{O}\left(mn^{-\epsilon/3}\right)$ edges, the second with $\tilde{O}(n^{1+\epsilon/3})$ edges, with high probability. If the first instance has $\tilde{O}(n^{1+\epsilon/3})$, then we are done. If not, then we can use reduction from Lemma 3.9 on the first instance, in a recursive manner. This results in a recursion of depth $O(\epsilon^{-1})$, which ends the proof of Lemma 3.6.

3.3.2 Solving sparse MST instances in parallel in Congested Clique. In this part of subsection 3.3, we argue that one can solve many MST instances simultaneously, if all of them are sufficiently sparse. In particular we show the following.

Lemma 3.10. *Given a set of $O(n^{1-\epsilon})$ instances of MST, such that each has $O(n^{1+\epsilon/3})$ edges, it is possible to solve all those instances simultaneously, in $O(1)$ rounds of* Congested Clique.

Proof. On the very top level, the MST algorithm for graphs with $O(n^{3/2})$ edges from [JN18] works as follows:

(1) we reduce sparse MST on m edge graph to $\frac{m}{n}$ instances of connected components via sorting,
(2) we reduce each instance of connected components to two instances, sparse (degree bounded by $\log\log n$) and small (division into $O(n/\log\log n)$ components),
(3) we reduce each sparse instance to a small instance; for each sparse instance we compute $\sqrt{n}$ random samples, each sample requires assigning a single player to it,
(4) we solve small instances by MST algorithm from [GP16].

With some changes as we explain next, we can make this algorithm work simultaneously on all $O(n^{1-\epsilon})$ instances, such that each has $\tilde{O}\left(n^{1+\epsilon/3}\right)$ edges.

In the step 1 of MST algorithm for graph $G = (V, E)$ in the Congested Clique we sort all edges, and order them by weight. Then, we split this set of edges into sets $U_1, U_2, \ldots, U_{m/n}$, such that U_1 contains $O(n)$ lightest edges from E, and U_i, for $i > 1$ contains $O(n)$ lightest edges from the set $E \setminus \bigcup_{j=1}^{i-1} U_j$. Then it is enough to find connected components on graphs $(V, \bigcup_{j=1}^{i} U_j)$, for $i \in \{1, 2, \ldots, m/n\}$. Therefore, the total number of edges in all instances of connected components is $O(m^2/n)$.

After applying KKT sampling, we reduced each of the $O(n^{1-\epsilon})$ instances to a sparse one – each contains only $\tilde{O}\left(n^{1+\epsilon/3}\right)$ edges. To perform this reduction from single MST problem to many connected component problems, for all instances simultaneously, we use sorting. Since total number of edges is $O(n^2)$ it can be done for all instances in parallel. Moreover, number of edges for each MST instance after reduction to many connected component instances is $\tilde{O}\left(n^{1+2\epsilon/3}\right) \cdot O(n^{1-\epsilon})$ which is still $O(n^2)$. At this point in the algorithm provided in [JN18] we have to perform load balancing in order to make the execution of all connected component instances in parallel possible. In the next paragraph, we provide a load balancing procedure, which ensures that all instances of connected components problem can be executed simultaneously. In contrast to a load balancing which was used in [JN18], this can be executed for $\tilde{O}\left(n^{1+\epsilon/3}\right)$ unrelated instances of connected components problems.

Load balancing: To properly describe the load balancing, we have to distinguish between *nodes*, which are nodes of the input graphs, *i–nodes* which are nodes in particular instances, and *players* which are nodes of a communication graph in the Congested Clique and perform computation / communication. We may think of i–nodes as pairs ⟨node, instance id⟩. Then, we provide the following:

Lemma 3.11. *Given a set of $O(n^{1-\epsilon})$ instances of MST, such that total number of edges in all instances is $O(n^2)$, it is possible to assign i–nodes to players in such a way that:*

- *total number of edges incident to i–nodes assigned to a single player is $O(n)$*
- *at most $O(n^{1-\epsilon})$ i–nodes were assigned to a single player*

Proof. In order to perform load balancing we can use the sorting procedure of Lenzen [Len13b]. Our goal is to estimate the degree of each i–node and use those to ensure that each player simulates a set of i–nodes with total number of incident edges in $O(n)$. For each instance of MST with id i in which edge $e_{u,v}$ is present, we make two tuples $(i, e_{u,v})$ and $(i, e_{v,u})$. If we sort all edges, we can compute for each node its degree in all instances. Each node announces its total degree to the whole network, and with that knowledge we can assign i–nodes to players. Since each player knows all the aggregated degrees, each player can do this locally. We can assign nodes to players in a greedy manner. If a node has aggregated a degree smaller than n, we assign to it the smallest non used natural number. To nodes of aggregated degree $d > n$, we assign d/n smallest non assigned numbers – the idea is to split set of i–nodes corresponding to this node into fragments such that in each fragment the total degree of i–nodes is $O(n)$. Then we assign to the ith player all i–nodes which have number $a \cdot n + i$ for any integer a. The largest number we use to assign i–nodes to players in the greedy procedure is $O(n)$, as each assignment reduces either the number of nodes by 1, or the number of edges by $\Theta(n)$, and there are only n nodes and $O(n^2)$ edges. Therefore, each player has $O(n)$ edges, each player has to simulate $O(1) \cdot O(n^{1-\epsilon})$ i–nodes. □

If we apply load balancing form Lemma 3.11, we can proceed with step 2 of the outline given above. In this step we reduce each instance of connected components problems to two instances of connected components – one of them is small, one of them is sparse. To do so, we perform two kinds of steps. The first kind requires sending a message to all neighbours, since each player has $O(n)$ edges in all instances, we can execute those by Lemma 3.4. The second kind of steps requires sending a message to some fixed node (coordinator). There is only one coordinator per connected components instance, therefore total number of coordinators is $O(n^{1-\epsilon})$. Hence, this can be done in $O(1)$ rounds, as each player has to send $O(n^{1-\epsilon})$ messages (one per i-node), and we have to be able to assign $O(n^{1-\epsilon})$ coordinators, one per instance.

In step 3, in the original version of the $O(1)$-round MST algorithm Jurdinski and Nowicki [JN18], for each instance the algorithm had to assign $\sqrt{n}$ special nodes (bosses), and each of them had to compute connected components of some random subgraph, thus we were able to reduce the number of components to $O(n/\log\log n)$, with very high probability. Here, it is enough to say that we can use $n^{\epsilon'}$ bosses for each instance, for any $\epsilon' \in \Theta(1)$, and we still have very high probability of reducing the number of components to $O(n/\log\log n)$. Therefore, if we pick $\epsilon' = \epsilon/2$, the total number of bosses is $O(n^{1-\epsilon/2})$. In the original algorithm, each i-node had to send up to $O(\log\log n)$ messages, to all bosses. Here, each i-node has to send $O(\log\log n)$ messages to all bosses assigned to its instance, therefore, total number of messages to send per player is $O(n^{1-\epsilon}) \cdot n^{\epsilon/2} \cdot O(\log\log n)$, which is $O(n)$. Thus, we can do this using $O(1)$ round routing procedure 3.4.

The last step, which is 4 in the outline above, can be executed even for $O(n/\operatorname{poly}\log n)$ instances in parallel. In this part, each i-node has to send some poly $\log n$ size messages, which can be done as each player has only $O(n^{1-\epsilon})$ assigned i-nodes. Also, each instance requires up to poly $\log n$ unique auxiliary nodes, to perform computing / gathering component-wise sketches.

Since all steps can be executed in parallel, we can find MST for $O(n^{1-\epsilon})$ instances, each with $\tilde{O}(n^{1+\epsilon/3})$ edges in $O(1)$ rounds of Congested Clique, which means that we can solve $n^{1-\epsilon}$ instances of the MST problem in $O(\epsilon^{-1})$ rounds for general graphs. □

3.4 Exact algorithm for graphs with small cuts

In this subsection we provide a final touch to the proof of Lemma 3.1, i.e, we provide an algorithm that, for any graph G, for any $c \in O\left(\frac{n^{1/3}}{\log^{14/3} n}\right)$,

- verifies whether G is c-connected or not, and
- if G is not c-connected returns the min-cut.

In particular we provide a version of the algorithm which can be executed in $\Theta(\log n)$ instances simultaneously, which provides the proof of Lemma 3.1, and completes the proof of Theorem 1.1.

The first step is to simulate $\Theta(n^{2/3}\log^{-1/3} n)$ contraction sequences, such that as a result we get graphs with $\Theta(n^{2/3}\log^{2/3} n)$ nodes. By Lemma 3.3, in a single contraction process which stops when there are $\Theta(n^{2/3}\log^{2/3} n)$ nodes, with probability $\Omega(n^{-2} \cdot n^{4/3}\log^{4/3} n) = \Omega(n^{-2/3}\log^{4/3} n)$ the min-cut survives. Therefore, if we execute $\Theta(n^{2/3}\log^{-1/3} n)$ contraction processes, the min-cut survives in at least one of them with high probability.

Since single contraction process can be simulated via MST computation, and by Theorem 3.5 we can compute $\Theta(n^{2/3}\log^{-1/3} n)$ in $O(1)$ rounds of Congested Clique, we can simulate $\Theta(n^{2/3}\log^{-1/3} n)$ contraction sequences in $O(1)$ rounds of Congested Clique. As a result we have $\Theta(n^{2/3}\log^{-1/3} n)$ divisions into components, corresponding to contracted graphs. Each of those divisions is known to a different player. Thus, in order to find the min-cut of G or decide that G is c-connected, it is enough to do so for all contracted graphs corresponding to division into components known to players.

To verify c-connectivity, or to find the min-cut if G is not c-connected, we use c-connectivity certificates introduced in [NI92] and [NP89]. In particular we use following lemma

Lemma 3.12. *Let F_0 be an empty set, and $F_1, F_2, \ldots, F_c$ are the subgraphs of G, such that F_i is a maximal spanning forest of $G \setminus \bigcup_{j=0}^{i-1} F_j$. Then graph $G_c = \bigcup_{i=1}^{c} F_i$ is c-connected if and only if G was c-connected. If G_c is not c-connected, its min-cut is also the min-cut of G.*

By Lemma 3.12, in order to verify whether it is enough to compute sequence of c spanning forests and verify c-connectivity of sum of those forests. The same approach was used in [AGM12], moreover in that paper authors provided a sketch based approach, which is useful for our algorithm. In order to verify c-connectivity of an n node graph, it is enough to gather $\Theta(c\log n)$ linear sketches for each node, each of size $\Theta(\log^4 n)$ bits, and then computation may be performed locally.

Here, we use fact that we have to find min-cuts on component graphs, and each of them has only $\Theta(n^{2/3}\log^{2/3} n)$ nodes. Therefore, by Lemma 3.8 we can compute component-wise sketches for all components in all instances simultaneously, then for each instance it is possible to gather all component-wise sketches, as total number of bits a single node has to gather is $\Theta(n^{2/3}\log^{2/3} n) \cdot O(n^{1/3}\log^{-14/3} n) \cdot \Theta(\log n) \cdot \Theta(\log^4 n) = O(n\log n)$, which fits into $O(n)$ messages. Therefore, by Lemma 3.4, we can gather all component-wise sketches in $O(1)$ rounds.

4 KARGER–STEIN ALGORITHM IN THE Congested Clique

Throughout this section, we provide the proof of Theorem 1.3. Namely, we prove that if the message sizes in the Congested Clique model are $O(d\log n)$ bits, then, we can compute an exact min-cut in $O\left(\frac{\log^3 n}{d}\right)$ rounds, when $d \in O(\log^2 n)$, and in $O\left(\log_{d'} n\right)$ rounds, when $d \in \Omega(\log^2 n)$ and $d' = \frac{d}{\log^2 n}$. This will be established by providing an adaptation of the Karger–Stein algorithm, for the Congested Clique model.

The Karger–Stein algorithm is a recursive algorithm based on Lemma 3.3. In particular, one of the corollaries from Lemma 3.3 is that if we run two random contraction sequences, such that the size of remaining graphs is $\lceil n/\sqrt{2}+1\rceil$, with probability at least 1/2, we have that one of those sequences preserved the min-cut, i.e. in one of smaller instances the min-cut corresponds to the min-cut of the input graph.

Then, the key observation is that we can find the min-cut on the smaller instances using the same algorithm, in a recursive manner. In the paper [KS96], the authors provide an analysis of procedure Recursive–Contract (Rec–Con), which finds the min-cut using this approach. In particular, they provide that probability of success of Rec–Con algorithm is $\Omega(1/\log n)$. Therefore, in order to find the min-cut with high probability, it is enough to execute $\Theta(\log^2 n)$ repetitions of Rec–Con.

In this section we provide an efficient implementation of the Karger–Stein algorithm in the Congested Clique model, i.e., we provide a proof of Theorem 1.2. Moreover, we prove Theorem 1.3, by showing how our algorithm can be sped up, if larger messages are allowed.

In our approximation algorithm, the difficult part was computing the min-cut for all contracted graph simultaneously. In particular, the number of divisions into component is so large that it is impossible to make all nodes know all divisions. For the approximation algorithm we used sketch based approach, in order to bypass this problem.

Here, we do not have such problem. The main idea, which allows to implement the exact algorithm efficiently, is that since we only execute two contraction sequences, we only have two division into components, therefore all nodes can know both divisions. Thus, we can compute smaller instances explicitly, and find the min-cut in recursive manner on both of them simultaneously.

In the subsection 4.1 we provide an $O(1)$ round procedure that reduces a single instance of size n to two instances of size $\lceil n/\sqrt{2}+1\rceil$. In the subsection 4.2 we show that we can execute all recursive calls simultaneously. Those two subsections prove Theorem 1.2. Finally, in the subsection 4.3, we prove Theorem 1.3, by providing a tradeoff between the message size and the number of rounds.

4.1 Finding contracted graphs

In this subsection we provide an $O(1)$ round procedure that reduces a single instance of the min-cut problem of size n to two instances of size $\lceil n/\sqrt{2}+1\rceil$. To emulate two contraction processes in parallel, we can use parallel MST algorithm we provided in Theorem 3.5. As a result we have two divisions into connected components. For each division we want to execute a contraction – replace all nodes in this component with a single node.

To restate the problem, we have two divisions into n/c–connected components, each is known to all nodes in the clique, and we have to compute contracted graphs i.e. replace each connected component with a single node, and replace multiple edges between components with a single edge with correspondingly larger weight. In this algorithm we process each division separately.

To compute the contracted graph it suffices to find the sum of weights of edges between each pair of components in a given division. For each edge, we make a tuple denoting ids of components incident to this edge and its weight. Then we can sort all those tuples, and aggregate weights for each pair of components. After aggregation there are $O\left(n^2/c^2\right)$ weighted edges and $O(n/c)$ nodes.

4.2 Simulation in the Congested Clique

In this subsection we explain how to simulate many smaller instances of Congested Clique in one large instance. This allows us to execute all recursive calls of the algorithm in parallel. In particular, we provide the following simulation result:

Lemma 4.1. *It is possible to simulate one round of c^2 separate* Congested Clique *instances, each of size $\left\lceil\frac{n}{c}\right\rceil$ in $O(1)$ rounds of* Congested Clique *of size n.*

Proof. To make this simulation work we can split nodes into c groups of size $\left\lceil\frac{n}{c}\right\rceil$. Each group can simulate c Congested Cliques of size $\left\lceil\frac{n}{c}\right\rceil$. Total number of messages each node has to send / receive is $\left\lceil\frac{n}{c}\right\rceil c \in O(n)$, as each original node simulates a member of clique of size $\frac{n}{c}$ in c such cliques. Therefore, simulating one round of communication can be done in $O(1)$ rounds by Lemma 3.4. □

4.3 Message size – round tradeoff

In this subsection we analyze the impact of the message size on the complexity of our algorithm. To do so, we allow the message size to be $d\log n$ bits, for some parameter d, and express round complexity of the algorithm as a function of n and d. The message size – round tradeoff for this implementation of the Karger–Stein algorithm relies on the fact that if we are allowed to have messages of size $d\log n$ we can basically use them to run d instances of Congested Clique with bandwidth $\log n$ simultaneously, which allows us either execute several instances of Rec–Con in parallel or to compute instances of smaller size during divide part of Rec–Con algorithm.

In the Karger–Stein algorithm we run $O(\log^2 n)$ repetitions of the Rec–Con algorithm, where each single instance is independent of the others. The first part of Theorem 1.3 follows from the fact that with $d\log n$ bit messages, we can simultaneously execute $O(d)$ repetitions of this algorithm, which already gives $O\left(\frac{\log^3 n}{d}\right)$ round complexity for any $d \in O(\log^2 n)$.

The second part of Theorem 1.3 follows from that a larger message size can be used to reduce the depth of recursion of the Karger–Stein algorithm. The key observation is that if we are able to compute larger number of subproblems in $O(1)$ rounds, we can reduce single instance to larger number of smaller instances i.e. we can reduce single instance of size n to d instances of size $\left\lceil\frac{n}{\sqrt{d}}\right\rceil$.

Again, by using d Congested Clique instances we can simultaneously compute d MST, which allows us to emulate d sequences of contractions in $O(1)$ rounds. Also, we can sort d sets of tuples in parallel, which allows us to compute edges for each of d contracted graphs in parallel, in $O(1)$ rounds. Therefore, we can reduce the size of a problem by a $\sqrt{d}$ factor in $O(1)$ rounds. This results with in a recursion of depth $\Theta(\log_d n)$.

In the corollary 4.2 we summarize the two points of presented tradeoff: (A) the smallest number of rounds we that we can get with polylogarithmic size messages, and (B) the smallest message size which allows to find min-cut in $O(1)$ rounds.

Corollary 4.2. *It is possible to find min-cut in* Congested Clique *problem in $O\left(\epsilon_1^{-1}\frac{\log n}{\log\log n}\right)$ rounds, with bandwidth $O(\log^{2+\epsilon_1} n)$, and in $O(\epsilon_2^{-1})$ rounds with bandwidth n^{ϵ_2} for any $\epsilon_1, \epsilon_2 \in \Theta(1)$.*

5 MINIMUM CUT IN $O(\log^2 n)$ ROUNDS OF Congested Clique

In this section, we present an $O(\log^2 n)$ round algorithm for the min-cut problem, thus proving Theorem 1.4. The algorithm is an implementation of Karger's algorithm based on a mixture of random sampling and tree packing [Kar00].

The algorithm is based on the fact that for a given graph G, with the min-cut of size λ, it is possible to find set of trees of size $O(\log n)$, such that each tree has assigned a weight, and a constant fraction (by weight) of them contains at most two edges of a min-cut. In more details, Karger proposes that for $G(p)$, where $p = 216\ln n/\lambda$, we can use tree packing algorithm based on [PST95]. Since the min-cut of $G(p)$ is $O(\log n)$, the tree packing algorithm requires only $\Theta(\log^2 n)$ MST computations. However, we have to execute them in a sequence, as weights of the edges are modified after each computed MST. The whole process is summarized in the Corollary 4.2 of [Kar00] and its proof.

Having $O(\log n)$ spanning trees, such that constant fraction (by weight) of them contains at most two edges of a min-cut, it is enough to compute the size of a cut determined by all pairs of edges in all those trees. The smallest of them has to be the min-cut of G.

The whole algorithm consists of two phases: In the first, we find appropriate tree packing, by adapting the PRAM algorithm proposed by Karger – we compute $O(\log^2 n)$ Minimum Spanning Trees, but computing each of them takes only $O(1)$ rounds, which allows us to find proper tree packing in $O(\log^2 n)$ of Congested Clique. In the second phase, which is described in details in subsection 5.1 for each tree T we have found, for each pair of edges $e_1, e_2 \in T$ we compute the size of a cut containing only those two edges from tree T, i.e cut which does not contain any $e \neq e_1 \wedge e \neq e_2 \wedge e \in T$. Since at least one tree has property that it contains at most two edges from a min-cut, if we check cuts for all pairs of edges in all trees we find the min-cut.

5.1 Treefix and finding a min-cut

In this subsection we describe $O(1)$ round Congested Clique procedure, which for a given tree T, and graph G, computes values of all cuts in G, such that they have at most 2 edges in T. More precisely we show the following

THEOREM 5.1. *Given a spanning tree T of graph G, let consider C_T, set of cuts of G, such that they share at most two edges with T. Then, we can find the size of all cuts in C_T in $O(1)$ rounds of the* Congested Clique.

PROOF. Let assume that as input one player knows whole tree T, and as an output some fixed node has to know the smallest cut defined by one or two edges of the given tree. In this subsection we briefly sketch Karger's algorithm and present $O(1)$ round algorithm solving this problem.

Let us assume that our tree T is rooted. For a given node v, by $v^{\downarrow}$ we denote subtree of v, by $v^{\uparrow}$ be the set of ancestors of v, including v. By the subtree of an edge $\{u, v\}$ we understand subtree of a node which is further away from the root, i.e subtree $\{u, v\}$ is $v^{\downarrow}$ iff $u \notin v^{\downarrow}$ and $u^{\downarrow}$ otherwise. There are three cases to consider consider, as the min-cut may contain

- A a single edge which is in T
- B two edges which are in T, one in the subtree of the other
- C two edges, such that none of them is in the subtree of the other

For a given function $f(v)$, which is defined for a node, we want to compute treefix function $f^{\downarrow}(v) = \sum_{u \in v^{\downarrow}} f(u)$. To use Karger's approach, which allows us to check all three cases, we have to compute those values:

(1) $\delta^{\downarrow}(v)$, where $\delta(v)$ is a weighted degree of v
(2) $\rho^{\downarrow}(v)$, where $\rho(v)$ is a total weight of edges whose endpoints' lower common ancestor is v
(3) $C^{\downarrow}(v)$, the size of the cut defined bu nodes in subtree of v
(4) $f_v^{\downarrow}(w)$, the total weight of edges from subtree of the node v to the node w
(5) $g_w^{\downarrow}(v)$, the total weight of edges from the subtree of v to the subtree of w

Computing 1 is simple. To compute $\delta^{\downarrow}(w)$ in the Congested Clique model, each node v locally computes $\delta(v)$, and announces its value to the whole network. Then each node w, aggregates values of $\delta(u)$ for all nodes $u \in w^{\downarrow}$, to get value of $\delta^{\downarrow}(w)$.

To compute 2, each node has to compute how much its incident edges contribute to $\rho\downarrow(v)$ for each v. Then all nodes can send their contribution to $\rho^{\downarrow}(v)$ to the node v. Since there are at most n different nodes, each node has to send / receive n values, therefore this can be done in $O(1)$ rounds, by Lemma 3.4. Then we can do the same thing as for computing $\delta^{\downarrow}(w)$, when we knew the value of δ for all nodes. Only difference is that we have to divide result by 2, a we counted each edge twice.

By Lemma 5.9 from [Kar00], we know that $C^{\downarrow}(v) = \delta^{\downarrow}(v) - 2\rho^{\downarrow}(v)$, and since each node v already knows $\delta^{\downarrow}(v)$ and $\rho^{\downarrow}(v)$, we can compute $C^{\downarrow}(v)$ locally.

The value of $f_v^{\downarrow}(w)$, we can compute in a similar way as $\rho^{\downarrow}(v)$. In the first place, each node w computes how much it contributes to value of $f_v^{\downarrow}(w)$. Since there are at most n nodes w and at most n subtrees $v^{\downarrow}$, each node has to send / receive up to n messages, which again can be done in $O(1)$ rounds, by Lemma 3.4. The same approach is applicable to $g_w^{\downarrow}(v)$.

Those are all building blocks we need to compute all cut values, such that one of them is a min-cut. Karger shows in [Kar00] that we can handle all cases A, B, C, just by using computed values. In particular, to handle the case A, all we have to know are values of $C^{\downarrow}(v)$. Let consider case B, let assume without loss of generality that v is in a subtree of w. The we can use following equation

$$\begin{aligned} C(w^{\downarrow} - v^{\downarrow}) &= C(w^{\downarrow}) - C(v^{\downarrow}) + 2C(v^{\downarrow}, w^{\uparrow} - v^{\uparrow}) \\ &= C(w^{\downarrow}) - C(v^{\downarrow}) + 2g_w^{\downarrow}(v) - 4\rho^{\downarrow}(v). \end{aligned}$$

For the case C we use the following equation:

$$C(w^{\downarrow} \cup v^{\downarrow}) = C(w^{\downarrow}) + C(v^{\downarrow}) - 2C(w^{\downarrow}, v^{\downarrow}) = C(w^{\downarrow}) + C(v^{\downarrow}) - 2g_w^{\downarrow}(v)$$

Therefore, for each pair of (v, w), we have to know only a constant number of values to compute the value of cut. We can assign to each player n such pairs, which means each player has to receive $O(n)$ values in order to be able to compute cut size for each assigned pair. Also, each player has to send only $O(n)$ messages. Each of values $g_w^{\downarrow}(v)$ is used only once, and a single player has n of them, which contributes at most $O(n)$ to the number of messages to send. Each of values $C(v^{\downarrow})$ and $\rho^{\downarrow}(v)$ is used n times, and each player has 1 of them, which also contributes at most $O(n)$ to the number of messages to the number of messages to send. Therefore, all messages can be exchanged by Lemma 3.4. □

From Theorem 5.1, we have that if we could find in some faster way a small set of trees, such that one of them contains at most two edges of the min-cut of G, then we would have fast exact algorithm for the min-cut problem. More precisely

Corollary 5.2. *Given an $f(n)$ round algorithm that produces $g(n)$ trees such that one of them contains at most two edges from a min-cut, we can find the min-cut in $O(f(n) + g(n))$ rounds.*

6 OPEN PROBLEMS

We presented an algorithm that finds a $1 + o(1)$ approximation of the min-cut in $O(1)$ rounds of the Congested Clique. Moreover, we showed that if the network graph has a min-cut of size $O\left(\frac{n^{1/3}}{\log^{14/3} n}\right)$, we can find an exact min-cut in $O(1)$ rounds. The first open question that we leave is whether there is an $O(1)$ round Congested Clique algorithm that solves the problem for general graphs.

To get the $1 + o(1)$ approximation algorithm, we proved that one can solve $O(n^{1-\epsilon})$ MST problems simultaneously, in $O(\epsilon^{-1})$ rounds of Congested Clique. This strengthens the recent result of Jurdziński and Nowicki [JN18] which solves one MST in $O(1)$ rounds. We think that this extension may be interesting on its own, as it shows that one can solve even a polynomial number of unrelated MST problems in $O(1)$ rounds. The second question that we leave is whether it is possible to solve $\tilde{O}(n)$ MSTs in $O(1)$ rounds of congested clique.

REFERENCES

[adHM98] Friedhelm Meyer auf der Heide and Gabriel Terán Martinez. Communication-efficient parallel multiway and approximate minimum cut computation. In *LATIN'98*, pages 316–330, 1998.

[AGM12] Kook Jin Ahn, Sudipto Guha, and Andrew McGregor. Analyzing graph structure via linear measurements. In *Proceedings of the twenty-third annual ACM-SIAM symposium on Discrete Algorithms*, pages 459–467. SIAM, 2012.

[BHP12] Andrew Berns, James Hegeman, and Sriram V Pemmaraju. Super-fast distributed algorithms for metric facility location. In *Automata, Languages, and Programming*, pages 428–439. Springer, 2012.

[BKKL17] Ruben Becker, Andreas Karrenbauer, Sebastian Krinninger, and Christoph Lenzen. Near-Optimal Approximate Shortest Paths and Transshipment in Distributed and Streaming Models. In Andréa W. Richa, editor, *31st International Symposium on Distributed Computing (DISC 2017)*, volume 91 of *Leibniz International Proceedings in Informatics (LIPIcs)*, pages 7:1–7:16. Schloss Dagstuhl–Leibniz-Zentrum fuer Informatik, 2017.

[CHKK+15] Keren Censor-Hillel, Petteri Kaski, Janne H. Korhonen, Christoph Lenzen, Ami Paz, and Jukka Suomela. Algebraic methods in the congested clique. In *the Proc. of the Int'l Symp. on Princ. of Dist. Comp. (PODC)*, pages 143–152. ACM, 2015.

[CLT18] Keren Censor-Hillel, Dean Leitersdorf, and Elia Turner. Sparse matrix multiplication with bandwidth restricted all-to-all communication. *CoRR*, abs/1802.04789, 2018.

[DG08] Jeffrey Dean and Sanjay Ghemawat. Mapreduce: simplified data processing on large clusters. *Communications of the ACM*, 51(1):107–113, 2008.

[DKO14a] Andrew Drucker, Fabian Kuhn, and Rotem Oshman. On the power of the congested clique model. In *the Proc. of the Int'l Symp. on Princ. of Dist. Comp. (PODC)*, pages 367–376. ACM, 2014.

[DKO14b] Andrew Drucker, Fabian Kuhn, and Rotem Oshman. On the power of the congested clique model. In *the Proc. of the Int'l Symp. on Princ. of Dist. Comp. (PODC)*, pages 367–376, 2014.

[DLP12] Danny Dolev, Christoph Lenzen, and Shir Peled. "tri, tri again": Finding triangles and small subgraphs in a distributed setting. In *Distributed Computing*, pages 195–209. Springer, 2012.

[EFS56] P. Elias, A. Feinstein, and C. Shannon. A note on the maximum flow through a network. *Information Theory, IEEE Transactions on*, 2(4):117–119, 1956.

[FF56] L. R. Ford and D. R. Fulkerson. Maximal flow through a network. *Canadian Journal of Mathematics*, 8:399–404, 1956.

[FF10] D. R. Ford and D. R. Fulkerson. *Flows in Networks*. Princeton University Press, Princeton, NJ, USA, 2010.

[Gab91] Harold N. Gabow. A matroid approach to finding edge connectivity and packing arborescences. In *Proc. of the Symp. on Theory of Comp. (STOC)*, pages 112–122. ACM, 1991.

[Gal16] François Le Gall. Further algebraic algorithms in the congested clique model and applications to graph-theoretic problems. In *DISC*, 2016.

[GGK+18] Mohsen Ghaffari, Themis Gouleakis, Christian Konrad, Slobodan Mitrović, and Ronitt Rubinfeld. Improved massively parallel computation algorithms for mis, matching, and vertex cover. In *the Proc. of the Int'l Symp. on Princ. of Dist. Comp. (PODC)*, 2018.

[Gha16] Mohsen Ghaffari. An improved distributed algorithm for maximal independent set. In *Pro. of ACM-SIAM Symp. on Disc. Alg. (SODA)*, 2016.

[Gha17] Mohsen Ghaffari. Distributed mis via all-to-all communication. In *the Proc. of the Int'l Symp. on Princ. of Dist. Comp. (PODC)*, pages 141–149, 2017.

[GP16] Mohsen Ghaffari and Merav Parter. MST in Log-Star Rounds of Congested Clique. In *the Proc. of the Int'l Symp. on Princ. of Dist. Comp. (PODC)*, 2016.

[HP14] James W Hegeman and Sriram V Pemmaraju. Lessons from the congested clique applied to MapReduce. In *the Proceedings of the International Colloquium on Structural Information and Communication Complexity*, pages 149–164. Springer, 2014.

[HPP+15a] James Hegeman, Gopal Pandurangan, Sriram Pemmaraju, Viveck Sardeshmuck, and Michele Scquizatto. Toward optimal bounds in the congested clique: Graph connectivity and MST. In *the Proc. of the Int'l Symp. on Princ. of Dist. Comp. (PODC)*, 2015.

[HPP+15b] James W. Hegeman, Gopal Pandurangan, Sriram V. Pemmaraju, Vivek B. Sardeshmukh, and Michele Scquizzato. Toward optimal bounds in the congested clique: Graph connectivity and MST. In *the Proc. of the Int'l Symp. on Princ. of Dist. Comp. (PODC)*, pages 91–100. ACM, 2015.

[HPS14] James W Hegeman, Sriram V Pemmaraju, and Vivek B Sardeshmukh. Near-constant-time distributed algorithms on a congested clique. In *Distributed Computing*, pages 514–530. Springer, 2014.

[JN18] Tomasz Jurdziński and Krzysztof Nowicki. MST in O(1) Rounds of Congested Clique. In *Pro. of ACM-SIAM Symp. on Disc. Alg. (SODA)*, pages 2620–2632, 2018.

[Kar93] David Karger. Global min-cuts in RNC and other ramifications of a simple mincut algorithm. In *Pro. of ACM-SIAM Symp. on Disc. Alg. (SODA)*, pages 21–30, 01 1993.

[Kar94] David R Karger. Random sampling in cut, flow, and network design problems. In *Proc. of the Symp. on Theory of Comp. (STOC)*, pages 648–657, 1994.

[Kar00] David R. Karger. Minimum cuts in near-linear time. *J. ACM*, 47(1):46–76, January 2000.

[KKT95] David R. Karger, Philip N. Klein, and Robert E. Tarjan. A randomized linear-time algorithm to find minimum spanning trees. *J. ACM*, 42(2):321–328, March 1995.

[Kru56] Joseph B. Kruskal. On the Shortest Spanning Subtree of a Graph and the Traveling Salesman Problem. *Proceedings of the American Mathematical Society*, 7(1):48–50, 1956.

[KS96] David R. Karger and Clifford Stein. A new approach to the minimum cut problem. *J. ACM*, 43(4):601–640, July 1996.

[KSV10] Howard Karloff, Siddharth Suri, and Sergei Vassilvitskii. A model of computation for mapreduce. In *Pro. of ACM-SIAM Symp. on Disc. Alg. (SODA)*, pages 938–948, 2010.

[Len13a] Christoph Lenzen. Optimal deterministic routing and sorting on the congested clique. In *the Proc. of the Int'l Symp. on Princ. of Dist. Comp. (PODC)*, pages 42–50, 2013.

[Len13b] Christoph Lenzen. Optimal deterministic routing and sorting on the congested clique. In *the Proc. of the Int'l Symp. on Princ. of Dist. Comp. (PODC)*, pages 42–50, 2013.

[LMSV11] Silvio Lattanzi, Benjamin Moseley, Siddharth Suri, and Sergei Vassilvitskii. Filtering: a method for solving graph problems in mapreduce. In *the Proceedings of the Symposium on Parallel Algorithms and Architectures*, pages 85–94, 2011.

[LPSPP05] Zvi Lotker, Boaz Patt-Shamir, Elan Pavlov, and David Peleg. Minimum-weight spanning tree construction in O(log log n) communication rounds. *SIAM Journal on Computing*, 35(1):120–131, 2005.

[MK13] M. Ghaffari and Fabian Kuhn. Distributed minimum cut approximation. In *Proc. of the Int'l Symp. on Dist. Comp. (DISC)*, pages 1–15, 2013.

[Nan14] Danupon Nanongkai. Distributed approximation algorithms for weighted shortest paths. In *Proc. of the Symp. on Theory of Comp. (STOC)*, 2014.

[NI92] Hiroshi Nagamochi and Toshihide Ibaraki. Computing edge-connectivity in multigraphs and capacitated graphs. *SIAM Journal on Discrete Mathematics*, 5(1):54–66, 1992.

[NP89] T. Nishizeki and S. Poljak. Highly connected factors with a small number of edges. *preprint*, 1989.

[NS14] Danupon Nanongkai and Hsin-Hao Su. Almost-tight distributed minimum cut algorithms. In *Proc. of the Int'l Symp. on Dist. Comp. (DISC)*, pages 439–453, 2014.

[PS16] Sriram V. Pemmaraju and Vivek B. Sardeshmukh. Super-Fast MST Algorithms in the Congested Clique Using o(m) Messages. In *FSTTCS 2016*, pages 47:1–47:15, 2016.

[PST95] Serge A. Plotkin, David B. Shmoys, and Éva Tardos. Fast approximation algorithms for fractional packing and covering problems. *Math. Oper. Res.*, 20(2):257–301, 1995.

[PST11] Boaz Patt-Shamir and Marat Teplitsky. The round complexity of distributed sorting. In *the Proc. of the Int'l Symp. on Princ. of Dist. Comp. (PODC)*, pages 249–256, 2011.

[PVZ12] Jeff M. Phillips, Elad Verbin, and Qin Zhang. Lower bounds for number-in-hand multiparty communication complexity, made easy. In *Pro. of ACM-SIAM Symp. on Disc. Alg. (SODA)*, pages 486–501, 2012.

[RVW16] Tim Roughgarden, Sergei Vassilvitskii, and Joshua R. Wang. Shuffles and circuits: (on lower bounds for modern parallel computation). In *the Proceedings of the Symposium on Parallel Algorithms and Architectures*, pages 1–12, 2016.

Locking Timestamps versus Locking Objects

Marcos K. Aguilera
VMware Research

Tudor David*
IBM Research, Zurich

Rachid Guerraoui
EPFL

Junxiong Wang
EPFL

ABSTRACT

We present *multiversion timestamp locking (MVTL)*, a new genre of multiversion concurrency control algorithms for serializable transactions. The key idea behind MVTL is simple: lock individual timestamps instead of locking objects. After presenting a generic MVTL algorithm, we demonstrate MVTL's expressiveness: we give several simple MVTL algorithms that address limitations of current multiversion schemes, by committing transactions that previous schemes would abort, by avoiding the problems of serial aborts or ghost aborts, and by offering a way to prioritize transactions that should not be aborted. We give evidence that, in practice, MVTL-based algorithms can outperform alternative concurrency control schemes.

ACM Reference Format:

Marcos K. Aguilera, Tudor David, Rachid Guerraoui, and Junxiong Wang. 2018. Locking Timestamps versus Locking Objects. In *PODC '18: ACM Symposium on Principles of Distributed Computing, July 23–27, 2018, Egham, United Kingdom.* ACM, New York, NY, USA, 10 pages. https://doi.org/10.1145/3212734.3212742

1 INTRODUCTION

Serializable transactions are a powerful paradigm available in many computing systems, such as transactional memory, database systems, and key-value storage systems. To ensure serializability, transactions require a scheme for concurrency control to handle any negative consequences of transaction interleaving.

The literature on concurrency control is rich [6, 26], and a particularly appealing class of algorithms is called *multiversion concurrency control* [5]. Briefly, these algorithms keep a *history* of each object, containing many versions of the data with associated timestamps. This history gives the system a *choice* of which version to use when an object is accessed. This choice permits more transactions to execute concurrently without blocking or aborting. For example, in some multiversion algorithms [6, 8], read-only transactions can execute without ever blocking or aborting, and update transactions can concurrently update the same object. Enabling more concurrency has become particularly important with the proliferation of multi-core and large-scale systems. Multiversion algorithms have wide application: they are used in database systems both commercial and academic [10, 19, 26, 27], and recent work has applied them to key-value storage systems and transactional memory (e.g., [11, 15–17, 22, 23]). In this paper, we do not restrict ourselves to particular applications, but rather study multiversion algorithms in their broadest scope.

There are three main genres of multiversion algorithms: *lock based*, *timestamp ordering*, and *serialization graph based* [6]. Lock-based algorithms (e.g., MV2PL [6]) acquire locks to avoid the ill-effects of concurrency; these algorithms are very simple. Timestamp ordering algorithms (e.g., MVTO [6]) assign a timestamp to each transaction, and then serialize transactions by timestamp; these algorithms permit read-only transactions to execute without ever aborting. Serialization graph algorithms (e.g., MVSGT [26]) detect cycles in the serialization graph to prevent a violation of serializability; these algorithms permit higher levels of concurrency than the alternatives.

Despite their many benefits, all types of multiversion algorithms have limitations. Lock-based algorithms significantly restrict the degree of concurrency. Timestamp ordering algorithms are susceptible to aborts, including *serial aborts*—aborts in serial executions—and *ghost aborts*—aborts caused by a conflict with a transaction that already aborted. Serialization graph algorithms are complex and incur significant computation overheads [3, 16, 20].

In this paper, we introduce a new genre of multiversion algorithms, called *multiversion timestamp locking* or MVTL in short. MVTL is based on a simple idea: use locks as in lock-based algorithms, but lock individual timestamps of objects, rather than entire objects at a time. A transaction is allowed to commit if it can find at least one timestamp that it managed to lock across all its objects. Intuitively, MVTL performs well because it uses locks with fine granularity: not only individual objects have separate locks, but individual timestamps within objects have their own locks. Locking at fine granularity increases parallelism and decreases blocking and aborting, as the system can explore many serialization points for each transaction.

Conceptually, MVTL keeps a lock state for each object and each timestamp, which amounts to an infinitely large lock state. However, in practice we can reduce the lock state significantly using interval compression, so that each object holds just a few lock intervals, and this state can be subsequently discarded when the associated versions are purged.

To precisely define MVTL, we give a generic algorithm (§4) that has several nondeterministic choices, such as what timestamps each operation tries to lock, and how locks are acquired (wait or give up on blocked locks). We prove that these choices do not affect safety: the generic algorithm is correct irrespective of them. However, the choices are crucial for performance.

We then propose several specific algorithms that specialize the generic MVTL algorithm by fixing these choices to obtain different benefits (§5). These algorithms are simple and address some important drawbacks of existing multiversion algorithms, such as serial aborts, ghost aborts, the lack of a priority scheme for transactions, and more. We also show that pessimistic and timestamp ordering

*Work done while the author was at VMware Research and EPFL.

PODC '18, July 23–27, 2018, Egham, United Kingdom

ACM ISBN 978-1-4503-5795-1/18/07...$15.00
https://doi.org/10.1145/3212734.3212742

algorithms can be seen as special cases of MVTL. Thus, in a precise sense, MVTL unifies these algorithms.

Next, we discuss some practical considerations around MVTL, such as how to compress the lock state (§6). We separate out these considerations because they are orthogonal to the concepts underlying the MVTL algorithm. However, they are important to using MVTL in practice.

Then, we show how to extend the basic MVTL algorithm to distributed transactions in a message-passing system (§7). We believe MVTL is particularly relevant in this setting as it can be quite communication efficient.

We implement an MVTL-based algorithm, and experimentally compare its behavior with multiversion and lock-based alternatives (§8). The results indicate significant advantages of MVTL in read-write workloads, and no disadvantages under read-only workloads.

To summarize, the contributions of this paper are the following:

- We propose a new genre of multiversion algorithms for transactions, called multiversion timestamp locking (MVTL), which is based on the idea of locking timestamps.
- We give several MVTL algorithms, which address various limitations of current multiversion algorithms.
- We show that MVTL generalizes both multiversion timestamp ordering and pessimistic multiversion algorithms.
- We discuss practical considerations for implementing MVTL, including techniques to compress the lock state.
- We describe a version of MVTL for distributed transactions.
- We implement an MVTL-based algorithm and demonstrate its advantages over alternatives.

The main contribution is conceptual in nature: locking individual timestamps is a new way to approach multiversion algorithms. The specific MVTL algorithms we present are simple and just scratch the surface; the investigation of additional MVTL algorithms is an exciting direction for future work. Also interesting is to implement MVTL in other types of transactional systems, such as software transactional memory, transactional key-value storage systems, transactional object systems, and database systems. While the fundamental MVTL algorithms we present are system agnostic, the details of how these algorithms can be best implemented depend on the system and deserve further study.

Due to space limitations, details of our contribution are omitted, including proofs and pseudo-code of some algorithms. They are given in the full paper [1].

2 MODEL

We consider a standard model for a multi-threaded concurrent system [13]. The system has processes that communicate via atomic shared memory. The system is asynchronous: there are no bounds on the relative speed of processes. We assume the existence of a discrete global clock, and processes may or may not have access to the global clock. More precisely, processes may have local clocks that match the global clock ("synchronized clocks") or that are within a known bound ϵ of the global clock ("ϵ-synchronized clocks").

We consider algorithms that implement a transactional storage system. Such a system maintains a set of objects and allows processes to manipulate the objects using transactions. Each object has a unique key (identifier) and, by abuse of language, we refer to the object and its key interchangeably. The system supports four operations with their usual semantics: BEGIN(tx) starts a transaction tx, COMMIT(tx) tries to commit tx and returns a success indication, READ(tx, k) reads key k within tx, and WRITE(tx, k, v) writes v to k within tx. Transactions are dynamic: their read and write operations can depend on the results of prior operations in the transaction.

Our correctness condition is *multiversion view serializability*, a form of serializability well-suited for multiversion algorithms. Roughly, this condition requires every multiversion schedule of the algorithm to be equivalent to a serial monoversion schedule [6, 26].

Some of our results refer to a *workload*, which specify the transactional work submitted to the system. More precisely, a workload is a sequence of operations indexed by the transaction they belong to, where each operation is *read*(k), *write*(k, v), or *commit*. We use workloads to study how different protocols react to the same inputs.

3 OVERVIEW

After recalling multiversion concurrency control, we introduce the notion of *timestamp locking* and explain how it addresses weaknesses of existing multiversion algorithms.

Multiversion concurrency control and the MVTO+ algorithm. A well-known genre of multiversion algorithms is multiversion timestamp ordering. Its basic idea is to assign a timestamp to each transaction and then use the timestamp to determine (a) what version the transaction reads from, (b) what version it writes to, and (c) the serialization order of transactions. This idea can lead to several slightly different algorithms. To focus the discussion, here we present a concrete algorithm denoted MVTO+, which is identical to the MVTO algorithm in [6] but with an improvement: it avoids cascading aborts by not reading uncommitted data. For each object, MVTO+ keeps many versions and a timestamp for each version. It is useful to think of each object as an evolving timeline with values. Each transaction tx has a unique timestamp t; when tx reads an object, it obtains the version of the object with the largest timestamp before t. When tx writes an object, tx does not immediately produce a new version but instead it stores the written value in a temporary area for the transaction. Upon commit, tx takes each written value in the temporary area and produces a new version with timestamp t.

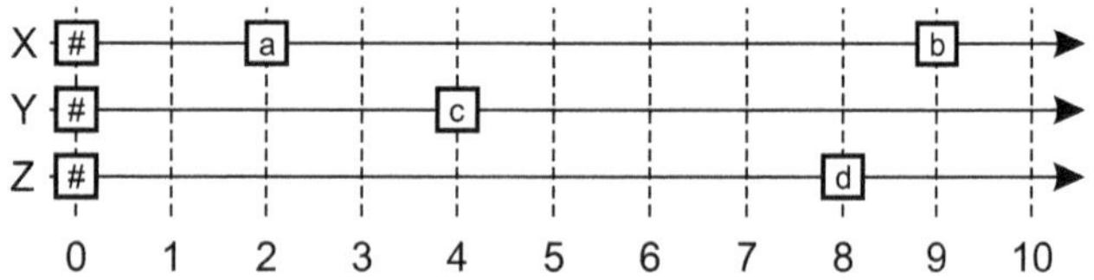

For example, the figure above depicts three objects X, Y, and Z. Each object has an initial version denoted #. In addition, X has two other versions with data a and b and timestamps 2 and 9; Y has data c with timestamp 4; and Z has data d with timestamp 8. Suppose a transaction tx is assigned timestamp 6. If tx reads X, it obtains a—the largest version with a timestamp before 6. Similarly, if tx reads Y, it obtains c. If tx writes e to Z and commits, then Z gets a new version with data e and timestamp 6.

Ultimately, transactions are serialized by the order of their timestamps. A key implication is that, after tx reads X and obtains a, another transaction should not produce a version of X with a timestamp between 2 and 6. To prevent this behavior, MVTO+ keeps a *read-timestamp* for each version: this is the largest timestamp with which the version was read by a transaction. In the example, after *tx* reads X and obtains a, the read-timestamp of a becomes 6 (if it was not already larger than 6).

Timestamp locking. We look at MVTO+ slightly differently, using our new notion of *timestamp locking*. This notion allows us to generalize MVTO+ into our new MVTL algorithm. Rather than read-timestamps, we can think that each object has several locks, one for each timestamp. When *tx* reads X, rather than updating the read-timestamp of a to 6, we can think that *tx* obtains a read-lock on each timestamp between 3 and 6. When another transaction wishes to write a version with timestamp, say 5, it must obtain the write-lock on that timestamp. But the read-locks by *tx* prevent this from happening, as required by MVTO+. We can now see the read-timestamp of a as simply a compact representation of the fact that there are read-locks between 3 and 6.

Thinking about timestamp locks has several advantages over read-timestamps. First, with read-timestamps, it is not clear what should happen if *tx* aborts: should the read-timestamp of a be updated to its previous value? But what is the previous value if several other transactions read a concurrently? This is a hard question, and MVTO+ avoids it altogether by taking an unnecessarily conservative approach: when *tx* aborts, it leaves the read-timestamp of a at 6. We show that this choice leads to ghost aborts. In contrast, timestamp locks provide a better alternative: if *tx* aborts, its read-locks are removed but the read-locks of other transactions remain.

Second, with timestamp locks, there is no reason that a transaction should be restricted to obtaining write-locks on just one timestamp, or obtaining read-locks on a range that ends with the transaction's timestamp. Permitting more choices allows the system to avoid serial aborts, as we explain later.

These advantages are captured by our MVTL algorithm, which we now briefly summarize. With MVTL, when a transaction wishes to read an object, it selects a version of the object to read and obtains read-locks on one or more timestamps adjacent to and immediately following that version. To write an object, the transaction obtains write-locks on one or more timestamps anywhere. To commit, the transaction must find a single common timestamp that is read-locked or write-locked across all objects read or written by the transaction, respectively. If such a timestamp exists, the transaction commits; otherwise, it aborts.

The exact timestamps that are locked by reads and writes depend on a *locking policy*. The algorithm remains correct for any locking policy, but a poorly chosen policy causes many aborts because there is no common locked timestamp. We present some simple but interesting algorithms using various locking policies, each with its own advantages.

4 GENERIC MVTL ALGORITHM

We now present our generic MVTL algorithm in detail. We start with some basic concepts (§4.1), explain a simple lock extension we use (§4.2), and cover the main algorithm (§4.3). We present a centralized version of MVTL designed for a single server. We later describe a distributed version of MVTL intended for distributed transactions. Some practical considerations for implementing MVTL, including how locks and data can be compacted, are discussed in §6.

4.1 Preamble

The system keeps many versions of data in an array *Values*$[k, t]$ where k is a key and t is a timestamp. To ensure processes pick distinct timestamps, we add a process id to a timestamp; thus, a timestamp is a pair (v, p) ordered lexicographically, where v is a number. There is a smallest timestamp denoted 0, and a special initial value denoted #, such that initially *Values*$[k, 0]$ = # for every k. It is also useful to assume that initially *Values*$[k, t] = \perp$ for every k and $t \neq 0$, representing an empty storage system.

4.2 Freezable locks

In the MVTL algorithm, each version of a key is a *write-once object*—an object initially set to $\perp$ that may change its state at most once. We define a simple variation of readers-writer locks, which we call freezable locks, which are appropriate for such objects and we use them in MVTL. A freezable lock is similar to a readers-writer lock, except that a lock holder can freeze the lock to indicate that it will never release it. Freezing is useful because it tells other processes that they should not wait to acquire the lock; we use this feature in several specialized MVTL algorithms. If a lock holder does not freeze a lock, it is expected to release it eventually.

We apply freezable locks to write-once objects as follows. A process acquires the lock in write mode if it intends to write the object. The process may ultimately fail to write if the transaction aborts, in which case it releases the lock; but if the transaction commits, the process freezes its lock to ensure other processes will not try to write the object again. Similarly, a process acquires the lock in read mode to read the object and it freezes the lock in case of a commit; if the object was not written (its state is $\perp$), this prevents other processes from writing to it, sealing its fate.

4.3 Algorithm

Algorithm 1 shows the main code of the generic MVTL algorithm. For clarity, we assume that the code in lines 17–19 is executed atomically, but we later remove this assumption (§6). To write a value into key k, a transaction obtains zero or more write-locks on timestamps for that key (function WRITE-LOCKS in line 4). Intuitively, a write-lock on a timestamp t for key k allows the transaction to commit with timestamp t as far as accesses to k are concerned. After getting the locks, the transaction remembers the key and value; the write is not visible to other transactions until the transaction commits.

To read a key, a transaction gets zero or more read-locks on timestamps for that key (function READ-LOCKS in line 7), with the requirement that these timestamps form a contiguous interval that starts immediately after the version that the read returns. For instance, if $[tr{+}1, te]$ denotes the read-locked timestamps, then the read must return the value committed with timestamp tr. This requirement is necessary for serializability: intuitively, the read locks permit the transaction to commit with any timestamp $t \in [tr{+}1, te]$ after having read v, by preventing other transactions from writing a different value with a timestamp between tr and te. After locking, the transaction remembers k and tr; knowledge of k is necessary

Algorithm 1 The generic MVTL algorithm (part 1/2): main code

```
1:  function BEGIN(tx)
2:      tx.readset ← ∅; tx.writeset ← ∅; tx.committs ← ⊥
3:  function WRITE(tx, k, v)                  ▷ write v to k in transaction tx
4:      WRITE-LOCKS(tx, k)            ▷ write lock some subset of timestamps
5:      add (k, v) to tx.writeset       ▷ remember key and value we wrote
6:  function READ(tx, k)                        ▷ read k in transaction tx
7:      tr ← READ-LOCKS(tx, k) ▷ read lock some interval [tr+1, . . .] with
                                                  Values[k, tr] ≠ ⊥
8:      if tr = ⊥ then return ⊥                              ▷ read failed
9:      add (k, tr) to tx.readset    ▷ remember key and version we read
10:     return Values[k, tr]                     ▷ return committed value
11: function COMMIT(tx)                     ▷ try to commit transaction tx
12:     COMMIT-LOCKS(tx)                   ▷ locks to acquire at commit time
13:     T ← {t : ∀k ∈ tx.readset.keys, tx has a lock on (k, t) and
              ∀k ∈ tx.writeset.keys, tx has a write-lock on (k, t)}
                                    ▷ try to find a locked timestamp for tx
14:     if T = ∅ then mark tx as aborted
15:     else
16:         tx.committs ← COMMIT-TS(T)        ▷ pick some timestamp in T
17:         for (k, v) ∈ tx.writeset do
18:             freeze write-lock for tx on (k, tx.committs)  ▷ freeze locks
19:             Values[k, tx.committs] ← v      ▷ expose committed value
20:         mark tx as committed
21:     if COMMIT-GC(tx) then GC(tx)                   ▷ invoke gc or not
22: function GC(tx)            ▷ garbage collect locks of tx after it ended
23:     if tx committed then
24:         for (k, tr) ∈ tx.readset do
25:             freeze read-locks for tx on [tr+1, tx.committs]
26:     release all unfrozen read- and write-locks for tx
```

Algorithm 2 The generic MVTL algorithm (part 2/2): policy

```
function WRITE-LOCKS(tx, k)
    acquire write-locks for tx on (k, T) for some set T
function READ-LOCKS(tx, k)                 ▷ returns a timestamp or ⊥
    acquire read-locks for tx on (k, T) for some T = [tr+1, . . .] where
            Values[k, tr] ≠ ⊥
    either return tr or return ⊥
function COMMIT-LOCKS(tx)
    acquire read- or write-locks for tx on some keys and timestamps
function COMMIT-TS(T) return some t ∈ T
function COMMIT-GC(tx) either return true or return false
```

to commit, and knowledge of both k and tr is needed to garbage collect the locks of the transaction.

To commit, a transaction gets zero or more additional locks (function COMMIT-LOCKS in line 12) and tries to find a commit timestamp t that is write-locked for every k in the write-set, and that is read- or write-locked for every k in the read-set. (A key in the read-set may be write-locked because the transaction read the key and then wrote it.) If there are many such timestamps, the transaction picks one (function COMMIT-TS in line 16). The transaction then freezes write-locks on that timestamp and records the written values so that they can be seen by other transactions. As an optional step (as determined by calling COMMIT-GC in line 21), the transaction may garbage collect the locks it holds. Doing so freezes the read locks between the version read and the commit timestamp, and releases all other locks. If the algorithm skips garbage collection on commit, garbage collection can be invoked any time later in the background; this is not shown in the code.

The algorithm depends on a policy of what locks to acquire, how to pick one of many possible commit timestamps, and whether to garbage collect during commit; these choices can depend on the transaction and other considerations. The choices are determined by the functions that we mentioned above: WRITE-LOCKS, READ-LOCKS, COMMIT-LOCKS, COMMIT-TS, and COMMIT-GC. The generic MVTL algorithm uses a generic policy that makes these choices nondeterministically (Algorithm 2). For example, to obtain write locks, the generic policy nondeterministically picks a set T of timestamps to lock. To obtain read locks, the policy picks an interval of timestamps starting immediately after a committed version.

We prove that the generic MVTL algorithm is correct with its nondeterministic choices. Naturally, this correctness carries over to any specialization that fixes the nondeterministic choices. These specializations lead to different algorithms (§5).

Some policies of the generic algorithm may cause deadlocks, where a process waits forever to acquire a lock. In such cases, standard techniques for deadlock detection can be used to abort the required transactions (e.g., cycle detection in the wait-for graph, timeout, etc). In the full paper, we show the following:

THEOREM 1. *The generic MVTL algorithm (Algorithms 1 and 2) ensures serializability.*

5 SIMPLE MVTL ALGORITHMS

We now give several simple algorithms that are instances of the generic MVTL algorithm, each with a different benefit. To specify these algorithms, we specialize the generic policy of MVTL (Algorithm 2). Due to limited space, we omit proofs and the detailed pseudo-code of some algorithms; they are provided in the full paper.

5.1 The preferential algorithm

Roughly speaking, our preferential algorithm, denoted MVTL-Pref, works with multiple timestamps for each transaction, where one of the timestamps is preferential. The algorithm tries to commit a transaction using its preferential timestamp, but if doing so would abort, it tries one of the other timestamps. To ensure viability of the other timestamps, the algorithm locks them as necessary during the execution.

More precisely, MVTL-Pref is parameterized by a function $A(t)$ that takes the transaction's preferential timestamp and returns a non-empty set of alternative timestamps different from t. $A(t)$ is a choice of the user of the algorithm. For example, $A(t) = \{t-10, t+10\}$ indicates that $t-10$ and $t+10$ are the alternative timestamps for a transaction with preferential timestamp t. The preferential timestamp itself comes from a clock, as in other timestamp-based protocols.

We assume that clock timestamps are unique (e.g., by appending the process id to each timestamp t) and that $A(t)$ also produces unique timestamps (e.g., by using the process id in t for each timestamp in $A(t)$).

When executing a read on a key k, the algorithm determines a version to return based on the preferential timestamp, and then read-locks contiguous timestamps of k to cover as many alternative timestamps as possible. When executing a write to key k, the algorithm obtains no locks; rather, locks are acquired at commit time, as follows. If the algorithm cannot obtain a write-lock for the preferential timestamp for each written key, it tries one of the alternative timestamps. If it manages to obtain read- and write-locks for all read and written objects at one of the timestamps, the transaction commits; otherwise it aborts.

Algorithm 3 The MVTL-Pref algorithm

```
function INITIALIZATION(tx)
    tx.PrefTS ← clock()
    tx.PossTS ← {tx.PrefTS} ∪ A(tx.PrefTS)
                                          ▹ possible timestamps for tx
function WRITE-LOCKS(tx, k) return ▹ lock write-set only on commit
function READ-LOCKS(tx, k)
    repeat
        tr ← max{t : t < tx.PrefTS and Values[k, t] ≠ ⊥}
                                          ▹ candidate value to read
        tmax ← max{t ∈ tx.PossTS :
                    no timestamps in [tr+1, t] are write frozen}
        for t ← tr+1 to tmax do  ▹ read-lock [tr+1, tx.TS] if possible
            try to acquire read-lock for tx on (k, t), waiting
                if timestamp is write-locked but not frozen
            if found frozen write-lock then
                release read-locks acquired above; break ▹ exit "for" loop
    until found no frozen locks in the for loop
    tx.PossTS ← tx.PossTS ∩ [tr, tmax]  ▹ update possible timestamps
    return tr
function COMMIT-LOCKS(tx)
    for t ∈ tx.PossTS do      ▹ Find a good timestamp. Loop order: first
                              tx.PrefTS then arbitrary for PossTS
        gotlocks ← true
        for (k, tr) ∈ tx.writeset do
            try to write-lock for tx on (k, t), without waiting if a
                timestamp is read-locked
            if write-lock not acquired then
                gotlocks ← false        ▹ this timestamp will not work
                release all write locks for tx
                break                   ▹ exit inner "for" loop
        if gotlocks then break ▹ found a timestamp for which we can
                                get write locks; exit outer "for" loop
    if gotlocks then tx.TS ← t             ▹ found good timestamp
    else tx.TS ← ⊥                         ▹ no good timestamps
function COMMIT-TS(T) return tx.TS
function COMMIT-GC(tx) return false
```

The pseudo-code of MVTL-Pref is given in Algorithm 3. We can show that if we choose the alternative timestamps $A(t)$ to be smaller than the preferential timestamps t, then the resulting MVTL-Pref algorithm aborts strictly fewer workloads compared to MVTO+. More precisely, we have the following:

THEOREM 2. *Suppose that* $\forall t' \in A(t), t' < t$. *(a) If a workload W produces no abort under MVTO+, then W produces no abort under MVTL-Pref. (b) There are infinitely many workloads that produce no aborts under MVTL-Pref but produce aborts under MVTO+.*

5.2 The prioritizer algorithm

Multiversion timestamp ordering provides no way for critical transactions to be prioritized over normal transactions. We explain how MVTL can do that, by using a policy that gives more locks to critical transactions. There are many ways to do that, but the simplest one is as follows. Normal transactions obtain their locks as in multiversion timestamp ordering using synchronized clocks, while critical transactions try to acquire all locks as in pessimistic concurrency control except that critical transactions do not block waiting for any of its locks. Both types of transactions garbage collect on commit. We give the detailed pseudo-code of the algorithm in the full paper.

THEOREM 3. *In the MVTL-Prio algorithm, transactions labeled critical are never aborted by transactions labeled normal.*

Given that high-priority transactions behave similarly to pessimistic concurrency control, they can cause deadlocks. However, transactions with normal priority behave identically to those in MVTO+, and thus never cause deadlocks.

5.3 The ϵ-clock algorithm

Multiversion timestamp ordering uses clocks to obtain its timestamps, but if clocks are not synchronized or monotonic[1], it is susceptible to *serial aborts*—aborts that occur in an execution that is completely serial. This is a concern in modern multicore machines that do not guarantee that clocks across cores are perfectly synchronized. For example, T_2 gets timestamp 2, reads an object X, and commits. Afterwards, T_1 gets a smaller timestamp 1, writes X, and tries to commit. This will cause T_1 to abort since the read-timestamp of X at version 0 is 2. This is the schedule:

T_2:	$R(X)$	C		
T_1:			$W(X)$	A

Here, time flows to the right and each line shows the operations of a transaction. R, W, C, and A indicate a read, write, commit, and abort; and X is the key. Thus, this schedule has two transactions T_1 and T_2, where T_2 reads X and commits, and then T_1 writes X and aborts.

The MVTL-ϵ-clock algorithm, which we now introduce, avoids serial aborts when used with ϵ-synchronized clocks. Briefly, when it starts, a transaction reads the clock, obtains a time t, and for each read and write tries to lock the interval $[t-\epsilon, t+\epsilon]$. At the end, it commits at the smallest common timestamp it locked for every accessed object. Before completing the commit, the transaction runs garbage collection. Algorithm 4 shows the detailed pseudo-code.

In a sequential execution, it is possible to show that *tx* picks a commit timestamp that is at most t, and thus it releases the lock on higher timestamps. As a result, the next transaction in the sequence will always have its own real time in the intersection of locked timestamps, and therefore does not abort.

THEOREM 4. *The MVTL-ϵ-clock algorithm is not susceptible to serial aborts when clocks are ϵ-synchronized.*

[1] A monotonic clock is one that ensures that it returns a higher timestamp if it is queried later in time. Monotonic clocks and time-synchronized clocks are equivalent for the purposes of this discussion.

Algorithm 4 The MVTL-ϵ-clock algorithm

```
function INITIALIZATION(tx)
    now ← clock()
    tx.TS ← [now − ε, now + ε]
function WRITE-LOCKS(tx, k)
    try to write-locks for tx on (k, tx.TS), waiting
        if a timestamp is read- or write-locked but not frozen
    tx.TS ← write-locks that tx could acquire
function READ-LOCKS(tx, k)
    if tx.TS = ∅ then return ⊥
    m ← max tx.TS
    repeat
        tr ← max{t : t < m and Values[k, t] ≠ ⊥}
        for t = tr+1 to m do ▹ read-lock interval [tr+1, m] if possible
            try to acquire read-lock for tx on (k, t), waiting
                if timestamp is write-locked but not frozen
            if found frozen write-lock then
                release read-locks acquired above; break ▹ exit "for" loop
    until found no frozen locks in the for loop
    tx.TS ← tx.TS ∩ [tr+1, m]
    return tr
function COMMIT-LOCKS(tx) return
function COMMIT-TS(T) return min T
function COMMIT-GC(tx) return true
```

5.4 Existing algorithms as special cases

We now show that MVTL generalizes two popular transactional algorithms, MVTO+ and pessimistic concurrency control. More precisely, we give two algorithms MVTL-TO and MVTL-Pessimistic, which specialize MVTL and behave exactly like MVTO+ and pessimistic concurrency control, respectively.

In MVTL-TO, each transaction obtains a timestamp t from a clock when the transaction starts. Writes do not lock anything, reads try to lock $[tr{+}1, t]$ (waiting for unfrozen locks) where tr is the largest timestamp before t for which $Values[k, tr] \neq \bot$, and commits lock t for each object in the transaction's write-set. Garbage collection is not invoked on commit. We give the detailed pseudo-code of the algorithm in the full paper.

Theorem 5. *The MVTL-TO algorithm behaves as the MVTO+ algorithm.*

Pessimistic concurrency control locks objects before accessing them, to prevent conflicting operations from executing concurrently. To emulate pessimistic concurrency, the MVTL-Pessimistic algorithm works as follows. Writes acquire write locks on all timestamps (blocking), while reads acquire read-locks on all timestamps in $[tr{+}1, \infty]$ (blocking). Garbage collection is invoked on commit.

Theorem 6. *The MVTL-Pessimistic algorithm behaves as the pessimistic concurrency control algorithm.*

5.5 The ghostbuster algorithm

Under multiversion timestamp ordering, a transaction may abort and later create a conflict with another transaction, causing it to abort. For example, suppose that T_1 starts with timestamp 1, T_2 starts with timestamp 2, and T_3 starts with timestamp 3. Then T_3 reads X and commits, T_2 reads Y, writes X, and tries to commit with its timestamp 2, but T_2 aborts because T_3 read X with timestamp 3. Next T_1 writes Y and tries to commit but aborts due to the read by T_2. This is a ghost abort, because the write of T_1 has a conflict with a transaction T_2 that had aborted before the write of T_1 started. This is the schedule:[2]

T_3:	$R(X)$	C					
T_2:			$R(Y)$	$W(X)$	A		
T_1:						$W(Y)$	A

We define ghost aborts precisely in the full paper.

While multiversion timestamp ordering has ghost aborts, MVTL-Ghostbuster can avoid that. MVTL-Ghostbuster is a simple modification to the MVTL-TO algorithm (§5.4): when a transaction commits, it performs garbage collection. This ensures that transactions that abort do not leave behind locks that cause ghost aborts. We thus have the following:

Theorem 7. *The MVTL-Ghostbuster algorithm is not susceptible to ghost aborts.*

6 PRACTICAL CONSIDERATIONS

Reducing lock state space. When we presented the generic MVTL algorithm, we defined a lock for each timestamp and object, which amounts to an infinite lock state space. We did not include mechanisms to compress this information, because they are orthogonal to the essence of the algorithm. However, a practical implementation should compress the lock state. To do so, we observe that MVTL algorithms usually acquire and release locks on a small number of points or contiguous intervals (this is true for all MVTL algorithms in this paper). Rather than keeping a lock state for each timestamp, an implementation can keep a single lock state for an entire interval. In the algorithms we presented, each object holds at most one lock interval per committed transaction. We evaluate the amount of lock state in §8.4.5. Furthermore, this state can be discarded when the associated version of the object is purged, as we discuss next.

Purging versions. By nature, a multiversion algorithm keeps multiple versions of each object. Doing so is feasible as storage prices fall. Disk systems such as database systems already use multiversion algorithms, but even memory systems can do so now. Nevertheless, multiversion algorithms need a way to purge old versions so that each object holds few versions—possibly just one after write activity on the object quiesces. We now explain how this can be done in MVTL. This is easy: at any time, the system can purge any version older than the latest committed one, without affecting the correctness of the algorithm. Transactions that need purged versions will abort, so in practice we purge versions older than a time limit chosen based on the duration of the longest expected transactions. In some MVTL algorithms, there is a lower bound on the timestamps that a transaction locks (e.g., ϵ-clock algorithm); we can purge versions with timestamps below the bound except the last one before the bound, without causing any side-effects. We evaluate the effectiveness and cost of garbage collection in §8.4.5.

Removing the atomic block. Algorithm 1 has an atomic block in lines 17–19, to avoid partially exposing the writes of a committing transaction when we assign to the array $Values[k, t]$. We can remove

[2]Here, transactions get a timestamp before their first operation, but one can construct a more complex schedule with the same problem even if transactions get a timestamp at the first operation.

this atomic block by (1) first storing a special value in *Values*$[k, t]$ for all timestamps in the for loop, (2) then storing the actual value v for all timestamps in the loop, and (3) having other processes wait if they read *Values* and see the special value.

7 DISTRIBUTED MVTL ALGORITHM

The MVTL algorithm of §4 works in a single machine, where multiple threads share lock state and data versions. We now explain how to extend that algorithm to distributed transactions, where clients in different machines execute transactions over the same data set. More precisely, the system consists of a set of clients who want to execute transactions, and a set of storage servers who keep the data, where clients and servers can be in different machines connected by a network. The data is partitioned across the servers by its key, and clients know how to find the server responsible for a key (e.g., by hashing the key or using a configuration map).

The basic idea of the distributed algorithm is that servers hold the state that is shared across clients: locks and data versions. Clients contact the servers to execute the steps of the algorithm in §4 that involve this state. More precisely, the server responsible for a key k keeps all versions and locks for k. A client contacts that server when it wishes to read k, create a new version for k, or manipulate k's lock state (obtain, freeze, or release locks on timestamps).

The system is subject to failures that may disrupt the algorithm. A failed client may leave write locks in an unfrozen state indefinitely, causing other transactions to block. A failed server can similarly cause indefinite waiting from clients.

To address these problems, we associate a *commitment* object with each transaction. This object solves consensus on the outcome of a transaction, which can be "abort" or "commit with a timestamp t", ensuring that clients and servers all agree on the outcome. The details of the algorithm are given in the full paper.

8 EXPERIMENTAL EVALUATION

We conduct a simple experimental evaluation of MVTL to answer some questions: Does MVTL enhance transaction concurrency and avoid aborts compared to alternatives? Does MVTL improve transaction throughput? On which workloads? Do the characteristics of the environment impact our conclusions? Does MVTL incur significant overheads in terms of state size?

To this end, we implement the distributed MVTL algorithm (§7) with a variant of the ϵ-clock algorithm (§5.3). In this variant, to execute a transaction T, a client obtains a timestamp t from its local clock and associates a timestamp interval $I = [t, t + \Delta]$ with T, where Δ is a small constant (we pick Δ = 5ms in the experiments). When accessing a key k, the client tries to lock the timestamps in I for key k. If the client cannot lock the entire interval I, but manages to lock some subinterval, then the client replaces I with that subinterval to reduce the amount of locking on subsequent keys. We call this algorithm MVTIL. This is similar to the ϵ-clock algorithm but we do not assume that clients have synchronized clocks and we shrink I when clients fail to obtain some locks, as described above. We consider two variants of MVTIL: (i) *MVTIL-early*, which at commit time picks the smallest timestamp in I to commit, and (ii) *MVTIL-late*, which picks the largest. We compare MVTIL to 2PL and MVTO+.

8.1 Implementation details

Keys and values are small strings of eight characters. Clients are multi-threaded, each thread running a different transaction. When a client realizes that an ongoing transaction will abort (because it does not have a single timestamp locked across all accessed keys), it has the option of aborting or restarting the transaction, with an interval I adjusted based on the state it has already seen at the servers. Servers are multi-threaded, with hundreds of threads, each responsible to handle a client request. A server stores version and lock state in a hash table indexed by key; for each key, the hash table stores two skip lists, one for version state, one for lock state. The version state is a list of value-timestamp pairs ordered by timestamp. The lock state is a list of timestamp-timestamp pairs representing a locked time interval, ordered by the first timestamp. To coordinate access across threads, we use a concurrent hash table (from the Intel TBB library [14]), with a latch per entry in the hash table. Latches are held while a thread changes the lock and version lists of a key. We use Apache Thrift [2] for communication between clients and servers,

A timestamp service periodically broadcasts a message with a time T in the past, equal to the service's current time minus a constant K; we use $K = 15s$ in the local test bed, and $K = 60s$ in the cloud test bed (§8.2). This message has two effects. First, it causes servers to purge old versions of keys, namely versions that meet two criteria: their timestamp is smaller than T and they are not the most recent version of a key. If clients have ongoing transactions that later try to access a purged version, those transactions are aborted. However, because T is an old timestamp, there will be few such transactions, if any. The second effect of broadcasting T is that clients advance their local clocks to T if they are behind—this ensures that clients with slow clocks do not start new transactions that need purged versions and subsequently get aborted.

Our implementations of MVTO+ and 2PL use the same framework, but run a different client protocol and keep a different server state: 2PL stores a single readers-writer lock per key, while MVTO+ stores a single skip list per key containing versions and associated locks. The implementations of all schemes are available at https://github.com/LPD-EPFL/MVTIL.

8.2 Test beds

We use two test beds for the experiments: a local test bed with dedicated servers, and a public cloud test bed with virtual machine instances. The local test bed represents an enterprise setting with higher-performance machines and network, while the cloud test bed represents a low-cost shared environment with a less predictable network.

On the local test bed, we use three machines: (a) a server with four 2.7 GHz Intel Xeon 12-core E7-4830v3 processors and 512 GB of RAM; (b) a server with two 2.8 GHz Intel Xeon 10-core E5-2680 v2 processors and 256 GB of RAM; and (c) a server with four 2.1 GHz AMD Opteron 6172 12-core Processors and 128 GB of RAM. Machines are connected by a 1 Gbps network.

The public cloud test bed consists of several hundred Amazon EC2 *t2.micro* instances with 1 vCPU each.

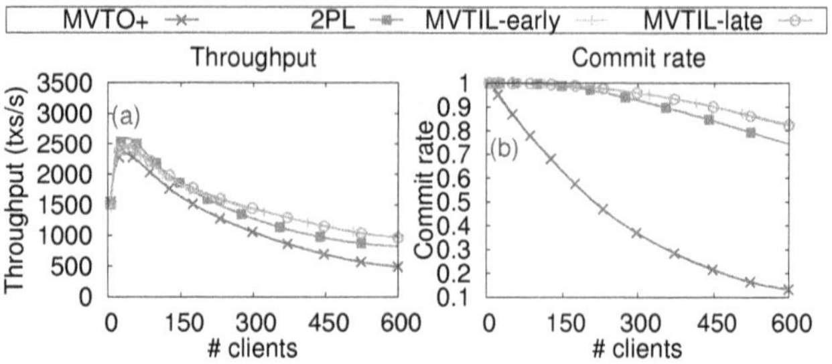

Figure 1: Effect of concurrency level on performance, local test bed.

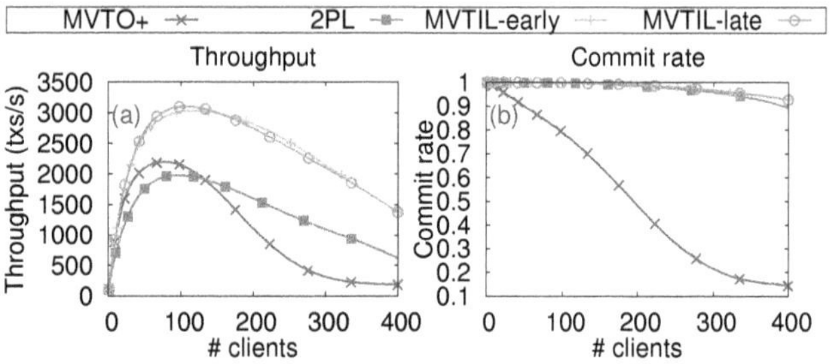

Figure 2: Effect of concurrency level on performance, cloud test bed.

8.3 Experiments

In an experiment, clients submit transactions repeatedly in a closed-loop. We measure the aggregate throughput of committed transactions and the commit rate, which is the fraction of transactions that commit. Before measuring, we run a warm-up stage of 40s to ensure all clients have started; we then measure the system for 20s. We repeat each experiment five times and report the average.

In each experiment, we fix the following parameters:

- algorithm (MVTIL, MVTO+, 2PL);
- number of clients, which determine the level of concurrency;
- size of transactions in number of operations;
- fraction of write operations in a transaction;
- size of the key space; and
- number of storage servers.

On the local test bed, which has three machines, we always run three servers on all machines, and we run client threads on a subset of the cores in those machines. For the cloud test bed, we run eight servers on eight different VM instances unless otherwise indicated, and we run each client on its own VM instance.

8.4 Results

We now present results regarding concurrency, fraction of write operations, transaction size, number of servers, and state size.

8.4.1 Level of concurrency. We study the effect of the level of concurrency on performance, under a workload where a majority of operations are reads—a common situation in practice. We vary the number of clients, while keeping the other parameters constant. We use transactions with 20 operations, 25% of which are writes. For the local test bed, we use 10K keys. For the larger cloud test bed, we use 50K keys.

Figures 1 and 2 show throughput and commit rates for the local and cloud test beds, respectively. We see that MVTIL outperforms MVTO+ and 2PL in both test beds. Moreover, when concurrency increases, the commit rate of MVTO+ drops due to conflicts, but this does not happen for MVTIL because it can commit at many serialization points. The inefficiency—due to aborts in MVTO+ and waiting for locks in 2PL—is the reason for the difference in throughout. This is more pronounced in the cloud test bed, where resources are scarce: there, MVTIL has roughly 2x better throughput than the alternatives. The difference is smaller on the local test bed.

The commit rate for 2PL is not 100% because transactions abort after a timeout. This prevents deadlocks and starving transactions from limiting throughput. We set the timeout value to maximize throughput.

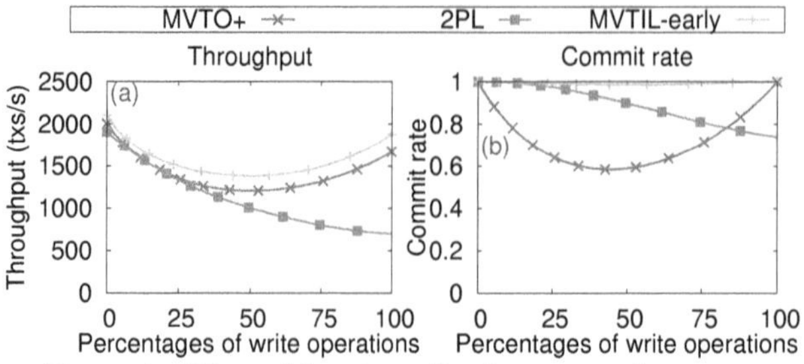

Figure 3: Effect of fraction of writes on performance.

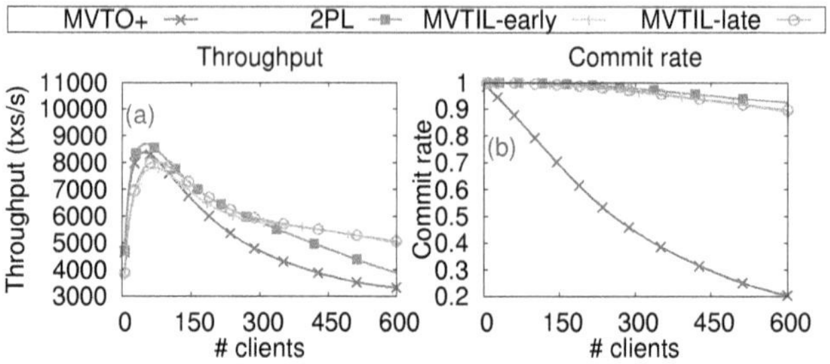

Figure 4: Effect of small transaction size on performance.

8.4.2 Write percentage. We next consider how the fraction of writes affect performance. We thus vary the fraction of writes and keep other parameters constant. We use the local test bed with 90 clients; transactions have 20 operations and 10K keys.

Figure 3 shows the results. For read-only transactions, the choice of protocol has little impact. Additionally, for write fractions close to 1, the workload consists mostly of blind writes, which allows multiversion protocols to commit nearly all transactions, as writes in such protocols do not conflict with each other. With a more balanced write fraction, MVTIL outperforms MVTO+ and 2PL. With 2PL, the more writes, the more time transactions wait for locks. MVTO+ has a high abort rate when the percentages of reads and writes are similar; this is where the chance of conflicts is highest in multiversion protocols. The issue impacts MVTIL less due to its ability to explore many serialization points to commit.

8.4.3 Transaction size. In previous experiments, we use transactions with 20 operations; we now consider smaller transactions with 8 operations. We vary the number of clients (level of concurrency) and observe the performance. We use the local test bed with a 50% fraction of writes and 10K keys.

Figure 4 shows the results. Under low concurrency, MVTIL behaves similar to MVTO+ and 2PL, but 2PL is ≈5% faster. This setting

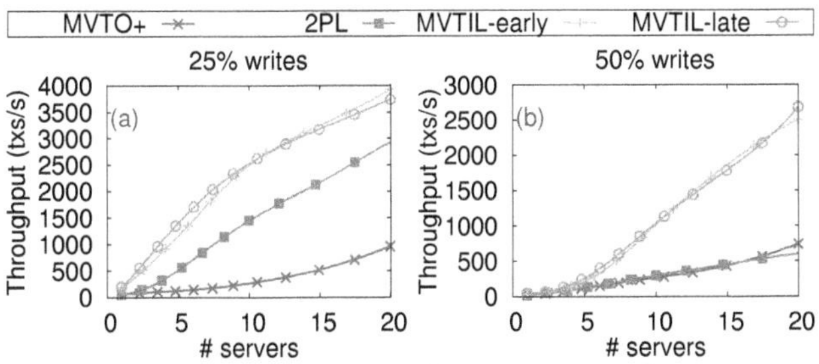

Figure 5: Effect of number of servers on performance.

with little concurrency, short transactions, and a local test bed with lots of resources is the only setting where MVTIL is worse than an alternative. However, as we increase concurrency, MVTIL again outperforms the others. This advantage is larger in the cloud test bed (not shown).

8.4.4 Number of servers. We now consider how the number of servers affect performance. Using the cloud test bed, we keep the number of clients constant to 400 and vary the number of server instances from 1 to 20. We use transactions with 20 operations with 25% or 50% writes, and 100K keys.

Figure 5 shows the results. The throughput of all protocols increases with the number of servers, but the scalability is better for MVTIL. MVTIL has a higher commit rate compared to MVTO+, and waits less for locks compared to 2PL; this is particularly visible with 50% writes.

8.4.5 State size. We now examine the size of the state kept by each algorithm, and the effectiveness of the garbage collection mechanisms. Most of the state of a multiversion protocol is the data versions and associated locks. We measure how the number of versions and locks evolve with time for MVTIL and MVTO+ without garbage collection, as well as MVTIL with garbage collection (MVTIL-GC) that activates every 15s to purge versions and locks. We use 50 clients running transactions with 20 operations, a fraction of 50% writes, and 8K keys, running on the local test bed.

Figure 6 shows the results. Without garbage collection, the state increases linearly with time. However, with garbage collection, the state size remains bounded in both the number of versions and locks. On average, there are ≈4 versions and ≈20 locks per key. Figure 7 shows how performance varies as time passes. Without garbage collection, throughput decreases after ≈5 minutes for MVTIL and MVTO+, because a larger state makes it slower to search for and access versions. Garbage collection removes this performance degradation. Moreover, comparing the performance with and without garbage collection at the beginning of the experiment, we see that the overhead of garbage collection is small.

8.5 Summary

We see that (i) with moderate contention, MVTIL outperforms alternatives, (ii) with no contention, MVTIL is at least as good as alternatives, and (iii) MVTIL's advantages are bigger in the cloud test bed that has limited processing power and unpredictable network latencies. MVTIL nevertheless represents just one of many MVTL-based algorithms. We believe that other MVTL algorithms will present different benefits on other workloads and environments.

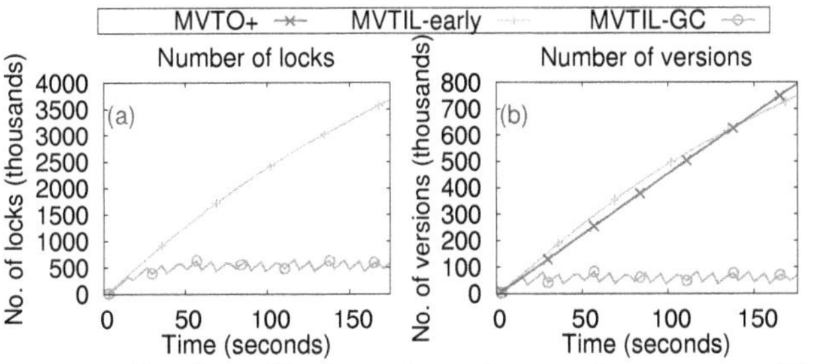

Figure 6: Number of locks and versions as time passes with garbage collection on and off.

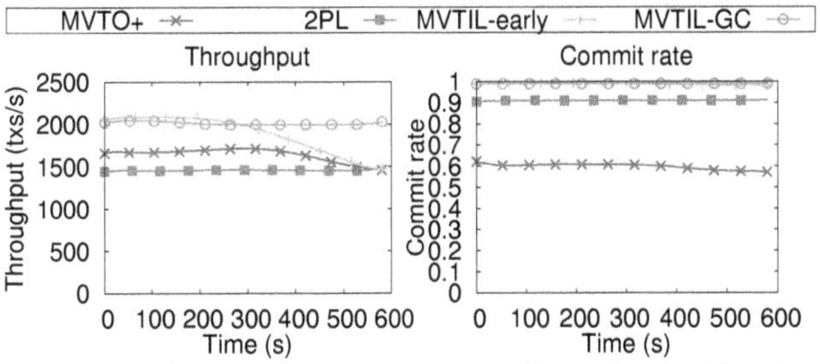

Figure 7: Performance as time passes with garbage collection on and off.

9 RELATED WORK

The main novelty of this work is the idea of locking individual timestamps, leading to a genre of multiversion algorithms called MVTL. No other work has proposed this idea, but because MVTL is a broad class, several existing algorithms become special cases of MVTL, leading to similarities in mechanism.

Multiversion concurrency control is an old idea [6] that has seen a resurgence in software transactional memory (STM) systems, several of which provide serializability [3, 7, 11, 15, 16, 20, 22–24]. Prior work in this space falls into three categories: (1) multiversion for read-only transactions, (2) conflict graph schemes, and (3) multiversion timestamp ordering algorithms. The first category [11, 22–24] are systems that use multiversion to benefit solely read-only transactions; update transactions rely on optimistic methods that, upon commit, validate the read-set and abort if any object has changed. While read-only transactions are important, these methods abort under simple concurrent update schedules, such as the following (where full multiversion schemes do not abort):

$$\begin{array}{llll} T_1: & R(X) & & W(Y) \\ T_2: & & W(X) & \end{array}$$

The second category (e.g., [3, 16, 20]) are multiversion systems that ensure serializability by detecting cycles in the *conflict graph*—a data structure that represents the conflicts across transactions—similarly to the MVSGT algorithm [26]. These algorithms have two drawbacks: they are complex and they incur significant computation overhead, as reported in some of these papers.

The third category are systems that extend multiversion timestamp ordering. Specifically, Kumar et al. [17] explain how to provide opacity, which is stronger than serializability. The algorithm suffers from the same drawbacks of multiversion timestamp ordering that we address in §5. It should be possible to extend MVTL to provide opacity using the ideas of Kumar et al., but this is future work.

Lomet et al. [19] introduce the multiversion timestamp range algorithm (MVTR). With MVTR, each transaction is assigned a range of timestamps, and this range shrinks as the transaction executes; at the end, MVTR commits if the range is non-empty. MVTR differs from MVTL because MVTR locks entire objects instead of timestamps. As a result, MVTR does not enjoy the full benefits of multiversion concurrency control, such as allowing two concurrent transactions to write the same object. Also, with MVTR one transaction manipulates the inner state of another transaction (e.g., by changing the range that another transaction uses), which requires careful synchronization of transactions using a scheduler or locks. Elastic transactions [12], aimed at search data structures, use timestamp ranges to determine if a transaction can commit based on its start time and when the accessed objects were written.

Snapshot isolation [4] is both an isolation property and a protocol. The protocol uses multiversioning and timestamps, similarly to multiversion timestamp ordering, but it does not provide serializability. Other protocols that use multiversioning and timestamps provide even weaker notions than snapshot isolation [25].

Optimistic concurrency control (OCC) [18] is another technique that can use multiversioning. With OCC, a transaction does not acquire locks when executing; to commit, the system checks that the versions that the transaction read are the latest. TicToc [28] optimizes OCC to serialize transactions based on the data they access. TicToc computes potential serialization points before the validation and commit phases. Thus, a transaction for which the read and write sets have been inspected might later abort. In contrast, MVTL ensures that once a serialization point has been found, the transaction commits. Bohm [10] is a multiversion protocol that pre-orders transactions before execution; in that sense, Bohm is more pessimistic than MVTL, which determines transaction ordering dynamically during execution. In addition, Bohm requires that the transaction be known ahead of time, and that its write-set be static.

Many practical systems with distributed transactions provide only snapshot isolation [9, 21] and abort on concurrent writes to the same object. Spanner [8] provides strict serializability using two-phase locking for read-write transactions, which limits parallelism.

10 CONCLUSION

This paper introduces a new genre of multiversion concurrency control algorithms called multiversion timestamp locking (MVTL). MVTL offers a new way to look at multiversion algorithms, based on locking individual timestamps. With this perspective, we find simple algorithms that improve the state of the art in different ways: by committing successfully more workloads than existing multiversion protocols, by avoiding the problems of serial aborts and ghost aborts, and by offering prioritized transactions. We can also view existing algorithms, such as MVTO and pessimistic concurrency control, as special cases of MVTL. We show how to realize MVTL in both centralized and distributed systems. Finally, we show experimental evidence of the benefits of MVTL in practice.

We believe that the algorithms proposed here are only a starting point for other possibilities opened up by MVTL. The design of other MVTL algorithms is a promising direction for future research.

Acknowledgements. We thank Dahlia Malkhi for valuable input early in the project. This work was supported in part by a VMware Fellowship.

REFERENCES

[1] M. K. Aguilera, T. David, R. Guerrraoui, and J. Wang. Locking timestamps versus locking objects. Technical report. https://infoscience.epfl.ch/record/229425, 2018.

[2] Apache thrift. https://thrift.apache.org.

[3] U. Aydonat and T. S. Abdelrahman. Serializability of transactions in software transactional memory. In *ACM SIGPLAN Workshop on Transactional Computing*, Feb. 2008.

[4] H. Berenson, P. Bernstein, J. Gray, J. Melton, E. O'Neil, and P. O'Neil. A critique of ANSI SQL isolation levels. In *International Conference on Management of Data*, pages 1–10, May 1995.

[5] P. A. Bernstein and N. Goodman. Concurrency control in distributed database systems. *ACM Computing Surveys*, 13(2):185–221, June 1981.

[6] P. A. Bernstein, V. Hadzilacos, and N. Goodman. *Concurrency control and recovery in database systems*. Addison-Wesley, 1987.

[7] J. Cachopo and A. Rito-Silva. Versioned boxes as the basis for memory transactions. *Science of Computer Programming*, 63(2):172–185, Dec. 2006.

[8] J. Corbett, J. Dean, M. Epstein, A. Fikes, C. Frost, J. Furman, S. Ghemawat, A. Gubarev, C. Heiser, P. Hochschild, W. Hsieh, S. Kanthak, E. Kogan, H. Li, A. Lloyd, S. Melnik, D. Mwaura, D. Nagle, S. Quinlan, R. Rao, L. Rolig, Y. Saito, M. Szymaniak, C. Taylor, R. Wang, and D. Woodford. Spanner: Google's globally-distributed database. In *Symposium on Operating Systems Design and Implementation*, pages 251–264, Oct. 2012.

[9] J. Du, S. Elnikety, and W. Zwaenepoel. Clock-SI: Snapshot isolation for partitioned data stores using loosely synchronized clocks. In *IEEE Symposium on Reliable Distributed Systems*, pages 173–184, Oct. 2013.

[10] J. M. Faleiro and D. J. Abadi. Rethinking serializable multiversion concurrency control. *Proceedings of the VLDB Endowment*, 8(11):1190–1201, July 2015.

[11] P. Felber, C. Fetzer, P. Marlier, and T. Riegel. Time-based software transactional memory. *IEEE Transactions on Parallel and Distributed Systems*, 21(12):1793–1807, 2010.

[12] P. Felber, V. Gramoli, and R. Guerraoui. Elastic transactions. *Journal of Parallel and Distributed Computing*, 100(C):103–127, Feb. 2017.

[13] M. Herlihy and N. Shavit. *The Art of Multiprocessor Programming, Revised First Edition*. Morgan Kaufmann, 2012.

[14] Intel TBB. https://www.threadingbuildingblocks.org.

[15] I. Keidar and D. Perelman. Multi-versioning in transactional memory. In *Transactional Memory. Foundations, Algorithms, Tools, and Applications*. Springer, 2015.

[16] I. Keidar and D. Perelman. On avoiding spare aborts in transactional memory. *ACM Transactions on Computer Systems*, 57(1):261–285, July 2015.

[17] P. Kumar, S. Peri, and K. Vidyasankar. A timestamp based multi-version STM algorithm. In *International Conference on Distributed Computing and Networking*, pages 212–226, 2014.

[18] H. T. Kung and J. T. Robinson. On optimistic methods for concurrency control. *ACM Transactions on Database Systems*, 6(2):213–226, June 1981.

[19] D. Lomet, A. Fekete, R. Wang, and P. Ward. Multi-version concurrency via timestamp range conflict management. In *International Conference on Data Engineering*, pages 714–725, Apr. 2012.

[20] J. Napper and L. Alvisi. Lock-free serializable transactions. Technical Report TR-05-04, University of Texas at Austin, Feb. 2005.

[21] D. Peng and F. Dabek. Large-scale incremental processing using distributed transactions and notifications. In *Symposium on Operating Systems Design and Implementation*, pages 251–264, Oct. 2010.

[22] D. Perelman, A. Byshevsky, O. Litmanovich, and I. Keidar. SMV: Selective multi-versioning STM. In *International Symposium on Distributed Computing*, pages 125–140, Sept. 2011.

[23] D. Perelman, R. Fan, and I. Keidar. On maintaining multiple versions in STM. In *ACM Symposium on Principles of Distributed Computing*, pages 16–25, July 2010.

[24] T. Riegel, P. Felber, and C. Fetzer. A lazy snapshot algorithm with eager validation. In *International Symposium on Distributed Computing*, pages 284–298, Sept. 2006.

[25] Y. Sovran, R. Power, M. K. Aguilera, and J. Li. Transactional storage for geo-replicated systems. In *ACM Symposium on Operating Systems Principles*, pages 385–400, Oct. 2011.

[26] G. Weikum and G. Vossen. *Transactional information systems: theory, algorithms, and the practice of concurrency control and recovery*. Morgan Kaufmann, 2001.

[27] Y. Wu, J. Arulraj, J. Lin, R. Xian, and A. Pavlo. An empirical evaluation of in-memory multi-version concurrency control. *Proceedings of the VLDB Endowment*, 10(7):781–792, Mar. 2017.

[28] X. Yu, A. Pavlo, D. Sanchez, and S. Devadas. TicToc: Time traveling optimistic concurrency control. In *International Conference on Management of Data*, pages 1629–1642, June 2016.

Relaxed Schedulers Can Efficiently Parallelize Iterative Algorithms

Dan Alistarh
IST Austria
dan.alistarh@ist.ac.at

Trevor Brown
IST Austria
me@tbrown.pro

Justin Kopinsky*
Massachusetts Institute of Technology
jkopin@mit.edu

Giorgi Nadiradze†
ETH Zurich
giorgi.nadiradze@inf.ethz.ch

ABSTRACT

There has been significant progress in understanding the parallelism inherent to iterative sequential algorithms: for many classic algorithms, the depth of the dependence structure is now well understood, and scheduling techniques have been developed to exploit this shallow dependence structure for efficient parallel implementations. A related, applied research strand has studied methods by which certain iterative task-based algorithms can be efficiently parallelized via relaxed concurrent priority schedulers. These allow for high concurrency when inserting and removing tasks, at the cost of executing superfluous work due to the relaxed semantics of the scheduler.

In this work, we take a step towards unifying these two research directions, by showing that there exists a family of relaxed priority schedulers that can efficiently and deterministically execute classic iterative algorithms such as greedy maximal independent set (MIS) and matching. Our primary result shows that, given a randomized scheduler with an expected relaxation factor of k in terms of the maximum allowed priority inversions on a task, and any graph on n vertices, the scheduler is able to execute greedy MIS with only an additive factor of poly(k) expected additional iterations compared to an exact (but not scalable) scheduler. This counter-intuitive result demonstrates that the overhead of relaxation when computing MIS is *not* dependent on the input size or structure of the input graph. Experimental results show that this overhead can be clearly offset by the gain in performance due to the highly scalable scheduler. In sum, we present an efficient method to deterministically parallelize iterative sequential algorithms, with provable runtime guarantees in terms of the number of executed tasks to completion.

*Justin's work was funded by the National Science Foundation, grant CCF-1563880 along with a generous grant from the Intel Corporation.
†Giorgi's work was funded by the Swiss National Fund Ambizione Project PZ00P2 161375.

PODC'18, July 23–27, 2018, Egham, United Kingdom

ACM ISBN 978-1-4503-5795-1/18/07...$15.00
https://doi.org/10.1145/3212734.3212756

ACM Reference Format:
Dan Alistarh, Trevor Brown, Justin Kopinsky, and Giorgi Nadiradze. 2018. Relaxed Schedulers Can Efficiently Parallelize Iterative Algorithms. In *Proceedings of ACM Symposium on Principles of Distributed Computing (PODC'18).* ACM, New York, NY, USA, 10 pages. https://doi.org/10.1145/3212734.3212756

1 INTRODUCTION

Given the now-pervasive nature of parallelism in computation, there has been a tremendous amount of research into efficient parallel algorithms for a wide range of tasks. A popular approach has been to map existing sequential algorithms to parallel architectures, by exploiting their *inherent parallelism.* In this paper, we will focus on two specific variants of this strategy.

The *deterministic* approach, e.g. [5–8, 18, 25] has been to study the directed-acyclic graph (DAG) step dependence in classic, widely-employed sequential algorithms, showing that, perhaps surprisingly, this dependence structure usually *has low depth.* One can then design schedulers which exploit this dependence structure for efficient execution on parallel architectures. As the name suggests, this approach ensures deterministic outputs (i.e. outputs uniquely determined by the input), and can yield good practical performance [7], but requires a non-trivial amount of knowledge about the problem at hand, and the use of carefully-constructed parallel schedulers [7].

To illustrate, let us consider the classic sequential greedy strategy for solving the maximal independent set (MIS) problem on arbitrary graphs: the algorithm examines the set of vertices in the graph following a fixed, random sequential priority order, adding a vertex to the independent set if and only if no neighbor of higher priority has already been added. The basic insight for parallelization is that the outcome at each node may only depend on a small subset of other nodes, namely its neighbors which are higher priority in the random order. Blelloch, Fineman and Shun [7] performed an in-depth study of the asymptotic properties of this dependence structure, proving that, for any graph, the maximal depth of a chain of dependences is in fact $O(\log^2 n)$ with high probability, where n is the number of nodes in the graph. Recently, an impressive analytic result by Fischer and Noever [13] provided tight $\Theta(\log n)$ bounds on the maximal dependency depth for greedy sequential MIS, effectively closing this problem for MIS. Beyond greedy MIS, there has been significant progress in analyzing the dependency structure of other fundamental sequential algorithms, such as algorithms for matching [7], list contraction [25], Knuth shuffle [25], linear programming [5], and graph connectivity [5].

An alternative approach has been to employ *relaxed data structures* to schedule task-based programs. Starting with Karp and Zhang [19], the general idea is that, in some applications, the scheduler can relax the strict order induced by following the sequential algorithm, and allow tasks to be processed speculatively ahead of their dependencies, without loss of correctness. A standard example is parallelizing Dijkstra's single-source shortest paths (SSSP) algorithm, e.g. [1, 20, 22]: the scheduler can retrieve vertices in relaxed order without breaking correctness, as the distance at each vertex is guaranteed to eventually converge to the minimum. The trade-off is between the performance gains arising from using simpler, more scalable schedulers, and the loss of determinism and the wasted work due to relaxed priority order. This approach is quite popular in practice, as several high-performance relaxed schedulers have been proposed, which can attain state-of-the-art results in settings such as graph processing and machine learning [14, 20]. At the same time, despite good empirical performance, this approach still lacks analytical bounds, and results are no longer deterministic.

In this paper, we ask: is it possible to achieve both the simplicity and good performance of relaxed schedulers *as well as* the predictable outputs and runtime upper bounds of the "deterministic" approach?

Contribution. In a nutshell, this work shows that a natural family of *fair relaxed schedulers*—providing upper bounds on the degree of relaxation, and on the number of inversions that a task can experience—can execute a range of iterative sequential algorithms *deterministically*, preserving the dependence structure, and *provably efficiently*, providing analytic upper bounds on the total work performed. Our results cover the classic greedy sequential graph algorithms for *maximal independent set (MIS)*, *matching*, and *coloring*, but also algorithms for *list contraction* and *generating permutations* via the Knuth shuffle. We call this class *iterative algorithms with explicit dependencies*. Our main technical result is that, for MIS and matching in particular, the overhead of relaxed scheduling is *independent of the graph size or structure*. This analytical result suggests that relaxed schedulers should be a viable alternative, a finding which is also supported by our preliminary concurrent implementation.

Specifically, we consider the following framework. Given an input, e.g., a graph, the sequential algorithm defines a set of *tasks*, e.g. one per graph vertex, which should be processed in order, respecting some fixed, arbitrary data dependencies, which can be specified as a DAG. Tasks will be accessible via a *scheduler*, which is *relaxed*, in the sense that it could return tasks *out of order*. This induces a sequential model,[1] where at each step, the scheduler returns a new task: for simplicity, assume for now that the scheduler returns at each step a task chosen *uniformly at random* among the top-k available tasks, in descending priority order. (We will model realistic relaxed schedulers [2, 21] precisely in the following section.)

Assume a thread receives a task from the scheduler. Crucially, the thread *cannot process the task* if it has data dependencies *on higher-priority tasks*: this way, determinism is enforced. (We call such a failed delete attempt by the thread a *wasted* step.) However, threads are free to process tasks which do not have such outstanding dependencies, potentially out-of-order (we call these *successful* steps.) We measure *work* in terms of the total number of scheduler queries needed to process the entire input, including both successful and unsuccessful removal steps.

We provide a simple yet general approach to analyze this relaxed scheduling process, by characterizing the interaction between the dependency structure induced by a given problem on an arbitrary input, and the relaxation factor k in the scheduling mechanism, which yields bounds on expected work when executing such algorithms via relaxed schedulers. Our approach extends to general iterative algorithms, as long as task dependencies are *explicit*, i.e., can be statically expressed given the input, and tasks can be randomly permuted initially.

The work efficiency of this framework will critically depend on the rate at which threads are able to successfully remove dependency-free tasks. Intuitively, this rate appears to be highly dependent on (1) the problem definition, (2) the scheduler relaxation factor k, but also on (3) the structure of the input. Indeed, we show that in the most general case, a k-relaxed scheduler can process an input described by a dependency graph G on n nodes and m edges and incur $O(\frac{m}{n}\,\mathrm{poly}(k))$ wasted steps, i.e. $n + O(\frac{m}{n}\,\mathrm{poly}(k))$ total steps. This result immediately implies a low "cost of relaxation" for problems whose dependency graph is inherently *sparse*, such as Greedy Coloring on sparse graphs, Knuth Shuffle and List Contraction, which are characterized by a dependency structure with only $m = O(n)$ edges. Hence, in general, such sparse problems incur negligible relaxation cost when $k \ll n$.

Our main technical result is a counter-intuitive bound for greedy MIS: our framework equipped with a k-relaxed scheduler can execute greedy MIS on *any* graph G and experience only poly(k) wasted steps (i.e. n + poly(k) total steps), *regardless of the size or structure of* G. This result is surprising as well as technically non-trivial, and demonstrates that for MIS on large graphs, operation-level speedups provided by relaxation come with a negligible global trade-off. A similar result holds for maximal matching.

In the broader context of the parallel scheduling literature, our results suggest that *task priorities* can be supported in a scalable manner, through relaxation, without loss of determinism or work efficiency. We believe this is the first time this observation is made. We validate our results empirically, via a preliminary implementation of the scheduling framework in C++, based on a lock-free extension of the MultiQueue relaxed schedulers [21]. Our broad finding is that this relaxed scheduling framework can ensure scalable execution, with minimal overheads due to contention and verifying task dependencies. For MIS on large graphs, we obtain a solution, with 6x speedup at 24 threads versus an optimized sequential baseline.

Related Work. Our work is inspired by the line of research by Blelloch et al. [5–7, 18, 25], as well as [11–13], whose broad goal has been to examine the dependency structure of a wide class of iterative algorithms, and to derive efficient scheduling mechanisms given such structure.

At the same time, there are several differences between these results and our work. First, at the conceptual level, [7, 25] start from

[1] We consider this sequential model, similar to [7], since there currently are no precise ways to model the contention experienced by concurrent threads on the scheduler. Instead, we validate our findings via a fully concurrent implementation.

analytical insights about the dependency structure of algorithms such as greedy MIS, and apply them to design scheduling mechanisms which can leverage this structure, which require problem-specific information. In some cases, e.g. [7], the scheduling mechanisms found to perform best in practice differ from the structure of the schedules analyzed. By contrast, we start from a realistic model of existing high-performance relaxed schedulers [21], and show that such schedulers can automatically and efficiently execute a broad set of iterative algorithms. Second, at the technical level, the methods we develop are *different*: for instance, the fact that the iterative algorithms we consider have low dependency depth [5, 7, 25] does not actually help our analysis, since a sequential algorithm could have low dependency depth and be inefficiently executable by a relaxed scheduler: the bad case here is when the dependency depth is low (logarithmic), but each "level" in a breadth-first traversal of the dependency graph has high fanout. Specifically, we emphasize that the notion of *prefix* defined in [7] to simplify analysis is *different* from the set of positions S which can be returned by the relaxed stochastic scheduler: for example, the parallel algorithm in [7] requires each prefix to be fully processed before being removed, whereas S acts like a sliding window of positions in our case. The third difference is in terms of analytic model: references such as [7] express work bounds in the CRCW PRAM model, whereas we count work in terms of number of tasks processing attempts. Our analysis is sequential, and we implement our algorithms on a shared memory architecture to demonstrate empirically good performance.

To our knowledge, the first instance of a relaxed scheduler is in work by Karp and Zhang [19], for parallelizing backtracking strategies in a (synchronous) PRAM model. This area has recently become extremely active, with several such schedulers (also called relaxed priority queues) being proposed over the past decade, see [1, 2, 4, 15, 20, 21, 23, 24, 26] for recent examples. In particular, we note that state-of-the-art packages for graph processing [20] and machine learning [14] implement such relaxed schedulers.

Recent work by a subset of the authors [2] showed that a simple and popular priority scheduling mechanism called the MultiQueue [14, 15, 21] enforces strong probabilistic guarantees on the rank of elements returned, in an idealized model. Concurrent work [3] proves that these guarantees in fact hold in asynchronous concurrent executions, under some analytic assumptions. Based on this result, our work bounds should hold when using MultiQueues as relaxed schedulers, in concurrent executions.

Parallel scheduling [9, 10] is an extremely vast area and a complete survey is beyond our scope. We do wish to emphasize that standard work-stealing schedulers *will not* provide this type of work bounds, since they do not provide any guarantees in terms of the *rank of elements removed*: the rank becomes unbounded over long executions, since a single random queue is sampled at every stealing step [2]. To our knowledge, there is only one previous attempt to add priorities to work-stealing schedulers [17], using a multi-level global queue of tasks, partitioned by priority. This technique is different, and provides no work guarantees.

2 EXECUTING ITERATIVE ALGORITHMS VIA PRIORITY SCHEDULERS

2.1 Modeling Relaxed Priority Schedulers

In the following, we will provide the sequential specification of a generic relaxed priority scheduler Q, which contains a set of $\langle task, priority\rangle$ pairs. A relaxed priority scheduler will provide the following methods:

- ApproxGetMin(), which returns a $\langle task, priority\rangle$ pair and deletes it from the structure, if a task is available, or $\perp$, otherwise. The relaxation guarantees of this operation are precisely defined below;
- Empty(), which returns whether the scheduler still has tasks or not;
- Insert($\langle task, priority\rangle$), which inserts a new task into Q.

Let $\mathsf{rank}(t)$ be the rank of the task which is returned by the tth ApproxGetMin operation, among all tasks present in Q. We say that task $u \in Q$ experiences a *priority inversion* at an ApproxGetMin step if a task v of *lower* priority than u is retrieved at that step. For any task u, let $\mathsf{inv}(u)$ be the number of inversions which the task u experiences before being removed.

Definition 2.1. Fix a relaxed priority scheduler Q, with parameters $k \geq 1$, the *rank bound*, and ϕ, the *fairness bound*. We say that Q is an (k, ϕ)-relaxed priority scheduler if it ensures the following:

(1) **Rank Bound.** For any time t, and any integer $\ell > 1$, $\Pr[\mathsf{rank}(t) \geq \ell] \leq \exp(-\ell/k)$.
(2) **Fairness Bound.** For any task u, and any integer $\ell \geq 1$, $\Pr[\mathsf{inv}(u) \geq \ell] \leq \exp(-\ell/\phi)$.

Relation to Practical Schedulers. Upon inspection, both the SprayList [1] and the MultiQueue [21] relaxed priority schedulers ensure these exponential tail bounds on both rank and fairness, under some analytic assumptions. These conditions are trivially ensured by deterministic implementations such as [26]. In particular, the SprayList ensures these bounds with parameters k and ϕ in $O(p \operatorname{polylog} p)$, where p is the number of processors [1]. MultiQueues ensure these bounds with parameters $k = O(m)$, and $\phi = O(m \log m)$, where m is the number of distinct priority queues [2]. This holds even in concurrent executions [3].

In the following, it will be convenient to assume a single parameter k, which upper bounds both the rank and the relaxation parameters. We call the (k, k)-relaxed scheduler simply a k-relaxed scheduler.

2.2 A General Scheduling Framework

We now present our framework for executing task-based sequential programs, whose pseudocode is given in Algorithm 1. We assume a permutation π which dictates an execution order on tasks. If u is the ith element in π, we will write $\pi(i) = u$ and $\ell(u) = i$ (ℓ for *label*). Algorithm 1 encapsulates a large number of common iterative algorithms on graphs, including Greedy Vertex Coloring, Greedy Matching, Greedy Maximal Independent Set, Dijkstra's SSSP algorithm, and even some algorithms which are not graph-based, such as List Contraction and Knuth Shuffle [5]. We show sample instantiations of the framework in Section 2.3.

Algorithm 1: Generic Task-based Framework

Data: *Dependency* Graph $G = (V, E)$
Data: Vertex permutation π
`// Q is an exact priority queue`
$Q \leftarrow$ vertices in V with priorities $\pi(V)$
for *each step t* **do**
    `// Get new element from the buffer`
    $v_t \leftarrow Q$.GetMin()
    Process(v)
    Remove v_t from Q
    if Q.empty() **then**
        break

Algorithm 2: Relaxed Scheduling Framework

Data: *Dependency* Graph $G = (V, E)$
Data: Vertex permutation π
Data: Parameter k
`// Q is a` k`-relaxed scheduler`
$Q \leftarrow$ vertices in random order
for *each step t* **do**
    `// Get new element from the buffer`
    $v_t \leftarrow Q$.ApproxGetMin()
    if v_t *has unprocessed predecessor* **then**
        $Q.insert(v_t, \pi(v_t))$ `// Failed; reinsert`
        continue
    else Process(v)
    if Q.empty() **then** break

Algorithm 2 gives a method for adapting Algorithm 1 to use a *relaxed* queue, given an explicit dependency graph $G = (V, E)$ whose nodes are the tasks, and whose edges are dependencies between tasks. Importantly, given the dependency graph G, Algorithm 2 gives the same output as Algorithm 1, irrespective of the relaxation factor k. As usual, we write $|V| = n$ and $|E| = m$. We assume that the permutation π represents a *priority order* so that an edge $e = (u, v) \in E$ means that v depends on u if $\ell(v) > \ell(u)$ and vice-versa. In the former case, we say that v is a *successor* of u and u is a *predecessor* of v.

Our main result regarding Algorithm 2, proven formally in Section 3.1, argues that if π is chosen uniformly at random from among all vertex permutations, then Algorithm 2 completes in at most $n + O(\frac{m}{n} poly(k))$ iterations (compared to exactly n for Algorithm 1). This result demonstrates that provided G is not too dense, the "cost of relaxation" is low for the class of problems which admit uniformly random task permutations. Notably, this class includes all of the problems mentioned above, except for Dijkstra's algorithm (since there, π needs to respect the ordering of nodes sorted by distance from the source).

2.3 Example Applications

Applying the sequential task-based framework of Algorithm 1 only requires an implementation of Process(v). Implementing the relaxed framework in Algorithm 2 further requires G (either explicitly or via a predecessor query method). We now give examples for Greedy Vertex Coloring and List Contraction, whose dependency graph is implicit.

Greedy Vertex Coloring. Vertex Coloring is the problem of assigning a *color* (represented by a natural number) to each vertex of the input graph, G, such that no adjacent vertices share a color. The Greedy Vertex Coloring algorithm simply processes the vertices in some permutation order, π, and assigns each vertex in turn the smallest available color. The implementation of Process(v) for Greedy Vertex Coloring needs to determine the color of v, which can be done as described below:

Algorithm 3: Greedy Vertex Coloring Process(v)

Data: Input Graph $G = (V, E)$
Data: Permutation π
Data: *Partial* coloring $c : V \rightarrow \mathbb{N}$
Function Process(v) :
    $S \leftarrow \emptyset$
    foreach $(u, v) \in G$, *s.t.* $\ell(u) < \ell(v)$ **do**
        $S \leftarrow S \cup \{c(u)\}$
    $c(v) \leftarrow \min_{i \in \mathbb{N}} i \notin S$

Since the underlying dependency graph is just the input graph with edge orientations given by π, this is all that needs to be provided.

List Contraction. List Contraction takes a doubly linked list, L, and iteratively *contracts* its nodes. Contracting a node v consists of swinging two pointers: v.next.previous $\leftarrow v$.previous and v.previous.next $\leftarrow v$.next, effectively removing v from the list. List Contraction is useful, e.g., for cycle counting. Although List Contraction is not inherently a graph problem, we can still construct a dependency graph G whose nodes are list elements and with an edge between elements which are adjacent in L. If we induce a priority order on list elements (e.g. uniformly at random), then there is an induced orientation of the edges of the dependency graph which forms a DAG. Then a predecessor query on v consists of checking whether either v.next or v.prev is an unprocessed predecessor. Process(v) can be implemented with just the two steps of contraction above (possibly along with the metrics the application is computing).

2.4 Greedy Maximal Independent Set

We give a variant of Algorithm 2 adapted for Greedy Maximal Independent Set (MIS), which makes use of some exploitable substructure. In particular, once some neighbor, u, of a vertex v is added to the MIS, then v can never be added to the MIS, at which point v's dependents no longer have to wait for v to be processed. Algorithm 4 implements MIS in the framework of Algorithm 2 while also making use of this observation. Interestingly, Algorithm 4 can also be used to find a maximal matching by taking the input graph G of the matching instance and converting it to a graph G', where G' has a vertex for each edge in G and there is an edge between vertices of G' if the corresponding edges of G share an incident vertex. (One can view matching as an "independent set" of edges, no two of which are incident to the same vertex.)

Algorithm 4: Relaxed Queue MIS

```
Data: Graph G = (V, E)
Data: Vertex permutation π
Data: Parameter k
// Q is a k-approximate priority queue
Q ← vertices in random order, all marked live
for each step t do
    // Get new element from the buffer
    v_t ← Q.ApproxGetMin()
    if v_t marked dead then continue
    else if v_t has live predecessor in Q then
        Q.insert(v_t, π(v_t)) // Failed; reinsert
        continue
    else
        Add v_t to MIS
        Mark all of v_t's neighbors dead
        Remove v_t from Q
    if Q.empty() then break
```

As we will show in Section 3, the simple improvement Algorithm 4 makes over Algorithm 2 results in only a negligible number of extra iterations due to relaxation.

3 ANALYSIS

In this section, we will bound the relaxation cost for the general framework (Algorithm 2) and for Maximal Independent Set (Algorithm 4). Algorithm 2 is easier to analyze and will serve as a warmup. Note that in both cases, n iterations are required to process all nodes and are necessary even with no relaxation. Thus, we can think of the "cost" of relaxation as the number of further iterations beyond the first n, which can be equivalently counted as the number of *re-insertions* performed by the algorithm. We will sometimes refer to executing such a re-insertion as a "failed delete" by Q.

Our primary goal will be to bound the number of iterations of the for loops in Algorithm 2 and 4 when running them sequentially with a k-relaxed priority queue. Although the initial analysis is sequential, the algorithms are parallel: threads can each run their own for loops concurrently and correctness is maintained. The difficulty in extending the analysis to the asynchronous setting is that it is not clear how to model failed deletes of dependents of a node that is being processed. The likelihood of such deletes depend on particulars of both the problem (i.e. how long processing and dependency checking steps actually take) and the thread scheduler and so are hard to model in our generic framework. Instead, we show empirically that our bounds hold in practice on a realistic asynchronous machine where threads run the loops fully in parallel.

The theorems we will prove are the following. Given a dependency graph $G = (V, E)$ with $|V| = n$ vertices and $|E| = m$ edges, we first bound the number of iterations of Algorithm 2:

Theorem 3.1. *Algorithm 2 runs for* $n + O\left(\frac{m}{n}\right)\text{poly}(k)$ *iterations in expectation.*

By contrast to Algorithm 2, we show that using a relaxed queue for computing Maximal Independent Sets on large graphs has essentially no cost at all, even for dense graphs! In particular, Algorithm 4 incurs a relaxation cost with no dependence at all on the size or structure of G, only on the relaxation factor k:

Theorem 3.2. *Algorithm 4 runs for* $n + \text{poly}(k)$ *iterations in expectation.*

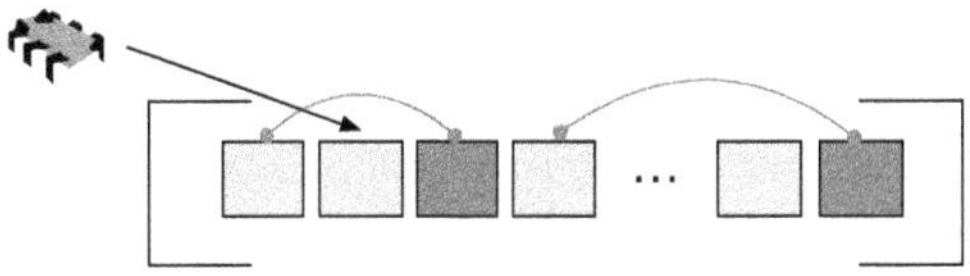

Figure 1: Simple illustration of the process. The blue thread queries the relaxed scheduler, which returns one of the top k tasks, on average (in brackets). Some of these tasks (green) can be processed immediately, as they have no dependencies. Tasks with dependencies (red) cannot be processed yet, and therefore result in failed deletes.

Before delving into the individual analyses, we first consider some key characteristics of a particular relaxed queue which will be at play, and quantify them in terms of the *fairness* and *rank error* of Q. As discussed in Section 2.1, we will assume that Q is k-relaxed: that is, Q provides exponential tail bounds on the rank error and on the number of inversions experienced by an element, in terms of the parameter k. Intuitively, it may help to think of a queue which returns a uniformly random element of the top-k at each step as the "canonical" k-relaxed Q. See Figure 1 for an illustration. (As discussed in Section 2.1, real schedulers have slightly different properties, which are captured in our framework.) We state and prove two technical lemmas parameterized by k.

First, we characterize the probability that, for some edge $e = (u, v)$ in the dependency graph where u is a predecessor of v, v experiences an inversion before u is processed. We say that vertex u experiences an inversion on or above node v at some point during the execution if $\ell(u) < \ell(v)$, but some node with label *at least* $\ell(v)$ is returned by Q before u is processed during the execution.

Lemma 3.3. *Consider running Algorithm 2 (or Algorithm 4) using a k-relaxed queue Q on input graph $G = (V, E)$. For a fixed edge $e = (u, v)$, the probability that u experiences an inversion on or above v during the execution is bounded by* $O(k^2 \log k/n)$.

Proof. We begin by proving a few immediate claims.

Claim 1. *At any time t, the probability of removing the element of top rank from Q is at least $1/k$.*

Proof. By the rank bound, we have that $\Pr[\text{rank}(t) \geq 2] \leq (1/e)^{2/k} < 1 - 1/k$. It therefore follows that $\Pr[rank(t) = 1] \geq 1/k$. □

Let t_u be the first time when u experiences an inversion, and let R_u be its rank at that time. Since an element of rank $\geq u$ must be chosen at t_u, we have that, for any $\ell \geq 1$,

$$\Pr[R_u \geq \ell] \leq \exp(-\ell/k).$$

In particular, $\Pr[R_u \geq ck \log k] \leq (1/k)^c$, for any constant $c \geq 1$. That is, u has rank $\leq ck \log k$ at the time where it experiences its first inversion, w.h.p. in k. We now wish to bound the number of removals between the point when u experiences its first inversion, and the point when u is removed. Let this random variable be Δ_k. By Claim 1, the top element is always removed within $O(k)$ trials in expectation, and hence we can show that

$$\Delta_k \geq (c+2)k^2 \log k, \text{ with probability at most } 1/k^c,$$

for $c \geq 1$, by bounding the time until all elements with rank $\geq u$ get removed, and connecting with the negative binomial distribution.

We now wish to know the probability that one of these steps is an inversion experienced by u on or above v. Fix a step t, and pessimistically assume that u is at the top of the queue at this time. Node v has lesser priority than u, chosen uniformly at random. Let j be the position of v, noting that $\Pr[j = \pi(u) + \ell] \leq 1/n$, for any integer $\ell \geq 1$.

Fixing j, we have that the probability that u experiences an inversion on or above v is $\leq (1/e)^{j/k}$. Fixing Δ_k, and bounding over all choices of j, we have that the probability that v is chosen is $\leq \sum_{j=1}^{n} \frac{1}{n} \left(\frac{1}{e}\right)^{j/k} = O(1/n)$.

Finally, bounding over all possible values of Δ_k and their probabilities, we get that the probability that u experiences an inversion on v during the execution is at most $O(k^2 \log k/n)$. □

Furthermore, the above proof directly implies the following corollary:

Corollary 3.4. *Consider running Algorithm 2 (or Algorithm 4) using a k-relaxed queue Q on input graph $G = (V, E)$. For a fixed edge $e = (u, v)$, the probability that u experiences an inversion on or above v during an execution on a random permutation π conditioned on $\ell(u) = t, \ell(v) > t$ is bounded by $O(k^2 \log k/(n-t))$.*

In Appendix A, we also prove a slightly tighter version of Lemma 3.3 for the case where the implementation of Q provides the further guarantee of *only* returning elements from the top-k. Note that such a queue is always k-rank bounded, but is not necessarily k-fair.

Our second technical lemma quantifies the expected number of *priority inversions* incurred by an element, u, of Q once u's dependencies have been processed—that is, the number of times an element of Q with lower priority than u is returned by GetApproxMin() before u is. If a vertex u has no predecessor in Q at some time t, we call u a *root.*

Lemma 3.5. *Consider running Algorithm 2 (or Algorithm 4) using a k-relaxed queue Q on input graph $G = (V, E)$. For a fixed node u, if u is a root at some time t, at most $O(k)$ other elements of Q with lower priority than u are deleted after t in expectation.*

Proof. Follows immediately from the k-fairness provided by Q. □

We stress that these two lemmas quantify the entire contribution of (the randomness of) the relaxation of Q to the analysis. The major burden of the analysis, particularly for MIS, is instead to manage the interaction between the randomness of the *permutation* π (which is not inherently related to the relaxation of Q) and the structure of G. Equipped with these lemmas, we are ready to do just that.

3.1 Algorithm 2: The General Case

The following theorem shows that the relaxed queue in Algorithm 2 has essentially no cost for sparse dependency graphs with $m = O(n)$ and still completes in $O(nk)$ iterations even for dense dependency graphs when $m = O(n^2)$. For example, Theorem 3.1 demonstrates that task-based problems which are inherently sparse such as Knuth Shuffle and List Contraction [5] incur only negligible "wasted work" when utilizing a k-relaxed queue with $k \ll n$. Furthermore, graph problems with edge dependencies such as greedy vertex coloring incur a cost proportional to the sparsity of the underlying graph. Although the result is not technically challenging, it is tight up to factors of k.

Theorem 3.1. *For a dependency graph $G = (V, E)$ with $|V| = n$ vertices and $|E| = m$ edges, Algorithm 2 runs for $n + O\left(\frac{m}{n}\right)\text{poly}(k)$ iterations.*

Proof. We will compute the expected number of failed deletes directly as follows: Whenever a failed delete occurs on a node w, charge it to the lexicographically first edge, $e = (u, v)$, for which u and v are both unprocessed and $\ell(v) \leq \ell(w)$ (i.e., with possibly $v = w$). Note that (1) such an edge must exist or else a failed delete could not have occurred, (2) the failed delete must represent a priority inversion on u, and (3) u must be a root (because e is lexicographically first). The first time an edge e is charged, we call e the *active* edge until u is processed. Since u is a root for the duration of e's status as active edge, by Lemma 3.5, u only experiences $O(k)$ priority inversions in expectation while e is active, which upper bounds the number of failed deletes charged to e.

Let A_e be the event that edge $e = (u, v)$ ever becomes active. A_e can only occur if u experiences an inversion on or above v during the execution, which is bounded by $O(k^2 \log k/n)$ by Lemma 3.3. Thus, the total expected cost of e is at most $\mathbb{E}[c(e)] = \Pr[A_e]\,\mathbb{E}[c(e)|A_e] = O(k^3 \log k)/n = \text{poly}(k)/n$. There are m edges so the total cost is $\Theta\left(\frac{m}{n}\right)\text{poly}(k)$ as claimed. □

Briefly, to see that Theorem 3.1 is tight (up to factors of k), consider executing a greedy graph coloring problem on a clique. In this case, at any step, only the highest priority node can ever be processed, and for each such node, u, it takes $O(k)$ delete attempts before u is processed. Thus in total, the algorithm runs for $O(nk)$ iterations.

3.2 Algorithm 4: Maximal Independent Set

The following theorem bounds the number of iterations of Algorithm 4. By contrast to Algorithm 2, we show that using a relaxed queue for computing Maximal Independent Sets on large graphs has essentially no cost at all, even for dense graphs! In particular, Algorithm 4 incurs a relaxation cost with no dependence on the size or structure of G, only on the relaxation factor k.

Theorem 3.2. *Algorithm 4 runs for $n + \text{poly}(k)$ iterations.*

Proof. Denote the lexicographically first MIS of G with respect to π as MIS_π. We first identify the key edges in the execution of Algorithm 4. We will say an edge $e = (u, v)$ is a *hot edge* w.r.t. π if u is the smallest labeled neighbor of v in MIS_π. Note that if (u, v) is a hot edge, v is not in MIS_π and u has a smaller label than v. Let H_e be the event that e is a hot edge w.r.t. π. Importantly, H_e depends only on the randomness of π and not on the randomness of the relaxation of Q. We make two key observations about hot edges that will allow us to prove the theorem:

Claim 2. *There is exactly one hot edge incident to each vertex $v \in V \setminus MIS_\pi$, and therefore the total number of hot edges is strictly less than n.*

This is clear from the condition that u is the smallest labeled neighbor of v in MIS_π and the fact that if v is not in the MIS_π, v must have at least one neighbor in MIS_π, or else MIS_π isn't maximal.

Claim 3. *A node w is only re-inserted by Algorithm 4 if there is at least one hot edge $e = (u, v)$ with u a root and $\ell(w) \geq \ell(v)$ (with possibly $v = w$). If e is such an edge, we say e is* active. *Furthermore, at least one active hot edge satisfies $\ell(u) < \ell(w)$.*

If w is re-inserted, then w must be live and adjacent to some smaller labeled live vertex u. Either u is a root, in which case (u, w) is the claimed hot edge, or else u must be adjacent to an even smaller labeled live vertex. In the latter case, we can recurse the argument down to u and eventually find a hot edge. In either case, both nodes incident to the discovered active hot edge will have a label no greater than w's.

Proof Outline. The strategy from here is a follows: whenever a failed delete occurs on a node w, we will charge it to an arbitrary hot edge $e = (u, v)$ with u a root and $\ell(w) \geq \ell(v)$ (of which there must be at least one by Claim 3). Similar to Theorem 3.1, we will say that e is active during the interval between the first time u experiences an inversion on or above v and the time u is processed. We say that the *cost*, $c(e)$, of an edge, e, is the number of failed deletes charged to it (which is notably 0 unless e is both hot and, at some point, active). We then separately bound (1) the expected number of active hot edges which ever exist over the execution of Algorithm 4 and (2) the expected number of failed deletes charged to an edge, given that it is an active hot edge. Combining these will give the result.

In order to quantify the distribution of hot edges, we will need one more definition. Fix $e = (u, v)$ and let G_e be the subgraph of G induced by $V' = V \setminus \{u, v\}$ and let π_e be π restricted to V'. Let $L_{e,t}$ be the event that neither u nor v has a neighbor $w \in MIS_{\pi_e}$ with $\ell_{\pi_e}(w) < t$. Informally, $L_{e,t}$ is the event that both u and v are still *live* in G after running Algorithm 4 with an exact queue ($k = 1$) for $t - 1$ iterations but with u, v excluded from Q. Like H_e, $L_{e,t}$ depends only on π and not on the randomness of the relaxation of Q; furthermore, $L_{e,t}$ is independent from $\ell(u)$ and $\ell(v)$. Using this definition, we can compute:

$$\Pr[H_e] = \sum_t \Pr[L_{e,t}] \Pr[\ell(u) = t] \Pr\left[\ell(v) > \ell(u) \middle| \ell(u) = t\right] = \sum_t \Pr[L_{e,t}] \frac{1}{n} \frac{n-t}{n-1}.$$

and

$$\Pr\left[\ell(u) = t \middle| H_e\right] = \frac{\Pr\left[H_e \middle| \ell(u) = t\right] \Pr[\ell(u) = t]}{\Pr[H_e]} = \frac{\Pr[L_{e,t}] \Pr\left[\ell(v) > t \middle| \ell(u) = t\right] \Pr[\ell(u) = t]}{\Pr[H_e]} = \frac{\Pr[L_{e,t}] \frac{n-t}{n-1} \frac{1}{n}}{\sum_{t'} \Pr\left[L_{e,t'}\right] \frac{1}{n} \frac{n-t'}{n-1}} = \frac{\Pr[L_{e,t}] (n-t)}{\sum_{t'} \Pr\left[L_{e,t'}\right] (n-t')}.$$

Next, we use the above formulations to bound the probability that a hot edge e is ever *active*. Suppose we are given that e is a hot edge and $\ell(u) = t$. Then e becomes active if and only if u suffers an inversion on or above v before u is processed by the algorithm. Let A_e be the event that e becomes active. At this point, we might wish to apply Lemma 3.3 directly, but unfortunately it is not clear that $\Pr[A_e]$ is independent from H_e, which we will need. However, note that H_e entails $\ell(v) > \ell(u)$ but given only that, $\ell(v)$ is otherwise independent from H_e. Thus, if we condition on $\ell(u) = t$ and $\ell(v) > \ell(u)$, then $\ell(u)$ is fixed and $\ell(v)$ is (conditionally) independent from H_e, and therefore A_e also becomes (conditionally) independent from H_e. Now we can apply Corollary 3.4, giving

$$\Pr\left[A_e \middle| \ell(u) = t, H_e\right] = \Pr\left[A_e \middle| \ell(u) = t, \ell(v) > \ell(u)\right] = O\left(\frac{k^2 \log k}{n-t}\right).$$

Then:

$$\Pr\left[A_e \middle| H_e\right] = \sum_t \Pr\left[\ell(u) = t \middle| H_e\right] \Pr\left[A_e \middle| \ell(u) = t, H_e\right] = \sum_t \frac{\Pr[L_{e,t}] (n-t)}{\sum_{t'} \Pr\left[L_{e,t'}\right] (n-t')} \frac{O(k^2 \log k)}{n-t} = O(k^2 \log k) \frac{\sum_t \Pr[L_{e,t}]}{\sum_{t'} \Pr\left[L_{e,t'}\right] (n-t')}.$$

Observe that for fixed $e = (u, v)$, $\Pr[L_{e,t}]$ is decreasing in t. In particular, for any permutation π in which the event $L_{e,t}$ occurs, $L_{e,t-1}$ occurs also, but the reverse is not true. Let $\mu = \frac{1}{n} \sum_t \Pr[L_{e,t}]$. Using *Chebyshev's sum inequality*, we obtain:

$$\Pr\left[A_e \middle| H_e\right] \leq O(k^2) \frac{n\mu}{\sum_{t'} \mu(n-t')} = O(k^2 \log k) \frac{n}{\sum_{t'} (n-t')} = O\left(\frac{k^2 \log k}{n}\right).$$

Finally, since u is a root and we only charge e for failed deletes on nodes with a larger label than v, and therefore a larger label than u as well, the number of times we charge e is upper bounded by the total number of priority inversions suffered by u while a root, which, by Lemma 3.5, is given by $O(k)$ in expectation. Thus $\mathbb{E}[c(e) \middle| A_e, H_e] = O(k)$.

Combining all the parts, we have a final bound on the total cost:

$$\mathbb{E}\left[\sum_e c(e)\right] = \sum_e \Pr[H_e] \Pr[A_e | H_e] \Pr[c(e) | A_e, H_e] = \sum_e \Pr[H_e] \cdot O\left(\frac{k^2 \log k}{n}\right) \cdot O(k)) = O\left(\frac{k^3 \log k}{n}\right) \mathbb{E}[\#\{H_e\}] \overset{\text{Claim 2}}{<} O\left(\frac{k^3 \log k}{n}\right) \cdot n = O(k^3 \log k) = \text{poly}(k), \text{ q.e.d.}$$

□

		k				
$\|V\|$	$\|E\|$	4	8	16	32	64
1000	10000	12.8	56.8	148.8	308.6	583.0
	30000	7.0	40.8	108.6	264.2	478.6
	100000	12.4	40.0	100.6	225.8	427.2
10000	10000	11.0	43.2	145.4	336.4	738.6
	30000	16.6	71.4	196.0	437.6	890.2
	100000	13.0	56.2	144.4	290.6	529.6

Table 1: Simulation results for varying parameters of Maximal Independent Set. k is the relaxation factor, n is the number of nodes and m is the number of edges. The number of extra iterations is averaged over 2 runs.

4 EXPERIMENTAL RESULTS

Synthetic Tests. To validate our analysis, we implemented the sequential relaxed framework described in Algorithm 2, and used it to solve instances of MIS, matching, Knuth Shuffle, and List Contraction using a relaxed scheduler which uses the MultiQueue algorithm [21], for various relaxation factors. We record the average number of extra relaxations, that is, the number of failed deletes during the entire execution, across five runs. Results are presented in Table 1. We considered graphs of various densities with 10^3 and 10^4 vertices. The results appear to confirm our analysis: the number of extra iterations required for MIS is low, and scales only in K and not in $|V| + |E|$. There is some variation for fixed K and varying $|V| + |E|$, but it is always within a factor of 2 for our trials and does not appear to be obviously correlated with $|V| + |E|$.

Concurrent Experiments. We implemented a simple version of our scheduling framework, using a variant of the MultiQueue [21] relaxed priority queue data structure. We assume a setting where the input, that is, the set of tasks, is loaded initially into the scheduler, and is removed by concurrent threads. We use lock-free lists to maintain the individual priority queues and we hold pointers to the adjacency lists of each node within the queue elements, in order to be able to efficiently check whether a task still has outstanding dependencies.

We compared to the exact scheduling framework using the Wait-free Queue as Fast as Fetch-and-Add [27]. Since there could still be some reordering of tasks due to concurrency, we elect to use a backoff scheme wherein if an unprocessed predecessor is encountered, we wait for the predecessor to process. In practice this rarely occurs.

Setup. Our experiments were run on an Intel Xeon Gold 6150 machine with 4 sockets, 18 cores per socket and 2 hyperthreads per core, for a total of 36 threads per socket, and 144 threads total. The machine has 512GB of memory, with 128GB *local* to each socket. Accesses to local memory are cheaper than accesses to remote memory. We pinned threads to avoid unnecessary context switches and to fill up sockets one at a time. The machine runs Ubuntu 14.04 LTS. We used the GNU C++ compiler (G++) 6.3.0 with optimization level -O3.

Experiments are performed on $G(n, p)$ random graphs in three classes; sparse graphs with 10^8 nodes and 10^9 edges, *small dense* graphs with 10^6 nodes and 10^9 edges, and *large dense* graphs with 10^7 nodes and 10^{10} edges. Our experiments were bottlenecked by graph generation and loading time so we were limited to these graph sizes.

For each data point, we run five trials. In each trial, a graph is generated in parallel by 144 threads, and then we measure the time for n threads to compute an MIS. Note that, even when $n = 1$, we generate the graph using 144 threads. To ensure that this does not change memory locality in a way that would invalidate our results, we used the `numactl` utility to cause memory to be allocated locally on *only* the sockets where n threads will compute the MIS. We verified that this yields the same behavior as experiments where the graph is generated with only n threads. (Without using *numactl*, we observed significant slowdowns in the sequential algorithm.)

The number of queues in the MultiQueue is 4× the number of threads. In our graphs, we plot the average run time on a logarithmic y-axis versus the number of concurrent threads. Error bars show *minimum* and *maximum* run times.

Discussion. Figure 2 shows that our framework using a relaxed scheduler scales with respect to the time to compute MIS over the target graph all the way up to max thread count. The exact framework using the fast wait-free queue also scales, but not as well. In the sparse graphs, the relaxed scheduler is up to ~ 18.2× faster than optimized sequential code, compared to the exact scheduler, which peaks at ~ 5.0× faster. In the small dense graphs, where the time spent traversing edges in the MIS algorithm dominates the minor cost of dequeuing nodes, the exact scheduler achieves a peak speedup of ~ 17.8× over the sequential algorithm, which is approaching the relaxed scheduler's peak speedup of ~ 24.6×. However, in the large dense graphs, even though many edges are still traversed by the MIS algorithm, there are sufficiently many nodes to be dequeued that the performance advantage of the relaxed scheduler shows through: it achieves speedup of up to ~ 16.3× compared to the exact scheduler, which manages only ~ 6.9×. Note that the single threaded performance of the relaxed scheduler is also quite close to the sequential algorithm. In contrast, the exact scheduler is orders of magnitude slower with a single thread.

5 FUTURE WORK

From a theoretical perspective, the natural next step would be to tighten the poly(k) bound on failed deletes, both for the generic algorithm and for MIS; in fact, we conjecture that the poly(k) bounds in both Theorems 3.1 and 3.2 can be replaced with $\Theta(k)$. However, proving such a bound seems to require a deep understanding of the interplay between the structure of G and the effects of the randomness of a k-relaxed queue, which we had to take care in our analysis to keep *separate*. Also of interest is to discover more applications, and perhaps more instances like MIS in which the bound in Theorem 3.1 can be improved on.

One shortcoming of our approach is the fact that our cost measure is the number of *vertex* accesses in the priority queue. Notice that in theory our bounds may be substantially different when expressed in other metrics, such as the number of edge accesses for the algorithm to terminate, which are closer to standard *work* bounds. We plan to investigate such cost measures in future work.

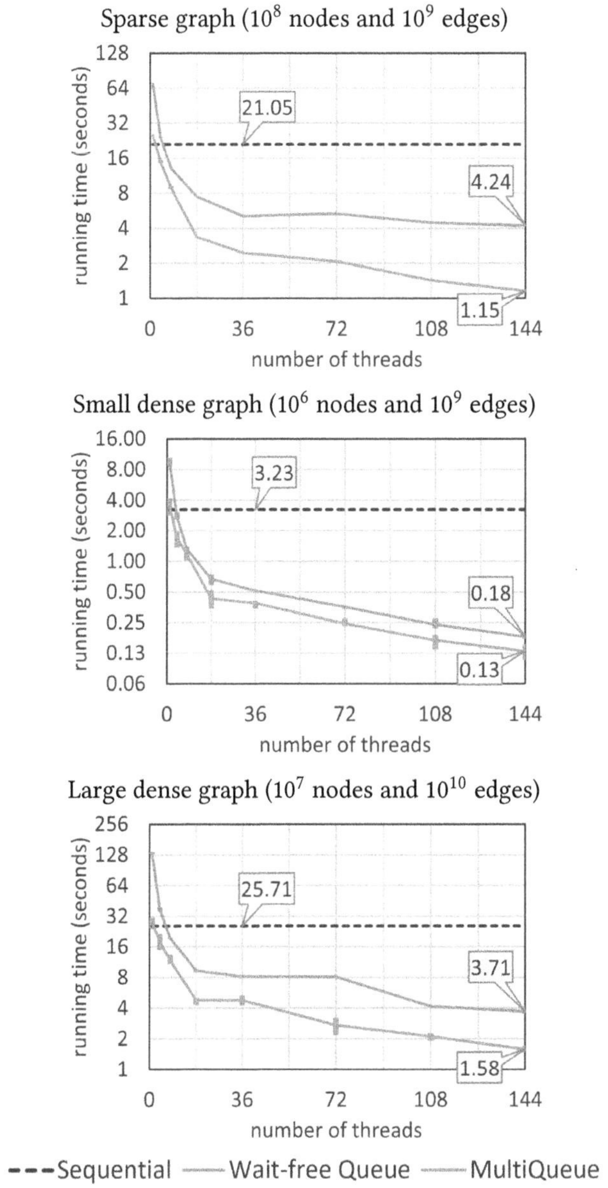

Figure 2: Results for concurrent MIS experiments.

From the practical perspective, the immediate step would to improve upon our preliminary results, and implement a high-performance variant of this scheduler, and use this framework in the context of more general graph processing packages.

REFERENCES

[1] Dan Alistarh, Justin Kopinsky, Jerry Li, and Nir Shavit. The spraylist: A scalable relaxed priority queue. In *20th ACM SIGPLAN Symposium on Principles and Practice of Parallel Programming*, PPoPP 2015, San Francisco, CA, USA, 2015. ACM.

[2] Dan Alistarh, Justin Kopinsky, Jerry Li, and Giorgi Nadiradze. The power of choice in priority scheduling. In *Proceedings of the ACM Symposium on Principles of Distributed Computing*, PODC '17, pages 283–292, New York, NY, USA, 2017. ACM. ISBN 978-1-4503-4992-5. doi: 10.1145/3087801.3087810. URL http://doi.acm.org/10.1145/3087801.3087810.

[3] Dan Alistarh, Trevor Brown, Justin Kopinsky, Jerry Li, and Giorgi Nadiradze. Distributionally linearlizable data structures. *Under Submission to SPAA 2018*, 2018.

[4] Dmitry Basin, Rui Fan, Idit Keidar, Ofer Kiselov, and Dmitri Perelman. CafÉ: Scalable task pools with adjustable fairness and contention. In *Proceedings of the 25th International Conference on Distributed Computing*, DISC'11, pages 475–488, Berlin, Heidelberg, 2011. Springer-Verlag. ISBN 978-3-642-24099-7. URL http://dl.acm.org/citation.cfm?id=2075029.2075087.

[5] Guy E Blelloch. Some sequential algorithms are almost always parallel. In *Proceedings of the 29th ACM Symposium on Parallelism in Algorithms and Architectures, SPAA*, pages 24–26, 2017.

[6] Guy E Blelloch, Jeremy T Fineman, Phillip B Gibbons, and Julian Shun. Internally deterministic parallel algorithms can be fast. In *ACM SIGPLAN Notices*, volume 47, pages 181–192. ACM, 2012.

[7] Guy E Blelloch, Jeremy T Fineman, and Julian Shun. Greedy sequential maximal independent set and matching are parallel on average. In *Proceedings of the twenty-fourth annual ACM symposium on Parallelism in algorithms and architectures*, pages 308–317. ACM, 2012.

[8] Guy E Blelloch, Yan Gu, Julian Shun, and Yihan Sun. Parallelism in randomized incremental algorithms. In *Proceedings of the 28th ACM Symposium on Parallelism in Algorithms and Architectures*, pages 467–478. ACM, 2016.

[9] Robert D Blumofe and Charles E Leiserson. Scheduling multithreaded computations by work stealing. *Journal of the ACM (JACM)*, 46(5):720–748, 1999.

[10] Robert D Blumofe, Christopher F Joerg, Bradley C Kuszmaul, Charles E Leiserson, Keith H Randall, and Yuli Zhou. Cilk: An efficient multithreaded runtime system. *Journal of parallel and distributed computing*, 37(1):55–69, 1996.

[11] Neil Calkin and Alan Frieze. Probabilistic analysis of a parallel algorithm for finding maximal independent sets. *Random Structures & Algorithms*, 1(1):39–50, 1990.

[12] Don Coppersmith, Prabhakar Raghavan, and Martin Tompa. Parallel graph algorithms that are efficient on average. In *Foundations of Computer Science, 1987., 28th Annual Symposium on*, pages 260–269. IEEE, 1987.

[13] Manuela Fischer and Andreas Noever. Tight analysis of parallel randomized greedy mis. In *Proceedings of the Twenty-Ninth Annual ACM-SIAM Symposium on Discrete Algorithms*, pages 2152–2160. SIAM, 2018.

[14] Joseph E Gonzalez, Yucheng Low, Haijie Gu, Danny Bickson, and Carlos Guestrin. Powergraph: distributed graph-parallel computation on natural graphs. In *OSDI*, volume 12, page 2, 2012.

[15] Andreas Haas, Michael Lippautz, Thomas A. Henzinger, Hannes Payer, Ana Sokolova, Christoph M. Kirsch, and Ali Sezgin. Distributed queues in shared memory: multicore performance and scalability through quantitative relaxation. In *Computing Frontiers Conference, CF'13, Ischia, Italy, May 14 - 16, 2013*, pages 17:1–17:9, 2013. doi: 10.1145/2482767.2482789. URL http://doi.acm.org/10.1145/2482767.2482789.

[16] Nick Harvey. Lecture notes in randomized algorithms. http://www.cs.ubc.ca/~nickhar/W12/Lecture3Notes.pdf, 2012.

[17] Shams Imam and Vivek Sarkar. Load balancing prioritized tasks via work-stealing. In *European Conference on Parallel Processing*, pages 222–234. Springer, 2015.

[18] Mark C Jeffrey, Suvinay Subramanian, Cong Yan, Joel Emer, and Daniel Sanchez. Unlocking ordered parallelism with the swarm architecture. *IEEE Micro*, 36(3): 105–117, 2016.

[19] R. M. Karp and Y. Zhang. Parallel algorithms for backtrack search and branch-and-bound. *Journal of the ACM*, 40(3):765–789, 1993.

[20] Donald Nguyen, Andrew Lenharth, and Keshav Pingali. A lightweight infrastructure for graph analytics. In *Proceedings of the Twenty-Fourth ACM Symposium on Operating Systems Principles*, SOSP '13, pages 456–471, New York, NY, USA, 2013. ACM. ISBN 978-1-4503-2388-8. doi: 10.1145/2517349.2522739. URL http://doi.acm.org/10.1145/2517349.2522739.

[21] Hamza Rihani, Peter Sanders, and Roman Dementiev. Brief announcement: Multiqueues: Simple relaxed concurrent priority queues. In *Proceedings of the 27th ACM Symposium on Parallelism in Algorithms and Architectures*, SPAA '15, pages 80–82, New York, NY, USA, 2015. ACM. ISBN 978-1-4503-3588-1. doi: 10.1145/2755573.2755616. URL http://doi.acm.org/10.1145/2755573.2755616.

[22] Konstantinos Sagonas and Kjell Winblad. The contention avoiding concurrent priority queue. In *International Workshop on Languages and Compilers for Parallel Computing*, pages 314–330. Springer, 2016.

[23] Konstantinos Sagonas and Kjell Winblad. A contention adapting approach to concurrent ordered sets. *Journal of Parallel and Distributed Computing*, 2017.

[24] Nir Shavit and Itay Lotan. Skiplist-based concurrent priority queues. In *Parallel and Distributed Processing Symposium, 2000. IPDPS 2000. Proceedings. 14th International*, pages 263–268. IEEE, 2000.

[25] Julian Shun, Yan Gu, Guy E Blelloch, Jeremy T Fineman, and Phillip B Gibbons. Sequential random permutation, list contraction and tree contraction are highly parallel. In *Proceedings of the twenty-sixth annual ACM-SIAM symposium on Discrete algorithms*, pages 431–448. SIAM, 2014.

[26] Martin Wimmer, Jakob Gruber, Jesper Larsson Träff, and Philippas Tsigas. The lock-free k-lsm relaxed priority queue. In *ACM SIGPLAN Notices*, volume 50, pages 277–278. ACM, 2015.

[27] Chaoran Yang and John Mellor-Crummey. A wait-free queue as fast as fetch-and-add. *SIGPLAN Not.*, 51(8):16:1–16:13, February 2016. ISSN 0362-1340. doi: 10.1145/3016078.2851168. URL http://doi.acm.org/10.1145/3016078.2851168.

A A TIGHTER VERSION OF LEMMA 3.3.

We now prove a slightly tighter version for the case where only elements from the top-k may be chosen by the scheduler Q. Note that the condition in the following Lemma (that u and v are simultaneously in the top-k) is a pre-requisite for u to experience an inversion on or above v, and thus the Lemma is slightly stronger than necessary.

LEMMA A.1. *Consider running Algorithm 2 (or Algorithm 4) using a k-relaxed queue Q on input graph $G = (V, E)$. For a fixed edge $e = (u, v)$, the probability that both u and v are simultaneously in the top-k of Q during any execution on a random permutation π is bounded by $O(k^2/n)$.*

PROOF. We will write $e \in$ top-k as shorthand for the event that u and v are simultaneously in the top-k of Q at some time. Note that no matter what dependencies exist in the top-k of Q, the entire top-k is flushed after the rank 1 element gets deleted k times. The number of iterations it takes to delete the rank 1 element k times after u enters the top-k (thereby flushing u with certainty) is a negative binomially distributed random variable X_u with mean k^2 and success probability $1/k$ (due to the fairness of Q), and similarly for X_v. Since S_e entails that either $\ell(u) < \ell(v) < \ell(u) + X_u$ or $\ell(v) < \ell(u) < \ell(v) + X_v$, we note that the two cases are symmetric and compute:

$$\begin{aligned}
\Pr[e \in \text{top-k}] &\leq \Pr[\ell(u) < \ell(v) < \ell(u) + X_u] \\
&\quad + \Pr[\ell(v) < \ell(u) < \ell(v) + X_v] \\
&= 2\Pr[\ell(u) < \ell(v) < \ell(u) + X_u] \\
&= 2\sum_r \Pr[X_u = r] \Pr[\ell(u) < \ell(v) < \ell(u) + r] \\
&= 2\sum_r \Pr[X_u = r] \frac{r}{n} \\
&\leq \frac{2ck^2}{n} \Pr\left[X_u \leq ck^2\right] + 2\sum_{r > ck^2} \Pr[X_u = r] \frac{r}{n} \\
&\leq O\left(\frac{k^2}{n}\right) + 2\sum_{r'} \Pr\left[X_u > r'k^2\right] \frac{(r'+1)k^2}{n} \\
&\leq O\left(\frac{k^2}{n}\right)\left(1 + \sum_{r'} e^{O(-r')}(r'+1)\right) \qquad (*) \\
&= O\left(\frac{k^2}{n}\right),
\end{aligned}$$

where (*) uses a standard tail bound on the Negative Binomial Distribution[2]. □

[2] See [16] for a derivation.

An Asynchronous Computability Theorem for Fair Adversaries

Petr Kuznetsov
LTCI, Télécom ParisTech
Université Paris-Saclay
Paris, France
petr.kuznetsov@telecom-paristech.fr

Thibault Rieutord
LTCI, Télécom ParisTech
Université Paris-Saclay
Paris, France
thibault.rieutord@telecom-paristech.fr

Yuan He
Computer Science Department
UCLA
Los Angeles, California, USA
yuan.he@cs.ucla.edu

ABSTRACT

This paper proposes a simple topological characterization of a large class of *fair* adversarial models via *affine tasks*: sub-complexes of the second iteration of the standard chromatic subdivision. We show that the task computability of a model in the class is precisely captured by iterations of the corresponding affine task. Fair adversaries include, but are not restricted to, the models of wait-freedom, t-resilience, and k-concurrency. Our results generalize and improve all previously derived topological characterizations of the ability of a model to solve distributed tasks.

CCS CONCEPTS

• **Theory of computation → Distributed computing models**;

KEYWORDS

adversarial models, affine tasks, topological characterization

ACM Reference Format:

Petr Kuznetsov, Thibault Rieutord, and Yuan He. 2018. An Asynchronous Computability Theorem for Fair Adversaries. In *PODC '18: ACM Symposium on Principles of Distributed Computing, July 23–27, 2018, Egham, United Kingdom.* ACM, New York, NY, USA, 10 pages. https://doi.org/10.1145/3212734.3212765

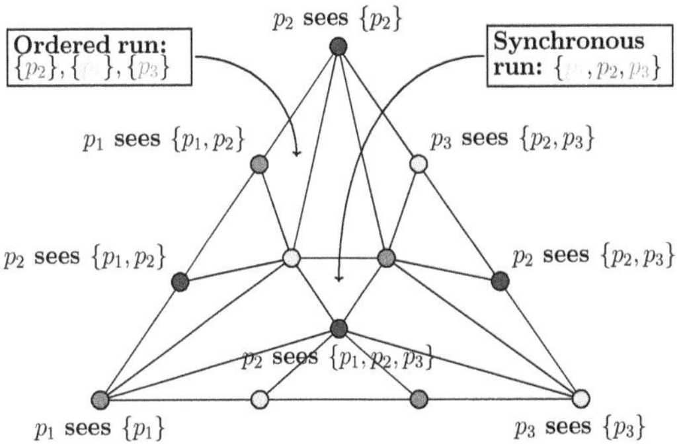

Figure 1: Chr(s), **the standard chromatic subdivision of a** 2-**simplex, the output complex of the** 3-**process** *IS* **task.**

1 INTRODUCTION

Distributed computing deals with a jungle of models, parameterized by types of failures, synchrony assumptions and communication primitives. Determining relative computability power of these models ("is model A more powerful than model B?") is an intriguing and important problem.

This paper deals with *shared-memory* models in which a set of *crash-prone asynchronous* processes communicate via invoking operations on a collection of shared objects, which, by default, include atomic read-write registers.

Topology of wait-freedom. The *wait-free* model [17] makes no assumptions on when and where failures might occur. Herlihy and Shavit proposed an elegant characterization of wait-free (read-write) task computability via the existence of a specific *simplicial* map from geometrical structures describing inputs and outputs [20].

A task T has a wait-free solution using read-write registers if and only if there exists a simplicial, chromatic map from some *subdivision* of the *input simplicial complex*, describing the inputs of T, to the *output simplicial complex*, describing the outputs of T, respecting the task specification Δ. In particular, we can choose this subdivision to be a number of iterations of the *standard chromatic* subdivision (denoted Chr, Figure 1). Therefore, the celebrated *Asynchronous Computability Theorem (ACT)* [20] can be formulated as:

> A task $T = (\mathcal{I}, \mathcal{O}, \Delta)$, where $\mathcal{I}$ is the input complex, $\mathcal{O}$ is an output complex, and Δ is a carrier map from $\mathcal{I}$ to sub-complexes of $\mathcal{O}$, is wait-free solvable if and only if there exists a natural number ℓ and a simplicial map $\phi : \mathrm{Chr}^{\ell}(\mathcal{I}) \to \mathcal{O}$ carried by Δ (informally, respecting the task specification Δ).

The output complex of the *immediate snapshot* (IS) task is precisely captured by Chr [5]. By solving the *IS* task iteratively, where the current iteration output is used as the input value for the next one, we obtain the *iterated* immediate snapshot (IIS) model, captured by iterations of Chr. The ACT theorem can thus be interpreted as: the set of wait-free (read-write) solvable task is precisely the set of tasks solvable in the IIS model. The ability of (iteratively) solving the *IS* task thus allows us to solve any task in the wait-free model. Hence, from the task computability perspective, the *IS* task is a finite representation of the wait-free model.

PODC '18, July 23–27, 2018, Egham, United Kingdom

ACM ISBN 978-1-4503-5795-1/18/07...$15.00
https://doi.org/10.1145/3212734.3212765

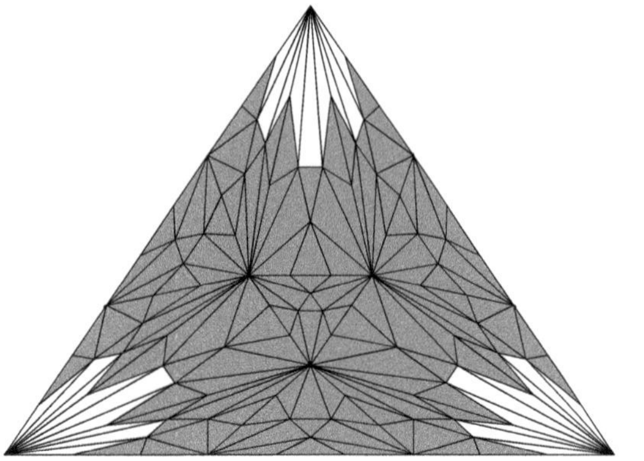

Figure 2: In blue, $\mathcal{R}_{1-res}$, the affine task of 1-resilience.

Adversaries. Given that many fundamental tasks are not solvable in the wait-free way [3, 20, 28], more general models were considered. Delporte et al. [9] introduced the notion of an *adversary*, a collection $\mathcal{A}$ of process subsets, called *live sets*. A run is in the corresponding *adversarial $\mathcal{A}$-model* if the set of processes taking infinitely many steps in it is a live set of $\mathcal{A}$. For example, the *t-resilient* n-process model is defined via an adversary $\mathcal{A}_{t-res}$ that consists of all process subsets of size $n - t$ or more. $\mathcal{A}_{t-res}$ is *superset-closed* [22], as it contains all supersets of its elements.

Saraph et al. [29] recently proposed a direct characterization of t-resilient task computability via a specific task $\mathcal{R}_{t-res}$. The task is defined as a restriction of the *double* immediate snapshot task: the output complex of the task is a sub-complex consisting of *all* simplices of the second degree of the standard chromatic subdivision of the task's input complex, except the simplices adjacent to the $(n - t - 1)$-skeleton of the input complex. Intuitively the output complex of $\mathcal{R}_{t-res}$ contains all of 2-round *IS* runs in which every process "sees" at least $n - t - 1$ other processes. We call such tasks *affine* [12, 15], as the geometrical representation of their output complexes are unions of affine spaces. An affine task consists in solving a (generalized) simplex agreement [5, 20] on the corresponding sub-complex of Chr^2 s.

Figure 2 depicts the output complex of $\mathcal{R}_{1-res}$, the affine task for the 3-process 1-resilient model.

Solving a task T in the t-resilient model is then equivalent to finding a map from iterations of $\mathcal{R}_{t-res}$ (applied to the input complex of T) to the output complex of T.

Similarly, the affine task of the *k-obstruction-free* adversary, consisting of all process subsets of size at most k, was recently determined by Gafni et al. [12]. Note that such an adversary is *symmetric* [31], as it only depends on the *sizes* of live sets, and not on process identifiers. Unlike $\mathcal{A}_{t-res}$ (which is also symmetric), the k-obstruction-free one is not superset-closed.

Topology of fair adversaries. In this paper, we present a compact topological characterization of the large class of *fair* adversarial models [23]. Informally, an adversary is fair if a subset of the participating processes P cannot achieve better set consensus than P. Fair adversaries subsume, but are not restricted to, symmetric and superset-closed ones.

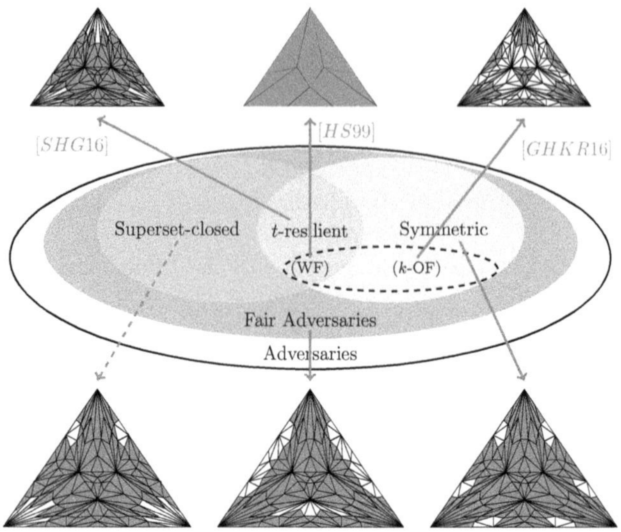

Figure 3: Earlier topological characterizations of the wait-free [20], t-resilient [29] and k-obstruction-free [12] models, and our contribution: affine tasks for all fair adversaries.

We define an affine task $\mathcal{R}_{\mathcal{A}}$ capturing the task computability of any fair (adversarial) $\mathcal{A}$-model. Our characterization can be put as the following generalization of the ACT [20]:

> A task $T = (\mathcal{I}, O, \Delta)$ is solvable in a fair adversarial $\mathcal{A}$-model if and only if there exists a natural number ℓ and a simplicial map $\phi : \mathcal{R}^{\ell}_{\mathcal{A}}(\mathcal{I}) \to O$ carried by Δ.

This result generalizes all existing topological characterizations of distributed computing models [12, 15, 20, 29], as it applies to *all* fair adversaries (and not only t-resilient and k-obstruction-free) and *all* tasks (and not only *colorless*).

Figure 3 shows adversary classes and summarizes the results of this paper along with earlier affine characterizations.

We believe that the results can be extended to all "practical" restrictions of the wait-free model, beyond fair adversaries, which may result in a complete computability theory for distributed computing shared-memory models.

Compact models. Our affine-task formalism enables a *compact* representation of a distributed computing model. Intuitively, assuming the conventional "longest-prefix" metric [2], a model M, as a set of infinite runs, is compact if it contains its limit points: if every prefix of an infinite run *complies* with M (i.e., can be extended to a run in M), then the run is in M. M can then be viewed as a *safety property* [27, Chap. 8]: to check if a run is in M, it is sufficient to check whether each of its finite prefixes complies with M.

Most adversarial models are non-compact. For example, the 1-obstruction-free 2-process model is compliant with all finite runs, but among the infinite ones—only those in which exactly one process runs solo from some point on are in the model. Similarly, consider an infinite solo run in which exactly one process takes steps. All finite prefixes of this run complies with the 1-resilient 3-process model, but the run itself is not in the model.

In contrast, the affine model L^*, defined as the subset of infinite IIS runs resulting by iterating an affine task L is, by construction, compact. By a simple application of König's lemma, we can easily show that every task solvable in an affine model is solvable in a *bounded* number of IIS rounds, i.e., in finitely many finite runs. In a non-compact model, such as the model of 1-resilience, many tasks can only be solved in arbitrarily long runs, hence, to check if a solution is correct, we might have to consider infinitely many infinite runs. Thus, working in an equivalent affine model may be attractive from the verification viewpoint.

Roadmap. Section 2 describes our model. Section 3 recalls the definitions of adversarial models and presents agreement functions. Section 4 defines the affine task $\mathcal{R}_{\mathcal{A}}$ for a fair adversary $\mathcal{A}$. In Section 5, we show that $\mathcal{R}^*_{\mathcal{A}}$ can be simulated in the adversarial $\mathcal{A}$-model. In Section 6, we show that any task solvable in the $\mathcal{A}$-model can be solved in $\mathcal{R}^*_{\mathcal{A}}$. Section 7 reviews related work and Section 8 concludes the paper. We encourage the reader to check the full version of this paper, with proofs and missing details [25].

2 PRELIMINARIES

We assume a system of n asynchronous processes, $\Pi = \{p_1, \ldots, p_n\}$. Two models of communication are considered: (1) *atomic snapshots* [1] and (2) *iterated immediate snapshots* [5, 20].

Atomic snapshot models. The atomic-snapshot (AS) memory is represented as a vector of n shared variables, where each process p_i is associated with the position i. The memory can be accessed with two operations: *update* and *snapshot.* An *update* operation performed by p_i modifies the value at position i and a *snapshot* returns the vector current state.

A *protocol* is a deterministic distributed automaton that, for each process and each its local state, stipulates which operation and state transition the process may perform. A *run* of a protocol is a possibly infinite sequence of alternating states and operations. An AS *model* is a set of infinite runs.

In an infinite run of the AS model, a process that takes only finitely many steps is called *faulty,* otherwise it is called *correct.* We assume that in its first step, a process shares its initial state using the *update* operation. If a process completed this first step in a given run, it is said to be *participating,* and the set of participating processes is called the *participating set.* Note that every correct process is participating.

Iterated Immediate Snapshot model. In the iterated immediate snapshot (IIS) model, processes proceed through an infinite sequence of independent memories $M_1, M_2, \ldots$. Each memory M_r is accessed by a process with a single *WriteSnapshot* operation [4]: the operation performed by p_i takes a value v_{ir} and returns a set V_{ir} of submitted values (w.l.o.g, values of different processes are distinct), satisfying the following properties (See Figure 4 for IS examples):

- self-inclusion: $v_{ir} \in V_{ir}$;
- containment: $(V_{ir} \subseteq V_{jr}) \vee (V_{jr} \subseteq V_{ir})$;
- immediacy: $v_{ir} \in V_{jr} \Rightarrow V_{ir} \subseteq V_{jr}$.

In the IIS communication model, we assume that processes run the *full-information* protocol, in which, the first value each process writes is its *initial state.* For each $r > 1$, the outcome of the WriteSnapshot operation on memory M_{r-1} is submitted as the input value for the WriteSnapshot operation on M_r. There are no failures in the IIS model, all processes go through infinitely many *IS* instances.

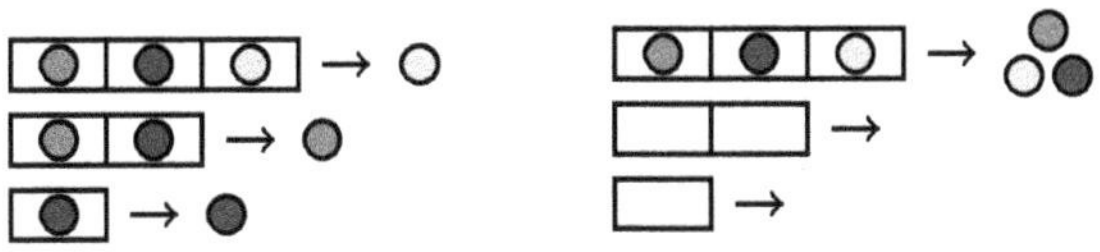

(a) Ordered run: $\{p_2\}, \{p_1\}, \{p_3\}$. **(b) Synchronous run:** $\{p_1, p_2, p_3\}$.

Figure 4: Examples of valid sets of IS outputs.

Note that the wait-free AS model and the IIS model are equivalent as regards task solvability [4, 18].

Tasks. In this paper, we focus on distributed *tasks* [20]. A process invokes a task with an *input* value and the task returns an *output* value, so that the inputs and the outputs across the processes respect the task specification. Formally, a *task* is defined through a set $\mathcal{I}$ of input vectors (one input value for each process), a set $\mathcal{O}$ of output vectors (one output value for each process), and a total relation $\Delta : \mathcal{I} \mapsto 2^{\mathcal{O}}$ that associates each input vector with a set of possible output vectors. We require that Δ is a *carrier* map: $\forall \rho, \sigma \in \mathcal{I}, \rho \subseteq \sigma$: $\Delta(\rho) \subseteq \Delta(\sigma)$. An input $\perp$ denotes a *non-participating* process and an output value $\perp$ denotes an *undecided* process. Check [18] for more details on the definition.

In the *k-set consensus* task [7], input values are in a set of values V ($|V| \geq k + 1$), output values are in V, and for each input vector I and output vector O, $(I, O) \in \Delta$ if the set of non-$\perp$ values in O is a subset of values in I of size at most k. The case of 1-set consensus is called *consensus* [10].

A protocol solves a task $T = (\mathcal{I}, \mathcal{O}, \Delta)$ in a model M, if it ensures that in every run of M in which processes start with an input vector $I \in \mathcal{I}$, there is a finite prefix R of the run in which: (1) decided values form a vector $O \in \mathcal{O}$ such that $(I, O) \in \Delta$, and (2) all correct processes decide. Hence, in the IIS model, all processes must decide.

Simplicial complexes. We use the standard language of *simplicial complexes* [18, 30] to give a combinatorial representation of the IIS model. A *simplicial complex* is defined as a set of *vertices* and an inclusion-closed set of vertex subsets, called *simplices.* The *dimension* of a simplex σ is $|\sigma| - 1$, and any subset of σ is one of its *faces.* We denote by $\mathbf{s}$ the *standard* $(n-1)$*-simplex*: a fixed set of n vertices and all its subsets.

Given a complex K and a simplex $\sigma \in K$, σ is a *facet* of K, denoted *facet*(σ, K), if σ is not a face of any stricly larger simplex in K. Let *facets*$(K) = \{\sigma \in K, \textit{facet}(\sigma, K)\}$. A simplicial complex is *pure* (of dimension n) if all its facets have dimension n. A simplicial complex is *chromatic* if it is equipped with a *coloring function* — a non-collapsing simplicial map χ from its vertices to $\mathbf{s}$, in one-to-one correspondence with n *colors.* In our setting, colors correspond to processes identifiers.

The *closure* of a set of simplices S, $Cl(S)$, is the complex formed by all faces of simplices in S, i.e., $\bigcup_{\sigma \in S} \textit{faces}(\sigma)$. Given a complex K, the *star* of $S \subseteq K$ in K, $St(S, K)$, is the set of all simplices in K having a simplex from S as a face, i.e., $\{\sigma \in K | \textit{faces}(\sigma) \cap S \neq \emptyset\}$. Given a pure complex K, we also define a new construct that we call the *pure complement* of $S \subseteq K$ in K, $Pc(S, K)$. It is the maximal pure sub-complex of K of the same dimension as K which does not intersect with S, i.e., $Cl(\{\sigma \in facets(K) | faces(\sigma) \cap S = \emptyset\})$.

Standard chromatic subdivision and IIS. The *standard chromatic subdivision* [20] of a complex K, $\mathrm{Chr}\, K$ ($\mathrm{Chr}\,\mathbf{s}$ is depicted in Figure 1), is a complex where vertices of $\mathrm{Chr}\, K$ are couples (c, σ), where c is a color and σ is a face of K containing a vertex of color c. Simplices of $\mathrm{Chr}\, K$ are the sets of vertices $(c_1, \sigma_1), \ldots, (c_m, \sigma_m)$ associated with distinct colors (i.e., $\forall i, j$, $c_i \neq c_j$) such that the σ_i satisfies the containment and immediacy properties of *IS*. It has been shown that Chr is a *subdivision* [21]. In particular, the geometric realization of $\mathrm{Chr}\,\mathbf{s}$, $|\mathrm{Chr}\,\mathbf{s}|$, is homeomorphic to $|\mathbf{s}|$, the geometric realization of $\mathbf{s}$ (i.e., the convex hull of its vertices). If we *iterate* this subdivision m times, each time applying Chr to all simplices, we obtain the mth chromatic subdivision, Chr^m. $\mathrm{Chr}^m\,\mathbf{s}$ captures the m-round IIS model, IS^m [5, 20].

Given a complex K and a subdivision of it $Sub(K)$, the carrier of a simplex $\sigma \in Sub(K)$ in K, $Car(\sigma, K)$, is the smallest simplex $\rho \in K$ such that the geometric realization of σ, $|\sigma|$, is contained in $|\rho|$: $|\sigma| \subseteq |\rho|$. The carrier of a vertex $(p, \sigma) \in \mathrm{Chr}\,\mathbf{s}$ is σ. In the matching *IS* task, the carrier corresponds to the snapshot returned by p, i.e., the set of processes *seen* by p. The carrier of a simplex $\rho \in \mathrm{Chr}\, K$ is simply the union (or, due to inclusion, the maximum) of the carriers of vertices in ρ. Given a simplex $\sigma \in \mathrm{Chr}^2\,\mathbf{s}$, $Car(\sigma, \mathbf{s})$ is equal to $Car(Car(\sigma, \mathrm{Chr}\,\mathbf{s}), \mathbf{s})$. $Car(\sigma, \mathrm{Chr}\,\mathbf{s})$ corresponds to the set of all snapshots seen by processes in $\chi(\sigma)$. Hence, $Car(\sigma, \mathbf{s})$ corresponds to the union of all these snapshots. Intuitively, it results in the set of all processes *seen* by processes in $\chi(\sigma)$ through the two successive immediate snapshots instances.

Simplex agreement and affine tasks. In the *simplex agreement task*, processes start on vertices of some complex K, forming a simplex $\sigma \in K$, and must output vertices of some subdivision of K, $Sub(K)$, so that outputs form a simplex ρ of $Sub(K)$ respecting carrier inclusion, i.e., $Car(\rho, K) \subseteq \sigma$. In the simplex agreement tasks considered in the characterization of wait-free task computability [5, 20], K is the standard simplex $\mathbf{s}$ and the subdivision is usually iterations of Chr.

An *affine task* is a generalization of the simplex agreement task, where $\mathbf{s}$ is fixed as the input complex and where the output complex is a pure non-empty sub-complex of some iteration of the standard chromatic subdivision, $\mathrm{Chr}^\ell\,\mathbf{s}$. Formally, let L be a pure non-empty sub-complex of $\mathrm{Chr}^\ell\,\mathbf{s}$ for some $\ell \in \mathbb{N}$. The affine task associated with L is then defined as $(\mathbf{s}, L, \Delta)$, where, for every face $\sigma \subseteq \mathbf{s}$, $\Delta(\sigma) = L \cap \mathrm{Chr}^\ell(\sigma)$. Note that $L \cap \mathrm{Chr}^\ell(\mathrm{t})$ can be empty, in which case the set of participating processes must increase before processes may produce outputs. Note that, since an affine task is characterized by its output complex, with a slight abuse of notation, we use L for both the affine task $(\mathbf{s}, L, \Delta)$ and its ouput complex.

By running m iterations of this task, we obtain L^m, a sub-complex of $\mathrm{Chr}^{\ell m}\,\mathbf{s}$, corresponding to a subset of $IS^{\ell m}$ runs (each of the m iterations includes ℓ *IS* rounds). The affine model associated with L, denoted L^*, corresponds to the set of infinite runs of the IIS model where every prefix restricted to a multiple of ℓ *IS* rounds belongs to the subset of $IS^{\ell m}$ runs associated with L^m. Note that the definition of the affine model L^* is done by satisfying a property on all its prefixes. Hence, affine models are, by construction, compact.

3 ADVERSARIES AND AGREEMENT FUNCTIONS

In this section, we introduce many results from [23] wich will be instrumental for our topological characterization.

Adversaries. It is convenient to model patterns in which process failures can occur using the formalism of *adversaries* [9]. An adversary $\mathcal{A}$ is defined as a set of possible correct process subsets, called *live sets*. An infinite run is *$\mathcal{A}$-compliant* if the set of processes that are correct in that run belongs to $\mathcal{A}$. An *(adversarial) $\mathcal{A}$-model* $\mathcal{A}$-model is thus defined as the set of $\mathcal{A}$-compliant runs.

An adversary is *superset-closed* [22] if each superset of a live set of $\mathcal{A}$ is also an element of $\mathcal{A}$, i.e., if $\forall S \in \mathcal{A}, \forall S' \subseteq \Pi, S \subseteq S' \implies S' \in \mathcal{A}$. Superset-closed adversaries provide a non-uniform generalization of the classical *t-resilient* adversaries. An adversary $\mathcal{A}$ is *symmetric* if it only depends on the *sizes* of live sets, and not on process identifiers: $\forall S \in \mathcal{A}, \forall S' \subseteq \Pi, |S'| = |S| \implies S' \in \mathcal{A}$. Introduced as symmetric progress conditions in [31], symmetric adversaries provide a generalization of t-resilience and k-obstruction-freedom.

The *agreement power* of a model, i.e., the smallest k such that k-set consensus is solvable, was determined for adversaries in [13] in order to characterize the power of adversaries in solving *colorless* tasks [4]. It is formalized as follows:

Definition 3.1. [Agreement power]

$$setcon(\mathcal{A}) = \begin{cases} 0 & \text{if } \mathcal{A} = \emptyset \\ \max\limits_{S \in \mathcal{A}}(\min\limits_{a \in S}(setcon(\mathcal{A}|_{S \setminus \{a\}}) + 1)) & \text{otherwise} \end{cases}$$

With $\mathcal{A}|_P$ the adversary composed of the live sets of $\mathcal{A}$ included in P. As previously shown in [14], for a superset-closed adversary $\mathcal{A}$, the agreement power of $\mathcal{A}$ is equal to $csize(\mathcal{A})$, where $csize(\mathcal{A})$ is the size of the minimal hitting set of $\mathcal{A}$, i.e., a set intersecting with each $L \in \mathcal{A}$. For a symmetric adversary $\mathcal{A}$, the agreement power formula reduces to $setcon(\mathcal{A}) = |\{k \in \{1, \ldots, n\} : \exists S \in \mathcal{A}, |S| = k\}|$.

Agreement functions. Consider an AS model M and a function α mapping subsets of Π to integers in $\{0, \ldots, n\}$. We say that α is the *agreement function* of M, if for each $P \in 2^\Pi$, $\alpha(P)$ is the agreement powe of the model $M|_P$ consisting of runs of M in which no process in $\Pi \setminus P$ participates [23]. Intuitively, $\alpha(P)$ is the best level of set consensus that can be solved adaptively in M. By convention, if $M|_P$ does not contain any run, then $\alpha(P)$ is equal to 0.

Let $P \subseteq P' \subseteq \Pi$. We can observe that, by construction, the agreement function of a model is *monotonic*, i.e., $\alpha(P) \leq \alpha(P')$ and of *bounded growth*, i.e., $\alpha(P') \leq \alpha(P) + |P' \setminus P|$.

It was shown in [23] that the agreement function of $\mathcal{A}$ can be defined using the *setcon* function: $\alpha(P) = setcon(\mathcal{A}|_P)$.

Fair adversaries. Informally, an adversary is *fair* [23] if a subset Q of participating processes P cannot achieve a better set consensus than P. For an adversary $\mathcal{A}$, and $Q \subseteq P \subseteq \Pi$, we define $\mathcal{A}|_{P,Q} = \{S \in \mathcal{A} : (S \subseteq P) \wedge (S \cap Q \neq \emptyset)\}$. When solving a task, only correct processes must output. Thus, for a task restricted to processes in Q, no process has to output in a run corresponding to a live set $L \in \mathcal{A}$ with $L \cap Q = \emptyset$.

Definition 3.2. [Fairness] An adversary $\mathcal{A}$ is *fair* if and only if:

$$\forall P \subseteq \Pi, \forall Q \subseteq P, setcon(\mathcal{A}|_{P,Q}) = min(|Q|, setcon(\mathcal{A}|_P)).$$

Superset-closed and symmetric adversaries are fair [23], as some others. Unfortunately, not all adversaries are fair.

The α-model. Generalizing the k-active-resilient model, the α-model was introduced to capture agreement functions ability to characterize the task computability of (some) models.

Definition 3.3. [α-model] The α-*model* is the AS model in which: if P is the participating set, then $\alpha(P) \geq 1$ and at most $\alpha(P) - 1$ processes in P are faulty.

Intuitively, the α-model is the weakest model with α as its agreement function. This allows us to use agreement functions to characterize models which are as weak as the corresponding α-model. It turns out that the task computability of a fair adversary is captured precisely by the corresponding α-model, i.e., they solve *the same* set of tasks.

THEOREM 3.4. *[23] For any fair adversary $\mathcal{A}$, a task is solvable in the $\mathcal{A}$-model if and only if it is solvable in the α-model.*

α-adaptive set consensus. The abstraction of *α-adaptive set consensus* [23] can be accessed with a single *propose*(v) operation. It ensures that (termination) every operation invoked by a correct process eventually returns, (validity) every returned value is the argument of a preceding *propose* invocation, and (α-agreement) at any point of the execution, the number of distinct returned values does not exceed $\alpha(P)$, with P the current participating set. This abstraction allows us to define yet another family of models, equivalent with α-model, and hence, with adversarial $\mathcal{A}$-models.

Definition 3.5. [α-set consensus model] The *α-set consensus* model is the AS model in which, if P is the participating set then $\alpha(P) \geq 1$, and processes have access to α-adaptive set-consensus objects.

THEOREM 3.6. *[23] A task is solvable in the α-model if and only if it is solvable in the α-set-consensus model.*

Hence, for a fair adversary $\mathcal{A}$ and its agreement function α the $\mathcal{A}$-model, the α-set-consensus model and the α-model can all be used interchangeably for task solvability issues.

4 DEFINING THE AFFINE TASK FOR A FAIR ADVERSARY

Given a fair adversary $\mathcal{A}$ and its agreement function α, we define the affine task $\mathcal{R}_{\mathcal{A}}$, a sub-complex of Chr^2 s, which will be shown to capture the task computability of the $\mathcal{A}$-model.

Agreement and contention simplices. We first show how to restrict Chr^2 s to obtain an affine task $\mathcal{R}_{k-OF}$, solvable in the k-obstruction-free model, and which allows, in $\mathcal{R}^*_{k-OF}$, any set of processes to solve k-set consensus among themselves. As in [12], the idea consists in specifying prohibited simplices and take their pure complement as the affine task.

For a vertex $v \in \mathrm{Chr}^2$ s, let $View^1(v)$ and $View^2(v)$ be the sets of processes seen by the process $\chi(v)$ in, respectively, the first and the second *IS* (we call these $View^1$ and $View^2$). Formally, $View^2(v) = Car(v, \mathrm{Chr}\, s)$ and $View^1(v) = Car(v', s)$ with $v' \in Car(v, \mathrm{Chr}\, s)$ such that $\chi(v) = \chi(v')$.

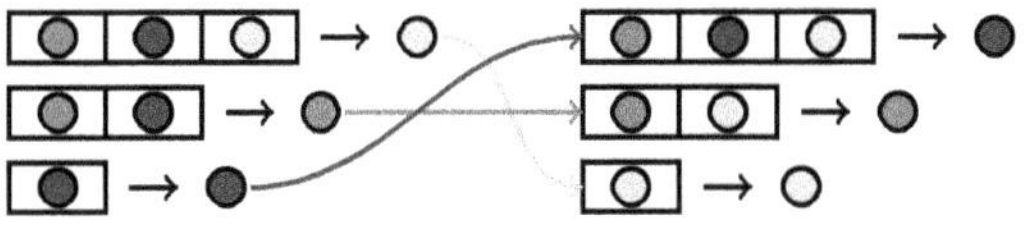

(a) Two reversed IS ordered runs: $\{p_2\}, \{p_1\}, \{p_3\}$ and $\{p_3\}, \{p_1\}, \{p_2\}$. Any set of processes is contending due to inverted execution orders.

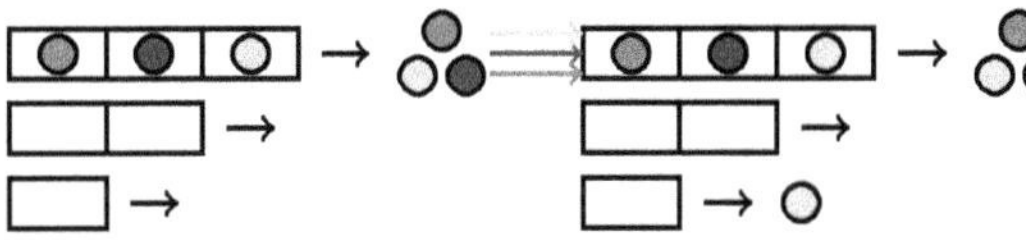

(b) Two synchronous IS runs: $\{p_1, p_2, p_3\}$ and $\{p_1, p_2, p_3\}$. Only singletons are contenting as all processes have the same IS ouputs.

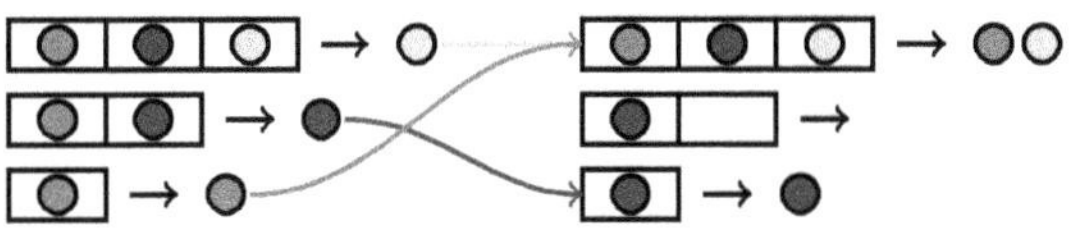

(c) Two ordered runs mixed orders: $\{p_1, p_2, p_3\}$ and $\{p_2\}, \{p_3, p_1\}$. The only couple of contending processes is $\{p_1, p_2\}$.

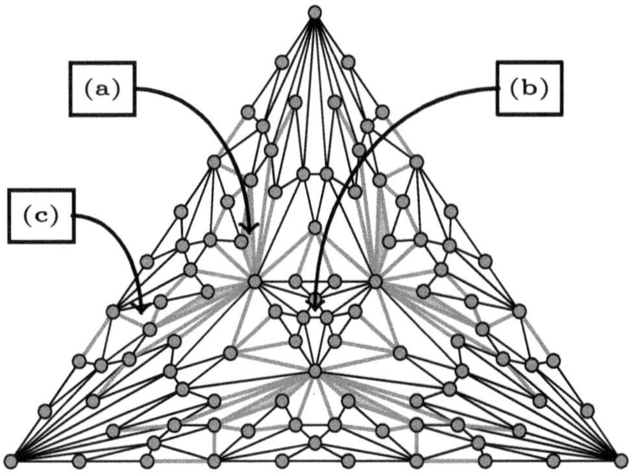

(d) The 2-contention complex shown in red.

Figure 5: Representation, in a 3-process system, of all 2-contention simplices in Chr^2 s and some detailled IS runs.

The idea behind the definition of these prohibited simplices is simple. In an execution, processes can only decide on the proposal they observed. Therefore, in an execution, if a process p sees only itself, other processes should return p's proposal to hope reaching an agreement with p. In Chr^2 s, if p is executed alone, then it has the smallest $View^1$ and $View^2$. Thus all processes would observe p's $View^1$. Therefore, a natural way to try to reach an agreement among processes is to adopt the proposal from the process observed with the smallest $View^1$. Moreover, as processes may share the same view, it is even better to deterministically select a value from the smallest $View^1$ itself.

We formalize this intuitive description as follows. In a simplex $\delta \in \mathrm{Chr}^2$ s, we say that vertices v and v' are *contending* if their $View^1$ and $View^2$ are ordered in the opposite way: $View^1(v)$

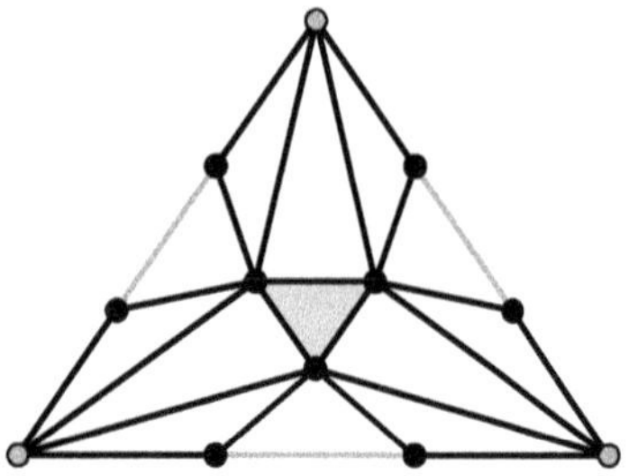

(a) For the α-model with $\alpha(P) = min(|P|, 1)$ (1-obstruction-freedom)

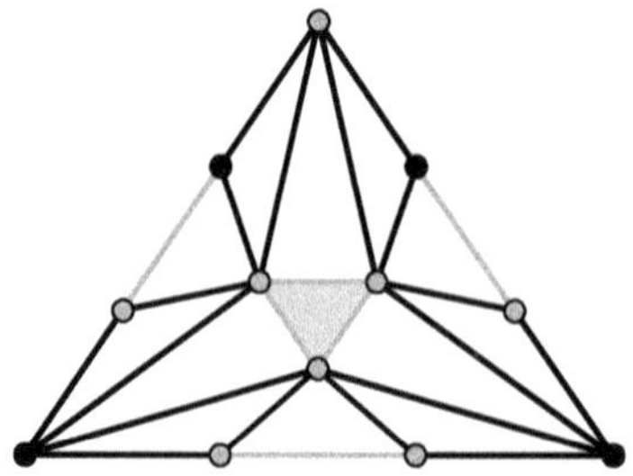

(b) For the adversary defined as $\{p_2\}$, $\{p_1, p_3\}$ plus all supersets.

Figure 6: Critical simplices are displayed in orange (with p_2 associated with the vertex on the top).

is a proper subset of $View^1(v')$ and $View^2(v')$ is a proper subset of $View^2(v)$, or vice versa. If every two vertices of δ are contending, then we say that δ is a 2-*contention* simplex. Let $Cont_2$ be the set of 2-contention simplices, formally:

Definition 4.1. $[Cont_2]$ $\sigma \in \text{Chr}^2\, \mathbf{s} : \forall v, v' \in \sigma, v \neq v' :$

$$((View^1(v) \subsetneq View^1(v')) \wedge (View^2(v') \subsetneq View^2(v)))\vee$$
$$((View^1(v') \subsetneq View^1(v)) \wedge (View^2(v) \subsetneq View^2(v'))).$$

$Cont_2$ is inclusion-closed: any face of a 2-contention simplex is also in $Cont_2$. Thus, $Cont_2$ is a complex: the 2-*contention complex* (depicted for a 3-process system in Figure 5d). Particular executions of two IS rounds are also depicted in Figure 5. In theses executions, one can see that a couple of processes is contending if the execution "order" is stricly reversed in the two IS runs.

Intuitively, a contention simplex of size k is one in which, in the corresponding run, all of the k processes have distinct $View^1$ and each one believes it had the smallest one among them. Thus, an execution for which all processes would return distinct proposals. Hence, $\mathcal{R}_{k-OF}$ is defined by prohibiting too large contending simplices:

Definition 4.2. [Affine task $\mathcal{R}_{k-OF}$]

$$\mathcal{R}_{k-OF} = Pc(\{\sigma \in Cont_2 | dim(\sigma) \geq k\}, \text{Chr}^2\, \mathbf{s}).$$

See Figure 8a for $\mathcal{R}_{1-OF}$ in a 3-process system. To see that $\mathcal{R}_{k-OF}$ indeed captures the k-obstruction-free adversary, one can check, which is not obvious, that the latter definition of $\mathcal{R}_{\mathcal{A}}$ reduces to $\mathcal{R}_{k-OF}$ when $\mathcal{A}$ is the k-obstruction-free adversary, or, alternatively, rely on the proofs from [12].

Agreement vs. participation. As described in Section 3, a fair adversary is characterized by its agreement function, i.e., the agreement power it has for all possible participation. Therefore, a natural generalization of $\mathcal{R}_{k-OF}$ would consist in adapting the size of allowed contention simplices with the participation, i.e., according to the carrier in $\mathbf{s}$ of a simplex.

The issue with this approach is that prioritizing processes with the smallest $View^1$ in order to limit contention conflicts with ensuring that processes have large enough views. To resolve this, instead of prioritizing processes with one of the smallest views, we prioritize the processes with the smallest view associated with a given agreement power. For example if the agreement function is equal to 1 for singletons or pairs and 2 for triplets or more, then a process with a view of size 1 or 3 is prioritized.

Unfortunately, it is possible that processes all obtain views of size 2, 4 or more. In this case, a process with a view of size 2 has the smallest view with an agreement power equal to 1, but it does not know it by its view alone. It must know that the other process it sees also has a view of size two, i.e., that it belongs to what we call a *critical simplex*.

Intuitively, a critical simplex is a set of processes with the same view P, which prohibits other processes to have a smallest view with an agreement power equal to $\alpha(P)$. Formally, $\sigma \in \text{Chr}\,\mathbf{s}$ is a critical if: (1) all its vertices share the same carrier; and (2) the agreement power of $\chi(Car(\sigma, \mathbf{s}))$ is strictly greater than the one of $\chi(Car(\sigma, \mathbf{s})) \setminus \chi(\sigma)$:

Definition 4.3. [Critical simplices]

$$CS_\alpha = \{\sigma \in \text{Chr}\,\mathbf{s} | (\forall v \in \sigma : Car(v, \mathbf{s}) = Car(\sigma, \mathbf{s}))\wedge$$
$$(\alpha(\chi(Car(\sigma, \mathbf{s})) \setminus \chi(\sigma)) < \alpha(\chi(Car(\sigma, \mathbf{s}))))\}.$$

Examples of critical simplices for 3-process models are depicted in Figure 6.

For $\sigma \in \text{Chr}^2\,\mathbf{s}$, let $\mathcal{CSM}_\alpha(\sigma)$ (critical simplices members of σ) be the set of vertices of σ which belong to some critical face of σ, i.e., $\mathcal{CSM}_\alpha(\sigma) = \cup_{\rho \in CS_\alpha \cap faces(\sigma)} \rho$. Similarly, let $\mathcal{CSV}_\alpha(\sigma)$ (critical simplices view) be the union of all processes observed by critical simplices in σ, i.e., $\mathcal{CSV}_\alpha(\sigma) = Car(\mathcal{CSM}_\alpha(\sigma), \mathbf{s})$.

Intuitively, α-adaptive set consensus is solved by making processes deterministically select a proposal from the $View^1$ of a critical simplex. If, however, critical sets do not offer proposals for some subset of processes, the size of the contention simplices in this subset should be adequately restricted. We define this restriction using the following map:

Definition 4.4. [Concurrency map] $\forall \sigma \in \text{Chr}\,\mathbf{s}$:

$$Conc_\alpha(\sigma) = max(0 \cup \{\alpha(\chi(Car(\tau, \mathbf{s}))), \tau \in CS_\alpha \cap faces(\sigma)\}).$$

The concurrency map is displayed in Figure 7 for examples of 3-process models. Each simplex of Chr s is associated with a concurrency level. One can observe that the set of simplices with a concurrency level equal to k corresponds to the simplices in the *star* of the critical simplices associated with an agreement power equal to k and which are not in the *star* of a critical simplex associated with a greater agreement power.

Affine task $\mathcal{R}_{\mathcal{A}}$. The affine task for a fair adversary $\mathcal{R}_{\mathcal{A}} \subseteq \text{Chr}^2\,\mathbf{s}$ is defined as follows:

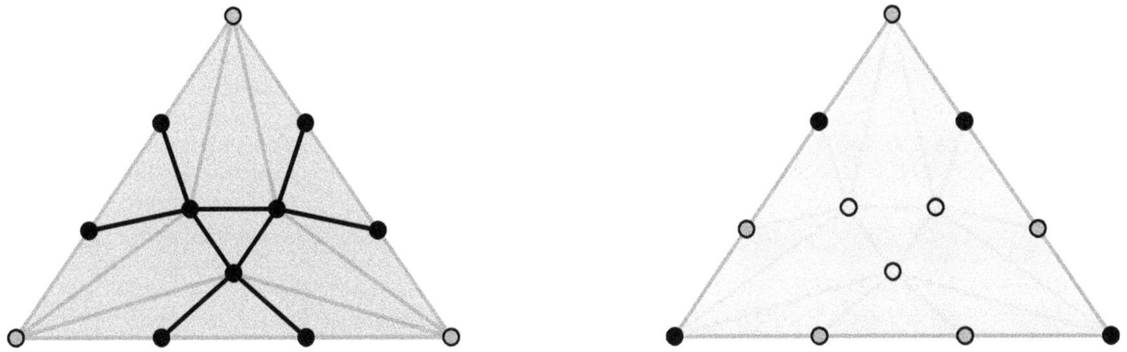

(a) For the α-model with $\alpha(P) = min(|P|, 1)$ (1-obstruction-freedom) (b) For the adversary defined as $\{p_2\}$, $\{p_1, p_3\}$ plus all supersets.

Figure 7: Simplices in black, orange and green are mapped to concurrency levels of 0, 1 and 2 respectively (with p_2 associated with the vertex on the top).

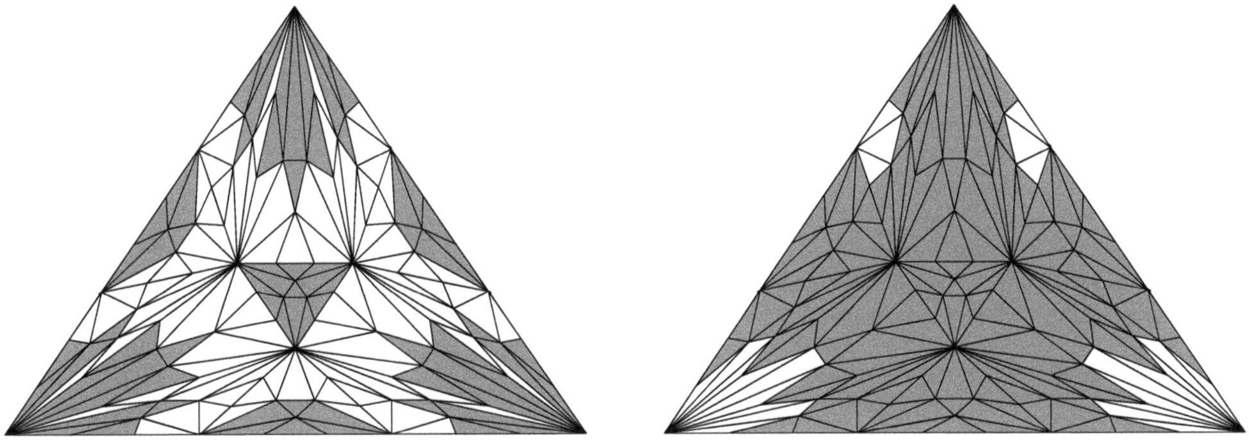

(a) For the α-model with $\alpha(P) = min(|P|, 1)$ (1-obstruction-freedom) (b) For the adversary defined as $\{p_2\}$, $\{p_1, p_3\}$ plus all supersets.

Figure 8: Some examples of affine tasks $\mathcal{R}_{\mathcal{A}}$ in blue (with p_2 associated with the vertex on the top).

Definition 4.5. $[\mathcal{R}_{\mathcal{A}}]$ $Cl(\sigma \in facets(\text{Chr}^2\, \mathbf{s}))$ with σ such that: $\forall \theta \in faces(\sigma)$, with $\tau = Car(\theta, \text{Chr}\, \mathbf{s})$ and $\rho = Car(\sigma, \text{Chr}\, \mathbf{s})$:

$$\theta \in Cont_2 \wedge (\chi(\theta) \cap \chi(\mathcal{CSM}_\alpha(\rho)) \cap \chi(\mathcal{CSV}_\alpha(\tau))) = \emptyset$$

$$\implies dim(\theta) < Conc_\alpha(\tau).$$

Intuitively, a simplex $\sigma \in \text{Chr}^2\, \mathbf{s}$ is in $\mathcal{R}_{\mathcal{A}}$ if and only if any of its "non-critical" subsets that cannot "rely" on the critical simplices in achieving α-adaptive set consensus has a sufficiently low contention level to solve α-adaptive set consensus on its own.

Examples of affine tasks for 3-process α-models are depicted in Figure 8.

5 FROM α-MODEL TO $\mathcal{R}_{\mathcal{A}}$

Let us fix a fair adversary $\mathcal{A}$, let α be its agreement function, and let T be any task that can be solved in $\mathcal{R}^*_{\mathcal{A}}$. To show that T is solvable in the $\mathcal{A}$-model, we present an algorithm that *solves* $\mathcal{R}_{\mathcal{A}}$ in the α-model. By iterating this task, we can simulate a run of $\mathcal{R}^*_{\mathcal{A}}$ and thus get a solution to T in the α-model and, by Theorem 3.4, in the $\mathcal{A}$-model.

Algorithm description. In our solution of $\mathcal{R}_{\mathcal{A}}$, presented in Algorithm 1, every process accesses two immediate snapshot objects: *FirstIS* to which it proposes its initial state, and *SecondIS* to which it proposes the outcome of *FirstIS*. Recall that outcomes of *SecondIS* form a simplex in $\text{Chr}^2\, \mathbf{s}$ [21]. To ensure that simplices are in $\mathcal{R}_{\mathcal{A}}$, after finishing *FirstIS*, processes wait for their turns to proceed to *SecondIS*.

In this *waiting phase* (Lines 7–10), processes check a specific condition on the *IS* outcomes that they share with each other in registers $IS1[1, \ldots, n]$ and $IS2[1, \ldots, n]$. Each process p_i periodically checks whether either (1) it belongs to a critical simplex by using the formula at Line 8, or (2) the number, computed at Line 9, of non-terminated processes ($IS2[j] = \emptyset$) which may have a smaller *FirstIS* output ($j \in IS1[i]$ and $IS1[j] \neq IS1[i]$) is smaller that some "level of concurrency". This level of concurrency is computed at Line 10 as the maximum between (1) the agreement power associated with the *View*[1] of the process itself ($\alpha(IS1[i])$) or (2) with the concurrency levels shared using the *Conc* registers by "terminated" critical simplices, i.e., a critical simplex with all its processes provided with *secondIS* outputs (Line 14).

Algorithm 1: Resolution of $R_{\mathcal{A}}$ in the α-model for process p_i.

1 **Shared:** Registers $IS1[1], \dots, IS1[n] \in 2^{\Pi}$, **initially** $\emptyset$;
2 $IS2[1], \dots, IS2[n] \in 2^{2^{\Pi}}$, **initially** $\emptyset$;
3 $Conc[1], \dots, Conc[n] \in \{0, \dots, n\}$, **initially** 0;
4 Immediate Snapshot Objects *FirstIS*, *SecondIS*;

5 $\mathcal{R}_{\mathcal{A}}(input_i)$:
6 $\quad IS1[i] \leftarrow FirstIS(\mathbf{input_i})$;
7 $\quad$ **wait until** $crit \vee (rank < conc)$ **with**
8 $\quad crit = (\alpha(IS1[i]) < \alpha(IS1[i] \setminus \{p_j \in \Pi : IS1[j] = IS1[i]\}))$
9 $\quad$ **and** $rank = |\{p_j \in IS1[i] : IS2[j] = \emptyset \wedge IS1[j] \neq IS1[i]\}|$
10 $\quad$ **and** $conc = \max\left(\alpha(IS1[i]), \max_{j \in \{1,\dots,n\}}(Conc[j])\right)$;

11 $\quad IS2[i] \leftarrow SecondIS(IS1[i])$;
12 $\quad sameView = \left\{p_j \in \Pi : (IS1[j] = IS1[i]) \wedge (IS2[j] \neq \emptyset)\right\}$;
13 $\quad$ **if** $(\alpha(IS1[i]) > \alpha(IS1[i] \setminus sameView))$ **then**
14 $\quad\quad Conc[i] \leftarrow \alpha(IS1[i])$
15 $\quad$ **return**$(IS2[i])$;
16 **End** $\mathcal{R}_{\mathcal{A}}$;

Intuitively, the waiting phase is used to ensure that *critical processes*, i.e., members of critical simplices, are prioritized to proceed with *SecondIS* over non-critical ones. A process may proceed to its *SecondIS* as soon as it knows that it belongs to some *critical* simplex ($crit = true$). A non-critical process is allowed to exit its waiting phase only when the number of potentially contending processes is smaller than the computed concurrency level ($rank < conc$). The proof relies mostly on showing that there are enough critical simplices to prevent non-critical processes from being blocked in the waiting phase.

THEOREM 5.1. *Algorithm 1 solves the task $\mathcal{R}_{\mathcal{A}}$ in the α-model.*

Proof sketch. Let us fix an execution with a participating set $P \in \Pi$ in which m processes crash before writing to *IS1*, and let $\sigma \in$ Chr s be the set of first *IS* outputs in that execution. We observe that, for any $\ell \in \mathbb{N}^+$, the minimal hitting set size of critical simplices in σ, associated with an agreement power greater than or equal to ℓ, is strictly greater than $\alpha(P) - \ell - m$, i.e.:

$$csize(\{\theta \in Crit_{\alpha}(\sigma), \alpha(\chi(Car(\theta, s))) \geq \ell\}) > \alpha(P) - \ell - m.$$

Recall that a hitting set of H is a set intersecting all $h \in H$.

Liveness. Suppose, by contradiction, that a correct process never terminates, i.e, it is *blocked* forever in the wait phase. Let p be the correct process blocked with the smallest *IS* view V. As p is blocked, we have $rank_p \geq conc_p$. Note that there are $rank_p$ crashed processes which could have obtained a *FirstIS* output smaller than V. Moreover, these $rank_p$ crashed processes cannot interfere with the number of critical simplices associated with an agreement power strictly greater than $\alpha(V)$. Thus, m can be replaced in the formula by m_1, the number of processes in $P \setminus V$ which failed before writing to *IS1*. Let m_2 the number of other faulty processes. Let $\ell = \alpha(P) - m_2 - m_1$ and assume that $\ell > \alpha(V)$, hence:

$$csize(\{\theta \in Crit_{\alpha}(\sigma), \alpha(\chi(Car(\theta, s))) \geq \ell\}) > m_2.$$

Thus, the members of a critical simplex whose *FirstIS* outputs are associated with an agreement power greater than or equal to ℓ must terminate and update the concurrency level. Indeed, to prevent all such critical simplices from terminating, at least one process in each of them must fail, forming a hitting set, which gives more than m_2 failures. Thus, if $\ell = \alpha(P) - m_2 - m_1 > \alpha(V)$, then $rank_p \geq conc_p \geq \ell$.

There are at most $\alpha(P) - 1$ failures in the α-model, so $m_1 + m_2 + rank_p < \alpha(P)$. Since $rank_p \geq conc_p$ and $conc_p \geq \alpha(V)$, we have $\alpha(P) - m_2 - m_1 > \alpha(V)$. So $rank_p \geq \ell = \alpha(P) - m_2 - m_1$, and hence, $m_1 + m_2 + rank_p \geq \alpha(P)$—a contradiction.

Safety. Processes must output vertices forming a simplex of $\mathcal{R}_{\mathcal{A}}$ respecting the affine task specification, i.e., ensuring carrier inclusion. By construction, since the outputs are provided using two successive immediate snapshots, they form a simplex of Chr^2 s which respects the carrier. Thus, we are left to check that the simplex they form is indeed in $\mathcal{R}_{\mathcal{A}}$: in any execution, non-critical processes do not form contention simplices of sizes greater than the concurrency level.

In order to form a contention simplex, processes must run concurrently *secondIS*. Therefore, if a contention simplex of size k is formed, a process must have exited the wait phase with a value of *conc* stricly greater than k.

If the value of *conc* is provided by a terminated critical simplex in Line 14, then, one can check that it indeed corresponds to the concurrency level from $\mathcal{R}_{\mathcal{A}}$ definition. Hence, that the contention simplex size is valid for $\mathcal{R}_{\mathcal{A}}$ for this execution.

Otherwise, $conc_p$ is equal to $\alpha(V)$. Let ℓ be the greatest agreement power associated with a terminated critical simplex, and σ the set of *FirstIS* outputs in this execution. Hence:

$$csize(\{\theta \in Crit_{\alpha}(\sigma), \alpha(\chi(Car(\theta, s))) \geq \ell + 1\}) > \alpha(V) - \ell - 1.$$

Thus, at least $\alpha(V) - \ell$ out of the processes counted in $rank_p$ are *critical*. Hence, p can form a contention simplex of non-critical processes of size at most $rank_p - \alpha(V) + \ell + 1$. But since $rank_p < conc_p = \alpha(V)$, it can be of size at most ℓ. Therefore, the contention simplex size is valid for $\mathcal{R}_{\mathcal{A}}$ for this execution.

A detailed proof of Theorem 5.1 is delegated to the technical report [25].

6 FROM $\mathcal{R}^*_{\mathcal{A}}$ TO THE FAIR ADVERSARIAL $\mathcal{A}$-MODEL

In this section, we discuss how to show that any task solvable in a fair adversarial $\mathcal{A}$-model can be solved in $\mathcal{R}^*_{\mathcal{A}}$. The proof is based on a *simulation*, in $\mathcal{R}^*_{\mathcal{A}}$, of any lock-free algorithm designed for the α-set-consensus model. We then use Theorem 3.6 to derive the solvability of any task from the $\mathcal{A}$-model. To simulate an algorithm running in the α-set-consensus model, we simulate accesses to (1) the AS memory and (2) instances of α-adaptive set-consensus, in an almost independent way. We sketch the simulation below, but a detailed description with a proof of correctness is delegated to the technical report [25].

Atomic-snapshot simulation. We rely upon the algorithm proposed in [16] that simulates a lock-free AS protocol in the *iterated AS* model (Defined as the IIS model, but with snapshots without the immediacy property). We treat the *view* a process obtains (i.e., the values of the carrier $Car(v, \mathbf{s})$ for its vertex v) after completing an iteration of $\mathcal{R}_{\mathcal{A}}$ as a snapshot, which gives us the iterated AS model that we are going to use for simulating the AS algorithm. Since the algorithm of [16] requires a non-terminated processes to have a pending AS operation, in our simulation a process with a pending access to a set-consensus instance keeps rewriting its last written value in each iteration.

Note that when a process completes a write operation, it linearizes all the pending write operations it sees. In particular, the first time a process completes a write operation, it linearizes initial write operations for a set of processes P, participating processes in the simulated run, such that $\alpha(P) > 0$.

Simulating α-adaptive set consensus in $\mathcal{R}^*_{\mathcal{A}}$. In our algorithm, every process continuously submits *decision estimates* to all simulated set-consensus instances it is aware of. Every decision estimate (initially the process's input) is recalculated after each iteration of $\mathcal{R}_{\mathcal{A}}$: the process adopts a decision estimate, if available, from a $View^1$ associated with a critical simplex or, otherwise, the smallest observed $View^1$.

As soon as *every* observed process involved in the considered instance of set consensus proposed a decision estimate during an iteration, the calculated estimate is considered to be *committed.* Before deciding on the committed value, the process proceeds to simulating an update operation (following the AS memory simulation described above), where the written value contains the inputs of all the processes it knows. Intuitively, the processes with these inputs then appear as participating in the simulated run, thus ensuring the desired properties of the simulated α-adaptive set consensus: the number of distinct decided values is properly related to the participating set.

Safety of the simulated α-adaptive set consensus instance relies mainly on the structure of the affine task: the set of known input states is always associated with an agreement power greater than the number of distinct committed values. Liveness follows from the fact that once a decision estimate is seen by all processes, all processes adopt a decision estimate. Then, once a decision estimate is adopted by all processes, they commit a value in the next iteration of $\mathcal{R}^*_{\mathcal{A}}$. For the rest we rely on the liveness of the AS memory simulation.

Combining the simulations. In the simulated algorithm, a process may have either a pending AS operation or a pending set-agreement operation. Liveness of the AS memory simulation ensures that some active (i.e., non-terminated) process completes infinitely many operations. Thus, progress is made unless all AS operations keep rewriting the same (bogus) value over and over again, hence, due to a pending set-consensus operation that never completes. But, as write completes, this process inputs are observed by all processes infinitely often, thus, eventually all processes must have a decision estimate, and hence, a value commited in the following round. Hence a distinct write value is proposed — a contradiction. Thus, our simulation is lock-free: at least one simulated process always makes progress. Inductively, we derive that in $\mathcal{R}^*_{\mathcal{A}}$, every process eventually outputs.

Combining our simulation with Theorem 5.1, we obtain:

THEOREM 6.1. *A task T is solvable in the fair adversarial $\mathcal{A}$-model if and only if T is solvable in $\mathcal{R}^*_{\mathcal{A}}$.*

We then can use König's lemma to show that, given a task, all processes must be provided outputs after a *bounded* number of iterations. Thus, we derive the following generalization of the ACT [20] to fair adversaries:

THEOREM 6.2. *[Fair ACT] A task $T = (\mathcal{I}, \mathcal{O}, \Delta)$ is solvable in a fair adversarial $\mathcal{A}$-model if and only if there exists a natural number ℓ and a simplicial map $\phi : \mathcal{R}^{\ell}_{\mathcal{A}}(\mathcal{I}) \to \mathcal{O}$ carried by Δ.*

7 RELATED WORK

Herlihy and Shavit [20] proposed a characterization of wait-free task computability through the existence of a simplicial map from a subdivision of the input complex of a task $\mathcal{I}$ to its output complex $\mathcal{O}$. (The reader is referred to [18] for a thorough discussion of the use of combinatorial topology in distributed computability.) Herlihy and Rajsbaum [19] studied colorless task computability in the special case of *superset-closed* adversaries. They show that the protocol complex of a superset-closed adversary with *minimal core size c* is $(c-2)$-connected. This result, obtained via an iterative application of the Nerve lemma, gives a combinatorial characterization of superset-closed adversaries. The characterization only applies to colorless tasks, and it does not allow us to express the adversary in an affine way.

Gafni et al. [15] introduced the notion of an affine task and characterized task computability in *iterated* adversarial models via infinite subdivisions of input complexes, assuming a limited notion of solvability that only guarantees outputs to "fast" processes [6, 11] (i.e., "seen" by every other process infinitely often). The liveness property defined in this paper for iterated models guarantees outputs for *every* process, which allowed us to establish a task-computability equivalence with conventional non-iterated models.

Saraph et al. [29] gave a compact combinatorial characterization of t-resilient task computability. Note that $\mathcal{A}_{t-res}$ is a superset-closed (and thus fair) adversary. Our solution of the affine task $\mathcal{R}_{\mathcal{A}}$ in the α-model is inspired by the t-resilient solution of $\mathcal{R}_{t-res}$ in [29]. Gafni et al. [12] presented affine tasks for the model of k-set consensus and, thus, k-concurrency and k-obstruction-freedom, which can be expressed as a symmetric and thus fair adversary.

The notions of agreement functions and a fair adversaries were introduced by the first two authors in [23]. One can determine the agreement function of any given adversary using the formula suggested earlier for the set consensus power [13]. It has been shown in [23] that agreement functions encode enough information to characterize the task computability of any fair adversary.

A short version of this paper appeared as a conference brief announcement [26], and an extended version with formal proofs can be found as a technical report [25].

8 CONCLUDING REMARKS

This paper generalizes all existing topological characterizations of distributed computing models [12, 15, 19, 20, 29]. It applies to all tasks (not necessarily colorless) and all *fair* adversarial models (not necessarily t-resilience or k-obstruction-freedom). Just as the wait-free characterization [20] implies that the *IS* task captures the wait-free model, our characterization equates any fair adversary with a (compact) affine task embedded in the second degree of the standard chromatic subdivision.

Interestingly, unlike [29], we cannot rely on the *shellability* [18] (and, thus, link-connectivity) of the affine task. Link-connectivity of a simplicial complex C allows us to work in the *point set* of its geometrical embedding $|C|$ and use continuous maps (as opposed to simplicial maps that maintain the simplicial structure). For example, the existence of a continuous map from $|\mathcal{R}_{\mathcal{A}_{t-res}}|$ to any $|\mathcal{R}^k_{\mathcal{A}_{t-res}}|$ implies that $\mathcal{R}_{\mathcal{A}_{t-res}}$ indeed captures the general task computability of $\mathcal{A}_{t-res}$ [29]. In general, however, the existence of a continuous map onto C only allows us to converge on a *single* vertex [18]. If C is not link-connected, converging on one vertex allows us to compute an output only for a single process, and not more. Unfortunately, only very special adversaries, such as $\mathcal{A}_{t-res}$, have link-connected counterparts (see, e.g., the affine task corresponding to 1-obstruction-freedom in Figure 8a). Instead of relying on link-connectivity, this paper takes an explicit algorithmic way of showing that iterations of $\mathcal{R}_{\mathcal{A}}$ simulate $\mathcal{A}$. An interesting question is to which extent point-set topology and continuous maps can be applied in affine characterizations.

Given that some models out of this class cannot be grasped by agreement functions (see [23] for examples), going beyond fair adversarial models is an important challenge. In particular, we should be able to account for models in which *coalitions* of participants can achieve better levels of set consensus than the whole set. Nailed down, this may allow us to compactly capture all "natural" models [12], such as, e.g., generic adversarial models or the *set consensus collections* models [8] for which only special cases of k-set consensus [12] and k-test-and-set [24] have been, in this sense, understood so far.

ACKNOWLEDGMENTS

This work has been supported by the Franco-German ANR-DFG Project DISCMAT (14-CE35-0010-02). The authors are grateful to Eli Gafni for asking the right questions at early stages of this work.

REFERENCES

[1] Yehuda Afek, Hagit Attiya, Danny Dolev, Eli Gafni, Michael Merritt, and Nir Shavit. 1993. Atomic Snapshots of Shared Memory. *J. ACM* 40, 4 (1993), 873–890.

[2] Bowen Alpern and Fred B. Schneider. 1985. Defining Liveness. *Inform. Process. Lett.* 21, 4 (Oct. 1985), 181–185.

[3] Elizabeth Borowsky and Eli Gafni. 1993. Generalized FLP impossibility result for t-resilient asynchronous computations. In *STOC*. 91–100.

[4] Elizabeth Borowsky and Eli Gafni. 1993. Immediate atomic snapshots and fast renaming. In *PODC*. 41–51.

[5] Elizabeth Borowsky and Eli Gafni. 1997. A simple algorithmically reasoned characterization of wait-free computation (extended abstract). In *PODC*. 189–198.

[6] Zohir Bouzid, Eli Gafni, and Petr Kuznetsov. 2014. Strong Equivalence Relations for Iterated Models. In *OPODIS*. 139–154.

[7] Soma Chaudhuri. 1990. Agreement is Harder than Consensus: Set Consensus Problems in Totally Asynchronous Systems. In *PODC*. 311–324.

[8] Carole Delporte-Gallet, Hugues Fauconnier, Eli Gafni, and Petr Kuznetsov:. 2016. Set-Consensus Collections are Decidable. In *OPODIS*. 7:1–7:15.

[9] Carole Delporte-Gallet, Hugues Fauconnier, Rachid Guerraoui, and Andreas Tielmann. 2011. The disagreement power of an adversary. *Distributed Computing* 24, 3-4 (2011), 137–147.

[10] Michael J. Fischer, Nancy A. Lynch, and Michael S. Paterson. 1985. Impossibility of Distributed Consensus with one Faulty Process. *J. ACM* 32, 2 (April 1985), 374–382.

[11] Eli Gafni. 1998. Round-by-Round Fault Detectors (extended abstract): Unifying Synchrony and Asynchrony. In *PODC*. 143–152.

[12] Eli Gafni, Yuan He, Petr Kuznetsov, and Thibault Rieutord. 2016. Read-Write Memory and k-Set Consensus as an Affine Task. In *OPODIS*. 6:1–6:17.

[13] Eli Gafni and Petr Kuznetsov. 2010. Turning Adversaries into Friends: Simplified, Made Constructive, and Extended. In *OPODIS*. 380–394.

[14] Eli Gafni and Petr Kuznetsov. 2011. Relating L-Resilience and Wait-Freedom via Hitting Sets. In *ICDCN*. 191–202.

[15] Eli Gafni, Petr Kuznetsov, and Ciprian Manolescu. 2014. A generalized asynchronous computability theorem. In *PODC*. 222–231.

[16] Eli Gafni and Sergio Rajsbaum. 2010. Distributed Programming with Tasks. In *OPODIS*. 205–218.

[17] Maurice Herlihy. 1991. Wait-free synchronization. *Transactions on Programming Languages and Systems* 13, 1 (Jan. 1991), 123–149.

[18] Maurice Herlihy, Dmitry N. Kozlov, and Sergio Rajsbaum. 2014. *Distributed Computing Through Combinatorial Topology*. Morgan Kaufmann.

[19] Maurice Herlihy and Sergio Rajsbaum. 2012. Simulations and reductions for colorless tasks. In *PODC*. 253–260.

[20] Maurice Herlihy and Nir Shavit. 1999. The topological structure of asynchronous computability. *J. ACM* 46, 2 (1999), 858–923.

[21] Dmitry N. Kozlov. 2012. Chromatic Subdivision of a Simplicial Complex. *Homology, Homotopy and Applications* 14, 1 (2012), 1–13.

[22] Petr Kuznetsov. 2012. Understanding Non-Uniform Failure Models. *Bulletin of the EATCS* 106 (2012), 53–77.

[23] Petr Kuznetsov and Thibault Rieutord. 2017. Agreement Functions for Distributed Computing Models. In *NETYS*. 175–190.

[24] Petr Kuznetsov and Thibault Rieutord. 2018. *Affine Tasks for k-Test-and-Set*. Technical Report. https://hal.archives-ouvertes.fr/hal-01810601.

[25] Petr Kuznetsov, Thibault Rieutord, and Yuan He. 2017. *An Asynchronous Computability Theorem for Fair Adversaries*. Technical Report. https://hal.archives-ouvertes.fr/hal-01572257v3.

[26] Petr Kuznetsov, Thibault Rieutord, and Yuan He. 2017. Brief Announcement: Compact Topology of Shared-Memory Adversaries. In *DISC*. 56:1–56:4.

[27] Nancy A. Lynch. 1996. *Distributed Algorithms*. Morgan Kaufmann.

[28] Michael Saks and Fotios Zaharoglou. 2000. Wait-Free k-Set Agreement Is Impossible: The Topology of Public Knowledge. *SIAM J. Comput.* 29 (2000), 1449–1483.

[29] Vikram Saraph, Maurice Herlihy, and Eli Gafni. 2016. Asynchronous Computability Theorems for t-Resilient Systems. In *DISC*. 428–441.

[30] Edwin H. Spanier. 1966. *Algebraic topology*. McGraw-Hill Book Co.

[31] Gadi Taubenfeld. 2010. The computational structure of progress conditions. In *DISC*. 221–235.

Population Stability: Regulating Size in the Presence of an Adversary

Shafi Goldwasser
MIT
shafi@csail.mit.edu

Rafail Ostrovsky
UCLA
rafail@cs.ucla.edu

Alessandra Scafuro
NCSU
ascafur@ncsu.edu

Adam Sealfon
MIT
asealfon@csail.mit.edu

ABSTRACT

We introduce a new coordination problem in distributed computing that we call the **population stability problem**. A system of agents each with limited memory and communication, as well as the ability to replicate and self-destruct, is subjected to attacks by a worst-case adversary that can at a bounded rate (1) delete agents chosen arbitrarily and (2) insert additional agents with arbitrary initial state into the system. The goal is perpetually to maintain a population whose size is within a constant factor of the target size N. The problem is inspired by the ability of complex biological systems composed of a multitude of memory-limited individual cells to maintain a stable population size in an adverse environment. Such biological mechanisms allow organisms to heal after trauma or to recover from excessive cell proliferation caused by inflammation, disease, or normal development.

We present a population stability protocol in a communication model that is a synchronous variant of the population model of Angluin et al. In each round, pairs of agents selected at random meet and exchange messages, where at least a constant fraction of agents is matched in each round. Our protocol uses three-bit messages and $\omega(\log^2 N)$ states per agent. We emphasize that our protocol can handle an adversary that can both insert and delete agents, a setting in which existing approximate counting techniques do not seem to apply. The protocol relies on a novel coloring strategy in which the population size is encoded in the *variance* of the distribution of colors. Individual agents can locally obtain a weak estimate of the population size by sampling from the distribution, and make individual decisions that robustly maintain a stable global population size.

ACM Reference Format:
Shafi Goldwasser, Rafail Ostrovsky, Alessandra Scafuro, and Adam Sealfon. 2018. Population Stability: Regulating Size in the Presence of an Adversary. In *PODC '18: ACM Symposium on Principles of Distributed Computing, July 23–27, 2018, Egham, United Kingdom.* ACM, New York, NY, USA, 10 pages. https://doi.org/10.1145/3212734.3212747

PODC '18, July 23–27, 2018, Egham, United Kingdom

ACM ISBN 978-1-4503-5795-1/18/07...$15.00
https://doi.org/10.1145/3212734.3212747

1 INTRODUCTION

A single fertilized mouse egg and a single fertilized human egg each develop into organisms of vastly different sizes and with vastly different numbers of cells. How do cellular mechanisms regulate the number of cells in complex biological systems? In order to function in adverse environments, organisms must maintain stability and be able to recover from unplanned circumstances. For example, a lizard that loses its tail can grow a new one, and internal organs require mechanisms to recover from cell loss caused by injury or from execessive cell proliferation due to development or disease. But how do individual cells know how to respond in order to reestablish the desired population size?

Regulation of population size may be achieved through a combination of internal programs running within each cell and intercellular communication. One approach could be for individual cells to count the population using a distributed protocol. But an interesting question is how to control the population size if each cell lacks sufficient memory to count. Understanding the mechanisms for regulating population size in an adversarial environment, in light of memory constraints of individual agents, is a natural computational question.

In this work, we study the problem of robustly maintaining a stable population size from the perspective of distributed computing. We introduce a new coordination question that we call the **population stability problem**. Consider a population of agents with the ability to replicate and self-destruct. How can such distributed systems detect and recover from adversarial deletions and insertions of agents so as to maintain the desired population size?

Our focus is on systems that consist of huge numbers of agents, where each agent individually has very limited memory and connective capability and can directly communicate with only a few other agents in the system. We model communication using a synchronous variant of the population model of Angluin et al. [4, 5]. In each round, a constant fraction of agents is matched at random and can exchange messages, where the matched agents are chosen independently in each round. Population size must be maintained in this setting in the presence of an adversary that observes the entire state of the system and can continually delete or insert agents. We describe the model in more detail below.

The population stability problem augments a growing body of work that uses the language and ideas of distributed computing to model biological systems consisting of a collection of resource-constrained components that collectively accomplish complex tasks.

Naturally, we do not claim direct relevance of our results to biological systems due to potential modeling differences. Regardless, the population stability problem makes sense in any system consisting of individual components with the ability to reproduce.

1.1 Contributions

Our main contributions are as follows.

A New Problem in Distributed Computing: The Population Stability Problem. We introduce a new problem in distributed computing. A population of N memory-constrained agents (i.e. processors with the ability to reproduce and self-destruct) is subjected to adversarial attacks. Whereas many attacks can be envisioned, we consider a worst-case adversary that can delete or insert agents at a bounded rate. The goal is to maintain a stable population size within a small multiplicative factor of the original size N. This problem appears fundamentally different from the classical problems of distributed computing, such as consensus, leader election, majority, common coin flipping, or computing general functions of the joint state of the parties.

Models for Communication and the Adversary. The communication model we consider is a synchronous variant of the population model of [4, 5]. That model was designed to represent sensor networks consisting of very limited mobile agents with no control over their own movement and whose goal is to compute some function of their inputs or evaluate a property of the system. Whereas [4] assumed that pairs of agents can communicate via pairwise interactions as scheduled by a uniformly random matching process, we assume in addition that agents are synchronized and interact with one another in rounds. Within each round, at least a γ fraction of agents participates in pairwise interactions, again scheduled uniformly at random. The agents additionally have the ability to self-destruct and to reproduce by producing a second identical copy of themselves.

It is clear that we cannot allow the adversary to delete most or all of the agents in a single round, since maintaining a stable population size in the presence of such an adversary is impossible. Consequently, we give the adversary a budget of K alterations to perform in each round, where an alteration consists of removing, inserting or modifying the memory of a single agent. We allow the adversary to observe the memory contents of *every* agent before determining its alterations for a round. Both γ and K are parameters of the model. The model is described in detail in Section 2.

Protocol for Population Stability. We present a protocol with three-bit messages requiring polylog(N) states (i.e. $\Theta(\log\log N)$ bits of memory) per agent that tolerates $K = N^{1/4-\epsilon}$ worst-case insertions or deletions in each round, for any constant $\epsilon > 0$. Formally, our main theorem is the following.

Theorem 1. *Let α, γ, ϵ be positive constants, where γ is a lower bound on the fraction of agents that is matched in each round. Then there exists a population stability protocol with three-bit messages and* polylog(N) *states per agent and guaranteeing that if the adversary inserts or deletes at most $K = O(N^{1/4-\epsilon})$ agents in each round, then with overwhelming probability*[1] *the population will remain between $(1-\alpha)N$ and $(1+\alpha)N$ for any polynomial number of rounds.*

New Techniques. The main idea employed in our construction is to *color* the agents with the values 0 and 1 in such a way that information about the population size is encoded in the distribution of colors. That is, given a set of agents with assigned colors in $\{0, 1\}$, consider the distribution specified by choosing an agent at random and observing its color. We are able to assign colors to agents in such a way that approximate population size is encoded in the *variance* of this distribution. Subsequently, each individual agent locally computes a very weak estimator of whether the variance is too large or too small, and makes a local decision of whether to reproduce or self-destruct. Although each individual agent's estimate is noisy, we show that in the aggregate, the local decisions are globally able to maintain a stable population size even in the presence of a powerful adversary.

We discuss the model and results further in Section 1.2. We provide a more in-depth overview of our techniques in Section 1.3 below. The model is described in further detail in Section 2. In Section 3 we provide a full description of the protocol, and in Section 4 we provide an overview of the analysis. Due to space limitations, the proof details are deferred to the full version [20].

1.2 Discussion and extensions

Challenges. The first obstacle we must confront in designing a protocol for population stability is the memory constraint. Each agent does not have sufficient memory to store a unique identifier or to count to the population target N. Yet collectively, they must have a good approximation of N and must individually decide whether to replicate if the population is too low or to self-destruct if the population is too high. Making their task even more challenging, these memory-constrained agents must correct deviations in the size of the population and make their decisions *while* the adversary is acting.

A second major challenge is that the adversary is very powerful. Although the number of agents inserted or deleted in each round is bounded, the adversary can observe the complete state of the system (i.e., read the memory contents of every agent) before deciding on its actions, and may insert agents of arbitrary initial state. These capabilities present difficulties for many standard techniques and abstractions used in distributed computing. For instance, many protocols are based on leader election, where a single leader processor is chosen to direct or facilitate the task at hand. However, since our adversary is able to observe the state of every agent, the adversary can simply wait for a leader to be chosen and then delete it. Furthermore, even without observing the internal memory of agents, the adversary could insert many additional agents that are all identical in state to the leader. Indeed, since agents can be in one of only polylog(N) distinct states and the adversary is able to insert $K = N^{1/4-\epsilon} \in$ poly(N) agents per round, the adversary can even insert many copies of *every possible* agent type in each round. Consequently any approach that relies on the existence of agents of unique or extremely special state, such as leader election, seems

[1] A function $\nu(x)$ is *negligible* if it is at most $1/x^{\omega(1)}$. Throughout this paper, we use the phrases "with high probability" and "with overwhelming probability" to mean with probability $1 - \nu(N)$ for some negligible function ν.

doomed to failure. This appears to render ineffectual a large part of the distributed computing toolbox.

Adversarial insertions. Recall that we allow the adversary to insert new agents with arbitrary initial state. Starting from that internal state, we assume that the inserted agents execute the same protocol as honest agents. We could instead consider an even stronger adversary that inserts agents running arbitrary malicious protocols specifying their subsequent behavior. However, the population stability problem as described above is clearly impossible in the face of this stronger adversary, since our model does not include the ability to destroy agents that do not cooperate. A malicious agent can simply ignore all interactions with other agents and replicate itself at every opportunity. Such malicious agents would quickly replicate themseves out of control, rapidly exceeding the population target.

One may consider a different model that allows agents not only to self-destruct but also to remove other agents it encounters. In such a setting, our protocol can be extended to achieve population stability even if the adversary is allowed to insert agents that execute arbitrary malicious programs, as long as there is a bound on how frequently malicious agents can replicate and an agent is able to detect when it encounters an agent whose program is different from its own. However, that setting is not the focus of this work.

Correction and detection. The objective in the population stability problem is to maintain a population size that is close to a target value N, and to correct the population if it deviates too far from this target. A closely related problem is that of simply *detecting* whether the population has deviated too far from the target or whether it has exceeded some threshold, objectives that seem very similar to the problem of approximate counting [25]. It would be natural to try to solve our problem by first detecting whether the population is too large or too small and then correcting appropriately. With a weaker adversary that can only delete agents but not insert additional ones (and additionally is oblivious to the internal states and coin flips of agents), this approach can be made to work using approximate counting techniques. In the adversarial model considered here, constructing approximate counters and detecting changes in population size are interesting open questions.

Synchrony. In this work we study a synchronous model, where all agents communicate and perform updates in rounds. As has commonly been the case across distributed computing, it is natural to study a new problem first in a synchronous setting to distill key ideas and techniques before adding additional complications in an asynchronous setting.

We note, however, that synchronization is far from an unreasonable assumption in biological systems. Indeed, many multicellular systems do achieve synchrony either through regular external stimuli such as sunlight or through chemical control mechanisms. For instance, heart cells maintained in culture were able to achieve a high degree of synchronization of their rhythmic contractions [21]. Neuronal cells too exhibit highly synchronized behavior. Even when grown in culture, specialized neuronal cells show the capacity to synchronize the release of particular hormones at regular time intervals [13]. Bacterial populations have also been shown to have the capability of producing coordinated oscillations [12, 24].

Nonetheless, an extremely natural and interesting question is how to solve the population stability problem in a setting without synchrony or with only partial synchrony. For instance, one could consider a setting where agents have clocks that have bounded drift relative to one another. Related to this is the typical random scheduler setting of population protocols [5], in which a single pair of agents at a time is chosen to interact and update state. By a concentration argument, this process allows agents to maintain clocks that do not drift too quickly relative to one another.

While the construction in this paper requires synchrony, there are some known techniques in the population protocol literature for maintaining approximate synchronization in a non-synchronous setting; see, for instance, the recent work of [2]. A natural extension is to show whether our techniques can be combined with synchronizers to achieve population stability in such settings.

Alternate communication models. Another very interesting question is to explore the population stability problem under a different communication model. In this paper, pairs of agents that communicate are chosen independently at random in each round. Alternatively, one could consider settings in which the neighbors of an agent are consistent over time, perhaps reflecting underlying geometric constraints.

One natural approach is to use a fixed sparse communication graph such as a grid graph or an expander. However, modeling problems arise in determining how connectivity changes upon agent replication, insertion, or deletion. In various settings along these lines, it is straightforward for the adversary to disconnect the communication graph and consequently to violate population stability. An alternate approach could be to associate agents with points in $\mathbb{R}^d$, and to allow each agent to communicate with a small number of the nearest other agents.

1.3 Technical overview

1.3.1 Preliminary attempts. We first describe two preliminary attempts at protocols for the population stability problem which, while unsound, will provide useful intuition toward the design of our actual protocol.

Attempt 1: non-interactive leader election. As a first attempt in the low-memory setting, consider the following approach, which is based on an idea from [1]. Each agent flips a biased coin where $\Pr[c = 1] = \frac{1}{N}$, where outcome 1 means that the agent is a leader. For $O(\text{polylog}(N))$ rounds, each agent sends any agent it encounters the bit 0 if its coin was zero and it has not received the message 1, and the bit 1 if its coin was 1 or it has received a 1 from another agent. In the absence of an adversary, this allows every agent to learn whether a 1 was obtained in any of the initial coin flips. The probability of this event differs noticeably depending on whether the population is too small or too large. After repeating to amplify the signal, with high probability the agents can detect if the population is too small or too large and can replicate or self-destruct accordingly. A protocol of this form can be shown to work in the presence of an adversary that can only delete and not insert agents, and is additionally oblivious to the coin flips made by the agents. However, in the adversary model considered here with insertion as well as deletion and full knowledge of the states of agents, the protocol will fail. The adversary can either insert an agent with coin value $c = 1$ in each phase, or else identify the agent or agents with coin value 1 and selectively remove these agents. Consequently the adversary can cause the population to grow or shrink arbitrarily.

This attempt highlights a fundamental difficulty in designing protocols in our adversarial model. The protocol relied on a non-interactive strategy related to leader election, where the presence or absence of a leader could be used to infer the approximate size of the population. However, as we have discussed above, the use of a special state with one or only a few agents of that state (in this case agents with coin value $c = 1$) provides the adversary with an easy avenue of attack, namely the deletion of agents of that state or the insertion of many additional agents of that state. Consequently, constructions of this flavor seem to have little promise in this adversarial setting.

Attempt 2: independent coloring. As a next attempt, consider the simple protocol in which each agent flips a fair coin, receiving at random a color $c \in \{0, 1\}$. For each agent, compare the colors of the next two agents encountered. If the colors are equal, then split, and otherwise self-destruct. Observe that if an agent encounters the same agent twice, the colors must be the same, while if an agent encounters two different agents, the colors are independently random. Consequently if the population currently has size m, then the probability of splitting is $\frac{1}{2} + \Theta(\frac{1}{m})$, which is slightly larger than the probability $\frac{1}{2} - \Theta(\frac{1}{m})$ of self-destructing, and so this protocol would cause the population to increase slightly over time. To compensate this, modify the protocol to split only with probability $1 - \Theta(\frac{1}{N})$ if the colors are equal while still self-destructing with probability 1 if the colors are unequal.[2]

Now, the population will stay the same size in expectation if its current size m is equal to the target N, will decrease in expectation if $m > N$, and will increase in expectation if $m < N$. Qualitatively, this is exactly the behavior that we want. However, tending in expectation to correct itself is insufficient for maintaining a stable population. In fact, despite a very weak bias to correct drifts in the population, the signal is overwhelmed by the noise, and the size of the population under this protocol will behave very much like a random walk. Even in the absence of an adversary, this protocol will cause the population to drift extremely far from its initial size.

In some sense the protocol we have just outlined behaves even worse than the empty protocol, in that it fails to maintain a stable population when there is no adversary at all. However, the protocol does have one intriguing feature. It entirely lacks any "special" agent types for the adversary to exploit. Consequently, if we could design a more sophisticated protocol along these lines that could maintain a stable population in the absence of an adversary, we might hope that it could do the same even in the presence of an adversary.

1.3.2 Overview of our protocol. We now describe our actual protocol. At a very high level, the idea behind our protocol is as follows. Through some *coloring process* which we will discuss below, agents are colored with the colors $\{0, 1\}$. After the agents are colored, agents run a step called the *evaluation phase* in which agents make the decision of whether to reproduce or self-destruct. The coloring process and evaluation phase are then repeated indefinitely. We will refer to each iteration of the coloring process followed by the evaluation phase as an *epoch*.

During the evaluation phase, each agent that is matched with another agent in this round compares its own color with the color of its *neighbor* (i.e. the agent to which it is matched). If the two agents have the same color, then the agent will replicate itself with some probability p_{split}. If the two agents have different colors, then the agent will self-destruct. Note that if the coloring process consisted of every agent tossing its own coin, then this would be essentially the same as Attempt 2 above. We will instead employ a more structured coloring process that results in agent colors that are not generated independently at random.

The coloring process will consist of two phases, a (noninteractive) *leader selection phase* and a *recruitment phase*. In the leader selection phase, $\Theta(1/\sqrt{N})$ of the agents will become "leaders"[3] and each leader will choose a random color in $\{0, 1\}$. In the recruitment phase, each leader will identify $\sqrt{N}$ uncolored agents and color each of them with its own color. We note that the leader will not directly encounter each of these $\sqrt{N}$ agents, but will directly color some agents which in turn will color other agents. To begin with, each leader activates the first inactive agent that it encounters, sharing its color with the new agent. Each agent is subsequently responsible for recruiting $\sqrt{N}/2$ inactive agents in the same manner, forming a recruitment tree of depth $\frac{1}{2}\log N$. By delegating the coloring in this manner, the recruitment process can be performed in only $O(\log^2 N)$ rounds.[4]

For each leader, at the end of the recruitment phase, $\sqrt{N}$ agents will have obtained a color based on the original coin toss of that leader. We will refer to these $\sqrt{N}$ agents as the *cluster* associated with the leader, and we will sometimes describe agents as belonging to the same cluster or different clusters. At the end of the recruitment phase and the beginning of the evaluation phase, a constant fraction of the population will have been colored having been recruited into the clusters of the various leaders, roughly half with color 0 and the other half with color 1.

Consider a particular agent in the evaluation phase. If the agent meets another agent from the same cluster, then they necessarily have the same color. If the agent meets an agent from a different cluster, then their colors are independently random. Consequently, if the current population size is m, then with probability $\frac{1}{2} + \Theta(\frac{\sqrt{N}}{m})$ the two agents will have the same color, and with probability $\frac{1}{2} - \Theta(\frac{\sqrt{N}}{m})$ the two agents will have different colors. We can choose the splitting probability $p_{\text{split}} = 1 - \Theta(1/\sqrt{N})$ so that the expected change in population is zero for $m = N$. For $m \gg N$ the expected change in population will be negative, and for $m \ll N$ the expected change in population will be positive. Moreover, unlike in Attempt 2 above, which behaved similarly to a random walk, here the effect

[2]Another perspective on why the protocol without this step cannot maintain a stable population is that the protocol run by each agent has no dependence on the population target N. Consequently, if agents are added or removed (either by the adversary, or even as a result of random drift) then the protocol should behave as if those agents were there to begin with and will not correct this deviation in the population.

[3]That is, each agent will become a leader with probability $\Theta(1/\sqrt{N})$.

[4]In order to achieve constant message size, our full protocol will be slightly different and will use additional rounds for the recruitment process.

is strong enough to maintain the population in a small interval around the target value N, with all but negligible probability.

Moreover, the adversary can do little to influence the result of the protocol. For a population size $m = \Theta(N)$, the number of leaders selected is $\sqrt{N}$, and so the standard deviation of the number of leaders with each color is roughly $N^{1/4}$. Consequently, an adversary that can insert or delete $o(N^{1/4})$ agents can do little to influence the distribution of colors. Even if the adversary selectively inserts or deletes agents that are leaders and have a particular color, the effect of the adversary on the distribution of colors is dominated by the random deviation of the sampling process. Unlike in Attempt 1 above, there are many leaders, and so the adversary is unable to delete enough of them or to insert enough additional leaders to overwhelm the protocol. As we will show, the adversary cannot cause substantial deviations in the size of the population.

Note that one strategy the adversary may attempt is inserting agents that do not know the correct round number within the epoch. In the protocol described so far, there is no mechanism for detecting and correcting this, and so over many rounds, adversarial insertions may lead to a population of agents attempting to execute different portions of the protocol. In order to address this, agents can exchange which round they are in, and self-destruct upon encountering an agent that is in a different round of the epoch. This results in the self-destruction of any agent with the wrong round number as soon as it encounters an agent with the correct round number. A corresponding number of correct agents are also destroyed, but we will show that the number of correct agents removed in this manner is sufficiently small.

As discussed briefly in Section 1.1, we can think of this protocol as encoding the population size in the variance of a distribution and then sampling from this distribution to obtain a weak estimate of the variance. Since the variance of the fraction of successes in many independent Bernoulli trials decreases as the number of trials increases, if the number of leaders is larger, then the fraction of colored agents with color 0 will be more closely concentrated around 1/2. On the other hand, if the number of leaders is smaller, then we expect the fraction of colored agents with color 0 to be farther from 1/2. Since the expected number of leaders is proportional to the current size of the population, an approximation to the population size is encoded in the fraction of agents of each color. Consider the distribution obtained by selecting an agent at random and reading its color. Comparing the colors of two agents serves as a very weak estimate of the variance of this distribution, while aggregating the results of many agents' individual choices of whether to replicate or self-destruct serves to amplify the accuracy of this estimate.

Achieving constant-size messages. The protocol described above involves messages of size $\Theta(\log\log N)$ bits, essentially as large as the entire memory of an agent. We now outline how to modify the protocol to use constant-size messages. The only large portions of the messages described so far consist of the current round in the epoch and the depth in the recruitment tree, each of which can be encoded in $\Theta(\log\log N)$ bits.

The current round in the epoch is sent to prevent the adversary from confusing the protocol by inserting agents with the wrong round number. However, rather than sending the exact round, we will instead send the single bit specifying whether or not the agent is currently in the evaluation round. If an agent is entering the evaluation round and its neighbor is not, then both agents will self-destruct. We can show that this suffices to maintain the invariant that a large majority of the agents are in the same round of the epoch.

The depth of the recruitment tree is sent to allow each leader to induce the recruitment of the correct number of agents. Note that we cannot simply recruit for $\frac{1}{2}\log N$ rounds, since recruiting agents may encounter other agents that are already colored and cannot recruit them. However, we can slow down the recruitment process to allow the depth in the recruitment tree to be determined as a function of the round number. To do this, we recruit for $\Theta(\log^3 N)$ rounds, divided into $\frac{1}{2}\log N$ subphases of $\log^2 N$ rounds each.[5] In a single subphase, a recruiting agent will recruit only the *first* inactive agent it sees even if it encounters many inactive agents in the subphase. This allows agents to determine their depth in the recruitment tree based on the round in which they were recruited. Since a subphase consists of $\omega(\log N)$ rounds, we will show that an inactive agent will be encountered with high probability.

This yields a population control protocol with constant-size messages, since messages consist of four binary values, namely an agent's color, whether or not it is active, whether or not it is recruiting, and whether or not it is currently in the evaluation round. In the analysis we will see how to achieve the same result with only three-bit messages.

1.4 Related work

Population Protocols. The population protocol model was introduced by Angluin et al. [3, 4]. In this model a collection of agents, which are modeled by finite state machines, move around unpredictably and have pairwise interactions. The original definition considers a worst-case environment/scheduler, while later formulations [5] consider the case where each interaction occurs between a pair of agents chosen uniformly at random. In a population protocol, agents start with an initial configuration, and the goal is to jointly compute a function of this input. Previous works have tried to identity the class of functions that can be computed in such a model [6], and the tradeoffs between the resources need to do so (e.g. [1]). In these works, the agents are always active throughout the execution of the protocol.

Another line of work expands the population model to the case in which agents can crash or undergo transient failures that corrupt their states. Delporte-Gallet et al. [14] consider a setting in which agents must compute a function of their inputs in presence of such failures. They construct a compiler that takes as input a protocol that works in the failure-free model, and outputs a protocol that works in the presense of failures as long as modifying a small number of inputs does not change the function output. Angluin et al. [7] incorporated the notion of self-stabilization into the population protocol model, giving self-stabilizing protocols for some classical problems such as leader election and token passing. They focus on the goal of stably maintaining some property such as having a unique leader or a legal coloring of the communication graph.

[5] We actually only require that subphases are $\omega(\log N)$ rounds, so it is sufficient to recruit for $\omega(\log^2 N)$ rounds.

Unlike these works, in our work agents have the ability to reproduce and self-destruct, and the goal of maintaining a consistent population size must be carried out in the presence of an adversary with the corresponding capability to insert and delete agents.

Approximate Counting. The problem of maintaining the population size of a collection of memory-constrained agents is related to the problem of counting N items when the available memory of the agents is less than $\log N$ bits. Approximate counters were introduced by Morris [25] as technique to accurately approximate a value N using only $\Theta(\log\log N)$ bits of memory. Techniques for approximate counting in the population model were developed in [1, 8].

A sequence of works by Di Luna et al. [22, 23] consider the problem of estimating the size of a network of agents that communicate according to a dynamic connection graph, in presence of an adversary that can add and remove *edges* in the graph.

Cellular Automata. Cellular automata were proposed by von Neumann [26] as a model to reason about artificial self-reproduction. A cellular automaton consists of a regular grid of cells, each assuming one of a finite number of states. Over time, the states of cells change according to some fixed rule (e.g. a mathematical function) that determines the new state of each cell in terms of the current state of the cell and the states of the cells in its neighborhood. Conway's Game of Life [17] is a cellular automaton that works with a simpler set of rules than von Neumann's rules, and was shown to be Turing-complete by Berlekamp, Conway and Guy [9]. Cook [10] proved that rule 110 (a binary, *one*-dimensional cellular automata) is Turing-complete.

Our setting is crucially different from the cellular automaton setting, since agents in our model do not simply change state but can be deleted from the system during the computation. Another difference between our setting and the cellular automaton setting is that we consider an *adversarial* model whereas in cellular automata cells deterministically change state. In some sense, in Conway's game, death "plays by the rules" while in our game death is sudden and unpredictable.

Dynamic Environments. A recent work of Goldreich and Ron [19] considers environments that evolve according to a fixed local rule. They define an *environment* as a collection of small components of a large system which interact in a local level, and change state according to a fixed rule. As an example, they focus on the model of a two-dimensional cellular automata. They ask how many queries a global observer must make about local components in order to test whether the evolution of the environment obeys a fixed known rule or to predict the state of the system at a given time and location. Although their work seems very different than ours, it bears some intellectual similarity in seeking information about a global property of the system from local information. However, whereas in [19] a global observer who can query a limited number of individual cells asks "does the global system obey a specific evolution rule," in our case individual agents need to decide locally what they should do to maintain the overall global property of population size.

Self-Stabilization. Also related to our question is the self-stabilization problem introduced by Dijkstra [15]. Given a system that starts in an arbitrary state, the goal of a stabilization algorithm is to eventually converge to the correct state. In this setting, however, deletion of system components is not considered. Super-stabilization [16] is the problem of achieving self stabilization in dynamic networks, that is, network where nodes are dynamically added and removed. While this setting is closer to ours, super-stabilization algorithms make additional assumptions about the system, such as that each node in the system is uniquely identified.

Distributed Algorithms Explaining Ant Colony Behaviors. A single ant has very limited communication and processing power, yet collectively a colony of ants can perform complex tasks such as consensus decision-making, leader election, and navigation. In [11] Cornejo et al. give a mathematical model for the problem of task allocation in ant colonies, and propose a very efficient protocol for satisfying this task. One of the main goals of their paper is to provide a formal model enabling the comparison of the various task allocation algorithms proposed in the biology literature. Similarly, in [18] Ghaffari et al. use techniques from distributed computing theory in order to gain insight into the *ant colony house-hunting problem*, where a set of agents need to identify potential nests, evaluate the quality of candidates, and reach consensus in a distributed manner.

2 THE POPULATION STABILITY PROBLEM

As discussed above, the population stability problem is concerned with a system of agents with bounded memory and the ability to reproduce and self-destruct. The system is subjected to adversarial attacks that delete or insert processors. The objective is to maintain a stable population size despite these adversarial attacks. In this section we give a formal description of the problem.

Parameters. The population stability problem is parameterized by the initial number of agents N, the number of distinct memory states M each agent can be in, the number of alterations K the adversary is allow to make in each round (where an alteration consists of removing or inserting a processor), a value α specifying how tightly concentrated the population size must remain around the target value N, and a value γ specifying a lower bound on the fraction of processors that are matched with other processors in each round. Below we describe each of these components of the problem.

Agents. We consider agents with bounded memory. Each agent can be in one of M possible states, so we can think of agents as having $\log M$ bits of memory. Agents can communicate by message-passing as specified by the connectivity structure of the system, which will be discussed further below. In our setting we will have $M \ll N$, so each individual agent has insufficient memory to count the total population, to posses a unique ID, or to address messages to a particular recipient. Each agent has the ability to flip unbiased coins, to split into two identical agents, or to self destruct. That is, in any round an agent may choose to split into two daughter agents which both inherit specified state from the parent agent, or it can decide to delete itself from the system.

Connectivity. As discussed above, we consider a *synchronous* version of the population model of Angluin et al. [3, 5], where we assume the existence of a global clock. We assume that the pairs of agents that are able to communicate in each round are selected by choosing a random matching of at least a γ fraction of surviving agents. We think of the parameter γ as a constant (e.g. $\gamma = 1/4$). That is, each agent is matched with at most one other agent (that we call its *neighbor*) in each round, and there is no consistency from round to round, since connectivity in different rounds is determined by sampling independently random matchings. The schedule of these matchings is unknown to the adversary in advance. Agents matched in a round may exchange messages in that round.

Adversary. We consider a worst-case, computationally unbounded adversary that can arbitrarily choose which agents to delete in each round and can insert agents with arbitrary state in each round. The adversary also can observe the entire history of agent interactions, including the memory contents of every agent. While the initial state of inserted agents is determined by the adversary, the newly inserted agents are assumed to follow the protocol (that is, the agents introduced by the adversary do not behave maliciously).

Objective. The goal in the population stability problem is to maintain a number of agents within a small interval $[(1-\alpha)N, (1+\alpha)N]$ around the initial population size N. That is, initially the system consists of N agents. In each round some agents may be removed or inserted by the adversary, and some agents may decide to replicate or to self-destruct. Let N_i denote the number of agents in the system after the ith round. The adversary wins in round i if $N_i \notin [(1-\alpha)N, (1+\alpha)N]$ at the end of the round. We say that protocol Π is a population stability protocol if for any polynomial p and any adversary, the probability that the adversary wins in at most $p(N)$ rounds is negligible in N.

3 THE PROTOCOL

We now provide a formal specification of the main protocol (Algorithm 1). Agents continually run the protocol throughout their lifetime. We will think of time as partitioned into epochs of $T = \frac{1}{2}\log^3 N$ rounds. Each epoch consists of three phases, the leader selection phase, the recruitment phase, and the evaluation phase. The recruitment phase consists of $\frac{1}{2}\log N$ subphases each consisting of roughly $T_{\mathsf{inner}} = \log^2 N$ rounds.[6] We will elaborate on each of these phases below.

Recall that agents have the ability to toss coins, to send and receive a message upon encountering another agent, to reproduce by splitting into two identical copies of itself, and to self-destruct. These capabilities are notated by the following functions. We denote flipping an unbiased coin by $x \overset{\$}{\leftarrow} \{0,1\}$. Agent splitting and death are implemented in commands SPLIT() and DIE(). Finally, the command $Z :=$ COMMUNICATE(X) sends message X to the neighboring agent in the present round, if any, simultaneously receiving in response message Z.[7] If the agent is unmatched in this round and has no neighboring agent, then the return value is assumed to be $\perp$. In the protocol below, messages will consist of four boolean values (inEvalPhase, active, color, recruiting). Upon receiving message Z, the value of each of these variables can be accessed by writing Z.inEvalPhase, Z.active, and so forth. If $Z = \perp$ then we will follow the convention that each of these components will also have value $\perp$.

The main variables that describe the state of an agent are round $\in [0, T-1]$ and four boolean variables active $\in \{0,1\}$ color $\in \{0,1\}$, recruiting $\in \{0,1\}$, and inEvalPhase $\in \{0,1\}$. The variable Nbr $\in \{0,1\}^4$ stores the most recent message received consisting of four boolean values (Nbr.inEvalPhase, Nbr.active, Nbr.color, Nbr.recruiting).An additional variable, to recruit $\in [0, \frac{1}{2}\log N]$, is not necessary for the protocol itself but is used in the analysis.We emphasize that these variables are local to a single agent, so that different agents have independent copies of each of these variables. Initially, at the onset of the system, for each agent we will have that all variables are set to zero.

The variable round keeps track of which round it is within the epoch. The variable is incremented modulo $T = \frac{1}{2}\log^3 N$ after each round, ensuring that agents begin and end each phase and each epoch at the same time.

The variables active and color specify whether an agent has been activated and colored, as well as the color of the agent. In the first round of each epoch, some of the agents will designate themselves as leaders and will become active, choosing at random a color color $\overset{\$}{\leftarrow} \{0,1\}$, while the rest of the agents remain inactive. During the recruitment phase, additional agents will become active and will receive colors in $\{0,1\}$, as inherited from a leader. The value of variable color is only relevant for active agents.

The variable recruiting specifies whether or not an active agent is trying to recruit in the present subphase. Each active agent should recruit only one additional agent in a single subphase, so this variable specifies whether or not the agent is still looking for an inactive agent to recruit in the subphase.

The variable inEvalPhase specifies whether the agent is currently in the evaluation phase, which is true exactly when round $= T-1$.

Finally, the variable to_recruit specifies the number of additional followers an active agent is tasked with recruiting directly, which is the logarithm of the total number of agents that should be activated as a result of the given agent. When a new leader first becomes active, it sets to_recruit $= \frac{1}{2}\log N$, indicating that it is tasked with recruiting a total of $2^{\text{to\_recruit}} = \sqrt{N}$ agents. Each time a new agent is recruited, the value of to_recruit is decremented and shared with the newly recruited agent, indicated that each of the two is responsible for recruiting only half of the total. For instance, after the first time a leader recruits another agent, both agents will have to_recruit $= \left(\frac{1}{2}\log N\right) - 1$, and so each of the two agents subsequently are responsible for recruiting only $\sqrt{N}/2$ agents. In this way a leader can induce the recruitment of $\sqrt{N}$ agents in roughly a logarithmic number of rounds. Although the variable is not used by the algorithm itself, we will refer to it in the analysis.

We first present the main procedure run by each agent in every round. Each agent first exchanges messages with its neighboring agent in this round, if any. The agent then performs a consistency check on its on state and the state of its neighbor. Then, depending on the value of variable round modulo T, the program calls the appropriate subroutine for the corresponding phase.

[6] More generally, we want $T = T_{\mathsf{inner}} \cdot \frac{1}{2}\log N$ for any $T_{\mathsf{inner}} = \omega(\log N)$. The first and last subphase will each be shorter by one round to account for the leader selection and evaluation phases.

[7] Recall that an agent's *neighbor* is the other agent it is randomly matched with in this round and that matchings in each round are independent and uniformly random.

Algorithm 1 Main protocol

```
procedure MainProtocolStep
    ExchangeMessages()
    CheckRoundConsistency()
    if round = 0 then              ▷ Handle initialization of leaders
        DetermineIfLeader()
        round := round + 1
    else if round < T − 1 then     ▷ Perform recruitment phase
        RecruitmentPhase()
        round := round + 1
    else            ▷ Final round of phase. Perform split or death.
        EvaluationPhase()
        round := 0
    end if
end procedure
```

We now describe the subroutine that exchanges messages with the neighboring agent, if any. An agent simply computes the indicator value of whether it is in the evaluation phase, and sends this information along with its activation state, color, and recruiting status. It receives a corresponding message from its neighbor, or the value $\perp$ if it has no neighbor in this round.

Algorithm 2 Subroutine to send and receive messages with neighboring agent

```
procedure ExchangeMessages
    if round = T − 1 then
        inEvalPhase := 1
    else
        inEvalPhase := 0
    end if
    MyStatus := (inEvalPhase, active, color, recruiting)
    Nbr := Communicate(MyStatus)
end procedure
```

We now describe the leader selection subroutine, which comprises the first round of each epoch. This is an entirely non-interactive process in which each agent becomes a leader with some fixed probability $1/(8\sqrt{N})$ by tossing its own coins, entirely independently of each other agent. With overwhelming probability, if the total number of agents is $\Theta(N)$, the number of leaders chosen in this phase will be $\Theta(\sqrt{N})$. Each newly activated leader chooses a random color in $\{0, 1\}$ and is tasked with recruiting $\sqrt{N}$ agents and assigning them this color.

Algorithm 3 Leader selection phase subroutine

```
procedure DetermineIfLeader
    active := TossBiasedCoin(log(8√N)).
                ▷ active = 1 w.p. 1/(8√N), and active = 0 otherwise.
    if active = 1 then
        color ←$ {0, 1}
        recruiting := 1
        to_recruit := (1/2) log(N)
    end if
end procedure
```

The leader selection phase, as well as the evaluation phase below, requires the ability to flip biased coins with bias $1/\text{poly}(N)$, in particular $1/\Theta(\sqrt{N})$, where bias refers to the probability of the coin having value 1 (so that a fair coin has bias 1/2). Recall that we assume only the ability to toss unbiased coins. We now give a simple procedure to obtain the desired bias using only $O(\log\log(N))$ bits of memory, assuming that $\log N$ is an even integer. More generally, we show how to obtain bias 2^{-a} for any integer a using $1 + \lceil \log a \rceil$ bits of memory. We note that it is sufficient to toss a coins and report 1 if they all landed heads and 1 otherwise. This requires counting to a, which can be done with $\log a$ memory.

Algorithm 4 Subroutine to toss a biased coin that equals 1 with probability 2^{-a} and equals 0 otherwise

```
procedure TossBiasedCoin(a)  ▷ Flip a biased coin with bias
        Pr[c = 1] = 2^(−a)
    c := 1
    for i = 1 to a do
        b ←$ {0, 1}
        if b = 0 then
            c := 0
        end if
    end for
    return c
end procedure
```

We now describe the recruitment phase, which is the second phase executed by each agent in every epoch and is the main source of interaction in the protocol. The phase lasts for $T = \Theta(\log^3 N)$ rounds, consisting of $\frac{1}{2}\log N$ subphases each of length $T_{\text{inner}} = \Theta(\log^2 N)$ rounds. As discussed above, during this phase each leader is tasked with finding $\sqrt{N}$ inactive agents (i.e. with active = 0) and coloring each of them with the color of the leader. We note again that the leader will not directly meet each of these $\sqrt{N}$ inactive agents, but rather that this is done by propagation, where the leader will activate some agents and each of these will activate additional agents. In each subphase each active agent will attempt to recruit a single nonactive agent, which will then start to recruit in the following subphase. Since there are $\frac{1}{2}\log N = \log\sqrt{N}$ subphases, if each attempt to recruit is successful, then a single leader will result in the activation of a total of $\sqrt{N}$ agents.

Algorithm 5 Recruitment phase subroutine

```
procedure RecruitmentPhase
    if Nbr.active = 0 and recruiting = 1 then    ▷ Other agent has been activated
        recruiting := 0
        to_recruit := to_recruit − 1
    else if active = 0 and Nbr.recruiting = 1 then    ▷ This agent must be activated
        active := 1
        color := Nbr.color
        recruiting := 0
        to_recruit := (1/2) log N − ⌈(round + 1)/T_inner⌉
    end if
    if round ≡ −1 (mod T_inner) then ▷ Prepare for next round
        recruiting := 1.
    end if
end procedure
```

The final phase of the algorithm is the evaluation phase, which occurs on the last round of each epoch. In this phase, each matched active agent compares its color to that of its neighbor and makes a decision of whether to replicate itself or to self-destruct.

Algorithm 6 Subroutine to perform splitting and self-destruction at the end of each phase

```
procedure EvaluationPhase
    if active = 1 and Nbr.active = 1 then
        if Nbr.color = color then    ▷ Colors same: split with probability 1 − 16/√N
            c := TossBiasedCoin(log(√N/16))
            if c = 0 then
                Split()
            end if
        else ▷ Colors different: self-destruct with probability 1
            Die()
        end if
    end if
    active := 0
    color := 0
    recruiting := 0
end procedure
```

Finally, we give the subroutine invoked at the very beginning of each round, that performs a consistency check on the round values of the agent and its neighbor. In the absence of adversarial insertions this subroutine is unnecessary, since agents will always have the correct round value in the epoch. However, it is necessary if the adversary is allowed to insert agents with an incorrect round value. If left to increase unchecked, the presence of many agents with different round values would interfere with the operation of the protocol. We will prevent this from happening by causing agents to self-destruct as soon as they encounter an agent with a different round value. However, implementing this exactly would require $\Theta(\log \log N)$-bit messages, since agents would need to exchange their round numbers. To avoid this, we will instead have agents exchange only an indicator variable for whether or not they are in the evaluation phase. An agent will self-destruct if it is in the evaluation phase and its neighbor is not, or if its neighbor is in the evaluation phase and it is not. This process deletes a small number of agents with the correct round number along with agents with the incorrect round number. This will ensure that there are few agents with the incorrect round number and that only a small number of agents with the correct round number will self-destruct as a result of this procedure.

Algorithm 7 Subroutine to determine if agent knows the correct round

```
procedure CheckRoundConsistency
    if Nbr ≠ ⊥ and inEvalPhase ≠ Nbr.inEvalPhase then
        Die()
    end if
end procedure
```

4 OVERVIEW OF ANALYSIS

In this section we outline the proof the main theorem. Due to space limitations, the formal proof is deferred to the full version [20].

THEOREM 2. *Let α, γ, ϵ be positive constants, where $\gamma \leq 1$ is a lower bound on the fraction of agents that is matched in each round. Then Algorithm 1 is a population stability protocol that can be implemented using $\omega(\log^2 N)$ states per agent and three-bit messages guaranteeing that if the adversary inserts and deletes at most $K = O(N^{1/4-\epsilon})$ agents in each round, then with all but negligible probability the population will remain between $(1-\alpha)N$ and $(1+\alpha)N$ for any polynomial number of rounds.*

For ease of presentation, the version of the protocol described above uses four-bit messages. However, we can reduce the message size to three bits, as follows. If the agent is in the evaluation phase (i.e. inEvalPhase = 1) then the message must contain the values active and color, but need not contain recruiting. If inEvalPhase = 0, then the message must contain the value color but not active if recruiting = 1 and the value active but not color if recruiting = 0. Consequently, the desired information can be encoded in only three bits.

For the memory requirements, $\log T$ bits are needed to store the variable round $\in \{0, 1\}$, and the other variables stored by each agent consist of eight boolean values. The invocations of the subroutine TossBiasedCoin() require $\log \log N$ bits of local memory. However, the subroutine is only invoked in two rounds of each epoch, the leader selection round and the evaluation round. Consequently, using additional indicator bits to specify whether an agent is in each of these those two rounds, the memory used to store the variable round can be used as the helper memory for the subroutine, and so additional memory is not necessary. For $T = \frac{1}{2}\log^3 N$, the total number of states is therefore $\Theta(\log^3 N)$. However, it suffices to have $T = T_{\text{inner}} \cdot \log N$ for any $T_{\text{inner}} = \omega(\log N)$, and so we can reduce the number of states to $\omega(\log^2 N)$.

Roadmap to proof. We must show that the population size will remain close to the target value N. We will do this by means of two key steps.

The first step is to show that in any single epoch the population size will be relatively stable. That is, we show that the population in the middle or end of an epoch will not be too much larger or smaller than the population at the beginning of the epoch. We achieve this by showing that irrespective of the adversary's actions, with overwhelming probability the number of agents of each color in the evaluation phase will be concentrated around one-sixteenth of the total number of agents.

The second step is to show that the population size will tend to correct itself if it has deviated too far from the target value N. More precisely, we show that if the population is far from N, then in expectation the population at the end of the phase will be substantially closer to N than the population at the start of the phase. This step highlights a key tension of the proof, namely the difficulty analyzing a system that contains both random components in the matching schedule and worst-case components in the adversary's insertions and deletions. Indeed, it is not even clear a priori what it means to discuss expectation in a system with a worst-case adversary.

Putting these two steps together will enable us to conclude the proof of the theorem. Consider the first epoch in which the population size lies outside the interval $[(1-\frac{\alpha}{2})N, (1+\frac{\alpha}{2})N]$. Since the population size does not deviate too much in a single epoch, the population at the start of the next epoch will be close to $(1 \pm \frac{\alpha}{2})N$. But for each epoch in which the population remains outside the interval $[(1-\frac{\alpha}{2})N, (1+\frac{\alpha}{2})N]$, in expectation the change in population will be in the direction of the target value N. Considering the next $N^{0.01}$ epochs, a Chernoff-Hoeffding bound then implies that with overwhelming probability the population will return to the interval $[(1-\frac{\alpha}{2})N, (1+\frac{\alpha}{2})N]$. Since the population does not change much in each epoch, it follows further that the population will remain inside the interval $[(1-\alpha)N, (1+\alpha)N]$ during these $N^{0.01}$ epochs. We will conclude that with all but negligible probability, the population will remain in the interval $[(1-\alpha)N, (1+\alpha)N]$ for any polynomial number of rounds.

5 ACKNOWLEDGMENTS

We thank the reviewers for their thoughtful comments. This work was done in part while visiting the Simons Institute for the Theory of Computing, supported by the Simons Foundation and by the DIMACS/Simons Collaboration in Cryptography through NSF grant CNS-1523467. Shafi Goldwasser and Adam Sealfon were supported by NSF MACS CNS-1413920, DARPA IBM W911NF-15-C-0236, and a Simons Investigator award agreement dated 6-5-12. Rafail Ostrovsky was supported in part by NSF grant 1619348, DARPA, US-Israel BSF grant 2012366, OKAWA Foundation Research Award, IBM Faculty Research Award, Xerox Faculty Research Award, B. John Garrick Foundation Award, Teradata Research Award, and Lockheed-Martin Corporation Research Award. Alessandra Scafuro was supported by NSF grant 1012798, and by Cisco Systems Inc. and Silicon Valley Community Foundation. Adam Sealfon was also supported by a DOE CSGF fellowship and the Center for Science of Information (CSoI), an NSF Science and Technology Center, under grant agreement CCF-0939370. The views expressed are those of the authors and do not reflect the position of the Department of Defense or the U.S. Government.

REFERENCES

[1] Dan Alistarh, James Aspnes, David Eisenstat, Rati Gelashvili, and Ronald L. Rivest. Time-space trade-offs in population protocols. In *SODA*, 2017.
[2] Dan Alistarh, James Aspnes, and Rati Gelashvili. Space-optimal majority in population protocols. In *SODA*, 2018.
[3] Dana Angluin, James Aspnes, Zoë Diamadi, Michael J. Fischer, and René Peralta. Computation in networks of passively mobile finite-state sensors. In *PODC*, 2004.
[4] Dana Angluin, James Aspnes, Zoë Diamadi, Michael J. Fischer, and René Peralta. Computation in networks of passively mobile finite-state sensors. *Distributed Computing*, 18(4), 2006.
[5] Dana Angluin, James Aspnes, and David Eisenstat. A simple population protocol for fast robust approximate majority. In *DISC*, 2007.
[6] Dana Angluin, James Aspnes, David Eisenstat, and Eric Ruppert. The computational power of population protocols. *Distributed Computing*, 20(4), 2007.
[7] Dana Angluin, James Aspnes, Michael J. Fischer, and Hong Jiang. Self-stabilizing population protocols. *TAAS*, 3(4), 2008.
[8] James Aspnes, Joffroy Beauquier, Janna Burman, and Devan Sohier. Time and space optimal counting in population protocols. In *OPODIS*, 2016.
[9] E. R Berlekamp, John Horton Conway, and R. K. Guy. Winning ways for your mathematical plays. In *A K Peters 1st Ed.*, 2001-2004.
[10] Matthew Cook. Universality in elementary cellular automata. In *Complex Systems*, 2004.
[11] Alejandro Cornejo, Anna R. Dornhaus, Nancy A. Lynch, and Radhika Nagpal. Task allocation in ant colonies. In *DISC*, 2014.
[12] Tal Danino, Octavio Mondragón-Palomino, Lev Tsimring, and Jeff Hasty. A synchronized quorum of genetic clocks. *Nature*, 463(7279), 2010.
[13] G Martinez De La Escalera, AL Choi, and Richard I Weiner. Generation and synchronization of gonadotropin-releasing hormone (gnrh) pulses: intrinsic properties of the gt1-1 gnrh neuronal cell line. *Proceedings of the National Academy of Sciences*, 89(5), 1992.
[14] Carole Delporte-Gallet, Hugues Fauconnier, Rachid Guerraoui, and Eric Ruppert. When birds die: Making population protocols fault-tolerant. In *DCOSS*, 2006.
[15] Edsger W. Dijkstra. Self-stabilizing systems in spite of distributed control. *Commun. ACM*, 1974.
[16] Shlomi Dolev and Ted Herman. Superstabilizing protocols for dynamic distributed systems. *Chicago J. Theor. Comput. Sci.*, 1997.
[17] Martin Gardner. The fantastic combinations of John Conway's new solitaire game "life". In *Scientific American*, 1970.
[18] Mohsen Ghaffari, Cameron Musco, Tsvetomira Radeva, and Nancy A. Lynch. Distributed house-hunting in ant colonies. In *PODC*, 2015.
[19] Oded Goldreich and Dana Ron. On learning and testing dynamic environments. *Journal of the ACM (JACM)*, 64(3), 2017.
[20] Shafi Goldwasser, Rafail Ostrovsky, Alessandra Scafuro, and Adam Sealfon. Population stability: regulating size in the presence of an adversary. *CoRR*, abs/1803.02540, 2018.
[21] HJ Jongsma, M Masson-Pevet, and L Tsjernina. The development of beat-rate synchronization of rat myocyte pairs in cell culture. *Basic research in cardiology*, 82(5), 1987.
[22] Giuseppe Antonio Di Luna, Roberto Baldoni, Silvia Bonomi, and Ioannis Chatzigiannakis. Conscious and unconscious counting on anonymous dynamic networks. In *ICDCN*, 2014.
[23] Giuseppe Antonio Di Luna, Roberto Baldoni, Silvia Bonomi, and Ioannis Chatzigiannakis. Counting in anonymous dynamic networks under worst-case adversary. In *ICDCS*, 2014.
[24] Joseph S Markson and Erin K O'Shea. The molecular clockwork of a protein-based circadian oscillator. *FEBS letters*, 583(24), 2009.
[25] Robert Morris. Counting large numbers of events in small registers. In *Commun. ACM*, 1978.
[26] John von Neumann. The general and logical theory of automata. In *Cerebral Mechanisms in Behavior*, 1951.

Brief Announcement: 2D-Stack – A Scalable Lock-Free Stack Design that Continuously Relaxes Semantics for Better Performance*

Adones Rukundo
Chalmers University of Technology, Sweden
adones@chalmers.se

Aras Atalar
Chalmers University of Technology, Sweden
aaras@chalmers.se

Philippas Tsigas
Chalmers University of Technology, Sweden
tsigas@chalmers.se

ABSTRACT

We briefly describe an efficient lock-free concurrent stack design with tunable and tenable relaxed semantics to allow for better performance. The design is tunable and allow for a continuous monotonic trade of weaker semantics for better throughput performance. Concurrent stacks have an inherent scalability bottleneck due to their single access point for both their operations. Elimination and semantics relaxation have been proposed in the literature to address this problem. Semantics relaxation has the potential to reach monotonically very high throughput by continuously trading relaxation for throughput. Previous solutions could not fully leverage this potential. We suggest a new two dimensional design that can achieve this by exploiting disjoint access parallelism in one dimension and locality in the other within tight accuracy bounds. The behaviour of the algorithm is tightly bound. We compare experimentally to previous work, with respect to throughput and relaxed behaviour observed, on different relaxation and concurrency settings. The experimental evaluation shows that our algorithm significantly outperform all other algorithms in terms of performance, also maintain better accuracy in contrast to other designs with relaxed semantics.

KEYWORDS

Lock-free, Data-structures, Relaxation, Distributed, Concurrency, Parallel, NUMA, Shared-Memory

1 INTRODUCTION

To improve performance scalability of concurrent data structures, recent research has focused on expanding the set of legal behaviours, including; weakening consistency and semantic relaxation for providing trade-offs between scalability and linearizability guarantees. Relaxed semantics definitions including; *k-Out-of-Order*, k-Lateness and k-Stuttering have been proposed in the literature [6, 11] as interesting relaxation models to consider. Distributing parts and hence access of the data-structure [4, 7, 13], has come out as a frequent technique used to implement relaxation. A given data-structure is split into multiple sub-structures (*horizontal*) with independent access points to improve on disjoint access parallelism. Operations are distributed over the sub-structures using different scheduling techniques; *thread* binding [13], random access [7], load-balancing [4], round robin and a combination of others. Until now, most proposed relaxed data-structures are one dimension, *horizontal* or *vertical*. *horizontal* for disjoint parallelism, *vertical* for locality.

Concurrent stacks, are fundamental data structures that suffer from an inherent scalability bottleneck, due to their single access point for both of their operations. Because of that, semantic relaxation is a promising approach to be used for improving their performance. We propose a lock-free concurrent design for stacks (*2D-Stack*) that leverages semantics relaxation through exploiting both disjoint access parallelism and locality leading to a two dimensional design. To achieve this, we implement a light weight synchronization mechanism that also maintains tight accuracy bounds. Our design, compared to previous solutions, would not only increase the performance for a given configuration but also give to the application the capability to monotonically trade accuracy for better performance, which was not possible before. We compare our design with known scheduling techniques and other stacks from the literature. Among the scheduling techniques, we compare with; random (*random*), random choice of two (*random-c2*) [7] and round-robin (*k-robin*). From the literature, we compare with segmented (*k-segment*), elimination (*elimination*) and Treiber stack (*treiber*). *2D-stack* significantly outperforms previous stack implementations as observed in the experimental evaluation Section 4.

2 RELATED WORK

Concurrent stacks suffer from their inherent single point access bottleneck. In the quest to improve performance scalability, disjoint access strategies have been proposed for designing concurrent stacks including; elimination trees [1, 9], combining funnels [10] and elimination back-off [3, 5]. Elimination back-off implements a collision array in which pop operations try to collide and cancel with concurrent push operations. Such operation pairs create disjoint collisions that are executed in parallel with operations accessing the main stack implementation. Elimination back-off mostly benefits symmetric workloads in which the numbers of push and pop operations are roughly equal, its performance deteriorates when workloads are asymmetric.

Recently, semantic relaxation has been proposed for data-structures that provide trade-offs between scalability and linearizability guarantees. Relaxation introduce an acceptable error within the legal

*This work was supported by the Swedish Research Council (Vetenskapsrådet) project "Models and Techniques for Energy-Efficient Concurrent Data Access Designs" Under Contract No.: 2016-05360 and SIDA/BRIGHT project 317 under the Makerere-Sweden bilateral research programme 2015-2020.

PODC '18, July 23–27, 2018, Egham, United Kingdom

ACM ISBN 978-1-4503-5795-1/18/07...$15.00
https://doi.org/10.1145/3212734.3212794

strict semantics of a given data-structure, i.e. the pop operation of a relaxed stack can return any of the k items of the stack. To quantify this error, relaxed semantic definitions have been introduced [6, 11]. Based on these definitions, a *k-Out-of-Order* stack has been proposed in [6], referred to as *k-segment*. It is composed of a linked list of memory segments whose size is defined by k number of indexes. The stack items can only be accessed through the topmost segment, where an operation pushes or pops an item from any k indexes. A *Push* operation adds a new segment if top segment is full whereas a *Pop* removes a segment if it is empty and not the last segment.

Other relaxed data-structures proposed in the literature include, priority queues [2, 7, 13] and distributed queues [4].

3 *2D-STACK*

Our stack is composed of multiple lock-free *sub-stacks*. An individual *sub-stack* is implemented using a linked list whose operations follow the Treiber stack design [12]. Each *sub-stack* has a unique *descriptor* that keeps track of the *sub-stack* information including; pointer to the topmost item and item-counter. A *descriptor* has a dedicated memory location accessed through an array (*stack-array*). Using a *CAE*[1] instruction we can update the descriptor contents in one atomic step to maintain correctness.

We introduce and implement an operational region (*window*) in which an operation can occur. It is defined by two parameters; *width* and *depth*. *width* defines the number of *sub-stacks* whereas *depth* defines the maximum number of items acceptable for a single *sub-stack* per *window*. We also implement a global counter (*Global*) that defines the maximum number of items per *sub-stack*. The *window* and *Global* together help us to tightly bound both relaxation and execution time.

To perform an operation, a *thread* searches for a *sub-stack* based on the *Global*. A *thread* selects a *sub-stack*, then, compares the *sub-stack* item-count with the *Global*. The *thread* can then proceed on the selected *sub-stack* only if the comparison evaluates to true. Otherwise the *thread* has to search for another *sub-stack*. For each operation, the *thread* starts from the previously known *sub-stack* on which it succeeded. First the *thread* tries a given number of random hops, then switches to round robin until a valid *sub-stack* is found, or the *thread* updates the *Global*, after failing on all *sub-stacks*. The *Global* is updated in relation to *depth*. If the *thread* detects contention on a *sub-stack*, a random hop to another *sub-stack* is performed. This is to reduce possible contention on consecutive *sub-stacks* that might arise from round robin hops.

During the search, the *thread* validates each *sub-stack* item-count against the *Global*. The item-count must be less than *Global* for *Push* or greater than the difference between *Global* and *depth* for *Pop*. If the item-count is zero, then the *sub-stack* is empty. If no valid *sub-stack* is found, the *Global* is updated atomically. *Push* adds whereas *Pop* subtracts a value ($shift$), $shift$ must be less than or equal to *depth*. Then the search is restarted with a fresh search count. If a valid *sub-stack* is found, the *thread* tries to operate on the it, on success the *sub-stack descriptor* is updated otherwise another *sub-stack* is searched for, starting from a random index. A successful *Push* increments whereas a *Push* decrements the item-counter by one. Also the topmost item pointer is updated. At this point, a *Push* adds an item whereas a *Pop* returns an item for a non empty *sub-stack* or NULL for empty. An empty *sub-stack* is represented by a NULL item pointer within the *descriptor*. As an optimization strategy, the *thread* keeps track of the *Global* for every hop during the search process, restarting for every *Global* change detected.

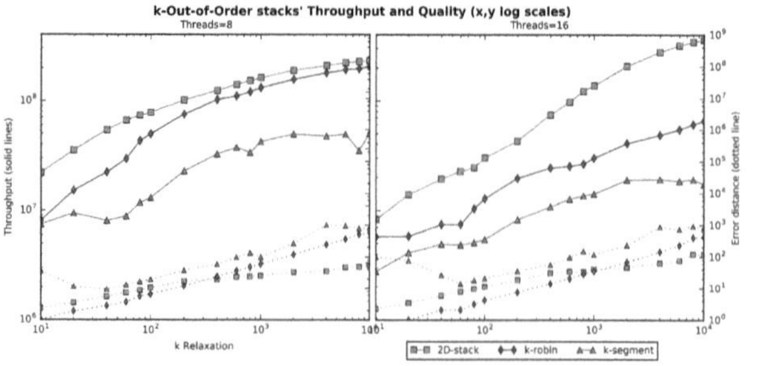

Figure 1: Throughput and observed accuracy as the k bound for relaxation increases. (k bounded algorithms).

2D-stack is correct with respect to *k-Out-of-Order* stack semantics. The deterministic bound for the relaxation is tunable, controlled by the parameters of our design, given by Theorem 1. Also, the step complexity analysis provide a tight bound for the algorithm [8].

Theorem 1. *2D-stack is linearizable with respect to k-Out-of-Order stack semantics, where* $k = (2shift + depth)(width - 1)$.

4 EXPERIMENTAL EVALUATION

We evaluate the performance of our implementation together with other existing stack designs including; the *k-segment* relaxed stack [6], *Elimination-Stack* (*elimination*) [5] and *Treiber-Stack* (*treiber*) [12]. All experiments run on an Intel Xeon CPU E5-2687W v2 machine with two 8-core Intel Xeon processors (2 threads per core). We pin one thread per core, filling one processor at a time up-to 16 threads before we switch to hyper-threading. Two NUMA settings are tested; intra-socket (1 to 8 threads) and inter-socket (9 to 16 threads). Threads select operations uniformly at random (*i.e.* with probability 1/2) from *Pop* and *Push* operations. To simulate high contention, we put no computational load between operations. For each experiment, the stack is initialized with 32,768 items, run for five seconds obtaining an average of five repeats. The stack algorithms are initialized in this way to avoid NULL returns that might arise from empty *sub-stacks*. Throughput is measured in terms of operations per second, whereas accuracy (quality) is measured in terms of error distance from the LIFO semantics.

To measure the quality, we adopt a similar method used in [2, 7]. A sequential linked list is run alongside the stack, for each *Push* or *Pop* a simultaneous insert or delete is performed on the list respectively. Items on the stack are duplicated on the list and can be identified by their unique labels. Insert operations happen at the head of the list similar to the push whereas the delete operation searches for the given item deletes it and returns its distance from the head (error distance). We then calculate the expected error distance for a given experiment run for 5 seconds with 5 repeats.

Scalability is evaluated on both increasing relaxation and concurrency, for different NUMA settings. Experiment results are then

[1]Compare and Exchange (*CAE*) atomically compares 16 bytes of memory content and exchanges it with new content on success.

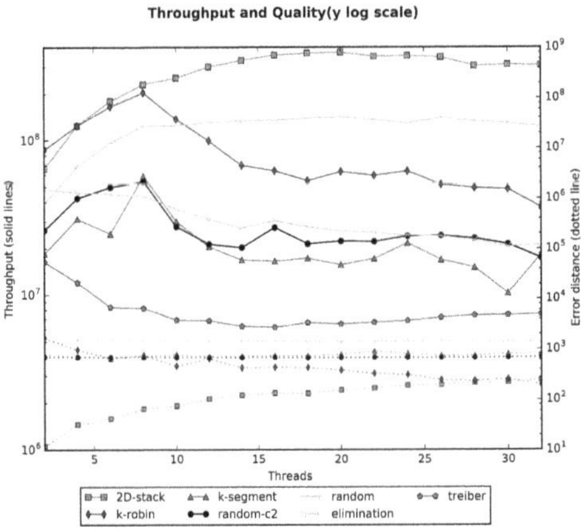

Figure 2: Throughput and observed accuracy as concurrency increases.

plotted using logarithmic scales, throughput (solid lines) and error distance (dotted lines) sharing the x-axis. Based on experimental observations and analysis presented in the full paper [8], we select $4P$ (P stands for number of threads and $width = 4P$) as the optimal performance configuration for *2D-stack width*. In Figure 1, we evaluate the performance of all algorithms, that are linearizable with respect to *k-Out-of-Order* stack (*k-robin,2D-stack* and *k-segment*), at different relaxation levels. We observe that *2D-stack* consistently outperforms the other algorithms. On low degree of relaxation, *2D-stack* avoids contention by hopping to another *sub-stack* on a failed *CAE*. This highly improves performance compared to *k-robin* that keeps retrying on the same *sub-stack*. As the relaxation increases, *2D-stack* combines contention avoidance with locality exploitation, a parameter exclusive to the *2D-stack* design as explained in [8]. While for the other algorithms the quality reduces almost linearly with the increase in relaxation, *2D-stack* maintains good quality with $width > 4P$ ($k > 200$ for $P = 8$ and $k > 600$ for $P = 16$). At this point, the algorithm switches from *horizontal* to *vertical* by increasing the depth. This change has a smaller negative impact on the quality, compared to the other algorithms. *2D-stack* continuously trades off quality for throughput by switching between relaxation dimensions for different relaxation levels. *k-segment* is mostly affected by the high cost of maintaining segments coupled with increased number of hops as relaxation increases.

We now configure the algorithms to obtain high throughput performance for both intra and inter-socket settings, Figure 2. Two "non-relaxed" algorithms *elimination* and *treiber* are also included in the experiment to compare the power of relaxation to improve performance compared to other strict semantics efficiency improvement techniques. We generally observe that, *2D-stack* is able to maintain the increase in throughput also while increasing the number of threads, even for the NUMA settings. As the number of threads increases, *random*, *random-c2* and *k-segment* maintain almost constant quality due to the fixed number of *sub-stacks*. *k-robin* and *2D-stack* vary the number of *sub-stacks* as the number of *threads* change. *k-robin* reduces number of *sub-stacks* with the increase in number of *threads* to keep the quality bound, this improves quality but hurts throughput due to the increased contention. Overall, *2D-stack* shows a full control to leverage the semantics relaxation to reach very high throughput in a continuous way. A property that was missing from previous solutions.

5 CONCLUSION AND FUTURE WORK

The aim of this work is to design an efficient lock-free stack algorithmic that can continuously relax *k-Out-of-Order* semantics to improve throughput through exploiting disjoint access parallelism and locality. We have achieved this through our two dimension relaxation technique that exploits disjoint access parallelism in one dimension and locality in the other. Our algorithm, *2D-stack*, uses also an efficient widows based synchronization that manages to keep the relaxation low without receding significantly performance achieved by disjoint access parallelism and locality. *2D-stack* significantly outperformed all the other stack implementations due to its capability to monotonically trade accuracy for better performance. In addition to *2D-stack*, we have implemented and tested a set of other possible relaxed stack designs:*random,random-c2* and *k-robin*. The full version of this paper further elaborates on a number of topics treated only briefly here, including complexity analysis, correctness, optimization but also Lock freedom and other experiments that due to space constraints have not been treated at all here [8].

As future work, we are working towards generalizing our design to work for other concurrent data structures.

REFERENCES

[1] Yehuda Afek, Guy Korland, Maria Natanzon, and Nir Shavit. 2010. Scalable producer-consumer pools based on elimination-diffraction trees. *Euro-Par 2010-Parallel Processing* (2010), 151–162.
[2] Dan Alistarh, Justin Kopinsky, Jerry Li, and Nir Shavit. 2015. The SprayList: a scalable relaxed priority queue. In *Proceedings of the 20th ACM SIGPLAN Symposium on Principles and Practice of Parallel Programming, PPoPP 2015, San Francisco, CA, USA, February 7-11, 2015.* 11–20.
[3] Gal Bar-Nissan, Danny Hendler, and Adi Suissa. 2011. A Dynamic Elimination-Combining Stack Algorithm. *CoRR* abs/1106.6304 (2011). arXiv:1106.6304 http://arxiv.org/abs/1106.6304
[4] Andreas Haas, Michael Lippautz, Thomas A. Henzinger, Hannes Payer, Ana Sokolova, Christoph M. Kirsch, and Ali Sezgin. 2013. Distributed Queues in Shared Memory: Multicore Performance and Scalability Through Quantitative Relaxation. In *Proceedings of the ACM International Conference on Computing Frontiers (CF '13)*. ACM, New York, NY, USA, Article 17, 9 pages.
[5] Danny Hendler, Nir Shavit, and Lena Yerushalmi. 2010. A scalable lock-free stack algorithm. *J. Parallel Distrib. Comput.* 70, 1 (2010), 1–12.
[6] Thomas A. Henzinger, Christoph M. Kirsch, Hannes Payer, Ali Sezgin, and Ana Sokolova. 2013. Quantitative relaxation of concurrent data structures. In *The 40th Annual ACM SIGPLAN-SIGACT Symposium on Principles of Programming Languages, POPL '13, Rome, Italy - January 23 - 25, 2013.* 317–328.
[7] Hamza Rihani, Peter Sanders, and Roman Dementiev. 2015. Brief announcement: Multiqueues: Simple relaxed concurrent priority queues. In *Proceedings of the 27th ACM symposium on Parallelism in Algorithms and Architectures*. ACM, 80–82.
[8] Adones Rukundo, Aras Atalar, and Philippas Tsigas. 2018. *2D-Stack: A scalable lock-free stack design that continuously relaxes semantics for better performance.* Technical Report 2018:06. Chalmers University of Technology.
[9] Nir Shavit and Dan Touitou. 1995. Elimination trees and the construction of pools and stacks: preliminary version. In *Proceedings of the seventh annual ACM symposium on Parallel algorithms and architectures*. ACM, 54–63.
[10] Nir Shavit and Asaph Zemach. 2000. Combining funnels: a dynamic approach to software combining. *J. Parallel and Distrib. Comput.* 60, 11 (2000), 1355–1387.
[11] Edward Talmage and Jennifer L. Welch. 2017. Relaxed Data Types as Consistency Conditions. In *Stabilization, Safety, and Security of Distributed Systems - 19th International Symposium, SSS 2017, Boston, MA, USA, November 5-8, 2017, Proceedings.* 142–156.
[12] R.K. Treiber. 1986. *Systems Programming: Coping with Parallelism.* International Business Machines Incorporated, Thomas J. Watson Research Center. https://books.google.se/books?id=YQg3HAAACAAJ
[13] Martin Wimmer, Jakob Gruber, Jesper Larsson Träff, and Philippas Tsigas. 2015. The lock-free k-LSM relaxed priority queue. In *Proceedings of the 20th ACM SIGPLAN Symposium on Principles and Practice of Parallel Programming, PPoPP 2015, San Francisco, CA, USA, February 7-11, 2015.* 277–278.

Brief Announcement: Performance Prediction for Coarse-Grained Locking

Vitaly Aksenov
ITMO University and Inria Paris

Dan Alistarh
IST Austria

Petr Kuznetsov
LCTI, Télécom ParisTech, Université Paris-Saclay

ABSTRACT

A standard design pattern found in many concurrent data structures, such as hash tables or ordered containers, is an alternation of parallelizable sections that incur no data conflicts and critical sections that must run sequentially and are protected with locks. A lock can be viewed as a *queue* that arbitrates the order in which the critical sections are executed, and a natural question is whether we can use *stochastic analysis* to predict the resulting throughput. As a preliminary evidence to the affirmative, we describe a simple model that can be used to predict the throughput of *coarse-grained* lock-based algorithms. We show that our model works well for CLH lock, and we expect it to work for other popular lock designs such as TTAS, MCS, etc.

ACM Reference Format:
Vitaly Aksenov, Dan Alistarh, and Petr Kuznetsov. 2018. Brief Announcement: Performance Prediction for Coarse-Grained Locking . In *PODC '18: ACM Symposium on Principles of Distributed Computing, July 23–27, 2018, Egham, United Kingdom.* ACM, New York, NY, USA, 3 pages. https://doi.org/10.1145/3212734.3212785

1 ABSTRACT COARSE-GRAINED SYNCHRONIZATION

Conventionally, the performance of a concurrent data structure is evaluated via experiments, and it is notoriously difficult to account for all significant experimental parameters so that the outcomes are meaningful. Our motivation here is to complement experimental evaluation with an analytical model that can be used to *predict* the performance rather than measure it. As a first step towards this goal, in this work, we attempt to predict the throughput of a class of algorithms that use *coarse-grained* synchronization.

Consider a concurrent system with N processes that obey the following simple *uniform* scheduler: at every time step, each process performs a step of computation. This scheduler, resembling the well-known PRAM model [3], appears to be a reasonable approximation of a real-life concurrent system. Suppose that the processes share a data structure exporting a single `operation()`. If the operation induces a work of size P and incurs no synchronization, the resulting throughput is $N \cdot \alpha / P$ operations in a unit of time: each process performs α / P operations in a unit of time, where α indicates the amount of work that can be performed by one process in a unit of time. One way to evaluate the constant α experimentally is to count the total number F of operations, each of work P, completed by N processes in time T. Then we get $\alpha = F/NP$. The longer is T, the more accurate is the estimation of α.

```
1 operation():
2   lock.lock()
3   for i in 1..C:
4     nop
5   lock.unlock()
6   for i in 1..P:
7     nop
```

Figure 1: The coarse-grained operation

Now suppose that, additionally, the operation performed by each process contains a *critical section* of size C. In the operation, described in Figure 1, every process takes a global lock, performs the critical section of size C, releases the lock and, finally, performs the *parallel section* of size P.

Here, as a unit of work, we take the number of CPU cycles spent during one iteration of the loop in Lines 3-4 or 6-7. The iteration consists of a `nop` instruction, an increment of a local variable and a conditional jump, giving us, approximately, *four* CPU cycles in total.

2 MODEL ASSUMPTIONS

Below we list basic assumptions on the abstract machine used for our analytical throughput prediction.

First, we assume that coherence of caches is maintained by a variant of MESI protocol [5]. Each cache line can be in one of four states: `Modified` (`M`), `Exclusive` (`E`), `Shared` (`S`) and `Invalid` (`I`). MESI regulates transitions between states of a cache line and responses depending on the request (read or write) to the cache line by a process or on the request to the memory bus. The important transitions for us are: (1) upon reading, the state of the cache line changes from any state to `S`, and, if the state was `I`, then a *read request* is sent to the bus; (2) upon writing, the state of the cache line becomes `M`, and, if the state was `S` or `I`, an *invalidation request* is sent to the bus.

We assume that the caches are *symmetric*: for each MESI state st, there exist two constants R_{st} and W_{st} such that any read from any cache line with status st takes R_{st} work and any write to a cache line with status st takes W_{st} work. David et al. [2] showed that for an Intel Xeon machine (similar to the one we use in our experimental validation below), given the relative location of a cache line with respect to the process (whether they are located on the same socket or not), the following hypotheses hold: (1) writes induce the same work, regardless of the state of the cache line; (2) swaps, not concurrent with other swaps, induce the same work as writes. Therefore, we assume that (1) $W = W_M = W_E = W_S = W_I$ and (2) any contention-free `swap` induces a work of size W.

PODC '18, July 23–27, 2018, Egham, United Kingdom

ACM ISBN 978-1-4503-5795-1/18/07.
https://doi.org/10.1145/3212734.3212785

```
1  class Node:
2    bool locked
3
4  Node head = new Node()  // global
5  Node my_node            // per process
6     my_node.locked ← true
7
8  operation():
9    Node next ← swap(&head, my_node)  // W or X
10   while (next.locked) {}            // R_I or 2 · R_I
11   for i in 1..C:                    // C
12     nop
13   my_node.locked ← false            // W
14   my_node ← next
15   my_node.locked ← true             // W
16   for i in 1..P:                    // P
17     nop
```

Figure 2: The coarse-grained operation with inlined lock and unlock functions

3 CLH LOCK

Multiple lock implementations have been previously proposed, from simple spinlocks and TTAS to more advanced MCS [4] and CLH [1]. For our analysis, we choose CLH, as the simplest lock among those considered to be efficient. In Figure 2, we inline `lock` and `unlock` calls to CLH lock in our abstract coarse-grained operation.

3.1 Cost of an operation

Let us zoom into what happens during the execution of the operation.

Note that at the beginning of an operation (unless it is the very first invocation), `my_node.locked` is loaded into the cache and the corresponding cache line is in state `M`, because of the set in Line 15 during the previous operation by the same process.

(1) The operation starts with `swap` (Line 9) that induces a work of size W, if not concurrent with other `swap`s, and a work of size at most X, otherwise.

(2) In Line 10, the algorithm loops on a field `next.locked`. During this loop one or two cache misses happens.

One cache miss can happen at the first iteration of the loop if the read of `locked` returns `true`. The last process that grabbed the lock already invalidated this cache line in Line 15 during its penultimate operation. MESI reloads the cache line and changes its state from `I` (or none if it was not loaded previously) to `S`.

The other cache miss happens in every execution when the operation reads `next.locked` and gets `false`. In this case, the cache line was invalidated in Line 13 during the last operation of the last process that grabbed the lock. MESI reloads the cache line and changes its state from `I` (or none) to `S`.

Each of the described cache misses induces the work of size R_I. Thus, the work induced in Line 10 is of size of R_I (if only the second miss happens) or $2 \cdot R_I$ (if both misses happen).

(3) In Lines 11-12, the critical section with work of size C is performed.

(4) In Line 13, `my_node.locked` is set to `false`. There are two cases: if `my_node.locked` is not yet loaded by any other process in Line 10 then the state remains `M`; otherwise, MESI changes the state from `S` to `M` and sends a signal to invalidate this cache line. In both cases, the induced work is of size W.

(5) In Line 14, the operation performs an assignment on local variables, without contributing to the total work.

(6) In Line 15, `my_node.locked` is set to `true`. From the end of the while loop at Line 10 the corresponding cache line is in state `S`. MESI changes the state to `M` and sends a signal to invalidate this cache line inducing work of size W.

(7) In Lines 16-17, the parallel work of size P is performed.

3.2 Evaluating throughput

To evaluate the throughput of the resulting program under the uniform scheduler, take a closer look on how N processes continuously perform the operation from Figure 2.

Process 1 executes: its first swap (taking at most X units); the critical section (blue, Lines 10-13): acknowledges the ownership of the lock by reading `false` in Line 10 (takes R_I units), performs the work of size C and releases the lock in Line 13 (takes W units); the parallel section (red, Lines 15-17 and 9): sets `my_node.locked` to `true` (takes W), performs the work of size P, performs a non-contended swap (takes W) and, possibly, reads `true` in Line 10 (takes R_I). (Here, the swap operation performed after the very first completed critical section is counted in the parallel work, as it is executed in the absence of contention.) Every other process i operates in the same way: it swaps as early as possible (taking at most X), waits until process $i-1$ releases the lock, and then performs its critical (blue) and parallel (red) sections.

Depending on the parameters N, C, P, W, and R_I, two types of executions are possible.

In case 1 (Figure 3a), at the moment when process 1 finishes its parallel section, process N already finished its critical section, i.e., $P + 2 \cdot W > (N-1) \cdot (C + R_I + W)$. Therefore, in the steady case, at every moment of time, each process do not wait and execute either the parallel or critical section, and the read in Line 10 cannot return `true` because the lock is already released. Thus, the throughput, measured as the number of operations completed in a unit of time, equals to $N \cdot \frac{\alpha}{(P+2\cdot W)+(C+R_I+W)}$.

In case 2 (Figure 3b), before proceeding to the next operation, process 1 has to wait until process N completes its critical section from the previous round of operations; process 2 waits for process 1, process 3 waits for process 2, etc. Thus, there is always some process in the critical section, giving the throughput of $\frac{\alpha}{C+R_I+W}$.

Therefore, given the number of processes N, the sizes C and P of critical and parallel sections, the throughput can be calculated as follows:

$$\begin{cases} \frac{\alpha}{C+R_I+W} & \text{if } P + 2 \cdot W \leq (N-1) \cdot (C + R_I + W) \\ \frac{\alpha \cdot N}{(P+2\cdot W)+(C+R_I+W))} & \text{otherwise} \end{cases}$$

4 EXPERIMENTS

For our measurements, we used a server with four 10-core Intel Xeon E7-4870 chips of 2.4 GHz (yielding 40 hardware processes in total), running Ubuntu Linux kernel v3.13.0-66-generic. We compiled the code with MinGW GCC 5.2.0 (with -O0 flag to avoid compiler optimizations, such as function inlining, that can screw up our benchmarking environment). The code is available at https://github.com/Aksenov239/complexity-lock-with-libslock.

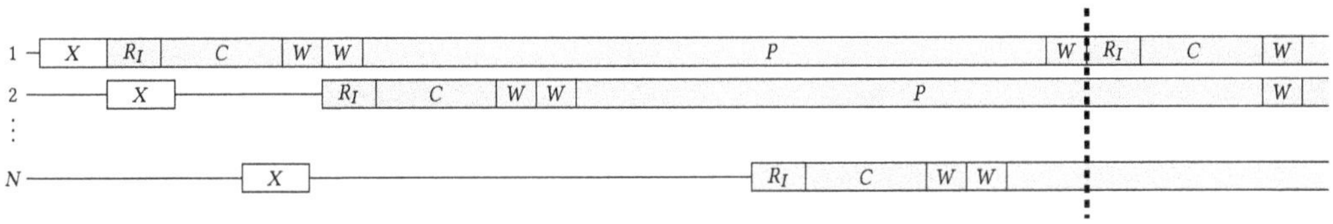

(a) **Case 1:** $W + P + W \geq (N-1) \cdot (R_I + C + W)$. **Each process enters the critical section without waiting in the queue.**

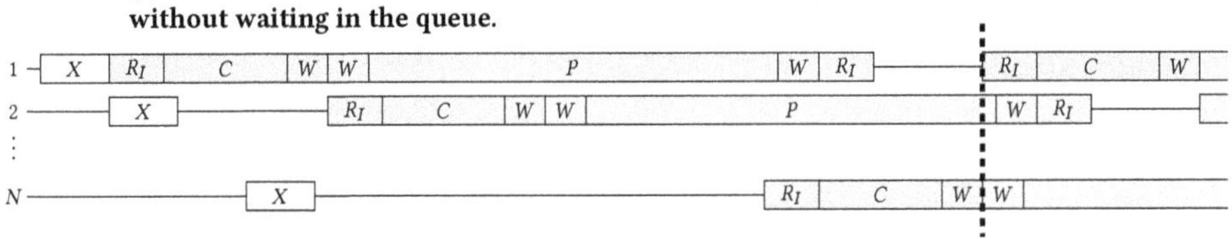

(b) **Case 2:** $W + P + W \leq (N-1) \cdot (R_I + C + W)$. **Each process waits in the queue before entering the critical section.**

Figure 3: Examples of executions of the coarse-grained algorithm from Figure 2. Blue intervals depict critical sections and red intervals depict parallel sections.

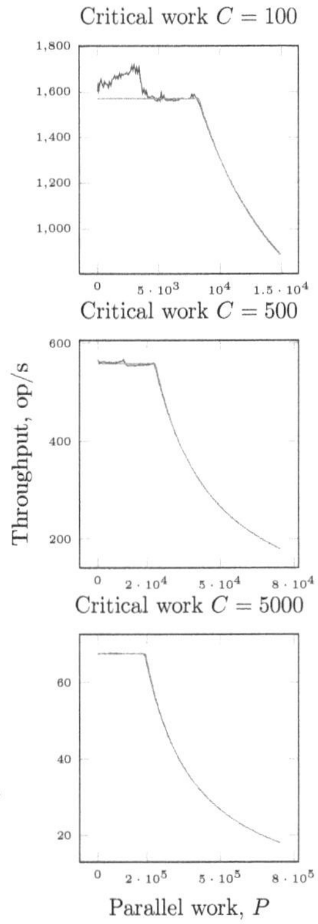

Figure 4: Throughput on 39 processes for $C \in \{100, 500, 5000\}$

We considered the following experimental settings: the number of processes $N \in \{5, 10, 20, 30, 39\}$; the size of the critical section $C \in \{100, 500, 1000, 5000, 10000\}$; and the multiplier $x \in [1, 150]$ (we choose all integer values) that determined the size of the parallel section $P = x \cdot C$. For each setting, we measured the throughput for 10 seconds. Our experimental evaluation gives $\alpha \approx 3.5 \cdot 10^5$, $W \approx 40$, and $R_I \approx 80$. The ratio between W and R_I correlates with the experimental results provided by David et al. [2].

In Figure 4 we show our experimental results for three settings with $N = 39$ and $C \in \{100, 500, 5000\}$ (blue curves) compared with our theoretical prediction (red curves). The two curves match very closely, except for the case of small C and P where our predicted throughput underestimates the real one. We relate this to the fact that we oversimplified the abstract machine: any write induces the work of constant size W, regardless of the relative location of the cache line with respect to the process. For small C and P two processes from the same socket are more likely to take the lock one after the other and, thus, on average, a write might induce less work than W, and, consequently, the throughput can be higher than predicted.

5 CONCLUSION

In this short note, we showed that a simple theoretical analysis may quite accurately predict the throughput of data structures implemented using coarse-grained synchronization. For the moment, our analysis is restricted to algorithms using CLH-based locking in systems obeying the uniform scheduler. In upcoming work, we intend extend the analysis to more realistic algorithm designs, lock implementations and architectures.

6 ACKNOWLEDGEMENTS

This research is partially supported by European Research Council (ERC-2012-StG-308246) and the Franco-German DFG-ANR Project DISCMAT (14-CE35-0010-02).

REFERENCES

[1] Travis Craig. 1993. *Building FIFO and priorityqueuing spin locks from atomic swap.* Technical Report. ftp://ftp.cs.washington.edu/tr/1993/02/UW-CSE-93-02-02.pdf

[2] Tudor David, Rachid Guerraoui, and Vasileios Trigonakis. 2013. Everything you always wanted to know about synchronization but were afraid to ask. In *Proceedings of the Twenty-Fourth ACM Symposium on Operating Systems Principles.* ACM, 33–48.

[3] Joseph JáJá. 1992. *An introduction to parallel algorithms.* Vol. 17. Addison-Wesley Reading.

[4] John M Mellor-Crummey and Michael L Scott. 1991. Algorithms for scalable synchronization on shared-memory multiprocessors. *ACM Transactions on Computer Systems (TOCS)* 9, 1 (1991), 21–65.

[5] Mark S Papamarcos and Janak H Patel. 1984. A low-overhead coherence solution for multiprocessors with private cache memories. In *ACM SIGARCH Computer Architecture News*, Vol. 12. ACM, 348–354.

Brief Announcement: Automatic Log Enhancement for Fault Diagnosis

Tong Jia
Peking University
jia.tong@pku.edu.cn

Ying Li
Peking University
li.ying@pku.edu.cn

Zhonghai Wu
Peking University
wuzh@ss.pku.edu.cn

ABSTRACT

When systems fail, logs are frequently the only evidence available for underlying fault diagnosis. Consequently, the quality of logs-how well system faults can be reflected by these log messages, is of significant importance. To improve the quality of logs, we propose a novel log enhancement approach which automatically identifies logging points that reflect anomalous behavior during system fault time. We further evaluate our approach with three popular open source projects. Results show that it can significantly improve over 50% accuracy of automatic fault diagnosis on average.[1]

CCS CONCEPTS

• **Software and its engineering** → **Extra-functional properties** → Software Reliability

KEYWORDS

Log enhancement; Automatic fault diagnosis; Control flow graph

ACM Reference format:

Tong Jia, Ying Li, Zhonghai Wu. 2018. Brief Announcement: Automatic Log Enhancement for Automatic Fault Diagnosis. In *Proceedings of ACM Symposium on Principles of Distributed Computing, Egham, United Kingdom, July 2018*, 3 pages. https://doi.org/10.1145/3212734.3212784

1 INTRODUCTION

Logs are common and important source of information for system fault diagnosis. Typically, administrators manually check log files and search for fault-related log lines. However, in large scale distributed systems, logs can be overwhelmingly large. Meanwhile, problems of distributed systems can be cross-component and it is hard to find root causes based on search certain "error" logs. Therefore, manually diagnosing system faults can be time consuming and error-prone.

To solve this problem, various automatic fault diagnosis models are proposed[5-6]. Through these models, machines can intelligently analyze large scale logs and detect anomalies automatically instead of tough human efforts. However, these models perform less satisfactorily in many cases. One of the major reasons is that currently logging is designed for humans rather than machines, that is, logging decisions are made by programmers mainly for debugging. Consequently, it is inadequate for accurate automatic fault diagnosis.

Driven by this problem, we propose a novel log enhancement approach for automatic fault diagnosis in this paper. Our approach leverages automatic fault diagnosis model, and identifies logging points that reflect anomalous behavior through the model during system fault time. Compared with other modern log enhancement methods[1-2], our approach has two major differences. First, enhanced logs are designed specifically for automatic fault diagnosis. Second, enhanced logs are designed automatically without any human knowledge. Our contributions include:

1. We propose a novel automatic log enhancement approach for automatic fault diagnosis. To the best of our knowledge, we are the first toward to enhancing machine oriented logs instead of human oriented.
2. We evaluate our approach with several popular open source software, and results show that it can significantly improve the performance of automatic fault diagnosis models.

2 LOG ENHANCEMENT APPROACH

To better illustrate the approach, we first briefly describe automatic fault diagnosis model. Automatic fault diagnosis model is a graph-based model that represents system request/transaction flow. Let us take time-weighted control flow graph(TCFG) model as an example[5-6] in the rest of this paper. It is a directed graph consisting of nodes, edges and time weights. Nodes are *logging points* and edges represent transition flows between nodes. A *logging point* is an abstraction of a logging statement in source code as summarization of multiple raw log lines. A time weight is added on each edge to record the transition time between two adjacent nodes.

Our log enhancement approach is designed based on the automatic fault diagnosis model. It includes a log enhancement kernel to generate appropriate fault-related logging points and two work modes defining the usage of these logging points in different situations.

2.1 Log Enhancement Kernel

As shown in Fig. 1, log enhancement kernel is composed of two key phases including anomaly flag detection and logging points generation. First, a TCFG model is mined from parsed logs (logging points generated from log parser) of a normal running system. If any system faults occur, input log stream is compared

ACM ISBN 978-1-4503-5795-1/18/07.
https://doi.org/10.1145/3212734.3212784

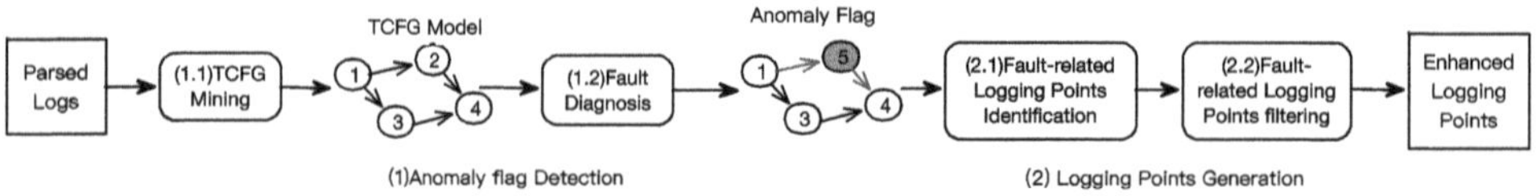

Figure 1. Log enhancement kernel

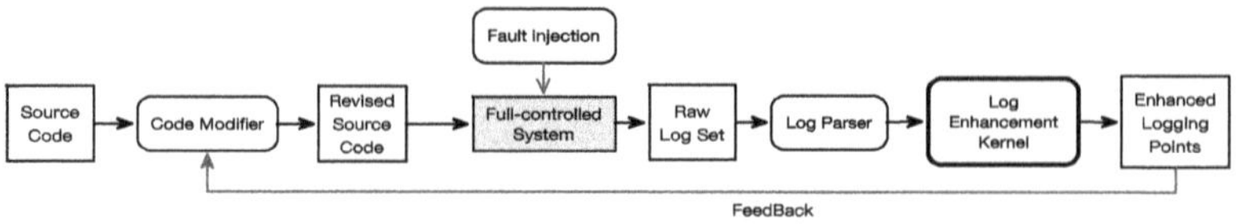

Figure 2 (a). Mode A: Fully controllable mode

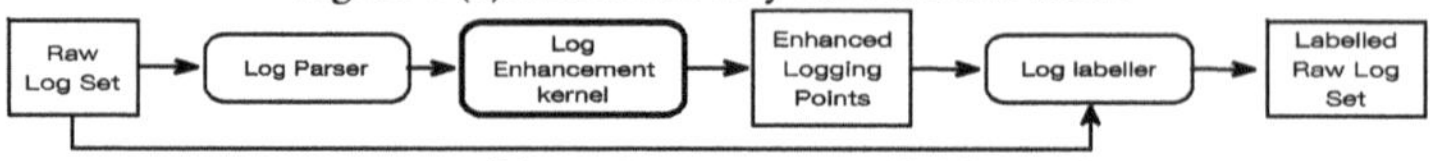

Figure 2 (b). Mode B: Uncontrollable mode

Figure 2. Two work modes

with the TCFG model and the anomaly flags are detected. Then, these flags are utilized to identify fault-related logging points. To reduce the number of identified logging points, log enhancement kernel further performs a filtering step. The output of filtering step is the final enhanced logging points.

2.1.1 Anomaly Flag Detection

(A) TCFG Mining

TCFG mining phase includes edge mining and time weight mining. Edge mining aims to mine transitions between nodes based on the sequence of logs in each request/transaction flow. First, each log is assumed to record a request ID. Logs with the same request ID are correlated together and sorted by their time stamps. Then, for each pair of adjacent logs with the same request ID, an edge is added from the logging point of prior one to the logging point of post one. Note that without request ID, edge mining is also available due to our prior work[5-6]. For each two adjacent logging points, the time weight is recorded as the maximum time difference in all pairs of occurrences.

(B) Fault Diagnosis

Three types of anomalies including *sequence anomaly*, *redundancy anomaly* and *latency anomaly* are defined for fault diagnosis. A *sequence anomaly* is raised when the log that follows the occurrence of a parent node can not be mapped to any of its children. A *redundancy anomaly* is raised when unexpected logs occur that cannot be mapped to any node in the temporal path of the TCFG. A *latency anomaly* is raised when the child of a parent node is seen but the interval time exceeds the time weight recorded on the edge. When anomalies are found, we flag a sub-structure of TCFG as the anomaly flag based on the anomaly types.

For *sequence anomaly*, we flag the minimal sub-tree starting with the parent node as well as the undesirable child node. For *redundancy anomaly*, we flag the unexpected node and its parent node due to the abnormal log stream. For *latency anomaly*, we flag the two adjacent nodes whose time interval exceeds the time weight recorded on the edge. Fig. 3 (a) is an example of TCFG with 7 nodes. When node 1 and node 2 suffer a latency anomaly, node 1, node 2 and the edge between them are recorded as the *anomaly flag*. Meanwhile, node 5 appears after node 2 unexpectedly and suffers a *sequence anomaly*, then the minimal sub-tree starting with node 2 (node 2, node 4, node 5 and the medial edges) is recorded as the anomaly flag. After that, unexpected node 8 appears after node 6, thus a redundancy anomaly occurs. Node 6 and node 8 are recorded as the *anomaly flag* correspondingly.

2.1.2 Fault-related Logging Points Generation

(A) Logging Points Identification

The purpose of log enhancement is to identify logging points as few as possible meanwhile they can reflect unusual behaviors when faults occur. Therefore, we define three rules for each type of anomaly to identify fault-related logging points from anomaly flags. For *sequence anomaly*, we choose the parent node with its unexpected child in the anomaly flag as fault-related logging points. The intuition behind is that no matter how TCFG changes, this unexpected child will always appear after the parent node when same fault occurs. For *redundancy anomaly*, only the redundant node is identified as the fault-related logging point. For latency anomaly, we choose the two adjacent nodes in the anomaly flag as the fault-related logging points. Fig. 3(c) shows the example of identified logging points.

(B)Logging Points Filtering

To further reduce the amount of fault-related logging points, we propose a filtering method based on information gain algorithm. Our objective is to find the least number of logging points that can distinguish as many types of fault as possible.

Let us denote all the system faults as $F = \{f_1, f_2, f_3, ..., f_m\}$ where m is the number of faults. The anomaly flags are formulated as $T = \{t_1, t_2, t_3, ..., t_n\}$ where n denotes the total number of anomaly flags. We define an $m \times n$ matrix $\mathcal{M}$ to record the relevance between faults and anomaly flags. Element in $\mathcal{M}$ is formulated as a_{ij} where $1 \le i \le m$ and $1 \le j \le n$. a_{ij} is assigned to 1 if anomaly flag t_j is caused by fault f_i, otherwise, it is assigned to 0:

$$a_{ij} = \begin{cases} 1 & if\ t_j\ is\ caused\ by\ f_i \\ 0 & otherwise \end{cases} \quad (1)$$

The input of our fault-related logging points filtering algorithm is an attribute-valued dataset D composed of $\mathcal{M}$ and F where F is denoted as the label vector of $\mathcal{M}$:

$$D = \begin{bmatrix} a_{11} & \cdots & a_{1n} & f_1 \\ \vdots & \ddots & \vdots & \vdots \\ a_{m1} & \cdots & a_{mn} & f_m \end{bmatrix} \quad (2)$$

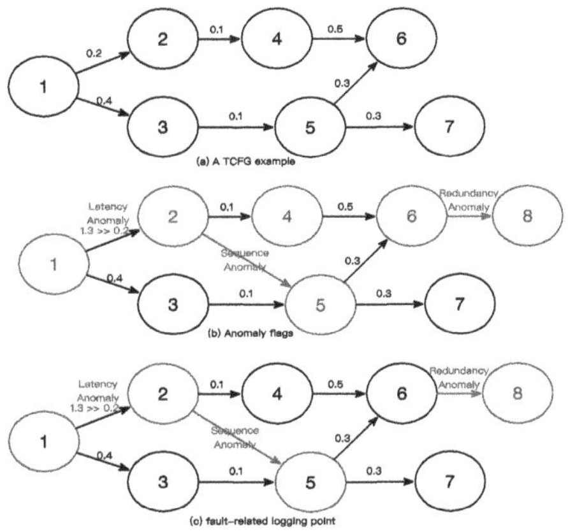

Figure 3. Example of fault diagnosis and fault-related logging points identification

The output is filtered anomaly flags. We consider information gain algorithm to solve this problem. Information gain is the change of information entropy *Info(D)* and conditional entropy $Info_A(D)$ on the condition of *A*.

$$Gain(A) = Info(D) - Info_A(D) \tag{3}$$

where condition A is a selected anomaly flag t_x. For each instance in *D*, value of a_{ix} can only be assigned to 0 or 1. Let us denote the number of instances where a_{ix} is assigned to 1 as m_1, and the number of instances where a_{ix} is assigned to 0 as m_0 where $m_0+m_1=m$. *Info(D)* and $Info_A(D)$ is computed as follows:

$$Info(\text{D}) = -\sum_{k=1}^{m} \frac{1}{m} log_2(\frac{1}{m}) \tag{4}$$

$$Info_A(\text{D}) = -\sum_{k=0}^{1} \frac{m_k}{m} log_2(\frac{m_k}{m}) \times \text{Info}(D_j) \tag{5}$$

Our algorithm is recursive. In each recursion, we compute the $Gain(t_x)$ for each *t* in *T* and then select the best feature t_{best} with the most information gain for current dataset. The value of t_{best} divides *D* into two subsets D_x and D_y, the algorithm then enters the next recursion to calculate the best feature of D_x and D_y. At last, we record all the t_{best} in every recursion as the filtered anomaly flags and the fault-related logging points in them are recorded as the final enhanced logging points.

2.2 Two Work Modes

To adapt our approach to different system situations, we propose two applicable modes denoted as mode A and mode B shown in Fig. 2. Mode A is designed for fully-controllable systems of which source code is accessible. Mode B is designed for uncontrollable systems of which source code is inaccessible.

In mode A, enhanced logging points from log enhancement kernel are utilized to modify system source code. The process of mode A is as follows. First, code modifier inserts logging statements to every execution path of system source code. Then the revised source code after insertion is built and deployed to a fully controllable environment to start a testing system. While the system is running, random faults are injected. Log parser collects logs from the system and identifies the logging point of each log. These logging points are fed into log enhancement kernel so as to generate enhanced logging points. At last, the enhanced logging points are fed back to code modifier, and code modifier insert these enhanced logging points into source code.

Table 1. Evaluation Results.

Project	Code Version	#Anomaly Flag	#Logging points	Fault Diagnosis Accuracy
AcmeAir	Original	5	35	3/19(15.79%)
	Enhanced	58	19	19/19(100%)
HDFS	Original	24	225	4/24(16.67%)
	Enhanced	107	65	18/24(75%)
Tensor flow	Original	12	125	6/26(23.07%)
	Enhanced	13	17	11/26(42.31%)

In mode B, log parser first collects logs printed from a black-box running system and identifies the logging point of each log through template mining[3]. Note that these logging points can not be mapped to source code in this situation. Then these logging points are fed into log enhancement kernel. At last, logs printed by the generated enhanced logging points are labeled. These labeled logs are highly correlated with system faults, thus are valuable for administrators to diagnose underlying fault causes.

3 EVALUATION

The proposed approach has been evaluated with three popular open source projects including AcmeAir, HDFS and Tensorflow. Result(Table. 1) shows that it can effectively generate fault-related logging points for different projects. Compared with original logging points, enhanced logging points are much less, but produce more types of anomaly flags on the contrary. For instance, there are 225 effective logging points in original HDFS source code. These logging points only produce 24 anomaly flags during fault time. Comparatively, our approach generates 65 logging points while producing 107 anomaly flags. More importantly, enhanced logging points perform much better accuracy of fault diagnosis than original ones (increasing 53.93% accuracy on average). In the best case (AcmeAir project), original logging points can only diagnose 3 of 19 injected faults(15.79% accuracy) while enhanced logging points can perfectly diagnose all faults(100% accuracy) increasing over 80% accuracy.

ACKNOWLEDGMENTS

This work was supported by PKU-Tencent Joint Innovation Lab.

REFERENCES

[1] Zhu, Jieming, et al. Learning to log: helping developers make informed logging decisions. *IEEE/ACM International Conference on Software Engineering IEEE.* 2015:415-425.

[2] Yuan, Ding, et al. Be conservative: enhancing failure diagnosis with proactive logging. *Usenix Conference on Operating Systems Design and Implementation.* USENIX Association, 2012:293-306.

[3] Fu Q, Lou J G, Wang Y, et al. Execution Anomaly Detection in Distributed Systems through Unstructured Log Analysis. *IEEE International Conference on Data Mining.* IEEE, 2009:149-158..

[4] He, Pinjia, et al. Drain: An Online Log Parsing Approach with Fixed Depth Tree. *IEEE International Conference on Web Services.*IEEE, 2017:33-40.

[5] Jia, Tong, et al. LogSed: Anomaly Diagnosis through Mining Time-Weighted Control Flow Graph in Logs. *IEEE International Conference on Cloud Computing.* IEEE, 2017:447-455.

[6] Jia, Tong, et al. An Approach for Anomaly Diagnosis Based on Hybrid Graph Model with Logs for Distributed Services. *IEEE International Conference on Web Services.*IEEE, 2017:25-32.

Distributed Coloring in Sparse Graphs with Fewer Colors*

Pierre Aboulker
Laboratoire G-SCOP (CNRS, Univ. Grenoble Alpes), Grenoble, France
pierre.aboulker@grenoble-inp.fr

Marthe Bonamy
LaBRI (CNRS, Université de Bordeaux), Bordeaux, France
marthe.bonamy@labri.fr

Nicolas Bousquet
Laboratoire G-SCOP (CNRS, Univ. Grenoble Alpes), Grenoble, France
nicolas.bousquet@grenoble-inp.fr

Louis Esperet
Laboratoire G-SCOP (CNRS, Univ. Grenoble Alpes), Grenoble, France
louis.esperet@grenoble-inp.fr

ABSTRACT

This paper is concerned with efficiently coloring sparse graphs in the distributed setting with as few colors as possible. According to the celebrated Four Color Theorem, planar graphs can be colored with at most 4 colors, and the proof gives a (sequential) quadratic algorithm finding such a coloring. A natural problem is to improve this complexity in the distributed setting. Using the fact that planar graphs contain linearly many vertices of degree at most 6, Goldberg, Plotkin, and Shannon obtained a deterministic distributed algorithm coloring n-vertex planar graphs with 7 colors in $O(\log n)$ rounds. Here, we show how to color planar graphs with 6 colors in polylog(n) rounds. Our algorithm indeed works more generally in the list-coloring setting and for sparse graphs (for such graphs we improve by at least one the number of colors resulting from an efficient algorithm of Barenboim and Elkin, at the expense of a slightly worst complexity). Our bounds on the number of colors turn out to be quite sharp in general. Among other results, we show that no distributed algorithm can color every n-vertex planar graph with 4 colors in $o(n)$ rounds.

CCS CONCEPTS

• **Mathematics of computing → Graph coloring**; **Graph algorithms**; • **Theory of computation → Distributed algorithms**;

KEYWORDS

Graph coloring; distributed algorithm; maximum average degree

ACM Reference Format:
Pierre Aboulker, Marthe Bonamy, Nicolas Bousquet, and Louis Esperet. 2018. Distributed Coloring in Sparse Graphs with Fewer Colors. In *PODC '18: ACM Symposium on Principles of Distributed Computing, July 23–27, 2018, Egham, United Kingdom.* ACM, New York, NY, USA, 7 pages. https://doi.org/10.1145/3212734.3212740

*A full version of the paper is available at arXiv:1802.05582.
Partially supported by ANR Projects STINT (ANR-13-BS02-0007) and GATO (ANR-16-CE40-0009-01), and LabEx PERSYVAL-Lab (ANR-11-LABX-0025).

PODC '18, July 23–27, 2018, Egham, United Kingdom

ACM ISBN 978-1-4503-5795-1/18/07...$15.00
https://doi.org/10.1145/3212734.3212740

1 INTRODUCTION

1.1 Coloring sparse graphs

This paper is devoted to the graph coloring problem in the distributed model of computation. Graph coloring plays a central role in distributed algorithms, see the recent survey book of Barenboim and Elkin [4] for more details and further references. Most of the research so far has focused on obtaining fast algorithms for coloring graphs of maximum degree Δ with $\Delta+1$ colors, or to allow more colors in order to obtain more efficient algorithms. Our approach here is quite the opposite. Instead, we are interested in proving "best possible" results (in terms of the number of colors), in a reasonable (say polylogarithmic) round complexity. By "best possible", we mean results that match the best known existential bounds or the best known bounds following from efficient sequential algorithms. A typical example is the case of planar graphs. The famous Four Color Theorem ensures that these graphs are 4-colorable (and the proof actually yields a quadratic algorithm), but coloring them using so few colors with an efficient distributed algorithm has remained elusive. Goldberg, Plotkin, and Shannon [13] (see also [3]) obtained a deterministic distributed algorithm coloring n-vertex planar graphs with 7 colors in $O(\log n)$ rounds, but it was not known[1] whether a polylogarithmic 6-coloring algorithm exists for planar graphs.

In this paper we give a simple deterministic distributed 6-coloring algorithm for planar graphs, of round complexity $O(\log^3 n)$. In fact, our algorithm works in the more general list-coloring setting, where each vertex has its own list of k colors (not necessarily integers from 1 to k). The algorithm also works more generally for sparse graphs, and the sparseness measure we consider here is the maximum average degree of a graph (see below for precise definitions), which seems to be more suited for coloring problems than arboricity, which had been previously considered [3, 12]. While it might seem at first sight that considering list-coloring instead of coloring is of little interest in distributed algorithms, one of the objectives of this paper is to show that instead it is particularly useful. This is a critical ingredient in our proof, which would most likely not work (or not as simply) without it.

[1]In [3], it is mentioned that a parallel algorithm of [13] that 5-colors plane graphs (embedded planar graphs) can be extended to the distributed setting, but this does not seem to be correct, since the algorithm relies on edge-contractions and some clusters might correspond to connected subgraphs of diameter linear in the order of the original graph. The authors of [3] acknowledged (private communication) that consequently, the problem of coloring planar graphs with 6-colors in polylogarithmic time was still open.

To state our result more precisely, we start with a couple of definitions and classic results on graph coloring.

1.2 Definitions

A *coloring* of a graph G is an assignment of colors to the vertices of G so that adjacent vertices are assigned different colors. The *chromatic number* of G, denoted by $\chi(G)$, is the minimum integer k so that G has a coloring using colors from $1, \ldots, k$. In this paper it will also be convenient to consider the following variant of graph coloring. A family of lists $(L(v))_{v \in G}$ is said to be a *k-list-assignment* if $|L(v)| \geqslant k$ for every vertex $v \in G$. Given such a list-assignment L, we say that G is *L-list-colorable* if G has a coloring c such that for every vertex $v \in G, c(v) \in L(v)$. We also say that G is *k-list-colorable*, if for any k-list-assignement L, the graph G is L-list-colorable. By a slight abuse of notation, we will sometimes write that our algorithm *finds a k-list-coloring of G*. This should be understood as: *for any k-list-assignment L, our algorithm finds an L-list-coloring of G.*

The *choice number* of G, denoted by $\mathrm{ch}(G)$, is the minimum integer k such that G is k-list-colorable. Note that if all lists $L(v)$ are equal, then G is L-list-colorable if and only if it is $|L(v)|$-colorable, and thus $\chi(G) \leqslant \mathrm{ch}(G)$ for any graph G. On the other hand, it is well known that complete bipartite graphs (and more generally graphs with arbitrary large average degree) have arbitrary large choice number.

The *average degree* of a graph $G = (V, E)$ is defined as the average of the degrees of the vertices of G (it is equal to 0 if V is empty and to $2|E|/|V|$ otherwise). The *maximum average degree* of a graph G, denoted by $\mathrm{mad}(G)$, is the maximum of the average degrees of the subgraphs of G. The maximum average degree is a standard measure of the sparseness of a graph. Note that if a graph G has $\mathrm{mad}(G) < k$, for some integer k, then any subgraph of G contains a vertex of degree at most $k - 1$, and in particular a simple greedy algorithm shows that G has (list)-chromatic number at most k. Therefore, for any graph G, $\chi(G) \leqslant \mathrm{ch}(G) \leqslant \lfloor \mathrm{mad}(G) \rfloor + 1$. This bound can be slightly improved when G does not contain a simple obstruction (a large clique), as will be explained below.

1.3 Previous results

Most of the research on distributed coloring of sparse graphs so far [3, 12] has focused on a different sparseness parameter: The *arboricity* of a graph G, denoted by $a(G)$, is the minimum number of edge-disjoint forests into which the edges of G can be partitioned. By a classic theorem of Nash-Williams [18], we have

$$a(G) = \max \left\{ \left\lceil \frac{|E(H)|}{|V(H)|-1} \right\rceil \mid H \subseteq G, |V(H)| \geqslant 2 \right\}.$$

From this result, it is not difficult to show that for any graph G, $2a(G) - 2 \leqslant \lceil \mathrm{mad}(G) \rceil \leqslant 2a(G)$ (the lower bound is attained for graphs whose maximum average degree is an even integer).

In [3], Barenboim and Elkin gave, for any $\epsilon > 0$, a deterministic distributed algorithm coloring n-vertex graphs of arboricity a with $\lfloor (2 + \epsilon)a \rfloor + 1$ colors in $O(\frac{a}{\epsilon} \log n)$ rounds. In particular, their algorithm colors n-vertex graphs of arboricity a with $2a + 1$ colors in $O(a^2 \log n)$ rounds.

1.4 Brooks theorem, Gallai trees, and list-coloring

A classic theorem of Brooks states that any connected graph of maximum degree Δ which is not an odd cycle or a clique has chromatic number at most Δ. This improves the simple bound of $\Delta + 1$ obtained from the greedy coloring algorithm. While most of the research in coloring in the distributed computing setting has focused on $(\Delta + 1)$-coloring, Panconesi and Srinivasan [19] gave a $O(\Delta \log^3 n / \log \Delta)$ deterministic distributed algorithm that given a connected graph G of maximum degree $\Delta \geqslant 3$ finds a clique $K_{\Delta+1}$ or a Δ-coloring. In Section 2 we show how to simply derive a list-version of this result from our main result, at the cost of an increased dependence in Δ (see Corollary 2.1).

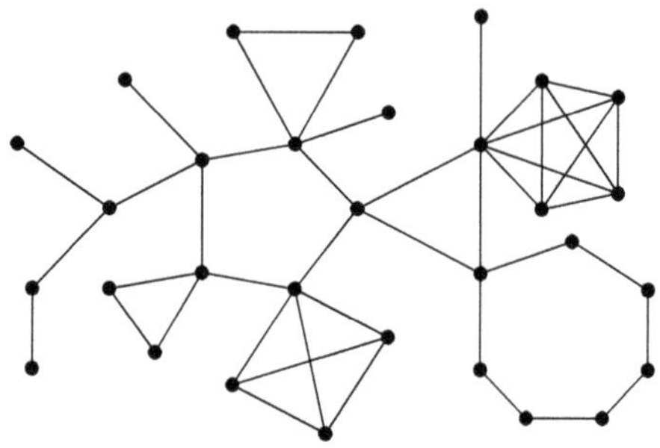

Figure 1: A Gallai tree.

A *block* of a graph G is a maximal 2-connected subgraph of G. A *Gallai tree* is a connected graph in which each block is an odd cycle or a clique, see Figure 1 for an example. Note that a tree is also a Gallai tree, since each block of a tree is an edge (i.e. a clique on two vertices). The degree of a vertex v in a graph G is denoted by $d_G(v)$. The proof of our main result is mainly based on the following classic theorem in graph theory proved independently by Borodin [5] and Erdős, Rubin, and Taylor [8], extending Brooks theorem (mentioned above) to the list-coloring setting.

THEOREM 1.1 ([5, 8]). *If a connected graph G is not a Gallai tree, then for any list-assignment L such that for every vertex $v \in G$, $|L(v)| \geqslant d_G(v)$, G is L-list-colorable.*

It is not difficult to prove that Theorem 1.1 implies Brooks theorem. We mentioned above that for any graph G, $\chi(G) \leqslant \mathrm{ch}(G) \leqslant \lfloor \mathrm{mad}(G) \rfloor + 1$. Let us now see how this can be slightly improved using Theorem 1.1 if we exclude a simple obstruction, in the spirit of Brooks theorem.

THEOREM 1.2 (FOLKLORE). *Let G be a graph and let $d = \lceil \mathrm{mad}(G) \rceil$. If $d \geqslant 3$ and G does not contain any $(d + 1)$-clique, then $\chi(G) \leqslant \mathrm{ch}(G) \leqslant d$.*

PROOF. We prove the result by induction on the number of vertices of G. We can assume that G is connected, since otherwise we can consider each connected component separately. If G contains a vertex v of degree at most $d - 1$, we remove it, color the graph by induction, and then choose for v a color that does not appear on any of its neighbors. Hence, we can assume that v has minimum degree at least d. Since G has average degree at most d, G is

d-regular. Note that the only d-regular Gallai trees (with $d \geqslant 3$) are the $(d+1)$-cliques[2], and thus it follows from Theorem 1.1 that G is d-list-colorable. □

1.5 Our results

Our main result is an efficient algorithmic counterpart of Theorem 1.2 in the LOCAL model of computation, which is standard in distributed graph algorithms. Each node of an n-vertex graph G has a unique identifier (an integer between 1 and n), and can exchange messages with its neighbors during synchronous rounds. Initially, each node only knows its own identifier, as well as n (the number of vertices) and sometimes some other parameters: in Theorem 1.3 below, each node knows its own list of d colors (in the list-coloring setting), or simply the integer d (if we are merely interested in coloring the graph with colors from 1 to d and there are no lists involved). With this information, each vertex has to output its own color in a proper coloring of the graph G. The *round complexity* of the algorithm is the number of rounds it takes for each vertex to choose a color.

Theorem 1.3 (Main result). *There is a deterministic distributed algorithm that given an n-vertex graph G, and an integer $d \geqslant \max(3, \mathrm{mad}(G))$, either finds a $(d+1)$-clique in G, or finds a d-list-coloring of G in $O(d^4 \log^3 n)$ rounds. Moreover, if every vertex has degree at most d, then the algorithm runs in $O(d^2 \log^3 n)$ rounds.*

Before we discuss some consequences of our result, let us first discuss its tightness. First, Theorem 1.3 improves the result of Barenboim and Elkin [3] mentioned above by at least one color in general, and by at least 3 colors in some cases (for instance for graphs whose maximum average degree is an even integer), and is best possible in general in terms of the number of colors (already from an existential point of view). On the other hand, the round complexity of our algorithm is slightly worst. Second, a classic result of Linial [17] showing that n-vertex paths cannot be 2-colored by a distributed algorithm using $o(n)$ rounds, also shows that we cannot omit the assumption that $d \geqslant 3$ in the statement of Theorem 1.3.

We also note that using network decompositions [20], we can replace the $O(d^4 \log^3 n)$ round complexity in Theorem 1.3 by $d^3 2^{O(\sqrt{\log n})}$, and the $O(d^2 \log^3 n)$ round complexity by $d 2^{O(\sqrt{\log n})}$ (the multiplicative factor of d is saved similarly as in [19]). These alternative bounds are not very satisfying, and in most of the applications we have in mind d is a constant anyway, so we omit the details. It remains interesting to obtain a bound on the round complexity that is sublinear in n regardless of the value of d.

In Section 2 we explore various consequences of our result. In particular, we prove that it gives a 6-(list-)coloring algorithm for planar graphs in $O(\log^3 n)$ rounds. On the other hand, we show that an efficient Four Color Theorem cannot be expected in the distributed setting.

Theorem 1.4. *No distributed algorithm can 4-color every n-vertex planar graph in $o(n)$ rounds.*

[2]This can be checked by considering a leaf block B of the Gallai tree: B is either a cycle (in which case the Gallai tree contains a vertex of degree 2) or a clique. If this clique contains a cut-vertex v, then the degree of v is larger than the degree of the other vertices of the clique, and thus the graph is not regular.

In Section 3, we give an overview of our algorithm. The proof of its correctness (and of its round complexity) follows from Lemmas 3.1 and 3.2, that are respectively proved in Sections 4 and 5.

2 CONSEQUENCES OF OUR MAIN RESULT

It was proved by Panconesi and Srinivasan [19] that there exists a deterministic distributed algorithm of round complexity $O(\frac{\Delta}{\log \Delta} \log^3 n)$ that given an n-vertex graph of maximum degree $\Delta \geqslant 3$ distinct from a clique on $\Delta + 1$ vertices, finds a Δ-coloring of G. Note that the following list-version of their result can be deduced as a simple corollary of our main result.

Corollary 2.1. *There is a deterministic distributed algorithm of round complexity $O(\Delta^2 \log^3 n)$ that given any n-vertex graph of maximum degree $\Delta \geqslant 3$, and any Δ-list-assignment L for the vertices of G, either finds an L-list-coloring of G, or finds that no such coloring exists.*

We note that Panconesi and Srinivasan [19] also gave a randomized variant of their algorithm working in $O(\frac{\log^3 n}{\log \Delta})$ rounds. In our case, it is not clear whether we can similarly avoid the multiplicative factor polynomial in Δ in a randomized version of our algorithm.

We now turn to consequences of our main result for sparse graphs (whose maximum average degree is independent of n). The *girth* of a graph G is the length of a shortest cycle in G. A simple consequence of Euler's formula is the following.

Proposition 2.2. *Every n-vertex planar graph of girth at least g has maximum average degree less than $\frac{2g}{g-2}$. In particular, planar graphs have maximum average degree less than 6, triangle-free planar graphs have maximum average degree less than 4, and planar graphs of girth at least 6 have maximum average degree less than 3.*

As a direct consequence of our main result, we obtain:

Corollary 2.3. *There is a deterministic distributed algorithm of round complexity $O(\log^3 n)$ that given an n-vertex planar graph G,*

(1) *finds a 6-(list-)coloring of G;*
(2) *finds a 4-(list-)coloring of G if G is triangle-free;*
(3) *finds a 3-(list-)coloring of G if G has girth at least 6.*

Let us discuss the tightness of our results. We first consider item 2 of Corollary 2.3, which turns out to be sharp in several ways. First, it is known that there exist triangle-free planar graphs that are not 3-list-colorable [23], so our 4-list-coloring algorithm is the best we can hope for (from an existential point of view). However, a classical theorem of Grötzsch [14] states that triangle-free planar graphs are 3-colorable, so a natural question is whether a distributed algorithm can find such a 3-coloring efficiently.

We now show that 3-coloring triangle-free planar graphs requires $\Omega(n)$ rounds, and even for rectangular grids (which are 2-colorable) finding such a 3-coloring requires $\Omega(\sqrt{n})$ rounds, which is significantly worst than our polylogarithmic complexity. The proof relies on the following observation, due to Linial [17], who first applied it to show that regular trees cannot be colored with a constant number of colors by a distributed algorithm using $o(\log n)$ rounds.

Observation 2.4. *Let G be a graph, and H be a graph in which each ball of radius at most r is isomorphic to some ball of radius at most r of G. Then no distributed algorithm can color G with less than $\chi(H)$ colors in at most r rounds.*

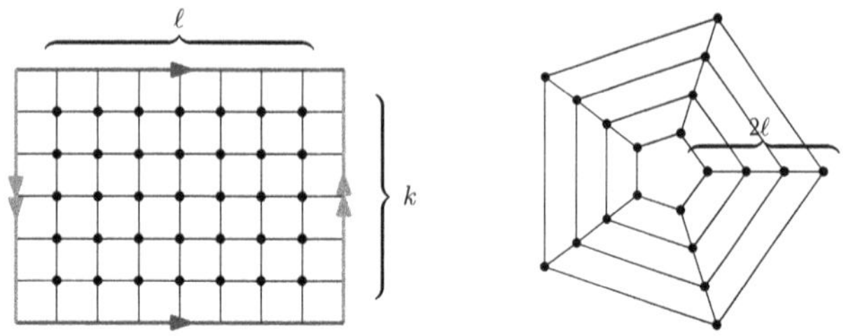

Figure 2: Left: A k by ℓ grid on the Klein bottle (the graph itself can be obtained by identifying the two blue segments (in the same direction), and the two red segments (in opposite directions)). Right: The planar triangle-free graph $H_{2\ell}$ (drawn here for $2\ell = 4$).

Let $G_{k,\ell}$ denote the k by ℓ rectangular grid on the Klein bottle (where k denotes the length of vertical cycles and ℓ denotes the length of horizontal cycles, see Figure 2, left). It was proved by Gallai [10] (see also [1, 16]) that for any k and ℓ, the graph $G_{2k+1,2\ell+1}$ is 4-chromatic. Observe that in $G_{2k+1,2k+1}$, any ball of radius less than k is isomorphic to a ball of the planar rectangular grid of size $2k+1$ by $2k+1$, and in $G_{5,2\ell+1}$, any ball of radius less than ℓ is isomorphic to a ball of a planar triangle-free graph (more precisely, a ball in the graph $H_{2\ell}$ depicted in Figure 2, right). Using Observation 2.4, this implies the following.

Theorem 2.5. *No distributed algorithm can 3-color the graph H_k in less than $k/2$ rounds. In particular, no distributed algorithm can 3-color every planar triangle-free graph on n vertices in $o(n)$ rounds.*

Theorem 2.6. *No distributed algorithm can 3-color the rectangular $k \times k$-grid in the plane in less than $k/2$ rounds. In particular, no distributed algorithm can 3-color every planar bipartite graph on n vertices in $o(\sqrt{n})$ rounds.*

It is an interesting problem to find an algorithm of round complexity matching this lower bound in the case of planar bipartite graphs.

Question 2.7. *Is there a distributed algorithm that can 3-color every n-vertex planar bipartite graph in $O(\sqrt{n})$ rounds?*

Consider now item (1) in Corollary 2.3. It is known that planar graphs are 5-list-colorable [21], so item (1) is not best possible (from an existential point of view). On the other hand, Voigt [22] proved that there exist planar graphs that are not 4-list-colorable. Fisk [9] proved that triangulations of surfaces in which all vertices have even degree except two adjacent vertices, are not 4-colorable. Such triangulations exist in the torus, see Figure 3, where the two vertices of odd degree are depicted in white. Versions of this graph on n vertices clearly exist for any $n \equiv 1 \pmod 3$, and in such a graph any ball of radius at most $\frac{n-1}{6} - 3$ induces a planar graph. Using Observation 2.4 again, this implies that no distributed algorithm

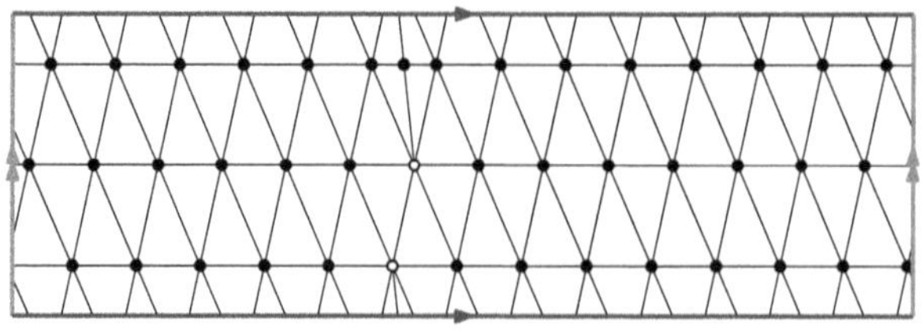

Figure 3: A toroidal triangulation that is not 4-colorable. The graph itself is obtained by identifying the two blue segments, and the two red segments.

can 4-color every planar graph on n vertices in $o(n)$ rounds, which proves Theorem 1.4. This raises the following natural question.

Question 2.8. *Is it true that there is a distributed algorithm 5-(list-)coloring planar graphs in a polylogarithmic number of rounds?*

It might be the case that the girth condition in item (3) of Corollary 2.3 is not best possible, so the following might very well have a positive answer.

Question 2.9. *Is it true that there is a distributed algorithm 3-(list-)coloring planar graphs of girth at least 5 in a polylogarithmic number of rounds?*

By the result of Linial [17] (mentioned above), stating that regular trees cannot be colored with a constant number of colors by a distributed algorithm within $o(\log n)$ rounds, there is no hope to obtain a better round complexity for the two questions above.

3 OVERVIEW OF THE PROOF OF THEOREM 1.3

We now recall the setting of Theorem 1.3. The graph G has n vertices, and maximum average degree at most d, for some integer $d \geqslant 3$. Moreover, G does not contain any clique on $d+1$ vertices (otherwise such a clique can be found in two rounds, and we are done). Any vertex v has a list $L(v)$ of d colors, and our goal is to efficiently find an L-list-coloring.

A first remark is that we can assume without loss of generality that $d \leqslant n$, since otherwise we can simply set $d := n$ in the theorem. This will be assumed implicitly throughout the proof (in fact it will only be needed towards the end of the proof of Proposition 4.1).

The proof of Theorem 1.3 goes as follows: in a polylogarithmic number of rounds, we identify some set A of vertices of G, representing a constant fraction of the vertex set, and such that any list-coloring of $G - A$ can be extended to A in a polylogarithmic number of rounds. By repeatedly removing such a set A (this can be done at most $O(\log n)$ times), we obtain a trivial graph (that can easily be colored) and then proceed to extend this coloring to each of the sets A that were removed, one by one (starting from the last one to the first one).

So the proof naturally breaks into two very different parts. In the first one, we find such a set A and show that it has linear size in n. We use purely graph theoretic arguments but we feel that some of our tools could be useful to design other distributed algorithms. In the second part, we show how to extend any coloring of $G - A$

to G in a polylogarithmic number of rounds. The analysis uses a combination of Theorem 1.1 and classic tools from distributed computing.

Let us now be more specific about the set A mentioned above. Let $c = \frac{12}{\log(6/5)}$ (this specific value will only be needed in the proof of Proposition 4.1, so anywhere else in the proof the reader can simply assume that c is any fixed constant). Given a vertex v and an integer r, the *ball centered in v of radius r*, denoted by $B^r(v)$, is the set of vertices at distance at most r from v. We will often consider balls of radius $r = \lceil c \log n \rceil$, in this case we will omit the superscript in $B^{\lceil c \log n \rceil}(v)$ and write $B(v)$ instead. Note that from now on we will omit floors and ceiling when they are not necessary in our discussions (we will write $c \log n$ instead of $\lceil c \log n \rceil$ and consider it as an integer). We will also be interested in balls within specific subgraphs of G. Given a subset R of vertices of G, $B^r_R(v)$ is the subset of vertices of G that are at distance at most r from v in $G[R]$ (the subgraph of G induced by R). Note that the ball $B^r_R(v)$ is empty if and only if $v \notin R$. Again, for convenience, we write $B_R(v)$ instead of $B_R^{c \log n}(v)$.

Any vertex of degree at most d in G is said to be *rich*, and the remaining vertices are said to be *poor*. Note that there are at most $\frac{d}{d+1} n$ poor vertices, and thus the set R of rich vertices has size at least $\frac{n}{d+1}$ (a formal proof will be provided at the end of the proof of Lemma 3.1). Our goal is to select a large set of vertices that can be easily (and efficiently) colored, given a partial coloring of the rest of the graph. Vertices v of degree at most $d-1$ certainly have this property, since their lists contain at least one more color than their degree (and then the coloring of $G - v$ can be extended). However, it might be the case that G contains few such vertices, or even no such vertex at all (if G is d-regular), and thus we also have to look for candidates in the set of vertices of degree precisely d. Indeed, we will not consider poor vertices (whose degree is at least $d+1$) as possible candidates. The ball $B_R(v)$ (as defined in the preceding paragraph) of a rich vertex v is called *the rich ball of v*. A rich vertex is said to be *happy* if its rich ball $B_R(v)$ contains a vertex of degree at most $d-1$ in G or is not a Gallai tree. Recall that this second option is equivalent to the fact that some block (2-connected component) of the subgraph of G induced by $B_R(v)$ is neither an odd cycle nor a clique. We denote by A the set of happy vertices. In Section 4, we prove the following result.

Lemma 3.1. *$|A| \geqslant \frac{n}{(3d)^3}$. Moreover, if there are no poor vertices in G, then $|A| \geqslant \frac{n}{12d+1}$.*

Our goal is then to prove that any coloring of $G - A$ can be efficiently extended to A.

Lemma 3.2. *Any L-list-coloring of $G - A$ can be extended to an L-list-coloring of G in $O(d \log^2 n)$ rounds.*

Lemma 3.2 will be proved in Section 5. In the remainder of this section, we show how to deduce Theorem 1.3 from Lemmas 3.1 and 3.2.

Proof of Theorem 1.3. Since being happy only depends on the ball of radius $c \log n$ around each vertex, the set A of happy vertices can be found in $O(\log n)$ rounds. We repeatedly remove sets $A_1, A_2, \ldots, A_k$ from G using Lemma 3.1 until G is empty. By Lemma 3.1, $k \leqslant \frac{\log n}{\log(1/(1-1/27d^3))} = O(d^3 \log n)$, and thus this part of the procedure takes $O(d^3 \log^2 n)$ rounds. If each vertex of G has degree at most d, then there are no poor vertices and it follows similarly from Lemma 3.1 that $k = O(d \log n)$ and this part of the procedure takes $O(d \log^2 n)$ rounds.

We then extend the list-coloring of the empty graph to $A_k, A_{k-1}, \ldots, A_1$ using Lemma 3.2. Each extension takes $O(d \log^2 n)$ rounds, so this part of the procedure runs in $O(kd \log^2 n) = O(d^4 \log^3 n)$ rounds. If each vertex of G has degree at most d, this part of the procedure runs in $O(kd \log^2 n) = O(d^2 \log^3 n)$ rounds. In the end, we obtain an L-list-coloring of G in $O(d^4 \log^3 n)$ rounds (or $O(d^2 \log^3 n)$ rounds if G has maximum degree at most d), as desired. This concludes the proof of Theorem 1.3. □

Observe that the proof above basically says that the round complexity in Theorem 1.3 is at most $O(\log n)$ times $O(d \log^2 n)$ (the complexity of Lemma 3.2) times $O(d^3)$ or $O(d)$ (the denominators in the bounds of Lemma 3.1). So any improvement in either of these two lemmas would yield an immediate improvement in Theorem 1.3.

4 *A* HAS LINEAR SIZE – PROOF OF LEMMA 3.1

The goal of this section is to prove that A, the set of happy vertices, has size linear in n.

Recall that a vertex is happy if it is rich (i.e. it has degree at most d) and its rich ball $B_R(v) = B_R^{c \log n}(v)$ contains a vertex of degree at most $d-1$ or is not a Gallai tree. Let $S = R \setminus A$ (here 'S' stands for 'Sad'). Note that S is the set of rich vertices whose rich ball contains only vertices of degree d (in G) and induces a Gallai tree. We will prove that S is not too large compared to A (Proposition 4.1 below), and since $R = A \cup S$ has size linear in n, this will prove Lemma 3.1.

The bulk of the proof of Lemma 3.1 is contained in the following technical proposition, whose proof is omitted here due to the lack of space (it is included in the full version of the paper).

Proposition 4.1. *There are at least $\frac{1}{12}|S|$ vertices of degree at most $d-1$ in $G[S]$.*

We are now ready to prove Lemma 3.1.

Proof of Lemma 3.1. By Proposition 4.1, there are at least $\frac{1}{12}|S|$ vertices of degree at most $d-1$ in $G[S]$. Since each vertex of S has degree d in G, this implies that there are also at least $\frac{1}{12}|S|$ edges leaving S. Let us divide these edges into two sets: $E(S,P)$, the set of edges with one end in S and the other in P, the set of poor vertices, and $E(S,A)$, the set of edges with one end in S and the other in A. Observe that since each vertex of A has degree at most d, we have $|A| \geqslant \frac{1}{d}|E(S,A)|$.

Since G has average degree at most d, we have $\sum_{v \in G}(d_G(v) - d) \leqslant 0$. Recall that P (the set of poor vertices) is precisely the set of vertices of degree at least $d+1$ in G, while A (the set of happy vertices) contains all the vertices of degree at most $d-1$ in G, and thus

$$d|A| \geqslant \sum_{v \in A}(d - d_G(v)) \geqslant \sum_{v \in P}(d_G(v) - d) \geqslant \max(|P|, |E(S,P)| - d|P|).$$

It follows that $|E(S,P)| \leqslant d|P| + d|A| \leqslant d(d+1)|A|$, and thus $|A| \geqslant \frac{1}{d(d+1)}|E(S,P)|$.

Summing up the inequalities we obtained on $|E(S, A)|$ and $|E(S, P)|$, we obtain

$$|A|(1+\frac{1}{d+1}) \geqslant |A|+\frac{1}{d+1}|A| \geqslant \frac{1}{d(d+1)}(|E(S,P)|+|E(S,A)|) \geqslant \frac{|S|/12}{d(d+1)},$$

and thus $|A| \geqslant \frac{|S|}{12d(d+2)}$.

Since G has average degree at most d, the set $R = A \cup S$ contains at least $\frac{n}{d+1}$ vertices and thus

$$|A| \geqslant \frac{n}{(d+1)(12d(d+2)+1)} \geqslant \frac{n}{(3d)^3},$$

where we used that $d \geqslant 3$ in the last inequality. This concludes the proof of the first part of Lemma 3.1.

Assume now that G has maximum degree at most d. Then P is empty, and so is $E(S, P)$. It follows that $|A| \geqslant \frac{1}{d}|E(S, A)| \geqslant \frac{1}{12d}|S|$. Since P is empty, $V(G) = R = A \cup S$ and thus $|A| \geqslant \frac{n}{12d+1}$, as desired. This concludes the proof of Lemma 3.1. □

5 THE COLORING CAN BE EXTENDED EFFICIENTLY – PROOF OF LEMMA 3.2

The goal of this section is to prove that any L-list-coloring of $G - A$ can be *efficiently* extended to A. (Actually our recoloring process might modify the colors of some vertices of $G \setminus A$). To show this, we will need the notion of an (α, β)-ruling forest, introduced by Awerbuch et al. in [2]. Given a graph H and a subset U of vertices of H, an *(α, β)-ruling forest with respect to U* is a family of vertex-disjoint rooted trees $(T_i, r_i)_{1 \leqslant i \leqslant t}$, such that

(1) each vertex of U lies in some tree T_i, and
(2) for each $1 \leqslant i < j \leqslant t$, the roots r_i and r_j are at distance at least α in H, and
(3) each rooted tree T_i has depth at most β (i.e. each vertex of T_i is at distance at most β from r_i in T_i).

Awerbuch et al. in [2] proved that a $(k, k \log n)$-ruling forest can be computed deterministically in the LOCAL model in a graph on at most n vertices in $O(k \log n)$ rounds. Note that ruling forests were also used by Panconesi and Srinivasan [19] in their "distributed" proof of Brooks theorem, but our application here is slightly different, essentially due to the fact that we have to consider a list-coloring problem rather than a coloring problem (and it is seems that their approach of switching colors cannot be applied in the list-coloring framework).

Consider a graph G', in which every vertex v starts with a list $L'(v)$ of size d, and assume that a subset U of vertices is precolored (i.e. each vertex of u is assigned a color from its list). Let H be the subgraph of G induced by the uncolored vertices (i.e. the vertices outside U), and for each $v \in H$, let $L_H(v)$ be the list obtained from $L'(v)$ by removing the colors of the precolored neighbors of v. Recall that $d_H(v)$ denotes the degree of a vertex v in H. The following simple observation will be crucial in our proof Lemma 3.2.

Observation 5.1. *For any vertex $v \in H$, $|L_H(v)| \geqslant d - d_{G'}(v) + d_H(v)$. In particular, if $d_{G'}(v) \leqslant d$ then $|L_H(v)| \geqslant d_H(v)$ and if $d_{G'}(v) \leqslant d-1$ then $|L_H(v)| \geqslant d_H(v)+1$.*

We can now proceed to the proof of Lemma 3.2.

Proof of Lemma 3.2. Recall that the vertex-set G is divided into two sets: R, the rich vertices (that have degree at most d), and P, the poor vertices (that have degree at least $d+1$) and the set R itself is divided into A (the happy vertices), and S (the set of rich vertices whose rich ball of radius $c \log n$ induces a Gallai tree and only contains vertices of degree d in G).

Consider some L-list-coloring of $G - A$, which we wish to extend to A.

Let $(T_i, r_i)_{1 \leqslant i \leqslant t}$ be a $(k, k \log n)$-ruling forest in $G[R]$ with respect to A, with $k = 2c \log n$. This ruling forest can be computed in $O(\log^2 n)$ rounds as proved in [2]. Let us denote by T the union of the vertices contained in some tree T_i. Note that T contains A (the set of vertices that are uncolored at this point), and also possibly some (colored) vertices of S. We uncolor all the vertices of $T \cap S$, and now T is precisely the set of uncolored vertices.

Let H be the subgraph of G induced by T. For each vertex $v \in T$, we start by removing from $L(v)$ the colors of the neighbors of v outside T. Let us denote by $L_H(v)$ the new list of each vertex v of H after this removal step. By construction, in order to extend the coloring of $G - A$ to A it is enough to (efficiently) find an L_H-list-coloring of H.

Since each vertex $v \in T$ has degree at most d in G, and starts with a list $L(v)$ of size d, it follows from Observation 5.1 that $|L_H(v)| \geqslant d_H(v)$. To find an L_H-list-coloring of H, we first compute a partition of H into $d+1$ stable sets $C_1, C_2, \ldots, C_{d+1}$. Since each vertex of T has degree at most d in G and thus in H, such a partition (which is exactly a proper $(d+1)$-coloring) can be computed deterministically in $O(d \log n)$ rounds [13]. Recall that each tree T_i has depth at most $k \log n = 2c \log^2 n$. We then proceed to L_H-list-color H as follows: for each i from $2c \log^2 n$ to 1, and for each j from 1 to $d+1$, we consider the vertices of C_j that are at distance precisely i from the root of their respective tree of the ruling forest (these vertices form a stable set of H and can thus be colored independently), and each of these vertices selects a color of its list L_H that does not appear on any of its colored neighbors in H. Since each such vertex v has at least one uncolored neighbor in H (its parent in the ruling forest, since we proceed from the leaves to the root), it has at most $d_H(v) - 1 \leqslant |L_H(v)| - 1$ colored neighbors and can thus select a suitable color from its list.

This procedure takes $O(d \log^2 n)$ steps, and all that remains to do is to find suitable colors for the roots r_i, $1 \leqslant i \leqslant t$. By the definition of a ruling forest, each root r_i lies in A, and thus the ball $B_R(r_i)$ (of radius $c \log n$) contains a vertex of degree at most $d-1$ or is not a Gallai tree. Moreover, it also follows from the defintion of our ruling forest that any two balls $B_R(r_i)$ and $B_R(r_j)$ are disjoint and have no edges between them. We then uncolor each of the balls $B_R(r_i)$ completely, and remove from the lists of the vertices inside these balls the colors assigned to their neighbors outside the balls. As before, it follows from Observation 5.1 that the list of remaining colors of each vertex v is as least as large as the number of uncolored neighbors of v. Moreover, if v has degree at most $d-1$ in G, the list of remaining colors for v is strictly larger than the number of uncolored neighbors of v. It thus follows from the definition of A that each vertex r_i can apply Theorem 1.1 to its ball $B_R(r_i)$, and thus extend the current L_H-list-coloring to these balls in $k \log n = 2c \log^2 n = O(\log^2 n)$ additional steps. This concludes the proof of Lemma 3.2. □

6 CONCLUSION

In Theorem 1.3, every vertex has the same number of colors in its list. However, as seen in Theorem 1.1, in the list-coloring setting, some results can be obtained when vertices have a varying number of colors. Indeed, many distributed $(\Delta + 1)$-coloring algorithms work in the more general $(\deg + 1)$-list-coloring setting, where each vertex v is given a list of $d(v) + 1$ colors, and the complexity of this specific problem plays an important role in the most efficient distributed $(\Delta + 1)$-coloring algorithms to date [6, 15].

There are obvious obstacles to an efficient version of Theorem 1.1 in the distributed setting: we cannot apply it to paths in $o(n)$ rounds. Paths are not the only difficult case to circumvent, as one could attach a clique to every vertex on a path and face similar issues. Therefore, we need to assume that every vertex v has a list $L(v)$ of size $d(v)$, except if $d(v) \leqslant 2$ or the neighbors of v form a clique, in which cases v has a list $L(v)$ of size $d(v)+1$. Such a list-assignment L is said to be *nice*. The same algorithm and proof go through merely by replacing d with the size of the given vertex' list. Indeed, every vertex is rich, and thus we obtain a complexity of $O(\Delta^2 \log^3 n)$ rounds.

THEOREM 6.1. *There is a deterministic distributed algorithm that given an n-vertex graph G of maximum degree Δ, and a nice list-assignment L for the vertices of G, finds an L-list-coloring of G in $O(\Delta^2 \log^3 n)$ rounds.*

We note that this also implies Corollary 2.1 and is another way to refine the result by Panconesi and Srinivasan [19] (which is faster by a factor of $\Delta \log \Delta$).

RECENT DEVELOPMENTS

Shortly after the submission of our manuscript, two related papers appeared on arXiv.

In [11], the authors were interested in d-coloring non-complete graphs of maximum degree at most d (this corresponds to the setting of our Corollary 2.1). They gave a deterministic distributed algorithm with round complexity $O(d^{1/2} \log^2 n)$ (improving our bound of $O(d^2 \log^3 n)$), and a randomized distributed algorithm with round complexity $d^{1/2+o(1)}(\log \log n)^2$. Using known lower bounds on the round complexity of the deterministic version of the problem (essentially $\Omega(\log n)$), this implies an exponential separation between the deterministic and randomized versions of the problem.

In [7], the authors were interested specifically in planar graphs. They gave deterministic distributed algorithms to 4-color triangle-free planar graphs and 6-color planar graphs in $O(\log n)$ rounds (improving our round complexity of $O(\log^3 n)$ from Corollary 2.3). They also gave a different proof of Theorem 1.4, based on similar ideas.

ACKNOWLEDGMENTS

The authors would like to thank Leonid Barenboim and Michael Elkin for the discussion about the parallel 5-coloring algorithm for planar graphs of [13] mentioned in [3], Jukka Suomela for providing helpful references, and Cyril Gavoille for his comments and suggestions.

REFERENCES

[1] D. Archdeacon, J. Hutchinson, A. Nakamoto, S. Negami, and K. Ota. 2001. Chromatic numbers of quadrangulations on closed surfaces. *J. Graph Theory* 37, 2 (2001), 100–114. https://doi.org/10.1002/jgt.1005

[2] B. Awerbuch, M. Luby, A. V. Goldberg, and S. A. Plotkin. 1989. Network decomposition and locality in distributed computation. In *30th Annual Symposium on Foundations of Computer Science.* 364–369. https://doi.org/10.1109/SFCS.1989.63504

[3] L. Barenboim and M. Elkin. 2010. Sublogarithmic distributed MIS algorithm for sparse graphs using Nash-Williams decomposition. *Distributed Computing* 22, 5 (01 Aug 2010), 363–379. https://doi.org/10.1007/s00446-009-0088-2

[4] L. Barenboim and M. Elkin. 2013. *Distributed Graph Coloring: Fundamentals and Recent Developments.* Morgan & Claypool. 171– pages. https://doi.org/10.2200/S00520ED1V01Y201307DCT011

[5] O. Borodin. 1977. Criterion of chromaticity of a degree prescription. In *Abstracts of IV All-Union Conf. on Th. Cybernetics.* 127–128.

[6] Y.-J. Chang, W. Li, and S. Pettie. 2018. An optimal distributed $(\Delta + 1)$-coloring algorithm?. In *Proceedings 50th ACM Symposium on Theory of Computing (STOC).*

[7] S. Chechik and D. Mukhtar. 2018. Optimal Distributed Coloring Algorithms for Planar Graphs in the LOCAL model. *CoRR* abs/1804.00137 (2018). arXiv:1804.00137 http://arxiv.org/abs/1804.00137

[8] P. Erdős, A. L. Rubin, and H. Taylor. 1980. Choosability in graphs. In *Proceedings of the West Coast Conference on Combinatorics, Graph Theory and Computing (Humboldt State Univ., Arcata, Calif., 1979) (Congress. Numer., XXVI).* Utilitas Math., Winnipeg, Man., 125–157.

[9] S. Fisk. 1978. The nonexistence of colorings. *J. Combin. Theory Ser. B* 24, 2 (1978), 247–248. https://doi.org/10.1016/0095-8956(78)90028-X

[10] T. Gallai. 1963. Kritische Graphen I. *Magyar Tud. Akad. Mat. Kutakó Int. Közl* 8 (1963), 165–192.

[11] M. Ghaffari, J. Hirvonen, F. Kuhn, and Y. Maus. 2018. Improved Distributed Δ-Coloring. *CoRR* abs/1803.03248 (2018). arXiv:1803.03248 http://arxiv.org/abs/1803.03248

[12] M. Ghaffari and C. Lymouri. 2017. Simple and Near-Optimal Distributed Coloring for Sparse Graphs. In *31st International Symposium on Distributed Computing, DISC 2017, October 16-20, 2017, Vienna, Austria.* 20:1–20:14. https://doi.org/10.4230/LIPIcs.DISC.2017.20

[13] A. V. Goldberg, S. A. Plotkin, and G. E. Shannon. 1988. Parallel Symmetry-Breaking in Sparse Graphs. *SIAM J. Discrete Math.* 1, 4 (1988), 434–446. https://doi.org/10.1137/0401044

[14] H. Grötzsch. 1959. Ein Dreifarbensatz für dreikreisfreie Netze auf der Kugel. *Wiss. Z. Martin-Luther-Univ. Halle-Wittenberg Math.-Natur. Reihe* 8 (1959), 109–120.

[15] D. G. Harris, J. Schneider, and H.-H. Su. 2016. Distributed $(\Delta + 1)$-coloring in sublogarithmic rounds. In *Proceedings of the 48th Annual ACM SIGACT Symposium on Theory of Computing, STOC 2016, Cambridge, MA, USA, June 18-21, 2016.* 465–478. https://doi.org/10.1145/2897518.2897533

[16] S. Klavzar and B. Mohar. 1995. The chromatic numbers of graph bundles over cycles. *Discrete Math.* 138, 1-3 (1995), 301–314. https://doi.org/10.1016/0012-365X(94)00212-2

[17] N. Linial. 1992. Locality in Distributed Graph Algorithms. *SIAM J. Comput.* 21, 1 (1992), 193–201. https://doi.org/10.1137/0221015

[18] C. St.J. A. Nash-Williams. 1964. Decomposition of Finite Graphs Into Forests. *J. London Math.Soc.* 1, 1 (1964), 12–12. https://doi.org/10.1112/jlms/s1-39.1.12

[19] A. Panconesi and A. Srinivasan. 1995. The Local Nature of Delta-Coloring and its Algorithmic Applications. *Combinatorica* 15, 2 (1995), 255–280. https://doi.org/10.1007/BF01200759

[20] A. Panconesi and A. Srinivasan. 1996. On the Complexity of Distributed Network Decomposition. *J. Algorithms* 20, 2 (1996), 356–374. https://doi.org/10.1006/jagm.1996.0017

[21] C. Thomassen. 1994. Every planar graph is 5-choosable. *J. Combin. Theory Ser. B* 62, 1 (1994), 180–181. https://doi.org/10.1006/jctb.1994.1062

[22] M. Voigt. 1993. List colourings of planar graphs. *Discrete Math.* 120, 1-3 (1993), 215–219. https://doi.org/10.1016/0012-365X(93)90579-I

[23] M. Voigt. 1995. A not 3-choosable planar graph without 3-cycles. *Discrete Math.* 146, 1-3 (1995), 325–328. https://doi.org/10.1016/0012-365X(94)00180-9

Improved Distributed Delta-Coloring

Mohsen Ghaffari
ETH Zürich
Zürich
ghaffari@inf.ethz.ch

Juho Hirvonen[*,†]
University of Freiburg
Freiburg
juho.hirvonen@cs.uni-freiburg.de

Fabian Kuhn[†]
University of Freiburg
Freiburg
kuhn@cs.uni-freiburg.de

Yannic Maus[†]
University of Freiburg
Freiburg
yannic.maus@cs.uni-freiburg.de

ABSTRACT

We present a randomized distributed algorithm that computes a Δ-coloring in any non-complete graph with maximum degree $\Delta \geq 4$ in $O(\log \Delta) + 2^{O(\sqrt{\log \log n})}$ rounds, as well as a randomized algorithm that computes a Δ-coloring in $O((\log \log n)^2)$ rounds when $\Delta \in [3, O(1)]$. Both these algorithms improve on an $O(\log^3 n / \log \Delta)$-round algorithm of Panconesi and Srinivasan [STOC'1993], which has remained the state of the art for the past 25 years. Moreover, the latter algorithm gets (exponentially) closer to an $\Omega(\log \log n)$ round lower bound of Brandt et al. [STOC'16].

CCS CONCEPTS

• **Mathematics of computing** → **Graph coloring**; • **Theory of computation** → **Distributed algorithms**;

KEYWORDS

distributed computing; distributed graph algorithms; graph coloring

ACM Reference Format:
Mohsen Ghaffari, Juho Hirvonen, Fabian Kuhn[†], and Yannic Maus[†]. 2018. Improved Distributed Delta-Coloring. In *PODC '18: ACM Symposium on Principles of Distributed Computing, July 23–27, 2018, Egham, United Kingdom.* ACM, New York, NY, USA, 10 pages. https://doi.org/10.1145/3212734.3212764

1 INTRODUCTION AND RELATED WORK

This paper presents faster distributed algorithms, in the LOCAL model, for computing a Δ-coloring of any non-clique graph with maximum degree $\Delta \geq 3$. Moreover, we also provide certain structural results on the locality of the Δ-coloring problem. To formally present our results and put them in the context of the area, let us start with recalling the model.

[*]Supported by ERC Grant No. 336495 (ACDC).
[†]Supported by Ulla Tuominen Foundation.

PODC '18, July 23–27, 2018, Egham, United Kingdom

ACM ISBN 978-1-4503-5795-1/18/07...$15.00
https://doi.org/10.1145/3212734.3212764

The LOCAL *Model of distributed computing [22, 28].* The graph is abstracted as an n-node network $G = (V, E)$ with maximum degree at most Δ. Communications happen in synchronous rounds. Per round, each node can send one (unbounded size) message to each of its neighbors. At the end, each node should know its own part of the output, e.g., its own color.

1.1 Background and State of the Art

Graph coloring—assigning colors to the vertices of the graph such that no two adjacent vertices have the same color—has been a central problem in the study of distributed graph algorithms. We refer to the *Distributed Graph Coloring* book by Barenboim and Elkin [4].

Much of the focus in this area has been on computing a coloring with $\Delta+1$ colors. Notice that any graph has a $(\Delta+1)$ coloring, which can be computed via a trivial sequential greedy method. Hence, in a sense, distributed $\Delta + 1$ coloring algorithms can all be viewed as attempts at parallelizing this greedy method. We are getting a better and better understanding of the complexity of this problem, see e.g., the very recent work of Chang et al. [12], which provides a $2^{O(\sqrt{\log \log n})}$-round randomized algorithm for $(\Delta + 1)$-coloring, and the references therein.

On the other hand, Δ-coloring is a problem of a very different nature. By a beautiful result of Brooks from 1941 [10], every connected graph admits a Δ coloring, unless it is exactly a complete graph or an odd cycle. The proof is of course far less trivial compared to that of $(\Delta + 1)$-coloring. See the 1975 work of Lovász [23] for a simplified proof, which also supplies a polynomial-time centralized algorithm for computing a Δ-coloring.

Why should we care about Δ-coloring? General Aspects. One can argue that this single color of difference between Δ-coloring and $(\Delta + 1)$-coloring is not relevant in practice. While that is probably true, we believe that there is a strong enough theoretical interest in investigating Δ-coloring. We view Δ-coloring as a clean and classic graph problem which reaches just outside the problems that we understand, and thus hopefully enables us to extend our understanding of the LOCAL model and to develop new algorithmic tools and techniques for it. The study of Δ-coloring has previously provided theoretical insight: (1) In the existential sense, Brooks' theorem and proofs of it are widely studied and covered throughout graph theory textbooks (see e.g., [25, Theorem 1.4] and [8, Theorem

14.4]), while $(\Delta + 1)$-coloring is usually passed over as a triviality. (2) There is a sizable literature on sequential and also parallel (PRAM) algorithms for computing (Δ) colorings. However, the sequential variant of $(\Delta+1)$-coloring is again ignored as being a mere triviality. Moreover, the study of $(\Delta + 1)$-coloring in the PRAM model effectively stopped with the MIS algorithms of Luby [24] and Alon et al. [2], which led to an $O(\log n)$-round algorithm for $(\Delta + 1)$-coloring.

We also note that the relation between $(\Delta + 1)$-coloring and Δ-coloring is similar to the relation between the two problems of $\Delta(1+o(1))$-coloring and $(\Delta + 1)$-coloring. One can argue that practically both are equally useful. However, the former can be solved easily in $2^{O(\sqrt{\log\log n})}$ rounds using methods of Barenboim et al. [6], while there is still ongoing research on $(\Delta + 1)$-coloring [12, 21], which only very recently led to a $2^{O(\sqrt{\log\log n})}$-round algorithm [12].

Why should we care about Δ-coloring? Technical Distributed Aspects. A concrete way of pointing out the difference between the two problems of Δ-coloring and $(\Delta + 1)$-coloring is as follows: any partial coloring of vertices with $\Delta + 1$ colors can be extended to a full coloring. However, this is not true for Δ-coloring: we cannot extend any partial Δ-coloring to a full coloring without changing the colors of some of the already colored vertices. This issue is one of the roots of our interest in understanding the complexity of this problem.

More concretely, many of the fast randomized algorithm for local graph problems developed over the past few years rely on the so-called *shattering* technique [6, 12, 14, 17, 20, 21]. In a rough sense, this method performs some randomized step which computes a partial solution such that the remaining part of the problem is made of several (disconnected) components, each of which is small, e.g., think of size poly$(\log n)$. Then, one can solve these smaller connected components using deterministic algorithms for graphs of size poly$(\log n)$. A crucial part here is that the partial solution is such that one can readily extend it to a full solution, in fact independently in each component, without needing to alter the already computed partial solution. The problem of Δ-coloring gives us one clean local problem that reaches outside this circle. In particular, it is not clear if one can do shattering for Δ-coloring, i.e., it is not clear whether there is a way of computing a partial Δ-coloring such that the remaining components are small and they can be colored on their own without altering the already colored part.

Furthermore, in contrast to $(\Delta + 1)$-coloring, Δ-coloring has an $\omega(\log^* n)$ lower bound, even for constant-degree graphs [9, 11]. The nature of this problem is very different from $(\Delta + 1)$-coloring which can be computed in $O(\log^* n)$ rounds in bounded degree graphs. Recently, in the context of lower bounds for the *Lovász Local Lemma problem*, Brandt et al. [9] proved that $\Omega(\log\log n)$-rounds are needed by any randomized Δ-coloring algorithm, even in constant-degree graphs. These results led to two problems which exhibit an exponential separation between their randomized and deterministic complexity. Sinkless orientation has an $\Omega(\log\log n)$ randomized lower bound [9] and an $\Omega(\log n)$ deterministic lower bound [9, 11], with matching randomized and deterministic upper bounds [20]. The other problem is Δ-coloring, which also has an $\Omega(\log\log n)$ randomized lower bound [9] and an $\Omega(\log n)$ deterministic lower bound [11]; however, finding matching upper bounds has remained mostly open.

State of the Art for distributed Δ-coloring. Panconesi and Srinivasan gave a randomized distributed algorithm for computing a Δ-coloring in $O(\log^3 n/\log\Delta)$ rounds [26, 27]. They also provided a deterministic variant of their algorithm with complexity $O(\Delta\log^2 n)$. Recently, Aboulker et al. [1] gave a more general algorithm for d-list coloring graphs of maximum average degree d in time $O(\Delta^4\log^3 n)$. In the special case of trees of large enough maximum degree, Chang et al. [11] give an $O(\log\log n)$-round randomized algorithm for computing a Δ-coloring. This, combined with their deterministic lower bound $\Omega(\log n)$ [11], gives an exponential separation on trees. Our algorithms establish this separation in the general bounded-degree case.

1.2 Our Results

Our first result is tailored to Δ-coloring constant-degree graphs.

Theorem 1. *There is a randomized distributed algorithm that, in any non-complete graph with maximum degree $\Delta \geq 3$, computes a Δ-coloring in $O\left(\sqrt{\Delta\log\Delta}\cdot\log^*\Delta\cdot\log^2\log n\right)$ rounds, w.h.p.**

Theorem 1 immediately implies an $O\big((\log\log n)^2\big)$ round algorithm for constant-degree graphs.

Corollary 2. *There is a randomized distributed algorithm that, in any non-complete graph G with maximum degree $\Delta \in [3, O(1)]$, computes a Δ-coloring of G in $O((\log\log n)^2)$ rounds, w.h.p..*

We comment that the condition of $\Delta \geq 3$ is necessary as 2-coloring graphs with $\Delta = 2$ needs $\Omega(n)$ rounds, even if possible, e.g., in the case of an even cycle [22, 26]. The round complexity of Corollary 2 gets significantly closer to the $\Omega(\log\log n)$ round lower bound of Brandt et al. [9]. Even in constant-degree graphs, the previous best known bound was the $O(\log^2 n)$-round algorithm of Panconesi and Srinivasan [26, 27].

Our second result applies to all graphs with $\Delta \geq 4$ and improves on the $O(\log^3 n/\log\Delta)$ round complexity of Panconesi and Srinivasan [26, 27]:

Theorem 3. *There is a randomized distributed algorithm that, in any non-complete graph $G = (V, E)$ with maximum degree $\Delta \geq 4$, computes a Δ-coloring in $O(\log\Delta) + 2^{O(\sqrt{\log\log n})}$ rounds, w.h.p.*

We also improve the deterministic complexity of Δ-coloring for graphs with $\Delta = 2^{o(\sqrt{\log n})}$.

Theorem 4 (Deterministic Δ-coloring). *Non-clique graphs of maximum degree $\Delta \geq 3$ can deterministically be Δ-colored in $O\big(\sqrt{\Delta}\cdot\log^{-3/2}\Delta\cdot\log^*\Delta\cdot\log^2 n\big)$ rounds.*

Note that Theorem 4 is close to the $\Omega(\log_\Delta n)$ deterministic lower bound of [11] when $\Delta = O(1)$.

*As standard, we use the phrase *with high probability* (w.h.p.) to indicate that an event happens with probability $1 - 1/n^c$ for a desirably large constant $c \geq 2$

1.3 Our Methods

Our algorithms are based on a structural result that essentially says that either a graph is easy to Δ-color locally, or it expands locally. This also yields a new proof of the distributed Brooks' Theorem by Panconesi and Srinivasan.

Theorem 5 (Distributed Brooks' Theorem). *Let G be a graph that is not a clique with maximum degree $\Delta \geq 3$, and let G be Δ-colored except for one node v. Now G can be Δ-colored by fixing the coloring inside the $(2\log_{\Delta-1} n)$-neighborhood of v.*

Our algorithms are based on a *layering technique*. In this technique we carefully choose a *base layer* $B_0 \subseteq V$ that is easy to color, and layers $B_1, \ldots, B_s$ where B_i consists of the nodes in distance i to B_0. To Δ-color all layers one can iteratively color the layers in *reverse order* while always respecting the already fixed colors. To Δ-color layer $B_i, i \neq 0$ we solve list coloring on the graph $G[B_i]$. Lists are of size $(\deg+1)$ as each node has an uncolored neighbor on a lower index layer. At the end layer B_0 is (usually) colored with different techniques.

The best way to understand the technique is the algorithm for Theorem 4. There the base layer B_0 consists of the nodes of a ruling set of G with large enough distance between nodes. The ruling property of B_0 implies that we only need few layers to cover the whole graph and due to their large distance the nodes in B_0 can be colored independently with Theorem 5.

In our algorithms we find such layers and remove them from the graph. Let H denote the *graph of remaining nodes*. In the algorithm explained above H is empty. In our randomized algorithms the layers do not always cover the whole graph and thus H might not be empty. However, the base layer is chosen such that our structural results (cf. Section 2.2) show that H expands: In particular, we identify all *small* node-induced subgraphs that are colorable regardless of colors outside the subgraphs, compute a ruling set of these subgraphs and put their nodes in the base layer B_0. Then the remaining graph H does not have any small subgraphs that are easy to color and our structural results show that H has to expand. We leverage the expansion by randomly placing *'slack'* in the graph, i.e., so called T-nodes and by removing – again with the layering technique – all nodes that find slack close by. Due to the expansion we can show that the probability to remain after the slack placement is $1/n^c$ for constant Δ, and $1/\operatorname{poly}(\Delta)$ for a suitable polynomial. In the second case standard shattering techniques (cf. Lemma 18) show that only *small* connected components remain which we color with a similar layering technique.

In the end we color the removed layers in reverse order via $(\deg+1)$ list colorings as explained in the layering technique. The base layer B_0 can be colored fast by definition as it consists of independent small and easy colorable subgraphs.

We emphasize that — to the best of our knowledge — our shattering is different from all previous shattering algorithms. Previous shattering algorithms compute a partial solution to shatter the graph into small unsolved components which are then solved to complete the partial solution. Here, the nodes in the small components are the last nodes to compute their output. Our algorithms shatter in a fundamentally different way. We shatter the graph by removing nodes from it. The nodes in remaining components are the first to compute their output. Only afterwards we add the removed nodes to the graph and let them compute their output last.

All missing proofs can be found in the full version [18].

2 GRAPH COLORABILITY AND STRUCTURAL RESULTS

In this section we study structural properties of graphs that are *not* degree-list colorable, at least locally. We will show several structural results about such graphs, which essentially tell that these graphs must expand exponentially. This will lead to a simplified proof of the "distributed" Brooks' theorem due to Panconesi and Srinivasan [27] in Section 2.3.

2.1 Definitions

Definition 6 (degree-choosability). A graph G is *degree-choosable*, if for every assignment of lists L, such that $|L(v)| \geq \deg(v)$ for all v, there exists a proper coloring of G with colors from L.

Definition 7 (Gallai-trees). A graph is a *Gallai-tree* if all of its maximal 2-connected components are either cliques or odd cycles.

It is known that Gallai-trees are exactly those graphs which are not degree-choosable.

Theorem 8 ([13, 30]). *A graph is not degree-choosable if and only if it is a Gallai-tree.*

Now, consider the problem of Δ-coloring. Assume that we color the graph partially but leave a 2-connected subgraph that is neither a clique nor an odd cycle uncolored. Then the coloring can be completed in this subgraph due to Theorem 8. These 2-connected subgraphs are called *degree-choosable components*.

Definition 9 (degree-choosable component). A node-induced subgraph is a *degree-choosable component* if it is 2-connected and not a clique nor an odd cycle.

We often write *DCC* instead of degree choosable component and the usual definitions for graphs can be extended to degree-choosable components. For example, the *diameter* of a degree-choosable component is the diameter of the node-induced subgraph.

A connected graph is a *nice graph* if it is neither a path, nor a cycle, nor a clique [27]. All nice graphs are Δ-colorable and we assume that all graphs throughout the paper are nice graphs.

A T-*node* is a node with two neighbors with the same color. In a partially colored graph, node u is a T-*node of* v if u is a T-node and there is an uncolored path from u to v.

2.2 Structure of Graphs with no Small Degree-Choosable Components

In this section we study graphs with no small degree-choosable components. Our goal is to prove that if such graphs are locally regular (and thus not easy to color locally), then these graphs must expand. Our general tool is to count the number of nodes in breadth-first search trees inside these graphs. Given a BFS tree $\mathrm{BFS}(v)$ rooted at node v of a graph G, we denote by $B_t(v)$ the set of nodes at distance t from v in this tree.

Lemma 10 (Unique BFS tree). *Let G be a graph with no degree-choosable components of radius r or less. The depth-r BFS tree rooted at an arbitrary $v \in V(G)$ is unique. In particular, any node $u \neq v$ on level $t \leq r$ has exactly one edge to the nodes on level $t-1$ of the BFS tree.*

Proof of Lemma 10. It is immediate that the zero and depth one BFS trees are unique. For larger depth consider the following proof by contradiction. For $t < r$ assume that u and u' are two nodes on the t-th level of the BFS tree that connect to the same node $w \notin B_{t-1} \cup B_t$, i.e., we assume that the next level of the BFS tree cannot be built uniquely. Then w is on level $t+1$. Let v' be the least common ancestor of u and u'. Then there is the even cycle $\{w, u'\}, \text{path}(u', v'), \text{path}(v', u), \{u, w\}$ that does not induce a clique as the nodes u, w, u' and w' lie on three different levels, a contradiction. □

For a node u in a BFS tree let $d(u)$ denote the number of children of u in the BFS tree.

Lemma 11 (BFS expansion lemma). *Let G be a graph without any DCC of radius at most r and $BFS(v)$ the unique depth-r BFS tree rooted at some node $v \in V(G)$. Let u' be a node of $BFS(v)$ with $\deg(u') \geq 3$ and u its immediate ancestor. Then $d(u) + d(u') \geq \min\{\deg(u), \deg(u')\}$ holds.*

For two nodes u, w of a BFS tree let $P(u, w)$ denote the unique path from u to w in the BFS tree.

Proof of Lemma 11. Let u be on some level $j \leq r-1$ of the BFS tree and u' on level $j+1 \leq r$. If $u = v$ the statement holds trivially as $d(u) = \deg(u)$. So assume that $u \neq v$. Due to the uniqueness of the BFS tree (cf. Lemma 10) $u \neq v$ has a single neighbor on level $j-1$ and $\deg(u)-1$ neighbors on level j and $j+1$. Similarly u is the only neighbor of u' on level j. For two nodes u, u' of the BFS tree let $P(u, u')$ denote the unique path in the BFS tree between u and u'. Let $\alpha = \min\{\deg(u), \deg(u')\}$. The result holds if $d(u) \geq \alpha$. We consider two cases for $d(u) < \alpha$.

Case $d(u) = \alpha - 1$: Assume that u' has one neighbor u'' in $N(u)$. We show that u' does not have a neighbor on its level that is not connected to u. So assume that u' also has a neighbor w on level $j+1$ that is not a child of u. Let v' denote the last common ancestor of u' and w in the BFS tree. The subgraph induced by the union of $\{u', w\} \cup \{u', u''\} \cup \{u, u''\} \cup \{\} \cup P(v', w) \cup P(v', u)$ is a DCC of radius at most r, a contradiction. Thus if, u' has one neighbor in $N(u)$ it has at most $\alpha - 2$ neighbors on its own level and we have $d(u') \geq \deg(u') - 1 - (\alpha - 2) = \deg(u') - \alpha + 1$. This implies $d(u) + d(u') \geq \alpha$.

Now assume that u' has no neighbor in $N(u)$. We show that it can have at most one neighbor on its own level. Assume that it has two neighbors w, w' on its own level. Let v' denote the last common ancestor of w and w'. Then the union of edges $P(v, w) \cup \{w, u'\} \cup \{u', w'\} \cup P(w', v)$ forms an even cycle that does not induce a clique, a contradiction. In this case we have $d(u') \geq \deg(u') - 2 \geq 1$ where the last inequality holds due to $\deg(u') \geq 3$. This implies $d(u) + d(u') \geq \alpha$.

Case $d(u) < \alpha - 1$: Because $d(u) < \deg(u) - 1$ node u must have a neighbor on level j that we denote with w. We first prove the following subclaim.

Claim: Node u' has no neighbor on level $j+1$ which is not connected to u.

Proof. Assume by contradiction that such a neighbor denoted with w' exists. Note that the edge $\{w, w'\}$ does not exist because otherwise the nodes u, u', w' and w would form a 4-cycle which does not induce a clique as $\{u, w'\} \notin E$.

Let v' be the last common ancestor of u, w, u' and w'. Then $\{u', w'\}, P_{w'v'}, P_{v'w}, \{w, u\}, \{u, u'\}$ forms an even cycle. The path $P_{w'v'}$ neither goes through w nor through u as the edges $\{w, w'\}$ and $\{u, w'\}$ do not exist. Thus the even cycle actually is a proper cycle and does not collapse. Furthermore it does not induce a clique as the nodes u, u', w and w' lie on three different levels of the BFS tree. Thus it induces a short even cycle, i.e., a DCC with radius at most r, a contradiction. □

Due to the claim all neighbors of u' in G that are on the same level as u' in the BFS tree are also connected to u in the BFS tree. As u has at most $d(u)$ children u' has at most $d(u) - 1$ neighbors on the same level and one neighbor in the level above. This implies $d(u') \geq \deg(u') - 1 - (d(u) - 1) = \deg(u') - d(u)$. That is, $d(u) + d(u') \geq \deg(u') \geq \alpha$. □

Informally, this lemma holds because if there are too many edges inside the local neighborhood of a node, then these edges must create a degree-choosable component.

Marking process. In our algorithms we apply the following marking process. Each node *selects* itself independently and uniformly at random with some probability p. Then, if there is another selected node within distance b (the *backoff distance*), the node unselects itself. Otherwise it picks two non-adjacent neighbors and colors them with color *one*. We call these neighbors *marked*. The selected node becomes a T-node. The following lemma shows that if we apply the marking process, the graph of the unmarked nodes expands deterministically.

Lemma 12. *Let $\Delta \geq 4$ and $G = (V, E)$ be a graph such that G does not contain any DCCs of radius at most r, for an even r. Apply the marking process to G with $b = 6$ and remove all marked nodes to obtain graph H. Consider an arbitrary node $v \in V(H)$. If $\Delta - 1 \leq \deg(u) \leq \Delta$ for each $u \in N_r(v)$, then the r-hop BFS tree around node $v \in V$ has at least $(\Delta - 2)^{r/2}$ nodes on level r.*

The proof is based on the previous Lemma 11. Due to the backoff distance b marked nodes cannot exist too close to each other if they do not form a T-node. Thus for every node on a level of the BFS tree that is blocked from expanding due to a marked node, there are many other nodes that are not blocked. We show that expansion also holds for $\Delta = 3$ if the backoff distance b between selected nodes is increased to 12. These proofs appear in the full version.

2.3 A Simplified Proof for the Distributed Brooks' Theorem

Panconesi and Srinivasan proved a distributed version of Brooks' Theorem (cf. Theorem 5). The goal of this section is to provide a simplified proof of the result. We begin by observing that if a graph does not have any small degree-choosable components, it is locally expanding. This result is easier to prove than Lemma 12 as it does not include the marking process.

Lemma 13. *Let G be a graph and $v \in V(G)$ be a node such that inside the r-radius neighborhood of v there are no degree-choosable components and every node has degree Δ. Then for each even r there are at least $(\Delta - 1)^{r/2}$ nodes at distance r from v.*

Now we can use previous lemmas to show that the uncolored node in the statement of Theorem 5 can fix its color as it sees a degree-choosable component or a node of degree $< \Delta$ inside its $O(\log_\Delta n)$-neighborhood.

Lemma 14. *Let G be a graph with maximum degree $\Delta \geq 3$. The $(2\log_{\Delta-1} n)$-neighborhood of any node contains a degree-choosable component or it contains a node of degree $< \Delta$.*

Proof. Fix a node $v \in V(G)$ and assume that its $r = 2\log_{\Delta-1} n$ neighborhood does not contain a degree-choosable component and that nodes in this neighborhood have degree Δ. By Lemma 13, the BFS tree has $|B_r(v)| \geq (\Delta - 1)^{r/2} \geq n$ nodes. Therefore the BFS tree cannot expand, and there is an edge to a lower level of BFS(v) from $B_r(v)$, or there is a node of degree $< \Delta$ in $B_r(v)$. □

Proof of Theorem 5. Let c denote the partial coloring G, with $c(v) = \bot$. We say that v has a *token*. We can always do the following operation: let u be an arbitrary neighbor of v. If v does not have a free color, that is, all of its Δ neighbors have Δ different colors, then we can move the token to u and color the node v with color $c(u)$. If v has a free color, it can choose that color and the token is eliminated. Now, if the $(2\log_{\Delta-1} n)$-neighborhood of v contains a node of smaller degree, we can move the token to that node, and it is guaranteed to have a free color. Now assume that no such node exists. By Lemma 14, there exists a degree-choosable component in the $(2\log_{\Delta-1} n)$-neighborhood of v. Let u be one of the closest nodes to v in the degree-choosable component B. We move the token from v to u by the shortest path. Next we uncolor the whole of B. By definition there exists a Δ-coloring of B compatible with the existing coloring in the rest of the graph. □

Remark 15. Theorem 5 implies an SLOCAL($O(\log_\Delta n)$) algorithm (cf. [19] for the model).

3 DETERMINISTIC Δ-COLORING (PROOF OF THEOREM 4)

In this section we present our deterministic Δ-coloring algorithm, exemplifying our layering technique.

Layering technique. In the layering technique there is a carefully chosen base layer B_0 that is easy to color and layers $B_1, \ldots, B_s$ where B_i consists of the nodes in distance i to B_0. This is particularly helpful for Δ-coloring as we can Δ-color the layers in reverse order while respecting the colored neighbors in layers with a larger index. To Δ-color layer B_i, $i \neq 0$ we need to solve a (deg +1) list coloring on the graph $G[B_i]$: A node $v \in B_i$ builds its list by removing the colors of neighbors in $B_{i+1} \cup \ldots \cup B_s$ from the set $\{1, \ldots, \Delta\}$. The size of this list is at least $\deg_{G[B_i]}(v) + 1$ as v has one neighbor in layer B_{i-1}. Then layer B_0 is colored after all other layers with different techniques as Δ-coloring B_0 while respecting already colored neighbors might not be a deg +1 list coloring instance. To make sure that we can still Δ-color B_0 efficiently (we might have to recolor previously colored nodes) it has to be chosen carefully.

This section uses the technique in a simple setting. We continue with list coloring results. In the (deg +1) list coloring problem each node v has a list $L(v)$ of available colors with $|L(v)| \geq \deg(v) + 1$. The objective is to properly color the graph such that each node picks a color from its list.

Theorem 16 ([15] +[5]). *There is a deterministic distributed* (deg +1) *list coloring algorithm with complexity $O\left(\sqrt{\Delta \log \Delta} \cdot \log^* \Delta\right)$ given a $O(\Delta^2)$ coloring of the graph.*

Theorem 17 (List Coloring [17]). *There is a randomized distributed algorithm that solves the* (deg +1)*-list coloring problem in $O\left(\log \Delta + 2^{O(\sqrt{\log \log n})}\right)$ rounds.*

We also use ruling set algorithms several times. A (α, β) ruling set of a graph G is a subset $M \subsetneq V(G)$ of the nodes such that $\text{dist}(v, M \setminus \{v\}) \geq \alpha$ for all $v \in M$ and $\text{dist}(v, M) \leq \beta$ for all $v \in V$. Table 1 summarizes the used distributed ruling set algorithms. Usually, when computing a ruling set it comes with a so called *ruling forest.* See [3, Definition 3] for a definition of ruling forests.

The following algorithm improves the deterministic complexity of distributed Δ-coloring. Its proof is based on the layering technique with $O(\log^2 n)$ layers and Theorem 5. The layer B_0 is chosen to be a ruling set such that Theorem 5 can be applied to color the nodes in B_0 independently. The runtime is dominated by the $O(\log^2 n)$ iterations of list coloring due to the layering technique.

Algorithm. First, color all nodes of G with $O(\Delta^2)$ colors with Linial's algorithm [22]. These colors are only used for symmetry breaking when applying list coloring algorithms and do not coincide with the desired Δ-coloring. Let $R := 4\log_{\Delta-1} n + 1 \leq 7\log n / \log \Delta$ and $z = 4 \cdot R^2$.

(1) (*Build layer* B_0) Compute a (R, z) ruling forest of G with part (2) of Table 1. Add all nodes of the ruling set to layer B_0.
(2) (*Remove layers* $B_0, \ldots, B_z$) Define layers $B_1, \ldots, B_z$ where $v \in B_i$ if the distance of v to B_0 is i. Remove all layers from the graph.
(3) (*Color layers* $B_z, \ldots, B_1$) Add the layers $B_z, \ldots, B_1$ to the graph one by one: When adding layer B_i color the nodes of B_i such that $G_{\uparrow i} = G[\bigcup_{j=i}^{z} B_j]$ is validly Δ-colored. Step $i = z, \ldots, 1$ is a deg +1 list coloring instance on $G_i = G[B_i]$ because a node $v \in B_i$ has an uncolored neighbor in B_{i-1}. We use Theorem 16 to solve each list coloring instance.
(4) (*Color layer* B_0) Use Theorem 5 to independently color the nodes in B_0 through recoloring nodes within distance at most $2\log_{\Delta-1} n < R/2$.

Proof of Theorem 4. By the definition of a ruling set every node of G is in distance at most z from its root in the ruling forest. Thus every node is contained in the $z + 1$ layers and is colored.

We formally show that coloring each layer is an instance of deg +1 list coloring in the graph G_i. Assume that we are in step i and want to color the nodes of B_i such that $G_{\uparrow i}$ is validly Δ-colored. Pick a node $v \in B_i$. The list of available colors of v is

Table 1: For any integers $k, \beta \geq 1$ there are the following ruling set algorithms.

(1)	$(2, \beta)$	Deterministic	[29]	$O(\beta\Delta^{2/\beta} + \log^* n)$
(2)	$(k, k^2\beta)$	Deterministic	[29] + [7]	$O(k^2 \cdot \beta\Delta^{2/\beta} + k \cdot \log^* n)$
(3)	$(2, O(\log\log n))$	Randomized	[16] +[29]	$O(\log\log n)$
(4)	$(2, \beta)$	Randomized	[17]	$O(\log^{1/\beta} \Delta + 2^{O(\sqrt{\log\log n})})$

$\{1, \ldots, \Delta\} \setminus F_v$ where F_v is the set of colors that have already been chosen by v's colored neighbors in $G_{\uparrow i}$. The size of F_v is at most $\deg_{G_{\uparrow i}}(v) - \deg_{G_i}(v)$. The degree $\deg_{G_{\uparrow i}}(v)$ is upper bounded by $\Delta - 1$ because at least one of v's neighbors in G is contained in L_{i-1}. Thus the list of available colors of v has size at least $\Delta - |F_v| \geq \Delta - (\deg_{G_{\uparrow i}}(v) - \deg_{G_i}(v)) \geq \deg_{G_i}(v) + 1$.

The runtime of the first step and the second step is

$$O\left(R^2 \cdot \sqrt{\Delta} + R \cdot \log^* n + z + \log^* n\right) = O\left(R^2 \cdot \sqrt{\Delta}\right).$$

The third step takes $O(\sqrt{\Delta \log \Delta} \log^* \Delta)$ rounds for each of the $z = O(R^2) = O(\log^2_\Delta n)$ iterations. The fourth step takes $O(R)$ rounds. In total the runtime is dominated by the third step. □

4 RANDOMIZED Δ-COLORING (PROOFS OF THEOREM 1 AND 3)

In this section we present our algorithm. The algorithm is split into two slightly different versions based on Δ: one version can handle any $\Delta \geq 4$ and the other any $3 \leq \Delta = O(1)$. We refer to these two versions as the *large-Δ* version and the *small-Δ* version. In this section we present the algorithms of Theorems 1 and 3 and their proofs.

Both variants share the same basic structure. We decompose the graph into layers $B_0, \ldots, B_s, C_0, \ldots, C_{2r}$ (and in some cases also layers $D_0, \ldots, D_\alpha$) of nodes such that all nodes are either colored or are in one of the layers. Then, the layers are iteratively colored in the reverse order that they were built. Coloring a single layer requires solving a (deg +1)-list coloring instance since we will guarantee that each node has an uncolored neighbor in a lower layer.

In Phase **I** we build layers $B_0, \ldots, B_s$: we identify the dense parts of the graph – the parts which are easy to color after the rest of the graph has been colored. These are removed from the graph, along with the nodes around them, to be colored later. Let H denote the remaining graph.

In Phase **II** we extract layers $C_0, \ldots, C_{2r}$ from H: The first phase guarantees that H does not contain any dense parts, and therefore the remaining graph must expand. We take advantage of this by randomly inserting *slack* into the graph. This means that we pick a set of well-separated nodes and color two of their neighbors with the same color: these nodes now effectively have decreased their degree and will be easy to color later. We again remove the nodes with slack along with the nodes around them to be colored later. Due to the expansion of H we can prove that the probability of each node to remain after this process is small.

Actually, in the small-Δ case we prove by union bound that with high probability no node remains after this process. In the large-Δ case we show that the graph formed by the remaining nodes has *shattered*: remaining connected components are of small size and can be colored efficiently with a similar layering technique using layers $D_0, \ldots, D_\alpha$ (cf. Phase **IIf**).

In Phase **III** we color the layers $C_0, \ldots, C_{2r}$ in reverse order. Then, in Phase **IV**, we color the layers $B_1, \ldots, B_s$ in the reverse order. By definition B_0 consists of (dense) parts that are easy to color if the remaining graph is colored, actually B_0 consists of DCCs and we can color the components of B_0 at the very end.

4.1 The Randomized Δ-Coloring Algorithms

First, we remove all degree-choosable components of radius r or less from the graph. This implies that the graph must expand locally (Lemma 14). The two versions differ in the radius r: in the small version we choose $r = O(\log\log n)$ and in the large version $r = O(1)$. Let $b = 6$ and $p = \Delta^{-b}$.

First, color all nodes of G with $O(\Delta^2)$ colors with Linial's algorithm [22]. These colors are only used for symmetry breaking when applying list coloring algorithms and do in no way coincide with the desired Δ-coloring.

I Removing Degree Choosable Components with Small Radius

(a) Each node that is contained in at least one degree choosable subgraph with radius at most r selects one such subgraph. Let $\mathcal{G}_{DCC}$ be the virtual graph that has a node for each selected degree choosable subgraph, and two subgraphs in $V(\mathcal{G}_{DCC})$ are connected in $\mathcal{G}_{DCC}$ by an edge if they share a vertex or if they are connected by an edge in G. The graph $\mathcal{G}_{DCC}$ has at most n nodes, maximum degree at most $\Delta^{2r+1} \leq \Delta^{3r}$, and one round of a distributed algorithm in it can be simulated in $O(r)$ rounds in G.
Runtime: $O(r)$.

(b) (*Build layer B_0*) Find a $(2, \beta)$ ruling set M of $\mathcal{G}_{DCC}$ with $\beta = 6 \cdot r$. Add all nodes of G that are in a component of M to the base layer B_0.
Runtime(n): Use the Table 1, (4) in time

$$O\left(\log^{1/\beta} \Delta + 2^{O(\sqrt{\log\log n})}\right).$$

Runtime(n, Δ): Use Table 1, (1) in time

$$O\left(r \cdot \beta \cdot \Delta^{2r/\beta} + \log^* n\right) = O\left(\Delta^{1/3} + \log^* n\right).$$

Runtime for small Δ: Use Table 1, (3) in time $O(r \cdot (O(\log\log n))) = O(\log^2 \log n)$.

(c) (*Remove layers $B_1, \ldots, B_s$*) For $s = \beta \cdot (r + 1)$ define layers $B_1, \ldots, B_s$. Layer B_i consists of the nodes of G that have the closest node with regard to distance in G in B_0 in distance exactly i. Remove all layers $B_0, \ldots, B_s$ from the graph.
Runtime for large Δ: $O(\beta \cdot r) = O(1)$.
Runtime for small Δ: $O(\beta \cdot r) = O(\log\log n)$.

Note that (besides potentially some other nodes) in particular all nodes that are in a degree choosable component with radius at most r are removed from the graph after phase **Ic**.

II Shattering of the Remaining Graph

(d) (*Random T-node creation*) Consider the remaining graph

$$H = G \setminus \left(\bigcup_{i=0}^{s} B_i \right) .$$

Each node of H becomes *selected* independently with probability p. Then, if there is another selected node within distance b, both become unselected. If not, the selected node picks a random pair of non-adjacent neigbors and colors them with color *one*. We call these neighbors *marked*.
Runtime: $O(1)$.

(e) (*Remove layers $C_0, \ldots, C_{2r}$*) We call a node *happy* if it has an uncolored path to a T-node in its r-neighborhood. By this definition we assign each happy node to its closest T-node in its r-neighborhood.
We define the *boundary* of graph H as the set of nodes with degree less than Δ in H. Nodes that are colored and have distance at most r steps away from the boundary now remove their color and each such node is assigned to its closest boundary node, breaking ties using identifiers. Now it might happen that a node v that is $r \leq \ell < 2r$ steps away from the boundary was assigned to a node w in the first round of assigning and that w is at most $r - 1$ steps away from the boundary. Due to the uncoloring w might not be a T-node anymore. However, w is assigned to a node w' on the boundary. Then there is an uncolored path of length at most $2r$ from v to w' through w and we assign v to w' as well.
Define layers $C_0, \ldots, C_{2r}$, where C_i consists of nodes of H that are at distance i from their respective assigned node. The layer C_0 consists of T-nodes, and all nodes that have degree $< \Delta$ in H. Remove the layers $C_0, \ldots, C_{2r}$ and the marked nodes from the graph.
In Section 4.4 we show that in the algorithm for small Δ, all nodes are removed after this phase with high probability. Hence this algorithm proceeds directly to Phase **IIIg**.
Runtime for large Δ: $O(r) = O(1)$.
Runtime for small Δ: $O(r) = O(\log \log n)$.

(f) (*Color Small Components*) Consider the remaining graph $L = H \setminus (C_0 \cup \ldots \cup C_{2r} \cup C')$ where C' are the marked nodes. In Section 4.2 we show that the probability for a node of H to remain in L is small and then the standard shattering technique (cf., e.g., [7] or Lemma 18) implies that L consists of small connected components of size at most $N := \text{poly}\, \Delta \cdot \log_\Delta n$.
Section 4.3 explains in detail how to color these small components. The core idea is that we can again handle the small components by constructing layers $D_0, \ldots, D_\alpha$ where $\alpha = O(\log^2 \log n)$. Besides some other nodes layer D_0 contains the nodes that have an uncolored neighbor in the layers $C_0 \cup C_1 \cup \ldots \cup C_{2r}$, i.e., they just did not get removed because the closest T-node was a little bit too far away. One can show that layer D_0 contains at least one node of each small component. However, then all nodes of the component are in one of the layers, because, assuming that a node v of a small component does not see a node of the first few layers, the BFS tree of v within the component expands so fast (basically due to Lemma 12) that it sees the whole component in $O(\log_\Delta N = O(\log \log n)$ hops, a contradiction.
Runtime(n): $2^{O(\sqrt{\log \log n})}$ based on network decompositions of the components.
Runtime(n, Δ): $O\left(\sqrt{\Delta \log \Delta} \log^* \Delta \cdot \log^2 \log n\right)$ due to the $O(\log^2 \log n)$ iterations of list coloring.

III Color Happy Nodes From the Shattering Process

(g) (*Color layers $C_{2r}, \ldots, C_0$*) Assume that the remaining small components are colored with Δ colors in Phase **IIf**. Go through the layers $C_{2r}, \ldots, C_0$ grown in step **IIe** in reverse order and Δ-color them one at a time while respecting the colors of nodes that are already colored. Coloring layer C_i corresponds to a $(\deg' + 1)$-list coloring instance on $H[C_i]$, since for each $i = 2r, \ldots, 1$ each node has a neighbor at a lower level and the nodes in C_0 have two neighbors of the same color.
Runtime(n): $O(\log \Delta + 2^{O(\sqrt{\log \log n})})$ with Theorem 17.
Runtime(n, Δ): $O(\sqrt{\Delta \log \Delta} \cdot \log^* \Delta)$ time with Theorem 16.
Runtime for small Δ: $O(\log \log n(\sqrt{\Delta \log \Delta} \cdot \log^* \Delta))$ with Theorem 16.

IV Color Degree Choosable Components

(h) (*Color layers $B_s, \ldots, B_1$*) Go through the layers $B_s, \ldots, B_1$ grown in step **Ic** and color each layer with Δ colors while respecting nodes colored previously: Coloring layer B_i forms a $(\deg' + 1)$-list coloring instance on $G[B_i]$, since each node has an uncolored neighbor in B_{i-1}.
Runtime(n): $O(\log \Delta + 2^{O(\sqrt{\log \log n})})$ with Theorem 17.
Runtime(n, Δ): $O(\sqrt{\Delta \log \Delta} \cdot \log^* \Delta)$ time with Theorem 16.
Runtime for small Δ: $O(\log \log n(\sqrt{\Delta \log \Delta} \cdot \log^* \Delta))$ with Theorem 16.

(i) (*Color layer B_0*) By definition, the components M selected in step **Ib**, i.e., the nodes in B_0, are Δ-list colorable and of radius $\leq r$. As there are no edges between different components in M by construction they can be handled independently. We find a coloring by brute forcing each component.
Runtime for large Δ: $O(r) = O(1)$.
Runtime for small Δ: $O(r) = O(\log \log n)$.

4.2 Shattering of the Remaining Graph (Phases IId-IIf)

In this section we show that the process of phase **IId** and **IIe** produce a graph with remaining components of size $O(\text{poly}(\Delta) \cdot \log n)$. In Section 4.3 we show how to color these small components fast. The nodes that are put into the layers in phase **IIe** are colored later in phase **IIIg**.

For a node v let $\mathcal{E}_v$ be the event that v is removed in the graph in phases **IId-IIe**. Let t be the radius such that the event $\mathcal{E}_v$ only depends on the random bits of nodes in radius t of v. The standard shattering technique (cf. Lemma 18) shows that the connected components of non-removed nodes are *small* if the probability of $\overline{\mathcal{E}_v}$ is upper bounded by $1/\,\text{poly}(\Delta)$ where the polynomial depends on the radius t.

Lemma 18 (The Shattering Lemma, [14, 18]). *Let $H = (V, E)$ be a graph with maximum degree Δ. Consider a process which generates a random subset $B \subseteq V$ where $P(v \in B) \leq \Delta^{-c_1}$, for some constant $c_1 \geq 1$, and that the random variables $1(v \in B)$ depend only on the randomness of nodes within at most c_2 hops from v, for all $v \in V$, for some constant $c_2 \geq 1$. Moreover, let $Z = H[2c_2 + 1, 4c_2 + 2]$ be the graph which contains an edge between u and v iff their distance in H is between $2c_2 + 1$ and $4c_2 + 2$. Let $L = H[B]$. Then with probability at least $1 - n^{-c_3}$, for any constant c_3 satisfying $c_1 > c_3 + 4c_2 + 2$, we have the following three properties:*

(P1) *$Z[B]$ has no connected component U with $|U| \geq \log_\Delta n$.*
(P2) *Each connected component of L has size at most $O(\log_\Delta n \cdot \Delta^{2c_2\Delta})$.*
(P3) *L admits a $(\lambda, O(\log^{1/\lambda} n \cdot \log^2 \log n))$ network decomposition, for any integer $\lambda \geq 1$, which can be computed by a randomized algorithm in $O\left(\lambda \log^{1/\lambda} n \cdot 2^{O(\sqrt{\log\log n})}\right)$ rounds, , w.h.p.*
(P4) *For any integer $R \geq 1$ there is a randomized algorithm to compute a $\left(2^{O(\sqrt{\log\log n})}, R \cdot 2^{O(\sqrt{\log\log n})}\right)$ network decomposition of L^R in $O(R \cdot 2^{O(\sqrt{\log\log n})})$ rounds, w.h.p.*

To show that the probability of $\overline{\mathcal{E}_v}$ is small enough we show that the BFS tree of uncolored nodes around v expands exponentially. Thus after $O(1)$ steps of expansion we see uncolored paths to enough nodes that independently form a T-node with probability $\Theta(p)$ and the probability that none of them actually is a T*−node* will be at most $1/\operatorname{poly}(\Delta)$ for a sufficiently small polynomial.

Now, we upper bound the probability that a given node does not become happy after the shattering process. Due to Lemma 12 the BFS tree around a node expands deterministically even after the marking process which implies the next lemma.

Lemma 19. *For every $0 < t \leq r$ and after the selection and marking process the t-neighborhood of every node v contains a boundary node or a set of nodes S_v with the following properties:*

(1) *$|S_v| \geq (\Delta - 2)^{t/2} \cdot \Delta^{-6}$,*
(2) *all nodes in S_v are reachable through uncolored nodes from v,*
(3) *for each $u \in S_v$ the probability that it is selected and creates a T-node that does not block the path to v is at least $1/3 \cdot p(1 - p)^{\Delta^6}$. The events are independent for distinct $u \in S_v$,*
(4) *For each $u \in S_v$ the event that it forms a T-node of the above type only depends on the random bits of nodes in radius $t + 7$ around v.*

Proof of Lemma 19. Let v be a fixed node. Due to Lemma 12 the BFS tree around v restricted to unmarked nodes contains at least $(\Delta - 2)^{t/2}$ nodes on level t. Let A_v be the set of these nodes. For each node $u \in A_v$ whose children in the BFS tree form a $\Delta - 1$ clique we remove u from A and add one of its children u' in the BFS tree to A_v. As the child has the $\Delta - 2$ nodes of the clique on its own level and u as parent it has only one child in the BFS tree. Thus the children of u' in the BFS tree cannot form a $\Delta - 1$ clique. Furthermore u' is distinct from all other nodes in A_v as the BFS tree is unique.

Now, we greedily add nodes of A_v to S_v. When we add a node $u \in A_v$ to S_v we remove the nodes from A_v that are in the 6-neighborhood of u; these are at most Δ^6 many. Thus the size of S_v is at least $|A_v| \cdot \Delta^{-6} = (\Delta - 2)^{t/2} \cdot \Delta^{-6}$ and nodes in S_v have pairwise distance at least 7.

We now compute the probability that a node $u \in S_v$ is selected and creates a T-node that does not block the path to v. To ensure that the path to v is not blocked we (1) condition on the event that certain nodes in the BFS tree around v are not uncolored (through the usage of Lemma 12) and (2) we ensure that none of the two nodes that u colors is the single neighbor u' of u that lies on the unique path in the BFS tree to v. Node u is selected with probability p and stays selected if no neighbor in its 6-neighborhood is selected, i.e., at least with probability $(1 - p)^{\Delta^6}$. As u does not have a $\Delta - 1$ clique on the next level of the BFS tree there are at least two non adjacent neighbors u_1 and u_2 of u that are distinct from u'. So the probability that u does not mark u' is at least $1/3$.

In this whole process we expanded for t steps to obtain the set A_v. The set S_v contains nodes in distance at most $t + 1$ from v and we use that nodes in distance 6 to nodes in S_v are not selected, i.e., the probabilities only depend on the $t + 7$ radius of v. The event whether distinct nodes in S_v can generate T*−nodes* are independent as they have pairwise distance at least 7. □

For any node v Lemma 19 provides a large set of independent nodes that have uncolored paths to v. Thus we can upper bound the probability that a node remains after the shattering process.

Lemma 20 (Shattering Probability). *Let $\Delta \geq 4$. There is an $r = O(1)$ such that every node finds an uncolored path of length at most $r - 7$ to a T-node with probability at least $1 - \left(\frac{1}{\Delta}\right)^{4r+4}$ using only the randomness in its t neighborhood. The constant r is independent from the graph.*

Proof. Let v be a node in H. Apply Lemma 19 with $t = r - 7$ and obtain a set S_v in which each node independently forms a T-node that is reachable from v through an uncolored path with probability $1/3 \cdot p(1 - p)^{\Delta^6}$. The probability that v remains after phase **IIe** is upper bounded by

$$\left(1 - \frac{1}{3}p(1 - p)^{\Delta^6}\right)^{|S_v|} \leq e^{-\frac{|S_v|}{3}p(1-p)^{\Delta^6}}$$
$$= e^{-\frac{(\Delta-2)^{t/2} \cdot \Delta^{-12}}{12}} \overset{(*)}{\leq} \Delta^{-4t-32},$$

where $(*)$ is satisfied if the exponent $-12^{-1}(\Delta - 2)^{t/2} \cdot \Delta^{-12}$ is smaller than $-(4t + 32) \cdot \ln \Delta$ which holds for some $t = O(1)$ and implies an $r = O(1)$ that is independent from v and the graph. □

Lemma 20 and the standard shattering technique (cf. Lemma 18) imply that the graph L that remains after phase **IIe** consists of connected components of size at most $\operatorname{poly}\Delta \cdot \log_\Delta n$. Section 4.3 explains in detail how these components can be Δ-colored while respecting the nodes colored with color *one* in phase **IId**. The algorithm for the small components relies on a layering technique with $O(\log^2 \log n)$ layers; after removing these layers no node is left.

4.3 Shattering: Coloring Small Remaining Components

We now explain how one can solve the small components that are left after the shattering process. Let C be a small component with size at most $N := \operatorname{poly}(\Delta) \cdot \log_\Delta n$. Call a node in C *free* if it has degree $< \Delta$ or at least one neighbor outside of C that is not colored with the first color after the shattering process.We color the nodes of C with the following algorithm where $R = 2\log_{\Delta-2} N + 1 = O(\log\log n)$. The algorithm is explained from the view of a single component.

(1) Each free node selects itself. Further, each node that is contained in at least one DCC with radius at most R selects one of these subgraphs. Let C_{DCC} be the virtual graph that has a node for each selected node and degree choosable subgraph. Any two subgraphs (or nodes) of C_{DCC} are connected in C_{DCC} if they share a vertex or are connected by an edge in G. The maximum degree of C_{DCC} is $\min\{N, O(\Delta^{O(R)})\}$ and it has at most $|C| = N$ nodes. One round of an algorithm on C_{DCC} can be executed in $O(R)$ steps in G.
(2) Find a $(2,\gamma)$ ruling set M' of C_{DCC} where $\gamma = O(R)$ such that $\Delta(C_{DCC})^{2/\gamma} \leq \Delta^{1/2}$.
Runtime(n): We use with Lemma 18 (P4) to compute a $\left(2^{O(\sqrt{\log\log n})}, 4R\cdot 2^{O(\sqrt{\log\log n})}\right)$ network decomposition of L^{4R}. Then each node assigns its color in this network decomposition to its corresponding selected node in C_{DCC}. This yields a $\left(2^{O(\sqrt{\log\log n})}, 2^{O(\sqrt{\log\log n})}\right)$ network decomposition of C_{DCC}. Then iterate through the colors of the network decomposition to compute the ruling set in time $O\left(R\cdot 2^{O(\sqrt{\log\log n})}\right) = 2^{O(\sqrt{\log\log n})}$.
Runtime(n, Δ): Use Table 1, (1) in time
$$O\left(R\cdot\gamma\cdot\Delta(C_{DCC})^{2/\gamma} + \log^* n\right) = O\left(\log^2\log n\cdot\sqrt{\Delta}\right).$$
(3) For $i = 0, \ldots, \gamma\cdot(R+1)+R$ define layers D_i where D_i consists of the nodes that are at distance i to the closest node that is contained in a component in M'.
(4) We color the layers in order $i = \gamma\cdot(R+1)+R, \ldots, 1$; each layer is a deg +1 list coloring instance. There are $R^2 + 2R$ layers and we obtain the following runtimes.
Runtime(n): In $O((R^2+2R)\cdot 2^{O(\sqrt{\log\log n})}) = 2^{O(\sqrt{\log\log n})}$ rounds via computing a single network decomposition for C with Lemma 18, (P3).
Runtime(n, Δ): If we first use Linial's algorithm to compute a $O(\Delta^2)$ coloring the runtime is $O\left((R^2+2R)\cdot\sqrt{\Delta\log\Delta}\cdot\log^*\Delta\right) = O\left(\log^2\log n\sqrt{\Delta\log\Delta}\cdot\log^*\Delta\right)$ time with Theorem 16.
(5) Now, we color the nodes that are in D_0. Each DCC is brute-forced independently in time $O(R)$. Each free node in D_0 can be colored in a single time unit as it has one uncolored neighbor outside the component it has a free color.
Runtime: $O(R) = O(\log\log n)$.

Lemma 21. *If D_0 is not empty each node of the component is in one of the layers.*

Proof. The layers $D_0, \ldots, D_{\gamma\cdot(R+1)}$ contain all free nodes, all nodes that are in a DCC with radius at most R and all nodes that have degree smaller Δ. The layers $D_0, \ldots, D_{\gamma\cdot(R+1)+R}$ additionally contain the nodes that have such a DCC or such a node in distance at most R. To show that all nodes are removed we assume that there is a node $v \in C$ that is in none of the layers. In particular it does not have a DCC or a free node in distance R, all nodes in its R-neighborhood have degree Δ or $\Delta - 1$. As the R-neighborhood of v does not contain a free node it can only hit the boundary of C at colored nodes, i.e., its R-neighborhood can be obtained from the marking process as described in Section 2.2. Thus we can apply Lemma 12 and obtain that the BFS tree around v and within the component expands and contains at least $(\Delta-2)^{R/2} > N$ nodes, a contradiction. □

Lemma 22. *D_0 is not empty.*

Proof. Assume that D_0 is empty. Let v be an arbitrary node of C. Its R-neighborhood neither contains a DCC of radius at most R nor a free node and all its nodes have degree Δ or $\Delta - 1$. As the R-neighborhood of v does not contain a free node it can only hit the boundary of C at colored nodes, i.e., its R-neighborhood can be obtained from the marking process as described in Section 2.2. Thus we can apply Lemma 12 and obtain that the BFS tree around v and within the component expands and contains at least $(\Delta-2)^{R/2} > N$ nodes, a contradiction. □

The above algorithm provides the following lemma.

Lemma 23. *Let $\Delta \geq 4$. Then the small components can, w.h.p., be Δ-colored in time*
$$\min\left\{2^{O(\sqrt{\log\log n})}, O\left(\log^2\log n\cdot\sqrt{\Delta\log\Delta\log^*\Delta}\right)\right\}.$$

Proof. Lemmas 21 and 22 imply that each node is colored. The proof that coloring a single layer in phase 4 is a a deg +1 list coloring instance is along similar lines as in the proof of Theorem 4. The components and free nodes in D_0 can be colored independently because the stem from the independent set M'. In both variants the runtime is dominated by phase 4 step which implies the result. □

Remark 24. The algorithm to solve the small components only uses randomization if it computes the network decomposition (Lemma 18).

4.4 Global Success After Marking Process for Small Δ

We will assume that locally all nodes in the remainder graph H have degree $\Delta = O(1)$, since nodes close to the boundary of H automatically become happy.

Lemmas 12 and its strenthened version imply that for $\Delta = O(1)$ we can choose an $r = \Theta(\log\log n)$ such that for an arbitrarily large constant c, we have $|B_r(v)| \geq c\log_\Delta n$ after the marking process.

Lemma 25. *Let u be a node such that there is an unmarked, unselected path from u to v. Then u or its child u' becomes a T-node of v with a constant probability.*

Note that the following analysis is done for $b = 12$. For $\Delta \geq 4$ we could equally well use $b = 6$ to optimize the constants.

Proof Sketch. A node u can become a T-node to node v if it has two non-adjacent neighbors that are also not on the path from u to v. Assume first that this is the case.

The children of u form at least two distinct cliques (including single nodes). There are $\Delta-1$ pairs that include the parent of u and at least $\Delta-2$ pairs that do not. Therefore if u can become a T-node of v

and if it is selected it becomes one with probability at least $1/3$. Node u succeeds with probability at least $p' = (p/3)(1-p)^{\Delta^{12}} = \Theta(1)$, since $\Delta = O(1)$. Now if the children of u form a clique, u cannot become a T-node of v. Its children must have a successor in the BFS tree, and therefore can become a T-node for v. The events that u or a child of u succeed are not independent but are disjoint, so the claim holds. □

Note that the event in Lemma 25 depends on randomness at distance at most 13.

Lemma 26. *The marking process generates a T-node for every node of the remainder graph H with high probability.*

Proof. Consider an arbitrary node $v \in V(H)$. By Lemma 12 and its strenthened version, for any $c > 0$ we can choose $r = O(\log\log n)$ such that at distance t from the root of any BFS tree, there are at least $c/p'\Delta^{13}\ln n$ nodes such that their path to u is unmarked and unselected. From this set find a set S of nodes as in Lemma 25, of size $c/p'\ln n$ such that they are at pairwise distance of at least 13 and can each produce a T-node for v with probability p'.

The events that each $u \in S$ become a T-node of v are independent due to the pairwise distance of the ndoes. Therefore no node of S becomes a T-node of v with probability at most

$$(1-p')^{c/p'\ln n} \leq e^{-c\ln n} \leq n^{-c}.$$

With a union bound over all nodes, all nodes of H are happy with probability at least $1 - 1/n^{c-1}$. □

REFERENCES

[1] Pierre Aboulker, Marthe Bonamy, Nicolas Bousquet, and Louis Esperet. 2018. Distributed coloring in sparse graphs with fewer colors. In *Proc. 37th ACM Symposium on Principles of Distributed Computing (PODC 2018)*. To appear.

[2] Noga Alon, László Babai, and Alon Itai. 1986. A fast and simple randomized parallel algorithm for the maximal independent set problem. *Journal of Algorithms* 7, 4 (1986), 567–583.

[3] B. Awerbuch, A. V. Goldberg, M. Luby, and S. A. Plotkin. 1989. Network Decomposition and Locality in Distributed Computation. In *Proc. 30th Symposium on Foundations of Computer Science (FOCS 1989)*. 364–369.

[4] Leonid Barenboim and Michael Elkin. 2013. Distributed graph coloring: Fundamentals and recent developments. *Synthesis Lectures on Distributed Computing Theory* 4, 1 (2013), 1–171.

[5] Leonid Barenboim, Michael Elkin, and Uri Goldenberg. 2018. Locally-Iterative Distributed ($\Delta + 1$)-Coloring below Szegedy-Vishwanathan Barrier, and Applications to Self-Stabilization and to Restricted-Bandwidth Models. In *Proc. 37th ACM Symposium on Principles of Distributed Computing (PODC 2018)*. To appear.

[6] Leonid Barenboim, Michael Elkin, Seth Pettie, and Johannes Schneider. 2012. The Locality of Distributed Symmetry Breaking. In *Proc. 53rd Symposium on Foundations of Computer Science (FOCS 2012)*. 321–330.

[7] Leonid Barenboim, Michael Elkin, Seth Pettie, and Johannes Schneider. 2016. The Locality of Distributed Symmetry Breaking. *Journal of the ACM* 63, 3, Article 20 (2016), 45 pages. https://doi.org/10.1145/2903137

[8] J.A. Bondy and U. Murty. 1976. *Graph Theory with Applications*. Elsevier.

[9] Sebastian Brandt, Orr Fischer, Juho Hirvonen, Barbara Keller, Tuomo Lempiäinen, Joel Rybicki, Jukka Suomela, and Jara Uitto. 2016. A lower bound for the distributed Lovász local lemma. In *Proc. 48th ACM Symposium on Theory of Computing (STOC 2016)*. ACM, 479–488.

[10] Rowland Leonard Brooks. 2009. On colouring the nodes of a network. In *Classic papers in combinatorics*. Springer, 118–121.

[11] Yi-Jun Chang, Tsvi Kopelowitz, and Seth Pettie. 2016. An exponential separation between randomized and deterministic complexity in the local model. In *Proc. 57th Symposium on Foundations of Computer Science (FOCS 2016)*. IEEE, 615–624.

[12] Yi-Jun Chang, Wenzheng Li, and Seth Pettie. 2018. An Optimal Distributed ($\Delta+1$)-Coloring Algorithm?. In *Proc. 50th ACM Symposium on Theory of Computing (STOC 2018)*. To appear.

[13] Paul Erdős, Arthur Rubin, and Herbert Taylor. 1979. Choosability in Graphs. In *Proc. West Coast Conference on Combinatorics, Graph Theory and Computing*, Vol. 26. Congressus Numerantium, 125–157.

[14] Manuela Fischer and Mohsen Ghaffari. 2017. Sublogarithmic Distributed Algorithms for Lovász Local Lemma, and the Complexity Hierarchy. In *Proc. 31st International Symposium on Distributed Computing (DISC 2017) (LIPIcs)*, Vol. 91. Schloss Dagstuhl - Leibniz-Zentrum fuer Informatik, 18:1–18:16.

[15] Pierre Fraigniaud, Marc Heinrich, and Adrian Kosowski. 2016. Local Conflict Coloring. In *Proc. 57th Symposium on Foundations of Computer Science (FOCS 2016)*. 625–634.

[16] Beat Gfeller and Elias Vicari. 2007. A Randomized Distributed Algorithm for the Maximal Independent Set Problem in Growth-bounded Graphs. In *Proc. 26th ACM Symposium on Principles of Distributed Computing (PODC 2007)*. ACM, New York, NY, USA, 53–60. https://doi.org/10.1145/1281100.1281111

[17] Mohsen Ghaffari. 2016. An Improved Distributed Algorithm for Maximal Independent Set. In *Proc. 27th ACM-SIAM Symposium on Discrete Algorithms (SODA 2016)*. 270–277. https://doi.org/10.1137/1.9781611974331.ch20

[18] Mohsen Ghaffari, Juho Hirvonen, Fabian Kuhn, and Yannic Maus. 2018. Improved Distributed Δ-Coloring. *CoRR* abs/1803.03248 (2018).

[19] Mohsen Ghaffari, Fabian Kuhn, and Yannic Maus. 2017. On the complexity of local distributed graph problems. In *Proc. 49th ACM Symposium on Theory of Computing (STOC 2017)*. ACM, 784–797.

[20] Mohsen Ghaffari and Hsin-Hao Su. 2017. Distributed degree splitting, edge coloring, and orientations. In *Proc. 28th ACM-SIAM Symposium on Discrete Algorithms (SODA 2017)*. Society for Industrial and Applied Mathematics, 2505–2523.

[21] David G Harris, Johannes Schneider, and Hsin-Hao Su. 2016. Distributed ($\Delta + 1$)-coloring in sublogarithmic rounds. In *Proc. 48th ACM Symposium on Theory of Computing (STOC 2016)*. ACM, 465–478.

[22] Nati Linial. 1992. Locality in Distributed Graph Algorithms. *SIAM J. Comput.* 21, 1 (1992), 193–201.

[23] László Lovász. 1975. Three short proofs in graph theory. *Journal of Combinatorial Theory, Series B* 19, 3 (1975), 269–271.

[24] Michael Luby. 1986. A simple parallel algorithm for the maximal independent set problem. *SIAM J. Comput.* 15, 4 (1986), 1036–1053.

[25] Michael Molloy and Bruce Reed. 2013. *Graph colouring and the probabilistic method*. Vol. 23. Springer Science & Business Media.

[26] Alessandro Panconesi and Aravind Srinivasan. 1992. Improved distributed algorithms for coloring and network decomposition problems. In *Proc. 24th ACM Symposium on Theory of Computing (STOC 1992)*. ACM, 581–592.

[27] Alessandro Panconesi and Aravind Srinivasan. 1995. The local nature of Δ-coloring and its algorithmic applications. *Combinatorica* 15, 2 (1995), 255–280. https://doi.org/10.1007/BF01200759

[28] David Peleg. 2000. Distributed computing. *SIAM Monographs on discrete mathematics and applications* 5 (2000).

[29] Johannes Schneider, Michael Elkin, and Roger Wattenhofer. 2013. Symmetry breaking depending on the chromatic number or the neighborhood growth. *Theoretical Computer Science* 509 (2013), 40–50.

[30] Vadim Vizing. 1976. Vextex coloring with given colors. *Metody Diskretn. Anal.* (1976), 29:3–10.

Locally-Iterative Distributed ($\Delta + 1$)-Coloring below Szegedy-Vishwanathan Barrier, and Applications to Self-Stabilization and to Restricted-Bandwidth Models*

Leonid Barenboim
Open University of Israel
Raanana, Israel
leonidb@openu.ac.il

Michael Elkin
Ben-Gurion University of the Negev
Beer-Sheva, Israel
elkinm@cs.bgu.ac.il

Uri Goldenberg
Open University of Israel
Raanana, Israel
uri.goldenberg@gmail.com

ABSTRACT

We consider graph coloring and related problems in the distributed message-passing model. *Locally-iterative algorithms* are especially important in this setting. These are algorithms in which each vertex decides about its next color only as a function of the current colors in its $1-hop-neighborhood$. In STOC'93 Szegedy and Vishwanathan showed that any locally-iterative ($\Delta + 1$)-coloring algorithm requires $\Omega(\Delta \log \Delta + \log^* n)$ rounds, unless there exists "a very special type of coloring that can be very efficiently reduced" [39]. No such special coloring has been found since then. This led researchers to believe that Szegedy-Vishwanathan barrier is an inherent limitation for locally-iterative algorithms, and to explore other approaches to the coloring problem [1, 2, 17, 29]. The latter gave rise to faster algorithms, but their heavy machinery which is of non-locally-iterative nature made them far less suitable to various settings. In this paper we obtain the aforementioned special type of coloring. Specifically, we devise a locally-iterative ($\Delta + 1$)-coloring algorithm with running time $O(\Delta + \log^* n)$, i.e., *below* Szegedy-Vishwanathan barrier. This demonstrates that this barrier is not an inherent limitation for locally-iterative algorithms. As a result, we also achieve significant improvements for dynamic, self-stabilizing and bandwidth-restricted settings. This includes the following results.

- We obtain self-stabilizing distributed algorithms for ($\Delta + 1$)-vertex-coloring, ($2\Delta - 1$)-edge-coloring, maximal independent set and maximal matching with $O(\Delta + \log^* n)$ time. This significantly improves previously-known results that have $O(n)$ or larger running times [21].
- We devise a ($2\Delta - 1$)-edge-coloring algorithm in the CONGEST model with $O(\Delta + \log^* n)$ time and $O(\Delta)$-edge-coloring in the Bit-Round model with $O(\Delta + \log n)$ time. The factors of $\log^* n$ and $\log n$ are unavoidable in the CONGEST and Bit-Round models, respectively. Previously-known algorithms had superlinear dependency on Δ for ($2\Delta - 1$)-edge-coloring in these models.
- We obtain an arbdefective coloring algorithm with running time $O(\sqrt{\Delta} + \log^* n)$. Such a coloring is not necessarily proper, but has certain helpful properties. We employ it in order to compute a proper $(1 + \epsilon)\Delta$-coloring within $O(\sqrt{\Delta} + \log^* n)$ time, and ($\Delta + 1$)-coloring within $O(\sqrt{\Delta \log \Delta} \log^* \Delta + \log^* n)$ time. This improves the recent state-of-the-art bounds of Barenboim from PODC'15 [1] and Fraigniaud et al. from FOCS'16 [17] by polylogarithmic factors.
- Our algorithms are applicable to the SET-LOCAL model [23] (also known as the weak LOCAL model). In this model a relatively strong lower bound of $\Omega(\Delta^{1/3})$ is known for ($\Delta + 1$)-coloring. However, most of the coloring algorithms do not work in this model. (In [23] only Linial's $O(\Delta^2)$-time algorithm and Kuhn-Wattenhofer $O(\Delta \log \Delta)$-time algorithms are shown to work in it.) We obtain the first linear-in-Δ algorithms that work also in this model.

ACM Reference Format:
Leonid Barenboim, Michael Elkin, and Uri Goldenberg. 2018. Locally-Iterative Distributed ($\Delta + 1$)-Coloring below Szegedy-Vishwanathan Barrier, and Applications to Self-Stabilization and to Restricted-Bandwidth Models. In *PODC '18: ACM Symposium on Principles of Distributed Computing, July 23–27, 2018, Egham, United Kingdom.* ACM, New York, NY, USA, 10 pages. https://doi.org/10.1145/3212734.3212769

1 INTRODUCTION

1.1 The Classical Model

Consider an n-vertex graph $G = (V, E)$ with maximum degree Δ whose vertices host processors. The vertices communicate with one another over the edges of G in *synchronous* rounds. The problem that we are studying is how many rounds (also known as *running time* in the *message-passing model of distributed computing*) are required for computing a proper[1] ($\Delta + 1$)-coloring of G. This is one of the most fundamental and well-studied distributed symmetry-breaking problems [1, 3–6, 8, 10, 17, 19, 30, 31, 39], and it has numerous applications to resource and channel allocation, scheduling, workload balancing, and to mutual exclusion [21, 29]. The study of distributed coloring algorithms on paths and cycles was initiated by Cole and Vishkin in 1986 [10], who devised a 3-coloring algorithm with $O(\log^* n)$ time[2]. The first distributed algorithm for the ($\Delta + 1$)-coloring problem on general graphs was devised by

*This research has been supported by ISF grant 724/15 and Open University of Israel research fund. The full version of this paper is available online [9]

PODC '18, July 23–27, 2018, Egham, United Kingdom

ACM ISBN 978-1-4503-5795-1/18/07...$15.00
https://doi.org/10.1145/3212734.3212769

[1] A coloring $\varphi : V \to [\Delta + 1]$ is called *proper*, if $\varphi(u) \neq \varphi(v)$, for every edge $e = (u, v) \in E$.
[2] Unless said otherwise, algorithms that we discuss are deterministic.

Goldberg and Plotkin in 1987 [19]. The running time of their algorithm is $2^{O(\Delta)} + O(\log^* n)$. ($\log^*$ is a very slow-growing function, defined formally in Section 2.) Goldberg, Plotkin and Shannon [20] improved this bound to $O(\Delta^2 + \log^* n)$. Linial [31] showed a lower bound of $\frac{1}{2}\log^* n - O(1)$. His lower bound applies to a more relaxed $f(\Delta)$-coloring problem, for any, possibly quickly-growing function $f()$. Linial also strengthened the upper bound of [20], and showed that an $O(\Delta^2)$-coloring can be computed in $\log^* n + O(1)$ time. (Via a standard color reduction, described e.g., in [5] Chapter 3, given an α-coloring one can compute a $(\Delta + 1)$-coloring in $\alpha - (\Delta + 1)$ rounds. Thus, Linial's algorithm also gives rise to $(\Delta + 1)$-coloring in $O(\Delta^2 + \log^* n)$ time.)

In STOC'93, Szegedy and Vishwanathan [39] studied *locally-iterative* coloring algorithms. An algorithm $\mathcal{A}$ is an α-to-β locally-iterative, for a pair of parameters $\alpha > \beta$, if it maintains a sequence $\varphi_1, \varphi_2, ..., \varphi_T$ of *proper* α-colorings, where φ_i is the coloring on round i, for every $1 \le i \le T$, the coloring φ_T is a β-coloring, and T is the running time of the algorithm. On each round i, every vertex v computes its new color $\varphi_{i+1}(v)$ based only on the colors $\{\varphi_i(u) \mid u \in \hat{\Gamma}(v)\}$, where $\hat{\Gamma}(v) = \{v\} \cup \{u \in V \mid (u, v) \in E\}$ is the $1 - hop - neighborhood$ of v. Szegedy and Vishwanathan showed upper and lower bounds on the quantity $\Psi(n, \Delta, D)$, which is the number of colors into which an n-vertex graph G of maximum degree Δ can be properly recolored within one single round, assuming that it was properly D-colored in the beginning of the round. Note, however, that for the lower bound of [39] to hold, the proper D-coloring of G is assumed to be *arbitrary*. As a corollary of their upper bound on $\Psi(n, \Delta, D)$, Szegedy and Vishwanathan [39] derived an improved upper bound of $O(\Delta \log \Delta + \log^* n)$ for locally-iterative $(\Delta+1)$-coloring. Specifically, they devised an $O(\Delta^2)$-to-$(\Delta + 1)$-locally-iterative algorithm with running time $O(\Delta \log \Delta)$. (This upper bound was later re-derived in a somewhat more explicit way by Kuhn and Wattenhofer [30].) As a corollary of their lower bound on $\Psi(n, \Delta, D)$, Szegedy and Vishwanathan [39] showed a *heuristic* lower bound on the number of rounds that a locally-iterative algorithm needs in order to compute a $(\Delta + 1)$-coloring from an $O(\Delta^2)$-coloring. Their lower bound (Theorem 12 in [39], marked as "heuristic") is $\Omega(\Delta \log \Delta)$. By Linial's lower bound [31], $\frac{1}{2}\log^* n - O(1)$ rounds are required to compute an $O(\Delta^2)$-coloring. All $(\Delta + 1)$-coloring algorithms developed before 2009 were locally iterative. (See Table 1 below for a summary of known locally-iterative algorithms.) In [2, 29] the first- and the second-named authors of the current paper, and independently Kuhn, devised an $O(\Delta + \log^* n)$-time $(\Delta + 1)$-coloring algorithm, using *defective colorings*. (See Section 2 for the definition of this notion.) The algorithms of [2, 6, 29] are, however, not locally-iterative. This direction was further pursued by the first-named author in [1], who devised an algorithm with running time $\tilde{O}(\Delta^{3/4} + \log^* n)$, using *arbdefective colorings*. (See Section 2; the notion originates from [3].) This result was further improved by Fraigniaud at al. [17], who devised the current state-of-the-art $(\Delta + 1)$-coloring with running time $O(\sqrt{\Delta}\log^{2.5}\Delta + \log^* n)$. The algorithms of [1, 2, 17, 29] are all not locally-iterative, as they all decompose the graph into many subgraphs, compute colorings for them, and carefully combine them into a single coloring for the original graph. In view of Szegedy-Vishwanathan's heuristic lower bound (henceforth, *SV barrier*), this seemed to be inevitable. In the current paper we show that this is not the case, and devise the first *locally-iterative* $(\Delta + 1)$-coloring algorithm with running time $O(\Delta + \log^* n)$, i.e., *below the SV barrier* of $\Omega(\Delta \log \Delta + \log^* n)$. Unlike previously locally-iterative algorithms, our algorithm does not necessarily reduces the number of employed colors in every round. Instead, if the initial number of colors is Δ^2, it can keep being $\Omega(\Delta^2)$ for almost the entire execution of the algorithm, and then "suddenly" reduce to $\Delta + 1$ in the last few rounds. The colorings $\varphi_1, \varphi_2, ..., \varphi_T$, $T = O(\Delta)$, that it computes on rounds $1, 2, ..., T$, respectively, are all proper, but they are *not at all arbitrary*. Rather they have some special properties that guarantee that in $O(\Delta)$ rounds the number of colors reduces to $(\Delta + 1)$.

Interestingly, in their seminar paper [39], Szegedy and Vishwanathan mention a possibility of such a phenomenon. In the preamble to their aforementioned "heuristic" theorem (Theorem 12) they wrote:

"There is a possibility, however, that after a few steps of iteration we arrive at a very special type of coloring that can be very efficiently reduced in steps thereafter. Assuming that this does not happen, the results of the previous section give the following theorem: Theorem 12 (heuristic): Let $1 \le b < a \le \Delta/2$. To decrease the number of colors from $a\Delta$ to $b\Delta$ it takes $\Theta(\Delta \log(a/b))$ steps. In particular, to decrease the number of colors from $\Delta^2/2$ to Δ requires $\Theta(\Delta \log \Delta)$ steps."[1]

We also use our new locally iterative technique to devise improved *not* locally-iterative coloring algorithms. Specifically, we obtain $(1 + \epsilon)\Delta$-coloring within $O(\sqrt{\Delta} + \log^* n)$ time, for an arbitrarily small constant $\epsilon > 0$, and a $(\Delta + 1)$-coloring within $O(\sqrt{\Delta \log \Delta}\log^* \Delta + \log^* n)$ time. This improves the best previously-known running time $O(\sqrt{\Delta}\log^{2.5}\Delta + \log^* n)$ of Fraigniaud et al. [17].

Running time	Reference
$2^{O(\Delta)} + O(\log^* n)$	Goldberg, Plotkin [19]
$O(\Delta^2) + \log^* n$	Linial [31]
$O(\Delta) \cdot \log n$	Goldberg at el. [20]
$O(\Delta^2) + \log^* n$	Goldberg et al. [20]
$O(\Delta \log \Delta) + \frac{1}{2}\log^* n$	Szegedy, Vishwanathan [39]
$O(\Delta \log \Delta) + \log^* n$	Kuhn, Wattenhofer [30]
$O(\Delta) + \log^* n$	**This paper**

Table 1: Known results for locally-iterative $(\Delta + 1)$-coloring.

1.2 Applications

In the Conclusions section of the paper [30] by Kuhn and Wattenhofer, the authors explain why locally-iterative algorithms are particularly important from practical perspective. They mention "emerging dynamic and mobile distributed systems such as peer-to-peer, ad-hoc, or sensor networks" as examples of networks for which such algorithms can be especially suitable. They also point out that locally-iterative algorithms are typically communication-efficient ones.

[1]The argument of [39] applies, in fact, to reducing the number of colors to $\Delta + 1$, as opposed to Δ.

In this paper we demonstrate that our novel locally-iterative algorithms indeed provide dramatically improved bounds for both the dynamic Self-Stabilizing scenarios and for scenarios in which communication-efficiency is crucial. In the next three subsections we discuss these applications of our locally-iterative technique one after another.

1.2.1 Self-Stabilizing Symmetry Breaking

The Self-Stabilizing setting was introduced by Dijkstra [11], and is being intensively studied since then. See, e.g., Dolev's monograph [12] and surveys by Herman [24], by Guelleti and Kheddouci [21]. Self-stabilization in dynamic systems was defined in [13]. In the context of $(\Delta+1)$-coloring, the setting we consider is the following one. Every vertex v of a graph $G=(V,E)$ of maximum degree at most Δ and at most n vertices has a unique ID number. The memory of each vertex consists of two areas. The *Read Only Memory* (henceforth, ROM) consists of hard-wired data such as vertex ID, degree bound Δ, vertices bound n, and program code. The ROM is faultless, but its contents cannot be changed during execution. The other area of the memory is *Random Access Memory* (henceforth, RAM). This memory may change during execution, and it is appropriate for storing variables, such as vertex colors. However, this memory area may change not only as a result of an algorithm instruction, but also as a result of faults. Such faults may make arbitrary and completely unpredictable changes in any round in the entire RAM. Moreover, in the *Fully-Dynamic Self-Stabilizing setting*, in each round vertices may crash, new vertices may appear and communication links between vertices may change arbitrarily, as long as the bounds on n and Δ hold[1]. For example, colors are stored in RAM, and as long as faults occur, vertices may hold arbitrary colors, possibly the same as those of their neighbors, no matter what operations are performed by an algorithm. The objective is to devise algorithms in which once faults stop occurring, the algorithm *self-stabilizes* quickly to a proper solution. The relevant notion of running time in this context is called *stabilization time* (also known as "quiescence" time), which is the maximum number T of rounds, so that T rounds after the last fault or dynamic change of the graph we are guaranteed that an algorithm arrives to a proper solution, e.g., the coloring of the graph is a proper $(\Delta+1)$-coloring. One can define analogously self-stabilizing variants of $(2\Delta-1)$-edge-coloring (see Section 1.2.2), of Maximal Independent Set (henceforth, MIS) and of Maximal Matching (henceforth, MM)[2].

Self-stabilizing symmetry-breaking problems were extensively studied [25–27, 38]. See also [21] for an excellent survey of self-stabilizing symmetry-breaking algorithms. However, all of them have prohibitively large stabilization time of $O(n)$ or more. In this paper we devise the first self-stabilizing algorithms with stabilization time of $O(\Delta+\log^* n)$ for all these four fundamental problems. We note that the fact that our algorithms are *deterministic* is particularly useful in this setting. Indeed, this prevents the possibility that adversarial faults will manipulate random bits of the algorithm.

[1] In fact, since the dependence of our algorithms' running time on n is just $\log^* n$, the bound for the number of vertices may be double- or triple-exponential in the real number of vertices, and still the running time will be affected by just an additive constant term.

[2] A subset $U \subseteq V$ of vertices is an *MIS* if there are no edges between pairs of vertices in U, and for every vertex $v \in V \setminus U$, there exists a neighbor $u \in U$. A subset $M \subseteq E$ of edges is an *MM* if no tow edges of M are incident, and for every $e \in E \setminus M$, there exists an edge $e' \in M$ incident on it.

1.2.2 Edge-Coloring

Another classical and extremely well-studied symmetry breaking problem is that of $(2\Delta-1)$-edge-coloring [4, 7, 8, 14–16, 18, 35, 36]. An *edge-coloring* φ of a graph $G=(V,E)$ is a function $\varphi: E \to N$. It is said to be *proper* if for every pair of incident edges $e, e' \in E$, $e \neq e'$, we have $\varphi(e) \neq \varphi(e')$. The classical theorem of Vizing [40] states that every graph is $(\Delta+1)$-edge-colorable. However, existing distributed deterministic solutions [4, 7, 8, 15, 16, 35] employ $(2\Delta-1)$ colors or more in general graphs. (There are efficient randomized distributed algorithms [8, 15] that compute $(1+\epsilon)\Delta$-edge-colorings in time close to $(\log n)/\Delta^{1-o(1)}$. This running time is incomparable to running time of the form $f(\Delta)+O(\log^* n)$, for some function $f()$, achieved by deterministic algorithms that we discuss here.) The first efficient deterministic algorithm for $(2\Delta-1)$-edge-coloring was devised by Panconesi and Rizzi [35]. Its running time is $O(\Delta+\log^* n)$.

In the LOCAL model of distributed computing, messages of arbitrary size are allowed. The $(2\Delta-1)$-edge-coloring problem for a graph G reduces to $(\Delta+1)$-vertex-coloring problem for the line graph $L(G)$ of G, and in the LOCAL model this reduction can be implemented without any overhead in running time. Therefore, the novel sublinear-in-Δ time algorithms for $(\Delta+1)$-vertex-coloring [1, 17] immediately give rise to sublinear-in-Δ time algorithms for $(2\Delta-1)$-edge-coloring. However, all these edge-coloring algorithms [1, 23, 35] are not locally iterative. Moreover, they do not apply (or require significantly more time) in the CONGEST model of distributed computing. In the latter model, every vertex v is allowed to send $O(\log n)$ bits of information to each of its neighbors in every round. Implementing Panconesi-Rizzi algorithm in the CONGEST model requires $O(\Delta^2+\log^* n)$ time. Simulating vertex-coloring for a line graph also yields a multiplicative overhead of factor at least Δ in the running time. Therefore, to the best of our understanding, the state-of-the-art solution for $(2\Delta-1)$-edge-coloring in the CONGEST model requires $\tilde{O}(\Delta^{3/2}+\log^* n)$ time, and it is not locally iterative. The best currently-known locally-iterative solution is even slower, and requires $O(\Delta^2\log\Delta+\log^* n)$ time. (It is achieved by simulating the locally-iterative $O(\Delta\log\Delta)$-time algorithm of [30, 39] in the line graph in the CONGEST model.) The problem of devising communication-efficient algorithms for symmetry-breaking problems was raised in a recent work by Pai et al. [34].

We adapt our locally-iterative algorithm for $(\Delta+1)$-vertex-coloring to work for $(2\Delta-1)$-edge-coloring directly, i.e., without simulation of the line graph. As a result we obtain a locally-iterative $(2\Delta-1)$-edge-coloring algorithm with running time $O(\Delta+\log^* n)$ in the CONGEST model. Moreover, we show that unlike previous solutions (that require stabilization time of $\Omega(n)$), our algorithm works in the self-stabilizing setting, still with small messages, with stabilization time $O(\Delta+\log^* n)$. Moreover, our algorithm is also applicable to the more restricted Bit-Round [28] model in which each vertex is only allowed to send 1 bit in each round over each edge.

1.2.3 SET-LOCAL Model

An additional application of our algorithms is in the SET-LOCAL model [23] that represents restricted networks in which vertices do not have IDs (but start from a proper coloring), and are not capable to distinguish between identical messages received from different neighbors. Since our algorithms are locally-iterative and compute the next colors based only on sets of current colors of 1-hop-neighborhoods, our algorithms are directly applicable to the SET-LOCAL model. Thus our algorithms compute proper $(\Delta + 1)$-coloring (and solve related problems) in $O(\Delta)$ time in the SET-LOCAL model starting from a proper $O(\Delta^2)$ coloring. The best previous algorithms in this model required $O(\Delta \log \Delta)$ time [23, 30, 39]. A lower bound of $\Omega(\Delta^{1/3})$ for $(\Delta + 1)$-coloring in this setting was obtained by Hefetz et al. [23].

1.2.4 Summary

We believe that these applications demonstrate the power of locally-iterative coloring. Bypassing Szegedy-Vishwanathan barrier via a locally-iterative algorithm does not only provide a surprising answer to a quarter-century-old open problem, but also provides new precious insights into distributed coloring in general. We are confident that these insights will be instrumental in achieving further breakthroughs in this important field.

1.3 Technical Overview

We start with describing our most basic subroutine, which we call *Additive Group algorithm*, or shortly, AG algorithm. The subroutine starts with a proper $(\Delta + 1)^2$-vertex-coloring φ of the input graph G, and produces its proper $(\Delta + 1)$-coloring in $O(\Delta)$ rounds, in a locally-iterative way. Assume (for simplicity of presentation) that $\Delta + 1 = p$ is a prime number. We represent every initial color $\varphi(v) = \varphi_0(v)$ as a pair $\langle a_v, b_v \rangle$, where a_v, b_v are from the field of integers with characteristic p, i.e., $a_v, b_v \in GF(p)$. Then every vertex $v \in V$ (in parallel) checks if there exists a neighbor $u \in \Gamma(v)$, with $b_u = b_v$. If there is no such a neighbor, then the vertex v *finalizes* its color, i.e., sets it to $\langle 0, b_v \rangle$. Otherwise, the vertex v sets its color to $\langle a_v, b_v + a_v \rangle$, where the addition is performed in $GF(p)$. We show (see Section 3) that when all vertices run this simple iterative step for $2p + 1 = 2(\Delta + 1) + 1$ rounds, the ultimate coloring ψ is a proper $(\Delta + 1)$-coloring. Moreover, at all times the graph is properly colored.

The simplicity and the uniformity of this iterative step makes it very powerful. In dynamic self-stabilizing environments vertices run this step forever in conjunction with an appropriate "check-and-fix" procedure, no matter what changes or faults occur in the network. It turns out that still, once faults stop occurring, within additional $O(\Delta)$ rounds the coloring converges to a proper $(\Delta + 1)$-coloring. In the edge-coloring scenario, every edge $e = (u, v)$ has a color $\varphi(e) = \langle a_e, b_e \rangle$, known to both endpoints. The endpoint u checks locally if there is an edge e_u incident on u, $e_u \neq e$, with $b_{e_u} = b_e$, and v makes an analogous test among edges incident on it. Then u and v communicate to one another *one single bit* each, which enables both of them to update the color of e. Therefore, this algorithm gives rise to the first communication- and time-efficient $(2\Delta - 1)$-edge-coloring algorithm. Moreover, this algorithm is extremely well suited to dynamic and self-stabilizing scenarios.

Some subtleties arise when $(\Delta+1)$ is not prime, and we overcome them by showing that in some cases the proof goes through even if the arithmetics is performed in an additive group $Z_{\Delta+1}$, rather than in a Galois field $GF(p)$. Another difficulty stems from the need to combine the AG algorithm with Linial's algorithm. The latter algorithm reduces the number of colors to $O(\Delta^2)$, and from there the AG algorithm takes over. However, in the self-stabilizing setting some vertices may run Linial's algorithm, while others have already proceeded to AG algorithm. Careful adaptations to both algorithms are required to handle such situations.

Finally, we also extend the AG algorithm to computing *arbdefective coloring*. For a pair of parameters α and β, a coloring φ is said to be *α-arbdefective β-coloring* if the β color classes of G induce subgraphs of arboricity at most α each. Arbdefective colorings were introduced by the first- and the second-named authors in [3], and they were shown to be extremely useful for efficient computation of proper colorings in [1, 3, 17]. Our extension of AG algorithm from proper to arbdefective colorings (we call the extended algorithm *ArbAG*) works very similarly to the AG algorithm. The only difference is that on each round, each vertex v tests if it has at most a certain number of neighbors u with $b_u = b_v$. (Recall that in AG algorithm, this threshold number is 0.) Other than that ArbAG has the same simple locally-iterative structure as algorithm AG, but the number of iterations of ArbAG is significantly smaller. (Note, however, that strictly speaking, a locally iterative algorithm is required to maintain a proper coloring on each round, while algorithm ArbAG maintains an arbdefective coloring.) This is in sharp contrast to previous methods [1, 3] of computing arbdefective colorings. The latter are far more involved, far less communication-efficient, and less time-efficient by polylogarithmic factors. As a result we also obtain improved (again, by polylogarithmic factors) algorithms for general (not necessarily locally-iterative) $(\Delta + 1)$-coloring and $(1 + \epsilon)\Delta$-coloring.

2 PRELIMINARIES

The function $\log^* n$ is the number of times the $\log_2$ function has to be applied iteratively starting from n, until we arrive at a number smaller than 2. The unique identity number (ID) of a vertex v in a graph G is denoted $id(v)$. The diameter $Diam(G)$ of a graph $G = (V, E)$ is the maximum (unweighted) distance between vertices $u, v \in V$. The *arboricity* $a = a(G)$ of a graph $G = (V, E)$ is the minimum number of forests into which the edge set E can be partitioned. A *d-defective p-coloring* is a vertex coloring using p colors such that each vertex has at most d neighbors colored by its color. A *b-arbdefective p-coloring* is a vertex coloring using p colors, such that each subgraph induced by vertices of the same color has arboricity at most b. We employ the following important fact. For any integer $\Delta > 0$, there exists a prime q in $[\Delta, 2\Delta]$. This is due to Bertrand-Chebyshev postulate. See, e.g., Theorem 418 in [22].

3 ADDITIVE-GROUP COLORING

In this section we present our main algorithm that computes a proper $O(\sqrt{k})$-coloring from a proper k-coloring, where $k = \Omega(\Delta^2)$. Consider a graph $G = (V, E)$ with a proper k-coloring ψ. For all vertices $v \in V$, we represent a color $\psi(v) = i$ by a pair $\langle a_v, b_v \rangle$. We do it by finding a prime number q, $\sqrt{k} \leq q \leq 2\sqrt{k}$. The color $\psi(v) = i$ is represented by the following pair $\psi(v) = \langle \lfloor i/q \rfloor, i \bmod q \rangle$. Our final goal is to eliminate the first coordinate, i.e., to change all nodes colors such that for every vertex $v \in V$, it will hold that $\psi(v) = \langle 0, b_v \rangle$, $0 \leq b_v < q$, and ψ is a proper q-coloring. Our algorithm proceeds in iterations, starting from the initial coloring ψ. In each iteration colors may change, but the coloring remains proper. We employ the following definition.

Definition 3.1. *Two neighbors u, v in G conflict with one another if and only if $\psi(v) = \langle a, b\rangle$ and $\psi(u) = \langle a', b\rangle$, where $0 \leq a, b, a' < q$.*

Denote $\psi(v) = \langle a, b\rangle$. We will refer to a as the first coordinate and to b as the second coordinate. Denote by $\psi_i(v)$ the color of $v \in V$ in round i. Our algorithm starts from a proper $k = \Omega(\Delta^2)$ coloring of the input graph $G = (V, E)$. In each round the algorithm performs the following step. For all $v \in V$ in parallel, if a node v conflicts with a neighboring node u, then the new color of v in the end of this round is $\psi_{i+1}(v) = \langle a, (b + a) \bmod q\rangle$. Otherwise (this means v does not conflict with any neighbor), we set $\psi_{i+1}(v) = \langle 0, b\rangle$, and the color of v becomes final and will not change anymore.[1] This completes the description of the algorithm. Note that a node does not have to send its new color to all of its neighbors. Rather it is enough to send only one bit indicating whether its color became final or that it changed according to the rule specified above. We will use this property later. Next, we prove correctness.

Lemma 3.2. *For each iteration i, the coloring $\psi_i(G)$ is proper.*

Proof. The proof is by induction on i. **Base: ($i = 0$):** holds trivially, since the initial coloring is proper.
Step: Assuming that in iteration i the coloring is proper, we prove that in iteration $i + 1$ it is proper as well. If a color of a node $v \in V$ is $\psi_i(v) = \langle a, b\rangle$, then for the next iteration the color is either $\psi_{i+1}(v) = \langle 0, b\rangle$ or $\psi_{i+1}(v) = \langle a, (b + a) \bmod q\rangle$. Consider an adjacent node u, i.e., $(u, v) \in E$. If $\psi_i(u) = \langle c, b\rangle$, where $0 \leq c < q$, then $c \neq a$, by the induction hypothesis. In this case, the new colors of the nodes will be $\psi_{i+1}(v) = \langle a, (b + a) \bmod q\rangle$ and $\psi_{i+1}(u) = \langle c, (b + c) \bmod q\rangle$ and since $c \neq a$ this means that the new colors of u and v are distinct. Otherwise, $\psi_i(u) = \langle c, d\rangle$, where $d \neq b$. If in iteration $i + 1$ it holds that $\psi_{i+1}(v) = \langle 0, b\rangle$ and $\psi_{i+1}(u) = \langle 0, d\rangle$, we are done since $b \neq d$. Otherwise, u or v had conflicts in iteration i. If exactly one of them had a conflict, then their colors in iteration $i + 1$ are distinct. (One of them has 0 in the first coordinate, while the other has not, in iteration $i + 1$.) It is left to consider the case that both had conflicts. Thus, $\psi_{i+1}(v) = \langle a, (b + a) \bmod q\rangle$ and $\psi_{i+1}(u) = \langle c, (d + c) \bmod q\rangle$. If $a \neq c$, we are done. Otherwise, $a = c$ and $b \neq d$, because ψ_i is proper. Thus, $b + a \not\equiv d + c \pmod q$, and $\psi_{i+1}(v) \neq \psi_{i+1}(u)$. □

We say that a vertex is in a *working* stage as long as its color $\langle a, b\rangle$ satisfies $a \neq 0$. Once a becomes 0, the vertex is in the *final* stage. In order to analyze the running time of the algorithm we observe in Lemmas 3.3, 3.4 and Corollary 3.5, assuming that q is sufficiently large, a pair of neighbors can conflict at most twice in q rounds. (Once in a working stage, and once in a final stage of one of the vertices.) Therefore, a vertex with less than $q/2$ neighbors will have a round out of q in which it conflicts with no neighbor. In this round it will select a final color. Since $q > 2 \cdot \Delta$, all vertices in the graph will select a color within q rounds. This gives rise to the following Corollary.

Lemma 3.3. *For $t \leq q$, suppose that our algorithm is executed for t rounds, and consider two neighboring nodes u, v in G that are in their respective working stages during these entire t rounds. Then u, v have the same second coordinate in their colors in the same round i, $0 \leq i < t$ (that is, $\psi_i(u) = \langle a, b\rangle$ and $\psi_i(v) = \langle c, b\rangle$, for some $0 \leq a, b, c < q$) at most once during these t consequent rounds.*

[1] Note, however, that a *finalized* vertex v, i.e., a vertex with $\psi_i(v) = \langle 0, b\rangle$, can keep running the same iterative step, and still its colors will stay unchanged.

Proof. Assume that in some iteration i it holds that $\psi_i(u) = \langle a, b\rangle$ and $\psi_i(v) = \langle c, b\rangle$. For each of the following iterations $j = i + 1, i + 2, \ldots$, the difference between the second coordinates is $(c - a) \cdot (j - i) \bmod q$. Note that since q is a prime and $a \neq c$ (since, by Lemma 3.2, the coloring is proper in all iterations, and in particular, ψ_i is a proper coloring), the equality $(c - a)(j - i) \bmod q = 0$ can only hold when $(j - i) \bmod q = 0$, i.e., only after additional q iterations. □

In the following lemma we complement Lemma 3.3.

Lemma 3.4. *For $t \leq q$, suppose that our algorithm is executed for t rounds, and consider two neighboring nodes u, v in G, such that u is in working stage and v is in final stage during these entire t rounds. Then u, v have the same second coordinate in their colors in the same round i, $0 \leq i < t$ (that is, $\psi_i(u) = \langle a, b\rangle$ and $\psi_i(v) = (0, b)$, for some $0 \leq a, b < q$) at most once during these t consequent rounds.*

Proof. Since v is in final stage, its color does not change during these t rounds. Indeed, it holds that $\langle 0, b\rangle = \langle 0, (b + 0) \bmod q\rangle$. On the other hand, u is in the working stage. If initially the color of v is $\langle c, d\rangle$, for some $0 \leq c, d < q$, then in the following t rounds it changes as follows: $\langle c, (d + c) \bmod q\rangle$, $\langle c, (d + 2c) \bmod q\rangle, \ldots, \langle c, (d + tc) \bmod q\rangle$. Since q is prime, all these values of the second coordinate are distinct in the field of integers modulo q. In other words, the equality $d + xc \equiv b \pmod q$ holds for exactly one element x of this field. Thus v conflicts with u at most once, in the round i where $d + ic \equiv b \pmod q$. □

Corollary 3.5. *Given a graph $G = (V, E)$ with a proper k-coloring, where $k = \Theta(\Delta^2)$, our Additive-Group Coloring algorithm produces a proper $O(\sqrt{k})$ coloring within $O(\Delta)$ rounds.*

Proof. By Lemma 3.3, for $q > 2\Delta$, two adjacent nodes in the working stage (whose colors are not final) cannot conflict with one other more than once during the first q rounds of the algorithm. However, two adjacent nodes can also conflict if exactly one of them has selected a final color. Once this happens, it will conflict with its neighbor that is still in the working stage at most once during these q rounds. (See Lemma 3.4.) Since any node starts from a working state, and once the state transits to final its color does not change anymore, a node cannot conflict with each of its neighbors more than twice. Therefore, for each node, within $q > 2 \cdot \Delta$ rounds, there must be a round in which it does not conflict with any of its neighbors. Hence, all nodes will reach a final stage within q rounds. Since $q \leq 2\sqrt{k} = O(\Delta)$, the statement about the running time of the corollary follows. A final color is of the form $\langle 0, b\rangle$, $0 \leq b < q$. Thus the number of employed colors is at most $q = O(\sqrt{k})$. □

Corollary 3.6. *Any graph $G = (V, E)$ can be colored with $\Delta + 1$ colors within $O(\Delta) + \log^* n$ rounds, by a locally-iterative algorithm.*

Proof. Running Linial's algorithm [31] on the input graph $G = (V, E)$ will produce a coloring $\varphi(G)$ using $O(\Delta^2)$ colors within $\log^* n + O(1)$ rounds. (Recall that Linial's algorithm is locally-iterative.)
At the second stage we run our Additive-Group algorithm on $\varphi(G)$.

This results in a new proper coloring $\psi(G)$ that employs $O(\Delta)$ colors. Computing the coloring ψ from φ requires $O(\Delta)$ rounds, by Corollary 3.5. At the last stage we reduce the number of colors to $\Delta + 1$ using the standard color reduction. This also requires $O(\Delta)$ time. Note that the standard color reduction is a locally-iterative algorithm as well. Therefore, the overall running time is $\log^* n + O(1) + O(\Delta) + O(\Delta) = O(\Delta + \log^* n)$. □

4 FULLY-DYNAMIC SELF-STABILIZING ALGORITHMS WITH $O(\Delta + \log^* n)$ ROUNDS

4.1 Fully-Dynamic Self-Stabilizing $O(\Delta)$-Coloring

In this section we employ a variant of Linial's algorithm for $O(\Delta^2)$-coloring that allows a vertex v to avoid being colored by colors from a given set $R(v)$ of size at most $O(\Delta)$ [1]. (This is useful when selecting a new color, to avoid collisions with some neighbors that have already obtained final colors.) We refer to this algorithm as Algorithm Excl-Linial.

Algorithm Excl-Linial is identical to Linial's original algorithm, except for the final stage that transforms a proper $O(\Delta^3)$-coloring into a proper $O(\Delta^2)$-coloring. In this stage each vertex v computes a polynomial $P_v(x)$ of degree 2 in a field of size $O(\Delta)$, and selects a color $\langle x, P_v(x)\rangle$, such that $\langle x, P_v(x)\rangle \neq \langle y, P_u(y)\rangle$, for any neighbor u of v and any y in that field. Since the degree of the polynomials in this stage is 2, each polynomial intersects with a neighboring node's polynomial in at most two points. Hence, there are at most 2Δ points on P_v that may intersect with some neighbor. If the field is of size $2\Delta + 1$, there must be a point such that $\langle x, P_v(x)\rangle \neq \langle y, P_u(y)\rangle$ for all neighbors u of v and all elements y in the field. Such a pair is selected by the original algorithm of Linial. In the modified variant, on the other hand, the field is of size greater than 3Δ. Consequently, if a set $R(v)$ of at most Δ forbidden colors is provided, there still exists an element x in that field, such that $\langle x, P_v(x)\rangle$ is not equal to any of the colors in the set $R(v)$, and neither to any $\langle y, P_u(y)\rangle$, for a neighbor u and an element y. Such a color is selected as a final color. Thus, we obtain an $O(\Delta^2)$-coloring were all colors belong to sets that exclude $O(\Delta)$ colors each, within $\log^* n + O(1)$ time. This completes the description of algorithm Excl-Linial.

Before describing our self-stabilizing algorithm, we define some notation, and describe yet another useful variant of Linial's algorithm, which we call Algorithm Mod-Linial. Let $r = \log^* n + O(1)$ denote the number of iterations in Linial's algorithm. Let $t_r = O((\Delta \log n)^2), t_{r-1} = O((\Delta(\log \Delta + \log\log n)^2), ..., t_1 = O(\Delta^2)$ denote upper bounds on the number of colors in the different iterations of Linial's algorithm. Define the intervals $I_0, I_1, I_2, ...$ as follows. $I_0 = [0, t_1 - 1], I_1 = [t_1, t_1 + t_2 - 1], ..., I_{r-1} = [t_1 + t_2 + ... + t_{r-1}, t_1 + t_2 + ... + t_r - 1], I_r = [t_1 + t_2 + ... + t_r, t_1 + t_2 + ... + t_r + n - 1]$. Since each such interval contains sufficient number of colors, we can map each color palette of each iteration of Linial's algorithm to one of the intervals defined above. Specifically, the palette of the first iteration is mapped to I_{r-1} (which is of size t_r), the palette of the second iteration is mapped to I_{r-2} (which is of size t_{r-1}), and so on, up to the last palette that is mapped to I_0. This way Linial's algorithm is modified, so that in each iteration $i = 1, 2, ..., r$ a coloring using a palette I_{r-i+1} is transformed into a coloring using the palette I_{r-i}. (The actual number of colors used from this palette is $O((\Delta \log^{(i)} n)^2)$.) The modified algorithm will be referred to as Mod-Linial. It accepts as input a color of a vertex v, a (sub)set of its neighbors colors, and a set of $O(\Delta)$ forbidden colors, and returns a new color for v. The range $I_r = [t_1 + t_2 + ... + t_r,\ t_1 + t_2 + ... + t_r + n - 1]$ will be used for an initial n-coloring obtained from IDs.

Our fully-dynamic self-stabilizing algorithm works as follows. The RAM of each vertex consists of a variable that holds a color in a range $\{0, 1, ..., t_1 + t_2 + ... + t_r + n - 1\}$. The ROM of each vertex holds the algorithm, the number of vertices n and the maximum degree Δ. In each round each vertex v checks whether it is in a proper state, i.e., its color is distinct from all colors of its neighbors. (See the pseudocode of Procedure Check-Error below.) If v is not in a proper state, the vertex returns to its initial state. (See lines 1- 3 of Procedure Self-Stabilizing-Coloring.) We define the initial state of a vertex with ID $j \in 0, 1, ..., n - 1$ by the color $t_1 + t_2 + ... + t_r + j$. Otherwise, the vertex is in a proper state. Then, the vertex v computes its next color or finalizes the current one. (See lines 4 - 20 of Procedure Self-Stabilizing-Coloring.) Specifically, as long as the vertex color belongs to an interval I_j for $j \geq 2$, i.e., the color is significantly larger than Δ^2, the vertex computes the next color from a smaller range using the algorithm Mod-Linial (lines 6-7 of Procedure Procedure Self-Stabilizing-Coloring). Once a color is in the interval I_1, the vertex must select a new color in the interval I_0 that is distinct from any neighboring color that is also in I_0. This is done in lines 9 - 11 of the procedure. The set S', computed in line 10 and provided as the third parameter of Procedure Mod-Linial in line 11, contains all possible colors that neighbors u of v that run already lines 12 - 18 (i.e., their colors are small enough) may obtain in the current iteration. Note that for each such $u \in \Gamma(v)$ there are at most 2 such colors. Finally, a color that is in the range I_0 either becomes final or changes to another color in I_0 according to Algorithm AG. See lines 12 - 18. This completes the description of the algorithm. Its pseudocode is provided below. Next, we analyze the algorithm.

Lemma 4.1. *Given an arbitrary graph $G = (V, E)$, our self-stabilizing algorithm produces a proper coloring $\psi(G)$ in each round, once faults no longer occur.*

Proof. Consider a round i. If a node $v \in V$ has a color that is equal to that of a neighbor u, i.e., $\psi_i(u) = \psi_i(v)$, then $\psi_{i+1}(v) = t_r + t_{r-1} + ... + t_1 + id(v) \neq \psi_{i+1}(u) = t_r + t_{r-1} + ... + t_1 + id(u)$. Otherwise, lines 3 - 20 are executed. Since it is assumed that no more faults will occur, we prove that lines 3-20 provide a proper coloring. If $j \geq 2$ (line 7) then $\psi_{i+1}(v)$ will be in the range I_{j-1}. (Any element in I_j is greater than any element in I_{j-1}, and thus numerical values of colors decrease as the algorithm proceeds. Also, all intervals are disjoint.) Therefore, all neighbors u with $\psi_i(u) \notin I_j$ will not select a new color $\psi_{i+1}(u)$ from I_{j-1}. For a neighbor u with $\psi_i(u) \in I_j$, its color belongs to Q, and Mod-Linial algorithm will produce a proper coloring.

If $j = 1$ then Mod-Linial algorithm works in the following way. It computes a new color from t_0, such that it is distinct from all neighbors' colors that transit from I_1 to I_0 in round i, and from all colors of the set S'. The latter set contains all possible colors that can be used in round $i + 1$ by neighbors of v with colors in the range I_0 in round i. Consequently, the new color of $\psi_{i+1}(v)$ of v is distinct from the new colors of such neighbors. Moreover, the new color is also distinct from new colors of the rest of the neighbors, since they were either in I_1 in round i, and do not collide with v in

round $i+1$ due to correctness of Mod-Linial, or in a higher range, and thus are not in I_0 in round $i+1$.
If $j = 0$, then lines 12 - 19 execute our Additive-Group algorithm (see Corollary 3.5), and produce a proper coloring for neighbors with $j = 0$. For neighbors with $j > 0$, the coloring is proper as well, by analysis of previous cases in this proof. □

Lemma 4.2. *Given an arbitrary graph $G = (V, E)$, our fully-dynamic self-stabilizing algorithm produces a proper $O(\Delta)$-coloring with $O(\Delta + \log^* n)$ stabilization-time.*

Proof. In the end of each round $i = 1, 2, \ldots$, counting from the moment that faults stop occurring, all colors are in the range $I_0 \cup I_1 \cup \ldots \cup I_{r+1-i}$. Therefore, within $r+1 = \log^* n + O(1)$ rounds, all colors are in the range I_0. From this moment and on, the procedure executes our Additive-Group algorithm in all vertices. Therefore, by Corollary 3.5, within $O(\Delta)$ additional rounds the number of colors becomes $O(\Delta)$. □

We also obtain a self-stabilizing algorithm that employs exactly $(\Delta + 1)$ colors. To this end, in each round each vertex v with a color of the from $< 0, b_v >$ whose all neighbors also have 0 in their first color coordinate performs the following. If b_v is greater then the colors of all v's neighbors, then v selects a new color $< 0, b'_v >$ such that $0 \le b'_v \le \Delta$, and $< 0, b'_v >$ is distinct from all colors of v's neighbors. Consequently, once all colors are of the form $< 0, b >$, $b = O(\Delta)$, at most $O(\Delta)$ additional rounds are required to arrive to a $(\Delta + 1)$- coloring, because at least one color is eliminated in each round. (This is the greatest color, as long as there are colors greater than Δ.) Further discussion about $(\Delta + 1)$-coloring appears in the full version of this paper [9]. We summarize this below.

Theorem 4.3. *Given an arbitrary graph $G = (V, E)$, our fully-dynamic self-stabilizing algorithm produces a proper $(\Delta + 1)$-coloring with $O(\Delta + \log^* n)$ stabilization time.*

4.2 Fully-Dynamic Self-Stabilizing MIS, MM, and $(2\Delta - 1)$-Edge-Coloring

We employ our self-stabilizing coloring algorithm from the previous section in order to compute MIS as follows. We add a bit μ_v to the RAM of each vertex $v \in V$. This bit represents whether v is in the MIS (if $\mu_v = 1$) or not in the MIS (if $\mu_v = 0$). We add the following instruction in the end of Procedure Self-Stabilizing-Coloring. If all neighbors u of v with smaller colors than that of v have $\mu_u = 0$, then we set $\mu_v = 1$. Otherwise, we set $\mu_v = 0$. This completes the description of the changes required to compute an MIS. The next lemma shows that within i rounds, for $i > 0$, after the stabilization of coloring, all vertices with colors $1, 2, \ldots, i$ induce a subgraph with a properly computed MIS. Consequently, within $O(\Delta)$ additional rounds an MIS of the entire input graph is achieved.

Proof. The proof is by induction on i. **Base (i = 0):** All vertices of color $< 0, 0 >$ do not have neighbors with smaller colors, and thus their μ bits become equal to 1. Since in this stage the coloring is proper, the set of such vertices is independent. Since it does not contain vertices of other colors in the current stage, the set is also maximal. (in other words, this set is an MIS of itself.)
Step: We consider the subset of vertices with the following colors: $\langle 0,0\rangle, \langle 0,1\rangle, \ldots., \langle 0,i\rangle$. By induction hypothesis, within i rounds from stabilization of the coloring, the subgraph induced by vertices of colors $\langle 0,0\rangle, \langle 0,1\rangle, \ldots., \langle 0,i-1\rangle$ has a properly computed MIS. Since colors do not change after stabilization, the μ bits of the vertices of this subgraph will not change in round $i+1$. In this round each vertex of color $\langle 0,i\rangle$ sets its μ bit to 1 if it has no neighbors with a smaller color in the MIS, and sets it to 0 otherwise. Consequently, there are no pair of neighbors with colors from $\{\langle 0,0\rangle, \langle 0,1\rangle, \ldots., \langle 0,i\rangle\}$, for which both their μ bits are set to 1. Moreover, each vertex of color smaller than $\langle 0,i\rangle$ for which $\mu = 0$ must have a neighbor with $\mu = 1$, by induction hypothesis. Each vertex of color $\langle 0,i\rangle$ for which $\mu = 0$ must have a neighbor with a smaller color and $\mu = 1$, according to the instruction that is executed in round $i+1$ after the stabilization of the coloring. Hence, after that round, the subgraph induced by $\langle 0,0\rangle, \langle 0,1\rangle, \ldots., \langle 0,i\rangle$ has a properly computed MIS. □

```
Check-Error (my_color, [neighbors_colors])
if my_color ∈ neighbors_colors then
    return error
end if
return valid
```

```
Self-Stabilizing-Coloring
1: if Check-Error(my_color, [neighbors_colors]) = error then
2:     my_color = t_1 + t_2 + ... + t_r + my_ID   /* initial state */
3: else
4:     Let I_j denote the range that my_color belongs to
5:     Let Q denote the subset of [neighbors_colors] of all colors
       that belong to I_j
6:     if j ≥ 2 then
7:         my_color = Mod-Linial(my_color, Q, ∅)
8:     else if j = 1 then
9:         Let S denote the subset of [neighbors_colors] of all colors
           that belong to I_0, represented as ordered pairs
10:        Let S' = {⟨a, (b+a) mod q⟩ | ⟨a,b⟩ ∈ S} ∪ {⟨0,b⟩ | ⟨a,b⟩ ∈
           S}
11:        my_color = Mod-Linial(my_color, Q, S') /* avoid collisions
           with S' */
12:    else if j = 0 then
13:        represent my_color as an ordered pair ⟨a, b⟩
14:        if ⟨a, b⟩ conflicts with a color in Q then
15:            my_color = ⟨a, (a + b) mod q⟩
16:        else
17:            my_color = ⟨0, b⟩ /* final color */
18:        end if
19:    end if
20: end if
```

Theorem 4.4. *Given an arbitrary graph $G = (V, E)$, our self-stabilizing algorithm produces a proper MIS within $O(\Delta + \log^* n)$ rounds after the last fault.*

Proof. Let $t_{cd} = O(\Delta + \log^* n)$ be the stabilization time of the coloring algorithm. (See Theorem 4.3.) Denote by U_i, $i = 1, 2, \ldots, \Delta+$

1, the set of vertices v that belong to MIS (i.e., have $\mu_v = 1$) at round $t_{cd} + i$ after faults stop occurring. Let ψ be the $(\Delta + 1)$-coloring maintained by the algorithm. (We know that t_{cd} rounds after the last fault occurred, ψ is indeed a proper $(\Delta + 1)$-coloring.)

We prove by induction on i that at time $t_{cd} + i$ after faults stop occurring, for $i = 1, 2, ..., \Delta + 1$, U_i is an MIS for the set $\hat{V}_i = \{v \mid 1 \leq \psi_i(v) \leq i\}$, where ψ_i is the coloring ψ maintained by the algorithm at that time.

Base (i = 1): All vertices of $\hat{V}_1$ form an independent set (because φ_1 is a proper $(\Delta + 1)$-coloring, because it is the coloring ψ more than t_{cd} rounds after the last fault occurred), and each of them joins MIS because they have no neighbors of smaller color.

Step: For some $i \leq \Delta$ we assume that U_i is an MIS for $\hat{V}_i$. Consider a vertex $v \in U_{i+1}$, i.e., $\psi_{i+1}(v) = i + 1$. This vertex had the same color $i+1$ for all the rounds $t_{cd}+1, t_{cd}+2, ..., t_{cd}+i+1$, counting from the moment T when faults stopped occurring. By end of round $T + t_{cd} + i$ or earlier, all its neighbors of smaller color (they also did not change their colors during the time interval $[T+t_{cd}, T+t_{cd}+i]$) have set their values μ_u. So in round $T + t_{cd} + i + 1$, if v has no smaller color neighbor in the MIS, it joins MIS. (It might have joined earlier, but it will anyway check again whether it has to join in round $T + t_{cd} + i + 1$.) Since vertices of $V_{i+1} = \{v \mid \psi_{i+1}(v) = i+1\}$ form an independent set, the resulting set U_{i+1} is an independent set for $\hat{V}_i \cup V_{i+1} = \hat{V}_{i+1}$. □

In the ordinary (non-stabilizing) setting it is possible to compute a maximal matching and an edge coloring by simulating the line-graph of the input graph, and computing an MIS and vertex-coloring of it. These solutions on the line graph directly provide solutions for maximal matching and edge coloring of the input graph within the same running time. This technique is applicable also to the self-stabilizing setting. Specifically, each vertex v simulates virtual vertices, one virtual vertex per edge adjacent on v. In the beginning of each round each vertex verifies whether the state of each of its virtual vertices that correspond to some edge equals to the state in the other endpoint of that edge. If this is not the case, the endpoint with a greater ID copies the state of the other endpoint for that virtual vertex. Consequently all edges have consistent representations, i.e., the same state in both their endpoints, in the entire graph. Now, a self-stabilizing MIS or vertex-coloring algorithm can be simulated correctly on the line graph in order to produce self-stabilizing maximal matching and edge-coloring of the input graph. In conjunction with Theorems 4.3, 4.4 this leads to the following result.

THEOREM 4.5. *Given an arbitrary graph $G = (V, E)$, our self-stabilizing algorithms produce a maximal matching and a proper $(2\Delta - 1)$-edge-coloring within $O(\Delta + \log^* n)$ stabilization time.*

5 EDGE COLORING WITHIN $O(\Delta + \log^* n)$ ROUNDS IN THE CONGEST MODEL AND $O(\Delta + \log n)$ ROUNDS IN THE BIT-ROUND MODEL

We employ our techniques in order to compute *edge colorings* using small messages. The algorithm consists of two stages. The first stage constructs an $O(\Delta^2)$-edge-coloring from scratch, and the second stage computes an $O(\Delta)$-coloring from this $O(\Delta^2)$-coloring. We remark that we cannot use the algorithm of Linial for the first stage, since its message complexity in the case of edge-coloring is quite large. Instead, we do the following. We invoke Kuhn's algorithm [29] for 2-defective Δ^2-edge coloring. This algorithm orients all edges towards endpoints with greater IDs. Then, each vertex assigns its outgoing edges distinct colors from the set $\{1, 2, ..., \Delta\}$. It also assigns its incoming edges distinct colors from the same range. Consequently, each edge obtains a pair of colors, one color from each of its endpoints. This is done within a single round by sending a message of size $O(\log n)$ per edge (in both directions).

Each color of an edge $e \in E$ can be represented as an ordered pair $\psi(e) = \langle i, j \rangle$, where $i, j \in \{1, 2, ..., \Delta\}$. Note that a set of edges with the same ψ-color consists of paths and cycles, since each vertex on such an edge has at most one another edge adjacent on it in this set. This is because the defect of ψ is 2. To remove the defect we run Cole and Vishkin coloring algorithm [10] on edges of each color class in parallel and assign a new color to each $e \in E$ in the form $\psi(e) = (i, j, k)$. The first two indices i, j are the result of the first stage, and the rightmost index $k \in \{1, 2, 3\}$ is the result of Cole-Vishkin's algorithm invocation.

Next, we compute an $O(\Delta)$-edge-coloring from the $O(\Delta^2)$-edge-coloring as follows. In each round both endpoints of an edge hold its color, that will be from now on represented as an ordered pair $\langle a, b \rangle$, $a, b \in O(\Delta)$, rather than a tuple. Consequently, each endpoint can check for conflicts of edges adjacent on it. For each edge with a conflict at an endpoint, the endpoint sends a message over this edge (consisting of a single bit) to notify the other endpoint about the conflict. Then, for each edge, both of its endpoint know whether it has a conflict with some adjacent edge or not. If the current edge color is $\langle a, b \rangle$, and there is a conflict, the new color becomes $\langle a, (a + b) \bmod q \rangle$. Otherwise, it becomes $\langle 0, b \rangle$. Both endpoints update the new color of their edge. This is done within a single round and by exchanging just a single bit on each edge. Then all vertices of the graph are ready to proceed to the next round and perform it in a similar way. The algorithm stops once all edges have colors of the from $\langle 0, b \rangle$, $0 \leq b < q = O(\Delta)$. (Here q is a prime number that satisfies that the original number of colors is at most q^2 and $q \geq 2\Delta - 1$.)

Lemma 5.1. *A proper $O(\Delta)$-edge coloring is obtained in $O(\Delta + \log^* n)$ rounds in the CONGEST model.*

PROOF. The algorithm starts with the invocation of Kuhn's algorithm that results in a 2-defective Δ^2-edge-coloring within $O(1)$ time. Then it is turned into a proper coloring using Cole-Vishkin algorithm within $O(\log^* n)$ time. Indeed, if prior to the execution of the latter algorithm a pair of adjacent edges had the same color $\langle i, j \rangle$, they now have distinct colors $\langle i, j, k \rangle$ and $\langle i, j, k' \rangle$, since Cole-Vishkin algorithm produces a proper 3-coloring of the edges in the set of color class $\langle i, j \rangle$. Next, in each round each color of an edge of the form $\langle a, b \rangle$ is transformed either into $\langle a, (a + b) \bmod q \rangle$ or into $\langle 0, b \rangle$. In both cases the new coloring is proper. See Lemma 3.5. Within $O(\Delta)$ rounds all colors obtain the form $\langle 0, b \rangle$. □

Lemma 5.2. *The bit complexity of our edge-coloring algorithm is $O(\Delta + \log n)$ per edge. If initially vertices know the IDs of their neighbors, then the bit complexity is $O(\Delta + \log \log n)$ per edge.*

Proof. Exchanging initial IDs between neighbors requires $O(\log n)$ bits. Exchanging the colors during the 2-defective Δ^2-edge-coloring requires $O(\log \Delta)$ bits. The first round of Cole-Vishkin algorithm is performed based on IDs of $O(\log n)$ bits. The second round of Cole-Vishkin algorithm requires $O(\log \log n)$ bits, the third one requires $O(\log \log \log n)$ bits, and so on. The last round of Cole-Vishkin algorithm requires a constant number of bits. The exchange between neighbors of the resulting proper $O(\Delta^2)$-edge coloring of the input graph requires $O(\log \Delta)$ bits. Each of the following $O(\Delta)$ rounds requires 1 bit. □

We can also produce edge-coloring with exactly $(2\Delta - 1)$-colors as follows. Once the stage of $O(\Delta)$-edge-coloring terminates, each vertex sends to its neighbors all colors that are used by edges adjacent on it. Since the range of colors is $O(\Delta)$, this can be done by sending a boolean array of length $O(\Delta)$. This requires $O(\Delta)$ bit-rounds. Then, each vertex knows whether an edge adjacent on its has a locally-maximal color. (I.e., greater than the colors of all other edges adjacent to that edge.) Each endpoint of such an edge selects the minimum color in the range $[0, 2 \cdot \Delta - 2]$ as the new proper color of that edge. Since both endpoints have the same set of forbidden colors of all adjacent edges, both of them select the same new edge-color. Then, endpoints of edges with color updates notify their neighbors about the new color. Since the set of color updates consists of non-adjacent edges, each vertex has to send information about a single color, which requires $O(\log \Delta)$ bits. After $O(\Delta)$ such iterations of maximal-color reductions, we arrive at a $(2\Delta - 1)$-edge-coloring. We summarize this below.

Theorem 5.3. *We compute $(2\Delta - 1)$-edge-coloring within $O(\Delta + \log^* n)$ rounds in the CONGEST model, within $O(\Delta \log \Delta + \log \log n)$ rounds in the Bit-Round model with knowledge of neighbors' IDs, and within $O(\Delta \log \Delta + \log n)$ time in the Bit-Round model without knowledge of neighbors' IDs.*

6 ARBDEFECTIVE $O(\frac{\Delta}{p})$-COLORING WITH DEFECT $O(p)$

Lovasz [32] showed that in a graph with maximum degree Δ, there exists a p-defective $\frac{\Delta}{p}$-coloring, where $1 \le p \le \Delta$. In this section we devise an algorithm for $O(\sqrt{\Delta})$-*arbdefective* $O(\sqrt{\Delta})$-coloring within $O(\sqrt{\Delta} + \log^* n)$ rounds. More generally, our algorithm computes an $O(p)$-arbdefective $O(\Delta/p)$-coloring within time $O(\Delta/p + \log^* n)$. (Definitions of defective- and arbdefective-colorings are found in Section 2.) Our algorithm starts with computing an $O(\sqrt{\Delta})$-defective $O(\Delta)$-coloring. This is done using the algorithm of [6] within $O(\log^* n)$ rounds. (More generally, the algorithm of [6] computes a p-defective $O((\Delta/p)^2)$-coloring, for any positive parameter p, in $\log^* n + O(1)$ time.) Then we perform $O(\Delta/p) = O(\sqrt{\Delta})$ rounds of color updates, rather than $O(\Delta)$ as in our Additive-Group algorithm. The update rule for arbdefective coloring is different from the rule for proper coloring. Specifically, we tolerate up to p conflicts. In other words, instead of setting $\psi_{i+1}(v) = \langle 0, b \rangle$ only if there are no neighbors with the same value b in the second coordinate, we set this if there are at most $p = \Theta(\sqrt{\Delta})$ neighbors of different original ψ-color with the same second coordinate b. We will show in the sequel that after $O(\Delta/p) = O(\sqrt{\Delta})$ rounds all colors are of the form $\langle 0, b \rangle$, and each color class induces a subgraph of arboricity $O(p)$. Thus, as a result we have an $O(\sqrt{\Delta})$-arbdefective $O(\sqrt{\Delta})$-coloring. The pseudocode of the algorithm is provided below. The next lemmas analyze its running time and show its correctness.

Arbdefective-Color($G, v, p = \sqrt{\Delta}$)

1: ψ = compute an $O(p)$-defective $O((\Delta/p)^2)$-coloring of G using [6] /* $O(\sqrt{\Delta})$-defective $O(\Delta)$-coloring */
2: represent $\psi_0(v)$ as an ordered pair $\langle a, b \rangle$, such that $a, b \in O(\Delta/p)$. /* $a, b \in O(\sqrt{\Delta})$ */
3: let $q = \Theta(\Delta/p)$ be the smallest prime such that q is greater than $2\lceil \Delta/p \rceil + 1$
4: **for** $i = 0, 1, , ...2\lceil \Delta/p \rceil$ **do**
5:   **if** v has at most p neighbors u of a different ψ-color, such that the second coordinate of $\psi_i(u)$ equals the second coordinate of $\psi_i(v)$ **then**
6:     $\psi_{i+1}(v) = \langle 0, b \rangle$
7:   **else**
8:     $\psi_{i+1}(v) = \langle a, (a + b) \bmod q \rangle$
9:   **end if**
10: **end for**

Lemma 6.1. *The produced coloring $\psi_{2\lceil \Delta/p \rceil+1}$ is of the form $\langle 0, b \rangle$, $0 \le b < q = \Theta(\Delta/p)$, for all $v \in V$.*

Proof. Consider a vertex $v \in V$. The vertex v can conflict at most twice with each neighbor u of different ψ-color within q rounds, i.e., at most once before u finalizes its color, and at most once after that. If v conflicts with more than p neighbors in each round, it means it has more than $\frac{1}{2} \cdot p \cdot (2\lceil \Delta/p \rceil + 1) > \Delta$ neighbors. This is a contradiction. Therefore, there is a round $i \in \{0, 1, ..., 2\lceil \Delta/p \rceil\}$ in which v conflicts with at most p neighbors. In this round its color finalizes, i.e., becomes of the form $\langle 0, b \rangle$. □

Lemma 6.2. *The resulting coloring $\psi_{2\lceil \Delta/p \rceil+1}$ has arbdefect at most $O(p) = O(\sqrt{\Delta})$.*

Proof. For the purpose of analysis, orient each edge $(u, v) \in E$ towards the endpoint that first set ψ_{i+1} to $\langle 0, b \rangle$. If both endpoints u, v did it in the same round, orient (u, v) towards the endpoint with greater ID. Let i denote the round in which v selects a color of the form $\langle 0, b \rangle$ for the first time. Observe that once a vertex v selects a color of the form $\langle 0, b \rangle$, its outgoing neighbors have already colors of the form $\langle 0, b' \rangle$. Thus, they will never change their colors from this moment and on. Moreover, the number of such neighbors of v of different original ψ-color and the same second coordinate of ψ_i is at most $p = \sqrt{\Delta}$. In addition, v may have at most $O(p)$ neighbors with the same original ψ-color, since the coloring ψ computed in line 1 is $O(p)$-defective. Thus, upon termination all vertices of the same $\psi_{2\lceil \Delta/p \rceil+1}$-color induce a subgraph with arboricity $O(p)$. This is because each vertex in such a subgraph has $O(p)$ outgoing edges, each of which can be assigned a distinct label from a range of size $O(p)$. Then, all edges of the same label form a forest, and the number of forests is $O(p)$. In other words, the resulting coloring has arbdefect at most $O(p)$. □

Lemma 6.3. *The running time of the algorithm is $O(\Delta/p + \log^* n) = O(\sqrt{\Delta} + \log^* n)$.*

Proof. Computing a defective-coloring in line 1 requires $O(\log^* n)$ time. Each iteration of the for-loop requires a single round. There are $O(\Delta/p) = O(\sqrt{\Delta})$ such iterations. □

The latter result gives rise to improved $(1+\epsilon)\Delta$-coloring and $(\Delta+1)$-coloring algorithms. This is summarized in the next theorem.

Theorem 6.4. *We compute $(1+\epsilon)\Delta$-coloring within $O(\sqrt{\Delta}+\log^* n)$ deterministic time, for an arbitrarilly small constant $\epsilon > 0$, and $(\Delta+1)$-coloring within $O(\sqrt{\Delta \log \Delta} \log^* \Delta + \log^* n)$ deterministic time.*

Proof. In [1] it was shown that given an $O(\sqrt{\Delta})$-arbdefective $O(\sqrt{\Delta})$-coloring one can compute a proper $(1+\epsilon)\Delta$-vertex-coloring within $O(\sqrt{\Delta} + \log^* n)$ deterministic time. (For more details, we refer the reader to the discussion in Section 3.4 of [1]. However, such an arbdefective coloring is computed in [1] only within time $(\sqrt{\Delta}\log^3 \Delta + \log^* n)$. See Lemma 3.5, Corollary 3.12, and the discussion preceding it in [1]. Consequently, the overall running time of the algorithm of [1] for $(1+\epsilon)\Delta$-coloring is $(\sqrt{\Delta}\log^3 \Delta + \log^* n)$ as well.) Our improved running time of arbdefective coloring (cf. Lemma 6.3) in conjunction with the procedure of [1] (i.e., by replacing the invocation of line 1 of Algorithm 1 of [1] by an invocation of our new algorithm Arbdefective-Color), gives rise to a deterministic $(1+\epsilon)\Delta$-coloring within $O(\sqrt{\Delta} + \log^* n)$ time.

It is shown in [17] that a deterministic $(\Delta+1)$-coloring is obtained in $O(\sqrt{\Delta}\log^{2.5} \Delta + \log^* n)$ time using arbdefective colorings. Specifically, the proof of Lemma 4.2 of [17] shows that given an β-arbdefective k-coloring algorithm with $O(k)$ running time, a proper $(\Delta+1)$-coloring is computed within time $O(\log^* n + T_A)$, where T_A is given by the recursive formula $T_A(\Delta) = O(k \log^* \Delta) + T_A(O(\beta^2 \log \Delta))$. By setting $\beta = \sqrt{\Delta/(c \log \Delta)}$ and $k = \sqrt{c\Delta \log \Delta}$, for a sufficiently large constant c, this recursive formula evaluates to $O(\sqrt{\Delta \log \Delta} \log^* \Delta)$. Moreover, we compute such β-arbdefective k-coloring within $O(\sqrt{\Delta \log \Delta} + \log^* n)$ time. (See Lemma 6.3.) Thus by using our Arbdefective-Color algorithm in conjunction with the procedure of [17], we obtain $(\Delta+1)$-coloring in $O(\sqrt{\Delta \log \Delta} \log^* \Delta + \log^* n)$ time. □

REFERENCES

[1] L. Barenboim. Deterministic $(\Delta+1)$-Coloring in Sublinear (in Δ) Time in Static, Dynamic and Faulty Networks. *Journal of the ACM*, 63(5) : 47, 2016.

[2] L. Barenboim, and M. Elkin. Distributed $(\Delta+1)$- coloring in linear (in Δ) time. In *Proc. of the 41st ACM Symp. on Theory of Computing*, pp. 111-120, 2009.

[3] L. Barenboim, and M. Elkin. Deterministic distributed vertex coloring in polylogarithmic time. In *Proc. 29th ACM Symp. on Principles of Distributed Computing*, pages 410-419, 2010.

[4] L. Barenboim, and M. Elkin. Distributed deterministic edge coloring using bounded neighborhood independence. In *Proc. of the 30th ACM Symp. on Principles of Distributed Computing*, pages 129 - 138, 2011.

[5] L. Barenboim, and M. Elkin. Distributed Graph Coloring: Fundamentals and Recent Developments. *Morgan and Claypool*, 2013.

[6] L. Barenboim, M. Elkin, and F. Kuhn. Distributed (Delta+1)-Coloring in Linear (in Delta) Time. *SIAM Journal on Computing*, 43(1): 72-95, 2014.

[7] L. Barenboim, M. Elkin, T. Maimon. Deterministic Distributed $(\Delta + o(\Delta))$-Edge-Coloring, and Vertex-Coloring of Graphs with Bounded Diversity. In *Proc. of the 36th ACM Symp. on Principles of Distributed Computing*, pages 175-184, 2017.

[8] L. Barenboim, M. Elkin, S. Pettie, and J. Schneider. The locality of distributed symmetry breaking. In *Proc. of the 53rd Annual Symp. on Foundations of Computer Science*, pages 321-330, 2012.

[9] L. Barenboim, M. Elkin U. Goldenberg. Locally-Iterative Distributed $(\Delta+1)$-Coloring below Szegedy-Vishwanathan Barrier, and Applications to Self-Stabilization and to Restricted-Bandwidth Models *https://arxiv.org/pdf/1712.00285.pdf*

[10] R. Cole, and U. Vishkin. Deterministic coin tossing with applications to optimal parallel list ranking. *Information and Control*, 70(1):32–53, 1986.

[11] E. Dijkstra. Self-stabilizing systems in spite of distributed control. *Communication of the ACM*, 17 (11): 643âĂŞ644, 1974.

[12] S. Dolev. Self-Stabilization. *MIT Press*, 2000.

[13] S. Dolev, and T. Herman. Superstabilizing Protocols for Dynamic Distributed Systems. *Chicago J. Theor. Comput. Sci.* 1997.

[14] D. Dubhashi, D. Grable, and A. Panconesi. Nearly-optimal distributed edge-colouring via the nibble method. *Theoretical Computer Science, a special issue for the best papers of ESA95*, 203(2):225–251, 1998.

[15] M. Elkin, S. Pettie, and H. Su. $(2\Delta-1)$-Edge-Coloring is Much Easier than Maximal Matching in the Distributed Setting. In *Proc. of the 26th ACM-SIAM Symp. on Discrete Algorithms*, pages 355-370, 2015.

[16] M. Fischer, M. Ghaffari, and F. Kuhn . Deterministic Distributed Edge Coloring via Hypergraph Maximal Matching. To appear in *58th Annual Symp on Foundations of Computer Science*, 2017.

[17] P. Fraigniaud, M. Heinrich, and A. Kosowski. Local Conflict Coloring. In *Proc. of the 57th Annual Symp. on Foundations of Computer Science*, pages 625 - 634, 2016.

[18] D. Grable, and A. Panconesi. Nearly optimal distributed edge colouring in O(log log n) rounds. *Random Structures and Algorithms*, 10(3): 385-405, 1997.

[19] A. Goldberg, and S. Plotkin. Parallel $(\Delta+1)$-Coloring of Constant-Degree Graphs. *Inf. Process. Lett.* 25(4): 241-245, 1987.

[20] A. Goldberg, S. Plotkin, and G. Shannon. Parallel symmetry-breaking in sparse graphs. *SIAM Journal on Discrete Mathematics*, 1(4):434–446, 1988.

[21] N. Guellati, and H. Kheddouci. A survey on self-stabilizing algorithms for independence, domination, coloring, and matching in graphs. *Journal of Parallel and Distributed Computing*, 70(4): 406-415, 2010.

[22] G. Hardy, and E. Wright. An introduction to the theory of numbers. *Oxford university press*, 5th edition, 1980.

[23] D. Hefetz, F. Kuhn, Y. Maus, and A. Steger. Polynomial Lower Bound for Distributed Graph Coloring in a Weak LOCAL Model. In *Proc. of the 30th International Symp. on DiStributed Computing*, pages 99 - 113, 2016.

[24] T. Herman. Self-stabilization bibliography: Access guide. *Chicago Journal of Theoretical Computer Science*, Working Paper WP-1, 2002.

[25] S.C. Hsu, S.T. Huang. A self-stabilizing algorithm for maximal matching. *Information Processing Letters*, 43 (2):7781, 1992 .

[26] M. Ikeda, S. Kamei, and H. Kakugawa. A space-optimal self-stabilizing algorithm for the maximal independent set problem. *In Proc. 3rd International Conference on Parallel and Distributed Computing, Applications and Technologies*, 2002.

[27] A. Kosowski, L. Kuszner. Self-stabilizing algorithms for graph coloring with improved performance guarantees. In *Proc. 8th International Conference on Artificial Intelligence and Soft Computing*, pages 1150-1159 2006.

[28] K. Kothapalli, C. Scheideler, M. Onus, and C. Schindelhauer. Distributed coloring in $O(\sqrt{\log n})$ bit rounds. In *Proc. of the 20th International Parallel and Distributed Processing Symp.*, 2006.

[29] F. Kuhn. Weak graph colorings: distributed algorithms and applications. In *Proc. of the 21st ACM Symp. on Parallel Algorithms and Architectures*, pages 138–144, 2009.

[30] F. Kuhn, and R. Wattenhofer. On the complexity of distributed graph coloring. In *Proc. 25th ACM Symp. Principles of Distributed Computing*, pp. 7–15, 2006.

[31] N. Linial. Distributive graph algorithms: Global solutions from local data In *Proc. 28th Symp. on Foundation of Computer Science*, pp. 331–335, 1987.

[32] L. Lovasz. On decompositions of graphs. *Studia Sci. Math. Hungar.*, 1:237âĂŞ238, 1966.

[33] M. Naor, and L. Stockmeyer. What can be computed locally? In *Proc. 25th ACM Symp. on Theory of Computing*, pages 184-193, 1993.

[34] S. Pai, G. Pandurangan, S. Pemmaraju, T. Riaz, and P. Robinson. Symmetry Breaking in the Congest Model: Time- and Message-Efficient Algorithms for Ruling Sets. https://arxiv.org/abs/1705.07861

[35] A. Panconesi, and R. Rizzi. Some simple distributed algorithms for sparse networks. *Distributed Computing*, 14(2):97–100, 2001.

[36] A. Panconesi, and A. Srinivasan. Randomized Distributed Edge Coloring via an Extension of the Chernoff-Hoeffding Bounds. *SIAM Journal on Computing*, 26(2):350-368, 1997.

[37] D. Peleg. *Distributed Computing: A Locality-Sensitive Approach.* SIAM, 2000.

[38] S. Sur, and P.K. Srimani. A self-stabilizing algorithm for coloring bipartite graphs. *Information Sciences*, 69, pages 219-227, 1993 .

[39] M. Szegedy, and S. Vishwanathan. Locality based graph coloring. In *Proc. 25th ACM Symp. on Theory of Computing*, pages 201-207, 1993.

[40] V. Vizing. On an estimate of the chromatic class of a p-graph. *Metody Diskret. Analiz*, 3: 25-30, 1964.

Lower Bounds for Searching Robots, some Faulty*

Andrey Kupavskii
University of Birmingham
Birmingham, UK
Moscow Institute of Physics and Technology
Moscow, Russia
kupavskii@ya.ru

Emo Welzl
Department of Computer Science
ETH Zurich
Zurich, Switzerland
emo@inf.ethz.ch

ABSTRACT

Suppose we are sending out k robots from 0 to search the real line at constant speed (with turns) to find a target at an unknown location; f of the robots are faulty, meaning that they fail to report the target although visiting its location (called crash type). The goal is to find the target in time at most $\lambda|d|$, if the target is located at d, $|d| \geq 1$, for λ as small as possible. We show that this cannot be achieved for

$$\lambda < 2\frac{\rho^\rho}{(\rho-1)^{\rho-1}} + 1, \ \rho := \frac{2(f+1)}{k},$$

which is tight due to earlier work (see J. Czyzowitz, E. Kranakis, D. Krizanc, L. Narayanan, J. Opatrny, PODC'16, where this problem was introduced). This also gives some better than previously known lower bounds for so-called Byzantine-type faulty robots that may actually wrongly report a target.

In the second part of the paper we deal with the m-rays generalization of the problem, where the hidden target is to be detected on m rays all emanating at the same point. Using a generalization of our methods, along with a useful relaxation of the original problem, we establish a tight lower for this setting as well (as above, with $\rho := m(f+1)/k$). When specialized to the case $f = 0$, this resolves the question on parallel search on m rays, posed by three groups of scientists some 15 to 30 years ago: by Baeza-Yates, Culberson, and Rawlins; by Kao, Ma, Sipser, and Yin; and by Bernstein, Finkelstein, and Zilberstein. The m-rays generalization is known to have connections to other, seemingly unrelated, problems, including hybrid algorithms for on-line problems, and so-called contract algorithms.

CCS CONCEPTS

• **Computing methodologies** → **Distributed algorithms**; • **Mathematics of computing** → *Combinatorial algorithms*; • **Computer systems organization** → *Robotics*; *Dependable and fault-tolerant systems and networks*;

*This research was initiated at the 15th Gremo's Workshop on Open Problems (GWOP), Pochtenalp, Switzerland, June 12-16, 2017.

PODC '18, July 23–27, 2018, Egham, United Kingdom

ACM ISBN 978-1-4503-5795-1/18/07.
https://doi.org/10.1145/3212734.3212745

KEYWORDS

m-ray search; cow-at-a-fence problem; hybrid algorithms; lower bounds

ACM Reference Format:
Andrey Kupavskii and Emo Welzl. 2018. Lower Bounds for Searching Robots, some Faulty. In *PODC '18: ACM Symposium on Principles of Distributed Computing, July 23–27, 2018, Egham, United Kingdom.* ACM, New York, NY, USA, 7 pages. https://doi.org/10.1145/3212734.3212745

1 INTRODUCTION

The following problem was raised in 1963 by Bellman [10] and addressed in the 60s by Beck [6–8] and Franck [18] (quoting from Beck's paper [6]):

> *"A man in an automobile searches for another man who is located at some point of a certain road. He starts at a given point and knows in advance the probability that the second man is at any given point of the road. Since the man being sought might be in either direction from the starting point, the searcher will, in general, have to turn around many times before finding his target. How does he search so as to minimize the expected distance traveled? When can this minimum expectation actually be achieved?"*

The authors were interested in proving the existence of and finding optimal strategies for different distributions, as well as proving non-existence results. In particular, in [8] it is shown that, without apriori knowledge of the distribution, we cannot hope the distance traveled to be smaller than 9 times the expected distance to the target.

A variant of the problem was rediscovered in the late 80s by computer scientists, and it became known as the cow path problem (or cow at a fence problem). Quoting from [4]:

> *"A cow comes to an infinitely long straight fence. The cow knows that there is a gate in the fence, and she wants to get to the other side. Unfortunately, she doesn't know where the gate is located. Assume that the gate is positioned in an integer number of steps away from the cow and that the cow can only recognize the gate when directly upon it. How can she optimally find the gate?"*

By optimality the authors mean the smallest worst-case ratio between the distance traveled and the distance to the gate (the *competitive ratio*). It is easy to see that the strategy in which the cow goes 1 to the left, then back and 2 to the right, then back and 4 to the left etc. gives the worst-case ratio of 9. It is shown in [4] (de-facto reproving one of the results of [8]) that one cannot hope for a better ratio.

The cow path problem gave rise to a significant line of research in computer science. Several variants of the problem were addressed ([12, 15]), as well as its planar variants [4, 5] that go back to another famous search problem, the lost at sea problem [9, 19]. We refer the reader to the book [2], in which many of the single robot search problems, including the cow path problem, are discussed. Motivated by numerous applications, different possible variants of collective search problems were considered in the context of random walks [1], forging [16], unmanned aerial vehicles [22].

In [13], [14] the authors proposed the following parallel search version of the cow path problem: We are sending out k robots from 0 to explore the real line $\mathbb{R}$, each one traveling at unit speed, changing directions according to some strategy we are free to prescribe. There is a target hidden at a point x of the real line, where $|x| \geq 1$. The robots may detect the target only when they arrive at the point where the target is hidden. Moreover, f robots are *faulty*. The problem is to determine the minimal *competitive ratio*: the supremum, over all possible target locations x, $|x| \geq 1$, of the ratio $\frac{\tau(x)}{|x|}$, for $\tau(x)$ the time taken for the non-faulty robots to be sure about the location of the target at x.

In [14] the authors focus on the faults of the *crash* type: When passing through the target, the robot does not detect it. We denote the competitive ratio in this setting by $A(k, f)$.

In [13] the authors study the faults of the *Byzantine* type: A faulty robot may stay silent even when it detects or visits the target, or may claim that it has found the target when, in fact, it has not found it. In this case we denote the competitive ratio by $B(k, f)$.

One of our contributions is the complete resolution of the case of faults of crash type (or *silent* robots):

Theorem 1.1. *Let us denote $s := 2(f + 1) - k$ and $\rho := \frac{2(f+1)}{k}$. If $0 < s \leq k$ (i.e. $1 < \rho \leq 2$) then we have*

$$A(k, f) = 2\sqrt[k]{\frac{(k+s)^{k+s}}{s^s k^k}} + 1 = 2\frac{\rho^\rho}{(\rho-1)^{\rho-1}} + 1\,. \tag{1}$$

We note that if $s \leq 0$, that is, $k \geq 2(f + 1)$, then by sending $f + 1$ of the robots to ∞ and $f + 1$ of the robots to $-\infty$ we achieve a competitive ratio 1. We also note that $s > k$, i.e. $f + 1 > k$, means that $k = f$, in which case we cannot find the target since all robots are faulty.

In [14] the authors exhibited a natural strategy which achieves the ratio in (1), as well as provided some lower bounds for $A(k, f)$. Thus, our contribution in Theorem 1.1 is the matching lower bound.

A lower bound for crash-type faulty robots is also a lower bound for Byzantine-type faulty robots. By this relation, our bounds also improve on the known bounds for Byzantine-type faulty robots, e.g. the bound of $B(3, 1) \geq 3.93$ from [13] is now at $B(3, 1) \geq \frac{8}{3}\sqrt[3]{4} + 1 \approx 5.23$.

More importantly, we develop a method which allows to deal with problems of this type. We demonstrate this in the proof of Theorem 1.1 in Section 2. In Section 3, we generalize Theorem 1.1 to the case of m rays, thus resolving an old question, which appeared in at least three different papers. We also give several useful relaxations of the original problem, which shed more light on this group of questions. Some of the less important proofs are deferred to Appendix.

2 PROOF OF THEOREM 1.1

We are given k robots, f of them faulty of crash type. To assure that the target at $x \in \mathbb{R}$ is found in time at most $\lambda|x|$, the point x has to be visited by at least $f + 1$ robots in time (otherwise the adversary will place the target there and choose the first f robots arriving at x to be faulty and stay silent). Therefore, for each pair of points $(x, -x)$, $x \in \mathbb{R}_{\geq 1}$, at least $2(f + 1) - k = s$ robots need to pass through both points before time λx elapses. If a robot visits both $(x, -x)$ in time λx, then we say that it *λ-covers* x. Similarly, if x is λ-covered s times by a group of several robots, we say that it is *s-fold λ-covered.* Since we are going to work with coverings in different settings, let us give the following general definition.

Definition 2.1. Fix $\lambda > 1$ and $s \in \mathbf{N}$. For a covering problem of a certain object with some set of rules (called *the setting*), and a certain set S we say that S is *λ-covered*, if for any point in S at distance x from the origin it was visited by the robot within time λx (where "visited" is interpreted within the setting, and should comply with the rules of the setting). We may also say that it is the *λ-covering of S*. Similarly, we say that a robot or set of robots we say that it produces an s-fold λ-covering of S (in some setting), if each point was λ-covered at least s times.

Note that this definition is strategy-dependent. Let us now formalize the covering setting that we are working with in this proof.

The symmetric line-cover setting: The goal is to cover $\mathbb{R}_{\geq 1}$. The robot (robots) moves on $\mathbb{R}$ with unit speed, starting from the origin. A point $x \in \mathbb{R}_{\geq 1}$ is covered by a robot r at the moment when r visited both x and $-x$, it is *λ-covered*, if that happens within time λx. A robot can cover any point at most once.

Throughout the proof we will be working with the s-fold λ-covering of $\mathbb{R}_{\geq 1}$ with k robots in the symmetric line-cover setting for fixed s and λ. Therefore, slightly abusing notation, we will use the term *$\pm$-covering* to refer to this covering problem.

By the above discussion, any valid strategy with competitive ratio λ for the original problem (of detecting a target with k robots, f of which are faulty of the crash type) is also a strategy for $\pm$-covering $\mathbb{R}_{\geq 1}$ with k robots. We actually obtain a lower bound as in (1) for the competitive ratio for the $\pm$-covering strategies. Our goal is to prove the following result.

Theorem 2.2. *It is impossible to $\pm$-cover $\mathbb{R}_{\geq 1}$ with k robots if*

$$\lambda < 2\sqrt[k]{\frac{(k+s)^{k+s}}{s^s k^k}} + 1\,.$$

For each individual robot r we will restrict ourselves to strategies described by an infinite nondecreasing sequence $T = T^{(r)} = (t_1, t_2, t_3, \ldots)$ over $\mathbb{R}_{\geq 1}$, with the interpretation that the robot is sent till $+t_1$ in the positive direction, till $-t_2$ in the negative direction, till $+t_3$ in the positive direction, etc. We argue that this carries no loss of generality.

First, it is clear that for $\pm$-covering, we may assume to start in the positive direction. Second, if the robot ever turns in territory that was visited before by this robot, we can shift the turning point in the direction where we came from (since we skip only parts of $\mathbb{R}$ which we have visited already, and any further visits occur now even earlier). These two observations restrict already to movements that alternate between turning at positive and negative numbers, actually with the positive turning points increasing and the absolute values of negative turning points increasing. Now suppose for $0 < x_2 < x_1$, the robot turns at x_1 and then at $-x_2$. Note that the interval $(x_2, x_1]$ is covered, but $[-x_1, x_2)$ is not, so as for $\pm$-covering, we may as well turn at x_2 instead of x_1 (since after turning at $-x_2$, we will return to $(x_2, x_1]$ before we actually extend our trip to points smaller than $-x_2$). Thus, we can transform any strategy to an at least as efficient strategy of the type as above.

Given a strategy $T = T^{(r)} = (t_1, t_2, t_3, \ldots)$ of a single robot r, it is easy to see that for x with $t_{i-1} < x \leq t_i$, it takes exactly $2(t_1 + t_2 + \cdots + t_i) + x$ time to visit both x and $-x$ (note that indeed the sum goes up to "t_i"). So in order for the robot to λ-cover x, we need

$$x \geq \frac{1}{\mu}(t_1 + t_2 + \cdots + t_i) \text{ for } \mu := \tfrac{\lambda-1}{2}. \tag{2}$$

Let us set

$$t_i'' := \max\left\{\frac{1}{\mu}(t_1 + t_2 + \cdots + t_i), t_{i-1}\right\} \tag{3}$$

unless this value exceeds t_i, when we leave t_i'' undefined. All i with t_i'' defined we call *fruitful*. It is clear that robot r λ-covers exactly

$$\mathrm{Cov}_\mu(T) := \bigcup_{i \text{ fruitful}} [t_i'', t_i]\ .$$

Note that if we skip a turn t_{i^*} in T, then, of course, we lose the interval $[t_{i^*}'', t_{i^*}]$, but following intervals (for $i > i^*$) extend even further to the left. That is, turning points that are not fruitful can be skipped, in this way definitely λ-covering at least as much. Moreover, it becomes clear that if $t_{i+1} = t_i$ (hence $t_{i+1}'' = t_{i+1}$, if defined), then we can skip t_{i+1} in the strategy thereby covering at least as much.

We move now to considering all robots, not just individual ones. If we are given a $\pm$-covering by k robots, then each point of $\mathbb{R}_{\geq 1}$ is contained in $\mathrm{Cov}_\mu(T^{(r)})$ for at least s (out of the k) robots. By truncating some of the intervals from $[t_i'', t_i]$ to half-open intervals $(t_i', t_i]$ (with $t_i'' \leq t_i' < t_i$) or even skipping some intervals we may assume that each point of $\mathbb{R}_{>1}$ is contained in *exactly* s such assigned intervals (of s different robots), and that the turning points of each robot coincide with the right ends of the corresponding intervals. Recall here, that if an interval is not needed, we can actually skip the corresponding turning point in the robot's strategy without affecting the validity of the other intervals used. We call the new half-open intervals $(t_i', t_i]$ *assigned intervals*. Let us emphasize, as a consequence of $t_i' \geq t_i''$ and (3), that

$$t_i' \geq \frac{1}{\mu}(t_1 + t_2 + \cdots + t_i) \tag{4}$$

or, equivalently,

$$t_i \leq \mu t_i' - (t_1 + t_2 + \cdots + t_{i-1})\ . \tag{5}$$

Next we accumulate all assigned intervals of all k robots in one sequence, sorted by their left endpoints, ties broken arbitrarily. Consider a prefix $\mathcal{P}$ of this sequence, long enough so that all robots have already some interval present in $\mathcal{P}$. What part of $\mathbb{R}_{>1}$ do these intervals cover, and how often? There is a value $a = a(\mathcal{P}) \geq 1$ such that $(1, a]$ is covered s times, and then there are points

$$a =: a_s \leq a_{s-1} \leq a_{s-2} \leq \ldots \leq a_1\ ,$$

such that every point in $(a_{j+1}, a_j]$ is covered exactly j times, $j = 1, \ldots, s-1$, and (a_1, ∞) is not yet covered. (Note that some of these intervals may be empty.) Associate with $\mathcal{P}$ the *multiset*

$$A(\mathcal{P}) := \{a_s, a_{s-1}, \ldots, a_1\}$$

(which can be seen as a description of the *covering situation* of $\mathcal{P}$).

We need one more notion. Define the *load*, $L^{(r)}(\mathcal{P})$, of robot r in $\mathcal{P}$ as the sum of all turning points occuring in the intervals of r in $\mathcal{P}$, i.e.

$$L^{(r)}(\mathcal{P}) := t_1^{(r)} + t_2^{(r)} + \cdots + t_{i_r}^{(r)} \text{ for } i_r \text{ s.t. } \begin{cases} (t_{i_r}'^{(r)}, t_{i_r}^{(r)}] \text{ in } \mathcal{P}, \text{ and} \\ (t_{i_r+1}'^{(r)}, t_{i_r+1}^{(r)}] \text{ not in } \mathcal{P}. \end{cases}$$

We immediately observe

$$L^{(r)}(\mathcal{P}) \leq \mu t_{i_r}'^{(r)} \leq \mu a \text{ (due to (4))}. \tag{6}$$

As we extend the prefix $\mathcal{P}$ by the next assigned interval, this interval has to be of the form $(t_i'^{(r^*)}, t_i^{(r^*)}]$, for some robot r^*. Note

$$t_i'^{(r^*)} = a \text{ and } t_i^{(r^*)} = \mu^* a - L^{(r^*)}(\mathcal{P})\ , \text{ for some } \mu^* \leq \mu \text{ (due to (5))}.$$

Set $\mathcal{P}^+$ to be the prefix with $\mathcal{P}$ extended by this next interval $(t_i'^{(r^*)}, t_i^{(r^*)}]$. We immediately see that loads of robots do not change as we move from $\mathcal{P}$ to $\mathcal{P}^+$, except for robot r^* for which we get

$$L^{(r^*)}(\mathcal{P}^+) = L^{(r^*)}(\mathcal{P}) + t_i^{(r^*)} = \mu^* a\ .$$

Also a_s in $A(\mathcal{P})$ gets replaced by $t_i^{(r^*)} = \mu^* a - L^{(r^*)}(\mathcal{P})$ in $A(\mathcal{P}^+)$, all other elements stay the same. (Note that still, $a(\mathcal{P}^+) = a(\mathcal{P})$ is a possibility if $a_s = a_{s-1}$.)

We want to analyze the function

$$f(\mathcal{P}) := \prod_{r=1}^{k} \left[\frac{\left(L^{(r)}(\mathcal{P})\right)^s}{\prod_{y \in A(\mathcal{P})} y}\right] \tag{7}$$

and understand how it changes as we move from $\mathcal{P}$ to $\mathcal{P}^+$. With $L^{(r)}(\mathcal{P}) \leq \mu a$ for all robots r and $y \geq a$ for all $y \in A(\mathcal{P})$ we get

$$f(\mathcal{P}) \leq \left(\frac{(\mu a)^s}{a^s}\right)^k = \mu^{ks}\ , \tag{8}$$

i.e. f stays bounded. With the changes of A and loads from $\mathcal{P}$ to $\mathcal{P}^+$ described, we see that

$$\frac{f(\mathcal{P}^+)}{f(\mathcal{P})} = \frac{a^k}{\left(L^{(r^*)}(\mathcal{P})\right)^s} \cdot \frac{(\mu^* a)^s}{\left(\mu^* a - L^{(r^*)}(\mathcal{P})\right)^k} = \frac{\mu^{*s}}{x^s(\mu^* - x)^k}$$

for $x := \frac{L^{(r^*)}(\mathcal{P})}{a}$, $0 < x < \mu^*$. We show that this ratio is larger than 1 if $\mu^* \leq \mu$ is too small, independent of x. We use the following lemma.

Lemma 2.3. *For $\mu^* > 0$ the polynomial $x^s(\mu^* - x)^k$ maximizes for $x = \frac{s\mu^*}{k+s}$ in the range $x \in \mathbb{R}$, $0 < x < \mu^*$.*

Proof. The derivative of the polynomial is $(\mu^*-x)^{k-1}x^{s-1}(s(\mu^*-x)-kx)$, which has only one zero $x=\frac{s\mu^*}{k+s}$ in $(0,\mu^*)$. Since the values at 0 and μ^* of the polynomial are 0, the zero of the derivative corresponds to the maximum of the function. □

Lemma 2.4. *For* $0<x<\mu^*$, $\frac{\mu^{*s}}{x^s(\mu^*-x)^k}\geq\frac{(k+s)^{k+s}}{s^sk^k\mu^{*k}}$ *and thus* $\frac{\mu^{*s}}{x^s(\mu^*-x)^k}\geq\delta$ *for* $\delta:=\frac{(k+s)^{k+s}}{s^sk^k\mu^k}>1$, *provided* $\mu<\sqrt[k]{\frac{(k+s)^{k+s}}{s^sk^k}}$.

Proof. The first inequality follows immediately from Lemma 2.3 after substituting the value $x=\frac{s\mu^*}{k+s}$. The second inequality is obvious since we know that $\mu^*\leq\mu$. □

Applying Lemma 2.4, we get that $\frac{f(\mathcal{P}^+)}{f(\mathcal{P})}\geq\delta>1$, provided $\mu<\sqrt[k]{\frac{(k+s)^{k+s}}{s^sk^k}}$. It implies that $f(\mathcal{P})$ is unbounded for larger and larger prefixes $\mathcal{P}$. This contradicts the bound on $f(\mathcal{P})$ from (8). Therefore, to have a valid strategy, one must have $\mu\geq\sqrt[k]{\frac{(k+s)^{k+s}}{s^sk^k}}$, which concludes the proof of the Theorem 2.2 and thus of Theorem 1.1.

3 GENERALIZATION TO m RAYS

The following natural generalization of the original cow-path problem was studied by several authors [5], [11], [20], [21], [23]. Consider m rays emanating from 0, and assume that there is a hidden target on one of the rays. We send a robot from 0 at unit speed, and the goal is to find (pass over) the target. It was shown in [4] that the best possible competitive ratio for the problem is $1+2\frac{m^m}{(m-1)^{m-1}}$, and this is tight.

This problem got a lot of attention due to its numerous connections to other, seemingly unrelated, problems. In particular, it is related to hybrid algorithms [3], [17], [20] for on-line problems. We quote from [20] (with "m" for "w" and "k" for "λ"):

> *"We study on-line strategies for solving problems with hybrid algorithms. There is a problem Q and m* basic *algorithms for solving Q. For some $k\leq m$, we have a computer with k disjoint memory areas, each of which can be used to run a basic algorithm and store its intermediate results. In the worst case, only one basic algorithm can solve Q in finite time, and all of the other basic algorithms run forever without solving Q. To solve Q with a* hybrid *algorithm constructed from the basic algorithms, we run a basic algorithm for some time, then switch to another, and continue this process until Q is solved. The goal is to solve Q in the least amount of time."*

Interpret the calculations done while performing the i-th basic algorithm as the i-th ray emanating at 0 (where 0 corresponds to the initial state). Then, being at a point x_i in the calculations of the i-th algorithm, it costs us at most x_i+x_j to pass from this point to the point x_j in the calculations of the j-th algorithm. This interpretation was given in [17], using which the authors exhibited an algorithm, which is competitive with respect to each of a given set of algorithms.

Another related field is contract algorithms. The connection was established in [11], and the setting is as follows. A processor is supposed to advance in m computational problems, until it is interrupted. Upon interruption, it is given the index $i\in\{1,\dots,m\}$, and is returns its most advanced computation on the i-th problem. Again, interpreting each problem as a ray emanating from 0, we easily see the connection to the m-path problem.

Both papers [11] and [20] were concerned with the variation of the m-path problem, in which k robots are conducting the search simultaneously. When introducing several robots, we may use two possible measures for competitive ratio: $\frac{T}{d}$ and $\frac{D}{d}$, where T is the time spent until the target was found (given that all robots travel at unit speed), and D is the total distance travelled by all robots until the target was found. The distance version of the problem was resolved in [20], in which the authors determined the optimal competitive ratio. Somewhat unfortunately, the optimal algorithm does not really use multiple robots simultaneously: all but one robot search on one ray each, while the last robot performs the search on all remaining rays. The time version of the problem was addressed in [11], where it was resolved for *cyclic strategies*. Informally speaking, a cyclic strategy is a strategy in which the advancements in the search on the rays is happening in cyclic order, and at each step each robot is assigned a farther distance to explore on a ray than it previously explored on other rays.

We address the natural faulty generalization of the problem, when we have m rays and k robots, f out of which are faulty. Let us denote the corresponding function by $A(m,k,f)$. That is, $A(k,f)=A(2,k,f)$. The following theorem gives the precise value of $A(m,k,f)$ in all (meaningful) cases. In particular, the $f=0$ case of our theorem answers the question posed in several research papers mentioned before. It strengthens the result from [11], answering their question whether their result is possible to generalize to all strategies, gives appropriate analogue of the result from [20] for the competitive ratios measured in terms of time, as well as answers the question posed by Baeza-Yates, Culberson, and Rawlins in [5].

Theorem 3.1. *Given that $f<k<m(f+1)$ and $q:=m(f+1)$, we have*

$$A(m,k,f)=\lambda_0:=2\sqrt[k]{\frac{q^q}{(q-k)^{q-k}k^k}}+1. \tag{9}$$

Note that the restriction on k simply excludes trivial cases: first, $f=k$ means that all robots are faulty. Second, if $k=m(f+1)$ (or larger), then sending $f+1$ robots on each of the m rays will guarantee a competitive ratio of 1.

It is easy to see that, substituting $m=2$ in (9), one gets (1).

The proof of the upper bound is deferred to the appendix. The proof of the lower bound uses the following covering relaxation of the original problem.

One-ray cover with returns (ORC) setting: The goal is to cover (a subset of) $\mathbb{R}_{\geq 1}$. The robot (robots) starts at 0 and move with unit speed along the ray $\mathbb{R}_{\geq 0}$. One robot may cover a point multiple times, but different coverings are only counted if the robot visited 0 in between.

Fix $k\in\mathbb{N}$ and $\lambda>1$. Then a q-fold λ-cover of $\mathbb{R}_{\geq 1}$ in the ORC setting may be seen as a relaxation of the m-ray cover problem. Indeed, in a sense we simply discard the labels of the rays, but still ask the robots to return to 0, imitating the change of the rays, which happened in the original problem. Thus, any strategy for searching a target on m rays with k robots, f out of which are faulty, with competitive ratio λ, induces a strategy for the q-fold λ-covering of $\mathbb{R}_{\geq 1}$ with k robots in the ORC setting, where $q = (f + 1)m$.

Let $C(k, q)$ be the infimum of all λ, for which there exists a strategy for a q-fold λ-covering of $\mathbb{R}_{\geq 1}$ with k robots in the ORC setting. We prove the following:

$$C(k, q) \geq 2\sqrt[k]{\frac{q^q}{(q-k)^{q-k}k^k}} + 1. \tag{10}$$

Clearly, $A(m, k, f) \geq C(k, m(f + 1))$, and thus the lower bound Theorem 3.1 follows from (10). At the same time, the bound (10) is tight, as follows from the "$\leq$" part of (9). Before proving (10), let us describe yet another covering problem, which is a fractional analogue of the multicovering problem in the ORC setting.

FRACTIONAL ONE-RAY RETRIEVAL WITH RETURNS: We are given a finite number of robots, of total weight 1 each of which moves with constant speed 1 along the ray $\mathbb{R}_{\geq 0}$. We are supposed to cover an unknown target at distance $x \geq 1$ with several robots of some prescribed total weight η, $\eta \in \mathbb{R}_{\geq 1}$. The same robot may cover any point any number of times, but different coverings are counted only if the robot visits 0 in between. We are interested in the worst-case competitive ratio $C(\eta)$ of the best algorithm for the problem.

Remark. Here's a related, but not equivalent formulation, which is closer to the original m-ray problem. We are given a finite number of robots, each of which moves with constant speed 1 along the ray $\mathbb{R}_{\geq 0}$ and is supposed to match an unknown target at distance $x \geq 1$ with one of the sample targets in a list of size η, $\eta \in \mathbb{R}_{\geq 1}$. The total size of the memory (that is, the total portion of the list they may carry) of all robots is fixed and is equal to 1. Robots may change the set of samples they carry only when visiting 0. In the worst case, the target is matched only after being compared with all samples. We are interested in the worst-case competitive ratio $C'(\eta)$ of the best algorithm for the problem.

The statement we prove is as follows:

$$C(\eta) = 2\frac{\eta^\eta}{(\eta-1)^{\eta-1}} + 1. \tag{11}$$

Naturally, the same equality holds for $C'(\eta)$ as well.

We defer the proof of the reduction of (11) to (9) to the appendix.

3.1 Proof of the lower bound in (10)

For technical reasons, we will prove the following slightly stronger statement about covering a finite part of $\mathbb{R}_{\geq 1}$: for any $\epsilon > 0$, there exists N, such that if k robots produce a q-fold λ-cover of $[1, N]$ in the ORC setting, then

$$\lambda \geq 2\sqrt[k]{\frac{q^q}{(q-k)^{q-k}k^k}} + 1 - \epsilon. \tag{12}$$

The main point here is that the needed N is independent of the strategy. Let us denote by $\mu(q, k)$ the root in the right hand side of the displayed inequality above. Note that $\mu(q, k) = \mu(cq, ck)$ for any $c > 0$ and thus $\mu(q, k) < \mu(q - 1, k - 1)$, provided that $q > k > 1$. Put

$$\epsilon' := 2\mu(q-1, k-1) - 2\mu(q, k).$$

In the rest of the proof we show the validity of (12).

The proof of the theorem follows similar steps as the proof of Theorem 1.1. We are presenting the proof in a somewhat contracted form, highlighting the changes one has to make in order to prove this theorem.

The proof goes by induction on k.[1] For $k = 1$ we of course will not use any inductive hypothesis. For $k \geq 2$, suppose by induction that the statement of (12) is valid for $k - 1$ and $q - 1$. Choose N', such that (12) holds for $k - 1$ and $q - 1$ with $N := N'$ and $\epsilon := \epsilon'$. In other words, for such choice of N' any $(q - 1)$-fold λ'-covering of $[1, N']$ by $k - 1$ robots in the ORC setting satisfies

$$\lambda' \geq 2\mu(q-1, k-1) + 1 - \epsilon' = 2\mu(q, k) + 1. \tag{13}$$

Fix $\epsilon > 0$ and a competitive ratio λ not satisfying (12) and put $\mu := (\lambda - 1)/2$. Fix a collective strategy of robots for k robots to produce a q-fold λ-covering of $[1, N]$ in the ORC setting (note that N is sufficiently large and would be chosen later).

Standardising the strategy. The *round* of a strategy for a robot is the period between two consecutive visits of 0. We can assume that in each round the robot turns exactly once at a turning point t. Therefore, we can describe a strategy by an infinite vector $T = (t_1, t_2, t_3, \ldots)$ of reals in $\mathbb{R}_{\geq 1}$, t_i the turning point in round i. Obviously, point $x \in \mathbb{R}_{\geq 1}$ is λ-covered in round i iff (i) $x \leq t_i$ and (ii) $2(t_1 + t_2 + \cdots + t_{i-1}) + x \leq \lambda x$ ($\Leftrightarrow x \geq 1/\mu(t_1 + t_2 + \cdots + t_{i-1})$ for $\mu := \lambda - 1/2$). We set $t_i'' := 1/\mu(t_1 + t_2 + \cdots + t_{i-1})$. If $t_i'' > t_i$, round i does not λ-cover any point, and we may as well skip this round (future rounds will λ-cover even more in this way). Otherwise, we call the round *fruitful* and the robot λ-covers exactly the interval $[t_i'', t_i]$ in round i. Clearly, we can assume that we are using only strategies with only fruitful rounds. Observe that the sequence $(t_1'', t_2'', t_3'', \ldots)$ is monotone increasing.

Suppose now we have k such strategies $T^{(r)} = (t_1^{(r)}, t_2^{(r)}, t_3^{(r)}, \ldots)$, $r = 1, 2, \ldots, k$, that establish a q-fold λ-covering of $\mathbb{R}_{\geq 1}$. Let us now assign truncated intervals $(t_i'^{(r)}, t_i^{(r)}] \subseteq [t_i''^{(r)}, t_i^{(r)}] \cap [1, \infty)$, in such a way that every point in $\mathbb{R}_{>1}$ is covered exactly q times, and such that each sequence $(t_1'^{(r)}, t_2'^{(r)}, t_3'^{(r)}, \ldots)$ is monotone increasing (this may actually also result in skipping some of the turning points).

Defining the function. Next we accumulate all assigned intervals of all k robots in one sequence, sorted by their left endpoints, ties broken arbitrarily. Consider a prefix $\mathcal{P}$ of this sequence, long enough so that all robots have already some interval present in $\mathcal{P}$. Clearly, it consists of all rounds of the strategy of the robot r up to some i_r, for each $r = 1, \ldots, k$. What part of $\mathbb{R}_{\geq 1}$ do these intervals cover, and how many times? There is a value $a = a(\mathcal{P}) \geq 1$ such that $(1, a]$ is covered q times, and then there are points

$$a =: a_q \leq a_{q-1} \leq a_{s-2} \leq \ldots \leq a_1\,,$$

such that every point in $(a_{j+1}, a_j]$ is covered exactly j times, $j = 1, \ldots, q-1$, and (a_1, ∞) is not yet covered. (Note that some of these intervals may be empty.) Associate with $\mathcal{P}$ the *multiset*

$$A(\mathcal{P}) := \{a_q, a_{q-1}, \ldots, a_1\}$$

(which can be seen as a description of the *covering situation* of $\mathcal{P}$).

[1] We remark that induction is needed only for one part of the proof, which is given in Case 2 below.

We need one more notion. Define the *load*, $L^{(r)}(\mathcal{P})$, of robot r in $\mathcal{P}$ as the sum of all turning points occurring in the intervals of r in $\mathcal{P}$, i.e.

$$L^{(r)}(\mathcal{P}) := t_1^{(r)} + t_2^{(r)} + \cdots + t_{i_r}^{(r)} \text{ for } i_r \text{ s.t. } \begin{cases} (t'^{(r)}_{i_r}, t^{(r)}_{i_r}] \text{ in } \mathcal{P}, \text{ and} \\ (t'^{(r)}_{i_r+1}, t^{(r)}_{i_r+1}] \text{ not in } \mathcal{P}. \end{cases}$$

Let $b^{(r)} := t'^{(r)}_{i_{r+1}}$ be the beginning of the first interval, assigned to robot r and which is not in $\mathcal{P}$. Then, clearly, the analogue of (6) is

$$L^{(r)}(\mathcal{P}) \leq \mu b^{(r)}. \tag{14}$$

The following function controls the situation:

$$f(\mathcal{P}) := \prod_{r=1}^{k} \left[\frac{\left(L^{(r)}(\mathcal{P})\right)^{q-k} (b^{(r)})^k}{\prod_{y \in A(\mathcal{P})} y} \right]. \tag{15}$$

Adding one interval. Add one new interval to $\mathcal{P}$, thus forming the covering situation $\mathcal{P}^+$. If the new interval is assigned to the robot r, then $b^{(r)} = a$. In $\mathcal{P}^+$, the beginning $b^{(r)}$ of the first non-included assigned interval to robot r is replaced by some b' (equal to $t'^{(r)}_{i_{r+2}}$); using (14), the load of r changes to $\mu^* b'$ for some $\mu^* \leq \mu$; at the same time, the element a is removed from $\mathcal{A}$ and replaced by the end of the new interval, which is $L^{(r)}(\mathcal{P}^+) - L^{(r)}(\mathcal{P}) = \mu^* b' - \mathcal{L}^{(r)}(\mathcal{P})$. Thus, in $f(\mathcal{P})$ the a^k multiple in the denominator is compensated by the $(b^{(r)})^k$ in the numerator, and we have

$$\frac{f(\mathcal{P}^+)}{f(\mathcal{P})} = \frac{(\mu^* b')^{q-k} \cdot b'^k}{\left(L^{(r)}(\mathcal{P})\right)^{q-k} \left(\mu^* b' - L^{(r)}(\mathcal{P})\right)^k} = \frac{\mu^{*q-k}}{x^{q-k}(\mu^* - x)^k}$$

for $x := \frac{L^{(r)}(\mathcal{P})}{b'}$, $0 < x < \mu^*$.

Making use of Lemma 2.4, we conclude is as follows: if the competitive λ does not satisfy (12) with ϵ, then there exists $\delta > 1$, such that

$$\frac{f(\mathcal{P}^+)}{f(\mathcal{P})} \geq \delta. \tag{16}$$

The last step of the proof is to conclude that, at the same time, $f(\mathcal{P})$ should be bounded (and that the number of intervals in the cover, and thus the number of such potential increments, is infinite). It is slightly more difficult in this case and is the reason why we use induction. We consider two cases.

Case 1. For any robot r and any two consecutive starting points $t'^{(r)}_i, t'^{(r)}_{i+1} \in \mathbb{R}_{\geq 1}$ of its assigned intervals, we have $t'^{(r)}_{i+1}/t'^{(r)}_i \leq C$, where C is an absolute constant, which we would specify later.

In this case, looking at (15), we have $b^{(r)} \leq C t'^{(r)}_{i_r} \leq Ca$, and thus $L^{(r)}(\mathcal{P}) \leq \mu Ca$. This allows us to bound $f(\mathcal{P})$:

$$f(\mathcal{P}) \leq C^{qk} \mu^{(q-k)k}.$$

Therefore, in a finite number of steps, we will get a contradiction with (16). At the same time, when passing from $\mathcal{P}$ to $\mathcal{P}^+$, the distance from the first point that is not q-covered to zero increases by at most C times. Thus, eventually, we get a contradiction. We can find the value of N needed in (12) based on these two simple facts.

Case 2. There exists a robot r and two consecutive starting points $t'^{(r)}_i, t'^{(r)}_{i+1} \in \mathbb{R}_{\geq 1}$ of its assigned intervals, such that $t'^{(r)}_{i+1}/t'^{(r)}_i \geq C$. Consider the interval

$$[\mu t'^{(r)}_i, C t'^{(r)}_i].$$

Then, due to (14), no endpoint of the first $i-1$ intervals assigned to r could have surpassed $\mu t'^{(r)}_i$. Thus, the interval displayed above is λ-covered by r at most once. It implies that the other $k-1$ robots produced a $(q-1)$-fold λ-covering of this interval in the ORC setting. Rescaling, we may assume that $k-1$ robots produced a $(q-1)$-fold λ-covering of the interval $[1, C/\mu]$. Using (13) and choosing C such that $C/\mu \geq N'$, we conclude that $\lambda \geq 2\mu(q,k) + 1$.

A APPENDIX

First, we give a proof of the upper bound in (10). We exhibit a so-called exponential strategy, similar to the many strategies that appeared for related problems. It is a fairly natural extension of the proofs of the upper bounds for some particular cases of our problem, exhibited in [14] and [11].

Proof of the upper bound in (10). It is sufficient, for each $x \in \mathbb{R}_{\geq 1}$, to produce an f-fold λ_0-covering each of points on the m rays at distance x.

Let us first do the *assignment* for each of the robots: to each robot r we assign intervals on different rays, which are supposed to be λ_0-covered by r. Fix $\alpha > 1$, which we optimize later. The assignment is as follows:

robot r λ_0-covers intervals $(\alpha^{k(i+mj)+m(r-f)}, \alpha^{k(i+mj)+mr}]$
for each $j = -2, -1, \ldots$ on ray i, $i = 1, \ldots, m$.

We start with $j = -2$ to ensure that before distance 1 on each ray, each of the robots has already done at least 1 pass on the ray. Let us first make sure that all the points at distance at least 1 from the origin are covered at least f times by such an assignment. Fix a ray i and a point on it, in the form α^x, where $x \geq 0$. Then x must fall into $(k(i+mj) + m(r-f), k(i+mj) + mr]$ for some j in order to be covered by r. It is equivalent to $y \in (kj + r - f, kj + r]$, where $y := \lceil \frac{x-ki}{m} \rceil$. Note that $y \geq -k$. Thus, y falls into the interval above if $y (\bmod k) \in (r - f (\bmod k), r (\bmod k)]$. This holds for $r \in [y(\bmod k), y + f(\bmod k))$. Thus, the point α^x was covered by the intervals assigned by the robots $y - f + 1, \ldots, y$ (modulo k).

Now let us describe a strategy for robots to cover these intervals, and calculate the corresponding competitive ratio. Each robot starts his tour with ray number 1, and visits the rays in cyclic order. When visiting ray i for the $(j+3)$-nd time (+3 is there since j starts from -2), he turns at the point $\alpha^{k(i+mj)+mr}$, returns to 0 and continues to the ray $i+1$. A point at distance $x \geq 1$ from the origin on ray i is covered for the f-th (and final) time by robot r, if it falls into the segment $(\alpha^{k(i+mj)+m(r-f)}, \alpha^{k(i+mj)+m(r-f+1)}]$ for some $j \in \mathbb{Z}$. Take $x \in (\alpha^{k(i+mj)+m(r-f)}, \alpha^{k(i+mj)+m(r-f+1)}]$. Then the time passed until robot r arrives at this point is at most

$$x + 2 \sum_{l=-2m}^{i+mj-1} \alpha^{kl+mr} < x + 2\frac{\alpha^{k(i+mj)+mr}}{\alpha^k - 1}.$$

Thus, the competitive ratio of such algorithm is $2\gamma + 1$, where γ is the maximum over all valid choices of x of the expression

$$\frac{\alpha^{k(i+mj)+mr}}{x(\alpha^k - 1)}.$$

This expression is clearly decreasing as x increases, therefore,

$$\gamma \leq \frac{\alpha^{k(i+mj)+mr}}{\alpha^{k(i+mj)+m(r-f)}(\alpha^k - 1)} = \frac{\alpha^{mf}}{\alpha^k - 1}.$$

Note that the last bound is independent of the choice of the ray and x. Applying Lemmas 2.3, 2.4 with $\mu^* = 1$, $x = \alpha^{-k}$, $s = \frac{mf-k}{k}$, we get that the displayed expression is minimised for $\alpha = \sqrt[k]{\frac{mf}{mf-k}}$, for which it is equal to $(\lambda_0 - 1)/2$. We conclude that the competitive value of the algorithm coincides with the right hand side of (9). □

Next, we give the reduction of (11) to (10).

Proof of (11). Let us first prove the "≤" direction: that the right hand side is an upper bound for the left hand side. Fix a sequence of rational numbers $\frac{q_i}{k_i}$, $i = 1, \ldots$, such that $\frac{q_i}{k_i} \geq \eta$ and $\lim_{i \to \infty} \frac{q_i}{k_i} = \eta$. Consider the strategy that gives the upper bound from Theorem 3.1 with $f := 1$, $k := k_i$, $m := q_i$. Then the competitive ratio is

$$2\sqrt[k_i]{\frac{q_i^{q_i}}{(q_i - k_i)^{q_i - k_i} k_i^{k_i}}} + 1 = 2\frac{\left(\frac{q_i}{k_i}\right)^{\frac{q_i}{k_i}}}{\left(\frac{q_i}{k_i} - 1\right)^{\frac{q_i}{k_i} - 1}} + 1 \to 2\frac{\eta^\eta}{(\eta - 1)^{\eta - 1}} + 1.$$

On the other hand, the strategy above can be clearly used to produce a fractional one-ray $\frac{q_i}{k_i}$-covering (and thus an η-covering): just split the weight between k_i robots in equal parts, and let them perform their strategy on one ray, ignoring the labels of the rays. Going to the limit, the "≤" part of (11) is proved.

The proof of the "≥" direction is similar. Fix $\epsilon > 0$ and consider a strategy S in the fractional problem, which achieves the competitive ratio $C(\eta) + \epsilon$. Assume that the weights of the robots used in the strategy are $w_1, \ldots, w_n$, $\sum_{i=1}^n w_i = 1$. Fix $\delta > 0$, which choice is specified later, and integers $q, k_1, \ldots, k_n$, such that $\frac{w_i}{\eta} \leq \frac{k_i}{q} \leq \frac{w_i}{\eta} + \delta$. Put $k := \sum_{i=1}^n k_i$. Thus, clearly, $\frac{k}{q} \geq \frac{1}{\eta}$. The requirement on δ is such that $\frac{k}{q} \leq \frac{1}{\eta - \epsilon}$.

Consider the strategy S' for the q-fold covering with k robots in the ORC setting, which is obtained as follows: the first k_1 robots repeat the actions of the first robot from strategy S, the next k_2 robots repeat the actions of the second robot from S etc. Clearly, the strategy produces the q-fold covering and has competitive ratio $C(\eta) + \epsilon$. On the other hand, using the lower bound from (10), it has competitive ratio at least

$$2\frac{(q/k)^{q/k}}{(q/k - 1)^{(q/k - 1)}} + 1 \geq 2\frac{(\eta - \epsilon)^{\eta - \epsilon}}{(\eta - \epsilon - 1)^{\eta - \epsilon - 1}} + 1.$$

This implies that for any $\epsilon > 0$ we have

$$C(\eta) \geq 2\frac{(\eta - \epsilon)^{\eta - \epsilon}}{(\eta - \epsilon - 1)^{\eta - \epsilon - 1}} + 1 - \epsilon.$$

Passing to the limit $\epsilon \to 0$ gives the result. □

ACKNOWLEDGMENTS

We thank Dániel Korándi, Alexander Pilz, Miloš Stojaković, and May Szedlak for discussions on and suggestions for the material covered in this paper, and Yoshio Okamoto for suggesting the problem.

The research of the first author was partially supported by the Swiss National Science Foundation grants no. 200020-162884 and 200021-175977 and by the EPSRC grant no. EP/N019504/1.

REFERENCES

[1] Noga Alon, Chen Avin, Michal Koucká̋ş, Gady Kozma, Zvi Lotker, and Mark R. Tuttle. 2011. Many random walks are faster than one. *Combinatorics, Probability and Computing* 20, 4 (2011), 481–502.
[2] Steve Alpern and Shmuel Gal. 2006. *The theory of search games and rendezvous.* Kluwer Academic Publishers, Boston.
[3] Yossi Azar, Andrei Z. Broder, and Mark S. Manasse. 1993. On-line Choice of On-line Algorithms. In *Proceedings of the Fourth Annual ACM-SIAM Symposium on Discrete Algorithms (SODA '93).* Society for Industrial and Applied Mathematics, Philadelphia, PA, USA, 432–440. http://dl.acm.org/citation.cfm?id=313559.313847
[4] Ricardo A. Baeza-Yates, Joseph C. Culberson, and Gregory J. E. Rawlins. 1988. Searching with uncertainty extended abstract. In *SWAT 88 (Lecture Notes in Computer Science).* Springer, Berlin, Heidelberg, 176–189. https://doi.org/10.1007/3-540-19487-8_20
[5] R. A. Baezayates, J. C. Culberson, and G. J. E. Rawlins. 1993. Searching in the Plane. *Information and Computation* 106, 2 (1993), 234–252. https://doi.org/10.1006/inco.1993.1054
[6] Anatole Beck. 1964. On the linear search problem. *Israel Journal of Mathematics* 2, 4 (1964), 221–228.
[7] Anatole Beck. 1965. More on the linear search problem. *Israel Journal of Mathematics* 3, 2 (1965), 61–70.
[8] Anatole Beck and D. J. Newman. 1970. Yet more on the linear search problem. *Israel Journal of Mathematics* 8, 4 (1970), 419–429.
[9] Richard Bellman. 1956. Minimization Problem. *Amer. Math. Soc.* 62, 4 (1956), 270.
[10] Richard Bellman. 1963. An Optimal Search. *SIAM Rev.* 5, 3 (1963), 274.
[11] Daniel S. Bernstein, Lev Finkelstein, and Shlomo Zilberstein. 2003. Contract algorithms and robots on rays: Unifying two scheduling problems. In *IJCAI.* 1211–1217.
[12] Prosenjit Bose, Jean-Lou De Carufel, and Stephane Durocher. 2013. Revisiting the problem of searching on a line. In *European Symposium on Algorithms.* Springer, 205–216.
[13] Jurek Czyzowicz, Konstantinos Georgiou, Evangelos Kranakis, Danny Krizanc, Lata Narayanan, Jaroslav Opatrny, and Sunil Shende. 2016. Search on a Line by Byzantine Robots. (2016). https://arxiv.org/abs/1611.08209
[14] Jurek Czyzowicz, Evangelos Kranakis, Danny Krizanc, Lata Narayanan, and Jaroslav Opatrny. 2016. Search on a Line with Faulty Robots. ACM Press, 405–414. https://doi.org/10.1145/2933057.2933102
[15] E. D. Demaine, S. P. Fekete, and S. Gal. 2006. Online searching with turn cost. *Theoretical Computer Science* 361, 2 (2006), 342–355.
[16] Ofer Feinerman, Amos Korman, Zvi Lotker, and Jean-Sébastien Sereni. 2012. Collaborative search on the plane without communication. In *Proceedings of the 2012 ACM symposium on Principles of distributed computing.* ACM, 77–86.
[17] Amos Fiat, Yuval Rabani, and Yiftach Ravid. 1994. Competitive k-server algorithms. *J. Comput. System Sci.* 48, 3 (1994), 410–428.
[18] Wallace Franck. 1965. An optimal search problem. *SIAM review* 7, 4 (1965), 503–512.
[19] J. R. Isbell. 1957. An optimal search pattern. *Naval Research Logistics Quarterly* 4, 4 (1957), 357–359. https://doi.org/10.1002/nav.3800040409
[20] Ming-Yang Kao, Yuan Ma, Michael Sipser, and Yiqun Yin. 2001. Optimal Constructions of Hybrid Algorithms. (2001). http://arxiv.org/abs/cs/0101028
[21] Ming-Yang Kao, John H. Reif, and Stephen R. Tate. 1996. Searching in an unknown environment: An optimal randomized algorithm for the cow-path problem. *Information and Computation* 131, 1 (1996), 63–79.
[22] M. M. Polycarpou, Yanli Yang, and K. M. Passino. 2001. A cooperative search framework for distributed agents. In *Proceedings of the 2001 IEEE International Symposium on Intelligent Control, 2001. (ISIC '01).* 1–6. https://doi.org/10.1109/ISIC.2001.971475
[23] Sven Schuierer. 2003. A Lower Bound for Randomized Searching on m Rays. In *Computer Science in Perspective.* Springer, Berlin, Heidelberg, 264–277. https://doi.org/10.1007/3-540-36477-3_20

Distributed Uniformity Testing

Orr Fischer
Tel-Aviv University
Tel-Aviv, Israel
orrfischer@mail.tau.ac.il

Uri Meir
Tel-Aviv University
Tel-Aviv, Israel
urimeir@mail.tau.ac.il

Rotem Oshman
Tel-Aviv University
Tel-Aviv, Israel
roshman@tau.ac.il

ABSTRACT

In the *uniformity testing* problem, we are given access to samples from some unknown distribution μ on a fixed domain $\{1, .., n\}$, and our goal is to distinguish the case where μ is the uniform distribution from the case where μ is ϵ-*far* from uniform in L_1 distance. Centralized uniformity testing has been extensively studied, and it is known that $\Theta(\sqrt{n}/\epsilon^2)$ samples are necessary and sufficient.

In this paper we study *distributed uniformity testing*: in a network of k nodes, each node i has access to s_i samples from the underlying distribution μ. Our goal is to test uniformity, while minimizing the number of samples per node, as well as the running time. We consider several distributed models: the LOCAL model, the CONGEST model, and a 0-round model where nodes cannot communicate with each other at all. We give upper bounds for each model, and a lower bound for the 0-round model. The key to our results is analyzing the centralized uniformity-testing problem in an unusual error regime, for which we give new upper and lower bounds.

CCS CONCEPTS

• **Theory of computation** → **Streaming, sublinear and near linear time algorithms**; *Lower bounds and information complexity*; • **Mathematics of computing** → *Information theory*; • **Networks** → *Network algorithms*;

ACM Reference Format:
Orr Fischer, Uri Meir, and Rotem Oshman. 2018. Distributed Uniformity Testing. In *PODC '18: ACM Symposium on Principles of Distributed Computing, July 23–27, 2018, Egham, United Kingdom.* ACM, New York, NY, USA, 10 pages. https://doi.org/10.1145/3212734.3212772

1 INTRODUCTION

Suppose we have a distributed network tasked with monitoring some environment or random process. Each network node draws *random samples* from its environment, and together the nodes must raise an alarm if the system's state deviates significantly from normal. For example, we could have several routers drawing random samples from the traffic they route, and trying to detect a denial-of-service attack; or a sensor network monitoring temperatures at a manufacturing plant, with their measurements subject to Gaussian noise. In each case, we have a "normal" or "expected" distribution η, and an unknown distribution μ; the network nodes draw samples from μ, and try to decide whether $\mu = \eta$ or whether μ is *far* from μ.

The problem we described above is a specific instance of *distribution testing*: we are given samples from some unknown distribution μ, and must decide whether μ satisfies some property or whether μ is *far* from all distributions that satisfy the property. Here, "far" is usually taken to mean a large L_1-distance, but other distance measures have also been considered in the literature. Distribution testing has been extensively studied, but to our knowledge, the distributed case has not been considered so far.

We take first steps towards understanding the possibilities and limitations of distributed testing of distributions. Specifically, we study *uniformity testing*, where we wish to determine whether our unknown distribution is the uniform distribution $\mathcal{U}_n$ on $\{1, \ldots, n\}$, or whether it is ϵ-far from $\mathcal{U}_n$ in L_1 distance, for a distance parameter ϵ. Uniformity testing is especially interesting because in the centralized setting, it is known that for any fixed distribution μ, the problem of testing equality to μ can be reduced to uniformity testing [10, 15]. This reduction continues to work in the distributed setting: it is a *filter* (essentially, a randomized mapping), which each node can independently apply to its samples using its own private randomness, and then call the uniformity tester.

We consider a network of k nodes, where each node receives s samples drawn independently from the unknown distribution μ. Our goal is to minimize the number of samples s that each node needs to draw, while also taking into consideration communication and round complexity.

In the centralized setting it is known that $\Theta(\sqrt{n}/\epsilon^2)$ samples are both necessary and sufficient for uniformity testing [21], so clearly we cannot have $s = o(\sqrt{n}/(\epsilon^2 k))$, otherwise the entire network does not have enough samples to decide. This gives us a lower bound on the number of samples at each node. At the other extreme, we know that we can always take $s = \Theta(\sqrt{n}/\epsilon^2)$, so that a single network node has enough samples to decide on its own. We ask whether there is a middle ground: when s is large enough that the total number of samples in the network is $s \cdot k = \Omega(\sqrt{n}/\epsilon^2)$, but too small for nodes to decide on their own (i.e., $s = o(\sqrt{n}/\epsilon^2)$), is there an efficient distributed algorithm that allows the nodes to decide whether the distribution is uniform or far from uniform?

We address this question in three models: the LOCAL model, the CONGEST model, and an intermediate "0-round model". Next we outline our results for each model.

0-round uniformity testing. We begin by studying a very simple model where the nodes cannot communicate with each other at all: each node examines its s samples, and decides whether to accept or reject. As usual in distributed decision, the network as a whole

ACM ISBN 978-1-4503-5795-1/18/07...$15.00
https://doi.org/10.1145/3212734.3212772

is said to *accept* if all nodes accepted; otherwise the network *rejects* ("some node raised an alarm"). We refer to this as the "AND" decision rule. Our goal is to ensure that if the underlying distribution is uniform, the network accepts with high probability, but if the distribution is far from uniform, the network rejects with high probability. Our main motivation for studying the 0-round model is that we can use it to develop uniformity testers for the LOCAL and CONGEST models: we *gather* as many samples as possible at as few nodes as possible, and then have these nodes use the 0-round tester to decide.

To solve uniformity testing in the 0-round model, we develop a single-node tester $\mathcal{A}_\delta$, which gives us a "very weak signal": for some very small parameter δ, when we give $\mathcal{A}_\delta$ samples from the uniform distribution $\mathcal{U}_n$, it accepts w.p. $1-\delta$; but when we give it samples from a distribution that is ϵ-far from $\mathcal{U}_n$, it rejects w.p. $\Theta(\delta)$ (i.e., small but noticeable probability). We show that we can implement $\mathcal{A}_\delta$ using $O(\sqrt{\delta n})$ samples, so when we take $\delta = o(1)$, we save on individual sample complexity.

If we set $\delta = \Theta(1/k)$, we expect that the uniform distribution will be accepted by all nodes, while an ϵ-far distribution will be rejected by at least one node. This is the behavior we are aiming for. Unfortunately, moving from having at least one node reject *in expectation* to having at least one node reject *with high probability* is not so easy. The "AND" decision rule, where we reject if at least one node wants to reject, is not robust where error probability is concerned: in some situations, there exists an efficient algorithm with success probability p, but if we want to increase the success probability to $p' > p$, we may not be able to do so efficiently [12]. The success probability we get by using $\mathcal{A}_\delta$ as outlined above depends on the distance parameter ϵ; it is roughly $1/2 + \Theta(\epsilon^2)$, and amplifying to a constant success probability is expensive.

Ultimately, we are able to show the following: for a constant C_p which depends on the desired success probability p,

Theorem 1.1. *There exists a 0-round ϵ-uniformity tester, with error probability at most p, which uses s samples per node, where*

$$s = \Theta\left((C_p/\epsilon^2) \cdot \sqrt{n/k^{\Theta(\epsilon^2/C_p)}}\right).$$

Motivated by the non-robustness of the standard "AND" decision rule, we also consider a setup where the network uses a *threshold rule* to decide: we fix some threshold $T \in [k]$, and the network is considered to *reject* iff at least T nodes want to reject. For this model we can use standard amplification techniques, and our result is substantially better:

Theorem 1.2. *There exists a 0-round ϵ-uniformity tester in the threshold decision model, with threshold $T = \Theta(1/\epsilon^4)$ that uses $\Theta(\sqrt{n/k}/\epsilon^2)$ samples per player.*

We later use the threshold 0-round tester to develop a (multi-round) tester for the CONGEST model.

For 0-round uniformity testing with the AND decision rule, we show the following lower bound, which matches Theorem 1.2 in term of number of samples, up to the dependence on ϵ:

Theorem 1.3. *For a sufficiently large constant $\epsilon \in (0, 1/2)$, any anonymous ϵ-uniformity tester that achieves error at most $1/3$ in network of size k, has sample complexity $\Omega(\sqrt{n/k}/\log(n))$ per node.*

An *anonymous* tester is one where all the nodes execute the same algorithm. Note, however, that the algorithm can be *randomized*, so the nodes can choose random identifiers from some large namespace, which will with high probability be unique.

0-round protocols with asymmetric costs. We develop an *asymmetric* version of our 0-round uniformity tester, where each node v can draw a different number of samples, s_v, and has a different cost per sample, c_v. Our goal now is to minimize the maximum cost paid by any node. We show, for example, that we can implement the 0-round threshold tester using $s = \Theta(\sqrt{n}/(\epsilon^2 \cdot \|T\|_2)$ samples, where T is the inverse cost vector defined by $T_v = 1/c_v$ for each $v \in V$, and $\|\cdot\|_2$ is the L_2-norm. Note that when all costs are equal to 1, we have $\|T\|_2 = \sqrt{k}$, so we recover the symmetric case (Theorem 1.2). We also analyze the asymmetric case with the AND-decision rule, and generalize Theorem 1.1.

The CONGEST *model.* Our algorithms for the LOCAL and the CONGEST model assume for simplicity that each node starts with a single sample ($s = 1$), and that there are enough samples in the whole network to solve uniformity (for $s = 1$, this means $k \geq \sqrt{n}/\epsilon^2$); the results generalize in a straightforward manner to larger s. We develop a "sample-gathering" protocol for the CONGEST model, which then allows us to use the 0-round uniformity tester from Theorem 1.2. This yields the following:

Theorem 1.4. *Uniformity testing can be solved in* CONGEST *in $O(D + n/(k\epsilon^4))$ rounds in k-node networks of diameter D.*

The LOCAL *model.* For the LOCAL model, we gives a simple strategy based on first finding a maximal independent set, and then gathering samples at the MIS nodes. Here again we suffer from the LOCAL model's inability to amplify success probabilities (without running for D rounds). Still, if each node initially has one sample, then r rounds suffice to get success probability $1 - p$, where

$$r = \Theta\left((C_p/\epsilon^2) \cdot \sqrt{n/k^{\Theta(\epsilon^2/C_p)}}\right)^{1/(1-\Theta(\epsilon^2/C_p))}.$$

This hairy expression tends to $\Theta(\sqrt{n}/\epsilon^2)$ as $\epsilon \to 0$, as in this case we cannot avoid collecting this many samples at one node (which will take a long time, in case the graph is, e.g., a line).

For lack of space, many technical details are omitted here, and will appear in the full version of the paper.

1.1 Related Work

Uniformity testing was the starting point for distribution testing. It was first considered implicitly in [13, 17], as part of a tester that estimated the *expansion* of a graph by testing whether the distribution of a short random walk in the graph is uniform, or far from uniform.

In [13, 17] it is shown that the number of samples needed for uniformity testing is $\Theta(\sqrt{n})$. Following this work, the first explicit study of property testing for distributions was in[4], which showed that testing whether two distributions are far from each other requires $\Theta(n^{2/3})$ samples. Later on, uniformity testing was shown to be complete for the problem of testing equality between an unknown input distribution and any fixed distribution [10, 15]. Distribution testing has expanded into a wide field of work, in which a large variety of properties of distributions were considered. We refer to [8, 11, 14, 16, 22] for background on property testing in general, and on distribution testing in particular.

A reduction between uniformity testing and the simultaneous communication complexity of Equality, using private randomness, was shown in [5]. We use this reduction to give a lower bound on distributed uniformity testing, but under a different error regime than the classical model. As for Equality itself, its simultaneous communication complexity with private randomness was studied in [3, 7, 19], and another optimal simultaneous protocol is given in [2]. In [6], the simultaneous Equality lower bound was revisited, using an information theoretic approach. We use the technique of [6] to prove a lower bound on simultaneous Equality with non-standard error.

Very recently, [1] studied testing properties of distributions (including uniformity testing) in a model similar to our 0-round model. The focus of [1] is mostly orthogonal to ours. In [1], each player receives only one sample, and can send a short message to a *referee*; the referee then decides whether the input distribution satisfies the property. The referee's output can be an arbitrary function of the messages it receives from the players. The focus in [1] is on the trade-off between number of players (which controls the number of samples) and communication per player. In contrast, our focus here is on the number of samples required per player for a given number of players, where each player is allowed to output only one bit (accept/reject). We do not allow the "referee" to apply any decision rule, and instead focus on the traditional "AND" rule, and on a threshold rule. As a result, our results and [1] do not overlap.

2 PRELIMINARIES

Distributed uniformity testing. In the distributed ϵ-uniformity testing problem, each network node $i \in V$ is given a set of s iid samples $S_i \sim \mu^s$ from an unknown distribution $\mu : \Omega \to [0,1]$. We assume that the domain Ω is known in advance, and let $n := |\Omega|$ be its size. (Our testers do not actually need to know Ω, only n, but our lower bound assumes that Ω is known as well.) The goal is to distinguish the case where μ is the uniform distribution $\mathcal{U}$ on Ω, from the case where μ has L_1 distance at least ϵ from $\mathcal{U}$. (The L_1 distance between a distribution μ and the uniform distribution is $\sum_{\omega\in\Omega} \left|\mu(\omega) - \frac{1}{n}\right|$.) We let $\mathcal{F}_\epsilon(\mathcal{U})$ denote the set of distributions on Ω that are at least ϵ-far from uniform.

Although we generally aim to develop testers with constant error probability, e.g. 1/3, along the way we construct testers with much higher, and often asymmetric, error. In particular, we often need to make sure that the uniform distribution is accepted with very high probability (so that all nodes accept it), but any ϵ-far distribution is only rejected with "not too small" probability (but much less than 1/2). This motivates the following definition, for centralized (i.e., single-node) testers with asymmetric error:

Definition 1 ((δ,α)-gap tester). *Fix $\delta \in (0,1)$ and $\alpha > 1$, and let $\mathcal{P}$ be a family of distributions. An algorithm $\mathcal{A}$ is said to be a (δ,α)-gap tester for $\mathcal{P}$ using s samples if for any distribution μ,*

(1) If $\mu \in \mathcal{P}$, then $\Pr_{S\sim\mu^s}[\mathcal{A}(S) = 1] \geq 1-\delta$, and
(2) If μ is ϵ-far from $\mathcal{P}$, then $\Pr_{S\sim\mu^s}[\mathcal{A}(S) = 1] \leq 1-\alpha\cdot\delta$.

Here, $\mathcal{A}(S)$ is the random variable denoting the output of $\mathcal{A}$ on samples S. We usually take α to be only slightly greater than 1.

When working with such a delicate error regime, the following lemma will be useful. It shows that in order to achieve the separation required for a (δ,α)-tester, some small but non-negligible amount of information is required:

Lemma 2.1. *Let B_p denote the Bernoulli distribution with probability p. For any $\delta \in (0,1/4)$ and $\tau \in (1,\frac{1}{\delta})$,*

$$D_{KL}\left(\mathsf{B}_{1-\delta} \parallel \mathsf{B}_{1-\tau\delta}\right) \geq \frac{\delta}{4}\left(\tau - 1 - \log\tau\right).$$

Here, $D_{KL}(\mu \parallel \eta) = \sum_x \mu(x)\log(\mu(x)/\eta(x))$ is the KL-divergence between distributions μ and η, a measure of how different they are from each other.

Distributed models. In addition to the standard distributed models, LOCAL and CONGEST, we consider a *0-round model*. In this model, each node outputs its decision without communicating with the other nodes. We consider two decision rules: the *AND rule*, where the network is said to accept iff all nodes accept; and the *threshold rule*, where we fix a threshold T, and the network is said to accept iff fewer than T nodes reject.

Simultaneous communication complexity. Our lower bound for uniformity testing takes a detour through *simultaneous communication complexity*. Here, we have three players: Alice, Bob, and a referee. Alice and Bob are given inputs $X, Y \in \{0,1\}^n$, and each player sends one message to the referee, who then outputs a value. The goal is for the referee to compute some function $f(X,Y)$ of Alice and Bob's inputs (which it cannot see directly). The *cost* of a simultaneous protocol is the worst-case maximum length of a message sent by Alice or Bob.

We are specifically interested in *private-coin* protocols, where Alice and Bob each have private randomness that is not shared with the other or with the referee. We let $\mathsf{SMP}_{\delta_0,\delta_1}(f)$ denote the minimum cost of a private-coin protocol, where if $f(X,Y) = 1$, the referee outputs 1 w.p. $\geq 1-\delta_1$; and if $f(X,Y) = 0$, the referee outputs 0 w.p. $\geq 1-\delta_0$.

3 0-ROUND DISTRIBUTED UNIFORMITY TESTING

We begin our investigation of distributed uniformity testing by studying the 0-round model, where no communication is allowed. We show that we can develop a tester where the number of samples at each node is much smaller than $\Theta(\sqrt{n}/\epsilon^2)$ (i.e., no single node can test uniformity on its own). Our strategy is to divide the responsibility for rejecting: we ask each node to reject an ϵ-far distribution with small (but noticeable) probability, but accept the uniform distribution with very high probability. This ensures that the network *as a whole* can distinguish an ϵ-far distribution from the uniform distribution.

First, we show that a single node using $s = \Theta(\sqrt{\delta n})$ samples is able to achieve probability $1-\delta$ of accepting the uniform distribution, and probability at least $(1+\Theta(\epsilon^2))\delta$ of rejecting any distribution that is ϵ-far from uniform.

3.1 The Collision-Based Tester, Revisited

It is well established (see, e.g., [16]) that when testing uniformity or any other symmetric property of distributions, all the relevant information is captured by the histogram of the samples: namely, one looks for *collisions* among the samples. Our challenge here is that we want to use a very small number of samples, such that the expected number of collisions is much smaller than one, and the probability of seeing *two* collisions is negligible. Unlike the optimal centralized uniformity tester [21], it is pointless for us to start *counting* collisions, because we will probably never see more than one.

For this reason, the tester we consider simply retrieves s samples from the oracle, and accepts (i.e., returns "uniform") if and only if all the samples are distinct. The question is: how large does s need to be, to guarantee the gap we need for a (δ, α)-gap uniformity tester? We show:

Theorem 3.1 (Gap tester, informal). *There is a $(\delta, 1 + \Theta(\epsilon^2))$-gap tester that uses $s = \Theta(\sqrt{\delta n})$ samples, provided δ is not too large compared to ϵ, and n is not too small.*

We then discuss ways of amplifying the success probability.

The more strict we get with the relations between δ, ϵ, n, the better gap we have. Specifically, for the distributed setting we will use a $(\delta, 1 + \epsilon^2/2)$-gap tester, that uses $s = \Theta(\sqrt{\delta n})$ samples, and works provided that $\delta < \epsilon^4/64$ and $n > 64/(\epsilon^4 \delta)$.

The analysis goes as follows: fix a distribution μ on a domain of n elements, and let χ be the collision probability of μ:

$$\chi = \chi(\mu) = \Pr_{X,Y\sim\mu}[X = Y] = \sum_{x \in \mathrm{Supp}(\mu)} \mu(x)^2.$$

The uniform distribution has $\chi(\mathcal{U}) = 1/n$. At the heart of collision-based uniformity testers is the following well-known property (see the textbook [16]):

Lemma 3.2. *If μ is ϵ-far from the uniform distribution, then $\chi(\mu) > (1 + \epsilon^2)/n$.*

Let s be such that $s(s - 1) = 2\delta n$; we assume that s is an integer (and will make sure that this assumption is satisfied when we use the tester).

In our analysis, we try to reach a gap as close as possible to $1 + \epsilon^2$, but in fact we only reach $1 + \gamma\epsilon^2$, where

$$\gamma := 1 - \frac{1}{s} - \sqrt{2\delta(1 + \epsilon^2)} - \frac{\frac{1}{s} + \sqrt{2\delta(1 + \epsilon^2)}}{\epsilon^2}. \tag{1}$$

This is a "slack term" that approaches 1 as $n/k \to \infty$.

Let $S \sim \mu^s$ be a set of s iid samples from μ, and let Z be an indicator for the event that there is a collision in S (that is, S contains two identical samples). Our tester outputs 0 iff $Z = 1$. Our analysis for the tester relies on a tight bound from [18] for the probability of getting a collision in a set of s samples:

Lemma 3.3 (Theorem 3, [18]). *For any distribution μ, we have $\Pr_{S\sim\mu^s}[Z = 0] \le e^{-(s-1)\cdot\sqrt{\chi}} \cdot (1 + (s - 1) \cdot \sqrt{\chi})$.*

Using this bound, we show:

Lemma 3.4. *The single-collision tester satisfies:*

(1) $(1 - \delta)$-completeness: if $\mu = \mathcal{U}$ is the uniform distribution, then $\Pr_{S\sim\mu^s}[Z = 0] \ge 1 - \delta$, and

(2) $(\alpha \cdot \delta)$-soundness: if μ is ϵ-far from the uniform distribution, then $\Pr_{S\sim\mu^s}[Z = 0] \le 1 - \alpha \cdot \delta$, where $\alpha = 1 + \Theta(\epsilon^2)$.

Proof sketch. Suppose $\mu = \mathcal{U}$ is the uniform distribution. What is the probability that we see no collisions? It turns out that Markov's inequality gives a tight bound in this case, since the probability for more than one collision is negligible. We have $\Pr[Z \ge 1] \le \mathrm{E}[Z]/1 = \binom{s}{2}/n$. Recall that we chose s so that $s(s - 1) = 2\delta n$, that is, $\binom{s}{2}/n = \delta$; thus, $\Pr[Z \ge 1] \le \delta$, as desired.

Now suppose μ is ϵ-far from uniform. Then Lemma 3.3, together with Lemma 3.2, yields

$$\Pr[Z = 0] \le e^{-(s-1)\sqrt{(1+\epsilon^2)/n}} \cdot \left(1 + (s - 1)\sqrt{\frac{1 + \epsilon^2}{n}}\right). \tag{2}$$

To analyze the expression in (2), let us denote $t := (s-1)\sqrt{(1 + \epsilon^2)/n}$, so that (2) takes the form: $\Pr[Z = 0] \le e^{-t}(t + 1)$. From the Taylor expansion $e^{-x} = 1-x+x^2/2-O(x^3)$ we know that $e^{-x} \le 1-x+x^2/2$ for all $x \ge 0$, so

$$\Pr[Z = 0] \le \left(1 - t + \frac{t^2}{2}\right)(1 + t) = 1 - \frac{1}{2}\left(t^2 - t^3\right). \tag{3}$$

Recall that we want to show that $\Pr[Z = 0] \le 1 - \alpha \cdot \delta$, where α is as large as we can make it — we are aiming for $\alpha = 1 + \Theta(\epsilon^2)$. Thus, our goal is to show that $\left(t^2 - t^3\right)/(2\delta) \ge 1 + \Theta(\epsilon^2)$. We compute the value of t^2, and obtain $t^2 = \left(1 - \frac{1}{s}\right)(1 + \epsilon^2) \cdot 2\delta$. As for t^3, we are able to bound it from above by $t^3 \le \sqrt{2\delta(1 + \epsilon^2)} \cdot t^2$. Plugging these bounds into (3) shows that $\Pr[Z = 0] \le 1 - (1 + \gamma\epsilon^2)\delta$, as required. □

3.2 From the Collision-Based Tester to a Distributed Algorithm

Let $\mathcal{A}_\delta$ be the $(\delta, 1 + \Theta(\epsilon^2))$-gap tester we developed in the previous section. This tester has very high failure probability: on a distribution that is ϵ-far from uniform, it almost certainly accepts, even though it should reject. We would like to use $\mathcal{A}_\delta$ to obtain a distributed 0-round algorithm in which the network as a whole has only *constant* (e.g., 1/3) failure probability.

We consider two different approaches: first, we adapt the tester to work with the "standard" distributed decision model, where on YES-instances we require all nodes to accept, and on NO-instances at least one node should reject. Unfortunately, this model is not amplification-friendly: it does not allow us to reduce the error probability by repeating our distributed tester several times and taking, say, the majority. (Here we mean the majority decision of the *entire network*, not the individual nodes.) Hence, the number of samples required degrades significantly when we aim for constant error.

The second model we consider is a *threshold decision* model, where we can set a threshold T, and define that the network has "accepted" an input if at least T nodes accepted, and otherwise we say that the network "rejected". This model *is* amenable to amplification using standard techniques. We will use our results for the threshold-decision model when we develop a multi-round tester for the CONGEST model.

3.2.1 The Standard Distributed Decision Model. Suppose we want the network to decide correctly with probability at least $1-p$ on any distribution. With the standard decision model, it suffices to require that if each node runs a tester $\mathcal{B}$,

- For the uniform distribution, the probability that $\mathcal{B}$ rejects is at most $\ln((1/(1-p))/(1-\beta))/k$, where $\beta := \ln(1/(1-p))/(2k)$ is a small slack term approaching 0 as $k \to \infty$.
- For any distribution that is ϵ-far from uniform, the probability that $\mathcal{B}$ rejects is at least $\ln(1/p)/k$.

Essentially, $\mathcal{B}$ needs to be a $(\Theta(1/k), 1+\Omega(1))$-gap tester, where the constant in the $\Omega(1)$ depends on the probability p. This ensures that the uniform distribution is accepted by all nodes with probability $1-p$, while for any distribution that is ϵ-far from uniform, with probability at least $1-p$ some node rejects.

Our tester from the previous section, $\mathcal{A}_\delta$, has a gap of only $1+\Theta(\epsilon^2)$. We need to increase the gap to at least C_p, where C_p is a constant that depends on the desired failure probability p. However, while doing so, we must preserve the very high acceptance probability for the uniform distribution, to make sure that w.h.p. the entire network accepts it.

A natural strategy to amplify the gap is to run the tester $\mathcal{A}_\delta$ independently m times, and reject iff all m trials rejected. To reach our desired gap of C_p, we need to take $m = \log_{1+\Theta(\epsilon^2)}(C_p) = \Theta(C_p/\epsilon^2)$ repetitions. However, the undesired side-effect of this strategy is that the acceptance probability is now decreased: if we started with probability δ of rejecting the uniform distribution, the probability that m independent trials all reject the uniform distribution is now δ^m. We require:

$$\left(1-\delta^m\right)^k \geq 1-p, \tag{4}$$

and therefore $\delta = \Theta(1/k^{1/m})$.

We instantiate this scheme by having every network node run $m = \Theta(C_p/\epsilon^2)$ independent repetitions of the tester $\mathcal{A}_\delta$ with $\delta = \Theta(1/k^{1/m})$. When k, n are sufficiently large compared to $1/\epsilon$, we obtain the tester described in Theorem 1.1. The full proof and the exact calculations are somewhat laborious, and are omitted from this text.

3.2.2 A Threshold-Based Tester. A significant improvement can be made when we change the decision rule to *threshold.* While asking each node to amplify its own gap by itself is very expensive, if we let the *whole network* work together, we can leverage the weak signal each node provides much more efficiently.

Proof of Theorem 1.2. We will again run the single-collision tester $\mathcal{A}_\delta$, but this time we set the parameters so as to create a large gap between the expected number of nodes that reject when the distribution is uniform, and the expected number of rejections when the distribution is ϵ-far from uniform.

Let R_v denote the event that node v rejects when it runs $\mathcal{A}_\delta$, and let R count the number of rejecting nodes in the network. Let $\eta(\mu) := \mathrm{E}_{S_1,\ldots,S_k\sim\mu^s}[R]$ denote the expected number of rejections when all nodes run $\mathcal{A}_\delta$ with samples drawn from μ. We simplify the notation by writing the distribution μ in the subscript, instead of the samples $S_1, \ldots, S_k \sim \mu^s$.

Recall that $\mathcal{A}_\delta$ is a $(\delta, 1+\gamma\epsilon^2)$-gap tester: that is, $\Pr_{\mathcal{U}}[R_v = 1] \leq \delta$, and for any $\mu \in \mathcal{F}_\epsilon(\mathcal{U})$ we have $\Pr_\mu[R_v = 1] \geq \left(1+\gamma\epsilon^2\right)\delta$. For our purposes here, it suffices to take $\gamma \geq 1/2$. Therefore, $\eta(\mathcal{U}) \leq k\cdot\delta$, and for all $\mu \in \mathcal{F}_\epsilon(\mathcal{U})$, $\eta(\mu) \geq k\cdot\left(1+\epsilon^2/2\right)\delta$. By Chernoff,

$$\Pr_{\mathcal{U}}[R \geq T] = \Pr_{\mathcal{U}}\left[R \geq \eta(\mathcal{U})\cdot\left(1+\frac{T-\eta(\mathcal{U})}{\eta(\mathcal{U})}\right)\right] \leq e^{-((T-\eta(\mathcal{U}))^2/(3\eta(\mathcal{U}))},$$

and for any $\mu \in \mathcal{F}_\epsilon(\mathcal{U})$,

$$\Pr_\mu[R < T] = \Pr_\mu\left[R < \eta(\mu)\cdot\left(1-\frac{\eta(\mu)-T}{\eta(\mu)}\right)\right] \leq e^{-(T-\eta(\mu))^2/(2\eta(\mu))}.$$

Of course, we would like to put the threshold T in between the two expectations $\eta(\mathcal{U})$ and $\eta(\mu)$ for any $\mu \in \mathcal{F}_\epsilon(\mathcal{U})$, such that the probabilities above are both bounded by $1/3$. It suffices to require (for all $\mu \in \mathcal{F}_\epsilon(\mathcal{U})$):

$$\eta(\mathcal{U}) + \sqrt{3\ln(3)\eta(\mathcal{U})} \leq T \leq \eta(\mu) - \sqrt{2\ln(3)\eta(\mu)}. \tag{5}$$

In order for a threshold T satisfying (5) to exist, we can take $\delta = \Theta(1/(\epsilon^4 k))$, which allows us to set $T = \Theta(1/\epsilon^4)$ (full details are omitted). Plugging this value of δ into Theorem 3.1, we see that $s = \Theta(\sqrt{n/k}/\epsilon^2)$ samples are sufficient. □

4 THE ASYMMETRIC CASE

We now generalize to the asymmetric case, where each node i can ask to draw s_i samples, at a cost of c_i per sample. The total cost of node i is therefore $s_i \cdot c_i$. We would like to minimize the *maximum individual cost*, $C := \max_i\{s_i \cdot c_i\}$.

For convenience, we denote $T_i := 1/c_i$. Our results will depend on various norms of the vector $T = (T_1, \ldots, T_k)$ of inverse costs.

The essential idea is to divide the *responsibility* we assign to each node in accordance with the cost it pays, in a way that allows "expensive nodes" (with high c_i) to draw fewer samples than "cheap nodes" (with low c_i). Here, the *responsibility* of node i corresponds to the part it plays in the network's decision.

Since we are interested in optimizing the maximum individual cost, $C = \max_i\{s_i \cdot c_i\}$, we may as well allow *all* nodes to use the same cost C (once we compute what C needs to be). Thus, for each node i, we will choose s_i so that $s_i \cdot c_i = C$, that is, $s_i = C \cdot T_i$.

We will use the collision-based tester fromSection 3, but now each node i will instantiate it with a different value δ_i. However, all nodes will still use the same value of α as in the symmetric case.

4.1 The AND Decision Rule

Let us compute the number of samples s_i that each node i must draw, when the final decision of the network is the AND of the nodes' individual decisions.

Each individual node will run a (δ_i, α_i)-gap tester. We will use the same gap, $\alpha_i = \alpha$, for all nodes, but different thresholds δ_i.

As we saw in the symmetric case, we can obtain a (δ_i, α)-gap tester by taking m repetitions of the tester $\mathcal{A}_{\delta_i'}$ from Section 3, with $\delta_i' = \delta_i^{1/m}$ and $m = \Theta(C_p/\epsilon^2)$. The number of samples required by node i is $s_i = m \cdot \sqrt{2\delta_i' n}$. Recalling that $s_i = C \cdot T_i$, we can express this as:

$$\delta_i = \frac{(C \cdot T_i)^{2m}}{(2n)^m m^{2m}}.$$

How are the various costs δ_i constrained? To ensure that the network accepts the uniform distribution with sufficiently high probability, we set the δ_is so that

$$\prod_{i=1}^{k}(1-\delta_i) = 1-p. \tag{6}$$

We show that if we set the δ_is so that (6) is satisfied, then *soundness* also holds: any distribution that is ϵ-far from uniform is rejected by at least one node, with probability at least $1-p$. Intuitively, this is because: the probability of accepting an ϵ-far distribution is given by $\prod_{i=1}^{k}(1-\alpha\delta_i)$. Under the constraint (6), this expression is maximized when when all δ_is take the same value, i.e., when we are back in the symmetric case. We know that in the symmetric case all players created a tester of the same δ and α, and soundness was satisfied; we show that taking asymmetric values for the δ_is but with all players using the same old α, can only *tighten* the bound, that is, *decrease* the probability that an ϵ-far distribution is accepted.

We prove this intuition using the following technical lemma:

Lemma 4.1. *Fix $c \in (0,1)$, $a \in (1, 1/(1-c))$ and $X = (x_1, \ldots, x_k) \in [0, 1-c]^k$ such that*

$$f_k(X) := \prod_{i=1}^{k}(1-x_i) = c.$$

Denote $Y_k := d_k \cdot (1, \ldots, 1) \in \mathbb{R}^k$, where $d_k := (1 - \sqrt[k]{c})$, so that $f_k(Y_k) = c$. Then the function $g_k(X) := \prod_{i=1}^{k}(1-ax_i)$ satisfies:

$$g_k(X) \leq g_k(Y_k).$$

Here, we are looking for a set $\{\delta_i\}_{i=1}^{k}$ satisfying (6) above. For simplicity, let us fix $p = 1/3$.

In the symmetric model, we ended up with each node being a (δ, α)-gap tester (recall the tester $\mathcal{B}$), where $\delta = \Theta(1/k)$ was the value that satisfied the completeness for the whole network. Meaning, $\prod_{i=1}^{k}(1-\delta) \approxeq 1 - 1/3$. We also had $\alpha = \ln(1/p)/\ln(1/(1-p))$ which we denoted as C_p, that was enough to satisfy the soundness of the whole network. For $p = 1/3$, this turns out to be $\alpha \approxeq 2.7$.

We can then use the lemma with $c = \prod_{i=1}^{k}(1-\delta) \approxeq 2/3$, $a = \alpha \approxeq 2.7 < 3 = 1/(1-c)$. The value d_k is (by definition) exactly the same value as δ, since $(1-d_k)^k = c = (1-\delta)^k$. We now apply the lemma with $X = (\delta_1, \ldots, \delta_k)$. Given that the probability of accepting the uniform distribution is good enough (i.e $\prod_{i=1}^{k}(1-\delta_i) = c$), we want to conclude the probability to accept ϵ-far distributions is not too large. Following the lemma, this is given by $g_k(X) = \prod_{i=1}^{k}(1-\alpha\delta_i)$.

Applying the lemma, we get

$$g_k(X) \leq g_k(Y_k) = \prod_{i=1}^{k}(1-\alpha d_k) = \prod_{i=1}^{k}(1-\alpha\delta)$$

This last term is exactly the soundness the whole network had when each player applied $\mathcal{B}$ in the symmetric case, which we know to be low enough, by our choosing of $\alpha = C_p$ for $p = 1/3$.

Thus we have our soundness for the asymmetric case "for free" when all players use the same α used in the symmetric case.

We now see that:

$$e^{ln(1-p)} = 1-p = \prod_{i=1}^{k}(1-\delta_i) \leq e^{-\sum\delta_i} = e^{-\frac{C^{2m}}{(2n)^m m^{2m}}\cdot(\sum T_i^{2m})}$$

And therefore our algorithm has the cost of:

$$C = \sqrt{2\sqrt[m]{ln(\frac{1}{1-p})}m\sqrt{n}} \cdot \frac{1}{||T||_{2m}}$$

where $m = \Theta(1/\epsilon^2)$. notice that for the symmetric case with k players, indeed we get $||T||_{2m} = \sqrt{k^{1/(2m)}} = \sqrt{k^{\Theta(\epsilon^2)}}$, as before.

We now turn to prove the lemma:

Proof of Lemma 4.1. We prove the lemma by induction on the dimension k.

For $k = 1$, the claim is trivial: we have a single-dimensional vector, that is, a scalar x, which by the conditions of the lemma satisfies $x = 1-c$. We also have $Y_1 = d_1 = 1-c$, and therefore $x = Y_1$ and $g_1(x) = g_1(Y_1)$.

Next, suppose the claim holds for all $j < k$, and let us prove it for k. First, note that $g_k(Y_k) \leq g_{k+1}(Y_{k+1})$. Also, we can assume that $x_i \neq 0$ for all $i \in [k]$, otherwise we can reduce the dimension to $k-1$ by eliminating the zero coordinates, and then apply the induction hypothesis.

Consider the compact cube $S = [0, 1-c]^k \subset \mathbb{R}^k$.

First, we look for solutions on the border of our constrained area, that is, the intersection of the manifold $f_k(X) = c$ and the border of S. We note that each point on the border must have $x_i \in \{0, 1-c\}$ for some i, but this implies that either $x_i = 0$ or otherwise $x_j = 0$ for all $j \neq i$. Thus, this case is handled again by the induction hypothesis, in a lower dimension.

Within the inner area of S, we apply the method of Lagrange multipliers over k variables and with $m = 1$ constraints, where our single constraint is $f_k(X) = c$. For brevity, from here and until the end of the proof, we omit the subscript and simply use f, g, Y, d instead.

We define $h(X, \lambda) := g(X) + \lambda \cdot (f(X) - c)$, and write the partial derivatives:

$$\frac{\partial f}{\partial x_i}(X) = -\Pi_{j\neq i}(1-x_j) = \frac{2/3}{x_i - 1},$$

$$\frac{\partial g}{\partial x_i}(X) = -a\Pi_{j\neq i}(1-ax_j) = \frac{-a \cdot g(X)}{(1-ax_i)}.$$

If X is a suspicious point inside of S, it must satisfy:

$$\forall i.\ 0 = \frac{\partial h}{\partial x_i}(X,\lambda) = \frac{\partial g}{\partial x_i}(X) + \lambda\frac{\partial f}{\partial x_i}(X) = \frac{-a \cdot g(X)}{(1-ax_i)} - + \frac{2/3\lambda}{x_i - 1},$$

which implies that for all i,

$$x_i = \frac{ag(X) + 2/3\lambda}{ag(X) + 2/3\lambda a}.$$

Since this holds for any i, and the r.h.s does not depend on i, we get that our point must satisfy $x_i = x_j$ for all $i \neq j$. In other words, if X is a suspicious point, then $X = m \cdot (1, \ldots, 1)$ for some m. Plugging in the last derivative, $\frac{\partial h}{\partial \lambda}(X,\lambda) = f(x) - C = 0$ (that is X is on the manifold $f(X) = c$), we get exactly that $X = Y$, and also $\lambda = \frac{-ag(Y)(1-d)}{2/3(1-ad)}$.

We have now shown that Y is the only suspicious point inside of S. To prove the lemma, we would like to show that Y is indeed an *extremal maximum* inside S. By the bordered Hessian method, a sufficient condition for this is that if we look at the sequence of growing submatrices of the bordered Hessian of $h(X, \lambda)$, the sequence of determinants alternates signs.

We first calculate

$$\frac{\partial^2 f}{\partial x_i \partial x_j}(X) = \Pi_{k \notin \{i,j\}}(1 - x_k) = \frac{2/3}{(1 - x_i)(1 - x_j)},$$

$$\frac{\partial^2 g}{\partial x_i \partial x_j}(X) = a^2 \Pi_{k \notin \{i,j\}}(1 - a x_k) = \frac{a^2 g(X)}{(1 - a x_i)(1 - a x_j)}.$$

Therefore, we have:

(1) $w := \frac{\partial^2 h}{\partial \lambda \partial x_i}(Y, \lambda) = \frac{\partial (f-c)}{\partial x_i}(Y, \lambda) = \frac{2/3}{d-1}$,

(2) $z := \frac{\partial^2 h}{\partial x_j \partial x_i}(Y, \lambda) = \frac{\partial^2 g}{\partial x_j \partial x_i}(Y) + \lambda \frac{\partial^2 f}{\partial x_j \partial x_i}(Y) = \frac{a^2 g(X)}{(1-a x_i)(1-a x_j)} + \lambda \frac{2/3}{(x_i - 1)(x_j - 1)}$,

(3) $\frac{\partial^2 h}{\partial x_i \partial x_i}(Y, \lambda) = \frac{\partial^2 g}{\partial x_i \partial x_i}(Y) + \lambda \frac{\partial^2 f}{\partial x_i \partial x_i}(Y) = 0.$

The bordered Hessian matrix is given by:

$$H(X, \lambda) = \begin{pmatrix} \frac{\partial^2 h}{\partial \lambda^2}(X, \lambda) & \frac{\partial^2 h}{\partial \lambda \partial X}(X, \lambda) \\ (\frac{\partial^2 h}{\partial \lambda \partial X}(X, \lambda))^\top & \frac{\partial^2 h}{\partial X^2}(X, \lambda) \end{pmatrix}$$

So at point (Y, λ), denoting $L := H(Y, \lambda)$ and using the equations above, we have

$$L(i,j) = \begin{cases} 0 & i = j, \\ w & i \neq j \wedge (i = 1 \vee j = 1), \\ z & \text{otherwise.} \end{cases}$$

Now, since we have only one constraint ($m = 1$), we need to look at the upper left submatrices of each size starting from $2m + 1 = 3$, and up to $k + m = k + 1$, and make sure the signs of their determinants are alternating. We note that each such submatrix preserves the structure of L itself. We now calculate the determinant for general matrix of that form and of size $t \times t$, which we will denote in L_t.

We know that the determinant can be viewed as a sum over all permutation of the parity of the said permutation, times the product of values in entries $(i, \sigma(i))$. Formally we can write:

$$\mathrm{Det}(L_t) := \sum_{\sigma \in S_t} (-1)^{\mathrm{sgn}(\sigma)} \Pi_{i=1}^{t} (L_t(i, \sigma(i))).$$

We notice a few facts that help us understand this expression:

(i) For any $\sigma \in S_t$ that has a fixpoint, we get a summand of 0, which we can disregard. Therefore we only sum over the derangements D_t (i.e., permutations with no fixpoint).
(ii) For any $\sigma \in D_t$, we must have $\sigma(1) \neq 1$, as well as $\sigma(j) = 1$ for some $j \neq 1$. So all pairs $(i, \sigma(i))$ are $(1, i_0, (i_1, 1)$ for $i_1, i_0 \neq 1$, and all the rest are (i, j) with $i \neq 1, j \neq 1$. Together with the form we have for L_t, we get that $\prod_{i=1}^{t} (L_t(i, \sigma(i))) = w^2 z^{t-2}$, for any $\sigma \in D_t$.
(iii) Letting $E(D_t)$ and $O(D_t)$ denote the number of even and odd derangements of size t, respectively, it is known [20] that $E(D_t) - O(D_t) = (-1)^{t-1}(t - 1)$.

Using these facts, we have:

$$\begin{aligned} \mathrm{Det}(L_t) &= \sum_{\sigma \in D_t} (-1)^{\mathrm{sgn}(\sigma)} \prod_{i=1}^{t} (L_t(i, \sigma(i))) \\ &= w^2 z^{t-2} \sum_{\sigma \in D_t} (-1)^{\mathrm{sgn}(\sigma)} = w^2 z^{t-2} (-1)^{t-1} (t - 1). \end{aligned}$$

Since $w, z, t - 1 > 0$, our sign only depends on the exponent of (-1), so we have $\mathrm{sgn}(\mathrm{Det}(L_t)) = (-1)^{t-1}$.

Starting at L_3, we get a positive determinant, and the signs of $\mathrm{Det}(L_4), \ldots, \mathrm{Det}(L_{k+m})$ alternate . According to the bordered Hessian condition, we get that Y is indeed an extremal maximum inside of S, proving the claim. □

4.2 The Threshold Model

In this model our solution let each player run $\mathcal{A}_{\delta_i}$. Following the same analysis and Chernoff bounds we had before, we need only to replace $k \cdot \delta$ by $\sum_i \delta_i$, and following the same calculations, we will now need:

$$\sum_i \delta_i = \Theta(1/\epsilon^4)$$

In that model, each δ_i required that we take $s_i = \sqrt{2\delta_i n}$ samples, and again setting $C = s_i / T_i$ for all players, we now get that $\delta_i = \frac{C^2 T_i^2}{2n}$, and we can write:

$$\Theta(1/\epsilon^4) = \sum_i \delta_i = \frac{S^2}{2n} \cdot \sum_i T_i^2$$

And therefore:

$$S = \Theta(\frac{\sqrt{n}}{\epsilon^2}) \cdot \frac{1}{||T||_2}$$

5 IMPLEMENTATION IN CONGEST

We now show how to solve uniformity testing in the CONGEST model. We assume for simplicity that each node has a single sample; generalizing to more samples is straightforward.

Our goal is to "concentrate" samples at a small number of nodes, who will then use our 0-round uniformity tester with the samples they collected. For this purpose, we define the τ-token-packaging problem.

Definition 2 (Token packaging). *Let $\tau \in \mathbb{N}$. In the τ-token packaging problem, each node $v \in V$ is initially given a single token $t_v \in [n]$. The goal is for the nodes to collectively output a set of multisets ("packages") of tokens, $S_1, \ldots, S_\ell \subseteq \{t_v \mid v \in V\}$, with each node outputting zero or more packages. (The number ℓ of packages is not fixed in advance.)*

We require the following:

(1) Each package is of size exactly τ.
(2) Each token t_v is included in at most one package (that is, we require $|\{i \mid t_v \in S_i\}| \leq 1$).
(3) All but at most $\tau - 1$ tokens are included in some package (that is, $|\{v \mid t_v \notin \bigcup_{i \in [\ell]} S_i\}| \leq \tau - 1$).

Note that even though we did not impose an explicit requirement on the number of packages, the problem definition implies that at most $\lfloor k/\tau \rfloor$ packages are produced, because we start out with n tokens and each token can belong to at most one package.

We also mention that even though the round complexity has the diameter D in it, the players does not need to know the value of D in advance in order to run the algorithm.

Theorem 5.1. *For any $\tau \geq 1$, the τ-token packaging problem can be solved in $O(D + \tau)$ rounds in* CONGEST.

We show how to solve τ-token packaging below, but first let us explain how we use it:

Proof of Theorem 1.4. We start out with k samples, one at each node. Fix a parameter τ for the package size. We package our k tokens into $\ell = \Theta(k/\tau)$ packages, and use the threshold-based tester from Theorem 1.2 with ℓ nodes and τ samples at each node, treating each package as a "virtual node". (If node v outputs $p(v)$ packages, then we have node v simulate $p(v)$ "virtual nodes".)

To use the threshold-based tester, the number of samples at each "virtual node" must satisfy $\tau = \Omega(\sqrt{n/\ell}/\epsilon^2)$. Recalling that $\ell = \Theta(k/\tau)$, we see that we should set $\tau = \Theta(n/(k\epsilon^4))$. Thus, the running time is $O(D + n/(k\epsilon^4))$ rounds: $O(D + \tau)$ rounds to solve τ-token packaging, and an additional D rounds to compute the threshold, by summing up the tree the number of virtual nodes that want to reject. Finally, the root rejects iff the number of rejecting nodes crosses the threshold, and the other nodes always accept. □

Solving token-packaging. The algorithm for token-packaging works as follows: first, the network identifies the vertex $r \in V$ with the largest identifier, and then constructs a BFS tree T rooted at node r. We will forward tokens up the tree: each tree node v that receives a total of $m(v)$ tokens from its subtree will keep $p(v) := \lfloor m(v)/\tau \rfloor$ full packages to itself (i.e., $p(v) \cdot \tau$ tokens), and send the rest of the tokens, $c(v) := m(v) \bmod \tau$, up the tree.

We begin by having each node v compute the number $c(v)$ of tokens it needs to sent upwards. The computation proceeds up the tree, as follows:

- If v is a leaf, then $c(v) = 1$.
- If v is not a leaf, and the children of v are $u_1, \ldots, u_d$, then

$$c(v) = \left(1 + \sum_{i=1}^{d} c(u_i)\right) \bmod \tau.$$

Next, for τ rounds, the nodes propagate tokens up the tree, with each node v passing the first $c(v)$ tokens it receives up to its parent, and keeping the rest for itself. Note that $c(v) < \tau$ for all $v \in V$. After τ rounds, the root r discards $c(r)$ tokens it received. Each node now has an integer multiple of τ tokens, which it packages and outputs.

Correctness of the algorithm. Recall that each tree node first forwards all $c(v)$ tokens it will *ever* forward up the tree, and then keeps the remaining tokens for itself. Intuitively, we show that tokens "pipeline" up the tree, so that every node has some new token to send in each round from the beginning of the algorithm until it has sent $c(v)$ tokens. Since $c(v) < \tau$, this means that after τ rounds, all nodes are done sending up the tree, and all tokens have reached their final destinations.

Let $h(v)$ denote the height of node v in the BFS tree (that is, the depth of its subtree, with leaves having depth one), let *children*(v) be the children of v.

We show that σ rounds are enough for each node v to receive and send up the $c(v) < \sigma$ tokens it needs to forward up the tree, and thereby establish the correctness of our algorithm. Formally, we argue by induction on the height $h(v)$ that:

Invariant 1. At any time $t \leq c(v)$,

(1) If $\ell_v(t) := |sent_v(t)|$ is the number of tokens v sent up to its parent by time t, then we have $\ell_v(t) = t$; and
(2) If $t < c(v)$, then at time t node v has $tokens_v(t) \neq \emptyset$.

(Recall that for the root, we interpret $\ell_v(t)$ as the number of tokens it discarded.)

This shows that at time $t = \sigma$, each node v has already sent on (or discarded, in the case of the root) $c(v)$ tokens, because $c(v) < \sigma$.

An easy induction up the tree shows that after the algorithm concludes, each node has an integer multiple of τ tokens, which it packages and outputs. Tokens are only ever discarded at the root, and the root r discards $c(r) < \tau$ tokens; therefore, all but at most $\tau - 1$ tokens are packaged. Thus, our algorithm solves τ-token packaging.

6 IMPLEMENTATION IN LOCAL

We assume again that each node initially has one sample. (This is not essential.)

As in the CONGEST tester, we want to concentrate samples at a small number of nodes, and then use the 0-round uniformity tester. Because we do not care about congestion, in the LOCAL model with $O(r)$ rounds, any node can send its sample to any node at distance $O(r)$.

Let $N^t(v)$ denote the t-neighborhood of $v \in V$. Our strategy is to first use Luby's MIS algorithm to find a maximal independent set on the graph G^r (where for any $u, v \in V$, we have $\{u, v\} \in E(G^r)$ iff the distance between u, v in G is at most r). Let S be the MIS we compute. Each non-MIS node $u \in V \setminus S$ must have some MIS node in its r-neighborhood; node u selects some MIS node $v \in S \cap N^r(u)$, and routes its sample to v, by asking the nodes in its r-neighborhood to forward the sample to v.

How many samples does each MIS node collect? For each $v \in S$, we know that there is no other MIS node in the $r/2$-neighborhood of v, otherwise S would not be an independent set of G^r. Therefore, all samples in $N^{r/2}(v)$ are routed to v. There are at least $r/2$ such samples: because the graph is connected, we have $|N^{r/2}(v)| \geq r/2$. This also implies that $|S| \leq \lfloor 2k/r \rfloor$.

Now we call the 0-round tester from Theorem 1.1, with $\lfloor 2k/r \rfloor$ "virtual nodes" (the MIS nodes), each having $r/2$ samples. If we take $r = \Theta\left(\left((C_p/\epsilon^2) \cdot \sqrt{n/k^{\Theta(\epsilon^2/C_p)}}\right)^{1/(1-\Theta(\epsilon^2/C_p))}\right)$, then by Theorem 1.1, we achieve success probability $1 - p$.

7 LOWER BOUND FOR ANONYMOUS 0-ROUND UNIFORMITY TESTING

In this section we show that any *anonymous* 0-round distributed uniformity tester requires at least $\Theta(\sqrt{n/k})$ samples at some network node in order to succeed with probability 2/3. An anonymous tester is one where all network nodes execute the same randomized algorithm. Note, however, that the nodes can make random choices, and in particular, they can choose a random identifier from any domain they desire. Technically, the anonymity requirement can be weakened further: what we need is that for any distribution μ that is ϵ-far from uniform, all network nodes have *the same probability* of rejecting μ.

Remark. The lower bound technique we use here cannot recover the dependence on the distance parameter ϵ, which we believe is $\Omega(1/\epsilon^2)$, in keeping with the centralized case. Throughout this section we mostly treat ϵ as a constant.

For the lower bound, we start by showing that in order for a single node to solve uniformity testing with $(1-\tau\delta, \delta)$-error, it must draw $\Omega(\sqrt{\delta n})$ samples. This lower bound is shown using the reduction from the 2-party Equality function given in [5]:

Theorem 7.1 ([5]). *Suppose we have a q-sample ϵ-uniformity tester, for a sufficiently small constant ϵ, with error (δ_0, δ_1). Then we must have* $\mathsf{SMP}_{\delta_0,\delta_1}(EQ) \le q \cdot \log n$.

Since we are interested in testers with asymmetric error, we study EQ in the asymmetric-error regime.

7.1 Lower Bound for Equality with Asymmetric Error

In this section we outline a lower bound on the simultaneous communication complexity of the Equality function: $\mathrm{EQ}(X, Y) = 1$ iff $X = Y$. Specifically, we are interested in the case where if $X = Y$, the protocol is *almost always right*: it outputs 1 w.p. at least $1-\delta$. But if $X \neq Y$, we allow the protocol to *almost always be wrong*, and we only require that it outputs 0 w.p. $\tau \cdot \delta$, for some constant $\tau > 1$. Note that this means the *gap* between the acceptance probability for YES-instances and for NO-instances is tiny, only $\Theta(\delta)$. Still, we can show the following lower bound: let $f(\tau) := \tau - 1 - \log(\tau)$.

Theorem 7.2. *Let $\tau > 1$ and $\delta < \min\{1/\tau, 1/4\}$. For any $\tau' > \tau$ we have* $\mathsf{SMP}_{(1-\tau'\delta),\delta}(EQ) = \Omega(\sqrt{f(\tau)\delta n})$.

We adapt the information-theoretic lower bound for EQ with constant error from [6] (fixing a mistake in [6] along the way). We give only a high-level overview of the proof here.

Proof sketch for Theorem 7.2. Fix a simultaneous private-coin protocol Π for equality, and let $\boldsymbol{M}_A, \boldsymbol{M}_B$ be the messages sent by Alice and Bob, respectively. (These are random variables, because the protocol is randomized.) Let $\pi(\eta)$ be the joint distribution of the players' messages, when their inputs are drawn from the distribution η. For a distribution μ on $\{0,1\}^n$, let $\mu_=$ denote the distribution on inputs $(\boldsymbol{X}, \boldsymbol{Y})$ where $\boldsymbol{X} \sim \mu$ and $X = Y$. And finally, let $\mu_\times$ be the distribution where $\boldsymbol{X}, \boldsymbol{Y}$ are drawn *independently* from μ.

We would like to find a "hard distribution" μ on $\{0,1\}^n$, such that: (1) when we draw the players' inputs independently, we have $\Pr_{\mu_\times}[X = Y] = o(1)$; but, (2) the distribution $\pi(\mu_=)$ of messages the referee sees when $(X, Y) \sim \mu_=$ is very similar to the distribution $\pi(\mu_\times)$ of messages it gets when $(X, Y) \sim \mu_\times$. Together, (1) and (2) mean the protocol has high error: the referee cannot distinguish the distribution $\mu_=$, where the inputs are *always* equal, from the distribution $\mu_\times$, where they are almost *never* equal.

For a starting point, we examine the protocol's behavior on the uniform distribution $\mathcal{U}$ on $\{0,1\}^n$. This distribution certainly satisfies (1), as $\Pr_{\mathcal{U}_\times}[X = Y] = 2^{-n}$. However, it does not necessarily satisfy (2). For example, if Alice and Bob each send the referee the parity of their input, then $\pi(\mu_=)$ looks very different from $\pi(\mu_\times)$. Thus, we modify the distribution, by *fixing* those parts of the input that "the players talk about" to some constant value. In our example, we would fix the parity of the input to, say, 0, and set our new distribution to be uniform *subject* to a parity of 0. After this fixing, the referee can no longer distinguish $\pi(\mu_=)$ from $\pi(\mu_\times)$, as in both cases it gets the bit '0' from each player.

Technically, we proceed as follows. We consider an "average" set of messages $B_1, \dots, B_m$ from Bob, and show that if we take $m = \Theta(|\boldsymbol{M}_A|/(f(\tau)\delta))$ messages and *condition* the input on these messages, then with good probability we "neutralize" all but at most $f(\tau) \cdot \delta$ of the difference, measured in KL-divergence [9] between $\pi(\mu_=)$ and $\pi(\mu_\times)$. Intuitively, after this many messages, we have probably already seen "everything Bob wants to say" that might significantly tie his input with Alice's message $\boldsymbol{M}_A$.

We also show that since the referee accepts w.p. $\ge 1-\delta$ on getting messages from $\pi(\mu_=)$, but accepts w.p. $\le 1-\tau\delta$ on seeing $\pi(\mu_\times)$, these two distributions need to be "different": they must have KL-divergence at least $f(\tau) \cdot \delta$ (see Lemma 2.1). Thus, we can fix a set of m messages from Bob and condition the input on them, such that the referee can no longer distinguish $\pi(\mu_=)$ from $\pi(\mu_\times)$ with a gap of $\Theta(\tau\delta)$.

So far we glossed over an important point: if we are too aggressive in fixing parts of the input, then we might violate our first requirement, that $\Pr_{\mu_\times}[X = Y]$ be very small. (For example, if we fix the *entire* input to 0^n, then of course we satisfy requirement (2), but at the cost of always having $\boldsymbol{X} = \boldsymbol{Y}$.) We must show that there is a set $B_1, \dots, B_m$ of messages from Bob that both "neutralizes" the dependence with Alice *and* has low probability that $\boldsymbol{X} = \boldsymbol{Y}$. To do this, we show that for "typical" messages $B_1, \dots, B_m$, when we condition on these messages, the resulting distribution only loses $O(m \cdot |\boldsymbol{M}_B|)$ bits of *collision-entropy*. The collision-entropy of a distribution η is defined as $\mathrm{H}_2(\eta) = -\log \Pr_{(\boldsymbol{A},\boldsymbol{B})\sim\eta_\times}[\boldsymbol{A} = \boldsymbol{B}]$, so high collision-entropy implies low probability of collision.[1] Recall that we started from the uniform distribution, which has $\mathrm{H}_2(\mathcal{U}) = n$, so if we make sure that $m \cdot |\boldsymbol{M}_B| \ll n$, we guarantee that the requirement (2) holds.

Combining our constraints we see that we require $m \ge |\boldsymbol{M}_A| \cdot f(\tau)\delta$ to make sure that the dependence between the players' inputs is sufficiently reduced, but we also need $m \cdot |\boldsymbol{M}_B| \ll n$ to guarantee small collision probability. If $|\boldsymbol{M}_A| \cdot |\boldsymbol{M}_B| = o(f(\tau)\delta n)$, then indeed there exists such an m, and we can construct our hard distribution which fools the protocol. Therefore, by contradiction, we must have $\max\{|\boldsymbol{M}_A|, |\boldsymbol{M}_B|\} = \Omega(\sqrt{f(\tau)\delta n})$. □

At this point we have proven the lower bound for simultaneous Equality with a gap of $\Theta(\delta)$. Since we see this problem as having independent interest, we show that the bound is tight:

Lemma 7.3. *Fix a constant $\tau > 1$. Then* $\mathsf{SMP}_{(1-\tau\delta),\delta}(EQ) = O(\sqrt{\delta n})$.

It is known that $\mathsf{SMP}_{1/3,1/3}(\mathrm{EQ}) = O(\sqrt{n})$ [2], so this claim would be trivial if we were interested in *expected* communication; but here we want small *worst-case* communication.

[1] The mistake in [6] is that they used Shannon entropy to make this argument, but high Shannon entropy does not imply low collision probability. We changed this part of the proof.

Proof of Lemma 7.3. We modify the protocol from [2].

Let m be an integer such that $3n \leq m \leq 4n$ and also $m = (6m_0)^2$ for some $m_0 \in \mathbb{N}$. (For sufficiently large n, there exists such m.)

The protocol uses the *Justesen error-correcting code*: a mapping $C : \{0,1\}^{m/3} \to \{0,1\}^m$, such that whenever $X \neq Y$, we have $\Delta(C(X), C(Y)) \geq m/6$ (that is, $C(X)$ and $C(Y)$ differ in at least $m/6$ places). Since $m = (6m_0)^2$, we can view each codeword as a table of size $(6m_0) \times (6m_0)$. We denote by $C(X)_{i,j}$ entry (i,j) of the table (that is, location $6m_0 \cdot i + j$ of $C(X)$). For convenience, we view the table as a *torus*, so that once we reach the last row or column we wrap-around back to the first row or column.

Now, let $t := \left\lceil \sqrt{24\tau\delta n} \right\rceil$. Alice and Bob receive inputs X, Y, and both compute $C(X), C(Y) \in \{0,1\}^m$. Alice picks a random entry $(a_1, a_2) \in [6m_0]^2$ of the matrix, and sends (a_1, a_2), together with a vertical "chunk" of t bits of her encoded input starting at (a_1, a_2): she sends

$$C(X)_{a_1,a_2}, C(X)_{a_1+1 \bmod (6m_0), a_2}, \ldots, C(X)_{a_1+t-1 \bmod (6m_0), a_2}.$$

Similarly, Bob picks a random entry $(b_1, b_2) \in [6m_0]^2$ of the matrix, and sends (b_1, b_2), together with a horizontal "chunk" of t bits: bits $C(X)_{b_1,b_2}, C(X)_{b_1+1 \bmod (6m_0), b_2}, \ldots, C(X)_{b_1+t-1 \bmod (6m_0), b_2}$.

The referee checks whether there is a location (i,j) sent by both players. If so, he compares this location, and accepts iff $C(X)_{i,j} = C(Y)_{i,j}$; otherwise he simply accepts. this protocol accepts "yes" instances with probability $1-\delta$, and rejects "no" instances with probability $\tau\delta$. □

7.2 Small-Gap Uniformity Testing

We now return to our original question: uniformity testing with asymmetric error. Using the reduction from [5] (Theorem 7.1), our Equality lower bound implies:

Corollary 7.4. *For a sufficiently large constant $\epsilon \in (0, 1/2)$, and for any $\delta < 1, \alpha > 1$, the query complexity of a (δ,α)-gap ϵ-uniformity tester is $\Omega\left(\sqrt{f(\alpha)\delta n}/\log(n)\right)$.*

Using a constant α, we can now prove our lower bound for distributed 0-round uniformity testing:

Proof of Theorem 7.2. Fix an anonymous distributed uniformity tester $\mathcal{A}$ with sample complexity s per node, which achieves error probability at most 1/3. Let us find lower bounds on δ and α, such that each network node must be a (δ,α)-gap tester.

When the distribution is uniform, the probability that the network accepts must satisfy $(1-\delta)^k \geq 2/3$, so we must have $\delta \leq 1-(2/3)^{1/k} \leq \ln(2/3)\frac{1}{k}$. On the other hand, when the distribution is ϵ-far from uniform, the probability that the network rejects should be $(1-\alpha\delta)^k \leq 1/3$, and so $\alpha\delta \geq 1-(1/3)^{1/k} \geq \ln(\sqrt{3})(1/k)$. We see that we must have $\alpha \geq (\ln(\sqrt{3})(1/k))/\delta > 5/4$. We now plug in these parameters into Corollary 7.4, and see that each node must draw $\Omega(\sqrt{n/k})$ samples. □

REFERENCES

[1] Jayadev Acharya, ClÃľment L. Canonne, and Himanshu Tyagi. 2018. *Distributed Simulation and Distributed Inference.* Technical Report arXiv:1804.06952. ArXiV. https://arxiv.org/abs/1804.06952

[2] A. Ambainis. 1996. Communication complexity in a 3-computer model. *Algorithmica* 16, 3 (1996), 298–301.

[3] L. Babai and P. G. Kimmel. 1997. Randomized Simultaneous Messages: Solution Of A Problem Of Yao In Communication Complexity. In *Proceedings of the 12th Annual IEEE Conference on Computational Complexity (CCC '97).* IEEE Computer Society, 239–.

[4] Tugkan Batu, Lance Fortnow, Ronitt Rubinfeld, Warren D. Smith, and Patrick White. 2000. Testing that distributions are close. In *41st Annual Symposium on Foundations of Computer Science, FOCS 2000, 12-14 November 2000, Redondo Beach, California, USA.* 259–269.

[5] Eric Blais, Clément L. Canonne, and Tom Gur. 2017. Distribution Testing Lower Bounds via Reductions from Communication Complexity. In *32nd Computational Complexity Conference, CCC 2017, July 6-9, 2017, Riga, Latvia.* 28:1–28:40.

[6] Ralph Bottesch, Dmitry Gavinsky, and Hartmut Klauck. 2015. Equality, Revisited. In *Mathematical Foundations of Computer Science 2015 - 40th International Symposium, MFCS 2015, Milan, Italy, August 24-28, 2015, Proceedings, Part II.* 127–138.

[7] J. Bourgain and A. Wigderson. [n. d.]. Personal communication (see [3]). ([n. d.]).

[8] Clément L. Canonne. 2015. A Survey on Distribution Testing: Your Data is Big. But is it Blue? *Electronic Colloquium on Computational Complexity (ECCC)* 22 (2015), 63.

[9] Thomas M. Cover and Joy A. Thomas. 2006. *Elements of Information Theory (Wiley Series in Telecommunications and Signal Processing).* Wiley-Interscience.

[10] Ilias Diakonikolas and Daniel M. Kane. 2016. A New Approach for Testing Properties of Discrete Distributions. In *IEEE 57th Annual Symposium on Foundations of Computer Science, FOCS 2016, 9-11 October 2016, Hyatt Regency, New Brunswick, New Jersey, USA.* 685–694.

[11] Eldar Fischer. 2001. The Art of Uninformed Decisions. *Bulletin of the EATCS* 75 (2001), 97.

[12] Pierre Fraigniaud, Amos Korman, and David Peleg. 2011. Local Distributed Decision. In *IEEE 52nd Annual Symposium on Foundations of Computer Science, FOCS 2011, Palm Springs, CA, USA, October 22-25, 2011.* 708–717.

[13] Goldreich and Ron. 2002. Property Testing in Bounded Degree Graphs. *Algorithmica* 32, 2 (01 Feb 2002), 302–343.

[14] Oded Goldreich. 1998. Combinatorial property testing – a survey. *Randomization Methods in Algorithm Design* (1998).

[15] Oded Goldreich. 2016. The uniform distribution is complete with respect to testing identity to a fixed distribution. *Electronic Colloquium on Computational Complexity (ECCC)* 23 (2016), 15.

[16] Oded Goldreich. 2017. *Introduction to Property Testing.* Cambridge University Press.

[17] Oded Goldreich and Dana Ron. 2000. On Testing Expansion in Bounded-Degree Graphs. *Electronic Colloquium on Computational Complexity (ECCC)* 7, 20 (2000).

[18] Michael J. Wiener. 2005. Bounds on Birthday Attack Times. 2005 (01 2005), 318.

[19] Ilan Newman and Mario Szegedy. 1996. Public vs. Private Coin Flips in One Round Communication Games (Extended Abstract). In *Proceedings of the Twenty-eighth Annual ACM Symposium on Theory of Computing (STOC '96).* 561–570.

[20] C.D. Olds. 1950. Odd and even derangements, Solution E907. *Amer. Math. Monthly* 57 (1950).

[21] L. Paninski. 2008. A Coincidence-Based Test for Uniformity Given Very Sparsely Sampled Discrete Data. *IEEE Transactions on Information Theory* 54, 10 (2008), 4750–4755.

[22] Dana Ron. 2009. Algorithmic and Analysis Techniques in Property Testing. *Foundations and Trends in Theoretical Computer Science* 5, 2 (2009), 73–205.

Minor Excluded Network Families Admit Fast Distributed Algorithms*

Bernhard Haeupler
Carnegie Mellon University
Pittsburgh, PA
haeupler@cs.cmu.edu

Jason Li
Carnegie Mellon University
Pittsburgh, PA
jmli@cs.cmu.edu

Goran Zuzic
Carnegie Mellon University
Pittsburgh, PA
gzuzic@cs.cmu.edu

ABSTRACT

Distributed network optimization problems, such as minimum spanning tree, minimum cut, and shortest path, are an active research area in distributed computing. This paper presents a fast distributed algorithm for such problems in the CONGEST model, on networks that exclude a fixed minor.

On general graphs, many optimization problems, including the ones mentioned above, require $\tilde{\Omega}(\sqrt{n})$ rounds of communication in the CONGEST model, even if the network graph has a much smaller diameter. Naturally, the next step in algorithm design is to design efficient algorithms which bypass this lower bound on a restricted class of graphs. Currently, the only known method of doing so uses the low-congestion shortcut framework of Ghaffari and Haeupler [SODA'16]. Building off of their work, this paper proves that excluded minor graphs admit high-quality shortcuts, leading to an $\tilde{O}(D^2)$ round algorithm for the aforementioned problems, where D is the diameter of the network graph. To work with excluded minor graph families, we utilize the Graph Structure Theorem of Robertson and Seymour. To the best of our knowledge, this is the first time the Graph Structure Theorem has been used for an algorithmic result in the distributed setting.

Even though the proof is involved, merely showing the existence of good shortcuts is sufficient to obtain simple, efficient distributed algorithms. In particular, the shortcut framework can efficiently construct near-optimal shortcuts and then use them to solve the optimization problems. This, combined with the very general family of excluded minor graphs, which includes most other important graph classes, makes this result of significant interest.

CCS CONCEPTS

• **Mathematics of computing → Graphs and surfaces**; • **Theory of computation →** *Distributed computing models*; *Distributed algorithms*;

KEYWORDS

Distributed Computing; CONGEST; Graph Structure Theorem; Minor Excluded Graphs; Shortcuts; Low-congestion Shortcuts

ACM Reference Format:
Bernhard Haeupler, Jason Li, and Goran Zuzic. 2018. Minor Excluded Network Families Admit Fast Distributed Algorithms. In *PODC '18: ACM Symposium on Principles of Distributed Computing, July 23–27, 2018, Egham, United Kingdom.* ACM, New York, NY, USA, 10 pages. https://doi.org/10.1145/3212734.3212776

1 INTRODUCTION

Network optimization problems in the CONGEST model, such as Minimum Spanning Tree, Min-Cut or Shortest Path are an active research area in theoretical distributed computing [8, 11, 22, 27]. This paper provides a fast distributed algorithm for such problems in excluded minor graphs in the CONGEST model.

Recently, lower bounds have been established on many distributed network optimization problems, including all of the mentioned ones [5]. More specifically, each of these problems in the CONGEST model require $\tilde{\Omega}(\sqrt{n})$[1] rounds of communication to solve. This holds even on graphs with small diameter, for example, when the diameter is logarithmic in the number of nodes n. The result is surprising since it is not immediately clear why a network of small diameter requires such a large number of communication rounds when solving an optimization problem.

On the positive side, the next major question in algorithmic design is to determine whether one can bypass this barrier by restricting the class of network graphs. One immediate question that arises is, what family of graphs should one consider? Ideally, such a class of graphs should be inclusive enough to admit most "realistic" networks, yet be restrictive enough to disallow the pathological lower bound instances.

In our search for a restricted graph family to study, we focus on three criteria. First, we desire a family with a *rich and rigorous mathematical theory*, so that our result is technically meaningful. Second, the family should capture many networks in practice. And finally, we want *robustness*: a graph with a few added or perturbed edges and vertices should still remain in the family. Robustness is an important goal, since we want our graph family to be resistant to noise. For example, planar graphs satisfy the first two criteria, but fail to be robust since often adding a single random edge will make the graph non-planar. Indeed, most algorithms on planar graphs fail completely when run on a planar graph with a few perturbed edges and vertices. Next, one might try genus-bounded graphs, but they

*Supported in part by NSF grants CCF-1527110, CCF-1618280 and NSF CAREER award CCF-1750808. The full version of the paper is available at https://arxiv.org/abs/1801.06237

PODC '18, July 23–27, 2018, Egham, United Kingdom

ACM ISBN 978-1-4503-5795-1/18/07...$15.00
https://doi.org/10.1145/3212734.3212776

[1]Throughout this paper, $\tilde{O}(\cdot)$ and $\tilde{\Omega}(\cdot)$ hide polylogarithmic factors in n, the number of nodes in the network.

also suffer from similar problems since adding a single randomly connected vertex can arbitrarily increase the genus.

A candidate graph family that fulfills all three conditions is the family of *excluded minor* graphs, namely the graphs which do not have a fixed graph H as a minor. This family encompasses several classes of naturally occuring networks. For example, trees which exclude K_3, planar graphs that capture the structure of two-dimensional maps exclude K_5 and $K_{3,3}$, and, series-parallel graphs that capture many network backbones exclude K_4 [1, 9]. Excluded minor graphs also have a history of deep results, including the series of Graph Minor papers by Robertson and Seymour.

In this paper, we provide efficient distributed algorithms for the class of excluded minor graphs which break the $\tilde{\Omega}(\sqrt{n} + D)$ lower bound for general graphs, giving evidence that most practical networks admit efficient distributed algorithms. We show an $\tilde{O}(D^2)$ algorithm for MST and $(1 + \epsilon)$ approximate min-cut, among other results. For networks having low diameter, such as $D = \text{poly}(\log n)$ or $D = n^{o(1)}$, our algorithms are optimal up to poly$(\log n)$ or $n^{o(1)}$ factors, respectively. This is a significant improvement over previous MST and min-cut algorithms, which run in $\Omega(\sqrt{n})$ time even on an excluded minor graph with $D = \text{poly}(\log n)$, such as a planar graph with an added vertex attached to every other node.

Our results use the framework of **low-congestion shortcuts**, introduced by [12] and built on by [15], which is a combinatorial abstraction to designing distributed algorithms. It introduces a simple, combinatorial problem involving **shortcuts** on a graph, and guarantees that a good **quality** solution to this combinatorial problem automatically translates to a simple, efficient distributed algorithm for MST and $(1 + \epsilon)$ approximate min-cut, among other problems; the concepts of shortcuts and quality will be defined later. Actually, the algorithm is the same regardless of the network or the graph family; the purpose of the combinatorial shortcuts problem is to prove that the algorithm runs *efficiently* on the graph or family.

To solve the shortcuts problem on excluded minor graphs, we appeal to the Graph Structure Theorem of Robertson and Seymour [29, 30]. At a high level, the Graph Structure Theorem decomposes every excluded minor graph into a set of almost-planar graphs connected in a tree-like fashion. Our solution to the shortcuts problem is in fact a series of results, one for each step in the structure decomposition. We remark that our result is, to the best of our knowledge, the first in distributed computing to make use of the Graph Structure Theorem to claim a distributed algorithm is fast. The absence of such a preceding result in distributed computing is unsurprising, since algorithms working with the Graph Structure Theorem generally require computing the required decomposition beforehand, and no efficient distributed algorithm to do so is known. Even the best classical algorithm still takes $O(n^3)$ time [21], so even a sublinear distributed algorithm is still out of reach. However, our result is unique in that we merely show the *existence* of a solution to the shortcuts problem in excluded minor graphs, and as a consequence, the simple algorithm of [15]—which does not look at any structure in the network graph, let alone compute a decomposition—is proven to run efficiently on excluded minor graphs.

The fact that this algorithm does not actually compute the Graph Structure Theorem should be stressed further. Since the framework of [15] computes a shortcut competitive to the optimal one, a consequence is that the running time of this algorithm rarely depends on the (large) constants appearing in the Graph Structure Theorem. In other words, while we can only *prove* that the constants in the running time are bounded by (some functions of) the constants in the Graph Structure Theorem, the actual running time of the algorithm is likely to be much smaller. In fact, for most excluded minor networks, we expect the running time to be $\tilde{O}(D^2)$ with a small constant, or even $\tilde{O}(D)$. In contrast, algorithms that explicitly compute a Graph Structure Theorem decomposition have an inherent bottleneck in the form of the potentially huge constants of the Graph Structure Theorem.

This paper is structured as follows. After the introduction, we begin with introducing the two main tools necessary for our main result, namely the Graph Structure Theorem and the low-congestion shortcuts framework. Then, we prove the existence of good shortcuts one step at a time, following the step-by-step construction in the Graph Structure Theorem.

1.1 Outline of the Proof

The goal of this section is to outline the proof of our main result, without delving into the technical details. Some concepts will be left undefined (e.g., shortcut quality, tree-restricted shortcuts), since the definitions are technical and require a lot of motivation beforehand. However, one can think of shortcuts as a combinatorial construction on a graph, and think of quality as a metric with which to measure a solution.

Theorem 1. *[Haeupler et al. [15, 16]] Suppose that a graph with diameter D admits tree-restricted shortcuts of quality $q : \mathbb{N} \to \mathbb{N}$. Then, there is an $\tilde{O}(q(D))$-round distributed algorithm for MST and $(1 + \epsilon)$-approximate min-cut for that graph.*

Our main technical result is showing the existence of good tree-restricted shortcuts in excluded minor graphs.

Theorem 2. *[Main Theorem] Every graph in a graph family excluding a fixed minor H admits tree-restricted shortcuts of quality $q(d) = \tilde{O}(d^2)$. The constants in the big-O depend only on the minor H.*

Combining the above Theorem 1 and Theorem 2, we get out main result.

Corollary 1. *There exists an $\tilde{O}(D^2)$-round distributed algorithm for MST and $(1 + \epsilon)$-approximate min-cut, for any $\epsilon > 0$, on graph networks excluding a fixed minor.*

For excluded minor graphs of diameter $n^{o(1)}$, as is the case for many practical networks, our algorithms also run in $n^{o(1)}$ time, which is optimal up to lower order terms. This is a significant improvement over the previously known $\tilde{\Omega}(\sqrt{n})$ time algorithms and it avoids the $\tilde{\Omega}(\sqrt{n})$ lower bound for general graphs, even when they have $n^{o(1)}$ diameter.

Corollary 2. *There exists an $n^{o(1)}$-round distributed algorithm for MST and $(1 + \epsilon)$-approximate min-cut, for any $\epsilon > 0$, on graph networks with diameter $n^{o(1)}$ and excluding a fixed minor.*

In order to work with excluded minor families, we appeal to the Robertson-Seymour Graph Structure Theorem. At a high level, this theorem states that every graph in an excluded minor family can be decomposed into a set of graph **almost embeddable** in a bounded genus surface that are glued together in a tree-like fashion. Naturally, our approach is to first construct good-quality shortcuts for the entire family of almost embeddable graphs, and then modify them in a robust manner as they are patched together in the composition. While this approach works in general, the patching required is very involved because of various interactions between the many ingredients involved in the decomposition. For example, one step in the construction of an almost embeddable graph is the addition of an "apex" vertex that connects arbitrarily to all previous vertices. While the addition of only one vertex appears harmless at first glance, observe that the diameter can shrink arbitrarily, e.g., to 2 if the apex is connected to all other vertices. If the graph without the apex has large diameter D, and its shortcuts solution leads to an $\tilde{O}(D^2)$-round algorithm, this same algorithm will not suffice on the graph with the apex, which can have diameter 2. A lot of technical effort goes into reconstructing shortcuts upon the addition of an apex, in order to handle the arbitrary decrease in graph diameter. Hence, as a consequence of all these difficulties, we settle for $\tilde{O}(d^2)$-quality shortcuts, and leave the improvement to $\tilde{O}(d)$-quality shortcuts as an open problem.

1.2 Related Work

Work on global network problems in the distributed setting was started by Gallager, Humblet and Spira [10] who gave a $O(n \log n)$-round algorithm to compute the MST. The algorithm was subsequently improved by Awerbuch [2] to an "optimal" $O(n)$ rounds. However, Peleg and Awerbuch [3] noted that a more useful notion of round complexity would parametrize on both the number of nodes n and the diameter D since $D \ll n$ for many practical networks. This influenced a substantial amount of work that followed, culminating in an $\tilde{O}(D + \sqrt{n})$ distributed algorithm for many optimizations problems in the CONGEST setting. Examples of such problems include the MST [8, 11, 22], $(1 + \epsilon)$-approximate Maximum Flow [13], Minimum Cut [14, 27], Shortest Paths, and Diameter [7, 18–20, 23, 24, 26]. The mentioned $\tilde{O}(D + \sqrt{n})$ round complexity is **existentially optimal** for all of these problems, as there exists a family of graphs for which any algorithm must take a matching $\tilde{\Omega}(D + \sqrt{n})$ rounds [5, 6].

Some early work that tried to circumvent the $\Omega(\sqrt{n})$ bound was done by Khan and Pandurangan[22] who argued that their MST algorithm performed in an **universally optimal** manner on some restricted classes of graphs. In particular, they gave a $\tilde{O}(D)$ round MST algorithm for (1) unit disk networks where weights match the distances, and (2) networks with IID random weights. Their approach used a novel parameter called "local shortest path diameter" that takes the edge weights into account. This makes their approach unsuitable for arbitrary weights and topologically constrained networks such as planar graphs.

However, an alternative approach has recently made progress for global optimization problems on restricted graph classes. Ghaffari and Haeupler showcased a distributed MST and $(1+\epsilon)$-approximate min-cut algorithm that runs in $\tilde{O}(D)$ rounds on planar graphs [12], which was later simplified and generalized to bounded treewidth graphs and bounded genus graphs [16]. All of these results use the aforementioned low-congestion shortcuts framework.

1.3 Preliminaries

For a graph G, let $V(G)$ and $E(G)$ denote the vertices and edges, respectively. Given $P \subseteq V(G)$, $G[P]$ denotes the induced subgraph, namely, the one obtained by removing $V(G) \setminus P$ from G. Finally, when G is the underlying network graph, we always assume that G is connected and contains no self-loops (which can be ignored in the distributed setting anyway).

Due to space constraints, we move the preliminary concerning the Graph Structure Theorem to Section 2; the reader is encouraged to review it to become familiar with the used terminology.

1.3.1 CONGEST model. While we only use the classical CONGEST model indirectly, via Theorem 1 of [15], we will state its assumptions for context. A network is given by a connected graph $G = (V, E)$ with n nodes and diameter D. Communication proceeds in synchronous rounds. In each round, each node can send a different $O(\log n)$ bit message to each of its neighbors. Local computations are free and require no time. Nodes have no initial knowledge of the topology G, except that we assume that they know n and D up to constants. One can easily remove these assumptions by distributively computing these parameters in $O(D)$ time, which is negligible in our context.

2 PRELIMINARY: GRAPH STRUCTURE THEOREM

In this section we introduce Robertson and Seymour's Graph Structure Theorem, following the survey of Lovász [25]. This theorem is instrumental in our shortcut construction, since it provides structure for all graphs that are H-free, for any minor H. At a high level, the theorem says that every H-free graph can be glued together in a tree-like fashion from graphs that can be "almost" embedded in a fixed surface. To elaborate on this statement, we need a few definitions. The first definition, k-clique-sum, captures the tree-like structure of the graph.

Definition 1 (k-clique-sum). *Let G_1 and G_2 be two graphs, and let $S_i \subseteq G_i$ be a k-clique for $i = 1, 2$. Let G be obtained by identifying S_1 with S_2 and deleting some (possibly none, possibly all) edges between the nodes in $S_1 = S_2$. We say that G is a **k-clique-sum** of G_1 and G_2. More generally, G is a k-clique-sum of $G_1, G_2, \ldots, G_\ell$ if G is formed by starting with G_1 and iteratively taking the k-clique-sum of the current graph with G_i, for $i = 2, \ldots, \ell$ in that order.*

The next few definitions classify the graphs which are almost embeddable on a surface. We start with the three main ingredients in constructing such a graph, and then define what it means to be almost-embeddable.

Definition 2 (Apex). *Define **adding an apex to graph** G as follows: create a new vertex called the **apex**, and connect it to an arbitrary subset of the vertices in G.*

Definition 3 (Surface of genus g). *A graph G has genus g if there is a **2-cell embedding** in a surface of genus g. In other words, this means: (i) there exists an oriented or unoriented surface (i.e., 2-manifold) Σ of genus g, (ii) vertices of G are mapped to distinct points of Σ, (iii) edges are mapped to simple paths whose interiors do not contain any vertices of G nor do path interiors mutually intersect, and (iv) each face defined by such embedding is homeomorphic to a unit disk, i.e., contains no holes or handles in it.*

Definition 4 (Vortex [25]). *Let G be a graph with a 2-cell embedding. Let C be a cycle in G that corresponds to a face on the surface. Call a continuous interval on the cycle an* ***arc****. Select a family of arcs on C so that each node is contained in at most k of these arcs. For each arc A, create a new node v_A and connect v_A to a subset of the vertices in C that lie on arc A. Such nodes v_A are called* ***internal vortex nodes****. Finally, for any two arcs A and B sharing a common vertex in C, we may add the edge $\{v_A, v_B\}$. We call this operation* ***adding a vortex of depth k to cycle C****.*

Definition 5. *A graph G is* ***(q, g, k, ℓ)-almost-embeddable*** *if it can be constructed according to the three steps below.*

(i) Start with a graph G' embedded on a surface of genus at most g.
(ii) We select at most ℓ faces of G' and add a vortex of depth at most k to each of them. Call the result G''.
(iii) We add q apices to G'', connected arbitrarily to vertices in G'' and to each other, and obtain the desired graph G.

For simpler notation, we say a graph is ***h-almost-embeddable*** *if it is (h, h, h, h)-almost embeddable.*

By this definition, the planar graphs are precisely the $(0, 0, 0, 0)$-almost-embeddable graphs, and the genus-g graphs are precisely the $(0, g, 0, 0)$-almost-embeddable graphs. Later on, we will study the planar graphs with added vortices, in particular the $(0, 0, k, \ell)$-almost-embeddable graphs for constants k and ℓ.

As a final ingredient to the Graph Structure Theorem, we construct a graph family $\mathcal{L}_k$ as follows.

Definition 6. *Let $\mathcal{L}_k$ denote all graphs that can be represented as a k-clique-sum of k-almost-embeddable graphs. That is, a graph G is in $\mathcal{L}_k$ if there exist k-almost-embeddable graphs $G_1, G_2, \ldots, G_\ell$ such that G is a k-clique-sum of $G_1, G_2, \ldots, G_\ell$.*

In other words, take any set of k-almost-embeddable graphs $G_1, G_2, \ldots, G_\ell$ for $\ell \geq 1$, and let G be their k-clique-sum. Construct a graph G by repeatedly taking a k-clique-sum operation between multiple G_i's constructed using step (i)–(iii) and connect them in a tree-like fashion. Define $\mathcal{L}_k$ as precisely all graphs G that can be constructed in this way.

Finally, we present the Graph Structure Theorem, which states that for any H, there is a k such that $\mathcal{L}_m$ includes (but does not exactly characterize) all graphs that are H-free [25].

Theorem 3 (Graph Structure Theorem). *For every graph H there is a fixed integer $k = k(H)$ such that any H-free graph G is contained in $\mathcal{L}_k$.*

Below, we include additional terminology on clique-sums and vortices used in the shortcut construction.

Definition 7 (Vortex terminology). *Let C be a cycle of G, and add a vortex of depth k to C, following Definition 4. Let $v_1, v_2, \ldots$ be the vertices created when adding a vortex of depth k to C. The vertices in C form the* ***vortex boundary****, and the added vertices $v_1, v_2, \ldots$ are called* ***inside the vortex*** *and* ***internal vortex*** *nodes. Moreover, suppose an internal vertex v_i corresponds to* ***arc*** *A_i of C in the vortex construction. Define the* ***vortex decomposition*** *to be the map $\mathcal{P}$ satisfying $\mathcal{P}(v_i) = A_i$. Finally, if G is embedded on a closed surface such that C forms a face in the embedding, then that face is called the* ***vortex face****.*

Definition 8 (k-Clique-sum decomposition tree). *Let the graph G be constructed as the k-clique-sum of subgraphs $B_1, B_2, \ldots, B_\ell$. The subgraphs $B_i \subseteq G$ are denoted as* ***bags****. A* ***k-clique-sum decomposition tree*** *of G is a tree $\mathbb{DT}$ whose vertices $V(\mathbb{DT})$ are identified with bags B_i. The edges of the decomposition $f \in E(\mathbb{DT})$ correspond to a clique in two of the bags, with possibly some removed edges. Therefore, we refer to them as* ***partial k-cliques*** *C_f. The decomposition satisfies the following properties:*

(1) $\bigcup_{i \in \mathbb{DT}} V(B_i) = V(G)$.
(2) For all $i \in V(\mathbb{DT})$, $B_i \subseteq G$.
(3) For all $f = \{i, j\} \in E(\mathbb{DT})$, $B_i \cap B_j = C_f$.
(4) For all $v \in V(G)$, the set $\{i \in V(\mathbb{DT}) \mid v \in V(B_i)\}$ is connected in $\mathbb{DT}$.
(5) For all $e \in E(G)$, there exists $i \in V(\mathbb{DT})$ with $e \in E(B_i)$.

We conclude with a statement that the above clique-sum decomposition tree captures all possible ways to take clique-sums of graphs.

Fact 1. *Let a graph G be the k-clique-sum of graphs from a family $\mathcal{F}$. Then, G has a k-clique-sum decomposition tree whose bags are graphs in $\mathcal{F}$.*

2.0.1 Tree-restricted Shortcuts.

This section introduces the shortcut framework from [12] and [15]. We state the definitions and concisely repeat the motivations behind them.

Imagine solving the following problem in a distributed manner: *Each node in the network is assigned a number x_v. The network is partitioned into a number of vertex disjoint individually-connected parts and each node wants to compute the minimum/maximum/sum of x_v between all nodes in its own part.* The above subproblem often occurs in algorithm design. Notably, it appears in Boruvka's Minimum Spanning Tree algorithm [28]. A naive solution would spread the information about x_v independently inside each part, because the problem statement basically makes them independent. However, this will incur performance penalties if the diameter of the parts in isolation is much larger than the diameter of the entire graph. For instance, a wheel graph has $\Theta(1)$ diameter, while a part containing all the outer nodes has $\Theta(n)$ diameter. This leads us to the idea of "helping" a part by assigning it additional edges that it can use to spread information. We call these edges "shortcuts".

Definition 9 (General Shortcuts). *Let $G = (V, E_G)$ be an undirected graph with vertices subdivided into* ***pairwise disjoint and connected*** *subsets $\mathcal{P} = (P_1, P_2, ..., P_{|\mathcal{P}|})$, $P_i \subseteq V$. In other words, $G[P_i]$ is connected and $P_i \cap P_j = \emptyset$ for $i \neq j$. The subsets P_i are called* ***parts****. We define a* ***shortcut*** *$\mathcal{H}$ as a tuple of* ***shortcut edges*** *$(H_1, H_2, \ldots, H_{|\mathcal{P}|})$, $H_i \subseteq E(G)$.*

The shortcut framework has particularly nice properties if the shortcut edges are restricted to some tree T, typically the BFS tree. In particular, they can be near-optimally constructed in a distributed and uniform manner on any network. We first define this structured version of shortcuts, enumerate the quality measures for them, and finally state the relevant theorems.

Definition 10 (Tree-Restricted Shortcuts). *Let $\mathcal{H} = (H_1, H_2, ..., H_{|\mathcal{P}|})$ be a shortcut on the graph $G = (V, E_G)$ with respect to the parts $\mathcal{P} = (P_i)_i$. Given a spanning tree $T = (V, E_T) \subseteq G$ we say that a* *shortcut $\mathcal{H}$ is T-**restricted** if for each part $P_i \in \mathcal{P}$, its shortcut edges $H_i \subseteq E_T$. In other words, every edge of H_i lies on the tree T.*

Note that the above definitions do not impose any hard condition on H_i with respect to P_i. We introduce these conditions implicitly by defining **congestion, block**, and **quality** parameters to measure how good they are (smaller is better).

Definition 11 (Congestion). *Let $\mathcal{H} = (H_1, H_2, ..., H_{|\mathcal{P}|})$ be a shortcut on $G = (V, E_G)$. Define a congestion over an edge e as $c_e := |\{i : e \in H_i\}|$, the number of shortcuts using an edge. Finally, define the **congestion of the shortcut** to be $\max_{e \in E_G} c_e$, the maximum congestion of any edge.*

Another beneficial property we would like is that the subgraphs $G[P_i]+H_i$ have small diameter. By $G[P_i]+H_i$ we mean the subgraph constructed by taking the induced subgraph $G[P_i]$ and then adding all the edges in H_i as well as any of their endpoints not contained in P_i. We will measure diameter of $G[P_i] + H_i$ indirectly, by defining a **block parameter** b that essentially measures the number of different subtrees (components) that exist in H_i. We use it in the following way: note that (1) $G[P_i]$ is connected by definition, (2) $G[P_i] + H_i$ effectively looks like b_i interconnected subtrees, (3) each subtree has diameter $O(D)$ since T is typically a spanning tree whose height is at most the diameter of G. From these properties we conclude that $G[P_i] + H_i$ has diameter $O(b_i D)$.

Definition12 (Block parameter). *For a shortcut $\mathcal{H}=(H_1, H_2, ..., H_{|\mathcal{P}|})$, fix a part P_i and consider the connected components of the spanning subgraph (V, H_i). If a connected component contains a node in P_i we call it a **block component**. They correspond to subtrees of T. We define that $\mathcal{H}$ has **block parameter** b if no part has more than b block components.*

*In general, for functions $b, c : \mathbb{N} \to \mathbb{N}$, a graph G is said to **admit** tree-restricted shortcuts with block parameter b and congestion c if for **any** spanning tree T with diameter at most d_T and any family of parts there exists a T-restricted shortcut with block parameter $b(d_T)$ and congestion $c(d_T)$. "Good" tree-restricted shortcuts typically have $\tilde{O}(1)$ block parameter and $\tilde{O}(d_T)$ congestion.*

Similarly, a family of graphs admits tree-restricted shortcuts with block parameter b and congestion c if all graphs in the family individually admit them.

We now define the **quality** of a tree-restricted shortcut. The terminology of admitting tree-restricted shortcuts carries over to quality.

Definition 13 (Quality). *The **quality** of a tree-restricted shortcut is the function $q : \mathbb{N} \to \mathbb{N}$ defined by $q(d) = b(d) \cdot d + c(d)$.*

We now restate the central theorem from the low-congestion shortcuts framework.

Theorem 1. *[Haeupler et al. [15, 16]] Suppose that a graph with diameter D admits tree-restricted shortcuts of quality $q : \mathbb{N} \to \mathbb{N}$. Then, there is an $\tilde{O}(q(D))$-round distributed algorithm for MST and $(1 + \epsilon)$-approximate min-cut for that graph.*

Note that D replaces d_T in the argument to the functions b and c. This is because the theorem takes T to be a BFS tree of the network graph, which has diameter at most D.

Finally, it is known from [12, 16] that good tree-restricted shortcuts exist in planar graphs and bounded treewidth graphs. We will be using this fact in a later section.

Theorem 4 ([12]). *The family of planar graphs admits tree-restricted shortcuts with block parameter $O(\log d_T)$ and congestion $O(d_T \log d_T)$.*

Theorem 5 ([16]). *The family of graphs of treewidth at most k admits tree-restricted shortcuts with block parameter $O(k)$ and congestion $O(k \log n)$.*

3 SHORTCUTS IN EXCLUDED MINOR GRAPHS

Our main result extends Theorem 4 and Theorem 5 to excluded minor graphs, showing that any family of graphs excluding a fixed minor has good tree-restricted shortcuts. We repeat Theorem 2 with a bit of extra detail.

Theorem 6. *[Main Theorem, Extended Version] The family of graphs excluding a fixed minor H admits tree-restricted shortcuts of quality $q(d) = \tilde{O}(d^2)$. More generally, the family admits block parameter $b(d) = O(d)$ and congestion $c(d) = O(d \log n + \log^2 n)$. The constants in the big-O depend only on the minor H.*

Using the shortcuts framework of Theorem 1, the above theorem translates to the algorithmic result of Corollary 1.

3.1 Two Parts of the Proof

Recall that the Graph Structure Theorem says that any excluded minor graph can be represented as a k-clique-sum of k-almost-embeddable graphs, for some constant k depending on the excluded minor. As with most results utilizing the Graph Structure Theorem, our proof is split into two parts, one handling the k-clique-sums and one for the k-almost-embeddable graphs.

Our proof has two main components, namely, Theorem 7 and Theorem 8 that we state below. It should be clear that they are sufficient to prove the main technical result, Theorem 6.

Clique Sums Part: In the k-clique-sums part, we show that if a family of graphs admits shortcuts with good quality, then so does any k-clique-sum of graphs from this family, for any constant k. In other words, having good tree-restricted shortcuts is a property robust under taking k-clique-sums for a fixed integer k. The theorem below is proved in Section 4.

Theorem 7. *[Shortcuts in Clique Sums] Let $\mathcal{F}$ be a family of graphs that admits tree-restricted shortcuts with block parameter $b_{\mathcal{F}}$ and congestion $c_{\mathcal{F}}$. Let G be a k-clique-sum of graphs in $\mathcal{F}$. Then G admits tree-restricted shortcuts with block parameter $b_G(d) \leq 2k + O(b_{\mathcal{F}}(d_T))$ and congestion $c_G(d) \leq O(k \log^2 n) + c_{\mathcal{F}}(d_T)$.*

On a high level, the proof relies on carefully charging the congestion to bags in the k-clique-sum decomposition. This leads to a bound that relies on the depth of the decomposition, which can be controlled by folding up long bag-paths in the decomposition.

To prove the full result, we use Theorem 7 with $\mathcal{F}$ as the family of k-almost-embeddable graphs, which we show admits tree-restricted shortcuts with block parameter and congestion $\tilde{O}(d)$. Plugging in these parameters, we obtain $b_G(d) = 2k + \tilde{O}(d)$ and $c_G(d) = O(k \log^2 n) + \tilde{O}(d)$ for the final result, which are both $\tilde{O}(d)$ since k

is a constant. Note that Theorem 7 does not assume that $\mathcal{F}$ is any particular family, so it may be of independent interest.

Almost Embeddable Part: The second part of the proof establishes good quality shortcuts for k-almost-embeddable graphs, namely the theorem below, proved in Section 5.

THEOREM 8. *[Shortcuts in Almost Embeddable Graphs] An (q, g, k, ℓ)-almost-embeddable graph G admits tree-restricted shortcuts with block parameter $b(d) = O(q + (g + 1)k\ell^2 d)$ and congestion $c(d) = O(q + k\ell^2 d(g + \log n))$.*

The proof is fairly technical and uses several novel ideas. The most prominent one is the construction of a structure we call the "combinatorial gate". Intuitively, when given a partition of a genus-bounded graph into balls of low diameter, there exists a small number of special vertices such that any subgraph that intersects many balls has to contain many of these special vertices. We use these combinatorial gates to set up a careful charging scheme that allows high-diameter parts to be given more shortcut edges without a catastrophic increase in the congestion.

Putting Them Together: The main theorem, restated below, follows immediately from Theorem 7 and Theorem 8.

THEOREM 6. *[Main Theorem, Extended Version] The family of graphs excluding a fixed minor H admits tree-restricted shortcuts of quality $q(d) = \tilde{O}(d^2)$. More generally, the family admits block parameter $b(d) = O(d)$ and congestion $c(d) = O(d \log n + \log^2 n)$. The constants in the big-O depend only on the minor H.*

PROOF. By Theorem 3, there is a constant k such that the family of H-free graphs is contained in $\mathcal{L}_k$, so it suffices to prove the claim for $\mathcal{L}_k$. Let $\mathcal{F}$ be the family of k-almost-embeddable graphs. By Theorem 8, $\mathcal{F}$ admits tree-restricted shortcuts with block parameter $b_{\mathcal{F}}(d) = O(d)$ and congestion $c_{\mathcal{F}}(d) = O(d \log n)$. Plugging in $\mathcal{F}$, $b_{\mathcal{F}}$, and $c_{\mathcal{F}}$ into Theorem 7, we conclude that $\mathcal{L}_k$ admits tree-restricted shortcuts with block parameter $O(d)$ and congestion $O(d \log n + \log^2 n)$, as desired. □

4 SHORTCUTS IN CLIQUE SUM GRAPHS

In this section, we prove Theorem 7, restated below.

THEOREM 7. *[Shortcuts in Clique Sums] Let $\mathcal{F}$ be a family of graphs that admits tree-restricted shortcuts with block parameter $b_{\mathcal{F}}$ and congestion $c_{\mathcal{F}}$. Let G be a k-clique-sum of graphs in $\mathcal{F}$. Then G admits tree-restricted shortcuts with block parameter $b_G(d) \leq 2k + O(b_{\mathcal{F}}(d_T))$ and congestion $c_G(d) \leq O(k \log^2 n) + c_{\mathcal{F}}(d_T)$.*

Local and Global Shortcuts: The intuition behind our construction is as follows. Let G be a k-clique-sum of graphs in $\mathcal{F}$, and consider a k-clique-sum decomposition tree $\mathbb{DT}$ of G. Its existence is guaranteed by Fact 1. Consider a part $P \subseteq V(G)$, which could either span much of a single bag in $\mathbb{DT}$, or traverse through multiple bags, or both. As a result, we construct two types of shortcuts—**local** shortcuts and **global** shortcuts—to handle each case separately. At a high level, local shortcuts, which are constrained within a single bag, are meant to deal with parts that behave wildly within a bag, while global shortcuts, which can span multiple bags, treat parts that stretch across many different bags. In particular, for each part P, we specify one bag on which we construct local shortcuts for P, and let global shortcuts handle the rest. The shortcut for P is simply the union of the local and global shortcuts.

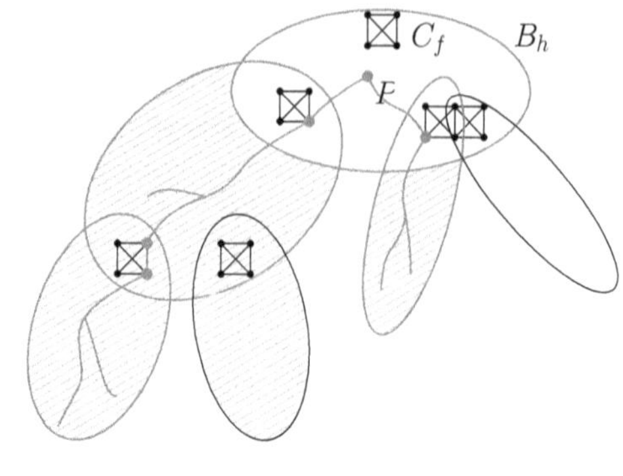

Figure 1: Global shortcut construction. The part P is shown in red. The global T-restricted shortcut is the intersection of T (not shown) with the shaded region. C_f denotes the partial clique leading to the parent of h, which is not used in the global shortcut.

Root $\mathbb{DT}$ at an arbitrary bag, and define $d_{\mathbb{DT}}$ to be the depth of the rooted tree $\mathbb{DT}$. We first prove a weaker result whose global shortcut depends on the value of $d_{\mathbb{DT}}$ in its congestion, then later show how to "compress" $\mathbb{DT}$ to a low depth independent of $d_{\mathbb{DT}}$, thereby removing the dependence of $d_{\mathbb{DT}}$.

Lemma 1. *Let $\mathcal{F}$ be a family of graphs that admits tree-restricted shortcuts with block parameter $b_{\mathcal{F}}$ and congestion $c_{\mathcal{F}}$. Let G be a k-clique-sum of graphs in $\mathcal{F}$ with decomposition tree $\mathbb{DT}$. Then G admits tree-restricted shortcuts with block parameter $b_G(d_T) \leq k + b_{\mathcal{F}}(d_T)$ and congestion $c_G(d_T) \leq kd_{\mathbb{DT}} + c_{\mathcal{F}}(d_T)$. (Note the dependence on $d_{\mathbb{DT}}$, the depth of the decomposition tree $\mathbb{DT}$, which is unrelated to d_T, the diameter of the spanning tree T.)*

PROOF. Let T be an arbitrarily rooted spanning tree of G of diameter d_T. Take a k-clique-sum decomposition tree $\mathbb{DT}$, root it at an arbitrary bag, and suppose that the rooted tree has depth $d_{\mathbb{DT}}$. In the rooted setting, define the set $\text{desc}(i) \subseteq V(\mathbb{DT})$ for $i \in V(\mathbb{DT})$ to be i along with all of its descendants in $\mathbb{DT}$.

Consider a part $P \subseteq V(G)$. Since P is connected, we know, by properties (4) and (5) of Definition 8, that the set of bags $S_P := \{j \in V(\mathbb{DT}) \mid V(B_j) \cap P \neq \emptyset\}$ is connected in $\mathbb{DT}$. Therefore, the lowest common ancestor, denoted by h_P, of S_P is also inside S_P. Similarly, for an edge $e \in E(G)$ we can define the set of bags that contain that edge $S_e := \{j \in V(\mathbb{DT}) \mid e \in E(B_j)\}$ and its lowest common ancestor $h_e \in S_e$.

Global Shortcuts: See Figure 1. The construction of the global shortcut is simple. For each edge f' to a child i of h_P such that $P \cap V(C_{f'}) \neq \emptyset$, allow part P to use all edges in $\left(\bigcup_{j \in \text{desc}(i)} E(B_j) \cap T \right) \setminus E(B_{h_P})$. Informally, the global shortcut "takes care" of all vertices in P except for those in B_{h_P}, which leaves constructing the local shortcut for P in B_{h_P}. More precisely, remember that T is rooted and consider the roots of the block components of P when using only the global shortcut: they are restricted to B_{h_P}.

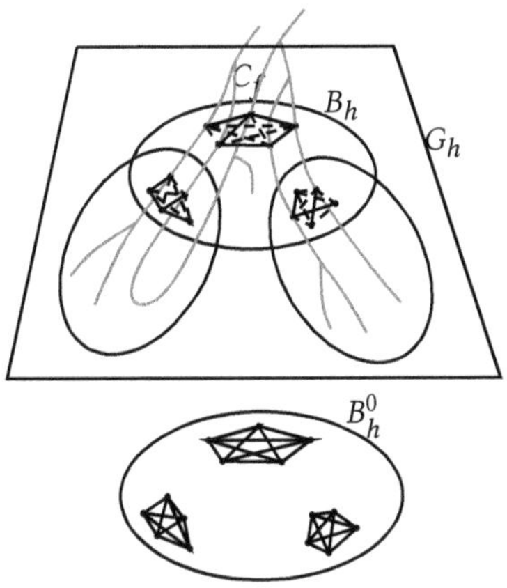

Figure 2: Local shortcut construction. On the left, T is solid red. Dotted black edges are edges absent from the partial k-cliques. On the right is B_h^0 for the B_h on the left.

We now argue about the congestion. Consider an edge $e \in E(G)$, and let $\mathcal{B}$ be the set of bags on the $\mathbb{DT}$-root-path to h_e, including h_e. Clearly, $|\mathcal{B}| \leq d_{\mathbb{DT}}$. Edge e can only be assigned to parts that contain a vertex in the partial-clique on a parent edge of a bag in $\mathcal{B}$. Hence its congestion is at most $k|\mathcal{B}| \leq kd_{\mathbb{DT}}$.

Local Shortcuts: See Figure 2. Let h be an arbitrary bag, we apply the following argument to all of them. We now focus on the local shortcut within B_h. Let $T_h^1 := T \cap B_h$ be the forest when we look at B_h in isolation (note that the tree T can become disconnected). We will repair T_h^1 in the next paragraph.

Let $B_h^0 \in \mathcal{F}$ be the original bag of B_h, which is B_h with all partial k-cliques involved in the clique-sum completed to full k-cliques (see Figure 2). In particular, $V(B_h) = V(B_h^0)$. We emphasize that $B_h^0 \in \mathcal{F}$ by the definition of partial-cliques.

In order to find a tree-restricted shortcut on B_h, we have to define the tree. The forest $T_h^1 := T \cap B_h^0$ might be disconnected, so we have to repair it. First, we define a **path contraction** operation between two vertices $s, t \in V(B_h^0)$. Consider the unique path between s and t in T, represented as a sequence of vertices $s = u_0, u_1, \ldots, u_* = t$. Delete any vertex $u_i \notin V(B_h)$ and one is left with (a sequence of vertices representing a) valid path in B_h^0 between s and t. Note that the contracted path is a graph minor of T.

We form the repaired tree T_h^2 in the following way: for every two $s, t \in V(B_h^0)$, take the path contraction between them and union it into T_h^2. It is clear that (1) T_h^2 is a subgraph of B_h^0, in fact, it is a spanning tree of B_h^0, (2) T_h^1 is a subgraph of T_h^2, and (3) T_h^2 is a contraction of T. The last property implies that T_h^2 is connected and that its diameter is at most d_T. Also, note that the same argument shows that for any part P, its restriction $B_h^0[P]$ is also connected since we can contract any path inside P and the resulting path is still in B_h^0 and contains only vertices in P—the only unimportant difference being that this path might be on T.

Next, construct a T_h^2-restricted shortcut, discard all edges in $T_h^2 \setminus T = T_h^2 \setminus T_h^1$, and discard all edges contained in C_f, where f is the parent $\mathbb{DT}$-edge of h. The resulting assignment is the local shortcut of B_h.

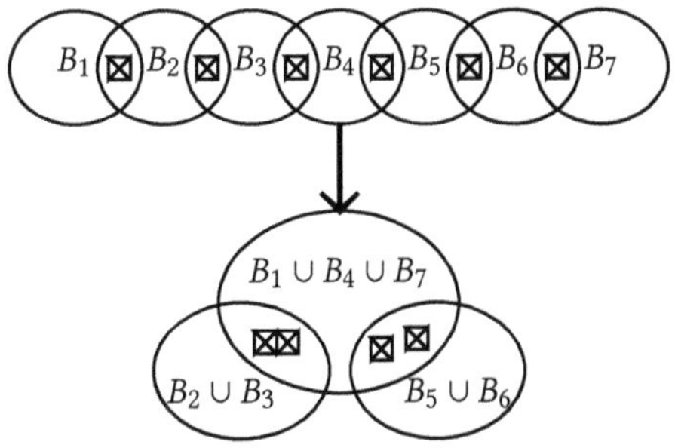

Figure 3: Compressing a k-clique-sum decomposition tree with high depth.

The congestion of the local shortcut is $c_{\mathcal{F}}(d_T)$. Fix an edge $e \in E(G)$, and note that it is only locally assigned in the bag h_e (due to discarding edge of C_f). But the local congestion of h_e is $c_{\mathcal{F}}(d_T)$, as claimed. The total congestion is at most the sum of the local and global one, hence it is at most $kd_{\mathbb{DT}} + c_{\mathcal{F}}(d_T)$.

Bounding the Block Parameter: With all shortcut edges established, we now upper bound the block parameter for each part $P \subseteq V(G)$. Remember that T is, arbitrarily, rooted. We will bound the number of nodes $v \in V(G)$ that are roots of block components. Note that $v \in B_{h_P}$ since otherwise the global shortcut assigns the T-parent edge of v to P. But in the lowest common ancestor B_{h_P}, v can be a block root only if either (a) it is a vertex in C_f, where f is the parent $\mathbb{DT}$-edge of h_P, or (b) it is a block root of a local shortcut inside B_{h_P}. Summing up the contributions of these two cases, the total number of block roots, and therefore block components, can be at most $k + b_{\mathcal{F}}(d_T)$.

□

To improve the $d_{\mathbb{DT}}$ factor in the congestion and prove the main result of this section, we compress the decomposition tree $\mathbb{DT}$ to reduce its depth to $O(\log^2 n)$, in a similar way to the compression scheme in [4] for treewidth decompositions.

Theorem 7. *[Shortcuts in Clique Sums] Let $\mathcal{F}$ be a family of graphs that admits tree-restricted shortcuts with block parameter $b_{\mathcal{F}}$ and congestion $c_{\mathcal{F}}$. Let G be a k-clique-sum of graphs in $\mathcal{F}$. Then G admits tree-restricted shortcuts with block parameter $b_G(d) \leq 2k + O(b_{\mathcal{F}}(d_T))$ and congestion $c_G(d) \leq O(k \log^2 n) + c_{\mathcal{F}}(d_T)$.*

Proof. Let $\mathbb{DT}$ be a k-clique-sum decomposition tree of G. To motivate the main proof, we first consider the case when $\mathbb{DT}$ is a single path from root to leaf. This case will directly help in the general case, in which we apply *heavy-light decomposition* to the tree, breaking it up into chains, and then treat each chain as a single path; we will present this general case next.

Case When $\mathbb{DT}$ Is a Path: Assume that $\mathbb{DT}$ is a rooted path with bags $B_1, \ldots, B_{d_{\mathbb{DT}}}$, in that order. We recursively construct a balanced binary decomposition tree $\mathbb{DT}'$ as follows.

(1) Group the bags $B_1, B_{\lceil d_{\mathbb{DT}}/2 \rceil}, B_{d_{\mathbb{DT}}}$ into a single bag B_r.
(2) Recursively solve the paths $B_2, \ldots, B_{\lceil d_{\mathbb{DT}}/2 \rceil - 1}$ and $B_{\lceil d_{\mathbb{DT}}/2 \rceil + 1}, \ldots, B_{d_{\mathbb{DT}}}$.

(3) Attach the two resulting trees as subtrees of B_r (see Figure 3).

We call this operation **folding** a path.

Call the new decomposition tree $\mathbb{DT}'$; it is almost a k-clique-sum decomposition tree, with one exception: an edge may no longer a partial k-clique, but a union of two partial k-cliques. We call such edges **double edges**. Note that, while we can add edges within each of the two partial k-cliques and keep the graph in the family $\mathcal{F}$, we cannot add edges between a vertex in one partial k-clique and a vertex in the other. Hence, we cannot simply treat the union of two partial k-cliques as a single partial $2k$-clique. However, a bag B_i can have at most two children connected by double edges.

Using the terminology of the above proof, let B_h^0 still be the bag B_h with all partial cliques filled in with edges (the union of two cliques in a double edge will not have edges between them). The only difference this incurs in the proof is the following: in the global shortcut, partial cliques on the edge of $\mathbb{DT}$ can now contain $2k$ vertices instead of k, doubling the congestion; and, in the local shortcut, a part restricted to to a bag $B_h^0[P]$ might not be connected anymore. However, we claim that it consists of at most $O(1)$ connected components: for each connected component we find a "representative vertex" in that component as follows. If (1) the component touches a partial clique in a double edge to a child, then the representative is the lowest numbered vertex in such a partial clique, and otherwise (2) we pick any vertex in the component. Now there will be at most $O(1)$ different representatives, thereby finishing the claim since no two different components can have the same representative. One can see this by arguing if (1) a part touches a partial clique in a double edge to a child, the it has at most 4 possibilities; otherwise (2) the part is already connected via the previous proof.

We construct local shortcuts considering connected components of the parts as separate (sub)parts and union the assignment in the end. This only decreases the congestion, and increases the block by a multiplicative $O(1)$ to a total of $2k + O(b_{\mathcal{F}}(d_T))$.

We now discuss the general case, when $\mathbb{DT}$ is an arbitrary tree. The main steps of the proof are as follows. First, we compute a *heavy-light decomposition* [17] of $\mathbb{DT}$. Then, we fold every chain in the heavy-light decomposition the same way we fold a single path, so that the resulting tree decomposition has depth $O(\log^2 n)$.

Heavy-Light Decomposition: The heavy-light decomposition is a decomposition of any rooted tree into vertex-disjoint paths, called **heavy chains**, such that any path from the root to a leaf changes at most $O(\log n)$ heavy chains, where n is the number of vertices in the tree. The decomposition is simple: for each non-leaf vertex of the tree, connect it to the child vertex with the largest number of vertices in its own subtree. On any path from root to leaf, if traveling from vertex u to vertex v changes heavy chains, then vertex u has at least twice as many vertices in its subtree than does v; such an event can only occur $\log_2 n$ times along the path.

Folding a Chain: Once we compute the heavy-light decomposition, we partition the vertices of $\mathbb{DT}$ into heavy chains, and then fold each chain independently. Then, we connect the resulting binary trees in the following natural way: if the root of chain C_1 is a child of some vertex v, then we connect the root of the binary tree of C_1 to v. Note that this is not a double edge. We get a rooted tree $\mathbb{DT}'$ of depth $O(\log^2 n)$ with the following key property: while every vertex in the new decomposition tree can have many children, it has at most two children connected via double edges. Therefore, the same argument for double edges in the single path case also applies here. With the depth of $\mathbb{DT}'$ reduced to $O(\log^2 n)$, the result follows. □

5 SHORTCUTS IN ALMOST EMBEDDABLE GRAPHS

In this section, we prove Theorem 8. In particular, we prove that k-almost-embeddable graphs admit good shortcuts. Recall that these graphs have bounded genus with an additional constant number of apices and vortices of constant depth added.

5.1 Apex Graphs

In this section, we add apices to $(0, g, k, l)$-almost-embeddable ("Genus + Vortex") graphs. At first glance, the addition of an apex to a graph might seem trivial, since the graph only changes by one vertex, and using that vertex can only make the shortcuts better. However, notice that the diameter of the graph can shrink arbitrarily with the addition of an apex, and our shortcuts on the apex graph must be competitive with the new diameter. Hence, we need ideas beyond our shortcut constructions for the graph without the apex. For a simple example, in a cycle graph, shortcuts with quality $\Theta(n)$ are considered good. However, by adding a single central vertex, we can transform the graph into the wheel graph where "good" shortcuts should have quality $\Theta(1)$. While good shortcuts actually do exist in the wheel graph, there are examples of graphs with good shortcuts where adding a apex makes good shortcuts impossible.

To streamline our arguments for (q, g, k, l)-almost-embeddable graphs ("Apex+Genus+Vortex") graphs, we will define a couple of intermediate properties which do not depend on the graph topology. More precisely, we will define the notions of **β-cell-assignment** and **s-combinatorial gates**. On a very high level, We will show that:

(1) A Genus+Vortex graph has an s-combinatorial gate, for an appropriately chosen s. (Section 5.3 and the Appendix)
(2) Graphs with s-combinatorial gate are β-cell-assignable, for appropriately chosen β and some technical stipulations. (Section 5.2)
(3) Graphs that are β-cell-assignable and each cell locally admits good tree-restricted shortcuts also globally admit good tree-restricted shortcuts, barring various technicalities. (Section 5.4)

In each part, we separately prove the statements with Genus+Vortex graphs replaced by planar graphs. It is recommended that the reader, in their first reading, focus only on the lemmas regarding planar graphs with a single apex, namely Lemmas 2, 3, 5, and 7.

5.2 Cell Partitions, β-Cell-Assignment and s-Combinatorial Gate

In this section, we first introduce the notions of "cell partitions", "β-cell-assignment" and "s-combinatorial gates". Second, we prove that the second property implies the first.

Definition 14. *A **cell partition** of G is simply a partition of V_G into disjoint, connected components with a small diameter, called the **cells**.*

Note that the diameter condition is the only thing differentiating it from the definition of parts. It is helpful to think of cells as low-diameter components, whereas parts may be long and skinny. A canonical example for a cell partition is the following. Given an apex graph of diameter D, remove the apex and start a concurrent BFS from each node adjacent to the removed apex. Each node in the graph (except the apex) gets assigned to exactly one BFS component. We call such BFS components cells. For most of this section, we will ignore any extra property that a cell partition might have and assuming nothing besides them being disjoint, connected and having a controlled diameter.

A graph is cell-assignable if we can relate its cells and parts in a way that no cell is assigned to too many parts and parts are assigned to **almost all** intersecting cells.

Definition 15. *A graph $G = (V_G, E_G)$ is β-cell-assignable if the following holds. For every valid family of parts $\mathcal{P}$ (as in Definition 9) and every valid cell partition C of diameter d there exists a relation $\mathcal{R} \subseteq C \times \mathcal{P}$ with the following properties:*

*(i) each part is in relation with **all** cells it intersects, **except** for at most 2 of them*

(ii) each cell is in relation with at most β parts

Note: β is a function of the cell diameter d.

We will not prove directly that Genus+Vortex graphs are β-cell-assignable. Instead, we focus on a combinatorial property that we show implies cell-assignment. This property is called a "combinatorial gate" and it intuitively asserts that every two touching cells have a "gate" that covers all the edges between them. Furthermore, the boundary of such a gate is called a "fence" and its size should be controlled. The reader is encouraged to review ?? for a mental picture of combinatorial gates on a planar graph.

Definition 16. *For a subset of vertices $S \subseteq V$, define the ∂S to be the set of vertices in S on the boundary of S, i.e., the vertices in S whose neighborhoods intersect $V \setminus S$.*

Definition 17. *Let $G = (V, E)$ be a graph from a family $\mathcal{F}$, and let C be a partition of G into cells. We define a s-**combinatorial gate** to be a collection $\mathcal{S} = \{(F_i, S_i)\}_i$ where $F \subseteq V$ are called **fences**, $S \subseteq V$ are **gates**, and the following properties hold:*

(1) Fences are a subset of their corresponding gates. I.e., $F \subseteq S$ for all $(F, S) \in \mathcal{S}$.

(2) The boundary of a gate are included in its fence. I.e., $\partial(S) \subseteq F$ for all $(F, S) \in \mathcal{S}$.

(3) Each edge $\{a, b\} \in E$ whose endpoints are in different cells must be covered by some gate. I.e., $a \in S \wedge b \in S$ for some gate S.

(4) Each gate S intersects at most two cells in C.

(5) The non-fence vertices of the gates are disjoint. I.e., for every $v \in V$ there is at most one $(F_i, S_i) \in \mathcal{S}$ s.t. $v \in S_i \setminus F_i$.

(6) The average size of fences compared to the number of cells is at most s. I.e., $\sum_{(F,S) \in \mathcal{S}} |F| \leq s|C|$.

Since this condition is entirely combinatorial, the proofs that imply β-cell-assignment are also combinatorial. Therefore, these results are self-contained and disregard any possible structure in the graph, for example, planarity. Next, we state that the s-combinatorial boundary implies β-cell-assignment via the following two lemmas. The proofs are omitted due to space constraints.

Lemma 2. *Suppose a graph G with cell partition C has an s-combinatorial gate $\mathcal{S}$. Then, for any collection of parts $\mathcal{P}$, either there exists a part intersecting at most two cells, or there exists a cell intersecting at most $2s$ parts.*

Lemma 3. *Let $\mathcal{F}$ be a family of graphs that is closed under taking minors. Suppose that there is a function $s(d) : \mathbb{N} \to \mathbb{N}$ such that every graph $G \in \mathcal{F}$ satisfies the following property:*

- *If G has a cell partition of diameter d, then there exists an $s(d)$-combinatorial gate $\mathcal{S}$ of subsets of $V(G)$.*

Then, every graph $G \in \mathcal{F}$ with a cell partition of diameter d is $2s(d)$-cell-assignable.

While Lemma 3 works well for planar graphs that are closed under taking minors, Genus+Vortex graphs do not have that property due to the existence of a bounded number of vortices. In particular, if one contracts an edge inside the vortex, the resulting graph is not Genus+Vortex. Therefore, we will deal with cells touching vortices as "special cells" that are not allowed to be contracted.

Lemma 4. *Let $\mathcal{F}$ be a family of graphs, not necessarily closed under taking minors. Suppose that there is a function $s(d) : \mathbb{N} \to \mathbb{N}$ such that every graph $G \in \mathcal{F}$ satisfies the following property:*

- *If G has a cell partition of diameter d, then there exists an $s(d)$-combinatorial gate $\mathcal{S}$ of subsets of $V(G)$.*

Consider a graph $G \in \mathcal{F}$ with a cell partition into two types of cells—normal cells and ℓ special cells—both of diameter d. Let E^* denote the set of edges in special cells. Assume that any graph G' obtained by deleting vertices and contracting edges outside of special cells is still in $\mathcal{F}$. Then, G is $2\ell s(d)$-cell-assignable with respect to a cell partition of only the normal cells.

5.3 Graphs with s-Combinatorial Gate Property

In this section, we show that Genus+Vortex graphs satisfy the s-combinatorial property. We highlight our main ideas by proving the statement for planar graphs before moving on to genus-bounded graphs.

Lemma 5. *Let G be a planar graph with a cell partition of diameter d. Then, there is an $36d$-combinatorial gate $\mathcal{S}$.*

Lemma 6. *Let G be a genus-g graph with (a possibly unbounded number of) vortices of depth k, and consider a cell partition of diameter d such that no vortex is split between more than one cell. Then, there exists an $O((g + 1)kd)$-combinatorial gate of G.*

5.4 Wrapping Up: From β-Cell-Assignment to Good Shortcuts

In this section, we finalize our proof for tree-restricted shortcuts in almost embeddable graphs. We do this by showing that if an $(0, g, k, l)$-almost-embeddable ("Genus+Vortex") graph is β-cell-assignable for small enough parameter β, then the same graph with q added apices admits good tree-restricted shortcuts. We first assume that the apex graph has exactly one apex, then establish a simple reduction from the multiple apices case. We begin with the same statement for $(1, 0, 0, 0)$-almost-embeddable ("Apex+Planar") graphs, continue with the full statement apart from the single apex, and finally finish with the most general statement. The proofs are omitted due to space constraints.

Lemma 7. *Let G be a planar graph with a single apex and a diameter d_T spanning tree T of G. For a given set of parts, there exists a T-restricted shortcut with block parameter $O(\log d_T)$ and congestion $O(d_T \log d_T)$.*

Lemma 8. *Let G be a genus-g graph with ℓ vortices of depth k and a single apex and T a spanning tree of G. For a given set of parts, there exists a T-restricted shortcut with block parameter $O((g+1)k\ell^2 d_T)$ and congestion $O(k\ell^2 d_T(g + \log n))$.*

Theorem 8. *[Shortcuts in Almost Embeddable Graphs] An (q, g, k, ℓ)-almost-embeddable graph G admits tree-restricted shortcuts with block parameter $b(d) = O(q + (g+1)k\ell^2 d)$ and congestion $c(d) = O(q + k\ell^2 d(g + \log n))$.*

Proof. Let G be the apex graph and T a the spanning tree of G. If a part contains one of the q apices, we give the entire tree T to the part. This increases the congestion by at most q. For the remaining parts, we do the following. First, add an auxiliary new vertex x that connects to each of the q apices; the diameter can grow by at most 1. Contract these $q+1$ vertices to a single apex to form graph G'; T might now contain cycles, so take a spanning subtree of depth d_T in the contracted T. Apply Lemma 8 to the single apex graph G'. If we extend the shortcuts for each part in the natural way to G, the congestion does not change any further. Furthermore, the block parameter increases by at most $q-1$ because a block component containing x splits into at most q block components. □

6 CONCLUSION AND OPEN PROBLEMS

We have proved all the ingredients we need to prove our main theorem, which we restate for convenience.

Theorem 6. *[Main Theorem, Extended Version] The family of graphs excluding a fixed minor H admits tree-restricted shortcuts of quality $q(d) = \tilde{O}(d^2)$. More generally, the family admits block parameter $b(d) = O(d)$ and congestion $c(d) = O(d \log n + \log^2 n)$. The constants in the big-O depend only on the minor H.*

An obvious open question is whether the block parameter $O(d_T)$ can be improved to $\tilde{O}(1)$, which would result in a near-optimal $\tilde{O}(D)$-round algorithm for MST and $(1+\epsilon)$-approximate mincut on excluded minor network graphs. The bottleneck in the current proof lies in the treewidth argument when arguing about Genus+Vortex graph, which produces the $O(d_T)$ block parameter. This treewidth argument cannot be improved due to lower bounds on treewidth-k graphs, as presented in [16]. Hence, an improvement on Genus+Vortex graphs requires a better understanding of vortices, beyond treating them as simply low-treewidth (or pathwidth) graphs.

REFERENCES

[1] Ittai Abraham and Cyril Gavoille. 2006. Object location using path separators. In *Proceedings of the twenty-fifth annual ACM symposium on Principles of distributed computing*. ACM, 188–197.

[2] Baruch Awerbuch. 1987. Optimal distributed algorithms for minimum weight spanning tree, counting, leader election, and related problems. In *Proceedings of the nineteenth annual ACM symposium on Theory of computing*. ACM, 230–240.

[3] Baruch Awerbuch. 1989. Randomized distributed shortest paths algorithms. In *Proceedings of the twenty-first annual ACM symposium on Theory of computing*. ACM, 490–500.

[4] Hans L Bodlaender. 1988. NC-algorithms for graphs with small treewidth. In *International Workshop on Graph-Theoretic Concepts in Computer Science*. Springer, 1–10.

[5] Atish Das Sarma, Stephan Holzer, Liah Kor, Amos Korman, Danupon Nanongkai, Gopal Pandurangan, David Peleg, and Roger Wattenhofer. 2012. Distributed verification and hardness of distributed approximation. *SIAM J. Comput.* 41, 5 (2012), 1235–1265.

[6] Michael Elkin. 2006. An unconditional lower bound on the time-approximation trade-off for the distributed minimum spanning tree problem. *SIAM J. Comput.* 36, 2 (2006), 433–456.

[7] Michael Elkin. 2017. Distributed exact shortest paths in sublinear time. In *Proceedings of the 49th Annual ACM SIGACT Symposium on Theory of Computing*. ACM, 757–770.

[8] Michael Elkin. 2017. A simple deterministic distributed MST algorithm, with near-optimal time and message complexities. *arXiv preprint arXiv:1703.02411* (2017).

[9] Paola Flocchini and Flaminia L Luccio. 2003. Routing in series parallel networks. *Theory of Computing Systems* 36, 2 (2003), 137–157.

[10] Robert G. Gallager, Pierre A. Humblet, and Philip M. Spira. 1983. A distributed algorithm for minimum-weight spanning trees. *ACM Transactions on Programming Languages and systems (TOPLAS)* 5, 1 (1983), 66–77.

[11] Juan A Garay, Shay Kutten, and David Peleg. 1998. A sublinear time distributed algorithm for minimum-weight spanning trees. *SIAM J. Comput.* 27, 1 (1998), 302–316.

[12] Mohsen Ghaffari and Bernhard Haeupler. 2016. Distributed algorithms for planar networks II: Low-congestion shortcuts, mst, and min-cut. In *Proceedings of the Twenty-Seventh Annual ACM-SIAM Symposium on Discrete Algorithms*. Society for Industrial and Applied Mathematics, 202–219.

[13] Mohsen Ghaffari, Andreas Karrenbauer, Fabian Kuhn, Christoph Lenzen, and Boaz Patt-Shamir. 2015. Near-optimal distributed maximum flow. In *Proceedings of the 2015 ACM Symposium on Principles of Distributed Computing*. ACM, 81–90.

[14] Mohsen Ghaffari and Fabian Kuhn. 2013. Distributed minimum cut approximation. In *International Symposium on Distributed Computing*. Springer, 1–15.

[15] Bernhard Haeupler, Taisuke Izumi, and Goran Zuzic. 2016. Low-congestion shortcuts without embedding. In *Proceedings of the 2016 ACM Symposium on Principles of Distributed Computing*. ACM, 451–460.

[16] Bernhard Haeupler, Taisuke Izumi, and Goran Zuzic. 2016. Near-Optimal Low-Congestion Shortcuts on Bounded Parameter Graphs. In *International Symposium on Distributed Computing*. Springer, 158–172.

[17] Dov Harel and Robert Endre Tarjan. 1984. Fast algorithms for finding nearest common ancestors. *siam Journal on Computing* 13, 2 (1984), 338–355.

[18] Monika Henzinger, Sebastian Krinninger, and Danupon Nanongkai. 2016. An almost-tight distributed algorithm for computing single-source shortest paths. In *Proceedings of the ACM Symposium on Theory of Computing*.

[19] Chien-Chung Huang, Danupon Nanongkai, and Thatchaphol Saranurak. 2017. Distributed Exact Weighted All-Pairs Shortest Paths in $\tilde{O}(n^{5/4})$ Rounds. *arXiv preprint arXiv:1708.03903* (2017).

[20] Taisuke Izumi and Roger Wattenhofer. 2014. Time Lower Bounds for Distributed Distance Oracles.. In *OPODIS*. 60–75.

[21] Ken-ichi Kawarabayashi and Paul Wollan. 2011. A simpler algorithm and shorter proof for the graph minor decomposition. In *Proceedings of the forty-third annual ACM symposium on Theory of computing*. ACM, 451–458.

[22] Maleq Khan and Gopal Pandurangan. 2008. A fast distributed approximation algorithm for minimum spanning trees. *Distributed Computing* 20, 6 (2008), 391–402.

[23] Christoph Lenzen and Boaz Patt-Shamir. 2015. Fast Partial Distance Estimation and Applications. 153–162.

[24] Christoph Lenzen and David Peleg. 2013. Efficient Distributed Source Detection with Limited Bandwidth. 375–382.

[25] László Lovász. 2006. Graph minor theory. *Bull. Amer. Math. Soc.* 43, 1 (2006), 75–86.

[26] Danupon Nanongkai. 2014. Distributed approximation algorithms for weighted shortest paths. In *Proceedings of the ACM Symposium on Theory of Computing*. 565–573.

[27] Danupon Nanongkai and Hsin-Hao Su. 2014. Almost-tight distributed minimum cut algorithms. In *International Symposium on Distributed Computing*. Springer, 439–453.

[28] Jaroslav Nešetřil, Eva Milková, and Helena Nešetřilová. 2001. Otakar Boruvka on minimum spanning tree problem translation of both the 1926 papers, comments, history. *Discrete mathematics* 233, 1-3 (2001), 3–36.

[29] Neil Robertson and Paul D Seymour. 1986. Graph minors. V. Excluding a planar graph. *Journal of Combinatorial Theory, Series B* 41, 1 (1986), 92–114.

[30] Neil Robertson and Paul D Seymour. 2003. Graph minors. XVI. Excluding a non-planar graph. *Journal of Combinatorial Theory, Series B* 89, 1 (2003), 43–76.

Brief Announcement: Population Protocols Are Fast

Adrian Kosowski
Inria Paris and IRIF
Paris, France
adrian.kosowski@inria.fr

Przemysław Uznański
ETH Zürich
Zürich, Switzerland
przemyslaw.uznanski@inf.ethz.ch

ABSTRACT

A population protocol describes a set of state change rules for a population of n indistinguishable finite-state agents (automata), undergoing random pairwise interactions. Within this very basic framework, it is possible to resolve a number of fundamental tasks in distributed computing, including: leader election, aggregate and threshold functions on the population, such as majority computation, and plurality consensus. For the first time, we show that solutions to all of these problems can be obtained *quickly* using finite-state protocols. For any input, the designed finite-state protocols converge under a fair random scheduler to an output which is correct with high probability in expected $O(\text{poly} \log n)$ parallel time. We also show protocols which always reach a valid solution, in expected parallel time $O(n^{\varepsilon})$, where the number of states depends only on the choice of $\varepsilon > 0$. The stated time bounds hold for *any* semi-linear predicate computable in the population protocol framework.

The key ingredient of our result is the decentralized design of a hierarchy of phase-clocks, which tick at different rates, with the rates of adjacent clocks separated by a factor of $\Theta(\log n)$. The construction of this clock hierarchy relies on a new protocol composition technique, combined with an adapted analysis of a self-organizing process of oscillatory dynamics. This clock hierarchy is used to provide nested synchronization primitives, which allow us to view the population in a global manner and design protocols using a high-level imperative programming language with a (limited) capacity for loops and branching instructions.

ACM Reference Format:
Adrian Kosowski and Przemysław Uznański. 2018. Brief Announcement: Population Protocols Are Fast. In *PODC '18: ACM Symposium on Principles of Distributed Computing, July 23–27, 2018, Egham, United Kingdom.* ACM, New York, NY, USA, 3 pages. https://doi.org/10.1145/3212734.3212788

1 INTRODUCTION

The model of population protocols was introduced by Angluin et al. [3]. A population consists of a large collection of indistinguishable agents that rely on very limited communication and computation power. Agents interact in a pairwise, sequential manner, governed by a scheduler. Rules of the protocol determine how agents update their states, and the update depends only on their states at the moment of interaction.

PODC '18, July 23–27, 2018, Egham, United Kingdom

ACM ISBN 978-1-4503-5795-1/18/07.
https://doi.org/10.1145/3212734.3212788

In this paper we look at the interplay between convergence time and the number of states of the agent's machine. The original formulation assumes that the agents are automata with a constant number of states [3]. Since then, this assumption has been frequently relaxed in the literature, making the number of states slightly dependent on the population size n. Such a relaxation has allowed for significant progress in the field, and specifically for designs of rapidly converging protocols for basic tasks. These results include majority computation in $O(\log^2 n)$ parallel time by the protocol of Alistarh et al. [2] using $O(\log n)$ states, and leader election in $O(\log^2 n)$ parallel time with the protocol of Gąsieniec and Stachowiak [9] using $O(\log \log n)$ states, under a fair random scheduler. Both these tasks can also be solved using finite-state agents, but the best known solutions to date required super-linear parallel time.

This paper shows that *it is possible to achieve fast computation in the finite-state model* of population protocols. Previously, results of this type were only known in the model variant with a unique pre-distinguished leader agent, which directly allows for a form of centralized control [4]. Here, we provide a completely leaderless approach to bypass the lack of synchronicity of the system, and consequently the lack of a common time measure for agents. This is achieved by creating a hierarchy of so-called *phase-clocks*, running at carefully tuned rates, which synchronize agents sufficiently to allow a form of imperative centralized program to be deployed on the system.

Our results. We provide a general framework for programming in what we call *a sequential code* for population protocols, and describe a way of compilation of such code to a set of rules ready for execution in the protocol environment. The language itself involves finite-depth loops of prescribed length (lasting a logarithmic number of rounds, w.h.p.) and branching instructions. It is meant to have sufficient expressive power on the one hand, and to bound the expected execution time of any finite-state protocol expressed in it, with the precise trade-off depending on the adopted variant of compilation.

The basic compilation scheme provides a simple way of achieving protocols which give results which are correct w.h.p., using $O(1)$ states and converging in expected polylogarithmic parallel time.

As a representative example, we express in the designed language protocols for two basic tasks: leader election and majority. *Leader election* is a problem in which all agents initially hold the same input state, and the goal is for the population to reach a configuration in which exactly one agent holds a distinguished output, labeled as the leader. *Majority* (in its generalized comparison version) is a problem in which some subset of agents holds initial state A, a disjoint subset of the population (of different cardinality) holds initial state B, and the population should converge to an identical boolean output for all agents, depending only on which of the initial sets is the larger one.

As a direct consequence of the formulation of our protocols within the framework (with no need for further analysis), we obtain the first constant-state protocols for leader election and majority, converging in polylogarithmic expected time w.h.p. to a w.h.p. correct result, under a fair scheduler. We remark that for majority, the high probability of correctness holds regardless of the gap between the sizes of the compared sets.

Next, the obtained solution to leader election allows us to exploit the leader-driven programming framework of [4], and to combine it with our framework. We apply protocols generated with (compiled within) this framework as a blackbox, composed with the solution to leader election. This allows us to compute any semi-linear predicate (i.e., one which can be resolved using population protocols with $O(1)$ states [3]) using a protocol converging in polylogarithmic time ($O(\log^5 n)$ rounds). Such predicates are much more general than the majority problem, including threshold estimation of the size of a set in relation to the entire population, as well as computation of modulo remainders. The task of *plurality consensus* (cf. [5, 6, 8]), in which the goal is to identify the largest of l input sets, can also be expressed using semi-linear predicates. A solution to plurality consensus is in fact obtained with a straightforward adaptation of our protocol for majority, with the same convergence time.

All the designed protocols can be made correct with certainty, converging in $O(n^\varepsilon)$ time, where $\varepsilon > 0$ is an arbitrarily chosen parameter, influencing the number of states of the agent. Alternatively, polylogarithmic running time can be preserved at the cost of using $O(\log \log n)$ states per agent.

The deterministically correct protocols which we present do not stand in contradiction to existing lower bounds on majority and leader election from Doty and Soloveichik [7], Alistarh et al. [1] and Alistarh et al. [2]. Those impossibility results were derived (and stated) conditioned on an assumption on *stable* computation – to state it briefly, that once the protocol has reached a state that is a valid output, it remains in this state indefinitely, under any sequence of interactions (see [7] for a formal definition of stability). This seemingly safe assumption is in fact prohibitive, as it prevents, e.g., an approach of using fast protocol to quickly compute an output that is correct with high probability, and combining it with a slow and always correct protocol (running in the "background") to make sure that the computation is always correct, eventually. This is precisely the way we proceed to solve both leader election and majority in our framework.

When speaking of convergence time, we must emphasize that detecting whether a population protocol has converged or not is not possible locally, in any model. Indeed, for most basic tasks, such as majority or leader election, no agent can decide whether convergence has already been achieved or whether the outputs of some agents will subsequently change, due to the properties of the random scheduler which may isolate some subset of agents for an arbitrarily long time with positive probability, regardless of the applied protocol.

2 PRELIMINARIES

Population protocols are expressed in the form of a set of rules, describing the state transitions of a pair of interacting agent. When designing protocols with $O(1)$ states, we use the convention that the state space of the agent is the Cartesian product of a certain number of boolean flags known as *state variables*, which may be set or unset for each agent (we use the symbol *on* to denote the truth value and *off* to denote the false value). A rule can then be conveniently described through bit-masks, i.e., by specifying a set of 4 boolean formulas $\Sigma_1, \Sigma_2, \Sigma_3, \Sigma_4$ on the state variables, written as follows: ▹ $(\Sigma_1) + (\Sigma_2) \rightarrow (\Sigma_3) + (\Sigma_4)$. Such a rule may be activated when the pair of interacting agents satisfy formulas Σ_1 and Σ_2 on their state variables, respectively. The execution of the rule corresponds to a minimal update of the states of the agents so that formulas Σ_3 and Σ_4 are satisfied by the states of the respective agents after the update. The special symbol (.) is used to denote the empty boolean formula, which matches any agent.

By convention, boolean variables associated with agents will be denoted by capital letters of the alphabet, such as A. The set of agents in the population for which A is set will be denoted by $\mathcal{A}$. The number of agents in the population is denoted by n.

Our constructions rely on the idea of composing multiple protocols. In the simplest setting, this is obtained by defining each protocol with its own ruleset, and putting the rulesets of the different protocols together into one. We call protocols which have been composed like this *threads*. We speak of *composing protocol P_2 on top of protocol P_1* if the ruleset of protocol P_2 does not affect the values of boolean variables used in protocol P_1. Intuitively, the (asymptotic) execution of a protocol is not affected by composing a constant number of other protocols on top of it.

3 PROTOCOL FORMULATION

Our simple language for writing sequential code is based on the following constructs and assumptions. The code of the protocol is a collection of threads, sharing the same pool of boolean state variables. Variables are defined and initialized at protocol startup, either as $X \leftarrow on$ or $X \leftarrow off$. The code of each thread is a finite-depth branching program with loops.

The only available control instructions are a branching instruction **if exists** (Σ): [block] **else**: [block], depending on whether at least one agent in the population holds a state matching formula Σ, and loops. These are given as **repeat**: [block] (without specifying the number of iterations) for the outermost control loop of a thread, and as **repeat** $\geq c \ln n$ **times**: [block] for possibly nested loops within a thread, where c is an explicitly stated positive integer. The only primitive instructions are **execute for** $\geq c \ln n$ **rounds ruleset**: [ruleset], followed by a set of primitive rules, and the assignment instruction $X := condition$, where X is a variable and *condition* is a boolean condition on local variables, updates the state of an agent to set X if and only if *condition* is true.

An informal description of the compilation process of the code is as follows. A certain (constant) number of threads are specified through code by the protocol designer. The remaining threads (also a constant number, dependent on the loop depth of the code formulation) are added internally to allow for clock operation and synchronization. For each thread, each agent runs its own control loop, which describes a finite state automaton. Starting from some moment of time, w.h.p. all agents have synchronized their operation, and the execution of iterations may be perceived as sequential w.h.p.. Such iterations are known as *good iterations*, and formalized in the full version of the paper [10].

We are now ready to state the main Theorem on the properties of the framework.

Theorem 3.1. *The programmed code can be compiled into a protocol, such that:*

(i) *The protocol always executes rules within its rule sets, and starting from some point never enters **if exists**(S) : blocks for an expression S which is no longer true for any agent;*
(ii) *After an initialization phase taking some number of rounds T_0, each of the subsequent $n^{\Omega(1)}$ iterations is good and takes at most $O(\text{poly}\log n)$ time;*
(iii) *Subject to a choice made at the time of compilation, we have $T_0 = O(n^\varepsilon)$, w.h.p. (for some choice of $\varepsilon > 0$ made at the time of compilation), with the outcome of compilation being a protocol with $O(1)$ states; or, we have $T_0 = O(\text{poly}\log n)$, w.h.p., with the outcome of compilation being a protocol with $O(\log\log n)$ states.*

4 DO-IT-YOURSELF: PROGRAMMING IN THE FRAMEWORK

Using the framework is easiest when the goal is to achieve w.h.p. correctness of the result. In this scenario, it will, in most cases, be sufficient to create one Main thread only. The execution of the code can be seen as follows: for some time, the provided rulesets will be executed in no particular order. Then, w.h.p., some number of iterations of the outermost loop of the code will be executed as designed, i.e., respecting all rules of sequential programming, conditions, and loop limits. At some point during such correct execution of the program, after a sufficient number of iterations are completed w.h.p., it may slow (or stop) without warning.

Thus, the following use of the framework is safe and recommended: the Main thread of the code should be given as "**repeat**: [Program]", where "Program" is a piece of code which is required to solve the problem correctly in a sequential setting, subject to the two additional constraints: (1) "Program" does not modify any of the states of the input of the protocol (if any), and resets any other variables it may use to a valid initialization if it detects their initialization to be invalid; (2) If the output variables computed in one execution of "Program" were a valid answer to the problem, then the next execution of "Program" in the next iteration of the outer "**repeat**:" loop should not alter the state of output variables for any agent.

In the above, constraint (1) eliminates the problem with the initial uncontrolled phase of the execution before its correct operation starts, and (2) handles the issue with the program stopping at an unpredictable moment (e.g., when writing output variables).

Protocols LeaderElection and Majority are provided in the form of pseudocode. Their analysis is deferred to the full version of the paper.

```
def protocol LeaderElection
var L ← on as output:

thread Main uses L:
    var D ← off, F ← on
    repeat:
        if exists (L):
            F := {on, off} chosen uniformly at random
            D := L ∧ F
            if exists (D):
                L := D
        else:
            L := on
```

```
def protocol Majority
var Y_A as output, A, B as input:

thread Main uses Y_A, reads A, B:
    var A* ← off, B* ← off, K ← off
    repeat:
        A* := A
        B* := B
        repeat ≥ c ln n times:
            execute for ≥ c ln n rounds ruleset:
                ▹ (A*) + (B*) → (¬ A*) + (¬ B*)
            K := off
            execute for ≥ c ln n rounds ruleset:
                ▹ (A* ∧ ¬ K) + (¬ A* ∧ ¬ B*)
                  → (A* ∧ K) + (A* ∧ K)
                ▹ (B* ∧ ¬ K) + (¬ A* ∧ ¬ B*)
                  → (B* ∧ K) + (B* ∧ K)
        if exists (A*):
            Y_A := on
        if exists (B*):
            Y_A := off
```

REFERENCES

[1] D. Alistarh, J. Aspnes, D. Eisenstat, R. Gelashvili, and R.L. Rivest. 2017. Time-Space Trade-offs in Population Protocols. In *SODA*. 2560–2579. https://doi.org/10.1137/1.9781611974782.169
[2] D. Alistarh, J. Aspnes, and R. Gelashvili. 2018. Space-Optimal Majority in Population Protocols. In *SODA*. 2221–2239. https://doi.org/10.1137/1.9781611975031.144
[3] Dana Angluin, James Aspnes, Zoë Diamadi, Michael J. Fischer, and René Peralta. 2006. Computation in networks of passively mobile finite-state sensors. *Distributed Computing* 18, 4 (2006), 235–253. https://doi.org/10.1007/s00446-005-0138-3
[4] Dana Angluin, James Aspnes, and David Eisenstat. 2008. Fast computation by population protocols with a leader. *Distributed Computing* 21, 3 (2008), 183–199. https://doi.org/10.1007/s00446-008-0067-z
[5] L. Becchetti, A.E.F. Clementi, E. Natale, F. Pasquale, and R. Silvestri. 2015. Plurality Consensus in the Gossip Model. In *SODA*. 371–390. https://doi.org/10.1137/1.9781611973730.27
[6] P. Berenbrink, T. Friedetzky, G. Giakkoupis, and P. Kling. 2016. Efficient Plurality Consensus, Or: the Benefits of Cleaning up from Time to Time. In *ICALP*. 136:1–136:14. https://doi.org/10.4230/LIPIcs.ICALP.2016.136
[7] D. Doty and D. Soloveichik. 2015. Stable Leader Election in Population Protocols Requires Linear Time. In *DISC*. 602–616. https://doi.org/10.1007/978-3-662-48653-5_40
[8] M. Ghaffari and M. Parter. 2016. A Polylogarithmic Gossip Algorithm for Plurality Consensus. In *PODC*. 117–126. https://doi.org/10.1145/2933057.2933097
[9] L. Gąsieniec and G. Stachowiak. 2018. Fast Space Optimal Leader Election in Population Protocols. In *SODA*. 2653–2667. https://doi.org/10.1137/1.9781611975031.169
[10] Adrian Kosowski and Przemysław Uznański. 2018. Population Protocols Are Fast. *CoRR* abs/1802.06872 (2018). arXiv:1802.06872 http://arxiv.org/abs/1802.06872

Brief Announcement: Space-Optimal Naming in Population Protocols*

Janna Burman
LRI, Université Paris-Sud, CNRS,
Université Paris-Saclay
Orsay, France
janna.burman@lri.fr

Joffroy Beauquier
LRI, Université Paris-Sud, CNRS,
Université Paris-Saclay
Orsay, France
joffroy.beauquier@lri.fr

Devan Sohier
LI-PaRAD, Université de Versailles,
Université Paris-Saclay
Versailles, France
devan.sohier@prism.uvsq.fr

ABSTRACT

This paper gives a brief presentation of a comprehensive study on the necessary and sufficient state space conditions for the deterministic *naming* task in the *population protocol* model. This problem is studied under various combinations of model assumptions: *weak or global fairness*, arbitrary or uniform initialization of agents, existence or absence of a distinguishable agent (arbitrarily initialized or not), possibility of breaking symmetry in pair-wise interactions (*symmetric or asymmetric transitions*). For each possible combination of these assumptions, either an impossibility is proven or the necessary *exact* number of states (per mobile agent) is determined and an appropriate space-optimal naming protocol is given.

CCS CONCEPTS

• **Theory of computation → Distributed computing models**; **Distributed algorithms**; *Design and analysis of algorithms*;

KEYWORDS

distributed algorithms; population protocols; self-stabilization; deterministic naming; exact space complexity; tight lower bounds

ACM Reference Format:
Janna Burman, Joffroy Beauquier, and Devan Sohier. 2018. Brief Announcement: Space-Optimal Naming in Population Protocols. In *PODC '18: ACM Symposium on Principles of Distributed Computing, July 23–27, 2018, Egham, United Kingdom.* ACM, New York, NY, USA, 3 pages. https://doi.org/10.1145/3212734.3212791

1 INTRODUCTION

The population protocol model was introduced by Angluin et al. as a minimalist model of finite-state agents interacting in pairs in an asynchronous way under the *global fairness* condition (which ensures that an infinitely often reachable configuration is unavoidable) [2]. The memory of agents is supposed to be constant, i.e., independent of the population size n. Due to this, agents are prohibited of storing unique identifiers. However, the interest in the model goes beyond this restriction, not only because of the related computational limitations (cf. [2]), but also because many practical motivating scenarios do not necessary impose such restriction. For example, many communicating devices are manufactured with (almost) unique identifiers. Together with that, there is a particular interest in a priori anonymous entities in studies of sociodynamic and economic phenomena (using social network models [5] or game theory [6]), and in which constant memory restriction is not obviously a necessity.

Additional negative results due to the severe memory restriction followed after [2]. For example, it was shown that *leader election* cannot be solved in sub-linear (*parallel*) time with only a fixed (constant) number of agent's states [12]. Many negative results have been established concerning constant space *self-stabilizing* [11] population protocols (converging from any starting configuration[1]). For example, at least n states and the knowledge of n are required for realizing self-stabilizing leader election (under global fairness and in complete graphs) [9]. Moreover, self-stabilizing *bipartition*, *counting*, *mutual exclusion*, and additional problems are impossible under *weak fairness* using a constant number of states (see [8]). Weak fairness (also considered in this work) is a classical fairness in distributed computing. It ensures that every pair of agents interacts infinitely often in an execution.

All these examples demonstrate the important limitation related to the memory restriction, to the design of population protocols and especially to the self-stabilizing ones. Whereas, in the context of limited-resource agents in population protocols (especially those inspired by biology, or by cheap mass-produced sensor devices), one should expect that agents naturally may be non-initialized and faulty (aspects dealt by self-stabilization).

Justified by the negative results and by a growing interest in the model, many extensions relaxing the state space restriction were proposed to overcome the impossibilities, augment its computational power, improve time complexity or tolerate faults (e.g., [1, 7, 13, 15]). Nevertheless, to the best of our knowledge, there are no previous studies dedicated to the task of naming in population protocols. Together with that, many self-stabilizing tasks have to use (at least) a linear (on n) space to be realized and the task of naming is frequently performed as a by-product or as an important design module (see, e.g., [3, 9, 10]). Furthermore, some fault-tolerant and self-stabilizing population protocols assume that names are given a priori, e.g., [13, 16].

*The full version of the paper is available in [8]. This work was partially supported by the Israeli-French Maïmonide and the INS2I PEPS JCJC research projects.

PODC '18, July 23–27, 2018, Egham, United Kingdom

ACM ISBN 978-1-4503-5795-1/18/07.
https://doi.org/10.1145/3212734.3212791

[1]We adopt the usual definitions for the protocol: *state* of an agent ($\in Q$), *configuration* (a vector of all the agents' states), *transition* (an atomic step in which two interacting agents exchange their states (s_1, s_2) and update them according to a *transition rule* $(s_1, s_2) \to (s_1', s_2')$), *execution* (a sequence of configurations where each next one is obtained by a transition from the previous), and execution is said to *terminate* or *converge* if a *terminal configuration* is reached, i.e., when no transition can change it.

These observations suggest that the task of naming in population protocols deserves to be studied thoroughly. The focus of this work is on deterministic protocol design useful whenever random behavior is inappropriate or deterministic guarantees are required.

We perform an *exact* state space analysis, in contrast to, e.g., the asymptotic one. The exact analysis received an important attention in population protocols, e.g., [3, 4, 14, 18]. On the practical side, the exact analysis is motivated, e.g., by extremely cheap resource-limited devices and by self-stabilization. The less volatile memory is used by a protocol, the less it is vulnerable to corruptions (dealt by self-stabilization). An important contribution of this work is that it shows, by performing a careful exact analysis and protocol design, that even in cases where an optimal-space naming (using only n states) is impossible, it is realizable using *only one* additional state (less than one bit), and thus very unlikely to be corrupted.

As in the related studies (e.g., [3, 4, 14]), we assume the existence of a known upper bound P on the number of agents n. Then, the space complexity is expressed in terms of the necessary number of states per agent with respect to P. Obviously, P is a lower bound for naming a population of at most P agents.

We study naming under various combinations of model parameters. The considered parameters affect the type and the level of difficulty of breaking symmetry or of achieving fault-tolerance. A first parameter of the model is the nature of the assumed fairness, weak or global. A second parameter is the symmetry nature of the (transition) rules of a protocol. With *symmetric rules*, two interacting agents in the same state, stay in identical states. With *asymmetric rules*, they can take different states. A third parameter is the presence or absence of a unique leader (a distinguishable agent). In the context of sensor networks, this agent may represent a base station, having augmented resources. From this perspective and similarly to the previous studies, we are not concerned with the space complexity of this agent. A fourth parameter is related to the initialization of system agents, i.e., of the leader (if present) and of the other agents (called here *mobile*). In case of mobile agents, if initialization is assumed, it is always *uniform*, i.e., to the same value for every mobile agent. Notice that, with weaker initialization assumption (only the leader is initialized, or nobody), the system is stronger against state corrupting transient faults, and is more adapted to repetitive execution of a task (requiring less or no re-initialization). In case of arbitrary initialization, the given solution is called self-stabilizing [11].

Considering all the possible combinations of the parameters described above, Table 1 gives a synthetic view of the results. For each case, it indicates first the proposition establishing the feasibility, either by proving impossibility or by construction of a space-optimal protocol. In the latter case, the table also indicates the optimal (used) number of states and the relevant statement of the lower-bound.

Notice that, first of all, the table concerns the case of *arbitrarily initialized mobile agents*. Together with that, it is also relevant to the case of *uniform initialization of mobile agents*. It is obvious for the positive results (the protocols stay correct). However, somewhat surprisingly, the impossibilities and lower bounds also hold under this stronger assumption, but with only one exception. The exception concerns symmetric rules under weak fairness and with an initialized leader, i.e., when a leader is present and can be initialized together with the other agents (refer to the table).

Table 1: Synthetic View of Results

	symmetric rules		asymmetric rules
	weak fairness	**global fairness**	**weak/global fairness**
no leader	impossible (Prop. 2.1)	Prop. 3.2, with $P+1$ states (Prop. 2.2)	Prop. 3.1, with P states
non-initialized leader	Prop. 3.4, with $P+1$ states (Prop. 2.3)	Prop. 3.2, with $P+1$ states (Prop. 2.3)	Prop. 3.1, with P states
initialized leader	*non-initialized agents:* Prop. 3.4, with $P+1$ states (Theorem 2.5); *initialized agents:* Prop. 3.3, with P states	Prop. 3.5, with P states	Prop. 3.1, with P states

Note: If not stated otherwise, the indicated results hold for both arbitrarily and uniformly initialized mobile agents.

2 NEGATIVE RESULTS

In this section, we clarify some boundaries on the possibility to obtain symmetric naming. They are useful for establishing the space-optimality (tightness) of the solutions presented in the next section. The first result is obtained by observing a weakly fair execution where symmetry breaking is impossible without a leader and using only symmetric transition rules.

PROPOSITION 2.1. *Under weak fairness and without leader (even with a uniform initialization of mobile agents), symmetric naming is impossible in the population protocol model.*

The following proposition holds because mobile agents cannot detect, without a leader, the existence of identical names (homonyms), using only P states and symmetric rules. The next proposition states that even with a leader such self-stabilizing naming is impossible.

PROPOSITION 2.2. *Even with a uniform initialization of agents, without a leader, and using only P states per agent, it is impossible to obtain symmetric naming in the population protocol model, under weak or global fairness.*

PROPOSITION 2.3. *There is no symmetric naming protocol with P states per agent with an arbitrarily initialized leader (or without it), under weak or global fairness.*

Now the goal is to prove that even with a properly initialized leader (still with arbitrarily initialized mobile agents), under weak fairness, there is no symmetric solution to the naming problem with only P states per agent. For proving this stronger intricate impossibility result, let us assume, for the sake of contradiction, that such a solution, denoted $Name$, exists. Some (additional necessary) properties of protocol $Name$ are proven and finally imply the impossibility of its existence, Theorem 2.5.

The next proposition establishes an important property of any protocol $Name$ - the existence of a unique state m, called *sink*. This particular state satisfies the following three conditions: (1) $(m, m) \rightarrow (m, m)$; (2) for every state $s \in Q$, there is a transition rule sequence $(s, s) \xrightarrow{*} (m, m)$[2]; (3) for any $n < P$, no mobile agent is assigned the name m at convergence (i.e., m does not appear infinitely often in executions with $n < P$).

PROPOSITION 2.4. *In any protocol Name, there is a sink state.*

[2]denotes an existing sequence of rules of a protocol s.t. $(s, s) \rightarrow (s_1, s_1), (s_1, s_1) \rightarrow (s_2, s_2), \ldots, (s_{j-1}, s_{j-1}) \rightarrow (s_j, s_j), (s_j, s_j) \rightarrow (m, m)$

The proof of Theorem 2.5 shows that *Name*, in a population of size P, can reach a terminal configuration C with an agent x in some state $s \neq m$, in such manner that the leader may be unaware of that. Then, the leader should manage to create the possibly missing s-agent for converging towards a configuration where the naming is realized. But, once created, this s-agent can disappear by a "reduction" with the "hidden" s-agent x, to the sink state m. This contradicts the fact that the reached configuration C is terminal.

THEOREM 2.5. *Under weak fairness, without the initialization of mobile agents, there is no symmetric naming protocol with P states per agent.*

3 POSITIVE RESULTS

Let us start by a proposition that illustrates the power of asymmetric transition rules. Basically, with such rules, a leader is not necessary for breaking symmetry, even under weak fairness. Moreover, P states are sufficient and no initialization is necessary, i.e., self-stabilizing space-optimal naming is possible. The proof is by construction of a protocol with a single asymmetric type of rule, $(s, s) \longrightarrow (s, s+1 \mod P)$. This idea is known in the literature, e.g., [4, 9]. We show that it can be used to obtain also asymmetric space-optimal naming under more general assumptions than considered there (with upper bound P, instead of exact knowledge of n, without a leader, and under both fairness assumptions).

PROPOSITION 3.1. *Even if agents cannot be initialized, asymmetric naming (under global or weak fairness) is possible using an optimal number of states (P) per agent and without leader.*

Now we consider one of the most difficult cases for symmetric protocols, without leader and initialization, impossible under weak fairness. Recall that global fairness mimics, in some sense, the behavior of randomized environments. The following proposition shows that this pseudo randomization is sufficient for breaking symmetry, and that a distinguishable agent is not needed for that. Thus, we propose below the first *symmetric space-optimal self-stabilizing* naming obtained without a leader. Notice, that by Proposition 2.2, at least $P + 1$ states per agent have to be used in this case.

PROPOSITION 3.2. *Even if agents cannot be initialized and without a leader, symmetric (self-stabilizing) naming under global fairness, for $n > 2$, is possible using $P + 1$ states per agent.*

PROOF SKETCH. Consider the following symmetric protocol defined by three types of transition rules:
1. $if\ s \neq P : (s, P) \longrightarrow (s, s+1 \mod P)$; **2.** $if\ s \neq P : (s, s) \longrightarrow (P, P)$; **3.** $(P, P) \longrightarrow (1, 1)$. □

Up to this point, we have covered the possible positive cases assuming that no leader is present. Now, we show that the impossibility results of Section 2 can be circumvented by the assumption of a distinguishable agent. This allows to obtain three space-optimal symmetric protocols: 1) a simple P state protocol with all agents being initialized, including the leader (Prop. 3.3); and two more intricate protocols: 2) a self-stabilizing one (with $P + 1$ states) under weak fairness (Prop. 3.4); and 3) a protocol using only P states under global fairness (Prop. 3.5).

PROPOSITION 3.3. *Given a unique initialized leader, and uniform initialization of mobile agents, naming is possible using only P states per agent, under weak or global fairness.*

The next two results (Prop. 3.4 and 3.5) exploit the existing space-optimal *counting* protocol from [3], which uses P states per mobile agent, and counts such non-initialized agents under weak fairness, assuming an initialized leader . Let us denote it by $Count_P$. It was not originally intended to be a naming protocol, neither a self-stabilizing one. However, it can be observed that, for the case of $n < P$, it performs (non self-stabilizing) naming (Th. 2 [3]).

By augmenting the mobile agents' state space to $P + 1$ and adapting $Count_P$ accordingly, one obtains a naming protocol (also correct in the case where $n = P$), though using a non-optimal $P + 1$ number of states. The resulting protocol, denoted by $Count_{P+1}$, is adapted further, using a *reset* technique [17] for solving the naming problem in a self-stabilizing way (Prop. 3.4).

The protocol proposed to prove Prop. 3.5 utilizes the global fairness assumption while modifying the original $Count_P$ of the leader for the case of $n = P$ only (for every $n < P$, $Count_P$ converges to a naming [3]). The resulting protocol is not self-stabilizing, as the leader is initialized (and otherwise impossible by Prop. 2.3).

PROPOSITION 3.4. *Self-stabilizing symmetric naming under weak fairness is possible using P + 1 states per mobile agent, given a unique (non-initialized) leader.*

PROPOSITION 3.5. *With an initialized leader (without initialization of mobile agents), symmetric naming under global fairness is possible using only P states per mobile agent.*

REFERENCES

[1] D. Alistarh, J. Aspnes, and R. Gelashvili. 2018. Space-Optimal Majority in Population Protocols. In *SODA 2018*. 2221–2239.
[2] D. Angluin, J. Aspnes, D. Eisenstat, and E. Ruppert. 2007. The computational power of population protocols. *Distributed Computing* 20, 4 (2007), 279–304.
[3] J. Beauquier, J. Burman, S. Clavière, and D. Sohier. 2015. Space-Optimal Counting in Population Protocols. In *DISC*. 631–646.
[4] J. Beauquier, J. Clement, S. Messika, L. Rosaz, and B. Rozoy. 2007. Self-Stabilizing Counting in Mobile Sensor Networks with a base station. In *DISC*. 63–76.
[5] L. Becchetti, L. Bergamini, F. Ficarola, and A. Vitaletti. 2012. Population protocols on real social networks. In *PE-WASUN 2012*. 17–24.
[6] O. Bournez, J. Chalopin, J. Cohen, and X. Koegler. 2008. Playing With Population Protocols. In *CSP 2008*. 3–15.
[7] O. Bournez, J. Cohen, and M. Rabie. 2018. Homonym Population Protocols. *Theory Comput. Syst.* 62, 5 (2018), 1318–1346.
[8] J. Burman, J. Beauquier, and D. Sohier. 2018. *Space-Optimal Naming in Population Protocols*. Research Report. LRI, Univ. Paris Sud. https://hal.inria.fr/hal-01790517
[9] S. Cai, T. Izumi, and K. Wada. 2012. How to Prove Impossibility Under Global Fairness: On Space Complexity of Self-Stabilizing Leader Election on a Population Protocol Model. *Theory Comput. Syst.* 50, 3 (2012), 433–445.
[10] I. Chatzigiannakis, O. Michail, S. Nikolaou, A. Pavlogiannis, and P. G. Spirakis. 2011. Passively mobile communicating machines that use restricted space. *Theor. Comput. Sci.* 412, 46 (2011), 6469–6483.
[11] E. W. Dijkstra. 1974. Self-stabilizing Systems in Spite of Distributed Control. *Commun. of the ACM* 17, 11 (Nov. 1974), 643–644.
[12] D. Doty and D. Soloveichik. 2015. Stable Leader Election in Population Protocols Requires Linear Time. In *DISC*. 602–616.
[13] R. Guerraoui and E. Ruppert. 2009. Names Trump Malice: Tiny Mobile Agents Can Tolerate Byzantine Failures. In *ICALP (2)*. 484–495.
[14] T. Izumi, K. Kinpara, T. Izumi, and K. Wada. 2014. Space-efficient self-stabilizing counting population protocols on mobile sensor networks. *Theor. Comput. Sci.* 552 (2014), 99–108.
[15] O. Michail, I. Chatzigiannakis, and P. G. Spirakis. 2011. *New Models for Population Protocols*. Morgan & Claypool Publishers.
[16] Y. Sudo, T. Masuzawa, A. K. Datta, and L. L. Larmore. 2016. The Same Speed Timer in Population Protocols. In *ICDCS 2016*. 252–261.
[17] G. Varghese. 1993. *Self-stabilization by local checking and correction*. Ph.D. Dissertation.
[18] H. Yasumi, F. Ooshita, K. Yamaguchi, and M. Inoue. 2017. Constant-Space Population Protocols for Uniform Bipartition. In *OPODIS 2017*. 19:1–19:17.

Brief Announcement: A Local Stochastic Algorithm for Separation in Heterogeneous Self-Organizing Particle Systems

Sarah Cannon*
Georgia Institute of Technology
Atlanta, GA, USA
sarah.cannon@gatech.edu

Joshua J. Daymude†
Arizona State University
Tempe, AZ, USA
jdaymude@asu.edu

Cem Gokmen‡
Georgia Institute of Technology
Atlanta, GA, USA
cgokmen@gatech.edu

Dana Randall§
Georgia Institute of Technology
Atlanta, GA, USA
randall@gatech.edu

Andréa W. Richa¶
Arizona State University
Tempe, AZ, USA
aricha@asu.edu

ABSTRACT

We investigate stochastic, distributed algorithms that can accomplish separation and integration behaviors in *self-organizing particle systems*, an abstraction of programmable matter. These particle systems are composed of individual computational units known as *particles* that have limited memory, strictly local communication abilities, and modest computational power, and which collectively solve system-wide problems of movement and coordination. In this work, we extend the usual notion of a particle system to treat *heterogeneous* systems by considering particles of different colors. We present a fully distributed, asynchronous, stochastic algorithm for *separation*, where the particle system self-organizes into segregated color classes using only local information about each particle's preference for being near others of the same color. Conversely, by simply changing the particles' preferences, the color classes become well-integrated. We rigorously analyze the convergence of our distributed, stochastic algorithm and prove that under certain conditions separation occurs. We also present simulations demonstrating our algorithm achieves both separation and integration.

CCS CONCEPTS

• **Theory of computation → Distributed algorithms**; *Random walks and Markov chains*; • **Computing methodologies →** *Self-organization*;

KEYWORDS

Programmable matter; self-organization; separation; distributed algorithms; stochastic algorithms; Markov chains

ACM Reference Format:
Sarah Cannon, Joshua J. Daymude, Cem Gokmen, Dana Randall, and Andréa W. Richa. 2018. Brief Announcement: A Local Stochastic Algorithm for Separation in Heterogeneous Self-Organizing Particle Systems. In *PODC '18: ACM Symposium on Principles of Distributed Computing, July 23–27, 2018, Egham, United Kingdom.* ACM, New York, NY, USA, 3 pages. https://doi.org/10.1145/3212734.3212792

1 INTRODUCTION

Examples of heterogeneous entities separating and integrating exist at many scales, from molecules exhibiting attraction and repulsion to inherent human biases that influence how we form and maintain social groups. Another example is species such as ants co-mingling peacefully when resources are plentiful but prioritizing the survival of their own colony when resources are scarce. This fundamental behavior of separation or integration in response to environmental stimuli spans remarkably diverse disciplines.

We focus on *programmable matter*, a physical material or substance that can intelligently respond to user input or environmental stimuli by changing its physical properties to achieve a goal. We abstractly envision programmable matter as a *self-organizing particle system*, an ensemble of simple active computational *particles* that individually execute distributed, local, asynchronous algorithms to cooperatively achieve macro-scale objectives. Here we consider *heterogeneous* particle systems — where particles have immutable *colors* — and seek local, distributed algorithms which result in *separation* of color classes.

To develop distributed algorithms for separation, we use concepts from stochastic processes. Of particular relevance is the Schelling model [11, 12] which explores how micro-motives can induce macro-phenomena such as racial segregation in residential neighborhoods. Stochastic dynamics for the Ising model of ferromagnetism from statistical physics [13] exhibit a similar dependence of global behavior on a single parameter controlling local preferences. Our work harnesses this interplay between local preferences and global behavior to develop a stochastic, distributed, asynchronous algorithm that provably accomplishes separation.

*This material is based on work supported by the National Science Foundation Graduate Research Fellowship Program under Grant No. NSF DGE-1650044. Any opinions, findings, and conclusions or recommendations expressed in this material are those of the author(s) and do not necessarily reflect the views of the National Science Foundation.
†Supported in part by NSF Awards CCF-1637393 and CCF-1733680.
‡Supported in part by NSF Award CCF-1733812.
§Supported in part by NSF Awards CCF-1637031 and CCF-1733812.
¶Supported in part by NSF Awards CCF-1637393 and CCF-1733680.

PODC '18, July 23–27, 2018, Egham, United Kingdom

ACM ISBN 978-1-4503-5795-1/18/07.
https://doi.org/10.1145/3212734.3212792

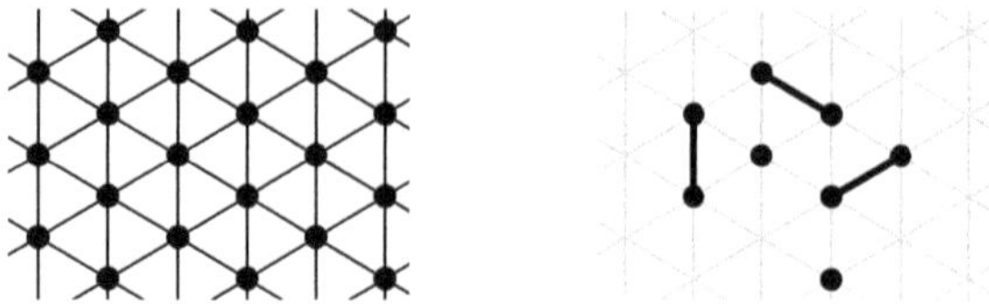

(a) (b)

Figure 1: (a) A section of the triangular lattice. (b) Contracted and expanded particles. The former are shown as black circles, and the latter as two black circles joined by a black line.

1.1 The Amoebot Model

In the *amoebot model*, programmable matter consists of individual, homogeneous computational elements called *particles*. A full description of the model is available online [6]. In the *geometric amoebot model*, we further assume the underlying geometry is the infinite triangular lattice (Fig. 1a). Each particle occupies a single node (it is *contracted*) or a pair of adjacent nodes (it is *expanded*); see Fig. 1b. Particles move via a series of *expansions* and *contractions*: a contracted particle can expand into an unoccupied adjacent node, and completes its movement by contracting to once again occupy a single node. Two particles occupying adjacent nodes are *neighbors*. A particle communicates only with its neighbors, has constant-size memory, and does not have any global information such as a coordinate system, orientation, or compass. A particle system is *connected* if the subgraph of the triangular lattice induced by its occupied nodes is connected. A *hole* of a particle system is a maximal finite, connected component of unoccupied nodes.

1.2 Systems of Heterogeneous Particles

We consider a particle system composed of n heterogeneous particles, generalizing previous work where particles were identical and indistinguishable [1, 5][1]. We model heterogeneity by assuming each particle P has a color $c(P) \in \{c_1, \ldots, c_k\}$ in its memory, visible to itself and its neighbors; we will assume $k = 2$. These colors can represent anything from differences in equipment between robots in multi-robot systems to demographic diversity in human communities. If particles P and Q are neighbors we say they are joined by an *edge*; this edge is *homogeneous* if $c(P) = c(Q)$ and *heterogeneous* otherwise.

We define a *swap move* under the amoebot model that enables adjacent particles of different colors to switch places. For two neighboring contracted particles P and Q, either P or Q can initiate a swap in one atomic action, which can be implemented as follows: P reads $x \leftarrow c(Q)$ from the memory of Q, overwrites $c(Q) \leftarrow c(P)$ in the memory of Q, and finally updates $c(P) \leftarrow x$. Implementing a swap as an exchange of in-memory attributes is purely for modeling convenience. When individuals have immutable "color" (e.g., ants from different colonies or robots with different hardware), swaps could be realized by a coordinated movement. Adding this natural swap move enables faster convergence of our algorithms in practice, but is not necessary for our results.

[1]A particle system with particles of different functional capabilities was considered in [7]; our particles all have the same capabilities regardless of color.

1.3 The Stochastic Approach

The stochastic (Markov chain) approach to self-organizing particle systems was introduced in [5] and further validated in [1]. Background on Markov chains can be found in standard textbooks (e.g., [9]) or in previous work [1, 5]. This approach is motivated by work in statistical physics that investigates the local micro-behavior causes of global macroscopic phenomena (e.g., [2, 3, 10]). Like a spring relaxing, physical systems favor configurations σ that minimize energy, determined by a *Hamiltonian* $H(\sigma)$. Each configuration is given a weight from the *Gibbs distribution*: $w(\sigma) = e^{-B \cdot H(\sigma)}/Z$, where B is inverse temperature and $Z = \sum_\sigma e^{-B \cdot H(\sigma)}$ is the normalizing constant (or *partition function*).

To achieve separation, we define a Hamiltonian where particle configurations with many edges and large monochromatic clusters have the lowest values. We then get Gibbs distribution that simplifies to $w(\sigma) = \lambda^{e(\sigma)} \cdot \gamma^{a(\sigma)}/Z$, where $e(\sigma)$ is the number of edges and $a(\sigma)$ is the number of homogeneous edges in σ. Larger λ favors more compressed configurations, while for smaller λ the opposite is true, just as in [5]. We expect γ to induce separation when large and integration when small.

Our main contribution is a Markov chain $\mathcal{M}$ whose stationary distribution π is exactly this Gibbs distribution. We run $\mathcal{M}$ indefinitely; once we reach π, we continue moving among different configurations but remain at this desirable distribution. Showing poorly separated configurations are exponentially unlikely in π is our main technical result. We carefully design $\mathcal{M}$ using a *Metropolis filter* [8], ensuring the probabilities of all transitions of $\mathcal{M}$ can be calculated with local information, which is necessary for translating $\mathcal{M}$ into a distributed algorithm.

2 ALGORITHM FOR SEPARATION

Starting at any connected, hole-free particle configuration, Markov chain $\mathcal{M}$ (Algorithm 1) for separation ensures the particle system remains connected and hole-free throughout its execution. We use the following notation. For a location ℓ, let $N_i(\ell)$ denote the set of particles of color c_i adjacent to location ℓ. For neighboring locations ℓ and ℓ', let $N_i(\ell \cup \ell')$ be the set $N_i(\ell) \cup N_i(\ell')$, excluding particles occupying ℓ and ℓ'. When ignoring color, let $N(\ell) = \bigcup_i N_i(\ell)$; define $N(\ell \cup \ell')$ analogously. Let $\mathbb{S} = N(\ell) \cap N(\ell')$ be the set of particles adjacent to both locations. The following locally-checkable properties ensure the particles stay connected and hole-free.

Property 1. *$|\mathbb{S}| \in \{1, 2\}$ and every particle in $N(\ell \cup \ell')$ is connected to exactly one particle in $\mathbb{S}$ by a path through $N(\ell \cup \ell')$.*

Property 2. *$|\mathbb{S}| = 0$, and both $N(\ell) \setminus \{\ell'\}$ and $N(\ell') \setminus \{\ell\}$ are nonempty and connected.*

To translate $\mathcal{M}$ into a fully local, distributed, asynchronous algorithm $\mathcal{A}$ run by each particle concurrently, we decompose the steps of $\mathcal{M}$ into individual particle activations, in which a single particle performs some computation and at most one movement [6]. This decouples a particle's expansion and contraction (Steps 4-7) and P and Q's coordinated swap (Steps 9-11) each into two particle activations. We use flag-locking mechanisms similar to [5] to ensure consistent snapshots of particle neighborhoods; details are omitted.

We prove the following results about $\mathcal{M}$, which then also hold for $\mathcal{A}$. Proofs can be found in [4].

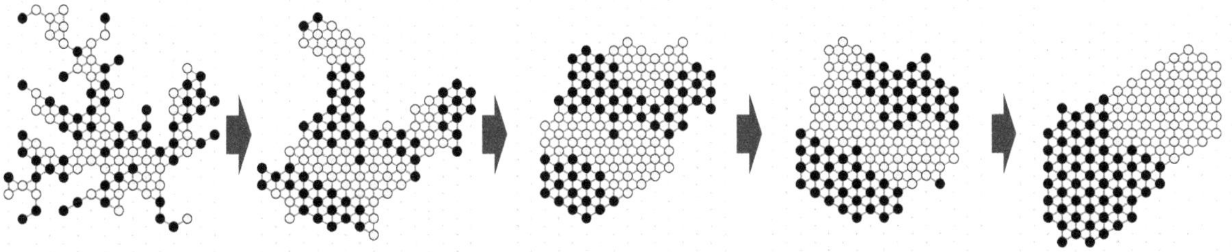

Figure 2: From left to right, a 2-color particle system after 0; 50,000; 1,050,000; 17,050,000; and 68,250,000 iterations of $\mathcal{M}$ with $\lambda = 4$ and $\gamma = 4$.

Algorithm 1 Markov Chain $\mathcal{M}$ for Separation and Integration

```
Choose a particle P uniformly at random from all n particles;
  let c_i be its color and ℓ its location.
Choose a neighboring location ℓ' and q ∈ (0, 1) uniformly at
  random.
if ℓ' is unoccupied then
    P expands to occupy both ℓ and ℓ'.
    if (i) ℓ and ℓ' satisfy Property 1 or 2 and (ii) q <
      λ^{|N(ℓ')|-|N(ℓ)|} · γ^{|N_i(ℓ')|-|N_i(ℓ)|} then
        P contracts to ℓ'.
    else P contracts back to ℓ.
else if ℓ' is occupied by particle Q of color c_j then
    P calculates |N_i(ℓ)| and |N_j(ℓ) \ {Q}| and sends them to Q.
    Q calculates |N_i(ℓ') \ {P}| and |N_j(ℓ')|.
    if q < γ^{|N_i(ℓ')\{P}|-|N_i(ℓ)|+|N_j(ℓ)\{Q}|-|N_j(ℓ')|} then Q
      swaps with P.
```

Lemma 2.1. *The particle system remains connected and hole-free throughout the execution of $\mathcal{M}$.*

Lemma 2.2. *$\mathcal{M}$ is ergodic, converging to unique stationary distribution π given by $\pi(\sigma) = \lambda^{e(\sigma)} \cdot \gamma^{a(\sigma)}/Z$, where $Z = \sum_\sigma \lambda^{e(\sigma)} \cdot \gamma^{a(\sigma)}$.*

Informally, a configuration with two colors is *separated* if there is a set R of particles such that most particles in R have color c_1, most particles in its complement $\overline{R}$ have color c_2, and the boundary between R and $\overline{R}$ is small. If this holds, R and $\overline{R}$ are *clusters*. Formally, a configuration is (β, δ)-clustered, for $\beta > 0$ and $\delta < 1/2$, if there are at most $\delta|R|$ particles of color c_2 in R, at most $\delta|\overline{R}|$ particles of color c_1 in $\overline{R}$, and the boundary between R and $\overline{R}$ is of size at most $\beta\sqrt{n}$, where n is the number of particles.

Theorem 2.3 (Informal). *Among the particle system configurations within an α factor of the minimum possible perimeter, for any $\beta > 4\alpha$ and $\delta < 1/2$, the probability $\mathcal{M}$ is not in a (β, δ)-clustered configuration at stationarity is exponentially small when λ, γ, and the number of particles are large enough.*

3 SIMULATIONS

We simulated $\mathcal{M}$ on a system of 100 particles with two colors. Fig. 2 shows the progression of $\mathcal{M}$ over time with parameters $\lambda = 4$ and $\gamma = 4$, the regime where we expect compression and separation. Fig. 3 shows the results of running $\mathcal{M}$ from the same initial configuration for the same number of iterations, varying only λ and γ; we observe four distinct phases: expanded-integrated, expanded-separated, compressed-integrated, and compressed-separated.

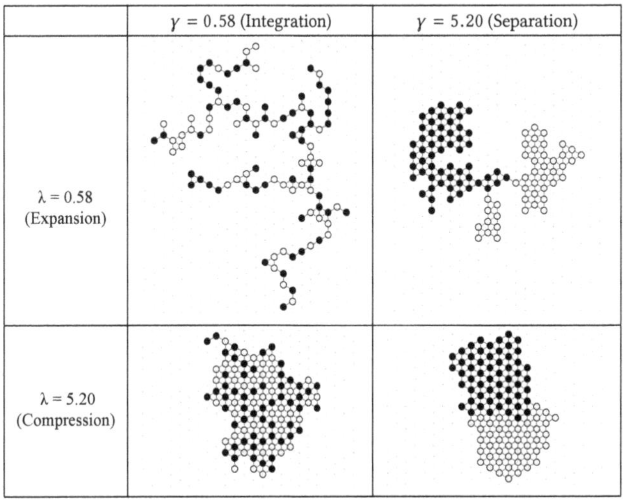

Figure 3: A 2-color particle system starting in the leftmost configuration of Fig. 2 after 50 million iterations of $\mathcal{M}$ for various λ and γ.

REFERENCES

[1] M. Andrés Arroyo, S. Cannon, J.J. Daymude, D. Randall, and A.W. Richa. 2017. A Stochastic Approach to Shortcut Bridging in Programmable Matter. In *DNA Computing and Molecular Programming — 23rd International Conference (DNA23)*. 122–138. A full and updated version is at https://arxiv.org/abs/1709.02425.

[2] R. J. Baxter, I. G. Enting, and S. K. Tsang. 1980. Hard-square lattice gas. *Journal of Statistical Physics* 22, 4 (01 Apr 1980), 465–489.

[3] A. Blanca, D. Galvin, D. Randall, and P. Tetali. 2013. Phase Coexistence and Slow Mixing for the Hard-Core Model on $\mathbb{Z}^2$. In *17th International Workshop on Randomization and Computation (RANDOM '13)*. 379–394.

[4] S. Cannon, J.J. Daymude, C Gokmen, D Randall, and A.W. Richa. 2018. A Local Stochastic Algorithm for Separation in Heterogeneous Self-Organizing Particle Systems. (2018). Available at https://arxiv.org/abs/1805.04599.

[5] S. Cannon, J.J. Daymude, D. Randall, and A.W. Richa. 2016. A Markov Chain Algorithm for Compression in Self-Organizing Particle Systems. In *Proceedings of the 2016 ACM Symposium on Principles of Distributed Computing (PODC '16)*. 279–288.

[6] J.J. Daymude, A.W. Richa, and C. Scheideler. 2017. The Amoebot Model. (2017). Available online at https://sops.engineering.asu.edu/sops/amoebot.

[7] G.A. Di Luna, P. Flocchini, G. Prencipe, N. Santoro, and G. Viglietta. 2018. Line Recovery by Programmable Particles. In *Proceedings of the 19th International Conference on Distributed Computing and Networking (ICDCN '18)*. 4:1–4:10.

[8] W. K. Hastings. 1970. Monte Carlo Sampling Methods Using Markov Chains and Their Applications. *Biometrika* 57 (1970), 97–109.

[9] D. Levin, Y. Peres, and E. Wilmer. 2009. *Markov chains and mixing times*. Providence, R.I. American Mathematical Society.

[10] R. Restrepo, J. Shin, P. Tetali, E. Vigoda, and L. Yang. 2013. Improving Mixing Conditions on the Grid for Counting and Sampling Independent Sets. *Probability Theory and Related Fields* 156 (2013), 75–99.

[11] T.C. Schelling. 1969. Models of Segregation. *The American Economic Review* 59, 2 (1969), 488–493.

[12] T.C. Schelling. 1971. Dynamic models of segregation. *The Journal of Mathematical Sociology* 1, 2 (1971), 143–186.

[13] D. Vinković and A. Kirman. 2006. A physical analogue of the Schelling model. *Proceedings of the National Academy of Sciences* 103, 51 (2006), 19261–19265.

A Brief Tutorial on Distributed and Concurrent Machine Learning

Dan Alistarh
IST Austria
dan.alistarh@ist.ac.at

ABSTRACT

The area of machine learning has made considerable progress over the past decade, enabled by the widespread availability of large datasets, as well as by improved algorithms and models. Given the large computational demands of machine learning workloads, *parallelism*, implemented either through single-node concurrency or through multi-node distribution, has been a third key ingredient to advances in machine learning.

The goal of this tutorial is to provide the audience with an overview of standard distribution techniques in machine learning, with an eye towards the intriguing trade-offs between synchronization and communication costs of distributed machine learning algorithms, on the one hand, and their convergence, on the other. The tutorial will focus on parallelization strategies for the fundamental *stochastic gradient descent (SGD)* algorithm, which is a key tool when training machine learning models, from classical instances such as linear regression, to state-of-the-art neural network architectures. The tutorial will describe the guarantees provided by this algorithm in the sequential case, and then move on to cover both *shared-memory* and *message-passing* parallelization strategies, together with the guarantees they provide, and corresponding trade-offs. The presentation will conclude with a broad overview of ongoing research in distributed and concurrent machine learning. The tutorial will assume no prior knowledge beyond familiarity with basic concepts in algebra and analysis.

CCS CONCEPTS

• **Mathematics of computing → Mathematical optimization**; • **Computing methodologies → Machine learning; Distributed algorithms**;

KEYWORDS

Machine Learning, Distributed Systems, Shared Memory, Message Passing, Stochastic Gradient Descent

ACM Reference Format:
Dan Alistarh. 2018. A Brief Tutorial on Distributed and Concurrent Machine Learning. In *PODC '18: ACM Symposium on Principles of Distributed Computing, July 23–27, 2018, Egham, United Kingdom.* ACM, New York, NY, USA, 2 pages. https://doi.org/10.1145/3212734.3212798

ACM ISBN 978-1-4503-5795-1/18/07.
https://doi.org/10.1145/3212734.3212798

1 INTRODUCTION

Machine learning and data science are areas of tremendous progress over the last decade, leading to exciting new research developments, and to potentially significant industrial impact. In particular, the last few years have seen the development of machine learning models which can reach human-level accuracy on challenging tasks such as image classification [5, 9], speech recognition [15], or strategic games [16]. Seen very broadly, progress in this area has been enabled by three main pillars: the rapidly increasing availability of data, better algorithms for learning from data, and large-scale computational platforms which enable researchers and practitioners to efficiently store, access, and train models on such immense datasets.

Efficient parallelization of machine learning computation is a key part of this third pillar, and will be the focus of this tutorial. For illustration purposes, we shall focus on the classic stochastic gradient descent (SGD) optimization algorithm [13], which provides the optimization backbone for a variety of models and applications, such as training neural networks for image classification and speech recognition, as well as fundamental data processing tools like regression.

The SGD algorithm works as follows. We are given a d-dimensional function $f : \mathbb{R}^d \to \mathbb{R}$ which we want to minimize. Intuitively, the reader can think of the arguments of f as the values of the weights in a neural network, and of its value as its error rate on a fixed dataset. Importantly, the algorithm should be able to differentiate this function with respect to its arguments, and will have access to random d-dimensional vectors $\tilde{g}(x)$ of this function at arbitrary points x, with the property that $\mathbb{E}[\tilde{g}(x)] = \nabla f(x)$. Assuming this setting, SGD then consists in the iteration

$$x_{t+1} = x_t - \alpha_t \tilde{g}(x_t),$$

where x_t is a d-dimensional vector which we will henceforth call the *model* (sometimes also called the *parameter*), encoding our current beliefs about the data, and α_t is the step size, which controls how "large" our updates in the direction of the gradient should be.

This somewhat abstract setting is instantiated in practice as follows. We are given a large dataset, consisting of M *labelled* data points $X_1, \ldots, X_M$. Each datapoint has an associated loss function $L_i : \mathbb{R}^d \to \mathbb{R}$, measuring the loss of any fixed model x at the data point X_i: this simply maps the difference between the prediction of the model x at X_i, and the true label corresponding to that point, to a quantifiable real number. A natural goal is to find a model $x^\star$ which minimizes the average loss over the dataset, that is, find

$$x^\star = \text{argmin}_x f(x) := \frac{1}{m} \sum_{i=1}^{m} L_i(x).$$

This setting corresponds to many natural supervised learning tasks, where we are given a large labeled dataset. The last step is to notice that SGD can proceed by simply picking a sample data point at every step, and updating the model estimate correspondingly. More precisely, in each iteration x_t, SGD takes the current version of the model x_t, computes the stochastic gradient $\tilde{g}(x_t)$ of this model with respect to the current sample by examining the derivative of the loss function at the point, given its label, and updates the model's components correspondingly. The last step is to check that the stochastic gradients $\tilde{g}(x_t)$ correspond to the gradient of the model x_t taken at a uniformly random data point X_i. Indeed, since the data point at which we compute the gradient is chosen uniformly at random, we have

$$\mathbb{E}[\tilde{g}(x)] = \frac{1}{m}\sum_{i=1}^{m} \nabla L_i(x) = \nabla f(x).$$

Parallel Machine Learning. In the last decade, a tremendous amount of research has gone into executing this simple process at extremely large scales, of up to tens of thousands of nodes [7, 9, 15]. The standard way to distribute SGD to multiple compute nodes is *data parallelism*: we are given a set of n computing nodes, and a dataset partitioned into n partitions. Nodes process samples in parallel, and synchronize periodically through a *shared model* x. In this tutorial, we will focus on two popular scenarios:

- Nodes are *threads*, communicating through *asynchronous shared memory*.
- Nodes are *processes*, communicating through *synchronous message passing*.

In parallel to practical applications, there is now a significant amount of literature studying the convergence properties of parallel optimization methods [1, 2, 6, 8, 10–12], going back to seminal work by Bertsekas and Tsitsiklis [3]. Although a complete survey is beyond our scope, we will attempt to provide a brief overview of the current state of this area.

2 TUTORIAL DESCRIPTION

2.1 Structure and Length

The total length of the tutorial is of *one hour*. The tutorial consists of the following parts:

- *Background on Stochastic Gradient Descent.* This part will consist of a formal definition of the optimization problem (similar to the above), along with its convergence guarantees in various scenarios.
- *Stochastic Gradient Descent in Shared Memory.* This part will cover the asynchronous shared-memory parallel variant of the algorithm, with a focus on the modeling and analytic challenges, and a statement of known convergence results.
- *Stochastic Gradient Descent in Message-Passing.* This part will cover the message-passing parallel variant of the algorithm, with a focus on the communication cost for large-scale models such as neural networks. We will briefly describe communication-reduction strategies, as well as their theoretical foundations.
- *Overview of Active Research Areas.* This part will provide a brief overview of active research areas in distributed machine learning not covered in the above sections, including Byzantine-Resilient Machine Learning, e.g. [4], and alternative optimization algorithms, e.g. [14].

2.2 Level of Detail

Due to time constraints, the presentation will focus primarily on the algorithm descriptions their guarantees, and their practical significance, and only provide brief proof sketches and intuition where necessary. We plan to provide separate time for in-depth follow-up questions, and a longer-form write-up covering tutorial material with pointers to complete proofs.

2.3 Intended Audience

The tutorial is aimed at researchers and practitioners in distributed computing, interested in machine learning. No prior knowledge of machine learning or optimization will be assumed, beyond familiarity with basic concepts in algebra and analysis. The tutorial aims to be self-contained.

REFERENCES

[1] Dan Alistarh, Christopher De Sa, and Nikola Konstantinov. 2018. The Convergence of Stochastic Gradient Descent in Asynchronous Shared Memory. *arXiv preprint arXiv:1803.08841* (2018).

[2] Dan Alistarh, Demjan Grubic, Jerry Li, Ryota Tomioka, and Milan Vojnovic. 2017. QSGD: Randomized Quantization for Communication-Efficient Stochastic Gradient Descent. In *Proceedings of NIPS 2017.*

[3] Dimitri P Bertsekas and John N Tsitsiklis. 1989. *Parallel and distributed computation: numerical methods.* Vol. 23. Prentice hall Englewood Cliffs, NJ.

[4] Peva Blanchard, El Mahdi El Mhamdi, Rachid Guerraoui, and Julien Stainer. 2017. Byzantine-tolerant machine learning. *arXiv preprint arXiv:1703.02757* (2017).

[5] Trishul M Chilimbi, Yutaka Suzue, Johnson Apacible, and Karthik Kalyanaraman. 2014. Project Adam: Building an Efficient and Scalable Deep Learning Training System.. In *OSDI*, Vol. 14. 571–582.

[6] Christopher M De Sa, Ce Zhang, Kunle Olukotun, and Christopher Ré. 2015. Taming the Wild: A Unified Analysis of Hogwild-style Algorithms. In *Advances in Neural Information Processing Systems.* 2674–2682.

[7] Jeffrey Dean, Greg Corrado, Rajat Monga, Kai Chen, Matthieu Devin, Mark Mao, Andrew Senior, Paul Tucker, Ke Yang, Quoc V Le, et al. 2012. Large scale distributed deep networks. In *Advances in neural information processing systems.* 1223–1231.

[8] John C Duchi, Sorathan Chaturapruek, and Christopher Ré. 2015. Asynchronous stochastic convex optimization. *arXiv preprint arXiv:1508.00882* (2015).

[9] Kaiming He, Xiangyu Zhang, Shaoqing Ren, and Jian Sun. 2016. Deep residual learning for image recognition. In *Proceedings of the IEEE conference on computer vision and pattern recognition.* 770–778.

[10] Rémi Leblond, Fabian Pederegosa, and Simon Lacoste-Julien. 2018. Improved asynchronous parallel optimization analysis for stochastic incremental methods. *arXiv preprint arXiv:1801.03749* (2018).

[11] Ji Liu and Stephen J Wright. 2015. Asynchronous stochastic coordinate descent: Parallelism and convergence properties. *SIAM Journal on Optimization* 25, 1 (2015), 351–376.

[12] Benjamin Recht, Christopher Re, Stephen Wright, and Feng Niu. 2011. Hogwild: A lock-free approach to parallelizing stochastic gradient descent. In *Advances in neural information processing systems.* 693–701.

[13] Herbert Robbins and Sutton Monro. 1951. A stochastic approximation method. *The Annals of Mathematical Statistics* (1951), 400–407.

[14] Tim Salimans, Jonathan Ho, Xi Chen, Szymon Sidor, and Ilya Sutskever. 2017. Evolution strategies as a scalable alternative to reinforcement learning. *arXiv preprint arXiv:1703.03864* (2017).

[15] F. Seide, H. Fu, L. G. Jasha, and D. Yu. 2014. 1-bit stochastic gradient descent and application to data-parallel distributed training of speech dnns. *Interspeech* (2014).

[16] David Silver, Aja Huang, Chris J Maddison, Arthur Guez, Laurent Sifre, George Van Den Driessche, Julian Schrittwieser, Ioannis Antonoglou, Veda Panneershelvam, Marc Lanctot, et al. 2016. Mastering the game of Go with deep neural networks and tree search. *nature* 529, 7587 (2016), 484–489.

Erasure Coding in Object Stores: Challenges and Opportunities

Lewis Tseng
Boston College
lewis.tseng@bc.edu

ABSTRACT

Recent years have seen a tremendous growth in the popularity of online services accessed over the Internet. Our daily lives are becoming more and more dependent on these online services, which generate and/or rely on huge amount of data. One core technique to deal with the unprecedented amount of data is the distributed storage systems that allow users/applications to read and write data in a distributed fashion and ensure fault-tolerance, durability, scalability, and availability. This tutorial will focus on the distributed key-value storage systems, i.e., read/write objects.

One common implementation of such a read/write object is via replicating data across multiple servers or even data-centers. The replication-based implementation has been studied in the literature, e.g., ABD [Attiya, Bar-Noy and Dolev '96] and LDR [Fan and Lynch '03], and adopted in practice e.g., Cassandra, MongoDB, and DynamoDB. One drawbacks of the replication-based mechanism is high storage cost and communication cost due to unnecessary redundancy.

To address the issue, there is an ongoing effort on applying erasure codes to distributed storage systems in both academia and industry. For example, Microsoft applies erasure coding across data-centers to build strongly consistent objects (Giza in Microsoft Azure Storage), and OpenStack provides erasure coding as a storage policy in their read/write object Swift. However, the field is still fairly young and has many interesting open problems.

This tutorial will focus on the challenges of using erasure codes in read/write objects that guarantee consistency. To begin with, I will introduce concepts on consistency models, erasure codes followed by some recent algorithms and existing practical systems. I will then discuss the state-of-the-art techniques in this field, and conclude the talk with potential challenges that lead to interesting research problems.

The talk will be accessible to anyone with a background a basic knowledge on algorithms or programming. First part of the results are done by Viveck Cadambe, Kishori Konwar, N. Prakash, Nancy Lynch, and Muriel Médard. In the end, I will also share our recent results.

CCS CONCEPTS

• **Computer systems organization** → *Cloud computing*;

ACM ISBN 978-1-4503-5795-1/18/07.
https://doi.org/10.1145/3212734.3212799

KEYWORDS

Erasure Code, Ditributed Storage, Read/Write Object

ACM Reference Format:
Lewis Tseng. 2018. Erasure Coding in Object Stores: Challenges and Opportunities. In *PODC '18: ACM Symposium on Principles of Distributed Computing, July 23–27, 2018, Egham, United Kingdom.* ACM, New York, NY, USA, 1 page. https://doi.org/10.1145/3212734.3212799

BIO

Lewis Tseng is currently an assistant professor in Computer Science department at Boston College. Before that, he spent a year and a half as a researcher at Toyota InfoTechnology Center. He received a B.S. and a Ph.D. degree both in Computer Science from the University of Illinois at Urbana-Champaign (UIUC) in 2010 and 2016, respectively. His research broadly lies in the intersection of fault-tolerant computing and distributed computing. Some recent research includes: (i) fault-tolerant primitives, such as broadcast and consensus, in directed and incomplete networks, (ii) scalable distributed shared storage systems that tolerate crash and Byzantine faults, and (iii) fundamental understanding of Blockchain-based systems.

Tutorial: Consistency Choices in Modern Distributed Systems

Alexey Gotsman
IMDEA Software Institute

ABSTRACT

Distributed systems underlying large-scale Internet services often guarantee immediate availability and tolerate network failures at the expense of providing only weak data consistency guarantees. This is compensated for by new programming constructs, such as replicated data types (aka CRDTs) and novel forms of transactions. Navigating the spectrum of possible consistency models and programming constructs is far from trivial. This tutorial surveys recent developments that help in this: formal definitions of consistency model semantics and methods for reasoning about how the weakness of consistency models affects the correctness of applications using them.

ACM Reference Format:
Alexey Gotsman. 2018. Tutorial: Consistency Choices in Modern Distributed Systems. In *PODC '18: ACM Symposium on Principles of Distributed Computing, July 23–27, 2018, Egham, United Kingdom.* ACM, New York, NY, USA, 1 page. https://doi.org/10.1145/3212734.3212800

PODC '18, July 23–27, 2018, Egham, United Kingdom

ACM ISBN 978-1-4503-5795-1/18/07.
https://doi.org/10.1145/3212734.3212800

BIO

Alexey Gotsman is an Associate Research Professor at the IMDEA Software Institute (Madrid, Spain), where he current holds an ERC Starting Grant. He obtained his PhD from the University of Cambridge, UK. Alexey's research interests are in methods and tools for developing correct concurrent and distributed software.

From Self-Stabilization to Self-Optimization: Principles of Distributed Network Design

Stefan Schmid
University of Vienna
Austria
stefan_schmid@univie.ac.at

ABSTRACT

The tutorial provides an overview of the principles and "pearls" of constructing, maintaining and optimizing network topologies, such as peer-to-peer overlays or datacenter interconnects. The tutorial consists of two parts:

- **Self-stabilization:** In the first part, we start simple by discussing basic mechanisms to reconfigure networks while maintaining connectivity. You will then learn how to design and analyze self-stabilizing algorithms for line topologies as well as more sophisticated networks such as hypercubes. A self-stabilizing algorithm guarantees that the network will automatically reconfigure to a "good topology" from an arbitrary initial state.
- **Self-optimization:** After we have learned how to design self-stabilizing networks, we will consider algorithms to design self-adjusting resp. "self-optimizing" networks: networks which not only "repair" themselves but also optimize themselves towards the demand. The study of such self-adjusting networks is motivated by emerging technologies in the context of datacenters and wide-area networks, allowing to reconfigure networks at runtime.

CCS CONCEPTS

• Networks → Network performance evaluation; • Theory of computation → Graph algorithms analysis;

KEYWORDS

Algorithms, Network Design, Self-Stabilization

ACM Reference Format:

Stefan Schmid. 2018. From Self-Stabilization to Self-Optimization: Principles of Distributed Network Design. In *PODC '18: ACM Symposium on Principles of Distributed Computing, July 23–27, 2018, Egham, United Kingdom.* ACM, New York, NY, USA, 1 page. https://doi.org/10.1145/3212734.3212801

PODC '18, July 23–27, 2018, Egham, United Kingdom

ACM ISBN 978-1-4503-5795-1/18/07.
https://doi.org/10.1145/3212734.3212801

1 MATERIAL AND LITERATURE

The tutorial is based on self-contained slides (please contact me to obtain a copy). Not all aspects of the tutorial are covered in existing literature. However, parts of the first part of the tutorial are based on concepts and techniques discussed in more depth in a chapter on overlay networks for peer-to-peer networks in the handbook [4] (as well as references therein), in the paper on self-stabilizing linearization by Gall et al. [2], and in the paper on self-stabilizing hypercubes by Jacob et al. [3]. The second part of the tutorial discusses approaches presented in the works by Avin et al. [1, 5] on self-adjusting datastructures.

REFERENCES

[1] Chen Avin, Kaushik Mondal, and Stefan Schmid. 2017. Demand-Aware Network Designs of Bounded Degree. In *Proc. International Symposium on Distributed Computing (DISC).*

[2] Dominik Gall, Riko Jacob, Andrea Richa, Christian Scheideler, Stefan Schmid, and Hanjo Taeubig. 2014. A Note on the Parallel Runtime of Self-Stabilizing Graph Linearization. *Theory of Computing Systems (TOCS)* (2014).

[3] Riko Jacob, Andrea Richa, Christian Scheideler, Stefan Schmid, and Hanjo Taeubig. 2014. SKIP+: A Self-Stabilizing Skip Graph. *Journal of the ACM (JACM)* (2014).

[4] Andrea Richa, Christian Scheideler, and Stefan Schmid. 2018. Chapter 72: Overlay Networks for Peer-to-Peer Networks. In *Handbook on Approximation Algorithms and Metaheuristics (AAM), 2nd Edition.*

[5] Stefan Schmid, Chen Avin, Christian Scheideler, Michael Borokhovich, Bernhard Haeupler, and Zvi Lotker. 2016. SplayNet: Towards Locally Self-Adjusting Networks. *IEEE/ACM Transactions on Networking (ToN)* (2016).

Author Index

www.ingramcontent.com/pod-product-compliance
Ingram Content Group UK Ltd.
Pitfield, Milton Keynes, MK11 3LW, UK
UKHW051414290926
15471UKWH00009B/1606

9 781450 359559